1981–1985 SUPPLEMENT TO
CRIME FICTION
1749–1980

GARLAND REFERENCE LIBRARY
OF THE HUMANITIES
(VOL. 766)

1981–1985 SUPPLEMENT TO
CRIME FICTION 1749–1980

Allen J. Hubin

GARLAND PUBLISHING, INC.
NEW YORK & LONDON
1988

© 1988 Allen J. Hubin
All rights reserved

Library of Congress Cataloging-in-Publication Data

Hubin, Allen J.
  1981–1985 supplement to Crime fiction, 1749–1980.

  (Garland reference library of the humanities ; vol. 766)
  Includes indexes.
  1. English fiction—Bibliography. 2. Detective and
mystery stories—Bibliography. 3. American fiction—
Bibliography. 4. Crime and criminals—Fiction—
Bibliography. 5. Detective and mystery plays—
Bibliography. 6. Gothic revival (Literature)—
Bibliography. I. Hubin, Allen J. Crime fiction,
1749–1980 II. Title. III. Series: Garland reference library of the humanities ; v. 766.
Z2014.F4H82 1984 Suppl.   016.823′0872   87-23637
[PR830.D4]
ISBN 0-8240-7596-X (alk. paper)

Printed on acid-free, 250-year-life paper
Manufactured in the United States of America

CONTENTS

Preface / vii

Introduction / ix

Introduction to 1984 Edition / xiii

Author Index / 1

Title Index / 135

Settings Index / 173

Series Index / 191

Movie Title Index / 197

Screenwriters Index / 213

Directors Index / 243

PREFACE

This 1981–1985 supplement to *Crime Fiction, 1749–1980* adds some 6,900 new book titles to the coverage of the field, and gives additional information about 4,300 titles cited in the original work. In addition, about 440 new series are identified, and further information is provided for some 270 series cited in the original work. And, as a new feature, about 3,200 theatrical films based on cited print fiction are identified, and the film title, producing studio, year of release, screenwriter(s), and director(s) are given.

INTRODUCTION

The purposes of this supplement to *Crime Fiction, 1749–1980* (herein identified as CF) are basically twofold:

1) To extend book coverage to the five years ending in 1985, using the same selection criteria (see the introduction to CF on page xiii), and to incorporate new information with respect to works published prior to that five-year period and to their authors. All features found in CF (with the exception of the Series Character Chronology) are present here, serving the same purposes and with the same general structure, though somewhat modified in certain cases, as identified below.

2) To provide an entirely new feature dealing with film adaptations of printed works coming within the purview of this bibliographic effort. The objective of this new feature is to identify all theatrical films, silent or in any language, based on a novel or short story cited either in CF or in this supplement, and where possible to give the movie title, producing studio, year of first release, screenwriter(s), and director(s), with appropriate indexing of all this film information.

AUTHOR INDEX

Here listed under the byline employed are works of crime fiction published from 1981 to 1985. In addition, works of crime fiction published prior to 1981 that have come to my attention since CF was published are listed. And in cases where new information about works or authors cited in CF has surfaced, this information is also provided here. This supplement is internally cross-referenced. Consult CF and its cross-references for authors' other bylines, real names, general reference work citations, and additional biographical information.

Those authors and book titles cited here that are also found in CF (which should generally be regarded in such cases as the primary reference) are marked with an asterisk.

As in CF, headnotes identify the general reference works in which an author is cited. The eight reference works used in CF also apply here, with one addition and three modifications:

1) A ninth reference work is incorporated in this feature: *1001 Midnights: The Aficionado's Guide to Mystery and Detective Fiction* (1986), by Bill Pronzini and Marcia Muller (abbreviation = TM).

2) Use of the continuing series *Contemporary Authors* is extended through Volume 119.

3) A new edition of *Mortal Consequences* by Julian Symons has appeared, titled *Bloody Murder* in both the United States and Great Britain (1985). This new edition has expanded author coverage, and authors included in this second edition are identified (abbreviation = BM).

4) A new edition of *Twentieth Century Crime and Mystery Writers*, edited by John M. Reilly, has also appeared (1985). This edition omits some authors covered in the first edition, adds others, and provides modified coverage for still others. These changes are identified for the affected authors in their headnotes in this supplement (abbreviation = TC2).

When a cited work of print fiction has been identified as the source of a theatrical film, that film is identified by giving, in this order, the producing studio, the year of first release, the movie title(s) (where different from the print work; when no movie title is specifically given, it is the same as that of the print source), the screenwriter(s) (abbreviation = scw), and the director(s) (abbreviation = dir).

When a given novel or short story has been filmed more than once, the films are listed chronologically. Silent films (generally made before 1929) are identified as such. Films made in languages other than English are identified, usually by giving first the non-English title, followed by the English translation or title of the release in English-speaking countries. When a film has been released under more than one title, as with different titles in United States and British release, the several titles are given. Some movies were found to be credited to an unidentified work by a given author, and these films are listed in the author headnote (prime example: Edgar Wallace).

Despite the extensive consultation of numerous primary reference works on movies (see "Sources and Acknowledgments" later in this Introduction), errors of omission and commission probably still persist, and in some cases a portion of the normal entry (such as the identity of the screenwriter) could not be found. Assistance in completing and correcting this feature of the bibliography, as well as in correcting or adding to author or book information, will be most welcome and will be acknowledged in the next edition.

TITLE INDEX

Here listed alphabetically are all book titles cited in the Author Index. Titles included both in this supplement and in CF are marked with an asterisk.

SETTINGS INDEX

Here listed alphabetically by setting are the authors and book titles identified with a specific setting in the Author Index. For completeness, even CF settings for which no new works have been identified in this supplement are listed.

SERIES INDEX

Here listed alphabetically are the series identified in the Author Index. Series also cited in CF are marked with an asterisk.

MOVIE INDEX

Here listed alphabetically (with initial article—"A," "An," "The"—removed for easier scanning) are the movie titles identified in the Author Index. In each case the author byline under which that movie may be found is given, and where the book title differs from the movie title the former is given as well to enable the user to quickly find the specific place in the Author Index where the movie is cited. Non-English movie titles are included in this index only in those few cases where no English translation or title for release in English-speaking countries was found.

SCREENWRITERS INDEX

Here listed alphabetically are the screenwriters identified in the Author Index. In each case following the screenwriter's name is an alphabetical list of his or her films, with identification of the byline (and book title, where different from the movie title) under which the film is listed in the Author Index.

DIRECTORS INDEX

Here listed alphabetically are the directors identified in the Author Index. In each case following the director's name is an alphabetical listing of his or her films, with identification of the byline (and book title, when different from the movie title) under which the film is listed in the Author Index.

SOURCES AND ACKNOWLEDGMENTS

Many of the reference works identified in the accompanying introduction to CF continued to be valuable resources in the compilation of this supplement. In addition, for checking or obtaining book and author information, the following further references were also consulted: *1001 Midnights* by Bill Pronzini and Marcia Muller; *Twentieth Century Crime and Mystery Writers*, Second Edition, edited by John M. Reilly; *Bloody Murder* by Julian Symons; *Campion's Career* by B.A. Pike; and *Paralittératures* by Yves Allard.

Reference works consulted in compiling the film information include *The British Film Catalogue 1895–1985* by Denis Gifford; *Filmed Books and Plays 1928–1983* by A.G.S. Ensor; volumes in the *A Title Guide to the Talkies* series by Richard Bertrand Dimmitt and by Andrew A. Aros; *Motion Picture Review Digest*; volumes in *The Film Yearbook* series by Al Clark; *British Films 1971–1983* by Linda Wood; *American Film Index 1908–1915* and *1916–1920* by Einar Lauritzen and Gunnar Lundquist; *American Film Institute Catalog Feature Films, 1921–1930*; *Variety Film Reviews 1907–1984* (18 volumes), plus individual issues of *Variety* after 1984; *Film Noir*, edited by Alain Silver and Elizabeth Ward; *The MGM Story* by John Douglas Eames; *The Films of 20th Century-Fox* by Tony Thomas and Aubrey Solomon; *The Paramount Story* by John Douglas Eames; *The Warner Bros. Story* by Clive Hirschhorn; *The Universal Story* by Clive Hirschhorn; *The RKO Story* by Richard B. Jewell with Vernon Harbin; *Halliwell's Film Guide* by Leslie Halliwell; *Halliwell's Filmgoer's Companion* by Leslie Halliwell; *The Psychotronic Encyclopedia of Film* by Michael Weldon; and *A Guide to American Screenwriters: The Sound Era, 1929–1982* by Larry Langman.

A number of the individuals who provided valued assistance in compiling CF continued their contributions as I worked on this supplement, and I am most grateful to them. In addition, I want particularly to thank Victor A. Berch for sharing the results of his persistent and remarkably resourceful bibliographic researches; Michael J. Tolley for information from his extensive explorations of Australian fiction; and Dory Christoffersen for her spontaneously offered and most helpful assistance in producing the final manuscript. Others whose supplying of bibliographic or author information for this supplement I also gratefully acknowledge include: William H. Adamson, Michel Amelin, Bob Anderson, Geoff Bradley, Carol Brenner, Richard Dalby, Greg Goode, Jim Goodrich, Tim Kelly, Cliff McCarty, Kathi Maio, Paul R. Moy, Rinehart S. Potts, Beth Pripstein, Frances R. Rogg, B.T. See, Gary E. Stevens, and Richard Williams.

ADDITIONAL ABBREVIATIONS

ABPC	= Associated British Picture Corporation
B&D	= British and Dominions Film Corporation
BM	= *Bloody Murder*
CF	= *Crime Fiction, 1749–1980: A Comprehensive Bibliography*
dir	= director
GFD	= General Film Distributors
NEL	= New English Library
scw	= screenwriter
TC2	= second edition of *Twentieth Century Crime and Mystery Writers*
TCF	= *Twentieth Century-Fox*

TM = *1001 Midnights: The Aficionado's Guide to Mystery and Detective Fiction*
WB-FN = *Warner Bros.-First National*

Allen J. Hubin
3656 Midland Ave.
White Bear Lake, MN 55110
July 7, 1987

INTRODUCTION TO 1984 EDITION

Crime fiction, for the purpose of this bibliography, is defined very broadly as fiction intended for adult readers, in which crime or the threat of crime is a major plot element. Thus included are mystery, detective, suspense, thriller, gothic (romantic suspense), police, and spy fiction. The intent is to cover all such fiction in the English language published in book form (both soft and hard covers) through the end of 1980. Magazine and dime novel fiction, juvenile and children's material, omnibus collections, and anthologies are not included.

Since fiction—all literature, in fact—can be thought of as a continuum, any attempt to carve out a portion of it, like crime fiction, is almost impossible and necessarily raises troublesome questions of the categorization of borderline material. Mysteries and tales of Royal Canadian Mounted Police (covered in this book) merge into adventure fiction (not covered); romantic suspense (covered) merges into straight romance, historical fiction, and supernatural or horror fiction (not covered); crime fiction merges into mainstream fiction, science fiction and fantasy, westerns, pornography, and nonfiction (not covered). Since the line between any of the covered and not covered types is a fine one involving subjective individual judgment, users of this bibliography will probably find that coverage is extended at least a small way into some of these other types of literature, especially where crime or detection is significantly present.

The alphabetization practice in this work is unusual only in that Mc, Mac, and M' entries are considered to be the same and are collected together before the other M's.

AUTHOR INDEX

The main body of this bibliography comprises the author index, to which all other sections refer. Here all authors identified with crime fiction published through the end of 1980 are arranged in alphabetical order. Books are listed alphabetically under the byline under which they were first published. Cross-referencing is provided to the author's real name, where different from the crime fiction byline, and to any other pseudonyms used for crime fiction.

The headnotes to byline entries provide author birth and death dates, where known. They also identify series characters (protagonists recurring in two or more books) and provide a means to show in which of the listed books the characters appear. When all appearances of a character are believed identified, the notation so indicates (with an equal sign); when unidentified appearances may exist, the headnote indicates this uncertainty ("in at least those titles marked . . .").

Headnotes also indicate settings used by the books listed under that byline when some general statement can be made. They identify any special way in which the titles are organized, as in the Rex Stout and James Reach entries.

In addition, headnotes identify in which of eight selected general reference works the author is significantly cited, or, if the author is not so cited, provide brief biographical information if such was obtained from other sources. The other sources include primarily the dust jackets of the author's books, and so the biographical information should be understood to relate principally to the author's active writing period; in a few other cases biographical information has come directly from the authors themselves. The identification of general reference works or provision of biographical information is done only once for an author: either in the headnote for the author's real name, when this was used for crime fiction, or in the headnote for the author's principal crime fiction pseudonym.

The general reference works (and the abbreviations) used are:

A Catalogue of Crime (CC), by Jacques Barzun and Wendell Hertig Taylor (1971)
Contemporary Authors (CA), Volumes 1-105
The Development of the Detective Novel (DD), by A.E. Murch (revised edition, 1968)
Encyclopedia of Mystery and Detection (EM), edited by Chris Steinbrunner and Otto Penzler (1976)
Masters of Mystery (MM), by H. Douglas Thomson (1931)
Mortal Consequences (MC), by Julian Symons (1972; published as *Bloody Murder* in England)
Murder for Pleasure (MP), by Howard Haycraft (1941)
Twentieth Century Crime and Mystery Writers (TC), edited by John M. Reilly (1980)

Numerous other studies of crime fiction have been published, both general and specific to single authors or types of fiction within the broad field. Those wishing to explore beyond the eight works cited here will find *What About Murder?* by Jon L. Breen (1981) a very valuable guide, and the compilations by Ronald Burt De Waal *(The World Bibliography of Sherlock Holmes and Dr. Watson*, 1974, and *The International Sherlock Holmes*, 1980) are indispensable to dealing with the abundant Sherlockian materials.

The books listed under each byline are normally identified with their first American publisher and date of first United States publication, and/or with their first British publisher and date of first British publication, depending on whether the books were published in both countries. When both British and American editions exist, the United States is given first when the book was intended primarily for the United States market, and the British first when Great Britain was the primary market. In most cases, this means that the authors were American and British, respectively.

The nature of the book content is also defined. Collections of short stories (ss), collections of novelets, plays (with the number of acts given when known), criminous book-length poetry, translations (with the original title and place and date of publication given when known), and novelizations of stage, radio, TV, or screen plays (with the original source given) are identified. Those not so identified can be understood to be un-derived novels.

Settings information is also given for each title where this was obtained. More than 25,000 volumes were examined for this purpose, either directly or indirectly. Many books have settings not clearly identified, or have changing settings, but those found to be set at least about 50% (by page count) in an identifiable city (understood as the entire metropolitan area), state, country, or region are noted by giving that setting in brackets with the title entry.

American authors most commonly use United States settings, so titles by such authors listed without setting may be assumed with some confidence to be set in the United States. British authors have the comparable tendency and the same assumption can be made. In addition, rather than attempting the individual identification of all books by British authors set in England, shorthand notation is used both in author index headnotes and in the settings index.

Many books have different titles in their various editions—for example, different titles in the United States and in England, and different titles relating to movie editions. All such variant titles are listed and cross-referenced to the original title, where publisher and date for all the editions are to be found.

A dash in front of a title indicates it to be either a marginal inclusion or one whose criminous content and eligibility for inclusion remain unconfirmed.

All titles are given in full in this index, as the title appears on the title page of the first edition. For compactness in presentation and to aid in scanning, titles having initial articles (A, An, The) omit those articles in all other sections of this bibliography.

All bylines are given in full in this index, as they appear on the title pages of the first editions, with parentheses used to identify portions of names not used in bylines. In all other sections of this bibliography, authors are identified only by last names and initials, except in those instances where giving the byline in full would remove an ambiguity produced by a coincidence of initials.

As indicated above, the appearance of an English-language book edition before the end of 1980 satisfies the time requirement for inclusion in this bibliography. Once this requirement is met, a later edition, such as a 1981 first appearance in England of a book published in 1980 in the United States, or a later retitled edition, is also identified.

Despite endless checking and cross-checking, errors doubtless persist in this bibliography. In addition, some titles were included based on incomplete or second-hand information, and all books could not be inspected for settings information. Corrections, additions, and recommended deletions which are based on first-hand information and come with supporting detail from users of this bibliography will be most welcome. Further settings information, or more specific settings identification, is also invited. Such confirmed contributions will be incorporated in future editions or supplements of this bibliography, and their contributors acknowledged.

TITLE INDEX

This lists alphabetically all titles given in the author index, and relates each title to the byline under which it first appeared, thus providing total title access to the principal index of this bibliography.

SETTINGS INDEX

This lists settings alphabetically, with appropriate cross-references to related or overlapping settings. It identifies—alphabetically by author, and alphabetically by title under the author—the books known to use each setting, and thus provides extensive guidance for those interested in fictional treatments of specific settings.

No book is cited for both a specific and a more general geographical setting, e.g., a book listed as set in Philadelphia is not also listed as set in Pennsylvania, although of course the latter is also true. To make this index reasonably compact, summary notations are used: when the number of books using a given setting under a single byline exceeds four this is stated rather than the specific titles themselves, and when all titles under a given byline share a common setting this also is stated instead of the specific titles. Reference to the author index will identify the individual titles in such cases.

Certain non-geographical settings are also identified, and in these instances the book may also be listed under a geographical setting. Non-geographical settings comprise those related to time (past and future, where date and place of setting are also given when known), as well as certain specialized settings (academia, aircraft, church, hospital, train, ship, theatre).

In the very few cases in which books use approximately equally two different geographical settings, the books are listed under both.

SERIES INDEX

Here listed alphabetically are all series and series characters identified in the author index, together with the byline(s) under which books forming part of these series are found, thus providing complete series access to the principal index of this bibliography. In addition, those characters such as Sherlock Holmes and Sexton Blake who are found in the works of large numbers of authors can best be traced to all those works through this index

SERIES CHARACTER CHRONOLOGY

A chronological listing of the more durable series characters may serve usefully to place a given series in time, to identify trends in types of characters, countries of origin, and types of publication, as well as to allow for comparisons in lengths of series.

These features are provided by this listing, in which "durable" series characters are defined as those having five or more book appearances through the end of 1980. The order of listing is by year, from oldest to most recent, with characters cited alphabetically within a given year.

The year of first book appearance is given for each character. When this year is in doubt, and may in fact be earlier, the year is given in parentheses.

Characters are categorized according to one of the following types, where information is available:

1. Adventurer (a character who acts out of love for intrigue or danger or revenge, rather than primarily for a fee; a knight-errant);
2. Amateur (a character whose activity—detection, primarily—arises out of abundant "accidental" encounters with crime and corpses, and who takes no fee);
3. Criminal;
4. Police (a member of a local, state, or national law enforcement agency);
5. Private (an investigator who seeks clients and takes a fee; a private eye or lawyer);
6. Spy.

It is important to note that each character is categorized here only according to his first appearance, and that changes in type can sometimes be observed in the books comprising a series. As examples: Peter Clancy is categorized as an amateur even though he functioned as such for only one book, and after a brief stint as a policeman he operated as a private detective for more than 50 books; other policemen have retired to private or amateur detection; spies have become private eyes in their later years; criminals have reformed and subsequently operated on the side of the godly.

The market for which each series was primarily written is identified (A = America; B = Britain, including Australian series; F = France; S = Sweden), as is the form of publication (hb = hardback; pb = paperback). Note that here too categorization is only according to initial appearance: some series have changed "nationalities" in midstream (such as J.M. Fox's stories about John Marshall), and others have moved from soft to hard covers (such as Ed McBain's 87th Precinct series, and John D. MacDonald's Travis McGee series) or switched from hard covers to paperback (such as the Johnny Liddell series by Frank Kane and the Mike Shayne series by B. Halliday).

When the number of appearances is in doubt, and may in fact be larger (but not smaller), it is given in parentheses. The byline(s) under which each series was issued is cited.

SOURCES AND ACKNOWLEDGMENTS

The primary sources of data for this bibliography were my own library of some 25,000 volumes of crime fiction, extensive researches in the reference literature, and the generous assistance of many knowledgeable students, readers, and authors of crime fiction.

Reference works consulted include *The National Union Catalogue, Cumulative Book Index, Paperback Books in Print, Cumulative Paperback Index 1939-1959* by R. Reginald and M.R. Burgess, *Forthcoming Books, British Museum Catalogue, English Catalogue, British National Bibliography, British Books in Print, Whitaker's Cumulative Book Lists, Contemporary Authors, A Catalogue of Crime* by Jacques Barzun and Wendell Hertig Taylor, *The Encyclopedia of Science Fiction and Fantasy* by Donald H. Tuck, *Encyclopedia of Mystery and Detection* edited by Chris Steinbrunner and Otto Penzler, *The Men Behind Boys' Fiction* by W.O.G. Lofts and D.J. Adley, *The Detective Short Story* by Ellery Queen, Victorian Detective Fiction by Eric Osborne, *A Gothic Bibliography* by Montague Summers, *The Detective Short Story: A Bibliography and Index* by E.H. Mundell and G. Jay Rausch, *The Science Fiction Encyclopedia* edited by Peter Nicholls, *The Paperback Price Guide* by Kevin Hancer, *The Complete Paperback Shopper, Drury's Guide to Best Plays* (Third Edition) by James M. Salem, *Twentieth Century Crime and Mystery Writers* edited by John M. Reilly, *Author Bibliographies Master Index, Sequels* by Frank Gardner, *Index to Full Length Plays, Twentieth Century Science Fiction Writers* edited by Curtis C. Smith, *A Spectrum of Fantasy* by George Locke, *Twentieth Century Romance and Gothic Writers* edited by James Vinson, *Gothic Novels of the Twentieth Century* by Elsa J. Radcliffe, *An Annotated Bibliography of California Fiction 1664-1970* by Newton D. Baird and Robert Greenwood, *The Checklist of Science-Fiction and Supernatural Fiction* by E.F. Bleiler, *Who's Who in Spy Fiction* by Donald McCormick, *Horror Literature* edited by Marshall B. Tymn, *The Bookseller, Publishers' Weekly*, and *Library Journal*.

Among individual contributors, I acknowledge particularly the pioneering bibliographic work of Ordean A. Hagen (*Who Done It?*, 1969), and the extensive assistance of Francis M. Nevins in preparing the first book version of this bibliography and my son Loren Hubin for invaluable help with the title index of that version. My sincere thanks also to the following and to all others who helped—this bibliography is much the more complete and accurate because of them: R.C.S. Adey, Helen Arvonen, Robert Aucott, Ivon Baker, John Ball, R. Jeff Banks, Jacques Barzun, Brian Bearshaw, Robert Beasecker, Tasman Beattie, Mrs. Otto Beeby, Norman Berrow, Peter E. Blau, E.F. Bleiler, Sydney Box, Jon L. Breen, Robert E. Briney, Douglas Browne, Joe Coffey, Kathryn Collins, J. Randolph Cox, Bill Crider, Michael Cropper, Ed Demchko, Richard Deming, Theodore Dukeshire, Bill Dunn, Herbert Eaton, Julie Ellis, Jim Finzel, L. Foulkes, James M. Fox, Niels H. Frandsen, Brian Garfield, Marilyn Granbeck, Douglas Greene, Elliott Greenfield, Mary Groff, John Hamister, Robert Hatch, Iwan Hedman, Daniel L. Higgins, Edward D. Hoch, Robert Hoffman, Don Ireland, Kenneth R. Johnson, Amnon Kabatchnik, Nancy Kingman, Herbert Kleist, Marvin Lachman, Richard M. Lackritz, Robert Lauritzen, Vernon Lay, Lionel Leventhal, Steve Lewis, Dennis Lien, Ethel Lindsay, George Locke, William R. Loeser, W.O.G. Lofts, William Lyles, Frank D. McSherry, Jr., James Malone, Mavis Marsh, Michael L. Masliah, Stephen Mertz, Jeff Meyerson, Harald Mogensen, Nigel Morland, Howard S. Mott, Will Murray, Ellen Nehr, Stanley Pachon, Lauran Paine, Madelyn Palmer, Angelo Panagos, Ruth Pattison, Hayford Peirce, Otto Penzler, B.A. Pike, Bill Pronzini, N.C. Ravenscroft, Becky Reineke, William Reynolds, W.E. Dan Ross, James Sandoe, W.A.S. Sarjeant, Tom and Enid Schantz, Stephen Schultheis, Arthur C. Scott, Charles Shibuk, Walter and Jean Shine, Patterson Smith, Aaron Marc Stein, Steven A. Stilwell, Ola Strom, Wendell H. Taylor, Michael J. Tolley, Valdis Treimanis, Edith Turner, John D. Vining, Howard Waterhouse, Charles G. Waugh, Hillary Waugh, J.F. Whitt, Camille Wolff, Neville W. Wood, and George Wuyek.

Allen J. Hubin
3656 Midland Ave.
White Bear Lake, MN 55110
June 5, 1983

ABBREVIATIONS

A = America
acad. = academia
Afghan. = Afghanistan
Afr. = Africa
Afr., E. = Africa, East
Afr., N. = Africa, North
Afr., W. = Africa, West
air. = aircraft
Ala. = Alabama
Alb. = Albania
Albuq. = Albuquerque, New Mexico
Amst. = Amsterdam, Holland
Arg. = Argentina
Ariz. = Arizona
Ark. = Arkansas
B = Britain
Balt. = Baltimore, Maryland
Bel. Congo = Belgian Congo
Belg. = Belgium
Brus. = Brussels, Belgium
Buch. = Bucharest, Rumania
Buda. = Budapest, Hungary
Buen. A. = Buenos Aires, Argentina
Bulg. = Bulgaria
CA = *Contemporary Authors*
ca. = circa
Calif. = California
Camb. = Cambodia
Can. = Canada
Can. Is. = Canary Islands
Capt. = Captain
Carib. = Caribbean
Casa. = Casablanca, Morocco
CC = *A Catalogue of Crime*
Cent. Am. = Central America
Cey. = Ceylon
Chan. Is. = Channel Islands
Chi. = Chicago, Illinois
Cin. = Cincinnati, Ohio
Cleve. = Cleveland, Ohio
Colo. = Colorado
Colom. = Colombia
Conn. = Connecticut
Copen. = Copenhagen, Denmark
Cors. = Corsica
Czech. = Czechoslovakia
D.A. = District Attorney
DD = *The Development of the Detective Novel*
Del. = Delaware

Den. = Denmark
Dep. = Deputy
Det. = Detroit, Michigan
Dom. Rep. = Dominican Republic
Dub. = Dublin, Ireland
Ecua. = Ecuador
Edin. = Edinburgh, Scotland
EM = *Encyclopedia of Mystery and Detection*
Eng. = England
Ethio. = Ethiopia
F = France
Fin. = Finland
Fla. = Florida
Fr. = France
Fr. Ant. = French Antilles
Frank. = Frankfurt, West Germany
Ga. = Georgia
Ger. = Germany
Gib. = Gibraltar
GM = Gold Medal (publisher)
Green. = Greenland
Guat. = Guatemala
H. Kong = Hong Kong
Hamb. = Hamburg, West Germany
Haw. = Hawaii
hb = hardback
Holl. = Holland
hosp. = hospital
Hung. = Hungary
Ia. = Iowa
Ice. = Iceland
Ida. = Idaho
Ill. = Illinois
Ind. = Indiana
Ind. O. = Indian Ocean
Indon. = Indonesia
Ire. = Ireland
Isr. = Israel
Istan. = Istanbul, Turkey
It. = Italy
Jack. = Jacksonville, Florida
Jam. = Jamaica
Jap. = Japan
Jerus. = Jerusalem, Palestine
Johan. = Johannesburg, South Africa
Kan. = Kansas
Kan. City = Kansas City, Missouri
Kor. = Korea
Kuw. = Kuwait

Abbreviations

Ky. = Kentucky
La. = Louisiana
L.A. = Los Angeles, California
Las Veg. = Las Vegas, Nevada
Leb. = Lebanon
Leip. = Leipzig, East Germany
L.I. = Long Island, New York
Lith. = Lithuania
Maced. = Macedonia
Maj. = Majorca
Mal. = Malaysia
Mars. = Marseilles, France
Mass. = Massachusetts
MC = *Mortal Consequences*
Md. = Maryland
Med. Is. = Mediterranean Island
Melb. = Melbourne, Australia
Mesop. = Mesopotamia
Mex. = Mexico
Mex. City = Mexico City, Mexico
Mich. = Michigan
Mid. East = Middle East
Midway Is. = Midway Island
Milw. = Milwaukee, Wisconsin
Minn. = Minnesota
Miss. = Mississippi
MM = *Masters of Mystery*
Mo. = Missouri
Mong. = Mongolia
Mont. = Montana
Montr. = Montreal, Canada
Mor. = Morocco
Mozam. = Mozambique
MP = *Murder for Pleasure*
Mpls. = Minneapolis, Minnesota
N.C. = North Carolina
n.d. = no date
N. Dak. = North Dakota
N.H. = New Hampshire
N.J. = New Jersey
N. Mex. = New Mexico
N.W. = northwest (United States)
N.Y. = New York (state)
N.Z. = New Zealand
NAL = New American Library (publisher)
Nashv. = Nashville, Tennessee
Neb. = Nebraska
Nev. = Nevada
New Eng. = New England
New Or. = New Orleans, Louisiana
Nic. = Nicaragua
Nig. = Nigeria
Nor. = Norway
NYC = New York City, New York
Okla. = Oklahoma
Okla. City = Oklahoma City, Oklahoma

Oreg. = Oregon
P. Rico = Puerto Rico
Pa. = Pennsylvania
Pak. = Pakistan
Pan. = Panama
Parag. = Paraguay
pb = paperback
PB = Pocket Books (publisher)
Phil. = Philadelphia, Pennsylvania
Philip. = Philippines
Pitt. = Pittsburgh, Pennsylvania
Pol. = Poland
Port. = Portugal
pp = pages
Prof. = Professor
R.I. = Rhode Island
Ref = reference(s)
Rhod. = Rhodesia
Rio de J. = Rio De Janeiro, Brazil
Roch. = Rochester, New York
Rum. = Rumania
Russ. = Russia
S = series
S = Sweden (in series chronology)
S. Afr. = South Africa
S. Am. = South America
S.C. = South Carolina
S. Dak. = South Dakota
S.F. = San Francisco, California
S. Pac. = South Pacific
S.W. = southwest (United States)
S.W. Africa = South West Africa
Sard. = Sardinia
Saud. Arab. = Saudi Arabia
SC = series character(s)
Scand. = Scandinavia
Scot. = Scotland
Sen. = Senegal
Set = setting(s)
Sgt. = Sergeant
Sic. = Sicily
Sing. = Singapore
Sol. Is. = Solomon Islands
Sp. = Spain
ss = short stories
Stock. = Stockholm, Sweden
Sum. = Sumatra
Supt. = Superintendent
Suri. = Surinam
Swed. = Sweden
Switz. = Switzerland
Syd. = Sydney, Australia
Syr. = Syria
Tang. = Tanganyika
Tanz. = Tanzania
Tas. = Tasmania
TC = *Twentieth Century Crime and Mystery Writers*

Abbreviations / xxi

Tenn. = Tennessee
Tex. = Texas
Thai. = Thailand
Tib. = Tibet
Trans. = Transvaal, South Africa
Trin. = Trinidad
Tun. = Tunisia
Turk. = Turkey
U = University
U.S. = United States
Urug. = Uruguay
Va. = Virginia
Van. = Vancouver, Canada
Venez. = Venezuela
Vir. Is. = Virgin Islands

Vt. = Vermont
W.I. = West Indies
W. Va. = West Virginia
Wash. = Washington (state)
Wash. D.C. = Washington, D.C.
WDL = World Distributors, Ltd. (publisher)
Wis. = Wisconsin
WWI = World War I
WWII = World War II
Wyo. = Wyoming
Yugos. = Yugoslavia
Zanz. = Zanzibar

Author Index

Author Index

*AARONS, EDWARD S(IDNEY). SC: Sam Durell, also in title marked SD below.
  *Assignment--The Cairo Dancer. ... Coronet, 1966
  Assignment Unicorn. GM, 1976 SD
*AARONS, WILL B. SC: Sam Durell, also in title below.
  Assignment: Death Ship. GM, 1983
AASHEIM, ASHLEY. 1942-   . Ref: CA.
  The Artemis Sanction. Dell, 1981; Muller, 1982
  A Stillness at Sea. Dell, 1983
  Vulcan Rising. Dell, 1982
*ABBEY, RUTH. Pseudonym of Ruth Pattison.
*ABBOT, ANTHONY. Ref also: TM.
  *About the Murder of the Circus Queen. Film: Columbia, 1933, as The Circus Queen Murder (scw: Jo Swerling; dir: Roy William Neill)
  *About the Murder of the Clergyman's Mistress. Also published as: Mysterious Murder of the Blonde Play-Girl. King Features, 193?
  *About the Murder of the Night Club Lady. Film: Columbia, 1932, as Night Club Lady (scw: Robert Riskin; dir: Irvin Cummings)
  Mysterious Murder of the Blonde Play-Girl; see *About the Murder of the Clergyman's Mistress
ABBOT, FRANCIS
  Dan Sanda. New Horizon, 1982
ABBOT, RICK. Pseudonym of *Jack Sharkey, q.v. Other pseudonym: Mike Johnson, q.v.
  "But Why Bump Off Barnaby?" French, 1981 (3-act play.)
  A Turn for the Nurse. French, 1980 (3-act play.)
*ABBOT, WILLIS J(OHN). Ref: CA.
ABBOTT, GEORGE, 1887-   , and JAMES GLEASON, 1886-   . See also: Dana Burnett; Philip (Hart) Dunning, 1892-   . Ref for Abbott: CA.
  The Fall Guy. French, 1928 (3-act play.) Film (RKO, 1930; released in England as Trust Your Wife (scw: Tim Whelan; dir: A. Leslie Pearce)
ABBOTT, MONICA. Joint pseudonym with Stanley Abbott: *Lesley Howard.
ABBOTT, RICHARD
  Dr. Jekyll and Mr. Hyde. French, 1941. (3-act play based on novel by *Robert Louis Stevenson, q.v.)
ABBOTT, STANLEY. Joint pseudonym with Monica Abbott: *Lesley Howard.
*ABDULLAH, ACHMED. Ref also: CA.
  *The Honorable Gentleman. Silent film (based on title story): Hodkinson, 1920, as Pagan Love (dir: Hugo Balin)
  *The Remittance Woman. Silent film: R-C, 1923 (scw: Carol Warren; dir: Wesley Ruggles)
*ABERCROMBIE, BARBARA (MATTES). 1939-   . Ref: CA.
  Run for Your Life. Morrow, 1984; Macdonald, 1984 <Calif.>
ABISH, WALTER. 1931-   . Ref: CA.
  How German Is It. New Directions, 1980; Faber, 1982
*ABLEMAN, PAUL
  *Shoestring. ... Parkhurst, 1984
  *Shoestring's Finest Hour. ... Parkhurst, 1985
*ABRAHAMS, DORIS CAROLINE. See: *Caryl Brahms.
*ABRAHAMS, PETER
  Tongues of Fire. Evans, 1982 <future>
ABSHIRE, RICHARD K. and WILLIAM R. CLAIR. Dallas police force veterans.
  Gants. SOS, 1985 <Dallas>
ACKROYD, PETER. 1949-   . Born in London, graduate of Cambridge, a Fellow at Yale; poet and critic; literary editor, managing editor of "Spectator".
  Hawksmoor. H. Hamilton, 1985; Harper, 1986
ADAMS, AGNES
  House of Shadows. Brown, 1961 (1-act play.)
*ADAMS, CLEVE F(RANKLIN). Ref also: CA, TM.
ADAMS, EVELYN V. and HOWARD C. WILSON
  On the Loose. Christopher, 1932 (3-act play.)
*ADAMS, FRANCIS (WILLIAM LAUDERDALE)
  *Strong As Death. <Australia>
*ADAMS, FRANK R(AMSEY)
  *Pleasure Island. Silent film: Universal, 1920, as The Brass Bullet (scw: Walter Woods; dir: Ben Wilson)
*ADAMS, FREDERICK UPHAM
  *The Bottom of the Well. Silent film: Vitagraph, 1917 (dir: John Robertson)
ADAMS, HAROLD. Lives in Mpls. SC: Carl Wilcox = CW.
  The Missing Moon. Ace, 1983
  Murder. Charter, 1981 CW <Minn., 1930's>
  The Naked Liar. Mysterious Press, 1985 CW <S. Dak., 1930s>
  Paint the Town Red. Charter, 1982 CW <S. Dak., 1930's>
*ADAMS, IAN. 1937-   . Born in Belgian Congo; newspaperman and journalist in Canada.
  *S--Portrait of a Spy. Gage, 1978; Ticknor, 1982 <Ottawa>
ADAMS, MORLEY
  Mudland. Manor, 1979 <Guyana>
ADAMS, RICHARD
  Warning Wings. Northwestern, 1941
*ADAMS, SAMUEL HOPKINS. Ref also: TM.
ADAMSON, BARTLETT
  Nice Day for a Murder and other stories. Caslon (Syd.), 1944 ss <Australia, 1800s>
ADAMSON, EWART. Pseudonym: *Dayle Douglas.
ADAMSON, JOHN ROBERT
  The Hidden Scar. Simpkin, 1900
ADCOCK, THOMAS LARRY. 1947-   . Police reporter, journalist; living in NYC. Pseudonym: Buck Sanders, q.v.
  Precinct 19. Doubleday, 1984 <NYC>
ADDERLEY, ALYS
  In Dread of the Law. Mellifont, 1936
*ADDYMAN, ELIZABETH
  *The Secret Tent. Film: Forward, 1956 (scw: Jan Reed; dir: Don Chaffey)
*ADE, GEORGE. Ref: CA.
ADLER, RENATA. 1938-   . Ref: CA.
  Pitch Dark. Knopf, 1983; H. Hamilton, 1984
*ADLER, TERRY. See: *Theo Durrant.
*ADLER, WARREN. Ref also: TM. SC: Fiona Fitzgerald = FF.
  American Quartet. Arbor, 1982; Severn, 1983 FF <Wash. D.C.>
  American Sextet. Arbor, 1983; Severn, 1983 FF <Wash. D.C.>
  *Trans-Siberian Express. Film: ITC, 1978 (existence of film not confirmed)
ADLER, WILLIAM A.
  -Some Rain Must Fall. Exposition, 1949
*AEBY, JACQUELYN
  The Elusive Clue. Dell, 1974
  Laurie's Legacy. Dell, 1974
  *The Pipes of Margaree. <Can.>
  *The Sign of the Blue Dragon.
*AFTEREM, GEORGE
  *Silken Threads. ... Published anonymously in England: Gardner, 1890
*AGNEW, SPIRO T(HEODORE). Ref: CA.

AGRY, ED
  Blowtorch: O'Reilly. Hale, 1982
*AHERN, JERRY. See also: *Nick Carter. SC: Dan Track = DT.
  The Armageddon Conspiracy. Gold Eagle, 1984 DT
  Atrocity. Gold Eagle, 1984 DT
  Captain Blood. Gold Eagle, 1985 DT <Russ.>
  Cocaine Run. Gold Eagle, 1985 DT <Cent. Am.>
  The D.E.A.T.H. Hunters. Gold Eagle, 1985 DT <Ida.>
  The Hard Way. Gold Eagle, 1984 DT <Las Veg.>
  Master of D.E.A.T.H. Gold Eagle, 1985 DT <Mex.>
  The Ninety Nine. Gold Eagle, 1984 DT
  Origin of a Vendetta. Gold Eagle, 1985 DT <Russ.>
  Revenge of the Master. Gold Eagle, 1985 DT
  The Takers. Gold Eagle, 1984
*AICKMAN, ROBERT (FORDYCE). 1914-1981.
*AIKEN, ALBERT W.
  *Chin Chin, the Chinese Detective. Ivers, 1901
  *Joe Phoenix, Private Detective; or, The League of Skeleton Keys. Ivers, 1901
  *Joe Phoenix, the Police Spy. Ivers, 1901
  *The Wolves of New York; or, Joe Phoenix's Greatest Manhunt. Ivers, 1901
*AIKEN, EDNAH (ROBINSON)
*AIKEN, JOAN. Ref also: BM.
  *Died on a Rainy Sunday. Film: Incite, 1986, as Mort un Dimanche de Pluie (Died on a Rainy Sunday) (scw: Joel Santoni, Philippe Setbon; dir: Santoni)
  -Foul Matter. Gollancz, 1983; Doubleday, 1983 <Fr.>
  The Girl from Paris; see The Young Lady from Paris
  A Whisper in the Night. Gollancz, 1982; Delacorte, 1984 ss
  The Young Lady from Paris. Gollancz, 1982. U.S. title: The Girl from Paris. Doubleday, 1982 <ca.1850>
AIKMAN, ANTHONY
  The Caves of Segada. Hale, 1985
AINSLEY, ALIX
  The House of Whispering Aspens. Zebra, 1985
*AINSWORTH, W(ILLIAM) HARRISON
  *Jack Sheppard. Silent film: Broadoak, 1923 (dir: Henry Cockraft Taylor)
  *Rookwood. Silent film: Stoll, 1922, as Dick Turpin's Ride to York (scw: Leslie Howard Gordon; dir: Maurice Elvey). Sound film: Stoll, 1933, as Dick Turpin (scw: Victor Kendall; dir: John Stafford, W. Victor Hanbury)
AINTREE. Pseudonym of *John Wallace, Q.v. Other pseudonym: *Gerald Grantham, q.v.
  -Beauty Wins. Crime Book (Melb.), 1939
  -Dead 'Un Wins. Crime Book (Melb.), 1940
*AIRD, CATHERINE. Ref (expanded): TC2; also: TM. SC: Insp. C. S. Sloan, also in title below marked CS.
  Harms Way. Collins, 1984; Doubleday, 1984
  *Henrietta Who. Film: Concorde, 1985, as De Prooi (The Prey) (scw: Vivian Pieters, Ton Ruys; dir: Pieters)
  Last Respects. Collins, 1982; Doubleday, 1982 CS
*AIRTH, RENNIE
  Once a Spy. Cape, 1981
  *Snatch. Film: Gaumont, 1976, as Le Grand Escogriffe (The Big Operator) (scw: Michel Audiard, Claude Pinoteau; dir: Pinoteau)
AKSYONOV, VASSILY (PAVLOVICH). 1932-   . Ref: CA.
  The Island of Crimea. Hutchinson, 1985 <Russ.> (Translation from the Russian.)

*ALBERT, MARVIN H(UBERT). Ref also: TC2, TM.
  *Goodbye Charlie. (Novelization of film: TCF, 1964; scw: Harry Kurnitz; dir: Vincente Minnelli)
  The Medusa Complex. Arbor, 1982
  Operation Lila. Arbor, 1983 <Fr., 1942>
  *Party Girl. (Novelization of film: MGM, 1958; scw: George Wells; dir: Nicholas Ray)
  *The Pink Panther. (Novelization of film: UA, 1964; scw: Blake Edwards, Maurice Richlin; dir: Edwards)

ALBERT, NED. Pseudonym of *Wilbur Braun, q.v. Other pseudonyms: Millard Crosby, Anthony Forsythe, qq.v.
  Dora, the Beautiful Dishwasher. French, 1951 (1-act play.)
  East Lynn. French, 1941 (3-act play based on novel by *Mrs. Henry Wood, 1814-1887, q.v.)
  Fireman, Save My Child! French, 1937 (1-act play.)

ALBERTS, DAVID
  Death by Arrangement. Bakers, 1981 (3-act play.)

*ALBRAND, MARTHA. Ref also: TM.
  *After Midnight. Film: Paramount, 1950; released in the U.S. as Captain Carey, U.S.A. (scw: Robert Thoeren; dir: Mitchell Leisen)
  *Desperate Moment. Film: BFM, 1953 (scw: Patrick Kirwan, George H. Brown; dir: Compton Bennett)

*ALDING, PETER. SC: Constable Kerr and Insp. Fusil, also in titles below.
  Betrayed by Death. Hale, 1982; Walker, 1982
  A Man Condemned. Hale, 1981; Walker, 1982
  One Man's Justice. Hale, 1983

*ALDANOV, MARK. Ref: CA.

*ALDOUS, ALLAN
  *Danger on the Map. <Australia>

*ALDRICH, THOMAS BAILEY. Ref also: CA.

*ALDRIDGE, (HAROLD EDWARD) JAMES
  I Wish He Would Not Die. Bodley, 1957 <Egypt>
  *A Sporting Proposition. criminous <Australia> Film: Disney, 1975, as Ride a Wild Pony (scw: Rosemary Ann Sisson; dir: Don Chaffey)
  *-The Statesman's Game. <Eng., China>
  *The Untouchable Juli. criminous <Australia>

*ALDYNE, NATHAN. Ref: TM. SC: Dan Valentine and Clarisse Lovelace, in *Vermilion, and in titles below.
  Cobalt. St. Martin's, 1982 <Cape Cod>
  Slate. Villard, 1984 <Boston>

*ALEXANDER, DAVID. Ref also: TM.

*ALEXANDER, HOLMES (MOSS). 1906-1985.

*ALEXANDER, IRENE
  *Villa Caprice. Delete: non criminous

*ALEXANDER, KARL. See also: John Mattera.
  *Time After Time. Film: Warner, 1979 (scw & dir: Nicholas Meyer)

ALEXANDER, MARC. 1929-   . Pseudonyms: Marcus Aylward, q.v.; *Mark Ronson.

*ALEXANDER, MARSHA. Pseudonym of Marsha Bourns.
  *Birthmark of Fear. <Calif.>
  *The Curtis Wives. <L.A.>

*ALEXANDER, PATRICK
  *Death of a Thin-Skinned Animal. Film: Cerito, 1981, as Le Professionel (The Professional) (scw: Michel Audiard; dir: Georges Lautner)
  Soldier on the Other Side. Heinemann, 1983

*ALEXANDER, RUTH
  *Blackmail. ... (Novelization of the play by Charles Bennett, 1899-   , q.v.)
  *The Man Who Knew Too Much. (Novelization of film: GFD, 1934; scw: A. R. Rawlinson, Charles Bennett, D. B. Wyndham Lewis, Edward Greenwood, Emlyn Williams; dir: Alfred Hitchcock)

*Rome Express. (Novelization of film: Gaumont, 1932; scw: Clifford Grey, Sidney Gilliat, Frank Vosper, Ralph Stock; dir: Walter Forde. Another film: Two Cities, 1948, as Sleeping Car to Trieste; scw: Allan MacKinnon, William Douglas Home; dir: John Paddy Carstairs.)

ALEXANDER, MRS. THOMAS
  Irene. Ponsonby, 1895

ALEXIS, KATINA. Pseudonym of Katina Parthemos Strauch, 1946- . Ref: CA.
  Young Blood. Pinnacle, 1982

ALGOZIN, BRUCE. See: *Nick Carter.

*ALINGTON, ADRIAN
  *The Amazing Test Match Crime. ... Hogarth, 1984

*ALLAIN, MARCEL. See: *Pierre Souvestre.

*ALLAN, DENNIS
  *The Case of the Headless Corpse. delete title: doesn't exist

*ALLAN, FRANCIS K. ca.1917-   . Born in Tex.; studied law.

ALLAN, OSWALD
  The Green Bushes. Aldine, 1889 <Ire.> (Novelization of play by J. B. Buckstone, q.v.)

*ALLAN, STELLA
  Arrow in the Dark. Collins, 1982
  The Communicating Door. Love Stories, 1986; Avon, 1981
  *No Marks for Trying. <Sp.>

ALLAN, TED. See: Roger MacDougall.

*ALLBEURY, TED. Ref also: TM. Settings where not otherwise indicated: usually Eng., which is also a shared setting in most other titles.
  All Our Tomorrows. Granada, 1982 <future>
  Children of Tender Years. NEL, 1985; Beaufort, 1985
  *Consequence of Fear. <Russ.>
  The Girl from Addis. Granada, 1984 <Ethio.>
  *Moscow Quadrille. <Russ.>
  No Place to Hide. NEL pb, 1984
  *The Only Good German. <Ger.>
  The Other Side of Silence. Granda, 1981; Scribner, 1981
  *Palomino Blonde. ... Reprinted in U.S. under British title: Perennial, 1983
  Pay Any Price. Granada, 1983 <U.S.>
  The Secret Whispers. Granada, 1981
  Shadow of Shadows. Granada, 1982; Scribner, 1982
  *The Special Collection. <Ger.>
  *The Twentieth Day of January. <U.S.>

*ALLEN, (CHARLES) GRANT (BLAIRFINDIE). Ref also: TC2.
  *The Beckoning Hand and other stories.   ss, some criminous
  *Desire of the Eyes and other stories.   ss, some criminous
  *The Scallywag. Silent film: Master, 1921 (scw: Walter Courtenay Rowden; dir: Challis Sanderson)
  *What's Bred in the Bone. Silent film: Master, 1916, as What's Bred ... Comes Out in the Flesh (scw & dir: Sidney Morgan)

ALLEN, HENRY. Editor for the Washington Post.
  Fool's Mercy. Houghton, 1982 <Wash. D.C.>

*ALLEN, MICHAEL (DEREK). SC: Supt. Ben Spence, also in title below.
  Spence at Marlby Manor. Walker, 1982

ALLEN, PETER
  Skyblazer. Hale, 1984

ALLEN, STEVE <STEPHEN VALENTINE PATRICK WILLIAM ALLEN>. 1921- . Ref: CA.
  The Talk Show Murders. Delacorte, 1982

*ALLEN, THOMAS B(ENTON)
  Ship of Gold, with Norman Polmar. Harper, 1982

ALLEN, WALTER (ERNEST). 1911-
  Ref: CA.

  Dead Man Over All. Joseph, 1950

*ALLEN, WOODY
  Side Effects. Ballantine, 1981; NEL pb, 1981 ss, one criminous

ALLENBY, PHILIP
  Baltic Wolf. Arrow, 1984

*ALLINGHAM, MARGERY (LOUISE). Ref also: TM. Pseudonym: *Maxwell March.
  Mr. Campion's Lady. Chatto, 1965 (Reprints 3 novels, and includes one ss in first book appearance)
  *The Tiger in the Smoke. Film: Rank, 1956 (scw: Anthony Pelissier; dir: Roy Baker)

ALLISON, E. M. A. Joint pseudonym of Eric W. and Mary Ann Allison, husband and wife living in N.Y.
  Through the Valley of Death. Doubleday, 1983; Hale, 1985 <Eng., 1379>

ALLISON, ERIC W. Joint pseudonym with Mary Ann Allison: E. M. A. Allison, q.v.

ALLISON, MARY ANN. Joint pseudonym with Eric W. Allison: E. M. A. Allison, q.v.

*ALLISON, WILLIAM. Probably a pseudonym of A. M. Williamson, 1869-1933, and/or C. N. Williamson, 1859-1920, qq.v.

*ALTMAN, THOMAS
  Black Christmas. Bantam, 1983; Corgi, 1984 <New Eng.>
  Dark Places. Bantam, 1984; Corgi, 1985 <NYC>
  The Intruder. Bantam, 1985 <Calif.>
  The True Bride. Bantam, 1982; Severn, 1986 <Phoenix>

*ALVERSON, CHARLES. Ref also: TM.

*AMBLER, DAIL. See: *Nat Karta.

*AMBLER, ERIC. Ref also: TM.
  The Care of Time. Weidenfeld, 1981; Farrar, 1981
  *Epitaph for a Spy. Film: RKO, 1944, as Hotel Reserve (scw: John Davenport; dir: Victor Hanbury, Lance Comfort, Max Greene)
  *Journey into Fear. Film: RKO, 1943 (scw: Orson Welles, Joseph Cotten; dir: Norman Foster)
  *The Light of Day. Film: United Artists, 1964, as Topkapi (scw: Monja Danischewsky; dir: Jules Dassin)
  *The Mask of Dimitrios. Film: Warner, 1944 (scw: Frank Gruber; dir: Jean Negulesco)
  *The Night-Comers. Film: Rank, 1959 (existence of film not confirmed)
  Uncommon Danger. Film: Warner, 1943, as Background to Danger (scw: W. R. Burnett; dir: Raoul Walsh)

*AMES, DELANO (L.). Ref also: CA, TC2.
  *Corpse Diplomatique. <Fr.>
  *She Shall Have Murder. Film: Concanen, 1950 (scw: Allen MacKinnon; dir: Daniel Birt)

*AMES, EDNA. Pseudonym of Andrew J. Collins.

*AMES, JENNIFER
  Shadow Across the Sun. Collins, 1955. U.S. title: Shadow over the Island, as by *Mary Douglas Warren. Arcadia, 1955 <Bermuda>

*AMES, LESLIE. These title written jointly with W. E. D. Ross, 1912-   , q.v.: *Bride of Donnybrook, *The Hidden Chapel, *The Hill of Ashes, *The Hungry Sea, *King's Castle.
  *Journey to Romance. ... No U.S. edition.
  *Sinister Love. ... No U.S. edition.
  *To Shadow Our Love. ... No U.S. edition.

AMESBURY, JAMES EDWARD. Englishman living in Calif.; TV scriptwriter. See also: Hyman Zore.
  A Sporting Chance. Dial, 1980 <Afr.>

AMIS, BRETON. Pseudonym of Rayleigh Breton Amis Best. Ref: CA.
  Terror Farm. International Publishing, 1947

They Walked In Fear. Fiction House, 1946

*AMIS, KINGSLEY (WILLIAM). Ref: not in TC2. Pseudonym: *Robert Markham.
*Russian Hide-and-Seek. <future>

AMIS, MARTIN. 1949- . Ref: CA.
Other People. Cape, 1981; Viking, 1981

AMSHEY, EDWARD. 1924-
Picnic in November. Pageant, 1956

ANDERS, K. T. <KATIE>
Legacy of Fear. Avon, 1985 <Paris>

*ANDERSCH, ALFRED
*The Redhead. Film: Europa, 1962, as Die Rote (The Redhead) (scw & dir: Helmut Kaeutner)

*ANDERSEN, U(ELL) S(TANLEY)
King of the Roses. St. Martin's, 1983; Macmillan (London), 1983 <Ky.>

*ANDERSON, EDWARD. 1906-1969.
*Thieves Like Us. Film: RKO, 1949, as They Live by Night; also known as The Twisted Road (scw: Charles Schnee; dir: Nicholas Ray). Also: United Artists, 1974 (scw: Calder Willingham, Joan Tewkesbury, Robert Altman; dir: Altman)

*ANDERSON, FREDERICK IRVING. Ref also: BM, TM. SC: Oliver Armiston, in all titles.
*The Notorious Sophie Lang. Film: Paramount, 1934 (scw: Anthony Veiller; dir: Ralph Murphy). Also: Paramount, 1936, as The Return of Sophie Lang (scw: Brian Marlow, Patterson McNutt; dir: George A. Archainbaud.) Also: Paramount, 1937, as Sophie Lang Goes West (scw: Doris Anderson, Brian Marlow, Robert Wyler; dir: Charles Riesner)

*ANDERSON, J(OHN) R(ICHARD) L(ANE). SC: Major Peter Blair, also in those marked PB below.
Death in a High Latitude. Gollancz, 1981. U.S. title: Death in the High Latitude. Scribner, 1984 PB
*Death in the City. ... Scribner, 1983 PB
*Death in the Greenhouse. ... Scribner, 1983 PB
Late Delivery. Gollancz, 1982

*ANDERSON, JAMES. Ref also: TM. SC: Insp. Wilkins, in *The Affair of the Blood-Stained Egg-Cosy, and in title marked W below; Jessica Fletcher (in novelizations of the "Murder, She Wrote" TV series) = JF.
The Affair of the Mutilated Mink Coat. Avon (London), 1983; Avon (NYC), 1981 W <Eng., 1930's>
Hooray for Homicide. Avon, 1985; Star, 1985 JF <Maine>
The Murder of Sherlock Holmes. Avon, 1985; Star, 1985 JF <Maine>

*ANDERSON, JESSICA
*An Ordinary Lunacy. <Syd.>

*ANDERSON, MAXWELL
*The Bad Seed. Film: Warner, 1956 (scw: John Lee Mahin; dir: Mervyn LeRoy).
-Key Largo. Anderson, 1939 (Play.) Film: Warner, 1948 (scw: Richard Brooks, John Huston; dir: Huston)

*ANDERSON, POUL (WILLIAM). Ref also: TM.
Earthman's Burden, with Gordon R(upert) Dickson, 1923- . Gnome, 1957 ss, including Sherlockian pastiche

ANDERSON, ROBERTA. 1942- . Joint pseudonym with Mary Kuczkir, 1933- : Fern Michaels, q.v.

ANDERTON, H. J. S.
The Dope King. Mellifont, 1937
The Golden Idol. Mellifont, 1936
The League of Death. Mellifont, 1934
The League of the Yellow Skull. Mellifont, 1932
"The Panther." Mellifont, 1933
The Quest of the Crimson Idol. Mellifont, 1932
Yellow Claws. Mellifont, 1934

*ANDRAU, MARIANNE
By Love Betrayed. Mystique, 1981 (Translation of "Mariage Eclair a Las Vegas". Paris, 1970.)
Dark Persuasion. Mystique, 1982 (Translation of "Cet Homme est a Moi." Paris, 1980.)
The Emerald Pool. Mystique, 1981 (Translation of "Le Rendez-Vous de l'Etang Vert." Paris, 1963.)
Mask of Destiny. Mystique, 1981 (Translation of "Un Charmant Vaurien." Paris, 1959.)

*ANDRE, ALIX
A Dangerous Affair. Mystique, 1981 (Translation of "Le Concerto de L'Empereur." Paris, 1979.)
Desperate Love. Mystique, 1981 (Translation of "Celle Qu'on n'Attend Pas." Paris, 1951.)
Pledge of Hatred. Mystique, 1981 (Translation of "Mon Seigneur de Cornouailles." Paris, 1967.)
Storm of Deception. Mystique, 1981 (Translation of "La Folle Aventure." Paris, 1964.)

ANDREWS, JOHN
Sexton Blake at the Varsity. Amalgamated, 1933 (Sexton Blake)

ANDREWS, JOHN MALCOLM. 1936- . Pseudonym: John Malcolm, q.v.

*ANDREWS, LUCILLA MATHEW. Pseudonym: *Joanna Marcus.

*ANDREWS, MICHAEL (ALFORD). 1939- . Ref: CA.

ANDREWS, SPIKE. All titles in Crisis Aversion Team (CAT) series.
Cult of the Damned. Warner, 1983 <NYC>
Kidnap Hotel. Warner, 1983 <NYC>
Tower of Blood. Warner, 1983 <NYC>

*ANDREWS, V(IRGINIA) C(LEO).
-1986. SC: Chris and Cathy Dollanganger, also in those marked D.
If There Be Thorns. PB, 1981; Piatkus, 1981 D <Calif.>
My Sweet Andrina. Poseidon, 1981; Piatkus, 1982
Seeds of Yesterday. PB, 1984; Piatkus, 1984 D <Va.>

*ANDREWS, VAL. SC: Sherlock Holmes, also in all titles below.
The Beekeeper. Magico, 1983
The Carriage Clock. Magico, 1983
The Case of the Chief Rabbi's Problem, with H. Penn. Magico, 1980
The Fair. Magico, 1983
The Fowlhaven Werewolf. Magico, 1983
The Last Reunion. Magico, 1983
Sherlock Holmes and a Theatrical Mystery, with H. Penn. Magico, 1980

*ANDRZEYEVSKI, JERZY (GEORGE)
*Ashes and Diamonds. Film: Film Polski, as Popiol y Diamant (Ashes and Diamonds) (scw & dir: Andrzej Wajda)

*ANGEL, ROSS
*One-Way Trip. (written by Donald Cresswell.)

*ANGELO, TONY. Pseudonym of Thomas Charles Packham Webb.

*ANGUS, SYLVIA. 1921-1982.

*ANGUS, WILLIAM. Pseudonym of Angus Moir.

*ANONYMOUS. SC: Tubby Haig = TH.
*Austenburn Castle. Minerva, 1776
*The Black Band. Blackett, 1876
The Boy Detective. Newnes, 1866
Caught and Bowled. Wright, 1888
*Caught in Mid-Ocean. delete
*The City of Purple Dreams (by *Edwin Baird). Silent film: Selig, 1918 (scw: Gilson Willets; dir: Colin Campbell)
The Cinema Crook. Newnes TH
*The Convict's Sweetheart. delete
Crimson Hairs. Grove, 1983
The Crook Who Came Back. Newnes TH
Death-Face, the Detective. Westbrook, 1920s
A Duel in the Dark. Newnes TH
*Ghost in the Bank of England. Hogg, 1888
A Great Gamble. Newnes TH
The Great Railway Mystery. Newnes TH
*Jack Sheppard, the Bandit King. delete
Jack's Mother. Arrowsmith, 1890
Jerry Abershaw; or, The Mother's Curse. Caffu, ca.1847-8
"Juliet." Stevens, 1907
The Living Clue. Newnes TH
Lost Man's Lane. Newnes, 1919
The Man in Wax. Newnes TH
The Man of Mystery. Newnes TH
Mantrap Manor. Long, 1908
Maria Marten; or, The Murder in the Red Barn. French, 1877 (2-act play.) Silent film: Harrison, 1902 (scw & dir: Dicky Winslow). Also: Haggar, 1908, as The Red Barn Crime. Also: Motograph, 1913 (scw & dir: Maurice Elvey). Also: QTS, 1928 (dir: Walter West). Sound film: George King, 1935 (scw: Randall Faye; dir: George King)
The Missing Airman. Newnes, 1917 TH
The Mystery of Marlborough House. Harrison, ca.1860 <ca.1800>
The Mystery of the Crooks' Contract. Newnes TH
Nothing New (by Dinah Maria Mulock, 1826-1887). Hurst, 1857; Harper, 1857 ss, one criminous
An Old Country House (by Catherine Maria Gray). Newby, 1850
The Old House (by The Master of Belhaven). Herbert Joseph, 1937
*On Trial for His Life. delete
The Policeman. Booker, 1841
*The President Vanishes. Film: Paramount, 1934 (scw: Carey Wilson, Cedric Worth, Lynn Starling; dir: William A. Wellman).
-The Private Memoirs and Confessions of a Justified Sinner (by James Hogg, 1770-1835, q.v.). Longman, 1824. Also published as: A Suicide's Grave. 1828. And as: The Confessions of a Fanatic. 1837
*The Queen of the Outlaw's Camp. delete; see *Olive Harper.
*The Queen of the Secret Seven. delete
*The Revelations of a Lady Detective. Booksellers, 1861. Also published as: The Experiences of a Lady Detective. Clarke, 1884 (Hayward authorship questionable.)
A Rogue of the Racecourse. Newnes TH
The Syndicate of Crooks. Newnes TH
Third Finger--Left Hand. Strothers, ca.1945 (ss; all by Edward Martell?)
*The Unclaimed Daughter. Whittaker, 1852
Winifred Power (by Bella Duffy). Bentley, 1883

ANSON, JAY. 1921-1980. Ref: CA.
666. Simon, 1981; Granada, 1982

ANSTEY, F. Pseudonym of Thomas Anstey Guthrie, 1856-1934. Ref: CA.
Salted Almonds. Smith, 1906 ss, one criminous

*ANSTRUTHER, GERALD
Dangerous Afternoon. English Theatre, 1951 (1-act play.) Film: Theatrecraft, 1961 (scw: Brandon Fleming; dir: Charles Saunders)
*Third Visiter. Film: Elvey, 1950 (scw: Gerald Anstruther, David Evans; dir: Maurice Elvey)

*ANTHONY, DAVID. Pseudonym of William Dale Smith, 1929-1986. Ref also: TM.
*The Midnight Lady and the Mourning Man. Film: Universal, 1974, as The Midnight Man (scw & dir: Roland Kibbee and Burt Lancaster)

*ANTHONY, EVELYN. Ref also: TM. SC: Davina Graham, in *The Defector, and in those marked DG.
Albatross. Hutchinson, 1982; Putnam, 1983 DG
The Avenue of the Dead. Hutchinson, 1981; Coward, 1982 DG <Wash. D.C>
The Company of Saints. Hutchinson, 1983; Putnam, 1984 DG
*The Silver Falcon. title correction (not The Silver Forest)
*The Tamarind Seed. Film: Jewel, 1974 (scw & dir: Blake Edwards)
Voices on the Wind. Hutchinson, 1985; Putnam, 1985 <Fr., WWII>

ANTHONY, MICHAEL. 1932- . Ref: CA.
All That Glitters. Deutsch (London & U.S.), 1981

*ANTHONY, PIERS and *ROBERTO FUENTES. SC: Jason Striker, also in title below.
The Bamboo Bloodbath. Berkley, 1974

ANZELON, ROBYN
The Goblin Tree. Mystique, 1981 <Calif.>

APFFEL, EDMUND R., JR. 1948- . Ref: CA.
Last Days at St. Saturn's. Holt, 1981 <acad.>

*APPEL, BENJAMIN
*Sweet Money Girl. Delete: non-criminous

APPEL, WILLIAM. 1939- . Ref: CA.
Housebound. Ballantine, 1982
The Watcher Within. GM, 1983

*APPLEBY, JOHN
*The Captive City. Film: Paramount, 1963 (scw: Guy Elmes, Eric Bercovici, Marc Brandel; dir: Joseph Anthony)

APPLEMAN, PHILIP (DEAN). 1926- Ref: CA.
Shame the Devil. Crown, 1981 <Ind.>

APPLETON, BARRY JOHN
A Walking Shadow. Hale, 1984

*APPLETON, G(EORGE) W(EBB)
*Catching a Tartar. criminous

*APPLIN, ARTHUR. 1883-1949.
*Wicked. Silent film: Samuelson, 1920, as All the Winners (dir: Geoffrey H. Malins)

*AQUIN, HUBERT
*The Antiphonary. ... Anasi (London), 1983
*Blackout. ... Anasi (London), 1983

ARATHORN, DAVID W. Pseudonym. Home: NYC.
Kamal. Harper, 1982; Macmillan (London), 1982

*ARD, WILLIAM (THOMAS). Ref also: TC2, TM.
*Hell Is a City. British title: *The Naked and the Innocent

*ARDIES, TOM
*Kosygin Is Coming. Film: ITC, 1975, as Russian Roulette (scw: Tom Ardies, Stanley Mann, Arnold Margolin; dir: Lou Lombardo)

*ARICHA, AMOS
Hour of the Clown. Signet, 1981
Journey Toward Death. Signet, 1984 <L.A.>

*ARLEN, MICHAEL
May Fair. Collins, 1925; Doran, 1925 ss Film (based on ss "The Gentleman from America"): Anglofilm, 1948, as The Fatal Night (scw: Gerald Butler, Kathleen Connors; dir: Mario Zampi)

*ARLEY, CATHERINE. See also: Ian Cullen.
Woman of Straw. Film: Novus, 1964 (scw: Michael Relph, Robert Muller, Stanley Mann; dir: Basil Dearden)

ARLT, ROBERTO. -1942.
The Seven Madmen. Godine, 1984 (Translation of "Siete Locos." Buenos Aires, 1929.)

ARMER, FRANK. Pseudonym: *Arthur Wallace, q.v.

*ARMOUR, TOBY (not Tony)

*ARMSTRONG, ANTHONY
*He Was Found in the Road. Film: Gibraltar, 1956, as The Man in the Road (scw: Guy Morgan; dir: Lance Comfort)
*The Strange Case of Mr. Pelham. Film: Excalibur, 1970, as The Man Who Haunted Himself (scw: Basil Dearden, Michael Relph; dir: Dearden)
*Ten Minute Alibi. Film: British Lion, 1935 (scw: Michael Hankinson, Vera Allinson; dir: Bernard Vorhaus)

*ARMSTRONG, CHARLOTTE. Ref also: TM.
*The Albatross. Film (based on ss "The Enemy"): MGM, 1952, as Talk About a Stranger (scw: Margaret Fitts; dir: David Bradley)
*The Balloon Man. Film: Films de la Boetie, 1970, as La Rupture (The Breakup) (scw & dir: Claude Chabrol)
*The Case of the Weird Sisters. Film: British National, 1948, as The Three Weird Sisters (scw: Louise Birt, Dylan Thomas, David Evans; dir: Dan Birt)
*Mischief. Film: TCF, 1952, as Don't Bother to Knock (scw: Daniel Taradash; dir: Roy Baker)
*Murder's Nest; see *The Better to Eat You
*The Unsuspected. Film: Warner, 1947 (scw: Ranald MacDougall; dir: Michael Curtiz)

ARMSTRONG, ELIZABETH
As the Clock Strikes. Row, 1933 (Play.)

ARMSTRONG, (FRANCIS) HAROLD COURTENAY (LUPIN). 1891- .
Hidden. Barker, 1938. Film: Welwyn, 1939, as Dead Men Are Dangerous (scw: Victor Kendall, Harry Hughes, Vernon Clancey; dir: Harold French)

*ARMSTRONG, RAYMOND. SC: J. Rockingham Stone, also in *The Sinister Widow Comes Back; Laura Scudamore, also in *The Widow and the Cavalier.

*ARNAUD, GEORGES. 1917-1987.
*The Wages of Fear. Film: Filmsonor, 1953, as Le Salaire de la Peur (The Wages of Fear) (scw & dir: H. G. Clouzot). Also: Paramount, 1977; released in U.S. as Sorcerer (scw: Walon Green; dir: William Friedkin)

ARNCLIFFE, ANDREW. Pseudonym of *Peter N(orman) Walker, q.v.
Murder After the Holidays. Hale, 1985

ARNETT, TOM. See: *Don(ald Eugene) Pendleton, Dick Stivers.

ARNEY, JAMES. Pseudonym of *Martin (James) Russell, q.v.
A View to Ransom. Hale, 1983

ARNOLD, ALLAN
Young Sherlock Holmes. PB, 1985; Dragon, 1986 (Novelization of the film: Paramount, 1985; scw: Chris Columbus; dir: Barry Levinson)

*ARNOLD, ELLIOTT
-The Commandos. Duell, 1942; Rich, 1944. Film: Columbia, 1943, as First Comes Courage (scw: Lewis Meltzer, Melvin Levy; dir: Dorothy Arzner)

*ARNOLD, MARGOT. Ref: TM. SC: Penelope Spring and Tobias Glendower, also in titles below.
*The Cape Cod Caper. ... Chivers, 1982
Death of a Voodoo Doll. Playboy, 1982 <New Or.>
Death on the Dragon's Tongue. Playboy, 1982 <Fr.>
*Exit Actors, Dying. ... Chivers, 1982

ARNOLD, WILLIAM. 1945-
China Gate. Villard, 1983; Macdonald, 1984 <1960s-1970s, Far East>

ARNOTT, HUGH
Mr. Hyde. Chapman, 1939

ARR, BILLY. See: Barry Sadler.

*ARRE, HELEN
*The Corpse by the River. <Reno>

*ARRIGHI, MEL. 1933-1986. Ref also: TM.
Alter Ego. St. Martin's, 1983; Quartet, 1984 <NYC>
Manhattan Gothic. St. Martin's, 1985 <NYC>
*Turkish White. <Istan.>

*ARTHUR, FRANK. Pseudonym of Arthur Frank Ebert, 1902-1984. Ref: not in TC2.

*ARTHUR, ROBERT. Ref: CA.
Mystery and More Mystery. Random, 1966 ss, including a Sherlockian pastiche

ASCANI, SPARKY (WILSON). 1928- Ref: CA.
Commune's Child. Tower, 1981

ASHBERY, JOHN (LAWRENCE). 1927- Ref: CA.
Three Plays. Z Press, 1978 (Plays, one criminous.)

*ASHBROOK, H(ARRIETTE CORA)
*The Murder of Steven Kester. Film: Chesterfield, 1934, as Green Eyes (scw: Andrew Moses; dir: Richard Thorpe)

ASHDOWN, OLIVIA
The Cupboard. Deane, 1960; Baker, 1960 (1-act play.)

*ASHE, ROSALIND
Dark Runner. Century, 1984

*ASHER, MIRIAM. Pseudonym of *Hester (Jane) Mundis.

ASHFORD, JANE
Cachet. GM, 1984

*ASHFORD, JEFFREY
Guilt with Honour. Collins, 1982; Walker, 1982
An Ideal Crime. Collins, 1985; Walker, 1986
The Loss of the Culion. Collins, 1981; Walker, 1981
Presumption of Guilt. Collins, 1984
A Sense of Loyalty. Collins, 1983; Walker, 1984

ASHFORTH, ALBERT. Has been on English faculties of universities in U.S. and Europe; teaches writing at Hofstra University.
Murder After the Fact. St. Martin's, 1984; Hale, 1985

ASHLEY, JACQUELINE
Secrets of the Heart. Harlequin, 1984 <Montana>

ASHTON, HENRY ALLEN
The Gordon Dock Mystery. Fleet, 1894

*ASHTON, MARK
All That Glistens. Hale, 1981
A Gilded Frame. Hale, 1981
That Infernal Triangle. Hale, 1981
When the Sky Falls. Hale, 1982

*ASIMOV, ISAAC. Ref also: TM. SC: Black Widowers, also in title marked BW below; Elijah Baley, also in titles marked EB below.
Banquets of the Black Widowers. Doubleday, 1984; Granada, 1985 ss BW
*The Caves of Steel. <NYC>
Robots and Empire. Doubleday, 1985; Granada, 1985 EB <future>
The Robots of Dawn. Doubleday, 1983; Granada, 1984 EB <future>
The Union Club Mysteries. Doubleday, 1983; Granada, 1984 ss

*ASKEW, ALICE and *CLAUDE ASKEW
*God's Clay. criminous. Silent film: Rooke, 1919 (scw & dir: Arthur Rooke). Also: First National, 1928 (scw: P. Maclean Rogers; dir: Graham Cutts)
*John Heriot's Wife. Silent film: Anglo-Hollandia, 1920 (scw & dir: B. E. Doxat-Pratt)
*Poison. criminous. Silent film: British Empire, 1916 (scw & dir: Albert Ward)
*The Shulamite. Silent film: London, 1915 (scw: Kenelm Foss; dir: George Loane Tucker). Also: Red Feather, 1916, as The Folly of Desire (scw & dir: George Loane Tucker). Also: Paramount, 1921, as Under the Lash (scw: J. E. Nash; dir: Sam Wood)

*ASKEW, CLAUDE. See: *Alice Askew.

*ASPLER, TONY. See: *Gordon Pape.

ASPRIN, ROBERT
Myth-ing Persons. Ace, 1984(?)

ASTRUP, HELEN, 1910- , and B(ERNARD) L(OUIS) JACOT (DE BOINOD). 1898-1977. Ref for Jacot: CA.
Night Has a Thousand Eyes. Macdonald, 1953. U.S. title: Oslo Intrigue. McGraw, 1954 (Novelized autobiography.) <Oslo>

*ASWAD, BETSY
  Family Passions. Dial, 1985 <Pa.>

*ASWELL, MARY LOUISE (WHITE). 1902-1984.

*ATHERTON, GERTRUDE (FRANKLIN HORN)
  *The Avalanche. Silent film: Artcraft, 1919 (scw: Ouida Bergere; dir: George Fitzmaurice)
  *Mrs. Balfame. Silent film: Powell, 1917 (scw & dir: Frank Powell)

*ATIYAH, EDWARD (SELIM)
  *The Thin Line. Film: Films de la Boetie, 1971, as Juste Avant la Nuit (Just Before Nightfall) (scw & dir: Claude Chabrol)

*ATKEY, PHILIP. 1908-1985. Pseudonym also: *Pat Merriman. Ref also: CA, TM.

*ATKINS, MEG ELIZABETH. SC: Insp. Henry Beaumont, also in title below.
  Palimpsest. Quartet, 1981; St. Martin's, 1982

ATKINSON, B. M., JR. Pseudonym: *Peter Duncan.

*ATKINSON, HUGH
  *Low Company. <Australia>
  *The Pink and the Brown. <Australia>
  *The Reckoning. ... McKay, 1972 <Australia> Film: Samson, 1978, as Weekend of Shadows (scw: Peter Yeldham; dir: Tom Jeffrey)

ATTENBOROUGH, BERNARD GEORGE. Pseudonym: James S. Rand, q.v.

*ATTIWILL, KEN(NETH)
  Reporter. Long, 1933. Film: Corfield, 1943 (scw: Maisie Sharman, Ralph Gilbert Bettinson; dir: John Harlow)
  *Sky Steward. Film: Gaumont, 1937, as Non-Stop New York (scw: Roland Pertwee, J. O. C. Orton, Kurt Siodmak, Derek Twist; dir: Robert Stevenson)

ATWOOD, MARGARET (ELEANOR). 1939-
  Ref: CA.
  Bodily Harm. Simon, 1982; Cape, 1982 <Carib.>

AUCHINCLOSS, BAYARD. Pseudonym: *Brian Negulesco.

*AUDEMARS, PIERRE. SC: Monsieur Pinaud, also in titles below.
  The Bitter Path of Death. Hale, 1982; Walker, 1983
  Gone to Her Death. Hale, 1981; Walker, 1981
  The Red Rust of Death. Hale, 1983
  A Small Slain Body. Hale, 1985

*AUDRENN, JOEL
  Chance Encounter. Mystique, 1981 (Translation of "La Dame en Rose." Paris, 1979.)

*AUGUST, JOHN. Pseudonym of Bernard Augustine DeVoto. Ref: CA.

*AUMONIER, STACY
  *Miss Bracegirdle and others. Silent film (from ss "Miss Bracegirdle Does Her Duty"): Gaumont, 1936, as Miss Bracegirdle Does Her Duty (dir: Edwin Greenwood). Sound film: London, 1936, as Miss Bracegirdle Does Her Duty (dir: Lee Grimes)
  Overheard. Heinemann, 1924; Doubleday, 1925 15 ss, a few criminous

*AUSLANDER, JOSEPH. Ref: CA.

AUSTER, PAUL. 1947- . Ref: CA.
  City of Glass. Sun and Moon, 1985 <NYC>

*AUSTIN, ALEX
  *Salt and Pepper. (Novelization of film: United Artists, 1968; scw: Michael Pertwee; dir: Richard Donner)

*AUSTIN, ANNE
  *A Wicked Woman. Film: MGM, 1934 (scw: Florence Ryerson, Zelda Sears; dir: Charles Brabin)

*AUSTIN, F(REDERICK) BRITTEN
  *On the Borderland. ss, some criminous Silent film (based on ss "Buried Treasure"): Cosmopolitan, 1921, as Buried Treasure (scw & dir: George D. Baker)

AUSTIN, RICHARD. All titles in the Guardians series. Set: future.
  Armageddon Run. Jove, 1985
  The Guardians. Jove, 1985
  Night of the Phoenix. Jove, 1985
  Thunder of Hell. Jove, 1985
  Trial by Fire. Jove, 1985

*AUSTWICK, JOHN. Ref: not in TC2.

*AVALLONE, MICHAEL. Ref also: TM. SC: Charlie Chan (following *Earl Derr Biggers, q.v.), in title marked CC.
  *A Bullet for Pretty Boy. (Novelization of film: American International, 1970; scw: Henry Rosenbaum; dir: Larry Buchanan)
  Charlie Chan and the Curse of the Dragon Queen. Pinnacle, 1981 CC (Novelization of film: American Cinema, 1980; scw: Stan Burns, David Axelrod; dir: Clive Donner)
  *Kaleidoscope. (Novelization of film: Warner, 1966; also released as The Bank Breaker; scw: Robert Carrington, Jane-Howard Carrington; dir: Jack Smight)
  *Madame X. (Novelization of film; see J. W. MacConaughy)
  *One More Time. (Novelization of film: United Artists, 1969; scw: Michael Pertwee; dir: Jerry Lewis)
  *Shock Corridor. (Novelization of film: Allied Artists, 1963; scw & dir: Samuel Fuller)

AVERELL, CLARA R.
  The Ghost's Retreat. Fitzgerald, 1927 (3-act play.)

*AVERY, ROBERT (J, JR.). ca.1911-1983. Ref: CA. All Joe Kelly titles identified.
  *A Fast Man with a Dollar. <Conn.>

AYLWARD, MARCUS. Pseudonym of Marc Alexander, 1929- . Other pseudonym: *Mark Ronson. Ref: CA. SC: Harper, in both titles.
  Harper's Folly. Barker, 1984
  Harper's Luck. Weidenfeld, 1985 <India>

BAAR, JAMES (A.). 1929- . Ref: CA.
  Great Free Enterprise Gambit. Houghton (NYC), 1980; Houghton (London), 1983

*BABBCOCK, DWIGHT V(INCENT). Ref: TM.

BABCOCK, NICHOLAS. Pseudonym of Tom Lewis, 1940- , q.v. Ref: CA.
  Billy's Army. Atheneum, 1982

BABE, THOMAS (JAMES). 1941- . Ref: CA.
  Billy Irish. Dramatists, 197? (3-act play.) <Vt.>
  A Prayer for My Daughter. French, 1977 (3-act play.)

*BABER, DOUGLAS GORDON
  My Death Is a Mockery. Heinemann, 1952. Film: Park Lane, 1952 (dir: Tony Young)

*BABSON, MARION. Pseudonym of Ruth Stenstreem. Ref also: TM.
  Bejeweled Death. Collins, 1981; Walker, 1982
  The Cruise of a Deathtime. Collins, 1983; Walker, 1984 <ship>
  Death Beside the Seaside. Collins, 1982; Walker, 1983, as Death Beside the Sea
  Death in Fashion. Collins, 1985; Walker, 1986
  Death Swap. Collins, 1984; Walker, 1985
  Death Warmed Up. Collins, 1982; Walker, 1982
  A Fool for Murder. Collins, 1983; Walker, 1984
  A Trail of Ashes. Collins, 1984; Walker, 1985 <New Eng.>
  *Unfair Exchange. ... Walker, 1986
  Weekend for Murder. Collins, 1985

*BACHELIN, ANITA
  *Mask of Death. ... Star, 1982

*BACHMAN, RICHARD. Pseudonym of *Stephen King.
  The Running Man. Signet, 1982; NEL pb, 1983 <future>
  Thinner. NAL, 1984; NEL, 1985. Also published as by Stephen King: Signet, 1985 <Conn.>

*BACHMANN, LAWRENCE P(AUL)
  -The Bitter Lake. Little, 1970; Collins, 1969 <Mid. East, hosp.>
  *The Kiss of Death. Film: MGM, 1952, as The Devil Makes Three (scw: Jerry Davis; dir: Andrew Marton)
  *The Lorelei. Film: Rank, 1959, as Whirlpool (scw: Lawrence P. Bachmann; dir: Lewis Allen)
  *The Phoenix. Film: UA, 1958, as Ten Seconds to Hell (scw: Robert Aldrich, Tedd Sherman; dir: Aldrich)

BACKER, JUNE MASTERS
  Echoes from the Past. Harvest House, 1985 <Ariz.>

*BACKHOUSE, (ENID) ELIZABETH
  *Death Came Uninvited. <Australia>

*BACKUS, JEAN LOUISE. 1914-1986.

*BAER, JILL. Pseudonym of Joan Gilbert.

BAGBEY, WILLIAM H.
  -Beyond the Wicked. Pageant, 1955

*BAGBY, GEORGE. Pseudonym of Aaron Marc Stein, 1906-1985, q.v. SC: Insp. Schmidt, also in titles below.
  The Golden Creep. Doubleday, 1982; Hale, 1982
  The Most Wanted. Doubleday, 1983; Hale, 1984 <NYC>
  A Question of Quarry. Doubleday, 1981; Hale, 1981
  Sitting Duck. Hale, 1982 (U.S. publicaton?)

*BAGLEY, DESMOND. Ref also: TM.
  Bahama Crisis. ... Summit, 1983
  *The Freedom Trap. Film: Columbia-Warner, 1973, as The Mackintosh Man (scw: Walter Hill; dir: John Huston, James Arnett)
  *The Golden Keel. <It.>
  Juggernaut. Collins, 1985 <Afr., W.>
  The Legacy. Collins, 1982 <Kenya>
  Night of Error. Collins, 1984
  Windfall. Collins, 1982; Summit, 1982 <Kenya>

BAGLEY, MICHAEL
  The Plutonium Factor. Allison, 1982; Allison (U.S.), 1985

*BAGNOLD, ENID
  *The Chalk Garden. Film: Quota, 1963 (scw: John Michael Hayes; dir: Ronald Neame)

BAILEY, E(LEANOR) M. 1937- . Born, educated, and living in Mass.
  The Quiet Murder and other stories. Vantage, 1975 ss

*BAILEY, H(ENRY) C(HRISTOPHER). Ref also: CA. See also: Alfred C. Ward.
  *Call Mr. Fortune. Dutton, 1921 (date correction)
  *Mr. Fortune Speaking. Ward, 1929 (date correction)

BAILEY, WILLIAM
  -The Powers. Putnam, 1982

*BAINBRIDGE, BERYL
  Watson's Apology. Duckworth, 1984; McGraw, 1985 <London, 1871>

*BAIRD, EDWIN. See: Anonymous.

BAKER, ARTHUR. Pseudonym of Arthur F. Giddings.
  The Short Term. Duell, 1948

BAKER, CHARLOTTE. 1910- . Ref: CA.
  House of the Roses. Dutton, 1942 <Mex. City>

BAKER, COLONEL
  Pool Ticket .025. Street, 1902 <NYC>

BAKER, F. ROBERT
  Warhead. Bantam, 1981

*BAKER, FRANK. 1908-1982.
  Stories of the Strange and Sinister. Kimber, 1983 ss

*BAKER, PETER
  Minnie Swan. Hodder, 1969 <Switz.>

*BAKER, ROBERT (MELVILLE) and *JOHN EMERSON
  *The Conspiracy. Silent film: Famous Players, 1914 (dir: Allan Dwan). Sound film: RKO, 1930, as Con-

spiracy (scw: Beulah Marie Dix; dir: Christy Cabanne)

*BAKER, W(ILLIAM ARTHUR) HOWARD. Pseudonym: *Nicola Devon, q.v. Correction: no listed books were written by Wilfred McNeilly.
*Crime Is My Business. Film: Searle, 1959, as Murder at Site Three (scw: Manning O'Brine; dir: Francis Searle)
Headcrash. Hale, 1984

BAKKER, KIT. Newspaper and magazine writer living in Ark.
Sea Treasure. Harlequin, 1985 <Miss.>

BALABAN, JOHN B. 1943- . Ref: CA.
Coming Down Again. Harcourt, 1985 <Far East>

*BALCHIN, NIGEL (MARLIN)
*Mine Own Executioner. Film: London-Harefield, 1947 (scw: Nigel Balchin; dir: Anthony Kimmins)
*The Small Back Room. Film: London Films, 1949 (scw & dir: Michael Powell, Emeric Pressburger)
*A Sort of Traitors. Film: Charter, 1960, as Suspect; released in the U.S. as The Risk (scw: Nigel Balchin, Roy Boulting, Jeffrey Dell; dir: Boulting)

*BALDERSTON, JOHN L(LOYD). 1889-1954. See: *Hamilton Deane.

BALDWIN, ALEX. Pseudonym of *William Edmund Butterworth III. Other pseudonym: Jack Dugan, q.v.
The Last Heroes. PB, 1985 <WWII>
The Secret Warriors. PB, 1985 <WWII>

BALDWIN, F. LEE
Crimes Stalk the Fan World. Entropy, 1960s (2 stories.)

BALDWIN, JOHN. 1944- . Raised in N.J.; has degrees in psychology; article writer.
Ice Pick. Morrow, 1983

*BALFOUR, HEARNDEN
*Anything Might Happen. Film: Real Art, 1934 (scw: H. Fowler Mear; dir: George A. Cooper)

*BALL, BRIAN N(EVILLE)
The Baker Street Boys. BBC, 1983 (Novelization of the TV series.)

BALL, DONNA. 1951- . Pseudonym: Rebecca Flanders, q.v.

*BALL, EUSTACE HALE
*Traffic in Souls. (Novelization of film: Imp, 1913; scw: Walter McNamara, George Loane Tucker; dir: Tucker)
*The Voice on the Wire. Silent film: Universal, 1917 (scw: J. Grubb Alexander; dir: Stuart Paton, Ben Wilson)

*BALL, JOHN (DUDLEY, JR.). Ref (revised): TC2; also: TM. SC: Jack Tallon, in *Police Chief, and in those marked JT below.
Chief Tallon and the S.O.R. Dodd, 1984 <Wash.> JT
*In the Heat of the Night. Film: UA, 1967 (scw: Stirling Silliphant; dir: Norman Jewison)
Trouble for Tallon. Doubleday, 1981; Hale, 1982 JT

BALL, PATRICIA. Pseudonym: Nan Hamilton, q.v.

BALLARD, (JOHN) FRED(ERICK). 1884- Ladies of the Jury. French, 1931 (3-act play.) <N.J.> Film: RKO, 1932 (scw: Marion Dix; dir: Lowell Sherman). Also: RKO, 1937, as We're on the Jury (scw: Franklin Coen; dir: Ben Holmes)

*BALLARD, W(ILLIS) T(ODHUNTER). Ref (revised and expanded): TC2; also: TM.
*Dealing Out Death. ... Banner, 1950s
Hollywood Troubleshooter. Popular Press, 1984 ss
*Murder Can't Stop. ... Banner, 1950s

*BALLEM, JOHN (BISHOP)
The Marigot Run. GM, 1984 <Carib.>

BALLING, L. CHRISTIAN
The Fourth Shot. Little, 1983; Gollancz, 1983 <1963>
Mallory's Gambit. Atlantic, 1985; Cape, 1986 <Berlin>

*BALLINGER, BILL (SANBORN). Ref also: TM.
*Portrait in Smoke. Film: Film Locations, 1956, as Wicked as They Come (scw: Ken Hughes, Robert Westerby, Sigmund Miller; dir: Hughes)
*Rafferty. Film from this and *The Night Watch by *Thomas Walsh, q.v.: Columbia, 1954, as Pushover (scw: Roy Huggins; dir: Richard Quine)
*The Wife of the Red-Haired Man. <NYC>

*BALMER, EDWIN. Ref also: CA.
*The Breath of Scandal. Silent film: Schulberg, 1924 (scw: Eve Unsell; dir: Louis Gasnier)
*Dangerous Business. Film: Victory, 1930, as Party Girl (scw: Monte Katterjohn, George Draney, Victor Halperin; dir: Halperin)
*That Royle Girl. Silent film: Paramount, 1925 (scw: Paul Schofield; dir: D. W. Griffith)

*BALZAC, HONORE DE
*Le Pere Goriot. Silent film: Metropolitan, 1926, as Paris at Midnight (scw: Francis Marion; dir: E. Mason Hopper)

BANATO, BURT
Doublecross Dame. 1950's.

*BANDY, (EUGENE) FRANKLIN (JR.). 1914-1987. Ref also: TM.

*BANGS, JOHN KENDRICK. Ref also: CA.

*BANKS, CAROLYN
The Girls on the Row. Crown, 1983 <Wash. D.C.>

BANKS, JOHN. Joint pseudonym with Jay Clarke and Richard Covell: Michael Slade, q.v.

BANKS, KELLEY. Pseudonym of James E. Eubank.
Ten--the Hard Way. Vantage, 1955

*BANKS, OLIVER (T.). 1941- . Ref: CA, TM. SC: Amos Hatcher, in *The Rembrandt Panel, and new title below.
The Caravaggio Obsession. Little, 1984; Gollancz, 1985 <Rome>
The Rembrandt File; see The Rembrandt Panel
*The Rembrandt Panel. British title: The Rembrandt File. Gollancz, 1984

BANNERMAN, DAVID. Pseudonym of *David (James) Hagberg, 1941- . Other pseudonyms: *Robert Pell, *Eric Ramsey. See also: Nick Carter. SC: Magic Man (Donald Briggs O'Meara), in at least those marked MM.
Call of Honor. Zebra, 1985 <S. Pac.>
The Gamov Factor. Zebra, 1983 MM <Moscow>
The Magic Man. Zebra, 1983 MM
Pipeline from Hell. Zebra, 1984 MM <Russia>

BANNISTER, JO. 1951- . Ref: CA, TM.
Striving with Gods. Hale, 1984; Doubleday, 1984

*BANNISTER, WILLIAM. Pseudonym of *William R. Gwinn.
*Countefeit Death. Lancer, 1968 (title and date correction) <Mex.>

*BANVILLE, JOHN. 1945- Ref: CA.

*BAOL, SAM
*The Man from the Diner's Club. (Novelization of film: Columbia, 1963; scw: Bill Blatty; dir: Frank Tashlin)

*BAR-ZOHAR, MICHAEL. Pseudonyms: *Michael Barak, Michael Hastings, qq.v.

BARAK, MICHAEL. Pseudonym of *Michael Bar-Zohar. Other pseudonym: Michael Hastings, q.v.
Double Cross. NAL, 1981
*The Enigma. Film: Archerwest, 1983 (scw: John Briley; dir: Jeannot Szwarc)

*BARBER, (CYRIL) ALEX (ANDER)

BARBER, FRANK DOUGLAS
The Last White Man. Allen, 1981 <Afr.>

BARBER, NOEL (JOHN LYSBERG). 1909- Ref: CA.
-A Women of Cairo. Hodder, 1984. U.S. title: Sakkara. Macmillan, 1985 <Egypt, 1940s>

BARBOUR, H. W. Pseudonym: *Jason Vaughn.

BARCLAY, ALTMAYER
The Man with the Glaring Eyes. Mellifont, 1936

BARCLAY, IAN. SC: Richard Dartley, in both titles.
The Crime Minister. Warner, 1984
Reprisal. Warner, 1985

BARCLAY, JOHN. Pseudonym of *Jack Matcha, 1919- . Other pseudonym: John Tanner, q.v.
Ask for Lois. Monarch, 1962

BARCLAY, NOEL
The Trail of the Three Lean Men. Dickson, 1932

*BARDIN, JOHN FRANKLIN. Ref also: TM.
*The Deadly Percheron. <NYC>
*The Last of Philip Banter. Film: Tesauro, 1986 (scw: Alvaro De La Huerta, Herve Hachuel; dir: Hachuel)

*BARDON, MINNA
His Best Girl. Arcadia, 1949

BARISH, STEVEN. Born and raised in N.Y.; employed at Gallaudet College for the deaf.
Reasonable Doubt. Hybar, 1985 <S.F.>

*BARKER, ALBERT (W.)
*The Diamond Hitch. (not The Diamond Fix)

BARKER, PAT. 1943- Ref: CA.
Blow Your House Down. Virago, 1984; Putnam, 1984

BARKER, WADE. House name. Titles written by Richard S. Meyers, q.v., marked #. All titles in Ninja Master series; SC: Brett Wallace.
Borderland of Hell. Warner, 1982
Death's Door. Warner, 1982 #
Dragon Rising. Warner, 1985; Futura, 1985 #
Lion's Fire. Warner, 1985 #
Million Dollar Massacre. Warner, 1982 #
Mountain of Fear. Warner, 1981 #
Only the Good Die. Warner, 1983 #
Serpent's Eye. Warner, 1985 #
The Skin Swindle. Warner, 1983
Vengeance Is His. Warner, 1981 (by *Stephen Smoke?)

BARKIN, CAROL. Joint pseudonym with Elizabeth James: Beverly Hastings, q.v.

*BARKLEY, DEANNE. 1931- . Ref: CA.

*BARLAY, STEPHEN
Cuban Confetti. H. Hamilton, 1981. U.S. title: In the Company of Spies. Summit, 1981 <1962>
The Price of Silence. H. Hamilton, 1983; H. Hamilton (U.S.), 1984
-The Ruling Passion. H. Hamilton, 1982

*BARLING, TOM
Bikini Red North. Eyre, 1981
Terminate with Prejudice. Methuen, 1982

*BARLOW, JAMES (HENRY STANLEY)
*The Burden of Proof. Film: EMI-MGM, 1971, as Villain (scw: Dick Clement, Ian La Frenais; dir: Michael Tuchner)
*Term of Trial. Film: Remus, 1962 (scw & dir: Peter Glenville)

BARNARD, CHRISTIAAN (NEETHLING), 1922- , and SIEGFRIED STANDER, 1935- . Ref (both authors): CA.
The Faith. Hutchinson, 1984

BARNARD, JACK
Mumbo-Jumbo. French, 1940 (3-act play.)

BARNARD, LESLIE T. Pseudonym: Jeff
    Stratton, q.v. See also: *Jeff
    Bogar, Greg Marlowe.
    The Interrupted Wedding. Boardman,
    1951
BARNARD, MARJORIE. Joint pseudonym with
    Flora Eldershaw: M. Barnard Elder-
    shaw. See: J. L. Rankin.
*BARNARD, ROBERT. Ref also: TC2, TM.
    SC: Insp. Perry Trethowan = PT.
    The Case of the Missing Bronte; see
        The Missing Bronte
    A Corpse in a Gilded Cage. Collins,
        1984; Scribner, 1984
    Death and the Princess. Collins,
        1982; Scribner, 1982   PT
    Death by Sheer Torture; see Sheer
        Torture
    Death of a Perfect Mother; see
        Mother's Boys
    The Disposal of the Living. Collins,
        1985. U.S. title: Fete Fatale.
        Scribner, 1985
    Fete Fatale; see The Disposal of the
        Living
    Little Victims. Collins, 1983. U.S.
        title: School for Murder. Scribner,
        1984   <acad.>
    The Missing Bronte. Collins, 1983.
        U.S. title: The Case of the Missing
        Bronte. Scribner, 1983   PT
    Mother's Boys. Collins, 1981. U.S.
        title: Death of a Perfect Mother.
        Scribner, 1981
    Out of the Blackout. Collins, 1985;
        Scribner, 1985
    School for Murder; see Little Victims
    Sheer Torture. Collins, 1981. U.S.
        title: Death by Sheer Torture.
        Scribner, 1982   PT
BARNATO, BART
    Dames Play Dumb. Self, 195?
    Rackets and Dames. Self, 195?
BARNES, JULIAN. 1946-   . Pseudonym:
    *Dan Kavanagh, q.v.
BARNES, LINDA J. Ref: TM. SC: Michael
    Spraggue, in all titles.
    Bitter Finish. St. Martin's, 1983;
        Severn, 1983   <Calif.>
    Blood Will Have Blood. Avon, 1982
    Dead Heat. St. Martin's, 1984;
        Severn, 1984   <Boston>
*BARNES, MICHAEL (GORELL). See: *Max
    Clinton, *Hyman Zore.
BARNES, STEVEN. See: *Larry Niven.
*BARNETT, JAMES. SC: Supt. Owen Smith,
    also in titles below.
    Diminished Responsibility. Secker,
        1984; Secker (U.S.), 1986
    The Firing Squad. Secker, 1981; Mor-
        row, 1981
    Marked for Destruction. Secker, 1982;
        Secker (U.S.), 1984
*BARONE, MIKE
    *Crazy Joe. (Novelization of film:
        Bright-Persky, 1973; scw: Lewis
        John Carlino; dir: Carlo Lizzani)
*BARONI, MAX
    Chicago Jungle. ca.1960
    I Hate Thee. Spencer, 1954
    This Time for Keeps. Spencer, 1953
*BARR, ROBERT. 1850-1912. Ref also:
    TC2.
BARRE, JEAN. Pseudonym: Lee Lindsay,
    q.v.
*BARRETT, FRANK
    *The Woman of the Iron Bracelets.
        Silent film: Progress, 1920 (scw
        & dir: Sidney Morgan)
*BARRETT, MAYE
    The Lady of Stantonwyck. Zebra, 1981
*BARRETT, MICHAEL (JOHN)
    *Appointment in Zahrein. Film: Para-
        mount, 1961, as Escape from Zahrein
        (scw: Robin Estridge; dir: Ronald
        Neame)
    *The Heroes of Yuca. Film: Paramount,
        1968, as The Invincible Six (ex-
        istence of film not confirmed)
    *The Reward. Film: TCF, 1965 (scw:
        Serge Bourguignon, Oscar Millard;
        dir: Bourguignon)
    *Stranger in Galah.   <Australia>

*BARRETT, SUSAN (MARY). 1938-   Ref:
    CA.
*BARRETT, WILLIAM E(DMUND). 1900-1986.
*BARRINGER, MICHAEL
    *Inquest. Film: Majestic, 1931 (scw:
        Michael Barringer; dir: G. B. Sam-
        uelson). Also: Charter, 1939 (scw:
        Francis Miller; dir: Roy Boulting)
*BARRINGTON, PAMELA. Film from uniden-
    tified novel: Major, 1957, as The
    Big Chance (scw & dir: Peter
    Graham Scott)
    *Account Rendered. Film: Major, 1957
        (scw: Barbara S. Harper; dir: Peter
        Graham Scott)
BARRIS, CHUCK. 1929-   . Ref: CA.
    Confessions of a Dangerous Mind. St.
        Martin's, 1984; Futura, 1985
*BARROLL, CLARE
    The Shadow Man. Avon, 1984 <Haw.>
*BARRON, ELWYN (ALFRED)
    *Marcel Levignet. Silent film: Para-
        mount, 1918, as The House of Si-
        lence (scw: Margaret Turnbull;
        dir: Donald Crisp)
*BARRON, HUGH. Pseudonym of *Burt
    Hirschfeld, q.v.
    The Big Score. Pyramid, 1969.
        Reprinted as by Burt Hirschfeld:
        Dell, 1984
    *Doll Baby. ... Pyramid, 1967.
        Reprinted as by Burt Hirschfeld:
        Dell, 1985
    *Fun City. ... Pyramid, 1968.
        Reprinted as by Burt Hirschfeld:
        Dell, 1985
    *The Goddess Game. ... Pyramid, 1970.
        Reprinted as by Burt Hirschfeld:
        Dell, 1985
    *The Love Thing. ... Pyramid, 1970.
        Reprinted as by Burt Hirschfeld:
        Dell, 1985
    *The Mercenary. ... Pyramid, 1969.
        Reprinted as by Burt Hirschfeld:
        Dell, 1985
*BARRY, BOB
    *Murder Among Friends. <NYC>
*BARRY, JOE. Pseudonym of Joe Barry
    Lake, 1909-
*BARRY, MIKE. Pseudonym of *Barry
    (Norman) Malzberg. Ref also: TC2,
    TM.
BARSTOW, PHYLLIS
    Dolphin Shore. Century, 1984
    Glacier Run. Century, 1983 <Switz.>
    Night Is for Hunting. Century, 1982
        <Kenya>
BART, SHELDON
    Ruby Sweetwater and the Ringo Kid.
        McGraw, 1981   <NYC, 1901>
*BARTH, RICHARD. Ref also: TM. SC:
    Margaret Binton, in *The Rag Bag
    Clan, and titles below.
    The Condo Kill. Scribner, 1985. Bri-
        tish title: The Co-Op Kill. Gol-
        lancz, 1986   <NYC>
    The Co-Op Kill; see The Condo Kill
    One Dollar Death. Dial, 1982; Gol-
        lancz, 1985   <NYC>
    *The Rag Bag Clan. ... Gollancz, 1983
    A Ragged Plot. Dial, 1981; Gollancz,
        1984   <NYC>
*BARTHOLOMEW, CECILIA
    *Second Sight. ... Hale, 1981. Re-
        printed as: The Dark Is Mine.
        Methuen pb, 1982
*BARTLETT, VERNON. 1894-1983.
BARTON, BILLY. 1927-   . Internation-
    ally famous circus performer as a
    trapeze artist.
    Past Murder Imperfect. Bilbar, 1981
BARTON, DONALD R(ICHMOND). 1913-
    -Once in Aleppo. Scribner, 1955;
        Museum, 1957   <Syr.>
*BARTON, ROBERT EUSTACE. Ref: CA.
*BARTRAM, GEORGE
    The Sunset Gun. Pinnacle, 1983;
        Arrow, 1986
    Under the Freeze. Pinnacle, 1984

*BASILE, GLORIA VITANZA
    Eye of the Eagle. Pinnacle, 1983
        <2000 A.D.>
    The Jackal Helix. Pinnacle, 1984
        <2000 A.D.>
    The Sting of the Scorpion. Pinnacle,
        1984   <future>
*BASS, RONALD (JAY)
    The Emerald Illusion. Morrow, 1984;
        Collins, 1985 <Paris, 1944> Film:
        MGM, 1985, as Code Name: Emerald
        (scw: Ronald Bass; dir: Jonathan
        Sanger)
    Lime's Crisis. Morrow, 1982   <1997>
BASSING, EILEEN (JOHNSTON). 1908-
    Home Before Dark. Random, 1957;
        Longmans, 1957. Film: Warner,
        1958 (scw: Eileen Bassing, Robert
        Bassing; dir: Mervy LeRoy)
*BATSON, GEORGE (DONALD)
    *Design for Murder. <NYC>
    *Gift of Murder! <Eng.>
    *The House on the Cliff.
    *Strange Boarders. <Mass.>
BATTIN, B(RINTON) W(ARNER). 1941-
    Ref: CA.
    Angel of Light. GM, 1983
    The Boogey Man. GM, 1984   <Denver>
    Programmed for Terror. GM, 1985
        <Kan. City>
*BAWDEN, NINA. Ref: not in TC2.
    *The Solitary Child. Film: Beacons-
        field, 1958 (scw: Robert Dunbar;
        dir: Gerald Thomas)
*BAX, ROGER
    *Came the Dawn. Film: MGM, 1953, as
        Never Let Me Go (scw: Ronald Mil-
        lar, George Froeschel; dir: Delmer
        Daves)
*BAXT, GEORGE
    The Dorothy Parker Murder Case. St.
        Martin's, 1984; Collins, 1985
        <NYC, 1920s>
    Process of Elimination. St. Martin's,
        1984
*BAXTER, JOHN
    Black Yacht. Jove, 1983
BAXTER, TERRY
    Hailstone. Zebra, 1984 <Wash. D.C.>
BAXTER, YOUNG. Pseudonym of W. I.
    James.
    Old Mortality, King of Detectives.
        Street, 1888
BAY, AUSTIN. Born in Houston, living in
    NYC; co-author of a book and author
    of over 70 articles; working on
    Ph.D. in English literature at
    Columbia Univ.
    The Coyote Cried Twice. Arbor, 1985
        <Tex.>
*BAYER, OLIVER WELD
    *Paper Chase. Film: MGM, 1945, as
        Dangerous Partners (scw: Marion
        Parsonnet; dir: Edward L. Cahn)
*BAYER, WILLIAM. Ref also: TM.
    Peregrine. Congdon, 1981; Severn,
        1982   <NYC>
    Switch. Linden, 1984; Joseph, 1985
        <NYC>
BAYLEY, BARRINGTON J(OHN). 1937-   .
    The Knights of the Limits. Allison,
        1978   ss, one criminous <future>
*BAYNE, SPENCER. Joint pseudonym of
    Floyd Albert Spencer, 1899-1978,
    and Paula Teresa Bayne Spencer,
    1907-   . FAS was born in Iowa,
    graduate of Univ. of Colo., Ph.D.
    from Univ. of Chicago; professor
    of Greek and classics at Ohio Wes-
    leyan Univ., Univ. of Ill., Roanoke
    College, New York Univ., Queens
    College. PTBS was born in Ill.;
    author.
*BAYNES, JACK. Pseudonym of Bertram
    B. Fowler.
BEACH, REX
    The Crimson Gardenia. Harper, 1916;
        Hodder, 1916 ss Silent film
        (based on title story): Goldwyn,
        1919 (dir: Reginald Barker)
BEAIRD, DICK
    Sweet Revenge. Zebra, 1982

*BEAL, M(ARY) F.
  *Angel Dance. <S.F.>

*BEAR, DAVID. 1949-   . Ref: CA.

*BEARDMORE, GEORGE (CEDRIC)
  *A Thousand Witnesses. <Fr.>

BEARDSLEY, CHARLES (NOEL). 1914-
  Ref: CA.
  Baksheesh and Roses. Mayflower, 1968

BEATON, ALLEN
  A Miser Is Murdered. Currawong
    (Syd.), 1945

BEATON, M. C. Pseudonym of Marion
  Chesney, 1936-   . Other pseudonym: Jennie Tremaine, q.v. Ref:
  CA.
  Death of a Gossip. St. Martin's,
    1985 <Scot.>

*BEATTIE, TASMAN
  Diamonds. Methuen, 1982

*BEATTY, ELIZABETH
  River in the Sun. Avalon, 1958
    <Fla.>

*BEATY, (ARTHUR) DAVID
  *Cone of Silence. Film: Baring,
    1960; released in U.S. as Trouble
    in the Sky (scw: Robert Westerby,
    Jeffrey Dell; dir: Charles Frend)

BEAVEN, E. W.
  Tales of the Divining Rod. Stockwell, 1899 ss, 1 or 2 criminous

BECK, K. K. Pseudonym of Kathrine
  Marris, who lives in Seattle, is
  regional vice president of
  Mystery Writers of America.
  Death in a Deck Chair. Walker, 1984
    <ship, 1927>

BECK, L(ILY MORESBY) ADAMS.   -1931.
  -The Openers of the Gate. Cosmopolitan, 1930 ss, some criminous

*BECK, ROBERT. Pseudonym: Iceberg
  Slim, q.v.

*BECKE, (GEORGE) LOUIS
  *Tom Gerrard. <Australia>

*BECKER, STEPHEN (DAVID). Ref also: TM.
  -The Blue-Eyed Shan. Random, 1982;
    Collins, 1982   <Burma>
  The Chinese Bandit. Random, 1975;
    Chatto, 1976   <China>
  *A Covenant with Death. Film: Warner,
    1967 (scw: Larry Marcus, Saul
    Levitt; dir: Lamont Johnson)
  *Juice.   <Fla.>

BECKNER, MORTON
  Money Plays. Simon, 1981 <Las Vegas>

BEDFORD, JESSIE. Pseudonym: Elizabeth
  Godfrey, q.v.

*BEDFORD, JOHN. Pseudonym of David
  Wiltshire.
  Moment in Time. Hale, 1983
  The Nemesis Concerto. Hale, 1982
  -The Titron Madness. Hale, 1984

BEDFORD, RUTH. See: J. L. Rankin.

BEE, (JOHN) DAVID (ASHFORD). 1931-
  Ref: CA.
  Our Fatal Shadows. Bles, 1964. U.S.
    title: Curse of Magira. Harper,
    1965 <Afr.>

BEECHCROFT, WILLIAM. Pseudonym of
  William Finn Hallstead, 1924-
  Ref: CA, TM.
  Image of Evil. Dodd, 1985 <Md.>
  Position of Ultimate Trust. Dodd,
    1981; Hale, 1982 <Fla.>

*BEECHING, JACK
  Death of a Terrorist. Constable, 1981

*BEEDING, FRANCIS. Ref also: TM.
  *The House of Dr. Edwardes. Film: UA,
    1945, as Spellbound (scw: Ben
    Hecht; dir: Alfred Hitchcock)
  *The Norwich Victims. Film: British
    National, 1939, as Dead Men Tell No
    Tales (scw: Walter Summers, Stafford Dickins, Doreen Montgomery,
    Emlyn Williams; dir: David
    Macdonald)

BEEK, JAMES R.
  Bradford's Trials. Carlton, 1969
    <Mich.>

BEERE, PETER
  The Crucifixion Squad. Arrow, 1984
  Urban Prey. Arrow, 1984

*BEESTON, L. J.
  *Every Night About Half-Past Eight.
    ss, mostly criminous

*BEEVOR, ANTHONY
  The Faustian Pact. Cape, 1983; Cape
    (U.S.), 1984
  For Reasons of State. Cape, 1981;
    Cape (U.S.), 1983

BEGG, KEN
  The Anvil Agreement. Pluto, 1985

*BEHM, MARC
  *The Eye of the Beholder. ... Zomba,
    1983. Film: Telema, 1983, as
    Mortelle Randonee (Deadly Circuit)
    (scw: Michel Audiard, Jacques
    Audiard; dir: Claude Miller)

*BEHN, NOEL
  *Big Stick-Up at Brink's! Film: Universal, 1978, as The Brink's Job
    (scw: Walon Green; dir: William
    Friedkin)
  *The Kremlin Letter. Film: TCF, 1969
    (scw: John Huston, Gladys Hill;
    dir: Huston)
  Seven Silent Men. Arbor, 1984; Pan,
    1984 <Mo., 1971>

*BEHREND, ARTHUR
  *The House of the Spaniard. Film:
    IPF, 1936 (scw: Basil Mason; dir:
    Reginald Denham)

BEILKE, EVAN A. 1924-
  The Big Steal. Vantage, 1954

*BELL, J(OHN) J(OY)
  Thread O'Scarlet. Gowans, 1923 (1-
    act play.) Film: Gaumont, 1930
    (scw: Ralph Gilbert Bettinson;
    dir: Peter Godfrey)

*BELL, JAY. Has been a sailor,
  steeplejack, bartender, actor,
  and commercial fisherman.

*BELL, JOSEPHINE. Ref also: TM. SC:
  Dr. David Wintringham, not in
  *Trouble at Wrekin Farm; Insp.
  Steven Mitchell, also in *Death
  on the Borough Council.
  *The Fennister Affair. <ship>
  A Deadly Place to Stay; see The
    Innocent
  The Innocent. Hodder, 1983. U.S.
    title: A Deadly Place to Stay.
    Walker, 1983

BELL, JOYCE. 1920-   . Ref: CA.
  Farmhouse by the Sea. Hale, 1972
  Garden of the Sun. Hale, 1971

BELL, MADISON SMARTT. 1957-   . Ref:
  CA.
  Waiting for the End of the World.
    Ticknor, 1985; Chatto, 1985 <NYC>
  The Washington Square Ensemble.
    Viking, 1983; Deutsch, 1983 <NYC>

BELL, NEAL
  Operation Midnight Climax. Dramatists, 1982 (1-act play.)
  Two Small Bodies. Dramatists, 1980
    (2-act play.)

BELL, QUENTIN (CLAUDIAN STEPHEN).
  1910-   . Ref: CA.
  The Brandon Papers. Chatto, 1985;
    Harcourt, 1985

*BELLAH, JAMES
  Imperial Express. Jove, 1982
    <Mex., 1937>

*BELLAIRS, GEORGE. Ref: not in TC2.
  *Close All Roads to Sospel. Gifford,
    1976 (date correction)
  *Corpses in Enderby.
    (title correction)

BELLAND, F. W.
  Fleshwound. Jove, 1981

*BELLEM, ROBERT LESLIE. Ref (revised):
  TC2; also: TM.
  Dan Turner, Hollywood Detective.
    Popular Press, 1983 ss <L.A.>

*BELLOC, (JOSEPH) HILAIRE (PIERRE
  RENE). Ref also: CA.

BELMONT, ELEANOR ROBSON, 1879-
  and *HARRIET FORD, q.v.
  In the Next Room. French, 1925 (3-
    act play based on *The Mystery of
    the Boule Cabinet, by *Burton
    Stevenson, q.v.) Film (partially
    based on this): First National,
    1930 (scw: James A. Starr; dir:
    Edward Cline)

BELSKY, DICK. City editor of New York
  Post.
  One for the Money. Academy Chicago,
    1985 <NYC>

BENATAR, STEPHEN (ROYCE). 1937-
  Ref: CA.
  -When I Was Otherwise. Bodley, 1983;
    St. Martin's, 1984

*BENCHLEY, NATHANIEL (GODDARD)
  *The Hunter's Moon. <New Eng.>
  *The Off-Islanders. Film: UA, 1966,
    as The Russians Are Coming, The
    Russians Are Coming (scw: William
    Rose; dir: Norman Jewison)
  *Sail a Crooked Ship. Film: Columbia,
    1961 (scw: Ruth Brooks Flippen,
    Bruce Geller; dir: Irving Brecher)

*BENEDICTUS, DAVID
  Who Killed the Prince Consort. Macmillan (London), 1982

BENEICH, DENIS. See: Theirry Breton.

BENFIELD, DEREK. 1926-   . Ref: CA.
  In for the Kill. French, 1981
    (Play.)
  Murder for the Asking. Evans, 1967
    (3-act play.)

BENFORD, TIMOTHY B(ARTHOLOMEW).
  1941-   . Ref: CA.
  Hitler's Daughter. Pinnacle, 1983
    <Wash. D.C.>

BENJAMIN, PAUL
  Squeeze Play. Avon, 1984 <NYC>

*BENNETT, ALFRED GORDON
  -The Forest of Fear. Unwin, 1924;
    Macaulay, 1924

*BENNETT, (ENOCH) ARNOLD. Ref also:
  BM, CA.
  *The Grand Babylon Hotel. Silent film:
    Hepworth, 1916 (dir: Frank Wilson)

*BENNETT, CHARLES
  *Blackmail. Film: British International, 1929 (scw: Alfred Hitchcock,
    Benn W. Levy, Charles Bennett,
    Garnett Weston; dir: Hitchcock)
  *The Last Hour. Film: Nettlefold, 1930
    (scw: H. Fowler Mear; dir: Walter
    Forde)

*BENNETT, DOROTHEA
  The Greek Girl. Hale, 1984
  *The Jigsaw Man. Film: Fisz, 1984
    (scw: Jo Eisinger; dir: Terence
    Young)

*BENNETT, DOROTHY
  *The Carrion Crows.   <W.I.>

BENNETT, F(RANCIS) I.
  -Glowing Emeralds. Wohlers, 1920

*BENNETT, GEOFFREY MARTIN. 1909-1983.

BENNETT, J(OHN) M(cGREW). Raised in
  NYC, graduate of Columbia Univ.,
  living in S.F.
  A Local Matter. Walker, 1985
    <Eng., 1914>

*BENNETT, JACK. Born in S. Afr.; reporter and newspaper editor; living
  in H. Kong in 1960s.
  *Dragon.   <H. Kong>
  *Ocean Road.   <Afr., E.>

*BENNETT, JAMES W(ILLIAM)
  Plum Blossoms and Blue Incense, with
    Soong Kwen-Ling. Commercial, 1926
    ss, some criminous

*BENNETT, JAY
  *Catacombs. Film: Parroch, 1964;
    released in U.S. as The Woman Who
    Wouldn't Die (scw: Dan Mainwaring;
    dir: Gordon Hessler)

BENNETT, R(ICHARD) A(LAN)
  Death Called at Night. Hale, 1983
  Death of a Dreamer. Hale, 1985
  Reason to Murder. Hale, 1984
  A Short Walk to Death. Hale, 1981
  Silence of Guilt. Hale, 1981

BENNETT, ROBERT D(ONALD). 1947-
 Ref: CA.
 Sector 12. GM, 1984 <Can.>

*BENNETTS, PAMELA
 Lucy's Cottage. Hale, 1981; St. Martin's, 1981, as by Margaret James

*BENNEY, MARK
 Low Company. Davies, 1936. U.S. title: Angels in Undress. Random, 1937

*BENSEN, D(ONALD) R.
 Irene, Good Night. Targ, 1982 (Sherlock Holmes)

*BENSON, BEN(JAMIN). Ref also: CA.
 *The Girl in the Cage. Film: Universal International, 1955, as Running Wild (scw: Leo Townsend; dir: Abner Biberman)

*BENSON, CRAIG
 Corpses Don't Kill. Gray, 195? <Chi.>

*BENSON, E(DWARD) F(REDERIC). Ref also: CA; not in TC2.
 *The Countess of Lowndes Square. ss, two criminous
 *The Room in the Tower and other stories. Film (from two ss, "The Room in the Tower" and "The Bus Conductor"): Ealing, 1945, as Dead of Night (scw: Angus MacPhail, John Baines, T. E. B. Clarke; dir: Basil Dearden)

*BENSON, EUGENE P(ATRICK). Born in Ireland, living in Canada since 1954; poet, essayist, playwright, opera librettist; professor of English.
 *The Bulls of Ronda. ... Methuen (U.S.), 1976 <Sp.>

*BENSON, O. G.
 *Cain's Woman. Reprinted as: Cain's Wife. Perennial, 1985

BENTHAM, JOSEPHINE. Pseudonym: *Serena Mayfield.

BENTINE, MICHAEL
 Smith and Son, Removers. Robson, 1981

*BENTLEY, E(DMUND) C(LERIHEW). Ref also: CA, TM.
 *Trent's Last Case. Silent film: Broadwest, 1920 (scw: P. L. Mannock; dir: Richard Garrick). Also (with partial sound): Fox, 1929 (scw: Scott Darling; dir: Howard Hawks). Sound film: British Lion, 1952 (scw: Pamela Wilcox Bower; dir: Herbert Wilcox)

*BENTLEY, JOHN
 *Rendezvous with Death. Film: WB-FN, 1943, as The Night Invader (scw: Brock Williams, Edward Dryhurst, Roland Pertwee; dir: Herbert Mason)

*BENTLEY, NICOLAS (CLERIHEW). Ref: not in TC2.
 *The Floating Dutchman. Film: Merton Park, 1953 (scw & dir: Vernon Sewell)
 *Third Party Risk. Film: Hammer, 1955; released in the U.S. as The Deadly Game (scw & dir: Daniel Birt)

*BENTLEY, PHYLLIS (ELEANOR). Ref: not in TC2.

BENTLEY, WILLIAM. Pseudonym: *John P. Radford.

BENTON, DICK
 Coffins Come All Sizes. Scion, 1952

BENTON, KENNETH (CARTER). SC: Peter Craig, also in *A Single Monstrous Act.

*BERCKMAN, EVELYN (DOMINICA)
 *The Blind Villain. <Phil.>
 *A Case in Nullity. Also published as: A Hidden Malice. Belmont, 19??
 *Do You Know This Voice? Film: British Lion, 19?? (existence of film not confirmed)
 *A Finger to Her Lips. <Ger., 1700s>

*BERCOVICI, ERIC
 So Little Cause for Caroline. Atheneum, 1981 <Calif.>

*BERESFORD, J(OHN) D(AVYS). Ref also: CA.

BERGER, PHIL. 1942- . Ref: CA.
 Deadly Kisses. Charter, 1984 <L.A.>

*BERGER, THOMAS (LOUIS). SC: Russel Wren, in *Who Killed Teddy Villanova?, and in title below.
 Nowhere. Delacorte, 1985; Methuen, 1986

BERGER, WALTER M.
 The Stroke of Twelve. Baker's, 1947 (Play.)

*BERGMAN, ANDREW. Ref: BM; not in TC2.

*BERKELEY, ANTHONY. Ref also: TM.
 *Trial and Error. Film: Warner, 1941, as Flight from Destiny (scw: Barry Trivers; dir: Vincent Sherman)

BERKELEY, REGINALD (CHEYNE). 1890-
 See: (John Gilbert) Bohun Lynch, 1884-

*BERLINER, ROSS. Lives in Balt.
 Hiding Places. Signet, 1985 <Balt., hosp.>

*BERNANOS, GEORGES
 *A Crime. Film: Solaris, 1984, as Un Delitto (A Crime) (scw: Vittorio Bonicelli; dir: Salvatore Nocita)

BERNE, KARIN. Joint pseudonym of Sue Bernell and Michaela Karni, two authors of Victorian romances, magazine articles, TV scripts and screenplays; living in Albuq. SC: Ellie Gordon, in both titles.
 Bare Acquaintances. Popular Library, 1985 <Calif.>
 Shock Value. Popular Library, 1985 <Calif.>

*BERNEDE, A(RTHUR)
 *The Haunted House. (Translation of "La Maison Hautee". Paris, 1928.)
 *The Mystery of the Louvre. (Translation of "Belphegor: Le Fantome Noir". Paris, 1927.)

BERNELL, SUE. Joint pseudonym with Michaela Karni: Karin Berne, q.v.

*BERRIDGE, ELIZABETH
 *Across the Common. Also published as: The Violent Past. Lancer, 1968

*BERROW, (CYRIL) NORMAN. Ref: TM.

BERT, CLAUDETTE
 A Touch of Terror. Mystique, 1981 (Translation of "Un Parfum d'Aventure." Paris, 1978.)

BERTIE, C. H. See: J. L. Rankin.

*BESSIE, ALVAH (CECIL). 1904-1985.
 *Bread and a Stone. Film: New World, 1986, as Hard Traveling (scw & dir: Dan Bessie)

BEST, RAYLEIGH BRETON AMIS. Pseudonym: Breton Amis, q.v.

*BESTER, ALFRED
 The Stars My Destination. Signet, 1957. British title: Tiger! Tiger! Sidgwick, 1956

*BETTAUER, HUGO
 *Viennese Love. Silent film: Sotar, 1925, as Die Freudlose Gasse (Joyless Street) (scw: Willy Haas; dir: G. L. Pabst). Sound film: Films Vog, 1938, as La Rue Sans Joie (Street Without Joy) (dir: Andre Hugon)

BETTS, DORIS (WAUGH). 1932- . Ref: CA.
 Heading West. Knopf, 1981

*BEYNON, JANE
 *Cypress Man. <L.A.>

*BEZZERIDES, A(LBERT) I(SAAC)
 Long Haul. Carrick, 1938; Cape, 1938. Film: Warner, 1940, as They Drive by Night; released in Britain as The Road to Frisco (scw: Jerry Wald, Richard Macaulay; dir: Raoul Walsh)
 *Thieves Market. Film: TCF, 1949, as Thieves' Highway (scw: A. I. Bezzerides; dir: Jules Dassin)

*BICKERS, RICHARD (LESLIE) TOWNSHEND
 Volunteers for Danger. Brown, 1960

*BICKERTON, DEREK
 *Payroll. Film: Lynx, 1961 (scw: George Baxt; dir: Sidney Hayers)

*BICKHAM, JACK
 Ariel. St. Martin's, 1984; Severn, 1985

BICKNELL, ARTHUR
 Moose Murders. French, 1984 (2-act play.)

BIDDLE, COLIN
 Deadly Misunderstanding. Hale, 1983

BIEDERMAN, MARCIA. 1949- . Raised in Conn., there a business editor of a newspaper chain; has degrees from Bryn Mawr College and San Francisco Univ.
 The Makeover. Academy Chicago, 1984 <S.F.>

BIEDERSTADT, LYNN
 The Eye of the Mind. Signet, 1982

BIGELOW, OTIS
 The Peacock Season. Dramatists, 1971 (3-act play.) <L.I.>

*BIGGERS, EARL DERR. Ref also: CA, TM. See also: *Michael Avallone.
 *The Agony Column. Silent film: Vitagraph, 1918, as The Blind Adventure (scw: George H. Plympton; dir: Wesley Ruggles). Also: Warner, 1926 (scw: Edward T. Lowe, Jr.; dir: Roy del Ruth). Sound film: Warner, 1930, as The Second Floor Mystery (scw: Joseph Jackson; dir: Roy del Ruth). Also: Warner, 1941, as Passage from Hong Kong (scw: Fred Niblo, Jr.; dir: D. Ross Lederman)
 *Behind That Curtain. Film: Fox, 1929 (scw: Sonya Levien, Clarke Silvernail; dir: Irving Cummings)
 *The Black Camel. Film: TCF, 1931 (scw: Barry Connors, Philip Klein; dir: Hamilton MacFadden)
 *Charlie Chan Carries On. Film: TCF, 1931 (scw: Philip Klein, Barry Connors; dir: Hamilton MacFadden). Also: TCF, 1940, as Charlie Chan's Murder Cruise (scw: Robertson White, Lester Ziffren; dir: Eugene Forde)
 *The Chinese Parrot. Silent film: Jewel, 1927 (scw: J. Grubb Alexander; dir: Paul Leni). Sound film: TCF, 1934, as Charlie Chan's Courage (scw: Seton I. Miller; dir: George Hadden)
 *Earl Derr Biggers Tells Ten Stories. Film (from ss, "Idle Hands"): Warner, 1931, as The Millionaire (scw: Julien Josephson, Booth Tarkington; dir: John Adolfi). Also: Warner, 1947, as That Way with Women (scw: Leo Townsend; dir: Frederick de Cordova)
 *Fifty Candles. Silent film: Willat, 1921 (dir: Irvin V. Willat)
 *The House Without a Key. Film: TCF, 1933, as Charlie Chan's Greatest Case (scw: Lester Cole, Marion Orth; dir: Hamilton MacFadden).
 *Inside the Lines. Silent film: World, 1918 (scw: Monte M. Katterjohn; dir: David M. Hartford). Sound film: RKO, 1930 (scw: Ewart Adamson, John Farrow; dir: Roy J. Pomeroy)
 *Love Insurance. Silent film: Paramount, 1920 (scw: Marion Fairfax; dir: Donald Crisp). Also: Universal, 1924, as The Reckless Age (scw: Rex Taylor; dir: Harry Pollard). Sound film: Universal, 1940, as One Night in the Tropics (scw: Gertrude Purcell, Charles Grayson; dir: A. Edward Sutherland)
 *Seven Keys to Baldpate. Silent film: Artcraft, 1917 (scw: George M. Cohen, Hugh Ford; dir: Ford). Also: Famous Players, 1925 (scw: Frank Griffin, Wade Boteler; dir: Fred Newmeyer). Sound film: RKO, 1930 (scw: Jane Murfin; dir: Reginald Barker). Also: RKO, 1935 (scw: Wallace Smith, Anthony Veiller; dir: William Hamilton, Edward Killy). Also: RKO, 1947 (scw: Lee Loeb; dir: Lew Landers). Also: Cannon, 1982, as House of the Long Shadows (scw: Michael Arm-

strong; dir: Peter Walker)
BILIR, KIM. Pseudonym of Arthur
 Hodgkin Scaife.
 Three Letters of Credit and other
 stories. Province Pub. Co., 1894
 ss, title story criminous

*BINDLOSS, HAROLD (EDWARD)
 -His One Talent. Ward, 1916.
 U.S. title: Brandon of the Engin-
 eers. Stokes, 1917 <S. Am.>

*BINGHAM, JOHN (MICHAEL WARD). SC:
 Supt. "Badger" Brock, in at least
 those marked BB.
 Brock. Gollancz, 1981 BB
 Brock and the Defector. Gollancz,
 1982; Doubleday, 1982 BB
 *A Fragment of Fear. Film: Columbia,
 1970 (scw: Paul Dehn; dir: Richard
 C. Sarafian)

BINGHAM, STELLA
 Charters and Caldicott. BBC, 1985
 (Novelization of the BBC TV
 serial.)

BINGLEY, MARGARET
 Children of the Night. Piatkus, 1985
 Piatkus, 1985
 The Devil's Child. Piatkus, 1983
 -Such Good Neighbours. Piatkus, 1984
 The Waiting Darkness. Piatkus, 1984

*BINKLEY, ANNE. Pseudonym of Anne Bink-
 ley Rand. Ref: CA.

BINYON, T(HOMAS) J(OHN). 1936-
 Ref: CA.
 Swan Song. H. Hamilton, 1982; Dial,
 1984 <Moscow, 1970s>

BIOY-CESARES, ADOLFO. See: *Jorge Luis
 Borges, 1899-1986.

BIRACREE, TOM
 The Red Berets. Pinnacle, 1983 <NYC>
 The Torch. Jove, 1983 <NYC>

*BIRCH, BRUCE
 *Subway in the Sky. (Novelization of
 film: Orbit, 1958; scw: Jack
 Andrews; dir: Muriel Box)

BIRCH, P. R. G.
 The Dead Collection. Hale, 1985

*BIRD, AL. Joint pseudonym of *Phillip
 Finch, q.v., and Leo N. Mandel.

*BIRD, MICHAEL J.
 *The Aphrodite Inheritance. (Noveli-
 zation of TV serial.) <Cyprus>
 Maelstrom. BBC, 1985 (Novelization
 of BBC TV serial.)

BIRD, SARAH McCABE. 1949-   Ref:
 CA.
 Do Evil Cheerfully. Avon, 1983
 <Texas>

BIRD, VERONICA. 1932-   . Ref: CA.
 Pressing Problems. Piatkus, 1982
 Wolf in Sheep's Clothing. Piatkus,
 1984

BIRDWELL, RUSSELL (JUAREZ). 1903-1977.
 Ref: CA.
 -I Ring Doorbells. Messner, 1939.
 Film: PRC, 1946 (scw: Dick Irving
 Hyland; dir: Frank Strayer)

BIRKBY, CAREL. See: *Charles Keary.

*BIRMINGHAM, GEORGE A.
 -Found Money.

*BIRMINGHAM, MAISIE. SC: Kate Weather-
 ley, in *The Heat of the Sun, and
 *You Can Help Me.

*BISHOP, CASEY. See: *Betty Black.

*BISHOP, GEORGE
 *Destination Death. Vega, 1961

*BISHOP, GEORGE
 The Shuttle People. Bantam, 1983
 <future>

BISHOP, LEONARD. 1922-   . Ref: CA.
 -The Everlasting. Poseidon, 1982

*BISHOP, MARY
 The Chill Winds of Ravenhall. Zebra,
 1981

*BISS, GERALD. 1876-1922.
 *Branded. Silent film: Gaumont-
 British, 1920 (scw: Paul Rooff;
 dir: C. C. Calvert)
 *The Fated Five. ... Brentano's, 1910

BISSON, ALEXANDRE (CHARLES AUGUSTE).
 1848-1912. See: J. W. MacConaughy.

*BLACK, BETTY and *CASEY BISHOP
 *The Sisterhood. Film: Heron Inter-
 national, 1986, as The Ladies
 Club (scw: Paul Mason, Fran Lewis
 Ebeling; dir: A. K. Allen)

*BLACK, CAMPBELL
 *Dressed to Kill. (Novelization of
 film: Cinema 77, 1980; scw & dir:
 Brian De Palma)
 Mr. Apology. Ballantine, 1984 <NYC>

*BLACK, GAVIN.
 *Dead Man Calling. <Jap.>
 The Fatal Shadow. Collins, 1983
 *A Moon for Killers. <Far East>

*BLACK, IAN STUART
 Creatures in a Dream. Constable,
 1985
 *The High Bright Sun. criminous
 Film: Rank, 1964; released in the
 U.S. as McGuire Go Home! (scw: Ian
 Stuart Black, Bryan Forbes; dir:
 Ralph Thomas)
 *In the Wake of a Stranger. Film:
 Crest, 1959 (scw: John Tully;
 dir: David Eady)
 *We Must Kill Toni. Film: Asher,
 1962, as She'll Have to
 Go (scw: John Waterhouse; dir:
 Robert Asher)

*BLACK, JOHN D. F.
 *Trouble Man. (Novelization of film:
 TCF, 1972; scw: John D. F. Black;
 dir: Ivan Nixon)

*BLACK, JONATHAN
 Dead Run. Jove, 1981 <NYC>

*BLACK, LAURA
 -Strathgallant. H. Hamilton, 1981;
 St. Martin's, 1982 <Eng., 1863>

*BLACK, LIONEL. Ref (expanded treat-
 ment): TC2; also: TM.
 Roumanian Circle. Collins, 1981

*BLACK, MANSELL
 *Dead on Course. Film: Hammer, 1952;
 released in Britain as Wings of
 Danger (scw: John Gilling; dir:
 Terence Fisher)

*BLACK, VERONICA
 *Fair Kilmeny. ... Berkley, 1972

*BLACKBURN, JOHN (FENWICK)
 The Bad Penny. Hale, 1985
 -A Beastly Business. Hale, 1982
 A Book of the Dead. Hale, 1984
 *Nothing But the Night. Film:
 Charlemagne, 1973 (scw: Brian
 Hughes; dir: Peter Sasdy)

*BLACKER, IRWIN R(OBERT). 1919-1985.

*BLACKSTOCK, CHARITY. Ref (revised):
 TC2; also: TM.
 The Encounter. Piatkus, 1981 <Czech.>

BLACKWELDER, STEPHEN and J. L. NEGRONI
 The Price of Heaven. Dell, 1984;
 Arrow, 1984 <NYC>

*BLACKWOOD, ALGERNON (HENRY). Ref (re-
 vised): TC2.
 The Listener and other stories.
 Nash, 1907; Vaughan, 1914 ss, at
 least one criminous

BLACKWOOD, CAROLINE. 1931-   . Ref:
 CA.
 Corrigan. Heinemann, 1984; Viking,
 1985
 The Fate of Mary Rose. Cape, 1981;
 Summit, 1981

*BLAGOWIDOW, GEORGE
 Operation Porterre. Hippocrene,
 1982. British title: Border Crossing. Piatkus, 1982. Reprinted in
 England under U.S. title: Sphere,
 1982 <WWII, Pol.>

BLAIR, ALPHA
 Through the Eyes of Evil. Leisure,
 1981 <Eng.>

*BLAIR, CHARLES F, JR. See: A(rthur)
 J(ames) Wallis.

BLAIR, CHRISTINA
 Crystal Destiny. Zebra, 1984 <West>

*BLAIR, MARCIA
 *The Final Fair. (title correction:
 not The Final Fear)

*BLAISDELL, ANNE. See also: *(Barbara)
 Elizabeth Linington.
 *Nightmare. Film: Hammer, 1965, as
 Die! Die! My Darling; released in
 Britain as Fanatic (scw: Richard
 Matheson; dir: Silvio Narizzano)

BLAKE, CAMERON
 Only Men on Board. Hodder, 1933 ss,
 some criminous

BLAKE, CECILIA M.
 Among the Water Lilies. Simpkin,
 1895

*BLAKE, CHRISTINA. SC: Insp. Ronald
 Dobbs, in *A Fragrant Death, and in
 title below.
 Deadly Legacy. Raven, 1981 <ship>

BLAKE, JENNIFER. Pseudonym of *Patricia
 (Anne Ponder) Maxwell.
 Midnight Waltz. Columbine, 1985
 <La., ca.1850>

*BLAKE, KEN. All titles are here also
 novelizations of "The Profession-
 als" TV series.
 Assassin! Sphere, 1982
 Cry Wolf. Sphere, 1981
 Foxhole. Sphere, 1982
 No Stone. Sphere, 1981
 Operation Susie. Sphere, 1982
 Spy Probe. Sphere, 1981
 The Untouchables. Sphere, 1982
 You'll Be All Right. Sphere, 1982.
 Reprinted as by Kenneth Bulmer:
 Severn, 1983

BLAKE, MARGARET. Pseudonym of Barbara
 Margaret Trimble, 1921-   . Other
 pseudonym: B. M. Gill, q.v.
 Apple of Discord. Hale, 1975
 Bright Sun, Dark Shadow. Hale, 1968
 Courier to Danger. Hale, 1973
 The Elusive Exile. Hale, 1971
 Flight from Fear. Hale, 1973
 The Rare and the Lovely. Hale, 1969
 Stranger at the Door. Hale, 1967
 Walk Softly and Beware. Hale, 1977

*BLAKE, NICHOLAS. Ref also: TM.
 *The Beast Must Die. Film: CFDC, 1969,
 as Que La Bete Meure (Let the Beast
 Die) (Killer) (scw: Paul Gegauff,
 Claude Chabrol; dir: Chabrol)

BLAKE, NICK
 Chainsaw Terror. Star, 1984. Also
 published as: Come the Night. Star,
 1985

*BLAKE, PATRICK
 Double Griffin. Jove, 1981 <NYC,
 1944>
 *Escape to Athena. (Novelization of
 film: ITC, 1979; scw: Edward Anhalt, Richard S. Lochte; dir:
 George Pan Cosmatos)

*BLAKE, ROGER. Pseudonym of John
 Trimble.

*BLAKE, VANESSA. Pseudonym of May
 Brown, 1913-   . Ref: CA.

*BLAKESLEY, STEPHEN
 The Cardinal and the Corpse. Fiction
 House, 1947
 A Case for the Cardinal. Fiction
 House, 1946
 The Case of the Alpha Murders. Fic-
 tion House, 1947
 The Proctor Case. Fiction House,
 1946
 Terrell in Trouble. Bear Hudson,
 1946

*BLAKESTON, OSWELL. 1907-1985(?).
 Ref: CA.

*BLANC, SUZANNE. Ref also: TM.

*BLANEY, CHARLES E. Note: Harry Clay
 Blaney was CEB's brother, not his
 pseudonym.
 *Across the Pacific. Silent film:
 World, 1914 (scw & dir: Edward
 Carewe). Also: Warner, 1926
 (scw: D. F. Zanuck; dir: Roy del
 Ruth)
 *The Curse of Drink. Silent film:
 Weber, 1922 (scw & dir: Harry O.
 Hoyt)

*The Dancer and the King. Silent
  film: World, 1914 (scw: Edwin
  Carewe; dir: E. Artaud)
*More to Be Pitied Than Scorned.
  Silent film: Waldorf, 1922 (dir:
  Edward Le Saint)
*Young Buffalo. delete

BLANKENSHIP, CATHERINE
  Murder Is Fun! French, 1941
  (1-act play.)

*BLANKENSHIP, WILLIAM D(OUGLAS)
  Brotherly Love. Arbor, 1982;
  Souvenir, 1982

*BLANKFORT, MICHAEL (SEYMOUR).
  Pseudonym: *Bryant Ford.

*BLASSINGAME, WYATT (RAINEY). 1909-
  1985.

BLATTY, WILLIAM PETER. 1928-
  Ref: CA. SC: Lt. Bill Kinderman,
  in both titles.
  -The Exorcist. Harper, 1971; Blond,
  1971. Film: Warner, 1973 (scw:
  William Peter Blatty; dir: Wil-
  liam Friedkin)
  Legion. Simon, 1983; Collins, 1983
  <Wash. D.C.>

BLAU, ERIC. 1921-   . Ref: CA.
  The Keys to Billy Tillo. Pinnacle,
  1984 <NYC>

*BLAYNE, SEBASTIAN. Pseudonym of Janet
  Huckins.

*BLEECK, OLIVER
  *The Procane Chronicle. Film: Warner,
  1973, as St. Ives (scw: Berry
  Beckerman; dir: J. Lee Thompson)

BLISS, RAYMOND
  Without Ransom. Veal, 1982

*BLOCH, ROBERT (ALBERT). Ref also: TM.
  SC: Norman Bates, in *Psycho, and
  in title marked NB below.
  *The Couch. (Novelization of film:
  Warner, 1962; scw: Robert Bloch;
  dir: Owen Crump)
  The Night of the Ripper. Doubleday,
  1984; Hale, 1986 <Eng., 1888>
  *Psycho. Film: Paramount, 1960 (scw:
  Joseph Stefano; dir: Alfred Hitch-
  cock)
  Psycho II. Warner, 1982; Corgi, 1983
  NB
  *The Skull of the Marquis de Sade and
  other stories. Film (based on title
  story): Amicus, 1965, as The
  Skull (scw: Milton Subotsky; dir:
  Freddie Francis)

*BLOCHMAN, LAWRENCE G(OLDTREE). Ref
  also: TM.
  *Bombay Mail. Film: Universal, 1934
  (scw: Tom Reed, L. G. Blochman;
  dir: Edwin L. Marin)
  *Pursuit. Film: MGM, 1935 (scw:
  Wells Root; dir: Edwin L. Marin)

*BLOCK, LAWRENCE. Ref (revised and ex-
  panded): TC2; also: TM. Pseudonym:
  *Chip Harrison, *Paul Kavanagh,
  qq.v. SC: Bernie Rhodenbarr,
  also in titles marked BR; Matthew
  Scudder, also in titles marked
  MS. Film (based on unidentified
  novel): Nightmare Honeymoon.
  MGM, 1972 (scw: S. Lee Pogostin;
  dir: Nicholas Roeg, Elliot Silver-
  stein). Film (based on the BR
  novels): Nelvana, 1987, as Burglar
  (scw: Joseph Loeb III, Matthew
  Weisman, Hugh Wilson; dir: Wilson)
  The Burglar Who Painted Like
  Mondrian. Arbor, 1983; Gollancz,
  1984 BR <NYC>
  The Burglar Who Studied Spinoza.
  Random, 1981; Hale, 1982 BR <NYC>
  Code of Arms, with *Harold King, q.v.
  Marek, 1981 <1940>
  Eight Million Ways to Die. Arbor,
  1982; Hale, 1983 MS <NYC> Film
  (also based on A Stab in the Dark,
  q.v.): PSO, 1985 (scw: Oliver
  Stone, David Lee Henry; dir: Hal
  Ashby)
  *The Girl with the Long Green Heart.
  <N.Y.>
  Like a Lamb to the Slaughter. Arbor,
  1984 ss, at least one with MS
  Sometimes They Bite. Arbor, 1983 ss,
  at least one with MS, one with BR
  A Stab in the Dark. Arbor, 1981;
  Hale, 1982 MS <NYC>

BLOCK, THOMAS H(ARRIS). 1945-
  Ref: CA.
  Forced Landing. Coward, 1983; NEL,
  1983 <ship>
  -Orbit. Coward, 1982; NEL, 1982

*BLODGETT, MICHAEL
  -Hero and the Terror. Harmony, 1982
  <L.A.>

*BLOM, K(ARL) ARNE. Ref also: BM.

*BLOODWORTH, DENNIS. 1919-

*BLOOM, MURRAY TEIGH
  *The 13th Man. Film: UA, 1979, as Last
  Embrace (scw: David Shaber; dir:
  Jonathan Demme)

*BLOOMFIELD, ROBERT
  *Stranger in Town. <Wis.>

BLOOMSTEIN, HENRY
  The Brothers Kresky. Brookdale, 1983

BLUMENTHAL, JOHN. Lives in L.A. SC:
  Mac Slade, in both titles.
  The Case of the Hardboiled Dicks.
  Fireside, 1985 <NYC>
  The Tinseltown Murders. Fireside,
  1985 <L.A.>

BLUNDELL, MRS. FRANCIS.   -1930.
  Pseudonym: M. E. Francis, q.v.

*BLYTH, JAMES
  Beset by Spies. White, 1913 <1904>

*BOARDMAN, NEIL (SERVIS)
  *The Wine of Violence. <Minn.>

*BOBKER, LEE R.
  Flight of a Dragon. Morrow, 1981
  <H. Kong>

BOBRICK, SAM. See: Ron Clark.

*BOCCA, GEOFFREY. 1923-1983. Ref: CA.

*BODELSEN, ANDERS
  *One Down. Film: A/S Nordisk, 1971, as
  Haendeligt Uheld (One of Those
  Things) (Hit and Run, Run, Run)
  (scw: Erik Balling, Anders
  Bodelsen; dir: Balling)
  *Operation Cobra. Film: Norsk, 1979,
  as Operasjon Cobra (Operation
  Cobra) (scw & dir: Ola Solum)
  *Think of a Number. Film: Nordisk,
  1969, as Taenk Paa et Tal (Think of
  a Number) (scw & dir: Palle
  Kjaerulff-Schmidt). Also: Carolco,
  1978, as The Silent Partner (scw:
  Curtis Hanson; dir: Daryl Duke)

*BODKIN, M(ATTHIAS) McDONNELL. Ref
  also: CA; not in TC2.

BODYAN, JESSE GLENN
  Midtown Aces. Playwrights, 1982
  (2-act play.)

*BOGAR, JEFF. House name.
  *Dinah for Danger. <U.S.> (Written
  by Leslie T. Barnard.)
  *Hoodman's Bait. (Written by Leslie T.
  Barnard.)
  Lady--Pass My Gat! hamilton, ca.1952
  *Payoff for Paula. <L.A.>

*BOGARD, DALE
  Don't Kill Me Twice. World Distributors, 1951

*BOGART, WILLIAM (G.). Ref: TM.
  *Hell on Friday. Also published as:
  *Murder Man.
  *Murder Man; see Hell on Friday
  *Singapore. (Novelization of film:
  Universal International, 1947;
  scw: Seton I. Miller, Robert
  Thoeren; dir: John Brahm)

BOGGIS, DAVID
  A Time to Betray. Macmillan (London),
  1981
  The Woman They Sent to Fight. Macmillan (London), 1983

BOGGS, MARCUS. 1947-   . Ref: CA.
  Scissors, Paper, Stone. Watts, 1981
  <South>

*BOGNAR, NORMAN
  *Snowman. Dell, 1978

*BOILEAU, PIERRE (PROSPER) and *THOMAS
  NARCEJAC. Ref also: TC2.
  *Faces in the Dark. Film: Pennington,
  1960 (scw: Ephraim Kogan, John
  Tully; dir: David Eady)

*The Living and the Dead. Film: Para-
  mount, 1958, as Vertigo (scw: Alec
  Coppel, Samuel Taylor; dir: Alfred
  Hitchcock)
*The Prisoner. Film: Rivers, 1957, as
  Les Louves (The She Wolves) (scw:
  Luis Saslavsky, Pierre Boileau,
  Thomas Narcejac; dir: Saslavsky).
  Also: Portman, 1985, as Les Louvres
  (Letters to an Unknown Lover) (scw:
  Pierre Boileau, Thomas Narcejac;
  dir: Peter Duffell)
*Spells of Evil. Film: SNEG, 1962, as
  Malefices (Sorcery) (scw: Claude
  Accursi, Albert Husson, Henri
  Decoin; dir: Decoin)
*The Woman Who Was. Film: Cinedis,
  1955, as Les Diaboliques (Diabo-
  lique; The Fiends) (scw: H. G.
  Clouzot, Jerome Geromini, Rene
  Masson, Frederic Grendel; dir:
  Clouzot)

*BOK
*Vampires of the China Coast. delete:
  non-fiction

BOK, CURTIS. 1897-1962.
  Star Wormwood. Knopf, 1959 <U.S.,
  1931>

*BOLAND, (BERTRAM) JOHN. Pseudonym:
  *James Trevor.
*The League of Gentlemen. Film: Allied
  Film, 1959 (scw: Bryan Forbes; dir:
  Basil Dearden)

*BOLDREWOOD, ROLF
  The Miner's Right. Macmillan (Lon-
  don), 1890 <Australia>
  Nevermore. Macmillan (London), 1892
  <Australia>
  *Robbery Under Arms. Film: Rank, 1957
  (scw: Alexander Baron, W. P. Lips-
  comb; dir: Jack Lee). Also: ITC,
  1985 (scw: Graeme Koestveld, Tony
  Morphett; dir: Ken Hannam, Donald
  Crombie)

*BOLES, PAUL DARCY. 1916-1984.

BOLLANS, GERTRUDE ELIZABETH
  The Crooked Courtship. Deane, 1955;
  Baker, 1955 (1-act play.)

*BOLT, BEN
  *-Diana of the Islands. (title cor-
  rection) Silent film: Clark, 1925,
  as Mutiny (dir: F. Martin Thornton)

BOLTON, MELVIN. Born in Eng.; has M.S.
  from London Univ.; wildlife manage-
  ment consultant; living in
  Australia.
  The Softener. Gollancz, 1984; Watts,
  1986

BOLTON, ROBERT L. and RUSS MUSARRA
  Sleep with the Angels. SNB, 1985
  <Cleve.>

BOMACK, ALAN. See: Don(ald Euguene)
  Pendleton.

*BOMBAL, MARIA LOUISA
  House of Mist. Belmont, 1964

BONAVIA, DAVID and JOHN BYRON. Bonavia
  is a journalist; Byron a pseudonym.
  The China Lovers. South China
  Morning Post, 1985 <China>

BOND, CHRISTOPHER
  A Policeman's Lot. Deane, 1957;
  Baker, 1957 (Play.)
  Sweeney Todd, the Demon Barber of
  Fleet Street. French, 1974
  (3-act play.) <London, early
  1800s>

*BOND, EVELYN
  Lady of Storm House. Lancer, 1965(?)

BOND, (THOMAS) MICHAEL. 1926-   . Ref:
  CA. SC: Monsieur Pamplemousse, in
  all titles. Set: Fr.
  Monsieur Pamplemousse. Hodder, 1983;
  Beaufort, 1985
  Monsieur Pamplemousse and the Secret
  Mission. Hodder, 1985; Beaufort,
  1986
  Monsieur Pamplemousse en Fete. Hod-
  der, 1984

BOND, MICHAEL. 1943-   . Has been
  candidate for U.S. senate, consultant to governments, environ-
  mental activist; living in Mont.
  Fire Like the Sun. St. Martin's,
  1985

B

*BONETT, EMERY. See also: *John
   Bonett.
  *High Pavement. Film: Burnham, 1948,
   as My Sister and I (scw: A. R.
   Rawlinson, Joan Rees, Michael
   Medwin, Robert Westerby; dir:
   Harold Huth)

*BONETT, JOHN. SC: Insp. Borges, also
   in title below.
   Perish the Thought. Hale, 1984

*BONETT, JOHN and EMERY. Ref (revised
   and expanded): TC2; also: TM.
  *A Banner for Pegasus. Reprinted in
   the U.S. under the British title:
   Perennial, 1982

*BONNAMY, FRANCIS. Ref: CA, TM.

*BONNER, GERALDINE
  *Miss Maitland, Private Secretary.
   Silent film: Hampton, 1920, as The
   Girl in the Web (scw: Waldemar
   Young; dir: Robert Thornby)

*BONNER, MARJORIE. Film actress in
   1930s; living in Beverley Hills in
   1980s.

*BOORSTIN, PAUL (TERRY)
   The Glory Hand, with Sharon Boorstin.
   Berkley, 1983; Sphere, 1984
   <Maine>

BOORSTIN, SHARON. See: *Paul (Terry)
   Boorstin.

*BOOTH, ANTHONY
   The Trial. French (London), 1972
   (1-act play.)

*BOOTH, CHARLES G(ORDON)
  *The General Died at Dawn. Film:
   Paramount, 1936 (scw: Clifford
   Odets; dir: Lewis Milestone)
  *Mr. Angel Comes Aboard. Film: RKO,
   1945, as Johnny Angel (scw: Steve
   Fisher, Frank Gruber; dir: Edwin
   L. Marin)

*BOOTH, CLARE
  *Margin for Error. Film: TCF, 1943
   (scw: Lillie Hayward; dir: Otto
   Preminger)

BOOTH, ROSEMARY FRANCES. 1928-   .
   Pseudonym: Frances Murray, q.v.

*BOOTHBY, GUY (NEWELL)
  *Across the World for a Wife. <Arg.,
   Cuba>
  *A Bid for Fortune. <ship> Silent
   film: Unity-Super, 1917 (scw &
   dir: Sidney Morgan)
  *Billy Binks, Hero. ss, at least one
   criminous
  *Bushigrams. criminous
  *Connie Burt. <Australia>
  *A Crime of the Under-Seas. <New
   Guinea, Australia>
  *-The Curse of the Snake.
  *'Farewell, Nikola'. <Venice>
  *A Lost Endeavor. delete: not cri-
   minous
  *For Love of Her. <Australia>
  *Love Made Manifest. delete: not
   criminous
  *The Man on the Crag. criminous
  *The Marriage of Esther: A Torres
   Straits Sketch. <Australia>
  *My Indian Queen. delete: not
   criminous
  *Pharos the Egyptian.
  *A Royal Affair and other stories.
   ss, one criminous <Australia>
  *A Sailor's Bride. delete: not
   criminous

*BOOTON, (CATHERINE) KAGE. Ref also:
   TM.

BORELLI, CASS <CESAR?>
   Downtown. Scion, 1954
   Get This Straight. Scion, 1951
   I Will Kill. Scion, 1953 (Written
   by *F. Dubrez Fawcett.)
   Million Dollar Babe. Scion, 1953

*BORER, MARY (IRENE) CATHCART. See:
   *Arnold Ridley.

*BORGENICHT, MIRIAM. Ref also: TM.
   Bad Medicine; see Fall from Grace
   Fall from Grace. St. Martin's, 1984.
      British title: Bad Medicine. Mac-
      millan (London), 1984 <NYC>
   False Colors. St. Martin's, 1985;
      Macmillan (London), 1986 <NYC>
   True or False. St. Martin's, 1982;
      Hale, 1983 <N.Y.>

*BORGES, JORGE LUIS. 1899-1986. Ref
   also: TM.
   Six Problems for Don Isidro Parodi,
   with Adolfo Bioy-Cesares. Dutton,
   1981. British title: Chronicles of
   Bustos Domecq. Lane, 1982 ss
   (Translation of "Seis Problemas
   para Don Isidro Parodi", as by H.
   Bustos Domecq. Buenos Aires, 1942.)

*BORNEMAN, ERNEST (WILLIAM JULIUS)
  *Tremolo. Film (?): Hammer, 1954, as
   Face the Music; released in the
   U.S. as The Black Glove (scw:
   Ernest Borneman; dir: Terence
   Fisher)

BORRIE, HERMINE. Singer and dancer on
   radio, TV, stage; later a model.
   The Golden Heron. Scorpion, 1984
   <1930s>

BORTHWICK, J. S. Lives in Maine. SC:
   Sarah Deane, Alex McKenzie, in both
   titles.
   The Case of the Hook-Billed Kites.
   St. Martin's, 1982; Gollancz, 1983
   <Tex.>
   The Down East Murders. St. Martin's,
   1985 <Maine>

BOSAK, STEVEN. Lives near Chicago and
   teaches in graduate writing program
   at Columbia College.
   Gammon. St. Martin's, 1985 <Port.>

*BOSSE, M(ALCOLM) J(OSEPH). Ref: CA.

BOST, PIERRE. 1901-   . See: Denis
   Cannan.

*BOSTON, CHARLES K.
  *The Silver Jackass. <L.A.>

BOSWELL, BEATRICE
   A Piper in the Street Today. Vantage,
   1969

BOSWORTH, DAVID. 1947-   . Ref: CA.
   The Death of Descartes. U. of Pittsburgh, 1981 ss, one criminous

*BOTTOME, PHYLLIS
   Eldorado Jane. Faber, 1956. U.S.
   title: Jane. Vanguard, 1957
   Jane; see Eldorado Jane
  *-The Lifeline. <Austria>
  *The Mortal Storm. Film: MGM, 1940
   (scw: Claudine West, George
   Froeschel, Andersen Ellis; dir:
   Frank Borzage)
  *Murder in the Bud. Film: Warner,
   1945, as Danger Signal (scw: Adele
   Commandini, C. Graham Baker; dir:
   Robert Florey)
  *The Rat. Silent film: Gainsborough,
   1925 (scw & dir: Graham Cutts).
   Sound film: Imperator, 1937 (scw:
   Hans Gulder Rameau, Marjorie Gaff-
   ney, Miles Malleson, Romney Brent;
   dir: Jack Raymond).

*BOUCHER, ANTHONY. Ref also: TM.
   Pseudonym: *H. H. Holmes, q.v. See
   also: Theo Durrant.
   Exeunt Murderers. Southern Illinois
   Univ. Press, 1983 ss

*BOUCICAULT, DION(YSIUS LARDNER)
   After Dark. <London>, 1868; Dramatic, 1868 (4-act play) Silent
   film: Kalem, 1913 (scw: Gene
   Gaunthier; dir: Sidney Olcott).
   Also: Buckland, 1915 (dir: Warwick Buckland). Also: World, 1915
   (dir: Frederick Thompson)
  *The Colleen Bawn. Lacy's, 1864
   (3-act play.) Silent film: Kalem,
   1911 (scw: Gene Gaunthier;
   dir: Sidney Olcott). Also: Stoll,
   1924; also released as The Loves of
   Colleen Bawn (scw: Eliot Stannard;
   dir: W. P. Kellino). Also: BIP,
   1929, as Lily of Kilarney (scw &
   dir: George Ridgwell). Sound film:
   Twickenham, 1934, as Lily of Kilarney; released in the U.S. as
   Bride of the Lake (scw: H. Fowler
   Mear; dir: Maurice Elvey)
   The Octoroon. Lacy's, 1859 (4-act
   play.) Silent film: Gaumont, 1903
   (scw: Dion Boucicault; dir: Dicky
   Winslow)

*BOULGER, MRS. DOROTHY HENRIETTA
   (HAVERS). 1847-1923.

*BOULLE, PIERRE
  *Ears of the Jungle. <Far East>

BOULTON, MATTHEW
   The Burglar and the Girl. French,
   1913 (1-act play.) Silent film:
   DeForest, 1928 (dir: Hugh Croise)

*BOURGEAU, ART. SC: Claude "Snake"
   Kirlin and F. T. Zevich, in *A
   Lonely Way to Die, and in all
   titles below.
   The Elvis Murders. Charter, 1985
   <Tenn.>
   The Most Likely Suspects. Charter,
   1981 <acad.>
   Murder at the Cheatin' Heart Motel.
   Charter, 1985 <Tenn.>

BOURNS, MARSHA. Pseudonym: Marsha
   Alexander, q.v.

BOWDLER, ROGER. 1934-   . Ref: CA.
   Hart to Hart. Mayflower, 1982
   (Novelization of TV series.)
   Magnum P.I. Mayflower, 1981 (Noveli-
   zation of the TV series.)

*BOWEN, (IVOR) IAN. 1908-1984.

BOWEN, JOHN (GRIFFITH). 1924-   . Ref:
   CA.
   The McGuffin. H. Hamilton, 1984;
   Atlantic, 1985 Film: BBC, 1985
   (scw: Michael Thomas; dir: Colin
   Bucksey)

*BOWEN, MARJORIE
  *Old Patch's Medley. ss, many crimin-
   ous <1690-1795, London>

*BOWEN-JUDD, SARA HUTTON. 1922-1986.

*BOWER, MARION and *LEON M. LION
  *The Chinese Puzzle. Silent film:
   Ideal, 1919 (scw & dir: Fred
   Goodwins). Sound film: Twickenham,
   1932 (scw: H. Fowler Mear; dir:
   Guy Newall)

BOWLAND, PETER
   Earnshaw's Evidence. Hale, 1983
   Kidnap. Hale, 1985

BOWSER, JIM. See: *Peter Winston.

*BOX, EDGAR. Ref also: TM.

*BOX, SYDNEY. 1907-1983.

BOYARSKY, ABRAHAM. Born in Poland;
   Canadian citizen and professor of
   mathematics at Concordia Univ. in
   Montreal.
   Shreiber. Beaufort, 1981 <Pol.,
   1945-6>

*BOYD, ERIC FORBES
  *The House of Whipplestaff. criminous

*BOYD, EUNICE MAYS. See: Theo Durrant.

BOYD, JOHN. Pseudonym of Boyd Upchurch,
   1919-   . Ref: CA.
   The Last Starship from Earth. Gollancz, 1968; Weybright, 1968
   <future>

*BOYER, RICK <RICHARD LEWIS>. Ref also:
   TM. SC: Charlie Adams, in both
   titles.
   Billingsgate Shoal. Houghton, 1982;
   Houghton (London), 1983 <Boston,
   Cape Cod>
   The Penny Ferry. Houghton, 1984;
   Gollancz, 1985 <Mass.>

BOYLAN, BRIAN RICHARD. 1936-   . Ref:
   CA.
   Final Trace. Bantam, 1983

*BOYLE, JACK. Ref also: TM; not in TC2.

*BOYLE, KAY
  *Avalanche. Film: Producers'
   Releasing Corp., 1946 (scw: Andrew
   Holt; dir: Irving Allen)

BOYLE, THOMAS. 1939-   . Ref: CA.
   The Cold Stove League. Academy Chicago, 1984; Hale, 1986 <Port.>
   Only the Dead Know Brooklyn. Godine,
   1985; Hodder, 1986 <NYC>

BOYLES, WILLIAM and HANK NUWER. SC:
   William (Tiny) Ryder (The Bounty
   Hunter), in all titles.
   Blood Mountain. Playboy, 1982
   The Deadliest Profession. Playboy,
   1981
   A Killing Trade. Playboy, 1981
   <New Or.>
   The Wild Ride. Playboy, 1981 <L.A.>

*BRACKEEN, STEVE. Pseudonym of *John Farris, q.v.

*BRACKETT, LEIGH. Ref also: TC2, TM.
*The Tiger Among Us. Film: Columbia, 1962, as 13 West Street (scw: Bernard C. Schoenfeld, Robert Presnell, Jr.; dir: Philip Leacock)

*BRADBURY, RAY (DOUGLAS). Ref: not in TC2.
Death Is a Lonely Business. Knopf, 1985; Grafton, 1986 <Calif., 1950>
Long After Midnight. Knopf, 1976; Hart-Davis, 1977 ss, some criminous
A Memory of Murder. Dell, 1984 ss

*BRADDON, M(ARY) E(LIZABETH). Ref also: CA. See also: George Roberts.
*Aurora Floyd. Silent film: Selig, 1912, as Her Bitter Lesson (dir: Hardee Kirkland). Also: Thanhauser, 1912 (scw & dir: Theodore Marston). Also: AB, 1915 (dir: Travers Vale)
*Lady Audley's Secret. Silent film: Walturdaw, 1906. Also: Kalem, 1908. Also: Imp, 1912 (dir: Otis Turner). Also: Fox, 1915 (scw: Mary Asquith; dir: Marshall Farnum). Also: Ideal, 1920 (scw: Eliot Stannard; dir: Jack Denton)

*BRADDON, RUSSELL (READING)
*End Play. Film: Roadshow, 1975 (scw & dir: Tim Burstall)
*Gabriel Comes to 24. <Australia>
*Out of the Storm. <Australia>

BRADFORD, ROY (HAMILTON). 1920- . Ref: CA.
Last Ditch. Blackstaff, 1982

BRADLEY, LILIAN TRIMBLE
What Happened Then? Gollancz, 1934 (3-act play.) Film: BIP, 1934 (scw & dir: Walter Summers)

*BRADLEY, MARION ZIMMER
The Inheritor. Tor, 1984

*BRADSHAW, GEORGE (FLOING)
*Practice to Deceive. ss

BRADY, CHARLES ANDREW. 1912- . Ref: CA.
-Viking Summer. Bruce, 1956

*BRADY, CYRUS TOWNSEND
The Man Who Won. McClurg, 1919; Jarrolds, 1924. Silent film: Vitagraph, 1919 (dir: Paul Scardon)

*BRADY, LEO. 1917-1984.
*Brother Orchid. Film: Warner, 1940 (scw: Earl Brady; dir: Lloyd Bacon)
*The Edge of Doom. Film: RKO, 1950; released in Britain as Stronger Than Fear (scw: Philip Yordan; dir: Mark Robson)

*BRADY, MATT. Pseudonym of *Joseph Shallitt.

*BRADY, MICHAEL
The Coda Alliance. Dell, 1981; Joseph, 1981

BRADY, WILLIAM S.
Death and the Jack Shade. Fontana, 1982

BRAGUNIER, MORDINA FLOYD. Pseudonym: *Mordie Floyd.

*BRAHMS, CARYL and *S. J. SIMON. Ref also for *Doris Caroline Abrahams: CA.

*BRALY, MALCOLM. Ref also: TM.
*The Master. (Novelization of film: Tomorrow, 1973, as Lady Ice; scw: Alan Trustman, Harold Clemens; dir: Tom Gries)
*On the Yard. Film: Midwest, 1978 (scw: Malcolm Braly; dir: Raphael D. Silver)

*BRAMAH, ERNEST. Ref also: TM. SC: Max Carrados, also in title below.
Short Stories. Harrap, 1929 ss, some criminous, including 3 about MC

*BRAMBLE, FORBES
Dead of Winter. H. Hamilton (London & U.S.), 1985

BRAMLEY-MOORE, ZELMA. See: Charles Neilson Gattey, 1921-

BRAMPTON, JOAN
Something Attempted. Deane, 1960; Baker, 1960 (3-act play.)

*BRAND, CHRISTIANNA. Ref also: TM.
The Brides of Aberdar. Joseph, 1982
*Death in High Heels. Film: Marylebone, 1947 (dir: Lionel Tomlinson)
*Green for Danger. Film: Individual, 1947 (scw: Sidney Gilliat, Claud Guerney; dir: Gilliat)

BRAND, HILARY. Pseudonym of *Stephen Francis, q.v. SC: Hilary Brand, in all titles.
All--or Something. Compact, 1965
Brand T. Compact, 1964
A Flair for Affairs. Compact, 1966
News Girl. Compact, 1963
Peak of Frenzy. Compact, 1964
Running Scared. Compact, 1966
Strictly Wild. Compact, 1966

*BRAND, MAX. Ref also: CA; not in TC2.
*Big Game. ... Henry, 1984

*BRANDEL, MARC. Ref also: CA.
The Ides of Summer; see *Rain Before Seven
A Life of Her Own. Houghton, 1984
*The Lizard's Tail. Also published as: The Hand. Berkley, 1981. Film: Orion, 1981, as The Hand (scw & dir: Oliver Stone)
Murder in the Family. Avon, 1985 <Conn.>
*Rain Before Seven. ... British title (?): The Ides of Summer. Eyre, 1948
*The Time of the Fire. Film: Columbia, 1963, as Maniac (scw: Jimmy Sangster; dir: Michael Carreras)

*BRANDNER, GARY
*The Howling. Film: AVCO, 1980 (scw: John Sayles, Terence H. Winkless; dir: Joe Dante)
*The Howling II. Film: Thorn EMI, 1985 (scw: Robert Sarns, Gary Brandner; dir: Philippe Mora)
-The Howling III: The Echoes. GM, 1985; Hamlyn, 1985

BRANDON, JAY (ROBERT). 1953- . Ref: CA.
Deadbolt. Bantam, 1985 <Tex.>

*BRANDON, JOHN G(ORDON). Ref also: CA; not in TC2.
Mystery of the Ice-Cream Man. Amalgamated, 1938 (Sexton Blake)
*The Silent House. Silent film (based on play): Nettlefold, 1929 (scw: H. Fowler Mear; dir: Walter Forde)

BRANDON, JOSEPH
Paradise in Flames. PB, 1976

BRANDON, SLIM
Hellbound. Gray, 195?

BRANDT, DIRK
Black Angel. Gray, 195?

BRANSON, CLIVE and *LARRY PRYCE
Men Who Robbed the Bank of England. Magread, 1982

*BRANSON, H(ENRY) C. ca.1905-1981. Ref also: TM. Attended Princeton Univ., graduated from Univ. of Mich.; lived in Ann Arbor.

BRASHLER, WILLIAM. 1947- . Ref: CA.
The Chosen Prey. Harper, 1982

BRASON, JOHN
The Fourth Arm. BBC, 1983 (Novelization of BBC TV series.) <WWII, Fr.>
Kessler. BBC, 1981 (Novelization of BBC TV series.)

BRAUDY, SUSAN (ORR). 1941- . Ref: CA.
Who Killed Sal Mineo? Wyndham, 1982 <L.A.>

*BRAUN, LILLIAN JACKSON. Ref: not in TC2.

*BRAUN, MAURICE-GILLES. Name sometimes given as Maurice-Georges Braun.

*BRAUN, R(EINHARD) A.
*Murder, Four Miles High. (title correction)

*BRAUN, WILBUR. Pseudonyms also: Ned Albert, q.v.; *Stephen Bristol; Millard Crosby, Anthony Forsythe, qq.v.

Her Fatal Beauty. French, 1940 (1-act play.)

*BRAUTIGAN, RICHARD. 1935-1984. Ref also: TM.

BRAWLEY, ERNEST. 1937- . Ref: CA.
The Rap. Atheneum, 1974; Secker, 1975. For: Lorimar, 1982, as Fast-Walking (scw & dir: James B. Harris)

BRAY, SANDRA
Strange Destiny. Mystique, 1981 (Translation of "Les Pieges de la Nuit." Paris, 1978.)

BREAM, FREDA
A Case of Art Failure. Hale, 1984
The Corpse on the Cruise. Hale, 1985 <ship>
Island of Fear. Hale, 1982
Murder in the Map Room. Hale, 1983
Sealed and Despatched. Hale, 1984
Vicar Done It. Hale, 1983
The Vicar Investigates. Hale, 1983
With Murder in Mind. Hale, 1985

*BREAN, HERBERT (J.). Ref also: TM.

BRECKLING, GRACE JAMISON
River of Fire. Pageant, 1959 <Cent. Am.>

*BREEM, WALLACE (WILFRED SWINBURNE). 1926- . Ref: CA.

BREEN, JON L(INN). 1943- . Ref: TC2, TM. SC: Jerry Brogan, in titles marked JB.
The Gathering Place. Walker, 1984; Macmillan (London), 1984 <L.A.>
Hair of the Sleuthhound. Scarecrow (U.S. and U.K.), 1982 ss
Listen for the Click. Walker, 1983. British title: Vicar's Roses. Macmillan (London), 1984 <Calif.> JB
Triple Crown. Walker, 1986; Macmillan, 1985 JB
Vicar's Roses; see Listen for the Click

*BREEN, RICHARD. 1935- . Ref: CA.
Made for TV. Beaufort, 1982

BREND, JULIAN. See: Wilfred Massey.

*BRENNAN, ALICE. Born in St. Louis; has been dancer, hat-check girl, secretary; living in Avoca, Mich., in 1960s.
*Litany of Evil. Lancer, 1969 (date correction)
*Thirty Days Hath July. <Mich.>

*BRENNAN, BILL
The Faster We Live. Monarch, 1962

BRENNAN, ELIZABETH
Whispering Walls. Metropolitan, 1948 <Ireland>

*BRENNAN, JOSEPH PAYNE. SC: Lucius Leffing, also in title marked LL below.
Act of Providence, with Donald M. Grant. Grant, 1979 LL
Evil Always Ends. Grant, 1982

BRENNAN, NOELLE. See: J. L. Rankin.

BRENNAN, PETER
Razorback. Jove, 1981; Fontana, 1982 <Australia> Film: McElroy, 1984 (scw: Everett De Roche; dir: Russell Mulcahy)
Sudden Death. Jove, 1978

*BRENT, MADELEINE
A Heritage of Shadows. Souvenir, 1983; Doubleday, 1984 <Eng., 1890s>
The Long Masquerade. Souvenir, 1981

*BRENT, PETER (LUDWIG). 1931-1984.

*BRESLIN, CATHERINE
*Unholy Child. ... Sphere, 1981 <Mpls.>

*BRESLIN, JIMMY
Forsaking All Others; see Kill the Bull!
*The Gang That Couldn't Shoot Straight. Film: MGM, 1971 (scw: Waldo Salt; dir: James Goldstone)
Kill the Bull! Simon, 1982. British title: Forsaking All Others. Macdonald, 1983 <NYC>

BRESLIN, PATRICK. 1940-
    Interventions. Doubleday, 1980
    <Chile>

BRETON, THIERRY and DENIS BENEICH
    Softwar. Holt, 1985 (Translation
    of "Softwar". Paris, 1984.)

*BRETONNE, ANNE-MARIE. Pseudonym of
    Arnold Berman (real name cor-
    rection)

BRETT, BARBARA. See: Hy Brett.

BRETT, HY and BARBARA
    Promises to Keep. Harper, 1981
    <N.H.>

BRETT, JOHN. Born in Eng., the son of
    an earl; living near Hollywood.
    Who'd Hire John Brett? St. Martin's,
    1981 <L.A.>

*BRETT, MICHAEL. 1928-   . Ref: TC2,
    TM.
    *Another Day, Another Stiff. PB,
        1968 (date correction)
    Jungle. Dell, 1976
    *Lie a Little, Die a Little. Film:
        Cambist, 1971, as Cry Uncle (scw:
        David Odell; dir: John G. Avild-
        sen)

*BRETT, SIMON (ANTHONY LEE). Ref (re-
    vised): TC2; also: TM. SC:
    Charles Paris, also in titles
    marked CP below.
    A Box of Tricks. Gollancz, 1985.
        U.S. title: Tickled to Death.
        Scribner, 1985 ss, one about CP
    Dead Giveaway. Gollancz, 1985;
        Scribner, 1986 CP
    Dead Romantic. Macmillan (London),
        1985; Scribner, 1986
    Murder in the Title. Gollancz, 1983;
        Scribner, 1983 <theatre> CP
    Murder Unprompted. Gollancz, 1982;
        Scribner, 1982 <theatre> CP
    Not Dead, Only Resting. Gollancz,
        1984; Scribner, 1984 CP
    A Shock to the System. Macmillan
        (London), 1984; Scribner, 1985 CP
    Situation Tragedy. Gollancz, 1981;
        Scribner, 1982 CP
    Tickled to Death; see A Box of
        Tricks

*BREUER, GUSTAV J. 1915-1985. Ref: CA.

*BREWER, GIL. 1922-1983. Ref also: TM.
    Pseudonym: *Elaine Evans.
    *Hell's Our Destination. Film: TCF,
        1957, as Lure of the Swamp (scw:
        William George; dir: Hubert Corn-
        field)
    *The Hungry One. <Fla.>
    *A Killer Is Loose. Film: M. Films,
        1986, as La Machine a Decoudre
        (The Unsewing Machine) (scw & dir:
        Jean-Pierre Mocky)
    *Memory of Passion. Lancer, 1962
        (date correction)
    *The Red Scarf. <Fla.>

*BREWER, JORDAN. Pseudonym of M. M.
    Marberry.

BREWIS, HAROLD
    The Body Was Missing. Leonard's,
        1953 (Play.)

BREZ, E. M.
    Those Dark Eyes. St. Martin's, 1984
    <NYC>

BRICE, SHIRLEY
    The Might of a Wrongdoer. Long, 1906

*BRIDGE, ANN. Ref: not in TC2.
    *The Tightening String (not The
        Tightening Screw)

*BRIDGES, ROY(AL)
    *The Alden Case. <Australia>
    *The Bubble Moon. <1700s>
    *Cloud. <Australia>
    *The House of Fendon. delete: not
        criminous
    *Legion. delete: not criminous
    *Merchandise. delete: not criminous
    *Negrohead. <Tas.>
    *Through Another Gate. Hutchinson,
        1927 (publisher correction)

*BRIDGES, VICTOR (GEORGE DE FREYNE).
    Ref: not in TC2.
    *Another Man's Shoes. Silent film:
        Essanay, 1916, as The Phantom
        Buccaneer (scw: H. Tipton Steck;
        dir: J. Charles Haydon). Also:

    Universal, 1922 (scw: Victor
        Bridges, Raymond L. Shrock; dir:
        Jack Conway)
    *Greensea Island. Silent film: Ideal,
        1923, as Through Fire and Water
        (scw: Eliot Stannard; dir:
        Thomas Bentley)
    *The Lady from Long Acre. Silent film:
        Fox, 1921 (scw: Paul Schofield;
        dir: George E. Marshall). Also:
        Fox, 1925, as Greater Than a Crown
        (scw: Wyndham Gittens; dir: Roy
        William Neill)
    *The Man from Nowhere. Silent film
        (?): Red Feather, 1916 (scw: Wil-
        liam M. Clifford; dir: Henry Otto)
    *Mr. Lyndon at Liberty. Silent film:
        London, 1915 (dir: Harold Shaw)

BRIENO, LINDA
    Brain Dead. Leisure, 1985

*BRIERLEY, DAVID. 1936-   . Ref: CA.
    SC: Cody, also in at least the
    title marked C.
    Big Bear, Little Bear. Faber, 1981;
        Scribner, 1981 <Berlin, 1948>
    *Blood Group O. ... Summit, 1984
        <Holl.>
    *Cold War. ... Summit, 1984
    Czechmate. Collins, 1984
    Shooting Star. Collins, 1983; Scrib-
        ner, 1983
    Skorpion's Death. Collins, 1985;
        Summit, 1986 <Afr., N.> C

BRIGGS, DESMOND (LAWTHER). 1931-
    Ref: CA.
    Standing into Danger. Secker, 1985;
        Secker (U.S.), 1986 <1960's>

BRILLIANT, JUDITH
    Dinner and Death. Truman, 1977

BRINKLEY, WILLIAM (CLARK). 1917-
    Ref: CA.
    Peeper. Viking, 1981; NEL, 1982

BRINTON, WILLIAM M.
    The Alaska Deception. Mercury House,
        1984

*BRISTOL, STEPHEN. Pseudonym of
    *Wilbur Braun, q.v. Other pseudo-
    nyms: Neb Albert, Millard Crosby,
    Anthony Forsthye, qq.v.

BRITTON, CHRISTOPHER (Q.). 1943-
    Ref: CA.
    -Paybacks. Fine, 1985 <San Diego,
        1971>

BRITTON, ERIC
    Blanche Fury. World Film, 1948
        (Novelization of the film; see
        *Joseph Shearing.)
    The October Man. World Film, 1947
        (Novelization of the film: Rank,
        1947; scw: Eric Ambler; dir:
        Roy Baker)

*BROADBRIDGE, HUGH
    *Moorland Terror. Film: Starcraft,
        1930, as The Road to Fortune
        (scw: Hugh Broadbridge; dir:
        Arthur Varney)

BRODERICK, JOHN. Leading Irish novel-
    ist; member of Irish Academy and
    awarded its prize for literature
    in 1975.
    A Prayer for Fair Weather. Boyars
        (London & NYC), 1984
    The Rose Tree. Boyars (London &
        NYC), 1985

*BRODEUR, PAUL
    *The Sick Fox. <Ger.>
    *The Stunt Man. Film: Simon, 1980
        (scw: Lawrence B. Marcus; dir:
        Richard Rush)

*BRODIE-INNES, JOHN WILLIAM. 1848-1923.

BRODY, PETER S. 1912-   . Pseudonym:
    David O. Wilderness, q.v.

*BROINOWSKI, ALISON
    *Take One Ambassador. <Jap.>

BROMELL, HENRY. 1947-   . Ref: CA.
    The Follower. Putnam, 1983; Hale,
        1985 <NYC>

*BROMLEY, GORDON. 1910-   . Ref: CA.

*BRONSON-HOWARD, GEORGE (FITZALAN).
    1884-1922.
    *Birds of Prey. Silent film: Columbia,
        1927 (scw: Dorothy Howell;
        dir: William James Craft)

    *The Black Book. Silent film: Trem
        Carr, 1928, as Man from Headquar-
        ters (scw: Arthur Hoerl; dir: Duke
        Worne)
    *The Devil's Chaplain. Silent film:
        Rayart, 1919 (scw: Arthur Hoerl;
        dir: Duke Worne). Also: Trem Carr,
        1929 (scw: Arthur Hoerl; dir:
        Duke Worne)
    *An Enemy to Society. Silent film:
        Metro, 1915 (dir: Edgar Jones)

BROOK, PETER (STEPHEN PAUL). 1925-
    Ref: CA.
    Box for One. Dramatic, 1971
        (1-act play.)

BROOK-SHEPHERD, (FREDERICK) GORDON.
    1918-   . Ref: CA.
    Eagle and Unicorn. Weidenfeld, 1966.
        U.S. title: The Eferding Diaries.
        Lippincott, 1967

*BROOKER, CLARE
    *Dark Mosaic. <Fr.>

*BROOKES, OWEN
    Deadly Communion. Holt, 1984; Futura,
        1985
    The Gatherer. Holt, 1983; Futura,
        1985 <Eng.>

BROOKS, ANN (TEDLOCK). 1905-   .
    -One Enchanted Summer. Arcadia, 1958
        <S.F.>

BROOKS, MAGGIE
    Loose Connections. Chatto, 1984

BROOKS, MEL. Professional name of Mel-
    vin Kaminsky, 1926-   . Ref: CA.
    See also: *William Johnston.
    Get Smart. Dramatic, 19??
        (3-act play based on TV series.)

BROOKS, RICHARD. 1912-   . Ref: CA.
    The Brick Foxhole. Harper, 1945.
        Film: RKO, 1947, as Crossfire
        (scw: John Paxton; dir: Edward
        Dmytryk)

*BROPHY, JOHN
    *The Day They Robbed the Bank of Eng-
        land. Film: Summit, 1960 (scw:
        Richard Maibaum, Howard Clewes;
        dir: John Guillermin)
    Turn the Key Softly. Collins, 1951.
        Film: Chiltern, 1953 (scw: John
        Brophy, Maurice Cowan; dir: Jack
        Lee)
    Waterfront. Cape, 1934; Macmillan,
        1934. Film: Conqueror, 1950;
        released in the U.S. as Waterfront
        Woman (scw: John Brophy, Paul
        Soskin; dir: Michael Anderson)

BROSNAN, JOHN
    Skyship. Hamlyn, 1981

BROSSARD, CHANDLER. 1922-   Pseudo-
    nym: Daniel Harper, q.v.

*BROTHERS, WILLIAM P. Military officer
    who has traveled widely; author of
    many articles and stories; living
    in S.F. area in 1950.

BROUGH, ROBERT B(ARNABAS). 1828-1860.
    Miss Brown, a Romance; and other
    tales. Ward, 1860 ss; title short
    novel is criminous

*BROWN, CARTER. Pseudonym of *Alan
    Geoffrey Yates, 1923-1985. Other
    pseudonym: *Paul Valdez. Ref
    also: TM. SC: Danny Boyd, also in
    titles marked DB below; Al Wheeler,
    also in titles marked AW below.
    Blonde Avalanche. Horwitz, 1984
    *Booty for a Babe. AW
    *Eve, It's Extortion. Also rewritten
        as published as: *Terror Comes
        Creeping, q.v.
    Kiss Michelle Goodbye. Horwitz, 1984;
        Tower, 1981 DB
    The Real Boyd. Horwitz, 1984 DB
    *The Savage Sisters. DB
    Stab in the Dark. Horwitz, 1984
    *Terror Comes Creeping. AW (SC
        correction)
    The Wicked Widow. Horwitz, 1981;
        Tower, 1981 AW

*BROWN, FREDRIC (WILLIAM). Ref also:
    TM.
    Before She Kills. McMillan, 1984 ss
    Carnival of Crime. Southern Illinois
        University, 1985 ss
    The Case of the Dancing Sandwiches.
        McMillan, 1985 (contains reprint
        of 1951 novelet and adds an unfin-
        ished novel based thereon)

The Freak Show Murders. McMillan, 1985 ss
Homicide Sanitarium. McMillan, 1984 ss
*Knock Three-One-Two. Film: M. Films, 1975, as L'Ibis Rouge (The Red Ibis) (scw: Jean-Pierre Mocky, Andre Ruellan; dir: Mocky)
Madman's Holiday. McMillan, 1985 ss Film (from title ss): RKO, 1946, as Crack-Up (scw: John Paxton, Ben Bengal, Ray Spencer; dir: Irving Reis)
The Screaming Mimi. Film: Columbia, 1957 (scw: Robert Blees; dir: Gerd Oswald)

*BROWN, HARRY JOE, JR.
*Duffy. (Novelization of film: Columbia, 1968; scw: Donald Cammell, Harry Joe Brown, Jr.; dir: Robert Parrish)

BROWN, HOSANNA
I Spy, You Die. Gollancz, 1984

BROWN, JOHN
Zaibatsu. Walrus (Sydney), 1983; Avon, 1985

*BROWN, MAY. 1913- . Pseudonym: *Vanessa Blake, q.v.

BROWN, PETER LANCASTER. 1927- Ref: CA.
Fjord of Silent Men. Hale, 1982

BROWN, R(OBERT) D. 1924- . Ref: CA.
Prime Suspect. Tower, 1981 <acad.>

*BROWN, ROBERT CARLTON. Ref also: CA.

*BROWN, ZENITH JONES. 1898-1983. Pseudonym also: Brenda Conrad, q.v.

*BROWNE, DOUGLAS G(ORDON)
*What Beckoning Ghost. ... Dover, 1986

*BROWNE, GERALD A(USTIN). Ref: TM.
*11 Harrowhouse. Film: TCF, 1974 (scw: Jeffrey Bloom, Charles Grodin; dir: Aram Avakian, Anthony Squire)
*Green Ice. Film: ITC, 1981 (scw: Edward Anhalt, Ray Hassett, Anthony Simmons, Robert de Laurentis; dir: Ernest Day)
19 Purchase Street. Arbor, 1982; Lane, 1983
Stone 588. Arbor, 1985; Viking (London), 1986

*BROWNE, HOWARD. Ref also: TC2, TM. SC: Paul Pine, also in title below.
The Paper Gun. McMillan, 1985 (novel and ss)

*BROWNE, K(ENNETH) R(OBERT) G(ORDON)
*Following Ann. Silent film: Universal, 1927, as The Cheerful Fraud (scw: Leigh Jacobson, Sam Mintz, Rex Taylor, William A. Seiter, Harvey Thew; dir: Seiter)

BROWNE, MARSHALL
City of Masks. Hale, 1981
Dark Harbour. Hale, 1984
Dragon Strike. Hale, 1981

BROWNE, PERCY
Dartmouth Drop. Merlin, 1982

BROWNE, WILLIAM DUNBAR. Canadian.
The Dew of Slumber. Christopher, 1955 <Calif.>

BROWNING, TOD. 1882-1962. Ref: CA.
The Mocking Bird. Jacobsen, 1926 (Novelization of film: MGM, 1926, as The Black Bird; scw: Waldemar Young; dir: Tod Browning)
Outside the Law. Jacobsen, 1926 (Novelization of film: Universal, 1930; scw: Tod Browning, Lucien Hubbard; dir: Browning)
-Where East Is East, with *(Harry) Sinclair Drago. Jacobsen, 1929 (Novelization of film: MGM, 1929; scw: Waldemar Young; dir: Tod Browning)

BRUCE, GRACE A.
Dark Secrets of the Manor. Castle, 1985

*BRUCE, JEAN
*Cold Spell. Film: Numbre One, 1967, as Cinq Gars pour Singapore (Five Ashore for Singapore) (scw: Bernard T. Michel, Pierre Kalfon; dir: Michel)

*Hot Line. Film: Valoria, 1966, as Atout Coeur a Tokyo pour OSS 117 (Heart Trump for OSS 117 in Tokyo) (scw: Pierre Foucaud, Terence Young, Marcel Mithois; dir: Michel Boisrond)
*Live Wire. Film: PAC-DA-MA, 1966, as OSS 117--Mission for a Killer (scw: Jean Halain, Pierre Foucaud, Andre Hunabelle; dir: Hunabelle)

*BRUCE, LEO
*Case with No Conclusion (not Case with No Solution). ... Academy Chicago, 1984
*Death at St. Asprey's School. ... Academy Chicago, 1984
*Furious Old Women. ... Academy Chicago, 1983
*Nothing Like Blood. ... Academy Chicago, 1985
*Our Jubilee Is Death. ... Academy Chicago, 1986

*BRUNNER, JOHN (KILIAN HOUSTON)
The Productions of Time. Signet, 1967; Penguin, 1970

*BRUTON, ERIC (MOORE). Ref (revised, expanded): TC2.

BRYAN, CHRISTOPHER. 1935- . Ref: CA.
Night of the Wolf. Harper, 1983; Lion, 1983

*BRYAN, MICHAEL. Pseudonym of Brian Moore, q.v. Other pseudonym: *Bernard Mara.
*Intent to Kill. Film: Zonic, 1958 (scw: Jimmy Sangster; dir: Jack Cardiff)

BRYANT, DOROTHY. 1930- , Ref: CA.
Killing Wonder. Ata, 1981; Women's Press, 1982 <Calif.>

*BRYANT, MARGUERITE
*The Redemption of Richard. Silent film: Universal, 1924, as The Breathless Moment (scw: Raymond L. Shrock, William E. Wing, Harvey Gates; dir: Robert F. Hill)

*BRYANT, PETER
*Two Hours to Doom. Film: Columbia, 1964, as Dr. Strangelove (scw: Stanley Kubrick, Terry Southern, Peter George; dir: Kubrick)

BRYSON, MADELENE
The Hitch-Hike Murders. Walker's Pond, 1977 <Boston>

BUCCI, MARK
The Court of the Stone Children. Dramatic, 1978 (Play.) <S.F.>

*BUCHAN, JOHN. Ref also: CA, TM.
*Huntingtower. Silent film: Welsh-Pearson, 1927 (scw: Charles E. Whittaker; dir: George Pearson)
*The Thirty-Nine Steps. Film: Gaumont British, 1935 (scw: Charles Bennett, Ian Hay, Alma Reville; dir: Alfred Hitchcock). Also: Rank, 1959 (scw: Frank Harvey, Charles Bennett, Ian Hay, Alma Reville; dir: Ralph Thomas). Also: Rank, 1978 (scw: Michael Robson; dir: Don Sharp)

*BUCHANAN, EILEEN-MARIE DUELL. 1922- . Pseudonym: *Clare Curzon, q.v., *Rhona Petrie.

*BUCHANAN, JAMES DAVID
The Prince of Malta. Constable, 1984 <Carib.>

*BUCK, CHARLES NEVILLE
*The Key to Yesterday. Silent film: Famous Players, 1914 (scw: Robert A. Dillon)

*BUCK, PAUL
*The Honeymoon Killers. (Novelization of film: Roxane, 1969; scw & dir: Leonard Kastle)

*BUCK, PEARL S.
Voices in the House. Brown, 1962

BUCK, PETER. SC: Marc Dean (The Mercenary). in all titles.
The Black Gold Briefing. Signet, 1982 <Mid. East>
The Deadly Birdman. Signet, 1981 <Haiti>
The Megadeath Option. Signet, 1983

Operation Icicle. Signet, 1981 <Russ.>
Passport to Peril. Signet, 1983 <Afr.>
Ready, Aim, Die. Signet, 1982
School for Slaughter. Signet, 1982 <Cors.>
The Secret of San Felipe. Signet, 1981
Thirteen for the Kill. Signet, 1981

BUCKLEY, JOHN
Beyond Murder. Carousel, 1980 <Calif.>

BUCKLEY, KATHLEEN. Joint pseudonym with Sharon Jarvis, 1943- : H. M. Major, q.v.

*BUCKLEY, WILLIAM F(RANK), JR. Ref also: TC2. SC: Blackford Oakes, also in all titles below.
Marco Polo, If You Can. Doubleday, 1982; Lane, 1982 <1959>
See You Later, Alligator. Doubleday, 1985; Arrow, 1985 <Cuba, 1962>
The Story of Henri Tod. Doubleday, 1984; Lane, 1984 <Berlin, 1961>

BUCKSTONE, J(OHN) B(ALDWIN). 1802-1879. See also: Oswald Allan.
The Green Bushes. National Acting, 1845 (3-act play.)
Jack Sheppard. Chapman, 1840 (4-act play.) Silent film: London Films, 1912 (dir: Percy Nash)

*BUDD, JACKSON
*A Convict Has Escaped. Film: Gloria-Alliance, 1947, as They Made Me a Fugitive; released in thhe U.S. as I Became a Criminal (scw: Noel Langley; dir: Alberto Cavalcanti)

*BUDE, JOHN. Ref also: CA.

*BUDRYS, ALGIS
*Who? Film: British Lion, 1974; released in the U.S. as Man Without a Face (scw: John Gould; dir: Jack Gold)

*BUELL, JOHN (EDWARD)
*The Pyx. Film: Cinerama, 1973 (scw: Robert Schlitt; dir: Harvey Hart)
*The Shrewsdale Exit. Film (?): Gaumont, 1975, as L'Agression (Act of Aggression) (scw: Jean-Patrick Mauchette, Gerard Pires; dir: Pires)

BUGLIOSI, VINCENT T., 1934- , and KEN HURWITZ, 1948- Ref (both authors): CA.
Shadow of Cain. Norton, 1981; Norton (London), 1982 <L.A.>

BUKOWSKI, CHARLES
Tales of Ordinary Madness. City Lights, 1983 ss, some criminous

*BULLETT, GERALD (WILLIAM)
*The Jury. Film: ACT, 1956, as The Last Man to Hang (scw: Ivor Montagu, Max Trell, Gerald Bullett, Maurice Elvey; dir: Terence Fisher)

*BULLIET, RICHARD (WILLIAMS)
The Gulf Scenario. St. Martin's, 1984

*BULLIVANT, CECIL H(ENRY)
*Blood Money. Silent film: Granger, 1921 (dir: Fred Goodwins)
*Whose Wife? Silent film: American, 1917 (dir: Rollin S. Sturgeon)
*The Wife Whom God Forgot. Silent film: Alliance, 1920; also released as Tangled Hearts (scw: Adrian Johnstone; dir: William J. Humphrey)
*The Woman Wins. Silent film: Broadwest, 1918 (scw: R. Byron-Webber, Kenelm Foss; dir: Frank Wilson)

*BULWER-LYTTON, EDWARD (GEORGE EARLE)
*Ernest Maltravers. Silent film: Gem, 1913, as The End of the Road (scw: Jack Byrne; dir: William Robert Daley). Also: AB, 1914 (scw: Travers Vale). Also: Ideal, 1920 (scw: Eliot Stannard; dir: Jack Denton)
*Eugene Aram. Silent film: Cricks, 1914 (scw & dir: Edwin J. Collins). Also: Edison, 1915 (scw & dir: Richard Ridgely). Also: Davidson, 1924 (scw: Kinchen Wood; dir: Arthur Rooke)
Night and Morning. Saunders, 1841;

BUNKER, EDWARD
-The Animal Factory. Viking, 1977
  Little Boy Blue. Viking, 1981 <L.A.>
*No Beast So Fierce. Film: Warner,
  1978, as Straight Time (scw: Alvin
  Sargent, Edward Bunker, Jeffrey
  Boam; dir: Ula Grosbard)

*BUNTLINE, NED
*Elfrida, the Red Rover's Daughter.
  (title correction)

BUONOCORE, BUD
  Shamrock Cohen and the Amorous Doppelganger. Magico, 1981 (two
  stories)

BURANELLI, VINCENT. 1919-   . See:
  Murray Wolfson, 1927-

BURCH, JAMES. Grew up in Tex., lived
  and traveled in Mex. and Europe;
  taught English in Paris; worked as
  commercial fisherman in Calif.;
  living in S.F.
  Lubyanka. Atheneum, 1983; Gollancz,
  1984 <Moscow, 1978>

BURDICK, EUGENE (LEONARD), 1918-1965,
  and JOHN HARVEY WHEELER, JR.,
  1918-   . Ref for Burdick: CA.
  Fail-Safe. McGraw, 1962; Hutchinson, 1963 <1967> Film: Columbia, 1964 (scw: Walter Bernstein;
  dir: Sidney Lumet)

*BURGE, REGINALD J.
*There Is a Destiny... <Fr.>

*BURGESS, ANTHONY
*A Clockwork Orange. Film: Warner,
  1971 (scw & dir: Stanley Kubrick)
-Honey for the Bears. Heinemann, 1963;
  Norton, 1964 <Russ.>

*BURGESS, (FRANK) GELETT. Ref also:
  CA; not in TC2.
*Find the Woman. Silent film: Fox,
  1920, as A Manhattan Knight (scw:
  Paul H. Sloane; dir: George A.
  Beranger)
*Two O'Clock Courage. Film: RKO, 1936,
  as Two in the Dark (scw: Seton I.
  Miller; dir: Ben Stoloff). Also:
  RKO, 1945 (scw: Robert E. Kent,
  Gordon Kahn; dir: Anthony Mann)
*The White Cat. Silent film: Bluebird,
  1918, as The Two-Soul Woman (scw &
  dir: Elmer Clifton). Also: Univer-
  sal, 1923, as The Untameable (scw:
  Hugh Hoffman; dir: Herbert Blache)

BURKE, ALAN DENNIS. 1949-   . Ref: CA.
  Getting Away with Murder. Little,
  1981

BURKE, JAMES. Born in Winnipeg; graduate of Univ. of Winnipeg; journalist.
  If It Weren't for Sex...I'd Have to
  Get a Job. NC Press, 1985 <Can.>
  (Dramatized cases of Canadian
  private investigator Arnold Man-
  weiler.)

*BURKE, JAMES WAKEFIELD
*Three Day Pass--to Kill. ... Berkley,
  1955

*BURKE, JOHN (FREDERICK)
*The Angry Silence. (Novelization of
  film: Beaver, 1960; scw: Bryan
  Forbes; dir: Guy Green)
  The Bill. Methuen, 1985 (Noveliza-
  tion of the TV series.)
*The Man Who Finally Died. (Noveliza-
  tion of film: Magna, 1962; scw:
  Lewis Greifer, Louis Marks; dir:
  Quentin Lawrence)
*-Privilege. (Novelization of film:
  Worldfilm, 1967; scw: Norman
  Bognor; dir: Peter Watkins)
*-The Trap. (Novelization of film:
  Parallel, 1966; scw: David Osborn;
  dir: Sidney Hayers)

*BURKE, JONATHAN
*Echo of Barbara. Film: Independent
  Artists, 1961 (scw: John Kruse;
  dir: Sidney Hayers)

BURKE, MARTYN. 1942-   .
  The Commissar's Report. Granada,
  1984; Houghton, 1984

*BURKE, RICHARD
*The Dead Take No Bows. Film: TCF,
  1941, as Dressed to Kill (scw:
  Stanley Rauh, Manning O'Connor;
  dir: Eugene Forde)

*BURKE, SIMON
  Death Is the Pay-Off. Scion, 1950
  (date correction)

*BURKE, STEWART
  Key to Murder. ... (3-act play.)

*BURKE, THOMAS. Ref also: CA.
*Limehouse Nights. Silent film (from
  "Gina of Chinatown" and "The Lamp
  in the Window"): Griffith, 1921,
  as Dream Street (scw: Roy Sin-
  clair; dir: D. W. Griffith).
  Also (from "The Chink and the
  Child"): Artcraft, 1917, as Broken
  Blossoms (scw & dir: D. W. Grif-
  fith). Sound film (from same ss):
  Twickenham, 1936, as Broken Blos-
  soms (scw: Emlyn Williams; dir:
  Hans Brahm). Also (from "Beryl,
  the Croucher, and the Rest of
  England"): Concanen, 1949, as No
  Way Back (scw: Stefan Osiecki,
  Derrick de Marney; dir: Osiecki)
*Night Pieces. ss, some criminous
*Whispering Windows. Silent film
  (from ss "Twelve Golden Curls"):
  Fox, 1924, as Curlytop (scw:
  Frederick Hatton; dir: Maurice
  Elvey)

BURKEY, DAVE
  Rain Lover. Ballantine, 1985 <Ill.>

*BURKHARDT, EVE. Joint pseudonym with
  *Robert F(erdinand) Burkhardt:
  Rob Eden, q.v.

*BURKHARDT, ROBERT F(ERDINAND). Joint
  pseudonym with *Eve Burkhardt:
  Rob Eden, q.v.

*BURKHOLZ, HERBERT. Born in NYC;
  lived in Spain for many years. SC:
  Eddie Mancuso and Vasily Borgneff,
  in *The Death Freak, as by *John
  Luckless, and in next title below.
*Mulligan's Seed. <Switz.>
  The Sleeping Spy, with *Clifford
  Irving. Atheneum, 1983; NEL, 1984

*BURLEY, W(ILLIAM) J(OHN). Ref also:
  TM. SC: Supt. Charles Wycliffe,
  also in titles marked CW below.
  The House of Care. Gollancz, 1981;
  Walker, 1982
  Wycliffe and the Beales. Gollancz,
  1983; Doubleday, 1984 CW
  Wycliffe and the Four Jacks. Gol-
  lancz, 1985; Doubleday, 1986 CW
*Wycliffe and the Scapegoat. ...
  Doubleday, 1979 (U.S. publisher
  correction.)
  Wycliffe's Wild-Goose Chase. Gol-
  lancz, 1982; Doubleday, 1982 CW

BURLINSON, RICHARD
  Concerto. New Horizon, 1981

*BURMEISTER, JON
*Running Scared. Film: Rank, 1978,
  as Tigers Don't Cry (existence of
  film not confirmed)

BURNET, DANA and GEORGE ABBOTT,
  1887-   , q.v.
  Four Walls. French (NYC), 1928 (3-
  act play.) Silent film: MGM,
  1928 (scw: Alice D. G. Miller;
  dir: William Nigh). Sound film:
  MGM, 1934, as Straight Is the Way
  (scw: Bernard Schubert; dir: Paul
  Sloane)

*BURNETT, W(ILLIAM) R(ILEY). Ref also:
  TM.
*The Asphalt Jungle. Film: MGM, 1950
  (scw: Ben Maddow, John Huston; dir:
  Huston). Also: MGM, 1958, as The
  Badlanders (scw: Richard Collins;
  dir: Delmer Daves). Also: MGM,
  1963, as Cairo (scw: Joanne Court;
  dir: Wolf Rilla). Also: MGM, 1972,
  as Cool Breeze (scw & dir: Barry
  Pollack)
*Dark Hazard. Film: First National,
  1934 (scw: Ralph Block, Brown
  Holmes; dir: Alfred E. Green).
  Also: Warner, 1937, as Wine, Women
  and Horses (scw: Roy Chanslor; dir:
  Louis King)
  Goodbye, Chicago. St. Martin's, 1981;
  Hale, 1982 <Chi., 1928>
-The Goodhues of Sinking Creek. Harper, 1934
*High Sierra. Film: First National,
  1941 (scw: John Huston, W. R. Burnett; dir: Raoul Walsh). Also: War-
  ner, 1949, as Colorado Territory
  (scw: John Twist, Edmund H. North;
  dir: Raoul Walsh). Also: Warner,
  1955, as I Died a Thousand Times
  (scw: W. R. Burnett; dir: Stuart
  Heisler)
*Little Caesar. Film: First National,
  1931 (scw: Francis Edward Faragoh;
  dir: Mervyn LeRoy)
*Nobody Lives Forever. Film: Warner,
  1946 (scw: W. R. Burnett; dir:
  Jean Negulesco)
*Vanity Row. Film: Republic, 1956, as
  Accused of Murder (scw: Bob
  Williams, W. R. Burnett; dir:
  Joe Kane)

BURNS, B(ERNARD) K.
-The Jury Woman. Burns, 1923 (3-act
  play.) Silent film: Associated
  First National, 1924, as The Love
  Racket (scw: Mary O'Hara; dir:
  Harry O. Hoyt). Sound film: War-
  ner, 1929, as The Love Racket
  (scw: John F. Goodrich; dir:
  William A. Seiter)

*BURNS, REX (RAOUL STEPHEN SCHLER).
  Ref also: TM. SC: Gabriel Wager,
  also in both titles below.
  The Avenging Angel. Viking, 1983;
  Penguin, 1984 <Colo.>
  Strip Search. Viking, 1984; Penguin,
  1985 <Denver>

BURNS, ROY
  Duckett's Condor. Hale, 1984
  Slate Secret. Hale, 1985

*BURROUGHS, EDGAR RICE
*The Oakdale Affair. Silent film:
  World, 1919 (dir: Oscar Apfel)

BURROUGHS, MILLY. Joint pseudonym with
  Robert Burroughs: Roberta
  Burroughs, q.v.

BURROUGHS, ROBERT. Joint pseudonym with
  Milly Burroughs: Roberta Burroughs,
  q.v.

BURROUGHS, ROBERTA. Joint pseudonym
  of Milly and Robert Burroughs.
  The Fugitive Feet. Gem, 1985
  <1944, Ida.>

BURROUGHS, WILLIAM (SEWARD). 1914-
  Ref: CA.
  Cities of the Red Night. Holt,
  1981; Calder, 1981
  The Last Words of Dutch Schultz.
  Viking, 1975; Calder, 1985

*BURTON, ANNE. SC: Richard Trenton,
  also in title below.
  Worse Than a Crime. Raven, 1981

*BURTON, ANTHONY
  Embrace of the Butcher. Dodd, 1982

BURTON, BRIAN J.
  East Lynne. Cambridge, 1965 (3-act
  play based on the novel by *Mrs.
  Henry Wood, q.v.)
  Lady Audley's Secret. Cambridge,
  1966 (3-act play adapted from the
  novel by *Mary Braddon, q.v.)
  The Murder of Maria Marten. Cam-
  bridge, 1964 (3-act play.)
  <Eng., 1827>
  Murder Play. French (London), 1981
  (1-act play.)
  Sweeney Todd the Barber. Cambridge,
  1962 (3-act play.)

*BURTON, MILES. Pseudonym of Cecil
  John Charles Street, 1884-1964.

BURTT, J. DOUGLAS
  Senseless. Tower, 1981

*BUSBY, ROGER (CHARLES)
  The Hunter. Collins, 1985

*BUSH, CHRISTOPHER. Ref: not in TC2.
  SC: Ludovic Travers, also in title
  marked LT below.
  The Case of the Happy Medium. Macdonald, 1952; Macmillan, 1952 LT
*Murder on Mondays. (title correc-
  tion)

BUSH, IAN. Has Ph.D. in physiology from
  Cambridge Univ.; lives in Vt.;
  Research Professor of Psychiatry
  and Physiology at Darmouth Univ.
  Medical School.

The Siberian Reservoir. Houghton (NYC and London), 1983

*BUTLER, GERALD (ALFRED)
  *Kiss the Blood Off My Hands. Film: Universal International, 1949; released in Britain as Blood on My Hands (scw: Leonardo Bercovici; dir: Norman Foster)
  *Mad with Much Heart. Film: RKO, 1952, as On Dangerous Ground (scw: A. I. Bezzerides; dir: Nicholas Ray)
  *They Cracked Her Glass Slipper. Film: Kenilworth, 1948, as Third Time Lucky (scw: Gerald Butler; dir: Gordon Parry)

*BUTLER, MICHAEL and *DENNIS SHRYACK
  *The Gauntlet. (Novelization of film: Warner, 1977; scw: Michael Butler, Dennis Shryack; dir: Clint Eastwood)

*BUTLER, (RAYMOND) RAGAN
  *Captain Nash and the Wroth Inheritance. ... Harwood, 1975

BUTLER, ROBERT OLEN (JR.). 1945- Ref: CA.
  Sun Dogs. Horizon, 1982 <Alaska>

*BUTLER, WILLIAM. Ref: CA.

*BUTLER, WILLIAM VIVIAN. SC: Commander George Gideon (following *J. J. Marric, q.v.), also in titles below.
  *Gideon's Force. ... Stein, 1985
  Gideon's Law. Hodder, 1981; Stein, 1985
  Gideon's Way. Hodder, 1983; Stein, 1986

*BUTTERWORTH, MICHAEL. Pseudonym: Michael Dobson, *Sarah Kemp, qq.v.
  The Man Who Broke the Bank at Monte Carlo. Collins, 1983; Doubleday, 1983 <Fr.>
  A Virgin on the Rocks. Collins, 1985; Doubleday, 1985 <Paris, 1933>

*BUTTERWORTH, W(ILLIAM) E(DMUND III). Pseudonyms: Alex Baldwin, Jack Dugan, qq.v.
  The Court-Martial. Signet, 1962 <Ger.>

*BUXTON, ANNE ARUNDEL. Pseudonym: *Anne Maybury, q.v.

BUZZELLI, ELIZABETH KANE
  Gift of Evil. Bantam, 1983

BYRD, MAX. Ref: TM. Teaches English at Univ. of Calif. at Davis. SC: Mike Haller, in all titles.
  California Thriller. Bantam, 1981; Allison, 1984 <S.F.>
  Finders Weepers. Bantam, 1983; Allison, 1985 <S.F.>
  Fly Away, Jill. Bantam, 1981; Allison, 1984 <Eng.>

BYRNE, DAVID. See: Gary Peterson.

*BYRNE, MURIEL ST. CLARE. 1895-1983. Ref: CA.

*BYRNE, ROBERT
  -The Dam. Atheneum, 1981; Coronet, 1983 <Calif.>
  Skyscraper. Atheneum, 1984 <NYC>

*BYROM, JAMES
  *Thou Shouldst Be Living. <U.S., acad.>

*BYRON, CHRISTOPHER. Associate editor for "Time" magazine; author of many articles on politics and culture of other nations; living in Conn.

BYRON, JOHN. Pseudonym. See: David Bonavia.

CABLE, MARY. 1920-   , Ref: CA.
  Avery's Knot. Putnam, 1981 <R.I., 1832>

CADBURY, G. J.
  When the Death Penalty Came Back. Macmillan (London), 1982

CADDY, LEONARD H.
  Jekyll and Hyde. French, 1981 (3-act play based on the story "The Strange Case of Dr. Jekyll and Mr. Hyde" by *Robert Louis Stevenson, q.v.)

CADE, STEVEN
  Slade's Marauders. Souvenir, 1980; Bantam, 1981 <Carib.>

CAGSON, BUD
  Come Clean, Baby. Ken, 1952

*CAIDIN, MARTIN
  Deathmate. Bantam, 1982
  Manfac. Dell, 1981

*CAILLOU, ALAN
  Assault on Agathon. Avon, 1972. Film: Nine Network, 1976 (scw: Alan Caillou; dir: Laslo Benedek)

*CAIN, JAMES M(ALLAHAN). Ref also: CA.
  The Baby in the Icebox. Holt, 1981; Hale, 1982 ss, plus *The Embezzler. Film (from title story): Paramount, 1934, as She Made Her Bed (scw: Casey Robinson, Frank R. Adams; dir: Ralph Murphy)
  *The Butterfly. Film: Par Par, 1981 (scw: John Goff, Matt Cimber; dir: Cimber)
  *Career in C Major and other stories. British publication of title story in: *Three of a Kind. Film (from title story): TCF, 1939, as Wife, Husband and Friend (scw: Nunnally Johnson; dir: Gregory Ratoff). Also (from ss "Everybody Does It"): TCF, 1949, as Everybody Does It (scw: Nunnally Johnson; dir: Edmund Goulding)
  Cloud Nine. Mysterious Press, 1984; Hale, 1985
  *Double Indemnity. Film: Paramount, 1944 (scw: Billy Wilder, Raymond Chandler; dir: Wilder)
  *The Embezzler; see The Baby in the Icebox
  The Enchanted Isle. Mysterious Press, 1985 <Balt.>
  *Love's Lovely Counterfeit. Film: RKO, 1956, as Slightly Scarlet (scw: Robert Blees; dir: Allan Dwan)
  *Mildred Pierce. Film: Warner, 1945 (scw: Ranald MacDougall; dir: Michael Curtiz)
  *The Postman Always Rings Twice. Film: Lux, 1939, as Le Dernier Tournant (The Last Turning) (scw: Charles Spaak; dir: Pierre Chenal). Also: MGM, 1946 (scw: Harry Raskin, Niven Busch; dir: Tay Garnett). Also: Paramount, 1981 (scw: David Mamet; dir: Bob Rafelson)
  *Serenade. Film: Universal, 1939, as When Tomorrow Comes (scw: Dwight Taylor; dir: John M. Stahl). Also: Warner, 1956 (scw: Ivan Goff, Ben Roberts, John Twist; dir: Anthony Mann). Also: Universal, 1957, as Interlude (scw: Daniel Fuchs, Franklin Coen; dir: Douglas Sirk). Also: Cocinor, 1959, as Ossessione (Obsession) (scw: Pietrangeli, Giuseppi De Santis, Mario Alicata, Gianni Fuccini, Luchino Visconti; dir: Visconti). Also: Columbia, 1968, as Interlude (scw: Lee Langley, Hugh Leonard; dir: Kevin Billington)

CAIN, JONATHAN. Pseudonym of Nick Uhernik. SC: Sgt. Mark Stryker (Saigon Commandos), in all titles.
  Boonie-Rat Body Burning. Zebra, 1984 <Saigon>
  Cherry-Boy Body Bag. Zebra, 1984 <Saigon>
  Code Zero: Shots Fired. Zebra, 1984
  Di Di Mau or Die. Zebra, 1984
  Dinky-Dau Death. Zebra, 1984 <Viet Nam>
  Mad Minute. Zebra, 1985
  Sac Mau, Victor Charlie. Zebra, 1985
  Saigon Commandos. Zebra, 1983 <Saigon>
  You Die, Du Ma! Zebra, 1985

*CAIN, PAUL. Ref: BM, TC2, TM.

CAINE, WILLIAM. 1873-1925.
  Lady Sheba's Last Stunt. Jenkins, 1924

CAIRNS, ALISON. Born in Scot.; living in Cornwall, where she lectures in sociology.
  New Year Resolution. Collins, 1984; St. Martin's, 1985
  Strained Relations. Collins, 1983; St. Martin's, 1984

*CAIRNS, COLLEEN
  *Great Gorme. <Carib.>

CALDECOTT, ANDREW. 1884-   .
  Not Exactly Ghosts. Arnold, 1947 ss

CALDER, JASON. Pseudonym of John Dunmore, 1923-   . Ref: CA.
  The O'Rourke Affair. Hale, 1979 <N.Z.>
  Target Margaret Thatcher. Hale, 1981

*CALDER, ROBERT. Pseudonym of Jerrold Mundis, 1941-   . Ref: CA.

CALDER-MARSHALL, ARTHUR. 1908-   Ref: CA.
  The Way to Santiago. Cape, 1940; Reynal, 1949 <Mex.>

CALDWELL, BETTY
  The Vanderleigh Legacy. Zebra, 1981 <N.J.>

*CALDWELL, (JANET MIRIAM) TAYLOR (HOLLAND). 1900-1985.

*CALEF, NOEL
  *Frantic. Film: Lux, 1958, as Ascenseur pour L'Echafaud (Elevator to the Gallows) (scw: Roger Nimier, Louis Malle; dir: Malle).

CALLAHAN, ROD
  Too Smart to Live. World, 1951

*CALLAN, MICHAEL FEENEY
  The Falcon Ring. Hale, 1981

*CALLARD, MAURICE
  *A Night in October. (2-act play.)

*CALTHROP, DION (WILLIAM PALGRAVE) CLAYTON. See also: *(Chambers) Haldane (Cooke) McFall.
  -Perpetua. Rivers, 1911; Lane, 1911. Silent film: Famous Players, 1922; released in the U.S. as Love's Boomerang (scw: Josephine Lovett, Helen Blizzard; dir: John S. Robertson, Tom Geraghty)

*CALVIN, HENRY
  *Boka Lives! <Afr.>

*CAMERON, KENNETH M.
  The Hundred and First. Dramatists, 19?? (1-act play.)

*CAMERON, LOU. See also: Dagmar.
  Dekker. Berkley, 1976
  The Hot Car. Avon, 1981 <L.A.>
  The Subway Stalker. Dell, 1980

*CAMERON, (COURTNEY) OWEN. Ref: TM.

*CAMP, (CHARLES) WADSWORTH
  *The Abandoned Room. Silent film: Jans, 1920, as Love Without Question (scw: Violet Clark; dir: B. A. Rolfe)
  *The Communicating Door. Silent film (from ss "Hate"): Metro, 1922, as Hate (scw: June Mathis; dir: Maxwell Karger)
  *The Gray Mask. Silent film: World, 1915 (dir: Frank Crane)
  *The House of Fear. Film (partial sound), 1928, as The Last Warning (scw: Alfred A. Cohn, Tom Reed; dir: Paul Leni). Also: Universal, 1939 (scw: Peter Milne; dir: Joe May)

*CAMPBELL, ALICE (ORMOND)
  *Juggernaut. Film: JH Productions, 1936 (scw: Cyril Campion, H. Fowler Mear, Heinrich Fraenkel; dir: Henry Edwards). Also: Bushey, 1949, as The Temptress (scw: Kathleen Butler; dir: Oswald Mitchell)

*CAMPBELL, SIR GILBERT (EDWARD)
  In the Shadow of Death. Blackett, 1888 <ca.1790>

*CAMPBELL, MARY E(LIZABETH). 1903-1984.

CAMPBELL, PATRICIA (PLATT). 1901-
  -Lush Valley. Superior, 1948 <1890's, Wash.>

*CAMPBELL, R. T.
  *Bodies in a Bookshop. ... Dover, 1984

*CAMPBELL, R(OBERT) WRIGHT. Pseudonym (?): F. G. Clinton, q.v.
  Malloy's Subway. Atheneum, 1981; Hale, 1982 <NYC>

C

C

*CAMPBELL, (JOHN) RAMSEY
  The Face That Must Die. Star, 1979; Scream Press, 1983
  The Nameless. Macmillan, 1981
  Watch the Birdie. Pardoe, 1984

*CAMPBELL, REGINALD
  *Death in Tiger Valley. Film: Republic, 1936, as Girl from Mandalay (scw: Wellyn Totman, Endre Boehm; dir: Howard Bretherton)

CAMPBELL, RONALD GRAYSON. Pseudonym: Rex Grayson, q.v.

*CAMPBELL, SCOTT
  *Below the Dead-Line. Silent films (based on ss): Edison, 1915, as The Banker's Double (scw: Langdon West); Edison, 1914, as The Man Who Vanished (dir: Langdon West); Edison, 1914, as Dickson's Diamonds (scw: Scott Campbell; dir: Langdon West); Edison, 1914, as The Case of the Vanished Bonds (dir: Langdon West)
  *The Woman in Red. Street, 1903

*CAMPION, CYRIL (THERON)
  Ask Beccles, with Edward Dignon. French (London), 1927 (3-act play.)

CAMPSIE, ALISTAIR (KEITH)
  Perfect Poison. Hale, 1985

*CAMPTON, DAVID
  Frankenstein. Miller, 1973 (2-act play based on novel by M. W. Shelley, q.v.)
  *Mutatis Mutandis. (Play.)

*CANADAY, JOHN EDWIN. 1907-1985.

CANARY, BRENDA BROWN
  Voice of the Clown. Avon (U.S.), 1982; Avon (London), 1983

CANAVOR, FREDERICK
  Rape One. Madrona, 1982 <NYC>

*CANDY, EDWARD. Ref: not in TC2.
  *Words for Murder Perhaps. ... Doubleday, 1984

CANFIELD, MARK
  -Madonna of Avenue A. Jacobsen, 1929 (Novelization of film: Warner, 1929; scw: Ray Doyle; dir: Michael Curtiz)

CANNAN, DENIS and PIERRE BOST, 1901- . Cannan is pseudonym of Dennis Pullein-Thompson, 1919-
  The Power and the Glory. French, 1959 (3-act play based on the novel by *Graham Greene, q.v.)

*CANNAN, JOANNA. Ref also: CA.

CANNELL, DOROTHY. Born in Eng., living in Ill. Ref: TM.
  Down the Garden Path. St. Martin's, 1985 <Eng.>
  The Thin Woman. St. Martin's, 1984 <Eng.>

*CANNING, VICTOR. 1911-1986. Ref also: TM. Pseudonym: Alan Gould, q.v.
  *Birdcage. <Port.>
  The Boy on Platform One. Heinemann, 1981. U.S. title: Memory Boy. Morrow, 1981 <Fr.>
  *The Burning Eye. <Afr., E.>
  *Castle Minerva. Film: Novus, 1964 as Masquerade (scw: Michael Relph, William Goldman; dir: Basil Dearden)
  Delay on Turtle, and other stories. Nel pb, 1962   3 stories
  -Fly Away, Paul. Hodder, 1936; Reynal, 1936
  *The Golden Salamander. Film: Pinewood, 1950 (scw: Ronald Neame, Victor Canning, Lesley Storm; dir: Neame)
  *His Bones Are Coral. Also published as: The Shark Run. NEL, 1968. Film: Heritage, 1969, as Shark (scw: Samuel Fuller, John Kingsbridge; dir: Fuller)
  *The House of the Seven Flies. Film: Coronado, 1959, as The House of the Seven Hawks (scw: Jo Eisinger; dir: Richard Thorpe)
  *The Limbo Line. Film: Trio, 1968 (scw: Donald James; dir: Samuel Gallu)
  Memory Boy; see The Boy on Platform One
  *Panther's Moon. Film: Universal International, 1950; released in the U.S. as Spy Hunt (scw: George Zuckerman, Leonard Lee; dir: George Sherman)
  *The Python Project. <Med. Is.>
  *The Rainbird Pattern. Film: Universal, 1976, as Family Plot (scw: Ernest Lehman; dir: Alfred Hitchcock)
  *The Scorpio Letters. Film: MGM, 1968 (scw: Adrian Spies, Jo Eisinger; dir: Richard Thorpe)
  Vanishing Point. Heinemann, 1982; Morrow, 1983
  *Venetian Bird. Film: British Film, 1952; released in the U.S. as The Assassin (scw: Victor Canning; dir: Ralph Thomas)
  *The Whip Hand. <Austria>

*CANNON, ELLIOTT
  The Life-Adjuster. Hale, 1981
  Nobody Loves Me. Hale, 1981
  A Question of Survival. Hale, 1981

CANNON, JOHN. Pseudonym of Michael Newton, 1951- . Other pseudonym: Vince Robinson, q.v.
  Death Cruise. Carousel, 1980
  Web of Terror. Carousel, 1980 <ship>

*CANON, JACK. See: *Nick Carter.

*CAPELLI, ACE. House name, first used by *Stephen D(aniel) Frances.
  Dead on Time. Stokes, 195?
  The Fix. Kaye, 1950
  Slaughter Street. Gaywood, 195?
  Trapped. Gaywood, 195?
  The Web. Gaywood, 1953
  Woman Trap. Stokes, 195?

*CAPON, (HARRY) PAUL
  *Death at Shinglestrand. (corrected title) Film: Luckwell, 1958, as Hidden Homicide (scw: Tony Young, Bill Luckwell; dir: Young)

*CAPOTE, TRUMAN. 1924-1984.
  *In Cold Blood. Film: Columbia, 1967 (scw & dir: Richard Brooks)

CAPPERTON, JANE
  In Safe Hands. GM, 1984

CAPUTI, ANTHONY (FRANCIS). 1924-
  Ref: CA.
  Storms and Son. Atheneum, 1985 <NYC>

CARDER, PETER
  The Well-Wisher. New Horizon, 1981

CARDONA-HINE, ALVARO. Pseudonym: *Ursula Sanford.

*CAREW, JEAN
  *Samantha. <Mass.>

*CAREY, ALFRED E.
  Sealed Orders. criminous

*CAREY, WEBSTER
  *Walking Tall: Part 2. (Novelization of film: American International, 1977; released in Britain as Legend of the Lawman; scw: Howard B. Kreitsek; dir: Earl Bellamy)

*CARGILL, LESLIE
  The Dead Are So Dumb. Gulliver, 1950
  *Matrimony Most Murderous. (title correction)

*CARGILL, MORRIS. 1914- . Joint pseudonym with *John Hearne, 1926- : John Morris, q.v.

CARGILL, PATRICK
  The Loving Elms. Fortune, 1952 (3-act play.)

*CARKEET, DAVID
  *Double Negative. ... Quartet, 1985

*CARLETON, MARJORIE (CHALMERS)
  *Cry Wolf. Film: Warner, 1947 (scw: Catherine Turney; dir: Peter Godfrey)
  *The Night of the Good Children. <New Eng.>

*CARLINO, LEWIS JOHN
  *The Brotherhood. (Novelization of film: Paramount, 1968; scw: Lewis John Carlino; dir: Martin Ritt)
  *The Mechanic. (Novelization of film: UA, 1972; scw: Lewis John Carlino; dir: Michael Winner)

*CARLON, PATRICIA (BERNADETTE)
  *Crime of Silence. <Australia>

CARLSON, P(ATRICIA) M(cEVOY). 1940- . Ref: CA. SC: Maggie Ryan, in both titles.
  Audition for Murder. Avon, 1985 <acad., N.Y.>
  Murder Is Academic. Avon, 1985 <acad., N.Y.>

CARLTON, GERALD. Pseudonyms: *Lieut. Carlton, *Bernard Wayde, qq.v.

*CARLTON, LIEUT. Pseudonym of Gerald Carlton. Other pseudonym: *Bernard Wayde, q.v.
  *After the Bribe Takers. Street, 1902
  *The Arm of the Law. Street, 1903
  *The Bank Note Plates. Street, 1903
  *The Corridor of Death. Street, 1903
  *A Counterfeiter's Wake. Street, 1904
  *A Government Spy. Street, 1903
  *The Haunt of the "Queer" Makers. Street, 1903
  *The Man in Stripes. Street, 1903
  *The Man in the Mail. Street, 1903
  *The Man with a Gun. Street, 1904
  *The Moonshiner's Dupe. Street, 1903
  *The Pirate's Retreat. Street, 1904
  *The Poisoned Arrow. Street, 1904

*CARLYLE, ANTHONY
  A Gamble with Hearts. Mills, 1922. Silent film: Master, 1923 (scw: Lucita Squiers; dir: Edwin J. Collins)

*CARMICHAEL, FRED(ERICK WALKER). SC: Crane Hammond = CH.
  *Any Number Can Die. <1920s>
  *Exit the Body. CH <Vt.>
  Exit Who? French, 1982 CH <Vt.> (3-act play.)
  Out of Sight--Out of Murder. French, 1983 (Play.)
  *Victoria's House. <ca.1900>
  Who Needs a Waltz. French, 19?? (3-act play.)

*CARNAC, CAROL
  *Clue Sinister. Macdonald, 1947 (date correction)

*CARNAC, NICHOLAS
  Indigo. H. Hamilton, 1982, St. Martin's, 1982 <India, 1857>

*CARNEY, DANIEL. Ref: CA.
  Macau. Century, 1985; Fine, 1985 <Macao>
  The Square Circle. Corgi, 1982; Firecrest, 1983. Also published as: Wild Geese II. Corgi, 1985 <Ger.> Film: Thorn EMI, 1985, as Wild Geese II (scw: Reginald Rose; dir: Peter Hunt)
  *The Whispering Death. Film: Lord & Eichberg, 1976 (scw: Juergen Goslar, Scot Finch; dir: Goslar)
  The Wild Geese. Heinemann, 1977; Bantam, 1978. Film: Rank, 1978 (scw: Reginald Rose; dir: Andrew V. McLaglen)

CARNEY, WILLIAM
  The Rose Exterminator. Everest, 1980 <San Diego>

CARO, DENNIS R.
  The Man in the Dark Suit. PB, 1980 <future>

*CAROL, JOHN. Pseudonym of *Frederick (Tom) Foden.

*CAROTHERS, A. J.
  *Hero at Large. (Novelization of film: MGM, 1980; scw: A. J. Carothers; dir: Martin Davidson)

*CARPENTER, CARLETON. Pseudonym: *Ivy Manchester.
  The Peabody Experience. Black Walnut, 1985 <Conn.>

*CARPENTER, EDWARD CHILDS. See also: *Laurence Gross.
  The Leopard Lady. French, 1928. Silent Film: DeMille, 1928 (scw: Beulah Marie Dix; dir: Rupert Julian)

*CARPENTER, MARGARET
  *Experiment Perilous. Film: RKO, 1944 (scw: Warren Duff; dir: Jacques Tourneur)

*CARR, A(LBERT) H. Z(OLATKOFF). Ref also: TM; not in TC2.

CARR, CAMERON
    The Other. Jenkins, 1938

*CARR, GLYN. SC: Abercrombie Lewker,
    also in title below.
    Murder of an Owl. Bles, 1956

CARR, JESS(E CROWE, JR.). Ref: CA.
    Murder on the Appalachian Trail.
    Commonwealth, 1985 <Va.>
    (Novelized true crime.)

*CARR, JOHN DICKSON. Ref also: TM.
    *The Burning Court. Film: UFA-Comaci-
    co, 1962, as Le Chambre Ardent (The
    Ardent Room) (scw: Charles Spaak,
    Julien Duvivier; dir: Duvivier)
    *Castle Skull. ... Stacey, 1973
    (British publisher correction)
    The Dead Sleep Lightly. Doubleday,
    1983 (radio plays) Film (based on
    radio play "Cabin B-13"): TCF,
    1953, as Dangerous Crossing (scw:
    Leo Townsend; dir: Joseph M.
    Newman)
    *The Emperor's Snuff Box. Film: Mon-
    arch, 1957, as That Woman Opposite
    (Britain) and City After Midnight
    (U.S.) (scw & dir: Compton Ben-
    nett)
    *The Lost Gallows. ... H. Hamilton,
    1931
    *The Third Bullet and other stories.
    Film (based on "The Gentleman from
    Paris"): MGM, 1951, as The Man with
    a Cloak (scw: Frank Fenton; dir:
    Fletcher Markle)

*CARR, KIRBY. Pseudonym of *Kin Platt.
    *You're Hired; You're Dead. <L.A.>

*CARR, MARGARET. Ref: not in TC2.

CARRAHER, PHILIP J.
    The Scarlet Wreath. Phian, 1985

CARROLL, JAMES
    Family Trade. Little, 1982; Collins,
    1982

CARROLL, JAY
    Baby Killer. PaperJacks, 1985
    <Chi., hosp.>

CARROLL, JOHN R.
    Murder Well Rehearsed. Baker's, 1976
    (1-act play.)

CARROLL, PERRY ORGAN. Pseudonym:
    *Perry Organ.

CARROLL, RICHARD
    The Xanadu Program. Hale, 1983

CARROLL, SIDNEY. Pseudonym: *Kendall
    Lane, q.v.

CARSON, AL
    Hell Let Loose. Gray, 195?
    Menace. Gray, 195?

*CARSON, BART. At least the following
    were written by William Maconachie:
    *Cuban Heel, *Murder Matinee,
    *Phone for a Hearse, and *Torment
    Was a Woman.

CARSON, MICHAEL
    The Experiment. Signet, 1984. British
    title: The Genesis Experiment.
    Star, 1985 <hosp.>

*CARTER, ANGELA
    Honeybuzzard; see Shadow Dance
    The Infernal Desire Machines
    of Doctor Hoffman. Hart-Davis,
    1972. U.S. title: The War of
    Dreams. Harcourt, 1974 <S. Am.>
    Shadow Dance. Heinemann, 1966. U.S.
    title: Honeybuzzard. Simon, 1967.
    Reprinted in Britain under U.S.
    title: Pan, 1968
    The War of Dreams; see The Infernal
    Desire Machines of Doctor Hoffman

*CARTER, JOHN FRANKLIN. Pseudonym:
    Jay Franklin, q.v.

CARTER, MARY (ARKLEY)
    The Minutes of the Night. Little,
    1965, Heinemann, 1966

*CARTER, NICHOLAS (M = Magnet below.)
    *The American Marquis. 1889 in Secret
    Service Series; 1897 in M
    *The Crime of a Countess. 1892 in
    Secret Service Series; 1897 in M
    *Fighting Against Millions. 1892 in
    Secret Service Series; 1897 in M
    *The Gambler's Syndicate. 1892 in
    Secret Service Series; 1897 in M
    *The Great Enigma. 1892 in Secret
    Service Series; 1897 in M
    *The Old Detective's Pupil. 1889 in
    Secret Service Series; 1898 in M
    *The Piano Box Mystery. 1892 in Secret
    Service Series; 1894 in Shield
    Series; 1897 in M
    *The Stolen Identity. 1892 in Secret
    Service Series; 1897 in M
    *A Wall Street Haul. 1889 in Secret
    Service Series; 1897 in M
    *A Woman's Hand. 1890 in Secret Ser-
    vice Series, as by John R. Coryell;
    1897 in M

*CARTER, NICK. SC: Nick Carter, in all
    titles.
    The Algarve Affair. Charter, 1984
    (by *Jack Canon)
    Appointment in Haiphong. Charter,
    1982 (by *David Hagberg, q.v.)
    The Assassin Convention. Charter,
    1985 (by *Joseph L. Gilmore, q.v.)
    Assignment: Rio. Charter, 1984
    <Rio de Jan.> (by *Jack Canon)
    Blood of the Scimitar. Charter, 1985
    (by *Jack Canon)
    The Blue Ice Affair. Charter, 1985
    (by Ron Felber)
    The Budapest Run. Charter, 1983
    (by *Jack Canon)
    Caribbean Coup. Charter, 1984
    <Carib.> (by Robert J. Randisi,
    1951-   , q.v.)
    Cauldron of Hell. Charter, 1981 (by
    *Michael Jahn, q.v.)
    Chessmaster. Charter, 1982 (by
    Robert J. Randisi, 1951-
    q.v.)
    The Christmas Kill. Charter, 1983
    <Jap.> (by *Joseph L. Gilmore)
    Circle of Scorpions. Charter, 1985
    (by *Jack Canon)
    The Coyote Connection. Charter, 1981
    (by Bill Crider, 1941-   , and
    Jack Davis)
    The Damocles Threat. Charter, 1982
    (by *David Hagberg, q.v.)
    Day of the Mahdi. Charter, 1984
    <Mid. East> (by *Dennis Lynds,
    q.v.)
    The Death Dealer. Charter, 1983 (by
    *Jack Canon)
    Death Hand Play. Charter, 1984
    <S. Am.> (by *David Hagberg, q.v.)
    Death Island. Charter, 1984 <S. Pac.>
    (by *David Hagberg, q.v.)
    The Death Star Affair. Charter, 1982
    (by *Jack Canon)
    Deathlight. Charter, 1982 (by
    *Jerry Ahern, q.v.)
    The Decoy Hit. Charter, 1983 (by
    *Robert J. Randisi, 1951-
    q.v.)
    Doctor DNA. Charter, 1982 (by Robert
    E. Vardeman)
    The Dominican Affair. Charter, 1982
    (by Bruce Algozin)
    The Dubrovnik Massacre. Charter, 1981
    <Czech.> (by Henry Rasof and
    Stephen Williamson)
    Earth Shaker. Charter, 1982 (by
    Robert E. Vardeman)
    Earthfire North. Charter, 1983 (by
    *David Hagberg, q.v.)
    The Execution Exchange. Charter,
    1985 (by Dennis Lynds, q.v.)
    The Golden Bull. Charter, 1981
    <Mex.> (by *John Stevenson)
    The Greek Summit. Charter, 1983 (by
    *Robert J. Randisi, 1951-
    q.v.)
    Hide and Go Die. Charter, 1983 (by
    *Jack Canon)
    The Hunter. Charter, 1982 (by
    *David Hagberg, q.v.)
    The Israeli Connection. Charter, 1982
    (by Robert Derek Steeley)
    The Istanbul Decision. Charter, 1983
    (by *David Hagberg, q.v.)
    The Kali Death Cult. Charter, 1983
    (by Robert E. Vardeman)
    The Kremlin Kill. Charter, 1984
    (by *Jack Canon)
    The Last Flight to Moscow. Charter,
    1985 (by *Joseph L. Gilmore,
    q.v.)
    The Last Samurai. Charter, 1982 (by
    Bruce Algozin)
    The Macao Massacre. Charter, 1985
    (by *Jack Canon)
    The Mayan Connection. Charter, 1984
    <Cent. Am.> (by *Dennis Lynds,
    q.v.)
    The Mendoza Manuscript. Charter, 1982
    (by Robert J. Randisi, 1951-
    q.v.)
    Night of the Warheads. Charter, 1984
    (by *Jack Canon)
    The Normandy Code. Charter, 1985 (by
    *Jack Canon)
    Norwegian Typhoon. Charter, 1982 (by
    Robert E. Vardeman)
    Operation: McMurdo Sound. Charter,
    1980 <Antarctic> (by *David
    Hagberg, q.v.)
    Operation Sharkbite. Charter, 1984
    (by *Jack Canon)
    Operation Vendetta. Charter, 1983
    (by *Joseph L. Gilmore, q.v.)
    The Ouster Conspiracy. Charter, 1981
    (by *David Hagberg, q.v.)
    The Outback Ghosts. Charter, 1983
    <Australia> (by Robert E. Vardeman)
    *The Pamplona Affair. ... Star, 1983
    The Parisian Affair. Charter, 1981
    <Paris> (by H. Edward Hunsburger)
    Pleasure Island. Charter, 1981 (by
    Robert J. Randisi, 1951-
    q.v.)
    The Puppet Master. Charter, 1982
    (by *David Hagberg, q.v.)
    Pursuit of the Eagle. Charter, 1985
    <Bulg.> (by *Dennis Lynds, q.v.)
    The Q-Man. Charter, 1981 (by *John
    Stevenson)
    *Race of Death. ... Star, 1982
    Retreat for Death. Charter, 1982
    (by *David Hagberg, q.v.)
    San Juan Inferno. Charter, 1984
    <P. Rico> (by *Joseph L. Gilmore,
    q.v.)
    Society of Nine. Charter, 1981
    (by *Jack Canon)
    The Solar Menace. Charter, 1981
    (by *Robert E. Vardeman)
    The Strontium Code. Charter, 1981
    (by *David Hagberg, q.v.)
    The Tarlov Cipher. Charter, 1985
    (by *Jack Canon)
    The Treason Game. Charter, 1982
    (by *Joseph L. Gilmore, q.v.)
    The Vengeance Game. Charter, 1985
    (by *David Hagberg, q.v.)
    White Death. Charter, 1985 <Antarc-
    tic> (by *Dennis Lynds, q.v.)
    The Yukon Target. Charter, 1983 (by
    Robert E. Vardeman)
    Zero Hour Strike Force. Charter, 1984
    (by *David Hagberg, q.v.)

*CARTMILL, CLEVE. See: *Henry Kuttner.

*CARVIC, HERON. Ref: not in TC2.

*CARY, (THOMAS) FALKLAND L(ITTON)
    *Madam Tic-Tac. Film: Gibraltar,
    1957, as No Road Back (scw:
    Charles A. Leeds, Montgomery Tully;
    dir: Tully)

*CARY, MORLAND
    *Love Rides the Rails. (3-act play.)

CARYL, WARREN H. 1920-   . Pseudonym:
    Moss Tadrack, q.v.

*CASBERG, MELVIN L. SC: Capt. Prem
    Narayan, in *Death Stalks the Pun-
    jab, and titles below.
    Dowry of Death. Strawberry Hill, 1984
    <India>
    Five Rivers to Death. Strawberry
    Hill, 1982 <India>

CASCIANI, PATRICIA
    Ice Planet. New Horizon, 1982

*CASE, DAVID. Ref: CA.
    *Fengriffen. Film: Amicus, 1974, as
    And Now the Screaming Starts (scw:
    Roger Marshall; dir: Roy Ward
    Baker)
    The Third Grave. Arkham, 1981

*CASEY, ROBERT J.
    *Hot Ice. Bobbs, 1933 (U.S. pub-
    lisher correction)

*CASPARY, VERA. Ref also: TM.
    *Bedelia. Film: Corfield, 1946
    (scw: Vera Caspary, Moie Charles,
    Herbert Victor, Roy Ridley, Isadore
    Goldsmith; dir: Lance Comfort)
    *Laura. Film: TCF, 1944 (scw: Jay
    Dratler, Samuel Hoffenstein, Betty
    Reinhardt; dir: Otto Preminger)

*CASSIDAY, BRUCE (BINGHAM). Pseudonym:
    *C. K. Fong.

CASSIDY, S. J.
    The Altar Boy. Jove, 1982 <Mass.>

*CASSILIS, ROBERT. Pseudonym of
    Michael F. H. Edwardes, 1923-
    Ref: CA.
    Madness of the People. H. Hamilton,
    1982 <future>

C

C

*CASTLE, AGNES (SWEETMAN) and *EGERTON CASTLE
Wolf-Lure. Cassell, 1917; Appleton, 1917 <Fr.>

*CASTLE, EGERTON. See: *Agnes (Sweetman) Castle.

*CASTLE, JOHN
*Flight into Danger. Film: Paramount, 1957, as Zero Hour! (scw: Arthur Hailey, John Champion, Hall Bartlett; dir: Bartlett)

CASTLE, RONALD
Back to Bandola. New Horizon, 1981

CASTOIRE, MARIE and *RICHARD POSNER
Castoire is a detective with the NYC Police Dept.
Gold Shield. Putnam, 1982; Sphere, 1983 <NYC>

*CATTO, MAX(WELL JEFFREY)
*The Banana Men. <Cuba>
-The Flanagan Boy. Harrap, 1949. Film: Hammer, 1953; released in the U.S. as Bad Blonde (scw: Richard Landau, Guy Elmes; dir: Reginald Leborg)
*The Killing Frost. Film: United Artists, 1956, as Trapeze (scw: James R. Webb; dir: Carol Reed)
*Mister Midas. Film: Ross-Talbot, 1964, as Mr. Moses (scw: Charles Beaumont, Monja Danischewsky; dir: Ronald Neame)
*A Prize of Gold. Film: Warwick, 1955 (scw: Robert Buckner, John Paxton; dir: Mark Robson)
They Walk Alone. Secker, 1939 (3-act play). Film: Kenilworth, 1947, as Daughter of Darkness (scw: Max Catto; dir: Lance Comfort)

CAUDWELL, SARAH. Pseudonym of a lawyer who works for Lloyds Bank in London. Ref: TM. SC: Hilary Tamar, in both titles.
The Shortest Way to Hades. Collins, 1984; Scribner, 1985
Thus Was Adonis Murdered. Collins, 1981; Scribner, 1981 <Venice>

CAUNITZ, WILLIAM J. 1935-   . Lieutenant in NYC police department.
One Police Plaza. Crown, 1984; Blond, 1984 <NYC>

CAVAL, PATRICE
-Girls in Bondage. Publishers Export, 1967 <Det.>

*CAVANAGH, ARTHUR
*The Children Are Gone. Film: Corona, 1971, as The Deadly Trap (scw: Sidney Buchman, Eleanor Perry; dir: Rene Clement)

*CAVE, EMMA
Cousin Henrietta. Collins, 1981; St. Martin's, 1982

*CAVE, PETER
Slow Burn. Hamlyn, 1981
Taggart: Murder in Season. Mainstream, 1985 (Novelization of the TV series.)

*CAVERHILL, WILLIAM MELVILLE. 1910-1983. Pseudonym: *Alan Melville, q.v.

CAWSE, RALPH THOMAS
Burglar in Petticoats. Condor (Syd.), 1943

*CAY, NOWELL. Pseudonym of *Herbert Flowerdew.

CAYER, D. M.
Scarborough Fear. Macdonald, 1982

CECIL, ALLAN
The Fifty Million Hijack. Hale, 1983

CECIL, INFRIEDE
All the Virtues of the Dead. Black Sun, 1985

*CECIL, HENRY. Ref also: CA. SC also: Colonel Brain = CB; Mr. Tewkesbury = T.
*Brothers in Law. Film: Tudor, 1957 (scw: Frank Harvey, Jeffrey Dell, Roy Boulting; dir: Boulting)
*Full Circle. ss
*Independent Witness. CB
*Much in Evidence. T
*Natural Causes. CB,T

*The Painswick Line. T
*Settled Out of Court. T

*CELESTIN, JACK and *JACK DE LEON
*The Man at Six. Film: BIP, 1931; released in the U.S. as The Gables Mystery (scw: Harry Hughes, Victor Kendall; dir: Hughes). Also: Welwyn, 1938, as The Gables Mystery (scw: Victor Kendall, Harry Hughes; dir: Hughes)

*CHABER, M. E. (not Chamber, as given in first printing of CF)
*The Man Inside. Film: Warwick, 1958 (scw: John Gilling, David Shaw, Richard Maibaum; dir: Gilling)

*CHABREY, F(RANCOIS)
*The Invisible Image. (Translation of "Le Vingt-Cinquieme Image." Paris, 1967.)

*CHACKO, DAVID
Brick Alley. Delacorte, 1981 <Pa., 1960>

*CHADWICK, JOSEPH L. Pseudonym:
*Elizabeth Grayson.

CHADWICK, VIVIENNE CHARLTON
The Invisible Line. British Columbia Centennial Committee, 1958; French, 1960 (1-act play.) <Can.>

CHAIS, PAMELA (HERBERT). 1930-
Ref: CA.
Final Cut. Simon, 1981; NEL, 1982 <L.A.>

*CHALLIS, MARY. SC: Jeremy Locke, also in titles below. Set: Eng.
The Ghost of an Idea. Raven, 1981
A Very Good Hater. Raven, 1981

CHALONER, JOHN (SEYMOUR). 1924-
Ref: CA.
Bottom Line. Severn, 1984; St. Martin's, 1984

*CHAMBERLAIN, ESTHER and *LUCIA
*The Coast of Chance. Silent film: Selig, 1913 (dir: Oscar Eagle)

*CHAMBERLAIN, GEORGE AGNEW
*The Red House. Film: Lesser, 1947 (scw & dir: Delmer Daves)

*CHAMBERLAIN, LUCIA. See also: *Esther Chamberlain.
*The Other Side of the Door. Silent film: American, 1916 (scw: Clifford Howard; dir: Thomas Ricketts)

CHAMBERS, BARBARA and BECKY GARDINER
New York. Jacobsen, 1927 (Novelization of film: Famous Players, 1927; scw: Forrest Halse; dir: Luther Reed)

*CHAMBERS, PETER. Pseudonym also: *Peter Chester. SC: Mark Preston, probably also in all titles below.
Bomb Scare: Flight 147. Hale, 1984
Dragons Can Be Dangerous. Hale, 1983
Female—Handle with Care. Hale, 1981
The Highly Explosive Case. Hale, 1982
Jail Bait. Hale, 1983
The Lady Who Never Was. Hale, 1981
A Long Time Dead. Hale, 1981
A Miniature Murder Mystery. Hale, 1982
The Moving Picture Writes. Hale, 1984
Murder Is Its Own Reward. Hale, 1982
The Vanishing Holes Murder. Hale, 1985

*CHAMBERS, ROBERT W(ILLIAM)
*In Secret. Silent film: Pathe, 1919-20, as The Black Secret (scw: Bertram Millhauser; dir: George B. Seitz)
*Secret Service Operator 13. Film: MGM, 1934, as Operator 13; released in Britain as Spy 13 (scw: Harvey Thew, Zelda Sears, Eve Greene; dir: Richard Boleslavsky)

*CHAMBERS, (ELWYN) WHITMAN
*The Campanile Murders. Film: Chesterfield, 1934, as Murder on the Campus (scw: Andrew Moses; dir: Richard Thorpe)
*The Come-On. criminous. Film: Anglo-Amalgamated, 1956 (scw: Warren Douglas, Whitman Chambers; dir: Russell Birdwell)
*Murder for a Wanton. Film: MGM, 1936, as Sinner Take All (scw: Leonard Lee, Walter Wise; dir: Errol Taggart)

*Once Too Often. Film: Film Classics, 1948, as Blonde Ice (scw: Kenneth Gamet; dir: Jack Bernhard)

*CHAMBERS, WILLIAM E.
*The Redemption Factor. <NYC>

CHAMPION, D'ARCY LYNDON. ca.1903-1968. Pseudonym: *Jack D'Arcy; *G. Wayman Jones, q.v.

*CHANCE, JOHN NEWTON. 1911-1983. Film (based on unidentified novel): Unifilms, 1962, as Crosstrap (scw: Philip Wrestler; dir: Robert Hartford-Davis).
The Bad Circle. Hale, 1985
The Black Widow. Hale, 1981
The Death Chemist. Hale, 1983
The Death Importer. Hale, 1981
The Hunting of Mr. Exe. Hale, 1982
Looking for Sampson. Hale, 1984
Madman's Will. Hale, 1982
The Mystery of Enda Favell. Hale, 1981
Nobody's Supposed to Murder the Butler. Hale, 1984
The Shadow in Pursuit. Hale, 1982
Terror Train. Hale, 1983
The Time Bomb. Hale, 1985
The Traditional Murders. Hale, 1983

CHANCE, LISBETH. 1946-   .
Cutting Edge. Walker, 1985 <Colo.>

*CHANDLER, BRYN. 1945-   . Ref: CA.
Behind the Badge. Ballantine, 1984 <Miami>

*CHANDLER, DAVID (LEON)
The Masters Connection. Arbor, 1981

*CHANDLER, RAYMOND (THORNTON). Ref also: TM. See also: Stuart Gordon.
*The Big Sleep. Film: Warner, 1946 (scw: William Faulkner, Leigh Brackett, Jules Furthman; dir: Howard Hawks). Also: UA, 1977 (scw & dir: Michael Winner)
*The Blue Dahlia. Film: Paramount, 1946 (scw: Raymond Chandler; dir: George Marshall)
*Farewell, My Lovely. Film: RKO, 1942, as The Falcon Takes Over (scw: Lynn Root, Frank Fenton; dir: Irving Reis). Also: RKO, 1945; released in the U.S. as Murder, My Sweet (scw: John Paxton; dir: Edward Dmytryk). Also: AVCO, 1975 (scw: David Zelag Goodman; dir: Dick Richards).
*The High Window. Film: TCF, 1942, as Time to Kill (scw: Clarence Upson Young; dir: Herbert I. Leeds). Also: MGM, 1947; released in the U.S. as The Brasher Doubloon (scw: Dorothy Hannah; dir: John Brahm)
*The Lady in the Lake. Film: MGM, 1946 (scw: Steve Fisher; dir: Robert Montgomery)
*The Little Sister. Film: MGM, 1969, as Marlowe (scw: Stirling Silliphant; dir: Paul Bogart)
*The Long Goodbye. Film: United Artists, 1973 (scw: Leigh Brackett; dir: Robert Altman)
Playback. Mysterious Press, 1985; Harrap, 1985 (screenplay)

*CHANG, LEE
*The Year of the Tiger. <S.F.>

*CHANNING, BRENT
Here Comes Trouble. Cooperbooks, 1952
Let the Dead Sleep On. World Distributors, 1951

*CHANSLOR, ROY
*Hazard. Film: Paramount, 1948 (scw: Arthur Sheekman, Roy Chanslor; dir: George Marshall)

CHAPMAN, RENATE
Evil in Waiting. Avalon, 1974
Milmorra House. Avalon, 1978?

*CHAPMAN, ROBERT (ALEC MARK)
*Behind the Headlines. Film: Kenilworth, 1956 (scw: Allan MacKinnon; dir: Charles Saunders)
*Murder for the Million. Film: Fortress, 1957, as Murder Reported (scw: Doreen Montgomery; dir: Charles Saunders)
*One Jump Ahead. Film: Kenilworth, 1955 (scw: Doreen Montgomery; dir: Charles Saunders)
*Winter Wears a Shroud. Film: Croydon, 1954, as The Delavine Affair (scw: George Fisher; dir: Douglas Pierce)

CHAPMAN, ROBIN
-My Vision's Enemy. Hodder, 1968

*CHARBONNEAU, LOUIS
The Brea File. Doubleday, 1982

CHARLES, CONN ALAN
Liar's Dice. Tor, 1985 <Cent. Am.>

*CHARLES, ROBERT. SC: Supt. Mark Nicolson, also in title below.
*The Prey of the Falcon. ... Pinnacle, 1976

CHARLES, ROBERT
Steel Killer. Jove, 1981 <Moscow, 1950>

CHARLES, WYNDHAM
-Dingane's War. Hale, 1983
Hogan's Last Case. Hale, 1982
No Love for Miss Stent. Hale, 1983

*CHARTERIS, LESLIE. Ref also: TM. SC: Simon Templar (The Saint), also in titles marked ST. Film (based on unidentified story): RKO, 1940, as The Saint's Double Trouble (scw: Ben Holmes; dir: Jack Hively). Also: RKO, 1941, as The Saint in Palm Springs (scw: Jerry Cady; dir: Jack Hively).
The Fantastic Saint. Hodder, 1983; Doubleday, 1982   6 ST ss reassembled from earlier collections
*Getaway. Film: RKO, 1941, as The Saint's Vacation (scw: Leslie Charteris, Jeffrey Dell; dir: Leslie Fenton)
*The Holy Terror. Film (from novelet "The Million Pound Day"): RKO, 1939, as The Saint in London (scw: Lynn Root, Frank Fenton; dir: John Paddy Carstairs)
*Lady on a Train. (Novelization of film: Universal, 1945; scw: Edmund Beloin, Robert O'Brien; dir: Charles David)
*Meet the Tiger. Film: RKO, 1941, as The Saint Meets the Tiger (scw: Leslie Arliss, Wolfgang Wilhelm, James Seymour; dir: Paul L. Stein)
*The Misfortunes of Mr. Teal. Also published as: The Saint in London. Hodder, 1952
The Saint in London; see *The Misfortunes of Mr. Teal
*The Saint in New York. Film: RKO, 1938 (scw: Charles Kaufman, Mortimer Offner; dir: Ben Holmes)
Salvage for the Saint. Hodder, 1983; Doubleday, 1983   ST
*She Was a Lady. Film: RKO, 1939, as The Saint Strikes Back (scw: John Twist; dir: John Farrow)

*CHARYN, JEROME
The Isaac Quartet. Zomba, 1984 (Contains all four of the Isaac Sidel novels published earlier in U.S.)

CHASE, BEATRICE. Pseudonym of Olive Katharine Parr, 1874-   .
Patricia Lancanster's Revenge. Longman's, 1928

*CHASE, BORDEN. Pseudonym of Frank G. Fowler, 1900-1971. Ref: CA.

*CHASE, JAMES HADLEY. Pseudonym of Rene Brabazon Raymond, 1906-1985. Ref also: CA, TM. SC: Helga Rolfe, also in title marked HR. Film (based on unidentified novel): Hamster, 1986, as Grandeure et Decadence d'un Petit Commerce de Cinema (The Grandeur and Decadence of a Small-Time Filmmaker) (scw & dir: Jean-Luc Godard)
*An Ace Up My Sleeve. Film: American-International, 1975, as Ace Up Your Sleeve; also released as Crime and Passion (scw: Jesse Lasky, Jr., Pat Silver; dir: Ivan Passer)
*Come Easy--Go Easy. Film: Paris Film, 1963, as Chair de Poule (Gooseflesh) (scw: Rene Barjaval, Julien Duvivier; dir: Duvivier)
*Eve. Film: Interopa, 1962, as Eve (scw: Hugo Butler, Evan Jones; dir: Joseph Losey)
*The Flesh of the Orchid. Film: Fox/Lira, 1975, as La Chair de L'Orchidee (The Flesh of the Orchid) (scw: Patrice Chereau, Jean-Claude Carriere; dir: Chereau)
Hand Me a Fig Leaf. Hale, 1981
Have a Nice Night. Hale, 1982
*Hit and Run. Film: Cinestar, 1985, as Rigged (scw: John Goff, Jill Gurr; dir: C. M. Cutry)
Hit Them Where It Hurts. Hale, 1984
*I Would Rather Stay Poor. Film: Atlas, 1974, as The Catamount Killing (scw: Julian More, Sheila More; dir: Krzysztof Zanussi)
*I'll Get You for This. Film: Kaydor, 1951; released in U.S. as Lucky Nick Cain (scw: George Callahan, William Rose; dir: Joseph M. Newman)
*Last Page. Film: Exclusive, 1952; released in the U.S. as Manbait (scw: Frederick Knott; dir: Terence Fisher)
Meet Helga Rolfe. Hale, 1984 HR
*Miss Callaghan Comes to Grief. Film: Corona, 1957, as Mefiez-Vous Fillettes (Look Out, Girls; Good Girls Beware; released in the U.S. as Young Girls Reward) (scw: Rene Wheeler, Jean Meckert; dir: Yves Allegret).
*Miss Shumway Waves a Wand. Film: Cocinor, 1963, as Une Blonde Comme Ca! (A Blonde Like That!) (scw: Jacques Robert, Felecien Marceau; dir: Jean Jabely)
*No Orchids for Miss Blandish. Also published as: The Villain and the Virgin. Novel Books, 19??. Film: Alliance, 1948 (scw & dir: St. John L. Clowes). Also: Cinerama, 1971, as The Grissom Gang (scw: Leon Griffiths; dir: Robert Aldrich)
Not My Thing. Hale, 1983
*Not Safe to Be Free. Film: Interfilm, 1968, as Le Demoniaque (The Woman Is a Stranger) (scw: Jean-Louis Curtiss; dir: Rene Gainville)
*One Bright Summer Morning. Film: Prodis, 1965, as Par un Beau Matin D'Ete (On a Nice Summer Day) (scw: Michel Audiard, Didier Goulard, Maurice Fabre, Georges Bardawill, Jacques Deray; dir: Deray)
*There's Always a Price Tag. Film: Rank, 1958 (existence of film not confirmed)
*Tiger by the Tail. Film: Cocinor, 1958, as L'Homme a L'Impermeable (The Man in the Raincoat) (scw: Rene Barjavel, Jules Duvivier; dir: Duvivier)
The Villain and the Virgin; see No Orchids for Miss Blandish
*The Way the Cookie Crumbles. Film: Films de Quadrangle, 1970, as Trop Petit Mon Ami (Too Small, My Friend) (scw: Saddy Rebbot, Jean-Claude Grimberg, Eddy Matalon; dir: Matalon)
We'll Share a Double Funeral. Hale, 1982
*The World in My Pocket. Film: British Lion, 1961; released in Britain as On Friday at Eleven (scw: Frank Harvey; dir: Alvin Rakoff)
*You Have Yourself a Deal. Film: Comacico, 1968, as La Blonde de Peking (The Blonde from Peking) (scw: Nicolas Gessner, Marc Behm, Jacques Vilfrid; dir: Gessner)

*CHASE, JOSEPHINE. 1883-1931. Pseudonym: *Martha Wickes.

*CHASE, OLIVE
*Driven to Murder. (3-act play.)

*CHASE, PHILIP.   SC: Aaron Eisenberg and William Kendall, in all titles.

*CHASTAIN, THOMAS. Ref: TC2, TM.   SC: Insp. Max Kauffman, also in title marked MK below; Robins family, in titles marked RF.
The Diamond Exchange. Doubleday, 1981; Hale, 1981 MK <NYC>
Nightscape. Atheneum, 1982 <NYC>
The Revenge of the Robins Family, with Bill Adler. Morrow, 1984 RF
Who Killed the Robins Family, with Bill Adler. Morrow, 1983; Joseph, 1983 RF

*CHATOR, ELIZABETH EILEEN. 1910-
Pseudonym: *Lee Chaytor.

*CHATTERTON, E(DWARD) KEBLE
The Marriages of Mayfair. Paul, 1909 (Novelization of play by Cecil Raleigh and Henry Hamilton.) Silent film: Metro, 1920, as The Fatal Hour (scw: Julia Burnham; dir: George W. Terwilliger)

*CHAYTOR, LEE. Pseudonym of Elizabeth Eileen Chater, 1910-   . Ref: CA.

*CHAZE, (LEWIS) ELLIOT. 1915-   . Ref: CA, TM. SC: Kiel St. James and Orson Boles = S&B.
*Black Wings Has My Angel. ... Also published in England as: One for the Money. Hale, 1985
Goodbye Goliath. Scribner, 1983; Hale, 1984 <Ala.>
Little David. Scribner, 1985 S&B <Ala.>
Mr. Yesterday. Scribner, 1984 S&B <Ala.>
One for the Money; see Black Wings Had My Angel
*Wettermark. ... Hale, 1984

CHEKHOV, ANTON (PAVLOVICH). 1860-1904. Ref: CA.
The Shooting Party. Paul, 1926; McKay, 1927. Film: United Artists, 1944, as Summer Storm (scw: Rowland Leigh; dir: Douglas Sirk)

CHENEY, THEODORE A(LBERT) REES. 1928-   . Ref: CA.
Day of Fate. Charter, 1981

CHERNENOK, MIKHAIL. Ref: TM. Member of Soviet Writers' Union; lives in Siberia; has written four novels about Anton Birnkov, who is featured in the novel below.
Losing Bet. Dial, 1984 <Russ.> (Translation of "Stavka na Proigrysh." Moscow, 1980)

CHERRY, KELLY. Ref: CA.
In the Wink of an Eye. Harcourt, 1983

*CHESBRO, GEORGE (CLARK). Ref also: TM. SC: Dr. Robert Frederickson (Mongo), also in title marked RF below.
The Beasts of Valhalla. Atheneum, 1985 RF
Turn Loose the Dragon. Ballantine, 1982; Severn, 1982 <Carib.>

CHESLEY, DONALD
Black Vendetta. Holloway, 1982

CHESNEY, MARION. 1936-   . Pseudonyms: M. C. Beaton, Jennie Tremaine, qq.v.

CHESNEY, P.
Protection of Democracy. Stockwell, 1985

CHESTER, CHARLIE. Pseudonym: *Carl Noone.

*CHESTER, GEORGE RANDOLPH
*Get-Rich-Quick Wallingford. Silent film: Pathe, 1915-16, as The New Adventures of J. Rufus Wallingford (dir: Theodore Wharton). Also: Paramount, 1921 (dir: Frank Borzage). Sound film: MGM, 1931, as The New Adventures of Get-Rich-Quick Wallingford (scw: Charles MacArthur; dir: Sam Wood)

*CHESTER, GILBERT
*Secret of the Snows. Amalgamated, 1938   (Sexton Blake)

*CHESTER, ROY
The Diamonds of Despair. Hale, 1982
The Winds of Pentecost. Hale, 1981

*CHESTERTON, G(ILBERT) K(EITH). Ref also: TM; TC2 (revised).
*The Innocence of Father Brown. Film (from ss "The Blue Cross"): Facet, 1954, as Father Brown; released in the U.S. as The Detective (scw: Thelma Schnee, Robert Hamer; dir: Hamer)
*The Man Who Knew Too Much and other stories. Film (from title story): GFD, 1934 (screen credits: see *Ruth Alexander)
*The Wisdom of Father Brown. Film: Paramount, 1935, as Father Brown, Detective (scw: Henry Myers, C. Gardner Sullivan; dir: Edward Sedgwick)

*CHETWYND-HAYES, R(EGINALD HENRY GLYNN) (corrected spelling)

*CHEVALIER, PAUL. Ref: CA.
More Deadly Than the Male. World Distributors, 1950. Film: U.N.A., 1959 (dir: Robert Bucknell)
The Shaft. Hodder, 1983

*CHEYNEY, PETER. Ref also: CA, TM. SC: Alonzo MacTavish, also in title marked AM; Slim Callaghan, also in title marked SC.

*The Best Stories of Peter Cheyney. Faber, 1954 ss (publisher correction)
*Calling Mr. Callaghan. Film: Atlantis, 1960 (existence of film not confirmed)
*Dames Don't Care. Film: CICO-Pathe, 1954, as Les Femmes S'En Balancent (Dames Get Along) (scw: Bernard Borderie, Jacques Vilfrid; dir: Borderie)
*I'll Say She Does. Film: Prodis, 1960, as Comment Qu'Elle Est (What a Girl!) (scw: Marc-Gilbert Sauvajon, Bernard Borderie; dir: Borderie)
*Lady in Green and other stories. ss AM
*Never a Dull Moment. SC also: SC
*Poison Ivy. Film: Pathe Consortium, 1953, as La Mome Vert de Gris (The Gun Moll) (scw: Jacques Berland, Bernard Borderie; dir: Borderie)
*Sinister Errand. Film: TCF, 1952, as Diplomatic Courier (scw: Casey Robinson, Liam O'Brien; dir: Henry Hathaway)
*This Man Is Dangerous. Film: Sonofilm, 1954, as Cet Homme Est Dangeureux (This Man Is Dangerous) (scw: Jacques Berland; dir: Jean Sacha)
*Uneasy Terms. Film: British National, 1948 (scw: Peter Cheyney; dir: Vernon Sewell)
*Your Deal, My Lovely. Film: Prodis, 1963, as A Toi de Faire Mignonne (You Do It, Cutie) (scw: Marc-Gilbert Sauvajon, Bernard Borderie; dir: Borderie)

*CHILD, RICHARD WASHBURN
*Fresh Waters and other stories. Silent film (from ss "Here's How"): Universal, 1925, as The Mad Whirl (scw: Frederic Hatton; dir: William A. Seiter).
*The Velvet Black. Silent film (from ss "A Whiff of Heliotrope"): Cosmopolitan, 1920, as Heliotrope (scw & dir: George D. Baker). Also: Paramount, 1928, as Forgotten Faces (scw: Howard Estabrook, Oliver H. P. Garrett; dir: Victor Schertzinger). Also (sound): Paramount, 1936, as Forgotten Faces (scw: Brian Marlow, Marguerite Roberts, Robert M. Yost; dir: E. A. Dupont). Also: United Artists, 1942, as A Gentleman After Dark (scw: Patterson McNutt, George Bruce; dir: Edwin L. Marin)

*CHILDERS, (ROBERT) ERSKINE. Ref also: CA.
*The Riddle of the Sands. Film: Rank, 1979 (scw: Tony Maylam, John Bailey; dir: Maylam)

*CHILDERS, JAMES S(AXON)
Enemy Outpost. Appleton, 1942 <Can.>

CHILDRESS, MARK
A World Made of Fire. Knopf, 1984; Hodder, 1985

*CHITTENDEN, F(RANK) A(LBERT)
*The Uninvited. Film: Tempean, 1957, as Stranger in Town (scw: Norman Hudis, Edward Dryhurst; dir: George Pollock)

CHITTENDEN, JONATHAN BRACE. 1864-1928.
Stolen Stamps. (NYC), 1926

*CHIU, TONY
Realm Seven. Bantam, 1984

*CHODOROV, EDWARD
*Kind Lady. Film: MGM, 1935; also released as House of Menace (scw: Bernard Schubert; dir: George B. Seitz). Also: MGM, 1951 (scw: Jerry Davis, Edward Chodorov, Charles Bennett; dir: John Sturges)

CHODOROV, JEROME, 1911-   , and NORMAN PANAMA, 1920-   . Ref (both): CA.
A Talent for Murder. French, 1982 (3-act play.)

CHRISTIANSEN, BENJAMIN. 1879-1959. Danish film director.
The Devil's Circus. Jacobsen, 1926 (Novelization of film: MGM, 1926; scw & dir: Benjamin Christiansen)

*CHRISTIANSEN, SIGURD (WESLEY)
*Two Living and One Dead. Film: Swan, 1961 (scw: Lindsey Galloway; dir: Anthony Asquith)

*CHRISTIE, AGATHA. Ref also: TM. SC: Supt. Battle, also in title marked SB; Mrs. Ariadne Oliver, with Hercule Poirot (= HP) in many titles and solo in *The Pale Horse; Jane Marple, also in title marked JM.
*The ABC Murders. Film: MGM, 1966, as The Alphabet Murders (scw: David Pursall, Jack Seddon; dir: Frank Tashlin)
*After the Funeral. Film: MGM, 1963, as Murder at the Gallop (scw: David Pursall, Jack Seddon, James P. Cavanagh; dir: George Pollock)
The Agatha Christie Hour. Collins, 1982 (9 ss from earlier collections, and 1 in first collected appearance in Eng.)
*Black Coffee. Film: Twickenham, 1931 (scw: Brock Williams, H. Fowler Mear; dir: Leslie Hiscott). Also: Haik, 1932, as Le Coffret de Laque (The Lacquered Box) (dir: Jean Kemm).
*Death on the Nile. Film: Paramount, 1978 (scw: Anthony Shaffer; dir: John Guillerman)
*Endless Night. Film: British Lion, 1971 (scw & dir: Sidney Gilliat)
*Evil Under the Sun. Film: EMI, 1982 (scw: Anthony Shaffer; dir: Guy Hamilton)
*4.50 from Paddington. Film: MGM, 1961, as Murder, She Said (scw: David Pursall, Jack Seddon, David Osborn; dir: George Pollock)
Hercule Poirot's Casebook. Dodd, 1984 (50 HP ss reassembled from earlier collections)
*The Listerdale Mystery. (correction: 8 ss appear in The Golden Ball and other stories.)
*Lord Edgware Dies. Film: Real Art, 1934 (scw: H. Fowler Mear; dir: Henry Edwards)
*The Mirror Crack'd from Side to Side. Film: EMI, 1980, as The Mirror Crack'd (scw: Jonathan Hales, Barry Sandler; dir: Guy Hamilton)
Miss Marple. Dodd, 1985 (All 20 JM ss assembled from earlier collections.)
*Mrs. McGinty's Dead. Film: MGM, 1964, as Murder Most Foul (scw: David Pursall, Jack Seddon; dir: George Pollock)
*The Murder of Roger Ackroyd. Film: Twickenham, 1931, as Alibi (scw: H. Fowler Mear; dir: Leslie Hiscott)
*Murder on the Orient Express. Film: EMI, 1974 (scw: Paul Dehn; dir: Sidney Lumet)
*The Mysterious Mr. Quin. Film (from ss "The Coming of Mr. Quin"): Strand, 1928, as The Passing of Mr. Quin (scw: Leslie Hiscott; dir: Julius Hagen)
*Ordeal by Innocence. Film: Cannon, 1984 (scw: Alexander Stuart; dir: Desmond Davis)
*The Secret Adversary. Silent film: studio?, as Die Abenteuer G.m.b.H. (Adventure, Inc.) (dir: Fred Sauer)
*Spider's Web. Film: Danziger, 1960 (scw: Albert G. Miller; dir: Godfrey Grayson)
*Ten Little Niggers. Film: TCF, 1945; released in the U.S. as And Then There Were None (scw: Dudley Nichols; dir: Rene Clair). Also: Seven Arts, 1965, as Ten Little Indians (scw: Peter Yeldham, Dudley Nichols; dir: George Pollock). Also: Copro, 1975, as Ten Little Indians (scw: Enrique Llovet, Erich Krohnke; dir: Peter Collinson)
*The Unexpected Guest. (3-act play.) <Wales>
*The Witness for the Prosecution. Film (from title story): United Artists, 1957 (scw: Billy Wilder, Harry Kurnitz; dir: Wilder)

*CHRISTIE, CAMPBELL. See: *Dorothy Christie.

*CHRISTIE, DOROTHY and *CAMPBELL
Carrington, V.C. French (London), 1954 (3-act play.) Film: Remus, 1954; released in the U.S. as Court Martial (scw: John Hunter; dir: Anthony Asquith)
*Grand National Night. Film: Talisman, 1953; released in the U.S. as Wicked Wife (scw: Dorothy Christie, Campbell Christie; dir: Bob McNaught)

*Someone at the Door. Film: BIP, 1936 (scw: Jack Davies, Marjorie Deans; dir: Herbert Brenon). Also: Hammer, 1950 (scw: A. R. Rawlinson; dir: Francis Searle)

*CHRISTOPHER, JAY
*Murder-Go-Round. <Paris>

*CHRISTOPHER, JOHN
*The Caves of Night. Film: Columbia (existence of film not confirmed)

CHRISTOPHER, WENDY
Clutch of Diamonds. Hale, 1978

*CHRISTY, HELEN
*Mr. Ace. (Novelization of film: Bogeaus, 1946; scw: Fred Finklehoff; dir: Edwin L. Marin)

CHRISTY, SARA
Flander's Folly. Mill, 1937

CHUBIN, BARRY. Executive of National Iranian Oil Co., member of inner circle of power around the Shah.
The Feet of a Snake. Hodder, 1984; Arbor, 1984 <Iran>

CHURCHILL, E. RICHARD. See: *Don(ald Eugene) Pendleton.

*CHURCHILL, LUANNA. Joint pseudonym of John and Frieda Dughman.

*CICELLIS, KAY
*The Day the Fish Came Out. (Novelization of film: TCF, 1967; scw & dir: Michael Cacoyannis)

CLAIR, WILLIAM R. See: Richard K. Abshire.

*CLAIRE, MARVIN. Pseudonym of Marvin Larson.

*CLANCY, AMBROSE
*Blind Pilot. (title correction)

CLANCY, TOM. 1947-   . Runs an insurance business in Md.
The Hunt for Red October. Naval Institute, 1984; Collins, 1985 <ship>

CLARINS, DANA. Pseudonym of *Thomas (Eugene) Gifford.
Quality Parties. Bantam, 1985
Woman in the Window. Bantam, 1984 <NYC>

*CLARK, AL C. Titles reprinted as by *Donald Goines.
*Crime Partners. <Detroit>
*Cry Revenge. <L.A.>
*Death List. <Detroit>
*Kenyatta's Escape. <Nevada>
*Kenyatta's Last Hit. <Las Vegas>

CLARK, ALAN R.
-The High Wall. Smith, 1936; Joseph, 1936. Film: MGM, 1947 (scw: Sydney Boehm, Lester Cole; dir: Curtis Bernhardt)

CLARK, ANNA C.
Passport to Peril. Lancer, 1967

CLARK, BRUCE
Deathstalk. Leisure, 1985 <Maine>

*CLARK, DOUGLAS (MALCOLM JACKSON). 1919-   . Ref: CA, TC2. SC: Insp./Supt. George Masters, also in all titles below.
Bouquet Garni. Gollancz, 1984
Dead Letter. Gollancz, 1984; Perennial, 1985
Doone Walk. Gollancz, 1985
*Dread and Water. ... Perennial, 1984
*Golden Rain. <acad.>
*Heberden's Seat. ... Perennial, 1984
Jewelled Eye. Gollancz, 1985; Gollancz (U.S.), 1986
The Longest Pleasure. Gollancz, 1981; Perennial, 1984
The Monday Theory. Gollancz, 1983; Perennial, 1985
Performance. Gollancz, 1985; Perennial, 1986
*Poacher's Bag. ... Perennial, 1983
Roast Eggs. Gollancz, 1981; Dodd, 1981
Shelf Life. Gollancz, 1982; Perennial, 1983
*Table D'Hote. ... Perennial, 1984
Vicious Circle. Gollancz, 1983; Perennial, 1985

*CLARK, ELLERY H(ARDING)
  *Loaded Dice. Silent film: Pathe, 1918 (scw: Gilson Willets; dir: Herbert Blache)

*CLARK, ERIC
  China Run; see Chinese Burn
  Chinese Burn. Hodder, 1984. U.S. title: China Run. Little, 1985 <Peking>
  Send in the Lions. Hodder, 1981; Atheneum, 1981 <1985>

CLARK, ERNEST
  Fatal Run. Dell, 1985

*CLARK, MARY HIGGINS. Ref also: TC2, TM.
  A Cry in the Night. Simon, 1982; Collins, 1983 <Minn.>
  Stillwatch. Simon, 1984; Collins, 1984 <Wash. D.C.>
  *A Stranger Is Watching. Film: MGM, 1981 (scw: Earl MacRauch, Victor Miller; dir: Sean S. Cunningham)
  *Where Are the Children? Film: Columbia, 1968 (scw: Jack Sholder; dir: Bruce Malmuth)

CLARK, RON and SAM BOBRICK
  Murder at the Howard Johnson's. French, 1980 (2-act play.)

*CLARK, WILLIAM (DONALDSON). 1916-1985.
  *Special Relationship. <1977>

*CLARKE, ANNA
  Desire to Kill. Hale, 1983; Doubleday, 1982
  Game, Set and Danger. Hale, 1983; Doubleday, 1981
  Last Judgement. Hale, 1986; Doubleday, 1985
  *The Last Voyage. ... St. Martin's, 1982 <Eng., 1939>
  *The Poisoned Web. ... St. Martin's, 1983
  Soon She Must Die. Hale, 1985; Doubleday, 1983
  We the Bereaved. Hale, 1984; Doubleday, 1982

*CLARKE, COLIN. 1940-
  K605. Sphere, 1985
  The Rat Box. Sphere, 1983

*CLARKE, DONALD HENDERSON
  Housekeeper's Daughter. Vanguard, 1938; Laurie, 1939. Film: United Artists, 1939 (scw: Rian James, Gordon Douglas; dir: Hal Roach)
  *Louis Beretti. Film: Fox, 1930; also released as Born Reckless (scw: Dudley Nichols; dir: John Ford)

CLARKE, JAY. Joint pseudonym with John Banks and Richard Covell: Michael Slade, q.v.

*CLARKE, LAURENCE (AYSCOUGH)
  Snowbird Paradine. Jarrolds, 1922 ss, some criminous

*CLARKE, MARCUS (ANDREW HISLOP)
  *His Natural Life. Silent film: Australasian, 1929, as For the Term of His Natural Life (scw & dir: Norman Dawn)

*CLARKE, T(HOMAS) E(RNEST) B(ENNETT)
  Grim Discovery. Hale, 1983
  Murder At Buckingham Palace. Hale, 1981; St. Martin's, 1982 <Eng., 1935>

CLARKE, THURSTON. 1946-   . Ref: CA.
  Thirteen O'Clock. Doubleday, 1984

CLARKSON, GEOFFREY
  Jihad. Pinnacle, 1981

*CLASON, CLYDE B. Ref also: TC2.

CLAUGHTON, RUSSELL
  Long Good Friday. Magnum, 1981 (Novelization of film: Calendar, 1981; scw: Barrie Keefe; dir: John MacKenzie)

CLAUSEN, DENNIS M(OURSE). 1943-
  Ref: CA.
  Ghost Lover. Bantam, 1981

*CLAUSSE, SUZANNE
  Bittersweet. Mystique, 1981 (Translation of "Te Reverrai-Je un Jour." Paris, 1964.)

CLAVELL, JAMES (DuMARESQ). 1924-
  Ref: CA.
  Noble House. Delacorte, 1981; Hodder, 1981 <H. Kong>

CLAYFORD, JAMES. See: *Arthur Wallace.

*CLEARY, C. P.
  *Death in the Life Department. <Dub.>

*CLEARY, JON (STEPHEN). Ref also: TM.
  The City of Fading Light. Collins, 1985; Morrow, 1986 <Berlin, 1939>
  *-The Climate of Courage. <Syd.>
  The Faraway Drums. Collins, 1981; Morrow, 1982 <India, 1911>
  The Golden Sabre. Collins, 1981; Morrow, 1981 <Russ., early 1900s>
  Helga's Web. Film: Cemp-Regent, 1975, as Scobie Malone (scw: Casey Robinson, Graham Woodlock, dir: Terry Ohlsson)
  *The High Commissioner. Film: Selmur, 1968; released in England as Nobody Runs Forever (scw: Wilfred Greatorex; dir: Ralph Thomas)
  *High Road to China. Film: Golden Harvest, 1983 (scw: Sandra Weintraub Roland, S. Lee Pogostin; dir: Brian G. Hutton)
  *Just Let Me Go. <Syd.>
  *Justin Bayard. Film: Warner, 1958, as Dust in the Sun (existence of film not confirmed)
  *The Long Shadow. <Australia>
  The Phoenix Tree. Collins, 1984 <Jap., 1945>
  -Spearfield's Daughter. Collins, 1982; Morrow, 1983 <NYC>
  You Can't See Round Corners. <Syd.> Film: Universal International, 1969 (scw: Richard Lane; dir: David Cahill)

CLEMEAU, CAROL. Pseudonym of Carol Clemeau Esler, 1935-   . Ref: CA.
  The Ariadne Clue. Scribner, 1982; Collins, 1983 <South, acad.>

*CLEMENS, BRIAN (HORACE)
  *The Edge of Darkness. criminous (3-act play.)

*CLEMENT, HENRY
  The Clairvoyant. Pinnacle, 1984 (Novelization of film; film not released?)
  *Darling Lili. (Novelization of film: Paramount, 1970; scw & dir: Blake Edwards)
  *Dillinger. (Novelization of film: American International, 1973; scw & dir: John Milius)
  *The Hearse. (Novelization of film: Marimark, 1980; scw: Bill Bleich; dir: George Bowers)
  *A Quiet Place in the Country. (Novelization of film: Pea Cinematografica, 1969; scw: Elio Petri, Luciano Vincenzoni; dir: Petri)
  *Slaughter. (Novelization of film: AIP, 1972; scw: Mark Hanna, Don Williams; dir: Jack Starrett)

*CLEMENTS, ABIGAIL. Pseudonym of Alice Skelton.

*CLERI, MARIO
  *Six Graves to Munich. Film: Carnation, 1983, as A Time to Die (scw: John Goff, Matt Cimber, William Russell; dir: Cimber)

*CLERK, ERNIE
  *Do You Like Tahiti. (Translation from the French.)

*CLEVELAND, JOHN
  *Minus One Corpse. <Calif.>

*CLEVELY, HUGH
  *Archer Plus 20. Film: RKO, 1939, as Meet Maxwell Archer; released in the U.S. as Maxwell Archer, Detective (scw: Hugh Clevely, Katherine Strueby; dir: John Paddy Carstairs)

*CLEWES, HOWARD (CHARLES VIVIAN)
  *An Epitaph for Love. <It.>
  *The Long Memory. Film: Europa, 1952 (scw: Robert Hamer, Frank Harvey; dir: Hamer)

*CLIFFORD, FRANCIS. Ref also: TM.
  *Act of Mercy. Film: Cavalcade, 1962; released in the U.S. as Guns of Darkness (scw: John Mortimer; dir: Anthony Asquith)

*The Naked Runner (incorrectly given as The Naked Spur in early printings of CF). Film: Artanis, 1967 (scw: Stanley Mann; dir: Sidney J. Furie)

CLIFFORD, MRS. W. K. <Lucy Lane Clifford>.   -1929.
  The Last Touches and other stories. Black, 1892; Macmillan, 1892 ss, one or two criminous
  -Mrs. Keith's Crime. Bentley, 1885; Harper, 1885

*CLIFT, DENNISON (HALLEY)
  *The Spy in the Room. ... Also published in Canada as: Espionage Agent. News Stand, 194?

CLINCH, CAPT.
  The Perth Amboy Mystery. Street, 1901 <N.J.>

*CLINE, C. TERRY (JR.)
  The Attorney Conspiracy. Arbor, 1983
  -Mindreader. Doubleday, 1981
  Missing Persons. Arbor, 1982; Sphere, 1983 <Fla.>
  Prey. NAL, 1985 <Ga.>

CLINTON, F. G. Pseudonym (?) of *R(obert) Wright Campbell, q.v.
  The Tin Cop. Pinnacle, 1983

*CLINTON, MAX
  *No Dame Wants to Die. (Written by *Michael Barnes.)

*CLINTON-BADDELEY, V(ICTOR VAUGHAN REYNOLDS GERAINT) C(LINTON)
  *To Study a Long Silence. ... Perennial, 1984

CLISSANT, EDOUARD
  The Ripening. Heinemann, 1985 (Translation.)

*CLIVE, JOHN
  Barossa. Granada, 1982; Delacorte, 1981 <Australia>

CLOTHIER, PETER (DEAN). 1936-
  Ref: CA.
  Chiaroscuro. St. Martin's, 1985

*CLOUSTON, J(OSEPH) STORER
  *His First Offense. Film: Lenauer, 1937, as Drole de Drame (Bizarre, Bizarre) (scw: Jacques Prevert; dir: Marcel Carne)
  *The Lunatic at Large. Silent film: Hepworth, 1921 (scw: George W. Dewhurst; dir: Henry Edwards). Also: First National, 1927 (scw: Ralph Spence; dir: Fred Newmeyer)
  *The Spy in Black. Film: Harefield, 1939; released in U.S. as U-Boat 29 (scw: Emeric Pressberger, Roland Pertwee; dir: Michael Powell)
  The Truthful Lady. Magico, 1984 (Sherlock Holmes)

CLOWES, ST. JOHN L(EGH)
  Dear Murderer. Evans, 1954 (3-act play.) Film: Gainsborough, 1947 (scw: Muriel Box, Sydney Box, Peter Rogers; dir: Arthur Crabtree)

*COATES, ROBERT M(YRON)
  *Wisteria Cottage. Film: United Artists, 1958, as Edge of Fury (scw: Robert Gurney; dir: Gurney, Peter Lerner)

*COBB, (GEOFFREY) BELTON. Ref: not in TC2.

*COBB, IRWIN S(HREWSBURY)
  *Back Home. ss, some criminous. Film: see Down Yonder with Judge Priest
  *Down Yonder with Judge Priest. Film (from "A Tree Full of Hoot Owls" and "Brer Fox and the Briar Patch", plus "Words and Music" from *Back Home): TCF, 1934, as Judge Priest (scw: Dudley Nichols, Lamar Trotti; dir: John Ford).
  *Old Judge Priest. Film (from ss "The Sun Shines Bright", "The Mob from Massac" and "The Lord Provides): Republic, 1953, as The Sun Shines Bright (scw: Laurence Stallings; dir: John Ford)

*COBB, THOMAS
  *Mrs. Erricker's Reputation. Silent film: Hepworth, 1920 (scw: Blanche McIntosh; dir: Cecil M. Hepworth)

*COBURN, ANDREW. Ref also: TC2.
-Company Secrets. Secker, 1982
*Off Duty. Film: Filmax, 1983, as Un Dimanche de Flics (A Cops' Sunday) (scw & dir: Michel Vianey)
Sweetheart. Macmillan, 1985; Secker, 1985 <Boston>
Widow's Walk. Secker, 1984 <New Eng.>

*COBURN, SAMMY
*Don't Tempt Me. Scion, 1950 (date correction)

*COCKRELL, FRANK and *MARIAN (BROWN) COCKRELL
*Dark Waters. Film: United Artists, 1944 (scw: Joan Harrison, Marian Cockrell; dir: Andre de Toth)

*COCKRELL, MARIAN (BROWN). See: *Frank Cockrell.

*CODY, LIZA. Ref: TM. SC: Anna Lee, in *Dupe, and titles below. Set: Eng.
Bad Company. Collins, 1982; Scribner, 1983
Head Case. Collins, 1985; Scribner, 1986
Stalker. Collins, 1984; Scribner, 1984

*COE, CHARLES FRANCIS
*Me--Gangster. Film: Fox, 1928 (scw: Charles Francis Coe; dir: Raoul Walsh)
*The River Pirate. Silent film: Fox, 1928 (scw: John Reinhardt, Benjamin Markson; dir: William K. Howard)

COFFARO, KATHERINE
Gently into Night. Harlequin, 1985 <NYC>

*COFFMAN, VIRGINIA (EDITH)
*The Curse of the Island Pool. ... Piatkus, 1986
*The Demon Tower. ... Piatkus, 1986 <It., 1808>
*A Fear of Heights. British title: Legacy of Fear. Piatkus, 1985
*From Satan, with Love. ... Piatkus, 1983
Legacy of Fear; see A Fear of Heights
The Lombard Heiress. Arbor, 1983; Severn, 1986
*The Looking-Glass. ... Piatkus, 1984
*The Master of Blue Mire. <Eng., 1814>
*Mistress Devon. ... Souvenir, 1982
The Orchid Tree. Arbor, 1984; Severn, 1985 <Haw., 1930s>
*Pacific Cavalcade. ... Severn, 1986
*The Rest Is Silence. ... Piatkus, 1985
*The Secret of Shower Tree. ... British title: Strange Secrets. Piatkus, 1984
Strange Secrets; see The Secret of Shower Tree

*COHAN, GEORGE M(ICHAEL). See also: *Max Marcin.
*The Tavern. (2-act play.)

COHAN, TONY. 1939-   . Ref: CA.
Canary. Doubleday, 1981
Opium. Simon, 1984; Granada, 1985 <H. Kong>

COHEN, ANTHEA. 1913-   . Ref: CA, TM. SC: Nurse Agnes Carmichael, in all titles. Set: Eng.
Angel of Death. Quartet, 1983; Doubleday, 1985
Angel of Vengeance. Quartet, 1982; Doubleday, 1984
Angel Without Mercy. Quartet, 1982; Doubleday, 1984
Fallen Angel. Quartet, 1984
Guardian Angel. Quartet, 1985; Doubleday, 1985

*COHEN, ARTHUR A(LLEN)
-A Hero in His Time. Random, 1976

*COHEN, BARNEY
The Taking of Satcon Station, with Jim Baen. Pinnacle, 1982 <future>

*COHEN, OCTAVUS ROY. Ref also: CA, TM.
*The Backstage Mystery. Film: Majestic, 1933, as Curtain at Eight (scw: Edward T. Lowe; dir: E. Mason Hopper)
*I Love You Again. Film: MGM, 1940 (scw: Charles Lederer, George Oppenheimer, Harry Kurnitz; dir: W. S. Van Dyke II)

*The Iron Chalice. Silent film: DeMille, 1926, as Red Dice (scw: Jeanie MacPherson, Douglas Zoty; dir: William K. Howard). Sound film: RKO, 1931, as The Big Gamble (scw: Walter DeLeon, F. McGrew Willis; dir: Fred Niblo)
*Jim Hanvey, Detective. Film: Republic, 1937 (scw: Joseph Krumgold, Olive Cooper; dir: Phil Rosen)
*The Outer Gate. Film: Monogram, 1937 (scw: A. Laurie Brazee; dir: Raymond Cannon)
*Romance in the First Degree. <NYC>

*COHEN, STANLEY. Ref also: TM.
Angel Face. St. Martin's, 1982; NEL, 1983 <NYC>

COHEN, WILLIAM S(EBASTIAN), 1940-   and GARY (WARREN) HART, 1936-   Ref (both): CA.
The Double Man. Morrow, 1985; Joseph, 1985 <Wash. D.C.>

*COHLER, DAVID KEITH. SC: Sam Knight, in *Gamemaker and title below.
Freemartin. Little, 1981 <NYC>

COHRS, TIMOTHY. Living in NYC.
Tendencies. St. Martin's, 1983

*COKE, PETER. SC: Brigadier Rayne, in *Midsummer Mink, and other title below.
Breath of Spring. French (London), 1959 (3-act play.) Film: Rank, 1960, as Make Mine Mink (scw: Michael Pertwee, Peter Blackmore; dir: Robert Asher)
*Midsummer Mink. (3-act play.)

COKER, CAROLYN. Ref: TM. TV personality and administrator, living in Calif.
The Other David. Dodd, 1984; Hale, 1986 <Florence>

COLBY, ERIC. Pseudonym of Peter Looney.
-The Bossa Nova Bed. Brandon, 1967 <Rio de J.>

*COLBY, LYDIA. Pseudonym of *W(illiam) E(dward) D(aniel) Ross.

COLDEWAY, ANTHONY
The Crimson City. Jacobsen, 1928 (Novelization of film: Warner, 1928; scw: Anthony Coldeway; dir: Archie Mayo)

COLE, ALEXANDER
The Auction. Jove, 1983

COLE, ALLISON. Pseudonym. Lives in Calif.
Back Toward Lisbon. Dodd, 1985

*COLE, DIANE. Pseudonym of Edith Copeland.

COLE, WILLIS VERNON
Park Avenue. Writers Guild, 1928 <NYC, future>

*COLEMAN, F(RANCIS) X(AVIER) J(EROME). 1939-   . Ref: CA.

COLERIDGE, NICHOLAS. 1957-   .
-Shooting Stars. Heinamann, 1984; Heinemann (U.S.), 1985

COLES, ENID
Nearly Four. Kenyon, 1975 (1-act play.)

*COLES, MANNING. Ref also: TM.

COLLEE, JOHN. 1955-   . Studied medicine in Edinburgh, practiced in Eng.; scriptwriter with BBC.
Kingsley's Touch. Allen Lane, 1984; St. Martin's, 1985 <Scot., hosp.>

*COLLIER, JOHN (HENRY NOYES). 1901-1980.

COLLIER, WILLIAM. 1868-   . See: Winchell Smith, 1871-1933.

*COLLINGWOOD, CHARLES (CUMMINGS). 1917-1985.

COLLINS, ANDREW J. Pseudonym: *Edna Ames.

*COLLINS, DALE
*Ordeal. Film: MGM, 1930, as The Ship from Shanghai (scw: John Howard Lawson; dir: Charles Brabin)
*Vulnerable. <ship>

*COLLINS, JACKIE. Pseudonym of Jacqueline Lerman.
The Bitch. Pan, 1979. Film: Spritebowl, 1979 (scw & dir: Gerry O'Hara)
-Hollywood Wives. Simon, 1983; Collins, 1983

*COLLINS, LARRY <John Lawrence Collins, Jr.>
Fall from Grace. Simon, 1985; Granada, 1985 <WWII>

*COLLINS, MAX ALLAN (JR.). Ref also: TM. SC: Nate Heller, in those marked NH; Mallory, in those marked M; Frank Nolan, also in those marked FN; Ms. Tree, in those marked T (comic strips).
The Baby Blue Rip Off. Walker, 1983; Hale, 1984 M <Ia.>
*The Broker. Also published as: Quarry. Foul Play, 1985
*The Broker's Wife. Also published as: Quarry's List. Foul Play, 1985
The Cold Dish. Renegade, 1985 T
*The Dealer. Also published as: Quarry's Deal. Foul Play, 1986
The Files of Ms. Tree. Renegade, 1985 T
Fly Paper. Pinnacle, 1981 FN
Hard Cash. Pinnacle, 1982 FN <Ia.>
Hush Money. Pinnacle, 1981 FN
Kill Your Darlings. Walker, 1984; Hale, 1986 <Chi.> M
No Cure for Death. Walker, 1983; Chivers, 1984 M <Iowa, 1974>
Quarry; see The Broker
Quarry's Cut; see The Slasher
Quarry's Deal; see The Dealer
Quarry's List; see The Broker's Wife
Scratch Fever. Pinnacle, 1982 FN
A Shroud for Aquarius. Walker, 1985 M <Ia.>
*The Slasher. Also published as: Quarry's Cut. Foul Play, 1986
True Crime. St. Martin's, 1985 NH <Chi., 1934>
True Detective. St. Martin's, 1983; Sphere, 1984 <Chi., 1920s> NH

*COLLINS, MICHAEL. SC: Dan Fortune, also in title below.
Freak. Dodd, 1983; Hale, 1983

*COLLINS, NORMAN (RICHARD)
London Belongs to Me. Collins, 1945. Film: GFD, 1948; released in the U.S. as Dulcimer Street (scw: Sidney Gilliat, J. B. Williams; dir; Gilliat)

*COLLINS, (WILLIAM) WILKIE. Ref also: TM. See also: *Tim J. Kelly.
*Armadale. Silent film: Gaumont, 1916 (dir: Richard Garrick)
*The Dead Secret. Silent film: Monopol, 1913 (dir: Stanner E. V. Taylor)
*The Moonstone. Silent film: Selig, 1909. Also: World, 1915 (scw: E. Magnus Ingleton; dir: Frank Crane). Sound film: Monarch, 1934 (scw: Adele Buffington; dir: Reginald Barker)
*The Woman in White. Silent film: Gem, 1912. Also: Thanhauser, 1912. Also: Fox, 1917, as Tangled Lives (scw: Mary Murillo; dir: J. Gordon Edwards). Also: Thanhauser, 1917 (scw: Lloyd Lonergan; dir: Ernest C. Warde). Also: Acme, 1919, as Twin Pawns (scw Leonce Perret). Also: B&D, 1929 (scw: Herbert Wilcox, Robert J. Cullen; dir: Wilcox). Sound film: Pennant, 1940, as Crimes at the Dark House (scw: Edward Dryhurst, Frederick Hayward, H. F. Maltby; dir: George King). Also: Warner, 1948 (scw: Stephen Morehouse Avery; dir: Peter Godfrey)
*The Yellow Mask. Paperback Library, 1967 (publisher correction)

*COLLIS, MAURICE (STEWART)
*The Dark Door. <Malaysia>

*COLLISON, WILSON
*Dark Dame. Film: MGM, 1939, as Maisie (scw: Mary McCall, Jr.; dir: Edwin L. Marin)
*Red-Haired Alibi. Film: Capital, 1932 (scw: Edward T. Lowe; dir: Christy Cabanne)

*COLOMBO, PAT. Pseudonym of G. Edward Mulgrue.

COLQUHOUN, KEITH. 1927-   . Ref: CA.
-Filthy Rich. Murray, 1982; Academy Chicago, 1983 <H. Kong>

*COLTER, FRANK. Pseudonym of *Dan(iel T.) Streib, q.v. Other pseudonym: *Mark Cruz.

COLTON, JAMES. Pseudonym of *Joseph Hansen, q.v.
-Known Homosexual. Brandon, 1968. Reprinted as: Stranger to Himself, as by Joseph Hansen. Major, 1977

*COLTON, MEL
*Big Woman. ⟨Havana⟩

COLVER, ALICE (MARY) ROSS. 1892- . Ref: CA.
The Dear Pretender. Penn, 1924; Hodder, 1925. Silent film: Warner, 1925, as On Thin Ice (scw: Darryl Francis Zanuck; dir: Mal St. Clair)

COMBE, MARTIN and DUNCAN LISLE
Arnold Robur. Chapman, 1886

COMBS, DAVID. 1934- . Ref: CA.
Sleepwalker. Avon, 1983 ⟨S.F.⟩

COMMINGS, JOSEPH
Operation Aphrodite. All Star, 1966

*COMO, LYNN
Ice in Her Eyes. Hamilton Stafford, 1952
*Stuttering Death. (Written by James McCormick.)

*COMPORT, BRIAN
*Mumsy, Nanny, Sonny and Girly. Film: Brigitte, 1969 (scw: Brian Comport; dir: Freddie Francis)

COMYNS, BARBARA ⟨Barbara Irene Veronica Comyns Carr⟩. 1912- . Ref: CA.
The Vet's Daughter. Heinemann, 1959

*CONAWAY, JIM C. Pseudonym: *Jake Quinn.

CONDE, NICHOLAS
-The Legend. NAL, 1984 ⟨Ariz.⟩
The Religion. NAL, 1983; Hutchinson, 1982 ⟨NYC⟩

*CONDON, RICHARD (THOMAS). Ref (revised, expanded): TC2; also: TM.
*The Manchurian Candidate. Film: United Artists, 1962 (scw: George Axelrod; dir: John Frankenheimer)
*The Oldest Confession. Film: United Artists, 1962, as The Happy Thieves (scw: John Gay; dir: George Marshall)
Prizzi's Honor. Coward, 1982; Joseph, 1982 ⟨NYC⟩ Film: TCF, 1985 (scw: Richard Condon, Janet Reach; dir: John Huston)
The Star Spangled Crunch. Bantam pb, 1974
*Winter Kills. Film: AVCO, 1979 (scw & dir: William Richert)

CONDOR, ELLIS. See: Whidden Graham.

*CONEY, MICHAEL G.
Charisma. Gollancz, 1975; Dell, 1979
The Girl with a Symphony in Her Fingers. Elmfield, 1975. U.S. title: The Jaws That Bite, The Claws That Catch. Daw, 1975
*Hello Summer, Goodbye. delete: not criminous
The Jaws That Bite, The Claws That Catch; see The Girl with a Symphony in Her Fingers
Monitor Found in Orbit. Daw, 1974 ss

CONIL, JEAN-EDMOND. Pseudonym: *Alain Page, q.v.

*CONNELL, RICHARD (EDWARD)
*Variety. Film (from ss "The Most Dangerous Game"): RKO, 1932, As The Most Dangerous Game; released in Britain as The Hounds of Zaroff (scw: James A. Creelman; dir: Ernest B. Schroedsack, Irving Pichel). Also: RKO, 1945, as A Game of Death (scw: Norman Houston; dir: Robert Wise). Also: United Artists, 1956, as Run for the Sun (scw: Dudley Nichols, Roy Boulting; dir: Boulting). Also: Cinegraf, 1961, as Bloodlust (scw & dir: Ralph Brooke)

*CONNOR, (PATRICK) REARDEN
-Shake Hands with the Devil. Dent, 1933; Morrow, 1934. Film: Pennebaker, 1959 (scw: Ivan Goff, Ben Roberts, Marian Thompson; dir: Michael Anderson)

*CONNERS, BERNARD F.
Dancehall. Bobbs, 1983; Star, 1983 ⟨N.Y.⟩

*CONNOLLY, COLM
The Voice. Souvenir, 1983; Beaufort, 1986 ⟨Dub.⟩

*CONNOLLY, RAY
The Sun Place. Avon, 1981; Avon (London), 1982 ⟨Bahamas⟩

*CONNOLLY, VIVIAN
Five Ports to Danger. Tower, 1980 ⟨ship⟩
The Prometheus Trap. Playboy, 1982

*CONNOR, RALPH. Ref: CA. SC: Sgt./Corp. Allan Cameron, in *Corporal Cameron, and in new title below.
*Corporal Cameron. Silent film: Hodkinson, 1922, as Cameron of the Mounted (dir: Henry MacRae)
The Patrol of the Sun Dance Trail. Hodder, 1914; Doran, 1914 ⟨Can.⟩

CONRAD, BARNABY
Keepers of the Secret, with Nico Mastorakis, q.v. Jove, 1983

*CONRAD, BRENDA. Pseudonym of Zenith Jones Brown, 1893-1983. Other pseudonyms: *Leslie Ford, *David Frome.
*The Stars Give Warning. ⟨Pan.⟩

*CONRAD, JOSEPH
*The Secret Agent. Film: Gaumont British, 1936, as Sabotage; released in U.S. as The Woman Alone (scw: Charles Bennett, Ian Hay, Alma Reville, Helen Simpson, E. V. H. Emmett; dir: Alfred Hitchcock)
*Under Western Eyes. Film: L'Alliance Cinematographie, 1936, as Sous Les Yeux D'Occident (Under Western Eyes; released in the U.S. as Razumov) (scw: H. Wilhelm, H. G. Lustig; dir: Marc Allegret)

*CONROY, ALBERT
*The Looters. Film: Valoria, 1967, as Estouffade a la Caraibe (Stew in the Caribbean) (scw: Pierre Foucard, Marcel Lebrun; dir: Jacques Bresnard)

*CONSTANTINE, K. C. Pseudonym of Carl Kosak, ca.1935- . Ref: TM. SC: Mario Balzac, also in titles below. Set: Pa.
Always a Body to Trade. Godine, 1983; Hodder, 1985
*The Blank Page. ... Kudos, 1984
The Man Who Liked Slow Tomatoes. Godine, 1982; Kudos, 1982
*The Man Who Liked to Look at Himself. ... Hodder, 1986
*The Rocksburg Railroad Murders. ... Kudos, 1984
Upon Some Midnights Clear. Godine, 1985; Hodder, 1986

*CONSTINER, (FRANCIS) MERLE. Ref: TM.
*Hearse of a Different Color. ⟨Tenn.⟩

*CONTENT, NIKKI. Pseudonym of *Frances Nichols Hanna.
*Hideaway. ... Also published as by Fan Nichols: Berkley, 1959

*CONTY, JEAN-PIERRE. Pseudonym of Conrad Kurt Walrafen.
*A Big Secret, Suzuki. ⟨Fla.⟩ (Translation of "Mr. Suzuki et le Grand Secret." Paris, 1968)

*CONWAY, HUGH
*Bound Together. ss, some criminous
*Called Back. Silent film: Thanhauser, 1912. Also: Gold Reel, 1914 (scw: James Dayton; dir: Otis Turner). Also: London, 1914 (dir: George L. Tucker). Also: Sound film: Real Art, 1933 (dir: Reginald Denham, Jack Harris)

*CONWAY, NORMAN. Pseudonym of Mark Rush.
*The Omega Operation. ⟨Fla.⟩

*CONWAY, PETER. Pseudonym of Peter Claudius Gautier-Smith.
Cryptic Clue. Hale, 1984
Dead Drunk. Hale, 1982
Fallen Angel. Hale, 1985
Mirror Image. Hale, 1982
Needle Track. Hale, 1981
Struck Dumb. Hale, 1983

CONWAY, STEVE. See: Douglas Trevern.

COOK, BOB
Disorderly Elements. Gollancz, 1985; St. Martin's, 1986

COOK, GLEN
A Matter of Time. Berkley, 1985

COOK, JUDITH
The Waste Remains. Pluto, 1984

*COOK, KENNETH. Born in Syd.; has been a journalist and film director.
*Wake in Fright. ⟨Australia⟩ Film: NIT, 1970, as Outback (scw: Evan Jones; dir: Ted Kotcheff)

*COOK, (JOHN) LENNOX. Ref: CA.
-Under Etna. Joseph, 1982

*COOK, ROBIN. Ref: CA.
Brain. Putnam, 1981; Macmillan (London), 1981 ⟨NYC⟩
*Coma. Film: MGM, 1978 (scw & dir: Michael Crichton)
Fever. Putnam, 1982; Macmillan (London), 1982 ⟨New Eng.⟩
Godplayer. Putnam, 1983; Macmillan (London), 1983
Mindbend. Putnam, 1985; Macmillan (London), 1985
*Sphinx. Film: Orion, 1981 (scw: John Byrum; dir: Franklin J. Schaffner)

COOK, STEPHEN. 1949- . Ref: CA.
Upperdown. Hodder (London & U.S.), 1985 ⟨acad.⟩

*COOK, SY and MARTHA MOFFETT. Both live in Fla. Cook has worked for over 30 years in electronics and telecommunications.
The Sharing. Avon, 1984 ⟨NYC⟩

*COOK, THOMAS H. 1947- . Ref: CA.
The Orchids. Houghton, 1982; Houghton (London), 1984 ⟨Ger.⟩
Tabernacle. Houghton, 1983 ⟨Salt Lake City⟩

COOK, (GEORGE) WHITFIELD. 1909- Ref: CA.
Taxi to Dubrovnik. Delacorte, 1981 ⟨Yugos.⟩

*COOK, WILLIAM WALLACE. Ref: CA.

*COOKE, H. O.
A Guilty Conscience. Street, 1904 (Magnet #371)
*The Sign of the Dagger. delete

COOKE, WILLIAM PEYTON
Orion's Shroud. Star, 1982

*COOKSON, CATHERINE (ANN McMULLEN)
*Rooney. Film: Rank, 1958 (scw: Patrick Kirwan; dir: George Pollock)

*COOLIDGE, ERWIN L. See: *Harry Mills.

*COOLRIDGE-RASK, MARIE
*London After Midnight. (Novelization of silent film: MGM, 1927; released in Britain as The Hypnotist; scw: Tod Browning, Waldemar Young; dir: Browning. Film remade: MGM, 1935, as Mark of the Vampire; scw: Guy Endore, Bernard Schubert; dir: Tod Browning)

*COONEY, CAROLINE B.
Sand Trap. Avon, 1983 ⟨N.C.⟩

*COONEY, RAY
Bang Bang Beirut, with Tony Hilton. English Theatre, 1971; Dramatists, 19?? (3-act play.) ⟨Beirut⟩

COOPER, (ALFRED) DUFF. 1890-1954.
-Operation Heartbreak. Hart-Davis, 1950; Viking, 1951

*COOPER, COLIN (SYMONS)
The Thunder and Lightning Man. Faber, 1968

*COOPER, EDMUND
*Prisoner of Fire. ⟨1990s⟩

*COOPER, JAMES FENIMORE
*The Spy. Silent film: Universal, 1914 (scw: James Dayton, Otis Turner; dir: Turner)
*The Ways of the Hour. ⟨N.Y.⟩

*COOPER, JOHN C.
*The Grip of the Strangler. (Novelization of film: Producer's Associates, 1958; released in the U.S. as

The Haunted Strangler; scw: Jan Read; dir: Robert Day)

*COOPER, LETTICE (ULPHA)
  The Lighted Room. Hodder, 1925 <Eng., 1600s>

COOPER, M(AE) K(LEIN). Ref: CA.
  -Lily Henry. Dutton, 1948; Muller, 1960, as by Nina Farewell

COOPER, MATTHEW HEALD. 1952-
  Ref: CA.
  To Ride a Tiger. Gollancz, 1984; Vanguard, 1985
  When Fish Begin to Smell. Gollancz, 1983; Vanguard, 1984 <London, 1951>

*COOPER, MORTON
  *High School Confidential. (Novelization of film: MGM, 1958; scw: Lewis Meltzer, Robert Blees; dir: Jack Arnold)
  *Young and Wild. (Novelization of film: Esla, 1958; scw: Arthur T. Horman; dir: William Witney)

*COOPER, RODERICK
  Chelsea Blues. Hale, 1984; Academy Chicago, 1986

COPE, EDDIE <EDWARD B. COPE>
  Agatha Christie Made Me Do It. Clark, 1975 (3-act play.)

COPELAND, EDITH. Pseudonym: *Diane Cole.

*COPELAND, RICHARD. Pseudonym of *Hugh (George) McLeave, q.v.

*COPP, DeWITT (S.). Pseudonym: *Sam Picard.

*COPPEE, FRANCOIS (EDOUARD JOACHIN)
  *The Guilty Man. Silent film: Paramount, 1918 (dir: Irwin Willat)

*COPPEL, ALEC
  *The Gazebo. (3-act play.) Film: MGM, 1959 (scw: George Wells; dir: George Marshall). Also: Trianon, 1971, as Jo (The Gazebo) (scw: Claude Magnier, Jacques Vilfrid; dir: Jean Girault)
  *I Killed the Count. Film: Grafton, 1939; released in U.S. as Who Is Guilty? (scw: Laurence Huntington, Alec Coppel; dir: Fred Zelnik)
  *A Man About a Dog. Film: Independent, 1949, as Obsession; released in U.S. as The Hidden Room (Alec Coppel; dir: Edward Dmytryk)
  *Mr. Denning Drives North. Film: British Lion, 1951 (scw: Alec Coppel; dir: Anthony Kimmins)
  *Moment to Moment. (Novelization of film: Universal, 1966; scw: John Lee Mahin, Alec Coppel; dir: Mervyn LeRoy)

*COPPER, BASIL. SC: Mike Faraday, also in all titles below.
  Dark Entry. Hale, 1981
  The Empty Silence. Hale, 1981
  The Far Horizon. Hale, 1982
  The Far Side of Fear. Hale, 1985
  Hang Loose. Hale, 1982
  Hard Contact. Hale, 1984
  The Hook. Hale, 1984
  The Long Rest. Hale, 1981
  The Narrow Corner. Hale, 1983
  Pressure-Point. Hale, 1983
  Shoot-Out. Hale, 1982
  Trigger Man. Hale, 1983
  Tuxedo Park. Hale, 1985
  You Only Die Once. Hale, 1984

*CORAM, CHRISTOPHER
  Prisoner on the Dam. Hale, 1982
  Prisoner on the Run. Hale, 1985

CORBETT, ANTHONY
  Cruise Breaker. Sidgwick, 1984

*CORBY, JANE
  A Nightmare Legacy. Lenox, 1970 <New Eng.>

CORDEAU, KATE MARIAN. Pseudonym: Daniel Dormer, q.v.

*CORDELL, ALEXANDER
  If You Believe the Soldiers. Hodder, 1973; Doubleday, 1974 <Eng., future>

*CORDELL, MELISSA. Pseudonym of Donald Roland.

*COREY, FRANK. Pseudonym of George Fox.

CORFIELD, WILLIAM E.
  Dead Spy, Dead Secret. Hale, 1981

*CORIOLA
  Cruel Betrayal. Mystique, 1981 (Translation of "Ouragan sur Maladenia." Paris, 1967.)
  Echoes of Innocence. Mystique, 1981 (Translation of "La Nuit de Feu." Paris, 1966.)

*CORMACK, BARTLETT
  *The Racket. Film: Silent film: Paramount, 1928 (scw: Bartlett Cormack, Harry Behn, Del Andrews; dir: Lewis Milestone). Sound film: RKO, 1951 (scw: William Wister Haines, W. R. Burnett; dir: John Cromwell)

*CORMIER, ROBERT. New England journalist and novelist; living in Mass.
  *After the First Death. <Mass.>

CORN, IRA (GEORGE), JR. 1921-1982. Ref: CA.
  Scalpel. Zebra, 1984

CORNABY, W(ILLIAM) ARTHUR. 1860-1921.
  A String of Chinese Peach Stones. Kelly, 1895   ss, some criminous

CORNELISEN, ANN. 1926- . Ref: CA.
  Any Four Women Could Rob the Bank of Italy. Holt, 1984; Severn, 1985 <It.>

CORNWALL, CLIVE
  One Man's Reality. Cornwall, 1985

CORR, REV. THOMAS J.
  Favilla: Tales, Essays and Poems. Paul, 1887   ss, one criminous

CORRIS, PETER. 1942- . SC: Cliff Hardy, in all titles except Pokerface.
  The Big Drop and other Cliff Hardy stories. Unwin (Syd.), 1985   ss <syd., S.F.>
  The Dying Trade. McGraw-Hill (Syd.), 1980; GM, 1986 <Syd.>
  The Empty Beach. Unwin (Syd.), 1983. Film: Jethro, 1985 (scw: Keith Dewhurst; dir: Chris Thomson) <Syd.>
  Heroin Annie and other Cliff Hardy stories. Unwin (Syd.), 1984   ss <Syd., S.F.>
  Make Me Rich. Pan, 1982; GM, 1987 <Syd.>
  The Marvelous Boy. Pan (Syd.), 1982 <Australia>
  Pokerface. Penguin (Australia), 1985 <Melb.>
  White Meat. Pan (Syd.), 1981; GM, 1986 <Australia>
  The Winning Side. Unwin (Syd.), 1984

CORT, NED. SC: Nick Chase (Boxer Unit--SS), in all titles. Set: WWII.
  Alpine Gambit. Warner, 1981 <Ger.>
  French Entrapment. Warner, 1981 <Fr.>
  Operation Counter-Scorch. Warner, 1982
  Partisan Demolition. Warner, 1982
  Target Norway. Warner, 1982

*CORTAZAR, JULIO. 1914-1984.

*CORY, DESMOND. Ref also: TM. SC correction: that identified as Laura Gray is a man named Gray.
  *Deadfall. Film: Salamander, 1967 (scw & dir: Bryan Forbes)
  *High Requiem. <Afr.>

*CORYELL, JOHN R(USSELL). See: *Nicholas Carter.

*COSGRAVE, PATRICK. Ref also: TC2. SC: Colonel Allen Cheyney, in the two previous titles and one below.
  Adventure of State. Anderson, 1984; St. Martin's, 1986

COSTANTINI, HUMBERTO
  The Gods, the Little Guys and the Police. Harper, 1984 <Arg.> (Translation of "De Dioses, Hombrecitos y Policias." Buenos Aires, 1984.)

COSTELLO, PETE
  Moll for the Morgue. Edwin Self, 1952
  Murder in Mink. Edwin Self, 1952

*COSTIGAN, LEE. Pseudonym of *Hank Searls, q.v.

*Never Kill a Cop. ... Reprinted as by Hank Searls: PB, 1977

*COTLER, GORDON
  *The Bottletop Affair. Film: MGM, 1962, as The Horizontal Lieutenant (scw: George Wells; dir: Richard Thorpe)
  *A Stranger Called the Blues. <Tib.>

COTTRELL, DOROTHY (WILKINSON). 1902-1957.
  The Silent Reefs. Morrow, 1953; Hodder, 1954. Film: TCF, 1960, as Secret of the Purple Reef (scw: Harold Yablonsky; dir: William Witney)

*COUGHLIN, WILLIAM J(EREMIAH). Pseudonym: *Sean A. Key, q.v.

*COULTER, STEPHEN. Ref also: CA.
  *Embassy. Film: Hemdale, 1972 (scw: William Fairchild, John Bird; dir: Gordon Hessler)

*COUNSEL, FIRTH
  *Juvenile Jungle. (Novelization of film: Coronado, 1958; scw: Arthur T. Horman; dir: William Witney)

*COUSINS, E(DMUND) G(EORGE)
  *Sapphire. (Novelization of film: Artna, 1959; scw: Janet Green; dir: Basil Dearden)

COVELL, RICHARD. Joint pseudonym with John Banks and Jay Clarke: Michael Slade, q.v.

*COVER, ARTHUR BYRON. 1950- . Ref: CA.

*COVERDALE, HARRY. Pseudonym of *Herman Landon, 1882-1960.

COVINGTON, JAMES
  The Operative. Belmont, 1981 <Swed.>

*COWEN, FRANCES. Ref: not in TC2.

COWEN, WILLIAM JOYCE
  They Gave Him a Gun. Smith, 1936; Heinemann, 1936. Film: MGM, 1937 (scw: Cyril Hume, Richard Maibaum, Maurice Rapf; dir: W. S. Van Dyke)

*COX, A(THONY) B(ERKELEY). Pseudonym: A. Monmouth Platts, q.v.

*COX, CONSTANCE
  *Lord Arthur Savile's Crime. (3-act play.)

COX, JONATHAN
  Kiss of the Raven. GM, 1981

*COX, RICHARD (HUBERT FRANCIS)
  Ground Zero. Secker, 1984; Stein, 1985 <Mid. East>
  The Ice Raid. Hutchinson, 1983
  The KGB Directive. Hutchinson, 1981; Viking, 1981

*COX, THOMAS R. Born in Indiana; has bachelor's and master's degrees from Indiana schools; teaching high school English and living in Indianapolis.
  *Shadows of One Another. <Midwest>

*COX, WILLIAM R(OBERT). Ref: TC2, TM.

COX, WILLIAM TREVOR. 1928- . Pseudonym: William Trevor, q.v.

*COXE, GEORGE HARMON. 1901-1984. Ref also: TM. SC: Jack Fenner, also in titles marked JF.
  *The Camera Clue. JF
  *The Candid Impostor. (spelling correction)
  *Flash Casey, Detective. (Not Flash Casey, Photographer, as given in first printing of CF.)
  *Murder with Pictures. JF   Film: Paramount, 1936 (scw: John C. Moffitt, Sidney Salkow; dir: Charles Barton)

COYNE, JOHN (P.). 1940- . Ref: CA.
  The Shroud. Berkley, 1983

COYNE, JOSEPH E. 1918- . Ref: CA.
  House of Exile. Bruce, 1964 <Mass.>

*CRAIG, ALISA. SC: Insp. Madoc Rhys, in *A Pint of Murder, and in title below marked MR; Osbert Monk = OM.
  The Grub-and-Stakers Move a Mountain. Doubleday, 1981   OM <Can.>

The Grub-and-Stakers Quilt a Bee.
  Doubleday, 1985 OM <Can.>
  Murder Goes Mumming. Doubleday, 1981
  MR <Can.>
  The Terrible Tide. Doubleday, 1983;
  Hale, 1985 <Can.>
*CRAIG, DAVID
  *Double Take. <Wales>
  *Whose Little Girl Are You? Film:
    Warner, 1977, as The Squeeze (scw:
    Leon Griffiths; dir: Michael Apted)
CRAIG, DORIN
  Mist in the Valley. Long, 1916. Si-
    lent film: Hepworth, 1923 (scw:
    George Dewhurst; dir: Cecil M.
    Hepworth)
*CRAIG, JONATHAN. Pseudonym of Frank E.
  Smith, 1919-1984. Ref also: CA, TM.
  *The Case of the Petticoat Murder.
    Also published as (in pirated edi-
    tion?): Wanton Wench, as by Mark
    Ryan. Zodiac, 1963
*CRAIG, M(ARY) S. Ref also: TM.
  Gillian's Chain. Dodd, 1983 <Chi.>
  *Ten Thousand Several Doors. <Calif.>
  The Third Blonde. Dodd, 1985 <Chi.>
  To Play the Fox. Dodd, 1982 <Calif.>
CRAIG, ROBERT. Lives in Calif.
  Trauma. Signet, 1984 <hosp.>
*CRANE, CAROLINE. Ref also: TM.
  Coast of Fear. Dodd, 1981 <Fr.>
  The Foretelling. Dodd, 1982 <N.Y.>
  Someone at the Door. Dodd, 1985
    <L.I.>
  Something Evil. Dodd, 1984 <N.Y.>
  The Third Passenger. Dodd, 1983;
    Hale, 1985 <N.Y.>
  Trick or Treat. Dodd, 1983 <N.Y.>
  Wife Found Slain. Dodd, 1981; Hale,
    1982 <NYC>
  Woman Vanishes. Dodd, 1984; Hale,
    1986
*CRANE, FRANCES. Ref also: TM. SC:
  Pat and Jean Abbott, also in *The
  Yellow Violet.
CRAWFORD, F(RANCIS) MARION. 1854-1909.
  Ref: CA.
  Whosoever Shall Offend... Macmillan
    (London & NYC), 1904. Silent film:
    Windsor, 1919 (scw: Kenelm Foss;
    dir: Arrigo Bocchi)
*CRAWFORD, JAMES TEMPLE. 1909-   .
  Killing Time. Arrow (N.Z.), 1980
    <N.Z.>
*CRAWFORD, OLIVER
  Blood on the Branches. Ace, 1956.
    Film: Republic, 1958, as Girl in
    the Woods (scw: Oliver Crawford,
    Marcel Klauber; dir: Tom Gries)
CREAGH, MONTY
  Nobask. Vantage, 1981
*CREASEY, JOHN. Ref also: TM. Pseudo-
  nyms: *Norman Deane, *Michael
  Halliday, qq.v.
  *Battle for Inspector West ... Lancer,
    1971
  *Hammer the Toff. Film: Butcher, 1952
    (dir: Maclean Rogers)
  *Salute the Toff. Film: Butcher, 1951
    (dir: Maclean Rogers)
  *The Toff and the Stolen Tresses.
    (Not The Toff and the Stolen
    Treasure, as in first printing of
    CF.)
*CREED, DAVID
  Travellers in a Antique Land. Secker,
    1982 <Beirut>
CREESE, ANNA
  Tales of Mystery and Suspense. New
    Horizon, 1983 ss
CRESSWELL, DONALD. See: *Ross Angel,
  *Nat Karta.
*CRICHTON, (JOHN) MICHAEL. Ref also:
  TM.
  *The Great Train Robbery. Film: UA,
    1979, as The First Great Train Rob-
    bery (scw & dir: Michael Crichton)
CRICHTON, WILLIAM
  -The Donnelly Murders. PaperJacks,
    1977 <1800s, U.S.>
CRIDER, (ALLEN) BILL(Y). 1941-
  Ref: CA. See: *Nick Carter.

CRIGHTON, RICHARD E. 1921-   . Ref:
  CA.
  The Million Dollar Lift. Avon, 1981
    <Calif.>
  Red for Terror. Dodd, 1982 <It.>
*CRISP, FRANK (ROBSON)
  *Fazackerley's Millions. <Java>
  *The Night Callers. Film: New Art,
    1965, as The Night Caller; released
    in the U.S. as Blood Beast from
    Outer Space (scw: Jim O'Connolly;
    dir: John Gilling)
*CRISP, N(ORMAN) J(AMES)
  The Brink. Macdonald, 1982; Viking,
    1982
  Festival. Macdonald, 1981
*CRISP, QUENTIN. Birth name: Dennis
  Pratt. Ref: CA.
CRISP, WILLIAM. 1942-   . Born in Va.;
  working in Vienna.
  The Compleat Agent. Macmillan (Lon-
    don), 1984
  Spytrap. Macmillan (London), 1982;
    Pantheon, 1983 <Vienna>
CRISPIN, A. C. See: Howard Weinstein.
*CRISPIN, EDMUND. Ref also: TM.
CROCKER, ARTHUR
  The Great Turon Mystery. Bookstall
    (Syd.), 1923
*CROFT-COOKE, RUPERT. Ref also: TM.
  *Clash by Night. Film: Eternal, 1963;
    released in the U.S. as Escape by
    Night (scw: Maurice J. Wilson,
    Montgomery Tully; dir: Tully)
  *Seven Thunders. Film: Dial, 1957;
    released in the U.S. as The Beast
    of Marseilles (scw: John Baines;
    dir: Hugo Fregonese)
*CROFTS, FREEMAN WILLS. Ref also: CA,
  TM.
*CRONIN, A(RCHIBALD) J(OSEPH)
  *Beyond This Place. Film: Georgefield,
    1959; released in U.S. as Web of
    Evidence (scw: Kenneth Taylor; dir:
    Jack Cardiff)
*CRONIN, MICHAEL
  The Killing of Quemada. Hale, 1981
  -The Mexican Stand-Off. Hale, 1985
  *Paid in Full. Film: Fancey, 1954, as
    Johnny on the Spot (scw & dir:
    Maclean Rogers)
  The Roker's Reef Affair. Hale, 1982
  The Tsurande Enterprise. Hale, 1983
  *You Pay Your Money. Film: Butcher,
    1957 (scw & dir: Maclean Rogers)
CRONLEY, JAY. 1943-   . Ref: CA.
  Cheap Shot. Atheneum, 1984 <NYC>
  Quick Change. Doubleday, 1981; NEL
    pb, 1984. Film: AMLF, 1985 (in
    French), as Hold-Up (scw: Francis
    Veber, Daniel Saint-Hamont, Alexan-
    dre Arcady; dir: Arcady)
CROSBY, JOHN (CAMPBELL). SC: Horatio
  Cassidy, in at least one earlier
  title and both titles below.
  Men in Arms. Stein, 1983; Constable,
    1984
  Take No Prisoners. Warner, 1985;
    Constable, 1986 <Cent. Am.>
CROSBY, MILLARD. Pseudonym of *Wilbur
  Braun, q.v. Other pseudonyms: Ned
  Albert, Anthony Forsythe, qq.v.
  The Ghostly Passenger. French, 1939
    (1-act play.)
  Who Murdered Who? French, 1941
    (1-act play.)
  Whodunit? French, 1942 (1-act play.)
*CROSS, AMANDA. Ref also: TM. SC:
  Kate Fansler, also in titles below.
  Death in a Tenured Position. Dutton,
    1981. British title: A Death in
    the Faculty. Gollancz, 1981
    <Boston>
  A Death in the Faculty; see Death in
    a Tenured Position
  Sweet Death, Kind Death. Dutton,
    1984; Gollancz, 1984 <acad., New
    Eng.>
CROSS, E. B.
  The Ninth Dragon. Pinnacle, 1985
    <Viet Nam>
*CROSS, GILBERT B. Pseudonyms: J. C.
  Winters, *Jon Winters, qq.v.

*CROSSEN, KENDALL FOSTER. Ref also: TM.
*CROTHERS, RACHEL. 1878-1958. Ref: CA.
*CROWCROFT, PETER
  *That Man Bolt. (Novelization of film:
    Universal, 1973; scw: Quentin
    Werty, Charles Johnson; dir: Henry
    Levin, David Lowell Rich)
CROWDER, KEN
  The Coulter Conspiracy. Zebra, 1984
  The Iron Web. Walker, 1985 <WWII,
    S. Afr.>
*CROWE, CECILY (TEAGUE). Ref: CA.
  Bloodrose House. St. Martin's, 1985
*CROWE, JOHN
  *Close to Death. ... Hale, 1983
*CROWTHER, BRUCE
  Black Wednesday. Hale, 1981
  Unholy Alliance. Hale, 1981
CRUGER, PAUL
  Black Phantom. Banner, 1932 (3-act
    play.)
  Easy Pickings. Banner, 1929 (3-act
    play.) Silent film: First Na-
    tional, 1929 (scw: Louis Stevens,
    William A. Burton; dir: George
    Archainbaud)
  The Sky Train. Banner, 1930 (3-act
    play.)
*CRUIKSHANK, CHARLES (GREIG)
  Kew for Murder. Hale, 1984
  Scotch Murder. Hale, 1985
*CRUMLEY, JAMES. Ref also: TC2, TM.
  SC: Milo Milodragovitch, in *The
  Wrong Case, and in title below.
  Dancing Bear. Random, 1983
*CRUZ, MARK. Pseudonym of *Dan(iel T.)
  Streib, q.v. Other pseudonym:
  *Frank Colter.
CUDLIP, DAVID R.
  Comprador. Dutton, 1984; Secker, 1985
    <U.S., future>
CULLEN, IAN and *CATHERINE ARLEY, q.v.
  Tantalus. Dramatists, 1982
  (2-act play based on Arley's novel
  *Woman of Straw, q.v.)
*CULLUM, RIDGWELL
  *The One-Way Trail. Silent film: Fox,
    1922, as The Yosemite Trail (scw:
    Jack Strumwasser; dir: Bernard
    J. Durning)
  *The Son of His Father. Silent film:
    Paramount, 1917 (dir: Victor
    Schertzinger)
  *The Way of the Strong. Silent film:
    Metro, 1919 (scw: June Mathis,
    Finis Fox; dir: Edwin Carewe)
CULVER, FREDERICK WILLIAM
  Double Exposure. Stockwell, 1956
    (1-act play.)
*CUMBERLAND, STEWART C.
  -The Rabbi's Spell. Appleton, 1885
*CUMMINGS, JACK <JOHN WILLIAM CUM-
  MINGS, JR.>. Ref: CA.
*CUMMINGS, RAY(MOND KING). Ref: CA.
*CUNNINGHAM, CHET. See also: Don(ald
  Eugene) Pendleton. SC: Team Three,
  in both titles.
  The Deadly Connection. American Art,
    1980
  Silent Murder. American Art, 1980
    <Calif.>
*CUNNINGHAM, E. V. SC: Sgt. Masao
  Masuto, also in all new titles
  below. Set: L.A.
  The Case of the Angry Actress; see
    Samantha
  The Case of the Kidnapped Angel.
    Delacorte, 1982; Gollancz, 1983
  The Case of the Murdered Mackenzie.
    Delacorte, 1984; Gollancz, 1985
  The Case of the Sliding Pool. Dela-
    corte, 1981; Gollancz, 1982
  *Penelope. Film: MGM, 1966 (scw:
    George Wells; dir: Arthur Hiller)
  *Samantha. Also published as: The
    Case of the Angry Actress. Dell,
    1984
  *Sylvia. Film: Paramount, 1965 (scw:
    Sydney Boehm; dir: Gordon Douglas)
*CUNNINGHAM, SCOTT
  Operation: Death Ray. Carousel, 1982

*CURRIE, BARTON (WOOD), 1878-1962, and *AUGUSTIN McHUGH. Ref for Currie: CA.
*Officer 666. Silent film: Kleine, 1914. Also: Goldwyn, 1920 (scw: Gerald C. Duffy; dir: Harry Beaumont)

*CURRY, ELLSWORTH
*The Happening. (Novelization of film: Horizon, 1967; scw: Frank R. Pierson, James D. Buchanan, Ronald Austin; dir: Eliot Silverstein)

*CURTIS, JAMES
*There Ain't No Justice. Film: Ealing, 1939 (scw: Pen Tennyson, Sergei Nolbandov, James Curtis; dir: Tennyson)
*They Drive by Night. criminous. Film: WB-FN, 1938 (scw: Derek Twist; dir: Arthur Woods)

*CURTIS, PETER. Pseudonym of Norah (Robinson) Lofts, 1904-1983.
*The Devil's Own. Film: Hammer, 1966, as The Witches; released in the U.S under the book title (scw: Nigel Kneale; dir: Cyril Frankel)
*You're Best Alone. Film: ABPC, 1950, as Guilt Is My Shadow (scw: Ivan Foxwell, Roy Kellino, John Gilling; dir: Kellino)

CURTIS, PHILIP (DELACOURT). 1920- Ref: CA.
A Sword to the Rescue. Heywood, 1951 (1-act play.)

*CURTIS, RICHARD (ALAN). 1937- .
Ref: CA. Pseudonym: Ray Lilly, q.v. Joint pseudonym with Paul Stevens: *Curtis Stevens, q.v.

*CURTIS, ROBERT (G.). (spelling correction)
*The Table. (Novelization of film script by *Edgar Wallace, q.v.)

*CURTIS, WADE
*Red Dragon. Reprinted as by *Jerry Pournelle: Charter, 1985
*Red Heroin. Reprinted as by *Jerry Pournelle: Charter, 1985

*CURTISS, URSULA (REILLY). 1923-1984. Ref also: TM.
Death of a Crow. Dodd, 1983; Macmillan (London), 1983 <Conn.>
Dog in the Manger. Dodd, 1982. British title: The Graveyard Shift. Macmillan (London), 1982 <Mass.>
*The Forbidden Garden. Film: Palomar, 1969, as Whatever Happened to Aunt Alice? (scw: Theodore Apstein; dir: Lee H. Katzin)
The Graveyard Shift; see Dog in the Manger
The House on Plymouth Street, and other stories. Dodd, 1985 ss
*Out of the Dark. Film: Universal, 1965, as I Saw What You Did (scw: William McGivern; dir: William Castle)

*CURWOOD, JAMES OLIVER
The Country Beyond. Cosmopolitan, 1922; Hodder, 1922. Silent film: Fox, 1926 (scw: Irving Cummings, Ernest Maas; dir: Cummings). Sound film: TCF, 1936 (scw: Lamar Trotti, Adele Comandini; dir: Eugene Forde)
The Flaming Forest. Cosmopolitan, 1921; Hodder, 1921. Silent film: Cosmopolitan, 1926 (scw: Waldemar Young; dir: Reginald Barker)
-The Gold Hunters. Bobbs, 1909. Silent film: Guaranteed, 1925 (dir: Paul Hurst). Sound film: Monogram, 1949, as Trail of the Yukon (scw: Oliver Drake; dir: William X. Crowley)
The Golden Snare. Cassell, 1918. Silent film: Hartford, 1921 (scw: James Oliver Curwood, David M. Hartford; dir: Hartford)
-The Hunted Woman. Doubleday, 1916. British title: The Valley of Gold. Cassell, 1916. Silent film: Vitagraph, 1916 (dir: S. Rankin Drew). Also: Fox, 1925 (scw: Robert N. Lee; dir: Jack Conway).
Isobel. Harper, 1913. Silent film: Selig, 1914, as In Defiance of the Law (scw & dir: Colin Campbell). Also: Davis, 1920 (scw & dir: Edwin Carewe)
-Kazan. Bobbs, 1914; Cassell, 1914. Silent film: Selig, 1921 (scw & dir: Bertram Bracken)
-Nomads of the North. Doubleday, 1919; Hodder, 1919. Silent film: First National, 1920 (scw: James Oliver Curwood, David M. Hartford)
The River's End. Cosmopolitan, 1919; Hodder, 1920. Silent film: First National, 1920 (scw: Marion Fairfax; dir: Marshall Neilan). Sound film: Warner, 1930 (scw: Charles Kenyon; dir: Michael Curtiz). Also: Warner, 1940; also released as Double Identity (scw: Barry Trivers, Bertram Milhauser; dir: Ray Enright)
*Philip Steele of the Royal Northwest Mounted Police. Silent film: Vitagraph, 1925, as Steele of the Royal Mounted (scw: Jay Pilcher; dir: David Smith)
The Valley of Gold; see The Hunted Woman
The Valley of Silent Men. Cosmopolitan, 1920; Hodder, 1921. Silent film: Paramount, 1922 (scw: John Lynch; dir: Frank Borzage)
-The Wolf Hunters. Bobbs, 1908; Cassell, 1917. Silent film: Ben Wilson, 1926 (dir: Stuart Paton). Sound film: Monogram, 1950 (scw: W. Scott Darling; dir: Oscar Boetticher)

*CURZON, CLARE. Pseudonym of Eileen-Marie Duell Buchanan, 1922- . Other pseudonym: *Rhona Petrie. SC: Supt. Mike Yeadings and Sgt. Angus Mott, in those marked Y&M.
I Give You Five Days. Collins, 1983 Y&M
Masks and Faces. Collins, 1984 Y&M
Special Occasion. Collins, 1981
Trojan Hearse. Collins, 1985

CURZON, DANIEL. Ref: CA.
From Violent Men. IGNA, 1983 <S.F.>

*CUSACK, (ELLEN) DYMPHNA. 1902-198?.
*Say No to Death. delete: not criminous

*CUSHING, E. LOUISE
*The Unexpected Corpse. <Toronto>

*CUSHMAN, DAN. Ref also: TM.
*Timberjack. Film: Republic, 1954 (scw: Allen Rivkin; dir: Joe Kane)

CUSHMAN, JANE. Pseudonym: Jane Sandford, q.v.

*CUSSLER, CLIVE (ERIC). SC: Dirk Pitt, also in all titles below.
Deep Six. Simon, 1984; H. Hamilton, 1984 <1989>
Night Probe! Bantam hc, 1981; Hodder, 1981 <1989>
Pacific Vortex. Bantam hc, 1983; Sphere, 1983 <ship>
*Raise the Titanic! Film: Associated Film, 1980 (scw: Adam Kennedy, Eric Hughes; dir: Jerry Jameson)

*CUTLER, ROLAND
The Seventh Sacrament. Dell, 1984

CUTLER, RON
The Medusa Syndrome. Signet, 1983 <N.Y.>

CUTTER, JOHN. SC: Jack Sullivan (The Specialist), in all titles.
American Vengeance. Signet, 1985 <Paris>
The Beirut Retaliation. Signet, 1985 <Beirut>
The Big One. Signet, 1984 <Carib.>
The Maltese Vengeance. Signet, 1984 <Malta>
Manhattan Revenge. Signet, 1984 <NYC>
One-Man Army. Signet, 1985
The Psycho Soldiers. Signet, 1984 <N.Y.>
Sullivan's Revenge. Signet, 1984 <N.W.>
A Talent for Revenge. Signet, 1984 <Fr.>
The Vendetta. Signet, 1985 <NYC>
Vengeance Mountain. Signet, 1985 <Mex.>

CUTTER, LEELA. Lives in Oakland, Calif. SC: Lettie Winterbottom, in all titles. Set: Eng.
Death of the Party. St. Martin's, 1985
Murder After Tea Time. St. Martin's, 1981
Who Stole Stonehenge? St. Martin's, 1983

*DACRE, CHARLOTTE

*Zofloya; or, The Moor. <It., 1400s>

*DAGMAR. Real name: Virginia Ruth Egnor. Both titles listed were ghost written by *Lou Cameron.

DAGMAR, PETER
Two Equals One. Book Guild, 1982

*D'AGNEAU, MARCEL
The Curse of the Nibelung. Arlington, 1981 (Sherlock Holmes)

*DAHL, ROALD. Ref: TM; not in TC2.

*DAKIN, W. J. See: J. L. Rankin.

*DALEY, ROBERT (BLAKE)
The Dangerous Edge. Simon, 1983; Hodder, 1983 <Fr., 1952>
Hands of a Stranger. Simon, 1985; Hodder, 1985 <NYC>
Year of the Dragon. Simon, 1981; Hodder, 1982 <NYC> Film: MGM, 1985 (scw: Oliver Stone, Michael Cimino; dir: Cimino)

DALMAS, JOHN. Pseudonym of John Robert Jones, 1926- . Ref: CA.
The Varkaus Conspiracy. Tor, 1983 <1995>

D'ALTON, MARTINA. Former editor with major NYC publisher; avid runner and marathon competitor.
Fatal Finish. Walker, 1982 <NYC>

*DALTON, MORAY. Real name (?): Arthur Caxton Hames.

*DALY, CARROLL JOHN. Ref also: TC2, TM.

*DALY, ELIZABETH. Ref also: TM.
*The House Without the Door. (corrected title)

*DALY, HAMLIN. Pseudonym of E. Hoffman Price.

*D'AMATO, BARBARA. SC: Dr. Garrett DeGraaf, in *The Hands of Healing Murder, and title below.
The Eyes on Utopia Murders. Charter, 1981 <Ariz.>

*DAMORE, LEO
*Cache. <Cape Cod>

*DANA, MARVIN
*The Master Mind. Silent film: Lasky, 1914 (scw: Clara Beranger; dir: Oscar Apfel)

*DANBY, FRANK
-The Copper Crash. Trischler, 1889

*DANE, CLEMENCE and *HELEN (DE GUERRY) SIMPSON. Ref (Dane): not in TC2.
*Enter Sir John. Film: British International, 1930, as Murder (scw: Alfred Hitchcock, Walter C. Mycroft, Alma Reville; dir: Hitchcock)

DANFORTH, LES. See: *Don(ald Eugene) Pendleton.

DANIEL, DAVID. 1945- .
Ark. Marek, 1984 <Turk.>

DANIEL, GLYN. Ref: not in TC2.

DANIEL, MARK. 1954- .
The Laughing Man. Joseph (London), 1954; Joseph (U.S.), 1955

*DANIEL, (WILLIAM) ROLAND. SC: Wu Fang, also in *Ruby of a Thousand Dreams, and in *The Society of the Spiders.
*The Man with the Magnetic Eyes. Film: British Foundation, 1945 (dir: Ronald Haines)

DANIELLE, MARIA. 1945- . Ref: CA.
Fieldwork. Avon, 1981

*DANIELS, A(LBERT) FREDERICK
High Tide. New Playwrights, 1982 (1-act play.)
The Patient in 4b. Deane, 1967; Baker's, 1967 (Play.)

*DANIELS, DOROTHY
Monte Carlo. Leisure, 1981; Star, 1981 <Fr., ca.1900>
Saratoga. Leisure, 1981; Star, 1981 <N. Y., 1880s>

*DANIELS, HAROLD R(OBERT). Ref also: TM.

*DANIELS, NORMAN A. Pseudonym: *Mark Reed, q.v. Ref also: TC2.
Bedroom in Hell! Rainbow, 195?

*DANIELS, PAUL. Pseudonym of *Paul W. Fairman.

*DANIELS, PHILIP
*Alibi of Guilt. ... Critic, 1986
Cinderella Spy. Hale, 1984; Critic, 1986
The Dracula Murders. Hale, 1983; Critic, 1986
Foolproof. Hale, 1981
A Genteel Little Murder. Hale, 1982; Academy Chicago, 1986
The Inconvenient Corpse. Hale, 1982
Nice Knight for Murder. Hale, 1982; Critic, 1986
Suspicious. Hale, 1981

DANIELS, VINCENT
Mendoza's Treasure. Leisure, 1980 <Carib.>

*DANNE, MAX HALLAN
*The Premature Burial. (Novelization of film: American International, 1961; scw: Charles Beaumont, Ray Russell; dir: Roger Corman)

*DANVERS, JACK
*The End of It All. delete: not criminous

*DARBON, LESLIE
*A Murder Is Announced. (2-act play.)

*DARBY, CATHERINE
*Season of the Falcon. <Eng., 1774>

DARBY, EDWARD
Two Bottles of Relish. Dramatic, 1967 (1-act play based on the ss by *Lord Dunsany.)

*D'ARCY, JACK. Pseudonym of D'Arcy Lyndon Champion, ca.1903-1968.

*DARK, JAMES. Pseudonym of James Edmund MacDonnell. Ref: CA.
*Assignment Tokyo; see *Operation Missat
*Operation Missat. U.S. title: *Assignment Tokyo

DARRELL, GEORGE
The Belle of the Bush. Bookstall (Syd.), 1916

DARRELL, WILLIAM
Compulsory Gangster. Fiction House, 1941
The Shadow of the Gestapo. Fiction House, 1940

DAVENPORT, JAMES
Murder at Bill's O' Jacks. Richardson, 1985 <Eng., 1832>

*DAVEY, JOCELYN. SC: Ambrose Usher, also in title below.
Murder in Paradise. Chatto, 1982; Walker, 1982 <Carib.>

*DAVID, KIRK. House name.

DAVID-NEEL, ALEXANDRA, 1868-1969, and LAMA (ALBERT ARTHUR) YONGDEN
-The Power of Nothingness. Houghton, 1982 (Translation of "La Puissance du Neant.")

DAVIDSON, ANDREA. Lives in Houston.
A Siren's Lure. Harlequin, 1985 <It.>

*DAVIDSON, AVRAM
Or All the Seas with Oysters. Berkley, 1962 ss, one criminous

*DAVIDSON, DAVID (ALBERT). 1908-1985.

*DAVIDSON, HUGH COLEMAN
*The Queen of the Black Hand. <Sp.>

DAVIDSON, JOHN. Pseudonym of *Charles (Alexander) Nuetzel. Other pseudonym: Alec Rivere, q.v.
-Mistress of the Damned. Anchor, 1965
-The Sex Cult Murders. Anchor, 1965 (Cover gives author as Fred MacDonald) <Calif.>

*DAVIDSON, LIONEL. Ref also: BM, TM.
*A Long Way to Shiloh. (title correction)
*Night of Wenceslas. Film: Rank, 1963, as Hot Enough for June; released in the U.S. as Agent 8 3/4 (scw: Lukas Heller; dir: Ralph Thomas)

*DAVIDSON, MURIEL. 1924-1983. Ref: CA.
'Til Death You Do Pay. Marek, 1981

*DAVIE-MARTIN, HUGH
Death's Bright Angel. Hale, 1982

DAVIES, COURTMAN. Pseudonym: Clifton Rank, q.v.

DAVIES, FRED
Stories Grave and Gray. Palatine, 1927 ss, at least one criminous (Sherlockian parody)

DAVIES, FREDERICK. 1916- .
Death of a Hit-Man. Hale, 1982; St. Martin's, 1983
Snow in Venice. Hale, 1983; Critic, 1985

*DAVIES, HUGH SYKES. 1909-1984. Ref: CA.

*DAVIES, JACK
*Esther, Ruth and Jennifer ... Also published as: *North Sea Hijack. Film: Universal, 1980, as North Sea Hijack; released in the U.S. as ffoulkes (scw: Jack Davies; dir: Andrew V. McLaglen)

DAVIES, JOHN. 1913-
The Savannah Syndrome. Hale, 1983

*DAVIES, JOHN EVAN WESTON. 1914-
Pseudonym: *Berkley Mather, q.v.

*DAVIES, L(ESLIE) P(URNELL)
-The Alien. Jenkins, 1968; Doubleday, 1971. Film: Universal, 1972, as The Groundstar Conspiracy (scw: Matthew Howard; dir: Lamont Johnson)
Morning Walk. Hale, 1983

DAVIES, LLOYD. 1922- .
Cult and Countercult. Artlook (Australia), 1984

DAVIES, (WILLIAM) ROBERTSON. 1913-
Ref: CA.
-What's Bred in the Bone. Viking, 1985; Viking (London), 1986

DAVIES, W. X. All titles in Countdown WWIII series.
Operation Black Sea. Berkley, 1984
Operation Choke Point. Berkley, 1984 <Guyana>
Operation North Africa. Berkley, 1984
Operation Persian Gulf. Berkley, 1984

DAVIS, BART. 1950- . Born in NYC, graduate of State University of New York at Stony Brook; brown belt in karate; licensed hypnotist; married to an attorney; living in N.Y.
Blind Prophet. Doubleday, 1983; Collins, 1984
A Conspiracy of Eagles. Bantam, 1984; Bantam (London), 1985 <S. Afr.>

*DAVIS, DOROTHY SALISBURY. Ref also: TM. SC: Julie Hayes, also in title below marked JH; Mrs. N., also in title marked N.
Lullaby of Murder. Scribner, 1984; Gollancz, 1984 JH <NYC>
Tales for a Stormy Night. Foul Play, 1984 ss, one about N
*A Town of Masks. <Mich.>

DAVIS, ELMER (HOLMES). 1890-1958.
Times Have Changed. McBride, 1923; Hodder, 1924. Silent film: Fox, 1923 (scw: Jack Strumwasser; dir: James Flood)

*DAVIS, FRANKLIN M(ILTON), JR.
*The Naked and the Lost. <Kor.>

*DAVIS, FREDERICK C(LYDE). Ref also: CA, TM.

*DAVIS, GERRY. See: *Kit Pedlar.

*DAVIS, GORDON
*Ring Around Rosy. Reprinted as: From Cuba with Love, as by E. Howard Hunt. Pinnacle, 1974

*DAVIS, GORDON. Pseudonym of *Leonard Levinson.

*DAVIS, HOWARD CHARLES
Poodle's Grave. Hale, 1981

DAVIS, JACK. See: *Nick Carter.

*DAVIS, JOHN GORDON
Fear No Evil. Macmillan, 1982; Collins, 1982 <NYC>

DAVIS, JOYCE ELLEN
Moonlight and Murder. Tiara, 1981

*DAVIS, KENN. Ref: TM. SC: Carver Bascombe, also in title marked CB below.
Dead to Rights. Avon, 1981 <N.W.>
Words Can Kill. GM, 1984 CB <Calif.>

*DAVIS, MEANS
*Murder Without Weapon. (title correction)

*DAVIS, MILDRED (B.). Ref also: TC2.
*The Invisible Boarder. (corrected spelling)

*DAVIS, NORBERT. 1909-1949. Ref: BM, TM.
*The Mouse in the Mountain. British title: *Rendezvous with Fear

*DAVIS, OWEN. See also: John P. Ritter.
*At 9:45. Film: WB-FN, 1934, as Nine Forty-Five (scw: Brock Williams; dir: George King)
*The Donovan Affair. Film: Columbia, 1929 (scw: Howard J. Green, Dorothy Howell; dir: Frank R. Capra)
Easy Come, Easy Go. French, 1926 (3-act play.) Silent film: Paramount, 1928 (scw: Florence Ryerson; dir: Frank Tuttle). Sound film: Paramount, 1930, as Only Saps Work (scw: Percy Health, Joseph L. Mankiewicz, Sam Mintz; dir: Edwin H. Knopf)
*The Haunted House. Film: First National, 1928 (scw: Richard Bee, Lajos Biro; dir: Benjamin Christiansen)
*Mr. & Mrs. North. Film: MGM, 1941 (scw: S. K. Lauren; dir: Robert B. Sinclair)
*The Ninth Guest. Film: Columbia, 1934 (scw: Garnett Weston; dir: Roy William Neill)

*DAVIS, PHIL
The Dancer's Death. Avon, 1981 <NYC>

*DAVIS, RICHARD HARDING. Ref also: TC2.
The Exile, and other stories. Harper, 1894; Osgood, 1894 ss Silent film (based on title story): Fox, 1923, as The Exiles (scw: Fred Jackson; dir: Edmund Mortimer). Sound film (based on same story): Fox, 1929, as Fugitives (scw: John Stone; dir: William Beaudine)
Gallegher, and other stories. Scribner, 1891; Osgood, 1891 ss, some criminous. Silent film (based on title story): DeMille, 1928, as Let 'Er Go Gallegher (scw: Elliott Clawson; dir: Elmer Clifton)
*In the Fog. Silent film: Edison, 1911, as How Sir Andrew Lost His Vote
The Lost Road. Scribner, 1913; Duckworth, 1914 ss, at least one criminous. Silent film (from ss "The Man of Zanzibar"): Fox, 1922, as The Man of Zanzibar (scw: Edward LeSaint; dir: Rowland V. Lee)
*The Scarlet Car. Silent film: Bluebird, 1917 (scw: William Parker; dir: Joseph DeGrasse). Also: Universal, 1923 (scw: George Randolph Chester; dir: Stuart Paton)
Somewhere in France. Scribner, 1915; Duckworth, 1916 ss Silent film (based on title ss): Triangle, 1916 (dir: Charles Giblyn)
*The White Mice. Silent film: Pinellas, 1926 (scw: Randolph Bartlett; dir: Edward H. Griffith)

DAVIS, ROBERT. 1927- .
Adria. Falmouth, 1955

*DAVIS, STRATFORD
*Death in Seven Hours. Film (?): Independent, 1953, as Death Goes to School (scw: Maisie Sharman, Stephen Clarkson; dir: Clarkson)
*One Man's Secret. Film: Merton Park, 1957, as Man in the Shadow (scw: Stratford Davis; dir: Montgomery Tully)

*DAVIS, TECH. Ref: TM.

DAVIS, WILLIAM F. Pseudonym: *Zeke Davis.

*DAVIS, YORKE
  *The Green Cloak. Silent film (?):
    Kleine, 1915 (scw: Owen Davis,
    Henry Kitchell Webster)

*DAVIS, ZEKE. Pseudonym of William F.
  Davis.

*DAVISON, GEOFFREY. Ref: CA.

*DAWE, (WILLIAM) CARLTON (LANYON)
  *The Black Spider. ⟨Fr.⟩ Silent
    film: B&C, 1920 (scw & dir: Wil-
    liam J. Humphrey). Also: Wild
    Gunning, 1922, as Foolish Monte
    Carlo (scw & dir: William
    Humphrey)
  *Claudia Pole. delete: not criminous
  *The Emu's Head. criminous ⟨Australia⟩
  *The Plotters of Peking. ss ⟨China⟩
  *The Shadow of Evil. Silent film:
    British Art, 1921 (scw: Harry
    Hughes; dir: James Readon)

DAWSON, LES
  The Spy Who Came... Star, 1976

DAY, DORIS M.
  A Will of Her Own. French, 1983
    (Play.)

*DEAL, BABS H(ODGES). Ref also: TM.

*DEAL, BORDEN. 1922-1985.
  A Long Way to Go. Doubleday, 1965;
    Joseph, 1966 ⟨South⟩

*DEAN, AMBER. 1902-1985. Ref: not in
  TC2.

DEAN, BURT
  Castle of the Sea. Vantage, 1954

DEAN, GEORGE. Pseudonym: *George
  Douglas.

*DEAN, ROBERT GEORGE. Pseudonym:
  *George Griswold.

DEAN, S. F. X. Pseudonym of Francis
  Smith, college professor who lives
  in Amherst, Mass. SC: Prof. Neil
  Kelly, in all titles.
  By Frequent Anguish. Walker, 1982;
    Collins, 1982 ⟨acad., New Eng.⟩
  Ceremony of Innocence. Walker, 1984;
    Gollancz, 1985 ⟨Eng.⟩
  Death and the Mad Heroine. Walker,
    1985; Gollancz, 1986 ⟨New Eng.⟩
  It Can't Be My Grave. Walker, 1984;
    Collins, 1983 ⟨Eng.⟩
  Such Pretty Toys. Walker, 1982;
    Collins, 1983 ⟨N. Mex.⟩

*DeANDREA, WILLIAM L(OUIS). Ref also:
  TM. Pseudonym: Philip DeGrave, q.v.
  SC: Matt Cobb, in *Killed in the
  Ratings, and in those titles
  marked MC below; Clifford Driscoll
  (= Bellman) = CD.
  Cronus. Mysterious Press, 1984 CD
  Five O'Clock Lightning. St. Mar-
    tin's, 1982 ⟨NYC, 1953⟩
  Killed in the Act. Doubleday, 1981
    MC ⟨NYC⟩
  Killed on the Ice. Doubleday, 1984
    MC ⟨NYC⟩
  Killed with a Passion. Doubleday,
    1983 MC ⟨N.Y.⟩
  Snark. Mysterious Press, 1985 CD
    ⟨Eng.⟩

*DEANE, HAMILTON and *JOHN L(OYD)
  BALDERSTON, 1889-1954.
  *Dracula. Film: Universal, 1979 (scw:
    W. D. Richter; dir: John Badham)

*DEANE, NORMAN. (Other titles were
  reprinted in England as by John
  Creasey.)
  *Incense of Death. SC: Bruce Murdoch.
    also at least in revised edition
    (NEL, 1969, as by John Creasey)

*DEARDEN, HAROLD. 1882(?)-1962. Ref:
  CA.

DE BEAUREGARD, G. and H. DE GORSSE
  The Stamp King. Gibbons, 1899

DE BECHEVET, LYDIA P.
  The Mystery of the Twisted Man.
    Hitchcock, 1927

*DE BORCHGRAVE, ARNAUD and ROBERT MOSS.
  Moss is Australian born; at age 22
  a univ. professor there; foreign
  correspondent and editor with "The
  Economist", later full-time fiction
  writer. SC: Robert Hockney, in *The
  Spike, and in title below.
  Monimbo. Simon, 1983   ⟨Miami⟩

*DE BOSSCHERE, JOHN. 1878-1953.

*DEBRETT, HAL
  *Before I Die. Film: Gibraltar, 1955;
    released in U.S. as Shadow of Fear
    (scw: Robert Westerby; dir: Al
    Rogell)

DECKER, JAKE. SC: Steve Sinclair (The
  Force), in all titles.
  Deadly Snow. Pinnacle, 1984 ⟨Thai.⟩
  Death Comes Home. Pinnacle, 1984
    ⟨Indiana⟩
  Death Gambit. Pinnacle, 1984 ⟨Ice.⟩
  Death's Little Sister. Pinnacle, 1984
    ⟨Wash. D.C.⟩

DE COURSEY, VIRGINIA. 1924-   . Ref:
  CA.
  Ever This Night. Dell, 1983
    ⟨Kan. City⟩

*DE CRESPIGNY, MRS. PHILIP CHAMPION
  *Tangled Evidence. Film: Real Art,
    1934 (scw: H. Fowler Mear; dir:
    George A. Cooper)

DEE, F. J.
  Captain Confetti. Simpkin, 1928 ss

*DE FELITTA, FRANK (PAUL)
  *Audrey Rose. Film: UA, 1977 (scw:
    Frank De Felitta; dir: Robert Wise)
  For Love of Audrey Rose. Warner,
    1982; NEL pb, 1982

DEFOE, DANIEL. 1660-1731.
  The Fortunate Mistress. Warner,
    1724; Knopf, 1924. Also published
    as: Roxana. Slater, 1742. And as:
    The Life and Adventures of Roxana.
    Whitefield, 1745
  The Fortunes and Misfortunes of the
    Famous Moll Flanders. Edling,
    1722; Nickerson, 1903. Also pub-
    lished as: Moll Flanders. Bell,
    1908; Small, 1926. Film: Para-
    mount, 1965, as The Amorous Adven-
    tures of Moll Flanders (scw: Denis
    Cannan, Roland Kibbee; dir: Terence
    Young)
  The History and Remarkable Life of
    the Truly Honourable Col. Jacque.
    Brotherton, 1723; Christy, 1844.
    Also published as: Life of Colonel
    Jack. Ballantyne, 1810

*DE FORD, MIRIAM ALLEN. Ref: TM; not in
  TC2.

*DE FRAGA, GEOFF
  *Murder at the Cookout. ⟨Australia⟩

DE FRANCQUEN, LEONARD
  The Eye-Witness. Deane, 1961 (Play.)

DE GORSSE, H. See: G. De Beauregard.

*DE GRAMONT, SANCHE
  *Lives to Give. (Translation of ...)
    ⟨Fr., WWII⟩

*DeGRAVE, PHILIP. Pseudonym of *William
  DeAndrea, q.v.
  Unholy Moses. Doubleday, 1985 ⟨NYC⟩

DE HARTOG, JAN. 1914-   . Ref: CA.
  -The Inspector. Atheneum, 1960; H.
    Hamilton, 1960. Film: Red Lion,
    1961; released in the U.S. as Lisa
    (scw: Nelson Gidding; dir: Phillip
    Dunne)

*DEIGHTON, LEN. Ref also: TM. SC:
  Bernard Samson = BS.
  Berlin Game. Hutchinson, 1983; Knopf,
    1983 BS
  *The Billion Dollar Brain. Film:
    Lowndes, 1967 (scw: John
    McGrath; dir: Ken Russell)
  *Funeral in Berlin. Film: Lowndes,
    1966 (scw: Evan Jones; dir: Guy
    Hamilton)
  *The Ipcress File. Film: Lowndes,
    1964 (scw: Bill Canaway, James
    Doran; dir: Sidney J. Furie)
  London Match. Hutchinson, 1985;
    Knopf, 1986 BS
  Mexico Set. Hutchinson, 1984; Knopf,
    1985 BS
  Only When I Larf. Sphere, 1968;
    Mysterious Press, 1987, as Only
    When I Laugh. Film: Beecord,
    1968 (scw: John Salmon; dir:
    Basil Dearden)
  Only When I Laugh; see Only When I
    Larf
  *Spy Story. Film: Shonteff, 1976
    (dir: Lindsay Shonteff)
  XPD. Hutchinson, 1981; Knopf, 1981

*DEJEANS, ELIZABETH
  *The Romance of a Million Dollars.
    Silent film: Bachmann, 1926 (scw:
    Arthur Hoerl; dir: Tom Terriss)
  *The Tiger's Coat. Silent film:
    Dial, 1920 (scw: Jack Cunningham;
    dir: Roy Clements)

*DEKKER, CARL. SC: Carl Dekker, in at
  least titles marked CD below.
  Blood on the Sand. Calvert   CD
  Danger Doll. Calvert   CD
  Double or Nothing. Calvert   CD
  Miss Deadly. Calvert
  Stab in the Dark. Calvert
  The Wax Museum. Calvert

*DEKKER, CARL. Cross-reference cor-
  rection: *Mark Sadler.

*DEKOBRA, MAURICE
  *Hell Is Sold Out. Film: Zelstro,
    1951 (scw: Guy Morgan, Moie
    Charles; dir: Michael Anderson)
  *The Madonna of the Sleeping Cars.
    Silent film (Russia): Natan, 1929
  *The Widow with the Pink Gloves.
    Film (in French): Davis, 1954, as
    Secret Document-Vienna (scw: Andre
    Legrand; dir: Andrew Haguet)

DELACORTA. Pseudonym of Daniel Odier,
  French novelist and screenwriter.
  SC: Serge Gorodish and Alba, in all
  titles.
  Diva. Summit, 1983; Lane, 1984
    ⟨Paris⟩   Film (in French): Galaxie,
    1981 (scw: Jean-Jacques Beineix,
    Jean Van Hamme; dir: Beineix)
  Lola. Summit, 1985; Viking (London),
    1986 ⟨Fr.⟩
  Luna. Summit, 1984; Viking (London),
    1985
  Nana. Summit, 1984; Lane, 1984
    ⟨Paris⟩
  Vida. Summit, 1985; Viking (London),
    1986 ⟨L.A.⟩

*DELACORTE, PETER
  Levantine. Norton, 1985 ⟨Mid. East⟩

DELACOUR, ALFRED CHARLEMAGNE LARTIGUE.
  1817-1883. See: Eugene Moreau,
  1806-1876.

DELAHAYE, MICHAEL
  On the Third Day; see Third Day
  The Sale of Lot 236. Constable, 1981
  Third Day. Constable, 1984. U.S.
    title: On the Third Day. Macmillan,
    1984 ⟨Mid. East, 1988⟩

*DE LA MARE, WALTER (JOHN). Ref: CA.

*DELANEY, LAURENCE. Former U.S. sub-
  marine officer; an actor, living
  in L.A.

*DE LARRABEITI, MICHAEL. Documentary
  cameraman, tour guide in Europe;
  living in England.

*DE LA TORRE, LILLIAN. Ref also: TM.
  SC: Dr. Sam: Johnson, also in
  title below.
  The Return of Dr. Sam: Johnson,
    Detector. International Polygonics,
    1984 ss

*DE LEON, JACK and *JACK CELESTIN, q.v.
  The Silent Witness. Play Rights,
    1936 (3-act play). Film: TCF,
    1932 (scw: Douglas Doty; dir:
    Marcel Varnel, R. L. Hough)

*DE LILLO, DON
  The Names. Knopf, 1982; Harvester,
    1983   ⟨Athens⟩

*DELL, AMEN. Pseudonym of Irving
  Mendell.

*DELL, JEFFREY. 1899-1985(?). Ref: CA.
  Official Secret. World Plays, 1938
    (2-act play). Film: British
    National, 1939, as Spies
    of the Air (scw: A. R. Raw-
    linson, Bridget Boland; dir:
    David Macdonald)
  *Payment Deferred. Film: MGM, 1932
    (scw: Ernest Vadja, Claudine West;
    dir: Lothar Mendez)

*DELLA, LEW
  *Ladies Sleep Alone. Archer, 1951

*DELLIGAN, WILLIAM. Pseudonym: *Ellen
  Orford.

*DELMAN, DAVID. Ref: CA, TM. SC: Lt.
  Jacob Horowitz, also in both
  titles below.

Death of a Nymph. Doubleday, 1985;
    Collins, 1986 ⟨acad, N.Y.⟩
Murder in the Family. Doubleday,
    1985   ⟨Lisbon⟩

DEL RIVO, LAURA. 1934-   .
    The Furnished Room. New Authors,
    1961; Doubleday, 1962. Film: Dial,
    1963, as West 11 (scw: Keith
    Waterhouse, Willis Hall; dir:
    Michael Winner)

DEL RUTH, HAMPTON
    Defenders of the Law. Jacobsen,
    1931 (Novelization of film:
    Standard, 1931; scw: Hampton Del
    Ruth, Louis Heifetz; dir: Joseph
    Levering)

DELUTRY, JEAN
    Victim of Love. Mystique, 1981
    (Translation of "D'Amour et de
    Champagne." Paris, 1978.)

*DELVING, MICHAEL. Ref also: TM.

*DE MARCO, GORDON. Grew up in Akron,
    Ohio; lived in S.F. after 1967. SC:
    Riley Kovacks, in *October Heat,
    and at least in title marked RK
    below.
    The Canvas Prison. Germinal, 1982;
        Germinal (London), 1984 ⟨L.A.,
        1949)   RK
    Frisco Blues. Pluto (U.S. and Lon-
        don), 1985   ⟨S.F.⟩
*October Heat. ... Pluto, 1984

*DEMARIS, OVID. Ref: not in TC2.
*Candyleg. Film: Columbia, 1970, as
    Machine Gun McCain (scw: Mino
    Roli; dir: Giuliano Montaldo)
*The Hoods Take Over. Film: TCF, 1958,
    as Gang War (scw: Louis Vittes;
    dir: Gene Fowler, Jr.)
The Vegas Legacy. Delacorte, 1983;
    Sphere, 1984 ⟨Las Veg.⟩

*DE MARNE, DENIS. See: *Ron Pember.

DE MARNEY, TERENCE. See: Percy
    Robinson, 1863-

*DE MARQUAND, ALIX. Pseudonym of
    Michael Skinner.

DEMESTICHAS, LOUIS
    Measure of Fear. Dorrance, 1955

*DE MILLE, JAMES. 1833-1880. (cor-
    rected birth year.)

*DE MILLE, NELSON
    Cathedral. Delacorte, 1981; Granada,
        1981 ⟨NYC⟩
    The Talbot Odyssey. Delacorte, 1984;
        Granada, 1984
    Word of Honor. Warner hc, 1985;
        Granada, 1985

*DEMING, RICHARD. 1915-1983. Ref also:
    TM.
*The Careful Man. Film: Paramount,
    1967, as Arrivederci, Baby!; re-
    leased in Britain as Drop Dead
    Darling (scw: Ken Hughes, Ronald
    Harwood; dir: Hughes)
*What's the Matter with Helen?
    (Novelization of film: Raymax,
    1971; scw: Henry Farrell; dir:
    Curtis Harrington)

DEMOREST, STEPHEN. 1949-   . Joint
    pseudonym with Michael Robert
    Gross, 1952-   : D. G. Devon,
    q.v.

DeMOSS, MARGUERITE
    The Scarlet Storm. Leisure, 1981

*DEMPSEY, AL
    Miss Finney Kills Now and Then.
        Pinnacle, 1982
    The Stendal Raid. Critics, 1985

DEMPSTER, CHRIS. 1943-   . Ref: CA.
    Contract! Corgi, 1983

*DENBY, EDWIN (ORR). Ref: CA.

*DENEVI, MARCO
    -Secret Ceremony. Time, 1961. Film:
    Universal, 1968 (scw: George
    Tabori; dir: Joseph Losey)

*DENHAM, BERTIE. SC: Derek Thyrde,
    in *The Man Who Lost His Shadow,
    and in title below.
    Two Thyrdes. Ross Anderson, 1983;
        St. Martin's, 1986

*DENHAM, REGINALD
    Minor Murder, with Mary Orr. French,
    1967 (2-act play.)   ⟨Australia⟩
*Recipe for a Crime. ⟨Mex.⟩

*DENIS, JOHN
*Hostage Tower. ... Crest, 1983

*DENKER, HENRY
    Outrage. Morrow, 1982; Allen, 1982
    A Place for the Mighty. McKay,
        1973; Allen, 1974 ⟨Wash. D.C.⟩
    -The Warfield Syndrome. Putnam, 1981;
        Macdonald, 1982 ⟨Wash. D.C.,
        hosp.⟩

*DENNING, MARK. SC: John Marshall,
    also in title below marked JM.
*Die Fast, Die Happy. ⟨Mex.⟩
    Din of Inequity. St. Martin's, 1984
        ⟨Reno⟩
    The Golden Lure. Tower, 1981 JM
*Shades of Gray. ⟨S.F.⟩
    The Swiss Abduction. Leisure, 1981
        ⟨Switz.⟩

*DENNIS, CHARLES
*The Next-to-Last Train Ride. Film:
    CBS Theatrical Films, 1984, as
    Finders Keepers (scw: Charles
    Dennis, Ronny Graham, Terence
    Marsh; dir: Richard Lester)

*DENNIS, RALPH. Ref: TM.
    Deadman's Game. Berkley, 1976

*DENNIS, ROBERT C. 1920-1983. Ref
    also: TM.

DENNISON, JANINE
    Attempt. Hale, 1974

*DENNISTON, ELINORE. Pseudonym:
    *Helen K. Maxwell.

DENNY, LESLEY
    Snap Judgement. Hale, 1981
    A Taste of Treachery. Hale, 1982

*DENT, LESTER. Ref also: CA, TM.

DENTINGER, JANE. Ref: TM. Graduate of
    Ithaca College in acting and di-
    recting; actress off Broadway and
    in regional theatres; lives in NYC
    and manages Murder Ink, the mystery
    bookstore. SC: Jocelyn O'Roarke
    & Phillip Gerard, in both titles.
    First Hit of the Season. Doubleday,
        1984; Gollancz, 1986 ⟨NYC,
        theatre⟩
    Murder on Cue. Doubleday, 1983; Gol-
        lancz, 1985 ⟨NYC, theatre⟩

*DE POLNAY, PETER. 1906-1984.
    The Moot Point. Creative Age, 1948;
        Hutchinson, 1948

*DERBY, E. C.
*A Counterfeiter's Roguery. Street,
    1903
*The Crossing of Clews. Street, 1904
*The Empty Mail Bags. Street, 1903
*Foiling a Counterfeiter. Street, 1903
*The Gold Maker's Secret. Street, 1904
*The Government's Man. Street, 1903
*In League with the Counterfeiters.
    Street, 1903
*The Mail Robber's Syndicate. Street,
    1903
*The Man in the Coach. Street, 1902
*A Master Stroke. Street, 1903
*A Nihilist's Vengeance. Street, 1903
*The Outlaw's Oath. Street, 1903
*A Smuggler's Fate. Street, 1904
*The Test of Anarchy. Street, 1903

*DERBY, MARK. Ref: TM.

*DERLETH, AUGUST (WILLIAM). Ref also:
    TM.

*DERRICK, LIONEL. SC: Mark Hardin
    (The Penetrator), also in titles
    below.
*Aryan Onslaught. ⟨Utah⟩
    Assassination Factor. Pinnacle, 1981
    Brotherhood of Blood. Pinnacle, 1983
        ⟨Calif.⟩
    City of the Dead. Pinnacle, 1984
        ⟨Bolivia⟩
    Deep Cover Blast-Off. Pinnacle, 1981
        ⟨Can.⟩
*Dixie Death Squad. ⟨Ga.⟩
*Dodge City Bombers. ⟨Kan.⟩
    Hell's Hostages. Pinnacle, 1981
        ⟨Mid. East⟩
    Inca Gold Hijack. Pinnacle, 1981
        ⟨Chi.⟩
    Jungle Blitz. Pinnacle, 1982
        ⟨Viet Nam⟩
    Neutron Nightmare. Pinnacle, 1983
    Orphan Army. Pinnacle, 1982
    Plundered Paradise. Pinnacle, 1983
    Quaking Terror. Pinnacle, 1982
    Rampage in Rio. Pinnacle, 1981
        ⟨Rio de J.⟩
    Satan's Swarm. Pinnacle, 1982
*The Skyhigh Betrayers. ⟨Calif.⟩
    Terrorist Torment. Pinnacle, 1982

DE ST. JEOR, OWANNA
    Bad Timing. Walker, 1984

*DE SAIX, TYLER. See: *H(enry)
    DeVere Stacpoole.

*DE SAVALLO, DONA TERESA
*The House of the Lost Court. Silent
    film: Edison, 1915 (dir: Charles
    Brabin)

*DES CARS, GUY
*The Brute. Film: B&A, 1954,
    as The Green Scarf (scw: Gordon
    Wellesley; dir: George More
    O'Ferrall)

DE SIMONE, DONALD
    A Kiss on Each Cheek. Pinnacle, 1981

*DETECTION CLUB
    Crime on the Coast, and No Flowers
    by Request. Gollancz, 1984
    (two novelets)
    The Scoop, and Behind the Screen.
    Gollancz, 1983; Harper, 1983
    (two novelets)

*DEUTCSH, ARTHUR V. Commanding officer
    of 70th Precinct in Brooklyn; has
    more than 20 years with NYC police;
    graduate of F.B.I. Academy, and has
    master's degree in public adminis-
    tration; assistant professor of
    police administration at City
    College of New York.

DEUTSCH, DAVID GEORGE
    Bend in the River. Target, 1985
    Danger on Target. Target, 1985

DEVANEY, ROBERT. Pseudonym: *Sarah
    MacIvers.

*DEVERELL, WILLIAM (HERBERT). Ref: CA.
    High Crimes. St. Martin's, 1982;
    Macmillan (London), 1983 ⟨ship⟩

*DE VILLIERS, GERARD
*The Angel of Vengeance. ⟨Urug.⟩
*Death in Santiago. ⟨Chile⟩
*Kill Kissinger. ⟨Kuw.⟩
*The Man from Kabul. ⟨Afghan.⟩

*DEVINE, DOMINIC. 1920-1980.
    This Is Your Death. Collins, 1981;
    St. Martin's, 1982 ⟨1962⟩

DEVON, D. G. Joint pseudonym of
    Michael Robert Gross, 1952-
    and Stephen Demorest, 1949-
    Ref (both): CA. SC: Temple Kent,
    in all titles.
    Precious Objects. Ballantine, 1984
    Shattered Mask. Ballantine, 1983
        ⟨NYC⟩
    Temple Kent. Ballantine, 1982;
        Hamlyn, 1984 ⟨NYC⟩

*DEVON, NICOLA. Pseudonym of
    *W(illiam Arthur) Howard Baker.

*DEWAR, EVELYN. Pseudonym of Evelyn
    Wilcock.

*DeWEESE, JEAN
    The Backhoe Gothic. Doubleday, 1981

*DEWEY, THOMAS B(LANCHARD). 1915-
    1981. Ref also: TM.

DE WOHL, LOUIS. 1903-1961. Ref: CA.
    Strange Daughter. Lawson, 1945

*DEWHURST, EILEEN (MARY). 1929-   .
    Ref: CA. SC: Insp. Neil Carter, in
    at least those marked NC.
*Curtain Fall. ... Doubleday, 1982
    The House That Jack Built. Collins,
        1983; Doubleday, 1984
    Playing Safe. Collins, 1985
    There Was a Little Girl. Collins,
        1984; Doubleday 1986 NC
    Trio in Three Flats. Collins, 1981;
        Doubleday, 1981 NC
    Whoever I Am. Collins, 1982; Double-
        day, 1983

DEWLEN, AL. 1921-   . Ref: CA.
    Twilight of Honor. McGraw, 1961;
    Longmans, 1962 ⟨Tex.⟩ Film:

MGM, 1963; released in Britain as The Charge Is Murder (scw: Henry Denker; dir: Boris Sagal)

*DEXTER, (NORMAN) COLIN. Ref also: TC2. SC: Insp. Morse, also in all titles below.
  The Dead of Jericho. Macmillan (London), 1981; St. Martin's, 1982
  The Riddle of the Third Mile. Macmillan (London), 1983; St. Martin's, 1984

DEXTER, PETE. 1943-   .
  God's Pocket. Random, 1984; Secker, 1985 <Phil.>

*DEY, FREDERIC MERRILL VAN RENSSELAER. Ref: CA.

DIAL, JOAN. 1937-   . Ref: CA.
  Echoes of War. St. Martin's, 1984; Piatkus, 1984 <Ger., WWII>

*DIAMOND, BRETT
  A Coffin for Clara. Spencer, 1952

*DIAMOND, FRANK
  *Love Me to Death. <Cape Cod>

DIBDIN-PITT, GEORGE. 1799-1855. See George Dibdin Pitt.

*DIBNER, MARTIN
  The Devil's Paintbrush. Doubleday, 1983

DiCHIARA, ROBERT
  Hard-Boiled. Godine, 1985 (3 puzzle novelets.)

DICK, KAY. 1915-   . Pseudonym: *Jeremy Scott.

*DICK, PHILIP K(ENDRED)
  -Clans of the Alphane Moon. Ace, 1964; Panther, 1975
  -Confessions of a Crap Artist. Entwhistle, 1978; Magnum, 1979
  -Counter-Clock World. Berkley, 1967; Sphere, 1968
  -Deus Irae, with Roger Zelazny. Doubleday, 1976; Gollancz, 1978
  -Do Androids Dream of Electric Sheep? Doubleday, 1968; Rapp, 1969. Film: Ladd, 1982, as Blade Runner (scw: Hampton Fancher, David People; dir: Ridley Scott)
  -Eye in the Sky. Ace, 1957; Arrow, 1971
  -The Golden Man. Berkley, 1960; Methuen, 1981 ss
  -The Man in High Castle. Putnam, 1962; Penguin, 1968
  -Our Friends from Frolix 8. Ace, 1970; Panther, 1976
  -Ubik. Doubleday, 1969; Rapp, 1970
  -The Variable Man and other stories. Ace, 1957; Sphere, 1969 ss

*DICKENS, CHARLES (JOHN HUFFHAM). Ref also: TM. See also: Walter Stephens.
  *Bleak House. Silent film: Walturdaw, 1910, as Jo, the Crossing Sweeper. Also: Barker, 1918, as Jo, the Crossing Sweeper (scw: Irene Miller; dir: Alexander Butler). Also: Ideal, 1920 (scw: William J. Elliott; dir: Maurice Elvey). Also: Master, 1922 (scw: Frank Miller; dir: H. B. Parkinson). Sound film: British Sound Film, 1928, as Grandfather Smallweed (dir: Hugh Croise)
  London Crimes. Academy Chicago, 1984 ss
  *The Mystery of Edwin Drood. Silent film: Gaumont, 1909 (dir: Arthur Gilbert). Also: Blache, 1914 (scw & dir: Tom Terriss). Sound film: Universal, 1935 (scw: John L. Balderston, Bradley King, Leopold Atlas, Gladys Unger; dir: Stuart Walker)

*DICKENS, FRANK
  Three Cheers for the Good Guys. Macmillan (London), 1984 <It.>

*DICKENS, MARY ANGELA
  Unveiled. Digby, 1906 5 stories, one criminous

*DICKENSON, FRED. 1909-1986. Ref: CA.

DICKEY, FRED
  Blood of the Eagle. Zebra, 1985

DICKEY, JAMES (LAFAYETTE). 1923-
  Deliverance. Houghton, 1970; H. Hamilton, 1970. Film: Warner, 1972 (scw: James Dickey; dir: John Boorman)

DICKEY, PAUL. 1885-1933. See: Charles William Goddard, 1879-1951.

*DICKINSON, PETER. Ref also: TM.
  Death of a Unicorn. Bodley, 1984; Pantheon, 1984
  Hindsight. Bodley, 1983; Pantheon, 1983 <acad.>
  The Last House Party. Bodley, 1982; Pantheon, 1982

DICKINSON, WILLIAM CROFT. 1897-1963. Ref: CA.
  -Dark Encounters. Harvill, 1963 ss

DICKSON, GORDON R(UPERT). 1923-
  See: *Poul (William) Anderson.

DICKSON, MARGARET (SMITH). 1947-
  Ref: CA.
  -Octavia's Hill. Houghton, 1983; Houghton (London), 1984 <Maine>

*DIDELOT, (ROGER) FRANCIS
  *The Seventh Juror. Film: Orex, 1962, as Le Sesptieme Jure (The Seventh Juror) (scw: Jacques Robert, Pierre Laroche; dir: Georges Lautner)

*DIEHL, WILLIAM (FRANCIS JR.)
  Chameleon. Random, 1982; Sphere, 1983
  Hooligans. Villard, 1984; Joseph, 1984 <Ga.>
  *Sharky's Machine. Film: Orion, 1981 (scw: Gerald DiPego; dir: Burt Reynolds)

DIETER, WILLIAM. 1929-   . Ref: CA.
  Beyond the Mountain. Atheneum, 1985 <Colo., 1920s>

DIGNON, EDWARD. See: *Cyril (Theron) Campion.

DILLINGER, JAMES
  Adrenaline. Signet, 1985 <L.A.>

*DIMENT, ADAM. Ref: not in TC2.

DIMICK, CHERYLLE LINDSEY. Pseudonym: Dawn Lindsey.

*DI MONA, JOSEPH
  *To the Eagle's Nest. Also published as: Eagle's Nest. Sphere, 1983

*DINELLI, MEL
  *The Man. Film: RKO, 1952, as Beware, My Lovely (scw: Mel Dinelli; dir: Harry Horner)

DINGLE, AYLWARD EDWARD. 1874- Pseudonym: Sinbad, q.v.

*DINNEEN, JOSEPH F(RANCIS)
  *The Anatomy of a Crime. Film: General Film, 1954, as Six Bridges to Cross (scw: Sidney Boehm; dir: Joseph Pevney)

*DINNER, WILLIAM and *WILLIAM MORUM
  *The Late Edwina Black. Film: General Film, 1951; released in the U.S. as Obsessed (scw: Charles Frank, David Evans; dir: Maurice Elvey)

*DI PEGO, GERALD F(RANCIS)
  Shadow of the Beast. Signet, 1984

*DISCH, THOMAS M(ICHAEL)
  The Businessman. Cape, 1984

*DISNEY, DORIS MILES. Ref also: TM.
  *Family Skeleton. Film: TCF, 1950, as Stella (scw & dir: Claude Binyon)
  *Straw Man. Film: Hedgerley, 1953 (scw & dir: Donald Taylor)

*DIVINE, DAVID
  *Boy on a Dolphin. Film: TCF, 1957 (scw: Ivan Moffat, Dwight Taylor; dir: Jean Negulsco)

*DIXON, H(ARRY) VERNOR
  *Too Rich to Die. <Calif.>

*DIXON, PETER L(EE) and *LAIRD P. KOENIG, q.v.
  *The Children Are Watching. Film: Adel, 1978, as Attention, Les Enfants Regardent (Attention, the Kids Are Watching) (scw: Christopher Frank, Serge Leroy; dir: Leroy)

*DOBBINS, PAUL H.
  *Murder Moon. <Ida.>

DOBKIN, KAYE <KATHLEEN HAMEL DOBKIN>. 1945-   . Ref: CA.
  -The White Rabbit. Dell, 1983

*DOBNER, MAEVA (PARK). 1918-1984.

DOBSON, WILLIAM. Pseudonym of *Michael Butterworth, q.v. Other pseudonym: *Sarah Kemp.
  The Child Player. Signet, 1981
  The Ripper. Signet, 1981

*DOBYNS, STEPHEN. SC: Charlie Bradshaw, in *Saratoga Longshot, and titles marked CB below.
  Dancer with One Leg. Dutton, 1983 <Boston, 1970s>
  Saratoga Headhunter. Viking, 1985; Allison, 1986 CB <N.Y.>
  Saratoga Swimmer. Atheneum, 1981; Allison, 1986 CB <N.Y.>

DODD, LEE WILSON. 1879-1933.
  Pals First. French, 1925 (3-act play.) Silent film: First National, 1926 (scw: F. P. Elliott, Olga Printzlau; dir: Edwin Carewe)

DODDS, STAN
  The Albanian Incident. Castle Books, 1983

*DODGE, DAVID (FRANCIS)
  *Plunder of the Sun. Film: Warner, 1953 (scw: Jonathan Latimer; dir: John Farrow)
  *To Catch a Thief. Film: Paramount, 1955 (scw: John Michael Hayes; dir: Alfred Hitchcock)

*DODSON, DANIEL B(OONE)
  Looking for Zoe. Dodd, 1981 <NYC>
  *The Man Who Ran Away. <Carib.>

*DOHERTY, EDWARD J.
  *The Broadway Murders. Film: Columbia, 1930, as Murder on the Roof (scw: F. Hugh Herbert; dir: George B. Seitz)

DOHERTY, P. C.
  The Death of a King. Hale, 1985; St. Martin's, 1986 <Eng., 1344>

*DOLINER, ROY
  The Twelfth of April. Crown, 1985 <1920-1958>

*DOLINSKY, MEYER
  *Hot Rod Gang Rumble. (Novelization of film: Nacirema, 1957, as Hot Rod Rumble; scw: Meyer Dolinsky; dir: Leslie H. Martinson)

*DOLSON, HILDEGARDE. Ref also: TM.

DOMATILLA, JOHN. Pseudonym.
  -The Last Crime. Atheneum, 1981 <Eng., future>

*DOMINIC, R. B. SC: Ben Safford, also in title below.
  Unexpected Developments. St. Martin's, 1984. British title: A Flaw in the System. Macmillan (London), 1983 <Wash. D.C.>

DONALDSON, STEPHEN R. Pseudonym: *Reed Stephens, q.v.

DORMER, DANIEL. Pseudonym of Kate Marian Cordeau.
  -The Mesmerist's Secret. Maxwell, 1888

*DORRANCE, ETHEL (ARNOLD SMITH) and *JAMES (FRENCH) DORRANCE
  *His Robe of Honor. Silent film: Paralta, 1918 (scw: Julian L. Lamothe; dir: Rex Ingram)

*DORRANCE, JAMES (FRENCH). See: *Ethel (Arnold Smith) Dorrance.

*DOSTOEVSKII, FEDOR MIKHAILOVITCH. See also: Alexander Hausvater.
  *The Brothers Karamazov. Film: Terra, 1931, as Der Moerderer (The Murderer). Also: Fincine, 1948, as I Fratelli Karamazov (The Brothers Karamazov) (scw: Giacomo Gentilomo, Gaspare Cataldo, Alberto Vecchietti, Giogio Pala; dir: Gentilomo). Also: MGM, 1957 (scw & dir: Richard Brooks). Also: Mosfilm, 1968, as Bratya Karamazovy (The Brothers Karamazov) (scw & dir: Ivan Piriev).

*Crime and Punishment. Silent film: Arrow, 1917 (dir: Lawrence McGill). Also: Newmann, 1923, as Raskolnikov (scw & dir: Robert Wiene). Also: Moscow Art Theatre, 1927. Sound film: Columbia, 1935 (scw: S. K. Lauren, Joseph Anthony; dir: Josef Von Sternberg). Also: General Productions, 1935, as Crime et Chatiment (Crime and Punishment) (scw: Marcel Ayme; dir: Pierre Chenal). Also: Monogram, 1946, as Fear (scw: Alfred Zeisler, Dennis Cooper; dir: Zeisler). Also: Terrafilm, 1948, in Swedish (scw: Bertil Malmberg, Sven Stople; dir: Hampe Faustman). Also: Pathe, 1957, as Crime et Chatiment (Crime and Punishment) (scw: Charles Spaak; dir: Georges Lampin). Also: Kingsley, 1958, as Most Dangerous Sin (existence of film not confirmed). Also: Allied Artists, 1958, as Crime and Punishment USA (scw: Walter Newman; dir: Denis Sanders). Also: Mosfilm, 1970, as Pestuplenie I Nakazanie (Crime and Punishment) (scw: Lev Kulijanov, Nikolai Figurovski; dir: Kulijanov). Also: Mostafa, 19??, as Sonya and the Madman (in Egyptian) (scw: Mahmoud Dyab; dir: Hossam El Dine Mostafa). Also: Villealfa, 1984, as Rikos Ja Rangaistus (Crime and Punishment) (scw: Aki Kaurismaki, Pauli Pentti; dir: Kaurismaki)

*DOUGHERTY, RICHARD. 1921-1987.
  *The Commissioner. Film: Universal, 1968, as Madigan (scw: Henri Simoun, Abraham Polonsky; dir: Don Siegel)

DOUGLAS, ARTHUR. 1926- .
  The Goods. Macmillan (London), 1985

DOUGLAS, AURIEL
  The Ghost of Staghorn. Pinnacle, 1981

DOUGLAS, BARNEY
  Brannigan's Lot. Castle, 1982

DOUGLAS, BEN
  Challenge at Castle Gap. Sunstone, 1984 <Tex., 1912>

*DOUGLAS, DAYLE. Pseudonym of Ewart Adamson.

*DOUGLAS, GEORGE. (Author of *The Case of the Greedy Rainmaker.) Pseudonym of George Dean.

*DOUGLAS, GRAEME
  The Prey. Hale, 1983

*DOUGLAS, HUDSON
  *A Million a Minute. Silent film: Quality, 1916 (scw: Howard Irving Young; dir: John W. Noble)

*DOUGLAS, MALCOLM
  *The Deadly Dames. (not The Deadly Games, as shown in early printings of CF)

DOUGLAS, RICHARD
  The Rig. Futura, 1975

*DOUGLASS, DONALD McNUTT. Ref also: TM.

DOUYAN, JACQUES. Pseudonym: *Adam St. Moore.

DOWLING, GREGORY. Born and educated in Bristol, studied at Christ Church, Oxford; living and teaching in Venice.
  Double Take. Severn, 1985; St. Martin's, 1985

*DOWLING, RICHARD
  *The Hidden Flame. criminous

*DOWNES, DONALD
  *The Easter Dinner. Film: Paramount, 1962, as The Pigeon That Took Rome (scw & dir: Melville Shavelson)
  *Orders to Kill. Film: Lynx, 1958 (scw: Paul Dehn, George St. George; dir: Anthony Asquith)

DOWNES, HUNDON
  The Opium Strategem. Bantam, 1973 <Far East>

*DOWNING, TODD. Ref: TM.

*DOWNING, WARWICK. Ref also: TM.

*DOYLE, (SIR) A(RTHUR) CONAN. Ref also: TM. See also: Paul Giovanni, John Hershey, *Tim J. Kelly, Alfred C. Ward.
  *The Adventures of Sherlock Holmes. Silent film (from ss "The Adventure of the Beryl Coronet"): Franco-British, 1912, as The Beryl Coronet (dir: Georges Treville). Also: Stoll, 1921, as The Beryl Coronet (scw: Charles Barnett; dir: Maurice Elvey). --- Silent film (from ss "The Adventure of the Blue Carbuncle"): Stoll, 1923, as The Blue Carbuncle (scw: Geoffrey H. Malins, Patrick L. Mannock; dir: George Ridgwell). --- Silent film (from ss "The Adventure of the Copper Beeches"): Franco-British, 1912, as The Copper Beeches (dir: Georges Treville). Also: Stoll, 1921, as The Copper Beeches (scw: William J. Elliott; dir: Maurice Elvey). --- Silent film (from ss "The Adventure of the Engineer's Thumb"): Stoll, 1922, as The Engineer's Thumb (scw: Patrick L. Mannock, Geoffrey H. Malins; dir: George Ridgwell). --- Silent film (from ss "The Adventure of the Noble Bachelor"): Stoll, 1921, as The Noble Bachelor (scw: William J. Elliott; dir: Maurice Elvey). --- Silent film (from ss "The Adventure of the Speckled Band"): Franco-British, 1912, as The Speckled Band (dir: Georges Treville). Also: Stoll, 1923, as The Speckled Band (scw: Geoffrey H. Malins, Patrick L. Mannock; dir: George Ridgwell). Sound film: British and Dominion, 1931, as The Speckled Band (scw: W. P. Lipscomb; dir: Jack Raymond). --- Silent film (from ss "The Boscombe Valley Mystery"): Franco-British, 1912, as The Mystery of Boscombe Vale (dir: Georges Treville). Also: Stoll, 1922, as The Boscombe Valley Mystery (scw: Patrick L. Mannock, Geoffrey H. Malins; dir: George Ridgwell). --- Silent film (from ss "A case of Identity"): Stoll, 1921 (scw: William J. Elliott; dir: Maurice Elvey). --- Sound film (from ss "The Five Orange Pips"): Universal, 1945, as The House of Fear (scw: Roy Chanslor; dir: Roy William Neill). --- Silent film (from ss "The Man with the Twisted Lip"): Stoll, 1921 (scw: William J. Elliott; dir: Maurice Elvey). Sound film: Telecine, 1951; also released as The Man Who Disappeared (dir: Richard M. Grey). --- Silent film (from ss "The Red-Headed League"): Stoll, 1921 (scw: William J. Elliott; dir: Maurice Elvey). --- Silent film (from ss "A Scandal in Bohemia"): Stoll, 1921 (scw: William J. Elliott; dir: Maurice Elvey)
  *The Casebook of Sherlock Holmes. Silent film (from ss "The Adventure of the Mazarin Stone"): Stoll, 1923, as The Mazarin Stone (scw: Geoffrey H. Malins, Patrick L. Mannock; dir: George Ridgwell). --- Silent film (from ss "The Adventure of Thor Bridge"): Stoll, 1923, as Thor Bridge (scw: Geoffrey H. Malins, Patrick L. Mannock; dir: George Ridgwell)
  *His Last Bow. Silent film (from ss "The Adventure of the Bruce-Partington Plans"): Stoll, 1922, as The Bruce-Partington Plans (scw: Patrick L. Mannock, Geoffrey H. Malins; dir: George Ridgwell). --- Silent film (from ss "The Adventure of the Cardboard Box"): Stoll, 1923, as The Cardboard Box (scw: Geoffrey H. Malins, Patrick L. Mannock; dir: George Ridgwell). --- Silent film (from ss "The Adventure of the Devil's Foot"): Stoll, 1921, as The Devil's Foot (scw: William J. Elliott; dir: Maurice Elvey). --- Silent film (from ss "The Adventure of the Dying Detective"): Stoll, 1921, as The Dying Detective (scw: William J. Elliott; dir: Maurice Elvey). Sound film (based on this and ss "His Last Bow"): Famous Players, 1929, as The Return of Sherlock Holmes (scw: Garrett Fort, Basil Dean; dir: Dean). --- Silent film (from ss "The Adventure of the Red Circle"): Stoll, 1922, as The Red Circle (scw: Patrick L. Mannock, Geoffrey H. Malins; dir: George Ridgwell). --- Silent film (from ss "The Disappearance of Lady Frances Carfax"): Stoll, 1923, as Lady Frances Carfax (scw: Geoffrey H. Malins, Patrick L. Mannock; dir: George Ridgwell). --- Silent film (from ss "His Last Bow"): Stoll, 1923, as The Last Bow (scw: Geofrey H. Malins, Patrick L. Mannock; dir: George Ridgwell). Sound film: Universal, 1942, as Sherlock Holmes and the Voice of Terror (scw: Lynn Riggs, John Bright; dir: John Rawlins)
  *The Hound of the Baskervilles. Silent film: Vitaskop, 1914, as Der Hund von Baskervilles (The Hound of the Baskervilles) (scw: Richard Oswald; dir: Rudolf Meinert). Also: Stoll, 1921, as The Devil's Foot (scw: William J. Elliott, Dorothy Westlake; dir: Maurice Elvey). Also: Erda-Film, 1929, as Der Hund von Baskervilles (The Hound of the Baskervilles) (scw: Herbert Juttke, G. C. Klaren; dir: Richard Oswald). Sound film: Gaumont, 1932 (scw: Edgar Wallace, V. Gareth Gundrey; dir: Gundrey). Also: Ondra-Lamac, 1937, as Der Hund von Baskervilles (The Hound of the Baskervilles) (scw: Carla von Stackelberg; dir: Karl Lamac). Also: TCF, 1939 (scw: Ernest Pascal; dir: Sidney Lanfield). Also: Universal, 1944, as The Scarlet Claw (scw: Edmund L. Hartmann, Roy William Neill; dir: Neill). Also: Hammer, 1959 (scw: Peter Bryan; dir: Terence Fisher). Also: Hemdale, 1978 (scw: Peter Cook, Dudley Moore, Paul Morrissey; dir: Morrissey). Also: Mapleton, 1983 (scw: Charles Pogue; dir: Douglas Hickox)
  Masterworks of Crime and Mystery. Dial, 1982 ss, taken from earlier collections
  *The Memoirs of Sherlock Holmes. Silent film (from ss "The Crooked Man"): Stoll, 1923 (scw: Geoffrey H. Malins, Patrick L. Mannock; dir: George Ridgwell). --- Silent film (from ss."The Final Problem"): Stoll, 1923 (scw: Geoffrey H. Malins, Patrick L. Mannock; dir: George Ridgwell). Sound film (based on this and "The Empty House" from *The Return of Sherlock Holmes): Twickenham, 1930, as The Sleeping Cardinal; released in the U.S. as Sherlock Holmes's Fatal Hour (scw: Cyril Twyford; dir: Leslie S. Hiscott). --- Silent film (from ss "The Gloria Scott"): Stoll, 1923 (scw: Geoffrey H. Malins, Patrick L. Mannock; dir: George Ridgwell). --- Silent film (from ss "The Greek Interpreter"): Stoll, 1922 (scw: Patrick L. Mannock, Geoffrey H. Malins; dir: George Ridgwell). --- Silent film (from ss "The Musgrave Ritual"): Franco-British, 1912 (dir: Georges Treville). Also: Stoll, 1922 (scw: Patrick L. Mannock, Geoffrey H. Malins; dir: George Ridgwell). Sound film: Universal, 1943, as Sherlock Holmes Faces Death (scw: Bertram Millhauser; dir: Roy William Neill). --- Silent film (from ss "The Naval Treaty"): Franco-British, 1912, as The Stolen Papers (scw: Georges Treville). Also: Stoll, 1922 (scw: Patrick L. Mannock, Geoffrey H. Malins; dir: George Ridgwell). --- Silent film (from ss "The Reigate Puzzle"): Franco-British, 1912, as The Reigate Squires (dir: Georges Treville). Also: Stoll, 1922, as The Reigate Squires (scw: Patrick L. Mannock, Geoffrey H. Malins; dir: George Ridgwell). --- Silent film (from ss "The Resident Patient"): Stoll, 1921 (scw: William J. Elliott; dir: Maurice Elvey). --- Silent film (from ss "Silver Blaze"): Franco-British, 1912 (dir: Georges Treville). Also: Stoll, 1923 (scw: Geoffrey H. Malins, Patrick L. Mannock; dir: George Ridgwell). Sound film: Twickenham, 1936; released in the U.S. as Murder at the Baskervilles (scw: H. Fowler Mear, Arthur Macrae; dir: Thomas Bentley). --- Silent film (from ss "The Stock-Broker's Clerk"): Stoll, 1922 (scw: Patrick L. Mannock, Geoffrey H. Malins; dir: George Ridgwell). --- Silent film (from ss "The Yellow Face"): Stoll, 1921 (scw: William J. Elliott; dir: Maurice Elvey)

D

D

*The Return of Sherlock Holmes. Silent film (from ss "The Adventure of Black Peter"): Stoll, 1922, as Black Peter (scw: Patrick L. Mannock, Geoffrey H. Malins; dir: George Ridgwell). --- Silent film (from ss "The Adventure of Charles Augustus Milverton"): Stoll, 1922, as Charles Augustus Milverton (scw: Patrick L. Mannock, Geoffrey H. Malins; dir: George Ridgwell). Sound film: Twickenham, 1932, as The Missing Rembrandt (scw: Leslie S. Hiscott, Cyril Twyford; dir: Hiscott). --- Silent film (from ss "The Adventure of the Abbey Grange"): Stoll, 1922, as The Abbey Grange (scw: Patrick L. Mannock, Geoffrey H. Malins; dir: George Ridgwell). --- Silent film (from ss "The Adventure of the Dancing Men"): Stoll, 1923, as The Dancing Men (scw: Geoffrey H. Malins, Patrick L. Mannock; dir: George Ridgwell). Sound film: Universal, 1943, as Sherlock Holmes and the Secret Weapon (scw: Edward T. Lowe, W. Scott Darling, Edmund L. Hartmann; dir: Roy William Neill). --- Silent film (from ss "The Adventure of the Empty House"): Stoll, 1921, as The Empty House (scw: William J. Elliott; dir: Maurice Elvey). See also: "The Final Problem" in *The Memoirs of Sherlock Holmes. --- Silent film (from ss "The Adventure of the Golden Pice-Nez"): Stoll, 1923, as The Golden Pince-Nez (scw: Geoffrey H. Malins, Patrick L. Mannock; dir: George Ridgwell). --- Silent film (from ss "The Adventure of the Missing Three-Quarter"): Stoll, 1923, as The Missing Three-Quarter (scw: Geoffrey H. Malins, Patrick L. Mannock; dir: George Ridgwell). --- Silent film (from ss "The Adventure of the Norwood Builder"): Stoll, 1922, as The Norwood Builder (scw: Patrick L. Mannock, Geoffrey H. Malins; dir: George Ridgwell). --- Silent film (from ss "The Adventure of the Priory School"): Stoll, 1921, as The Priory School (scw: Charles Barnett; dir: Maurice Elvey). --- Silent film (from ss "The Adventure of the Second Stain"): Stoll, 1922, as The Second Stain (scw: Patrick L. Mannock, Geoffrey H. Malins; dir: George Ridgwell). --- Silent film (from ss "The Adventure of the Six Napoleons"): Stoll, 1922, as The Six Napoleons (scw: Patrick L. Mannock, Geoffrey H. Malins; dir: George Ridgwell). Sound film: Universal, 1944, as The Pearl of Death (scw: Bertram Millhauser; dir: Roy William Neill). --- Silent film (from ss "The Adventure of the Solitary Cyclist"): Stoll, 1921, as The Solitary Cyclist (scw: William J. Elliott; dir: Maurice Elvey). --- Silent film (from ss "The Adventure of the Three Students"): Stoll, 1923, as The Three Students (scw: Geoffrey H. Malins, Patrick L. Mannock; dir: George Ridgwell).
*The Sign of the Four. Silent film: Thanhauser, 1913. Also: Stoll, 1923 (scw & dir: Maurice Elvey). Sound film: ATP, 1932 (scw: W. P. Lipscomb; dir: Graham Cutts, Rowland V. Lee). Also: Mapleton, 1983 (scw: Charles Pogue; dir: Desmond Davis)
*A Study in Scarlet. Silent film: Samuelson, 1914 (scw: Harry Engholm; dir: George Pearson). Also: Gold Seal, 1914 (scw: Grace Cunard; dir: Francis Ford). Sound film: World Wide, 1933; also released as The Scarlet Ring (scw: Robert Florey, Reginald Owen; dir: Edward L. Marin). Also: Universal, 1944, as Sherlock Holmes and the Spider Woman (scw: Bertram Millhauser; dir: Roy William Neill)
The Uncollected Stories. Doubleday, 1984 ss
The Unknown Conan Doyle. Secker, 1982 ss
*The Valley of Fear. Silent film: Samuelson, 1916 (scw: Harry Engholm; dir: Alexander Butler). Sound film: Real Art, 1934, as The Triumph of Sherlock Holmes (scw: H. Fowler Mear, Cyril Twyford; dir: Leslie S. Hiscott)

*DOYLE, MONTE
  *Signpost to Murder. Film: MGM, 1964 (scw: Sally Benson; dir: George Englund)

*DOYLE, RICHARD
  Pacific Clipper. Arlington, 1985

DOYLE, RUBY M.
  -The Mystery of the Hills. Penfold (Syd.), 1919 <Australia>
  -The Winning of Miriam Heron. Edwards (Syd.), 1924 <Australia>

*DRACHMAN, THEODORE S(OLOMON)
  The Deadly Dream. Eriksson, 1982
  *Something for the Birds. <N.Y.>

*DRAGO, (HARRY) SINCLAIR. Ref: CA.

*DRAKE, ARNOLD
  *The Steel Noose. <NYC>

DRAKE, DAVID (ALLEN). 1945- . Ref: CA. See also: Janet (Ellen) Morris, 1946-
  Skyripper. Tor, 1983

*DRAKE, H(ENRY) B(URGESS)
  The Remedy. Long, 1925. U.S. title: *The Shadowy Thing

DRAKE, LISA with OTTO PENZLER. Drake is the pseudonym of a "well known mystery writer".
  The Medical Center Murders. PB, 1984 <NYC>

*DRAKE, MAURICE
  *-The Salving of a Derelict. Silent film: Davidson, 1924, as Nets of Destiny (scw: Eliot Stannard; dir: Arthur Rooke)

DRAKE, NATHAN. 1766-1836.
  Winter Nights; or, Fire-Side Lucubrations. Longman, 1820 (includes criminous novel-length story)

DRAKE, STAN. See: Leonard Starr.

*DRAPER, ALFRED (ERNEST)
  *The Death Penalty. Film: Lira Elephant, 1984, as A Mort l'Arbitre (Kill the Referee) (scw: Jean-Pierre Mocky, Jacques Dreux; dir: Mocky)

*DRATLER, JAY J. 1911-1968.
  *The Pitfall. Film: United Artists, 1948 (scw: Karl Lamb; dir: Andre De Toth)

DRAYTON, MARY
  The Playroom. French, 1965 (3-act play.)

*DRAYTON, RICKY
  *Hell's Belles! <N.J.>
  Nothing to Lose. Milestone, 1952

*DREISER, THEODORE. Ref also: CA.

DRESSER, MARY. Pseudonym: *Mary Savage.

*DREW, JOHN H. Lives in San Diego; writer of TV and radio commercials.
  *Edge of the Tightrope. <Calif.>

DREYER, MYRTA M.
  Beckoning Hands. Herold, 1930 <Mich.>

DRIGGS, LAURENCE LA TOURETTE. 1876- .
  On Secret Air Service. Little, 1930. British title: The Secret Squadron. Hamilton, 1930

*DRISCOLL, PETER (JOHN)
  -Heritage. Granada, 1982; Doubleday, 1982 <Algeria, 1945-62>
  *Pangolin. <H. Kong>
  *The White Lie Assignment. (title misprint correction)
  *The Wilby Conspiracy. Film: Optimus, 1975 (scw: Rod Amateau, Harold Nebenzal; dir: Ralph Nelson)

DROWN, MERLE. 1943- . Ref: CA.
  Plowing Up a Snake. Dial, 1982 <N.H., 1956>

DRUMMOND, CHARLES H.
  To Hinder Their Coming. Selwyn, 1943

*DRUMMOND, J. Pseudonym of John Newton Chance, 1911-1983.

*DRUMMOND, JOHN. Ref: CA.

DRUMMOND, JOHN KEITH. Living in S.F.
  Thy Sting, Oh Death. St. Martin's, 1985 <Calif.>

*DRUMMOND, JUNE
  *I Saw Him Die. <S. Afr.>
  The Trojan Mule. Gollancz (London & NYC), 1982 <NYC>

*DRUMMOND, WILLIAM. Pseudonym of Arthur Calder Marshall.
  *-Life for Ruth. (Novelization of film: Allied, 1962; released in the U.S. as Condemned to Life; scw: Janet Green, John McCormick; dir: Basil Dearden)
  *Midnight Lace. (Novelization of film; see *Matilda Shouted Fire, by *Janet Green)
  *Night Must Fall. (Novelization of film; see *Emlyn Williams)
  *Victim. (Novelization of film: Allied, 1961; scw: Janet Green, John McCormick; dir: Basil Dearden)

DRURY, ALLEN (STUART). 1918- . Ref: CA.
  Decision. Doubleday, 1983; Joseph, 1983 <Wash. D.C.>

DRURY, HARRY
  A Viennese Snuffbox. Hale, 1984

*DRYER, BERNARD VICTOR
  *Port Afrique. Film: Coronado, 1956 (scw: Frank Partos, John Cresswell; dir: Rudolph Mate)

DUBAY, SANDRA. 1954- . Ref: CA.
  The Claverleigh Curse. Zebra, 1982

*DU BOIS, THEODORA (McCORMICK)
  *The Listener. <NYC>

*DU BOISGOBEY, FORTUNE (HIPPOLYTE AUGUSTE)
  *The Angel of the Bells. Also published as The Angel of the Chimes. Vizetelly, 1886

DU BROCK, NEAL
  Countess Dracula. French, 19?? (3-act play.)

*DUDLEY, ERNEST
  *The Harassed Hero. Film: Corsair, 1954 (scw: Brock Williams; dir: Maurice Elvey)

DUDLEY, WILLIAM E.
  The Untold Sherlock Holmes. Magico, 1983 ss (Sherlock Holmes)

*DUERRENMATT, FRIEDRICH. Ref also: TM.
  *A Dangerous Game. <Switz.>
  Episode on an Autumn Evening. Dramatic, 1959 (1-act play.) (Translation of "Abendstunde im Spat-Herbst.")
  *The Judge and His Hangman. Film: MFG-T.R.A., 1975, as Murder on the Bridge; also released as End of the Game) (scw: Maximillian Schell, Arlene Sellers; dir: Schell)
  *The Pledge. Film: Praesens, 1958, as Es Geshah am Belichten Tag (It Happens in Broad Daylight) (scw: Friedrich Duerrenmatt, Hans Jacoby, Ladislav Vajda; dir: Vajda)
  The Visit. Random, 1958; Cape, 1962 (3-act play.) (Translation of "Der Besuch der Alten Dame." Zurich, 1956.) Film: TCF, 1964 (scw: Ben Barzman; dir: Bernhard Wicki)

*DUFF, DAVID (SKENE). Ref: CA.

DUFFIELD, ANNE (TATE). 1895- . Ref: CA.
  Lovable Stranger. Macrae, 1949

DUFFIELD, (SILAS) BRAINERD
  The Lottery. Dramatic, 1953 (1-act play based on the ss by *Shirley Jackson, q.v.)

DUFFY, BELLA. See: Anonymous.

*DUFFY, MAUREEN. Ref: CA.
  I Want to Go to Moscow. Hodder, 1973. U.S. title: All Heaven in a Rage. Knopf, 1973

DUGAN, JACK. Pseudonym of *William Edmund Butterworth III q.v. Other pseudonym: Alex Baldwin, q.v.
  The Deep Kill. Charter, 1984

DUGGAN, C. R.
  The GG-2 Deception. Tower, 1981

DUGHMAN, FRIEDA. Joint pseudonym with John Dughman: *Luanna Churchill.

DUGHMAN, JOHN. Joint pseudonym with Frieda Dughman: *Luanna Churchill.

*DUKE, MADELAINE (ELIZABETH). Ref also: TC2.
Flashpoint. Joseph, 1982

*DUMAS, CHARLES (LOUIS) ROBERT -1946.
*Second Bureau. Film: Compagnie Francaise, 1935, as Deuxieme Bureau (Second Bureau) (scw: Bernard Zimmer; dir: Pierre Billon). Also: Premier-Stafford, 1936 (scw: Akos Tolnay; dir: W. Victor Hanbury)

*DU MAURIER, DAPHNE. Ref also: TM.
*The Apple Tree. Film (from ss "The Birds"): Universal, 1963, as The Birds (scw: Evan Hunter; dir: Alfred Hitchcock)
*Jamaica Inn. Film: Mayflower, 1939 (scw: Sidney Gilliat, Joan Harrison, J. B. Priestley; dir: Alfred Hitchcock)
*My Cousin Rachel. Film: TCF, 1952 (scw: Nunally Johnson; dir; Henry Koster)
*Not After Midnight. Film (from ss "Don't Look Now"): Casey, 1973, as Don't Look Now (scw: Allan Scott, Chris Bryant; dir: Nicolas Roeg)
*Rebecca. Film: United Artists, 1940 (scw: Robert E. Sherwood, Joan Harrison; dir: Alfred Hitchcock)
*The Scapegoat. Film: MGM, 1959 (scw: Gore Vidal, Robert Hamer; dir: Hamer)

DUNANT, PETER
Exterminating Angels. Deutsch, 1983

DUNCAN, J. R.
Switchback City. Hale, 1985

*DUNCAN, PETER. Pseudonym of B. M. Atkinson, Jr.

*DUNCAN, ROBERT L(IPSCOMB). Ref: CA. Joint pseudonym with Wanda Duncan: W. R. Duncan, q.v.
In the Blood. Dell, 1984; Inner Circle, 1985 <Pa.>
In the Enemy Camp. Delacorte, 1985 <Indon.>

DUNCAN, W. R. Joint pseudonym of *Robert L(ipscomb) Duncan, q.v., and Wanda Duncan.
The Queen's Messenger. Delacorte, 1982; Joseph, 1982 <Thai.>

DUNCAN, WANDA. Joint pseudonym with *Robert L(ipscomb) Duncan, q.v.: W. R. Duncan, q.v.

DUNHAM, DONALD (CARL). 1908- Ref: CA.
Zone of Violence. Belmont, 1962

DUNKERLEY, WILLIAM ARTHUR. 1852-1941. Pseudonym: John Oxenham, q.v.

DUNLAP, SUSAN. Lives in Calif. Ref: TM. SC: Vejay Haskell = VH; Jill Smith = JS.
As a Favor. St. Martin's, 1984; Hale, 1986 JS <S.F.>
The Bohemian Connection. St. Martin's, 1985 <Calif.> VH
An Equal Opportunity Death. St. Martin's, 1984; Hale, 1986 VH <Calif.>
Karma. Raven, 1981
Not Exactly a Brahmin. St. Martin's, 1985 JS <S.F.>

DUNMORE, JOHN. 1923- . Pseudonym: Jason Calder, q.v.

DUNMORE, SPENCER (SAMBROOK). 1928- Ref: CA.
-The Sound of Wings. Heinemann, 1984; Macmillan, 1985

DUNN, CHRISTOPHER
Deadlines. Heinemann, 1981

DUNNE, COLIN
Ratcatcher. Secker, 1985; Secker (U.S.), 1986
Retrieval. Secker, 1984; Bantam, 1985 <Ger.>

DUNNE, DOMINICK
-The Two Mrs. Grenvilles. Crown, 1985; Sidgwick, 1986

DUNNE, H. P.
Daughter of Darkness. Signet, 1981

*DUNNE, JOHN GREGORY. Ref: not in TC2.
Dutch Shea, Jr. Linden, 1982; Weidenfeld, 1982
*True Confessions. Film: United Artists, 1981 (scw: John Gregory Dunne, Joan Didion; dir: Ula Grosbard)

*DUNNETT, DOROTHY. SC: Johnson Johnson, also in new title below (earlier titles in *Dorothy Halliday entry in CF).
Dolly and the Bird of Paradise. Joseph, 1983; Knopf, 1984
*Dolly and the Starry Bird. <It.>

DUNNING, FRANCES. See: Philip (Hart) Dunning, 1892-

*DUNNING, JOHN
Deadline. GM, 1981; Gollancz, 1982

*DUNNING, LAWRENCE
Taking Liberty. Avon, 1981

DUNNING, PHILIP (HART). 1892-
Broadway, with George Abbott, 1887- , q.v. Doran, 1927; Hutchinson, 1928. 3-act play version: Doran, 1927. Film: Universal, 1929 (scw: Edward T. Lowe, Jr., Charles Furthman; dir: Paul Fejos). Also: Universal, 1942 (scw: Felix Jackson, John Bright; dir: William A. Seiter).
Night Hostess, with Frances Dunning. French, 1928 (Play.) Film: MGM, 1930, as The Woman Racket (scw: Albert Shelby LeVino; dir: Robert Ober, A. Kelly)
Sequel to a Verdict. Dramatists, 1962 (3-act play.)

*DUNSANY, LORD. See also: Edward Darby.

DURAND, LOUP
The Angkor Massacre. Morrow, 1983

*DURAND, ROBERT
*Lady in a Cage. (Novelization of film: Paramount, 1964; scw: Luther Davis; dir: Walter Grauman)

*DURAS, MARGUERITE
L'Amante Anglais. Hamilton, 1968; Grove, 1968
*Ten-Thirty on a Summer Night. Film: United Artists, 1966, as 10:30 P.M. Summer (scw: Jules Dassin, Marguerite Duras; dir: Dassin)

*DURBRIDGE, FRANCIS (HENRY)
Breakaway. Hodder, 1981
The Doll. Hodder, 1982
*News of Paul Temple. Film: Nettlefold, 1950, as Paul Temple's Triumph (scw: A. R. Rawlinson; dir: Maclean Rogers)
*Portrait of Alison. Film (based on radio serial which preceded the novel): Insignia, 1955; released in the U.S. as Postmark for Danger (scw: Guy Green, Ken Hughes; dir: Green)

DURING, STELLA M.
The Temptation of Carlton Earle. Ward, 1920. Silent film: British Actors, 1923 (scw: S. H. Herkomer; dir: Wilfred Noy)

*DURIS, GENE
*Real Endings. <NYC>

*DURRANT, THEO. Joint pseudonym of *Terry Adler, *Anthony Boucher, *Eunice Mays Boyd, Florence Ostern Faulkner, Allen Hymson, *(John) Cary Lucas, *(Mabel) Dana Lyon, *Lenore Glen Offord, *Virginia Rath, *Richard Shattuck, *Darwin L. Teilhet, *William Worley.
*The Marble Forest. Film: Allied Artists, 1958, as Macabre (scw: Robb White; dir: William Castle)

DURRELL, LAWRENCE (GEORGE). 1912- Ref: CA.
White Eagles Over Serbia. Criterion, 1957; Faber, 1957 <Yugos.>

*DU SOE, ROBERT C(OLEMAN)
*The Devil Thumbs a Ride. Film: RKO, 1947 (scw & dir: Felix Feist)

*DUTTON, JAMES S., JR.
*Underground. <Can.>

DVORKIN, DAVID. 1943- Ref: CA.
Time for Sherlock Holmes. Dodd, 1983 (Sherlock Holmes)

*DWYER, K. R.
*Chase. Film (?): Viaduc, 1977, as Les Passagers (The Passengers) (scw: Serge Leroy, Christopher Rank; dir: Leroy)

DYAR, RALPH E.
A Voice in the Dark. (Spokane), 1946 (3-act play.) Silent film: Goldwyn, 1921 (scw: Arthur F. Statter; dir: Frank Lloyd)

*DYER, GEORGE (BELL)
*The Five Fragments. Film: Warner, 1934, as Fog Over Frisco (scw: Robert N. Lee, Eugene Solow; dir: William Dieterle). Also: Warner, 1942, as Spy Ship (scw: Robert E. Kent; dir: B. Reeves Eason)

*DYSON, JOHN
Blue Hurricane. Futura, 1983

*"E-7."
*Romance of a Spy. <Fr., WWII>

EARL, C. K.
The Shadow of a Crime. Abbott, 1892

EARLY, JACK. Pseudonym of *Sandra Scoppettone. Ref: TM.
A Creative Kind of Killer. Watts, 1984
Razzamatazz. Watts, 1985 <L.I.>

EASTERMAN, DANIEL. Professor of Islamic studies at a univ. in Eng.
The Last Assassin. Hodder, 1984; Doubleday, 1985 <Iran>

EASTON, JACK OSBORNE
Defence of the Realm. Macdonald, 1985

*EASTWOOD, JAMES
*Deadline. criminous (Novelization of film: TCF, 1952; released in the U.S. as Deadline U.S.A.; scw & dir: Richard Brooks)

*EBERHART, MIGNON G(OOD). Ref also: TM. Film (based on unidentified Eberhart story): TCF, 1937, as The Great Hospital Mystery (scw: Bess Meredyth, William Conselman, Jerry Cady; dir: James Tinling)
Alpine Condo Cross Fire. Random, 1984; Collins, 1985
Family Affair. Random, 1981; Collins, 1981 <NYC>
*From This Dark Stairway. Film: First National, 1936, as The Murder of Dr. Harrigan (scw: Peter Milne, Sy Bartlett; dir: Frank McDonald). Also: WB-FN, 1938, as The Dark Stairway (scw: Brock Williams, Basil Dillon; dir: Arthur Woods)
*Hasty Wedding. Film: Republic, 1945, as Three's a Crowd (scw: Dane Lussier; dir: Lesley Selander)
*Murder by an Aristocrat. Film: First National, 1936 (scw: Luci Ward, Roy Chanslor, Mignon G. Eberhart; dir: Frank McDonald)
*The Mystery of Hunting's End. Film: Warner, 1938, as Mystery House (scw: Sherman L. Lowe, Robertson White; dir: Noel Smith)
Next of Kin. Random, 1982; Collins, 1983 <NYC>
The Patient in Cabin C. Random, 1983; Collins, 1983 <ship>
*The Patient in Room 18. Film: Warner, 1938 (scw: Eugene Solow, Robertson White; dir: Bobby Connolly, Crane Wilbur)
*While the Patient Slept. Film: First National, 1935 (scw: Robert N. Lee, Eugene Solow, Brown Holmes; dir: Ray Enright)
*The White Cockatoo. Film: Warner, 1935 (scw: Ben Markson, Lillie Hayward; dir: Alan Crosland)

*EBERSOHN, WESSEL (SCHALK). Ref also: TC2, TM. SC: Yudel Gordon, in *A Lonely Place to Die, and title below.
Divide the Night. Gollancz, 1981; Pantheon, 1981 <S. Afr.>

EBERSTADT, ISABEL
Natural Victims. Knopf, 1983; Hogarth, 1984 <Paris>

E

*EBERT, ARTHUR FRANK. 1902-1984.
    Pseudonym: *Frank Arthur, q.v.

EBERT, VIRGINIA
    Broken Image. Morrow, 1951

*EBY, LOIS (CHRISTINE) and JOHN
    C(HESTER) FLEMING
    *The Velvet Fleece. Film: Universal,
    1948, as Larceny (scw: Herbert F.
    Margolis, Louis Morheim, William
    Bowers; dir: George Sherman)

*ECHARD, MARGARET
    *The Dark Fantastic. <Midwest, 1870s>
    Film: Warner, 1951, as Lightning
    Strikes Twice (scw: Lenore Coffee;
    dir: King Vidor)

ECKERT, ALLAN W. 1931-   . Ref: CA.
    The Scarlet Mansion. Little, 1985
    <Chi., 1800s>

ECO, UMBERTO. 1932-   . Ref: BM, CA.
    The Name of the Rose. Secker, 1983;
    Harcourt, 1983 <It., 1327> (Translation of Il Nome della Rose. Milan, 1983.) Film: TCF, 1986 (scw:
    Andrew Birkin, Gerard Brach, Howard Franklin, Alain Godard; dir:
    Jean-Jacques Annaud)

*EDELMAN, MAURICE. See: Jerome Lawrence, 1915-

*EDEN, DOROTHY (ENID). Ref: not in TC2.

*EDEN, MATTHEW. SC: Marc Savage (spelling correction)
    *The Gilt-Edged Traitor.   <Vienna>

EDEN, ROB. Joint pseudonym of *Eve
    Burkhardt and *Robert F(erdinand)
    Burkhardt.
    Love Comes Flying. Gramercy, 1940
    A New Friend. Gramercy, 1949
    Short Skirts. Grosset, 1930 <L.A.>

*EDGAR, KEITH
    *The Incendiary Blonde. ss

*EDGLEY, LESLIE
    *False Face. <Wis.>
    *Fear No More. Film: Scaramouche,
    1961 (no credits found)

*EDINGTONS, THE
    *The Studio Murder Mystery. Film:
    Paramount, 1929 (scw & dir: Frank
    Tuttle)

EDLER, PETER. 1934-   . Ref: CA.
    The Dooming Eye. Smith, 1978

*EDMONDS, HARRY
    *The Death Ship.   <ship>
    *The Red Desert.   <Mid. East>

EDMONDSON, G. C., 1922-   , and C. M.
    KOTLAN. Ref for Edmondson: CA.
    The Takeover. Ace, 1984 <future>

*EDWARD, MARIE ELAINE. Pseudonym of
    *Blanche Y. Mosler.

EDWARDES, MICHAEL F. H. 1923-   .
    Pseudonym: *Robert Cassilis, q.v.

*EDWARDS, ALEXANDER. Pseudonym of
    *Leonore Fleischer. Ref: CA.
    *The Black Bird. (Novelization of
    film: Columbia, 1975; scw &
    dir: David Giler)
    *The Last of Sheila. (Novelization of
    film: Warner, 1973; scw: Stephen
    Sondheim, Anthony Perkins; dir:
    Herbert Ross)
    *McQ. (Novelization of film: Warner,
    1974; scw: Lawrence Roman; dir:
    John Sturges)

EDWARDS, AMELIA (ANN) B(LANFORD).
    1831-1892.
    -In the Days of My Youth. Hurst,
    1873; Porter, 1874

*EDWARDS, JAMES G.
    *Murder in the Surgery. Film: Universal, 1939, as Mystery of the White
    Room (scw: Alex Gottlieb; dir:
    Otis Garrett)

*EDWARDS. PAUL
    *The Glyphs of Gold. <Mex.>

EDWARDS, R. T. with OTTO PENZLER
    Prize Meets Murder. PB, 1984. British
    title: This Prize Is Dangerous.
    Target, 1985

EDWARDS, RUTH DUDLEY. 1944-   . Ref:
    CA. SC: Robert Amiss, in both
    titles. Set: Eng.
    Corridors of Death. Quartet, 1981;
    St. Martin's, 1982
    The St. Valentine's Day Murders.
    Quartet, 1984; St. Martin's, 1985

EEDY, CLARICE
    Can It Be True? Hodder, 1938

*EGAN, LESLEY. SC: Jesse Falkenstein,
    also in those marked JF below; Vic
    Varallo, also in those marked VV
    below. Set: L.A.
    Chain of Violence. Doubleday, 1985;
    Gollancz, 1985
    Crime for Christmas. Doubleday, 1984;
    Gollancz, 1984 VV
    Little Boy Lost. Doubleday, 1983;
    Gollancz, 1984 JF
    The Miser. Doubleday, 1981; Gollancz, 1982 JF
    Random Death. Doubleday, 1982; Gollancz, 1982 VV
    The Wine of Life. Doubleday, 1985;
    Gollancz, 1986

*EGGLESTON, EDWARD. Ref: CA.

*EGLETON, CLIVE (FREDERICK). SC:
    Charles Winter, in at least those
    marked CW.
    A Conflict of Interests. Hodder,
    1984; Atheneum, 1983
    A Different Drummer. Hodder, 1985;
    Stein, 1986
    The Eisenhower Deception; see The
    Winter Touch
    A Falcon for the Hawks. Hodder, 1982;
    Walker, 1984
    The Russian Enigma. Hodder, 1983;
    Atheneum, 1982 CW <1962>
    *Seven Days to a Killing. Film: Universal, 1974, as The Black Windmill
    (scw: Leigh Vance; dir: Don
    Siegel)
    Troika. Hodder, 1984; Atheneum, 1984
    The Winter Touch. Hodder, 1981. U.S.
    title: The Eisenhower Deception.
    Atheneum, 1981 CW <1956>

EGNOR, VIRGINIA RUTH. Professional
    name: Dagmar, q.v.

*EHRLICH, MAX (SIMON). 1909-1983.
    -The Big Boys. Houghton, 1981 <Mass.>
    *First Train to Babylon. Film: Glass,
    1961, as The Naked Edge (scw:
    Joseph Stefano; dir: Michael
    Anderson)
    *The Reincarnation of Peter Proud.
    Film: Crosby, 1974 (scw: Max
    Ehrlich; dir: J. Lee Thompson)
    Shaitan. Arbor, 1982; Severn, 1982
    *Spin the Glass Web. Film: Universal,
    1953, as The Glass Web (scw: Robert
    Blees, Leonard Lee; dir: Jack
    Arnold)

EIDEN, PAUL. See: *Peter Winston.

*EINSTEIN, CHARLES
    *The Bloody Spur. Film: RKO, 1956, as
    While the City Sleeps (scw: Casey
    Robinson; dir: Fritz Lang)

*EISINGER, JO
    *The Walls Came Tumbling Down. Film:
    Columbia, 1946 (scw: Wilfrid H.
    Pettitt; dir: Lothar Mendez)

EKERT-ROTHOLZ, ALICE (MARIA)
    Checkpoint Orinoco. Fromm, 1983
    <Venez.> Translation of "Funf
    Uhr Nachmittag." Hamburg, 1983.)

EKSTROM, JAN. 1923-
    The Ancestral Precipice. Macmillan
    (London), 1983. U.S. title: Deadly
    Reunion. Scribner, 1983 (Translation of "Attestupan". Stockholm,
    1975.)

EL SAADAWI, NAWAL. 1931-   . Ref: CA.
    Woman at Point Zero. Zed, 1983
    (Translation from the Arabic.)

*ELDER, MICHAEL
    *The Phantom in the Wings. <theatre>

ELDERSHAW, FLORA. Joint pseudonym with
    Marjorie Barnard: M. Barnard
    Eldershaw. See: J. L. Rankin.

ELDERSHAW, M. BARNARD. Joint pseudonym
    of Flora Eldershaw and Marjorie
    Barnard. See: J. L. Rankin.

*ELDRIDGE, MARK. Architect, engineer;
    born in Wis., living in Calif.
    *Lightning May Strike Anywhere.
    <L.A.>

ELGIN, (PATRICIA ANNE) SUZETTE HADEN.
    1936-   . Ref: CA.
    Star-Anchored, Star-Angered. Doubleday, 1979 <future>

*ELIADE, MIRCEA. 1907-1986.

*ELIOT, MAJOR GEORGE F(IELDING)
    *Federal Bullets. Film: Monogram,
    1937 (scw & dir: Karl Brown)

ELKINS, AARON J. Ref: TM. Professor
    of Anthropology, author of papers
    in that field; living in Calif. SC:
    Gideon Oliver, in all titles.
    The Dark Place. Walker, 1983; Hale,
    1986 <Wash.>
    Fellowship of Fear. Walker, 1982
    <Ger.>
    Murder in the Queen's Armes. Walker,
    1985 <Eng.>

ELKOFF, MARVIN. 1926-
    After the Race. Simon, 1983

ELLER, JOHN. 1935-   . Ref: CA. SC:
    Charlie Rope, in both titles.
    Charlie and the Iceman. St. Martin's,
    1981 <NYC>
    Rage of Heaven. St. Martin's, 1983
    <NYC>

*ELLERBECK, ROSEMARY (ANNE L'ESTRANGE).
    Ref: CA.

ELLI, FRANK
    Riot. Coward, 1967; Heinemann, 1967.
    Film: Paramount, 1969 (scw: James
    Poe; dir: Buzz Kulik)

*ELLIN, STANLEY (BERNARD). 1916-1986.
    Ref also: TM.
    *The Bind. Film: Hemdale, 1979, as
    Sunburn (scw: John Daly, Stephen
    Oliver, James Booth; dir: Richard
    C. Sarafian)
    The Dark Fantastic. Mysterious Press,
    1983; Deutsch, 1983 <NYC>
    *Dreadful Summit. Film: United Artists, 1951, as The Big Night (scw:
    Stanley Ellin, Joseph Losey; dir:
    Losey)
    *House of Cards. Film: Universal,
    1969 (scw: James P. Bonner; dir:
    John Guillermin)
    *The Key to Nicholas Street. Film (in
    French): CCFC, 1959, as A Double
    Tour (Web of Passion) (scw: Paul
    Gegauff; dir: Claude Chabrol)
    *Mystery Stories. Film (from ss "The
    Best of Everything"): Domino, 1963,
    as Nothing But the Best (scw:
    Frederic Raphael; dir: Clive
    Donner)
    Very Old Money. Arbor, 1985; Deutsch,
    1985 <NYC>

ELLIOTT, ELTON. Joint pseudonym with
    Richard Geis: Richard Elliott, q.v.

*ELLIOTT, FRANCIS PERRY
    *The Haunted Pajamas. Silent film:
    Metro, 1917 (scw & dir: Fred J.
    Balshofer)

*ELLIOTT, JANE. Pseudonym of Peter
    Miner.

*ELLIOTT, PEERS
    *The Mystery of the Black Dagger.
    <Australia>

*ELLIOTT, R(OBERT) C(OWELL)

ELLIOTT, RICHARD. Joint pseudonym of
    Richard Geis and Elton Elliott.
    The Sword of Allah. GM, 1984

*ELLIOTT, SUMNER LOCKE
    *Careful, He Might Hear You.
    <Australia> Film: Syme, 1983
    (scw: Michael Jenkins; dir: Carl
    Schultz)

*ELLIOTT, W. GERALD
    *Nine Days' Blunder. Film: B&D, 1935,
    as Cross Currents (scw: Adrian
    Brunel, Pelham Leigh Amann; dir:
    Brunel)

*ELLIS, J(OHN) BRECKENRIDGE
    The Picture on the Wall. Burton,
    1920. Silent film: Gotham, 1925,
    as The Shadow on the Wall (scw:
    Henry McCarty; dir: Reeves Eason)

ELLIS, JAMES J(OSEPH)
    A Bad Name. Author's Cooperative,
    1890

*ELLIS, JULIE. 1933-   . Ref: CA.

*ELLIS, KENNETH
 *The Trial of Vivienne Ware. Film: Fox, 1932 (scw: Philip Klein, Barry Connors; dir: William K. Howard)

ELLIS, LEIGH. 1959- . Ref: CA.
 Green Lady. Avon, 1981

ELLIS, PETER BERRESFORD. 1943- .
 Pseudonym: Peter Tremayne, q.v.

ELLIS, WALTER W. 1874- .
 S.O.S. French, 1929 (3-act play.)
 Silent film: Strand, 1928 (dir: Leslie Hiscott)

*ELLISON, EARL
 Angels Are So Few. Spencer, 1952
 The Tomb of Horror. Hamilton, ca. 1948 <Egypt>

*ELLISON, HAL
 *Games. (Novelization of film: Universal, 1967; scw: Gene Kearney; dir: Curtis Harrington)
 *Tomboy. Film: Cinedis, 1960, as Terrain Vague (The Waste-Land) (scw: Henri-Francois Rey, Marcel Carne; dir: Carne)

ELLROY, JAMES. 1948- . SC: Sgt. Lloyd Hopkins, in those marked LH.
 Because of the Night. Mysterious Press, 1984 LH <L.A.>
 Blood on the Moon. Mysterious Press, 1984; Allison, 1985 LH <L.A.>
 Brown's Requiem. Avon, 1981; Allison, 1983 <L.A.>
 Clandestine. Avon, 1982; Allison, 1984 <L.A., ca.1951>

*ELMAN, RICHARD (M.) SC: Prof. Robert Harmon, in *The Breadfruit Lotteries, and in title below.
 The Menu Cypher. Macmillan, 1982 <Nic.>

ELMBLAD, MARY (B.). 1927- . Ref: CA.
 Little Company. Avon, 1982 <Seattle>
 Outrageous Fortune. Avon, 1981 <Eng.>

ELMORE, CLARA
 A Buried Crime. Abbott, 1892

ELON, AMOS
 -Timetable. Doubleday, 1980; Hutchinson, 1981 <1944>

ELSER, DONALD
 Special Guest. Row, 1948 (1-act play.)

ELWARD, JAMES JOSEPH. 1928- .
 Pseudonym: *Rebecca James.

*ELY, DAVID. Ref also: TM.
 *Seconds. Film: Paramount, 1966 (scw: Lewis John Carlino; dir: John Frankenheimer)

EMERSON, EARL W. A firefighter in Seattle. SC: Thomas Black, in both titles.
 Poverty Bay. Avon, 1985 <Seattle>
 The Rainy City. Avon, 1985 <Seattle>

*EMERSON, JOHN. See: *Robert (Melville) Baker.

*EMERY, CHARLES
 The Red Key. French, 1949 (1-act play.)
 Tiger Lily. French, 1954 (1-act play.)

EMMERTON, ANTON
 Blood Red Sky. Zebra, 1985

EMMETT, ROBERT. SC: Mike McVeigh (American Avenger), in all titles.
 Beat a Distant Drum. Signet, 1981 <Berlin>
 The Devil's Finger. Signet, 1982 <Libya>
 King, Bishop, Knight. Signet, 1982 <Mid. East>
 Ride the Tiger. Signet, 1982 <Thai.>
 Trojan Horses. Signet, 1982 <Greece>

ENDERS, RICHARD. Pseudonym of Robert Fenster, 1946- . Ref: CA.
 Slow Twitch. PB, 1982
 Tight Squeeze. PB, 1982 <L.A.>

*ENDORE, GUY
 *Methinks the Lady--. Film: TCF, 1950, as Whirlpool (scw: Ben Hecht, Andrew Solt; dir: Otto Preminger)

 *The Werewolf of Paris. Film: Hotspur, 1961, as The Curse of the Werewolf (scw: John Elder; dir: Terence Fisher)

*ENEFER, DOUGLAS
 The Deadly Streak. Hale, 1982
 The Last Leap. Hale, 1983

ENGEL, HOWARD. 1931- . Ref: CA, TM. SC: Benny Cooperman, in all titles. Set: Can.
 Murder on Location. Clarke, 1982; Gollancz, 1983; St. Martin's, 1985
 Murder Sees the Light. Penguin, 1984; 1985; St. Martin's, 1985
 The Ransom Game. Clarke, 1981; Gollancz, 1982; St. Martin's, 1984
 The Suicide Murders. Clarke, 1980; Gollancz, 1984; St. Martin's, 1984

ENGEL, PETER (H.). 1935- . Ref: CA.
 Tender Offers. St. Martin's, 1983; Macdonald, 1984

*ENGLAND, GEORGE ALLAN. Ref: CA.
 *The Alibi. Silent film: Vitagraph, 1916 (scw: George H. Plympton; dir: Paul Scardon)
 *The Gift Supreme. Silent film: Macaulay, 1920 (dir: Ollie L. Sellers)

ENGLEMAN, PAUL
 Dead in Center Field. Ballantine, 1983 <N.J., 1961>

*ENGLISH, ARNOLD. Pseudonym of *Morris Hershman.

*ENGSTRAND, STUART (DAVID)
 Beyond the Forest. Creative Age, 1948; Cape, 1950. Film: Warner, 1949 (scw: Lenore Coffee; dir: King Vidor)
 Norwegian Spring; see Spring 1940
 *The Sling and the Arrow. ... Barker, 1962
 Spring 1940. Doubleday, 1941. British title: Norwegian Spring. Secker, 1940 <Nor.>

EPSTEIN, JULIUS J., 1909- , PHILIP G. EPSTEIN, 1909-1952, and HOWARD KOCH, 1902- . Ref for each: CA.
 Casablanca. Overlook, 1973; Pan, 1974 (Screenplay of film: Warner, 1942; dir: Michael Curtiz)

EPSTEIN, PHILIP G. 1909-1952. See: Julius J. Epstein, 1909- .

*ERDMAN, PAUL E(MIL)
 The Last Days of America. Simon, 1981; Secker, 1981 <Switz.>
 *The Silver Bears. Film: EMI, 1977 (scw: Peter Stone; dir: Ivan Passer)

ERICKSON, LYNN
 Gentle Betrayal. PB, 1982

*ERICSON, WALTER
 *Fallen Angel. Film: Universal, 1965, as Mirage (scw: Peter Stone; dir: Edward Dmytryk). Also: Universal, 1968, as Jigsaw (scw: Quentin Werty; dir: James Goldstone)

*ERSKINE, LAURIE YORK
 *The Confidence Man. Silent film: Famous Players, 1924 (scw: Paul Sloane; dir: Victor Heerman)

*ERSKINE, MARGARET. Pseudonym of Margaret Wetherby Williams, -1984. Ref also: TM.

*ESCOTT, JONATHAN. Pseudonym: *Jack S. Scott, q.v.
 Landfall in Sefton Carey. Hale, 1976

ESKAPA, SHIRLEY. Has degree in sociology and psychology from univ. in Johannesburg; later living in Geneva and London.
 Blood Fugue. Quartet, 1981; Academy, 1986 <S. Afr.>
 -The Secret-Keeper. Quartet, 1982; St. Martin's, 1983 <Geneva>

ESLER, CAROL CLEMEAU. 1935- .
 Pseudonym: Carol Clemeau, q.v.

*ESSER, ROBIN
 *The Paper Chase. <Ger.>

ESSEX, PETER
 The Exile. Collins, 1984 <Afr.>

*ESTEY, DALE
 The Bonner Deception. St. Martin's, 1983 <Can.>

*ESTLEMAN, LOREN D. Ref also: TC2, TM. SC: Amos Walker, in *Motor City Blue, and in titles marked AW below; Peter Macklin = PM.
 Angel Eyes. Houghton, 1981; Hale, 1982 AW <Det.>
 The Glass Highway. Houghton, 1983; Hale, 1984 AW <Det.>
 Kill Zone. Mysterious Press, 1984 <Det.> PM
 The Midnight Man. Houghton, 1982; Hale, 1983 AW <Det.>
 Roses Are Dead. Mysterious Press, 1985 PM <Det.>
 Sugartown. Houghton, 1985; Macmillan (London), 1986 AW <Det.>

ETCHISON, DENNIS WILLIAM. 1943-
 Pseudonym: Jack Martin, q.v.

EUBANK, JAMES E. Pseudonym: Kelley Banks, q.v.

EULO, ELENA YATES
 Ice Orchids. Berkley, 1984; Star, 1984 <acad.>

EULO, KEN. 1939- . Ref: CA.
 -The Ghost of Veronica Gray. PB, 1985
 Nocturnal. PB, 1983; Coronet, 1985 <NYC>

*EUSTACE, ROBERT. Ref: not in TC2.

*EUSTIS, HELEN
 *The Fool Killer. Film: Allied Artists, 1965 (scw: Morton Fine, David Friedkin; dir: Servando Gonzalez)

EVANS, AUDREY
 So Pitifully Slain. Brown, 1982 (1-act play.) <Eng., 1500s>

*EVANS, E(DWARD) EVERETT. Ref: CA.

*EVANS, ELAINE. Pseudonym of *Gil Brewer, 1922-1983.

EVANS, GEORGE EWART. 1909- . Ref: CA.
 The Turnpike. Paxton, 1950 (1-act play.)

*EVANS, GWYN(FIL ARTHUR). Fleet Street journalist.
 *The Clue of the Missing Link. 2 stories
 *The Mysterious Miss Death. 3 stories

*EVANS, JOHN
 *If You Have Tears. Also published as: The Blonde Dies First. Horwitz, 1956

*EVANS, JOHN P. and *JOHN B. MANNION
 The Vanishing Vector. GM, 1981 <Wash. D.C.>

*EVANS, JONATHAN. Pseudonym of *Brian (Harry) Freemantle, q.v.
 Chairman of the Board. Joseph, 1982. U.S. title: Takeover. Tor, 1982
 The Kremlin Correction. Tor, 1984 (British title?)
 The Laundryman. Joseph, 1985
 The Midas Men. Joseph, 1981. U.S. title: The Sagomi Gambit. Tor, 1983 <Russ., 1984>
 Monopoly. Joseph, 1984
 The Sagomi Gambit; see The Midas Men
 The Solitary Man. Tor, 1983 (British title?)
 Takeover; see Chairman of the Board

*EVANS, PETER. 1933- .
 The Englishman's Daughter. Lane, 1983; Random, 1983 <Moscow>

*EVANS, STUART. Ref: CA.

EVANS, WILLIAM PARKER
 The Double Cross Squadron. Bantam, 1982 <Ger., WWII>

EVENS, HODGE
 Three for Passion. Falcon, 195?

*EVERETT, PETER
 A Death in Ireland. Little, 1981 <Ire.>
 *Negatives. Film: Kettledrum, 1968 (scw: Peter Everett, Roger Lowry; dir: Peter Medak)

*EVERETT-GREEN, E(VELYN). Ref: CA.

EVERTON, FRANK
    The Battle of Jericho Street. Hale, 1984

*EWINGS, MICHAEL. See: *Frank Ross.

*EXBRAYAT, CHARLES
    *The Ravishing Idiot. Film: Belles Rives, 1964, as Une Ravissante Idiote (A Ravishing Idiot) (scw: Edouard Molinaro, Andre Tabet, Georges Tabet; dir: Molinaro)

EYEN, TOM. Ref: CA.
    Ten Plays. French, 1971 (Plays, including at least one 3-act criminous play: Grand Tenement/November 22.)

EYSMAN, HARVEY A(LLEN). 1939-   Ref: CA.
    Courier's Fist. Beaufort, 1981

FABER, DORIS (GREENBERG). 1924-
    Ref: CA.
    Quest for Love. Mystique, 1981 (Translation of "Le Chemin de Lumiere." Paris, 1969.)

FACKLER, ELIZABETH. 1947-   Ref: CA.
    Arson. Dodd, 1983 <Midwest>

FAHY, CHRISTOPHER. 1937-   . Ref: CA.
    Nightflier. Jove, 1982; Corgi, 1982

*FAIRBAIRN, DOUGLAS
    *Shoot. Film: AVCO, 1976 (scw: Dick Berg; dir: Harvey Hart)

FAIRBAIRNS, ZOE (ANN). 1948-   Ref: CA.
    Here Today. Methuen, 1984; Avon, 1984

*FAIRBURN, ELRANOR. Pseudonym: *Elena Lyons.

*FAIRCHILD, WILLIAM
    *The Sound of Murder. Film: Lippert, 1970, as The Last Shot You Hear (scw: Tim Shields; dir: Gordon Hessler)

*FAIRFAX-BLAKEBOROUGH, J(OHN FREEMAN). 1883-1976.

FAIRLEIGH, RUNA. Pseudonym of L(arry) A(lan) Morse, 1945-   , q.v.
    An Old-Fashioned Mystery. Avon, 1983

*FAIRLIE, GERARD. 1899-1983. Ref also: CA.
    *Calling Bulldog Drummond. Film: MGM, 1951 (scw: Howard Emmett Rogers, Gerard Fairlie, Arthur Wimperis; dir: Victor Saville)
    *Scissors Cut Paper. Film: ABPC, 1940, as Bulldog Sees It Through (scw: Doreen Montgomery; dir: Harold Huth)
    *Shot in the Dark. Film: Real Art, 1933 (scw: H. Fowler Mear; dir: George Pearson)
    *They Found Each Other. <Fr., WWII>

*FAIRMAN, PAUL W. Ref: CA. Pseudonym: *Paul Daniels.
    *Coffy. (Novelization of film: American International, 1973; scw & dir: Jack Hill)

FAITH, BARBARA <BARBARA FAITH COVARRUBIAS>. 1932-   . Ref: CA.
    Kill Me Gently, Darling. Manor, 1978

*FALKNER, LEONARD
    *M. <Ohio>

FALKSON, BARRY
    Fatal Friend. Morrow, 1985

FALLON, TOM
    Craftsmen in Crime. Muller, 1956 (Dramatized true crime stories.)

FANTONI, BARRY. SC: Mike Dime, in *Mike Dime, and new title below.
    *Mike Dime. Hodder, 1980; Watts, 1981 (dates wrong in first printings of CF)
    Stickman. Hodder, 1982

*FARHI, (MUSA) MORIS
    The Last of Days. Crown, 1983; Bodley, 1983 <Mid. East>

*FARJEON, B(ENJAMIN) L(EOPOLD)
    *The Golden Land. <Australia>
    *Grif. <Australia>
    *-Miriam Rozella. Silent film: Astra, 1924 (scw & dir: Sidney Morgan)

*FARJEON, J(OSEPH) JEFFERSON
    *Holiday Express. Film (?): Twickenham, 1935, as The Last Journey (scw: H. Fowler Mear, John Soutar; dir: Bernard Vorhaus)
    *The House Opposite. Film: BIP, 1931 (scw & dir: Walter Summers)
    *No. 17. Silent film (sound added later: Fellner, 1928 (dir: Geza M. Bolvary). Sound film: BIP, 1932 (scw: Alfred Hitchcock, Alma Reville, Rodney Ackland; dir: Hitchcock)

*FARMER, PHILIP JOSE
    *The Image of the Beast. criminous

*FARNOL, (JOHN) JEFFERY
    *The Amateur Gentleman. Silent film: Stoll, 1920 (dir: Maurice Elvey). Also: First National, 1926 (scw: Lillie Hayward; dir: Sidney Olcott). Sound film: Criterion, 1936 (scw: Clemence Dane, Sergei Nolbandov, Edward Knoblock; dir: Thornton Freeland)
    *The Definite Object. criminous. Silent film: Eros, 1920 (scw & dir: Edgar J. Camiller). Also: Famous Players, 1924, as Manhattan (scw: Paul Sloane, Frank W. Tuttle; dir: R. H. Burnside)
    *The Money Moon. Silent film: Alliance, 1920 (scw: Adrian Johnstone; dir: Fred Paul)

*FARNSWORTH, MONA. Pseudonym of Muriel Newhall.

FARRAR, FRANCIS. Pseudonym of R. W. Francis.
    The Great Mine Mystery. Donohue, 1895

*FARRELL, HENRY. Ref: TM.
    *Such a Gorgeous Kid Like Me. Film: Films Du Carosse, 1972, as Une Belle Fille Come Moi (Such a Lovely Kid Like Me) (scw: Francois Truffaut, Jean-Louis Dahadie; dir: Truffaut)
    What Ever Happened to Baby Jane? Film: Seven Arts, 1962 (scw: Lukas Heller; dir: Robert Aldrich)

FARRELL, JOHNNY
    Curves and Angles. Milestone, 1953
    Sugar, You're Swell. Scion, 1952

*FARRER, KATHERINE (DOROTHY). Ref: not in TC2.

*FARRERE, CLAUDE
    *The Man Who Killed. Silent film: Paramount, 1920, as The Right to Love (scw: Ouida Bergere; dir: George Fitzmaurice). Sound film: Terra, 1931, as Der Mann Der den Mord Beging (The Man Who Murdered) (scw: Heinz Goldberg, Herman Kosterlitz, Harry Kahn; dir: Kurt Bernhardt)

*FARRIS, JOHN. Pseudonym: *Steve Brackeen.
    -Catacombs. Delacorte, 1981; Hodder, 1982
    *The Fury. Film: TCF, 1978 (scw: John Farris; dir: Brian DePalma)
    The Minotaur. Tor, 1985; NEL pb, 1985
    Son of the Endless Night. St. Martin's, 1985; Hodder, 1985

FAST, CHARLES
    Ride the Golden Tiger. Lancer, 1973 (book exists?)

*FAST, HOWARD (MELVIN). Ref also: TM.
    *The Winston Affair. Film: Pennebaker, 1963, as Man in the Middle (scw: Keith Waterhouse, Willis Hall; dir: Guy Hamilton)

*FAULEY, WILBUR FINLEY
    *Queenie. Silent film: Fox, 1921 (scw: Dorothy Yost; dir: Howard M. Mitchell)

FAULKNER, FLORENCE OSTERN. See: Theo Durrant.

*FAULKNER, WILLIAM. Ref also: TM.
    *Intruder in the Dust. Film: MGM, 1949 (scw: Ben Maddow; dir: Clarence Brown)
    *Knight's Gambit. Film (from ss): Filmgroup, 1972, as Tomorrow (scw: Horton Foote; dir: Joseph Anthony)
    *Sanctuary. Film: Paramount, 1933, as The Story of Temple Drake (scw: Oliver H. P. Garrett; dir: Stephen Roberts). Also: TCF, 1961 (scw: James Poe; dir: Tony Richardson)

FAULKS, SEBASTIAN
    A Trick of the Light. Bodley, 1984

*FAUST, RON. Ref: TM.
    *The Burning Sky. British title: The Killing Game. NEL pb, 1981

FAVORS, JEAN M.
    Programmed for Danger. Ballantine, 1985

*FAWCETTE, F. DUBREZ. See: Cass Borelli, *Duke Linton.

FAWCETTE, STEVE
    Computer Criminals...It Began at the World's Fair. HC Publishing, 1984 <New Or.>
    Murder at the 1984 Summer Games. HC Publishing, 1984 <L.A.>
    Time Runs Out at the Democratic Convention. HC Publishing, 1984 <S.F.>

FAYET, CLAUDETTE
    Beyond Desire. Mystique, 1981 (Translation of "La Belle-Herbe." Paris, 1968.)
    The Spider's Eye. Mystique, 1981 (Translation of "Fiancailles Rompues." Paris, 1976.)

*FEARING, KENNETH (FLEXNER). Ref also: TM.
    *The Big Clock. Film: Paramount, 1948 (scw: Jonathan Latimer; dir: John Farrow)

*FEEGEL, JOHN R(ICHARD)
    *Autopsy. ... Avon (London), 1983 <Fla.>
    The Dance Card. Dial, 1981 <Atlanta>
    Malpractice. NAL, 1981 <Ga.>
    Not a Stranger. NAL, 1983 <Ala.>

*FEELY, TERENCE (JOHN). 1928-   . Ref: CA.
    Limelight. Sidgwick, 1984; Morrow, 1984
    Murder in Mind. French, 1982 (Play.)

*FEIBLEMAN, PETER S(TEINAM). Ref: CA.

*FEIFFER, JULES
    Little Murders. French, 1968; Cape, 1970   (2-act play.) Film: TCF, 1971 (scw: Jules Feiffer; dir: Alan Arkin)
    The White House Murder Case. French, 1970   (2-act play.) <Wash. D.C.>

FEINMAN, JEFFREY. 1943-   . Ref: CA.
    Black Narc. Manor, 1977

*FEIST, AUBREY (NOEL LYDSTON)
    Crime at the Cedars. Kenyon, 1972 (1-act play.)

FELBER, RON. See: *Nick Carter.

FELDMAN, ELLEN BETTE. 1941-   .
    Pseudonym: Elizabeth Villars, q.v.

FELL, DORIS ELAINE. See: Carole Gift Page, 1942-

FELTON, ARTHUR
    The Purple Plant. Houghton, 1932

*FENADY, ANDREW J.
    *The Man with Bogart's Face. Film: TCF, 1980 (scw: Andrew J. Fenady; dir: Robert Day)

*FENISONG, RUTH. Ref also: TM.

FENNELL, GEORGE. SC: Mike Brent, in both titles.
    Blood Patrol. Pinnacle, 1970
    Killer Patrol. Pinnacle, 1970 <Cent. Am.>

*FENNELLY, PARKER (W.)
    *Cuckoos on the Hearth. <Maine>

FENNELLY, TONY. 1945-   . Ref: CA.
    The Glory Hole Murders. Carroll, 1985; Arlington, 1986 <New Or.>

FENSTER, ROBERT. 1946-   . Pseudonym: Richard Enders, q.v.

*FENTY, PHILIP
    *Super Fly. (Novelization of film: Warner, 1972; scw: Philip Fenty; dir: Gordon Parks, Jr.)

*FERGUSON, MARGARET
    *The Sign of the Ram. Film: Columbia, 1948 (scw: Charles Bennett; dir: John Sturgis)

FERGUSON, NANCY
  Black Coral. Charter, 1985 <Carib.>

FERGUSON, RACHEL. 1893-1957.
  Nymphs and Satires. Benn, 1932 ss, one criminous (Sherlockian parody)

*FERGUSON, W(ILLIAM) B(LAIR) M(ORTON)
  *Crackerjack. Film: Gainsborough, 1938; released in the U.S. as Man with 100 Faces (scw: A. R. Rawlinson, Michael Pertwee, Basil Mason; dir: Albert de Courville)

*FERNAND, ROLAND (F.)
  Shadow of a Dream. Dramatic, 1947 (1-act play.)

*FERRAND, GEORGINA
  -Assignment in Venice. Hale, 1982
  Moonmist. Ballantine, 1976 (British title?) <Eng., 1840>

*FERRARS, ELIZABETH. Ref also: BM, TM. SC: Andrew Basnet, in at least those marked AB; Virginia Freer, also in at least those marked VF.
  The Crime and the Crystal. Collins, 1985; Doubleday, 1985 AB
  Death of Minor Character. Collins, 1983; Doubleday, 1983 VF
  Experiment with Death. Collins, 1981; Doubleday, 1981
  I Met Murder. Collins, 1985; Doubleday, 1986 VF
  Root of All Evil. Collins, 1984; Doubleday, 1984 AB
  Skeleton in Search of a Cupboard. Collins, 1982; Doubleday, 1982
  Something Wicked. Collins, 1983; Doubleday, 1984 AB
  Thinner Than Water. Collins, 1981; Doubleday, 1982

FERRIS, MONK
  Let's Murder Martha. French, 1984 (Play.)

*FERRIS, PAUL (FREDERICK)
  A Distant Country. Weidenfeld, 1983

*FERRIS, WALLY
  *Across 110th. Film: United Artists, 1972 (scw: Luther Davis; dir: Barry Shear)

FERRIS, WALTER
  Death Takes a Holiday. French, 1930 (3-act play.) Film: Paramount, 1934 (scw: Maxwell Anderson, Gladys Lehman; dir: Mitchell Leisen)

*FETHALAND, JOHN. Pseudonym of Leonard Inkster.

FEUER, LEWIS (SAMUEL). 1912-   Ref: CA.
  The Case of the Revolutionist's Daughter. Prometheus, 1983 (Sherlock Holmes) <Eng., 1881>

FEZANDIE, HECTOR. 1856-1943. Pseudonym: *Edgar Morette.

*FICK, CARL
  A Disturbance in Paris. Little, 1982; Gollancz, 1983 <Paris>

*FICKLING, G. G. Ref: TM.

FIELD, EVAN. Joint pseudonym of two "well-known film authorities."
  What Nigel Knew. Potter, 1981 <NYC>

*FIELD, MEDORA
  *Blood on Her Shoe. Film: Republic, 1944, as The Girl Who Dared (screen credits not found)
  *Who Killed Aunt Maggie? Film: Republic, 1940 (scw: Stuart Palmer; dir: Arthur Lubin)

FIELDE, ADELE M(ARION). 1839-1916.
  Chinese Nights' Entertainment. Putnam, 1893. Also published as: Chinese Fairy Tales. Putnam, 1912 ss, some criminous

FIELDHOUSE, WILLIAM. See: Gar Wilson.

*FIELDING, A. Ref: not in TC2.

*FIELDING, JOY
  Kiss Mommy Goodbye. Doubleday, 1981; Piatkus, 1981
  Life Penalty. Doubleday, 1984

FILBRUN, J. S.
  Gemini Rising. GM, 1982 <1998>

FINCH, PHILLIP. Joint pseudonym with Leo N. Mandel: Al Bird, q.v. Former reporter; novelist living in Wash. D.C.
  In a Place Dark and Secret. Watts, 1985 <Md.>

*FINDLEY, FERGUSON
  *Waterfront. Film: Columbia, 1951, as The Mob; released in Britain as Remember That Face! (scw: William Bowers; dir: Robert Parrish)

*FINDLEY, TIMOTHY
  Famous Last Words. Delacorte, 1982 <WWII>

*FINE, PETER HEATH
  Troubled Waters. Pinnacle, 1981 <Calif.>

FINER, ALEX. 1947-   . Born in London; has law degrees from London School of Economics and U. of Calif.; journalist; now Special Projects Editor of the Illustrated London News.
  Deepwater. Hutchinson, 1983; Doubleday, 1985 <ship>

FINLAY, D. G.
  Watchman. Century, 1984; Century (U.S.), 1986

FINLEY, GLENNA. Pseudonym of Glenna Finley Witte, 1925-   . Ref: CA.
  Kiss a Stranger. Signet, 1972 <Wales>

*FINNEGAN, ROBERT. Ref also: CA.

*FINNEY, JACK. Ref: TM.
  *Assault on a Queen. Film: Paramount, 1966 (scw: Rod Serling; dir: Jack Donahue)
  *Five Against the House. Film: Columbia, 1955 (scw: Stirling Silliphant, William Bowers, John Barnwell; dir: Phil Karlson)
  *The House of Numbers. Film: MGM, 1957 (scw: Russell Rouse, Don M. Mankiewicz; dir: Rouse)

*FIRTH, N. WESLEY
  Studio Revels. Hamilton, 1952

FISCHER, BRUNO. Ref also: TM.

FISCHER, CINDY
  The Adventure of the Copper Beeches. Last Bow, 1978 (Sherlock Holmes)

*FISH, ROBERT L(LOYD). Ref also: TM.

FISHER, CHARLES
  Some Unaccountable Exploits of Sherlock Holmes. <Author>, 1956 ss (Sherlock Holmes)

*FISHER, DAVID E(LIMELECH)
  Grace for the Dead. Hale, 1985
  Katie's Terror. Morrow, 1982; Hale, 1983 <NYC>
  The Man You Sleep With; see Variations on a Theme
  Variations on a Theme. Doubleday, 1981. British title: The Man You Sleep With. Quartet, 1981 <N.Y.>

*FISHER, GRAHAM. Pseudonym: *Dean Morgan.

FISHER, MICHAEL (JOHN). 1933-   Ref: CA.
  Bethnel Green. Cassell, 1961; Holt, 1961. Film: Excalibur, 1963, as A Place to Go (scw: Michael Relph, Clive Exton; dir: Basil Dearden)

*FISHER, RUDOLPH. Ref: CA.

*FISHER, STEVE. Ref also: TM.
  *I Wake Up Screaming. Film: TCF, 1941; released in Britain as Hot Spot (scw: Dwight Taylor; dir: H. Bruce Humberstone). Also: TCF, 1953, as Vicki (scw: Dwight Taylor; dir: Harry Horner)

*FISHMAN, HAL and *BARRY SCHIFF
  Flight 902 Is Down! St. Martin's, 1982; Allen, 1982

*FISKE, DORSEY
  *Academic Murder. ... St. Martin's, 1986

FITCH, (WILLIAM) CLYDE. 1865-1909. Ref: CA.
  The Woman in the Case. Little, 1915 (4-act play.) Silent film: Famous Players, 1916 (scw: Anthony P. Kelly; dir: Hugh Ford). Also: Famous Players, 1922, as The Law and the Woman (scw: Albert Shelby LeVino; dir: Penrhyn Stanlaws). Sound film: Paramount, 1932, as The Wiser Sex (scw: Caroline Francke, Harry Hervey; dir: Berthold Viertel)

*FITT, MARY. Ref: CA.

*FITZGERALD, ARLENE J.
  *Pamela's Palace. Macfadden, 1971

FITZGERALD, KITTY
  Marge. Sheba, 1984

*FITZSIMMONS, CORTLAND
  *Death on the Diamond. Film: MGM, 1934 (scw: Harvey Thew, Joseph Sherman, Ralph Spence; dir: Edward Sedgwick)
  *70,000 Witnesses. Film: Paramount, 1932 (scw: Garrett Fort, Robert N. Lee, William McGrath; dir: Ralph Murphy)
  *The Whispering Window. Film: MGM, 1936, as The Longest Night (scw: Robert Andrews; dir: Errol Taggart)

*FLAHERTY, JOE. ca.1936-1983.

FLANAGAN, JIM
  The Crossing. GM, 1983

FLANDERS, REBECCA. Pseudonym of Donna Ball, 1951-   . Ref: CA.
  Easy Access. Harlequin, 1985 <Kan.>
  The Key. Harlequin, 1984 <Midwest>
  Silver Threads. Harlequin, 1984 <Fla.>

FLANNAGAN, ROY (CATESBY). 1897-1952.
  County Court. Doubleday, 1937; Heinemann, 1938 <Va.>

*FLANNERY, SEAN. SC: John Mahoney = JM.
  Broken Idols. Charter, 1985 JM
  False Prophets. Charter, 1983 JM
  The Hollow Men. Charter, 1982
  The Trinity Factor. Charter, 1981 <WWII>

*FLAVIN, MARTIN
  The Criminal Code. Liveright, 1929 (3-act play.) Film: Columbia (scw: Fred Niblo, Jr., Seton I. Miller; dir: William Hawks). Also: Columbia, 1938, as Penitentiary (scw: Fred Niblo, Jr., Seton I. Miller; dir: John Brahm). Also: Columbia, 1950, as Convicted (scw: William Bowers, Fred Niblo, Jr., Seton I. Miller; dir: Henry Levin)

*FLEETWOOD, HUGH (NIGEL). Ref: CA, BM.
  *The Order of Death. Film: Vigo, 1983 (scw: Robert Faenza, Ennio de Concini, Hugh Fleetwood; dir: Faenza)
  A Young Fair God. H. Hamilton (London & U.S.), 1982 <Mex.>

FLEISCHER, RICHARD. 1916-   .
  The Narrow Margin. Ungar, 1985 (Screenplay of film: RKO, 1952; scw: Earl Felton; dir: Richard Fleischer)

*FLEISCHMAN, A(LBERT) S(IDNEY)
  *Counterspy Express. Film: Allied Artists. 1958. as Spy in the Sky (scw: Myles Wilder; dir: W. Lee Wilder)

*FLEMING, BRANDON
  *Pillory. Film: Gaumont, 1924, as Eleventh Commandment (scw: Brandon Fleming; dir: George A. Cooper)

*FLEMING, IAN (LANCASTER). Ref also: TM.
  *Casino Royale. Film: Famous Artists, 1967 (scw: Wolf Mankowitz, John Law, Michael Sayers; dir: John Huston, Ken Hughes, Val Guest, Robert Parrish, Joe McGrath)
  *Diamonds Are Forever. Film: United Artists, 1971 (scw: Richard Maibaum, Tom Mankiewicz; dir: Guy Hamilton)
  *Doctor No. Film: United Artists, 1962 (scw: Richard Maibaum, Johanna Harwood, Berkely Mather; dir: Terence Young)
  *From Russia with Love. Film: United Artists, 1963 (scw: Richard Maibaum; dir: Terence Young)

*Goldfinger. Film: United Artists, 1964 (scw: Richard Maibaum, Paul Dehn; dir: Guy Hamilton)
*Live and Let Die. Film: United Artists, 1973 (scw: Tom Mankiewicz; dir: Guy Hamilton)
*The Man with the Golden Gun. Film: United Artists, 1974 (scw: Richard Maibaum, Tom Mankiewicz; dir: Guy Hamilton)
*Octopussy and The Living Daylights. Film (based on "Octopussy" and "The Property of a Lady"): Eon, 1983, as Octopussy (scw: George MacDonald Fraser, Richard Maibaum, Michael G. Wilson; dir: John Glen)
*On Her Majesty's Secret Service. Film: Eon, 1969 (scw: Richard Maibaum; dir: Peter Hunt)
*Thunderball. Film: United Artists, 1964 (scw: Richard Maibaum, John Hopkins; dir: Terence Young). Also: Woodcote, 1983, as Never Say Never Again (scw: Lorenzo Semple, Jr.; dir: Irvin Kershner)
*You Only Live Twice. Film: Eon, 1967 (scw: Roald Dahl, Harry Jack Bloom; dir: Lewis Gilbert)

*FLEMING, JOAN (MARGARET)
*The Deeds of Dr. Deadcert. Film: Templar, 1957, as Family Doctor; released in the U.S. as Rx Murder (scw & dir: Derek Twist)

*FLEMING, JOHN C(HESTER). See: *Lois (Christine) Eby.

*FLEMING, MAY AGNES
*Erminie; or, The Gipsy Queen's Vow. (title correction) Also published as: The Gipsy Queen's Vow. Beadle, 1870

*FLEMING, THOMAS F.
Dreams of Glory. Warner, 1983; Star, 1983 <Charleston, 1780>

*FLETCHER, AARON. SC: Philip Magellan = PM (see also *Frank Scarpetta, *Peter McCurtin); Bounty Hunter, in at least those marked BH.
Blood Money. Leisure, 1977 BH
Bounty Hunter. Leisure, 1977 BH
Icepick. Leisure, 1982
The Microwave Factor. Leisure, 1983
Outback. Leisure, 1978
Project Jael. Leisure, 1985
The Reckoning. Leisure, 1981 PM

*FLETCHER, DAVID
On Suspicion. Macmillan (London), 1985
Rainbow in Hell. Macmillan (London), 1983
Rainbows End in Tears. Macmillan (London), 1984

*FLETCHER, DOROTHY
*Beyond Recall. <Calif.>

*FLETCHER, HENRY. 1856-1932.

*FLETCHER, J(OSEPH) S(MITH). Ref also: CA, TM.
*Dead Men's Money. (title correction)
The Golden Venture. Nash.
*The Marriage Lines. Silent film: Master, 1921 (scw & dir: Wilfred Noy)
Morrison's Machine. Hutchinson, 1900
*The Root of All Evil. Film: Gainsborough, 1947 (scw & dir: Brock Williams)

*FLETCHER, LUCILLE
*Blindfold. Film: Univeral, 1966 (scw: Philip Dunne, W. H. Menger; dir: Dunne)
*Eighty Dollars to Stamford. Film: Comworld, 1982, as Hit and Run; also released as Revenge Squad (scw: Don Enright; dir: Charles Braverman)
*Night Watch. <NYC> Film: Avco Embassy, 1973 (scw: Tony Williamson, Evan Jones; dir: Brian G. Hutton)
*Sorry Wrong Number. Film: Paramount, 1948 (scw: Lucille Fletcher; dir: Anatole Litvak)

FLETCHER, OMAR
Black Against the Mob. Holloway, 1977
Black Godfather. Holloway, 1977

FLETCHER-ALLEN, EDGAR
After Midnight. Readers Library, 1928 (Novelization of film: MGM, 1927; scw & dir: Monta Bell)

*FLORA, FLETCHER. Ref also: TM.

FLORENCE, RONALD. 1942-   . Ref: CA.
-Zeppelin. Arbor, 1982

*FLOWER, PAT(RICIA MARY BRYSON)
*Slyboots. ... Stein, 1977 (date correction)

*FLOWERDEW, HERBERT. Pseudonym: *Nowell Cay.

FLOYD, HERBERT LEROY. Pseudonym of R. H. Floyd, 1886-   .
The Rugged Trail. Humphries, 1949

FLOYD, JOHN
Wooden Kimono. French, 1933 (3-act play.)

*FLOYD, MORDIE. Pseudonym of Mordina Floyd Bragunier.

FLOYD, R. H. 1886-   . Pseudonym: Herbert Leroy Floyd, q.v.

FLUKE, JOANNE
Cold Judgment. Dell, 1985
Winter Chill. Dell, 1984 <Minn.>

FLUSSER, MARTIN. 1947-   . Ref: CA.
The Squeal Man. Morrow, 1977 <L.I.> (Novelized true crime.)

FLYNN, CAROL HOULIHAN. 1945-   Ref: CA.
Washed in the Blood. Seaview, 1983 <L.A., 1938>

FLYNN, DON(ALD ROBERT). 1928-   . Ref: CA. SC: Ed Fitzgerald, in both titles.
Murder Isn't Enough. Walker, 1983; Hale, 1986 <NYC>
Murder on the Hudson. Walker, 1985 <NYC>

*FLYNN, JAY. Ref: TM.
*The Action Man. Film: Comacico, 1967, as Le Soleil des Voyous (Hoodlum's Sun) (Action Man) (scw: Alphonse Boudard, Jean Delannoy; dir: Delannoy)

FLYNN, LOUIS
Madness on Madrona Drive. French, 1977 (3-act play.)

*FLYNN, WILLIAM J(AMES)
*Eagle's Eye. Silent film: Foursquare, 1918 (scw: Courtney Riley Cooper; dir: George A. Lessey, Wellington Playter)

*FODEN, FREDERICK (TOM). Pseudonym: *John Carol.

FODOR, LASZLO <LADISLAUS>. 1896-
Jewel Robbery. French (NYC), 1932 (3-act play.) Film: Warner, 1932 (scw: Erwin Gelsey; dir: William Dieterle). Also: Warner, 1942, as The Peterville Diamond (scw: Brock Williams, Gordon Wellesley; dir: Walter Forde)

*FOLDES, YOLANDA
Golden Earrings. Hale, 1945; Morrow, 1946. Film: Paramount, 1947 (scw: Abraham Polonsky, Frank Butler, Helen Deutsch; dir: Mitchell Leisen)

*FOLEY, LORETTE
Murder in Burgos. Hale, 1981

*FOLEY, RAE. Ref: TC2 (revised and expanded); TM.
*Where Is Mary Bostwick? (title correction) Also published as: Escape to Fear (publisher, date?)

*FOLLETT, JAMES. Ref: CA.
Dominator. Methuen, 1984; Doubleday, 1986
The Tiptoe Boys. Corgi, 1982. Film: Rank, 1982, as Who Dares Wins (scw: Reginald Rose; dir: Ian Sharp)

*FOLLETT, KEN(NETH MARTIN). Ref also: TC2, TM. Pseudonym also: *Zachary Stone, q.v.
Lie Down with Lions. H. Hamilton, 1985; Morrow, 1986 <Afghan.>
The Man from St. Petersburg. H. Hamilton, 1982; Morrow, 1982 <Eng., 1914>
*Storm Island. Film: King's Road, 1981 as Eye of the Needle (scw: Stanley Mann; dir: Richard Marquand)

*FOLLIOTT, DORIA
*Signpost to Murder. (Novelization of film; see: *Monte Doyle.)

*FONBLANQUE, ALBANY (DE GRENIER)
*Tom Rocket. ss, some criminous

*FONG, C. K. Pseudonym of *Bruce (Bingham) Cassiday.

*FOOTE, HORTON
*The Chase. Film: Columbia, 1966 (scw: Lillian Hellman; dir: Arthur Penn)
The Traveling Lady. Dramatists, 1955 (3-act play.) Film: Columbia, 1965, as Baby, the Rain Must Fall (scw: Horton Foote; dir: Robert Mulligan). Novelization under film title: Popular Library, 1965

*FOOTMAN, DAVID (JOHN). 1895-1983. Ref: CA.

*FOOTNER, (WILLIAM) HULBERT. Ref also: CA.
*The Fur-Bringers. <Can.>
*The Huntress. Silent film: Associated First National, 1923 (scw: Percy Heath; dir: Lynn Reynolds)
*Jack Chanty. <Can.> Silent film: Alliance, 1915 (scw: Elliott Clawson; dir: Max Figman)
*Ramshackle House. Silent film: Tilford, 1924 (scw: Coolidge Streeter; dir: Harmon Weight)

*FORBES, COLIN. SC: Tweed and Bob Newman = T&N.
*Avalanche Express. Film: Lorimar, 1979 (scw: Abraham Polonsky; dir: Mark Robson)
Cover Story. Collins, 1985; Atheneum, 1986 T&N <Scand.>
Double Jeopardy. Collins, 1982
The Leader and the Damned. Collins, 1983; Atheneum, 1984 <Ger., WWII>
The Stockholm Syndicate. Collins, 1981; Dutton, 1982
*The Stone Leopard. Film: ITC, 1978 (existence of film not confirmed)
Terminal. Collins, 1984; Atheneum, 1985 T&N <Switz.>

*FORBES, MURRAY. ca.1908-1987. Radio actor; for many years the voice of Willy Fitz on "Ma Perkins" radio program.
*Hollow Triumph. Also published as: The Big Fake. Pyramid, 1953. Film: Eagle-Lion, 1948; also released as The Scar (scw: Daniel Fuchs; dir: Steve Sekely)

*FORBES, (JOAN) ROSITA (TORR). 1893-1967. Ref: CA.

*FORBES, STANTON. Ref also: TM.
*Go to Thy Death Bed. Film: Columbia, 1971, as Reflection of Fear (scw: Edward Hume, Lewis John Carlino; dir: William A. Fraker)

*FORBES, WILLIAM G.
*Ben Bradley's Puzzle. Street, 1907 (Magnet #483)
*Ben Bradley's Weirdest Case. Street, 1906 (Magnet #475)
*Fight to a Finish. Street, 1906 (Magnet #463)
*Fighting an Unknown Power. Street, 1906 (Magnet #469)
*From Despair to Triumph. Street, 1906 (Magnet #457)
*Into the Jaws of Death. Street, 1906 (Magnet #451)

*FORD, BRYANT. Pseudonym of *Michael (Seymour) Blankfort.

*FORD, COREY
Three Rousing Cheers for the Rollo Boys. Doran, 1925 ss, including a Sherlockian parody

*FORD, ELBUR
*Such Bitter Business. <Eng., 1800s>

*FORD, HARRIET. See also: Eleanor Robson Belmont, 1879-   .
*The Argyle Case. (4-act play.) Silent film: Warwick, 1917 (scw: Frederic Chapin, Ralph Ince; dir: Ince). Sound film: Warner, 1929 (scw: Harvey Thew; dir: Howard Bretherton)

*FORD, JEREMY. Pseudonym of William Levine.

*FORD, LESLIE. Pseudonym of Zenith
   Jones Brown, 1898-1983. Pseudonym
   also: *Brenda Conrad. Ref also:
   TM.
 *The Capital Crime; see Old Lover's
   Ghost
 *The Murder of a Fifth Columnist.
   not = *The Capital Crime
 *Old Lover's Ghost. British title:
   *A Capital Crime

*FORD, PAUL LEICESTER
 *The Great K&A Train Robbery. Silent
   film: Fox, 1926 (scw: John Stone;
   dir: Lewis Seiler)

FORD, RICHARD. 1944-   . Ref: CA.
   The Ultimate Good Luck. Houghton,
   1981 <Mex.>

FORDE, GERTRUDE
   -Rupert Alison; or, Broken Lights.
   Hurst, 1891

*FORDE, NICHOLAS
   Urgent Conference. Hale, 1981

*FORES, JOHN
   The Last Adventure. Hale, 1985
 *The Springboard. Film: Ealing, 1955,
   as Out of the Clouds (scw: Michael
   Relph, John Eldridge, Rex Reinits;
   dir: Basil Dearden)

FOREST, REGAN. Living in Ariz.
   One Step Ahead. Harlequin, 1985
   <Colo.>

FORESTAL, SEAN
   Dark Angel. Dell, 1982

FORESTER, BRUCE M(ICHAEL). 1939-
   Ref: CA.
   In Strict Confidence. Ashley, 1982
   <NYC>
   Signs and Omens. Dodd, 1984

*FORESTER, C(ECIL) S(COTT). Ref also:
   BM, TM.

FORREST, ANTHONY. Pseudonym. SC: Capt.
   John Valcourt Justice, in all
   titles.
   A Balance of Dangers. Lane, 1984;
   Hill, 1984 <ca.1804>
   Captain Justice. Lane, 1981; Hill,
   1981 <Fr., 1804>
   The Pandora Secret. Lane, 1982; Hill,
   1982 <Eng., 1804>

FORREST, DAVID
   Touch of Violence. News Stand, 1949

*FORREST, DAVID
 *The Great Dinosaur Robbery. Film:
   Disney, 1975, as One of Our
   Dinosaurs Is Missing (scw: Bill
   Walsh; dir: Robert Stevenson)

FORREST, KATHERINE V.
   Amateur City. Naiad, 1984 <L.A.>

*FORREST, RICHARD (STOCKTON). Ref:
   TC2, TM. SC: Lyon Wentworth, also
   in titles below.
   The Death at Yew Corner. Holt, 1980;
   Hale, 1981 <Conn.>
   Death Under the Lilacs. St. Martin's,
   1985 <Conn.>

*FORREST, WILLIAM. Pseudonym: *Wilma
   Forrest.

*FORREST, WILMA. Pseudonym of *William
   Forrest.

*FORRESTER, IZOLA L(OUISE)
 *The Dangerous Inheritance. Silent
   film: B.B. Productions, 1922, as
   How Women Love (scw: Dorothy Far-
   num, George Farnum; dir: Kenneth
   Webb)

*FORRESTER, LARRY
 *A Girl Called Fathom. Film: TCF,
   1967, as Fathom (scw: Lorenzo
   Semple, Jr.; dir: Leslie H.
   Martinson)

*FORSYTH, FREDERICK. Ref also: BM, TM.
 *The Day of the Jackal. Film: Univer-
   sal, 1973 (scw: Kenneth Ross; dir:
   Fred Zinnemann)
 *The Devil's Alternative. <1982>
 *The Dogs of War. Film: United
   Artists, 1980 (scw: Gary DeVore,
   George Malko; dir: John Irvin)
   The Fourth Protocol. Hutchinson,
   1984; Viking, 1984 <1988> Film:
   Rank, 1987 (scw: Frederick
   Forsyth; dir: John Mackenzie)

   No Comebacks. Hutchinson, 1982;
   Viking, 1982 ss
 *The Odessa File. Film: Columbia,
   1974 (scw: Kenneth Ross, George
   Markstein; dir: Ronald Neame)

FORSYTHE, ANTHONY. Pseudonym of *Wilbur
   Braun, q.v. Other pseudonyms:
   Ned Albert, Millard Crosby, qq.v.
   No Mother to Guide Her. French,
   1955 (3-act play.)

*FORVE, GUY
 *Ofanu. <Jap.>

FORWARD, ROBERT L(ULL). 1932-   .
   Ref: CA.
   The Owl. Pinnacle, 1984 <L.A.>

FOSBURGH, LACEY. 1942-   . Ref: CA.
   Old Money. Doubleday, 1983;
   Deutsch, 1983

FOSTER, DAVID (MANNING). 1944-
   Ref: CA.
   Dog Rock. Penguin, 1985 <Australia>

*FOSTER, DIRK
   Pam Slipped Up. Gaywood, 1952
   Small Town Big Shot. Gaywood, 195?

*FOSTER, MAXIMILIAN
 *The Trap. Silent film: Goldwyn,
   1921, as The Highest Bidder (scw:
   Lloyd Lonergan; dir: Wallace
   Worsley)

*FOSTER, R(EGINALD) FRANCIS. Ref:
   CA.

FOSTER, TONY
   The Money Burn. Methuen (Canada),
   1984; Critic, 1986

FOUNTAIN, NIGEL
   Days Like These. Pluto, 1985

FOWLER, BERTRAM B. Pseudonym: *Jack
   Baynes.

FOWLER, FRANK G. 1900-1971. Pseudonym:
   *Borden Chase.

FOWLER, GUY. 1893?-1966.
   The Last of Mrs. Cheyney. Grosset,
   1929 (Novelization of play by
   *Frederick Lonsdale, q.v.)

FOWLER, HELEN (MARJORIE). 1910-   .
   The Shades Will Not Vanish. Angus
   (Sydney), 1952. U.S. title:
   The Intruder. Morrow, 1953. Film:
   Anglo-Amalgamated, 1957, as
   Strange Intruder (scw: David
   Evans, Warren Douglas; dir:
   Irving Rapper)

*FOWLER, SYDNEY
 *Three Witnesses. Film: Twickenham,
   1935 (scw: Michael Barringer;
   dir: Leslie Hiscott)

*FOWLES, ANTHONY
   Rough Trade. Magnum, 1981

*FOWLES, JOHN. See also: David
   Parker.
 *The Collector. Film: Columbia, 1965
   (scw: Stanley Mann, John Kohn;
   dir: William Wyler)
  -A Maggot. Cape, 1985; Little, 1985
   <1700s>

FOWLKES, FRANK. 1941-   .
   The Peruvian Contracts. Putnam, 1976

*FOX, ANTHONY. Pseudonym of Anthony
   Fullerton. Served in submarines in
   British Navy; has been a Russian
   interpreter; living in Ire.
 *Kingfisher Scream. ... Viking, 1981
   (date correction)

FOX, CHARLES. 1942-   .
   The Noble Enemy. Doubleday, 1980;
   Granada, 1981

FOX, GEORGE. Pseudonym: *Frank Corey.

*FOX, GEORGE (RICHARD)
   Amok. Simon, 1978; Secker, 1978
   <Philip.>
   Warlord's Hill. Times, 1982 <N.J.,
   1940s>

*FOX, JAMES M. Ref also: TC2.
   The Coven. Raven, 1981

*FOX, PETER (F.)
   Kensington Gore. Macmillan (London),

   1983. U.S. title (?): The Trail
   of the Reaper. St. Martin's, 1983
   <acad.>
   Satan's Messenger. Macmillan (London), 1981
   The Trail of the Reaper; see Kensington Gore

FOX, TERRY CURTIS. 1948-   . Ref: CA.
   Cops. French, 1978   (3-act play.)
   <Chi.>

*FOX, COLONEL VICTOR J.
 *The Pentagon Case. <Wash. D.C.>

*FOXALL, P(ETER) A(UGUSTUS)
   The A4 Murder. Hale, 1985
   The Champagne Bandits. Hale, 1983
   The Circle of Death. Hale, 1982
   Counterstrike. Hale, 1983
   The Drugs Farm. Hale, 1984
   The Face of Fury. Hale, 1982
   On Course for Murder. Hale, 1982
   The Silent Informer. Hale, 1981
   The War Chest. Hale, 1985
   The Wild Card. Hale, 1981

FOY, GEORGE. 1952-   . Ref: CA, TM.
   Asia Rip. Viking, 1984. British
   title (?): Tidal Race. Collins,
   1985 <Cape Cod, NYC>

*FRANCES, STEPHEN D(ANIEL). See also:
   *Ace Capelli, *Hank Janson.
   The Day the Island Almost Sank.
   Consul, 1964 (Novelization of
   "The Naked City" TV series.)
  -One Man in His Time. Pendulum, 1946.
   Reprinted as by Hank Janson: New
   Fiction, 1953

FRANCIS, CLARE. 1946-   . Ref: CA.
   Night Sky. Heinemann, 1983; Morrow,
   1984 <1935-1945>
   Red Crystal. Heinemann, 1985

*FRANCIS, DICK. Ref also: TM.
   Banker. Joseph, 1982; Putnam, 1983
   Break In. Joseph, 1985; Putnam, 1986
   The Danger. Joseph, 1983; Putnam,
   1984
 *Dead Cert. Film: Woodfall, 1974 (scw:
   Tony Richardson, John Oaksey; dir:
   Richardson)
   Proof. Joseph, 1984; Putnam, 1985
   Twice Shy. Joseph, 1981; Putnam, 1982

FRANCIS, M. E. Pseudonym of Mrs. Francis Blundell,   -1930.
   Lychgate Hall. Longmans, 1904

FRANCIS, R. W. Pseudonym: Francis
   Farrar, q.v.

*FRANCIS, RICHARD H.
   The Enormous Dwarf. Panther, 1982
   The Whispering Gallery. Deutsch,
   1984; Norton, 1984

FRANCIS, STEPHEN. Pseudonym: Hilary
   Brand, q.v.
   Day of Terror. Consul, 1962

*FRANK, LEONHARD. Ref: CA.

FRANK, WALTER I.
   The Diner on the Other Track. Vantage, 1956
   Good for One More Ride. Vantage,
   1956 <early 1900s, L.A.>

*FRANKEL, SANDOR
 *The Aleph Solution. <NYC>

FRANKLIN, JAY. Pseudonym of *John
   Franklin Carter.
   Rat Race. Fantasy Publishing Co.,
   1950 <future>

*FRANKLIN, MAX
 *The Destructors. (Novelization of
   film: Kettledrum, 1974; scw: Judd
   Bernard; dir: Robert Parrish)
 *The 5th of November. (Novelization of
   film: Marseilles, 1975; released in
   Britain as Hennessy; scw: John Gay;
   dir: Don Sharp)
 *Good Buys Wear Black. (Novelization
   of film: American Cinema, 1978;
   scw: Bruce Cohn, Mark Medoff; dir:
   Ted Post)
 *99 44/100% Dead. (Novelization of
   film: TCF, 1974, as 99 and 44/100%
   Dead; also released as Call Harry
   Crown; scw: Robert Dillon; dir:
   John Frankenheimer)

FRANKLIN, (STELLA MARIA) MILES (LAMPE).
   1879-1954. Ref: CA.
   Bring the Monkey. Endeavor, 1933

FRANZEN, JON and KATHY SIEBERT
  The Fig Connection. Dramatic, 19??
    (1-act play.)

*FRASER, ANTHEA. SC: Chief Insp. Webb,
    in both titles below.
  A Necessary End. Collins, 1985;
    Walker, 1986
  A Shroud for Delilah. Collins, 1984;
    Doubleday, 1986

*FRASER, ANTONIA. Ref also: TM. SC:
    Jemima Shore, also in all titles
    below.
  Cool Repentance. Weidenfeld, 1982;
    Norton, 1983
  Oxford Blood. Weidenfeld, 1985;
    Norton, 1985
  A Splash of Red. Weidenfeld, 1981;
    Norton, 1982

*FRASER, GUY
  The Blackhope Legend. Hale, 1982
  The Man Who Stole the Sun. Hale, 1982
  Monster. Hale, 1981

*FRASER, JEAN
  In the Bleak Midwinter. Hale, 1983

*FRASER, JOHN
  In Place of Reason. Macmillan (Lon-
    don), 1985 <It.>

FRASER, JOHN CRAWFORD
  The Ace of Spades. Skeffington, 1919.
    Film: Real Art, 1935 (scw: Gerard
    Fairlie; dir: George Pearson)

FRASER, MARY CRAWFORD, 1851-1922, and
    J. I. STAHLMANN
  The Satanist. Hutchinson, 1912
    <It.>

*FRASER-SIMPSON, C(ICELY DEVENISH)
  *Footsteps in the Night. Film: ATP,
    1931; released in Britain as A
    Honeymoon Adventure (scw: Rupert
    Downing, John Paddy Carstairs;
    dir: Maurice Elvey)

FRATTI, MARIO. 1927-   . Ref: CA.
  The Refrigerators. Dramatic (Johan-
    nesburg), 1972; French, 1977
    (3-act play.)
  The Return. Dramatic (Johannesburg),
    1972; French, 1977 (1-act play.)
  Victim. Dramatic (Johannesburg),
    1972; French, 1978 (3-act play.)

*FRAZEE, (CHARLES) STEVE. Ref also:
    TM.
  *Running Target. Film: United Artists,
    1956 (scw: Marvin R. Weinstein,
    Jack C. Couffer, Conrad Hall; dir:
    Weinstein)

*FREDERICKS, ARNOLD
  *The Ivory Snuff Box. Silent film:
    World, 1915 (scw: E. M. Ingleton;
    dir: Maurice Tourneur)

*FREED, DONALD
  *The China Card. <1984>

FREEDMAN, RALPH
  Divided. Dutton, 1948

*FREELING, NICOLAS. Ref also: TM.
    SC: Henri Castang, also in
    those titles marked HC; Arlette
    Van Der Valk, also in title
    marked AV.
  Arlette; see One Damn Thing After
    Another
  The Back of the North Wind. Heine-
    mann, 1983; Viking, 1983 HC <Fr.>
  *Because of the Cats. Film: Cine-Vog,
    1973, as Niet Voor de Poesen (Be-
    cause of the Cats) (The Rape) (scw:
    Hugo Claus; dir: Fons Rademakers)
  A City Solitary. Heinemann, 1985;
    Viking, 1985 <Fr.>
  *Love in Amsterdam. Film: Trio,
    1968, as Amsterdam Affair (scw:
    Edmund Ward; dir: Gerry O'Hara)
  No Part in Your Death. Heinemann,
    1984; Viking, 1984 HC <Fr.>
  One Damn Thing After Another. Heine-
    mann, 1981. U.S. title: Arlette.
    Pantheon, 1981 AV <Fr.>
  Wolfnet. Heinemann, 1982; Pantheon,
    1982 HC <Fr.>

FREEMAN, GILLIAN. 1929-   . Ref: CA.
  An Easter Egg Hunt. H. Hamilton,
    1981; Congdon, 1981

*FREEMAN, R(ICHARD) AUSTIN. Ref also:
    CA, TM. See: Alfred C. Ward.

*FREEMANTLE, BRIAN (HARRY). Pseudonym:
    *Jonathan Evans, q.v. SC: Charlie
    Muffin, also in titles marked CM.
  *Charlie Muffin. Film: Euston, 1979,
    as Charlie Muggin (existence of
    film not confirmed)
  Charlie Muffin and Russian Rose. Cen-
    tury, 1985 CM
  Deaken's War. Hutchinson, 1982; Tor,
    1985
  The Lost American; see Rules of
    Engagement
  Madrigal for Charlie Muffin. Hutchin-
    son, 1981 CM
  Rules of Engagement. Century, 1984.
    U.S. title (?): The Lost American.
    Tor, 1984 <Moscow>

*FREMLIN, CELIA. Ref also: BM, TM.
  A Lovely Day to Die, and other sto-
    ries. Gollancz, 1984, Doubleday,
    1984 ss
  The Parasite Person. Gollancz, 1982;
    Doubleday, 1982

FRENTZEN, JEFFREY. 1956-   . See:
    Buck Sanders.

FRESHMAN, BRUCE JACK
  The Master Plan. Bobbs, 1981

FREWER, GLYN MERVYN. Pseudonym:
    *Mervyn Lewis.

FREY, JAMES N.
  The Armageddon Game. Zebra, 1985
  The Last Patriot. Zebra, 1984

FRIEDMAN, HAL <HAROLD LEE>. 1942-
    Ref: CA.
  Crib. PB, 1982

FRIEDMAN, MICHAELE THOMPSON. 1944-
    Pseudonym: Mickey Friedman, q.v.

FRIEDMAN, MICKEY. Pseudonym of Michaele
    Thompson Friedman, 1944-   .
    Ref: CA, TM.
  The Fault Tree. Dutton, 1984 <India>
  Hurricane Season. Dutton, 1983
    <Fla., 1950s>

*FRIEDMAN, PHILIP
  *Rage. (Novelization of film: Warner,
    1972; scw: Philip Friedman, Dan
    Kleinman; dir: George C. Scott)

*FRIEND, ED
  *The Corpse in the Castle and *The
    Most Deadly Game are the same book
    (title and subtitle)

FRIMMER, STEVEN. 1928-   . Ref: CA.
  Dead Matter. Holt, 1982; Hale, 1983
    <NYC>

FRISCH, LARRY
  The Dream-Boaters. Exposition, 1953

FRISCH, MAX (RUDOLF). 1911-   Ref:
    CA.
  Bluebeard. Harcourt, 1983; Methuen,
    1983 (Translation of "Blaubart."
    Frankfurt, 1982.)

FRISSELL, WILLIAM DONALD. Pseudonym:
    *Jason Morgan.

FRITH, STAN
  Step in the Right Direction. New
    Horizon, 1983

*FRIZELL, BERNARD
  *Timetable for the General. <WWII>

*FROEST, FRANK
  *The Grell Mystery. Silent film:
    Vitagraph, 1917 (dir: Paul Scardon)

*FROME, DAVID. Pseudonym of Zenith
    Jones Brown, 1898-1983. Other
    pseudonym: *Brenda Conrad.

*FROST, BARBARA <BARBARA FROST SHIVELY>
    (spelling correction)
  *Innocent Bystander. <NYC>

FROST, G. H. See: Dick Stivers.

FROST, JASON. Pseudonym of Raymond
    Obstfeld, 1952-   , q.v. SC:
    Warlord = W (set: future).
  Invasion U.S.A. Pinnacle, 1985 (No-
    velization of film: Cannon, 1985;
    scw: James Bruner, Chuck Norris;
    dir: Joseph Zito)
  Badlands. Zebra, 1984 W
  The Cutthroat. Zebra, 1984 W
  Prisonland. Zebra, 1984 W
  The Warlord. Zebra, 1983 W <Calif.>

FROST, JOAN VAN EVERY
  Portrait in Black. GM, 1985 <Calif.>

*FROST, LESLEY. 1899-1983.

*FRUTTERO, C(ARLO) and *FRANCO LUCEN-
    TINI
  *The Sunday Woman. Film: TCF Europa,
    1976, as La Donna Della Domenica
    (The Sunday Woman) (scw: Agi and
    Scarpelli)

*FRY, ALAN
  *The Revenge of Annie Charlie.
    criminous

FRY, PAMELA. 1917-
  Harsh Evidence. Wingate, 1953; Roy,
    1956 <Can.>

*FRYERS, AUSTIN
  -A Pauper Millionaire. Pearson, 1899

FUCHS, DANIEL. 1909-   . Ref: CA.
  Low Company. Vanguard, 1937. Film:
    Allied Artists, 1947, as The Gang-
    ster (scw: Daniel Fuchs; dir:
    Gordon Wiles)

*FUENTES, ROBERTO. See: *Piers Anthony.

FULANI, DAN
  Deafman No Hear. Safari, 1983
  No Condition Is Permanent. Spectrum,
    1981
  -Flight 800. Spectrum, 1983

*FULLER, ALBERT (CHARLES). See: *Clyde
    North.

*FULLER, BLAIR
  *A Far Place. <Afr.>

FULLER, CHARLES (H., JR.). 1939-
    Ref: CA.
  A Soldier's Play. Hill, 1982
    (2-act play.) <La., 1944> Film:
    Caldix, 1984, as A Soldier's
    Story (scw: Charles Fuller; dir:
    Norman Jewison)
  Zooman and the Sign. French, 1982
    (3-act play.) <Phil.>

FULLER, DEAN
  Passage. Dodd, 1983; Hale, 1984

FULLER, JACK. Editor/reporter for
    Chicago Tribune.
  Convergence. Doubleday, 1982; Hod-
    der, 1983
  Mass. Morrow, 1985; Hodder, 1985

FULLER, JOHN
  Flying to Nowhere. Salamander, 1983;
    Braziller, 1984

*FULLER, ROGER
  *On the Double. (Novelization of film:
    Deni-Capri, 1961; scw: Jack Rose,
    Melville Shavelson; dir: Shavelson)

*FULLER, ROY (BROADBENT)
  *Fantasy and Fugue. Also published as:
    Murder in Mind. Academy Chicago,
    1987

*FULLER, SAMUEL (MICHAEL). Ref also:
    CA, TM; not in TC2.
  *The Dark Page. Film: Columbia, 1952;
    released in the U.S. as Scandal
    Sheet (scw: Ted Sherdeman, Eugene
    Ling, James Poe; dir: Phil Karl-
    son)
  *Dead Pigeon on Beethoven Street.
    (Novelization of film: Bavaria
    Atelier, 1972; scw & dir: Samuel
    Fuller)
  *The Naked Kiss. (Novelization of
    film: Allied Artists, 1965; scw &
    dir: Samuel Fuller)

*FULLER, TIMOTHY. Ref also: TM.

*FULLER, WILLIAM. Ref: TM.

*FULLERTON, ALEXANDER
  The Aphrodite Cargo. Joseph, 1985

FULLERTON, ANTHONY. Pseudonym:
    *Anthony Fox, q.v.

FULTON, E. G.
  Vengeance, My Love. Pinnacle, 1982
    <Mid. East>

FURMAN, LAURA. Ref: CA.
  The Shadow Line. Viking, 1982
    <Houston>

*FURST, ALAN. SC: Roger Levin, also in
    title marked RL below.

The Caribbean Account. Delacorte, 1981; Quartet, 1983 RL
*The Paris Drop. ... Quartet, 1983
Shadow Trade. Delacorte, 1983; Quartet, 1984 <NYC>

*FUTRELLE, JACQUES. Ref also: CA, TM.
*The Chase of the Golden Plate. Film: Rock, 1936, as The Man Behind the Mask (scw: Ian Hay, Syd Courtenay, Jack Byrd, Stanley Haynes; dir: Michael Powell)
*The Diamond Master. Burt, 19?? (This reprint includes "The Haunted Bell", with SC Prof. Augustus S. F. X. Van Dusen, apparently in its first book appearance; subsequently included in *Great Cases of the Thinking Machine.) Silent film (based on "The Haunted Bell"): Imp, 1916, as The Haunted Bell (scw: J. Grubb Alexander; dir: Henry Otto)
*Elusive Isabel. Silent film: Eclair, 1914, as Adventures of Diplomacy. Also: Bluebird, 1916, as Elusive Isabel (scw: Raymond L. Shrock; dir: Stuart Paton)
*The High Hand. Silent film: Favorite Players, 1915 (dir: William D. Taylor)
*My Lady's Garter. Silent film: Tourneur, 1920 (scw: Lloyd Lonergan; dir: Maurice Tourneur)

*FUTRELLE, MAY (PEEL)
*Secretary of Frivolous Affairs. Silent film: American, 1915 (scw & dir: Thomas Ricketts)

⅛"G-MAN." Pseudonym of Gordon Holmes Landsborough.

*GABORIAU, EMILE. Ref also: TM. Film (based on unidentified novel): World, 1919, as The Scar (scw: Hamilton Smith; dir: Frank Crane).
*The Clique of Gold. Silent film: Bluebird, 1916, as The Evil Women Do (scw: E. J. Clawson; dir: Rupert Julien)
*File No. 113. Silent film: AB, 1915. Also: Fox, 1917, as Thou Shalt Not Steal (scw: Adrian Johnson; dir: William Nigh). Sound film: Allied, 1932, as File 113 (scw: J. Francis Natteford; dir: Chester M. Franklin)
*Monsieur Lecoq. Silent film: Thanhauser, 1914.
*The Mystery of Orcival. Silent film: AB, 1916 (dir: J. Farrell MacDonald)
*Other People's Money. Silent film: Thanhauser, 1916 (dir: William Parke)

*GADNEY, REG. Ref (revised, expanded): TC2.

*GAGE, NICHOLAS
-Eleni. Random, 1983; Collins, 1983 <Greece> Film: Warner, 1985 (scw: Steve Tesich; dir: Peter Yates)

GAGNON, MAURICE
Inner Ring. Collins, 1985

*GAINES, ROBERT
*Final Night. Film: Lewis, 1953, as Front Page Story (scw: Jay Lewis, Jack Howells, William Fairchild, Guy Morgan; dir: Gordon Parry)

*GAINHAM, SARAH
*A Place in the Country. <Austria, 1946>
The Tiger, Life. Methuen, 1983 <Berlin>

GAINSBOROUGH, LOUIS
Of Dope and Dervishes. Rapollo, 1980

GAITHER, FRANCES ORMOND (JONES). 1889-1955.
Double Muscadine. Macmillan, 1948; Joseph, 1949 <South, 1850s>

GALBALLY, FRANK and ROBERT MACKLIN
Juryman. O'Neill (Australia), 1982 <Melb.>

*GALE, ADELA. Joint pseudonym of Gale and Adela Maritano.

GALE, CHARLES
Golden Eyes. Target, 1985

*GALE, JOHN. Pseudonym of Richard Gaze, 1917-ca.1983.

GALGUT, DAMON
A Sinless Season. Penguin, 1985 <S. Afr.>

*GALL, SANDY
Chasing the Dragon. Collins, 1981

GALLAGHER, MARY. 1947-   . Ref: CA.
Quicksilver. Putnam, 1982; Futura, 1984 <NYC>

GALLAGHER, STEPHEN
-Chimera. Sphere, 1982; St. Martin's, 1982
Follower. Sphere, 1984

*GALLICO, PAUL (WILLIAM)
*Trial by Terror. Film: Columbia, 1952, as Assignment--Paris (scw: William Bowers; dir: Robert Parrish)

GALLO, DIANE
Sin in the South. Bakers, 1982 (1-act play.) <South>

*GALLON, TOM
*Boden's Boy.   delete: not criminous
*The Great Gay Road.   delete: not criminous
*The Lackey and the Lady. Silent film: British Actors, 1919 (scw & dir: Thomas Bentley)
*The Man in Motley. criminous. Silent film: London, 1916 (dir: Ralph Dewsbury)
*Meg the Lady. Silent film: London-Diploma, 1916 (dir: Maurice Elvey)
*The Princess of Happy Choice.   delete: not criminous
*A Rogue in Love. Silent film: London, 1916 (scw & dir: Bannister Merwin). Also: Diamond, 1922 (scw: Harry Hughes; dir: Albert Brouett)
*Tatterly. Silent film: Lucoque, 1916 (scw: Nellie E. Lucoque; dir: H. Lisle Lucoque)
*The Touch of the Child. Silent film (from title ss): Hepworth, 1918 (scw: Blanche McIntosh; dir: Cecil M. Hepworth)
*Young Eve and Old Adam. Silent film: Union, 1920.

GALSWORTHY, JOHN. 1867-1933.
Escape. Duckworth, 1926; Scribner, 1927 (2-act play.) Film: ATP, 1930 (scw & dir: Basil Dean). Also: TCF, 1948 (scw: Philip Dunne; dir: Joseph L. Mankiewicz).
Five Tales. Heinemann, 1918; Scribner, 1918 ss, at least one criminous. Silent film (based on ss "The First and the Last"): Paramount, 1924, as The Stranger (dir: Joseph Henabery). Sound film (based on same ss): London, 1937, as The First and the Last; also released as 21 Days; released in the U.S. as 21 Days Together (scw: Graham Greene; dir: Basil Dean)
Justice. Duckworth, 1910; Scribner, 1910 (4-act play.) Silent film: Ideal, 1917 (scw: Eliot Stannard; dir: Maurice Elvey)
-Loyalties. Duckworth, 1922; Scribner, 1922 (3-act play.) Film: ATP, 1933 (scw: W. P. Lipscomb; dir: Basil Dean)

*GALTON, RAY(MOND PERCY) and *ALAN (FRANCIS) SIMPSON
*The Spy with a Cold Nose. (Novelization of film: Embassy, 1966; scw: Ray Galton, Alan Simpson; dir: Daniel Petrie)

*GANDOLFI, SIMON
France Security. Blond, 1981

*GANN, ERNEST K(ELLOGG)
-Fiddler's Green. Sloan, 1950; Hodder, 1954. Film: Universal, 1951, as The Raging Tide (scw: Ernest K. Gann; dir: George Sherman)

*GANPAT
-The Speakers in Silence. Hodder, 1929 <India>
-Walls Have Eyes. Hodder, 1930

*GANT, NORMAN. Pseudonym of *George Wolk.
*Burn. (Novelization of film: Grimaldi, 1970; scw: Franco Solinas, Giorgio Arlorio; dir: Gillo Pontecorvo)

*GARBO, NORMAN
Gaynor's Passion. Houghton, 1985.

British title: A Sudden Madness. Allen, 1985
A Sudden Madness; see Gaynor's Passion
Turner's Wife. Norton, 1983; Allen, 1982

GARDEN, GRAEME. 1943-   . Ref: CA.
The Seventh Man. Eyre, 1981

*GARDEN, JOHN
*All on a Summer's Day. Film: Reynolds, 1950, as Double Confession (scw: William Templeton, Ralph Keene; dir: Ken Annakin)

GARDINER, BECKY. See: Barbara Chambers.

*GARDINER, DOROTHY. Ref also: TM.

GARDINER, JUDY. 1922-   . Ref: CA.
The Big Goodnight. Hamlyn, 1983
-Who Was Sylvia? Severn, 1982; St. Martin's, 1983

*GARDNER, ERLE STANLEY. Ref also: TM.
*The Case of the Caretaker's Cat. Film: First National, 1936, as The Case of the Black Cat (scw: F. Hugh Herbert; dir: William McGann)
*The Case of the Curious Bride. Film: First National, 1935 (scw: Tom Reed; dir: Michael Curtiz)
*The Case of the Howling Dog. Film: Warner, 1934 (scw: Ben Markson; dir: Alan Crosland)
*The Case of the Lucky Legs. Film: First National, 1935 (scw: Brown Holmes, Ben Markson, Jerry Chodorov; dir: Archie L. Mayo)
*The Case of the Mischievous Doll. (incorrectly rendered "Moll" in first printings of CF)
*The Case of the Stuttering Bishop. Film: First National, 1937 (scw: Don Ryan, Kenneth Gamet; dir: William Clemens)
*The Case of the Velvet Claws. Film: First National, 1936 (scw: Tom Reed; dir: William Clemens)
The Human Factor. Morrow, 1981 ss, one criminous

*GARDNER, JOHN (EDMUND). Ref also: TM. SC: James Bond (following *Ian Fleming, q.v.): JB; Herbie Kruger, also in title marked HK.
*A Complete State of Death. Film: Columbia, 1973, as The Stone Killer (scw: Gerald Wilson; dir: Michael Winner)
Flamingo. Hodder, 1983 <Shanghai, 1930s>
For Special Services. Cape, 1982; Coward, 1982 JB <Tex.>
*Founder Member. Muller, 1969 (publisher correction)
Icebreaker. Cape, 1983; Putnam, 1983 JB <Fin.>
License Renewed. Cape, 1981; Marek, 1981 JB
*The Liquidator. Film: MGM, 1965 (scw: Peter Yeldham; dir: Jack Cardiff)
The Quiet Dogs. Hodder, 1982 HK
Role of Honour. Cape, 1984; Putnam, 1984 JB
The Secret Generations. Heinemann, 1985; Putnam, 1985 <1909-1935>

GARDNER, RICHARD (M.). 1931-   . Ref: CA.
The Dragon Breath Papers. Viking, 1976

*GARFIELD, BRIAN (FRANCIS WYNNE). Ref also: TM.
Checkpoint Charlie. Mysterious Press, 1981 ss
*Deep Cover. <Tucson>
*Death Wish. Film: Paramount, 1974 (scw: Wendell Mayes; dir: Michael Winner)
*Hopscotch. Film: AVCO, 1980 (scw: Brian Garfield, Bryan Forbes; dir: Ronald Neame)
*Line of Succession. <Wash. D.C.>
Necessity. St. Martin's, 1984; Macmillan (London), 1984 <Calif.>

*GARFIELD, LEON
The House of Cards. Bodley, 1981; St. Martin's, 1983

GARLAND, LAWRENCE. Joint pseudonym of Lawrence Toppman and Steven Garland.
The Affair of the Unprincipled Publisher. Oak Knoll, 1983 (Sherlock Holmes)

G

G

*GARLAND, NICHOLAS
A Crime of Innocence. Berkley, 1982; Fontana, 1983 <South>

GARLAND, STEVEN. Joint pseudonym with Lawrence Toppman: Lawrence Garland, q.v.

*GARNER, HUGH
*Murder Has Your Number. ... PaperJacks (U.S.), 1984
*The Sin Sniper. Film: Dimension, 1980, as Stone Cold Dead (scw & dir: George Mendeluk)

*GARNER, WILLIAM
Rats' Alley. Heinemann, 1984
Think Big, Think Dirty. Heinemann, 1983; St. Martin's, 1983
Zones of Silence. Heinemann, 1985

GARNET, A. H. Joint pseudonym of a teacher at a Michigan university and author of children's books; and a retired university professor who has taught television and radio. SC: Cyrus Wilson, in both titles.
Maze. Ticknor, 1982; Gollancz, 1983 <acad., Mich.>
The Santa Claus Killer. Ticknor, 1981; Gollancz, 1982 <Det.>

GARNETT, BILL <WILLIAM JOHN>. 1941-   . Ref: CA.
-The Crone. Sphere, 1984
The Shadow. Sphere, 1982

*GARRETT, RANDALL (PHILLIPS). Ref: TM. SC: Lord Darcy, also in titles below.
The Best of Randall Garrett. Timescape, 1982 ss, including one previously uncollected LD story, plus one other detective story
Lord Darcy Investigates. Ace, 1981 ss

*GARRETT, WILLIAM (A.)
*The Secret of the Hills. Silent film: Vitagraph, 1921 (scw: E. Magnus Ingleton; dir: Chester Bennett).
*The Professional Guest. Film: King, 1931 (scw: H. Fowler Mear; dir: George King)

GARRIGUES, EDUARDO. Spanish career diplomat stationed in Kenya 1974-6; living in Madrid and serving as Deputy Director General of Africa for Spain.
The Grass Rain. Macmillan, 1984 <Kenya>   (Translation of "Lluvias de Hierba.")

*GARRISON, CHRISTIAN (BASCOM). SC: Ace Chaney, in *Snake Doctor, and title below.
Paragon Man. Avon, 1981 <South>

*GARRISON, JIM (C.). Ref: CA.

*GARTH, DAVID
*Eastward in Eden. <Egypt>
*Four Men and a Prayer. Film: TCF, 1938 (scw: Richard Sherman, Sonya Levien, Walter Ferris; dir: John Ford). Also: TCF, 1948, as Fury at Furnace Creek (scw: Charles G. Booth; dir: H. Bruce Humberstone)
*Three Roads to a Star. <Morocco>

*GARTH, ED. Pseudonym of *William Johnston.

GARTH-THORNTON, ELMOND
For Love and Duty. Remington, 1884

*GARVE, ANDREW. Ref also: TM.
*Death and the Sky Above. Film: Playpont, 1962, as Two-Letter Alibi (scw: Roger Marshall; dir: Robert Lynn)
*The Megstone Plot. Film: Foxwell, 1959, as A Touch of Larceny (scw: Roger MacDougall, Guy Hamilton, Paul Winterton, Ivan Foxwell; dir: Hamilton)

*GARVICE, CHARLES
Diana and Destiny. Hodder, 1906. U.S. title: Diana's Destiny. American News, 1905. Silent film: Windsor, 1916, as Diana and Destiny (dir: F. Martin Thornton)
The Verdict of the Heart. Newnes, 1912. Silent film: Clarenden, 1915 (dir: Wilfred Noy)

GARYS, WALTER
The Detonator. Tower, 1981 <NYC>

GASH, JOE. Pseudonym of *Bill Granger, q.v. Other pseudonym: Bill Griffith, q.v. SC: Terry Flynn, in both titles below, and in *Public Murders, as by *Bill Granger.
Newspaper Murders. Holt, 1985 <Chi.>
Priestly Murders. Holt, 1984 <Chi.>

*GASH, JONATHAN. Ref also: TC2, TM. Pseudonym of *John Grant. Other pseudonym: Graham Gaunt, q.v. SC: Lovejoy, also in all titles below.
Firefly Gadroon. Collins, 1982; St. Martin's, 1984
The Gondola Scam. Collins, 1984; St. Martin's, 1984 <Venice>
Pearlhanger. Collins, 1985; St. Martin's, 1985
The Sleepers of Erin. Collins, 1983; Dutton, 1983
The Vatican Rip. Collins, 1981; Ticknor, 1982 <Rome>

*GASKELL, MRS. ELIZABETH (CLEGHORN STEVENSON)
Mary Barton. Chapman, 1848; Harper, 1848

*GASKIN, CATHERINE. Ref: not in TC2.
*The File on Devlin. <Switz.>

*GAST, KELLY P. Ref: CA.

*GASTON, BILL
-Winter and the Widowmakers. Hale, 1984
-Winter and the Wild Rover. Hale, 1982

GAT, DIMITRI (VSEVOLOD). 1936-   . Ref: CA. SC: Yuri Nevsky, in both titles.
Nevsky's Demon. Avon, 1983
Nevsky's Return. Avon, 1982 <Pitt.>

GATER, DILYS. 1944-   . Pseudonym: Clover Sinclair, q.v.

*GATES, H(ENRY) L(EYFORD)
*The Red Dancer of Moscow. Film: Fox, 1928, as The Red Dance (scw: James Ashmore Creelman; dir: Raoul Walsh)

*GATES, TUDOR
Who Saw Him Die. French (London), 1975   (3-act play.)

GATTEY, CHARLES NEILSON, 1921-   , and ZELMA BRAMLEY-MOORE. Ref for Gattey: CA.
The Eleventh Hour. Deane, 1952; Baker's, 1952 (3-act play.)
Fair Cops. Deane, 1965; Baker's, 1965 (1-act play.)

*GAULT, WILLIAM CAMPBELL. Ref also: TM. SC: Brock Callahan, also in titles below.
The Dead Seed. Walker, 1985; Hale, 1986 <Calif.>
Death in Donegal Bay. Walker, 1984 <Calif.>

GAUNT, GRAHAM. Pseudonym of *John Grant. Other pseudonym: *Jonathan Gash, q.v.
The Incomer. Collins, 1981; Doubleday, 1982

*GAYET, CAROLINE
Mirror of Darkness. Mystique, 1981 (Translation of "Chanson Pour un Amour". Paris, 1969.)
Passionate Stranger. Mystique, 1981 (Translation of "La Double Enigma." Paris, 1979.)

*GAYLORD, OTIS H.
*The Rise and Fall of Legs Diamond. (Novelization of film: Warner, 1960; scw: Joseph Landon; dir: Budd Boetticher)

*GAZE, RICHARD. 1917-ca.1983.

*GEARON, JOHN
*The Velvet Well. Film: Action, 1978, as Un Papillon Sur L'Epaule (A Butterfly on the Shoulder) (scw: Jean-Claude Carriere, Tonino Guerra; dir: Jacques Deray)

*GEDDES, PAUL. SC: Ludovic Fender, in *High Game and *A November Wind, and in title below.
A State of Corruption. Bodley, 1985; Holt, 1986   <Rome>

GEE, MAGGIE
Dying, in Other Words. Harvester, 1981

*GEE, MAURICE (GOUGH)
*Games of Choice. <N.Z.>
A Glorious Morning, Comrade. Auckland Univ. Press, 1975 ss <N.Z.>
*In My Father's Den. <N.Z.>
Plumb. Faber, 1978 <N.Z.>
A Special Flower. Hutchinson, 1975 <N.Z.>

GEIS, RICHARD. Joint pseudonym with Elton Elliott: Richard Elliott, q.v.

GEISER, ROBERT LEE. 1931-   . Pseudonym: Stephen Peters, q.v.

GELINET, CLAUDE. Pseudonym: *Jean Giltene.

*GELLER, STEPHEN. Born and raised in L.A.; has degrees from Dartmouth and Yale Drama School; author of screenplays; living in Rome.
*She Let Him Continue. Film: TCF, 1968, as Pretty Poison (scw: Lorenzo Semple, Jr.; dir: Noel Black)

*GENET, JEAN
*The Balcony. Film: Reade-Sterling, 1963 (scw: Ben Maddow; dir: Joseph Strick)
The Maids and Deathwatch. Grove, 1954 (2 plays; second is translation of "Haute Surveillance." Paris, 1949). Second play published separately in Britain: Faber, 1961. Film (based on first play): Mantis, 1976, as The Maids (scw: Robert Enders, Christopher Miles; dir: Miles)

GENTLE, LIONEL
Pacific Interlude. Stockwell, 1983

*GEORGE, CHARLES
The Darkest Hour. French, 1935 (1-act play.)

GEORGE, KARA. Newspaper and magazine writer.
Murder at Tomorrow. Walker, 1982; Hale, 1983

GERAGHTY, TONY
Freefall Factor. Macmillan (London), 1985

*GERARD, MAURICE
*The Secret of the Moor. Silent film: British Lion, 1919 (dir: Lewis Willoughby)

GERHARD, H. HARRIS. See: Leslie Alan Horvitz.

*GERMESHAUSEN, ANNA LOUISE. Ref: CA.

GERON, FRANK
The Geneva Transfer. Zebra, 1983

*GERRITY, DAVID J(AMES). 1923-1984. Ref: TM.

*GERSON, JACK. Born and educated in Glasgow; contributor to TV programs and creator of two TV series.
The Back of the Tiger. Allen, 1984; Beaufort, 1985
Treachery Game. BBC, 1981
The Whitehall Sanction. Allen, 1983; Beaufort, 1984

GETHIN, DAVID. SC: Wyatt, in those marked W.
Jack Lane's Browning. Gollancz, 1984. U.S. title: Point of Honor. Scribner, 1985
Point of Honor; see Jack Lane's Browning
Wyatt. Gollancz, 1983; St. Martin's, 1983 W
Wyatt and the Moresby Legacy. Gollancz, 1983; St. Martin's, 1984 W
Wyatt's Orphan. Gollancz, 1985 W

GETTEL, RONALD. 1931-   . Ref: CA.
Twice Burned. Walker, 1983; Hale, 1986   <Chi.>

GHOSE, ZULFIKAR. 1935-   . Ref: CA.
Don Bueno. Hutchinson, 1983; Holt, 1984 <Brazil>

GIALANELLA, VICTOR
Frankenstein. Dramatists, 1982 (2-act play based on the novel by *M. W. Shelley, q.v.) <Switz.>

GIANCOL, ANTHONY
The Three Racketeers. Vantage, 1955 <1920s>

*GIBBON, PERCEVAL. SC: Miss Gregory, in *The Adventures of Miss Gregory, and one ss in *The Second Class Passenger, and other stories.

GIBBONS, HARRY (SCOTT)
The Hunter Equation. Dell, 1981

GIBBONS, SCOTT
Peacock. GM, 1980

*GIBBS, GEORGE F(ORT)
*Paradise Garden. Silent film: Metro, 1917 (scw: Fred J. Balshofer, Richard V. Spencer; dir: Balshofer)
*The Silent Battle. Silent film: Bluebird, 1916 (scw: F. McGrew Willis; dir: Jack Conway)
*The Splendid Outcast. Silent film: Fox, 1922, as Honors First (scw: Joseph Franklin Poland; dir: Jerome Storm)
*The Yellow Dove. Silent film: Kane, 1926, as The Great Deception (scw: Paul Bern; dir: Howard Higgin)

GIBBS, NORAH. Pseudonym: *Dallas Romaine.

*GIBBS, PHILIP (HAMILTON)
The Law-Breakers. Hutchinson, 1963

*GIBBS-SMITH, C(HARLES) H(ARVARD). 1909-1981.

GIBSON, FRANK E.
Cloak-and-Doctor. Exposition, 1974

GIBSON, H(ARRY) N(ORMAN). See: Freda M(argaret) Kelsall.

GIBSON, MILES. 1947-   . Ref: CA.
The Sandman. Heinemann, 1984; St. Martin's, 1985

*GIBSON, WALTER B(ROWN), 1897-1985. Ref also: CA, TM. SC: Lamont Cranston (The Shadow), also in titles below.
The Golden Master; see The Shadow and the Golden Master
House of Ghosts; see The Shadow: Jade Dragon and House of Ghosts
Jade Dragon; see The Shadow: Jade Dragon and House of Ghosts
The Shadow and the Golden Master. Mysterious Press, 1984 (Contains two novels: The Golden Master, and Shiwan Khan Returns)
The Shadow: Jade Dragon and House of Ghosts. Doubleday, 1981
Shiwan Khan Returns; see The Shadow and the Golden Master

GIBSON, WILLIAM. 1948-   .
Neuromancer. Gollancz, 1984; Ace, 1984 <future>

GIBSON-COWAN, W. L.
Fantoccini. Danegold, 1927 ss, some criminous

GIDDINGS, ARTHUR F. Pseudonym: Arthur Baker, q.v.

*GIELGUD, VAL (HENRY)
*Death at Broadcasting House. (out of alphabetical order) Film: Phoenix, 1934; released in the U.S. as Death at a Broadcast (scw: Basil Mason; dir: Reginald Denham)

*GIESY, J(OHN) U(LRICH). Ref: CA.

*GIFFORD, THOMAS (EUGENE). Pseudonym: Dana Clarins, q.v.
*The Glendower Legacy. Film: Filmplan, 1980, as Dirty Tricks (scw: William Norton, Sr., Eleanor Elias Norton, Thomas Gifford, Camille Gifford; dir: Alvin Rakoff)

*GILBERT, ANNA. Ref: CA.
The Long Shadow. Piatkus, 1983; St. Martin's, 1985
Miss Bede Is Staying. Piatkus, 1982; St. Martin's, 1983 <Eng., 1800s>

*GILBERT, ANTHONY. Ref also: TM.
*Death Lifts the Latch. ... Smith & Durrell, 1946 (publisher correction)
*The Mouse Who Wouldn't Play Ball. Film: British National, 1944, as Candles at Nine (scw: Basil Mason, John Harlow; dir: Harlow)
*The Vanishing Corpse. Film: IP-Excelsior, 1943, as They Met in the Dark (scw: Anatole de Grunwald, Miles Malleson, Basil Bartlett, Victor MacClure, James Seymour; dir: Karel Lamac)
*The Woman in Red. Film: Columbia, 1945, as My Name Is Julia Ross (scw: Muriel Roy Bolton; dir: Joseph H. Lewis)

GILBERT, JOAN. Pseudonym: *Jill Baer.

*GILBERT, MICHAEL (FRANCIS). Ref also: TM.
*Amateur in Violence. Film (based on ss): Argo, 1960, as The Unstoppable Man (scw: Alun Falconer, Manning O'Brine; dir: Terry Bishop)
The Black Seraphim. Hodder, 1983; Harper, 1984
*Death Has Deep Roots. Film: Gibraltar, 1956, as Guilty? (scw: Maurice J. Wilson, Ernest Dudley; dir: Edmond T. Greville)
*Death in Captivity. Film: Lesslie 1959, as Danger Within; released in U.S. as Blackout (scw: Bryan Forbes, Frank Harvey; dir: Don Chaffey)
End-Game; see The Final Throw
The Final Throw. Hodder, 1982. U.S. title: End-Game. Harper, 1982
The Long Journey Home. Hodder, 1985; Harper, 1985
Mr. Calder and Mr. Behrens. Hodder, 1982; Penguin, 1983

GILBERT, MICHAEL A. 1945-   . Born in Brooklyn; associate professor of philosophy at York Univ. in Ontario, Can.
Office Party. Linden, 1981; Hale, 1984 <Ohio>
Yellow Angel. PB, 1985

GILBERT, NICHOLAS
Not on the Agenda. New Horizon, 1982

*GILBERT, (WILLIAM) STEPHEN
*Ratman's Notebooks. Film: Crosby, 1971, as Willard (scw: Gilbert A. Ralston; dir: Daniel Mann)

*GILBERT, WILLIAM
De Profundis. Strahan, 1864
Doctor Austin's Guests. Strahan, 1866 ss, some criminous

*GILBERT, WILLIE. See: *Jack Weinstock.

GILCHRIST, ANDREW (GRAHAM). 1910-
The Russian Professor. Hale, 1984; Critic, 1985
The Watercress File. Hale, 1985; Critic, 1986

*GILCHRIST, R(OBERT) MURRAY
*Weird Wedlock. criminous

GILCHRIST, TOM
Committed Agent. Hale, 1983

GILES, JANICE (HOLT). 1909-1979. Ref: CA.
-The Plum Thicket. Houghton, 1954 <Ark.>

GILES, MERTON BARNETT
-A City Office Mystery. Johnson (Syd.), 1946

*GILES, RAYMOND
*Shamus. (Novelization of film: Columbia, 1973; scw: Barry Beckerman; dir: Buzz Kulik)

*GILL, B(ARBARA) M. Pseudonym of Barbara Margaret Trimble, 1921-   . Other pseudonyms: Margaret Blake, q.v. Ref: TC2.
Seminar for Murder. Hodder, 1985; Scribner, 1986
The Twelfth Juror. Hodder, 1984; Scribner, 1984

*GILL, BARTHOLOMEW. SC: Insp. McGarr, also in all titles below.
McGarr and the Method of Descartes. Viking, 1984 <Ire.>
McGarr and the P.M. of Belgrave Square. Viking, 1983; Penguin, 1986 <Ire.>

*GILL, JOHN
*The Tenant. Reprinted in the U.S. under British title: Academy Chicago, 1985

*GILLER, NORMAN. See: *Jimmy Greaves.

*GILLESPIE, ROBERT (BRYNE). 1917-   . Ref: CA. SC: Ralph Simmons, in both titles.
Heads You Lose. Dodd, 1985
Print-Out. Dodd, 1983 <NYC>

GILLETTE, (JAY) MICHAEL. 1939-
Ref: CA.
The Cortez Letter. Avon, 1983

*GILLETTE, PAUL J.
*The Cat O'Nine Tails. (Novelization of film: Spettacoli, 1971; scw & dir: Dario Argento)
*Play Misty for Me. (Novelization of film: Universal, 1971; scw: Jo Heims, Dean Riesner; dir: Don Siegel)

*GILLETTE, WILLIAM (HOOKER)
*Secret Service. Silent film: Paramount, 1919 (scw: Beulah Marie Dix; dir: Hugh Ford). Sound film: RKO, 1931 (scw: Bernard Schubert; dir: J. Walter Ruben)
*Sherlock Holmes. Silent film: Essanay, 1916 (scw: H. S. Sheldon; dir: Arthur Berthelet). Also: Goldwyn, 1922; released in Britain as Moriarty (scw: Marion Fairfax, Earle Brown; dir: Albert Parker). Sound film: Fox, 1932 (scw: Bertram Millhauser; dir: William K. Howard). Also: TCF, 1939; released in the U.S. as The Adventures of Sherlock Holmes (scw: Edwin Blum, William Drake; dir: Alfred Werker)

GILLIAT, SIDNEY, 1908-   . See: Frank Launder, 1907-

*GILLMORE, RUFUS (HAMILTON)
*The Alster Case. Silent film: Essanay, 1915 (dir: J. Charles Haydon)

GILLOTTI, ALBERT F. Pseudonym: Thomas Henege, q.v.

*GILMAN, DOROTHY. Ref also: TM. SC: Mrs. Emily Pollifax, also in titles below.
Mrs. Pollifax and the Hong Kong Buddha. Doubleday, 1985; Hale, 1986 <H. Kong>
Mrs. Pollifax on the China Station. Doubleday, 1983; Hale, 1983 <China>
*The Unexpected Mrs. Pollifax. Film: United Artists, 1970, as Mrs. Pollifax, Spy (scw: C. A. McKnight; dir: Leslie Martinson)

*GILMER, J. LANCE
Hell Is Forever. Holloway, 1977 <S.F.>
-The Last Touchdown. Holloway, 1978

*GILMORE, CHRISTOPHER COOK
The Bad Room. Avon, 1983; Avon (U.K.), 1983 <N.J.>

*GILMORE, JOSEPH (LEE). See also: *Nick Carter.
Blue Flame. Dodd, 1982 <Boston>

*GILMOUR, H. B.
*The Eyes of Laura Mars. (Novelization of film: Columbia, 1978; scw: John Carpenter, David Zelag Goodman; dir: Irvin Kershner)
*Windows. (Novelization of film: United Artists, 1980; scw: Barry Siegel; dir: Gordon Willis)

GILROY, FRANK (DANIEL). 1925-
Ref: CA.
That Summer, That Fall, and Far Rockaway. Random, 1967 (2 plays, the second criminous; 1-act)

*GILTENE, JEAN. Pseudonym of Claude Gelinet.

GILTSPAR, NETHERSOLE
A Bag o' Gold. Houghton, 1887

GIOVANNETTI, ALBERTO. 1913-   .
Ref: CA.
Requiem for a Spy. Doubleday, 1983 <NYC> (Translation of "Requiem per una Spia.")

GIOVANNI, PAUL
The Crucifer of Blood. French, 1979 (3-act play based on *The Sign of Four, by *A. Conan Doyle, q.v.) (Sherlock Holmes) <1887>

*GIPE, GEORGE
*Coney Island Quickstep. <NYC, 1891>

GIRARD, KENNETH
  Altered Egos. Pinnacle, 1983

GIROUX, E. X. Pseudonym of *Doris
  Shannon, q.v. SC: Robert Forsythe,
  in all titles. Set: Eng.
  A Death for a Dancer. St. Martin's,
  1985
  A Death for a Darling. St. Martin's,
  1985
  A Death for Adonis. St. Martin's,
  1984; Hale, 1986

GIROUX, LEO, JR.
  The Rishi. Evans, 1985; Grafton,
  1986 <Boston>

GISKES, H. J. 1896-
  London Calling North Pole. Kember,
  1953; British Book Centre, 1953.
  Film: Allied Artists, 1959, as The
  House of Intrigue (scw: Duilio
  Coletti, Ennio De Concini, Giuseppi
  Scoponi, Massimo Mida; dir:
  Coletti)

GLADE, MERTON
  Days of Wine and Murder. Dedalus,
  1984; Hippocrene, 1985

GLADSTONE, EVE. Pseudonym of Herma
  Werner, 1926-   . Ref: CA.
  A Taste of Deception. Harlequin, 1985
  <NYC>

GLASBY, JOHN S. 1928-   . Pseudonym:
  *A. J. Merak.

*GLASMON, KUBEC and *JOHN BRIGHT
  *The Public Enemy. (Novelization of
  film: Warner, 1931; released in
  Britain as Enemies of the Public;
  scw: Harvey Thew, Kubec Glasmon,
  John Bright; dir: William
  Wellman)

*GLASPELL, SUSAN (KEATING). Ref: CA.

GLAZIER, STEPHEN. 1947-   . Ref: CA.
  The Lost Provinces. Avon, 1981
  <Fr., 1907-1911>

*GLAZNER, JOSEPH MARK. SC: Billy
  Nevers, also in titles below.
  Big Apple Money Is Rotten to the
  Core. Warner, 1981 <NYC>
  Hot Money Can Cook Your Goose.
  Warner, 1981

GLEASON, JAMES. 1886-   . See:
  George Abbott, 1887-

GLEASON, WILLIAM
  The Calamityville Terror. Dramatic,
  1981 (2-act play.)
  No Crime Like the Present. Dramatic,
  1982 (3-act play.)
  The Pink Panther Strikes Again.
  Dramatic, 1981 (2-act play based
  on the film.)
  The Prime Time Crime. Dramatic, 1977
  (3-act play.)

*GLEIG, CHARLES. See: *Edwin (William)
  Pugh.

GLENDINNING, RALPH
  Death Match. Jove, 1985 <Haw.>
  The Ultimate Game. Wyndham, 1981;
  NEL, 1981 <Conn.>

GLENNON, GORDON
  Gathering Storm. Rylee, 1952 (3-act
  play.) Film: Leontine, 1952, as
  A Killer Walks (scw & dir: Ronald
  Drake)

*GLINTO, DARCY
  Blonde, Cute and Wicked. Moring, 1952
  Born to Die. Moring, 1952
  Dames Are Deadly. Moring, 1952
  Protection Payoff. Racecourse, 19??

*GLOAG, JULIAN
  Blood for Blood. H. Hamilton, 1985;
  Holt, 1985
  *Our Mother's House. Film: Heron, 1967
  (scw: Jeremy Brooks, Haya Hara-
  reet; dir: Jack Clayton)

*GLORE, CHARLES
  *Moonshine Mountain. (Novelization of
  film: ?   1967; scw: Charles
  Glore.)

*GLUCK, SINCLAIR
  *The Last Trap. Film: Chesterfield,
  1936, as The Dark Hour (scw: Ewart
  Adamson; dir: Charles Lamont)

*GLUCKMAN, JANET
  Rite of the Dragon. Leisure, 1982;
  Star, 1982

*GLUYAS, CONSTANCE. Ref: CA.

*GOBER, DON. Pseudonym of *Joseph G.
  Nazel (Jr.), q.v.

*GODDARD, ANTHEA
  The Brown Satin Bomb. Severn, 1985
  The Love Murders. Magnum, 1981

GODDARD, CHARLES WILLIAM. 1879-1951.
  The Ghost Breaker. Hearst, 1915
  (Novelization of unpublished play
  by Goddard and Paul Dickey, 1885-
  1933.) Silent film: Lasky, 1914
  (scw: James Montgomery, Cecil B.
  DeMille; dir: Oscar Apfel). Also:
  Famous Players, 1922 (scw: Jack
  Cunningham, Walter DeLeon; dir:
  Alfred E. Green). Sound film:
  Paramount, 1940 (scw: Walter
  DeLeon, dir: George Marshall).
  Also: Paramount, 1953, as Scared
  Stiff (scw: Herbert Baker, Walter
  DeLeon; dir: George Marshall)

GODDARD, KENNETH (WILLIAM).
  1946-   . Ref: CA.
  The Alchemist. Bantam hc, 1985;
  Bantam (London), 1986 <Calif.>
  Balefire. Bantam, 1983; Corgi, 1983
  <L.A., 1984>

*GODDARD, NORMAN (MOLYNEUX)

*GODDEN, JON. 1906-1984.
  In Her Garden. Knopf, 1981

*GODEY, JOHN. Ref also: TM.
  Fatal Beauty. Atheneum, 1984;
  Methuen, 1985 <It.>
  Nella. Delacorte, 1981; Severn, 1982
  <NYC>
  *The Taking of Pelham One Two Three.
  Film: United Artists, 1974 (scw:
  Peter Stone; dir: Joseph Sargent)
  *A Thrill a Minute with Jack Albany.
  Film: Buena Vista, 1967, as Never
  a Dull Moment (scw: A. J. Caro-
  thers; dir: Jerry Paris)

GODFREY, ELIZABETH. Pseudonym of
  Jessie Bedford.
  A Stolen Idea. Jarrolds, 1899

*GODFREY, ELLEN. 1942-   . Ref: CA.
  By Reason of Doubt. Clarke, 1982

GOERTZ, ALEXANDER. See: Ruth Goertz.

GOERTZ, RUTH and ALEXANDER
  The Hidden River. Dramatists, 19??
  (3-act play based on the novel by
  *Storm Jameson, q.v.)

GOETZ, AUSTIN B. Pseudonym: Kathleen
  O'Neill, q.v.
  "Beyond Reason." Northwestern, 1935
  (3-act play.)
  "Black Magic." Northwestern, 1938
  (3-act play.)
  Murder in Rehearsal. French, 1936
  (3-act play.)
  "The Panther's Claw." Northwestern,
  1934 (3-act play.)
  Shadow of Terror. <Syracuse>, 1935
  (Play.)

*GOFF, IVAN and *BEN ROBERTS
  *Portrait in Black. Film: Universal,
  1960 (scw: Ivan Goff, Ben Roberts;
  dir: Michael Gordon)

*GOINES, DONALD. 1937-1974. Ref: CA,
  TC2. Pseudonym: *Al C. Clark, q.v.
  *Black Gangster. <Detroit>
  *Eldorado Red. <Detroit>
  *Street Players. <Detroit>
  *White Man's Justice: Black Man's
  Grief. <Detroit>
  *Whoreson. <Detroit>

GOLAN, MATTI. 1936-   . Ref: CA.
  The Geneva Crisis. A&W, 1981 <Geneva>

*GOLDBERG, GERALD JAY
  -Heart Payments. Viking, 1982
  <L.A., 1966>

GOLDBERG, LEE. Joint pseudonym with
  *Lewis Perdue, q.v.: Ian Ludlow,
  q.v.

*GOLDIE, BERTHA (BARRE)
  *The Piper of Arristoun. <Scot.>

*GOLDING, LOUIS
  The Loving Brothers. Hutchinson, 1952

*GOLDMAN, JAMES (A.)
  Waldorf. Random, 1965; Joseph, 1966
  <Costa Rica>

*GOLDMAN, LAWRENCE
  *Black Fire. <Havana>

*GOLDMAN, WILLIAM. Ref also: TM.
  Control. Delacorte, 1982; Hodder,
  1982
  Edged Weapons; see Heat
  Heat. Warner hc, 1985. British title:
  Edged Weapons. Granada, 1985
  <Las Veg.> Film: Escalante, 1987
  (scw: William Goldman; dir: R. M.
  Richards)
  -Magic. Delacorte, 1976; Macmillan
  (London), 1976. Film:
  LeVine, 1978 (scw: William
  Goldman; dir: Richard Atten-
  borough)
  *Marathon Man. Film: Paramount, 1976
  (scw: William Goldman; dir: John
  Schlesinger)

*GOLDSMITH, JOHN
  Bullion. Sidgwick, 1982; A&W, 1983

*GOLDSMITH, MARTIN M.
  *Detour. Film: Producers Releasing,
  1946 (scw: Martin Goldsmith; dir:
  Edgar G. Ulmer)

*GOLDSTEIN, ARTHUR D(AVID). Ref: not
  in TC2.

GOLDSTEIN, STANLEY B. 1937-   .
  Pseudonym: *Bob Randall, q.v.

*GOLDSTEIN, WILLIAM (ISAAC)
  *Dr. Phibes. (Novelization of film:
  AIP, 1971, as The Abominable Dr.
  Phibes; scw: James Whiton, William
  Goldstein; dir: Robert Fuest)
  *Dr. Phibes Rises Again. (Novelization
  of film: AIP, 1972; scw: Robert
  Fuest, Robert Blees; dir: Fuest)

*GOLDTHWAITE, EATON K(ENNETH)
  The Case of the Nameless Corpse; see
  Don't Mention My Name
  *Don't Mention My Name. Also published
  as: The Case of the Nameless
  Corpse. Death House, 1944
  First You Have to Find Him. Double-
  day, 1981; Hale, 1982 <L.I.>

*GOLLER, NICHOLAS. Has degree in
  mathematics; works in operations
  research for England's National
  Coal Board.

*GOLLIN, JAMES. SC: Alan French (The
  Antigua Players), in *The Philomel
  Foundation, and both titles below.
  Eliza's Galiardo. St. Martin's, 1983
  <NYC>
  The Verona Passamezzo. Doubleday,
  1985

GONZALES, LAURENCE. 1947-   .
  The Last Deal. Atheneum, 1981

GONZALEZ, GLORIA. 1940-   . Ref: CA.
  Curtains. Dramatists, 1976
  (1-act play.)

GOOCH, ALAN
  Miller's Deal. Hale, 1984

*GOODCHILD, GEORGE
  *The Black Orchid. <Far East>
  *Colorado Jim. Silent film: Fox, 1921,
  as Colorado Pluck (scw & dir:
  Jules Furthman)
  *Jack O'Lantern. Film: Twickenham,
  1932, as Condemned to Death
  (scw: Bernard Merivale, Harry
  Fowler Mear, Brock Williams; dir:
  Walter Forde)
  *No Exit. Film: Pathe Welwyn, 1936, as
  No Escape (dir: Norman Lee)
  *The Splendid Crime. Film: RKO, 1931,
  as The Public Defender (scw: Ber-
  nard Schubert; dir: J. Walter
  Ruben)
  *Trooper O'Neill. Silent film: Fox,
  1922 (scw: William K. Howard; dir:
  C. R. Wallace, Scott Dunlap)

*GOODCHILD, GEORGE and *(CARL ERIC)
  BECHHOFER ROBERTS
  *The Dear Old Gentleman. <Scot.>

*GOODE, GEORGE W.
  *King Dan, the Factory Detective. (by
  *Erwin L. Coolidge.) <Mass.>

*GOODIS, DAVID (LOEB). Ref also: TM.
  *Black Friday. Film (also based on
  *Somebody's Done For): (studio?),

1972, as La Course du Lievre a Travers les Champs (And Hope to Die) (scw: Sebastian Japrisot; dir: Rene Clement)
*The Burglar. Film: Columbia, 1957 (scw: David Goodis; dir: Paul Wendkos). Also: Verneuil, 1971, as Le Casse (The Burglars) (scw: Vahe Katcha; dir: Henri Verneuil)
*Dark Passage. Film: Warner, 1947 (scw & dir: Delmar Daves)
*Down There. Film: Cocinor, 1960, as Tiruz sur le Pianiste (Shoot the Piano Player) (scw: Marcel Moussy, Francois Truffaut; dir: Truffaut)
*The Moon in the Gutter. ... Zomba, 1983, in David Goodis Omnibus. Film: Gaumont, 1983, as La Lune dans le Canivaux (The Moon in the Gutter) (scw: Jean-Jacques Beineix)
*Nightfall. Film: Columbia, 1957 (scw: Stirling Silliphant; dir: Jacques Tourneur)
*Of Missing Persons. Film: (studio?), 1956, as Section des Disparus (dir: Pierre Chenal)
*Somebody's Done For; see *Black Friday
*Street of the Lost. Film: Films de la Tour, 1984, as Rue Barbare (Barbarous Street) (scw: Gilles Behat, Jean Vautrin; dir: Behat)
*The Wounded and the Slain. Film: Partner's, 1986, as Descente aux Enfers (Descent into Hell) (scw: Francis Girod, Jean-Loup Dabadie; dir: Girod)

GOODMAN, ABRAHAM. Birth name of: *Abby Mann.

*GOODRUM, CHARLES A(LVIN). Ref also: TM.

GOODSPEED, D. J. Pseudonym: *Dougal McLeish.

GOODWIN, HOPE
-Home for the heart. Manor, 1979 <Oreg.>

*GOODWIN, JOHN
*The Avenger. Film: Monogram, 1933 (scw: Brown Holmes; dir: Edwin L. Marin)
*The House of Marney. Silent film: Nettlefold, 1926 (scw: Harry Hughes; dir: Cecil M. Hepworth)
*Paid in Full. Silent film: Banner, 1926, as Brooding Eyes (scw: Mary Alice Scully, Pierre Gendron; dir: Edward J. Le Saint)

*GORDON, ALEX
*The Cipher. Film: Donen, 1966, as Arabesque (scw: Julian Mitchell, Stanley Price, Pierre Marton; dir: Stanley Donen)

GORDON, ARTHUR
Pitchblende Quarry. Edwards, 1946 novelet and ss, former criminous

*GORDON, ARTHUR
*Reprisal. Film: Columbia, 1956 (scw: David P. Harmon; dir: George Sherman)

GORDON, DON
Tropic Equations. Macquarie (Syd.), 1933 <New Guinea>

*GORDON, JAMES
-Of Our Time. Dobson, 1946. U.S. title: Collision. Farrar, 1947

*GORDON, KURTZ
*The Bride's Bouquet. <N.Y.>
Jumpin' Jupiter. Dramatists, 1942 (3-act play.) <NYC>

*GORDON, MILDRED. 1905-1979.

*GORDON, NEIL
*The Shakespeare Murders. Film: Fox British, 1934, as The Third Clue (scw: Michael Barringer, Lance Sieveking, Frank Atkinson; dir: Albert Parker). Also: Fox British, 1938, as The Clayton Treasure Mystery (scw: Edward Dryhurst; dir: Manning Haynes)

*GORDON, R(ICHARD) L(AURENCE). 1920- . Ref: CA.

*GORDON, RICHARD. Pseudonym of Gordon Stanley Ostlere. Ref: CA, TM.
*The Medical Witness. <Eng., 1936>
The Private Life of Dr. Crippin. Heinemann, 1981. U.S. title: A Question of Guilt. Atheneum, 1981 <Eng., 1909>
A Question of Guilt; see The Private Life of Dr. Crippin

GORDON, STUART and CAROLYN PURDY-GORDON
The Little Sister. Dramatic, 19?? (3-act play based on the novel by *Raymond Chandler.)

GORDONE, CHARLES. 1925- . Ref: CA.
No Place to Be Somebody. Bobbs, 1969 (3-act play.)

*GORDONS, THE. Ref also: TM.
*Case File: FBI. Film: United Artists, 1954, as Down Three Dark Streets (scw: The Gordons, Bernard C. Schoenfeld; dir: Arnold Laven)
*Make Haste to Live. Film: Republic, 1954 (scw: Warren Duff; dir: William A. Seiter)
*Operation Terror. Film: Columbia, 1962, as Experiment in Terror; released in Britain as The Grip of Fear (scw: The Gordons; dir: Blake Edwards)
Race for the Golden Tide. Doubleday, 1983 (by Gordon Gordon and Mary Dorr.)
*Undercover Cat. Film: Disney, 1965, as That Darn Cat (scw: The Gordons, Bill Walsh; dir: Robert Stevenson)

*GORE-BROWN, ROBERT. See also: Harold Marsh Harwood, 1874- .
*An Imperfect Lover. Also published as: Cynara. Grosset, 1933. Film: Goldwyn, 1933, as Cynara (scw: Frances Marion, Lynn Starling; dir: King Vidor)

*GORES, JOE <JOSEPH NICHOLAS GORES>. Ref also: TM.
*Hammett. Film: Zeotrope, 1982 (scw: Ross Thomas, Dennis O'Flaherty; dir: Wim Wenders)

GORMAN, EDWARD. 1942- . Pseudonym: Daniel Ransom, q.v. Runs advertising agency in Cedar Rapids, Ia.; author of short fiction and criticism in magazines; has written documentaries and commercials for TV.
New Improved Murder. St. Martin's, 1985
Roughcut. St. Martin's, 1985

*GOSHGARIAN, GARY. 1942- . Ref: CA.

*GOSLING, PAULA. 1939- . Ref: CA, TC2, TM. Pseudonym: *Ainslee Skinner.
*A Running Duck. Film: Cannon, 1986, as Cobra (scw: Sylvester Stallone; dir: George Pan Cosmatos)
The Woman in Red. Macmillan (London), 1983; Doubleday, 1984 <Sp.>

GOSS, SUSAN WILLS
Memory's Dancer. Harvester, 1985

GOTLIEB, SONDRA. 1936- . Ref: CA.
A Woman of Consequence. St. Martin's, 1983

*GOTTLIEB, NATHAN
The Zukovka Experiment. Zebra, 1984

*GOTTLIEB, PAUL
*Agency. Film: RSI, 1980 (scw: Noel Hynd; dir: George Kaczender)

*GOULART, RON(ALD JOSEPH). Ref also: TM.
Big Bang. DAW, 1982 <2003>
Brainz, Inc. Daw, 1985 <future>
The Chameleon Corps. Macmillan, 1972 ss, criminous in part <future>
*Cleopatra Jones. (Novelization of film: Warner, 1973; scw: Max Julien, Sheldon Keller; dir: Jack Starrett)
*Cleopatra Jones and the Casino of Gold. (Novelization of film: Warner, 1975; scw: William Tennant; dir: Chuck Ball)
A Graveyard of My Own. Walker, 1985 <Conn.>
Upside Downside. DAW, 1982

GOULD, ALAN. Pseudonym of *Victor Canning, 1911-1986, q.v.
-Every Creature of God Is Good. Hodder, 1939

*GOULD, CHESTER. 1900-1985.

*GOULD, HEYWOOD
Fort Apache, the Bronx. Warner, 1981; Sphere, 1981 <NYC> (Novelization of film: TCF, 1981; scw: Heywood Gould; dir: Daniel Petrie)
*Glitterburn. ... Granada, 1983

*GOULD, JAY REID
The Long Silence. Dramatic, 1960 (1-act play.) <Maine>

*GOULD, NAT(HANIEL)
*A Dead Certainty. Silent film: Broadwest, 1920 (scw: P. L. Mannock; dir: George Dewhurst)
*The Doctor's Double. <Australia>
*A Lad of Mettle. <Australia>
A Rank Outsider. Routledge, 1900. Silent film: Broadwest, 1920 (scw: Patrick L. Mannock; dir: Richard Garrick)
*The Stolen Racer. (title correction) criminous <Australia>
*A Turf Conspiracy. Silent film: Broadwest, 1918 (scw: Bannister Merwin; dir: Frank Wilson)

GOURIET, JOHN
Checkmate Mr. President! Maclellan, 1981

GOW, GREGSON
Unravelled Skeins: Tales for the Twilight. Blackie, 1882 ss, some criminous

*GOYNE, RICHARD
*Parisian Nights. (Novelization of silent film: Gothic, 1925; scw: Kennedy Myton; dir: Al Santell)

*GRADY, JAMES (THOMAS). Pseudonym: *Brit Shelby, q.v. Ref also: TM. SC: James Rankin = JR.
Hard Bargains. Macmillan, 1985 JR <Wash. D.C.>
Razor Game. Bantam, 1985 <Balt.>
Runner in the Street. Macmillan, 1984 <Wash. D.C.> JR
*Six Days of the Condor. Film: Paramount, 1975, as Three Days of the Condor (scw: Lorenzo Semple, Jr., David Rayfiel; dir: Sydney Pollack)

GRAE, CAMARIN
The Winged Dancer. Blazon, 1983 <S. Am.>

*GRAEME, BRUCE. SC: Insp. Stevens also makes cameo appearance in title marked IS.
*Blackshirt. Film: WB-FN, 1935, as Black Mask (scw: Paul Gangelin, Frank Launder, Michael Barringer; dir: Ralph Ince)
*Disappearance of Roger Tremayne. Film: Asher, 1939, as Ten Days in Paris; released in the U.S. as Missing Ten Days, and as Spy in the Pantry (scw: John Meehan, Jr., James Curtis; dir: Tim Whelan)
*Fog for a Killer. Film: Eternal, 1962, as Out of the Fog (scw & dir: Montgomery Tully)
*Hate Ship. Film: British International, 1929 (scw: Monckton Hoffe, Eliot Stannard, Benn W. Levy; dir: Norman Walker)
*La Belle Laurine. <Fr.>
*Lord Blackshirt. IS
*Suspense. Film: Gibraltar, 1956, as Face in the Night; released in the U.S. as Menace in the Night (scw: Norman Hudis, John Sherman; dir: Lance Comfort)
*The Trail of the White Knight. <Hung., 1919>
*The Way Out. Film: Merton Park, 1955, as Dial 999; released in U.S. under book title (scw & dir: Montgomery Tully)

*GRAFTON, C(ORNELIUS) W(ARREN). Ref: TC2, TM.
*Beyond a Reasonable Doubt. <Ky.>
*The Rope Began to Hang the Butcher. <Ky., 1941>

GRAFTON, SUE. 1940- . Ref: CA, TM. SC: Kinsey Millhone, in both titles.
"A" Is for Alibi. Holt, 1982; Macmillan (London), 1986 <Calif.>
"B" Is for Burglar. Holt, 1985; Macmillan (London), 1986 <Calif.>

*GRAHAM, ALAN
*Follow the Little Pictures! ... Little, 1920 <Scot.>

*GRAHAM, BURTON
*Spy or Die. <Mid. East>

GRAHAM, CAROLINE. 1931-   . Ref: CA.
  The Envy of the Stranger. Century, 1984

*GRAHAM, JAMES
  *The Wrath of God. Film: MGM, 1972 (scw & dir: Ralph Nelson)

GRAHAM, JAMES M.
  A World Bewitched. Harper, 1898

GRAHAM, LYNN
  Dangerous Fragrance. Stockwell, 1984

*GRAHAM, WHIDDEN
  *Crimson Hairs. Also published as by Ellis Condor: Bee-Line, 1968 <NYC>

*GRAHAM, (MATILDA) WINIFRED (MURIEL). 1873-1950.

*GRAHAM, WINSTON (MAWDSLEY)
  *Fortune Is a Woman. Film: Harvel, 1957; released in the U.S. as She Played with Fire (scw: Sidney Gilliat, Frank Launder, Val Valentine; dir: Gilliat)
  *Marnie. Film: Universal, 1964 (scw: Jay Presson Allen; dir: Alfred Hitchcock)
  *Night Without Stars. Film: Europa, 1951 (scw: Winston Graham; dir: Anthony Pelissier)
  *Take My Life. Film: Cineguild, 1947 (scw: Winston Graham, Valerie Taylor, Margaret Kennedy; dir: David Lean)
  *The Walking Stick. Film: Winkast, 1970 (scw: George Bluestone; dir: Eric Till)

*GRAM, DEWEY
  *Boulevard Nights. (Novelization of film: Warner, 1979; scw: Desmond Nakano; dir: Michael Pressman)

*GRANBECK, MARILYN. Pseudonym: M. R. Henderson, q.v.

*GRANGER, BILL. Pseudonyms: Joe Gash, Bill Griffith, qq.v. SC: Devereaux, in *The November Man, and in titles below marked D.
  The British Cross. Crown, 1983; Sphere, 1985 D <Helskinki>
  Queen's Crossing. GM, 1982 <ship>
  Schism. Crown, 1981; NEL, 1982 D <Fla.>
  The Shattered Eye. Crown, 1982; NEL, 1984 D <Fr.>
  The Zurich Numbers. Crown, 1984; Sphere, 1986 D

*GRANT, CHARLES L.
  *The Hour of the Oxrun Dead. <Conn.>

GRANT, DONALD M. See: *Joseph Payne Brennan.

*GRANT, DOUGLAS
  *The Fifth Ace. Silent film: Universal, 1919, as The Red Glove (scw: Hope Loring; dir: J. D. McGowan)

*GRANT, JAMES. SC: Mace, in both titles below.
  Mace! Piatkus, 1984; Critic, 1986 <L.A.>
  Mace's Luck. Piatkus, 1985

*GRANT, JAMES EDWARD. 1905-1966. Ref: CA.
  *The Green Shadow. Film: RKO, 1936, as Muss 'Em Up; released in Britain as The House of Fate (scw: Erwin Gelsey; dir: Charles Vidor)

*GRANT, JOHN. Pseudonyms: Jonathan Gash, Graham Gaunt, qq.v.

*GRANT, MAXWELL
  *Shadow Beware. ... Starbooks (Syd.), n.d.

GRANT, NEIL (FORBES). 1882-   .
  Dusty Ermine. French (London), 1937 (3-act play.) Film: Twickenham, 1936; released in the U.S. as Hideout in the Alps (scw: L. DuGarde Peach, Michael Hankinson, Arthur Macrae, Paul Hervey Fox, H. Fowler Mear; dir: Bernard Vorhaus)
  The Nelson Touch. French, 1933. (Play.) Film: Gaumont British, 1937, as His Lordship; released in the U.S. as Man of Affairs (scw: Maude T. Howell, L. DuGarde Peach; dir: Herbert Mason)

*GRANT, RODERICK. Ref: CA.

GRANT-ADAMSON, LESLEY. Former newspaper reporter; author of fiction and screenplays.
  Death on Widow's Walk; see Patterns in the Dust
  The Face of Death. Faber, 1985; Scribner, 1986
  Patterns in the Dust. Faber, 1985. U.S. title: Death on Widow's Walk. Scribner, 1985

*GRANTHAM, GERALD. Pseudonym of *John Wallace.
  *Dope Runners. Popular Publications, 1940
  *The Mystery of the S.S. Timor. Popular Publications, 1940

GRAVE, STEPHEN. Both titles are novelizations of the Miami Vice TV series. Set: Miami.
  The Florida Burn. Avon, 1985; Star, 1986
  The Vengeance Game. Avon, 1985; Star, 1985

GRAVERSEN, PAT. 1935-   . Ref: CA.
  The Fagin. A&W, 1982

*GRAVES, CHARLES (PATRICK RANKE). 1899-1971.

*GRAVES, RICHARD L(ATSHAW)
  *The Platinum Bullet. <Bahamas, Colom.>

GRAVES, WARREN. 1933-   .
  The Mumberley Inheritance. Playwright's, 1971 (2-act play.) <Eng., 1900>

*GRAY, BERKELEY
  *Dare-Devil Conquest. Film: B&A, 1953, as Police Plaza 605; released in the U.S. as Norman Conquest (scw: Bernard Knowles, Albert Fennell, Bertram Ostrer, Clifford Witting; dir: Knowles)

GRAY, CATHARINE MARIA. See: Anonymous.

*GRAY, DULCIE
  *No Quarter for a Star. <theatre>

*GRAY, MAXWELL. Pseudonym of Mary Gleed Tuttiett,   -1923.

*GRAY, SIMON (JAMES HALLIDAY)
  Molly. French, 1979 (3-act play.)
  Wise Child. Faber, 1968; White, 1968 (3-act play.)

*GRAYSON, ELIZABETH. Pseudonym of *Joseph L. Chadwick.

GRAYSON, LAURA
  -Tomorrow for the Roses. Hale, 1981

GRAYSON, REX. Pseudonym of Ronald Grayson Campbell.
  -Snatch and Grab. Longmans, 1938

*GRAYSON, RICHARD. SC: Insp. Gautier, also in those marked G.
  Crime Without Passion. Gollancz, 1983; St. Martin's, 1983 G <Paris, ca.1900>
  The Death of the Abbe Didier. Gollancz, 1981; St. Martin's, 1981 G <Paris, ca.1900>
  Death Stalk. Gollancz, 1982; St. Martin's, 1983 G as by Richard Grindal <Hebrides>
  The Montmartre Murders. Gollancz, 1982; St. Martin's, 1982 G <Paris, ca.1900>
  The Whisky Murders. Gollancz, 1984; Walker, 1987, as by Richard Grindal <Scot.>

*GREATOREX, WILFRED
  The Button Zone. Macdonald, 1984; Macmillan, 1984

*GREAVES, JIMMY and *NORMAN GILLER
  The Boss. Barker, 1981
  -The Second Half. Barker, 1981

*GRECCO, JOHNNY
  Manhattan Massacre. Kaye, 1952 <NYC>
  Smart Dame. Gaywood, 1952
  A Sucker for Dames. Kaye, 1950

GREELEY, ANDREW (MORAN). 1928-   . Ref: CA. SC: Monsignor John Blackwood Ryan, in both titles.
  Happy Are the Meek. Warner, 1985; Macdonald, 1986 <Chi.>
  Virgin and Martyr. Warner hc, 1985; Macdonald, 1985

*GREEN, MRS. See: *W. G. Wills.

GREEN, ALAN (BAER). Ref also: TM.

*GREEN, ANNA KATHARINE. Ref also: CA, TM.
  *The Leavenworth Case. Silent film: Bennett, 1923 (scw: Eve Stuyvesant; dir: Charles Giblyn). Sound film: Republic, 1936 (scw: Albert DeMond, Sidney Sutherland; dir: Lewis D. Collins)
  *The Mayor's Wife. Silent film: Pyramid, 1922, as His Wife's Husband (scw: Dorothy Farnum; dir: Kenneth Webb)
  *The Millionaire Baby. Silent film: Selig, 1915 (scw: Gilson Willets; dir: Lawrence Marston)
  *A Strange Disappearance. Silent film: Imp, 1915 (scw: Raymond L. Shrock; dir: George A. Lessey)

*GREEN, EDITH PINERO. Ref also: TM. SC: Dearborn V. Pinch, also in title below.
  Perfect Fools. Dutton, 1982 <Havana>

*GREEN, F(REDERICK) L(AWRENCE)
  *Odd Man Out. Film: Two Cities, 1947; released in the U.S. as Gang War (scw: F. L. Green, R. C. Sherriff; dir: Carol Reed). Also: Universal, 1969, as The Lost Man (scw & dir: Robert Alan Aurthur)
  *On the Night of the Fire. Film: GFD, 1939; released in the U.S. as The Fugitive (scw: Brian Desmond Hurst, Patrick Kirwan, Terence Young; dir: Hurst)

*GREEN, GERALD
  The Heartless Light. Scribner, 1961; Longmans, 1962 <L.A.>
  Karpov's Brain. Morrow, 1983; NEL, 1984 <Moscow>

GREEN, HILARY
  The Fidelio Affair. Hale, 1985
  A Woman Called Omega. Hale, 1984

GREEN, HOWARD J. 1893?-1965.
  -The Melody Man. Jacobsen, 1930 (Novelization of film: Columbia, 1930; scw: Howard J. Green; dir: William Neill)

*GREEN, JANET
  Matilda Shouted Fire. Dramatists, 1961 (3-act play.) Film: Universal, 1960, as Midnight Lace; also released as Murder, My Sweet Matilda (scw: Ivan Goff, Ben Roberts; dir: David Miller)
  *Murder Mistaken. (Novelization of Janet Green's play, Gently Does It) Film: Frobisher, 1955, as Cast a Dark Shadow (scw: John Cresswell; dir: Lewis Gilbert)

GREEN, MICHAEL (FREDERICK). 1927-   Ref: CA.
  Four Plays for Coarse Actors. French, 1978 (Four plays, one, "Streuth", a 1-act play, is criminous.)

*GREEN, THOMAS J(OHN). 1946-   . Ref: CA.

GREEN, WALTON (ATWATER). 1881-   .
  Corsair. Doubleday, 1931. Film: United Artists, 1931 (scw: Josephine Lovett; dir: Roland West)

*GREEN, WILLIAM M(ARK)
  The Romanov Connection. Beaufort, 1984; Murray, 1985 <Russ., ca. 1920>

*GREENAN, RUSSELL H(ENRY). Ref: TM.

*GREENBURG, DAN
  *Philly. Film: Farley, 1981, as Private Lessons (scw: Dan Greenburg; dir: Alan Myerson)

*GREENE, FRANCES NIMMO
  *The Devil to Pay. Silent film: Pathe, 1920 (scw: Jack Cunningham; dir: Ernest C. Warde)
  *One Clear Call. <Ala.>

*GREENE, GRAHAM. Ref also: TM. See also: Denis Cannan. Film (based on unidentified ss): New World, 1937, as Four Dark Hours; also released as The Green Cockatoo; and as Race Gang (scw: Edward O. Berkman, Arthur Wimperis; dir: William Cameron Menzies)

*The Basement Room and other stories. Film (from title ss): British Lion, 1948, as The Fallen Idol; released in the U.S. as The Lost Illusion (scw: Graham Greene, Leslie Storm, William Templeton; dir: Carol Reed)
*Brighton Rock. Film: APL, 1947; released in the U.S. as Young Scarface (scw: Graham Greene, Terence Rattigan; dir: John Boulting)
*The Comedians. Film: MGM, 1967 (scw: Graham Greene; dir: Peter Glenville)
*The Confidential Agent. Film: Warner, 1945 (scw: Robert Buckner; dir: Herman Shumlin)
*The End of the Affair. Film: Coronado, 1955 (scw: Lenore Coffee; dir: Edward Dmytryk)
*England Made Me. Film: Hemdale, 1972 (scw: Peter Duffell, Desmond Cory; dir: Duffell)
*A Gun for Sale. Film: Paramount, 1942, as This Gun for Hire (scw: Albert Maltz, W. R. Burnett; dir: Frank Tuttle). Also: Paramount, 1957, as Short Cut to Hell (scw: Ted Berkman, Raphael Blau; dir: James Cagney)
*The Heart of the Matter. Film: London, 1953 (scw: Ian Dalrymple, Lesley Storm; dir: George More O'Ferrell)
*The Honorary Consul. Film: World Film, 1983; released in the U.S. as Beyond the Limit (scw: Christopher Hampton; dir: John Mackenzie)
*The Human Factor. Film: Rank, 1979 (scw: Tom Stoppard; dir: Otto Preminger)
*Loser Takes All. Film: IFP, 1956 (scw: Graham Greene; dir: Ken Annakin)
*The Man Within. Film: Production Film, 1947; released in the U.S. as The Smugglers (scw: Muriel Box, Sydney Box; dir: Bernard Knowles)
*The Ministry of Fear. Film: Paramount, 1944 (scw: Seton I. Miller; dir: Fritz Lang)
*Nineteen Stories. Film (from ss Across the Bridge): IPF, 1957, as Across the Bridge (scw: Guy Elmes, Enis Freeman; dir: Ken Annakin)
*Our Man in Havana. Film: Kingsmead, 1960 (scw: Graham Greene; dir: Carol Reed)
*The Power and the Glory. Film: RKO, 1947, as The Fugitive (scw: Dudley Nichols; dir: John Ford)
*The Quiet American. Film: United Artists, 1957 (scw & dir: Joseph L. Mankiewicz)
*Stamboul Train. Film: TCF, 1934, as Orient Express (scw: Paul Martin, Carl Hovey, Oscar Levant; dir: Martin)
The Tenth Man. Bodley, 1985; Simon, 1985 <Fr., 1945>
*The Third Man. Film: British Lion, 1949 (scw: Graham Greene; dir: Carol Reed)
*Travels with My Aunt. Film: MGM, 1972 (scw: Jay Presson Allen, Hugh Wheeler; dir: George Cukor)

*GREENE, HARRIS (CARL)
Inference of Guilt. Doubleday, 1982; Hale, 1982
The Thieves of Tumbutu. Doubleday, 1968 <Afr.>

*GREENE, JOSIAH E. 1911-1955. Ref: TM.
-A Bridge at Branfield. Macmillan, 1948 <Conn.>

GREENE, L. L.
Sleeping Beauty. Signet, 1982

GREENE, STEVEN. Pseudonym of *John (Thomas) Lutz, q.v.
Exiled! Popular Library, 1982

*GREENE, WARD
*Death in the Deep South. Film: Warner, 1937, as They Won't Forget (scw: Aben Kandel, Robert Rossen; dir: Mervyn LeRoy)

*GREENER, WILLIAM OLIVER. SC: Jo Salis, in both titles.

*GREENFIELD, IRVING A.
Agent Out of Place. Charter, 1982

GREENLEAF, JEANNE M. Lives in Maine.
Above All, Love. Walker, 1984; Star, 1985

*GREENLEAF, STEPHEN (HOWELL). Ref also: TC2, TM. SC: John Marshall Tanner, also in titles marked JT below.
*Death Bed. ... NEL, 1982
The Ditto List. Villard, 1985; Collins, 1985 <L.A.>
Fatal Obsession. Dial, 1983; Hale, 1984 <Ia.> JT
State's Evidence. Dial, 1982; NEL, 1983 <Calif.> JT

*GREENLEE, SAM
*The Spook Who Sat by the Door. Film: United Artists, 1973 (scw: Sam Greenlee, Melvin Clay; dir: Ivan Dixon)

*GREENOUGH, MRS. (SARA DANA LORING)
*In Extremis. Roberts, 1872 (date correction)

GREENWALD, HARRY J.
Knock Twice. Hale, 1981

*GREENWALD, NANCY
*Ladycat. (one word, not two)

GREENWOOD, DUNCAN, 1919-   , and ROBERT KING, 1947-   , q.v. Ref for Greenwood: CA.
Murder by the Book. French, 1982 (Play.)

GREENWOOD, JAMES
-Reminiscences of a Raven. Warne, 1866

GREENWOOD, JOHN. Pseudonym of *John Buxton Hilton, 1921-1986, q.v. SC: Insp. Mosley, in all titles. Set: Eng.
The Missing Mr. Mosley; see Mosley Went to Mow
Mosley by Moonlight. Quartet, 1984; Walker, 1985
Mosley Went to Mow. Quartet, 1985. U.S. title: The Missing Mr. Mosley. Walker, 1985
Murder, Mr. Mosley. Quartet, 1983; Walker, 1983

GREER, GEORGE
Call in the Feds. 1950's (exists?)

GREGG, MARTIN. Pseudonym of *Wilfred (Glassford) McNeilly, q.v.
Dhow Patrol. Hale, 1983; Walker, 1984 <ship>

*GREGOR, MANFRED
*Town Without Pity. Film: United Artists, 1961 (scw: Silvia Reinhardt, Georg Hurdalek; dir: Gottfried Reinhardt)

GREGORY, FRANK. See: Reginald Simpson.

*GREGORY, JACKSON
*Ladyfingers. Silent film: Metro, 1921; also released as Alias Ladyfingers (scw: Lenore J. Coffee; dir: Bayard Veiller)
The Maid of the Mountain. Scribner, 1925 <Calif.>
*Mystery at Spanish Hacienda. Film: Republic, 1944, as The Laramie Trail (scw: J. Benton Cheney)

GRENIER, RICHARD. 1926-   .
The Marrakesh One-Two. Houghton, 1983; Macdonald, 1984 <Morocco>

GRESHAM, STEPHEN
Rockabye Baby. Zebra, 1984

*GRESHAM, WILLIAM LINDSAY. Ref: TM.
*Nightmare Alley. Film: TCF, 1947 (scw: Jules Furthman; dir: Edmund Goulding)

GRESSON, R. SHELTON
The Strange Adventure of Anelay Moreland. Remington, 1893

*GRETH, LeROMA
*Nightmare! <Fla.>

GRETTON, MARY STURGE
Crumplin! Benn, 1932 <1491, Eng.>

*GREX, LEO. Pseudonym of Leonard (Reginald) Gribble, 1908-1985, q.v.
Hot Ice. Hale, 1983
*Stolen Death. Film: 20th Century, 1939, as Inspector Hornleigh on Holiday (scw: Frank Launder, Sidney Gilliat; dir: Walter Forde)

GREY, CHRIS
Wake Up and Die. Cooperbooks, 1952

*GREY, HARRY. Ref: TM.
*The Hoods. Film: Ladd, 1984, as Once Upon a Time in America (scw: Leonardo Benvenuti, Piero De Bernardi, Enrico Medioli, Franco Arcalli, Franco Ferrini; dir: Sergio Leone)
*Portrait of a Mobster. Film: Warner, 1961 (scw: Howard Browne; dir: Joseph Pevney)

GREY, JOHN W. See: *Arthur B(enjamin) Reeve.

*GRIBBLE, LEONARD (REGINALD). 1908-1985.
*The Arsenal Stadium Mystery. Film: GFD, 1939 (scw: Thorold Dickinson, Donald Bull; dir: Dickinson)
The Dead Don't Scream. Hale, 1983
Dead End in Mayfair. Hale, 1981

GRIEG, JAN
The Sign of the Flying Fox. Vantage, 1976

*GRIERSON, EDWARD (DOBBYN)
*Reputation for a Song. Film: MGM, 1970, as My Lover, My Son (scw: William Marchant, Jenni Hall, Brian Degas, Tudor Gates; dir: John Newland)

*GRIFFIN, JOHN. SC: Richard Raven, also in title below.
A Flame from Persepolis. Hale, 1981

GRIFFITH, BILL. Pseudonym of *Bill Granger, q.v. Other pseudonym: Joe Gash, q.v.
Time for Frankie Coolin. Random, 1982 <Chi.>

GRIFFITHS, ELLA
Murder on Page Three. Quartet, 1984

GRIFFITHS, JOHN. 1942-   .
A Loyal and Dedicated Servant. Playboy, 1981
The Memory Man. Playboy, 1981

GRIFFITHS, JOHN C(HARLES). 1934-   . Ref: CA.
The Queen of Spades. Deutsch, 1983 <Afghan.>

GRIMES, MARTHA. Ref: CA, TM. SC: Insp. Richard Jury, in all titles. Set: Eng.
The Anodyne Necklace. Little, 1983; Little (London), 1984
The Deer Leap. Little, 1985
The Dirty Duck. Little, 1984; O'Mara, 1986
Help the Poor Struggler. Little, 1985
Jerusalem Inn. Little, 1984
The Man with a Load of Mischief. Little, 1981
The Old Fox Deceiv'd. Little, 1982; Little (London), 1982

GRIMWOOD, KEN
The Voice Outside. Doubleday, 1982 <La.>

*GRINDAL, RICHARD. Pseudonym: Richard Grayson, q.v.

GRISMAN, ARNOLD
The Winning Streak. St. Martin's, 1985

GROSS, JOEL. 1951-   . Ref: CA.
-This Year in Jerusalem. Putnam, 1983; Piatkus, 1984 <Jerus.>

*GROSS, LAURENCE and *EDWARD CHILDS CARPENTER
*Whistling in the Dark. Film: MGM, 1933 (scw & dir: Elliott Nugent). Also: MGM, 1941 (scw: Robert MacGunigle, Harry Clork, Albert Mannheimer; dir: S. Sylvan Simon)

GROSS, LEONARD. See: *Pierre (Emile George) Salinger.

GROSS, MICHAEL ROBERT. 1952-   . Joint pseudonym with Stephen Demorest, 1949-   : D. g. Devon, q.v.

*GROSSBACH, ROBERT
*...And Justice for All. (Novelization of film: Columbia, 1979; scw: Valerie Curtin, Barry Levinson; dir: Norman Jewison)
*The Cheap Detective. (Novelization of film: Columbia, 1978; scw: Neil Simon; dir: Robert Moore)

GROSSMAN, ARNOLD. See: Richard Lamm.

*GRUBB, DAVIS (ALEXANDER)
   *Fool's Parade. Film: Columbia, 1971;
    released in Britain as Dynamite Man
    from Glory Jail (scw: James Lee
    Barrett; dir: Andrew V. McLaglen).
   *The Night of the Hunter. Film: United
    Artists, 1955 (scw: James Agee;
    dir: Charles Laughton)
   *Shadow of My Brother. criminous
    <South>

*GRUBER, FRANK. Ref also: TM.
   *Beagle Scented Murder. Rinehart, 1946
    (date correction)
   *Brass Knuckles. Film (from ss "Dog
    Show Murder"): Paramount, 1939, as
    Death of a Champion (scw: Stuart
    Palmer, Cortland Fitzsimmons; dir:
    Robert Florey)
   *The French Key. Film: Republic, 1946
    (scw: Frank Gruber; dir: Walter
    Colmes)
   *The Lock and the Key. Film: RKO,
    1957, as Man in the Vault
    (scw: Burt Kennedy; dir: Andrew
    V. McLaglen)
   *Simon Lash, Private Detective. Film:
    Pathe, 1946, as Accomplice (scw:
    Irving Elman, Frank Gruber; dir:
    Walter Colmes)
   *Twenty Plus Two. Film: Allied
    Artists, 1961; released in Britain
    as It Started in Tokyo (scw: Frank
    Gruber; dir: Joseph M. Newman)

GUARE, JOHN. 1938-   . Ref: CA.
    Landscape of the Body. Dramatists,
    1978 (3-act play.) <NYC>

*GUILD, NICHOLAS (M.). SC: Ray Guin-
    ness, also in title marked RG
    below.
    The Berlin Warning. Putnam, 1984;
    Collins, 1985 <1941>
    Chain Reaction. St. Martin's, 1983
    <1944>
    The Favor. St. Martin's, 1981; Hale,
    1983 <Amst.> RG
    The Linz Tattoo. McGraw, 1985;
    Piatkus, 1986
    Old Acquaintance. ... Magnum, 1982
    The President's Man. St. Martin's,
    1982 <Wash. D.C.>

*GULL, C(YRIL ARTHUR EDWARD) RANGER
   *The Lost Judge. Silent film (?):
    Barker, 1919, as The Disappear-
    ance of the Judge (dir: Alexander
    Butler)

GULLIVER, NICOL
    Floating on an Ice Cloud. New Hori-
    zon, 1983

*GUNN, JAMES (EDWARD)
   *Deadlier Than the Male. Film: RKO,
    1947, as Born to Kill (scw: Eve
    Greene, Richard Macaulay; dir:
    Robert Wise). Also: Films du
    Semaphore, 1986, as Corps et
    Biens (With All Hands) (scw &
    dir: Benoit Jacquot)

*GUNN, JAMES (EDWIN)
    Star Bridge, with Jack Williamson.
    Gnome, 1955 <future>

*GUNN, VICTOR
   *Ironsides Sees Red. Collins, 1943
   *Murder on Ice. (three novelets)
   *Road to Murder. (three novelets)
   *Three Dates with Death. (three
    novelets)

GUNNING, WID
    The Hawk's Nest. Jacobsen, 1928
    (Novelization of silent film:
    First National, 1928; scw: James
    T. O'Donohoe; dir: Benjamin
    Christiansen)

*GUNTER, ARCHIBALD CLAVERING
   *Mr. Barnes of New York. Silent film:
    Vitagraph, 1914 (scw: Eugene
    Mullin; dir: Maurice Costello,
    Robert Gaillord). Also: Goldwyn,
    1921, as Vendetta (scw: George
    Jacoby, Leo Lasko; dir: Jacoby).
    Also: Goldwyn, 1922 (scw: Gerald
    Duffy; dir: Victor Schertzinger)
   *Mr. Potter of Texas. Home, 1887
    (publisher correction) Silent
    film: San Antonio, 1922 (scw:
    George Rader; dir: Leopold
    Wharton)
   *The Surprises of an Empty Hotel.
    Silent film: Vitagraph, 1916 (scw:
    Jasper E. Brady; dir: Theodore
    Marston)

*GURR, DAVID
    A Woman Called Scylla. Viking, 1981
GUTCHEON, BETH (RICHARDSON). 1945-
    Ref: CA.
    Still Missing. Putnam, 1981; Joseph,
    1981 <Boston> Film: TCF, 1983, as
    Without a Trace (scw: Beth
    Gutcheon; dir: Stanley R. Jaffe)

*GUTHRIE, A(LFRED) B(ERTRAM), JR. Ref
    also: TM. SC: Sheriff Chick
    Charleston, also in title below.
    Playing Catch-Up. Houghton, 1985
    <Mont.>

GUTHRIE, THOMAS ANSTEY. 1856-1934.
    Pseudonym: F. Anstey, q.v.

GUY, DAVID. 1948-   . Ref: CA.
    The Man Who Loved Dirty Books. NAL,
    1983

*GWINN, WILLIAM R. Pseudonym:
   *William Bannister.

GWYN, ANNE BAXTER
    In a Turkish Garden. Greening, 1910

*GWYNNE, P. N.
    Pushkin Shove. Dutton, 1984

*HABE, HANS
   *Agent of the Devil. Film: Dalton,
    1962, as The Devil's Agent (scw:
    Robert Westerby; dir: John Paddy
    Carstairs)

*HACKETT, WALTER
   *The Barton Mystery. Silent film:
    Stoll, 1920 (scw: R. Byron-Webber;
    dir: Harry Roberts). Sound film:
    B&D, 1932 (dir: Henry Edwards)
    Captain Applejack. French, 1925
    (Play.) Silent film: Mayer, 1923,
    as Strangers of the Night (scw:
    Bess Meredyth; dir: Fred Niblo).
    Sound film: Warner, 1931 (scw:
    Maude Fulton; dir: Hobart Henley)
   *The Fugitives. Film: TCF, 1937, as
    Love Under Fire (scw: Gene Fowler,
    Allen Rivkin, Ernest Pascal; dir:
    George Marshall)
   *The Gay Adventure. Film: Grosvenor,
    1936 (scw: D. B. Wyndham Lewis;
    dir: Sinclair Hill)
    Other Men's Wives. French, 1929
    (Play.) Film: First National,
    1930, as Sweethearts and Wives
    (scw: Forrest Halsey; dir: Clarence
    Badger)
   *Road House. Film: Gaumont, 1934 (scw:
    Austin Melford, Leslie Arliss; dir:
    Maurice Elvey)
    77, Park Lane. Film: Famous Players,
    1931 (scw: Michael Powell, Reginald
    Berkeley). Also: Albert de Cour-
    ville). Also: United Artists,
    1931, as 77 Rue Chalgrin (scw: A.
    Seabourne; dir: Albert de
    Courville)
    Sorry You've Been Troubled. French,
    1931 (3-act play.) Novelization:
    Readers Library, 1930. Film: B&D
    Paramount, 1932; also released as
    Life Goes On (dir: Jack Raymond)

*HACKETT, WALTER ANTHONY
    Air Tight Alibi. Baker, 1945 (1-act
    play.)

*HACKSTAFF, RICHARD
   *Tracked by a Pin. Street, 1903 (Mag-
    net #295)

HADLEY, J. B. Both titles are in the
    Point Team series.
    The Point Team. Warner, 1984; Warner
    (London), 1985
    Viper Squad. Warner, 1985

*HAEDRICH, MARCEL
   *Crack in the Mirror. Film: TCF, 1960
    (scw: Mark Canfield; dir: Richard
    Fleischer)

HAGAN, CHET. 1922-   . Pseudonym:
    Colin John, q.v.

HAGAN, PATRICIA. Pseudonym of Patricia
    Hagan Howell, 1939-   . Ref: CA.
    Dark Journey Home. Avon, 1983 <Fla.>
    Winds of Terror. Avon, 1983 <Ala.>

HAGAR, JUDITH. Lives in Portugal.
    Shadow of the Eagle. Hale, 1982;
    Walker, 1984 <Pol.>

*HAGBERG, DAVID (JAMES). 1941-
    Pseudonyms: David Bannerman,

    *Robert Pell, *Eric Ramsey, qq.v.
    See also: *Nick Carter. Ref: CA.
    The Heartland. Pinnacle, 1983
    Heroes. Tor, 1985

*HAGEN, LORINDA
    Winter Roses. Leisure, 1985 <Nev.>

*HAGEN, MIRIAM-ANN. 1903-1984.

*HAGENBACH, KEITH
    The Fat Cat Affair. Allen, 1982
    The Rat Quotient. Allen, 1981

*HAGER, JEAN
    Terror in the Sunlight. Walker, 1984

*HAGGARD, (SIR) H(ENRY) RIDER. Ref
    also: TM.
   *Mr. Meeson's Will. Silent film:
    Thanhauser, 1915 (dir: Frederick
    Sullivan). Also: Bluebird, 1916,
    as The Grasp of Greed (scw: Ida
    May Park; dir: Joseph De Grasse)

*HAGGARD, RAYMOND (GORDON RIDER). Ref:
    CA.

*HAGGARD, WILLIAM. SC: Col. Charles
    Russell, also in at least those
    titles marked CR below.
    The Heirloom. Hodder, 1983
    The Meritocrats. Hodder, 1985
    The Mischief Makers. Hodder, 1982;
    Walker, 1982 CR
    The Money Men. Hodder, 1981; Walker,
    1981 CR
    The Need to Know. Hodder, 1984 CR

HAIGH, RAYMOND
    Colder Than the Grave. Hale, 1984
    Death Care. Hale, 1984

HAILEY, HAZEL ROSS
    Lure! Grosset, 1932 <L.I.>

*HAIM, VICTOR. See: *Victor Vicas.

*HAINING, PETER
   *The Hero. <future>

*HALE, CHRISTOPHER
   *Dead of Winter. ... Boardman, 1943.
    Not the same as: Going, Going,
    Gone
   *Going, Going, Gone. Published only
    in England. <Ohio>

*HALE, JENNIFER
   *House of Strangers. Lancer, 1972
    (publisher correction)
    The Secret of Devil's Cave. Lancer,
    1973 <Calif.>

*HALE, JOHN (BARRY)
    The Whistle Blower. Cape, 1984;
    Atheneum, 1985. Film: Portreeve,
    1986 (scw: Julian Bond; dir:
    Simon Langton)

HALEY, ANDREA
    The Velvet Shadows of Justin Wood.
    Zebra, 1982

HALEY, RICHARD
    The Beckford Don. Hale, 1984

HALFF, ALMA MURPHY
    A Ghost on the Loose. Baker, 1948
    (3-act play.)

*HALIDOM, M. Y.
   *A Son of Desolation. <Sp.>
   -A Weird Transformation. Burleigh,
    1904

HALKIN, JOHN
    Fatal Odds. Hale, 1981; Leisure, 1981

*HALL, ADAM. SC: Quiller, also in the
    titles below.
   *The Berlin Memorandum. Film: Foxwell,
    1966, as The Quiller Memorandum
    (scw: Harold Pinter; dir: Michael
    Anderson)
    Northlight. Allen, 1985. U.S. title:
    Quiller. Tor, 1985 <Russ.>
    The Pekin Target. Collins, 1981;
    Playboy, 1982, as The Peking
    Target <Far East>
    Quiller; see Northlight

*HALL, ANGUS
   *The Late Boy Wonder. Film: New Realm,
    1970, as Three in a Cellar; re-
    leased in the U.S. as Up in the
    Cellar (scw & dir: Theodore J.
    Flicker)
   *Live Like a Hero. criminous
   *Qualtrough. Film: AIP, 1974, as

Madhouse (scw: Greg Morrison, Ken
Levison; dir: Jim Clark
Self-Destruct. Severn, 1985

HALL, BOB and DAVID RICHMOND
The Passion of Dracula. French, 1979
(3-act play based on *Dracula by
*Bram Stoker.) <Eng., 1911>

*HALL, DOUGLAS. Born, educated and
living in Toronto; graduate in
business of Univ. of Toronto; has
worked in TV, been a free-lance
writer, and an information representative for IBM.

HALL, EMMETT CAMPBELL
-The Beloved Adventurer. Lubin, 1914
(Novelization of silent film:
Lubin, 1914; scw: Emmett Campbell
Hall; dir:, Joseph Smiley, John
Ince)
The Exposure of Land Swindlers.
Kalem, 1913 (3-act play.)

HALL, HOWARD
-The Waif's Paradise. Ogilvie, 1904
(Novelization of unpublished play.)

*HALL, HOLWORTHY
The Valiant, with Robert M. Middle-
mass. French, 1925 (1-act
play.) Film: Fox, 1929 (scw: John
Hunter Booth, Tom Barry; dir:
William K. Howard, in both titles.
Also: TCF, 1940, as The Man Who Wouldn't Talk
(scw: Robert Ellis, Helen Logan,
Lester Ziffren, Edward Ettinger;
dir: David Burton)

HALL, JENNI(FER ANTOINETTE)
*Ask Agamemnon. Film: Shaftel, 1970,
as Goodbye Gemini (scw: Edmund
Ward; dir: Alan Gibson)

HALL, UNITY
Passage Through Midnight. Pinnacle,
1984

*HALL, WARNER
*Even Jericho. <Alaska>

*HALLAHAN, WILLIAM H(ENRY). Ref: CA,
TM.
The Trade. Morrow, 1981; Gollancz,
1981 <Ger.>

HALLERAN, TUCKER. President of marketing consulting firm in Fla. SC:
Cam MacCardle, in both titles.
A Cool Clear Death. St. Martin's,
1984 <Fla.>
Sudden Death Finish. St. Martin's,
1985 <Fla.>

*HALLIDAY, BRETT. Ref also: TM.
*Murder Is My Business. Film: PRC,
1946 (scw: Fred Myton; dir:
Sam Newfield)
*The Private Practice of Michael
Shayne. Film: TCF, 1940, as Michael
Shayne, Private Detective (scw:
Stanley Rauh, Manning O'Connor;
dir: Eugene Forde)
*Target: Mike Shayne. (misspelling
corrected)

*HALLIDAY, DOROTHY. See: Dorothy
Dunnett. Ref also: TM.

*HALLIDAY, FRED
Ambler. Simon, 1983 <NYC>

*HALLIDAY, MICHAEL
*Cat and Mouse. Film: Anvil, 1958;
also released as The Desperate Men
(scw & dir: Paul Rotha)
*Murder in the Stars. ... World, 1972,
as by John Creasey

HALLIFAX, PEGGY
Ma's Bar. Deane, 1957; Baker, 1957
(1-act play.)

HALLIWELL, LESLIE. 1929-   . Ref: CA.
The Ghost of Sherlock Holmes. Granada pb, 1984; Academy Chicago,
1984   ss

HALLSTEAD, WILLIAM FINN. 1924-   .
Pseudonym: William Beechcroft, q.v.

*HALSEY, FORREST
*The Stain. Silent film: Eclectic,
1914 (dir: Frank Powell)

HAMBLY, BARBARA
The Quirinal Hill Affair. St. Martin's, 1983   <Rome, 116 A.D.>

HAMBY, WILLIAM H(ENRY). 1876-   .
The Seventh Hunch. Hutchinson, 1925

HAMES, ARTHUR CAXTON. Pseudonym (?):
*Moray Dalton.

*HAMILL, DENIS. 1951-   . Ref: CA.
Machine. Delacorte, 1984   <NYC>
*Stomping Ground. ... NEL pb, 1984

*HAMILL, PETE. Ref also: TM.
The Guns of Heaven. Bantam, 1983
<NYC>

*HAMILTON, ADAM
*The Wyss Pursuit.   <Far East>

*HAMILTON, ALISTAIR
Holding Pattern. Hamlyn, 1981

*HAMILTON, (ARTHUR DOUGLAS) BRUCE.
1900-1974. Ref also: CA.
*The Brighton Murder Trial. <future:
1940s>

*HAMILTON, CLARE
Seadrift House. Tower, 1981

HAMILTON, COSMO.   -1942.
-The Princess of New York. Bren-
tano's, 1911; Hutchinson, 1911.
Silent film: Famous Players, 1921
(scw: Margaret Turnbull; dir:
Donald Crisp)

*HAMILTON, DONALD (BENGTSSON). Ref
also: TM. SC: Matt Helm, also in
new titles below.
*The Ambushers. ... Muller, 1964
(British publisher correction).
Film: Columbia, 1967 (scw: Herbert
Baker; dir: Henry Levin)
The Annihilators. GM, 1983 <S. Am.>
*Assignment: Murder. Film: United
Artists, 1957, as Five Steps to
Danger (scw & dir: Henry S.
Kessler)
*Death of a Citizen; see *The Silen-
cers
The Detonators. GM, 1985; Futura,
1986
The Infiltrators. GM, 1984
*Murderer's Row. Film: Columbia, 1966
(scw: Herbert Baker; dir: Henry
Levin)
*Night Walker. Film: Columbia, 1954,
as Rough Company (existence of
film not confirmed)
The Revengers. GM, 1982
*The Silencers. Film: Columbia, 1966
(based also on *Death of a Citi-
zen) (scw: Oscar Saul; dir: Phil
Karlson)
*The Wrecking Crew. Film: Columbia,
1968 (scw: William P. McGivern;
dir: Phil Karlson)

HAMILTON, KELLY
Trixie True, Teen Detective. French,
19??   (3-act play.)

HAMILTON, NAN. Pseudonym of Patricia
Ball. Wife of *John (Dudley)
Ball (Jr.), q.v. Ref: TM.
Killer's Rights. Walker, 1984;
Hale, 1986   <L.A.>

*HAMILTON, (ANTHONY WALTER) PATRICK.
Ref also: CA.
*Gas Light. <Eng., 1800s> Film: Bri-
tish National, 1940; released in
the U.S. as Angel Street (scw: A.
R. Rawlinson, Briget Boland; dir:
Thorold Dickinson). Also: MGM,
1944; released in Britain as The
Murder in Thornton Square (scw:
John Van Druten, Walter Reisch,
John L. Balderston; dir: George
Cukor)
*Hangover Square. Film: TCF, 1945
(scw: Barre Lyndon; dir: John
Brahm)
*Money with Menaces, and To the Public
Danger. Film (of second play): Gen-
eral Film, 1948 (scw: T. J. Morri-
son, Arthur Reid; dir: Terence
Fisher)
*Rope. Film: Warner, 1948 (scw: Arthur
Laurents; dir: Alfred Hitchcock)

HAMILTON, WILLIAM. 1939-   . Ref: CA.
The Charlatan. Simon, 1985; Weidenfeld, 1986

HAMIZRACHI, YORAM. 1942-   . Ref: CA.
The Golden Lion and the Sun. Dutton,
1982 <Iran>   (Translation from
the Hebrew.)

HAMMAN, HENRY (LONGLEY). 1946-
Ref: CA.
Lapis. Academy Chicago, 1984
<Afghan.>

*HAMMETT, (SAMUEL) DASHIELL. Ref also:
TM.
*The Glass Key. Film: Paramount, 1935
(scw: Kathryn Scola, Kubec Glasmon;
dir: Frank Tuttle). Also: Para-
mount, 1942 (scw: Jonathan Latimer;
dir: Stuart Heisler)
*The Maltese Falcon. Film: Warner,
1931 (scw: Maude Fulton, Lucien
Hubbard, Brown Holmes; dir: Roy del
Ruth). Also: Warner, 1936, as Satan
Met a Lady (scw: Brown Holmes; dir:
William Dieterle). Also: Warner,
1941 (scw & dir: John Huston)
*Red Harvest. Film: Paramount, 1930,
as Roadhouse Nights (scw: Garrett
Fort; dir: Hobart Henley)
*The Thin Man. Film: MGM, 1934 (scw:
Albert Hackett, Frances Goodrich;
dir: W. S. Van Dyke)

*HAMMIL, JOEL. 1909-   Ref: CA.

HAMMOND, CLARKE. Pseudonym of *Sam(uel
Kimball) Merwin, Jr.
-So Violent My Love. Brandon, 1966
<NYC>

*HAMMOND, GERALD (ARTHUR DOUGLAS).
Ref: CA. SC: Keith Calder, in
*Dead Game, *The Reward Game, and
in those marked KC below. Set for
*Dead Game: Scot.
Cousin Once Removed. Macmillan (Lon-
don), 1984; St. Martin's, 1984 KC
<Scot.>
Fair Game. Macmillan (London), 1982;
St. Martin's, 1982 <Scot.>   KC
Fred in Situ. Hodder, 1965
The Game. Macmillan (London), 1982;
St. Martin's, 1983 <Scot.>   KC
Pursuit of Arms. Macmillan (London),
1985; St. Martin's, 1986 KC
<Scot.>
The Revenge Game. Macmillan (London),
1981; St. Martin's, 1981 KC <Scot.>
Sauce for the Pigeon. Macmillan (Lon-
don), 1984; St. Martin's, 1985 KC
<Scot.>

*HAMMOND, MARC
The Spandau Wager. Futura, 1981
*The Theseus Code. ... Jove, 1984
<Crete, 1943, 1978>

HAMMOND, MARY ANN
Land of Gold. PB, 1984 <S.F., 1800s>

HAMMONDS, MICHAEL (GALEN). 1942-
Ref: CA.
The OPEC Objective. Tower, 1981
<Calif.>

HAMMONS, CORNEL I. California-born
poet.
Looking for a Kidnapper. Vantage,
1984

HAMRICK, SAMUEL J., JR. 1929-
Pseudonym: *W. T. Tyler, q.v.

*HANCOCK, HARRIE I(RVING). Pseudonym:
Richard Ashton Wainwright, q.v.
*Inspector Henderson, the Central
Office Detective. Ogilvie, 1891
<Boston>

*HANDLEY, ALFRED
The Vortex Assignment. Hale, 1981

HANEY, RICHARD
Maelstrom. Corgi, 1982

HANNA, DAVID. 1917-   . Ref: CA.
The Opera House Murders. Leisure,
1985 <theatre>

*HANNA, FRANCES NICHOLS. Pseudonym
also: *Nikki Content, q.v.

HANNA, STEVE
Angela. Hale, 1983

*HANNAH, BARRY. 1942-   . Ref: CA.
*Nightwatchman. <Miss., acad.>

HANNIBAL, EDWARD. 1936-   . Ref: CA.
A Trace of Red. Dial, 1982

*HANNON, EZRA
*Doors. Reprinted as by Ed McBain:
Warner, 1976

*HANSEN, JOSEPH. Ref also: BM, TM.
Pseudonym also: James Colton, q.v.
SC: Dave Brandstetter, also in

those marked DB.
Backtrack. Countryman, 1982 <L.A.>
Brandstetter and Others. Foul Play, 1984 ss, some about DB
Gravedigger. Holt, 1982; Owen, 1982 <L.A.>
Nightwork. Holt, 1984; Owen, 1984 DB
Steps Going Down. Countryman, 1985; Arlington, 1986 <Calif.>
*Stranger to Himself. (published under Colton byline, q.v.)

*HANSEN, ROBERT P(OWELL)
*Walk a Wicked Mile. (title correction)

*HANSHEW, THOMAS W. Ref also: CA.
*The World's Finger. <Eng.>

HANSL, ARTHUR
Freeze-Frame. Signet, 1985

*HANSOM, MARK
*The Shadow on the House. ... Godwin, 1935

*HANSON, V. J. Byline also: *Vic J. Hanson. See also: *Duke Linton, *Brad Shannon, *Hyman Zore.

*HANSON, VIC J. Byline also: *V. J. Hanson. See also: *Duke Linton, *Brad Shannon, *Hyman Zore.

*HARCOURT, PALMA. Joint pseudonym with husband Jack H. Trotman: John Penn, q.v.
*Climate for Conspiracy. ... Jove, 1986
-A Cloud of Doves. Collins, 1985
*Dance for Diplomats. ... Jove, 1986
The Distant Stranger. Collins, 1984; Beaufort, 1984
Shadows of Doubt. Collins, 1983; Beaufort, 1985
*A Sleep of Spies. ... Jove, 1986
A Turn of Traitors. Collins, 1981; Scribner, 1982
The Twisted Tree. Collins, 1982 <Afr., W.>

*HARDIN, PETER. Pseudonym of Louis Charles Vaczek, 1913-1983.

*HARDING, HARRY
*The Hawk of Rede. Silent film: Ideal, 1923, as Hutch Stirs 'Em Up (scw: Eliot Stannard; dir: Frank H. Crane)

HARDING, MIKE
Killer Budgies. Robson, 1983

HARDING, RICHARD. Pseudonym of *Robert Tine, q.v. SC: Bonner (Outrider), in all titles. Set: future.
Bay City Burnout. Pinnacle, 1985 <Calif.>
Blood Highway. Pinnacle, 1984
Fire and Ice. Pinnacle, 1984
The Outrider. Pinnacle, 1984

HARDING, WADE GARRISON. Pseudonym: *Wade Garrison.

*HARDINGE, REX
*Beyond the Skyline. <Afr.>
*The Blazing Launch Murder. Film: Fox British, 1935, as Sexton Blake and the Bearded Doctor (dir: George A. Cooper)

HARDWICK, ELIZABETH
The Simple Truth. Harcourt, 1955; Weidenfeld, 1955

*HARDWICK, (JOHN) MICHAEL (DRINKROW). SC: Bergerac, in title marked B below; see also: Andrew Saville.
Bergerac. BBC, 1981; St. Martin's, 1982 B (Novelization of the TV series.)
The Chinese Detective. BBC pb, 1981
The Private Life of Dr. Watson. Weidenfeld, 1985; Dutton, 1983 <Past>
*The Private Life of Sherlock Holmes. (Novelization of film: United Artists, 1970; scw: Billy Wilder, I. A. L. Diamond; dir: Wilder)
Sherlock Holmes: My Life and Crimes. Harvill, 1984; Doubleday, 1984

*HARDWICK, MOLLIE. SC: Insp. Jean Darblay, in *Juliet Bravo, and in title below.
Calling Juliet Bravo. BBC, 1981 (Novelization of the TV series.)

*HARDY, IZA DUFFUS
*A New Othello. White, 1890 (date correction)

*HARDY, J(OCELYN) L(EE)
*Everything Is Thunder. Film: Gaumont, 1936 (scw: Marion Dix, John Orton; dir: Milton Rosmer)
*Recoil. <Ger.>

*HARDY, LINDSAY
*Requiem for a Redhead. Film: Anglo Amalgamated, 1962, as Million Dollar Manhunt (existence of film not confirmed)

*HARDY, ROBIN and *ANTHONY (JOSHUA) SHAFFER, q.v.
*The Wicker Man. Film: British Lion, 1973 (scw: Anthony Shaffer; dir: Robin Hardy)

*HARDY, RONALD (HAROLD)
*The Face of Jalanath. <Far East>
Rivers of Darkness. Putnam, 1979; H. Hamilton, 1979 <Mozam.>

*HARDY, WILLIAM M(ARION)
*Lady Killer. Reprinted as: Malice Domestic. Detective Book Club, 1957

*HARE, CYRIL. Ref also: CA, TM.
*Best Detective Stories of Cyril Hare. Also published as: Death Among Friends and other detective stories. Perennial, 1984

HARE, DAVID. 1947-   . Ref: CA.
Knuckle. Faber, 1974 (3-act play.)

HARING, FIRTH. 1937-   . Ref: CA.
Greek Revival. Dutton, 1985 <N.Y.>
The Woman Who Went Away. Holt, 1981; Severn, 1985

*HARKINS, STERLING. Pseudonym of Danny Pyles.

HARMAN, NEAL
Blackmail Incorporated. Hale, 1983
Carlos Is Dead. Hale, 1984
Fall Guy. Hale, 1981

HARPER, DANIEL. Pseudonym of Chandler Brossard, 1922-   . Ref: CA.
The Wrong Turn. Avon, 1954

*HARPER, DAVID
*Hijacked. Film: MGM, 1972, as Skyjacked (scw: Stanley R. Greenberg; dir: John Guillermin)

HARPER, EDWARD M. Pseudonym: Edward McGhee. See: *Robin Moore.

*HARPER, HENRY G.
*The Silent Stranger. Street, 1903

*HARPER, OLIVE
It's Never Too Late to Mend. Ogilvie, 1907 <NYC>
The Queen of the Outlaw's Camp. Ogilvie, 1909
The Shoemaker. Ogilvie, 1907
Tony, the Bootblack. Ogilvie, 1907

*HARPER, RICHARD. Ref also: TM.
*Death to the Dancing Masters. ... Hale, 1985
The Kill Factor. GM, 1983; Hale, 1983 <Ariz.>

HARPUR, PATRICK. 1950-   . Ref: CA.
The Serpent's Circle. Macmillan (London), 1985; St. Martin's, 1985 <church>

*HARRAGAN, STEVE
*Cuban Heel. <Havana>
*Sin Is a Redhead. <NYC>

HARRELL, ANDREW
Kickback. Hale, 1984
Rivermist. Hale, 1983
A Touch of Jade. Hale, 1985
Trailersnatch! Hale, 1983
The Twin Bridges Murder. Hale, 1982

*HARRINGTON, JOSEPH. Ref: not in TC2.
*The Last Known Address. Film: Valoria, 1970, as Dernier Domicile Connu (Last Known Address) (scw & dir: Jose Giovanni)

*HARRINGTON, JOYCE. Ref also: TM.
Family Reunion. St. Martin's, 1982; Severn, 1983 <South>

*HARRINGTON, R(OBERT) E(DWARD)
-The Doomsday Game. Secker, 1981
Aswan High, with James A. Young. Secker (London & U.S.), 1983 <Egypt, 1984>

*HARRINGTON, WILLIAM
The English Lady. Seaview, 1982; Severn, 1984 <Ger., 1931-WWII>
*Mister Target. <NYC>
*Partners. <Tex.>
*The Power. <Ohio>
Skin Deep. Putnam, 1983 <Conn.>

HARRIOTT, TED <EDWIN THOMAS HARRIOTT>. 1933-   . Ref: CA.
No Sanctuary. Secker, 1983

*HARRIS, A. L.
*The Fatal Request. Street, 1902 (Magnet #253)

*HARRIS, ALFRED
*Baroni. Film: GEF, 1980, as Pile ou Face (Heads or Tails) (scw: Robert Enrico, Marcel Julian, Michel Audiard; dir: Enrico)

HARRIS, CHARLAINE. 1951-   . Ref: CA, TM.
Dead Dog; see Sweet and Deadly
A Secret Rage. Houghton, 1984; Severn, 1984 <South>
Sweet and Deadly. Houghton, 1981. British title: Dead Dog. Hale, 1982 <La.>

*HARRIS, CHARLES AVERY
-Broad Players. Holloway, 1983
Fast Track. Holloway, 1978
*Macking Gangster. (title correction) <Balt>

HARRIS, DAVID (VICTOR). 1946-   . Ref: CA.
The Last Scam. Delacorte, 1981 <Mex.>

*HARRIS, ELMER BANEY
*Johnny Belinda. French, 1956

*HARRIS, EVELYN
The Black Candle. Hale, 1983
Deadly Green. Hale, 1981; St. Martin's, 1981
The Disposal Job. Hale, 1984
From Hex to Hemlock. Hale, 1982
Largely Luck. Hale, 1985

*HARRIS, JOHN. Ref also: TC2.
The Fox from His Lair. Hutchinson, 1978; Walker, 1984 <WWII>
A Funny Place to Hold a War. Hutchinson, 1984 <Sierra Leone>
*Road to the Coast. <ship>
*The Sea Shall Not Have Them. Film: Apollo, 1954 (scw: Lewis Gilbert, Vernon Harris; dir: Gilbert)
Up for Grabs. Hutchinson, 1985

*HARRIS, LEONARD
The Hamptons. Wyndham, 1981 <L.I.>
*The Masada Plan. <1979>

*HARRIS, RICHARD
Honor Bound. Marek, 1982. British title (?): Death of a Friend. Severn, 1983 <NYC>

HARRIS, RICHARD. 1934-   . Ref: CA.
The Business of Murder. French, 1981 (Play.)

*HARRIS, THOMAS. Ref: CA, TM.
*Black Sunday. Film: Paramount, 1977 (scw: Ernest Lehman, Kenneth Ross, Ivan Moffat; dir: John Frankenheimer)
Red Dragon. Putnam, 1981; Bodley, 1982. Also published as: Manhunter. Bantam, 1986. Film: De Laurentis, 1986, as Manhunter (scw & dir: Michael Mann)

*HARRIS-BURLAND, J(OHN) B(URLAND)
*The White Rook. Silent film: Paramount, 1920, as His Wife's Friend (scw: R. Cecil Smith; dir: Joseph De Grasse)

*HARRISON, CHIP. Pseudonym of *Lawrence Block, q.v.
*Make Out with Murder. Also published as: The Five Little Rich Girls. Schocken, 1984; Allison, 1984, as by Lawrence Block
*The Topless Tulip Caper. ... Allison, 1984, as by Lawrence Block

HARRISON, CRAIG
  Quiet Earth. Hodder, 1981

*HARRISON, HARRY (MAX). SC: Slippery Jim Di Griz, also in titles marked JD below.
  The Daleth Effect. Faber, 1970; Putnam, 1972
  The Stainless Steel Rat for President. Sphere, 1982; Bantam, 1982 <30th century> JD
  A Stainless Steel Rat Is Born. Sphere, 1985; Bantam, 1985 <30th century> JD

HARRISON, RAY. Educated at Cambridge; worked for some years on fraud squad of the Inland Revenue. SC: Sgt. Joseph Bragg and Constable James Morton, in all titles. Set: Eng., 1890's.
  Death of a Dancing Lady. Quartet, 1985; Scribner, 1986
  Death of an Honourable Member. Quartet, 1984; Scribner, 1985
  Deathwatch. Quartet, 1985; Scribner, 1986
  French Ordinary Murder. Quartet, 1983. U.S. title: Why Kill Arthur Potter? Scribner, 1984
  Why Kill Arthur Potter?; see French Ordinary Murder

*HARRISON, WILLIAM (J.)
  Savannah Blue. Marek, 1981; Severn, 1982 <Afr.>

HARRISS, WILL(ARD IRVIN). 1922-   . Ref: CA.
  The Bay Psalm Book Murder. Walker, 1983; Hale, 1983 <Calif.>

*HART, CAROLYN G(IMPEL)
  Castle Rock. Hale, 1983
  Death by Surprise. Hale, 1983
  -Escape from Paris. Hale, 1982; St. Martin's, 1983 <Paris, 1940>
  The Rich Die Young. Hale, 1983
  Skulduggery. Hale, 1984

*HART, FRANCES (NEWBOLD) NOYES. Ref also: CA, TM.
  *The Bellamy Trial. <N.Y.> Film (partial sound): MGM, 1928 (scw & dir: Monta Bell)

HART, GARY (WARREN). 1936-   . See: William S(ebastian) Cohen, 1940-

HART, J. P.
  The Freemason; or, The Secret of the Lodge Room. Pattie, ca.1839 (2-act play.)

HART, JEFFREY. Pseudonym: *Geoffrey St. George, q.v.

HART, ROY
  A Position of Trust. Hale, 1985; St. Martin's, 1985

*HART, STAN. 1929-   . Ref: CA.

*HART-DAVIS, DUFF
  Fire Falcon. Cape, 1983 <Scot.>
  Level Five. Cape, 1982; Atheneum, 1982 <Ger.>
  -The Man-Eater of Jassapur. Cape, 1985 <India>

HARTE, (FRANCIS) BRET. 1836-1902. Ref: CA.
  Condensed Novels. Second Series. Houghton, 1902; Chatto, 1902 ss, including Sherlockian parody

HARTE, SAMANTHA. Pseudonym of Sandra Lynn Housby, 1948-   . Ref: CA.
  The Snows of Craggmoor. Avon, 1978

HARTLAND, MICHAEL. 1941-   . Ref: CA. SC: David Nairn, in both titles.
  Down Among the Dead Men. Hodder, 1983; Macmillan, 1983 <H. Kong, 1970s>
  Seven Steps to Treason. Hodder, 1984; Macmillan, 1984

HARTLEY, L(ESLIE) P(OLES). 1895-1972.
  The Travelling Grave and other stories. Arkham, 1948; Barrie, 1951 ss, two criminous

*HARTLEY, NORMAN
  Hard Rain. Collins, 1984
  Shadowplay. Collins, 1983; Atheneum, 1982

HARTLEY, REX
  Murder in Mind. Massey, 1957 (3-act play.)

HARTMAN, DANE. House name. SC: Dirty Harry Callahan, in all titles. Those by Richard S. Meyers marked #.
  Blood of the Strangers. Warner, 1982
  City of Blood. Warner, 1982; NEL pb, 1984 <S.F.>
  The Dealer of Death. Warner, 1983
  Death in the Air. Warner, 1983 <S.F.>
  Death on the Docks. Warner, 1981; NEL pb, 1982 <S.F.> (by Leslie Horvitz)
  Duel for Cannons. Warner, 1981; NEL pb, 1982 <S.F.>
  Family Skeletons. Warner, 1982; NEL pb, 1983 <Boston>
  Hatchet Men. Warner, 1982 #
  The Killing Connection. Warner, 1983 #
  The Long Death. Warner, 1981; NEL pb, 1982 #
  Massacre at Russian River. Warner, 1982 <Calif.>
  The Mexico Kill. Warner, 1982; NEL pb, 1983 <Mex.>

*HARTMANN, MICHAEL
  *Game for Vultures. Film: Columbia, 1979 (scw: Philip Baird; dir: James Fargo)

*HARTSHORNE
  Whisper of Treason. Hale, 1981

HARVEY, FRANK, JR. 1885-   .
  Saloon Bar. Deane, 1942 (3-act play.) Film: Ealing, 1940 (scw: Angus MacPhail, John Dighton; dir; Walter Forde)

*HARVEY, JOHN. SC: Scott Mitchell, also in *Neon Madman.
  Blind. Eyre, 1981

HARVEY, JOHN. 1942-   .
  Coup D'Etat. Collins, 1985; Atheneum, 1985 <Greece>

HARVEY, LINDA. Pseudonym: Christina Vail, q.v.

*HARVEY, WILLIAM F(RYER). Ref: TM.
  *The Beast with Five Fingers. Film: Warner, 1947 (scw: Curt Siodmak; dir: Robert Florey)

HARWELL, KING M.
  The Killbride Mystery. Story Book, 1954

HARWOOD, HAROLD MARSH. 1874-   .
  Cynara. Benn, 1930 (3-act play based on *An Imperfect Lover, by *Robert Gore-Brown, q.v.)

HASHIAN, JACK
  Mamigon. Coward, 1982

HASHIAN, JAMES T. ca.1926-   . See: Trevanian.

*HASLUCK, NICHOLAS (P.)
  Bellarmine Jug. Penguin, 1985

HASSLER, JON (FRANCIS). 1933-   . Ref: CA.
  The Love Hunter. Morrow, 1981; Weidenfeld, 1982

HASSLER, KENNETH L. Pseudonym: *Jeananne St. Clair.

HASTINGS, BEVERLY. Joint pseudonym of Carol Barkin and Elizabeth James.
  Don't Walk Home Alone. Jove, 1985 <N.Y.>
  Secrets. Jove, 1983

*HASTINGS, CHARLOTTE
  *Bonaventure. <hosp.> Film: Universal International, 1951; released in the U.S. as Thunder on the Hill (scw: Oscar Brodney, Andrew Solt; dir: Douglas Sirk)

*HASTINGS, MACDONALD. 1909-1982.

*HASTINGS, MICHAEL (GERALD TAILOR)
  *The Nightcomers. (Novelization of film: Scimitar, 1972; scw: Michael Hastings; dir: Michael Winner)

HASTINGS, MICHAEL. Pseudonym of *Michael Bar-Zohar.
  A Spy in Winter. Macmillan, 1984

HASTINGS, PATRICK. 1880-1952.
  The Blind Goddess. French (London), 1948 (3-act play.) Film: Gainsborough, 1948 (scw: Muriel Box, Sydney Box; dir: Harold French) Novel based on film: Allen, 1948

HATFIELD, MICHAEL (VERNON). 1935-   . Ref: CA.
  Spy Fever. Quartet, 1981 <past>

*HATTON, CHARLES
  Much Ado About Mowbray. Long, 1951

*HATTON, JOSEPH
  *John Needham's Double. Silent film: Bluebird, 1916 (scw: Olga Printzlau; dir: Lois Weber, Philipps Smalley)

HATVARY, GEORGE EGON. Ref: CA.
  The Suitor. Avon, 1981 <NYC>

*HAUBOLD, CLEVE (ERNST)
  Sherlock Holmes and the Curious Adventure of the Clockwork Prince. French, 19?? (3-act play.) <London, 1899> (Sherlock Holmes)

*HAUGHEY, THOMAS BRACE. 1943-   . Ref: CA. SC: Geoffrey Weston, also in title below.
  The Case of the Hijacked Moon. Bethany, 1981 <Eng.>

HAUSER, THOMAS. 1946-   . Ref: CA.
  Agatha's Friends. Avon, 1983. British title: Friends. Futura, 1984 <NYC>
  The Beethoven Conspiracy. Macmillan, 1984; Futura, 1985 <NYC>
  Friends; see Agatha's Friends
  Hanneman's War. Ballantine, 1984 <Nepal>

HAUSVATER, ALEXANDER
  The Crime and Punishment Show. Playwrights, 1978 (2-act play based on the novel by *Fedor Mikhailovitch Dostoevskii, q.v.)

HAVARD, LEZLEY
  Hide and Seek. Dramatists, 1980 (3-act play.)

HAWKES, ELLEN. Taught modern literature and women's studies at Stanford and Boston; author of essays and reviews on Virginia Woolf.
  The Shadow of the Moth. Marek, 1983 <London, 1917>

*HAWKEY, RAYMOND
  It. NEL, 1983; Stein, 1986

*HAWKINS, JOHN and *WARD HAWKINS
  *The Floods of Fear. Film: Rank, 1958 (scw: Charles Crichton, Vivienne Knight; dir: Crichton)

*HAWKINS, WARD. See: *John Hawkins.

*HAWTHORNE, NATHANIEL
  *Twice Told Tales. Film (from ss "Dr. Heidegger's Experiment," "Rappacini's Daughter," and "The House of the Seven Gables"): Admiral, 1963, as Twice Told Tales (scw: Robert E. Kent; dir: Sidney Salkow)

*HAY, WILLIAM (GOSSE)
  *The Escape of the Notorious Sir William Heans. <Tas.>
  *The Mystery of Alfred Doubt. <Australia>

*HAYES, JOSEPH (ARNOLD). Ref also: TM.
  *The Deep End. <NYC>
  *The Desperate Hours. Film: Paramount, 1955 (scw: Joseph Hayes; dir: William Wyler)
  No Escape. Delacorte, 1982; Deutsch, 1982 <Fla.>
  *The Third Day. Film: Warner, 1965 (scw: Burton Wohl, Robert Presnell, Jr.; dir: Jack Smight)
  Tomorrow Is Too Late; see The Ways of Darkness
  The Ways of Darkness. Morrow, 1985. British title: Tomorrow Is Too Late. Allen, 1986 <Vt.>

*HAYES, RALPH (EUGENE). See also:
  *Nick Carter.
  Deadly Reunion. Leisure, 1984
  Illegal Entry. Leisure, 1984 <Haiti>
  *The Satan Stone. <S. Afr.>
  The Scorpio Cipher. Leisure, 1983 <Iran>

A Sudden Madness. Tower, 1981
*A Taste for Blood. (title correction)

HAYES, STEPHEN K.
Tulku. Contemporary, 1985 <Japan>

HAYES, STEVE
The Osprey Dilemma. Dell, 1983

*HAYES, WILLIAM EDWARD
*The Black Doll. Film: Universal, 1938 (scw: Harold Buckley; dir: Otis Garrett)

HAYMON, S. T. Ref: TM. Living in Norwich, Eng.; author of biographies, an historical novel, and a history of Norwich. SC: Insp. Ben Jurnet, in *Death and the Pregnant Virgin, and the titles below. Set: Eng.
Ritual Murder. Constable, 1982; St. Martin's, 1982
Stately Homicide. Constable, 1984; St. Martin's, 1984

*HAYNES, BRIAN. 1939-   . Ref: CA. See: *Tom Keene.

*HAYS, LEE
A Deadly State of Mind. Popular Library, 1976 (Novelization of the "Columbo" TV series.)
Once Upon a Time in America. Signet, 1984; Sphere, 1984 (Novelization of the movie; see *Harry Gray.) <NYC, 1933-1968>

*HAYTHORNE, JOHN. Ref: TM. SC: Mandrake, in titles marked M.
Mandrake in Granada. Anderson, 1984 M
Mandrake in the Monastery. Anderson, 1985 M
The Strelsau Dimension. Quartet, 1981

*HAYWARD, DAVID
The Strasbourg Connection. Hale, 1981

*HAZELTINE, HORACE
*The Sable Lorcha. Silent film: Triangle, 1915 (scw: Chester B. Clapp; dir: Lloyd Ingraham)

HAZLEWOOD, C(OLIN) H(ENRY)
The Female Detective. DeWitt, 187? (3-act play.)

*HEAD, (JOANNE) LEE. 1931-1983.

*HEAD, MATTHEW. Pseudonym of John Edwin Canaday, 1907-1985. Ref also: TM.

*HEAL, ANTHONY
Hydra. Sphere, 1982
The Million Cut. Sycamore, 1982

HEALD, AYA
Shadows Under White Face. Vantage, 1956 <N.Y.>

*HEALD, TIM(OTHY VILLIERS). SC: Simon Bognor, also in titles marked SB below.
-Class Distinctions. Hutchinson, 1984
Masterstroke. Hutchinson, 1982. U.S. title: A Small Masterpiece. Doubleday, 1982 <acad.> SB
Murder at Moose Jaw. Hutchinson, 1981; Doubleday, 1981 <Can.> SB
Red Herrings. Macmillan (London), 1985; Doubleday, 1986 SB
A Small Masterpiece; see Masterstroke

*HEALEY, BEN(JAMIN JAMES). Ref also: TM. SC: Paul Hedley, also in at least the title below marked PH; Harcourt d'Espinal, also in at least the title below marked HE.
Last Ferry from the Lido. Hale, 1981. U.S. title: Midnight Ferry to Venice. Walker, 1982 PH & HE <Venice>
Midnight Ferry to Venice; see Last Ferry from the Lido
*Waiting for a Tiger. Film: Trio 1969, as Taste of Excitement (scw: Brian Carton, Don Sharp; dir: Sharp)
The Week of the Scorpion. Hale, 1981

HEALY, J(EREMIAH) M. 1948-   . Lawyer in Boston. Ref: TM.
Blunt Darts. Walker, 1984; Macmillan (London), 1986 <Mass.>

HEARD, GERALD. See: H(enry) F(itzgerald) Heard.

*HEARD, H(ENRY) F(ITZGERALD). Byline for all titles in England: Gerald Heard. Ref also: TM.
*The Great Fog and other weird tales. Also published as: Weird Tales of Terror and Detection. Sun Dial, 1946
*A Taste of Honey. Film: Amicus, 1967, as The Deadly Bees (scw: Robert Bloch, Anthony Marriott; dir: Freddie Francis)
Weird Tales of Terror and Detection; see The Great Fog and other weird tales

*HEARNE, JOHN. 1926-   . Joint pseudonym with *Morris Cargill, 1914-   : John Morris, q.v.

HEATH, CHARLES. Pseudonym of Ron Renauld, q.v. All titles are novelizations of "The A-Team" TV series.
The A-Team. Dell, 1984; Star, 1983 <Mex.>
Old Scores to Settle. Dell, 1984; Target, 1984 <L.A.>
Operation Desert Sun: The Untold Story. Dell, 1984; Target, 1985 <Mid. East>
Small But Deadly Wars. Dell, 1984; Target, 1985 <L.A.>
Ten Percent of Trouble. Dell, 1984; Target, 1984
When You Comin' Back, Range Rider. Dell, 1984; Target, 1984 <Ariz.>

*HEATH, ERIC
*Murder of a Mystery Writer. Arcadia, 1953 (date correction)
*The Murder Pool. <L.A.>

*HEATH, PERCY
*Slightly Scarlet. (Novelization of film: Paramount, 1930; scw: Howard Estabrook, Joseph L. Mankiewicz, Percy Heath; dir: Louis Gasnier)

*HEATH, ROY A(UBREY) K(ELVIN) 1926-   . Ref: CA.

*HEATH, W(ILLIAM) L(EDBETTER)
*Violent Saturday. Film: TCF, 1955 (scw: Sydney Boehm; dir: Richard Fleischer)

*HEATTER, BASIL. (Entry scrambled in first printing of CF, so reproduced here in full correctly, with updates.) 1918-   . Born on L.I., the son of radio commentator Gabriel Heatter; was advertising copywriter in 1970s living on a boat off Fla., and racing and chartering. SC: Timothy Devlin = TD.
*Act of Violence. Lion, 1954 <N.H.>
*Any Man's Girl. GM, 1961; Muller pb, 1962
*-The Better Part of Valor. Doubleday, 1964
*Devlin's Triangle. Pinnacle, 1976 TD <Carib.>
The Einstein Plot. Dell, 1982 <1941>
*The Golden Stag. Pinnacle, 1976 TD <Boston>
*Harry and the Bikini Bandits. GM, 1971
The London Gun. Dell, 1984; Severn, 1985 <WWII>
*The Mutilator. GM, 1962; Muller pb, 1962 <Fr.>
*The Naked Island. Trident, 1968; Hale, 1970 <Bahamas>
*-Sailor's Luck. Lion, 1953
*The Scarred Man. GM, 1973 <Fla.>
*Virgin Cay. GM, 1963; Muller pb, 1964

*HEAVEN, CONSTANCE (FECHER)
-The Ravensley Touch. Heinemann, 1982; Coward, 1982
The Wildcliffe Bird. Heinemann, 1981; Coward, 1983

*HEBDEN, MARK. SC: Insp. Clovis Pel, also in all new titles below. Set: Fr.
*Death Set to Music. ... Walker, 1983
*The Eyewitness. Film: Allen, 1970; released in the U.S. as Sudden Terror (scw: Ronald Harwood; dir: John Hough)
Pel and the Bombers. H. Hamilton, 1982; Walker, 1983
*Pel and the Faceless Corpse. ... Walker, 1982
Pel and the Pirates. H. Hamilton, 1984
Pel and the Predators. H. Hamilton, 1984; Walker, 1985
Pel and the Prowler. H. Hamilton, 1985; Walker, 1986
Pel and the Staghound. H. Hamilton, 1982; Walker, 1984
Pel Is Puzzled. H. Hamilton, 1981
*Pel Under Pressure. ... Walker, 1983
*What Changed Charley Farthing. Film: Patina, 1975 (scw: David Pursall, Jack Seddon; dir: Sidney Hayers)

*HEBERDEN, M(ARY) V(IOLET). Ref also: TM.
*To What Dread End. Also published as: The Doctor Was a Lady. (publisher/date?)

HEBERT, ANNE. 1916-   . Ref: CA.
In the Shadow of the Wind. Stoddart (Toronto), 1983; Beaufort, 1984 <Fr., 1936> (Translation of "Les Fous de Basson." Paris, 1982)

*HECHT, BEN. Ref also: TM.
*The Collected Stories of Ben Hecht. Film (from ss "Crime Without Passion"): Paramount, 1934, as Crime Without Passion (scw & dir: Ben Hecht, Charles MacArthur)
*The Florentine Dagger. Film: Warner, 1935 (scw: Tom Reed, Brown Holmes; dir: Robert Florey)
*I Hate Actors. Film: Septembre, 1986, as Je Hais les Acteurs (I Hate Actors) (scw & dir: Gerard Krawozyk)
*1001 Afternoons in New York. Viking, 1941

*HEDDON, JAMES
*Love and Bullets. (Novelization of film: ITC, 1978; scw: Wendell Mayes, John Melson; dir: Stuart Rosenberg)

*HEED, RUFUS
*Ghosts Never Die. <Chi.>

HEELAN, KEVIN
Heartland. French, 1982 (2-act play.) <Midwest>

*HEFFERNAN, WILLIAM (A.)
Caging the Raven. Wyndham, 1981 <Wash. D.C.>
The Corsican. Simon, 1983; Granada, 1983 <Far East>

HEINLEIN, ROBERT A(NSON), 1907-   Ref: CA.
The Unpleasant Profession of Jonathan Hoag. Gnome, 1959; Dobson, 1961 novel and ss, criminous in part

*HELDMAN, GLADYS M. Has been tournament level tennis player, author of many tennis books, founded "World Tennis" magazine, established Virginia Slims and Futures circuits; living in Tex.

HELDMAN, RICHARD B. 1867-1915. Pseudonym: *Richard Marsh, q.v.

HELFER, HAROLD
The Big Hamburger. Vantage, 1956

HELFGOTT, DANIEL. 1952-   . Ref: CA.
The Buried. Avon, 1981 <Peru>

*HELITZER, FLORENCE (SAPERSTEIN)
*Hans, Who Goes There? <Ger.>

*HELLER, FRANK. SC: Mr. Collin, also in *The Grand Duke's Finances.

HELLER, KEITH. 1949-   . Ref: CA. SC: George Man, in both titles.
Man's Illegal Life. Collins, 1985; Scribner, 1985 <London, 1722>
Man's Storm. Collins, 1985; Scribner, 1986 <London, 1703>

HELLERSTEIN, HARRY. 1939-   . Lawyer, graduate of Boston U. and Harvard Law School; federal public defender in S.F.
Wired. St. Martin's, 1982; Severn, 1982 <S.F.>

HELM, ERIC. SC: Mack Gerber (The Scorpion Squad), in all titles, set in Viet Nam.
Body Count. Pinnacle, 1984
Chopper Command. Pinnacle, 1985
The Nhu Sting. Pinnacle, 1984
River Raid. Pinnacle, 1985

*HELM, PETER (JAMES)
The Brainpicker. Hale, 1981

*HELSETH, HENRY EDWARD
*The Chair for Martin Rome. Film: TCF, 1948, as Cry of the City (scw: Richard Murphy; dir: Robert Siodmak). Also: Valoria, 1971, as Un Aller Simple (One Way Ticket) (scw & dir: Jose Giovanni)

*HELVICK, JAMES
*Beat the Devil. Film: Romulus, 1953 (scw: Truman Capote, John Huston; dir: Huston)

*HELWIG, DAVID (GORDON)
-A Sound Like Laughter. Stoddart (Toronto), 1983; Beaufort, 1983 ⟨Can.⟩

HELY, SARA
The Sign of the Serpent. Deutsch, 1984; St. Martin's, 1984 ⟨Ire., 1700s⟩

HEMINGWAY, AMANDA
Tantalus. H. Hamilton, 1984; Arbor, 1984

HEMINGWAY, ERNEST. 1899-1961. Ref: CA.
Men Without Women. Scribner, 1927; Cape, 1928 ss, at least one criminous. Film (from ss "The Killers"): Universal, 1946, as The Killers (scw: Anthony Veiller; dir: Robert Siodmak). Also: Universal, 1964 (scw: Gene L. Coon; dir: Don Siegel)
To Have and Have Not. Scribner, 1937; Cape, 1937. Film: Warner, 1945 (scw: Jules Furthman, William Faulkner; dir: Howard Hawks). Also: Warner, 1950, as The Breaking Point (scw: Ranald MacDougall; dir: Michael Curtiz). Also: United Artists, 1958, as The Gun Runners (scw: Daniel Mainwaring, Paul Monash; dir: Don Siegel)

*HEMINGWAY, JOAN and *PAUL BONNECARRERE
*Rosebud. Film: United Artists, 1975 (scw: Erik Lee Preminger; dir: Otto Preminger)

HENDERSON, DON
Bomb Two. Buchan, 1983

HENDERSON, HAROLD H(ALE). 1928-
Ref: CA.
Queen of Spades. Permanent Press, 1983 ⟨West⟩

*HENDERSON, LAURENCE
*Sitting Target. Film: MGM-EMI, 1972 (scw: Alexander Jacobs; dir: Douglas Hickox)

HENDERSON, M. R. Pseudonym of *Marilyn Granbeck.
If I Should Die. Doubleday, 1985 ⟨Calif.⟩

HENDRICKSON, R. J.
Hear the Children Cry. Leisure, 1981

*HENDRYX, JAMES B(EARDSLEY). Ref: TM.

HENEGE, THOMAS. Pseudonym of Albert F. Gillotti, V.P. of Europe Credit Group of Banker's Trust Company.
A Cargo of Tin; see Death of a Shipowner
Death of a Shipowner. Dodd, 1981; British title: A Cargo of Tin. Deutsch, 1982 ⟨Oslo⟩
Skim. St. Martin's, 1984 ⟨Afr., W.⟩

HENLEY, WALLACE (BOYNTON). 1941-
Ref: CA.
The Roman Solution. Tyndale, 1984 ⟨Wash. D.C.⟩

*HENRY, CHARLES
*The Hostage. Film: Heartland, 1966 (scw: Robert Laning; dir: Russell S. Doughten, Jr.)

*HENRY, JOAN
*Yield to the Night. Film: Kenwood, 1956; released in the U.S. as Blonde Sinner (scw: John Cresswell, Joan Henry; dir: J. Lee Thompson)

*HENRY, O. Ref also: TM.

*HENRY, VERA
*Mystery of Cedar Valley. Also published as: Portrait in Fear. Caravelle, 1967

*HENSLEY, JOE L. Ref also: TC2, TM. SC: Donald Robak, also in titles marked DR below. Set: Ind.
*Color Him Guilty; see The Color of Hate
*The Color of Hate. Revised version: Color Him Guilty. Walker, 1987
Final Doors. Doubleday, 1981 ss
Outcasts. Doubleday, 1981 DR
Robak's Cross. Doubleday, 1985 DR

HENSTELL, DIANA. Pseudonym of Diana Levine, formerly editor-in-chief at NAL.
The Other Side. Bantam, 1984; Fontana, 1984

HENTOFF, NAT(HAN IRVING). 1925- .
Ref: CA. SC: Noah Green, in both titles.
Blues for Charlie Darwin. Morrow, 1982; Constable, 1983 ⟨NYC⟩
The Man from Internal Affairs. Mysterious Press, 1985 ⟨NYC⟩

*HENTY, G(EORGE) A(LFRED). Ref: CA.

HEPPENSTALL, (JOHN) RAYNER. 1911-1981.
Ref: CA.
The Pier. Schocken, 1985 ⟨Eng.⟩

HERALD, HEINZ and GEZA HERCZEG
The Burning Bush. Collier, 1947 (3-act play.) Film: United Artists, 1948, as The Vicious Circle (scw: Heinz Herald, Guy Endore; dir: W. Lee Wilder)

*HERBERT, A(LAN) P(ATRICK)
*The House by the River. Film: Fidelity, 1950 (scw: Mel Dinelli; dir: Fritz Lang)

HERBERT, ALBERT. See: Roger Myers.

*HERBERT, FRANK (PATRICK). 1920-1986.
The White Plague. Berkley, 1983; Gollancz, 1983

*HERBERT, JAMES
-The Jonah. NEL, 1981; Signet, 1981
*The Rats. Film: Northshore, 1982 (scw: Charles Eglee; dir: Robert Clouse)
*The Survivor. Film: Tuesday, 1981 (scw: David Ambrose; dir: David Hemmings)

HERCZEG, GEZA. See: Heinz Herald.

*HERLIN, HANS. 1925- . In journalism and publishing until 1972, full-time book author since; born in Ger., living in Fr.
*Friends. ⟨Ger.⟩
The Last Spring in Paris. Deutsch, 1985; Doubleday, 1985 (Translation of "Der Letzte Fruhling in Paris." Dusseldorf, 1983.) ⟨Paris, 1944⟩
Solo Run. Collins, 1983; Doubleday, 1983 ⟨Ger., ca.1975⟩ (Translation of "Satan Ist auf Gottes Seite.")

*HERMAN, HENRY
Hearts of Gold and Hearts of Steel. Newnes, 1893
*The Sword of Fate. Silent film: Screen Plays, 1921 (scw: Frances E. Grant, Kate Gurney; dir: Grant)

HERMES, MARGARET. Living in St. Louis.
The Phoenix Nest. Contemporary, 1981 ⟨Maine⟩

*HERON-MAXWELL, BEATRICE
The Fifth Wheel, with F(lorence) E(thel) Eastwick. Ward, 1916

*HERRICK, MARIAN J. and *J. TRUMBELL ROGERS
*When Last Seen... ⟨NYC, Paris⟩

HERRICK, WILLIAM. 1915- . Ref: CA.
Love and Terror. New Directions, 1981

HERRING, ROBERT (HERSCHEL). 1938-
Ref: CA.
Hub. Viking, 1981 ⟨Ark.⟩

HERSHEY, JOHN
The Phantom Gentleman. French, 1940 (1-act play.)
The Sign of the Four. French, 1937 (1-act play based on the novel by *A. C. Doyle, q.v.) (Sherlock Holmes)

*HERSHMAN, MORRIS. Pseudonym: Sam Victor, q.v.

*HERTZ, GEORGE
*The Foreign Harry Complot. ⟨Fr., Algiers⟩

HERVEY, EVELYN. Pseudonym of *H(enry) R(eymond) F(itzwalter) Keating, q.v. SC: Harriet Unwin, in both titles.
The Governess. Weidenfeld, 1984; Doubleday, 1983 ⟨Eng., 1870⟩
The Man of Gold. Weidenfeld, 1985; Doubleday, 1985 ⟨Eng., 1874⟩

HESLA, STEPHEN
The Hawthorn Conspiracy. Dembner, 1984 ⟨Guyana⟩

*HESS, KAMELLE
Death Goes to the Bahamas. Laura, 1979 ⟨Bahamas⟩

*HETH, EDWARD HARRIS
*Any Number Can Play. Film: MGM, 1949 (scw: Richard Brooks; dir: Mervyn LeRoy)

HEWLETT, MAURICE (HENRY). 1861-1923.
Ref: CA.
The Spanish Jade. Cassell, 1908; Doubleday, 1908. Silent film: Paramount, 1915 (scw: Josephine Lovett; dir: Tom J. Geraghty)

*HEYER, GEORGETTE. Ref also: TM.
*Footsteps in the Dark. ... Berkley, 1986

*HEYES, DOUGLAS
The Kill. Ballantine, 1985 ⟨L.A., 1938⟩

*HEYM, STEFAN
*Hostages. Film: Paramount, 1943 (scw: Lester Cole, Frank Butler; dir: Frank Tuttle)

*HEYMAN, EVAN LEE
*Dead Heat on a Merry-Go-Round. (Novelization of film: Columbia, 1968; scw & dir: Bernard Girard)
*The Thomas Crown Affair. (Novelization of film: United Artists, 1968; scw: Alan R. Trustman; dir: Norman Jewison)

HEYS, JO
No Clear Evidence. Hale, 1983
Taken in Vein. Hale, 1984

*HEYWARD, DOROTHY (HARTZEL KUHNS). Ref: CA.

HIAASEN, CARL, 1953- . See: William D(aniel) Montalbano.

*HICHENS, ROBERT (SMYTHE)
*After the Verdict. Silent film: Tschechowa, 1929 (scw: Alma Reville; dir: Henrik Galeen)
-Bella Donna. Heinemann, 1909; Lippincott, 1909. Silent film: Famous Players, 1915 (scw: Hugh Ford; dir: Ford, Edwin S. Porter). Also: Famous Players, 1923 (scw: Ouida Bergere; dir: George Fitzmaurice). Sound film: Twickenham, 1934 (scw: Vera Allinson, H. Fowler Mear; dir: Robert Milton). Also: Universal, 1946, as Temptation (scw: Robert Thoeren; dir: Irving Pichel)
*Doctor Artz. ... Cosmopolitan, 1929
*The Paradine Case. Film: British Lion, 1947 (scw: David O. Selznick; dir: Alfred Hitchcock)

HICKS, HELEN B.
Castle at Jade Cove. Harlequin, 1984 ⟨Calif., 1884⟩

*HIGGINS, GEORGE V(INCENT). Ref also: BM, TM. SC: Jerry Kennedy, in *Kennedy for the Defence, and titles marked JK below.
A Choice of Enemies. Knopf, 1983; Secker, 1984 ⟨Boston⟩
*The Friends of Eddie Coyle. Film: Paramount, 1973 (scw: Paul Monash; dir: Peter Yates)
The Patriot Game. Knopf, 1982; Secker, 1982 ⟨Boston⟩
Penance for Jerry Kennedy. Knopf, 1985; Deutsch, 1985 JK ⟨Boston⟩
The Rat on Fire. Knopf, 1981; Secker, 1981 ⟨Boston⟩ JK

*HIGGINS, JACK. SC: Liam Devlin, in *The Eagle Has Landed, and in titles below marked LD.
Confessional. Collins, 1985; Stein, 1985 LD ⟨Ire.⟩

*The Eagle Has Landed. Film, ITC, 1976 (scw: Tom Mankiewicz; dir: John Sturges)
Exocet. Collins, 1983; Stein, 1983
Luciano's Luck. Collins, 1981; Stein, 1981
Touch the Devil. Collins, 1982; Stein, 1982 LD

HIGGS, ERIC C. Former naval officer living in Calif.
The Happy Man. St. Martin's, 1985 <San Diego>

*HIGHSMITH, (MARY) PATRICIA (PLAUGMAN). Ref also: TM.
*The Animal-Lover's Book of Beastly Murder. ... Mysterious Press, 1986
The Black House and other stories. Heinemann, 1981 ss
*The Blunderer. Film: Cocinor, 1963, as Le Meurtrier (The Murderer; Enough Rope) (scw: Jean Aurenche, Pierre Bost; dir: Claude Autant-Lara)
*Deep Water. Film: Hamster, 1981, as Eaux Profondes (Deep Water) (scw: Michel Deville, Florence Delay, Christopher Frank; dir: Deville)
*Edith's Diary. Film: Geissendoerfer, 1983, as Edith's Tagebuch (Edith's Diary) (scw & dir: Hans W. Geissendoerfer)
*The Glass Cell. Film: Roxy/Solaris, 1978, as Die Glaeserne Zelle (The Glass Cell) (scw: Hans C. Geissendoerfer, Klaus Baedekerl; dir: Geissendoerfer)
*Little Tales of Misogyny. ... Penzler, 1986
Mermaids on the Golfcourse. Heinemann, 1985
-The People Who Knock on the Door. Heinemann, 1982; Penzler, 1985
*Ripley Underground; see *Ripley's Game
*Ripley's Game. Film (based also on *Ripley Underground): Filmverlag der Autoren, 1977, as Der Amerikanische Freund (The American Friend) (scw & dir: Wim Wenders)
*Slowly, Slowly in the Wind. ... Penzler, 1985
*Strangers on a Train. Film: Warner, 1951 (scw: Raymond Chandler, Czenzi Ormonde; dir: Alfred Hitchcock). Also: Warner, 1969, as Once You Kiss a Stranger (scw: Frank Tarloff, Norman Katkov; dir: Robert Sparr)
*The Talented Mr. Ripley. Film: CCFC, 1960, as Plein Soleil (Broad Daylight; Purple Noon) (scw: Paul Gegauff, Rene Clement; dir: Clement)
*This Sweet Sickness. Film: AMLF, 1977, as Dites Lui Que Je L'Aime (Tell Him I Love Him) (scw: Claude Miller, Luc Beraud; dir: Miller)
*The Two Faces of January. Film: Monaco, 1986, as Die Zwei Gesichter des Januar (The Two Faces of January) (scw: Karl Heinz Willschrei, Wolfgang Storch; dir: Storch)

HIGMAN, DENNIS
Pranks. Leisure, 1983 <Wash.>

HILBORN, ANN. 1942-   . Ref: CA.
Personal Justice. Avon, 1982; Avon (U.K.), 1983 <Houston>

HILD, JACK. SC: Nile Barrabas (SOB's), in all titles.
The Barrabas Run. Gold Eagle, 1983 <Afr.> (by Jack Canon, Robin Hardy, and Alan Bomack.)
Butchers of Eden. Gold Eagle, 1984 (by Alan Philipson.) <Sri Lanka>
Eye of the Fire. Gold Eagle, 1985 (by Robin Hardy.) <Cuba>
Gulag War. Gold Eagle, 1985 (by Alan Philipson.) <Russ.>
The Plains of Fire. Gold Eagle, 1984 <Iran> (by Alan Philipson.)
Red Hammer Down. Gold Eagle, 1985 (by Alan Philipson.) <Maj.>
Rivers of Flesh. Gold Eagle, 1985 <Camb.>
Some Chose Hell. Gold Eagle, 1985 (by Robin Hardy) <S. Afr.>

*HILDICK, (EDMUND) WALLACE. Ref: not in TC2.

HILL, F(REDERIC) S(TANHOPE). 1805-1850.
The Six Degrees of Crime. French, 1834(?)   (Play.)

*HILL, FREDERICK TREVOR
*The Thirteenth Juror. Silent film: Jewel, 1927 (dir: Edward Laemmle)

*HILL, H. HAVERSTOCK
*Spoil of the Desert. <Australia>

*HILL, K(ATE) F.
*Sarah Brown, Detective. Westbrook, 1920
*The Twin Detectives. Street, 1899

*HILL, R. LANCE
*The Evil That Men Do. Film: ITC, 1984 (scw: David Lee Henry, John Crowther; dir: J. Lee Thompson)

*HILL, REGINALD (CHARLES). Ref also: BM, TM. SC: Supt. Andrew Dalziel, also in those titles marked AD. Set: Eng.
*An Advancement of Learning. ... Foul Play, 1985
*An April Shroud. ... Foul Play, 1986 AD
*A Clubbable Woman. ... Foul Play, 1984
Deadheads. Collins, 1983; Macmillan, 1984 AD
Exit Lines. Collins, 1984; Macmillan, 1985 AD
*A Fairly Dangerous Thing. ... Foul Play, 1983
*Fell of Dark. ... Signet, 1986
Guardians of the Prince; see Who Guards a Prince
-No Man's Land. Collins, 1985; St. Martin's, 1985
Traitor's Blood. Collins, 1983; Foul Play, 1986
*A Very Good Hater. ... Foul Play, 1982
Who Guards a Prince? Collins, 1982; Pantheon, 1982. Also published as: Guardians of the Prince. Fontana, 1983

HILL, ROGER. See: Glen A. Larson, 1937(?)-

HILL, ROSA
House of Green Dragons. Methuen, 1982; St. Martin's, 1983

*HILL, SAM. Pseudonym of Harvey S. Turner.

*HILLERMAN, TONY. Ref also: BM, TM. SC: Sgt. Jim Chee, in *People of Darkness, and in titles below marked JC.
*Dance Hall of the Dead. ... Pluto, 1985
The Dark Wind. Harper, 1982; Gollancz, 1983 JC   <N. Mex.>
The Ghost Way. McMillan, 1984; Gollancz, 1985 JC   <N. Mex.>
*People of Darkness. ... Gollancz, 1982

*HILTON, CHRISTOPHER
Moves on an Old Board. Hale, 1981

*HILTON, JAMES. Ref: not in TC2.
Knight Without Armour. Benn, 1933. U.S. title: Without Armor. Morrow, 1934 <Russ., ca.1915> Film: London, 1937, as Knight Without Armour (scw: Frances Marion, Lajos Biro, Arthur Wimperis; dir: Jacques Feyder)
-Rage in Heaven. King, 1932. Film: MGM, 1941 (scw: Christopher Isherwood, Robert Thoeren; dir: Robert Sinclair, W. S. Van Dyke)
-We Are Not Alone. Macmillan (London), 1937; Morrow, 1937. Film: First National, 1939 (scw: James Hilton, Milton Krims; dir: Edmund Goulding)
Without Armor; see Knight Without Armour

*HILTON, JOHN BUXTON. 1921-1986. Pseudonym: John Greenwood, q.v. Ref also: TM. SC: Supt. Simon Kenworthy, also in titles below marked SK; Insp. Thomas Brunt, also in titles below marked TB. Set: Eng.
The Asking Price. Collins, 1983; St. Martin's, 1983 SK
Corridors of Guilt. Collins, 1984; St. Martin's, 1984 SK
The Green Frontier. Collins, 1982; St. Martin's, 1982 SK
The Hobbema Prospect. Collins, 1984; St. Martin's, 1984 SK
Mr. Fred. Collins, 1983; St. Martin's, 1983 TB
Passion in the Peak. Collins, 1985;
St. Martin's, 1985 SK
Playground of Death. Collins, 1981; St. Martin's, 1981 SK
The Quiet Stranger. Collins, 1985; St. Martin's, 1985 TB
The Sunset Law. Collins, 1982; St. Martin's, 1982 SK <Fla.>
Surrender Value. Collins, 1981; St. Martin's, 1981 SK

HILTON, TONY. See: *Ray Cooney.

*HIMES, CHESTER (BOMAR). 1909-1984. Ref also: TM.
*Cotton Comes to Harlem. Film: United Artists, 1969 (scw: Arnold Perl, Ossie Davis; dir: Davis)
*The Heat's On. Film: Warner, 1972, as Come Back, Charleston Blue (scw: Bontche Schweig, Peggy Elliott; dir: Mark Warren)

*HIMMEL, RICHARD
Echo Chambers. Delacorte, 1982

*HINCKS, CYRIL MALCOLM
Pincher in Peace and War. Pearson, 1916 ss

HIND, GRAHAM
Table for Two and other stories. New Horizon, 1981 ss

*HINE, AL. Pseudonym: *Bradford Street, q.v.
*Juggernaut. (Novelization of film: United Artists, 1974; scw: Richard Alan Simmons; dir: Richard Lester)

*HINKEMEYER, MICHAEL T(HOMAS). Ref also: TM. SC: Sheriff Emil Whippletree, in *The Fields of Eden, and in titles below marked EW.
Fourth Down, Death. St. Martin's, 1985 EW <Minn.>
Lilac Night. Crown, 1981 <L.I.>
A Time to Reap. St. Martin's, 1984 EW <Minn.>

*HINKLE, VERNON. 1935-   . Ref: CA.

*HINTZE, NAOMI A(GANS). (Last name misspelled in first printing of CF.) Ref also: TM.
*You'll Like My Mother. Film: Universal, 1972 (scw: Jo Heims; dir: Lamont Johnson)

*HINXMAN, MARGARET. Former film critic with London Daily Mail.
The Boy from Nowhere. Collins, 1985
The Corpse Now Arriving. Collins, 1983
The Night They Murdered Chelsea. Collins, 1984; Dodd, 1985
The Telephone Never Tells. Collins, 1982

*HIRSCHBERG, CORNELIUS. Ref also: TM; not in TC2.

*HIRSCHFELD, BURT. Ref: CA. Pseudonym: *Hugh Barron, q.v.
*Bonnie and Clyde. (Novelization of film: Warner, 1967; scw: David Newman, Robert Benton; dir: Arthur Penn)
Flawless. Freundlich, 1984; Severn, 1985
*-Gas. (Novelization of film: American International, 1970; scw: Graham Armitage; dir: Roger Corman)
The Verdugo Affair. Dell, 1984

HIRT, HOWARD. Prof. of Geography at Framingham State College; has spent several years in India, including one as Fulbright Lecturer.
The Heat of Winter. Harcourt, 1984; Weidenfeld, 1984 <India, 1952>

HISCHAK, THOMAS
Murder by Membership Only. Clark, 1980 (2-act play.)

*HISCOTT, LESLIE
*The Bishop's Move. <Fr.>

HITCHCOCK, LYDIA
The Ducetti Lair. Columbine, 1981 <It.>
The Geneva Touch. Columbine, 1983

*HITCHCOCK, RAYMOND (JOHN)
Archangel 006. Constable, 1984; St. Martin's, 1983

*HITCHENS, (HU)BERT (ALLEN) and (JULIA CLARA CATHERINE) DOLORES (BIRK OLSEN), q.v. Ref also: TM.

*HITCHENS, (JULIA CLARA CATHERINE) DOLORES (BIRK OLSEN)
*Fools' Gold. Film: Anouchka, 1964, as Bande a Part (Band of Outsiders) (scw: & dir: Jean-Luc Godard)

HITCHINS, J.
Which Side Gave In? and other stories. Skeffington, 1894 ss, some criminous

*HITTLEMAN, CARL K.
*36 Hours. (Novelization of film: MGM, 1964; scw & dir: George Seaton)

*HJORTSBERG, WILLIAM (REINHOLD). Ref also: TM.
*Falling Angel. Film: Tri-Star, 1987, as Angel Heart (scw & dir: Alan Parker)

HOBBS, STERLING
The Black Angels. Holloway, 1982

*HOBHOUSE, ADAM. Pseudonym.
*The Hangover Murders. Film: Universal, 1935, as Remember Last Night? (scw: Doris Malloy, Harry Clork, Dan Totheroh; dir: James Whale)

HOBSON, B. Pseudonym of Bert James, q.v.
The Mystery of the Boxing Contest. Bookstall (Syd.), 1910

*HOCH, EDWARD D(ENTINGER). Ref also: BM, TM. SC: Simon Ark, also in title marked SA below; Nick Velvet, also in title marked NV below.
Leopold's Way. Southern Ill. Univ., 1985 ss
The Quests of Simon Ark. Mysterious Press, 1984 16 ss SA
The Theft of the Persian Slipper. Mysterious Press, 1978 (A NV ss separately issued in limited edition for promotional purposes.)

*HOCKING, ANNE. Pseudonym of *Mona (Naomi Anne Hocking) Messer, 189?-1966.
Death in the Cup; see There's Death in the Cup
*There's Death in the Cup. Reprinted as: Death in the Cup. Severn, 1984
*The Wicked Flee. Film: Gibraltar, 1957, as The Surgeon's Knife (scw: Robert Westerby; dir: Gordon Parry)

*HOCKING, SILAS (KITTO)
-The Shadow Between. Warne, 1908. Silent film: Seal, 1920 (scw & dir: George Dewhurst)

*HODDINOTT, DEREK
*Murder in Style.   (2-act play.)

HODGE, WILLIAM T(HOMAS). 1874-1932.
Straight Through the Door. French, 1929   (3-act play.)

*HODGES, CARL G.
*Crime on My Hands. ... Moring, 1951

HODGES, HORACE and T(HOMAS) WIGNEY PERCYVAL
Grumpy. French, 1921 (4-act play.) Silent film: Famous Players, 1923 (scw: Clara Beranger; dir: William De Mille). Sound film: Paramount, 1930 (scw: Doris Anderson; dir: George Cukor, Cyril Gardner)

HODGSON, ANTHONY
The Golden Ballast. Mystery House, 1956 <Eng.>

*HODGSON, WILLIAM HOPE. Ref also: CA.

*HOFFENBERG, JACK
A Thunder at Dawn. Dutton, 1965; Barker, 1965

*HOFFMAN, WILLIAM
Godfires. Viking, 1985 <Va.>

HOFRICHTER, PAUL. Seee: *Bruno Rossi, *Frank Scarpetta, Dick Stivers.

*HOGAN, JAMES P.
The Proteus Operation. Bantam hc, 1985; Century, 1986 <1939>

HOGAN, LOU RAND. Pseudonym: *Lou Rand, q.v.

*HOGAN, ROBERT J. SC: G-8, also in title below.

Scourge of the Steel Mask. Dimedia, 1985

HOGG, JAMES. 1770-1835. See also: Anonymous.
Tales of Love and Mystery. Canongate, 1985 ss
Winter Evening Tales, Collected Among the Cottagers in the South of England. Oliver, 1820; Kirk, 1820 ss, a few criminous

HOILE, EDWARD (VICTOR). See: Guy Paxton.

*HOLDEN, ANNE
*The Witnesses. Film: DEG, 1987, as The Bedroom Window (scw & dir: Curtis Hanson)

*HOLDEN, GENEVIEVE. Ref also: CA.
*Sound an Alarm. (not South an Alarm, as shown in first printing of CF)

*HOLDEN, RICHARD
*Snow Fury. <N.H.>

*HOLDING, ELISABETH SANXAY. Ref also: CA, TM.
*The Blank Wall. Film: Columbia, 1949, as The Reckless Moment (scw: Henry Garson, Robert W. Soderberg; dir: Max Opuls)

*HOLLAND, HESTER
Week-Ends with Henry. (title correction) criminous

*HOLLAND, ISABELLE
*Cecily. ... Severn, 1985
A Death at St. Anselm's. Doubleday, 1984; Severn, 1985 <NYC, church>
Flight of the Archangel. Doubleday, 1985; Severn, 1986 <N.Y.>
The Lost Madonna. Rawson, 1981; Collins, 1982 <It.>

HOLLAND, JACK. Ref: CA.
The Prisoner's Wife. Dodd, 1981; Hale, 1982 <Belfast>

*HOLLAND, MARTY. Pseudonym of Mary Holland.
*Fallen Angel. Film: TCF, 1945 (scw: Harry Kleiner; dir: Otto Preminger)

HOLLAND, MARY. Pseudonym: *Marty Holland, q.v.

*HOLLAND, RUTH
Laburnum Grove. Heinemann, 1936 (Novelization of the play by *J. B. Priestley, q.v.)

HOLLANDER, CARL. Pseudonym: *Eddie Stone.

HOLLANDER, LESLIE
The Exhibit. Pinnacle, 1981 <NYC>

*HOLLES, ROBERT (OWENS)
Sun Blight. H. Hamilton, 1982

HOLLIDAY, DOLORES
The Seventh Gate. Mystique, 1981

HOLLOWAY, RUPERT
The Terrorist Conspiracy. Book Guild, 1983

*HOLLOWAY, TERESA (BRAGUNIER)
Lady Lawyer. Avalon, 1964
-Rosemary King, Government Girl. Avalon, 1957

*HOLLY, J. HUNTER. Pseudonym of *Joan Carol Holly, 1932-1982.
The Mind Traders. Avalon, 1966 <future>

*HOLLY, JOAN CAROL. 1932-1982.

HOLLYOCK, DULCIE
An Innocent Madness. Harlequin, 1984 <Ire., 1838>

*HOLMAN, (CLARENCE) HUGH. Ref: not in TC2.

*HOLME, TIMOTHY. Ref: TM. SC: Insp. Achille Peroni, in *The Neopolitan Streak, and in titles below.
The Assisi Murders. Macmillan (London), 1985 <Venice>
The Devil and the Dolce Vita. Macmillan (London), 1982 <Venice>
A Funeral of Gondolas. Macmillan (London), 1981; Coward, 1982 <Venice>

HOLMES, CLARA H.
Floating Fancies Among the Weird and the Occult. Neely, 1898 ss, some criminous

*HOLMES, DAVID C(HARLES)
*The Velvet Ape. <Cent. Am.>

*HOLMES, H. H.
*Nine Times Nine. ... Zomba, 1984, in Four Novels by Anthony Boucher
*Rocket to the Morgue. ... Zomba, 1984, in Four Novels by Anthony Boucher

*HOLMES, CAPTAIN HOWARD
*The Never-Fail Detective. Westbrook, 1920 (date correction)

*HOLMES, MRS. M. E.
*Her Fatal Sin. Silent film (?): Strand, 1915 (no credits found)

*HOLMES, PAUL A(LLEN). 1901-1985.

*HOLT, HENRY
*The Midnight Mail. Film: Admiral, 1939, as The Spider (scw: Victor M. Greene, Kenneth Horne, Reginald Long; dir: Maurice Elvey)

HOLT, RICHARD. 1917-   .
The Asian Affair. New Horizon, 1982

*HOLT, VICTORIA. Ref also: TC2, TM.
-The Demon Lover. Collins, 1982; Doubleday, 1982 <Paris, 1800s>
The Judas Kiss. Collins, 1981; Doubleday, 1981
The Landower Legacy. Collins, 1984; Doubleday, 1984
-The Road to Paradise Island. Collins, 1985; Doubleday, 1985 <Eng., 1800s>
The Time of the Hunter's Moon. Collins, 1983; Doubleday, 1983 <Eng., 1800s>

HOLZER, ERIKA. Graduate of Cornell Univ. and NYU School of Law; author of articles, interviews, editorials and reviews; newspaper columnist.
Double Crossing. Putnam, 1983

*HOLTON, LEONARD. Pseudonym of Leonard (Patrick O'Connor) Wibberley, 1915-1983.

*HOME, MICHAEL. SC: John Benham, in *The Auber File, and at least one other title.
-The Place of Little Birds. Methuen, 1941. U.S. title: Attack in the Desert. Morrow, 1942 <Libya>

*HOMES, GEOFFREY. Ref also: TM.
*Build My Gallows High. Film: RKO, 1947; released in the U.S. as Out of the Past (scw: Geoffrey Homes; dir: Jacques Tourneur). Also: Columbia, 1984, as Against All Odds (scw: Eric Hughes; dir: Taylor Hackford).
*Forty Whacks. Film: Warner, 1944, as Crime by Night (scw: Richard Weil, Joel Malone; dir: William Clemens)
*No Hands on the Clock. Film: Paramount, 1941 (scw: Maxwell Shane; dir: Frank McDonald)

HOMESLEY, LEATRICE
Blondy's Boy Friend. Chelsea, 1930 <Conn.>

HOMEWOOD, CHARLES H. 1914(?)-1984. Pseudonym: *Harry Homewood, q.v.

*HOMEWOOD, HARRY. Pseudonym of Charles H. Homewood, 1914(?)-1984. Ref: CA.

*HONE, JOSEPH. Ref also: TC2. SC: Peter Marlow, also in the title below.
The Valley of the Fox. Secker, 1982; St. Martin's, 1984

*HONEYCOMBE, GORDON
*Neither the Sea Nor the Sand. Film: Tigon, 1972 (scw: Gordon Honeycombe, Rosemary Davies; dir: Fred Burnley)

HONEYWOOD, JOHN
The Dying Breath. Hale, 1981
The Terrorist's Woman. Hale, 1981

*HOOKE, NINA WARNER
  *Darkness I Leave You. Film: Rank, 1958, as The Gypsy and the Gentleman (scw: Janet Green; dir: Joseph Losey)
  *Deadly Record. Film: Independent Artists, 1959 (scw: Vivian A. Cox, Lawrence Huntington; dir: Huntington)

*HOPKINS, JOHN (RICHARD)
  *This Story of Yours. Film: Tantallon, 1973, as The Offence (scw: John Hopkins; dir: Sidney Lumet)

*HOPKINS, R(OBERT) THURSTON. 1883-1958.

*HOPKINS, ROBERT (SYDNEY). Ref: CA.

*HOPKINS, STANLEY, JR. Pseudonym of Blythe Morley, 1923-   ; daughter of *Christopher (Darlington) Morley.

*HOPLEY, GEORGE
  *Night Has a Thousand Eyes. Film: Paramount, 1948 (scw: Barre Lyndon, Jonathan Latimer; dir: John Farrow)

HORAN, DON. See: *Norman Stahl.

*HORAN, JAMES D(AVID)
  -The Blue Messiah. Crown, 1971
  The Peking Agent. Crown, 1982

HORGAN, McCALL
  Dames Is My Undoing. Editorial Services, ca.1950 <L.A.>
  The Lady Was Loaded. Editorial Services, 1950s
  12:15 A.M.: I'm Blasted. Editorial Services, 1950s

*HORLER, SYDNEY. Ref also: TM.
  *The House of Secrets. Film: Chesterfield, 1936 (scw: Adeline Leitzbach; dir: Edmund Lawrence)
  *In the Dark. Film: Continental, 1929, as A Life for Sale (existence of film not confirmed)
  *The Thirteenth Hour. (Novelization of silent film: MGM, 1927; scw: Maximilian Fabian; dir: C. M. Franklin.)

*HORNBLOW, ARTHUR. See also: *Charles Klein.
  *The Lion and the Mouse. Silent film (based on play): Lubin, 1914 (scw: E. W. Sargent; dir: Barry O'Neil). Also: Vitagraph, 1919 (scw & dir: Tom Terriss)
  *The Mask. Silent film: Selig, 1921 (scw: Bertram Bracken, Arthur Lavon; dir: Bracken)
  *The Third Degree. Silent film: Lubin, 1914 (scw: Clay M. Greene; dir: Barry O'Neil). Also: Vitagraph, 1919 (scw: Phil Lang; dir: Tom Terriss). Also: Warner, 1926 (scw: C. Graham Baker; dir: Michael Curtiz)

HORNE, KENNETH. 1900-1975. Ref: CA.
  A Lady Mislaid. English Theatre, 1950 (2-act play.) Film: Welwyn, 1958 (scw: Frederick Gotfurt; dir: David Macdonald)

HORNIG, DOUG. 1943-   . Ref: CA, TM. SC: Loren Swift, in both titles.
  Foul Shot. Scribner, 1984 <Va.>
  Hardball. Scribner, 1985; Macmillan (London), 1986 <Va.>

*HORNIMAN, ROY
  *Israel Rank. Film: Ealing, 1949, as Kind Hearts and Coronets (scw: Robert Hamer, John Dighton; dir: Hamer)
  A Nonconformist Parson. Sisley's, 1907. Silent film: British Lion, 1919; also released as Heart and Soul (scw: Eliot Stannard; dir: A. V. Bramble)

*HORNUNG, E(RNEST) W(ILLIAM). See also: Peter Tremayne. Ref: all except MM. Film (from Raffles stories): Markham, 1932, as The Return of Raffles (scw: W. J. Balef; dir: Mansfield Markham)
  *The Amateur Cracksman. Silent film: Weber, 1917, as Raffles (scw: Anthony Kelly; dir: George Irving). Also: Universal, 1925, as Raffles, the Amateur Cracksman (scw: Harvey Thew; dir: King Baggott). Sound film: United Artists, 1930, as Raffles (scw: Sidney Howard; dir: Harry D'Arrast, George Fitzmaurice). Also: United Artists, 1939, as Raffles (scw: John Van Druton, Sidney Howard; dir: Sam Wood)
  *The Boss of Taroomba. <Australia>
  *A Bride from the Bush. delete: not criminous
  *Dead Men Tell No Tales. Silent film: Vitagraph, 1920 (scw: Lillian Chester, George Randolph Chester; dir: Tom Terriss)
  *Denis Dent. <Australia>
  *Irralie's Bushranger. ss, some criminous <Australia>
  *Mr. Justice Raffles. Silent film: Hepworth, 1921 (scw: Blanche McIntosh; dir: Gerald Ames, Gaston Quiribet)
  *The Rogue's March. <Australia>
  *The Shadow of the Rope. Silent film: Paramount, 1919, as Out of the Shadow (scw: Eve Unsell; dir: Emile Chautard)
  *Stingaree. Silent film: Kalem, 1915-6 (scw & dir: James W. Horne). Sound film: RKO, 1934 (scw: Becky Gardiner; dir: William A. Wellman)
  *Tiny Luttrell. delete: not criminous

HOROVITZ, ISRAEL. 1939-   . Ref: CA.
  The Indian Wants the Bronx. Dramatists, 1968 (1-act play.) <NYC>

HORTON, FOREST W., JR.
  The Technocrats. Leisure, 1980 <Wash. D.C.>

*HORTON, MILESON (DENIS JAMES) and *THOMAS PEMBROKE
  *Photocrimes. ... Hillman, 1937

HORVITZ, LESLIE ALAN and H. HARRIS GERHARD. For Horvitz, see also: Dane Hartman.
  The Donors. Signet, 1982; Star, 1983
  Double-Blinded. Signet, 1984; Star, 1985

*HOSKEN, CLIFFORD (JAMES WHEELER). Ref: not in TC2.
  *The Shadow Syndicate. Reprinted as by Richard Keverne: Penguin, ca.1945

*HOSKINS, ROBERT. See: Gar Wilson.

HOSPITAL, JANETTE TURNER. 1942-   . Ref: CA.
  Borderline. Dutton, 1985; Hodder, 1985

*HOSSENT, HARRY. See: *Ray Stahl.

*HOSTOVSKY, EGON
  *The Midnight Patient. Film: Cinedis, 1958, as Les Espions (The Spies) (scw: H. G. Clouzot, Jerome Jeronimi; dir: Clouzot)

*HOTCHNER, A(ARON) E(DWARD)
  The Man Who Lived at the Ritz. Putnam, 1981; Weidenfeld, 1982 <Paris, 1940>

HOTCHNER, STEPHEN. 1941-   .
  Dracula. Hanbury, 1978 (Play based on the novel by *Bram Stoker, q.v.)

HOUGAN, CAROLYN. Born in La., educated at Univ. of Wis., has worked in journalism, publishing, and politics; lives near Wash. D.C.
  Shooting in the Dark. Simon, 1984 <Amst.>

*HOUGH, S(TANLEY) B(ENNETT)
  *Fear Fortune, Father. ... Perennial, 1984
  *Sweet Sister Seduced. ... Perennial, 1983

HOUGHTON, DENNIS
  The Cerberus Gambit. Malvern, 1985

*HOULT, NORAH. 1898-1984. Ref: CA.

HOUSBY, SANDRA LYNN. 1948-   . Pseudonym: Samantha Harte, q.v.

*HOUSE, RON
  *Bullshot Crummond. Film: HandMade, 1983, as Bullshot (scw: Ron House, Diz White, Alan Shearman; dir: Dick Clement)

*HOUSEHOLD, GEOFFREY (EDWARD WEST). Ref also: TM. SC: Raymond Ingelram, in *Rogue Male, and title marked RI below.
  The Adversary; see Dance of the Dwarfs
  Capricorn and Cancer. Joseph, 1981 ss
  *Dance of the Dwarfs. Also published as: The Adversary. Dell, 1970. Film: Dove, 1982 (existence of film not confirmed)
  Rogue Justice. Joseph, 1982; Little, 1982 RI
  *Rogue Male. Film: TCF, 1941, as Man Hunt (scw: Dudley Nichols; dir: Fritz Lang)
  *A Rough Shoot. Film: United Artists, 1953; released in U.S. as Shoot First (scw: Eric Ambler; dir: Robert Parrish)
  Summon the Bright Water. Joseph, 1981; Little, 1981
  *Tales of Adventurers. Film (from ss "Brandy for the Parson"): Group Three, 1952, as Brandy for the Parson (scw: John Dighton, Walter Meade, Alfred O'Shaughnessy; dir: John Eldridge)

*HOUSTON, ROBERT. Ref: TM.
  Ararat. Avon, 1982; Avon (London), 1983
  Blood Tango. Avon, 1984 <Arg.>
  Cholo. Avon, 1981 <Lima>
  The 16th of September Game. Ballantine, 1985

HOVLAND, BONNIE L. Pseudonym: Bonnie Lee, q.v.

*HOWARD, CLARK. Ref: TC2.

*HOWARD, COLIN. Pseudonym of *(Colin) Howard Shaw, q.v.

HOWARD, HAMPTON (W.)
  War Toys. Stein, 1983 <Paris>

*HOWARD, HARTLEY
  *Department K. Film: Mazurka, 1967, as Assignment K (scw: Val Guest, Bill Strutton, Maurice Foster; dir: Guest)

*HOWARD, JAMES A.
  Death Audit. Raven, 1981 <Calif.>
  Friday Is a Killing Day. Raven, 1981
  *I Like It Tough. <Colo.>

*HOWARD, LEIGH
  *Blind Date. Film: Independent Artists, 1959; released in the U.S. as Chance Meeting (scw: Ben Barzman, Millard Lampell; dir: Joseph Losey)

*HOWARD, LESLEY. Joint pseudonym of Stanley and Monica Abbott.

*HOWATCH, SUSAN (STURT)
  -The Wheel of Fortune. Simon, 1984; H. Hamilton, 1984

*HOWE, GEORGE (LOCKE)
  *Call It Treason. Film: TCF, 1951, as Decision Before Dawn (scw: Peter Viertel; dir: Anatole Litvak)

HOWELL, DAVID
  After-Shock. Jove, 1981

HOWELL, JEAN
  To Love a Stranger. Leisure, 1985

HOWELL, PATRICIA HAGAN. 1939-   . Pseudonym: Patricia Hagan, q.v.

*HOWES, ROYCE
  *Murder at Maneuvers. <Mich.>

HOWLETT, ANTHONY
  Bristow's Wreck. Hale, 1985
  Pursuit of the Owl. Hale, 1982
  The Ultimate Judge. Hale, 1985
  Whirlpool. Hale, 1984

*HOWLETT, JOHN (REGINALD)
  Murder of a Moderate Man. Arrow, 1985; St. Martin's, 1987
  Orange. Hutchinson, 1985

*HOYLE, TREVOR
  The Last Gasp. Sphere, 1984; Crown, 1983
  Vail. Calder, 1984; Riverrun, 1984 <Eng., future>

*HOYT, RICHARD. Ref: TC2, TM. SC: John Denson, in *Decoys, and at least in titles marked JD below; James Burlane = JB.
  Cool Runnings. Viking, 1984 <NYC>
  Fish Story. Viking, 1985; Hale, 1986 <Seattle> JD

Head of State. Tor, 1985; Severn, 1986 JB <Russ.>
The Manna Enzyme. Morrow, 1982 <Oreg.>
The Siskiyou Two-Step. Morrow, 1983; Hale, 1986 JD <Oreg.>
30 for a Harry. Evans, 1981; Hale, 1982 JD <Seattle>
Trotsky's Run. Morrow, 1982 JB

*HRABEL, BAHUMIL. Ref: CA.

*HUBER, FREDERICK VINCENT. 1941-   .
Apple Crunch. Seaview, 1981; Sphere, 1982 <NYC>

*HUCH, RICARDA (OCTAVIA). Ref: CA.

HUCKINS, JANET. Pseudonym: *Sebastian Blayne.

HUDSEN, DICK
Get Going Sister! Gannet, 1952

HUDNER, KENNEDY. Graduate of Yale Law School; practicing attorney in Conn.
Heirs of the Kingdom. Holt, 1981 <future>

*HUDSON, CHRISTOPHER
*The Final Act. Film: Sawbuck, 1980 (existence of film not confirmed)
Insider Out. Joseph, 1982 <Wash. D.C.>

*HUDSON, JEFFERY
*A Case of Need. Film: MGM, 1972, as The Carey Treatment (scw: James P. Bonner; dir: Blake Edwards)

*HUFF, T(OM) E.
*Nine Bucks Row. Reprinted as: Susannah, Beware. Dell, 1976

*HUGGINS, ROY. Ref also: TM.
*The Double Take. Film: Columbia, 1947, as I Love Trouble (scw: Roy Huggins; dir: S. Sylvan Simon)
*Too Late for Tears. Film: United Artists, 1949 (scw: Roy Huggins; dir: Byron Haskin)

HUGHES, ALISON
Appointment with Danger. Hale, 1982

HUGHES, (JOHN) DAVID. 1930-   . Ref: CA.
The Pork Butcher. Constable, 1984; Schocken, 1985 <Fr.>

*HUGHES, DENNIS T(ALBOT)

*HUGHES, DOROTHY B(ELLE FLANAGAN). Ref also: TM.
*The Expendable Man. Film: Rank, 1964, as The Hanged Man (existence of film not confirmed)
*The Fallen Sparrow. Film: RKO, 1943 (scw: Warren Duff; dir: Richard Wallace)
*In a Lonely Place. Film: Columbia, 1950 (scw: Andrew Solt; dir: Nicholas Ray)
*Ride the Pink Horse. Film: Universal International, 1947 (scw: Ben Hecht, Charles Lederer; dir: Robert Montgomery)

*HUGHES, KEN(NETH GRAHAM)
*High Wray. Film: Hammer, 1954; released in the U.S. as Heatwave (scw & dir: Ken Hughes)

*HUGHES, MICHAEL
The Gironde Incident. Allen, 1983; Zebra, 1984
The Infiltrator. Allen, 1982
The Sleeper; see The Sleeper Awakes
*The Sleeper Awakes. Reprinted as: The Sleeper. Star, 1981
Spectre of Maralinga. Star, 1985

HUGHES, RICHARD (EDMUND). 1927-   Ref: CA.
Unholy Communion. Doubleday, 1982; Hale, 1983 <Vt.>

HUGHES, ROBERT
School Days. Charter, 1982

*HUGHES, RUPERT
*Ladies' Man. Film: Paramount, 1931 (scw: Herman J. Mankiewicz; dir: Lothar Mendes)

HUGHES, TERENCE J. 1938-   .
Queen's Mate. Hodder, 1982. U.S. title: The Day They Stole the Queen Mary. Morrow, 1983 <ship, 1943>

*HUGHES, WILLIAM. SC: George Willis, also in at least the title below marked GW.
*Aces High. delete: not criminous
*Blind Terror. (Novelization of film: Filmways, 1971; released in the U.S. as See No Evil; scw: Brian Clemens; dir: Richard Fleischer)
Call or Fold. Magread, 1982
*Connecting Rooms. delete: not criminous
Cover Zero. Magread, 1981 GW
*Deathsport. (Novelization of film: New World, 1978; scw: Henry Suso, Donald Stewart; dir: Suso, Allan Arkush)
French Deal. Magread, 1982
*Inside Out. (Novelization of film: Warner, 1975; also released as Hitler's Gold; scw: Judd Bernard, Stephen Schneck; dir: Peter Duffell)
*Secret Ceremony. (Novelization of film; see *Marco Denevi.)

HUGHES, ZACH. Pseudonym of *Hugh Zachary, q.v. Other pseudonym: Zachary Hughes, q.v.
Pressure Man. Signet, 1980

HUGHES, ZACHARY. Pseudonym of *Hugh Zachary, q.v. Other pseudonym: Zach Hughes, q.v.
The Adlon Link. Jove, 1981 <Berlin>
The Fires of Paris. Jove, 1981 <Paris>
Fortress London. Jove, 1981 <Eng.>
Tower of Treason. Jove, 1982

*HUGHSTON, DANA
*You Stand Accused. <Calif.>

HUGO, RICHARD. 1923-1982. Ref: CA, TM.
Death and the Good Life. St. Martin's, 1981; Hale, 1982 <Mont.>

HUGO, RICHARD. 1947-   . Lawyer living in Eng.
The Hitler Diaries. Macmillan (London), 1982; Morrow, 1983
Last Judgement. Macmillan (London), 1984; Stein, 1986

HUIE, WILLIAM B(RADFORD). 1910-   Ref: CA.
-In the Hours of Night. Delacorte, 1975

HULL, J. H.
Nicole. Richardson, 1985

HULL, RAYMOND. 1919-1985. Ref: CA.
Sweeney Todd. Pioneer, 1980 (1-act play.)

*HULL, RICHARD. Ref also: TM.
*My Own Murderer. (Not The Own Murderer, as given in first printing of CF)

*HUME, DAVID
*Crime Unlimited. Film: WB-FN, 1935 (scw: Brock Williams, Ralph Smart; dir: Ralph Ince)
*They Called Him Death. Film: Rialto, 1941, as This Man Is Dangerous; also released as The Patient Vanishes (scw: John Argyle, Edward Dryhurst; dir: Lawrence Huntington)
*Too Dangerous to Live. Film: WB-FN, 1939 (scw: Paul Gangelin, Connery Chappell, Leslie Arliss; dir: Anthony Hankey, Leslie Norman)

HUME, DAVID. 1931-   .
Outbid. Heinemann, 1984

*HUME, FERGUS(ON WRIGHT). Ref also: CA.
*The Devil Stick. U.S. title: *For the Defense
*The Mystery of a Hansom Cab. Silent film: B&C, 1915 (scw: Eliot Stannard; dir: Harold Weston)
*The Other Person. Silent film: Granger, 1921 (scw: Benedict James; dir: B. E. Doxat-Pratt)
*The Top Dog. Silent film: Windsor, 1918 (scw: Kenelm Foss; dir: Arrigo Bocchi)
*A Traitor in London. <Eng., S. Afr.>
*Whom God Hath Joined. delete: not criminous

HUMES, H(AROLD) L(OUIS). 1926-   Ref: CA.
-The Underground City. Random, 1958; Heinemann, 1958 <Fr., WWII>

HUMPHREYS, JAMES
"Through the Eyes of a Pig." Sphere, 1981

HUMPHREYS, JOEL DON
Vendetta. Macmillan, 1982

HUNSBURGER, H. EDWARD. See: *Nick Carter.

HUNT, ALETHIA
-Girl at Sea. Hale, 1983
-The Hadleigh Inheritance. Hale, 1980
-Girl in the Dark. Hale, 1981
-Mystery in Mdina. Hale, 1982

*HUNT, CHARLOTTE
*Gemini Revenged. ... Magna, 1985
*Tremayne's Wife. ... Magna, 1983

*HUNT, (EVERETTE) HOWARD. Ref also: TM. Pseudonym: *Gordon Davis, q.v.
Cozumel. Stein, 1985
The Gaza Intercept. Stein, 1981
The Kremlin Conspiracy. Stein, 1985 <Moscow>
*Maelstrom. <Mex.>
*Whisper Her Name. <Cuba>

*HUNTER, ALAN (JAMES HERBERT). Ref also: TM. SC: Supt. Gently, also in all titles below.
Amorous Leander. Constable, 1983. U.S. title: Death on the Broadlands. Walker, 1984
The Chelsea Ghost. Constable, 1985
Death on the Broadlands; see Amorous Leander
Death on the Heath; see Fields of Heather
Fields of Heather. Constable, 1981. U.S. title: Death on the Heath. Walker, 1982
Gabrielle's Way. Constable, 1981. U.S. title: The Scottish Decision. Walker, 1981 <Scot.>
Gently Between Tides. Constable, 1982; Walker, 1983
"Once a Prostitute." Constable, 1984
The Scottish Decision; see Gabrielle's Way
The Unhanged Man; see The Unhung Man
The Unhung Man. Constable, 1984. U.S. title: The Unhanged Man. Walker, 1984

*HUNTER, EVAN. Ref also: TM.
*The Blackboard Jungle. Film: MGM, 1955 (scw & dir: Richard Brooks)
*Every Little Crook and Nanny. Film: MGM, 1972 (scw: Cy Howard, Jonathan Axelrod, Robert Klane; dir: Howard)
*A Horse's Head. <NYC>
Lizzie. Arbor, 1984; H. Hamilton, 1984 <U.S., 1890s>
*A Matter of Conviction. Film: United Artists, 1961, as The Young Savages (scw: Edward Anhalt, J. P. Miller; dir: John Frankenheimer)

*HUNTER, JACK D(AYTON)
Florida Is Closed Today. Leisure, 1982 <Fla.>
The Tin Cravat. Harper, 1981; Sidgwick, 1981 <Ger., 1945>

HUNTER, R. WILKES
Crusade into Crime. Australasian (Syd.), 1948

HUNTER, ROBIN. 1935-   .
The Fourth Angel. Macmillan (London), 1985; Arbor, 1986

*HUNTER, STEPHEN
The Second Saladin. Morrow, 1982; Collins, 1983
The Spanish Gambit. Crown, 1985 <Sp., 1930s>
Target. Warner, 1985; Corgi, 1986 (Novelization of film: Warner, 1985; scw: Howard Berk, Don Peterson; dir: Arthur Penn)

*HURD, DOUGLAS (RICHARD). See: *Andrew Osmond.

HURWITZ, KEN. 1948-   . See: Vincent T. Bugliosi, 1934-

*HURWOOD, BERNHARDT J. 1926-1987.

HUSON, PAUL (ANTHONY). 1942-   Ref: CA.
The Keepsake. Warner, 1981; Severn, 1982

HUTCHINSON, MARY JANE. 1924-   Ref: CA.
Red Ice. Avon, 1981

*HUTTER, A. D. Psychoanalyst, and professor at UCLA.

HUTTON, ANN. 1929-   . Ref: CA.
  Edge of the Deep. Hale, 1977 <Carib.>
  The Ivory Slave. Hale, 1981 <H. Kong>
  Passport to Peril. Hale, 1975 <Kenya>
  Search for Simon. Hale, 1982

*HUTTON, JOHN (HARWOOD). Ref: CA.
  Accidental Crimes. Bodley, 1983;
    Bodley (U.S.), 1984

*HUTTON, MALCOLM. 1921-   . Ref: CA.
  Address Unknown. Hale, 1981; St. Martin's, 1981
  The Chinese Girl. Hale, 1985 <China>
  Georgina and Georgette. Hale, 1984;
    St. Martin's, 1984
  -Mark Peterson's Daughter. Hale, 1982
  -Tara. Hale, 1984

*HUXLEY, ALDOUS (LEONARD)
  *Mortal Coils. Film (from ss "The Gioconda Smile"): Universal International, 1947, as A Woman's Vengeance (scw: Aldous Huxley; dir: Zoltan Korda)

*HUXLEY, ELSPETH (JOCELYN GRANT). Ref also: TM.
  -The Prince Buys the Manor. Chatto, 1982

HYAMS, JOE <JOSEPH>. 1923-   . Ref: CA.
  Murder at the Academy Awards. St. Martin's, 1983 <L.A.>

HYDE, ANTHONY. Lives in Ottawa, Can.
  The Red Fox. Knopf, 1985; H. Hamilton, 1985

*HYDE, CHRISTOPHER
  The Icarus Seal. Houghton, 1982; Hodder, 1983 <Can.>
  Maxwell's Train. Villard, 1985;
    Hutchinson, 1985 <train>
  Styx. Severn, 1982
  The Tenth Crusade. Houghton, 1983;
    Hodder, 1984

HYDE, JOHN
  The Prediction. PB, 1983

*HYLAND, (HENRY) STANLEY. Ref: not in TC2.

*HYLTON, SARA
  The Carradice Chain. Hutchinson, 1981. U.S. title: Jacintha. St. Martin's, 1982 <Eng., WWI>
  The Crimson Falcon. Hutchinson, 1983; St. Martin's, 1983 <Vienna, ca.1900>
  Jacintha; see The Carradice Chain
  -The Talisman of Set. Hutchinson, 1984
  -Whispering Glade. Century, 1985

HYMAN, (VERNON) TOM. Editor with NYC publisher turned full-time writer.
  Giant Killer. Marek, 1981 <1984>
  Riches and Honor. Viking, 1985;
    Viking (London), 1986
  The Russian Woman. St. Martin's, 1983; Hodder, 1984 <Wash. D.C.>

HYMSON, ALLEN. See: *Theo Durrant.

*HYND, NOEL
  Flowers from Berlin. Dial, 1985;
    Allen, 1985 <U.S., 1939>

*HYNE, C(HARLES) J(OHN) CUTCLIFFE (WRIGHT). Ref also: CA.
  *Adventures of Captain Kettle. Silent film: Kettle, 1922 (dir: Meyrick Milton)
  *Fireman Hot. ss, some with OK

*IAMS, JACK
  *A Corpse of the Old School. <Conn.> (setting correction)

*IANNUZZI, JOHN N(ICHOLAS)
  *Courthouse. <NYC>

IBANEZ, VICENTE BLASCO. 1867-1928. Ref: CA.
  The Mad Virgins, and other stories. Butterworth, 1926 ss, some criminous

IBARGUENGOITIA, JORGE. 1928-1983. Ref: CA.
  The Dead Girls. Avon, 1983; Chatto, 1983 (Translation of "Las Muertas." Mexico City, 1977.) <Mex.>
  Two Crimes. Godine, 1984; Chatto, 1984 <Mex.> (Translation of "Dos Crimenes." Mexico City, 1979)

IDRIESS, ION L(LEWELLYN). 1890-1979. Ref: CA.
  Nemarluk, King of the Wilds. Angus, 1941 <Australia>

IHARA, TONI. See: Ralph Warner.

*ILES, FRANCIS
  *Before the Fact. Film: RKO, 1941, as Suspicion (scw: Samson Raphaelson, Joan Harrison, Alma Reville; dir: Alfred Hitchcock)

INCHBALD, PETER. SC: Insp. Franco Corti, in all titles.
  Or the Bambino Dies. Collins, 1985; Doubleday, 1985 <It.>
  Short Break in Venice. Collins, 1983; Doubleday, 1983 <Venice>
  The Sweet Short Grass. Collins, 1982; Doubleday, 1982 <Venice>
  Tondo for Short. Collins, 1981; Doubleday, 1982 <Venice>

*ING, DEAN. 1931-   . Ref: CA.

INKSTER, LEONARD. Pseudonym: *John Fethaland.

*INMAN, H(ERBERT) ESCOTT
  A Tear of Kalee, with Hartley Aspden. Chatto, 1902

*INNES, (RALPH) HAMMOND. Ref also: BM, TM. SC: Peter Deveril, in *Air Disaster, and in others.
  The Black Tide. Collins, 1982; Doubleday, 1983 <Afghan., ship>
  *Campbell's Kingdom. Film: Rank, 1957 (scw: Robin Estridge, Hammond Innes; dir: Ralph Thomas)
  High Stand. Collins, 1985; Atheneum, 1986 <Can.>
  *The Lonely Skier. Film: Gainsborough, 1948, as Snowbound (scw: David Evans, Keith Campbell; dir: David Macdonald)
  *The Mary Deare. Film: MGM, 1959, as The Wreck of the Mary Deare (scw: Eric Ambler; dir: Michael Anderson)
  *The White South. Film: Warwick, 1954, as Hell Below Zero (scw: Alec Coppel, Max Trell, Richard Maibaum; dir: Mark Robson)

*INNES, MICHAEL. SC: John Appleby, also in titles belowmarked JA; Charles Honeybath, also in titles below marked CH. Set: Eng.
  Appleby and Honeybath. Gollancz, 1983; Dodd, 1983 JA,CH
  *Appleby Talking. Detective Book Club reprint as Dead Man's Shoes omits 3 ss and adds one.
  Carson's Conspiracy. Gollancz, 1984; Dodd, 1984 JA
  *Christmas at Candleshoe. Film: Disney, 1977, as Candleshoe (scw: David Swift, Rosemary Anne Sisson; dir: Norman Tokar)
  *The Journeying Boy. <Ire.>
  Lord Mullion's Secret. Gollancz, 1981; Dodd, 1982 CH
  Sheiks and Adders. Gollancz, 1982; Dodd, 1983 JA

*IRISH, WILLIAM
  After-Dinner Story. Film (from ss "Rear Window"): Paramount, 1954, as Rear Window (scw: John Michael Hayes; dir: Alfred Hitchcock)
  *The Dancing Detective. Film (from ss "Two Fellows in a Furnished Room"): Monogram, 1947, as The Guilty (scw: Robert R. Presnell, Sr.; dir: John Reinhardt)
  *Borrowed Crime. Film (from ss "Chance"): Columbia, 1944, as Mark of the Whistler (scw: George Bricker; dir: William Castle)
  *Dead Man Blues. Film (from ss "Fire Escape"): RKO, 1949, as The Window (scw: Mel Dinelli; dir: Ted Tetzlaff). Also: Universal International, 1966, as The Boy Cried Murder (scw: Robin Estridge; dir: George Breakston). Film (from ss "If the Dead Could Talk"): Pathe, 1954, as Obsession (scw: Antoine Blondin, Roland Laudenbach, Jean Delannoy; dir: Delannoy). Also: Carr, 1984, as Cloak and Dagger (scw: Tom Holland; dir: Richard Franklin)
  *Deadline at Dawn. Film: RKO, 1946 (scw: Clifford Odets; dir: Harold Clurman)
  *Eyes That Watch You. Film (from ss "All at Once, No Alice"): Columbia, 1948, as Return of the Whistler (scw: Edward Bock, Maurice Tombragel; dir: D. Ross Lederman)
  *I Married a Dead Man. Film: Paramount, 1950, as No Man of Her Own (scw: Sally Benson, Catherine Turney; dir: Mitchell Leisen). Also: Sara, 1983, as J'Ai Epouse une Ombre (I Married a Dead Man) (scw: Davis Laurent, Patrick Laurent; dir: Robin Davis)
  *I Wouldn't Be in Your Shoes. Film (from title ss): Monogram, 1948, as I Wouldn't Be in Your Shoes (scw: Steve Fisher; dir: William Nigh). Film (from ss "Nightmare"): Paramount, 1947, as Fear in the Night (scw & dir: Maxwell Shane)
  *Phantom Lady. Film: Universal, 1944 (scw: Bernard C. Schoenfeld; dir: Robert Siodmak)
  *Six Nights of Mystery. Film (from ss "One Night in New York"): Columbia, 1938, as Convicted (scw: Edgar Edwards; dir: Leon Barsha)
  *Waltz into Darkness. Film: United Artists, 1969, as La Sirene du Mississippi (Mississippi Mermaid) (scw & dir: Francois Truffaut)

IRONS, GENEVIEVE
  The Mystery of the Priest's Parlour. Sands, 1911; Herder, n.d.

IRONSIDE, ELIZABETH
  A Very Private Enterprise. Hodder, 1984; Hodder (U.S.), 1985 <India>

IRVINE, E. MARIE. See: J. L. Rankin.

*IRVINE, R(OBERT) R(ALSTONE). Ref also: TM. All earlier appearances of SC Bob Christopher are identified; he appears also in the title below.
  Ratings Are Murder. Walker, 1985 <L.A.>

*IRVING, CLIFFORD (MICHAEL). See also: *Herbert Burkholz.
  The Angel of Zin. Stein, 1984; Hodder, 1984 <Pol., 1943>

*IRVING, CLIVE
  *Axis. <1936-1940>

*IRWIN, THEODORE D.
  *Collusion. Film: Majestic, 1934, as Unknown Blonde (scw: Leonard Field, David Silverstein; dir: Hobart Henley). Also: MGM, 1935, as Age of Indiscretion (scw: Leonore Coffee; dir: Edward Ludwig)

*ISAACS, SUSAN
  *Compromising Positions. Film: Paramount, 1985 (scw: Susan Isaacs; dir: Frank Perry)

ISDALE, MARK
  Mrs. Burlington. Gleniffer, 1983

*ISHAM, FREDERIC S(TEWART)
  *Half a Chance. Silent film: Reliance, 1913 (dir: Oscar Apfel). Also: Hampton, 1920 (scw: Fred Myton; dir: Robert Thornby)
  *A Man and His Money. Silent film: Goldwyn, 1919 (dir: Harry Beaumont)
  *The Social Buccaneer. Silent film: Bluebird, 1916 (scw: Fred Myton; dir: Jack Conway)
  Three Live Ghosts. Bobbs, 1918. 3-act play version, with *Max Marcin, q.v.: French, 1922. Film: Schenck, 1929 (scw: Helen Hallett; dir: Thornton Freeland)

*ISRAEL, CHARLES E(DWARD)
  *The Mark. Film: Stross, 1961 (scw: Sidney Buchman, Stanley Mann; dir: Guy Green)

*IVES, JOHN
  *Fear in a Handful of Dust. Also published as by Brian Garfield: Mysterious Press, 1985. Film: Amiritraj, 1984, as Fleshburn (scw: Beth Gage, George Gage; dir: George Gage)

*JACKMAN, STUART (BROOKE). Ref: not in TC2.

*JACKS, JEFF. Ref: TM.
  *Murder on the Wild Side. Film: Warner, 1974, as Black Eye (scw: Mark Haggard, Jim Martin; dir: Jack Arnold)

*JACKSON, BASIL
  Crooked Flight. St. Martin's, 1985;

Hale, 1984
The Night Manhattan Burned. Norton, 1979; Hale, 1980
State of Emergency. Norton, 1982; Hale, 1983

*JACKSON, BRUCE. 1936-   . Director of Studies in American Culture, Professor of English and Comparative Literature, and Adjunct Professor of Law at the State Univ. of N.Y. at Buffalo.

JACKSON, CHARLES REGINALD. 1903-1968. Ref: CA.
The Outer Edges. Reinhart, 1948; Nevill, 1950

JACKSON, DELMAR. 1921-   .
The Cut of the Ax. Harcourt, 1953; Hart-Davis, 1954. Reprinted as: The Night Is My Undoing. Popular Library, 1954 <West>

JACKSON, FRANCIS. See: J. L. Rankin.

*JACKSON, FREDERICK
*The Bishop Misbehaves. Film: MGM, 1935; released in Britain as The Bishop's Misadventures (scw: Leon Gordon, George Auerbach; dir: E. A. Dupont)

JACKSON, ROBERT. 1941-   . SC: Yoeman, in all titles.
-Hunter Squadron. Weidenfeld, 1984
-Hurricane Squadron. Barker, 1978; Walker, 1984
-Korean Combat. Barker, 1983
-The Last Battle. Barker, 1982
-Malta Victory. Barker, 1980
-Mosquito Squadron. Barker, 1981
-Operation Diver. Barker, 1981
-Operation Firedog. Barker, 1982
-Squadron Scramble. Barker, 1978; Walker, 1985
-Target Tobruk. Barker, 1979
-Tempest Squadron. Barker, 1981
-Venom Squadron. Barker, 1983

*JACKSON, SHIRLEY. Ref: not in TC2. See also: (Silas) Brainerd Duffield.
*The Bird's Nest. Film (from title ss): MGM, 1957, as Lizzie (scw: Mel Dinelli; dir: Hugo Haas)
*The Haunting of Hill House. Film: Argyle, 1963, as The Haunting (scw: Nelson Gidding; dir: Robert Wise)

JACOBS, HARVEY. 1930-   . Ref: CA.
The Juror. Watts, 1980 <NYC>

*JACOBS, T(HOMAS) C(URTIS) H(ICKS)
*Traitor Spy. Film: Rialto, 1939; released in the U.S. as The Torso Murder Mystery (scw: Walter Summers, John Argyle, Jan Van Lusil, Ralph Gilbert Bettinson; dir: Summers)

*JACOBS, W(ILLIAM) W(YMARK)
*The Lady of the Barge. Silent film (from ss "The Monkey's Paw"): Magnet, 1915, as The Monkey's Paw (dir: Sidney Northcote). Also: Artistic, 1923, as The Monkey's Paw (scw: Lydia Hayward; dir: Manning Haynes). Sound film: RKO, 1933, as The Monkey's Paw (scw: Graham John; dir: Wesley Ruggles). Also: Kay, 1948, as The Monkey's Paw (scw: Norman Lee, Barbara Toy; dir: Lee)
*Sea Whispers. Film (from ss "The Interruption"): Film Locations, 1955, as Footsteps in the Fog (scw: Lenore Coffee, Dorothy Reed, Arthur Pierson; dir: Arthur Lubin)

*JACOBSEN, JULIUS
*The Revelations of a Police Court Inspector. criminous ss

JACOBSON, DAN. 1929-   . Ref: CA.
A Dance in the Sun. Weidenfeld, 1956; Harcourt, 1956 <S. Afr.>

JACOT, (DE BOINOD) B(ERNARD) L(OUIS). 1898-1977. See: Helen Astrup, 1910-

*JACQUEMARD, YVES. 1943-1981.

*JACQUES, NORBERT
*Dr. Mabuse, Master of Mystery. Silent film: Ufa, 1922, as Doktor Mabuse, Der Spieler (Dr. Mabuse, Gambler) (scw: Thea von Harbou; dir: Fritz Lang). Also: Decla-Bioscop, 1927 (credits not found)

*JAEDIKER, KERMIT. ca.1912-1986. Ref: CA.

*JAFFE, SUSAN
*The Other Anne Fletcher. ... Sphere, 1983

JAGGER, ARTHUR
Murder Intended. (London) pb, ca. 1950

JAGNINSKI, TOM. See: *Don(ald Eugene) Pendleton.

*JAHN, (JOSEPH) MICHAEL. Ref also: TM. See also: *Nick Carter.
Night Rituals. Norton, 1982 <NYC>

*JAKES, JOHN (WILLIAM). Ref also: TM.

JAMES, BERT. Pseudonym of B. Hobson, q.v.
The Loser Pays. States (Syd.), 1925

JAMES, BILL
You'd Better Believe It. Constable, 1985; St. Martin's, 1986

*JAMES, DONALD
The Fall of the Russian Empire. Putnam, 1982; Granada, 1983 <Russ., 1986>

JAMES, ELIZABETH. Joint pseudonym with Carol Barkin: Beverly Hastings, q.v.

*JAMES, FRANKIE-LEE. 1908-   .
Pseudonym: *Saliee O'Brien.

JAMES, GEOFFREY
At Break of Dawn. Drane, 1906

JAMES, GERTIE DE S. WENTWORTH
The Devil's Profession. Everett, 1914. Silent film: Arrow, 1915 (scw & dir: F. C. S. Tudor)

*JAMES, HENRY. See also: Ken Whitmore.
-The Aspern Papers. Macmillan (NYC & London), 1888. Film: Universal, 1947, as The Lost Moment (scw: Leonardo Bercovici; dir: Martin Gabel). Also: Oxala (Portugal), 1981, as Aspern (scw: Michael Graham; dir: Eduardo de Grigorio)
The Princess Casamassina. Macmillan (NYC & London), 1886
*The Turn of the Screw. Film: Achilles, 1960, as The Innocents (scw: William Archibald, Truman Capote, John Mortimer; dir: Jack Clayton). Also: Guarko, 1985, as Otra Vuelta de Tuerca (The Turn of the Screw) (scw: Gonzalo Golkoetxea, Eloy de la Iglesia, Angel Sastre; dir: de la Iglesia)

*JAMES, MARGARET. Pseudonym of *Pamela Bennetts, q.v.

*JAMES, P(HYLLIS) D(OROTHY). Ref also: BM, TM. SC: Cordelia Gray, in *An Unsuitable Job for a Woman, and in title marked CG below. Set: Eng.
The Skull Beneath the Skin. Faber, 1982; Scribner, 1982 CG
*An Unsuitable Job for a Woman. Film: Boyd, 1981 (scw: Elizabeth MacKay, Brian Scobie, Christopher Petit; dir: Petit)

JAMES, PETER. 1948-   .
Atom Bomb Angel. Allen, 1982
-Billionaire. Allen, 1983
Dead Letter Drop. Allen, 1981
Traveling Man. Star, 1984 (Novelization of TV series.)

*JAMES, REBECCA. Pseudonym of James Joseph Elward, 1928-   . Ref: CA.

JAMES, RIAN. 1899-   . Brooklyn newspaperman.
Love Is a Racket. King, 1931. Film: Warner, 1932 (scw: Courtney Terrett; dir: William A. Wellman)
Some Call It Love. King, 1933. Film: Warner, 1933, as The Parachute Jumper (scw: John Francis Larkin; dir: Alfred E. Green)

*JAMES, STUART
*Jack the Ripper. (Novelization of film: Mid Century, 1958; scw: Jimmy Sangster; dir: Robert S. Baker)
*The Stranglers of Bombay. (Novelization of film: Hammer, 1959; scw: David Z. Goodman; dir: Terence Fisher)

JAMESON, FRANK
Green Fire. Hodder, 1984 <S. Am., 1968>

*JAMESON, (MARGARET) STORM. See also: Ruth Goertz.
*Before the Crossing. <Eng., 1939>
The Hidden River. Macmillan (London), 1955; Harper, 1955

JANCE, J(UDITH) A(NN). 1944-   . Ref: CA.
Until Proven Guilty. Avon, 1985 <Seattle>

JANES, J. ROBERT
The Watcher. PaperJacks, 1982 <Can.>

JANESHUTZ, TRISH. 1947-   . Born and raised in Caracaz, Venez.; living in south Florida.
In Shadows. Ballantine, 1985 <acad., Miami>

*JANSON, HANK. House name. So much new information is available that the entry, as amended, is here produced in full; no reference to CF is necessary. Titles by *Stephen D(aniel) Francis, 1917-   , q.v., are marked "by SF". Titles by *Harry Hobson, 1908-   , are marked "by HH"; other Hobson pseudonym: *Hank Hobson. Titles by *James Moffatt, 1922-   , are marked "by JM". Titles by Colin Simpson are marked "by CS". Titles by *Harold Ernest Kelly, 1900-1969, are marked "by HK"; other Kelly pseudonyms: *Eugene Ascher, *Darcy Glinto, *Gordon Holt, *Buck Toler. Titles by *Victor George Charles Norwood, 1920-1983, are marked "by VN"; other Norwood pseudonyms: *Shane Baxter, *Johnny Dark, *Mark Hampton, *Nat Karta. SC: Hank Janson, in at least those titles marked HJ. Note that at least those titles published by Gold Star are copyrighted by G. Gold and D. Warburton.
*Abomination. Compact, 1965 by JM
Accused. New Ficton, 1952
*The Affairs of Paula. Gold Star, 1965 HJ <Chi.>
All Tramps Are Trouble. Roberts, 1960
Amok. New Fiction, 1953. Reprinted as: Fireball. Roberts, 1960?
*Amorous Captive. Moring, 1958-9 (3 volumes)
*Angel Astray. Roberts, 1962
*Angel, Shoot to Kill. Frances, 1949. Reprinted as: Outcast. Roberts, 1961 by SF
*Auctioned. New Fiction, 1952
*Avenging Nymph. Moring, 1958
*Baby, Don't Dare Squeal. Frances, 1951. Reprinted as: Cool Sugar. Roberts, 1960 by SF
*Backlash of Infamy. Compact, 1965 by JM
*Bad Girl; see Frails Can Be So Tough
*Beauty and the Heat. Roberts, 1962 by HH
*Becky. Gold Star, 1965
*Beloved Traitor; see Lady Toll That Bell
Berlin Briefing. Compact, 1965 by HH
Bewitched. Moring, 1957?
*Bid for Beauty. Compact, 1966 by CS
*The Big H. Compact, 1966 by HH
The Big Lie. Moring, 1956
The Big Round Bed. Compact, 1970 by HH
*Blonde on the Spot. Frances, 1949 by SF
*Blood Bath. Rroberts, 1962 by VN
*Brand Image. Compact, 1963 by SF
*Brazen Seductress. Gold Star, 1963 HJ
*Break for a Lovely. Roberts, 1961
*The Bride Wore Weeds. Frances, 1950 by SF
Bring Me Sorrow; see *Skirts Bring Me Sorrow
*Broads Don't Scare Easy. New Fiction, 1951. Reprinted as: Don't Scare Easy. Moring, 1956 by SF
Cactus. Moring, 1956
Caribbean Caper. Compact, 1971 by HH
Casino Strip. Compact, 1967 by HH
*Casinopoly. Compact, 1967 by HH
*Catch Me a Renegade. Compact, 1965 by JM

J

Cat's Paw. Compact, 1969 by CS
*Chicago Chick. Roberts, 1962 <Chi.> by HH
*Cold Dead Coed. Gold Star, 1964 HJ
*Come Quickly, Honey; see *Sweetie, Hold Me Tight
*Conflict. New Fiction, 1952
*Contraband. Moring, 1955
*Cool Sugar; see Baby, Don't Dare Squeal
Corruption. Top Fiction, 1952. Reprinted as: *Secret Session. Roberts, 1960
*Counter-Feat. Compact, 1965
Covering Fire. Compact, 1969 by CS
*Crime on My Hands. Roberts, 1962
*Crimebeat Crisis. Compact, 1964 by HH
*Crowns Can Kill. Roberts, 1961 by HH
Crunch. Compact, 1968 by CS
Cupid Turns Killer. Roberts, 1960
*Cutie on Call. Roberts, 1960
*Darling Delinquent. Compact, 1966 by HH
*Dateline Darlene. Roberts, 1963 by HH
*Dateline Debbie. Compact, 1963 by HH
*Dateline Diane. Roberts, 1962 by HH
*Daughter of Shame. Compact, 1963 by SF
*Dead Certainty. Compact, 1966
Deadly Horse-Race. Compact, 1967 by HH
*Deadly Mission. Top Fiction, 1953?
*Death Wore a Petticoat. Frances, 1951 by SF
*Delicious Danger; see *Sadie Don't Cry Now
Depravity. Compact, 1964 by JM
*Desert Fury. New Fiction, 1953
*Design for Dupes. Compact, 1964
*Destination Dames. Roberts, 1961
*The Devil and the Deep. Compact, 1965 by JM
*Devil's Highway. Moring, 1956
*Dig Those Heels. Roberts, 1962
The Dish Ran Away. Compact, 1964 by JM
*Doctor Fix. Compact, 1964 by HH
Don't Cry Now; see *Sadie, Don't Cry Now
*Don't Dare Me, Sugar. Frances, 1950 by SF
*Don't Mourn Me, Toots. Frances, 1951 by SF
*Don't Scare Easy; see Broads Don't Scare Easy
*Double Take. Compact, 1964
*Downtown Doll; see Lola Brought Her Wreath
*Ecstacy. Roberts, 1960
Enemy of Man. Moring, 1957
*Escalation. Compact, 1966 by HH
*Escape. Moring, 1956
*Exclusive. Roberts, 1962
*The Exotic Seductress. Gold Star, 1964 HJ
*Expectant Nymph. Gold Star, 1964 HJ
F.E.U.D. Compact, 1966 by HH
*Fan Fare. Compact, 1964 by HH
*Fanny. Gold Star, 1964 HJ
*Fast Buck. Compact, 1963 by HH
*The Filly Wore a Rod. New Fiction, 1952. Reprinted as: Lose This Gun. Moring, 1958
*Fireball; see Amok
*Flashpoint. Compact, 1965 by HH
*Flight from Fear; see Pursuit
*Flower of Desire. Compact, 1964
*48 Hours. Moring, 1955
*Frails Can Be So Tough. New Fiction, 1951. Reprinted as: Bad Girl. Turton, 1959 by SF
Frame and Fortune. Compact, 1970 by CS
*Framed. Moring, 1955
*Furtive Flame. Compact, 1965
*A Girl in Hand. Compact, 1964
Globe Probe. Compact, 1969 by HH
*Go with a Jerk. Roberts, 1962 by VN
*Grape Vine. Roberts, 1962 by HH
Grass Widow. Compact, 1971 by CS
*Gun Moll for Hire. Frances, 1948 by SF
*Gunsmoke in Her Eyes. Frances, 1949 by SF
*Hate; see *Women Hate Till Death
*Heartache. Compact, 1963
Hell Brood. Compact, 1967 by CS
Hell of a Dame. Roberts, 1960
Hellcat. Moring, 1957
*Helldorado. Compact, 1966 by HH
*Hell's Angel. Moring, 1956; Gold Star, 1964 HJ
*Hell's Belles. Roberts, 1961
*Her Weapon Is Passion. Gold Star, 1964 HJ

*Hilary's Terms. Compact, 1963
*Honey for Me. Roberts, 1962
*Honey, Take My Gun. Frances, 1949 by SF
*Hot House. Gold Star, 1964 HJ
*Hot Line. Compact, 1963 by HK
*Hotsy, You'll Be Chilled. Frances, 1951 by SF
*I for Intrigue. Roberts, 1963
Infiltrators. Compact, 1970 by HH
*Invasion. Moring, 1959
*It's Always Eve That Weeps. Frances, 1951 by SF
*It's Bedtime, Baby! Gold Star, 1964 HJ
*Jack Spot. Moring, 1958
*The Jane with Green Eyes. Frances, 1950 by SF
*Janson, Go Home. Roberts, 1961 HJ by HH
*Jazz Jungle. Compact, 1965
*Junk Market. Compact, 1965
The Kay Assignation. Compact, 1971 by HH
*Kill Her If You Can. New Fiction, 1952 by SF
*Kill Her with Passion. Gold Star, 1963 HJ
*Kill Me for Kicks. Roberts, 1962 by VN
*Kill This Man. Moring, 1958
Killer. New Fiction, 1952
*Krush. Compact, 1966
*The Lady Has a Scar. Frances, 1950. Reprinted as: *Sentence for Sin. Roberts, 1960 by SF
*Lady, Lie Low. Roberts, 1961
*Lady, Mind That Corpse. Frances, 1948; Checker, 1949 by SF
*Lady, Toll That Bell. Frances, 1950. Reprinted as: *Beloved Traitor. Roberts, 1960 by SF
*Ladybirds Are In. Compact, 1967 by HH
*Lake Loot. Compact, 1964 by HH
Lament for a Lover. Compact, 1970 by HH
*The Last Lady. Compact, 1964 by JM
*Late Last Night. Roberts, 1961
*Like Crazy. Roberts, 1962 by HH
*Like Lethal. Roberts, 1962 by HH
*Like Poison. Roberts, 1962 by HH
*Lilies for My Lovely. Frances, 1949 by SF
Limbo Lover. Compact, 1964 by HH
*Liquor Is Quicker. Compact, 1966 by HH
The Liz Assignation. Compact, 1971 by HH
*Lola Brought Her Wreath. Frances, 1950. Reprinted as: *Downtown Doll. Roberts, 1961 by SF
The Long Arm. Compact, 1970 by HH
*Lose This Gun; see The Filly Wore a Rod
Love-In and Lamentation. Compact, 1963 by HH
*The Love Makers. Compact, 1963 by HH
*The Love Secretaries. Compact, 1964 by JM
*Lover. Gold Star, 1963 HJ
*Lust for Vengeance. Compact, 1965
*Make Mine Mink. Compact, 1966 by HH
*Master Mind. Roberts, 1961 by HH
*Mayfair Slayride. Compact, 1966 by HH
*Menace. Moring, 1955
Micro Kill. Compact, 1968 by CS
*Milady Took the Rap. New Fiction, 1951 by SF
*Missile Mob. Compact, 1965 by HH
*Mistress of Fear. Moring, 1958
*Model in Mayhem. Compact, 1965 by JM
*Murder. New Fiction, 1952
*Nefarious Quest. Compact, 1966
Nerve Center. Compact, 1963
*A Nice Way to Die. Gold Star, 1963 HJ <Chi.>
*No Regrets for Clara. Frances, 1949. Reprinted as: Rave for a Roughneck. Roberts, 1962 by SF
Nyloned Avenger. Top Fiction, 1953. Reprinted as: *The Sultry Avenger. Moring, 1959
Nymph in the Night. Roberts, 1962
*A Nympho Named Silvia. Gold Star, 1965 HJ
Obsession. Roberts, 1959?
One Against Time. Moring, 1956
*One Man in His Time; see Stephen D. Frances entry
One-Way Split. Compact, 1967 by HH
Operation Obliterate. Compact, 1967 by HH
*Outcast; see Angel, Shoot to Kill
*Passion Pact. Roberts, 1963
*Passionate Playmate. Gold Star, 1964 HJ
*Passionate Waif. Roberts, 1960
*Patterned Rape. Compact, 1964 by JM

Perfumed Nemesis. Top Fiction, 1953
Persian Pride. Top Fiction, 1953
*Physical Attraction. Compact, 1966 by HH
*Play It Quiet; see Some Look Better Dead
Playgirl. Compact, 1963 by VN
*Prey for a Newshawk; see Sister, Don't Hate Me
Pursuit. New Ficton, 1953. Reprinted as: Flight from Fear. Moring, 1958
*Quiet Waits the Grave. Roberts, 1960
*Rave for a Roughneck; see No Regrets for Clara
*Reluctant Hostess. Roberts, 1961
Revolt. Moring, 1957
*Ripe for Rapture. Roberts, 1960
*Riviera Showdown. Compact, 1966 by HH
*Roxy by Proxy. Compact, 1965 by HH
*Run for Lover. Roberts, 1962
*Sadie, Don't Cry Now. New Fiction, 1952. Reprinted as: Don't Cry Now. Moring, 1957? And as: *Delicious Danger. Roberts, 1961 by SF
*Same Difference. Compact, 1967 by HH
*Savage Sequel. Roberts, 1962
*Say It with Candy. Compact, 1965
*Scent from Heaven. Roberts, 1961
*Second String. Roberts, 1963 by SF
*Secret Session; see Corruption
Sensuality. Compact, 1963 by VN
*Sentence for Sin; see The Lady Has a Scar
*Sex Angle. Compact, 1964
*The Sexy Vixen. Gold Star, 1964 HJ
Shalom, My Love. Compact, 1968 by HH
*She Sleeps to Conquer. Roberts, 1961
She Waif. Roberts, 1962
*Short-Term Wife. Roberts, 1961
Silken Menace. Top Fiction, 1953. Reprinted as: *Silken Snare. Moring, 1959
*Silken Snare; see Silken Menace
Sinister Rapture. Moring, 1957
*Sister, Don't Hate Me. Frances, 1949. Reprinted as: *Prey for a Newshawk. Roberts, 1961 by SF
*Situation, Grave!; see *Sweetheart, Here's Your Grave
*Skirts Bring Me Sorrow. New Fiction, 1952. Reprinted as: Bring Me Sorrow. Moring, 1956 by SF
Slaves for Seduction. Roberts, 1960
*Slay-Ride for Cutie. Frances, 1949 by SF
*Smart Girls Don't Talk. Frances, 1949 by SF
*Soft Cargo. Compact, 1964
*Some Look Better Dead. Frances, 1950. Reprinted as: *Play It Quiet. Roberts, 1962 by SF
Sprung! Compact, 1968 by HH
The Spy in My Bed. Compact, 1969 by HH
*Square One. Compact, 1964 by HH
Strange Destiny. Moring, 1956
Strange Ritual. Compact, 1963
*Suddenly, It's Sin; see Torment for Trixie
*Sugar and Vice. Moring, 1958
*The Sultry Avenger; see Nyloned Avenger
Suspense. New Fiction, 1952
Sweet Fury. Moring, 1957?
*Sweet Talk. Compact, 1965 by JM
*Sweetheart, Here's Your Grave! Frances, 1949. Reprinted as: *Situation, Grave! Moring, 1958 by SF
*Sweetie, Hold Me Tight. Frances, 1950. Reprinted as: *Come Quickly, Honey. Roberts, 1960 by SF
*Tailsting. Compact, 1965 by HH
*Take This--Sweetie. Roberts, 1962 by HH
Take Two Blondes. Compact, 1967 by CS
*Tension. New Fiction, 1952
*That Brain Again. Compact, 1964 by HH
They Die Alone. Moring, 1956
*This Dame Dies Soon. Frances, 1951. Reprinted as: Too Soon to Die. Moring, 1958 by SF
*This Hood for Hire; see Vengeance
This Wicked Sex. Roberts, 1960
*This Woman Is Death. Frances, 1948 by SF
*Tigress. Compact, 1963
*Tomorrow and a Day. Moring, 1955
*Too Soon to Die; see This Dame Dies Soon
*Top Ten. Compact, 1964 by VN
Torment. New Fiction, 1953
*Torment for Trixie. Frances, 1950. Reprinted as: Suddenly It's Sin. Roberts, 1961 by SF
*Torrid Temptress. Turton, 1959
Twilight Tigress. Compact, 1970

by CS
*Twist for Two. Roberts, 1962
  Ultimate Deterrent. Compact, 1970
    by HH
*Uncommon Market. Roberts, 1962 by HH
*Uncover Agent. Roberts, 1962 by HH
*The Unseen Assassin. Top Fiction,
  1953 <future>
  Untamed. Moring, 1955?
*V for Vitality. Compact, 1963
*Vagabond Vamp. Roberts, 1962
  Vengeance. New Fiction, 1953. Re-
    printed as: *This Hood for Hire.
    Roberts, 1960
*Venus Makes Three. Roberts, 1961
  Villon of the Piece. Compact, 1970
    by HH
*Visit from a Broad. Compact, 1963
    by HH
*Voodoo Violence. Compact, 1964
*Way Out Wanton. Roberts, 1962
*When Dames Get Tough. Ward & Hitchon,
    1946
*Whiplash. New Fiction, 1952
*Why Should Sylvia? Compact, 1965
    by JM
*Wild Girl. Turton, 1959
*Will-Power. Compact, 1964 by VN
  Woman Trap. Top Fiction, 1953
*Women Hate Till Death. New Fiction,
  1951. Reprinted as: Hate. Moring,
  1958 by SF
*The Young Wolves. Compact, 1967
    by CS
*Zero Takes All. Compact, 1967 by HH

*JAPRISOT, SEBASTIEN
*The Lady in the Car with Glasses and
  a Gun. Film: Lira, 1970, as La
  Dame Dans L'Auto Avec des Lunettes
  et un Fusel (The Lady in the Car
  with Glasses and a Gun) (scw:
  Richard Harris, Eleanor Perry; dir:
  Anatole Litvak)
*One Deadly Summer. Film: SNC, 1983,
  as L'Ete Meurtrier (One Deadly Sum-
  mer) (scw: Sebastien Japrisot; dir:
  Jean Becker)
*The 10:30 from Marseilles. Film:
  Seven Arts, 1965, as Compartment
  Tueurs (The Sleeping Car Murders)
  (scw: Sebastien Japrisot, Costa
  Gavras; dir: Gavras)
*Trap for Cinderella. Film: Gaumont,
  1965, as Piege pour Cendrillon
  (Trap for Cinderella) (scw: Se-
  bastien Japrisot, J. B. Rossi,
  Jean Anouilh, Andre Cayatte; dir
  Cayatte)

*JARDINE, WARWICK. Pseudonym of Francis
  Alister Warwick.

JARREAU, LESLIE
  Hanky Panky. Pinnacle, 1982 (Noveli-
    zation of film: Columbia, 1982;
    scw: Henry Rosenbaum, David Taylor;
    dir: Sidney Poitier)

*JARRETT, CORA (HARDY). Ref: not in
  TC2.

JARRETT, PAUL
  The Throwaway Man. Hale, 1985 <1943>

JARVIS, SHARON. 1943-   . Joint pseudonym with Kathleen Buckley:
  H. M. Major, q.v.

JASON, PAUL and JEFFREY SAGER
  Entangled. NAL, 1982; Severn, 1983
    <NYC>

*JASON, STUART. SC: The Butcher, also
  in all titles below, written by
  *Michael (Angelo) Avallone, q.v.
  Coffin Corner. Pinnacle, 1981
  Death in Yellow. Pinnacle, 1981
  Go Die in Afghanistan. Pinnacle, 1982
    <Afghan.>
  Gotham Gore. Pinnacle, 1982
  The Hoodoo Horror. Pinnacle, 1981
  The Man from White Hat. Pinnacle,
    1982 <S. Am.>

*JAUNIERE, CLAUDETTE
  Captive Heart. Mystique, 1981 (Trans-
    lation of "Mariage Manque." Paris,
    1965.)
  Heart of Deception. Mystique, 1981
    (Translation of "Le Sourire aux
    Levres." Paris, 1961.)
  Heart's Revenge. Mystique, 1981
    (Translation of "Des Mots Pour
    Rever." Paris, 1964.)
  Journey of Fear. Mystique, 1982
    (Translation of "La Folle Impru-
    dence." Paris, 1975.)
  Marry into Danger. Mystique, 1982
    (Translation of "L'Amour S'Em
    Va..." Paris, 1954.)

*JAY, CHARLOTTE. Ref: TM.
*The Knife Is Dangerous. <Australia>

*JEFFERIES, IAN
*It Wasn't Me! criminous

*JEFFERIS, BARBARA (TARLTON)
*Beloved Lady. <Eng., 1400s>
*Solo for Several Players.
  <Australia>
*Undercurrent. <Syd.>
*The Wild Grapes. <Australia>

*JEFFERS, H(ARRY) PAUL. Ref also: TM.
  SC: Harry MacNeil = HM.
  Murder Most Irregular. St. Martin's,
    1983; Hale, 1984 <Eng.>
  Murder on Mike. St. Martin's, 1984
    HM <NYC, 1939>
  -A Portrait in Murder and Gay Colors.
    Knights, 1985
  The Rubout at the Onyx. Ticknor, 1981
    HM <NYC, 1935>

*JEFFERSON, ROLAND S. 1939-   . Ref:
  CA.
*The School on 103rd Street. ... Also
  published as: The Secret Below
  103rd Street. Holloway, 1983

JEFFREY, WILLIAM. Joint pseudonym of
  *Bill Pronzini, q.v., and *Jeffrey
  M(iner) Wallmann.
  Day of the Moon. Hale, 1983

*JEFFREYS, J. G. See: *Jeremy Stur-
  rock.

*JEFFRIES, GRAHAM MONTAGUE. 1900-1982.

*JEFFRIES, RODERIC (GRAEME). Ref
  also: TM. SC: Insp. Alvarez, also
  in all titles below. Set: Majorca.
  Deadly Petard. Collins, 1983; St.
    Martin's, 1984
  Layers of Deceit. Collins, 1985; St.
    Martin's, 1985
  Three and One Make Five. Collins,
    1984; St. Martin's, 1984
  Unseemly End. Collins, 1981; St.
    Martin's, 1982

JEFKINS, FRANK (WILLIAM). 1920-
  Ref: CA.
  Wanted on Holiday. Hodder, 1960

*JENKINS, CECIL. Ref also: CA.

*JENKINS, GEOFFREY
  Fireprint. Collins, 1984 <future>
  -A Ravel of Waters. Collins, 1981
 *A Twist of Sand. Film: Christina,
    1967 (scw: Marvin H. Albert;
    dir: Don Chaffey)
  The Unripe Gold. Collins, 1983

*JENKINS, JERRY (BRUCE). SC: Margo
  Franklin Spence and Philip Spence
  also in titles marked S below;
  Jennifer Grey, in titles marked JG.
  Allyson. Moody, 1981 S
  The Calling. Victor, 1984 JG <Chi.>
  Courtney. Moody, 1983 <Ill.> S
  Erin. Moody, 1983 <Chi.> S
  Gateway. Victor, 1983 JG <Chi.>
  Heartbeat. Victor, 1983 JG <Chi.>
 *Hilary. <Ill.>
  Janell. Moody, 1983 <Chi.>   S
 *Karlyn. <Ill.>
  Lindsey. Moody, 1983 S
  Lyssa. Moody, 1984 <Chi.>
 *Margo. <Chi.>
  Margo's Reunion. Moody, 1984 S
    <Chi.>
  Meagham. Moody, 1983 S
  Paige. Moody, 1981 <Ill.> S
  Shannon. Moody, 1982 <Chi.> S
  Three Days in Winter. Victor, 1983
    JG <Chi.>
  Too Late to Tell. Victor, 1984 JG
    <Chi.>
  Veiled Threat. Victor, 1985 JG
    <Chi.>

JENKINS, PRISCILLA
  Black Wedding. Hutchinson, 1983

*JENKINS, WILL(IAM) F(ITZGERALD). Ref
  also: TM.

JENKINSON, E(DWARD) J(AMES)
  The Gates of Doom. Stockwell, ca.1930
    <India>

*JENKS, GEORGE C(HARLES). Ref: CA.

*JENSEN, RUBY JEAN
  Home Sweet Home. Zebra, 1985

*JEPSON, EDGAR (ALFRED). SC: Lord Bar-
  radine, in *Barradine Detects, and
  *The Four Green Fish.
 *Arsene Lupin. Silent film: London,
    1916 (scw: Kenelm Foss; dir: George
    L. Tucker). Also: Vitagraph, 1917
    (scw: Garfield Thompson, Paul
    Potter; dir: Paul Scardon).
 *The Loudwater Mystery. Silent film:
    Broadwest, 1921 (scw & dir: Norman
    Macdonald)

*JEPSON, SELWYN
 *Man Running. Film: WB-FN, 1950, as
    Stage Fright (scw: Whitfield Cook,
    Alma Reville, James Bridie; dir:
    Alfred Hitchcock)
 *The Qualified Adventurer. Silent
    film: Stoll, 1925 (scw & dir:
    Sinclair Hill)

*JEROME, GILBERT
 *The Filibuster's Warning. Street,
    1903

JESSEY, CORNELIA. Pseudonym of Cornelia
  Silver Sussman, 1914-   . Ref: CA.
  The Treasures of Darkness. Noonday,
    1953; Collins, 1955 <Ariz.>

*JESSUP, RICHARD. Ref also: CA.
 *The Cunning and the Haunted. <Ga.>
 *The Deadly Duo. Film: United Artists,
    1962 (scw: Owen Harris; dir:
    Reginald LeBorg)
 *The Man in Charge = *The Young Don't
    Cry
  Threat. Viking, 1981; Gollancz, 1981
    <NYC>
 *The Young Don't Cry = *The Man in
    Charge. Film: Columbia, 1957 (scw:
    Richard Jessup; dir: Alfred L.
    Werker)

*JEVONS, MARSHALL. SC: Henry Spearman,
  in *Murder at the Margin, and in
  title below.
  The Fatal Equilibrium. MIT (U.S. &
    U.K.), 1985 <acad.>

JOB, THOMAS
  Uncle Harry. French, 1942 (3-act
    play.) Film: Universal, 1945, as
    The Strange Affair of Uncle Harry;
    also released as Uncle Harry (scw:
    Stephen Longstreet, Keith Winter;
    dir: Robert Siodmak)

JOBSON, A. E.
  The Adventures of Russell Howard.
    Bookstall (Syd.), 1909 ss

*JOBSON, HAMILTON
  Don't Tell the Press. Hale, 1981
  The Sleeping Tiger. Hale, 1982

*JOEY (BLACK).   -1982.

JOHN, COLIN. Pseudonym of Chet Hagan,
  1922-   . Ref: CA.
  The Witching. Tower, 1982 <Pa.>

*JOHN, KATHERINE. See: *Romilly John.

*JOHN, OWEN. Ref: CA.

*JOHN, ROMILLY and KATHERINE
*Death by Request. ... Hogarth, 1984

JOHNS, ALLAN
  The Hit Girl. Hale, 1983

*JOHNS, DEREK
*The Beatrice Mystery. ... Secker
    (U.S.), 1983 <It.>

*JOHNS, LARRY
  The Dongola Script. Hale, 1981
  A Time to Die. Hale, 1981

*JOHNS, VERONICA PARKER. Ref also: TC2,
  TM.

JOHNSON, AUDREY P(IKE). 1915-
  Ref: CA.
  Hush, Winifred Is Dead. Avalon,
    1976 <N.Y.>

JOHNSON, CHRISTINE. 1953-   .
  Clinic. Alexandrian, 1985 <Calif.>

*JOHNSON, E(MIL) RICHARD. Ref also:
  TM.

JOHNSON, ENID. Joint pseudonym with
  Margaret Lane: *Jennifer Jones.

*JOHNSON, GEORGE CLAYTON and *JACK GOLDEN RUSSELL
*Ocean's 11. (Novelization of film: Warner, 1960; scw: Harry Brown, Charles Lederer; dir: Lewis Milestone)

JOHNSON, GLADYS (ETTA). 1891- .
Moon Country. Penn, 1924 <Calif.>

JOHNSON, LOUIS OMOTAYO
Black Maria. Spectrum, 1981
Murder at Dawn. Spectrum, 1981
The Oil Pirates. Spectrum, 1983

JOHNSON, MICHAEL J.
Death and Lila Fell. Tower, 1981

*JOHNSON, MIKE. Pseudonym of *Jack Sharkey, q.v. Other pseudonym: Rick Abbot, q.v.
*The Clone People. French, 1978 (3-act play.) <L.A.>
Return of the Maniac. French, 1981 (3-act play.)

JOHNSON, NORMA (TADLOCK)
Inca Gold. Walker, 1984
-Too Hot to Handle. Walker, 1985

*JOHNSON, SANDY
Walk a Winter Beach. Delacorte, 1982 <L.I.>

JOHNSON, SHEILA
Goldilocks. Collins, 1983
Of Wilful Intent. Collins, 1982
Suffer Little Children. Collins, 1981

*JOHNSON, STANLEY (PATRICK)
The Marburg Virus. Heinemann (London & U.S.), 1982
Tunnel. Heinemann (London & U.S.), 1984

JOHNSON, UWE. 1934-1984. Ref: CA.
-Speculations About Jacob. Grove, 1963 (Translation of "Mutmassungen uber Jakob." Frankfurt, 1959.)

*JOHNSON, WILLIAM OSCAR
Hammered Gold. PB, 1982; Star, 1983 <L.A., 1984>

*JOHNSTON, (WILLIAM) DENIS. 1901-1984. Ref: CA.

*JOHNSTON, GEORGE H(ENRY). Pseudonym: *Shane Martin.

JOHNSTON, IVAN
Sergeant on Trial. Hale, 1982
Special Drug Squad. Hale, 1982

JOHNSTON, JANE. 1927- . Former teacher living in NYC.
Pray for Ricky Foster. St. Martin's, 1985 <NYC>

*JOHNSTON, VELDA. Ref: TC2, TM.
The Crystal Cat. Dodd, 1985 <Conn.>
The Fateful Summer. Dodd, 1981; Chivers, 1983 <L.I., 1910>
The Other Karen. Dodd, 1983 <Maine>
*A Presence in an Empty Room. ... Allen, 1982
Shadow Behind the Curtain. Dodd, 1985; Severn, 1986 <N. Mex.>
*The Stone Maiden. ... Chivers, 1983
Voice in the Night. Dodd, 1984; Chivers, 1985 <Ariz.>

*JOHNSTON, WILLIAM (ANDREW)
*The House of Whispers. Silent film: Hankinson, 1920 (scw: Jack Cunningham; dir: Ernest C. Warde).
*The Innocent Murderers, with Paul West. ... Low, 1910

*JOHNSTON, WILLIAM. See also: Mel Brooks. Pseudonym: *Ed Garth.
*-Angel, Angel, Down We Go. (Novelization of film: American International, 1969; scw & dir: Robert Thom)
*Asylum. (Novelization of film: Amicus, 1972; scw: Robert Bloch; dir: Roy Ward Baker)
*Klute. (Novelization of film: Warner, 1971; scw: Andy Lewis, Dave Lewis; dir: Alan J. Pakula)
*Then Came Bronson. (Novelization of TV pilot, released as theatre film outside the U.S.: MGM, 1970; scw: Denne Bart Petticlerc; dir: William Graham)

JOHNSTONE, WILLIAM W.
Blood in the Ashes. Zebra, 1985
The Initiation. Zebra, 1982
The Sanction. Zebra, 1981

JON, MONTAGUE. SC: Stephen Kale, in both titles. Set: Eng.
A Question of Law. Macmillan (London), 1981; St. Martin's, 1982
The Wallington Case. Macmillan (London), 1981; St. Martin's, 1982

JONES, BRUCE
Tarotown. Leisure, 1982; Star, 1982

*JONES, CHARLES REED
*The King Murder. Film: Chesterfield, 1932 (scw: Charles Reed Jones; dir: Richard Thorpe)

JONES, CLEO. An ex-Mormon living in Calif. Ref: TM.
Prophet Motive. St. Martin's, 1984 <Utah>

*JONES, CRAIG
Fatal Attraction. Crown, 1983; Futura, 1984

JONES, DENNIS. 1945- .
Rubicon One. Beaufort, 1983; Hutchinson, 1984 <Mid. East, 1986>
Russian Spring. Beaufort, 1984; Hutchinson, 1985 <Moscow>

JONES, FRANK. 1937- . Ref: CA.
Master and Maid. Irwin, 1985 <Toronto, 1915>

JONES, FRED
The Man on the Landing. Cape, 1984

*JONES, G. WAYMAN. Listed title is by D'Arcy Lyndon Champion, ca.1903-1968; born in Melb.

JONES, GWYN(ETH A.). 1952-
-Up Will Go Parliament. New Horizon, 1981
Up with Your Hands. New Horizon, 1982

JONES, H. LLOYD
Temporary A.S.P. Smith and other stories. Albion (Ceylon), ca.1935 ss

*JONES, HENRY ARTHUR. Ref: CA.
*The Silver King. Silent film: Paramount, 1919 (scw: Burns Mantle; dir: George Irving). Also: Welsh-Pearson, 1929 (scw: Fenn Sherie; dir: T. Hayes Hunter)

*JONES, JACK
Baja. GM, 1982

*JONES, JENNIFER. Joint pseudonym of Margaret Lane and Enid Johnson.

JONES, JOHN ROBERT. 1926- . Pseudonym: John Dalmas, q.v.

*JONES, L. Q.
*The Brotherhood of Satan. (Novelization of film: Four Star, 1970; scw: William Welch; dir: Bernard McEveety)

*JONES, MADISON (PERCY, JR.)
An Exile. Viking, 1967; Deutsch, 1970. Film: Columbia, 1970, as I Wal': the Line (scw: Alvin Sargent; dir: John Frankenheimer)
Season of the Strangler. Doubleday, 1982 <Ala., 1969>

JONES, MARGARET. Australian journalist, foreign correspondent, stationed for two years in Peking; now based in London.
The Conficius Enigma. Collins (Sydney), 1981; St. Martin's, 1982 <Peking>

*JONES, MERVYN
Two Women and Their Man. Deutsch, 1981; St. Martin's, 1982 <Wales>

JONES, R. D.
The Fenris Option. Tower, 1981 <WWII>

*JONES, ROBERT PAGE
*The Heisters. Film(?): Prodis, 1966, as L'Homme de Marrakech (The Man from Marrakech; That Was George) (scw: H. Lanoe, Jose Giovanni, Jacques Deray; dir: Deray)

JONES, RUDOLPH CLIFFORD. 1912-1987. Pseudonym (?): *John Ross, q.v.

JONES, RUSS. Pseudonym: *Jack Younger.

JORDAN, CATHLEEN. Editor-in-chief of Alfred Hitchcock's Mystery Magazine; living in NYC.
A Carol in the Dark. Walker, 1984 <S. Dak., acad.>

*JORDAN, DAVID
Double Red. Deutsch, 1981
*Nile Green. <Egypt>

JORDAN, LAURA
Hidden Fires. PB, 1982 <Tex., ca.1900>

JORDAN, LEE
Cat's Eyes. Hodder, 1981; NAL, 1982

*JORDAN, LEONARD
Without Mercy. Zebra, 1981

*JOSEPH, MARIE. Ref: CA.

JOSEPH, ROBERT F.
The Aquarius Transfer. GM, 1982

JOSHEE, O(M) K(UMAR). 1934- . Ref: CA, TM.
Mr. Surie. St. Martin's, 1984 <Bombay>

*JOYCE, CYRIL
A Bullet for Betty. Hale, 1981
A Calculated Risk. Hale, 1981
Errant Sleuth. Hale, 1983
Errant Target. Hale, 1982
Errant Witness. Hale, 1981
From the Grave to the Cradle. Hale, 1982
Murder Is a Pendulum. Hale, 1983
Widow's Beads. Hale, 1984

*JOYCE, T. ROBERT
*S.P.Y.S. (Novelization of film: TCF, 1974, as S*P*Y*S; scw: Malcolm Marmorstein, Lawrence J. Cohen, Fred Freeman; dir: Irvin Kershner)

*JUDD, HARRISON
*Shadow of a Doubt. Film (?): CIC, 1978, as Le Temoin (The Witness) (scw: Rodolfo Sonego; dir: Jean-Pierre Mocky)

*JUDD, MARGARET
*Husband of the Corpse. <Vt.>

*JUDGE, JAMES P.
*Square Crooks. Silent film: Fox, 1928 (scw: Becky Gardiner; dir: Lewis Seiler). Sound film: Fox, 1934, as Baby, Take a Bow (scw: Philip Klein, E. E. Paramore, Jr.; dir: Harry Lachman)

JUDGE, MICHAEL
The Killing Trade. Hale, 1983
Operation Smokescreen. Hale, 1984
Without Fear. Hale, 1983

*JUDSON, JEANNE. Pseudonym: *Emily Thorne, q.v.

*JUDSON, WILLIAM
Cold River. Mason, 1975. Film: Cold River, 1982 (scw & dir: Fred G. Sullivan)

JULIAN, ROBERT. Pseudonym of *Saul Wernick.
Murder in Focus. Raven, 1981 <New Eng.>

JUPP, KENNETH. 1938- . Ref: CA.
Echo. Little, 1981; Deutsch, 1980

*JUTE, ANDRE
-The Zaharoff Commission. Hyland (Melbourne), 1981; Secker, 1982 <Ger., WWII>

KABAL, A. M.
The Adversary. Allison, 1985 <Egypt>

KADES, HANES. Pseudonym of Hans Werlberger, 1906- .
The House of Crystal. Angus, 1957 (Translation of "Monte Cristallo." Vienna, 1956.)

*KAHN, JAMES. 1947- . Ref: CA

*KAHN, STEVE
The Mall. PB, 1983 <Conn.>

KALISH, ROBERT. SC: Skipper Gould, in all titles.
Bloodmoon. Avon, 1985 <Mass.>
Bloodrun. Avon, 1984 <Bangkok>
Bloodtide. Avon, 1985 <Maine>

*KALLEN, LUCILLE. Ref also: TC2, TM. SC: C. B. Greenfield, also in

titles below.
No Lady in the House. Wyndham, 1982;
  Collins, 1982
The Piano Bird. Random, 1984; Col-
  lins, 1984 <Fla.>

*KAMINSKY, HOWARD. Joint pseudonym
  with Susan Stanwood Kaminsky:
  *Brooks Stanwood.

KAMINSKY, MELVIN. 1926-   . Professional name: Mel Brooks, q.v.

*KAMINSKY, STUART M(ELVIN). Ref also:
  TC2, TM. SC: Toby Peters, also in
  those marked TP below; Insp.
  Porfiry Rostnikov, in those marked
  PR (PR titles set in Moscow).
  Black Knight in Red Square. Charter,
    1984 PR
  Catch a Falling Clown. St. Martin's,
    1982 TP <Calif., ca.1942>
  Death of a Dissident. Charter, 1981.
    British title: Rostnikov's Corpse.
    Macmillan (London), 1981 PR
  Down for the Count. St. Martin's,
    1985 TP <L.A., 1942>
  Exercise in Terror. St. Martin's,
    1985
  The Fala Factor. St. Martin's, 1984
    TP <L.A., ca.1942>
  He Done Her Wrong. St. Martin's, 1983
    TP <L.A., ca.1942>
  High Midnight. St. Martin's, 1981;
    Severn, 1982 TP <L.A., 1942>
  Red Chameleon. Scribner, 1985 PR
  Rostnikov's Corpse; see Death of a
    Dissident
  When the Dark Man Calls. St. Mar-
    tin's, 1983; Firecrest, 1985 <Chi.>

*KAMINSKY, SUSAN STANWOOD. 1937-
  Joint pseudonym with *Howard
  Kaminsky: *Brooks Stanwood.

KAMITSES, ZOE. 1941-   . Ref: CA.
  Moondreamer. Little, 1983

*KAMM, (JAN) DORINDA
  The Kingsroads Legacy. Zebra, 1981

*KANE, ABEL
  *Slaughter's Big Rip-Off. (Noveliza-
    tion of film: American Interna-
    tional, 1973; scw: Charles
    Johnson; dir: Gordon Douglas)

*KANE, FRANK. Ref also: TM.
  *Key Witness. Film: MGM, 1960 (scw:
    Alfred Brenner, Sidney Michaels;
    dir: Phil Karlson)

*KANE, HENRY. Ref also: TM. Pseudo-
  nyms: Kenneth R. McKay, q.v.,
  *Mario J. Sagola.
  Don't Just Die There. Lancer, 1963
  *Edge of Panic. <NYC>
  The Little Red Phone. Arbor, 1982
    <Maine>

KANFER, STEFAN. 1933-   . Ref: CA.
  Fear Itself. Putnam, 1981

*KANTOR, HAL
  The Big Stopper. Popular Library,
    1982 <Chi., 1920s>

KANTOR, LEONARD. ca.1925-1984. Ref:
  CA.
  Dead Pigeon. French, 19?? (3-act
    play.) Film: Columbia, 1955, as
    Tight Spot (scw: William Bowers;
    dir: Phil Karlson)

*KANTOR, MacKINLAY
  *Author's Choice. Film (from ss "Gun
    Crazy"): United Artists, 1949, as
    Deadly Is the Female; also re-
    leased as Gun Crazy (scw: MacKin-
    lay Kantor, Millard Kaufman; dir:
    Joseph H. Lewis). Film (from
    ss "Mountain Music"): Paramount,
    1937, as Mountain Music (scw: Duke
    Atteberry, Russell Crouse, Charles
    Lederer, John C. Moffitt; dir:
    Robert Florey)

*KAPLAN, ANDREW. Raised in NYC; has
  been journalist in Europe and Africa; fought in Six-Day War as member
  of Israeli army; living in L.A.
  *The Hour of the Assassins. <S. Am.>

*KAPLAN, ARTHUR. Ref also: TM.

KARL, M. S.
  The Mobius Man. Leisure, 1982 <Mex.>

KARLIN, WAYNE
  Crossover. Harcourt, 1984; Methuen,
    1984 <Yugos., train>

*KARNEY, JACK. Born in NYC; worked in
  NYC D.A.'s office.

KARNI, MICHAELA. Joint pseudonym with
  Sue Bernell: Karin Berne, q.v.

*KARP, DAVID
  *Hardman. <NYC>

*KARTA, NAT
  *Brother Rat. (by *Victor Norwood.)
  *Climax. (by *Victor Norwood.)
  *The Foolish Virgin Returns. (by
    Donald Cresswell.)
  *Love Me, Hurt Me. Scion, 1952 (date
    correction)
  *Sinister Lovely. (by Terry Stanford.)
  *Some Dame. (by *Dail Ambler.)
  *We the Condemned. (by Norman Lazen-
    by.)

KARTUN, DEREK. SC: Alfred Baum, in
  those titles marked AB.
  Beaver to Fox. Century, 1983; St.
    Martin's, 1984 <Paris> AB
  The Courier. Century, 1985; St. Mar-
    tin's, 1985 <1940, Fr.>
  Flittermouse. Century, 1984 AB

*KASTLE, HERBERT D(AVID)
  *Cross-Country. Film: Filmline, 1983
    (scw: John Hunter, William Gray;
    dir: Paul Lynch)
  -David's War. Allen, 1982

KATA, ELIZABETH. Born in Syd. of
  Scottish descent; married to Ja-
  panese citizen and living in Japan
  when WWII began; moved back to
  Australia after the war.
  The Death of Ruth. Pan (Sydney),
    1981; Severn, 1982; St. Martin's,
    1982

*KATCHER, LEO
  *Hard Man. Film: Columbia, 1957 (scw:
    Leo Katcher; dir: George Sherman)

KATKOV, NORMAN. 1918-   . Ref: CA.
  Blood and Orchids. St. Martin's,
    1983; Bodley, 1984 <Haw., 1930>

*KATZ, ROBERT
  *The Cassandra Crossing. (Novelization
    of film: AVCO, 1977; scw:
    Tom Mankiewicz, Robert Katz,
    George Pan Cosmatos; dir:
    Cosmatos)

KATZ, SHELLEY
  The Shadow President. Dell, 1982

*KATZ, WILLIAM
  Copperhead. Deutsch, 1982 (= Red
    Heat?)
  *North Star Crusade. Film: ITC, 1978
    (existence of film not confirmed)
  Open House. McGraw, 1985; Hale,
    1986 <NYC>
  Red Heat. Dell, 1982
  Surprise Party. McGraw, 1984; Hale,
    1985 <NYC>
  Visions of Terror. Warner, 1981;
    Arrow, 1981

KATZENBACH, JOHN. 1950-   . Ref: CA.
  In the Heat of the Summer. Atheneum,
    1982; Joseph, 1982. Also published
    as: The Mean Season. Ballantine,
    1985. Film: Orion, 1985, as The
    Mean Season (scw: Leon Piedmont;
    dir: Philip Borsos)

KAUFELT, DAVID A(LLAN). 1939-
  Ref: CA.
  Souvenir. NAL, 1983; Piatkus, 1984
    <Paris, 1942>

*KAUFFMAN, (ROY) FRANKLIN
  *The Coconut Wireless. <Mal.>

*KAUFFMAN, REGINALD WRIGHT
  *Money to Burn. Silent film: Gotham,
    1926 (scw: James R. Smith; dir:
    Walter Lang)
  *The Spider's Web. Silent film:
    Gotham, 1928, as Midnight Life
    (scw: Adele Buffington; dir: Scott
    Dunlap)

*KAUFFMANN, LANE
  *The Perfectionist. Also published as:
    Kill the Beloved. Lion, 1956

*KAUFMAN, GEORGE S(IMON). See:
  *Alexander (Humphries) Woollcott.

*KAUFMAN, LENARD
  The Color of Green. Ace, 1957;
    Davies, 1957

*KAUFMAN, MICHAEL T.
  *The Nickel Ride. (Novelization of
    film: TCF, 1975; scw: Eric Roth;
    dir: Robert Mulligan)

*KAVALER, REBECCA
  Doubting Castle. Schochen, 1984
    <late 1800s>

*KAVANAGH, DAN. Pseudonym of Julian
  Barnes, 1946-   . Ref: CA. SC:
  Nick Duffy, in *Duffy, and in
  titles below.
  *Duffy. ... Pantheon pb, 1986
  Fiddle City. Cape, 1981; Pantheon pb,
    1986
  Putting the Boot In. Cape, 1985

*KAVANAGH, PAUL
  *Not Comin' Home to You. Reprinted as
    by Lawrence Block: Foul Play, 1986
  *The Triumph of Evil. Reprinted as by
    Lawrence Block: Foul Play, 1986

KAVANAUGH, KATHERINE <KATHERINE KAVA-
  NAUGH ZIEGFELD>. 1875-   .
  The Phantom Pilot. Dramatic, 1930
    (3-act play.)
  Second Story Peggy. Dramatic, 1929
    (3-act play.)

KAY, MALCOLM
  Sugar for the Inspector. Methodist
    Youth, 1957   (1-act play.)

KAY, MAXINE AMY
  "Henry." Deane, 1961; Baker, 1961
    (1-act play.)
  A Loop of String. Deane, 1964; Baker,
    1964 (1-act play.)

KAY, TERRY <TERRENCE>. 1918-   Ref:
  CA.
  After Eli. Houghton, 1981 <Ga., 1939>
  Dark Thirty. Poseidon, 1984; Granada,
    1985 <Ga.>

*KAYE, M(ARY) M(ARGARET). Ref also: TM.
  Death in Berlin; see Death Walked in
    Berlin
  Death in Cyprus; see Death Walked in
    Cyprus
  Death in Kenya; see Later Than You
    Think
  Death in the Andamans; see Night on
    the Island
  *Death in Zanzibar; see The House of
    Shade
  *Death Walked in Berlin. U.S. title:
    Death in Berlin. St. Martin's,
    1985. Reprinted in Britain under
    U.S. title: Viking, 1985
  *Death Walked in Cyprus. U.S. title:
    Death in Cyprus. St. Martin's,
    1984. Reprinted in Britain under
    U.S. title: Penguin, 1985
  *Death Walked in Kashmir. U.S. title:
    Death in Kashmir. St. Martin's,
    1984. Reprinted in Britain under
    U.S. title: Viking, 1984
  *The House of Shade. Revised edition:
    *Death in Zanzibar. ... Lane, 1983
  *Later Than You Think. Also published
    as: Death in Kenya. Lane, 1983
  *Night on the Island. Reprinted as:
    Death in the Andamans. Viking (Lon-
    don), 1985; St. Martin's, 1986

*KAYE, MARVIN (NATHAN). Ref also: TM.
  SC: Hilary Quayle, also in title
  below.
  The Soap Opera Slaughters. Doubleday,
    1982

KAYE, WILLIAM
  Wrong Target. Leisure, 1981

KAZAN, ELIA. 1909-   . Ref: CA.
  The Assassins. Stein, 1972; Collins,
    1972 <New Mex.>

*KEAREY, CHARLES
  The Black Box, with Carel Birkby.
    Collins, 1971 <Afr.>
  Overload, with Carel Birkby. Collins,
    1970 <Afr.>

KEAST, FRANCIS
  Sunburst. Hale, 1984

*KEATING, H(ENRY) R(EYMOND) F(ITZWAL-
  TER). Ref (revised, expanded)
  TC2, TM. Pseudonym: Evelyn Hervey,
  q.v. SC: Insp. Ganesh Ghote, also
  in those marked GG below; Mrs.
  Craggs, in *Death of a Fat God,
  and in title marked C below.
  Go West, Inspector Ghote. Collins,
    1981; Doubleday, 1981 <L.A.> GG
  Mrs. Craggs: Crimes Cleaned Up.

Buchan, 1985; St. Martin's, 1986 ss C
*A Rush on the Ultimate. ... Doubleday, 1982
The Sheriff of Bombay. Collins, 1984; Doubleday, 1984 GG <Bombay>

*KEATING, HENRY
*Murder by Death. (Novelization of film: Columbia, 1976; scw: Neil Simon; dir: Robert Moore)

KEDDELL, SCUD. See: *Hyman Zore.

KEEFFE, BARRIE. 1945- .
Sus. Eyre, 1979 (3-scene play.)

*KEELER, HARRY STEPHEN. Ref also: TM.
*Sing Sing Nights. Film: Monogram, 1935 (scw: Marion North, Charles Logue; dir: Lew Collins). Also: Monogram, 1935, as The Mysterious Mr. Wong (scw: Nina Howatt; dir: William Nigh)

*KEENAN, JAMES. Pseudonym: *J. J. Montague.

*KEENE, DAY. Ref also: TM.
*Chautauqua. Film: MGM, 1969, as The Trouble with Girls (scw: Arnold Peyser, Lois Peyser; dir: Peter Tewkesbury)
*His Father's Wife. <New Eng.>
*Joy House. Film: MGM, 1964; also known as The Love Cage (scw: Pascal Jardin, Charles Williams, Rene Clement; dir: Clement)
*My Flesh Is Sweet. <S.W.>
*Strange Witness. Film: UFA-Comacico, 1961, as Cause Toujours Mon Lapin (Keep Talking, Baby) (scw: Roger Boussinot, Yvon Samuel, Guy Le Frane; dir: Le Frane)

*KEENE, TOM
Earthrace. Lane, 1982 <Afr.>
The Fuse. Lane, 1984; Charter, 1986
Skyshroud, with *Brian Haynes, q.v. Lane, 1981

KEITGES, JULIE. 1940- . Ref: CA.
Dawn and Vengeance. Avon, 1983 <Ecua.>

*KEITH, DAVID
*Blue Harpsichord. Reprinted as by Francis Steegmuller: Carroll, 1984

KELAART, PIERS
Midas. Futura, 1981; Signet, 1982 <Switz.>

KELLAN, JIM
Honey Drop That Weed. Gannet, 1952
She's Dynamite! Gannet, 1953

*KELLAND, CLARENCE BUDINGTON. Ref also: TM; not in TC2.
Archibald the Great. Harper, 1943; World's Work, 1950 <Ariz.>
*The Case of the Nameless Corpse. Also published as: The Nameless Corpse. Detective Book Club, 1957
*The Cat's Paw. Film: Lloyd, 1934 (scw & dir: Sam Taylor)
*Conflict. Silent film: Universal, 1921 (scw: George C. Hull; dir: Stuart Paton)
*Contraband. Silent film: Famous Players, 1925 (scw: Jack Cunningham; dir: Alan Crosland)
*Counterfeit Gentleman. <Phoenix>
The Hidden Spring. Harper, 1916. Silent film: Yorke-Metro, 1917 (scw: Fred J. Balshofer; dir: E. Mason Hopper)
The Nameless Corpse; see *The Case of the Nameless Corpse
*Scattergood Baines. Film: RKO, 1941 (scw: Michael L. Simmons, Edward T. Lowe; dir: Christy Cabanne)
Silver Spoon. Harper, 1941. Film: RKO, 1942, as Highways by Night (scw: Lynn Root, Frank Fenton; dir: Peter Godfrey)
This Is My Son. Harper, 1948; Museum, 1950 <Ariz.>

KELLER, KIRK
Final Landscapes. Leisure, 1981 <Utah>

KELLERMAN, DAN. Pseudonym of Dan Schmidt. SC: Jesse Heller, in both titles. Set: Tex.
Blood Run. Pinnacle, 1985
Hellrider. Pinnacle, 1985

KELLERMAN, JONATHAN. 1946- . Ref: CA.
When the Bough Breaks. Atheneum, 1985. British title: Shrunken Heads. Macdonald, 1985 <L.A.>

*KELLEY, LEO P(ATRICK). Ref: CA.

KELLEY, PATRICK A. A professional magician.
Sleightly Murder. Avon, 1985 <Pa.>

KELLEY, WILLIAM, 1929- , and EARL W. WALLACE. Ref for Kelley: CA.
The Witness. PB, 1985; NEL pb, 1985 (Novelization of film: Paramount, 1985; scw: Earl W. Wallace, William Kelley; dir: Peter Weir)

*KELLY, ANTHONY PAUL
*Three Faces East. Silent film: Producer's Distributing, 1926 (scw: C. Gardner Sullivan, Monte Katterjohn; dir: Rupert Julian). Sound film: Warner, 1930 (scw: Oliver H. P. Garrett, Arthur Caesar; dir: Roy del Ruth). Also: Warner, 1940, as British Intelligence; released in Britain as Enemy Agent (scw: Lee Katz; dir: Terry Morse)

KELLY, JAMES
Music from Another Room. Leisure, 1980 <Mex.>
-No Rest for the Dying. Leisure, 1981

KELLY, JOAN COLLINGS. 1890- . Pseudonym: Joan Sutherland, q.v.

KELLY, NORA. An American historian.
In the Shadow of King's. St. Martin's, 1985; Collins, 1984 <Eng., acad.>

*KELLY, PATRICK
The Lonely Margins. Granada, 1981

KELLY, ROBERT. 1935- . Ref: CA.
A Transparent Tree. McPherson, 1985 ss, one or two criminous

KELLY, SUSAN. Lives in Cambridge, Mass.; teaches at Howard Univ. School of Business and at the Cambridge Police Academy.
The Gemini Man. Walker, 1985 <Boston>

*KELLY, TIM J.
A-Haunting We Will Go. Dramatic, 1981 (2-act play.)
The Adventure of the Clouded Crystal. French, 1981 (1-act play.)
The Adventure of the Speckled Band. Clark, 1981 (2-act play based on the ss by *A. Conan Doyle, q.v. (Sherlock Holmes)
Beast of the Baskervilles. Pioneer, 1984; Hanbury, 1985 (1-act play.)
Bloody Jack. Clark, 1981 (2-act play.)
The Butler Did It. Baker's, 1977 (Play.) Musical version: Baker's, 1986
Case of the Curious Moonstone. Bakers, 1978 (2-act play based on *The Moonstone by *Wilkie Collins, q.v.)
Country Gothic. Baker's, 1977 (1-act play.)
Cry of the Banshee. Pioneer, 1977; Hanbury, 1984 (2-act play.)
Dark Deeds at Swan's Place. French, 1981 (2-act play.)
Dracula. Clark, 1978 (2-act play based on the novel by *Bram Stoker, q.v.)
Enter Pharaoh Nussbaum. Baker's, 1978 (2-act play.)
The Fall of the House of Usher. Clarke, 1979 (2-act play based on the ss by *Edgar A. Poe, q.v.)
*Frankenstein. <Switz.>
The Green Archer. Baker's, 1980 (2-act play based on the novel by *Edgar Wallace, q.v.)
Horror High. Baker's, 1982 (2-act play.)
If Sherlock Holmes Were a Woman. Baker's, 1970 (1-act play.)
Lady Dracula. Pioneer, 1977; Hanbury, 1980 (2-act play.)
The Last of Sherlock Holmes. Baker's, 1970 (1-act play.)
Life on the Bowery. French, 1985 (2-act play.)
Little Miss Christie. Pioneer, 1981 (2-act musical play.)
*Lizzie Borden of Fall River. ... Hanbury, 1986
Lost in Space and the Mortgage Due. Eldridge, 1979 (2-act play.) <future>
Lucky, Lucky Hudson and the 12th St. Gang. Contemporary Drama, 1983 (2-act play.)
Merry Murders at Montmarie. Baker's, 1972 (2-act play.)
Murder by Natural Causes. Dramatic, 1985 (2-act play.)
Murder Game. Broadway, 1985 (2-act play.)
Murder in the Magnolias. Baker's, 1980 (2-act play.) <South>
Murder Takes a Holiday. Clark, 1984 (2-act play.)
The Mystery of the Black Abbot. Baker's, 1982 (2-act play based on the novel by *Edgar Wallace, q.v.)
Oliver Twisted. Contemporary Drama, 1983 (1-act play.)
The Omelet Murder Case. Dramatists, 1984 (1-act play.)
Reunion on Gallows Hill. Pioneer, 1984 (1-act play.)
Seven Wives for Dracula. Pioneer, 1973; Hanbury, 1985 (1-act play.)
Sherlock Holmes' First Case. Baker's, 1976 (2-act play.) (Sherlock Holmes)
Sherlock Holmes Meets the Phantom. Pioneer, 1975; Hanbury, 1985 (1-act play.) (Sherlock Holmes)
The Soapy Murder Case. Baker's, 1979 (2-act play.)
The Speckled Band. Clark, 1981 (2-act play based on ss by *A. Conan Doyle, q.v.) (Sherlock Holmes)
Squad Room. Pioneer, 1984 (2-act play.)
Sweeney Todd. Clark, 1978 (2-act play based on *The String of Pearls by *Thomas Preskett Prest.)
Terror by Gaslight. Dramatists, 1981 (2-act play.) <Phil., 1800s>
Under Jekyll's Hyde. Pioneer, 1980; Hanbury, 1984 (1-act play.)
The Uninvited. Dramatists, 1979 (2-act play based on the novel by Dorothy Macardle, q.v.)
Widow's Walk. Harper, 1963 (3-act play.)
The Witch Who Wouldn't Hang. Baker's, 1972 (1-act play.)
The Zombie. French, 1983 (3-act play.)

KELSALL, FREDA M(ARGARET) and H(ARRY) N(ORMAN) GIBSON
Double, Double. Allen, 1965

KELSO, JACK
The Ghost Skier. Grayling, ca.1945 <Switz.>

KELTON, ELMER. 1926- . Ref: CA.
Stand Proud. Doubleday, 1984 <Tex., ca.1905>

KEMAL, YASHAR. 1923- . Ref: CA.
The Sea-Crossed Fisherman. Braziller, 1985; Harvill, 1985 <Turk.>

*KEMELMAN, HARRY. Ref also: BM, TM. SC: Rabbi David Small, also in title below.
Someday the Rabbi Will Leave. Morrow, 1985; Hutchinson, 1985 <Mass.>

KEMENY, JEAN ALEXANDER. 1930- . Ref: CA.
Strands of War. Houghton, 1984 <Ger., WWII>

*KEMP, SARAH. Pseudonym of *Michael Butterworth, q.v. Other pseudonym: William Dobson, q.v.
No Escape. Century, 1985; Doubleday, 1984

*KEMPLEY, WALTER
*The Probability Factor. Film(?): Imperia, 1976, as L'Ordinateur des Pompes Funebres (The Undertaker Parlor Computer) (scw: Jean-Patrick Manchette, Gerard Pires; dir: Pires)

KENAN, AMOS. 1927- .
The Road to Ein Harod. Al Saqi, 1985 <Isr.> (Translated from the Hebrew.)

*KENDRICK, BAYNARD (HARDWICK). Ref also: TM.
*The Last Express. Film: Universal, 1938 (scw: Edmund L. Hartmann; dir: Otis Garrett)
*Odor of Violets. Film: MGM, 1942, as Eyes in the Night (scw: Guy Trosper, Howard Emmett Rogers; dir: Fred Zinnemann)

*KENEALLY, THOMAS (MITCHELL)
  *The Chant of Jimmie Blacksmith. <Australia> Film: Film House, 1978 (scw & dir: Fred Schepsi)
  *The Fear. <Australia>
  *The Survivor. <Antarctic> (setting correction)

*KENNAWAY, JAMES (PEBLES EWING)
  *The Mind Benders. Film: Novus, 1962 (scw: James Kennaway; dir: Basil Dearden)

*KENNEDY, ADAM. Ref also: CA. SC: Roy Tucker, in *The Domino Principle, and in title marked RT below.
  Debt of Honor. Delacorte, 1981; Allen, 1981 <Wash. D.C.>
  *The Domino Principle. Film: Associated General, 1977; released in Britain as The Domino Killings (scw: Adam Kennedy; dir: Stanley Kramer)
  The Domino Vendetta. Beaufort, 1984; Allen, 1982 RT

KENNEDY, BARBARA
  The Uninvited Guest. GM, 1981 <Fla.>

KENNEDY, GEORGE. The TV and movie actor. Books below reportedly ghosted by *Walter J. Sheldon, q.v. SC: George Kennedy, in both titles.
  Murder on High. Avon, 1984 <air.>
  Murder on Location. Avon, 1983; Hale, 1985 <Mex.>

*KENNEDY, JAY RICHARD
  *The Chairman. Film: Apjac, 1969; released in Britain as The Most Dangerous Man in the World (scw: Ben Maddow; dir: J. Lee Thompson)

KENNEDY, THOMAS. 1920-   . Ref: CA.
  Die a Little. Macmillan (London), 1982

KENNEDY, WILLIAM P.
  Code Conquistador. PB, 1982

KENNEY, SUSAN (McILVAINE). 1941-   . Ref: CA. SC: Roz Howard, in both titles.
  Garden of Malice. Scribner, 1983; Hale, 1985 <Eng.>
  Graves in Academe. Viking, 1985 <Maine, acad.>

*KENNINGTON, (GILBERT) ALAN
  *The Night Has Eyes. Film: ABPC, 1942; released in the U.S. as Terror House (scw: John Argyle, Leslie Arliss; dir: Arliss)
  *She Died Young. Film: Forth, 1956, as You Can't Escape (scw: Robert Hall, Doreen Montgomery; dir: Wilfred Eades)

*KENRICK, TONY. Ref also: TM.
  Blast. Signet, 1984 <NYC>
  Faraday's Flowers. Doubleday, 1985. Also published as: Shanghai Surprise. Penguin, 1986. <Shanghai, 1940> Film: MGM, 1986, as Shanghai Surprise (scw: John Kohn, Robert Bentley; dir: Jim Goddard)
  *Two for the Price of One. Film: Columbia, 1981, as Nobody's Perfekt (scw: Tony Kenrick; dir: Peter Bonerz)

*KENT, FORTUNE. Pseudonym of John Toombs, 1927-   . Ref: CA.

KENT, JOHN. Pseudonym of Arthur George Balbernie, 1893-
  Give Me Liberty. Ward, 1939

*KENT, LARRY
  Baby Doll Blues. Cleveland (Australia), 1970
  The Beautiful Bait. Cleveland (Australia), 1970
  The Cyanide Girl. Cleveland (Australia), 1965
  Dames Die Hard. Cleveland (Australia), 1965
  Minx Manx. Cleveland (Australia), 1965

*KENT, SIMON
  *The Lions at the Kill. Film: TCF, 1960, as Seven Thieves (scw: Sidney Boehm; dir: Henry Hathaway)

*KENT, WILLIS
  *A Woman in Purple Pajamas. Film: MGM, 1932, as A Scarlet Weekend (scw: Oliver Blake, William Nobles; dir: George Melford)

*KENYON, MICHAEL. Ref also: TM. SC: Insp. Harry Peckover, in all titles below. Set: Eng.
  The Elgar Variation; see Zigzag
  A Free Range Wife. Collins, 1983; Doubleday, 1983
  God Squad Bod. Collins, 1982. U.S. title: The Man at the Wheel. Doubleday, 1982
  The Man at the Wheel; see God Squad Bod
  Zigzag. Collins, 1981. U.S. title: The Elgar Variation. Coward, 1981

KEON, (JAMES) MICHAEL. 1918-
  The Durian Tree. Simon, 1960; H. Hamilton, 1960 <Mal.>

*KEPPEL, CHARLOTTE
  *The Villains. ... St. Martin's, 1982 <Eng., 1744>

*KERNAHAN, MRS. COULSON
  *The Gate of Sinners. criminous
  *No Vindication. criminous

KEROUAC, JACK <JOHN>. 1922-1969.
  Doctor Sax. Grove, 1959

*KERR, GEOFFREY (KEMBLE GRINHAM)
  Cottages to Let. French (London), 1941 (3-act play.) Film: Gainsborough, 1941, as Cottage to Let; released in the U.S. as Bombsight Stolen (scw: Anatole de Grunwald, J. O. C. Orton; dir: Anthony Asquith)

KERR, ROLPH WHITESIDE. 1887-   .
  Princess of Steel. Exposition, 1958

*KERR, SOPHIE
  -As Tall As Pride. Rinehart, 1949
  *The Blue Envelope. Silent film: Vitagraph, 1916, as The Blue Envelope Mystery (scw: Helen Duey and/or A. Von Buren Powell; dir: Wilfred North)

KERRIGAN, PHILIP. 1959-   . Born and living in Eng.; graduate of Norfolk College of Arts and Technology.
  Dead Ground. Macmillan (London), 1985; St. Martin's, 1986

KERRUISH, JESSIE DOUGLAS. 1890?-1949.
  The Undying Monster. Heath Cranton, 1922; Macmillan, 1936. Film: TCF, 1942; released in Britain as The Hammond Mystery (scw: Lillie Hayward, Michel Jacoby; dir: John Brahm)

*KERSH, GERALD
  *Jews Without Jehovah. criminous
  *Night and the City. Film: TCF, 1950 (scw: Jo Eisinger; dir: Jules Dassin)

KESSELMAN, WENDY (ANN)
  My Sister in This House. French, 1982 (1-act play.)

*KESSELRING, JOSEPH (OTTO)
  *Arsenic and Old Lace. Film: Warner, 1944 (scw: Julius J. Epstein, Philip G. Epstein; dir: Frank Capra)

KESSNER, LAWRENCE. 1957-   . Ref: CA.
  The Spy Next Door. Arlington, 1981 <N.Y.>

*KETCHUM, PHILIP. Pseudonym: *Miriam Leslie.

KEY, L. J.
  -The Spawn. Dell, 1983

*KEY, SEAN A. Pseudonym of *William J(eremiah) Coughlin. SC: Cain, in *The Mark of Cain, and in title below.
  Cain's Chinese Puzzle. Dell, 1981 <H. Kong>

*KEY, (SAM)UEL (WHITTELL)
  The Broken Fang and Other Experiences of a Specialist in Spooks. Hodder, 1920 ss of occult detection

KEYES, DANIEL. 1927-   . Ref: CA.
  -The Fifth Sally. Little, 1980; Hale, 1981

KEYES, EDWARD. 1927-   . Ref: CA.
  Double Dare. McGraw, 1981 <NYC>

KICKHAM, CHARLES (JOSEPH). ca.1826-1882.
  -Knocknagow. Duffy, 1879 <Ire.>
    Silent film: Film. Co. of Ireland, 1918 (scw: N. F. Patton; dir: Fred O'Donovan)

KIDMAN, FIONA. 1940-   .
  Paddy's Puzzle. Heinemann, 1984

*KIEFER, WARREN (DAVID). Ref also: TM.

*KIELY, BENEDICT
  Honey Seems Bitter. Dutton, 1952; Methuen, 1954. Reprinted as: The Evil Men Do. Dell, 1954

*KIENZLE, WILLIAM X(AVIER). Ref also: TC2, TM. SC: Father Bob Koesler, also in all titles below.
  Assault with Intent. Andrews, 1982 <Det.>
  Kill and Tell. Andrews, 1984; Chivers, 1985 <Det.>
  Mind Over Murder. Andrews, 1981; Hodder, 1981 <Det.>
  Shadow of Death. Andrews, 1983; Chivers, 1983 <Det.>
  Sudden Death. Andrews, 1985; Hale, 1986 <Det.>

*KILGORE, AXEL. SC: Hank Frost (The Mercenary), also in all titles below.
  The Afghanistan Penetration. Zebra, 1983
  Assassin's Express. Zebra, 1982
  Buckingham Blowout. Zebra, 1984 <Eng.>
  Bush Warfare. Zebra, 1982 <Afr.>
  Canadian Killing Ground. Zebra, 1981 <Can.>
  China Bloodhunt. Zebra, 1983 <China>
  Death Lust! Zebra, 1982
  Eye for Eye. Zebra, 1984
  The Hard Man. Zebra, 1984
  Naked Blade, Naked Gun. Zebra, 1983
  The Opium Hunter. Zebra, 1981 <Burma>
  The Siberian Alternative. Zebra, 1983
  The Slaughter Run. Zebra, 1981
  Slave of the Warmonger. Zebra, 1981
  The Terror Contract. Zebra, 1982
  Vengeance Army. Zebra, 1981

KILGORE, KATHRYN
  Something for Nothing. Seaview, 1981 <N.J.>

KILIAN, MICHAEL
  Blood of the Czars. St. Martin's, 1984; Allen, 1985 <Russ.>
  Northern Exposure. St. Martin's, 1983 <Ottawa, future>
  The Valkyrie Project. St. Martin's, 1981; Hamlyn, 1982 <Ice.>

*KILLOUGH, (KAREN) LEE
  Deadly Silents. Ballantine, 1981

*KILPATRICK, SARAH. Pseudonym of Mavis Eileen Underwood, 1916-   . Ref: CA.

*KIMBROUGH, KATHRYN. All new titles also in Phenwick Women series.
  Alexandra, the Ambivalent. Popular Library, 1981
  *Barbara, the Valiant. <Ga., 1859>
  Iris, the Bewitched. Popular Library, 1982
  Laura, the Emperiled. Popular Library, 1981
  Letitia, the Dreamer. Popular Library, 1981
  *Millijoy, the Determined. <Ga., 1858>
  *Patricia, the Beautiful. <Va., 1787>
  *Rachel, the Possessed. <Maine, 1798>
  Romula, the Dedicated. Popular Library, 1981
  *Susannah, the Righteous. <Boston, 1807>

*KIMMINS, ANTHONY (MARTIN)
  *Lugs O'Leary. <Australia>

*KING, C(HARLES) DALY. Ref also: TM. SC: Michael Lord, also in *Obelists at Sea.

*KING, (JAMES) CLIFFORD
  *Bitter Springs. (Novelization of film: Ealing, 1950; scw: Monja Danischewsky, W. P. Lipscomb; dir: Ralph Smart)

KING, ELLIOTT
  Kill Me Softly. Hale, 1984

*KING, FRANCIS (HENRY). Ref also: BM.
  Act of Darkness. Hutchinson, 1983; Little, 1983 <India, 1930s>

*KING, FRANK
  *The Ghoul. Film: Gaumont, 1933 (scw: Roland Pertwee, John Hastings Turner, Frank King, Leonard Hines, L. DuGarde Peach, Rupert Downing; dir: T. Hayes Hunter). Also: New World, 1961, as What a Carve Up! (also released as: No Place Like Homicide?) (scw: Ray Cooney, Tony Hilton; dir: Pat Jackson)

*KING, HAROLD. See also: *Lawrence Block.
  The Hahnemann Sequela. Arbor, 1984 <N.Y.>

KING, PAULINE. 1917- . Ref: CA.
  Snares of the Enemy. Collins, 1985; Scribner, 1986 <acad.>

*KING, PHILIP
  *Elementary, My Dear. (3-act play.)

KING, RAMONA
  Steal Away. French, 1982 (2-act play.) <Chi., 1930s>

KING, ROBERT. 1947- . See also: Duncan Greenwood, 1919- .
  Red Spy at Night. French, 1972 (1-act play.) <Fr.>

*KING, RUFUS (FREDERICK). Ref also: TM.
  *The Case of the Constant God. Film: Universal, 1936, as Love Letters of a Star (scw: Lewis R. Foster, Milton Carruth, James Mulhauser; dir: Foster and Carruth)
  *Invitation to a Murder. Film: Warner, 1942, as The Hidden Hand (scw: Anthony Coldeway; dir: Ben Stoloff)
  *Murder by the Clock. Film: Paramount, 1931 (scw: Henry Myers; dir: Edward Sloman)
  *Museum Piece No. 13. Film: Universal International, 1948, as The Secret Beyond the Door (scw: Sylvia Richards; dir: Fritz Lang)

KING, (RAYMOND) SHERWOOD
  *If I Die Before I Wake. Film: Columbia, 1948, as The Lady from Shanghai (scw & dir: Orson Welles)

*KING, STEPHEN. Pseudonym: *Richard Bachman.
  *The Dead Zone. Film: EMI, 1984 (scw: Jeffrey Boam; dir: David Cronenberg)
  Different Seasons. Viking, 1982; Macdonald, 1982 (4 novelets, 3 criminous) Film (from novelet "Children of the Corn"): Gatlin, 1984 (scw: George Goldsmith; dir: Fritz Kiersch)
  *Firestarter. criminous. Film: Universal, 1984 (scw: Stanley Mann; dir: Mark L. Lester)

KING, TABITHA. 1949- . Ref: CA.
  Caretakers. Macmillan, 1983; Methuen, 1984
  The Trap. Macmillan, 1985. British title (?): Wolves at the Door. Granada, 1985
  Wolves at the Door; see The Trap

*KINGERY, DON
  *Paula. <Tex.>

KINGSBURY, CARL LOUIS
  The Mystery at the Carrol Ranch. Cook, 1910 <S.W.>

*KINGSLEY, GERRY
  *The Cat and the Canary. (Novelization of film; see *John Willard)

KINGSLEY, HENRY. 1830-1876.
  Geoffrey Hamlyn; see The Recollections of Geoffrey Hamlyn
  -Ravenshoe. Macmillan (London), 1862; Ticknor, 1862
  The Recollections of Geoffrey Hamlyn. Macmillan (London), 1859; Ticknor, 1859. Reprinted as: Geoffrey Hamlyn. Chapman, 1874

*KINGSLEY, SIDNEY
  *Dead End. Film: United Artists, 1937 (scw: Lillian Hellman; dir: William Wyler)
  *Detective Story. Film: Paramount, 1951 (scw: Philip Yordan, Robert Wyler; dir: William Wyler)

*KINGSLEY-SMITH, TERENCE
  The Murder of an Old-Time Movie Star. Pinnacle, 1983 <L.A., 1930s>

KINGSTON, ROBERT
  None Should Look. M. C. Publications, ca.1950

KINNEY, JEFFERSON
  A Locket for Tawi. Vantage, 1958 <S. Pac.>

KINSLEY, LAWRENCE
  The Red-Light Victim. Tower, 1981 <Boston>

*KINSLEY, PETER
  The Pistolero. Hale, 1983

KINSOLVING, WILLIAM
  Raven. Putnam, 1983; Collins, 1983

KIPPEN, JANE M.
  The Laird's Deed of Settlement. Digby, 1983

*KIRK, LYDIA (CHAPIN). 1896-1984. Ref: CA.

*KIRK, MICHAEL. Pseudonym of *Bill Knox, q.v. Other pseudonyms: *Robert MacLeod, q.v., *Noah Webster.

*KIRK, PHILIP. Pseudonym of *Leonard Levinson. SC: Butler, in all five previous titles and in all titles below.
  Chinese Roulette. Leisure, 1979
  Dead Fall. Leisure, 1982
  The Killer Virus. Leisure, 1983
  Laser Shuttle. Leisure, 1982
  The Midas Kill. Leisure, 1984
  The Q Factor. Leisure, 1984
  The Paris Kill. Leisure, 1983

*KIRKPATRICK, JOHN (ALEXANDER)
  Ah, Sweet Mystery! French, 1947 (1-act play.)
  *The Woman at Dead Oaks. <Conn.>

*KIRKWOOD, JAMES
  *Some Kind of Hero. Film: Paramount, 1982 (scw: James Kirkwood, Robert Boris; dir: Michael Pressman)

KIRKWOOD, THOMAS
  The Quiet Assassin. Fine, 1985 <Berlin>

*KIRST, HANS HELLMUT. Ref also: TM.
  *The Night of the Generals. Film: Horizon, 1966 (scw: Joseph Kessel, Paul Dehn; dir: Anatole Litvak)

KIRTON, JAMES
  Greek Fire. Hale, 1985 <Greece>
  Time for Murder. Hale, 1985

KISNER, JAMES (MARTIN, JR.). 1947- . Ref: CA.
  Nero's Vice. Beaufort, 1981
  Slice of Life. Zebra, 1982 <Chi., 1945>

*KISTLER, MARY
  *The Night of the Tiger. ... Piatkus, 1982

KITCHENER, JAMES A. G.
  The Argosy Project. Hale, 1983

*KITCHIN, C(LIFFORD) H(ENRY) B(ENN)
  *Death of His Uncle. ... Perennial, 1984

*KLASNE, WILLIAM. Chicago policeman turned writer; newspaperman; living in N.C.

*KLAUSNER, LAWRENCE D(AVID). 1939- . Ref: CA.
  Conclave. McGraw, 1981

KLAVIN, ANDREW. Joint pseudonym with Laurence Klavin: Margaret Tracy, q.v.

KLAVIN, LAURENCE. Joint pseudonym with Andrew Klavin: Margaret Tracy, q.v.

KLAWANS, HAROLD L(EO), M.D. 1937- . Ref: CA.
  Sins of Commission. Contemporary, 1982 <Chi., hosp.>

KLEIN, ALEXANDER. 1918- . Ref: CA.
  The Counterfeit Traitor. Holt, 1958; Muller, 1958. Film: Paramount, 1962 (scw & dir: George Seaton)

*KLEIN, CHARLES
  The Gamblers. French, 1910 (3-act play.) Novelization with *Arthur Hornblow: Dillingham, 1911; Unwin, 1911. Silent film: Lubin, 1914 (scw: George W. Terwilliger; dir: Barry O'Neil). Also: Vitagraph, 1919 (scw: Sam Taylor, Lucien Hubbard; dir: Paul Scardon). Sound film: Warner, 1929 (scw: J. Grubb Alexander; dir: Michael Curtiz)

KLEIN, DANIEL M(ARTIN). 1939- . Rev: CA.
  Wavelengths. Doubleday, 1982; NEL pb, 1983

*KLEIN, DAVE. SC: Butch Lewis, in *Blind Side, and in title below.
  Hit and Run. Charter, 1982

KLEIN, EDWARD. 1936- . Ref: CA.
  The Parachutists. Doubleday, 1981; Gollancz, 1981 <Hung., 1944>

KLINE, OTIS ADELBERT. 1891-1946.
  The Man Who Limped and other stories. Chartered, 1946 ss

*KLINGER, HENRY. Ref: not in TC2.

*KLUGE, P(AUL) F(REDERICK)
  *Eddie and the Cruisers. Film: Aurora, 1983 (scw: Martin Davidson, Arlene Davidson; dir: Martin Davidson)

KNEALE, BRUCE
  Appointment in Cairo. Evans, 1950 <Cairo>

*KNEBEL, FLETCHER
  Crossing in Berlin. Doubleday, 1981; Deutsch, 1982 <Berlin>
  Poker Game. Doubleday, 1983; Hale, 1984
  *Seven Days in May. Film: Paramount, 1964 (scw: Rod Serling; dir: John Frankenheimer)
  *Vanished. <Wash. D.C.>

KNEESHAW, J(OHN) W(ILLIAM)
  A Black Shadow. Express, 1894

*KNICKMEYER, STEVE. Ref also: TM.

*KNIGHT, CLIFFORD (REYNOLDS). Ref also: TC2.

*KNIGHT, KATHLEEN MOORE. ca.1890-1984. Ref also: TC2, TM.
  Death Wears a Bridal Veil; see Seven Were Veiled
  *Seven Were Veiled. Also published as: Death Wears a Bridal Veil. Mystery Novel Classics, 194?
  *They're Going to Kill Me. Reprinted as by Alan Amos: Detective Book Club, 1956

*KNIGHT, LEONARD A(LFRED)
  Murder Story. Low, 1943

*KNIGHT, STEPHEN. 1951-1985.

KNOPP, JEROME M.
  The Eternal Reich. Tower, 1981 <Ger.>

*KNOTT, FREDERICK (M. P.)
  *Dial "M" for Murder. Film: Warner, 1954 (scw: Frederick Knott; dir: Alfred Hitchcock)
  *Wait Until Dark. (3-act play.) <NYC> Film: Warner, 1967 (scw: Robert Carrington, Jane-Howard Carrington; dir: Terence Young)
  *Write Me a Murder. <Eng.>

KNOTT, WILLIAM CECIL. 1927-
  Pseudonym: Brian Swift, q.v.

*KNOWLTON, ROBERT A(LMY)
  *Court of Crows. <N.C.>

*KNOX, BILL. Pseudonyms: *Robert MacLeod, q.v., *Michael Kirk, *Noah Webster. Ref also: TM. SC: Colin Thane and Phil Moss, also at least in the title marked T&M; Webb Carrick, also in at least those titles marked WC.
  Bloodtide. Hutchinson, 1982; Doubleday, 1983 WC <Scot.>
  The Hanging Tree. Hutchinson, 1983; Doubleday, 1984 T&M <Glasgow>
  A Killing in Antiques. Hutchinson, 1981; Doubleday, 1981
  Wavecrest. Hutchinson, 1985; Doubleday, 1985 WC <Scot.>

*KNOX, E(DMUND GEORGE) VALPY. 1881-1971. Ref: CA.

*KNOX, RONALD A(RBUTHNOTT). Ref also: CA, TM.

*Doublecross Purposes. ... Dover, 1986
*KOCH, CHRISTOPHER J.
  The Boys in the Island. H. Hamilton, 1958 <Tas., Melb.>
  *The Year of Living Dangerously. ... Nelson, 1978 <Indon.>
KOCH, HOWARD. 1902-   . See: Julius J. Epstein, 1909-
*KOENIG, LAIRD (P.). See also: *Peter L(ee) Dixon.
  *The Little Girl Who Lives Down the Lane. Film: Braun, 1976 (scw: Laird Koenig; dir: Nicolas Gessner)
  Rockabye. St. Martin's, 1981; Piatkus, 1982   <NYC>
*KONING, HANS
  De Witt's War. Pantheon, 1983 <Holl., 1941>
  -The Kleber Flight. Atheneum, 1981
*KONRAD, JAMES. Pseudonym of Charles MacLean, 1946-   , q.v.
KONSALIK, HEINZ G. 1921-   .
  Strike Force Ten. Macmillan (London), 1981; Charter, 1984 <Russ., 1945> (Translation of "Sie Waren Zehn." Munich, 1979.)
*KONVITZ, JEFFREY
  *The Sentinel. Film: Universal, 1976 (scw: Michael Winner, Jeffrey Konvitz; dir: Winner)
*KOONTZ, DEAN R(AY). Ref: CA, TC2, TM. Pseudonyms: Richard Paige, Owen West, qq.v.
  Hanging On. Evans, 1973; Barrie, 1974 <Fr., WWII>
  Phantoms. Putnam, 1983; Allen, 1983 <Calif.>
*KOOTZ, (SAMUEL MELVIN). Ref: CA.
*KOPERWAS, SAM
  Easy Money. Morrow, 1983   <Fla.>
KOPIT, ARTHUR (LEE). 1937-   . Ref: CA.
  The Day the Whores Came Out to Play Tennis, and other plays. Hill, 1965. British title: Chamber Music, and other plays. Methuen, 1969 (Plays, one--"The Questioning of Nick"--criminous.)
*KORMAN, KEITH
  *Swan Dive. ... Hale, 1982
*KORNBLUTH, C(YRIL) M. Pseudonym: Jordan Park, q.v. See also: *Frederik Pohl.
KOROTYUKOV, ALEXEI
  It's Hard to Be a Russian Spy. Long Shadow, 1985 <Russ.> (Translation of "Nelegko byt Runskim Shpionom.")
KOSAK, CARL. ca.1935-   . Pseudonym: K. C. Constantine, q.v.
KOTANI, ERIC. See: John Maddox Roberts.
KOTLAN, C. M. See: G. C. Edmondson.
*KOTZWINKLE, WILLIAM
  Seduction in Berlin. Putnam, 1985 <Berlin>
  Trouble in Bugland. Godine, 1983 ss, Sherlockian parodies
*KOZHEVNIKOV, VADIM
  *Shield and Sword. <Ger., WWII>
KRANES, DAVID
  Criminals. Charter, 1981
*KRASNA, NORMAN. ca.1909-1984. Ref: CA.
  Small Miracle. French, 1935 (3-act play.) Film: Paramount, 1935, as Four Hours to Kill (scw: Norman Krasna; dir: Mitchell Leisen)
  Who Was That Lady I Saw You With? Film: Columbia, 1960, as Who Was That Lady? (scw: Norman Krasna; dir: George Sidney)
*KRASNER, WILLIAM. SC: Sam Birge, also in the titles below.
  Death of a Minor Poet. Scribner, 1984; Chivers, 1985   <Mo.>
  Resort to Murder. Scribner, 1985 <Mo.>

KRAUTH, NIGEL
  Matilda, My Darling. Allen (Syd.), 1982; Allen, 1984; Watts, 1985 <Australia, 1890s>
KRAUZER, STEVEN. See: *Don(ald Eugene) Pendleton.
KRELL, EDWIN D. and MAJOR J.J. VASEL
  Killer Cops. Manor, 1979 <St. Louis>
KRENTZ, JAYNE ANN. Lives in Seattle.
  Legacy. Harlequin, 1985 <Calif.>
KREPPS, ROBERT W(ILSON). 1919-1980. Ref: CA.
  The Field of Night. Rinehart, 1948
KRIZ, JOSEPH
  The Karsten's Flats. Vantage, 1976 <Tex., 1938>
KROETSCH, ROBERT. 1927-   . Ref: CA.
  Alibi. Beaufort, 1983
KRUEGER, TERRY
  -Night Cries. Dell, 1985
  Vectors. Dell, 1984
*KRUGER, PAUL. Ref also: TM.
KRUSE, JOHN. 1919-   . Ref: CA.
  Red Omega. Bodley, 1981; Random, 1981 <1951>
KUCZKIR, MARY. 1933-   . Joint pseudonym with Roberta Anderson, 1942-   : Fern Michaels, q.v.
*KUMMER, FREDERIC ARNOLD
  *The Brute. Silent film: Famous Players, 1914
  *The Green God. Silent film: Vitagraph, 1918 (dir: Paul Scardon)
  *The Painted Woman. Silent film: Famous Players, 1917, as The Slave Market (scw: Clara S. Beranger; dir: Hugh Ford)
  *A Song of Sixpence. Silent film: Art Dramas, 1917 (dir: Ralph Dean)
*KURLAND, MICHAEL (J.). Ref also: TM.
  Death by Gaslight. Signet, 1982 <Eng., ca.1890> (Sherlock Holmes)
*KURNITZ, HARRY. Ref also: TM.
  *A Shot in the Dark. Film: United Artists, 1964 (scw: Blake Edwards, William Peter Blatty; dir: Edwards)
*KUTAK, ROSEMARY
  *I Am the Cat.   <L. I.>
*KUTTNER, HENRY. Ref also: CA, TM.
  *Man Drowning. Ghosted by *Cleve Cartmill.
  *The Murder of Ann Avery. ... Banner, 1950s
*KUTTNER, PAUL
  Absolute Proof. Dawnwood, 1984 <S.F.>
  -Condemned. Dawnwood, 1983
*KWEN-LING, SOONG. See: *James W(illiam) Bennett.
KYDD, DERMOTT
  The Konigsberg Assignment. Hale, 1982
*KYLE, DUNCAN. Ref also: TC2, TM.
  The Dancing Men. Collins, 1985; Holt, 1986
  The King's Commissar. Collins, 1983; St. Martin's, 1984 <Russ., 1918; contemporary London>
  The Stalking Point. Collins, 1981; St. Martin's, 1982 <WWII>
*KYLE, ELIZABETH
  *Carolina House. ... Nelson, 1955 criminous
*KYLE, SEFTON. SC: Insp. J. Rason, also in *Guilty, But---.
*LA BERN, ARTHUR (JOSEPH). Ref: not in TC2.
  *Goodbye Piccadilly, Farewell Leicester Square. Film: Universal, 1972, as Frenzy (scw: Anthony Shaffer; dir: Alfred Hitchcock)
  *It Always Rains on Sunday. Film: Ealing, 1947 (scw: Angus MacPhail, Robert Hamer, Henry Cornelius; dir: Hamer)
  *Night Darkens the Streets. Film: Triton, 1948, as Good Time Girl (scw: Muriel Box, Sydney Box,

Ted Willis; dir: David Macdonald)
  Paper Orchid. Marlowe, 1948. Film: Ganesh, 1949 (scw: Val Guest; dir: Roy Baker)
LABUS, MARTA HAAKE. 1943-   . Pseudonym: Claire McCormick, q.v.
LA CROIX, ARDA
  The Yankee Doodle Detective. Ogilvie, 1909
*LACY, ED. Ref also: TM.
*LAFORE, LAURENCE (DAVIS). 1917-1985.
*LA FOUNTAINE, GEORGE
  *Flashpoint. Film: HBO Pictures, 1984 (scw: Dennis Shryack, Michael Butler; dir: William Tannen)
  *Two Minute Warning. Film: Universal, 1976 (scw: Edward Hume; dir: Larry Peerce)
*LAIDLAW, ROSS. 1931-   . Ref: CA.
  The Linton Porcupine. Canongate, 1984 <Eng., 1500s>
*LAINE, ANNABEL
  The Melancholy Virgin. Macdonald, 1981; St. Martin's, 1982 <Eng., 1800s>
*LAIT, JACK
  *Beast of the City. (Novelization of film: MGM, 1932; scw: John Lee Mahin; dir: Charles Brabin)
  *Big House. (Novelization of film: MGM, 1930; scw: Frances Marion; dir: George Hill)
  *Put on the Spot. Film: RKO, 1931, as Bad Company (scw: Thomas Buckingham, Tay Garnett; dir: Garnett)
LAJEUNESSE, C. R.
  Dead Man Running. Hale, 1981
LAKE, JOE BARRY. 1909-   . Pseudonym: *Joe Barry.
LAMARTINE, EUGENE
  Web of Intrigue. Phoenix (London), 1954
*LAMB, J. J. Ref: TM. SC: Zach Rolfe (spelling correction)
  *Losers Take All. <Can.>
LAMB, MARGARET. 1936-   . Born in N. Dak., educated at Vassar and NYU; living in NYC; author of plays, articles and scholarly works on Shakespeare.
  Chains of Gold. St. Martin's, 1985 <Conn.>
*LAMB, MAX and *HARRY SANFORD
  *The Last Nazi. <Sp.>
*LAMBERT, DEREK (WILLIAM). Ref also: TC2, TM.
  The Golden Express. H. Hamilton, 1984; Stein, 1984 <train, 1940>
  The Judas Code. H. Hamilton, 1983; Stein, 1984 <Lisbon, 1941>
  The Man Who Was Saturday. H. Hamilton, 1985; Stein, 1985 <Russ.>
  The Red Dove. H. Hamilton, 1982; Stein, 1983
  *Touch the Lion's Paw. Film: Paramount, 1980, as Rough Cut (scw: Francis Burns; dir: Donald Siegel)
  Trance. Arlington, 1981 <Wash. D.C.>
*LAMBERT, ERIC
  *The Ballarat. criminous <Australia>
  *The Dark Backward. delete: not criminous
  *Dolphin. delete: not criminous
  *The Drip Dry Man. criminous
  The Five Bright Stars. Australasian, 1954 <Australia>
  *Glory Thrown In. delete: not criminous
  *Hiroshima Reef. delete: not criminous
  *Kelly. criminous <Australia>
  *The Long White Night. delete: not criminous
  *A Short Walk to the Stars. delete: not criminous
  *The Twenty Thousand Thieves. delete: not criminous
  *The Veterans. <New Guinea>
  *Waterman. delete: not criminous
*LAMBERT, LEE
  The Balinese Pearls. Hale, 1982
*LAMBOT, ISOBEL (MARY)
  Rooney's Gold. Hale, 1984

L

LAMM, RICHARD and ARNOLD GROSSMAN.
    Lamm is 3-term governor of Colo.;
    Grossman is a creator of media
    campaigns for politicians.
    1988. St. Martin's, 1985; Severn,
    1986   <1988>

L'AMOUR, LOUIS (DEARBORN). 1908-
    Ref: CA.
    The Hills of Homicide. Carroll, 1983;
    Corgi, 1985   ss

LAMPARD, DAVID
    A Present from Peking. Doubleday,
    1965

LANCASTER, G. B. Pseudonym of Edith
    J. Lyttleton.
    The Law Bringers. Doran, 1913; Hod-
    der, 1913. Silent film: Metro,
    1923, as Eternal Struggle (scw: J.
    G. Hawks, Monte Katterjohn; dir:
    Reginald Barker)

*LAND, JANE
    *These Tiger's Hearts. <1860s, Vienna>

LAND, JON
    The Doomsday Spiral. Zebra, 1983
    -The Lucifer Directive. Zebra, 1984
    Vortex. Zebra, 1984

*LANDON, CHRISTOPHER (GUY)
    *Ice-Cold in Alex. Film: ABPC, 1958;
    released in the U.S. as Desert
    Attack (scw: J. Lee Thompson,
    Christopher Landon; dir: Thompson)

*LANDON, HERMAN. 1882-1960. Pseudonym:
    *Harry Coverdale.

*LANDON, HILARY
    Choose Your Own Verdict. Gifford,
    1949

LANDSBOROUGH, GORDON HOLMES. Pseudonym:
    "G-Man."

LANDSTONE, CHARLES. 1897-   .
    The Man from Butler's. Murray, 1930
    ss, some criminous

LANE, ALLISON
    Revelations. Jove, 1981   <Israel>

LANE, JIM R.
    Static. Avon, 1984   <Neb.>

*LANE, KENDALL. Pseudonym of Sidney
    Carroll.
    *Gambit. ... Coronet, 1966
    (Novelization of film: Universal,
    1966; scw: Jack Davies, Alvin
    Sargent; dir: Ronald Neame)

LANE, MARGARET. Joint pseudonym with
    Enid Johnson: *Jennifer Jones.

*LANE, W.
    Sherlock Holmes and the Wood Green
    Empire Mystery. Magico, 1985
    (Sherlock Holmes)

*LANG, ANDREW. Ref: CA.

*LANG, JOHN
    *Botany Bay. ss, mostly criminous
    The Forger's Wife. Ward, 1855
    <Australia>

LANG, (ALEXANDER) MATHESON. 1879-
    The Purple Mask. French, 1923
    (5-act play.)

*LANGE, JOHN
    *Binary.   <San Diego>

*LANGHAM, JAMES R.
    *Sing a Song of Homicide. Film: Para-
    mount, 1942, as A Night in New
    Orleans (scw: Jonathan Latimer;
    dir: William Clemens)

LANGHORN, FRANCES
    Murder at Midday. New Playwrights,
    1981   (Play.)

*LANGLEY, BOB
    Autumn Tiger. Joseph, 1981; Walker,
    1986
    Conquistadores. Joseph, 1985. U.S.
    title: Falklands Gambit. Walker,
    1985   <Arg.>
    East of Everest. Joseph, 1984; Jo-
    seph (U.S.), 1985   <Tibet>
    Falklands Gambit; see Conquistadores
    Hour of the Gaucho. Joseph, 1983

*LANGTON, JANE (GILLSON). Ref also:
    TC2, TM. SC: Homer Kelly, also in
    titles below.

Emily Dickinson Is Dead. St. Mar-
    tin's, 1984   <Mass.>
Natural Enemy. Ticknor, 1982   <Mass.>

*LANHAM, EDWIN (MOULTRIE). Ref also:
    TM.
    *It Shouldn't Happen to a Dog. Film:
    TCF, 1946 (scw: Eugene Ling, Frank
    Gabrielson; dir: Herbert I. Leeds)

LANIGAN, CATHERINE. 1947-   . Ref: CA.
    Bound by Love. Avon, 1981   <1914>

LANSDALE, JOE R(ICHARD). 1951-
    Ref: CA.
    Act of Love. Zebra, 1981   <Houston>

*LANSDALE, NINA. Pseudonym of Marilyn
    Meeske Sorel.

LANSING, JOHN. SC: Black Eagles, in
    all titles.
    AK-47 Firefight. Zebra, 1985   <Viet
    Nam>
    Beyond the DMZ. Zebra, 1985   <Viet
    Nam>
    Boocoo Death. Zebra, 1985   <Viet Nam>
    Hanoi Hellground. Zebra, 1983;
    Sphere, 1985   <Viet Nam>
    Mekong Massacre. Zebra, 1983, Sphere,
    1985   <Viet Nam>
    Nightmare in Laos. Zebra, 1984;
    Sphere, 1985   <Laos>
    Pungi Patrol. Zebra, 1984   <Viet Nam>
    Saigon Slaughter. Zebra, 1984   <Sai-
    gon>

LA PLANTE, LYNDA. Both titles are
    novelizations of a TV series.
    The Widows. Sphere, 1983
    The Widows II. Thames, 1985

*LARANY, DAVID
    *The Big Red Sun. <Peking>

LARSEN, ERNEST. 1946-   . Ref: CA.
    Not a Through Street. Random, 1981;
    Pluto, 1985   <NYC>

*LARSEN, GAYLORD D. 1932-   . Ref:
    CA. SC: Henry Garrett, in *The
    Kilbourne Connection, and in title
    below.
    Trouble Crossing the Pyrenees. Regal,
    1983

*LARSON, CHARLES. Ref also: TM. SC:
    Nils-Frederik Blixen, also in
    title below.
    The Portland Murders. Doubleday,
    1983; Chivers, 1985   <Portland>

LARSON, GLEN A., 1937(?)-   , and
    ROGER HILL. Ref for Larson: CA. SC:
    Michael Long, in all titles (novel-
    izations of the "Knight Rider" TV
    series).
    Hearts of Stone. Pinnacle, 1984;
    Target, 1984
    Knight Rider. Pinnacle, 1983; Star,
    1984
    Mirror Image. Target, 1985
    Trust Doesn't Rust. Pinnacle, 1984;
    Star, 1984
    The 24-Caret Assassin. Target, 1984

LARSON, MARVIN. Pseudonym: *Marvin
    Claire.

LA SERRE, EDWARD. See: Malcolm Watson.

LASKER, MICHAEL and RICHARD ALAN SIM-
    MONS
    The Gangster Chronicles. Jove, 1981
    (Novelization of the TV series.)

LASSITER, ADAM. SC: Dennison, in all
    titles.
    Conte's Run. Bantam, 1985
    Dennison's War. Bantam, 1984; Bantam
    (London), 1986
    Hell on Wheels. Bantam, 1985
    King of the Mountain. Bantam, 1985
    <Mont.>
    Triangle. Bantam, 1985   <Viet Nam>

LATHAM, BRAD. SC: Bill Lockwood (The
    Hook), in all titles.
    Corpses in the Cellar. Warner, 1982
    <NYC>
    The Death of Lorenzo Jones. Warner,
    1982
    The Gilded Canary. Warner, 1981
    <NYC, 1930s>
    Hate Is Thicker Than Blood. Warner,
    1981
    Sight Unseen. Warner, 1981

*LATHEN, EMMA. Ref also: TM. SC:
    John Putnam Thatcher, also in both
    titles below.

Going for the Gold. Simon, 1981;
    Gollancz, 1981   <N.Y.>
Green Grow the Dollars. Simon, 1982;
    Gollancz, 1982

*LATIMER, JONATHAN (WYATT). Ref also:
    CA, TM.
    *The Dead Don't Care. Film: Universal,
    1938, as The Last Warning (scw:
    Edmund L. Hartmann; dir: Al
    Rogell)
    *Headed for a Hearse. Film: Universal,
    1937, as The Westland Case (scw:
    Robertson White; dir: Christy
    Cabanne)
    *The Lady in the Morgue. Film: Univer-
    sal, 1938; released in Britain as
    The Case of the Missing Blonde
    (scw: Eric Taylor, Robertson White;
    dir: Otis Garrett)

*LA TOURRETTE, JACQUELINE
    The House on Octavia Street. Beau-
    fort, 1984   <S.F., 1899>

*LAUBEN, PHILIP. SC: Capt. Homer Clay,
    in at least those marked HC.
    A Nice Sound Alibi. Hale, 1981; St.
    Martin's, 1981   <Ky.>   HC
    A Sort of Tragedy. Hale, 1985
    A Surfeit of Alibis. Hale, 1982; St.
    Martin's, 1983   <Ky.>   HC

*LAUMER, (JOHN) KEITH
    *Deadfall. Film: TCF, 1975, as Peeper
    (scw: W. D. Richter; dir: Peter
    Hyams)
    Once There Was a Giant. Tor, 1984
    <future>

LAUNDER, FRANK, 1907-   , and SIDNEY
    GILLIAT, 1908-   .
    Meet a Body. French (London), 1955
    (3-act play.) Film: British Lion,
    1956, as The Green Man (scw: Sid-
    ney Gilliat, Frank Launder; dir:
    Robert Day)

LAURANCE, ANDREW
    The Black Hotel. Star, 1983
    Ouija. Star, 1982

LAURIE, JESSICA
    The Mistress of Harrowgate. Zebra,
    1981

*LAW, JANICE. Ref also: TM. SC: Anna
    Peters, also in title below.
    Death Under Par. Houghton, 1981;
    Houghton (London), 1982   <Scot.>

LAWMAN, ANTHONY
    The Hounds of Spring. Hale, 1984
    <Holl., 1940>

*LAWRENCE, H(ENRY) L(IONEL)
    *The Children of Light. Film: British
    Lion, 1961, as The Damned; released
    in the U.S. as These Are the Damned
    (scw: Evan Jones; dir: Joseph
    Losey)

*LAWRENCE, HILDA. Ref also: TM.
    *Duet of Death. One novelet, *The
    House, also published separately
    under that title: Avon, 1971

LAWRENCE, JAMES E.
    The Case of the Phantom Baseball.
    Theatre World, 1978   (3-act play.)

LAWRENCE, JEROME, 1915-   , and
    ROBERT E(DWIN) LEE, 1918-
    Ref for both: CA.
    A Call on Kuprin. French, 1962
    (3-act play based on the novel by
    *Maurice Edelman.)

LAWRENCE, JOHN. 1920-   .
    Love Is the Victim. New Horizon, 1982

*LAWRENCE, MARGERY (H.)
    *The Madonna of the Seven Moons. Film:
    Gainsborough, 1944 (scw: Brock
    Williams, Roland Pertwee; dir:
    Arthur Crabtree)

LAWRENCE, MARJORIE K.
    Intruder. Maiden, 1961

LAWTON, CEDRIC
    Double Fix. Blackstaff, 1985   <Dub.>
    The Master Theron. New Horizon, 1981

*LAYMON, RICHARD
    *The Cellar.   delete: not criminous
    Out Are the Lights. Warner, 1983;
    NEL pb, 1982

LAYNE, MARION MARGERY. Joint pseudonym
    of Marion Woolf, Margery Papich,
    and Layne Torkelson. Woolf is from

N. Mex., has a degree in architecture; an executive recruiter in S.F. Papich was raised in the East, attended Northwestern Univ.; magazine editor, freelance author of ss and articles; living in Albuq. Torkelson has been a reporter and magazine writer and has worked in public relations in N. Mex.
  The Balloon Affair. Dodd, 1981 <N. Mex.>

LAZENBY, NORMAN. See: *Nat Karta.

*LEACH, CHRISTOPHER
  The Black Unicorns. Dent, 1983
  Blood Games. Dent, 1981.
    U.S. title: Texas Station. Harcourt, 1983 <Tex.>
  -A Killing Frost. Dent, 1982
  Texas Station; see Blood Games

*LEADER, CHARLES. SC: David Chan, also in title below.
  *A Wreath of Cherry Blossoms. <Jap.>

LEAMER, LAURENCE (ALLEN). 1941- . Ref: CA.
  Assignment. Dial, 1981; Hodder, 1981 <Peru>

LEARNING, WALTER. See: Alden Nowlan.

*LEASOR, (THOMAS) JAMES. SC: Aristo Autos, also in *Host of Extras.
  -Open Secret. Collins, 1982
  *Passport to Oblivion. Film: MGM, 1965, as Where the Spies Are (scw: Wolf Mankowitz, Val Guest, James Leasor; dir: Guest)
  Ship of Gold. Collins, 1984
  *The Yang Meridian; see Passport in Suspense (corrected cross reference)

LEBLANC, MAURICE (MARIE EMILE). Ref also: CA. Silent film (from unidentified stories): Edison, 1908, as The Gentleman Burglar (scw & dir: Edwin S. Porter). Also: Vitagraph, 1917, as Arsene Lupin (scw: Garfield Thompson, Paul Potter; dir: Paul Scardon)
  *813. Silent film: Robertson-Cole, 1921 (scw: W. Scott Darling; dir: Scott Sidney)
  *The Girl with the Green Eyes. Film: MGM, 1932, as Arsene Lupin (scw: Carey Wilson, Bayard Veiller, Lenore Coffee; dir: Jack Conway). Also: Universal, 1944, as Enter Arsene Lupin (scw: Bertram Millhauser; dir: Forbe Beebe)
  *The Teeth of the Tiger. Silent film: Paramount, 1919 (scw: Roy Somerville; dir: Chet Withey)
  *The Woman of Mystery; see *The Bomb-Shell (cross-reference correction)

*LE CARRE, JOHN. Ref also: TM.
  *Call for the Dead. Film: Lumet, 1966, as The Deadly Affair (scw: Paul Dehn; dir: Sidney Lumet)
  The Little Drummer Girl. Hodder, 1983; Knopf, 1983. Film: Pan Arts, 1984 (scw: Loring Mandel; dir: George Roy Hill)
  *The Looking Glass War. Film: Frankovich, 1969 (scw & dir: Frank R. Pierson)
  *The Spy Who Came in from the Cold. Film: Paramount, 1966 (scw: Paul Dehn, Guy Trosper; dir: Martin Ritt)

*LECOMBER, BRIAN
  *Dead Weight. <W.I.>
  *Turn Killer. Simon, 1975 <W.I.> (corrected U.S. publisher)

LEDERER, PAUL JOSEPH. 1944- .
  Pseudonym: Elizabeth Wolfe, q.v.

LEE, BONNIE. Pseudonym of Bonnie L. Hovland.
  The Shadows of Cliffside. Lenox, 1975

LEE, EDNA (L. MOONEY). 1890- .
  -The Queen Bee. Appleton, 1949; Hurst, 1951 <Atlanta>

*LEE, ELSIE
  *The Masque of the Red Death. (Novelization of film: Alta Vista, 1964; scw: Charles Beaumont, R. Wright Campbell; dir: Roger Corman)
  *-Muscle Beach Party. (Novelization of film: American International,

1964; scw: Robert Dillon; dir: William Asher)

*LEE, GYPSY ROSE. Pseudonym of *Rose Louise Hovick. Ref also: CA.
  *The G-String Murders. Film: Universal, 1943, as Lady of Burlesque; released in Britain as Striptease Lady (scw: James Gunn; dir: William Wellman)

*LEE, H. W. (correction of middle initial)

LEE, (NELLE) HARPER. 1926- . Ref: CA.
  -To Kill a Mockingbird. Lippincott, 1960; Heinemann, 1961. Film: Universal, 1962 (scw: Horton Foote; dir: Robert Mulligan)

*LEE, JOHN (DARRELL)
  -Lake of the Diamond. Doubleday, 1979 <WWII>
  -Night of the Fox. Doubleday, 1980; Sphere, 1984

LEE, ROBERT E(DWIN). 1918- . See: Jerome Lawrence, 1915- .

LEE, STAN(LEY R.). 1922- . Birth name: Stanley Martin Lieber. Ref: CA.
  Dunn's Conundrum. Harper, 1985; Joseph, 1985 <Wash. D.C., future>

*LEE, SUSAN, 1944- , and *SONDRA TILL ROBINSON. Ref for Lee: CA.
  *Dear John. ... Sphere, 1982

*LEE, THOMAS
  The House of Montague. Lee, 1888 <New Or.>

LEEDS, WENDY
  Cameo. Leisure, 1982
  The Child Sellers. Leisure, 1981

*LEEK, MARGARET. SC: Stephen Marryat, also in title below.
  Voice of the Past. Raven, 1981

LEEMING, JOHN F(ISHWICK). 1900- .
  Ref: CA.
  A Girl Like Wigan. Harrap, 1961

*LEES, HANNAH
  *Death in the Doll's House. Film: MGM, 1949, as Shadow on the Wall (scw: William Ludwig; dir: Patrick Jackson)

LEES, R. H.
  Death for an Emerald. Hale, 1983
  A Question of Murder. Hale, 1981

*LE FANU, JOSEPH SHERIDAN
  *Chronicles of Golden Friars. novels, criminous in part
  Ghost Stories and Tales of Mystery. McGlashan, 1851 ss, 2 of 5 criminous
  *In a Glass Darkly. Reprinted (with omission of one story): Newnes, n.d., as Green tea. Film (from ss "Carmilla"): Dreyer, 1931, as Vampyr (The Strange Adventure of David Gray) (scw: Carl Theodore Dreyer, Christian Jul; dir: Dreyer). Also: E.G.E, 1961, as Et Mourir de Plaisir (Blood and Roses) (scw: Roger Vadim, Roger Vailland, Claude Brule, Claude Martin; dir: Vadim). Also: Morgana, 1972, as La Novia Ensangrentada (The Blood-Spattered Bride) (scw & dir: Vicente Aranda)
  *Uncle Silas. Film: Two Cities, 1947; released in the U.S. as The Inheritance (scw: Ben Travers; dir: Charles Frank)

*LEFFLAND, ELLA. Ref also: TM.

*LEHMAN, ERNEST (PAUL)
  -Farewell Performance. McGraw, 1982; Severn, 1984

LEIBEE, LOUIS
  Prayer of a Chance. Vantage, 1958

LEIGH, ROBERT. 1933- .
  The Cheap Dream. Macmillan (London), 1982. U.S. title (?): First and Last Murder. St. Martin's, 1983
  First and Last Murder; see The Cheap Dream
  The Girl with the Bright Head. Macmillan (London), 1982

*LEIGHTON, FLORENCE
  *As Strange a Maze. <Bermuda>

*LEIGHTON, MARIE (FLORA BARBARA) CONNOR.
  *Convict 99. Silent film: Gaumont, 1909 (dir: Arthur Gilbert). Also: Samuelson, 1919 (dir: G. B. Samuelson)

*LEIGHTON, TOM
  *The Phoenix Formula. <WWII>

*LEINSTER, MURRAY
  *Murder Will Out. Film: First National, 1930 (scw: J. Grubb Alexander; dir: Clarence Badger)

LEITCH, MAURICE. 1933- . Ref: CA.
  Silver's City. Secker, 1981

LELAND, CHRISTOPHER T(OWNE). 1951- Ref: CA.
  Mean Time. Random, 1982 <S.W.>

LE LITT, D.
  Gwen-Amyia. Stockwell, 1925

*LEMARCHAND, ELIZABETH (WHARTON). Ref also: TM. SC: Insp. Tom Pollard (not Wharton, as given wrongly in first printings of CF), also in all titles below.
  *The Affacombe Affair. ... Walker, 1985
  *Alibi for a Corpse. ... Walker, 1986
  Light Through Glass. Piatkus, 1984; Walker, 1986 <acad.>
  Nothing to Do with the Case. Piatkus, 1981; Walker, 1981
  Troubled Waters. Piatkus, 1982; Walker, 1983
  The Wheel Turns. Piatkus, 1983; Walker, 1984

*LE MAY, ALAN. Ref: CA.

LEMON, MARK. 1809-1870.
  Leyton Hall, and other tales. Hurst, 1867; Peterson, 186? ss, some criminous

L'ENGLE, MADELEINE. 1918- . Ref: CA.
  -A Severed Wasp. Farrar, 1982; Farrar (London), 1984 <NYC, church>

LENNOX, TERRY
  Danger Draws a Wild Card. Hale, 1985

LENZ, SIEGFRIED. 1926- . Ref: CA.
  The Lightship. Heinemann, 1962; Hill, 1962 (Translation of "Das Feuerschiff." Hamburg, 1960.)

LEODAS, GUS
  The Forgotten Mission. Zebra, 1982

*LEONARD, ELMORE. Ref: TC2, TM.
  *The Big Bounce. <Mich.> Film: Warner, 1969 (scw: Robert Dozier; dir: Alex March)
  Cat Chaser. Arbor, 1982; Viking (London), 1986 <Miami>
  *Fifty-Two Pickup. Film: Cannon, 1984, as The Ambassador (scw: Max Jack; dir: J. Lee Thompson). Also: Cannon, 1986 (scw: Elmore Leonard, John Steppling; dir: John Frankenheimer)
  Glitz. Arbor, 1985; Viking (London), 1985 <N.J.>
  -Gold Coast. Bantam, 1980; Allen, 1982
  *The Hunted. Dell, 1977 (publisher correction)
  La Brava. Arbor, 1984; Viking (London), 1984 <Miami>
  *Mr. Majestyk. (Novelization of film: United Artists, 1974; scw: Elmore Leonard; dir: Richard Fleischer)
  *The Moonshine War. Film: MGM, 1970 (scw: Elmore Leonard; dir: Richard Quine)
  Ryan's Rules; see Swag
  Split Images. Arbor, 1982; Allen, 1983 <Fla.>
  Stick. Arbor, 1983; Lane, 1984 <Fla.> Film: Universal, 1985 (scw: Elmore Leonard, Joseph C. Stinson; dir: Burt Reynolds)
  *Swag. ... Penguin, 1985. Also published as: *Ryan's Rules (title correction)
  *Valdez Is Coming. Film: United Artists, 1971 (scw: Roland Kibbee, David Rayfiel; dir: Edwin Sherin)

*LEONARD, GEORGE (BURR). 1946- Ref: CA.
  The Ice Cathedral. Simon, 1984 <L.I.>

*LEOPOLD, CHRISTOPHER
  The Night Fishers of Antibes. H. Hamilton, 1981

LEOPOLD, KEITH
  My Brow Is Wet. Angus, 1970
    <Australia>
  When We Ran. Rigby (Adelaide), 1984.
    Film: South Australian Film, 1984,
    as Reunion (scw: Graham Hartley;
    dir: Chris Langman)

LE PRETRE, WILLIAM
  The Hypocrite. Houghton (London),
    1934

*LEQUEUX, WILLIAM (TUFNELL). Ref also:
    CA, TM.
  *Sons of Satan. Silent film: London,
    1915 (dir: George Loane Tucker)
  *The White Lie. Silent film: Gaumont,
    1914 (existence of film not con-
    firmed)

LERMAN, JACQUELINE. Pseudonym: Jackie
    Collins, q.v.

*LERMINA, JULES (HYPPOLYTE)
  *The Chase. <South>

*LEROUX, GASTON. Ref also: CA, TM. See
    also: Gene Traylor.
  *Balaoo. Silent film: Fox, 1927, as
    The Wizard (scw: Harry O. Hoyt,
    Andrew Bennison; dir: Richard
    Rosson)
  *Cheri-Bibi. Film: Distribution Pari-
    sienne, 1938 (in French) (dir:
    Leon Mathot). Also: Ariel, 1955
    (in French) (scw: Paul Mesnier;
    dir: Marcello Pagliero)
  *Cheri-Bibi and Cecily. Film: MGM,
    1931, as The Phantom of Paris (scw:
    Bess Meredyth, John Meehan, Edwin
    Justus Mayer; dir: John S.
    Robertson)
  *Cheri-Bibi, Mystery Man. (Transla-
    tion of "Palas et Cheri-Bibi,"
    part one of "Nouvelles Aventures
    de Cheri-Bibi." Paris, 1921.)
  *The Dancing Girl. (Translation of
    "Fatalitas!," part two of "Nou-
    velles Aventures de Cheri-Bibi."
    Paris, 1921.)
  *The Double Life. (Translation of
    "La Double Vie de Theophraste
    Longuet." Paris, 1904.)
  *The Man of a Hundred Masks. Film (in
    French): Universelle Cinematogra-
    phique, 1936, as Mister Flow (scw:
    Henri Jeanson; dir: Robert
    Siodmak)
  *The Mystery of the Yellow Room. Si-
    lent film: Realart, 1919 (scw
    & dir: Emile Chautard). Sound
    film: Osso, 1931, as Le
    Mystere de la Chambre Jaune (The
    Mystery of the Yellow Room)
    (dir: Marcel L'Herbier)
  *The Perfume of the Lady in Black.
    Film: Osso, 1931, as Parfum de la
    Dame en Noir (The Perfume of the
    Lady in Black) (dir: Marcel
    L'Herbier)
  *The Phantom of the Opera. Silent
    film: Universal, 1925 (scw: Raymond
    Shrock, Elliot Clawson; dir: Rupert
    Julian). Film (partial sound): Uni-
    versal, 1929 (dir: E. J. Clawson;
    dir: Rupert Julian). Sound film:
    Universal, 1943 (scw: Eric Taylor,
    Samuel Hoffenstein; dir: Arthur
    Lubin). Also: Hammer, 1962 (scw:
    John Elder; dir: Terence Fisher)

LESLIE, JULIA
  Perahera. Gollancz, 1983 <Ceylon>

*LESLIE, MIRIAM. Pseudonym of *Philip
    Ketchum.

*LESLIE, PETER. See also: *Don(ald
    Eugene) Pendleton.
  *The Bastard Brigade. <Fr., WWII>

LESSING, DORIS (MAY). 1919-   . Ref:
    CA.
  The Good Terrorist. Knopf, 1985;
    Cape, 1985

LESTIENNE, VOLDEMAR. 1932-   .
  Furioso. Allen, 1972; St. Martin's,
    1973 <Fr., WWII> (Translation
    of "Furioso." Paris, 1971.)

LEUCI, BOB. 1940-   . Retired from
    NYC police in 1981 after 20 years;
    has lectured and done residencies
    at 30 universities and law schools.
  Doyle's Disciples. Freundlich, 1984;
    Fontana, 1986 <NYC>
  Odessa Beach. Freundlich, 1985 <NYC>

LEVATINO, ANTHONY J.
  The Black Market Soldiers. Dell, 1983

*LEVEL, MAURICE. Film (from unidenti-
    fied novel): RKO, 1932, as The
    Roadhouse Murder (scw: J. Walter
    Ruben, Gene Fowler; dir: Rubin)

*LEVERAGE, HENRY
  *Whispering Wires. Silent film: Fox,
    1926 (scw: L. G. Rigby; dir:
    Albert Ray)

LEVEY, MICHAEL. 1927-   . Ref: CA.
  An Affair on the Appian Way. H. Ham-
    ilton, 1984 <ancient Rome>

*LEVI, PETER (CHAD TIGAR)
  Grave Witness. Quartet, 1985; St.
    Martin's, 1985

*LEVIN, IRA. Ref also: BM, TM.
  *The Boys from Brazil. Film: TCF, 1978
    (scw: Heywood Gould; dir: Franklin
    J. Schaffner)
  *Deathtrap. Film: Warner, 1982 (scw:
    Jay Presson Allen; dir: Sidney
    Lumet)
  *Dr. Cook's Garden. (3-act play.)
    <Vt.>
  *A Kiss Before Dying. Film: United
    Artists, 1956 (scw: Lawrence
    Roman; dir: Gerd Oswald)
  *Rosemary's Baby. Film: Paramount,
    1968 (scw & dir: Roman Polanski)
  *The Stepford Wives. Film: Fadsin,
    1975 (scw: William Goldman; dir:
    Bryan Forbes)

LEVIN, JENIFER. 1955-   . Ref: CA.
  Snow. Poseidon, 1984 <Carib.>

LEVIN, JOHN. 1944-   . See: *Frank
    M(alcolm) Robinson.

*LEVIN, MEYER
  *Compulsion. Film: TCF, 1959 (scw:
    Richard Murphy; dir: Richard
    Fleischer)

LEVINE, DIANA. Pseudonym: Diana
    Henstell, q.v.

LEVINE, RICHARD M.
  Bad Blood. Random, 1982 <Calif.>

LEVINE, WILLIAM. Pseudonym: *Jeremy
    Ford.

*LEVINSON, LEONARD. Pseudonyms:
    *Gordon Davis; Philip Kirk, q.v.

*LEVINSON, RICHARD, 1934-1987, and
    *WILLIAM LINK, 1934-   .
  Guilty Conscience. French, 1985
    (2-act play.)
  The Playhouse. Charter, 1985
    <Calif.>

*LEVY, D(AVID) LAWRENCE

LEWIN, ELSA. Ref: CA.
  I, Anna. Penzler, 1985

*LEWIN, MICHAEL Z(INN). Ref also:
    TM. SC: Lt. Leroy Powder,
    in *Night Cover, and in
    titles marked LP below; Albert
    Samson, also in titles marked AS
    below.
  Hard Line. Morrow, 1982; Macmillan
    (London), 1983 LP <Indianapolis>
  Missing Woman. Knopf, 1981; Hale,
    1982 AS <Indiana>
  *The Next Man. (Novelization of film:
    Artists Entertainment, 1976; scw:
    Mort Fine, Alan R. Trustman, David
    M. Wolf, Michael Chapman; dir:
    Richard C. Sarafian)
  Out of Season. Morrow, 1984. British
    title: Out of Time. Macmillan
    (London), 1984 AS, LP (in very
    minor role) <Indianapolis>
  Out of Time; see Out of Season

*LEWIS, COLIN
  Acid Test. Hamlyn, 1982
  Hot Rain. Hamlyn, 1983

*LEWIS, DAVID. Pseudonym of David Lewis
    Patton.

*LEWIS, ELLIOTT. SC: Fred Bennett,
    also in all titles below.
  Bennett's Bomb. Pinnacle, 1982
  Death and the Single Girl. Pinnacle,
    1983 <Calif.>
  Double Trouble. Pinnacle, 1981
  Here Today, Dead Tomorrow. Pinnacle,
    1983 <Calif.>
  People in Glass Houses. Pinnacle,
    1981

*LEWIS, FREDERICK
  *The Strange Case of Mary Page. Silent
    film: Essanay, 1916 (scw: Frederick
    Lewis; dir: J. Charles Haydon)

*LEWIS, FLORENCE JAY
  *The Climax. (Novelization of film:
    Universal, 1944; scw: Curt Siodmak,
    Lynn Starling; dir: George Waggner)

LEWIS, HELEN PROTHERO
  -Love and the Whirlwind. Hutchinson,
    1916. Silent film: Alliance, 1922
    (dir: Duncan Macrae, Harold Shaw)
  -The Silver Bridge. Hutchinson, 1918.
    Silent film: Cairns, 1920 (scw:
    Eliot Stannard; dir: Dallas Cairns)

*LEWIS, HERSHELL G.
  *Two Thousand Maniacs. (Novelization
    of film: studio?, 1964; scw:
    Hershell G. Lewis.)

*LEWIS, MERVYN. Pseudonym of Glyn Mer-
    vyn Louis Frewer. Ref: CA.

*LEWIS, NORMAN. Ref also: TM.
  Cuban Passage. Collins, 1982; Pan-
    theon, 1982 <Cuba, 1959>
  The Man in the Middle; see A Suitable
    Case for Corruption
  A Suitable Case for Corruption. H.
    Hamilton, 1984. U.S. title: The
    Man in the Middle. Pantheon, 1984
    <Libya>
  *Within the Labyrinth. ... Carroll,
    1986

*LEWIS, (JOHN) ROY(STON). Ref also:
    TM. SC: Eric Ward, in *A Certain
    Blindness, and in at least those
    titles marked EW below; Arnold
    Landon, in titles marked AL; Insp.
    John Crow, in earlier titles as
    indicated in CF.
  A Blurred Reality. Collins, 1985; St.
    Martin's, 1985 EW
  Dwell in Danger. Collins, 1982; St.
    Martin's, 1982 EW
  A Gathering of Ghosts. Collins, 1982;
    St. Martin's, 1983 AL
  A Limited Vision. Collins, 1983; St.
    Martin's, 1984 EW
  Most Cunning Workmen. Collins, 1984;
    St. Martin's, 1985 AL
  Once Dying, Twice Dead. Collins,
    1984; St. Martin's, 1985 EW
  A Relative Distance. Collins, 1981
  Seek for Justice. Collins, 1981

LEWIS, RICHARD. 1945-   . Pseudonym:
    Alan Radnor, q.v.
  -Night Killers. Hamlyn, 1983

*LEWIS, ROY HARLEY. Ref: TM. SC:
    Matthew Coll, in *A Cracking of
    Spines, and in titles marked MC
    below. Set: Eng.
  *A Cracking of Spines. St. Martin's,
    1982 (U.S. publisher correction)
  The Manuscript Murders. Hale, 1981;
    St. Martin's, 1982 MC
  A Pension for Death. Hale, 1983; St.
    Martin's, 1983 MC
  Where Agents Fear to Tread. Hale,
    1984; St. Martin's, 1984 <Pak.>

LEWIS, STEPHEN
  Cowboy Blues. Alyson, 1985; Alyson
    (London), 1986 <L.A.>

*LEWIS, TED
  *Billy Rags. criminous
  *Jack's Return Home. Film: MGM, 1970,
    as Get Carter (scw & dir: Mike
    Hodges). Also: MGM, 1972, as Hit
    Man (scw & dir: George Armitage)

LEWIS, TOM. 1940-   . Ref: CA. Pseu-
    donym: Nicholas Babcock, q.v.
  Rooftops. Evans, 1981 <NYC>

*LEY, ALICE CHETWYND
  A Reputation Dies. Methuen, 1984;
    St. Martin's, 1985 <London, 1816>

*LIDDY, G(EORGE) GORDON (BATTLE). Ref:
    CA.

LIEBER, STANLEY MARTIN. See: Stan(ley
    R.) Lee, 1922-   .

*LIEBERMAN, HERBERT (HENRY)
  -Brilliant Kids. Macmillan, 1975;
    Arrow, 1982
  Night Call from a Distant Time Zone.
    Crown, 1982; Hutchinson, 1982
  Nightbloom. Putnam, 1984; Hutchinson,
    1984 <NYC>

LIEBMAN, RON
 Grand Jury. Ballantine, 1983
 <Phil.>

LILLO, GEORGE. 1693-1739.
 The London Merchant. Gray, 1731
 (5-act play.) Silent film: Hepworth, 1913, as George Barnwell,
 the London Apprentice (scw: Ivan
 Patrick Gore; dir: Hay Plumb)

LILLY, RAY. Pseudonym of *Richard
 (Alan) Curtis, 1937-   . Joint
 pseudonym with Paul Stevens:
 *Curtis Stevens, q.v.
 The Sunday Alibi. Manor, 1977

*LINCOLN, JOSEPH C(ROSBY)
 *Blair's Attic. <Mass.>

*LINCOLN, NATALIE SUMNER
 *The Man Inside. Silent film: Uni-
 versal, 1916 (scw: Raymond L.
 Shrock; dir: John G. Adolfi)

*LINDALL, EDWARD
 *A Gathering of Eagles. <Australia>
 *A Kind of Justice. delete: not
 criminous
 *Stranger Among Friends. delete: not
 criminous
 *A Time Too Soon. criminous <New
 Guinea>

*LINDEN, CATHERINE. 1939-   . Ref: CA.

*LINDQUIST, DONALD
 The Red Gods. Delacorte, 1981;
 Hamlyn, 1981

*LINDOP, AUDREY ERSKINE. SC: Father
 Keogh, in at least those marked K.
 *I Start Counting. Film: Triumverate,
 1969 (scw: Richard Harris;
 dir: David Greene)
 *I Thank a Fool. MGM, 1962 (scw:
 Karl Tunberg; dir: Robert Stevens)
 -The Judas Figures. Heinemann, 1956;
 Appleton, 1956 K <Mex.>
 -The Singer Not the Song. Heinemann,
 1953; Appleton, 1953 K <Mex.>
 *The Tall Headlines. Film: Grafton,
 1952; released in the U.S. as The
 Frightened Bride (scw: Audrey
 Erskine Lindop, Dudley Leslie; dir:
 Terence Young)

*LINDSAY, DAVID T.
 *-The Temple of the Flaming God.

LINDSAY, FREDERIC
 Brond. Macdonald, 1983

*LINDSAY, HOWARD
 *Remains to Be Seen. Film: MGM, 1953
 (scw: Sidney Sheldon; dir: Don
 Weis)

LINDSAY, LEE. Pseudonym of Jean Barre.
 The Three Buccaneers. Wright, 1934

LINDSEY, DAVID L. Ref: TM. Book editor
 living in Austin, Tex. SC: Stuart
 Haydon, in titles marked SH.
 Black Gold, Red Death. GM, 1983
 <Mex.>
 A Cold Mind. Harper, 1983; Arlington,
 1984 SH <Houston>
 Heat from Another Sun. Harper, 1984;
 Arlington, 1985 SH <Houston>

*LINDSEY, DAWN. Pseudonym of Cherylle
 Lindsey Dimick.

*LININGTON, (BARBARA) ELIZABETH. Ref
 also: TM. SC: Ivor Maddox, also in
 titles below. Set: L.A.
 Felony Report. Doubleday, 1984; Gollancz, 1985, as by Anne Blaisdell
 Skeletons in the Closet. Doubleday,
 1982; Gollancz, 1983, as by Anne
 Blaisdell

*LINK, WILLIAM and *RICHARD LEVINSON,
 1934-1987, q.v.
 *Prescription: Murder.   <NYC>

*LINKLATER, ERIC (ROBERT RUSSELL)
 The House of Gair. Cape, 1953; Harcourt, 1954 <Scot.>

LINSCOTT, GILLIAN. SC: Birdie Linnett
 and Nimue Hawthorne, in both
 titles.
 A Healthy Body. Macmillan (London),
 1984; St. Martin's, 1984 <Fr.>
 Murder Makes Tracks. Macmillan (London), 1985; St. Martin's, 1985
 <It.>

*LINTON, DUKE. House name.
 *Hold Everything. (by *F. Dubrez
 Fawcett.)
 *Killer Bait. (by *Victor J. Hanson.)
 Poison. Scion, 1953 (by *Victor J.
 Hanson.)
 *Sinner. (by *Gray Usher.)
 *So Dead, So Sweet. (by *Victor J.
 Hanson.)
 *Strip Tease Angel. (by *Victor J.
 Hanson.)
 *Who's Sorry Now. (by *Victor J.
 Hanson.)

*LINZEE, DAVID (AUGUSTINE ANTHONY).
 Ref also: TM.
 *Belgravia. <Eng.>

LIPATOV, VIL (VLADIMIROVICH)
 A Village Detective. Progress Pub-
 lishers (Moscow), 1970 ss
 <Russ.> (Translation of
 "Derevenskii Detektiv.")

LIPEZ, RICHARD. 1938-   . Pseudonym:
 Richard Stevenson, q.v.

*LIPMAN, CLAYRE and *MICHEL LIPMAN
 *House of Evil. <S.F.>

*LIPMAN, MICHEL. See: *Clayre Lipman.

*LIPMAN, WILLIAM (R.)
 *Yonder Grow the Daisies. Film: Fox,
 1930, as Double Cross Roads (scw:
 George Brooks, Howard Estabrook;
 dir: Alfred L. Werker)

*LIPPINCOTT, DAVID (McCORD)
 The Home. Dell, 1984 <Fla.>
 The Nursery. Dell, 1983; Corgi, 1984
 <Md.>
 Unholy Mourning. Dell, 1982; Corgi,
 1983 <Mich.>
 *The Voice of Armageddon. Film: Lira,
 1977, as Armaguedon (Armageddon)
 (scw & dir: Alain Jessua)

*LIPPINCOTT, NORMAN
 *Murder at Glen Athol. Film: In-
 vincible, 1935; also released as
 Criminal Within (scw: John W.
 Krafft; dir: Frank R. Strayer)

*LIPSKY, ELEAZAR.
 *The Kiss of Death. Film: TCF, 1947
 (scw: Ben Hecht, Charles Lederer;
 dir: Henry Hathaway). Also: TCF,
 1958, as The Fiend Who Walked the
 West (scw: Harry Brown, Philip
 Yordan; dir: Gordon Douglas)
 *The People Against O'Hara. <NYC>
 Film: MGM, 1951 (scw: John Monks,
 Jr.; dir: John Sturges)
 *The Scientists. <N.Y.>

LISH, GORDON (JAY). 1934-   . Ref:
 CA.
 Dear Mr. Capote. Holt, 1983

LISLE, DUNCAN. See: Martin Combe.

LITCHFIELD, MICHAEL. 1939-
 Murder Circus. Hale, 1985
 Nailed! Hale, 1985
 See How They Run. Hale, 1984

*LITTELL, ROBERT. Ref: BM, CA, TC2.
 The Amateur. Simon, 1981; Cape, 1981
 <Czech.> Film: TCF, 1982 (scw:
 Robert Littell, Diana Maddox; dir:
 Charles Jarrott)

*LITTLE, CONSTANCE, 1899-1980, and
 GWENYTH, 1903-1986. Ref also: TM.

*LITTLE, GWENYTH. 1903-1986. See:
 *Constance Little, 1899-1980.

*LITTLE, PHILIP
 *Who Was He? Street, 1904 (Magnet
 #367)

*LITVINOFF, EMANUEL. 1915-   . Ref:
 CA.
 Falls the Shadow. Joseph, 1983;
 Stein, 1983 <Tel Aviv>

*LITVINOFF, IVY. Ref: not in TC2.

LIVINGSTON, JACK. Ref: TM. SC: Joe
 Birney, in both titles.
 Die Again, Macready. St. Martin's,
 1984; Macmillan (London), 1984
 <NYC>
 A Piece of the Silence. St. Mar-
 tin's, 1982; Hale, 1983 <NYC>

*LIVINGSTON, M. JAY
 The Synapse Function. Signet, 1984;
 Futura, 1985

LIVINGSTON, NANCY
 The Trouble at Aquitaine. Gollancz,
 1985; St. Martin's, 1986

*LLEWELLYN, RICHARD. Pseudonym of
 *Richard David Vivian Llewellyn
 Lloyd, 1906-1983.
 Mr. Hamish Gleave. Joseph, 1956;
 Doubleday, 1956
 *Poison Pen. Film: APBC, 1939
 (scw: William Freshman, Doreen
 Montgomery, N. C. Hunter, Esther
 McCracken; dir: Paul L. Stein)

*LLOYD, RICHARD DAVID VIVIAN LLEWELLYN.
 1906-1983.

LOCHTE, DICK <RICHARD SAMUEL>.
 1937-   . Ref: CA.
 Sleeping Dog. Arbor, 1985; Macmillan
 (London), 1986 <L.A.>

*LOCKE, W(ILLIAM) J(OHN)
 *The Joyous Adventures of Aristide
 Pujol. Silent film: Foss, 1920
 (scw & dir: Frank Miller)

LOCKHART, (ROBERT) H(AMILTON) BRUCE.
 1886-1970. Ref: CA.
 Memoirs of a British Agent. Putnam
 (London & NYC), 1932 (Novelized
 autobiography.) Film: Warner,
 1934, as British Agent (scw: Laird
 Doyle; dir: Michael Curtiz)

*LOCKRIDGE, FRANCES (LOUISE DAVIS),
 and RICHARD (ORSON) LOCKRIDGE.
 Ref also: TM.

LOCKWOOD, ELEANOR STANLEY
 Fatal Shadows. Humphries, 1949

*LOCKWOOD, ETHEL
 House in the Hollow. Lenox, 1972;
 Remploy, 1975

*LODWICK, JOHN
 *Love Bade Me Welcome. <Paris>

LOEWINSOHN, RON(ALD WILLIAM).
 1937-   . Ref: CA.
 Magnetic Field(s). Knopf, 1983

*LOFTS, NORAH (ROBINSON). 1904-1983.
 Ref: not in TC2. Pseudonym:
 *Peter Curtis, q.v.
 The Claw. Hodder, 1981; Doubleday,
 1982
 Jassy. Joseph, 1944; Knopf, 1945
 <Eng., 1800s> Film: General Film,
 1947 (scw: Dorothy Christie,
 Campbell Christie, Geoffrey Kerr;
 dir: Bernard Knowles)

LOGAN, MAX
 Dressed to Kill. Gray, 195?
 Hellcat. Gray, 195?
 The Reckoning. Gray, 195?

LOGHRY, LIZABETH
 The Cursed Inheritance. Zebra, 1981

*LOGUE, JOHN. SC: John Moore, in
 *Follow the Leader, and in title
 below.
 Replay: Murder. Ballantine, 1983
 <South>

LOKEN, CHRIS. Former actor and playwright; operates family fruit farm
 in upstate N.Y.
 The Boy Next Door. Dodd, 1985 <Wis.>

*LOMBARD, NAP. Ref: BM. SC: Lord
 Winterstone (Lord Pig), in both
 titles (*Murder's a Swine, and
 *Tidy Death).

LONDON, BELLE E.
 Room on Floor One. French, 1979
 (1-act play.)

LONDON, DARRYL
 Respect. Lloyds, 1984

*LONDON, JACK <JOHN GRIFFITH LONDON>.
 Ref also: CA.
 The Assassination Bureau. Film:
 Heathfield, 1969 (scw: Michael
 Relph, Wolf Mankowitz; dir: Basil
 Dearden)

*LONG, AMELIA REYNOLDS. Ref: TM. SC:
 Peter Piper, also in title marked
 PP below.
 *The Lady Saw Red. <theatre> PP
 *Murder by Magic. ... Grafton, 1946
 (date correction)

*LONG, FREDA M(ARGARET)
 -Poison in Putney. Hale, 1981

LONG, H(ERBERT) KINGSLEY
"G" Men. Readers Library, 1935 (Novelization of film: Warner, 1935; scw: Seton I. Miller; dir: William Keighley)

*LONG, HARMAN. SC: Franklyn Keene, also in *The Corpse Can't Walk.

*LONG, LYDA BELKNAP
*The Witch Tree. <S.C.>

*LONGBAUGH, HARRY
*No Way to Treat a Lady. Film: Paramount, 1968 (scw: John Gay; dir: Jack Smight)

LONGFELLOW, ALICE
A Rose for This Day's Madness. SOS, 1985

LONGLEY, W. B. Pseudonym of *Robert J(oseph) Randisi, 1951-   , q.v. Both titles are in Angel Eyes series.
Death's Angel. PaperJacks, 1985
The Miracle of Revenge. PaperJacks, 1985

*LONGRIGG, ROGER (ERSKINE). Ref: TM. Pseudonyms: *Ivor Drummond; *Frank Parrish, Domini Taylor, qq.v.

*LONGSTREET, STEPHEN
*The Ambassador. <Rome>

*LONSDALE, FREDERICK. See also: Guy Fowler.
The Last of Mrs. Cheyney. Collins, 1925. (3-act play.) Film: MGM, 1929 (scw: Hans Kraly, Claudine West; dir: Sidney Franklin). Also: MGM, 1937 (scw: Leon Gordon, Samson Raphaelson, Monckton Hoffe; dir: Richard Boleslawski). Also: MGM, 1951, as The Law and the Lady (scw: Leonard Spigelgass, Karl Tunberg; dir: Edwin H. Knopf)

*LOOKABEE, EMMITT
*A Twist of Yarn. Pageant, 1956 (date correction)

LOOMIS, PAUL
For Her C-h-e-ild's Sake. French, 1940 (3-act play.)
Pure As the Driven Snow. French, 1939 (3-act play.) <Vt.>

LOONEY, PETER. Pseudonym: Eric Colby, q.v.

*LORAC, E. C. R. Ref also: CA.
*The Last Escape; see *Dishonour Among Thieves

*LORAINE, PHILIP. Ref also: TM.
*The Break in the Circle. Film: Hammer, 1954 (scw: Robert Westerby, Val Guest; dir: Guest). Also: TCF, 1957 (scw & dir: Val Guest)
*Day of the Arrow. Film: Filmways, 1966, as Eye of the Devil (scw: Robin Estridge, Dennis Murphy; dir: J. Lee Thompson)
Death Wishes. Collins, 1983; St. Martin's, 1983 <Fr.>
*The Dublin Nightmare. Film: Penington, 1958 (scw: John Tully; dir: John Pomeroy)
Loaded Questions. Collins, 1985; St. Martin's, 1986
Sea-Change. Collins, 1982; St. Martin's, 1983
*W.I.L. One to Curtis. Film: AVCO, 1975, as Permission to Kill (scw: Robin Estridge; dir: Cyril Frankel)

*LORD, DANIEL A(LOYSIUS)
Red Arrows in the Night. Queen's Work, 1941

*LORD, GABRIELLE. 1946-   . Ref: CA.
Tooth and Claw. Bodley, 1983; Vanguard, 1983 <Australia>

*LORD, GRAHAM (JOHN)
-The Nostradamus Horoscope. Hutchinson, 1981

LORD, JAMES. See: *Don(ald Eugene) Pendleton.

LORING, EMILIE (BAKER)
-What Then Is Love. Little, 1956; Hale, 1965

LORRAH, JEAN. Ref: CA.
The Vulcan Academy Murders. PB, 1984 (Part of series of Star Trek TV novelizations.)

LOTH, DAVID (GOLDSMITH). 1899-
Ref: CA.
Gold Brick Cassie. GM, 1954; Fawcett (London), 1958

LOTHAR, ERNEST
-The Mills of God. Secker, 1935. U.S. title: The Loom of Justice. Putnam, 1935. Film: Universal International, 1949, as An Act of Murder; also released as Live Today for Tomorrow (scw: Michael Blankfort, Robert Thoeren; dir: Michael Gordon)

LOUGHMAN, JOS. A.
-Who Shall Win? Charing Cross, 1878

LOUGHRAN, PETER. 1938-   . Ref: CA.
Jacqui. Panther, 1984. U.S. title (?): The Third Beast. Stein, 1985

LOURIE, RICHARD. 1940-   . Living in Mass; prize-winning fiction writer; translator from Russian and Polish.
First Loyalty. Harcourt, 1985; Macmillan (London), 1986 <NYC>

LOVEGROVE, ARTHUR
Nasty Things, Murders. French, 1974 (1-act play.)

*LOVEGROVE, PETER. Pseudonym of John Philip Ray, 1929-   . Ref: CA.

LOVELADY, GORDON KEITH
Beyond the Rim. Greenwich, 1958 <Can.>

*LOVELL, MARC. SC: Appleton Porter, in *The Spy Game, and in those titles marked AP below.
Apple Spy in the Sky. Doubleday, 1983 AP <Sp.>
Apple to the Core. Doubleday, 1983 AP
How Green Was My Apple. Doubleday, 1984 AP
The Last Seance. Hale, 1982
The Only Good Apple in a Barrel of Spies. Doubleday, 1984 AP
Spy on the Run. Doubleday, 1982 AP
The Spy Who Got His Feet Wet. Doubleday, 1985 AP <Dub.>
The Spy with His Head in the Clouds. Doubleday, 1982; Hale, 1982 AP

*LOVESEY, PETER (HARMER). Ref also: TM.
Butchers and other stories of crime. Macmillan (London), 1985 ss
The False Inspector Dew. Macmillan (London), 1982; Pantheon, 1982 <ship, 1921>
Keystone. Macmillan (London), 1983; Pantheon, 1983 <L.A., 1915>

*LOWDEN, DESMOND (SCOTT)
*Bandersnatch. <ship>
Cry Havoc. Macmillan (London), 1984
Sunspot. Macmillan (London), 1981; Holt, 1982

LOWE, STEVE. Graduate of Boston College; then French teacher, producer and host of "Our Time" radio program; living in Mass.
Aurora. Dodd, 1985 <U.S., 1987>

*LOWNDES, MARIE BELLOC. Ref also: CA, TM.
*The Chink in the Armour. Silent film: Astra, 1922, as The House of Peril (scw & dir: Kenelm Foss)
Duchess Laura; Certain Days of Her Life. Ward, 1929. U.S. title: The Duchess Intervenes. Putnam, 1933 ss. some crimmison ss
*Letty Lynton. Film: MGM, 1932 (scw: John Meehan, Wanda Tuchock; dir: Clarence Brown)
*The Lodger. Silent film: Gainsborough, 1926; released in the U.S as The Case of Jonathan Drew (scw: Eliot Stannard, Alfred Hitchcock; dir: Hitchcock). Sound film: Twickenham, 1932; released in the U.S. as The Phantom Fiend (scw: Miles Mander, Paul Rotha, Ivor Novello; dir: Maurice Elvey). Also: TCF, 1944 (scw: Barre Lyndon; dir: John Brahm). Also: TCF, 1953, as Man in the Attic (scw: Robert Presnell, Jr., Barre Lyndon; dir: Hugo Fregonese)
*The Story of Ivy. Film: Universal, 1947, as Ivy (scw: Charles Bennett; dir: Sam Wood)
Studies in Love and Terror. Methuen, 1913; Scribner, 1913 ss

*LOWELL, J. R.
The Irish Game. Prentice, 1967 <Ire., 1939>

*LUARD, NICHOLAS (LAMBERT). Ref also: TC2.
*The Orion Line. (title correction)

*LUCAS, (JOHN) CARY. See: *Theo Durrant.

LUCAS, CURTIS
Angel. Lion, 1953

LUCAS, JAMES
Battle Group Peiper. Sphere, 1985
Red Eagle. Sphere, 1983

LUCAS, RUTH. 1909-   . Ref: CA.
Who Dare to Live. Houghton, 1965; Gollancz, 1965 <Ger., WWII>

*LUCENTINI, FRANCO. See: *C(arlo) Fruttero.

*LUCKLESS, JOHN. See: *Herbert Burkholz.

*LUDDECKE, WERNER J(ORG)
*Morituri. Film: TCF, 1965; also released as The Saboteur (scw: Daniel Taradash; dir: Bernard Wicki)

LUDI, GERARD
Operation Atlantis. Nasionale Boekhandel (Cape Town), 1967
Operation Q-018. Nasionale Boekhandel (Cape Town), 1969

LUDLOW, GEOFFREY. Pseudonym of *Laurence (Walter) Meynell, q.v.
-Inside Out! or, Mad As a Hatter! Harrap, 1934

LUDLAM, HARRY. See: Paul Lund.

LUDLOW, IAN. Joint pseudonym of *Lewis Perdue, q.v., and Lee Goldberg. SC: Brett Macklin (Vigilante), in all titles.
Make Them Pay. Pinnacle, 1985 <L.A.>
.357 Vigilante. Pinnacle, 1985 <L.A.>
White Wash. Pinnacle, 1985 <L.A.>

*LUDLUM, ROBERT. Ref also: TM.
The Acquitaine Progression. Random, 1984; Granada, 1984
*The Gemini Contenders. Film: ITC, 1978 (existence of film not confirmed)
*The Holcroft Covenant. Film: Thorn EMI, 1985 (scw: George Axelrod, Edward Anhalt, John Hopkins; dir: John Frankenheimer)
*The Osterman Weekend. Film: Davis-Panzer, 1983 (scw: Alan Sharp, Ian Masters; dir: Sam Peckinpah)
The Parsifal Mosaic. Random, 1982; Granada, 1982

*LUGAR, HANS.   (spelling correction)

*LUKE, THOMAS
Condor. Allen, 1984

*LUND, JAMES. Pseudonym of John Thomson Stonehouse, 1925-   , q.v.

LUND, PAUL and HARRY LUDLAM
-Icekill. Hale, 1984

LUNDEEN, RICHARD
Hunter's Orange. Laranmark, 1982

LUNDY, MIKE. Pseudonym of a former NYC policeman.
Raven. Stuart, 1985

LUPOFF, RICHARD A(LLEN). 1935-   . Ref: CA.
-Lovecraft's Book. Arkham, 1985 <1927>

*LUSTBADER, ERIC VAN. 1946-
Ref: CA.
Black Heart. Dutton, 1984; Granada, 1984 <Far East>
Jian. Villard, 1985; Granada, 1985 <H. Kong>
The Miko. Villard, 1984; Granada, 1984 <Tokyo>
*The Ninja. Evans, 1980; Granada, 1980 <NYC>
Sirens. Evans, 1981; Granada, 1981

*LUSTGARTEN, EDGAR (MARCUS)
*Game for Three Losers. Film: Merton Park, 1965 (scw: Roger Marshall; dir: Gerry O'Hara)

*LUTZ, JOHN (THOMAS). See also: *Bill Pronzini. Pseudonym: Steven Greene, q.v. Ref also: TM; TC2 (expanded). SC: Al Nudger, in *Buyer Beware, and in title marked AN below.
Nightlines. St. Martin's, 1985; Macmillan (London), 1986 AN <St. Louis>
The Shadow Man. Morrow, 1981

*LYALL, GAVIN (TUDOR). SC: Major Harry Maxim, in *The Secret Servant, and in titles below.
The Conduct of Major Maxim. Hodder, 1982; Viking, 1983
The Crocus List. Hodder, 1985; Viking, 1986

LYKIARD, ALEXIS (CONSTANTINE). 1940-   . Ref: CA.
Last Throes. Panther, 1976

*LYLE-SMITH, ALLAN. Pseudonym: Alex Webb, q.v.

*LYMINGTON, JOHN. Pseudonym of John Newton Chance, 1911-1983.
The Green Drift. Hodder, 1965

LYNCH, (JOHN GILBERT) BOHUN, 1884- and REGINALD (CHEYNE) BERKELEY, 1890-   .
Decorations and Absurdities. Collins, 1923 ss, including a Sherlockian pastiche

LYNCH, J. BERNARD
Props, Tales of the Pawnshop and other stories. Meador, 1932 ss, at least one criminous

LYNCH, JACK. Ref: TM. SC: Peter Bragg, in all titles.
Bragg's Hunch. GM, 1982 <S.F.>
The Missing and the Dead. GM, 1982
Monterey. Warner, 1985 <Calif.>
Pieces of Death. GM, 1982
San Quentin. Warner, 1984 <Calif.>
Sausalito. Warner, 1984 <Calif.>
Seattle. Warner, 1985 <Seattle>

*LYNCH, MIRIAM
*Pale Hand of Danger. <Mass.>

LYNCH, WILLIAM
The Intimate Stranger. Lion, 1950

*LYNDE, FRANCIS
*Stranded in Arcady. Silent film: Astra, 1917 (scw: Philip Bartholomae; dir: Frank Crane)

*LYNDON, BARRE
*The Amazing Dr. Clitterhouse. Film: First National, 1938 (scw: John Wexley, John Huston; dir: Anatole Litvak)
*The Man in Half Moon Street. Film: Paramount, 1944 (scw: Charles Kenyon; dir: Ralph Murphy). Also: Hammer, 1959, as The Man Who Could Cheat Death (scw: Jimmy Sangster; dir: Terence Fisher)
*They Came by Night. Film: TCF, 1940 (scw: Sidney Gilliat, Roland Pertwee, Frank Launder, Michael Hogan; dir: Harry Lachman)

*LYNDS, DENNIS. Ref also: TM. See also: *Nick Carter. Pseudonyms: *Michael Collins, Sheila McErlean, *Mark Sadler, qq.v.

*LYNN, JACK
The Factory. Harper, 1982; Robson, 1982

*LYNN, MARGARET. Ref: CA, TM.

*LYON, (MABEL) DANA. See also: *Theo Durrant.
*The Frightened Child. Film: TCF, 1951, as House on Telegraph Hill (scw: Elick Moll, Frank Partos; dir: Robert Wise)

*LYON, WINSTON. Pseudonym of *William Woolfolk, 1917-   , q.v.
*Batman vs. the Fearsome Foursome. (Novelization of film: TCF, 1966, as Batman; scw: Lorenzo Semple, Jr.; dir: Leslie Martinson)

LYONS, AMY
Black Country Sketches. Stock, 1901 ss, some criminous

*LYONS, ARTHUR (JR.). Ref also: TC2, TM. SC: Jacob Asch, also in all titles.
At the Hands of Another. Holt, 1983 <Calif.>
*Castles Burning. ... Hale, 1983
*Dead Ringer. ... Hale, 1983
Hard Trade. Holt, 1981; Hale, 1984 <L.A.>
Three with a Bullet. Holt, 1985

*LYONS, DELPHINE. Pseudonym of Evelyn E. Smith. Ref: CA.

*LYONS, ELENA. Pseudonym of *Eleanor Fairburn.

*LYONS, IVAN. See *Nan Lyons.

LYONS, JOSEPH,   -1917, and *CECIL RALEIGH
The Master Crime. Cassell, 1907

*LYONS, NAN and *IVAN LYONS
-Sold! Coward, 1982; Sphere, 1985
*Someone Is Killing the Great Chefs of Europe. Film: Warner, 1978, as Who Is Killing the Great Chefs of Europe?; released in Britain as Too Many Chefs (scw: Peter Stone; dir: Ted Kotcheff)

LYPSYTE, ROBERT. Born, raised, educated in NYC; with New York Times for 14 years; fiction writer, lecturer, teacher.
Liberty Two. Simon, 1974

LYSAGHT, BRIAN. An L.A. attorney. SC: Ben O'Malley, in both titles.
Special Circumstances. St. Martin's, 1983; Severn, 1983 <L.A.>
Sweet Deals. St. Martin's, 1985 <L.A.>

LYTTLETON, EDITH J. Pseudonym: G. B. Lancaster, q.v.

McADAM, PRESTON. SC: Michael Sheriff (The Shield), in all titles.
African Assignment. Avon, 1985
Arabian Assault. Avon, 1985 <Mid. East>
Island Intrigue. Avon, 1985

MacALAN, PETER
-The Confession. Allen, 1985

McALLISTER, BRIAN. Professional pilot; teaches counter-insurgency, anti-terrorist and air transport bush flying techniques.
Bullion Run 101. Golden Eagle (U.S. and Eng.), 1984 <Afr.>
Desert of the Damned. Golden Eagle (U.S. and Eng.), 1985

MacANTHONY, JOE
Prime Target. Arrow, 1982

*MACARDLE, DOROTHY. See also: *Tim J. Kelly.
*Uneasy Freehold. Film: Paramount, 1944, as The Uninvited (scw: Dodie Smith, Frank Partos; dir: Lewis Allen)

McCARTER, JIM <JAMES WILLIAM>
Love's Lunatic. Denton (Syd.), 1933 <Australia>
-Shoot to Kill. Johnson (Syd.), 1942

*MACAULAY, PAULINE
The Creeper. French, 1966 (3-act play.)

McAULAY, SARA
Chance. Knopf, 1982

*McAULIFFE, FRANK (MALACHI). 1926-   Ref also: TC2, TM.

MacAVOY, R(OBERTA) A(NN). 1949-   Ref: CA.
Tea with the Black Dragon. Bantam, (U.S. and London), 1983 <S.F.>

*McBAIN, ED. SC: Matthew Hope, in *Goldilocks, and in titles marked MH below; the men of the 87th Precinct, also in those marked P below.
Beauty and the Beast. Holt, 1983; H. Hamilton, 1982 <Fla.> MH
*Blood Relatives. Film: Filmel, 1978 (scw: Claude Chabrol, R. Sydeny; dir: Chabrol)
*Cop Hater. Film: Barbizon, 1957 (scw: Henry Kane; dir: William Berke)
Eight Black Horses. Arbor, 1985; H. Hamilton, 1985 P
*Fuzz. Film: United Artists, 1972 (scw: Evan Hunter; dir: Richard A. Colla)
Heat. Viking, 1981; H. Hamilton, 1981 P
Ice. Arbor, 1983; H. Hamilton, 1983 P
Jack and the Beanstalk. Holt, 1984; H. Hamilton, 1984 MH <Fla.>
*King's Ransom. Film: Toho, 1962, as Tengoku To-Jogoku (High and Low) (scw: Akira Kurosawa, Ryuzo Kikushima, Eijiro Hisaita, Hideo Oguni; dir: Kurosawa)
*Lady, Lady, I Did It! Film: Toho, 1982, as Kofuku (Lonely Hearts) (scw: Masaya Hidaka, Ikuko Oya, Kon Ichikawa; dir: Ichikawa)
Lightning. Arbor, 1984; H. Hamilton, 1984 P
The McBain Brief. Arbor, 1983; H. Hamilton, 1982 ss
*The Mugger. Film: Barbizon, 1958 (scw: Henry Kane; dir: William Berke)
*The Pusher. Film: United Artists, 1960 (scw: Harold Robbins; dir: Gene Milford)
Rumpelstiltskin. Viking, 1981; H. Hamilton, 1981 MH <Fla.>
Snow White and Rose Red. Holt, 1985; H. Hamilton, 1985 MH <Fla.>
*Ten Plus One. Film: Valoria, 1971, as Sans Mobile Apparent (Without Apparent Motive) (scw: Philippe Labro, Jacques Lenzmann; dir: Labro)

MacBETH, GEORGE (MANN). 1932-   Ref: CA.
A Kind of Treason. Hodder, 1981. U.S. title: The Katana. Simon, 1982 <Singapore, ca.1940>

*McCAFFREY, ANNE (INEZ)
Stitch in Snow. Tor, 1985; Corgi, 1985 <Denver>

*McCAGUE, JAMES
*To Be a Hero. criminous

McCALL, DAN (ELLIOTT). 1940-   .
-Bluebird Canyon. Congdon, 1983

McCANDLESS, ANTHONY
The Burke Foundation. Macmillan (London), 1985; Stein, 1986

*McCARRY, CHARLES. Ref also: BM; revised and expanded: TC2. SC: Paul Christopher, also in new title below.
*The Better Angels. Film: Columbia, 1982, as Wrong Is Right; released in Britain as The Man with the Deadly Lens (scw & dir: Richard Brooks)
The Last Supper. Dutton, 1983; Hutchinson, 1983
*The Tears of Autumn. <1963>

McCARTAN, DOMINIC
Operation Emerald. Pluto, 1985; Dembner, 1986 <Ire.>

*McCARTHY, JANE. Pseudonym of *Ruth McCarthy Sears.

McCLENAGHAN, JACK. 1928-   . Born in N.Z.; article writer and newspaper editor.
Moving Target. Gollancz, 1966; Harcourt, 1966 <N.Z.>

*McCLOY, HELEN (WORRELL CLARKSON). Ref also: TM.
*The Impostor. (spelling correction)

*McCLURE, JAMES. Ref also: BM, TM; revised and expanded: TC2. SC: Lt. Kramer and Sgt Zondi, also in title below.
The Artful Egg. Macmillan (London), 1984; Pantheon, 1985 <S. Afr.>

*MacCLURE, VICTOR. SC: Archie Burford, also in title marked AB below.
*Death on the Set. Film: Twickenham, 1935 (scw: Michael Barringer; dir: Leslie S. Hiscott)
The Case of the Dead Producer. Newnes, ca.1930 AB

McCOLM, ALEC
Something Missing. Hale, 1981

McCOLLUM, ROBERT. Born in Calif., living in Austin, Tex.; English teacher turned salesman.
And Then They Die. St. Martin's, 1985 <Tex.>

MacCONAUGHY, J. W.
Madame X. Fly, 1910; Readers Library, 1930 (Novelization of

play by Alexandre Bisson, 1848-1912). Silent film (based on play): Gold Rooster, 1916 (scw: William Elliot Burlock; dir: George F. Marion). Also: Goldwyn, 1920 (scw: J. E. Nash, Frank Lloyd; dir: Lloyd). Sound film: MGM, 1929 (scw: Willard Mack; dir: Lionel Barrymore). Also: MGM, 1937 (scw: John Meehan; dir: Sam Wood). Also: Invicta, 1948, as The Trial of Madame X (scw & dir: Paul England). Also: Universal, 1965 (scw: Jean Holloway; dir: David Lowell Rich)

McCONNELL, FRANK D(eMAY). 1942- Ref: CA.
Murder Among Friends. Walker, 1983 <Chi.>

*McCONNELL, MALCOLM. 1939- . Ref: CA.
Just Causes. Viking, 1981

*McCONNOR, VINCENT. ca.1907- . Ref: CA. SC: Insp. Damiot, in *The Province Puzzle, and in titles marked D below.
I Am Vidocq. Dodd, 1985 <Paris, 1823>
The Paris Puzzle. Macmillan, 1982 D <Paris>
The Riviera Puzzle. Macmillan, 1981 D <Fr.>

McCORKLE, JILL. 1958- .
July 7th. Algonquin, 1984 <South>

McCORMACK, TOM
Strictly Amateur. Pinnacle, 1982 <NYC>

McCORMICK, CLAIRE. Pseudonym of Marta Haake Labus, 1943- . Ref: CA. SC: John Waltz, in all titles.
The Club Paradis Murders. Walker, 1983 <Tahiti>
Murder in Cowboy Bronze. Walker, 1985 <Ariz.>
Resume for Murder. Walker, 1982 <Pa., acad.>

McCORMICK, JAMES. See: *Lynn Como, *Greg Marlowe. Pseudonym: Jim Mack, q.v.

*McCOY, ANDREW. Ref: CA.
Blood Ivory. Secker, 1983; Secker (U.S.), 1984 <Afr.>

*McCOY, HORACE. Ref also: CA, TM.
*I Should Have Stayed Home. <L.A.>
*Kiss Tomorrow Goodbye. Film: Warner, 1950 (scw: Harry Brown; dir: Gordon Douglas)
*No Pockets in a Shroud. Film: Balzac, 1975, as Un Linceul N'a Pas de Poches (No Pockets in a Shroud) (scw: Jean-Pierre Mocky, Alain Moury; dir: Mocky)
*Scalpel. Film: Columbia, 1953, as Bad for Each Other (scw: Irving Wallace, Horace McCoy; dir: Irving Rapper)
*They Shoot Horses, Don't They? Film: Cinerama, 1969 (scw: James Poe, Robert E. Thompson; dir: Sydney Pollack)

McCOY, MADELEINE. Pseudonym: *Merlda Mace.

McCRAY, MIKE. SC: Black Berets, in all titles.
The Black Berets. Dell, 1984
The Black Palm. Dell, 1984 <Carib.>
Cold Vengeance. Dell, 1984
Contract: White Lady. Dell, 1984
Deadly Reunion. Dell, 1984 <Viet Nam>
The Death Machine Contract. Dell, 1985 <Cent. Am.>
Louisiana Firestorm. Dell, 1985 <La.>
The Red Man Contract. Dell, 1985 <Nev.>

*McCRUM, ROBERT
A Loss of Heart. H. Hamilton, 1982; Viking, 1982

McCRUMB, SHARYN. Living in Va.
Lovely in Her Bones. Avon, 1985 <Va.>
Sick of Shadows. Avon, 1984 <Ga.>

*McCULLEY, JOHNSTON. Ref: CA.
*Broadway Bab. Silent film: Pathe, 1920, as Ruth of the Rockies (dir: George Marshall)

McCURDY, JAMES KYRLE
A Little Girl in a Big City. Ogilvie, 1915. Silent film: Lumas, 1925 (scw: Victoria Moore; dir: Burton King)

*McCURTIN, PETER. SC: Jim Rainey, also in at least those titles marked JR.
Blood Island. Leisure, 1985 JR
Bloodbath. Leisure, 1985 JR <Haw.>
Death Squad. Leisure, 1985 JR
Golden Triangle. Leisure, 1984 JR <Viet Nam>
Green Hell. Leisure, 1984 JR <Ire.>
Kalahari. Leisure, 1984 JR <Afr.>
Moro. Leisure, 1984 JR <Philip.>
Rockwell. Leisure, 1982
Somali Smashout. Leisure, 1985 JR <Ethio.>
Yellow Rain. Leisure, 1984 JR <Afghan.>

*McCUTCHAN, PHILIP (DONALD). Ref also: TM. SC: Commander Esmonde Shaw, also in titles marked ES; Simon Shard, also in titles marked SS.
The Hoof. Hodder, 1983 ES
Rollerball. Hodder (London and U.S.), 1984 ES
Shard at Bay. Hodder (London & U.S.), 1985 SS
Shard Calls the Tune. Hodder, 1981 SS
Werewolf. Hodder, 1982 ES

*McCUTCHEON, GEORGE BARR
-Green Fancy. Dodd, 1917; Hodder, 1918. Silent film: Paramount, 1919, as The Mystery Girl (scw: Marion Fairfax; dir: William D. DeMille)
-The Hollow of Her Hand. Dodd, 1912; Stevens, 1917. Silent film: Select, 1919, as In the Hollow of Her Hand (scw & dir: Charles Maigne)

*McCUTCHEON, HUGH (DAVIE-MARTIN)
*To Dusty Death. Film: Butcher, 1961, as Pit of Darkness (scw & dir: Lance Comfort)

*McDANIEL, DAVID (EDWARD)
The Prisoner #3. Dobson, 1981 (Novelization of the TV series.)

*McDERMID, FINLAY. ca.1905-1987.

McDERMOTT, BRIAN
Who Killed Robin Cock? Hale, 1981

McDONALD, ALICE
Black Deeds in Whitehorse. French, 19?? (3-act play.) <Can.>

MacDONALD, CHARLES B., JR.
The Riddle of the Veiled Song. Pageant, 1954

MacDONALD, FRED. See: John Davidson.

*McDONALD, GREGORY (CHRISTOPHER). Ref also: TM. SC: Irwin M. Fletcher (Fletch), also in titles marked F; Francis Xavier Flynn, also in titles marked FF.
The Buck Passes Flynn. Ballantine, 1981; Gollancz, 1982 FF <Tex.>
Carioca Fletch. Warner, 1984; Gollancz, 1984 F <Brazil>
*Fletch. Film: Universal, 1985 (scw: Andrew Bergman; dir: Michael Ritchie)
Fletch and the Man Who. Warner, 1983; Gollancz, 1983 F
Fletch and the Widow Bradley. Warner, 1981; Gollancz, 1981 F
Fletch Won. Warner hc, 1985; Gollancz, 1985 F <L.A.>
Fletch's Moxie. Warner, 1982; Gollancz, 1983 F <L.A.>
Flynn's In. Mysterious Press, 1984; Gollancz, 1985 FF
*Running Scared. Film: Paramount, 1972 (scw: Clive Exton, David Hemmings; dir: Hemmings)
Safekeeping. Mysterious Press, 1985; Gollancz, 1986 <NYC, 1940s>

*MACDONALD, JOHN
*The Moving Target. Film: Warner, 1967, as Harper; released in Britain under book title (scw: William Goldman; dir: Jack Smight)

*MacDONALD, JOHN D(ANN). 1916-1986. Ref also: TM; expanded: TC2. SC: Travis McGee, also in titles marked TM below.
Cinnamon Skin. Harper, 1982; Collins, 1982 TM
*Darker Than Amber. Film: National General, 1970 (scw: Ed Waters; dir: Robert Clouse)
*The Executioners. Film: Universal International, 1962, as Cape Fear (scw: James R. Webb; dir: J. Lee Thompson)
*A Flash of Green. Film: Spectrafilm, 1984 (scw & dir: Victor Nunez)
Free Fall in Crimson. Harper, 1981; Collins, 1982 TM <Fla.>
*The Girl, the Gold Watch, and Everything. ... Muller, 1964 (British publisher correction)
The Good Old Stuff. Harper, 1982; Collins, 1984 ss
The Lonely Silver Rain. Knopf, 1985; Hodder, 1985 TM <Fla.>
More Good Old Stuff. Knopf, 1984 ss
*Soft Touch. Film: Paramount, 1961, as Man-Trap (scw: Ed Waters; dir: Edmund O'Brien)
Two. Carroll, 1983 2 stories

*MACDONALD, JOHN ROSS
*The Drowning Pool. Film: Warner, 1975 (scw: Tracy Keenan Wynn, Lorenzo Semple, Jr., Walter Hill; dir: Stuart Rosenberg)

MacDONALD, PATRICIA J.
The Unforgiven. Dell, 1981

*MacDONALD, PHILIP. Ref also: TM.
*The List of Adrian Messenger. Film: Universal International, 1963 (scw: Anthony Veiller; dir: John Huston)
*The Nursemaid Who Disappeared. Film: WB-FN, 1939 (scw: Paul Gangelin, Connery Chappell; dir: Arthur Woods). Also: TCF, 1956, as 23 Paces to Baker Street (scw: Nigel Balchin; dir: Henry Hathaway)
*R.I.P. Film: Paramount, 1934, as Menace (scw: Anthony Veiller; dir: Ralph Murphy)
*The Rasp. Film: Film Engineering, 1931 (scw: J. Jefferson Farjeon; dir: Michael Powell)
*Rynox. Film: Film Engineering, 1931 (scw: J. Jefferson Farjeon; dir: Michael Powell). Also: WB-FN, 1937, as Who Killed John Savage? (scw: Basil Dillon; dir: Maurice Elvey)

*MACDONELL, A(RCHIBALD) G(ORDON)
The Crew of the Anaconda. Macmillan (London), 1940

*McDONELL, GORDON
*Jump for Glory. Film: Criterion, 1937; released in the U.S as When Thief Meets Thief (scw: John Meehan, Jr., Harold French; dir: Raoul Walsh)
*They Won't Believe Me. Film: RKO, 1947 (scw: Jonathan Latimer; dir: Irving Pichel)

MacDONNELL, JAMES EDMUND. Pseudonym: *James Dark, q.v.

MacDOUGALL, ROGER and TED ALLAN
Double Image. French (London), 1957 (3-act play based on ss by *Roy Vickers, q.v.)

*McDOWELL, MICHAEL
Jack and Susan in 1953. Ballantine, 1985 <1953>
Katie. Avon, 1982; Avon (U.K.), 1983 <NYC, 1871>
Toplin. Scream Press, 1985

*McELFRESH, (ELIZABETH) ADELINE. Pseudonym: *Elizabeth Wesley, q.v.

*McENERY, JOHN
*A Black Inheritance. <Russ.>

McERLEAN, SHEILA. Pseudonym of *Dennis Lynds. Other pseudonyms: *Michael Collins, Mark Sadler, qq.v. See also: *Nick Carter.
Mask of Silence. Lancer, 1968 <Eng.>

McEVOY, CHARLES (ALFRED)
Brass Faces. Paul, 1912; Houghton, 1913

McFADDEN, ELIZABETH (APTHORP). 1875- .
Double Door. French, 1934 (3-act play.) Film: Paramount, 1934 (scw: Gladys Lehman, Jack Cunningham; dir: Charles Vidor)

*McFALL, (CHAMBERS) HALDANE (COOKE), and *DION (WILLIAM PALGRAVE) CLAYTON CALTHROP
*Rouge. ss, one criminous

McFARLANE, IAN
 The Jerusalem Conspiracy. Rigby, 1984 <Israel>

*McFARLANE, LESLIE. 1902-1977. Ref: CA.

*McGARRITY, MARK. Ref also: TC2.

McGARVEY, ROBERT. 1948-   . Pseudonym: Steve White, q.v.

MacGAUGHY, DUDLEY DEAN. Pseudonym: Dean Owen, q.v.

*McGERR, PATRICIA. 1917-1985. Ref also: TM.
 *Follow, As the Night. Film: Sirius, 1955, as Bonnes a Tuer (Rope for Killing; One Step to Eternity) (scw: Henri Decoin, Jacques de Baroncelli, J. C. Eger; dir: Decoin)

*McGHEE, EDWARD. Pseudonym: Edward M. Harper. See: *Robin Moore.

*McGILL, GORDON
 See No Evil. Sphere, 1981; Firecrest, 1983

McGILLIVRAY, DAVID and WALTER ZERLIN, JR.
 The Farndale Avenue Housing Estate Townswoman's Guild Dramatic Society Murder Mystery. French, 1981 (Play.)

*McGINLEY, PATRICK. Ref: TM.
 Goosefoot. Weidenfeld, 1983; Dutton, 1982 <Dublin> Film: ITC, 1986, as The Fantasist (scw & dir: Robin Hardy)
 The Trick of the Ga Bolga. Cape, 1985; St. Martin's, 1985 <Ire.>

*McGIVERN, WILLIAM P(ETER). Ref also: TM.
 *The Big Heat. Film: Columbia, 1953 (scw: Sydney Boehm; dir: Fritz Lang)
 *The Caper of the Golden Bulls. Film: Embassy, 1967; released in Britain as Carnival of Thieves (scw: Ed Waters, David Moessinger; dir: Russell Rouse)
 *A Choice of Assassins. Film: Rome Paris, 1967, as Un Choix d'Assassins (A Choice of Assassins) (scw: Remo Forlani, Philippe Fourastie; dir: Fourastie)
 *The Darkest Hour. Film: Warner, 1955, as Hell on Frisco Bay (scw: Sydney Boehm, Martin Rackin; dir: Frank Tuttle)
 A Matter of Honor. Arbor, 1984 <Chi.>
 *Night of the Juggler. Film: Columbia, 1980 (scw: Bill Norton, Sr., Rick Natkin; dir: Robert Butler)
 *Odds Against Tomorrow. Film: United Artists, 1959 (scw: John O. Killens; dir: Robert Wise)
 *Rogue Cop. Film: MGM, 1954 (scw: Sydney Boehm; dir: Roy Rowland)
 *Shield for Murder. Film: United Artists, 1954 (scw: Richard Alan Simmons, John C. Higgins; dir: Edmund O'Brien)
 Summitt. Arbor, 1982; Collins, 1983 <Tenn.>

*McGOVERN, JAMES
 *Fraulein. Also published as: Erika. Popular Library, 1957. Film: TCF, 1958, as Fraulein (scw: Leo Townsend; dir: Henry Koster)

MacGOWAN, JONATHAN
 The Nature of the Beast. Hale, 1985

McGOWN, JILL
 A Perfect Match. Macmillan (London), 1983; St. Martin's, 1983
 Record of Sin. Macmillan (London), 1985

*MacGRATH, HAROLD
 *The Carpet from Bagdad. Silent film: Selig, 1915 (scw & dir: Colin Campbell)
 *The Drums of Jeopardy. Silent film: Hoffman, 1923 (scw: Arthur Hoerl; dir: Roland G. Edwards). Sound film: Tiffany, 1931 (scw: Florence Ryerson; dir: George B. Seitz)
 *The Girl in His House. Silent film: Vitagraph, 1918 (scw: Katharine Reed; dir: Tom Mills)
 *The Luck of the Irish. Silent film: Mayflower, 1920 (dir: Allan Dwan)
 *The Man on the Box. Silent film: Lasky, 1914 (scw: Clara Beranger; dir: Cecil B. DeMille, Oscar Apfel, Wilfred Buckland). Also: Warner, 1925 (scw: Charles A. Logue; dir: Charles Reisner)
 *The Million Dollar Mystery. (Novelization of film: Thanhauser, 1914; scw: Lloyd F. Lonegan; dir: Howell Hansel)
 -Parrot & Co. Bobbs, 1913. Silent film: Bennett, 1921, as Not Guilty (scw: J. Grubb Alexander; dir: Sidney A. Franklin)
 *Pidgin Island. Silent film: Metro, 1916 (scw: Richard V. Spencer, Fred J. Balshofer; dir: Balshofer)
 -A Splendid Hazard. Bobbs, 1910; Ward, 1910. Silent film: First National, 1920 (dir: Alan Dwan)
 *The Voice in the Fog. Silent film: Lasky, 1915 (scw: Hector Turnbull; dir: Frank Reicher)
 *The Yellow Typhoon. Silent film: First National, 1920 (scw: Monty Katterhorn; dir: Edward Jose)

McGRATH, JOHN (PETER). 1935-   Ref: CA.
 -Bakke's Night of Fame. Davis-Poynter, 1973 (3-act play based on *"A Danish Gambit" by *William Dinner)

*McGUIRE, (DOMINIC) PAUL. 1903-1978.

*McHALE, TOM. Ref also: TM.

*MacHARG, WILLIAM (BRIGGS). Ref also: TM.
 *The Blind Man's Eyes. Silent film: Metro, 1919 (scw: June Mathis; dir: John Ince)

*McHUGH, AUGUSTIN. See: *Barton (Wood) Currie.

*McILVANNEY, WILLIAM. Ref also: TC2, TM. SC: Insp. Jack Laidlaw, in *Laidlaw, and in title below.
 The Papers of Tony Veitch. Hodder, 1983; Pantheon, 1983 <Glasgow>

*McINERNY, RALPH (MATTHEW). Pseudonym: Monica Quill, q.v. Ref also: TC2. SC: Father Roger Dowling, also in titles marked RD below.
 Getting a Way with Murder. Vanguard, 1984 RD <Ill.>
 The Grass Widow. Vanguard, 1983 RD <Ill.>
 A Loss of Patients. Vanguard, 1983 RD <Ill.>
 The Noonday Devil. Atheneum, 1985 <NYC>
 Rest in Pieces. Vanguard, 1985 RD <Ill.>
 Thicker Than Water. Vanguard, 1981; Hale, 1982 RD

*MacINNES, HELEN (CLARK). 1907-1985. Ref also: TM. SC: Robert Renwick, in *The Hidden Target, and in title marked RR below.
 *Above Suspicion. Film: MGM, 1943 (scw: Keith Winter, Melville Baker, Patricia Coleman; dir: Richard Thorpe)
 *Assignment in Brittany. Film: MGM, 1943 (scw: Anthony Veiller, William H. Wright, Howard Emmett Rogers; dir: Jack Conway)
 Cloak of Darkness. Harcourt, 1982; Collins, 1982 RR
 Ride a Pale Horse. Harcourt, 1984; Collins, 1984
 *The Salzburg Connection. Film: TCF, 1972 (scw: Oscar Millard; dir: Lee H. Katzin)
 *The Venetian Affair. Film: MGM, 1966 (scw: E. Jack Neuman; dir: Jerry Thorpe)

*McINTYRE, JOHN (THOMAS). Silent film (based on unidentified story): Gold Rooster, 1915, as An Affair of Three Nations (dir: Arnold Daly, Ashley Miller)

McIVER, N. J.
 Come Back, Alice Smythereene! St. Martin's, 1985 <NYC>

*MacIVERS, SARAH. Pseudonym of *Robert Devaney.

*MacKAY, AMANDA. Ref: TM. SC: Hannah Land, in *Death is Academic, and in title below.
 Death on the Eno. Little, 1981. British title: Death on the River. Gollancz, 1983 <N.C.>

*McKAY, KENNETH R. Pseudonym of *Henry Kane.
 Indecent Relations. Playboy, 1982

McKEE-WRIGHT, APRIL
 Murder in the Markets. London (Syd.), 1944
 -Stop Press. New Order (Syd.), 1944

MacKELLAR, SINCLAIR
 Prompt for Murder. Raven, 1981

McKENNA, ALFRED
 Goddess on the Gate. Artlook (Australia), 1984

*McKENNA, MARTHE
 *Lancer Spy. Film: TCF, 1937 (scw: Philip Dunne; dir: Gregory Ratoff)

*McKENNEY, KENNETH
 The Terminator. Franklin, 1972

*MacKENZIE, DONALD. SC: John Raven, also in titles below marked JR.
 Harrier! Granada pb, 1983
 The Last of the Boatriders. Macmillan (London), 1981
 *Nowhere to Go. Film: Ealing, 1958 (scw: Seth Holt, Kenneth Tynan; dir: Holt)
 Raven's Longest Night. Macmillan (London), 1984; Doubleday, 1984 <Port.> JR
 Raven's Revenge. Macmillan (London), 1982; Houghton, 1982 JR
 Raven's Shadow. Macmillan (London), 1984; Doubleday, 1985 JR
 *Scent of Danger. Film: Associated British, 1960, as Moment of Danger; released in the U.S. as Malaga (scw: David Osborn, Donald Ogden Stewart; dir: Laslo Benedek)

MACKIE, PHILIP. 1918-1985. Ref: CA.
 The Whole Truth. Evans, 1956; Dramatic, 1963 (3-act play.) Film: Valiant, 1958 (scw: Jonathan Latimer; dir: John Guillermin)

McKINNEY, ROBERT L.
 The Kamchatka Incident. Dembner, 1985 <Russ., 1993>

*McLAREN, JACK
 *Stories of Fear. <S. Pac.>

*MacLAREN-ROSS, J(ULIAN). 1913-1964.

*McLAUGHLIN, W(ILLIAM) R(AFFAN) D(AVIDSON)
 Sabotage at Sea. Mayflower, 1978

*MacLEAN, ALISTAIR. 1922-1987. Ref also: TM.
 *Bear Island. Film: Columbia, 1980 (scw: Don Sharp, David Butler, Murray Smith; dir: Sharp)
 *Breakheart Pass. Film: United Artists, 1975 (scw: Alistair MacLean; dir: Tom Gries)
 *Caravan to Vaccares. Film: Rank, 1974 (scw: Paul Wheeler, Joseph Forest; dir: Geoffrey Reeve)
 *Fear Is the Key. Film: EMI, 1972 (scw: Robert Carrington; dir: Michael Tuchner)
 Floodgate. Collins, 1983; Doubleday, 1984 <Holl.>
 *Force 10 from Navarone. Film: AIP, 1978 (scw: Robin Chapman, Carl Foreman, George MacDonald Fraser; dir: Guy Hamilton)
 *The Golden Gate. Film: ITC, 1978 (existence of film not confirmed)
 *The Golden Rendezvous. Film: Film Trust, 1977 (scw: Stanley Price; dir: Ashley Lazarus)
 *The Guns of Navarone. Film: Open Road 1961 (scw: Carl Foreman; dir: J. Lee Thompson)
 *Ice Station Zebra. Film: MGM, 1968 (scw: Douglas Heyes; dir: John Sturgis)
 *The Last Frontier. Film: Universal International, 1960, as The Secret Ways (scw: Jean Hazlewood; dir: Phil Karlson)
 The Lonely Sea. Collins, 1985; Doubleday, 1986 ss
 Partisans. Collins, 1982; Doubleday, 1983 <Yugos., 1943>
 *Puppet on a Chain. Film: Big City, 1970 (scw: Alistair MacLean, Don Sharp, Paul Wheeler; dir: Sharp, Geoffrey Reeve)
 River of Death. Collins, 1981; Doubleday, 1982 <Brazil>
 San Andreas. Collins, 1984; Doubleday, 1985 <ship, WWII>

*South by Java Head. Film: TCF, 1959
  (existence of film not confirmed)
*When Eight Bells Toll. Film: Rank,
  1971 (scw: Alistair MacLean; dir:
  Etienne Perier)
*Where Eagles Dare. (title given in-
  correctly as Where Eagles Fly in
  first printings of CF) Film:
  Winkast, 1968 (scw: Alistair
  MacLean; dir: Brian G. Hutton)

MacLEAN, CHARLES. 1946-   . Ref: CA.
  Pseudonym: *James Konrad.
  The Watcher. Lane, 1983; Simon, 1983

*McLEAVE, HUGH (GEORGE). SC: Dr. Ste-
  phen Armitage, in *No Face in the
  Mirror, as by *Richard Copeland,
  and in title marked SA below; Dr.
  Gregor Maclean, also in title
  marked GM.
  Death Masque. Hale, 1985; Walker,
    1986 GM
  The Icarus Threat. Gollancz, 1984.
    U.S. title (?): The Life and Death
    of Liam Faulds. St. Martin's, 1984
  The Life and Death of Liam Faulds;
    see The Icarus Threat
  Second Time Round. Hale, 1981;
    Walker, 1981 SA

*McLEISH, DOUGAL. Pseudonym of D. J.
  Goodspeed.

McLELLAN, C(HARLES) M(ORTON) S(TEWART).
  1865-1916.
  Leah Kleschna. French, 1920 (5-act
    play). Silent film: Famous Players,
    1913 (dir: J. Searle Dawley). Also:
    Paramount, 1918, as The Woman Who
    Came Back (scw: Beulah Marie Dix;
    dir: Robert G. Vignola). Also:
    Famous Players, 1924, as The Moral
    Sinner (scw: J. Clarkson Miller;
    dir: Ralph Ince)
  The Shirkers. French, 1951
    (1-act play).

*McLENDON, JAMES
  *Eddie Macon's Run. Film: Universal,
    1983 (scw & dir: Jeff Kanen)

*MacLEOD, CHARLOTTE (MATILDA HUGHES).
  Ref also: TC2, TM. SC: Sarah Kel-
  ling, also in titles marked SK
  below; Prof. Peter Shandy, also in
  titles marked PS below.
  The Bilbao Looking Glass. Doubleday,
    1983; Collins, 1983 SK <Mass.>
  The Convivial Codfish. Doubleday,
    1984; Collins, 1984 SK <Mass.>
  The Curse of the Giant Hogweed.
    Doubleday, 1985 PS <Wales>
  The Palace Guard. Doubleday, 1981;
    Collins, 1982 SK <Boston>
  The Plain Old Man. Doubleday, 1985;
    Collins, 1985 SK <Mass.>
  Something the Cat Dragged In. Double-
    day, 1983; Collins, 1984 PS
    <Mass.>
  Wrack and Rune. Doubleday, 1982;
    Collins, 1982 PS <Mass.>

*MacLEOD, ROBERT. SC: Jonathan Gaunt,
  also in titles below marked JG;
  Andrew Laird, also in titles below
  marked AL.
  A Cut in Diamonds. Century, 1985;
    Doubleday, 1986, as by Michael
    Kirk AL
  A Legacy from Tenerife. Hutchinson,
    1984; Doubleday, 1984, as by Noah
    Webster JG <Can. Is.>
  Mayday from Malaga. Hutchinson, 1983;
    Doubleday, 1983, as by Michael Kirk
    AL <Sp.>
  A Problem in Prague. Hutchinson,
    1981; Doubleday, 1981, as by Noah
    Webster JG <Prague>

McMAHON, LUELLA E.
  The Charge Is Murder. Dramatic, 19??
    (1-act play.)
  The People vs. Maxine Lowe. Dramatic,
    1955 (3-act play.)

McMANUS, JAMES. 1951-   . Ref: CA.
  Out of the Blue. Crown, 1984 <Chi.>

McMASTER, ALISON
  Nothing Ever Happens Here. Heywood,
    1955 (1-act play.)
  The Ready-Made Man. Deane, 1958;
    Baker's, 1958 (3-act play.)

*McMORDIE, TABER (L.). Was Navy pilot,
  tool designer, law student, head of
  banking trust operation in U.S.
  southwest, professional photographer, screenwriter; author of a
  business book.

*McMULLEN, MARY. Pseudonym of Mary
  Reilly Wilson. Ref also: CA, TM;
  revised, expanded: TC2.
  Better Off Dead. Doubleday, 1982;
    Macmillan (London), 1983
  The Gift Horse. Doubleday, 1985;
    Macmillan (London), 1985 <N. Mex.>
  A Grave Without Flowers. Doubleday,
    1983; Macmillan (London), 1983
    <Eng.>
  Other Shoe. Doubleday, 1981; Collins,
    1982
  Until Death Do Us Part. Doubleday,
    1982; Macmillan (London), 1983
    <NYC>

McNAB, TOM <THOMAS>. 1933-   Ref:
  CA.
  Rings of Sand. Hodder, 1984

McNALLY, JOHN
  Paper Chase. French, 1926 (3-act
    play.) Film: Samuelson, 1931, as
    The Wickham Mystery (dir: G. B.
    Samuelson)

*McNALLY, TERRENCE
  Sweet Eros, and Witness. Dramatists,
    1969 (two 1-act plays, the latter
    criminous)

McNAMARA, JOSEPH D. Chief of Police in
  San Jose, Calif. Ref: TM.
  The First Directive. Crown, 1984;
    Collins, 1985 <Calif.>

*McNAMARA, MICHAEL M.
  *The Sovereign Solution. <Ire.>

*McNEAR, ROBERT. ca.1930-1985. Ref:
  CA.

*McNEIL, JOHN
  Little Brother. Century, 1983;
    Coward, 1983 <Boston>

*McNEILE, H(ERMAN) C(RYIL). SC:
  Bulldog Drummond, also in title
  marked BD.
  *The Black Gang. Film: BIP, 1934,
    as The Return of Bulldog Drummond
    (scw & dir: Walter Summers)
  *Bulldog Drummond. Silent film:
    Astra, 1922 (scw: B. E. Doxat-
    Pratt; dir: Oscar Apfel). Sound
    film: Goldwyn, 1929 (scw:
    Wallace Smith, Sidney Howard; dir:
    F. Richard Jones)
  *Bulldog Drummond at Bay. Film:
    ABPC, 1937 (scw: James Parrish,
    Patrick Kirwan; dir: Norman Lee).
    Also: Columbia, 1947 (scw: Frank
    Gruber)
  *Challenge. Film: Paramount, 1938, as
    Bulldog Drummond in Africa (scw:
    Garnett Weston; dir: Louis King).
    Also: Reliance, 1948, as The Chal-
    lenge (scw: Frank Gruber, Irving
    Elman; dir: Jean Yarbrough)
  *The Female of the Species. Film:
    Paramount, 1937, as Bulldog Drum-
    mond Comes Back (scw: Edward T.
    Lowe; dir: Louis King)
  *The Final Count. Film: Paramount,
    1939, as Arrest Bulldog Drummond
    (scw: Stuart Palmer; dir: James
    Hogan)
  *Knock-Out. Film: United Artists,
    1934, as Bulldog Drummond Strikes
    Back (scw: Nunnally Johnson; dir:
    Roy Del Ruth). Also: Columbia,
    1947, as Bulldog Drummond Strikes
    Back (scw: Edna Anhalt, Edward
    Anhalt)
  *The Return of Bulldog Drummond.
    Film: Paramount, 1937, as Bulldog
    Drummond's Revenge (scw: Edward
    T. Lowe; dir: Louis King)
  "Sapper": The Best Short Stories.
    Dent, 1984 ss, including 5 pre-
    viously uncollected stories about
    BD
  *Temple Tower. Film: Fox, 1930 (scw:
    Llewellyn Hughes; dir: Donald
    Gallagher). Also: Paramount, 1939,
    as Bulldog Drummond's Secret
    Police (scw: Garnett Weston; dir:
    James Hogan)
  *The Third Round. Silent film: Astra,
    1925, as Bulldog Drummond's Third
    Round (scw & dir: Sidney Morgan).
    Sound film: Paramount, 1938, as
    Bulldog Drummond's Peril (scw:
    Stuart Palmer; dir: James Hogan)
  *-Three of a Kind. Film: ATP, 1932,
    as Love on the Spot (scw: John
    Paddy Carstairs, Reginald Purdell;
    dir: Graham Cutts)

*McNEILLY, WILFRED (GLASSFORD). Con-
  trary to CF, has not used pseudonym
  *W(illiam) Howard Baker. Pseudonym:
  Martin Gregg, q.v.

McNEISH, JAMES. 1931-   . Ref: CA.
  The Glass Zoo. Hodder, 1976; St.
    Martin's, 1976

MacNICHOL, KENNETH
  The Nose of Papa Hilaire, with other
    curious comedies. Blackwood,
    1925 ss, at least one criminous

MACONACHIE, WILLIAM. See: *Bart Carson,
  *Ray Stahl.

*McPARTLAND, JOHN
  *The Kingdom of Johnny Cool. Film:
    United Artists, 1963, as Johnny
    Cool (scw: Joseph Landon; dir:
    William Asher)
  *No Down Payment. Film: TCF, 1957
    (scw: Philip Yordan; dir: Martin
    Ritt)
  *The Wild Party. Film: United Artists,
    1956 (scw: John McPartland; dir:
    Harry Horner)

McPHERSON, GEORGE A. 1897-   .
  The Fugitive Three. Vantage, 1980

*MacPHERSON, MALCOLM (COOK)
  The Lucifer Key. Dutton, 1981;
    Hamlyn, 1982

McPHILEMY, SEAN
  Bust! Macmillan (London), 1985

McQUAY, MIKE. Graduate of Univ. of
  Dallas; teaches science fiction
  writing course at Okla. Central
  State Univ. SC: Matthew Swain, in
  those titles marked MS (set in
  21st century).
  The Deadliest Show in Town. Bantam,
    1982 MS
  Escape from New York. Bantam, 1981
    <NYC, 1977> (Novelization of the
    movie.)
  Hot Time in Old Town. Bantam, 1981
    MS
  The Odds Are Murder. Bantam, 1982
    MS
  When Trouble Beckons. Bantam, 1981
    MS

MacQUEEN, HECTOR
  Strange Voyage. Heywood, 1951
    (3-act play.)

*McQUINN, DONALD E.
  Shadow of Lies. Tor, 1985 <Seattle>
  Wake in Darkness. Macmillan, 1982
    <Manila>

McQUOID, ALAN. 1935-   . Born in L.A.;
  vice president of firm which is
  member of New York Stock Exchange.
  The Puppet Master. Vantage, 1971
    <Berlin>

*McRAE, G. R(OY)
  *The Passing of Mr. Quinn. (Noveliza-
    tion of film; see *Agatha
    Christie.)

*McSHANE, MARK. Ref also: TM.
  -The Halcyon Way. Manor, 1979; Hale,
    1982
  *The Passing of Evil. Film: National
    General, 1969, as The Grasshopper
    (scw: Jerry Belson, Garry Mar-
    shall; dir: Jerry Paris)
  *Seance on a Wet Afternoon. Film:
    AFM, 1964 (scw & dir: Bryan
    Forbes)

*McVEAN, JAMES
  Seabird Nine. Macdonald, 1981;
    Coward, 1981 <Arctic>

*MacVEIGH, SUE
  *Grand Central Murder. Film: MGM,
    1942 (scw: Peter Ruric; dir: S.
    Sylvan Simon)

*MacVICAR, ANGUS
  *Stranger at Christmas. criminous

*M--, MR.
  *The Chest of Opium. <China>
  2 stories

*MACAO, MARSHALL. At least the follow-
  ing titles were written by Thaddeus
  Francis Tuleja, 1944-   . Ref: CA.
  The Devil's Triangle. Freeway, 1974
  *The Kak-Abdullah Conspiracy
  *Mark of the Vulture.

*MACE, MERLDA. Pseudonym of Madeleine McCoy.

*MACHEN, ARTHUR
 The Terror. Duckworth, 1917; McBride, 1917

MACHIN, MEREDITH LAND. Living in Haw.
 Outrageous Fortune. St. Martin's, 1985 <Wis.>

MACK, JIM. Pseudonym of James McCormick.
 Faust of the F.B.I. Hamilton Stafford, 1953

*MACK, JOHNNY
 *Faust of the F.B.I. delete; wrong byline

*MACK, WILLARD
 *Kick-In. Silent film: Astra, 1917 (dir: George Fitzmaurice). Also: Famous Players, 1923 (scw: Ouida Bergere; dir: George Fitzmaurice). Sound film: Paramount, 1931 (scw: Bartlett Cormack; dir: Richard Wallace)
 Tiger Rose. Belasco, 1917 (3-act play.) Silent film: Warner, 1923 (scw: Edmund Goulding, Millard Webb; dir: Sidney Franklin). Sound film: Warner, 1929 (scw: Harvey Thew, Gordon Rigby; dir: George Fitzmaurice)

MACKLIN, ROBERT. See: Frank Galbally.

*MACKWORTH, JOHN (DOLBEN)
 Blood-Amber. Diamond, 1927

MACY, DORA. Pseudonym of *Grace (Perkins) Oursler.
 Night Nurse. Brentano's, 1930; Shaylor, 1931. Film: Warner, 1931 (scw: Oliver H. P. Garrett, Charles Kenyon; dir: William A. Wellman)

MADDOX, LEE
 The Muskrat Ramble. Hale, 1985
 Star-Cluster Kill. Hale, 1984

MADISON, JOYCE. Pseudonym of Joyce Lois Mintz, 1933- . Ref: CA.
 Run If You Can. Pinnacle, 1981

*MAGALI
 All That Glitters. Mystique, 1982 (Translation of "Belle-de-Mai." Paris, 1962.)
 The Healing Heart. Mystique, 1982 (Translation of "Le Bonheur est Pour Demain." Paris, 1980.)
 Love in Jeopardy. Mystique, 1981 (Translation of "Le Chateau des Coeurs Perdus." Paris, 1963.)
 Pact of Love. Mystique, 1981 (Translation of "Sa Derniere Soiree." Paris, 1961.)
 Tender Fate. Mystique, 1981 (Translation of "La Voyageuse Clandestine." Paris, 1953.)

MAGDALANY, PHILIP. ca.1936-1985. Ref: CA.
 Criss-Crossing. Dramatists, 1970 (1-act play.)

MAGDALEN, I. I. Pseudonym of a former member of British Intelligence who under his own name is a well-known novelist and correspondent for one of England's leading newspapers.
 Ana P. World's Work, 1983; Overlook, 1985
 The Search for Anderson. World's Work, 1982; St. Martin's, 1982 <1963>

MAGEE, BILL and CRAIG SCHENK. SC: Columbo, also in title below.
 Columbo and the Samurai Sword. Black, 1980 <L.A.>

*MAGNUSON, TEODORE
 Dead Weight. Star, 1982

*MAHANNAH, FLOYD. 1911- . Ref: TM.

MAHON, THOMAS (CAVAN). 1944- . Ref: CA.
 The Fandango Involvement. GM, 1981

*MAI, DENISE
 Invitation to Danger. Mystique, 1981 (Translation of "Les Invites de Delila." Paris, 1968.)
 The Ruins of Love. Mystique, 1981 (Translation of "La Serre aux Orchidees." Paris, 1977.)

*MAILER, NORMAN
 -An American Dream. Dial, 1965; Deutsch, 1965. Film: Warner, 1966; released in Britain as See You in Hell, Darling (scw: Mann Rubin; dir: Robert Gist)
 Tough Guys Don't Dance. Random, 1984; Joseph, 1984 <Mass.>

*MAIR, JOSEPH
 *Never Come Back. Film: Tempean, 1955, as Tiger by the Tail; released in the U.S. as Cross Up (scw: John Gilling, Willis Goldbeck; dir: Gilling)

MAJESKI, BILL <WILLIAM>. 1927- Ref: CA.
 The Very Great Grandson of Sherlock Holmes. Dramatic, 1976 (3-act play.)

MAJOR, H. M. Joint pseudonym of Sharon Jarvis, 1943- , and Kathleen Buckley. Ref for Jarvis: CA.
 The Alien Trace. Signet, 1984 <future>

*MAKIN, WILLIAM J(AMES)
 *Murder at Covent Garden. Film: Twickenham, 1932 (scw: Michael Barringer, H. Fowler Mear; dir: Barringer, Leslie Hiscott)

MALCOLM, JOHN. Pseudonym of John Malcolm Andrews, 1936- . Ref: CA. SC: Tim Simpson, in all titles. Set: Eng.
 A Back Room in Somers Town. Collins, 1984; Scribner, 1985
 The Godwin Sideboard. Collins, 1984; Scribner, 1985
 The Gwen John Sculpture. Collins, 1985; Scribner, 1986

*MALING, ARTHUR (GORDON). Ref also: TM. SC: Brock Potter, also in title marked BP.
 From Thunder Bay. Harper, 1981 <Can.>
 A Taste of Treason. Harper, 1983; Gollancz, 1983 BP

*MALLORY, PETER
 A Killing Matter. Hale, 1981

MALLOY, LESTER. SC: Martin Moon, in at least those marked MM.
 Beware the Yellow Packard. Hale, 1982
 The Bullet-Proof Toga. Hale, 1984 MM
 The Happiest Ghost in Town. Hale, 1981 MM
 JoJo and the Private Eye. Hale, 1981
 So Help Me Hannah. Hale, 1982 MM

MALONE, MICHAEL (CHRISTOPHER). 1942- . Ref: CA.
 Uncivil Seasons. Delacorte, 1983; Chatto, 1984 <N.C.>

MALONEY, J(OSEPH) J(OHN). 1940- Ref: CA.
 I Speak for the Dead. Andrews, 1982 <Kan. City>

MALOUF, DAVID. 1934- . Ref: CA.
 Child's Play. Braziller, 1981; Chatto, 1982

*MALZBERG, BARRY (NORMAN). Pseudonym: *Mike Barry, q.v.

MAN, JOHN. 1941- . Ref: CA.
 The Lion's Share. Corgi, 1982; St. Martin's, 1982 <1976>

*MANCHESTER, IVY. Pseudonym of *Carleton Carpenter, q.v.

MANCHESTER, JOE
 Run, Thief, Run! Dramatists, 1964 (1-act play.) <NYC>

MANDEL, LEO N. Joint pseudonym with *Phillip Finch, q.v.: Al Bird, q.v.

MANDELL, MARK. SC: Curt Jaeger (Nazi Hunter), in all titles.
 Butcher Block. Pinnacle, 1982 <S.F.>
 Hell Nest. Pinnacle, 1983
 Killer Instinct. Pinnacle, 1982 <L.A.>
 Nazi Hunter. Pinnacle, 1981
 Slaughter Summit. Pinnacle, 1982

*MANER, WILLIAM
 What's Left of Fred. Hale, 1984

MANGAN, MICHAEL
 Murder, Inspector. Duffy, 1959 (3-act play.)

*MANKIEWICZ, DON M(ARTIN)
 *Trial. Film: MGM, 1955 (scw: Don M. Mankiewicz; dir: Mark Robson)

*MANKTELOW, BETTINE
 *Death Walked In. (2-act play.)

*MANN, ABBY. 1927- . Birth name: Abraham Goodman. Ref: CA.

MANN, EDWARD BEVERLY. 1902- . Pseudonym: Hugh Neban, q.v.

MANN, JAMES
 Endgame. NEL, 1981

*MANN, JESSICA. Ref also: TM; revised: TC2.
 Funeral Sites. Macmillan (London), 1981; Doubleday, 1982
 Grave Goods. Macmillan (London), 1984; Doubleday, 1985
 No Man's Island. Macmillan (London), 1983; Doubleday, 1983
 *The Sting of Death. ... Doubleday, 1983

*MANN, PATRICK
 *Dog Day Afternoon. Film: Warner, 1975 (scw: Frank Pierson; dir: Sidney Lumet)

*MANNERS, DAVID X. Ref: CA.

*MANNERS, WILLIAM. 1907-
 -Wharf Girl. Lion, 1954

*MANNIN, ETHEL (EDITH). 1900-1984.

*MANNION, JOHN B. See: *John P. Evans.

MANRIQUE, JAIME
 Columbian Gold. Potter, 1983 <Colom.>

*MANTELL, LAURIE. Ref: TM. SC: Sgt. Steve Arrow, also in at least the title marked SA.
 Murder in Vain. Gollancz, 1984 <N.Z.>
 Murder to Burn. Gollancz, 1983 SA <N.Z.>

*MANTZ, LEW
 Alias the Maestro. Hamilton Stafford, 1952 (by *Thomas Hector Martin.)

*MARA, BERNARD. Pseudonym of *Brian Moore. Other pseudonym: *Michael Bryan.

MARACOTTA, LINDSAY. Lives in NYC.
 Caribe. Jove, 1980
 Hide-and-Seek. PB, 1982 <NYC>

*MARASCO, ROBERT
 *Burnt Offerings. Film: PEA Films, 1976 (scw: William F. Nolan, Dan Curtis; dir: Curtis)
 *Child's Play. <acad.> Film: Paramount, 1972 (scw: Leon Prochnik; dir: Sidney Lumet)

MARBERRY, M. M. Pseudonym: *Jordan Brewer.

*MARCH, MAXWELL. Pseudonym of *Margery (Louise) Allingham, q.v.

*MARCH, WILLIAM. Ref: CA, TM.

*MARCHANT, SIR HERBERT (STANLEY). Ref: CA.

*MARCHETTI, VICTOR. Ref: CA.

*MARCHMONT, ARTHUR W(ILLIAM)
 *By Snare of Love. <Mid. East>

*MARCIN, MAX. See also: *Frederic S(tewart) Isham.
 *Cheating Cheaters. Silent film: Young, 1919 (scw: Kathryn Stuart; dir: Allen Dwan). Also: Universal, 1927 (scw: Charles A. Logue; dir: Edward Laemmle). Sound film: Universal, 1934 (scw: Gladys Unger, Allen Rivkin; dir: Richard Thorpe)
 The House of Glass, with George M. Cohan. Cohan, 1916 (4-act play.) Silent film: Select, 1918 (scw: Charles E. Whittaker; dir: Emile Chautard)
 *The Nightcap. Silent film: Universal, 1925, as Secrets of the Night (scw: Edward J. Montagne; dir: Herbert Blache)
 *The Substitute Prisoner. Silent film: Bacon, 1919, as Sun-Up (scw: Basil Dickey; dir: Oliver D. Bailey)

*MARCUS, JOANNA. Pseudonym of *Lucilla Mathew Andrews. Ref: CA.

M

MARDON, DEIRDE
   In for a Penny. Harlequin, 1984 <NYC>
   With Penalty and Interest. Harlequin, 1985 <Conn.>

*MARGOLIN, PHILLIP M.
   The Last Innocent Man. Little, 1982; Macmillan (London), 1982 <Portland>

MARINO, JAMES
   The Asgard Solution. Avon, 1983

*MARION, FRANCES
   *The Secret Six. (Novelization of film: MGM, 1931; scw: Frances Marion; dir: George Hill)

MARITANO, ADELA. Joint pseudonym with Gale Maritano: *Adela Gale.

MARITANO, GALE. Joint pseudonym with Adela Maritano: *Adela Gale.

MARKHAM, STEVE
   Alcatraz Break. Art Publicity, 1950
   Dames Can't Wait. Art Publicity, 1950
   The Hideout. Art Publicity, 1950

*MARKHAM, VIRGIL. Ref also: TM.

*MARKO, ZEKIAL. Pseudonym: *John Trinian, q.v.
   *Scratch a Thief. delete entry

MARKS, PETER. See: Walter Marks.

MARKS, WALTER and PETER
   The Butler Did It. Dramatists, 1981 (3-act play.)

*MARKSTEIN, GEORGE. 1929-1987. Ref: TC2.
   *Chance Awakening. Film: Cathala, 1982, as Espion Leve-Toi (Rise Up, Spy) (scw: Claude Veillot, Yves Boisset, Michel Audiard; dir: Boisset)
   Ferret. Hodder, 1983; Ballantine, 1983
   The Ultimate Issue. NEL, 1981; Ballantine, 1981 <1961>

*MARLOWE, ANN
   The Red Rocking Bird. St. Martin's, 1985; NEL, 1984 <Fr.>

*MARLOWE, DAN J(AMES). 1914-1986. Ref also: TM. See: Gar Wilson.

*MARLOWE, DEREK. Ref also: BM, TM.
   *A Dandy in Aspic. Film: Columbia, 1968 (scw: Derek Marlowe; dir: Anthony Mann, Laurence Harvey)
   *Echoes of Celandine. Film: Hemmings, 1977, as The Disappearance (scw: Paul Mayersberg; dir: Stuart Cooper)

*MARLOWE, GREG. House name.
   *Behind the Enemy. (by Leslie T. Barnard.)
   *Death Mask of War. (by Leslie T. Barnard.)
   *Espionage. (by James McCormick.)

*MARLOWE, HUGH
   *A Candle for the Dead. Film: Trio, 1969, as The Violent Enemy (scw: Edmund Ward; dir: Don Sharp)

MARLOWE, JOHN
   Trouble in Muristan. Cresset, 1957

MARLOWE, MARCH. Pseudonym of *Manning Lee Stokes.
   F.B.I. Girl. Arcadia, 1959 <Midwest>

*MARLOWE, STEPHEN. Ref also: TM.
   1956. Arbor, 1981; NEL, 1982 <1956>

MARMOR, ARNOLD
   The Secret Past. SOS, 1985 <NYC>
   The 13 Sinners. Merit, 1960 <NYC>

MARON, MARGARET. Living in N.C. SC: Lt. Sigrid Harald = SH.
   Bloody Kin. Doubleday, 1985 <N.C.>
   Death in Blue Folders. Doubleday, 1985 SH <NYC>
   Death of a Butterfly. Doubleday, 1984 SH <NYC>
   One Coffee With. Raven, 1981 SH <NYC>

*MARQUAND, JOHN P(HILLIPS). Ref also: TM.
   *Stopover: Tokyo. Film: TCF, 1957 (scw: Richard L. Breen, Walter Reisch; dir: Breen)
   *Thank You, Mr. Moto. TCF, 1937 (scw: Norman Foster, Willis Cooper; dir: Foster)
   *Think Fast, Mr. Moto. Film: TCF, 1937 (scw: Norman Foster, Howard Ellis Smith; dir: Foster)

MARQUEZ, GABRIEL GARCIA. 1928- Ref: CA.
   Chronicle of a Death Foretold. Knopf, 1983 (Translation of "Cronica de una Muerta Anunciada." Buenos Aires, 1981.)

MARR, REED
   Women Without Men. GM, 1957

*MARRIC, J. J.
   *Gideon's Day. Film: Columbia, 1958; released in the U.S. as Gideon of Scotland Yard (scw: T. E. B. Clarke; dir: John Ford)

MARRIOTT, ANTHONY. SC: Frank Marker, also in title by *Audley Southcott, q.v.
   Marker Calls the Tune. Fontana, 1968 (Novelization of the "Public Eye" TV series.)

MARRIS, KATHRINE. Pseudonym: K. K. Beck, q.v.

MARRYAT, CAPTAIN (FREDERICK). 1792-1848.
   The Phantom Ship. Colburn, 1839; Weeks, 1839
   Snarleyow; or, The Dog Fiend. Colburn, 1837; Colyer, 1837

*MARRYAT, FLORENCE
   -Mount Eden. White, 1889; Lovell, 1889

*MARS, ALISTAIR. 1915-1985. Ref: CA.

MARS-JONES, ADAM. 1954- . Ref: CA.
   Lantern Lecture, and other stories. Faber, 1981 3 stories, 1 criminous

MARSH, EILEEN
   Coroner's Jury. Metropolitan, 1949

*MARSH, (EDITH) NGAIO. Ref also: TM. SC: Roderick Allyn, also in title below.
   Light Thickens. Collins, 1982; Little, 1982 <theatre>

MARSH, PETER
   The Devil's Daughter. Swift, 1942; Harborough, 1951 <NYC>

*MARSH, RICHARD. Pseudonym of Richard B. Heldmann, 1867-1915.
   *The Beetle. Silent film: Barker, 1919 (scw: Helen Blizzard; dir: Alexander Butler)
   *In Full Cry. Silent film: Broadwest, 1921 (scw: Benedict James, Frank Fowell; dir: Einer J. Bruun)
   *Miss Arnott's Marriage. criminous

MARSHALL, ARTHUR CALDER. Pseudonym: *William Drummond, q.v.

*MARSHALL, BRUCE
   -Vespers in Vienna. Houghton, 1947. British title: The Red Danube. Constable, 1947. Film: MGM, 1949, as The Red Danube (scw: Gina Kaus, Arthur Wimperis; dir: George Sidney)

*MARSHALL, JOSEPH R.
   Carla. GM, 1961

*MARSHALL, LOVAT. SC: Sugar Kane, not in *Murder Town.

*MARSHALL, RAYMOND
   *Hit and Run. Film: Groupe des Quatre, 1959, as Delit de Fuite (Hit and Run) (scw: Jean Aurel; dir: Bernard Borderie)
   *Mission to Siena. Film: Rialto, 1964, as Wartezimmer zum Jenseits (Waiting Room for the Other Side) (scw: Eberhard Keindorff, Johanna Sibelius; dir: Alfred Vohrer)
   *Mission to Venice. Film: Cocinor, 1964, as Voir Venise et Crever (See Venice and Die) (scw: Jacques Robert, Andre Versini; dir: Versini)
   *A Short Time to Live. Film: Gaumont International, 1968, as La Petite Vertu (The Little Virtuous) (scw: Claude Sautet, Michel Audiard; dir: Serge Korber)
   *The Things Men Do. Film: Imperia, 1959, as Ca N'Arrive Qu'Aux Vivants (It Only Happens to the Living) (scw: Pierre Larey, Jean Cosmos; dir: Tony Saytor)

*MARSHALL, WILLIAM (LEONARD). Ref: TC2, TM. SC: Insp. Harry Feiffer (not Peiffer, as given in first printings of CF), also in new titles below, all set in H. Kong.
   *The Age of Death. delete: not criminous
   The Far Away Man. Secker, 1984; Holt, 1985
   Perfect End. H. Hamilton, 1981; Holt, 1983
   Roadshow. Secker, 1985; Holt, 1985
   Sci Fi. H. Hamilton, 1981; Holt, 1981
   War Machine. H. Hamilton, 1982

*MARSLAND, AMY (LOUISE)
   A Classic Death. Doubleday, 1985 <Fr.>

*MARSTEN, RICHARD
   *Murder in the Navy. ... Muller, 1956

MARTELL, EDWARD. See: Anonymous.

*MARTENS, ANNE (LOUISE) COULTER
   The High Road. French, 1971 (1-act play.)
   Whodunit. Dramatic, 19?? (1-act play.)
   You, the Jury. Dramatic, 1965 (1-act play.)

*MARTIN, A(RCHIBALD) E(DWARD)
   Common People. Consolidated (Syd.), 1944 <Australia>
   *The Outsiders. Film: Hammer, 1955, as The Glass Cage; released in the U.S. as The Glass Tomb (scw: Richard Landau; dir: Montgomery Tully)

MARTIN, C. H. Lives in Mich.; director of mental health for state of Mich.; a clinical psychologist.
   The PK Factor. Unicorn-Star, 1984 <Mich.>

*MARTIN, DON
   *"Shed No Tears." Film: Pathe, 1948 (scw: Brown Holmes, Virginia Cook; dir: Jean Yarbrough)

MARTIN, GEORGE R(AYMOND) R(ICHARD). 1948- . Ref: CA.
   The Armageddon Rag. Poseidon, 1983; NEL pb, 1984

MARTIN, JACK. Pseudonym of Dennis William Etchison, 1943- . Ref: CA.
   Halloween II. Zebra, 1981 (Novelization of film: Universal, 1981; scw: Carpenter Hill; dir: Rick Rosenthal)

MARTIN, LEE. Pseudonym of Martha G. Webb, 1943- , q.v.
   Too Sane a Murder. St. Martin's, 1984; Quartet, 1986 <Tex.>

MARTIN, MARIAN
   Dangerous Stranger. Tiara, 1981
   The Ravens of Rockhurst. Harlequin, 1983 <Wash.>

*MARTIN, RALPH
   *The Man Who Haunted Himself. (Novelization of film; see *Anthony Armstrong.)

*MARTIN, ROBERT (LEE). Ref also: TM.

MARTIN, ROY PETER. 1931- . Pseudonym: James Melville, q.v.

MARTIN, RUSSELL W.
   The Resurrection of Candy Sterling. Playboy, 1982

*MARTIN, SHANE. Pseudonym of *George H(enry) Johnston.

*MARTIN, THOMAS HECTOR. 1913-1985. See: Lew Mantz.

MARTIN, TREVOR
   The Terminal Transfer. Avon, 1984

*MARTIN, TROY KENNEDY
   *The Italian Job. (Novelization of film: Oakhurst, 1969; scw: Troy Kennedy Martin; dir: Peter Collinson)

*MARTIN, WILLIAM. Lives in Mass.
   *Back Bay. (title correction) ... Futura, 1985
   Nerve Endings. Crown, 1984; Futura, 1985

MARTINDALE, JESSE CARR
    Makepeace Not War. Futura, 1985 (Novelization of the TV series.)

MARTINS, JOYCE F.
    Rosemary for Remembrance. French, 19?? (1-act play.)

*MARTON, GEORGE
    *Catch Me a Spy. Film: Ludgate, 1971 (scw: Dick Clement, Ian La Frenais; dir: Clement)

*MARTYN, WYNDHAM
    *All the World to Nothing. Silent film: Pathe, 1916 (scw: Stephen Fox; dir: Henry King)
    *The Mysterious Mr. Garland. Silent film: Berwilla, 1921, as The Star Reporter (dir: Duke Worne)
    *The Secret of the Silver Car. Silent film: Vitagraph, 1921, as The Silver Car (scw: Wyndham Martyn; dir: David Smith)

MARVAL, HELEN
    At Devil's Bridge. Mystique, 1981 (Translation of "Le Secret du Pont d'Enfer." Paris, 1976.)

*MASON, A(LFRED) E(DWARD) W(OODLEY). Ref also: TM.
    *At the Villa Rose. Silent film: Stoll, 1920 (scw: Sinclair Hill; dir: Maurice Elvey). Sound film: Haik, 1930, as Mystere de la Villa Rose (Mystery of the Villa Rose) (scw: Louis d'Yvre; dir: Louis Mercanton, Renee Hervil). Also: Twickenham, 1930, as Mystery at the Villa Rose (scw: Cyril Twyford; dir: Leslie Hiscott). Also: ABPC, 1939; released in the U.S. as House of Mystery (scw: Doreen Montgomery; dir: Walter Summers)
    *The House of the Arrow. Film: Twickenham, 1930 (scw: Cyril Twyford; dir: Leslie Hiscott). Also: ABPC, 1940 (scw: Doreen Montgomery; dir: Harold French). Also: ABPC, 1953 (scw: Edward Dryhurst; dir: Michael Anderson)
    *Running Water. Silent film: Stoll, 1922 (scw: Kinchen Wood; dir: Maurice Elvey)
    *The Summons. <Sp.>
    *The Winding Stair. Silent film: Fox, 1926 (dir: John Griffith Wray)
    *The Witness for the Defence. Silent film: Artcraft, 1919 (scw: Ouida Bergere; dir: George Fitzmaurice)

*MASON, BURNHAM F.
    *The Stroke of a Knife. Street, 1903 (Magnet #281)

MASON, CLIFFORD. Living in NYC.
    The Case of the Ashanti Gold. St. Martin's, 1985 <NYC>

*MASON, HOWARD
    *Photo Finish. Film: Cavalcade, 1960, as Follow That Horse (scw: Alfred Shaughnessy, William Douglas Home, Howard Mason; dir: Alan Bromly)

MASON, RICHARD (LAKIN). 1919-   . Ref: CA.
    The Fever Tree. World, 1962; Collins, 1962 <Nepal>

MASON, SARAH J. Born in Eng.; graduate of St. Andrew's University.
    Let's Talk of Wills. Collins, 1985; St. Martin's, 1986

*MASON, (FRANCIS) VAN WYCK. Ref also: TM.

MASON, WILLIAM
    Dagger. Zebra, 1984
    Eagle Down. Zebra, 1985

MASSEY, WILFRED
    Crime at the Club. Massey, 1943 (3-act play.)
    Dangerous Company. Massey, 1944 (3-act play.)
    Dead Loss, with Julian Brend. Massey, 1965 (3-act play.)
    Leap in the Dark. Massey, 1953 (3-act play.)
    A Long Shot. Northumberland, 1947 (1-act play, part of Crime at the Club, q.v.)
    The Master Key. French, 1939 (1-act play.)
    Murder No Object. Northumberland, 1947 (1-act play, part of Crime at the Club, q.v.)
    Such Things Happen. Northumberland, 1947 (3-act play.)
    The Two Mrs. Hemingways. Massey, 1946 (3-act play.)

MASSIE, ALLAN. 1938-
    The Death of Men. Bodley, 1981; Houghton, 1982 <Rome, 1978>
    One Night in Winter. Bodley, 1984

*MASSIE, CHRIS
    *The Confessions of a Vagabond. delete: non-fiction
    *Corridor of Mirrors. Film: Apollo, 1948 (scw: Rudolph Cartier, Edana Romney; dir: Terence Young)
    *Pity My Simplicity. Film: Paramount, 1945, as Love Letters (scw: Ayn Rand; dir: William Dieterle)

MASTERO STORYTELLER
    Welcome to the Torture Chamber. Vantage, 1983 <Egypt>

MASTERS, ANTHONY. All titles are novelizations of the TV series.
    Minder. Sphere, 1984
    Minder--Back Again. Sphere, 1984
    Minder--Yet Again. Sphere, 1985

MASTERS, DOUG. SC: Anthony Nicholas Twin, in all titles.
    The Beast. Charter, 1985
    The Devil's Claw. Charter, 1985
    Spiral of Death. Charter, 1985 <Parag.>
    TNT. Charter, 1985

*MASTERS, JOHN. 1914-1983. Ref: CA.

*MASTERSON, WHIT. Ref also: TM.
    *All Through the Night. Film: Warner, 1956, as A Cry in the Night (scw: David Dortort; dir: Frank Tuttle)
    *Badge of Evil. Film: Universal, 1958, as Touch of Evil (scw & dir: Orson Welles)
    *Evil Come, Evil Go. Film: TCF, 1963, as The Yellow Canary (scw: Rod Serling; dir: Buzz Kulik)
    *711--Officer Needs Help. Film: Paramount, 1967, as Warning Shot (scw: Mann Rubin; dir: Buzz Kulik)

MASTERTON, GRAHAM. 1946-   . Ref: CA.
    Condor. Tor, 1985 <WWII>
    Famine. Ace, 1981; Sphere, 1981
    Ikon. Tor, 1984; Allen, 1983 <1962>
    Sacrifice. Tor, 1986; Allen, 1985
    Tengu. Tor, 1983; Sphere, 1984 <L.A.>

MASTORAKIS, NICO and *BARNABY CONRAD, q.v.
    Fire Down Below. Dell, 1981

*MASUR, HAROLD Q. Ref also: TM; expanded: TC2. SC: Scott Jordan, also in title marked SJ below.
    The Broker. St. Martin's, 1981; Souvenir, 1981
    The Mourning After. Raven, 1981; Gollancz, 1983 SJ <NYC>

*MATCHA, JACK. Pseudonyms: John Barclay, John Tanner, qq.v.
    *Ask for Lois. delete
    *Gambler's Girl. delete

*MATHER, ARTHUR (R.). Living in Melbourne.
    The Duplicate. Sphere, 1985

*MATHER, BERKLEY. Pseudonym of John Evan Weston Davies, 1914-   . Ref also: CA; revised: TC2. SC: Stafford family, in all titles below.
    Hour of the Dog. Collins, 1982; St. Martin's, 1982 <H. Kong, 1941>
    The Midnight Gun. Collins, 1981; St. Martin's, 1984 <Far East>
    The Pagoda Tree. Collins, 1979; Scribner, 1980

*MATHERS, HELEN B(UCKINGHAM)
    The Sin of Hagar. Hutchinson, 1896

*MATHESON, RICHARD (BURTON). Ref also: TM.
    *Fury on Sunday. <NYC>
    *Hell House. Film: Pilgrim, 1973, as The Legend of Hell House (scw: Richard Matheson; dir: Jean Hough)
    *Ride the Nightmare. Film: Corona, 1971, as De la Port des Copains (From the Boys) (scw: Shimon Wincelberg; dir: Terence Young)
    *Someone Is Bleeding. Film: Fox-Lira, 1974, as Les Seins de Glace (Icy Breasts) (scw & dir: Georges Lautner)

MATHEWS, WILLIAM C.
    King Cobra. Avon, 1983 <Mex., San Diego>

*MATHEWSON, JOSEPH. SC: Alicia Von Helsing, in *Alicia's Trump, and in title below.
    Death Turns Right. Avon, 1982 <NYC>

MATHEWSON, WILLIAM (GLEN, JR.). 1940-   . Ref: CA.
    Immediate Release. Simon, 1982 <W.I.>

MATHIS, EDWARD. 1927-   . Ref: CA.
    From a High Place. Scribner, 1985 <Tex.>

MATTERA, JOHN
    Abra Cadaver. Dramatic, 19?? (1-act play.)
    Dracula. Dramatic, 1980 (3-act play based on the novel by *Bram Stoker, q.v.)
    Frankenstein, with Stephen Barrows. Dramatic, 1981 (7 scene play based on the novel by *M. Shelley, q.v.)
    An Open and Shut Case. Dramatic, 1981 (1-act play.)
    Time After Time. Dramatic, 19?? (3-act play based on the novel by *Karl Alexander, q.v.)

MATTHEWS, CHRISTOPHER. 1954-
    Al Jazzar. Allen, 1982

*MATTHEWS, CLAYTON (HARTLEY). See also: *Patricia Matthews.
    *Dive into Death. Sherbourne, 1969 (publisher/date correction)

MATTHEWS, JOHN
    Basikasingo. Arrow, 1982
    The Crescents of the Moon. Arrow, 1984

*MATTHEWS, PATRICIA and *CLAYTON
    Midnight Whispers. Bantam, 1981

MATTHEWS, SEYMOUR
    Anagram of Murder. French, 1984 (Play)

MATTHIAS, LEE A. Living in Milw.; head of a motion picture properties marketing firm.
    The Pandora Plague. Leisure, 1981 <Eng., 1902> (Sherlock Holmes)

MAUDSLEY, JERE
    Hunter. Permanent Press, 1985

*MAUGHAM, ROBIN. Ref: not in TC2.
    *Line on Ginger. Film: Foxwell, 1953, as The Intruder (scw: Robin Maugham, John Hunter, Anthony Squire; dir: Guy Hamilton)

*MAUGHAM, W(ILLIAM) SOMERSET. Ref also: TM.
    *Ashenden. Film: Gaumont British, 1936, as The Secret Agent (scw: Charles Bennett, Ian Hay, Jesse Lasky, Jr., Alma Reville; dir: Alfred Hitchcock)
    The Letter. Doran, 1925; Heinemann, 1927 (3-act play.) Silent film: Paramount, 1929 (scw: Garret Fort; dir: Jean De Limur). Sound film: Paramount Publix, 1930, as La Lettre (The Letter) (dir: Louis Mercanton). Also: First National, 1940 (scw: Howard Koch; dir: William Wyler). Also: Warner, 1947, as The Unfaithful (scw: David Goodis, James Gunn; dir: Vincent Sherman)

MAULE, DONOVAN
    Philippa Sees It Through. Modern, ca.1930

MAULE, FOX
    The Madhouse on the Moors. Mellifont, 1936

MAUZENS, FREDERIC
    The Living Strong-Box. Richards, 1909 (Translation of "Le Coffre-Fort Vivant." Paris, 1907)

*MAXFIELD, HENRY S.
    *Legacy of a Spy. Also published as: Double Man. Panther, 1966. Film: Albion, 1967, as The Double Man (scw: Frank Tarloff, Alfred Hayes; dir: Franklin J. Schaffner)

MAXIM, JOHN (R.). 1937-   . Ref: CA.
    Abel/Baker/Charley. Houghton, 1983;
    Panther, 1985 <NYC>
MAXWELL, A. E. Joint pseudonym of Ann
    Elizabeth Lowell Maxwell, 1944-   ,
    and Evan Maxwell. Ref for AELM: CA.
    Just Another Day in Paradise. Double-
    day, 1985 <Calif.>
    Steal the Sun. Marek, 1982
    <N. Mex., 1945>
MAXWELL, ANN ELIZABETH LOWELL.
    1944-   . Joint pseudonym with
    Evan Maxwell: A. E. Maxwell, q.v.
MAXWELL, EVAN. Joint pseudonym with
    Ann Elizabeth Lowell Maxwell,
    1944-   : A. E. Maxwell, q.v.
*MAXWELL, HELEN K. Pseudonym of *Eli-
    nore Denniston.
*MAXWELL, PATRICIA (ANNE PONDER).
    Pseudonyms: Jennifer Blake, q.v.;
    *Patricia Ponder.
MAXWELL, WILLIAM (KEEPERS, JR.).
    1908-   . Ref: CA.
    So Long, See You Tomorrow. Knopf,
    1980 <Ill., 1920s>
MAXXE, ROBERT. Pseudonym of *Robert
    (J.) Rosenblum.
    Arcade. Doubleday, 1984 <L.I.>
MAY, CLARA
    Forbidden Love. Mystique, 1981
    (Translation of "Le Solitaire de
    L'Ile Grecque." Paris, 1979.)
MAY, PETER. 1951-   .
    Hidden Faces. Piatkus, 1981. U.S.
    title: The Man with No Face. St.
    Martin's, 1981 <Brus.>
*MAYBURY, ANNE. Pseudonym of Anne
    Arundel Buxton. Ref: CA.
    *Ride a White Dolphin. <Venice>
*MAYFIELD, SERENA. Pseudonym of
    Josephine Bentham.
*MAYHEW, GEORGE A.
    *Murder at Daybreak. <Mich.>
MAYO, DIANE. Living in Montauk, N.Y.
    Murder at Bean and Beluga. Perma-
    nent, 1983
    Murder at the Big Store. St. Mar-
    tin's, 1984 <NYC>
MAYO, J. K.
    The Hunting Season. Collins, 1985;
    Holt, 1986
*MAYO, JAMES
    *Hammerhead. Film: Allen, 1968
    (scw: William Bast, Herbert Baker,
    John Briley; dir: David Miller)
*MAYOR, F(LORA) M(acDONALD). 1872-
    1932.
*MAYSE, ARTHUR
    *The Desperate Search. Film: MGM,
    1952 (scw: Walter Doniger; dir:
    Joseph Lewis)
MEACHAM, LEILA. 1938-   .
    Crowning Design. Walker, 1984
*MEAD, RUSSELL. SC: Dr. Peter Casey,
    in *The Moses Bottle, and in titles
    below.
    The Nightingale Trivet. Raven, 1981
    <Cape Cod>
    The Third One. Raven, 1981
*MEADE, L. T. Ref also: CA.
MEAGHER, ALICE ELIZABETH
    The Moving Finger. Macquarie (Syd.),
    1934 <Australia>
*MEAKER, MARIJANE. 1927-   Pseudo-
    nym: *Vin Packer.
MEAR, H(ARRY) FOWLER. See: William C.
    Stone.
MEARS, A(MELIA) GARLAND
    The Story of a Trust and other tales.
    Simpkin, 1893 ss, one criminous
MEEK, M(ARGARET) R(EID) D(UNCAN).
    1918-   . Born in Scot.; educated
    in law at London Univ. and a
    solicitor after 1967. SC: Lennox
    Kemp, in at least those marked LK.
    Hang the Consequences. Collins, 1984;
    Scribner, 1985 LK

The Sitting Ducks. Collins, 1984
The Split Second. Collins, 1985;
    Scribner, 1987 LK <Scot.>
With Flowers That Fell. Hale, 1983

*MEGGS, BROWN (MOORE). Ref: not in TC2.

*MEGRUE, ROI COOPER
    *Under Cover. Silent film: Famous
    Players, 1916 (scw: Doty Hobart;
    dir: Robert Vignola)

*MEIRING, DESMOND
    The Brinkman. Hodder, 1964; Houghton,
    1965 <Laos, 1960>
    A Talk with the Angels. Secker, 1985;
    St. Martin's, 1986 <Mid. East>

*MELCHIOR, IB (JORGEN)
    Eva. Dodd, 1984 <Ger., 1944>
    The Tombstone Cipher. Bantam, 1983
    V-3. Dodd, 1985 <Ger.>

*MELVILLE, ALAN. Pseudonym of William
    Melville Caverhill, 1910-1983.
    *Weekend at Thrackley. Film: Present
    Day, 1952, as Hot Ice (scw & dir:
    Kenneth Hume)

*MELVILLE, JAMES. Pseudonym of Roy
    Peter Martin, 1931-   . Ref: TC2,
    TM. SC: Supt. Otani, also in titles
    below. All set in Jap.
    The Death Ceremony. Secker, 1985;
    St. Martin's, 1985
    Death of a Daimyo. Secker, 1984; St.
    Martin's, 1985
    The Ninth Netsuke. Secker, 1982; St.
    Martin's, 1982
    Sayonara, Sweet Amaryllis. Secker,
    1983; St. Martin's, 1985
    A Sort of Samurai. Secker, 1981; St.
    Martin's, 1982

*MELVILLE, JENNIE. SC: Charmian Dan-
    iels, also in title marked CD
    below.
    The Hand of Glass. Macmillan (Lon-
    don), 1983
    Murder Has a Pretty Face. Macmillan
    (London), 1981 CD
    The Painted Castle. Macmillan
    (London), 1982

*MELVILLE-ROSS, ANTONY. SC: Tre-
    lawney, also in title marked T
    below.
    Backlash. Collins, 1979
    Command. Collins, 1985
    Shadow. Collins, 1984
    Talon. Collins, 1983
    Tightrope. Collins, 1981 T
    Trigger. Collins, 1982; Ballantine,
    1982

MENDELL, IRVING. Pseudonym: *Amen
    Dell.

MENUHIN, GERARD. Son of Yehudi Menuhin.
    Elmer. Hutchinson, 1985

*MERAK, A. J. Pseudonym of John S.
    Glasby, 1928-

MERCER, JUNE
    Death-Line. Hale, 1983

MEREDITH, D(ORIS) R. Ref: TM. Born in
    Okla.; operates a bookstore in
    Dumas, Tex. SC: Sheriff Charles
    Timothy Matthews, in both titles.
    The Sheriff and the Branding Iron
    Murders. Walker, 1985 <Tex.>
    The Sheriff and the Panhandle Mur-
    ders. Walker, 1984 <Tex.>

MERKIN, ROBERT (BRUCE). 1947-
    Ref: CA.
    The South Florida Book of the Dead.
    Morrow, 1982 <Fla.>

*MERLE, ROBERT (JEAN GEORGES)
    *The Day of the Dolphin. Film: AVCO
    Embassy, 1973 (scw: Buck Henry;
    dir: Mike Nichols)

*MERLIN, CHRISTINA
    Sword of Mithras. Hale, 1982

MERRELL, BARBARA
    Sign of Death. Zebra, 1981 <Eng.>

*MERRIMAN, PAT. Pseudonym of *Philip
    Atkey, 1908-1985.

*MERRITT, A(BRAHAM). SC: Dr. Lowell,
    in *Burn, Witch, Burn!, and in
    *Creep, Shadow!
    *Burn, Witch, Burn! Film: MGM, 1936,
        as The Devil-Doll (scw: Tod Brown-
        ing, Garrett Fort, Erich Von
        Stroheim, Guy Endore; dir: Brown-
        ing)
    *Seven Footprints to Satan. Film:
        First National, 1929 (scw: Richard
        Bee; dir: Benjamin Christensen)

MERRITT, DON. 1945-   . Ref: CA.
    My Sister's Keeper. Coward, 1983
    <1960s>
    One Easy Piece. Coward, 1981

*MERTZ, STEPHEN. See: *Don(ald Eugene)
    Pendleton.

*MERWIN, SAM(UEL KIMBALL), JR. Ref:
    TM. Pseudonym: Clarke Hammond,
    q.v.

MESKIL, PAUL
    Sin Pit. Lion, 1954 <St. Louis>

*MESSER, MONA (NAOMI ANNE HOCKING).
    189?-1966. Pseudonym: *Ann
    Hocking, q.v.

*MESSMANN, JON (J.). Pseudonyms:
    *Claude Nicole, *Claudia Nicole.
    SC: Jefferson Boone (The
    Handyman), also in title
    marked JB below.
    *The Game of Terror. ... Pyramid,
    1973 JB
    *Ransom! <S. Am.>

METCALFE, FELICIA. Pseudonym:
    *Whitaker Metcalfe.

*METCALFE, WHITAKER. Pseudonym of
    Felicia Metcalfe.

METTLER, GEORGE
    Down Home. GM, 1981 <Ga.>

MEWBURN, ROBERT
    The Tangled Skein. New Horizon, 1981

*MEWSHAW, MICHAEL
    The Year of the Gun. Atheneum, 1984;
    Severn, 1985 <Rome>

MEYER, GEOFFREY
    Final Exam. Pinnacle, 1981 (Noveli-
    zation of film: Motion Picture
    Marketing, 1981; scw & dir: Jimmy
    Huston)

MEYER, KARL
    The Bishop's Room. Manor, 1978
    <Rome>

*MEYER, NICHOLAS. Ref also: TM.
    *The Seven-Per-Cent Solution. Film:
    Universal, 1976 (scw: Nicholas
    Meyer; dir: Herbert Ross)

*MEYERS, MANNY
    *The Last Mystery of Edgar Allan Poe.
    Also published as: The Troy
    Dossier. Mysterious Press, 1986

*MEYERS, MARTIN
    *Reunion for Death. <NYC>

MEYERS, RICHARD S. See: Wade Barker,
    Dane Hartman.

*MEYNELL, LAURENCE (WALTER). Pseudonym:
    Geoffrey Ludlow, q.v. SC: Hooky
    Heffernan, in those marked HH.
    The Affair at Barwold. Macmillan
    (London), 1985 HH
    -Bandaberry. Bodley, 1960
    *The Breaking Point. Film: Butcher,
    1960; released in the U.S. as The
    Great Armored Car Swindle (scw:
    Peter Lambert; dir: Lance Comfort)
    *The Creaking Chair. Film: Anglo-
    Amalgamated, 1953, as Street of
    Shadows; released in the U.S. as
    Shadow Man (scw & dir: Richard
    Vernon)
    Hooky Goes to Blazes. Macmillan (Lon-
    don), 1981 HH
    *The House in Marsh Road. Film: Eter-
    nal, 1960 (scw: Maurice J. Wilson;
    dir: Montgomery Tully)
    *The Mystery at Newton Ferry. (title
    correction)
    *One Step from Murder. Film: Eternal,
    1960, as The Price of Silence
    (scw: Maurice J. Wilson; dir:
    Montgomery Tully)
    The Open Door. Macmillan (London),
    1984 HH
    The Secret of the Pit. Macmillan
    (London), 1982
    Silver Guilt. Macmillan (London),
    1983
    *Third Time Unlucky. Film: WB-FN,

1936, as Crown v. Stevens (scw: Brock Williams; dir: Michael Powell)
*The Thirteen Trumpeters. <It.>

MICHAEL, IAN. Pseudonym: *David Serafin, q.v.

MICHAELIS, ALAN
Ingram Intervenes. Robertson (Melb.), 1933 <Australia>

*MICHAELS, BARBARA. Ref also: TM; slightly expanded: TC2.
Be Buried in the Rain. Atheneum, 1985; Piatkus, 1986 <Va.>
Black Rainbow. Congdon, 1982; Souvenir, 1983 <Eng., 1855>
The Grey Beginning. Congdon, 1984; Souvenir, 1986 <Florence>
Here I Stay. Congdon, 1983; Souvenir, 1984 <Md.>
Someone in the House. Dodd, 1981; Souvenir, 1982 <Pa.>

MICHAELS, FERN. Joint pseudonym of Roberta Anderson, 1942- , and Mary Kuczkir, 1933- . Ref for both: CA.
Panda Bear Is Critical. Macmillan, 1982

MICHAELS, PHILIP. Pseudonym of *Philippe van Rjndt.
Come, Follow Me. Avon, 1983; Coronet, 1984 <NYC>

*MICHAELS, STEVE
*-The Main Attraction. (Novelization of film: Seven Arts, 1963; scw: John Patrick; dir: Daniel Petrie)

*MICHELSON, BENNETT
The Chosen People. Tower, 1982

*MICHELSON, MIRIAM
-In the Bishop's Carriage. Bobbs, 1904; Constable, 1904

MICKLE, ALAN
The Execution of Necome Bowles. Australasian (Syd.), 1948

MIDDLEMASS, ROBERT M. See: *Holworthy Hall.

*MIDDLEMISS, ROBERT (WILLIAM)
The Pelican's Clock. GM, 1981

MIDDLETON, GEORGE (M.). 1880-1967. Ref: CA. See also: Stuart Olivier, 1880- .
Blood Money. French, 1929 (3-act play.)

*MIDGLEY, JOHN
Despair and Die. Hale, 1983
The Kremlin Directive. Hale, 1981
The Stone Killer. Hale, 1982

*MIGLIS, JOHN
Killing Eyes. GM, 1984

MIKHANOVSKY, V(LADIMIR) N(AUMOVICH)
The Doubles. Progress, 1981; Central Books, 1982 (Translation from the Russian.)

*MILBURN, ELLEN. Pseudonym of Milburn Smith.

MILES, DORIEN KLEIN. 1915- . Joint pseudonym with Sylvia Mularchy: Sylvia Miles, q.v.

MILES, GRAHAM
Evil Mark. Hale, 1985; St. Martin's, 1985 <1820s, Eng.>

*MILES, JOHN. Ref: TM.
*The Silver Bullet Gang. <Calif.>

*MILES, RICHARD
*Angel Loves Nobody. Prentice-Hall, 1967
*That Cold Day in the Park. Delacorte, 1965, Souvenir, 1966. Film: Commonwealth, 1969 (scw: Gillian Freeman; dir: Robert Altman)

MILES, SYLVIA. Joint pseudonym of Sylvia Mularchy and Dorien Klein Miles, 1915- . Ref for Miles: CA.
Shadow over Beauclaire. Bouregy, 1975
Terror of Heartbreak House. Bouregy, 1979

*MILLAR, KENNETH. Ref also: TM.
*Blue City. Film: Paramount, 1986 (scw: Lukas Heller, Walter Hill; dir: Michelle Manning)
*The Three Roads. Film: Quandrant, 1980, as Double Negative (scw: Thomas Hedley, Jr., Charles Dennis, Janis Allen; dir: George Bloomfield)

*MILLAR, MARGARET (ELLIS STURM). Ref also: TM. SC: Tom Aragon, also in title marked TA below.
Banshee. Morrow, 1983; Gollancz, 1983 <Calif.>
*The Cannibal Heart. <Calif.>
Mermaid. Morrow, 1982; Gollancz, 1982 TA

*MILLARD, JOE
*The Hunting Party. (Novelization of film: United Artists, 1971; scw: William Norton, Gilbert Alexander, Lou Morheim; dir: Don Medford)
*Mansion of Evil. <Pa.>
*Thunderbolt and Lightfoot. (Novelization of film: United Artists, 1974; scw & dir: Michael Cimino)

MILLER, A. W.
The Destroyers. Leisure, 1980

*MILLER, ALICE DUERR
*Manslaughter. Silent film: Famous Players, 1922 (scw: Jeanie MacPherson; dir: Cecil B. DeMille). Sound film: Paramount, 1930 (scw & dir: George Abbott). Also: Paramount, 1931, as Le Requisitoire (Public Prosecutor's Speech) (dir: Dimitri Buchowetzki)

*MILLER, BEN E.
*Death Deal. <NYC>

MILLER, BEULAH MONTGOMERY. 1917- . Ref: CA.
The Fires of Heaven. Douglas-West, 1974

*MILLER, BILL. Ref: CA.

MILLER, DAVID C. See: John H. Way, M.D.

MILLER, GEOFFREY (SAMUEL). 1945- . Ref: CA.
The Black Glove. Viking, 1981 <L.A.>

MILLER, HELEN T(OPPING). 1884-1960. Ref: CA.
Sheridan Road. Appleton, 1942

MILLER, JUDI. 1941- . Ref: CA.
Hush Little Baby. PB, 1983
I'll Be Wearing a White Carnation. Avon, 1985 <NYC>
Save the Last Dance for Me. PB, 1981; Star, 1981 <NYC, theatre>

*MILLER, MARC
Widow, Weep for Me. Arcadia, 1960

MILLER, MAX (CARLTON). 1899-1967. Ref: CA.
-I Cover the Waterfront. Dutton, 1932. Film: United Artists, 1933 (scw: Wells Root, Jack Jevne, Max Miller; dir: James Cruze). Also: United Artists, 1961, as Secret of Deep Harbor (scw: Owen Harris, Wells Root; dir: Edward L. Cahn)

*MILLER, VICTOR B(ROOKE). 1940- . Ref: CA.
Angel's Blood. Playboy, 1981 <L.A.>

*MILLER, WADE. Ref also: TM.
*Guilty Bystander. Film: Film Classics, 1950 (scw: Don Ettlinger; dir: Joseph Lerner)
*Kitten with a Whip. Film: Universal, 1964 (scw & dir: Douglas Heyes)

*MILLER, WARREN
*The Banker's Millions. Street, 1903 (Magnet #275)
*The Confessions of a Thug. Street, 1904 (Magnet #339)
*The Crimson Glove. Street, 1903 (Magnet #283)
*The Deed of a Night. Street, 1904 (Magnet #345)
*In Terror's Grasp. Street, 1903 (Magnet, #291)
*The Man Who Made Diamonds. Street, 1902 (Magnet, #257)
*A Midnight Vigil. Street, 1903 (Magnet #317)
*The Missing Bullet. Street, 1904 (Magnet #321)
*The Power of a Villain. Street, 1903 (Magnet #309)
*The Price of Protection. Street, 1904 (Magnet #329)
*The Sleepless Eye. Street, 1903 (Magnet #299)
*An Unfortunate Rogue. Street, 1902 (Magnet #267)

*MILLS, HARRY
*The Mossbank Murder. (title correction) (by *Erwin L. Coolidge) <N.Y.>

*MILLS, JAMES (SPENCER)
*The Panic in Needle Park. Film: TCF, 1971 (scw: Joan Didion, John Gregory Dunne; dir: Jerry Schatzberg)
*Report to the Commissioner. Film: United Artists, 1974; released in Britain as Operation Undercover (scw: Abby Mann, Ernest Tidyman; dir: Milton Katselas)

*MILLS, (WILLIAM) MERVYN
*The Long Haul. Film: Marksman, 1957 (scw & dir: Ken Hughes)

*MILN, LOUISE JORDAN
*Mr. Wu. Silent film (based on play): Stoll, 1922 (scw: Frederick Blatchford; dir: Maurice Elvey)

*MILNE, A(LAN) A(LEXANDER). See also: Ruth Perry. Ref also: TM.
*Four Days' Wonder. Film: Universal, 1937 (scw: Harvey Thew, Michael H. Uris; dir: Sidney Salkow)
*The Fourth Wall. Film: ATP, 1931, as Birds of Prey; released in the U.S as The Perfect Alibi (scw: Basil Dean, A. A. Milne; dir: Dean)

MILNE, JOHN. 1952- .
London Fields. H. Hamilton, 1983
Out of the Blue. H. Hamilton, 1985; H. Hamilton (U.S.), 1986
-Tyro. H. Hamilton, 1982

*MILNER, GEORGE
A Bloody Scandal. St. Martin's, 1985

MILTON, NANCY DALL. Taught at Peking First Foreign Languages Institute from 1964 to 1969; author of books and articles on Asia and China; living and teaching in S.F.
The China Option. Pantheon, 1982; Pluto, 1984 <China, future>

MINAHAN, JOHN. 1933- . Ref: CA. SC: "Little John" Rawlings, in those titles marked JR.
Eyewitness. Avon, 1981. British title: The Janitor. Futura, 1981 (Novelization of film: TCF, 1981); scw: Steve Tesich; dir: Peter Yates) <NYC>
The Great Diamond Robbery. Norton, 1984 JR <NYC>
The Great Hotel Robbery. Norton, 1982 JR <NYC>

MINEHAN, MIKE
Only the Strong. Star, 1981

MINER, PETER. Pseudonym: *Jane Elliott.

MINER, VALERIE. 1947- . Ref: CA.
Murder in the English Department. Women's Press (U.S. and London), 1982 <S.F., acad.>

*MINNEY, R(UBEIGH) J(AMES). 1895-1979.

*MINTON, PAULA
*Thunder over the Reefs. <S.F.>

MINTZ, JOYCE LOIS. 1933- . Pseudonym: Joyce Madison, q.v.

MITCHELL, ADRIAN. 1932- . Ref: CA.
The Bodyguard. Cape, 1970; Doubleday, 1971 <future>
Wartime. Cape, 1973; Doubleday, 1975

MITCHELL, BRIAN. 1948- .
-Code Name Harlequin. New Horizon, 1982

*MITCHELL, GLADYS (MAUDE WINIFRED). 1901-1983. SC: Mrs. Adela Beatrice Lestrange Bradley, also in all new titles below.
Cold, Lone and Still. Joseph, 1983; Joseph (U.S.), 1984
The Crozier Pharaohs. Joseph, 1984; Joseph (U.S.), 1985
*The Dancing Druids. ... St. Martin's,

M

1986
  The Death-Cap Dancers. Joseph, 1981;
    St. Martin's, 1981
  Death of a Burrowing Mole. Joseph,
    1982
  *Faintly Speaking. ... St. Martin's,
    1986
  The Greenstone Griffins. Joseph, 1983
  Here Lies Gloria Mundy. Joseph, 1982;
    St. Martin's, 1983
  Lovers, Make Moan. Joseph, 1981
  No Winding-Sheet. Joseph, 1984
  *The Rising of the Moon. ... St. Martin's, 1984
  *St. Peter's Finger. ... St. Martin's,
    1987
  *Uncoffin'd Clay. ... St. Martin's,
    1982

*MITCHELL, JAMES (WILLIAM). Ref also:
  TC2.
  The Evil Ones. H. Hamilton, 1982
  *A Magnum for Schneider. Film: EMI,
    1974, as Callan (scw: James
    Mitchell; dir: Don Sharp)
  Sometimes You Could Die. H. Hamilton,
    1985

MITCHELMORE, GARRY
  A Natural Weapon. Tower, 1981 <La.>

MITFORD, NANCY. 1904-1973. Ref: CA.
  -Pigeon Pie. H. Hamilton, 1940

MITGANG, HERBERT. 1920- . Ref: CA.
  SC: Sam Linkum, in both titles.
  Kings in the Counting House. Arbor,
    1983
  The Montauk Fault. Arbor, 1981.

MIX, TERENCE and VICTOR J. ROSEN. Mix
  is a lawyer in Calif.; former
  president of the L.A. Trial Lawyers Association. Rosen is a
  medical doctor.
  A Question of Judgement. Bantam, 1985
    <hosp., Conn.>

M

MOCHAN, BEN
  The Assassin Code. Jove, 1985
  Brass Knuckles. Jove, 1984; NEL pb,
    1985 <NYC>

MODIANO, PATRICK (JEAN). 1945-
  Ref: CA.
  Missing Person. Cape, 1980 (Translation of "Rue des Boutiques Obscures." Paris. 1978.)

*MOFFAT, GWEN. SC: Melinda Pink, also
  in titles below.
  Die Like a Dog. Gollancz (London &
    U.S.), 1982 <Wales>
  Grizzly Trail. Gollancz (London &
    U.S.), 1984 <Mont.>
  Last Chance Country. Gollancz (London
    & U.S.), 1983 <Ariz.>

*MOFFETT, CLEVELAND (LANGSTON)
  *Through the Wall. Silent film: Vitagraph, 1916 (scw: Marguerite
    Bertsch; dir: Rollin S. Sturgeon)

MOFFETT, MARTHA. See: *Sy Cook.

MOFFITT, IAN
  The Retreat of Radiance. Collins,
    1983; Stein, 1985 <Far East>

MOIR, ANGUS. Pseudonym: *William Angus.

*MOISEWITSCH, MAURICE
  *The Sleeping Tiger. Film: Insignia,
    1954 (scw: Carl Foreman, Harold
    Buchman; dir: Joseph Losey)

*MOLL, ELICK
  *Night Without Sleep. Film: TCF, 1952
    (scw: Frank Partos, Elick Moll;
    dir: Roy Baker)

MOLLOY, MICHAEL
  The Black Dwarf. Hodder, 1985;
    Hodder (U.S.), 1987

*MONETTE, PAUL
  The Long Shot. Avon, 1981

MONNINGER, JOSEPH. Pseudonym: Brennan
  Patrick, q.v.

MONROE, STANLEY C. and ROBERT J.
  SZILAGYE, q.v.
  The Trident Tragedy. Dell, 1983

*MONSARRAT, NICHOLAS (JOHN TURNEY)
  *The Ship That Died of Shame. Film
    (based on title ss): Ealing, 1955;
    released in the U.S. as PT Raiders
    (scw: John Whiting, Michael
    Relph, Basil Dearden; dir:
    Dearden)
  *Something to Hide. Film: Avton,
    1973 (scw & dir: Alastair Reid)

*MONTAGUE, J. J. Pseudonym of *James
  Keenan.

MONTAGUE, JEANNE. Pseudonym of Jeanne
  Frances Treasure Yarde, 1925- .
  Ref: CA.
  The Clock Tower. Century, 1983; St.
    Martin's, 1984 <Eng., 1900>

MONTAGUE, MARGARET PRESCOTT. 1828-
  1955.
  -In Calvert's Valley. Baker, 1908.
    Silent film: Fox, 1922, as Calvert's Valley (scw: Jules Furthman;
    dir: Jack Dillon)

MONTALBAN, MANUEL VAZQUEZ. 1939-
  Born and living in Barcelona;
  journalist; member of Catalan
  Communist Party; has written on
  political theory, culinary practice. Title below is fourth to
  feature series detective Pepe
  Carvalho, but first translated
  into English.
  Murder in the Central Committee.
    Pluto, 1984; Academy Chicago, 1985
    <Sp.> Translation of "Asesinato
    en el Comite Centrale." 1981.)
    Film: Morgana, 1982, as Asesinato
    en el Comite Centrale (Murder in
    the Central Committee) (scw & dir:
    Vicente Aranda)

*MONTALBANO, WILLIAM D(ANIEL), and CARL
  HIAASEN, 1953- . Ref for both:
  CA.
  A Death in China. Scribner, 1984;
    Sidgwick, 1985 <China>
  Powder Burn. Atheneum, 1981 <Miami>
  Trap Line. Atheneum, 1982

*MONTANA, RON
  Deathcalls. GM, 1981

*MONTEILHET, HUBERT. Ref also: CA.
  *The Praying Mantises. Film: Portman,
    1982, as Praying Mantis (scw:
    Philip Mackie; dir: Jack Gold)
  *Return from the Ashes. Film: Mirisch,
    1965 (scw: Julius J. Epstein,
    Charles Blair; dir: J. Lee
    Thompson)

*MONTROSS, DAVID. Pseudonym of Jean
  Louise Backus, 1914-1986.

*MOODY, LAURENCE
  The Ruthless Ones. Hale, 1969.
    Film: Palomar, 1972, as What Became
    of Jack and Jill? (scw: Roger
    Marshall; dir: Bill Bain)

*MOODY, RON. 1924- . Ref: CA.

MOODY, SUSAN. SC: Penny Wanawake, in
  all titles.
  Penny Black. Macmillan (London),
    1984; GM, 1986
  Penny Dreadful. Macmillan (London),
    1984; GM, 1986
  Penny Post. Macmillan (London), 1985;
    GM, 1986

MOOERS, DE SACIA
  The Blonde Vampire. Moffat, 1920
    (Novelization of silent film:
    Physioc, 1922; dir: Wray Physioc)

*MOORE, AMOS
  *Royce of the Royal Mounted. Macaulay,
    1932; Harrap, 1933

MOORE, ARTHUR
  Archers of the Long Bow. Constable,
    1904
  The Eyes of Light. Arrowsmith, 1901

MOORE, BARBARA <BARBARA MOORE LEE>.
  1934- . Ref: CA, TM.
  The Doberman Wore Black. St. Martin's, 1983 <Colo.>

*MOORE, BRIAN. Pseudonyms: *Michael
  Bryan, q.v.,*Bernard Mara.
  Sailor's Leave; see *Wreath for a
    Redhead
  *Wreath for a Redhead. Also published
    as: Sailor's Leave. Pyramid, 1953
    <Montr.>

*MOORE, CARLYLE. See also: Roland
  West.
  *Stop Thief! Silent film: Kleine,
    1915 (dir: George Fitzmaurice).
    Also: Goldwyn, 1920 (scw: Charles
    Kenyon; dir: Harry Beaumont)

MOORE, CHRISTOPHER. 1946- . Trained
  in law at Oxford Univ.; was professor of law at Univ. of British
  Columbia; living in NYC.
  His Lordship's Arsenal. Freundlich,
    1985 <Vancouver>

MOORE, DAN TYLER. 1908-
  The Terrible Game. Farrar, 1957.
    Film: MGM, 1985 (scw: Charles
    Robert Carnes; dir: Robert Clouse)

MOORE, DORIS O. Joint pseudonym with
  Mary Alice Philips: *Philips
  Moore.

*MOORE, F(RANK) FRANKFORT
  Well, After All... Hutchinson,
    1899; Dodd, 1899
  Where the Rail Runs Now. Ward, 1876

MOORE, GEORGINA MARY GALBRAITH.
  1930- . Pseudonym: *Helena
  Osborne.

*MOORE, PHILIPS. Joint pseudonym of
  Doris O. Moore and Mary Alice
  Philips.

*MOORE, ROBIN
  *The Chinese Ultimatum. Actually
    written only by Edward McGhee
    (pseudonym of Edward M. Harper).
  *The Establishment. ... Severn, 1982
  *French Connection II. (Novelization
    of film: TCF, 1975; scw: Robert
    Dillon, Laurie Dillon, Alexander
    Jacobs; dir: John Frankenheimer)

*MOORHOUSE, FRANK. 1938- . Ref:
  CA.

MORAN, CARY
  Killer's Caress. Valhalla, 1936 <NYC>

*MORAY, HELGA
  That Woman. Hale, 1982 <Fr., ca.
    1790>

MOREAU, EUGENE, 1806-1876, PAUL SIRAUDIN, 1813-1883, and ALFRED
  CHARLEMAGNE LARTIGUE DELACOUR,
  1817-1883.
  The Courier of Lyons. Lacy, 1856
    (4-act play.) Silent film: Samuelson, 1915, as The True Story of the
    Lyons Mail (scw: Harry Engholm;
    dir: George Pearson). Also: Ideal,
    1916, as The Lyons Mail (scw: Benedict James; dir: Fred Paul). Sound
    film: Twickenham, 1931, as The
    Lyons Mail (scw: H. Fowler Mear;
    dir: Arthur Maude)

MORELL, MAX
  Apartment Hotel. Aldor, 1946

*MORELLI, SPIKE. Pseudonym of *William
  (Simpson) Newton, q.v.
  *Coffin for a Cutie. ... Archer, 195?
  *You'll Never Get Me. ... Kaywin, 1952

*MORETTE, EDGAR. Pseudonym of Hector
  Fezandie, 1856-1943.

*MORGAN, BRIAN STANFORD
  Vain Citadels. Heinemann, 1947;
    Little, 1948

MORGAN, CHARLES (LANBRIDGE). 1894-1958.
  The Judge's Story. Macmillan (London & NYC), 1947

*MORGAN, DEAN. Pseudonym of *Graham
  Fisher.

*MORGAN, DIANA
  *My Cousin Rachel. Dramatists, 1980
    (3-act play based on novel by
    *Daphne Du Maurier.)

*MORGAN, JASON. Pseudonym of William
  Donald Frissell.

MORGAN, JOAN. 1905- . Ref: CA.
  This Was a Woman. Fortune, 1946
    (Play.) Film: Excelsior, 1948
    (scw: Val Valentine; dir: Tim
    Whelan)

*MORGAN, MICHAEL. Ref: TM.

*MORGAN, MURRAY C(ROMWELL). Ref: CA.

*MORGAN, STANLEY
  The Dark Side of Destiny. GM, 1982

*MORGAN, WESLEY
 *The Enforcer. (Novelization of film: Warner, 1976; scw: Stirling Silliphant, Dean Riesner; dir: James Fargo)

*MORGULAS, JERROLD
 The Twelfth Power of Evil. Seaview, 1981; Sphere, 1983 <1944>

*MORICE, ANNE. Ref also: TM. SC: Tessa Crichton, also in all titles below.
 Dead on Cue. Macmillan (London), 1985; St. Martin's, 1985
 Getting Away with Murder. Macmillan (London), 1984; St. Martin's, 1985
 Hollow Vengeance. Macmillan (London), 1982; St. Martin's, 1982
 The Men in Her Death. Macmillan (London), 1981; St. Martin's, 1981
 Murder Post-Dated. Macmillan (London), 1983; St. Martin's, 1984
 Sleep of Death. Macmillan (London), 1982; St. Martin's, 1983 <theatre>

MORISON, B(ETTY) J(ANE). 1924-   . Born in Maine; owns and operates the Criterion Theatre in Bar Harbor, Maine. SC: Elizabeth Lamb Worthington, in all titles.
 Beer and Skittles. Thorndike, 1985 <Maine, 1972>
 Champagne and a Gardener. Thorndike, 1983 <Maine>
 Port and a Star Boarder. Thorndike, 1984 <Maine>

*MORLAND, NIGEL. 1905-1986. Film (based on unidentifies story): Hurley, 1939, as Mrs. Pym of Scotland Yard (scw: Fred Elles, Nigel Morland, Peggy Barnwell; dir: Elles)

*MORLEY, BLYTHE. 1923-   . Pseudonym: *Stanley Hopkins, Jr.

*MORLEY, CHARLES
 *Archie; or, The Confessions of an Old Burglar. Westminster Gazette, 1897 ss

*MORLEY, CHRISTOPHER (DARLINGTON). Ref also: CA, TM.

*MOROSO, JOHN A(NTONIO)
 *The People Against Nancy Preston. Silent film: Stromberg, 1925, as The People vs. Nancy Preston (scw: Marion Orth; dir: Tom Forman)
 *The Quarry. Silent film: Selig, 1915 (scw: Gilson Willets; dir: Lawrence Marston). Also: Lasky, 1921, as City of Silent Men (scw: Frank Condon; dir: Tom Forman). Sound film: Paramount, 1930, as Shadow of the Law (scw: Max Marcin; dir: Louis Gasnier)

*MORRELL, DAVID. Ref also: TM.
 Blood Oath. St. Martin's, 1982; Pan, 1983 <Fr.>
 The Brotherhood of the Rose. St. Martin's, 1984; NEL, 1985
 *First Blood. Film: Orion, 1982 (scw: Michael Kozoll, William Sackheim, Sylvester Stallone; dir: Ted Kotcheff)
 The Fraternity of the Stone. St. Martin's, 1985; NEL, 1986
 Rambo: First Blood Part II. Jove, 1985; Arrow, 1985 (Novelization of film: Tri-Star, 1985; scw: Sylvester Stallone, James Cameron; dir: George Pan Cosmatos)
 *-The Totem.

MORRIESON, RONALD HUGH. 1922-
 The Scarecrow. Angus (Sydney), 1963; Angus (London), 1964. Film: Oasis, 1984 (scw: Michael Heath, Sam Pilsbury; dir: Pilsbury)

MORRIS, CHRIS(TOPHER). 1938-   . Ref: CA. See: (Janet) (Ellen) Morris, 1946-   .

MORRIS, EARL J.
 The Cop. Exposition, 1951

MORRIS, GILBERT (LESLIE). 1929-   Ref: CA.
 Delaney. Living Books, 1984 <Ark.>

MORRIS, GORDON
 The Midnight Call. French, 1936 (1-act play.)

*MORRIS, GOUVERNEUR
 *Yellow Men and Gold. Silent film: Goldwyn, 1922 (scw: Irvin Willat, L. V. Jefferson; dir: Willat)

MORRIS, JANET (ELLEN). 1946-   .
 Active Measures, with David (Allen) Drake, 1945-   , q.v. Baen, 1985 <future>
 The Forty-Minute War, with Chris(topher) Morris, 1938-   . Baen, 1984 <future>

*MORRIS, JOHN. Joint pseudonym of *John Hearne, 1926-   , and *Morris Cargill, 1914-   . Ref for Hearne: CA. Cargill has family roots going back 300 years in Jamaica; owner of banana plantation; writer for Jamaica press and a radio commentator.

MORRIS, MARGARET JEAN. 1924-   . Pseudonym: *Kenneth O'Hara, q.v.

*MORRIS, THOMAS BADEN
 *Deserted Night. (3-act play.)

*MORRISON, ARTHUR. Ref also: TM.
 The Best Martin Hewitt Detective Stories. Dover, 1976 ss reassembled from earlier collections
 *The Dorrington Deed Box. ... New Amsterdam, 1900
 Fiddle O'Dreams and more. Hutchinson, 1933 ss, some criminous

MORRISON, NICK. 1939-   . Business consultant living in Idaho.
 Intercept. Pace, 1981

MORRISON, R(IDDELL) P(RESTON)
 Sacrife. Rich, 1939

MORSE, L(ARRY) A(LAN). 1945-   . Ref: CA, TM. Pseudonym: Runa Fairleigh, q.v. SC: Sam Hunter, in those titles marked SH.
 The Big Enchilada. Avon, 1982; Avon (U.K.), 1983 <L.A.> SH
 The Old Dick. Avon, 1981; Avon (U.K.), 1982 <L.A.>
 Slease. Avon, 1985 <L.A.> SH

*MORTIMER, JOHN (CLIFFORD). Ref also: TC2. SC: Rumpole, also in those marked R below.
 -Charade. Bodley, 1947; Viking, 1947
 Regina v Rumpole. Lane, 1981 (Contains first hardcover publication of *Rumpole's Return, plus 7 previously unpublished ss. These 7 subsequently published as: Rumpole for the Defence. Penguin, 1982 R
 Rumpole and the Golden Thread. Penguin, 1983; Penguin (U.S.), 1984 ss R
 Rumpole for the Defence; see R v Rumpole
 *Rumpole of the Bailey. ss
 *Rumpole's Return; see Regina v Rumpole
 Three Plays. Elek, 1958; Grove, 1962 (plays, two criminous: I Spy, and The Dock Brief.) Film (based on The Dock Brief): MGM, 1962; released in the U.S. as Trial and Error (scw: Pierre Rouve; dir: James Hill)
 *The Trials of Rumpole. ss

MORTON, JOYCE
 Speak No Evil. Avalon, 1978

*MORTON, MICHAEL
 Alibi. French, 1929 (3-act play.) Film: Twickenham, 1931 (H. Fowler Mear; dir: Leslie S. Hiscott)

*MORTON, PATRICIA
 Daughter of Evil. Lancer, 1973

*MORTON, VICTORIA
 *The Whirlpool. Silent film: Select, 1918 (scw: Eve Unsell; dir: Alan Crosland)
 *The Yellow Ticket. Silent film: Astra, 1918 (scw: Tom Cushing; dir: William Parke). Sound film: Fox, 1931; released in Britain as The Yellow Passport (scw: Jules Furthman, Guy Bolton; dir: Raoul Walsh)

*MORUM, WILLIAM. See: *William Dinner.

*MOSER, MAURICE and *CHARLES F. RIDEAL
 *Stories from Scotland Yard. Routledge, 1890
 *True Detective Stories (from Scotland Yard). Trischler, 1889; Lovell, 1890

MOSIMAN, BILLIE SUE. 1947-   . Ref: CA.
 Wireman. PaperJacks, 1984 <Houston>

*MOSLER, BLANCHE Y. Pseudonym: *Marie Elaine Edward.

*MOSLEY, LEONARD O(SWALD). Ref: CA.
 -The Cat and the Mice. Barker, 1958; Harper, 1958. Also published as: Foxhole in Cairo. Hamilton, 1960. <Cairo> Film: British Lion, 1960, as Foxhole in Cairo (scw: Leonard Mosley, Donald Taylor; dir: John Moxey)

*MOSS, JACK
 *The Arson Job. <Omaha>

*MOSS, ROBERT (JOHN). 1946-   . Ref: CA. See also: *Arnaud De Borchgrave.
 Death Beam. Crown, 1981; Weidenfeld, 1981
 Moscow Rules. Villard, 1985; Hodder, 1985 <Moscow>

*MOTLEY, WILLARD (FRANCIS). 1912-1965. Ref: CA, TM.
 Knock on Any Door. Appleton, 1947; Collins, 1948. Film: Columbia, 1949 (scw: Daniel Taradash, John Monks, Jr.; dir: Nicholas Ray)
 Let No Man Write My Epitaph. Random, 1958; Longmans, 1959. Film: Columbia, 1960 (scw: Robert Presnell, Jr.; dir: Philip Leacock)

*MOULTON, H(UGH LAURENCE) FLETCHER
 *The Unofficial Executor. criminous

MOUNTFORD, A(LEXANDER) MACDONALD
 Beneath the Night Sky. Wright, 1956 <Carib.>

MOUNTFORD, GEORGE F(REDERICK). 1890-
 Crooks for a Month. Denison, 1926 (3-act play.)

*MOWERY, WILLIAM BYRON
 Heart of the North. Doubleday, 1930; Paul, 1931. Film: First National, 1938 (scw: Lee Katz, Vincent Sherman; dir: Lewis Seiler)
 Vengeance Trail. Methuen, 1937 <Can.>

MOXON, GEOFFREY
 Spycracker. Merlin, 1984

*MOYES, PATRICIA. Ref also: TM; expanded: TC2. SC: Henry and Emmy Tibbett, also in both titles below.
 Night Ferry to Death. Collins, 1985; Holt, 1985
 A Six-Letter Word for Death. Collins, 1983; Holt, 1983

*MOYZISCH, L(UDWIG) C(ARL)
 *Operation Cicero. Film: TCF, 1952, as Five Fingers (scw: Michael Wilson; dir: Joseph L. Mankiewicz)

MUIR, ALAN
 Tumbledown Farm. Munro, 1885; Blackett, 1889

MUIR, DOUGLAS
 American Reich. Charter, 1985

MUIR, J. K.
 Lady Middletower and the Red Dagger. Kenyon, 1975 (1-act play.)

*MUKERJI, DHAN GOPAL. Ref: CA.

MULARCHY, SYLVIA. Joint pseudonym with Dorien Klein Miles, 1915-   : Sylvia Miles, q.v.

MULGRUE, G. EDWARD. Pseudonym: *Pat Colombo.

MULISCH, HARRY. 1927-   . Ref: CA.
 -The Assault. Pantheon, 1985. (Translation of "De Aanslag." Amsterdam, 1982.)

*MULLER, MARCIA. Ref also: TC2, TM. See also: *Bill Pronzini. SC: Sharon McCone, in *Edwin of the Iron Shoes, and in titles below marked SM; Elena Olivarez = EO.
 Ask the Cards a Question. St. Martin's, 1982; Hale, 1983 SM <S.F.>
 The Cheshire Cat's Eye. St. Martin's, 1983; Hale, 1983 SM <S.F.>

Games to Keep the Dark Away. St. Martin's, 1984; Severn, 1985 SM <S.F.>
Leave a Message for Willie. St. Martin's, 1984; Severn, 1985 SM <S.F.>
The Legend of the Slain Soldiers. Walker, 1985; Hale, 1986 EO <Calif.>
There's Nothing to Be Afraid Of. St. Martin's, 1985 SM <S.F.>
The Tree of Death. Walker, 1983; Hale, 1986 EO <Calif.>

MULLIN, CHRIS
A Very British Coup. Hodder, 1982 <Eng., 1989>

MULLINER, ERNEST
"Declined with Thanks." Henry, 1893 ss, two criminous

MULOCK, DINAH MARIA. 1826-1887. See: Anonymous.

MUNDER, LAURA. Clinical psychologist in Wash. D.C.
Therapy for Murder. St. Martin's, 1984 <hosp., Wash. D.C.>

*MUNDIS, HESTER (JANE). Pseudonyms: *Miriam Asher, *Aynn Westminster.

*MUNDIS, JERROLD. 1941-   . Pseudonym also: *Robert Calder. Lives in NYC.
The Retreat. Popular Library, 1985

*MUNDY, TALBOT
*King of the Khyber Rifles. Film: Fox, 1929, as The Black Watch (scw: John Stone; dir: John Ford). Also: TCF, 1954 (scw: Ivan Goff, Ben Roberts; dir: Henry King)
*The Woman Ayisha. U.S. edition contained in *The Hundred Days

MUNN, VELLA
Touch a Wild Heart. Harlequin, 1984 <Oreg.>

*MUNRO, JAMES
*The Innocent Bystanders. Film: Sagittarius, 1972 (scw: James Mitchell; dir: Peter Collinson)

MUNRO, JOHN
The Catwalk Kill. Hale, 1985

MUNSEY, FRANK A(NDREW). 1854-1925.
A Tragedy of Errors. Munsey, 1889

*MURARI, T(IMERI) N.
The Shooter. Hodder, 1984; Dell, 1986

MURDOCH, MORDECAI
Wroclaw Dracula. Caedmon, 1985

MURDOCH, WALTER. See: J. L. Rankin.

MURE, DAVID
The Last Temptation. Buchan, 1984

*MURPHY, AGATHA. Pseudonym of Charlotte Murphy.

MURPHY, BRIAN. 1939-   . Ref: CA.
The Enigma Variations. Scribner, 1981; Blond, 1982 <acad.>

MURPHY, CHARLOTTE. Pseudonym: *Agatha Murphy.

MURPHY, CHRISTOPHER. SC: Sparrow, in at least those marked S.
Dance for a Diamond. Secker, 1985; Walker, 1986 <Afr.>
I, Said the Sparrow. Secker, 1984 S
The Jericho Rumble. Secker, 1982
Scream at the Sea. Secker, 1981; St. Martin's, 1982 S

*MURPHY, JAMES F, JR.
Night Watcher. Avon, 1982

*MURPHY, TOM
The Panther Throne. Signet, 1982

MURPHY, WALTER F(RANCIS). 1929-   Ref: CA.
The Roman Enigma. Macmillan, 1981 <Rome>

*MURPHY, WARREN B. Ref also: TC2, TM. SC: Remo Williams (The Destroyer), also in titles marked RW; Julian Burroughs (The Digger) = JB; Devlin Tracy = DT.
The Arms of Kali, with *Richard Sapir, q.v. Signet, 1984 RM (by Murphy and Sapir)
Balance of Power. Pinnacle, 1981 RW (by Murphy and Molly Cochran)
The Ceiling of Hell. GM, 1984
Date with Death. Pinnacle, 1984 RW <N. Mex.> (by Murphy and Molly Cochran)
Dead Letter. PB, 1982 JB <New Eng., acad.>
Dying Space. Pinnacle, 1982 RW (by Murphy and Molly Cochran)
Encounter Group. Pinnacle, 1984 RW (by Murphy and Will Murray)
The End of the Game, with *Richard Sapir, q.v. Signet, 1985 RW (by Murphy and Sapir)
Fool's Flight. PB, 1982 JB
Fool's Gold, with *Richard Sapir, q.v. Pinnacle, 1983 RW
Grandmaster, with Molly Cochran. Pinnacle, 1984; Futura, 1985
Killing Time. Pinnacle, 1982 RW (by Murphy and Molly Cochran)
Last Drop. Pinnacle, 1983 RW (by Murphy and Molly Cochran)
Lords of the Earth, with *Richard Sapir, q.v. Signet, 1985 RW (by Murphy and Sapir)
Lucifer's Weekend. PB, 1982 JB <Pa.>
Master's Challenge. Pinnacle, 1984 RW <Peru> (by Murphy, *Richard Sapir, *Molly Cochran)
Midnight Man. Pinnacle, 1981 RW (by Murphy and *Robert J. Randisi, q.v.)
Next of Kin. Pinnacle, 1981 RW (by Murphy and Molly Cochran)
Once a Mutt. Signet, 1985 DT
Pigs Get Fat. Signet, 1985 DT <S.F.>
Profit Motive. Pinnacle, 1982 RW (by Murphy and *Richard Sapir, q.v.)
The Red Moon. GM, 1982
Remo: The First Adventure, with *Richard Sapir, q.v. signet, 1985; Futura, 1986 <NYC> (by Sapir alone) (Novelization of film: Orion, 1985 (scw: Christopher Wood; dir: Guy Hamilton)
The Seventh Stone, with *Richard Sapir, q.v.. Signet, 1985 RW (by Murphy and Sapir)
Shock Value. Pinnacle, 1983 RW (by Murphy and Molly Cochran)
Skin Deep. Pinnacle, 1982 RW (by Murphy and Molly Cochran)
The Sky Is Falling. Signet, 1985 RW (by *Richard Sapir, q.v., and Will Murray)
Smoked Out. PB, 1982 JB <L.A.>
Spoils of War. Pinnacle, 1981 RW (by Murphy and Molly Cochran)
Time Trial. Pinnacle, 1983 RW <Guat.> (by Murphy and Molly Cochran)
Total Recall. Pinnacle, 1984 RW (by Murphy and *Robert J. Randisi, q.v.)
Trace. Signet, 1983 DT <N.J.>
Trace and 47 Miles of Rope. Signet, 1984 DT <Las Veg.>
Two Steps from Three East. Signet, 1983 DT <Las Veg.>
When Elephants Forget. Signet, 1984 DT <NYC>

*MURRAY, DAVID CHRISTIE
*In His Grip. Silent film: Gaumont, 1921 (scw: Paul Rooff; dir: C. C. Calvert).
*The Penniless Millionaire. Silent film: Broadwest, 1921 (scw: Frank Fowell; dir: Einar J. Bruun)

MURRAY, FRANCES. Pseudonym of Rosemary Frances Booth, 1928-   . Ref: CA.
-The Belchamber Scandal. Hodder, 1985; St. Martin's, 1985 <Eng., 1860s>

MURRAY, HAL
Death Deals in Diamonds. Hale, 1982

MURRAY, HELEN
Ski Lift to Love. Tiara, 1980

*MURRAY, LIEUTENANT M. M.
*The Dog Detective and His Young Master. <Boston>

*MURRAY, MAX(WELL)
*The Neat Little Corpse. Film: Paramount, 1953, as Jamaica Run (scw & dir: Lewis R. Foster)

MURRAY, STEWART
Chinese Justice. Hale, 1984
The Death Merchants. Hale, 1984
Tropical Murder. Hale, 1983

MURRAY, WILLIAM. See: *Chuck Scarborough.

*MURRAY, WILLIAM (BUCKLEY). SC: Lou (Shifty) Anderson, in titles marked LA.
The Hard Knocker's Luck. Viking, 1985 <Calif.> LA
-The Sweet Ride. NAL, 1967; Allen, 1967. Film: TCF, 1968 (scw: Tom Mankiewicz; dir: Harvey Hart)
Tip on a Dead Crab. Viking, 1984; Penguin, 1985 <Calif.> LA

MUSARRA, RUSS. See: Robert L. Bolton.

*MUSTO, BARRY. Ref: CA.

MUUSMANN, CARL (QUISTGAARD). 1863-1936.
Sherlock Holmes at Elsinore. Baker Street Irregulars, 1956 (Sherlock Holmes)

MWANGI, MEJA. 1948-
Kill Me Quick. Heinemann, 1973 <Kenya>

MYERS, ELIZABETH. 1912-1947.
Mrs. Christopher. Chapman, 1946. Film: General Film, 1950, as Blackmailed (scw: Hugh Mills, Roger Vadim; dir: Marc Allegret)

MYERS, PAUL
Deadly Variations. Constable, 1985; Vanguard, 1986

MYERS, ROGER and ALBERT HERBERT
The Last Survivor. Manor, 1976

*MYKEL, A. W.
The Salamandra Glass. St. Martin's, 1983; Corgi, 1984 <Fr.>

MYRTLE, WILLIAM
The Plagiarist. Oliphant, 1897

*NABARRO, DERRICK
*The Seeds of Destruction. criminous

NABB, MAGDALEN. 1947-   . A potter turned writer; has lived in Florence since 1975. SC: Marshall Guarnaccia, in all titles, set in Florence.
Death in Autumn. Collins, 1985; Scribner, 1985
Death in Springtime. Collins, 1983; Scribner, 1984
Death of a Dutchman. Collins, 1982; Scribner, 1983
Death of an Englishman. Collins, 1981; Scribner, 1982

*NABOKOFF-SIRIN, VLADIMIR (VLADIMIROVICH)
*Despair. Film: Bavaria Atelier, 1978 (scw: Tom Stoppard; dir: Rainer Werner Fassbinder)

NAHE, ED. 1950-   . Ref: CA.
The Paradise Plot. Bantam, 1980
The Suicide Plague. Bantam, 1982

*NAHUM, LUCIEN. 1930(?)-1983. Ref: CA.

*NAPIER, GEOFFREY
*The Wrong Box. (Novelization of film; see *Robert Louis Stevenson.)

*NAPIER, MARY
Forbidden Places. Collins, 1981; Coward, 1981 <Alb.>
-State of Fear. Hutchinson, 1984; Hutchinson (U.S.), 1986

NAPIER, S. ELLIOTT. See: J. L. Rankin.

*NARCEJAC, THOMAS. See: *Pierre (Prosper) Boileau.

NASH, JAY ROBERT. 1937-   . Ref: CA. SC: Jack Journey = JJ.
A Crime Story. Delacorte, 1981 JJ <Chi.>
The Dark Fountain. A&W, 1982 <Calif., 1927>
The Mafia Diaries. Delacorte, 1984 JJ

*NASH, N(ATHAN) RICHARD
Radiance. Doubleday, 1983 <L.A.>

NASH, PADDER. Pseudonym of Alan Sewart, 1928-   , q.v. Other pseudonym: Alan Stewart Well, q.v. SC: Grass, apparently in all titles.
Coup de Grass. Hale, 1983
Grass. Hale, 1982

Grass and Supergrass. Hale, 1984
Grass in Idleness. Hale, 1983
Grass Makes Hay. Hale, 1985
Grass's Fancy. Hale, 1982
Wayward Seeds of Grass. Hale, 1983

*NASH, SIMON
*Dead of a Counterplot. ... Perennial, 1985

*NASON, LEONARD H(ASTINGS). 1895-1970. Ref: CA.

NASSIVERA, JOHN. 1950-   . Ref: CA.
The Penultimate Problem of Sherlock Holmes. French, 1980 (2-act play.) (Sherlock Holmes)

NATALE, RICHARD
Butcher, Baker, Nightmare Maker. PB, 1981 (Novelization of film; not released?)

NATHANSON, JOSEPH
A Puzzle for Experts. SOS, 1985 <L.A.>

NATSUKI, SHIZUKO. 1938-   . Best-selling Japanese mystery writer; she's written over 80 novels, ss and serials, 40 of which have been made into Japanese TV movies.
Murder at Mt. Fuji. St. Martin's, 1984 <Jap.>

*NAUGHTON, EDMUND
*McCabe. Film: Warner, 1971, as McCabe and Mrs. Miller (scw: Robert Altman, Brian McKay; dir: Altman)

NAYBARD, HUGH
The Red Dagger. Murray, 1912

*NAZEL, JOSEPH (JR.). Pseudonym: *Don Gober.
Delta Crossing. Holloway, 1984 <La.>
Devil Dolls. Holloway, 1984 <L.A.>
-Satan's Master. Holloway, 1983
-The Wolves of Summer. Holloway, 1984

NEARY, PATRICK. See: *Don(ald Eugene) Pendleton.

NEBAN, HUGH. Pseudonym of Edward Beverly Mann, 1902-   .
The Crucible of Courage. Lane, 1936 <Ariz.>

*NEBEL, (LOUIS) FREDERICK. Ref also: TM.
*Fifty Roads to Town. Film: TCF, 1937 (scw: George Marion, Jr., William Counselman; dir: Norman Taurog)
*Sleepers East. Film: TCF, 1934 (scw: Lester Cole; dir: Kenneth MacKenna). Also: TCF, 1941, as Sleepers West (scw: Lou Breslow, Stanley Rauh; dir: Eugene Forde)

*NEEBEL, RICHARD
Immediate Action. Charter, 1982 <S. Am.>

NEELY, ESTHER JANE
Chateau Laurens. Tower, 1980 <Fla.>

*NEELY, RICHARD. Ref: TC2, TM.
-An Accidental Woman. Holt, 1981; Sphere, 1982
*The Damned Innocents. Film: Les Films La Boetie, 1975, as Les Innocents aux Mains Sales (The Innocents with Dirty Hands; Dirty Hands) (scw & dir: Claude Chabrol)
Shadows from the Past. Delacorte, 1983 <NYC, 1942>

NEGGERS, CARLA A(MALIA). 1955-   . Ref: CA.
The Knotted Skein. Avon, 1984
The Venus Shoe. Avon, 1984

NEGRONI, J. L. See: Stephen Blackwelder.

*NEGULESCO, BRIAN. Pseudonym of Bayard Auchincloss.

*NEIDER, CHARLES
*The Authentic Death of Hendry Jones. Film: Paramount, 1961, as One-Eyed Jacks (scw: Guy Trosper, Calder Willingham; dir: Marlon Brando)

NEIDERMAN, ANDREW. 1940-   . Ref: CA.
Brainchild. PB, 1981; Arrow, 1983 <N.Y.>
Imp. PB, 1985; Severn, 1985
-Pin. PB, 1981; Arrow, 1982
Someone's Watching. PB, 1983; Arrow, 1984 <N.Y.>
Tender, Loving Care. PB, 1984; Arrow, 1985

*NEIDIG, WILLIAM J(ONATHAN)
*The Fire Flingers. Silent film: Jewel, 1919 (scw: Waldemar Young; dir: Rupert Julian)

NEILD, MARY (RODEN). See: Tom Neild.

NEILD, TOM <THOMAS DAWSON NEILD> and MARY (RODEN) NEILD
The Man in the Lane. Deane, 1962; Baker, 1962 (Play.)

NEILSON, ANDREW. 1946-   . Ref: CA.
Braking Point. Allen, 1983; GM, 1986
Dead Straight. Allen, 1983
The Monza Protest. Allen, 1985

*NELMS, HENNING
Only an Orphan Girl. Dramatists, 1944 (4-act play.)

*NELSON, HUGH LAWRENCE. Ref also: TM.

*NELSON, JACK. See: *Clyde North.

*NEMEC, DAVID
Mad Blood. Dial, 1983 <NYC>
The Systems of Mr. M. R. Shurnas. Riverrun, 1984; Calder, 1985

*NESBIT, E(DITH) <EDITH NESBIT BLAND>. Ref also: CA. Joint pseudonym with *Hubert Bland: *Fabian Bland.

*NESSEN, RON(ALD HAROLD). Ref: CA.

*NEUBAUER, WILLIAM (ARTHUR)
The Golden Heel. Arcadia, 1965

NEUGEBOREN, JAY. 1938-   . Ref: CA.
The Stolen Jew. Holt, 1981

*NEUMAN, FREDRIC (JAY)
Maneuvers. Dial, 1983; Gollancz, 1984 <Ger., 1962>

*NEVILLE, MARGOT. SC note: Insp. Grogan is a Syd. policeman.
*Drop Dead. <Syd.>
*Murder and Gardenias. <Syd.>

*NEVINS, FRANCIS M(ICHAEL). Ref also: TM.

NEVITT, BRIAN
The Texts of Dime. International, 1978 (Play.)

*NEW, CHRISTOPHER. Ref: CA.

NEWHALL, MURIEL. Pseudonym: *Mona Farnsworth.

NEWING, DeWITT
The Unseen Way. Co-National, 1930 (3-act play.)

NEWLAND, SIMPSON. 1835-1925.
Blood Tracks of the Bush. Gay, 1900

*NEWMAN, BERNARD (CHARLES)
*The Travelling Executioner. <Ger.>

*NEWMAN, G(ORDON) F. Ref also: TC2.
Law and Order. Sphere, 1977
The Men with the Guns. Secker (London & U.S.), 1982 <NYC>
*The Player and the Guest. criminous
*Sir, You Bastard. Film: Columbia, 1974, as The Take (scw: Del Reisman, Franklin Coen; dir: Robert Hartford-Davis)

NEWMAN, JOEL. 1951-   .
Dead Man's Tears. Beaufort, 1981 <Montr.>

NEWMAN, OSCAR. 1935-   . Ref: CA.
Unmasking a King. Macmillan, 1981 <NYC>

NEWMAN, PAUL GLEN. See: Gar Wilson.

*NEWTON, (WILFRID) DOUGLAS
*Sookey. delete: not criminous

NEWTON, JOSEPH EMERSON
Java Edge. Humphries, 1955 <Far East>

NEWTON, MICHAEL. 1951-   . Ref: CA. Pseudonyms: John Cannon, Vince Robinson, qq.v. See also: *Don(ald Eugene) Pendleton.
1984 <N.Y.>

*NEWTON, WILLIAM (SIMPSON). Pseudonym: *Spike Morelli, q.v.
Death Is for Losers. Hale, 1981
Don't Hold Your Breath. Hale, 1983
It Never Comes Easy. Hale, 1981
The Rio Contract. Hale, 1982
The Set-Up. Hale, 1981
The Way to Get Dead. Hale, 1982
You Can Go Feet First. Hale, 1984

NEZNANSKY, FRIDRIKH and EDWARD TOPOL. Authors are recent emigres from Russ. to U.S.
Deadly Games. Quartet (London & U.S.), 1984 <Moscow> (Translation of "Zhurnalist dlia Brezhneva." 1981.)

NGUGI WA THIONG'O. 1938-   . Ref: CA.
Petals of Blood. Heinemann, 1977 <Kenya>

*NIALL, IAN
No Resting Place. Heinemann, 1948; Knopf, 1948. Film: Lesslie, 1951 (scw: Paul Rotha, Colin Lessliek, Michael Orrom, Gerald Healy; dir: Rotha)

*NIALL, MICHAEL
*Bad Day at Black Rock. Film: MGM, 1955 (scw: Millard Kaufman; dir: John Sturges)

NICHOLAS, JAMES
Blind Drop. Hale, 1981

*NICHOLS, (JOHN) BEVERLEY. 1899-1983.

*NICHOLS, FAN. Other pseudonym: *Nikki Content, q.v. Ref: TM.
*Hideaway. delete

*NICHOLS, LEIGH
The Eyes of Darkness. PB, 1981; Piatkus, 1982 <Las Veg.>
The House of Thunder. PB, 1982; Piatkus, 1983
The Servants of Twilight; see Twilight
Twilight. PB, 1984. British title: The Servants of Twilight. Piatkus, 1985 <Calif.>

*NICHOLSON, MEREDITH
*The House of a Thousand Candles. Silent film: Selig, 1915 (scw: Gilson Willets; dir: T. N. Heffron). Sound film: Republic, 1936 (scw: H. W. Hanemann, Endre Boehm; dir: Arthur Lubin)
*The Port of Missing Men. Silent film: Famous Players, 1914

*NICHOLSON, MICHAEL. TV journalist.

NICHOLSON, ROBIN
A Passion for Treason. Jove, 1981 <Ger., WWII>

*NICOLAYSEN, BRUCE
*Perilous Passage. <Fr., WWII> Film: Hemdale, 1979, as The Passage (scw: Bruce Nicolaysen; dir: J. Lee Thompson)

*NICOLE, CHRISTOPHER (ROBIN). SC: Jonathan Anders = JA.
The Longest Pleasure. Hutchinson, 1970
Operation Destruct. Dell, 1972 JA
Operation Manhunt. Dell, 1974 JA (book exists?)
Operation Neptune. Dell, 1973 JA?

*NICOLE, CLAUDE. Pseudonym of *Jon (J.) Messmann, q.v. Other pseudonym: *Claudia Nicole.

*NICOLE, CLAUDIA. Pseudonym of *Jon (J.) Messmann, q.v. Other pseudonym: *Claude Nicole.

NICOLE, MARIE. Pseudonym of Marie Rydzynski. Lives in Calif.; author of numerous romances.
Code Name: Love. Harlequin, 1985 <NYC>
Thick As Thieves. Harlequin, 1985 <W. Va.>

*NIELSEN, HELEN (BERNICE). Ref also: TM.
*Gold Coast Nocturne. Film: Hammer, 1954, as Murder by Proxy; released in the U.S. as Blackout (scw: Richard Landau; dir: Terence Fisher)

N

*NIELSEN, TORBEN. 1918-ca.1984. Ref: CA.
*19 Red Roses. Filmed in 1974 (credits not found)

*NIESEWAND, PETER
Fallback. Granada, 1982; Morrow, 1982 <Russ.>
Scimitar. Granada, 1983; Stein, 1984 <Afghan.>
*The Underground Connection. ... Stein, 1985
The Word of a Gentleman. Secker, 1981; Stein, 1985

NIMSE, GORDON
Take What You Want. Hale, 1984. U.S. title (?): Once We Were Men. Critics, 1985 <Burma>

NISBET, JIM
The Gourmet. Pinnacle, 1981 <S.F.>

*NIVEN, LARRY
Dream Park, with Steven Barnes. Ace, 1981 <future>

*NOEL, DENISE
Bitter Heritage. Mystique, 1981 (Translation of "D'Un Couer a L'Autre." Paris, 1963.)
Season of Anguish. Mystique, 1982 (Translation of "Pas D'Imprudences, Veronique." Paris, 1962.)
Secret Love. Mystique, 1981 (Translation of "Les Filles de Chanteloube." Paris, 1964.)

*NOEL, STERLING. 1903-1984. Ref: CA.
*House of Secrets. Film: Rank, 1956; released in the U.S. as Triple Deception (scw: Robert Buckner, Bryan Forbes; dir: Guy Green)

*NOLAN, FREDERICK (W.)
*The Oshawa Project. Film: MGM, 1978, as Brass Target (scw: Alvin Boretz; dir: John Hough)
Wolf Trap. Piatkus, 1983; St. Martin's, 1984 <Ger., WWII>

*NOLAN, WILLIAM F(RANCIS). SC: Space, in *Space for Hire, and in title below.
Look Out for Space. International Polygonics, 1985 <future>

NOLDER, ANN
Dream of Danger. Tiara, 1981; Star, 1981

NOONAN, MICHAEL
Magwitch. Hodder, 1982; St. Martin's, 1983 <Australia, ca.1850>

*NOONE, CARL. Pseudonym of Charlie Chester, radio comedian in Eng.

*NOONE, JOHN. Ref: CA.

NORFOLK, WILLIAM
The Lights Are Warm and Coloured. French, 19?? (3-act play.)

*NORMAN, EARL. Pseudonym of Norman Thomson. SC: Burns Bannion, also at least in title marked BB below.
Hang Me in Hong Kong. Jade Orient (Tokyo), 1976 <H. Kong>
Kill Me in Roppongi. Erle (Tokyo), 1967 BB <Jap.>

*NORMAN, FRANK
The Baskerville Caper. Macdonald, 1981

NORMAN, GEOFFREY. Has been editor at Playboy and Esquire magazines; columnist for Esquire; lives in Vt. and Gulf Coast.
Midnight Water. Dutton, 1983 <Fla.>

*NORMAN, YVONNE. Pseudonym of Norma Seely, 1942-   . Ref: CA.

NORRIS, (BENJAMIN) FRANK(LIN). 1870-1902. Ref: CA.
Shanghaied. Richards, 1899 <ship>

NORRIS, PAT
Virtue Triumphant. French, 1979 (3-act play.)

*NORTH, CLYDE, *ALBERT C(HARLES) FULLER, and *JACK NELSON
*Remote Control. Film: MGM, 1930 (scw: Frank Butler; dir: Malcolm St. Clair, Nick Grinde)

*NORTH, ERIC
*A Chip on My Shoulder. <Australia>

*NORTH, JESSICA
Mask of the Jaguar. Coward, 1981

NORTHAN, IRENE
Miss Astbury and Milordo. Hale, 1981

*NORTHWAY, COLIN. See: *Frank Ross.

*NORTON, ANDRE
At Sword's Point. Harcourt, 1954 <Holl.>

*NORTON, PATRICIA. delete entry

NORVILLE, WARREN. 1923-   . Ref: CA.
Death Tide. Jove, 1979; NEL pb, 1981

NORWOOD, FRANK
The Pope Must Die. Charter, 1985 <Rome>

*NORWOOD, VICTOR. See: *Nat Karta.

NOWAK, JACQUELYN. Art historian, instructor in art history, newspaper columnist, playwright; living in Tucson.
Death at the Crossings. Dodd, 1985 <acad., Midwest>

NOWLAN, ALDEN and WALTER LEARNING. Ref for Nowlan: CA.
Frankenstein. Clarke, 1976 (3-act play based on the novel by *M. Shelley, q.v.)
The Incredible Murder of Cardinal Tosca. Learning Productions, 1979 (3-act play.) (Sherlock Holmes)

NOYE, NICK
No City of Angels. Hale, 1983 <Bangkok>

NOYES, ALFRED. 1880-1958. Ref: CA.
The Hidden Player. Hodder, 1924; Stokes, 1924 ss, some criminous

*NUETZEL, CHARLES (ALEXANDER). Pseudonyms: John Davidson, Alec Rivere, qq.v.

NUNN, FRANK
Blue Haze. New Century (Syd.), 1944 <Far East>
Java Sea Mystery. New Century (Syd.), 1941

NUNN, KEM
-Tapping the Source. Delacorte, 1984; Joseph, 1984 <Calif.>

NUWER, HANK. See: William Boyles.

NYBERG, MARY, 1900-   , and ROBERT NYBERG, 1929-   .
The Call of the East. Exposition, 1956 ss

NYBERG, ROBERT. 1929-   . See: Mary Nyberg, 1900-   .

OATES, JOYCE CAROL. 1938-   . Ref: CA.
Angel of Light. Dutton, 1981; Cape, 1982
The Mysteries of Winterthurn. Dutton, 1984; Cape, 1984 <N.Y., 1800s> 3 linked stories

O'BRIEN, LARRY. Following titles reportedly published in 1950s.
A Dame Ain't Safe.
Frisco Rock.
Swan Song for Paolo.

*O'BRIEN, SALIEE. Pseudonym of *Frankie-Lee James, 1908-   . Ref: CA.

*O'BRINE, (PADRAIC) MANNING. 1915-ca.1973.
*Corpse to Cairo. <ship> (setting correction)
*Crambo. <Alb.>
*Dagger Before Me. <Mid. East>
*Deadly Interlude. <Tangier>
*Dodos Don't Duck. <Ind. O.>
*No Earth for Foxes. <It.>
*Passport to Treason. <Maj.> Film: Mid-Century, 1956 (scw: Kenneth Hayles, Norman Hudis; dir: Robert S. Baker)

*OBSTFELD, RAYMOND. 1952-   . Ref: CA. Pseudonyms: Jason Frost, Carl Stevens. See also: Don(ald Eugene) Pendleton. SC: Harry Gould, also in titles marked HG below.
Dead Bolt. Charter, 1982 HG
Dead Heat. Charter, 1981 HG
The Remington Factor. Charter, 1985

*O'CALLAGHAN, MAXINE. SC: Delilah West, in *Death Is Forever, and in title below.
Run from Nightmare. Raven, 1981

O'CALLAGHAN, SEAN
Terror of the Triads. Star, 1982

O'CONNOR, BRIAN
The One-Shot War. Times, 1980 <Wash. D.C.>

OCORK, SHANNON. Ref: TM. SC: T. T. Baldwin, in *Sports Freak, and in titles below.
End of the Line. St. Martin's, 1981; Gollancz, 1984 <N.Y.>
Hell Bent for Heaven. St. Martin's, 1983 <NYC>

O'DELL, J. W. Ref: TM.
Loan Shark. Belmont, 1975 <NYC>

ODETS, CLIFFORD. 1906-1963. Ref: CA.
The Big Knife. Random, 1946 (Play.) Film: United Artists, 1955 (scw: James Poe; dir: Robert Aldrich)

ODIER, DANIEL. Pseudonym: Delacorta, q.v.

*ODLUM, JEROME
*Each Dawn I Die. Film: Warner, 1939 (scw: Norman Reilly Raine, Warren Duff, Charles Perry; dir: William Keighley)
*The Morgue Is Always Open. Film: Republic, 1943, as A Scream in the Dark (scw: Gerald Schnitzer, Anthony Coldeway; dir: George Sherman)
*Nine Lives Are Not Enough. Film: Warner, 1941 (scw: Fred Niblo, Jr.; dir: A. Edward Sutherland)

*O'DONNELL, LILLIAN (UDVARDY). Ref also: TM. SC: Norah Mulcahaney, also in new titles below.
Casual Affairs. Putnam, 1985 <NYC>
The Children's Zoo. Putnam, 1981; Hale, 1982 <NYC>
Cop Without a Shield. Putnam, 1983 <Pa.>
Ladykiller. Putnam, 1984 <NYC>
*The Sleeping Beauty Murders. <N.Y.>
*Wicked Designs. ... Hale, 1983

O'DONNELL, MICHAEL
The Devil's Prison. Gollancz, 1982

*O'DONNELL, PETER. Ref also: CA, TM. SC: Modesty Blaise, also in new titles marked MB below.
*The Black Pearl and The Vikings. (title correcton) 2 stories
Dead Man's Handle. Souvenir, 1985; Mysterious Press, 1986 MB <Greece>
*Dragon's Claw. ... Mysterious Press, 1985
The Gabriel Set-Up. Titan, 1985 (comic strips) MB
*Last Day in Limbo. ... Mysterious Press, 1985 <Guat.>
Mr. Fothergill's Murder. English Theatre, 1983 (2-act play.)
Mr. Sun. Titan, 1985 (comic strips) MB
*Modesty Blaise. Film: TCF, 1966 (scw: Evan Jones; dir: Joseph Losey)
The Night of Morningstar. Souvenir, 1982; Mysterious Press 1987 MB
*Pieces of Modesty. ... Mysterious Press, 1986
*The Silver Mistress. ... Mysterious Press, 1985
The Xanadu Talisman. Souvenir, 1981; Mysterious Press, 1984 MB

O'DONOGHUE, JOHN
Sergeant Horn's Murder Trap. Hale, 1984

O'DONOHOE, NICK
April Snow. Raven, 1981

*OEMLER, MARIE CONWAY
-Slippy McGee. Century, 1917; Heinemann, 1918. Film: Republic, 1948 (scw: Norman S. Hall, Jerry Gruskin; dir: Albert Kelley)

O'FAOLAIN, JULIA. 1932-   . Ref: CA.
The Irish Signorina. Viking (London), 1984; Adler, 1986

O'FARRELL, WILLIAM. Ref: TC2.
*Repeat Performance. Film: Pathe, 1947 (scw: Walter Bullock; dir: Alfred Werker)

*OFFORD, LENORE GLEN. Ref also: TM. See also: *Theo Durrant.

*O'FLAHERTY, LIAM. 1896-1984.
*The Informer. Film: BIP, 1929 (scw: Benn W. Levy, Rolfe E. Vanlo; dir: Arthur Robinson). Also: RKO, 1935 (scw: Dudley Nichols; dir: John Ford). Also: Paramount, 1968, as Uptight (scw: Jules Dassin, Ruby Dee, Julian Mayfield; dir: Dassin)

*OGAN, GEORGE (F.). 1912-1982. SC: Johnny Bordelon, also in title below.
Murder by Proxy. Raven, 1981

OGDEN, DAVID
Jones '38. Akira, 1985

OGILVIE, C. H.
The Bristol Express Mystery. Mellifont, 1934
Death at 8 P.M. Mellifont, 1936
The Night Mall Mystery. Mellifont, 1934
Who Killed Ferraby? Mellifont, 1935

*OGILVIE, ELIZABETH
The Silent Ones. McGraw, 1981; Chivers, 1983 <Scot.>

OGNIBENE, PETER J(OHN). 1941- Ref: CA.
The Big Byte. Ballantine, 1984

O'GRADY, LESLIE
Lady Jade. St. Martin's, 1981; Piatkus, 1982 <China, ca.1900>

*O'GRADY, ROHAN
The Curse of the Montrolfes; see *Pippin's Journal
*Let's Kill Uncle. Film: Universal, 1966 (scw: Mark Rodgers; dir: William Castle)
*Pippin's Journal. Also published as: The Curse of the Montrolfes. Second Chance, 1983

*O'HANLON, JAMES D. Ref: TM.
*As Good As Murdered. Film: TCF, 1942, as Over My Dead Body (scw: Edward James; dir: Malcolm St. Clair)

*O'HARA, BORIS
*The St. Valentine's Day Massacre. (Novelization of film: Corman, 1967; scw: Howard Browne; dir: Roger Corman)

O'HARA, GEORGE. See: *Mal(colm) St. Clair, 1897-1952.

*O'HARA, KENNETH. Pseudonym of Margaret Jean Morris, 1924- . Ref also: CA.
Nightmare's Nest. Gollancz, 1982; Doubleday, 1983

*O'HIGGINS, HARVEY J(ERROLD)
*The Dummy. Silent film: Famous Players, 1917 (scw: Eve Unsell; dir: Francis E. Grandon). Sound film: Parmount, 1929 (scw: Herman J. Mankiewicz; dir: Robert Milton)

*OHNET, GEORGES
*Doctor Rameau. Silent film: Fox, 1915 (scw & dir: Will S. Davis)
*The Woman of Mystery. Silent film: AB, 1916 (dir: Travers Vale)

OLCOTT, ANTHONY. 1950- . Ref: CA. SC: Ivan Kuvakin, in both titles.
May Day in Magadan. Bantam hc, 1983; Macmillan (London), 1984 <Russ.>
Murder at the Red October. Academy Chicago, 1981; Hodder, 1982 <Moscow>

*OLD SLEUTH
*Amzi, the Detective. Also published as: *Night and Morning. Ogilvie, 1900
*The Beautiful Fugitive. Also published as: Saved by a Detective. Ogilvie, 1900
*The Bicycle Detective; see Bicycle Jim
*Bicycle Jim. Also published as: *The Bicycle Detective. Ogilvie, 1900
Brant Adams, the Emperor of Detectives. Street, 1887. Also published as by Judson R. Taylor: Street (Magnet #86), 1899
*Bruce Angelo, the City Detective. Street, 1887. Also published as by Judson R. Taylor: Street (Magnet #102), 1899
*Cool Tom, the Sailor Boy Detective. Ogilvie, 1897
*The Cowboy Detective. Also published as: *A Little Cowboy in New York. Ogilvie, 1897
*Daring Maddie; see *A Weird Sea Mystery
Desmond Dare. Ogilvie, 1897. Also published as: *A Desperate Chance. Ogilvie, 1900
*A Desperate Chance; see Desmond Dare
*Detective Payne. Also published as: *Detective Payne's Shadow. Ogilvie, 1900
*Detective Payne's Shadow; see Detective Payne
*Detective Thrash, the Trapper of Criminals; see *The Man Trapper
*A Detective Trio. Also published as: *The Three Boy Detectives. Ogilvie, 1897
*A Detective's Enigma. Also published as: *A Puzzling Shadow. Ogilvie, 1900
*Dick, the Boy Detective; see Magic Dick, a Boy Detective
*The Ex-Pugilist Detective; see Yankee Rue, the Ex-Pugilist Detective
A Fatal Resemblance; see *A Marvelous Escape
*Fighting for a Fortune; see *A Straight-Out Detective
*Fighting His Way. Also published as: Variety Jack. Royal, 1898
*A Final Triumph. Ogilvie, 1900
*Fire-Bomb Jack. Also published as: The Mystery Man. Ogilvie, 1900
From the Streets to the Footlights; see *Snap and Jerry
*The Giant Athlete. Also published as: *A Little Giant. Ogilvie, 1897. And as: The Giant Detective. Ogilvie, 1900
The Giant Detective; see *The Giant Athlete
*The Giant Detective Among the Italian Brigands. Also published as: *Old Ironsides Among the Italian Brigands. Royal, 1897
*Jack and Gil. Ogilvie, 1898 (title correction)
Jack the Juggler's Ordeal; see *Tricks and Triumphs
*Jolly Jess. Ogilvie, 1897. Also published as: *Winning a Princess. Ogilvie, 1900
*Kingsley, the Detective. Also published as: *A Single Clue. Ogilvie, 1900
*A League of Three. Ogilvie, 1897
*A Little Cowboy in New York; see The Cowboy Detective
*A Little Giant; see The Giant Athlete
*Magic Dick, a Boy Detective. Ogilvie, 1898. Also published as: *Dick, the Boy Detective. Ogilvie, 1900
Malcolm. Ogilvie, 1897
*A Man of Mystery. Ogilvie, 1900
*The Man Trapper. Munro, 1894. Also published as: *Detective Thrash, the Trapper of Criminals. Royal, 1908
*The Man Who Vanished. Royal, 1908
*A Marvelous Escape. Also published as: A Fatal Resemblance. Ogilvie, 1900
*Murray, the Detective; see *A Mystery of One Night
*The Mysteries and Miseries of New York. Royal, 1897 (title correction)
The Mystery Man; see Fire-Bomb Jack
*A Mystery of One Night. Also published as: *Murray, the Detective. Ogilvie, 1900
*Night and Morning; see *Amzi, the Detective
*Nimble Ike, the Detective. Ogilvie, 1900
*Old Ironsides Among the Italian Brigands; see The Giant Detective Among the Italian Brigands
*Oscar, the Detective. Parlor Car, 1897 (title correction)
*Preston Jayne. Ogilvie, 1897
*A Puzzling Shadow; see A Detective's Enigma
*The Runaway. Ogilvie, 1897. Also published as: The West Point Detective. Ogilvie, 1900
Saved by a Detective; see The Beautiful Fugitive
*Shadowed to His Doom. <NYC>
*Snap and Jerry. Parlor Car, 1895. Also published as: From the Streets to the Footlights. Street, 1900
*A Straight-Out Detective. Also published as: *Fighting for a Fortune. Royal, 1897
*A Startling Discovery; see A Tragic Mystery
Tales from a Gilded Palace. Ogilvie, 1900
*The Three Boy Detectives; see *A Detective Trio
*A Tragic Mystery. Royal, 1897. Also published as: *A Startling Discovery. Royal, 1908
*Tricks and Triumphs. Parlor Car, 1896. Also published as: Jack the Juggler's Ordeal. Ogilvie, 1900
*The Twin Ventriloquists. Also published as: *The Ventriloquist Detectives. Ogilvie, 1900
*Van, the Government Detective. Street, 1897. Also published as by Judson R. Taylor: Street (Magnet #92), 1899
Variety Jack; see Fighting His Way
*The Ventriloquist Detectives; see The Twin Ventriloquists
*A Weird Sea Mystery. Ogilvie, 1900. Contains: *Cool Tom, the Sailor Boy Detective, q.v., and *Daring Maddie
The West Point Detective; see *The Runaway
*Winning a Princess; see Jolly Jess
*Woodchuck Jerry, the Country Detective. Ogilvie, 1897
*Yankee Rue, the Ex-Pugilist Detective. Ogilvie, 1897. Also published as: *The Ex-Pugilist Detective. Ogilvie, 1900

*OLD SPICER
*A Deadly Witness. Street, 1903 (Magnet #287) (title correction)
*A Desperate Game. Street, 1903 (Magnet #307)
*A High Class Swindler. Street, 1903 (Magnet #271)
*In the Shadow. Street, 1903 (Magnet, #315)
*A Matter of Thousands. Street, 1902 (Magnet #261)
*On the Brink of Ruin. Street, 1903 (Magnet #279)
*The Palace of Chance. Street, 1904 (Magnet #337)
*A Question of Evidence. Street, 1904 (Magnet #333)
*The Shadow of Guilt. Street, 1903 (Magnet #297)
*The Sport of Fate. Street, 1902 (Magnet #255)
*The Stolen Jewels. Street, 1904 (Magnet #343)
*The Tattooed Wrist. Street, 1904 (Magnet #327)
*The Three Finger Marks. Street, 1902 (Magnet #265)
*Tightening of the Coils. Street, 1903 (Magnet #319)

*OLDEN, MARC. Ref: TM. SC: Robert Sand, also in title marked RS below.
*Cocaine. Lancer, 1973
Dai-Sho. Arbor, 1983; Corgi, 1985 <Jap.>
-A Dangerous Glamour. GM, 1982; Hamlyn, 1984
Giri. Arbor, 1982; Corgi, 1984 <NYC>
*The Golden Kill. RS <Eng.>

*OLDFELD, PETER. Joint pseudonym of *Per Jacobsson, 1894-1963, and *Vernon Bartlett, 1894-1983.

OLDFIELD, MARY
Please Communicate. Dramatists, 1956 (3-act play.)

OLDHAM, H. R
Dames Spell Homicide. Hamilton, 1952

OLIPHANT, ELEANA
The Haunting at Lost Lake. Leisure, 1985

*OLIVER, ANTHONY. SC: Lizzie Thomas and Insp. John Webber, in *The Pew Group, and in both titles below.
The Property of a Lady. Heinemann, 1983; Doubleday, 1983
The Elberg Collection. Heinemann, 1985; Doubleday, 1985

OLIVIER, STUART. 1880- .
The Bride, with George (M.) Middleton, 1880-1967, q.v. French, 1926 (Play.) Silent film: Metropolitan, 1926 (scw: Finis Fox; dir: Edward Dillon)

*OLSEN, JACK
    Have You Seen My Son? Atheneum, 1982;
      Hale, 1983
    Missing Persons. Atheneum, 1981;
      Hale, 1982   <N.W.>

OLSHAKER, MARK. 1951-   . Ref: CA.
    Einstein's Brain. Evans, 1981; Hamlyn, 1982

OLSON, D. J.
    A Dram of Evil. Award, 1967

OLSON, OSCAR NILS
    Mountie on Trial. Ryerson (Toronto),
      1953; Bouregy, 1954   <Can.>

OLSON, SELMA
    Ana Mistral. Domina, 1975

*O'MALLEY, PATRICK. Pseudonym of *Frank
    O'Rourke. Ref: TM.

O'MARIE, SISTER CAROL ANNE. Entered
    Sisters of St. Joseph of Carondelet in 1951, made vows in 1954;
    has worked as teacher, administrator, editor; is director of development of a high school; lives in
    Calif.
    A Novena for Murder. Scribner, 1984
      <S.F., acad.>

*O'NAIR, MAIRI
    Peggy Paradine, House Agent. Mills,
      1935

O'NEILL, FRANK. 1943-   . Born in
    Atlanta, graduate of Oxford, living
    in Charleston, S.C.; magazine
    writer.
    Agents of Sympathy. Putnam, 1985;
      Hodder, 1985   <Afr., N.>

*O'NEILL, JAMES
    *The Molly Maguires. (Novelization of
      film: Tamm, 1970; scw: Walter
      Bernstein; dir: Martin Ritt.)

O'NEILL, KATHLEEN. Pseudonym of Austin
    B. Goetz, q.v.
    The Kitten's Necklace. Baker, 1948
      (3-act play.)
    Out of This World. Baker, 1946
      (3-act play.)

*O'NEILL, WILL(IAM DANIEL III)
    *The Libyan Kill.   <Lib.>

*OPERATOR 1384
    *The Black Arab.   <Isr.>
    *The Catacombs of Death.   <Tun.>

*OPPENHEIM, E(DWARD) PHILLIPS. Ref
    also: TM. Silent film (based
    on unidentified story):
    Famous Players, 1921, as Dangerous
    Lies (scw: Mary O'Connor; dir:
    Paul Powell). Also: Mutual, 1914,
    as The Floor Above (dir: James
    Kirkwood)
    *The Amazing Partnership. Silent film:
      Stoll, 1921 (scw: Charles Barnett;
      dir: George Ridgwell)
    *The Amazing Quest of Mr. Ernest
      Bliss. Silent film: Hepworth. 1920
      (dir: Henry Edwards). Sound film:
      Klement, 1936; released in the U.S.
      as Romance and Riches (scw: John L.
      Balderston; dir: Alfred Zeisler)
    *Anna the Adventuress. Silent film:
      Hepworth, 1920 (scw: Blanche
      McIntosh; dir: Cecil M. Hepworth)
    *The Black Box. (Novelization of
      silent film: Universal, 1915; scw
      & dir: Otis Turner.)
    *Conspirators. Silent film: Stoll,
      1924; also released as The Barnes
      Murder Case (scw & dir: Sinclair
      Hill)
    *The Double Life of Mr. Alfred Burton.
      Silent film: Lucky Cat, 1919 (scw:
      Kenelm Foss; dir: Arthur Rooke)
    *The Ex-Duke. Silent film: First National, 1926, as The Prince of
      Tempters (scw: Paul Bern; dir:
      Lothar Mendez)
    *Expiation. Silent film: Stoll, 1922
      (scw & dir: Sinclair Hill)
    *False Evidence. Silent film: Stoll,
      1922 (scw: Frank Miller; dir:
      Harold Shaw)
    *The Game of Liberty. Silent film:
      London, 1916; released in the U.S.
      as Under Suspicion (dir: George
      Loane Tucker)
    *The Great Awakening. Silent film:
      Metro, 1917, as A Sleeping Memory
      (scw: Albert Shelby Le Vino; dir:
      George D. Baker)
    *The Great Impersonation. Silent film:
      Famous Players, 1921 (scw: Monte
      Katterjohn; dir: George Melford).
      Sound film: Universal, 1935 (scw:
      Frank Wood, Eve Greene; dir: Alan
      Crosland). Also: Universal, 1942
      (scw: W. Scott Darling; dir: John
      Rawlins)
    *The Great Prince Shan. Silent film:
      Stoll, 1924 (scw & dir: A. E.
      Coleby)
    *The Hillman. Silent film: Vitagraph,
      1917, as In the Balance (scw: Garfield Thompson; dir: Paul Scardon).
      Also: Vitagraph, 1924, as Behold
      This Woman (scw: Marian Constance;
      dir: J. Stuart Blackton)
    *The Illustrious Prince. Silent film:
      Hawarth, 1919 (dir: William
      Worthington)
    *The Inevitable Millionaires. Silent
      film: Warner, 1926, as Millionaires (scw: Raymond L. Shrock; dir:
      Herman Raymaker)
    *Jeanne of the Marshes. Silent film:
      Famous Players, 1921, as Behind
      Masks; also released as Jeanne of
      the Marshes (scw: Katherine Stuart;
      dir: Frank Reicher). Sound film
      (?): Columbia, 1932, as Behind the
      Mask (scw: Jo Swerling; dir: John
      Francis Dillon)
    *The Lion and the Lamb. Film: Columbia, 1931 (scw: Matt Taylor; dir:
      George B. Seitz).
    *The Long Arm. Silent film: National
      Film, 1919, as The Long Arm of Mannister (dir: Bertram Bracken)
    *A Lost Leader. Silent film: Stoll,
      1922 (scw: William J. Elliott; dir:
      George Ridgwell)
    *The Master Mummer. Silent film: Edison, 1915 (scw & dir: Walter Edwin)
    *Master of Men. Silent film: Harma,
      1917 (dir: Wilfred Noy)
    *The Missioner. Silent film: Stoll,
      1922 (scw: Paul Rooff; dir: George
      Ridgwell)
    *Mr. Billingham, the Marquis and Madelon. Film (from ss "The Numbers of
      Death"): Monogram, 1934, as Monte
      Carlo Nights (scw: Norman Houston;
      dir: William Nigh)
    *Mr. Grex of Monte Carlo. Silent film:
      Lasky, 1915 (scw: Marion Fairfax;
      dir: Frank Reicher)
    *Mr. Wingrave, Millionaire. Silent
      film: Paramount, 1919, as The
      Test of Honor (scw: Eve Unsell;
      dir: John S. Robertson)
    *The Mystery of Mr. Bernard Brown.
      Silent film: Stoll, 1921 (scw:
      Mrs. Sydney Groome; dir: Sinclair
      Hill)
    *The Mystery Road. Silent film:
      Famous Players, 1921 (scw: Margaret
      Turnbull, Mary O'Connor; dir:
      Paul Powell)
    *The Other Romilly. Silent film: Cosmopolitan, 1920, as The Cinema Murder (scw: Frances Marion; dir:
      George D. Baker)
    *The Passionate Quest. Silent film:
      Warner, 1926 (scw: Marian Constance, J. Stuart Blackton; dir:
      Blackton)
    *The Plunderers. Silent film: Garrick,
      1920, as The Golden Web (scw:
      Milton Rosmer; dir: Geoffrey H.
      Malins). Also: Gotham, 1926, as
      The Golden Web (scw: James Bell
      Smith; dir: Walter Lang)
    *Seeing Life. Silent film: Selznick,
      1917, as The Silent Master (scw &
      dir: Leonce Perret)
    *The Strange Boarders of Palace Crescent. Film: Gainsborough, 1938,
      as Strange Boarders (scw: Sidney
      Gilliat, A. R. Rawlinson; dir:
      Herbert Mason)
    *The Temptation of Tavernake. Silent
      film: Trem Car, 1928, as Sisters of
      Eve (scw: Arthur Hoerl; dir: Scott
      Pembroke)
    *The World's Great Snare. Silent
      film: Famous Players, 1916 (dir:
      Joseph Kaufman)

*ORCZY, BARONESS (EMMUSKA). Ref also:
    TM.
    *The Celestial City. Silent film:
      British Instructional, 1929 (scw
      & dir: Joe Orton)
    The Emperor's Candlesticks. Pearson,
      1899; Doscher, 1908. Film: MGM,
      1937 (scw: Monckton Hoffe, Harold
      Goldman; dir: George Fitzmaurice)
    *The Old Man in the Corner. Silent
      films: Stoll, 1924, as The Affair
      at the Novelty Theatre; The
      Brighton Mystery; The Hocussing of
      Cigarette; The Kensington Mystery;
      The Mystery of Brudenell Court;
      The Mystery of Dogstooth Cliff;
      The Mystery of the Khaki Tunic;
      The Northern Mystery; The Regent's
      Park Mystery; The Tragedy of Barnsdale Manor; The Tremarne Case;
      The York Mystery (scw & dir: Hugh
      Croise)
    *Unravelled Knots. Film (based on ss
      "A Moorland Tragedy"): GEM, 1933,
      as A Moorland Tragedy (scw: Allen
      Francis; dir: M. A. Wetherell)

*ORDE, LEWIS
    -Deadfall. Zebra, 1984
    Eagles. Arbor, 1984; Piatkus, 1984
      <Eng.>
    Heritage. Arbor, 1981; Piatkus,
      1985   <Eng., 1934-1954>
    -The Lion's Way. Arbor, 1981;
      Piatkus, 1985
    Munich 10. Arbor, 1982; Piatkus,
      1986   <Munich>

*ORDE-POWLETT, NIGEL (AMYAS). 1900-
    1963.

*ORDWAY, PETER
    The Final Safari. Barker, 1983 <Afr.>

*O'REILLY, JOHN BOYLE. 1844-1890.
    Moondyne. Pilot, 1879; Routledge,
      1889   <Australia>

ORENSTEIN, FRANK (EVERETT). 1919-   .
    Ref: CA. SC: Ev Franklin, in both
    titles.
    The Man in the Gray Flannel Shroud.
      St. Martin's, 1984   <NYC>
    Murder on Madison Avenue. St. Martin's, 1983   <NYC>

*ORFORD, ELLEN. Pseudonym of *William
    Delligan.

*ORGAN, PERRY. Pseudonym of Perry
    Organ Carroll.

*ORGILL, DOUGLAS (WILLIAM)
    -Brother Esau. Bodley, 1982; Harper,
      1982

*ORMEROD, ROGER. Ref also: TM; revised and expanded: TC2. SC: David
    Mallin, also in title marked DM
    below.
    Dead Ringer. Constable, 1985;
      Scribner, 1986
    Face Value. Constable, 1983. U.S.
      title: The Hanging Doll Murder.
      Scribner, 1984
    The Hanging Doll Murder; see Face
      Value
    One Deathless Hour. Hale, 1981 DM
    Seeing Red. Constable, 1984; Scribner, 1985   <Wales>

*O'ROURKE, FRANK. Pseudonym also:
    *Patrick O'Malley.

*ORR, CLIFFORD
    *The Dartmouth Murders. Film: Chesterfield, 1935, as A Shot in the Dark
      (scw: Charles Belden; dir: Charles
      Lamont)

ORR, MARY. See: *Reginald Denham.

*ORTON, JOE
    Entertaining Mr. Sloane. H. Hamilton,
      1964; Grove, 1965 (3-act play.)
      Film: Canterbury, 1970 (scw: Clive
      Exton; dir: Douglas Hickox)
    Funeral Games. Methuen, 1970 (1-act
      play.)
    *Loot. Film: Performing Arts, 1970
      (scw: Ray Galton, Alan Simpson;
      dir: Silvio Narizzano)

*ORUM, POUL. Ref also: CA.
    *Nothing But the Truth. Film: Crone,
      1975, as Kun Sandheden (Nothing
      But the Truth) (dir: Henning
      Oernbak)

*OSBORN, DAVID (D.). Ref: CA.
    Heads. Bantam (NYC & London), 1985
    Love and Treason. NAL, 1982; Granada,
      1982   <Wash. D.C.>

OSBORN, JOHN JAY, JR. 1945-   . Ref:
    CA.
    The Man Who Owned New York. Houghton,
      1981; Hale, 1982   <NYC>

*OSBORNE, GEOFFREY. Ref: CA.

*OSBORNE, HELENA. Pseudonym of Georgina
    Mary Galbraith Moore, 1930-
    Ref: CA.

*OSBORNE, WILLIAM HAMILTON
  *The Boomerang. Silent film: KB, 1913
    (scw: C. Gardner Sullivan; dir:
    Thomas H. Ince). Also: National,
    1919 (scw: Franklyn Hall; dir:
    Bertram Bracken)
  *The Catspaw. Silent film: Edison,
    1916 (dir: George A. Wright)
  *The Red Mouse. Silent film: Columbia,
    1916, as The Half Million Bribe
    (scw: Harry O. Hoyt; dir: Edgar
    Jones)
  *The Running Fight. Silent film:
    Paramount, 1915.

OSBOURNE, IVOR
  Prodigal. Akira, 1985

O'SHEA, SEAN. Pseudonym of *(Stanley)
  Robert Tralins, 1926-   .
  Operation Boudoir. Belmont, 1967

OSMAN, GEORGE
  Une Affaire Mysterieuse. New Horizon,
  1981

*OSMOND, ANDREW
  War Without Frontiers, with *Douglas
  (Richard) Hurd. Hodder, 1982

OSMOND, MARION (WALLACE)
  -The Chinese Bungalow. Long, 1923.
    Silent film: Stoll, 1926 (dir:
    Sinclair Hill). Sound film: Neo-
    Art, 1930 (dir: J. B. Williams,
    Arthur W. Barnes). Also: Pennant,
    1940; released in the U.S. as
    Chinese Den (scw: A. R. Rawlinson,
    George Wellesley; dir: George King)
  -The Curtains of Solomon. Long, 1924
    <Mid. East>

OSTER, JERRY. 1943-   . Ref: CA.
  Sweet Justice. Harper, 1985. British
  title: Rough Justice. Collins,
  1985 <NYC>

*OSTLERE, GORDON STANLEY. Pseudonym:
  *Richard Gordon, q.v.

*OSTRANDER, ISOBEL (EGERTON)
  *At One-Thirty. <NYC>
  *Island of Intrigue. Silent film:
    Metro, 1919 (scw: June Mathis, A.
    S. Le Vino; dir: Henry Otto)
  *Suspense. Silent film: Reicher,
    1919 (scw: Eve Unsell; dir: Frank
    Reicher)

*O'SULLIVAN, J(AMES) B(RENDAN). SC:
  Steve Silk, also in *Casket of
  Death.

*O'SULLIVAN, VINCENT
  -A Dissertation Upon Second Fiddles.
    Richards, 1902

OTFINOSKI, STEVEN
  Barracuda Run. Ballantine, 1985

*O'TOOLE, GEORGE. Former CIA agent.
  Poor Richard's Game. Delacorte, 1982

*OTTOLENGUI, RODRIGUES. SC: John
  Barnes, in all listed titles.

*OURSLER, (CHARLES) FULTON
  *The Spider. Film: TCF, 1931 (scw:
    Barry Connors, Philip Klein; dir:
    W. C. Menzies, Kenneth MacKenna).
    Also: TCF, 1945 (scw: Jo Eisinger,
    W. Scott Darling; dir: Robert
    Webb)

*OURSLER, GRACE (PERKINS). Pseudonym:
  Dora Macy, q.v.

*OURSLER, WILL(IAM CHARLES). 1913-
  1985.

*OVERHOLSER, STEPHEN. SC: Molly Owens,
  in *Molly and the Confidence Man,
  and title below (western detective
  series).
  Molly and the Gold Baron. Bantam,
  1981 <Colo.>

OWEN, DEAN. Pseudonym of Dudley Dean
  MacGaughy.
  Juice Town. Monarch, 1962 <Calif.>

OWEN, GUY (JR.). 1925-1981. Ref: CA.
  -The Ballad of the Flim Flam Man.
    Macmillan, 1965. Film: TCF, 1967,
    as The Flim Flam Man; released in
    Britain as One Born Every Minute
    (scw: William Rose; dir: Irvin
    Kershner, Yakima Canutt).

*OWEN, HANS C.
  *Ways of Death = *Fit to Kill

OWEN, HARRISON. 1890-
  The Mount Marunga Mystery. Bookstall
  (Syd.), 1919

OWEN, WALTER. 1884-   .
  -"More Things in Heaven..." Dakers,
    1947

OXENHAM, JOHN. Pseudonym of William
  Arthur Dunkerley, 1852-1941.
  -A Maid of the Silver Sea. Hodder,
    1910. Silent film: Clark, 1922
    (scw & dir: Guy Newall)

OXFORD, JAMES. "Best-selling author
  author writing under a pseudonym."
  The Night of the Falcon. St. Martin's, 1981; Hale, 1983

*OZAKI, MILTON K. Ref also: TM.
  Pseudonym: *Robert O. Saber, q.v.

P., K. U. Pseudonym of Katherine Ursula Parrott, 1902-   .
  Gentleman's Fate. Cape & Smith, 1931.
  Film: MGM, 1931 (scw: Leonard Praskins; dir: Mervyn Le Roy)

*PACE, TOM. 1929-

*PACKARD, FRANK (LUCIUS)
  *The Adventures of Jimmie Dale. Silent
    film: Monmouth, 1917, as Jimmy
    Dale, Alias "The Grey Seal" (scw:
    Mildred Considine; dir: Henry
    McRae Webster)
  *From Now On. Silent film: Fox, 1920
    (scw & dir: Raoul Walsh)
  *The Miracle Man. Film: Silent film:
    Paramount, 1919 (scw & dir: George
    Loane Tucker). Sound film: Para-
    mount, 1932 (scw: Waldemar Young;
    dir: Norman McLeod)
  *The Night Operator. Silent film
    (based on ss "The Wrecking Boss"):
    First National, 1928, as The Crash
    (scw: Charles Kenyon; dir: Eddie
    Cline)
  *Pawned. Silent film: Select, 1922
    (scw: Frank L. Packard; dir: Irvin
    V. Willat)
  *The Sin That Was His. Silent film:
    Selznick, 1920 (scw: Edmund Gould-
    ing; dir: Hobart Henley)
  *The White Moll. Silent film: Fox,
    1920 (scw: E. Lloyd Sheldon; dir:
    Harry Millarde)

*PACKER, VIN. Pseudonym of *Marijane
  Meaker, 1927-   . Ref: CA.

PACOTTI, PAMELA
  The Last Heiress of Merriott Manor.
  Zebra, 1982

*PAGANO, JO. Born in Denver; commercial
  illustrator, art critic, scenario
  writer; living in L.A. in 1947.
  *The Condemned. Film: United Artists,
    1951, as Try and Get Me; released
    in Britain as The Sound of the
    Fury (scw: Jo Pagano; dir: Cyril
    Endfield)

*PAGE, ALAIN. Pseudonym of Jean-Edmond
  Conil.
  Hook. International, 1969 (Transla-
    tion of "Le Grappin." Paris, 1966.)

PAGE, CAROLE GIFT, 1942-   , and DORIS
  ELAINE FELL. Ref for Page: CA.
  Mist over Morro Bay. Harvest House,
    1985 <Calif.>

*PAGE, EMMA. Ref also: CA; not in TC2.
  SC: Insp. Kelsey, in all titles
  below.
  Cold Light of Day. Collins, 1983;
    Walker, 1984
  Every Second Thursday. Collins, 1981;
    Walker, 1981
  Last Walk Home. Collins, 1982;
    Walker, 1983
  Scent of Death. Collins, 1985;
    Doubleday, 1986

*PAGE, MARCO
  *Fast Company. Film: MGM, 1938 (scw:
    Marco Page, Harold Tarshis; dir:
    Edward Buzzell)

*PAGE, MARTIN
  Set a Thief. Bodley, 1984. U.S.
  title: The Man Who Stole the Mona
  Lisa. Pantheon, 1984 <Paris, 1911>

PAIGE, RICHARD. Pseudonym of *Dean
  R(ay) Koontz, q.v. Other pseudonym:
  Owen West, q.v.
  The Door to December. Signet, 1985
  <L.A.>

*PAIN, BARRY (ERIC ODELL). Ref also:
  CA.

*PALEY, FRANK
  *Rumble on the Docks. <NYC> Film:
    Columbia, 1956 (scw: Lou Morheim,
    Jack DeWitt; dir: Fred F. Sears)

PALINURIS. Pseudonym.
  The Paper Boat. Bowden, 1897
  ss, one or two criminous

PALKA, KURT
  Rose Garden. Allen, 1982

*PALMER, LILLI. Pseudonym of Maria
  Lilli Peiser, 1914-1986. Ref: CA.
  Night Music. Weidenfeld, 1982
  <Ger.> (Translation of "Nacht-
  musik.")

PALMER, MICHAEL (STEPHEN). 1942-
  Ref: CA.
  Side Effects. Bantam (NYC & London),
    1985 <Boston>
  The Sisterhood. Bantam, 1982; Hodder,
    1982 <Boston, hosp.>

*PALMER, (CHARLES) STUART. Ref also:
  TM. Film (based on uniden-
  tified story): RKO, 1936,
  as The Plot Thickens; released in
  Britain as The Swinging Pearl
  Mystery (scw: Clarence Upson Young,
  Jack Townley; dir: Ben Holmes).
  Also (based on another unidentified
  story): RKO, 1937, as Forty Naughty
  Girls (scw: John Grey; dir: Edward
  Cline)
  *Murder on the Blackboard. Film: RKO,
    1934 (scw: Willis Goldbeck; dir:
    George Archainbaud)
  *The Penguin Pool Murder. Film: RKO,
    1932; released in Britain as The
    Penguin Pool Mystery (scw: Willis
    Goldbeck; dir: George Archainbaud)
  *The Puzzle of the Pepper Tree. Film:
    RKO, 1935, as Murder on a Honeymoon
    (scw: Seton I. Miller, Robert
    Benchley; dir: Lloyd Corrigan)
  *The Puzzle of the Red Stallion. Film:
    RKO, 1936, as Murder on a Bridle
    Path (scw: Dorothy Yost, Thomas
    Lennon, Edmund North, James Gow;
    dir: Edward Killy, William Hamil-
    ton)

PALMER, THOMAS. 1955-   . Ref: CA.
  The Transfer. Ticknor, 1983; Collins,
  1983 <Miami>

PALMER, TONY. 1941-   . Ref: CA.
  Wasting Assets. Malvern, 1984

PALMERIO, A. J.
  Jackey. Allen, 1982

PANATI, CHARLES. 1943-   . Ref: CA.
  The Pleasuring of Rory Malone. St.
  Martin's, 1982 <NYC>

PANGER, DANIEL. 1926-   . Ref: CA.
  -The Mask of Abraham Morgenstern. SOS,
    1985 <L.A.>
  -You Can't Kill a Dead Man. Leisure,
    1982

PAPAZOGLOU, ORANIA. 1951-   . Former
  Vassar student and English profes-
  sor. Ref: TM. SC: Patience Campbell
  McKenna, in both titles.
  Sweet, Savage Death. Doubleday, 1984
    <NYC>
  Wicked, Loving Murder. Doubleday,
    1985 <NYC>

*PAPE, GORDON and *TONY ASPLER
  The Music Wars. Beaufort, 1985
  <Moscow>

PAPICH, MARGERY. Joint pseudonym with
  Marion Woolf and Layne Torkelson:
  Marion Margery Layne, q.v.

PARETSKY, SARA. 1947-   . Born in
  Ames, Ia.; has B.A. in political
  science from Univ. of Kansas, MBA
  in finance and Ph.D. in history
  from Univ. of Chi.; an insurance
  executive in Chi. Ref: TM. SC: V.
  I. Warshawski, in all titles.
  Deadlock. Dial, 1984; Gollancz, 1984
    <Chi.>
  Indemnity Only. Dial, 1982; Gollancz,
    1982 <Chi.>
  Killing Orders. Morrow, 1985; Gol-
    lancz, 1986 <Chi.>

PARETTI, SANDRA. Ref: CA.
  Maria Canossa. St. Martin's, 1981
  <Rome, 1943> (Translation of
  "Maria Canossa." Germany, 1979.)

*PARGETER, EDITH (MARY)
  *The Assize of the Dying. Film: Wentworth, 1958, as The Spaniard's
  Curse (scw: Kenneth Hyde; dir:
  Ralph Kemplen)

PARIS, ALAIN
  Teeth of the Wolf. Holt, 1983;
  Sidgwick, 1983 <Ger., 1945>
  (Translation of "Commando des
  Salopards." Paris, 1980.)

*PARISH, JAMES. 1904-1973. Ref: CA.
  The Hour of the Unicorn. Collins,
  1969 <Ger.>

PARK, JORDAN. Pseudonym of *C(yril) M.
  Kornbluth. See also: *Frederik
  Pohl.
  -Sorority House. Lion, 1956 <acad.>

PARKER, DAVID
  The Collector. French, 1973 (3-act
  play based on the novel by *John
  Fowles, q.v.)

PARKER, GORDON. 1940-   . Ref: CA.
  The Action of the Tiger. Macdonald,
  1981

*PARKER, PERCY SPURLARK. Ref also: TM.

*PARKER, ROBERT B(ROWN). Ref also:
  BM, TM. SC: Spenser, also in all
  titles below.
  A Catskill Eagle. Delacorte, 1985;
  Viking (London), 1986
  Ceremony. Delacorte, 1982; Piatkus,
  1983 <Boston>
  Early Autumn. Delacorte, 1981; Penguin, 1985 <Maine>
  *Looking for Rachel Wallace. ... Piatkus, 1982
  A Savage Place. Delacorte, 1981;
  Piatkus, 1982 <L.A.>
  Surrogate. Lord John, 1982 one ss
  Valediction. Delacorte, 1984; Penguin, 1985 <Boston>
  The Widening Gyre. Delacorte, 1983

PARKER, T. JEFFERSON. Journalist, editor, and magazine writer; living
  in Calif.
  Laguna Heat. St. Martin's, 1985;
  Bodley, 1986 <L.A.>

PARNELL, MICHAEL
  Shannon. Granada pb, 1982

PARR, OLIVE KATHARINE. 1874-   . Pseudonym: Beatrice Chase, q.v.

*PARRISH, FRANK. Pseudonym of *Roger
  (Erskine) Longrigg. Other pseudonyms: *Ivor Drummond; Domini
  Taylor, q.v. SC: Dan Mallet, also
  in all titles below.
  Bait on the Hook. Constable, 1983;
  Dodd, 1983
  Death in the Rain; see Face at the
  Window
  Face at the Window. Constable, 1984.
  U.S. title: Death in the Rain.
  Dodd, 1984
  Snare in the Dark. Constable, 1982;
  Dodd, 1981

PARRISH, PATT. 1942-   . Living in
  Va.
  -The Amberley Affair. Hale, 1983
  Escape the Past. Walker, 1985 <Iowa>

*PARRISH, RANDALL
  *The Strange Case of Cavendish. Silent
  film: Universal, 1926, as The Lion
  Man (scw: Karl L. Coolidge, Joe
  Brandt, William Pigott; dir: Jack
  Wells, Albert Russell)

PARROTT, KATHERINE URSULA. 1902-
  Pseudonym: K. U. P., q.v.

PARRY-ELLIS, ROBERT
  Dear Murderer. Axtell, 1947

PARSONS, ELMER M. Pseudonym: *Philip
  Race.

*PARTRIDGE, ANTHONY
  *Passers-By. Silent film: Frothingham, 1921, as Pilgrims of the
  Night (scw & dir: Edward Sloman)

PARTRIDGE, (EDWARD) BELLAMY. 1877-
  Lawyer born in N.Y.

The Ainsley Case. Random, 1955
  <N.Y., 1885> (Novelized true
  crime.)

*PARVIN, BRIAN
  Then There Was Murder. Hale, 1980
  Wreath for a Ragman. Hale, 1981

PASCAL, FRANCINE (P). 1938-   . Ref:
  CA.
  Save Johanna! Morrow, 1981

*PATCH, DAN E. L. Setting, all books:
  Mich.

*PATERNOSTER, (GEORGE) SIDNEY
  *The Hand of the Spoiler. Silent
  film: Barker, 1916, as In the Hands
  of the Spoilers (dir: Leon Bary)

*PATERSON, (JAMES EDMOND) NEIL
  *Man on a Tight Rope. Film: TCF,
  1953 (scw: Robert E. Sherwood; dir:
  Elia Kazan)

*PATON, RAYMOND
  *-The Autobiography of a Blackguard.
  Silent film: UFA, 1925, as The
  Blackguard (scw: Alfred Hitchcock;
  dir: Graham Cutts)

PATRICK, BRENNAN. Pseudonym of Joseph
  Monninger.
  The Night Caller. Dell, 1981

*PATRICK, Q. Ref also: TM.

*PATRICK, VINCENT
  Family Business. Poseidon, 1985
  <NYC>
  *The Pope of Greenwich Village. Film:
  MGM, 1984 (scw: Vincent Patrick;
  dir: Stuart Rosenberg)

PATRICK, WILLIAM
  Spirals. Houghton, 1983; Sphere,
  1985 <Mass.>

*PATTERSON, HARRY. Ref also: TM; revised: TC2.
  Dillinger. Hutchinson, 1983; Stein,
  1983 <Mex., 1934>
  *To Catch a King. Film; Gaylord,
  1983 (existence of film not confirmed)

*PATTERSON, JOHN M(cREADY). 1913-1983.
  Ref: CA.

*PATTERSON, RICHARD NORTH
  Escape the Night. Random, 1983 <NYC>
  The Outside Man. Little, 1981 <Ala.>
  Private Screening. Villard, 1985;
  Joseph, 1986

*PATTERSON, ROBERT
  *Man with a Past. criminous

*PATTINSON, JAMES
  The Antwerp Appointment. Hale, 1981
  A Car for Mr. Bradley. Hale, 1983
  -Come Home, Toby Brown. Hale, 1985
  *The Courier Job. ... Critic, 1986
  Dead of Winter. Hale, 1984
  A Fatal Errand. Hale, 1982
  Flight to the Sea. Hale, 1983
  Homecoming. Hale, 1985; Critic, 1986
  *The Honeymoon Caper. ... Critic, 1986
  The Kavulu Lion. Hale, 1983
  Lethal Orders. Hale, 1982; Critic,
  1986
  -Life-Preserver. Hale, 1985
  Precious Cargo. Hale, 1984 <ship>
  The Saigon Merchant. Hale, 1984
  The Seven Sleepers. Hale, 1981
  The Stalking Horse. Hale, 1982;
  Critic, 1986
  Stride. Hale, 1981

PATTON, DAVID LEWIS. Pseudonym: *David
  Lewis.

PAUL, (JOHN) ANTHONY. 1941-   . Ref:
  CA.
  A Present from Hugo. Collins, 1966
  <Mid. East>

*PAUL, BARBARA. Lives in Pitt. SC:
  Enrico Caruso = EC.
  A Cadenza for Caruso. St. Martin's,
  1984 <NYC, 1910, theatre> EC
  *First Gravedigger. ... Collins, 1982
  Kill Fee. Scribner, 1985; Collins,
  1985
  Prima Donna at Large. St. Martin's,
  1985 EC <1915, NYC, theatre>
  The Renewable Virgin. Scribners,
  1985; Collins, 1984 <NYC>
  Your Eyelids Are Growing Heavy.
  Doubleday, 1981; Collins, 1982

*PAUL, ELLIOT (HAROLD). Ref also: CA,
  TM.

*PAUL, JOHN
  Oil by Murder. <Can.>

*PAUL, RAYMOND. 1940-   . Ref: CA.
  The Thomas Street Horror. Viking,
  1982 <NYC, 1836>
  The Tragedy at Tiverton. Viking,
  1984 <New Eng., 1832>

PAUL, WILLIAM
  Seasons of Revenge. Severn, 1985

*PAULSEN, GARY. SC: Lt. Ronnie Gold,
  in *The Sweeper, and in title
  marked RG below.
  Clutterkill. Raven, 1981 RG <Chi.>
  Compkill. Pinnacle, 1981
  *The Death Specialists. <Venez.>

PAXTON, GUY and EDWARD (VICTOR)
  HOILE
  Merely Murder. Deane, 1953; Baker,
  1953 (3-act play.)

*PAYES, RACHEL (RUTH) C(OSGROVE)
  The Silent Place. Ace, 1969

*PAYN, JAMES
  High Spirits. Chatto, 1879; Harper,
  1879 ss, some criminous

PAYNE, L. R. See: Dick Stivers.

*PAYNE, LAURENCE. Ref also: TC2. SC:
  Mark Savage, in titles marked MS;
  John Tibbet, in *Spy for Sale, and
  in title marked JT; Chief Insp.
  Sam Birkett, also in title marked
  SB.
  Dead for a Ducat. Hodder, 1985;
  Doubleday, 1986 SB, MS
  Even My Foot's Asleep. Hodder, 1971
  JT
  Malice in Camera. Hodder, 1983;
  Doubleday, 1985 MS
  *The Nose on My Face. Film: Viewfinder, 1963, as Girl in the
  Headlines; released in the U.S. as
  The Model Murder Case (scw:
  Vivienne Knight, Patrick Campbell;
  dir: Michael Truman)
  Take the Money and Run. Hodder, 1982;
  Doubleday, 1984 <Wales> MS
  Vienna Blood. Hodder, 1984; Doubleday, 1986 MS <Vienna>

PAYTON, CORAL
  The Gold Key. Hale, 1984

PEACH, LAWRENCE DU GARDE. 1890-1974.
  Ref: CA.
  Danger on the Right. French, 1960
  (1-act play.)
  The White Sheep of the Family, with
  Ian Hay (pseudonym of John Hay
  Beith, 1876-1952). French, 1953
  (3-act play.)

*PEACOCK, F(ERDINAND) M(ANSEL)
  Ronald the Fusilier. Gale, 1892

*PEARL, JACK
  *Lepke. (Novelization of film: Warner,
  1975; scw: Wesley Lau, Tamar Hoffs;
  dir: Menachem Golan)
  *Our Man Flint. (Novelization of film:
  TCF, 1965; scw: Hal Fimberg, Ben
  Starr; dir: Daniel Mann)
  *Robin and the Seven Hoods. (Novelization of film: Warner, 1964; scw:
  David R. Schwartz; dir: Gordon
  Douglas.)

*PEARLMAN, GILBERT
  *The Adventures of Sherlock Holmes'
  Smarter Brother. (Novelization of
  film: TCF, 1975; scw & dir:
  Gene Wilder.)

PEARSON, ANNE
  Dracula. Company, 1978 (Play based
  on the novel by *Bram Stoker, q.v.)

PEARSON, JOHN. 1930-   . Living in
  London.
  The Kindness of Dr. Avicenna. MacMillan (London), 1982; Holt, 1982
  <Rome>

PEARSON, RIDLEY. Musician, songwriter,
  composer of scores for films;
  living in Idaho.
  Never Look Back. St. Martin's, 1985;
  Hale, 1986

*PEARSON, WILLIAM
  Chessplayer. Viking, 1984; Viking
  (U.K.), 1984 <Moscow, Wash. D.C.>

PEART, ROBERT
    Angels of Death. Fontana, 1982; Pinnacle, 1984 <Fr., 1942>
    -Danger Signal. Fontana, 1985

PEASE, HOWARD. 1894-1974. Ref: CA.
    Borderland Studies. Mawson, 1893
        ss, two criminous
    Tales of Northumbria. Methuen, 1899
        ss, some criminous

*PEDLAR, KIT and *GERRY DAVIS
    *Brainrack. (title correction)

PEDNEAU, DAVE
    Presumption of Innocence. Avon, 1985 <W. Va.>

*PEDRICK, GALE
    *Meet the Rev. Film: Hammer, 1949, as Meet Simon Cherry (scw: Gale Pedrick, Godfrey Grayson, A. R. Rawlinson; dir: Grayson)

*PEEL, COLIN D(UDLEY). Ref: CA.
    Firestorm. Hale, 1983; Doubleday, 1984
    Snowtrap. Hale, 1981; Doubleday, 1985 <Australia>

PEEL, KENDAL J(OHN). 1940- . Ref: CA.
    The Twelfth Night of Ramadan. Heinemann, 1983; Vanguard, 1984 <Saud. Arab.>

PEISER, MARIA LILLI. 1914-1986. Pseudonym: *Lilli Palmer, q.v.

*PELL, ROBERT. Pseudonym of *David (James) Hagberg, q.v. Other pseudonyms: David Bannerman, q.v.; *Eric Ramsey. See also: *Nick Carter.

*PEMBER, RON and *DENIS DE MARNE
    *Jack the Ripper. <London, 1888>

*PEMBERTON, MAX. Ref: not in TC2.
    *Kronstadt. Silent film: Gaumont, 1919 (scw: Max Pemberton)

PENDARK, ROBERT
    The Butler Did It. Arcade, 1983

*PENDLETON, DON(ALD EUGENE). Ref also: TM. SC: Mack Bolan (The Executioner), also in all titles below. Note: Actual or collaborative authors identified in parenthesis below.
    Ambush on Blood River. Gold Eagle, 1983; Mills, 1985 <Belg. Congo> (by Alan Bomack)
    Appointment in Kabul. Gold Eagle, 1985 <Afghan.> (by *Stephen Mertz)
    *Arizona Ambush. (coauthored by Michael Newton, q.v.)
    Beirut Playback. Gold Eagle, 1984 <Beirut> (by *Stephen Mertz)
    Blood Dues. Gold Eagle, 1984 <Miami> (by Michael Newton, q.v.)
    Bloodsport. Gold Eagle, 1982; Mills, 1984 <Ger.> (by Raymond Obstfeld, q.v.)
    The Bone Yard. Gold Eagle, 1985; Mills, 1985 <Las Veg.> (by Michael Newton, q.v.)
    Brothers in Blood. Gold Eagle, 1983; Mills, 1984 <Idaho> (by Steven Krauzer)
    Cambodian Clash. Gold Eagle, 1984 <Camb.> (by Tom Jagninski)
    *Cleveland Pipeline. (coauthored by *Stephen Mertz and Michael Newton, q.v., with Don Pendleton)
    *Command Strike. (Coauthored by *Stephen Mertz and Michael Newton, q.v., with Don Pendleton)
    Council of Kings. Gold Eagle, 1985; Mills, 1985 <Oreg.> (by *Chet Cunningham, q.v., and Les Danforth)
    Crude Kill. Gold Eagle, 1983; Mills, 1985 <ship> (by *Chet Cunningham, q.v.)
    Day of Mourning. Gold Eagle, 1984; Mills, 1986 <Va.> (by *Stephen Mertz)
    Dead Man Running. Gold Eagle, 1984; Mills, 1986 <Wash. D.C.> (by *Stephen Mertz)
    Death Games. Gold Eagle, 1985; Mills, 1985 (by Tom Arnett)
    Dirty War. Gold Eagle, 1985 <Viet Nam> (by *Stephen Mertz)
    Doomsday Disciples. Gold Eagle, 1983; Mills, 1984 <S.F.> (by Michael Newton, q.v.)
    Double Crossfire. Gold Eagle, 1982; Mills, 1985 (by Steve Krauzer) <Turk.>
    Fastburn. Gold Eagle, 1985 <China> (by James Lord)
    Flesh Wounds. Gold Eagle, 1983; Mills, 1985 <Pa.> (by *Raymond Obstfeld, q.v.)
    Hammerhead Reef. Gold Eagle, 1985; Mills, 1986 <Fla.> (by Alan Bomack)
    Hellbinder. Gold Eagle, 1985 <Isr.> (by *Chet Cunningham, q.v.)
    Hollywood Hell. Gold Eagle, 1985 Mills, 1985 <L.A.> (by Michael Newton, q.v.)
    Ice Cold Kill. Gold Eagle, 1984 <Russ.> (by Peter Leslie)
    The Invisible Assassins. Gold Eagle, 1983; Mills, 1985 <Jap.> (by Alan Bomack)
    The Iranian Hit. Gold Eagle, 1982; Mills, 1984 (by *Stephen Mertz) <Md.>
    Island Deathtrap. Gold Eagle, 1983; Mills, 1985 <Maine> (by E. Richard Churchill)
    The Libya Connection. Gold Eagle, 1982; Mills, 1984 (by *Stephen Mertz) <Libya>
    Missouri Deathwatch. Gold Eagle, 1985 <St. Louis> (by Michael Newton, q.v.)
    Mountain Rampage. Gold Eagle, 1983; Mills, 1985 <Colo.> (by E. Richard Churchill)
    The New War. Gold Eagle, 1981; Mills, 1985 (by Saul Wernick) <Cent. Am.>
    Orbiting Omega. Gold Eagle, 1984 <Ariz.> (by *Chet Cunningham, q.v.)
    Paradine's Gauntlet. Gold Eagle, 1983 <Fr.> (by Michael Newton, q.v.)
    Paramilitary Plot. Gold Eagle, 1982; Mills, 1984 (by Michael Newton, q.v.) <Fla.>
    Prairie Fire. Gold Eagle, 1984 <Kan.> (by Michael Newton, q.v.)
    Renegade Agent. Gold Eagle, 1982; Mills, 1984 (by Steven Krauzer)
    Resurrection Day. Gold Eagle, 1985; Mills, 1986 <San Diego> (by *Chet Cunningham, q.v.)
    Return to Vietnam. Gold Eagle, 1982; Mills, 1984 (by *Stephen Mertz) <Viet Nam>
    Running Hot. Gold Eagle, 1985; Mills, 1985 <Fr.>
    Savannah Swingsaw. Gold Eagle, 1985 <Ga.> (by *Raymond Obstfeld, q.v.)
    Shock Waves. Gold Eagle, 1985; Mills, 1985 <NYC> (by *Michael Newton, q.v.)
    Skysweeper. Gold Eagle, 1984 <Calif.> (by *Chet Cunningham, q.v.)
    Sold for Slaughter. Gold Eagle, 1983; Mills, 1985 (by Michael Newton, q.v.)
    Stony Man Doctrine. Gold Eagle, 1983; Mills, 1984 (by Dick Stivers, q.v.)
    Teheran Wipeout. Gold Eagle, 1985
    *Tennessee Smash. (coauthored by Michael Newton, q.v.)
    Terminal Velocity. Gold Eagle, 1984 <Russ.> (by Alan Bomack)
    Terrorist Summit. Gold Eagle, 1982; Mills, 1984 <Afr.> (by Steven Krauzer)
    Tiger War. Gold Eagle, 1984; Mills, 1985 <Thai.> (by Tom Jagninski)
    Tuscany Terror. Gold Eagle, 1983; Mills, 1984 <It.> (by *Stephen Mertz)
    The Violent Streets. Gold Eagle, 1982; Mills, 1984 <Minn.> (by Michael Newton, q.v.)
    Vulture's Vengeance. Gold Eagle, 1983; Mills, 1984 <air> (by Patrick Neary)

PENN, H. See: *Val Andrews.

PENN, JOHN. Joint pseudonym of *Palma Harcourt, q.v., and her husband Jack H. Trotman. SC: Insp. George Thorne and Sgt. Bill Abbot = T&A. Set: Eng.
    An Ad for Murder; see Notice of Death
    A Deadly Sickness. Collins, 1985; Scribner, 1985 T&A
    Deceitful Death. Collins, 1983. U.S. title: Stag Dinner Death. Scribner, 1984
    Mortal Term. Collins, 1984; Scribner, 1985 <acad.> T&A
    Notice of Death. Collins, 1982. U.S. title: An Ad for Murder. Scribner, 1983
    Stag Dinner Death; see Deceitful Death
    A Will to Kill. Collins, 1983; Scribner, 1984

*PENTECOST, HUGH. SC: George Crowder, also in titles marked GC; Pierre Chambrun, also in titles marked PC; Julian Quist, also in titles marked JQ.
    The Copycat Killings. Dodd, 1983; Hale, 1984 GC <Conn.>
    Murder in High Places. Dodd, 1983; Hale, 1983 PC <NYC>
    Murder in Luxury. Dodd, 1981; Hale, 1981 PC <NYC>
    Murder Out of Wedlock. Dodd, 1983; Hale, 1985 JQ (PC in cameo role) <NYC>
    Murder Round the Clock. Dodd, 1985 PC ss <NYC>
    Murder Sweet and Sour. Dodd, 1985 GC <Conn.>
    The Party Killer. Dodd, 1985 JQ <New Eng.>
    Past, Present, and Murder. Dodd, 1982; Hale, 1983 JQ <NYC>
    The Price of Silence. Dodd, 1984 GC <Conn.>
    Remember to Kill Me. Dodd, 1984; Hale, 1985 PC <NYC>
    Sow Death, Reap Death. Dodd, 1981; Hale, 1982 JQ <L.I.>
    Substitute Victim. Dodd, 1984; Hale, 1986 JQ
    With Intent to Kill. Dodd, 1982; Hale, 1983 PC <NYC>

PENZLER, OTTO. 1942- . See: Lisa Drake, R. T. Edwards.

*PERCY, EDWARD
    *Ladies in Retirement. Film: Columbia, 1941 (scw: Garrett Fort, Reginald Denham; dir: Charles Vidor). Also: Columbia, 1969, as The Mad Room (scw: Bernard Girard, A. Z. Martin; dir: Girard)
    *Play with Fire. Film: British Lion, 1946, as The Shop at Sly Corner; released in the U.S. as The Code of Scotland Yard (scw: Katherine Strueby; dir: George King)
    *Trunk Crime. Film: Charter, 1939; released in the U.S. as Design for Murder (scw: Francis Miller; dir: Roy Boulting)

PERCYVAL, T(HOMAS) WIGNEY. See: Horace Hodges.

*PERDUE, LEWIS. Joint pseudonym with Lee Goldberg: Ian Ludlow, q.v.
    The Da Vinci Legacy. Pinnacle, 1983
    The Delphi Betrayal. Pinnacle, 1982
    The Linz Testament. Fine, 1985
    Queen's Gate Reckoning. Pinnacle, 1982; Coronet, 1984
    The Tesla Bequest. Pinnacle, 1984

*PERDUE, VIRGINIA
    *He Fell Down Dead. Film: Warner, 1946, as Shadow of a Woman (scw: Whitman Chambers, C. Graham Baker; dir: Joseph Santley)

PERELMAN, LAURA (WEST)
    The Night Before Christmas, with *S(idney) J(oseph) Perelman. French, 1942 (3-act play.) Film: Warner, 1942, as Larceny, Inc. (scw: Everett Freeman, Edwin Gilbert; dir: Lloyd Bacon)

*PEREIRA, MICHAEL (NICHOLAS O'DONNELL).
    *An Angel Came Down. <Mid. East>
    *Pigeon's Blood. <H. Kong, Sing.>

*PEROWNE, BARRY
    *Raffles After Dark. 3 novelets
    *Ten Words of Poison. Mystery House, 1941 (publisher correction)

*PERRAULT, E(RNEST) G. Born and raised in Vancouver; has worked in advertising and public relations; author of ss, plays, novels, articles and film documentaries.

*PERRAULT, GILLES
    *Dossier 51. Film: Elefilm, 1978, as Le Dossier 51 (The 51 File; Dossier 51) (scw: Gilles Perrault, Michel Deville; dir: Deville)

*PERRELLI, NICK
    Take It Easy. Milestone, 1952

PERRIN, NEIL H.
    Death by My Destiny. News Stand, 1950

*PERRY, ANNE. Ref also: TM. SC: Charlotte Ellison (Pitt) and Insp. Thomas Pitt, also in all titles below. Set (all titles): Eng., 1880s.

Bluegate Fields. St. Martin's, 1984
Death in the Devil's Acre. St. Martin's, 1985
Paragon Walk. St. Martin's, 1981
Resurrection Row. St. Martin's, 1981
Rutland Place. St. Martin's, 1983

*PERRY, RITCHIE (JOHN ALLEN). Ref: TM. SC: Philis, also in titles marked P below.
Fool's Mate. Collins, 1981; Pantheon, 1981 <Fr.> P
Foul Up. Hale, 1985; Doubleday, 1982 P
Kolwezi. Hale, 1986; Doubleday, 1985 P
MacAlester. Doubleday, 1984

*PERRY, ROLAND. Freelance journalist in England; documentary scriptwriter, commentator, interviewer.

*PERRY, RUTH
The Red House Mystery. Dramatic, 1956 (3-act play based on the novel by *A. A. Milne, q.v.)

PERRY, STEVE. See also: J. Michael Reaves.
The Tularemia Gambit. GM, 1981

PERRY, THOMAS. Assistant coordinator of General Education program at Univ. of Southern Calif.; has Ph.D. in English from Univ. of Rochester. Ref: TM.
Big Fish. Scribner, 1985; Collins, 1986 <L.A.>
The Butcher's Boy. Scribner, 1982; Constable, 1982 <Las Veg.>
Metzger's Dog. Scribner, 1983; Collins, 1984 <L.A.>

*PERSICO, JOSEPH E(DWARD)
Never Forgive Never Forget. Allen, 1984

*PERTWEE, MICHAEL (HENRY ROLAND). See also: *Roland Pertwee.
*Night Was Our Friend. Film: Act, 1951 (scw: Michael Pertwee; dir: Michael Anderson)

*PERTWEE, ROLAND
Honours Easy. French (London), 1932 (3-act play.) Film: BIP, 1935 (dir: Herbert Brenon)
*Interference. Film: Paramount, 1928 (scw: Hope Loring, Ernest Pascal; dir: Lothar Mendes, Roy J. Pomeroy). Also: Paramount, 1935, as Without Regret (scw: Doris Anderson, Charles Bennett; dir: Harold Young)
Out to Win. Cassell, 1922. Silent film: Ideal, 1923 (scw & dir: Denison Clift)
The Paragon, with *Michael Pertwee, q.v. English Theatre, 1949 (2-act play.) Film: Independent, 1949, as Silent Dust (scw: Michael Pertwee; dir: Lance Comfort)
*Pink String and Sealing Wax. Film: Ealing, 1945 (scw: Diana Morgan, Robert Hamer; dir: Hamer)
*A South Sea Bubble. Silent film: Gainsborough, 1928 (scw: Angus MacPhail, Alma Reville; dir: T. Hayes Hunter)

*PETERS, ELIZABETH. SC: Vicky Bliss, also in title marked VB; Jacqueline Kirby, also in titles marked JK; Amelia Peabody Emerson, in *Crocodile on the Sandbank, and in titles marked AE below.
The Copenhagen Connection. Congdon, 1982; Souvenir, 1983 <Copen.>
The Curse of the Pharoahs. Dodd, 1981; Souvenir, 1982 <Egypt, ca.1900> AE
Die for Love. Congdon, 1984; Souvenir, 1985 JK <NYC>
*The Love Talker. JK
The Mummy Case. Congdon, 1985; Souvenir, 1986 AE <Egypt, late 1800s>
Silhouette in Scarlet. Congdon, 1983; Souvenir, 1984 VB <Swed.>

*PETERS, ELLIS. SC: Brother Cadfael, also in all titles below, set in 12th century Eng.
Dead Man's Ransom. Macmillan (London), 1984; Morrow, 1985
The Devil's Novice. Macmillan (London), 1983; Morrow, 1984
An Excellent Mystery. Macmillan (London), 1985; Morrow, 1986

The Leper of Saint Giles. Macmillan (London), 1981; Morrow, 1982
The Pilgrim of Hate. Macmillan (London), 1984
Saint Peter's Fair. Macmillan (London), 1981; Morrow, 1981
The Sanctuary Sparrow. Macmillan (London), 1983; Morrow, 1983
The Virgin in the Ice. Macmillan (London), 1982; Morrow, 1983

*PETERS, LUDOVIC
*Out by the River. <Balkans>

PETERS, RALPH. 1952- . Has been rock musician and professional soldier; living in Europe.
Bravo Romeo. Marek, 1981 <Ger.>

PETERS, STEPHEN. Pseudonym of Robert Lee Geiser, 1931- . Ref: CA.
The Park Is Mine. Doubleday, 1981; Blond, 1982 <NYC>

*PETERSEN, HERMAN. Ref: TM.

*PETERSON, BERNARD
The Marseilles Connection. Hale, 1985
*The Peripheral Spy. <Paris>

PETERSON, GARY and DAVID BYRNE
Klondike Kalamity. Dramatic, 19?? (3-act play.) <Can., 1888>

PETERSON, JACK
Balance of Power. Leisure, 1984 <Wash. D.C.>

*PETERSON, JAMES. Pseudonym of Henry A. Zeiger.
*Arrivederci, Baby! (Novelization of film: see *Richard Deming.)

PETIEVICH, GERALD. 1944- . Ref: CA, TM.
Money Men and One-Shot Deal. Harcourt, 1981; NEL, 1982 <L.A.> 2 novelets
The Quality of the Informant. Arbor, 1985 <Calif.>
To Die in Beverly Hills. Arbor, 1983 <L.A.>
To Live and Die in L.A. Arbor, 1984 <L.A.> Film: MGM, 1985 (scw: William Friedkin, Gerald Petievich; dir: Friedkin)

PETRI, DAVID
The Curtain of Night. Rotabook, 1982; Dell, 1983

*PETRIE, GLEN
The Tondeau of Chartres. Macmillan (London), 1981

PETTITT, WILFRID H(ENRY)
Nine Girls. Dramatic, 1943 (2-act play.) Film: Columbia, 1944 (scw: Karen DeWolf, Connie Lee; dir: Leigh Jason)

*PETTY, BARBARA
Don't Tell Daddy. Dell, 1982

PHARR, ROBERT DEANE. 1916- . Ref: CA.
-The Book of Numbers. Doubleday, 1969. Film: AVCO, 1973 (scw: Larry Spiegel; dir: Raymond St. Jacques)

*PHELAN, JIM
Ten-A-Penny People. Gollancz, 1938. Film: British National, 1938, as Night Journey (scw: Jim Phelan, Maisie Sharman; dir: Oswald Mitchell)

PHELPS, WINIFRED
Temptation Sordid. French, 1960 (1-act play.)

PHILBIN, TOM
Precinct #1: Siberia. GM, 1985 <NYC>
The Yearbook Killer. GM, 1981 <L.I.>

PHILBRICK, W. R. Lives in N.H. Ref: TM.
Shadow Kills. Beaufort, 1985. British title (?): Slow Grave. Hale, 1986 <Boston>
Slow Dancer. St. Martin's, 1984; Hale, 1986 <Maine>
Slow Grave; see Shadow Kills

*PHILIPS, (JOHN) AUSTIN (DRURY)
A Columbo Night. Mills, 1926 ss, some criminous

*PHILIPS, JUDSON (PENTECOST). Ref also: TM; revised: TC2. SC: Peter Styles, also in both titles below.
Murder As the Curtain Rises. Dodd, 1981 <Conn.>
Target for Tragedy. Dodd, 1982; Hale, 1983 <Conn.>

PHILIPS, MARY ALICE. Joint pseudonym with Doris O. Moore: *Philips Moore.

*PHILIPS, PAGE
*At Bay. Silent film based on play: Gold Rooster, 1915 (dir: George Fitzmaurice)

PHILIPSON, ALAN. See: Jack Hild.

*PHILLIPS, CLYDE B.
*The Driver. (Novelization of film: TCF, 1978; scw & dir: Walter Hill.)
*Somebody Killed Her Husband. (Novelization of film: Columbia, 1978; scw: Reginald Rose; dir: Lamont Johnson.)

*PHILLIPS, CONRAD
*Walk in the Dark. ... Roy, 1956

PHILLIPS, EDWARD
Death Is Relative. Avon, 1985. British title: Where There's a Will. Macmillan (London), 1985 <Montr.>

PHILLIPS, HUBERT. 1891- .
Heptameron. Eyre, 1945 ss, including six detective stories

*PHILLIPS, JAMES ATLEE. Ref also: TM.

*PHILLIPS, JEAN. Pseudonym of *Francis Swann.

PHILLIPS, JENNIFER
Bombshell. Allen, 1985

*PHILLIPS, LEON
Ritual Fire Dance. Hale, 1981

PHILLIPS, MARY. 1915- .
Catchee Chinaman. Henry, 1982

PHILLIPS, MEREDITH. 1943- . Author of a parent's guidebook to the S.F. Bay Area, has written for local and national publications; living in Calif.; founder and sole employee of Perseverance Press, dedicated to the publishing of mystery fiction.
Death Spiral. Perseverance, 1984 <Calif.>

*PHILLIPS, STELLA.
*Death in Sheep's Clothing. ... Walker, 1983

*PHILLPOTTS, EDEN
*The American Prisoner. Film: BIP, 1929 (scw: Eliot Stannard, Garnett Weston; dir: Thomas Bentley)
-The Drums of Dombali. Hutchinson, 1945
Fall of the House of Heron. Hutchinson, 1948
*George and Georgina. <Barbados>
*The Master of Merripit. Silent film: Clarendon, 1915 (dir: Wilfred Noy)
*There Was an Old Man. delete: not criminous

PHILO, THOMAS
Judgement by Fire. Bantam, 1985

PHIPPS, CONSTANTINE
Careful with the Sharks. Cape, 1985; Cape (U.S.), 1986

*PICARD, SAM. Pseudonym of *DeWitt (S.) Copp.

*PICI, J. R.
The Papa Legacy. Raven, 1981

PICKARD, NANCY. Lives in Kan. ref: TM. SC: Jenny Cain, in both titles.
Generous Death. Avon, 1984 <Mass.>
Say No to Murder. Avon, 1985 <Mass.>

PICKERING, PAUL
Wild About Harry. Atheneum, 1985; Weidenfeld, 1985 <Parag.>

PIECZENIK, STEVE R.
The Mind Palace. Simon, 1985 <Moscow>

PIERCY, MARGE. 1936- . Ref: CA.
-Fly Away Home. Summit, 1984; Chatto, 1984

PIERLAIN, NELL
    Cruel Triumph. Mystique, 1981
    (Translation of "La Divine." Paris,
    1978.)

PIKE, PETER
    Fool's Blooding. Hale, 1984

*PIKE, ROBERT
    *Mute Witness. Film: Warner, 1968, as
    Bullitt (scw: Alan R. Trustman,
    Harry Kleiner; dir: Peter Yates)

PIKSER, JEREMY. Playwright living in
    NYC.
    Junk on the Hill. Carroll, 1985;
    Pluto, 1984 <N.J.>

*PILPEL, ROBERT H(ARRY)
    *High Anxiety. (Novelization of film:
    TCF, 1977; scw: Mel Brooks, Ron
    Clark, Rudy DeLuca, Barry Levinson;
    dir: Brooks)

PINES, PAUL (ANDRE). 1941-   . Ref:
    CA.
    The Tin Angel. Morrow, 1983 <NYC>

*PINKERTON, ALLAN
    *The Molly Maguires and the
    Detectives. ... Haskell, 1983

PINTER, HAROLD. 1930-   . Ref: CA.
    The Dumb Waiter. Dramatists, 1960;
    French (London), 1960
    (1-act play.)

*PIPER, EVELYN
    *Bunny Lake Is Missing. <NYC> Film:
    Wheel, 1965 (scw: John Mortimer,
    Penelope Mortimer; dir: Otto
    Preminger)
    *The Lady and Her Doctor. <N.Y.>
    *The Nanny. Film: Hammer, 1965 (scw:
    Jimmy Sangster; dir: Seth Holt)

*PIPER, H(ENRY) BEAM. Ref: CA.

*PIRKIS, C(ATHERINE) L(OUISA)
    *The Experiences of Loveday Brooke,
    Detective. U.S. title: Loveday
    Brooke. Dover, 1986

PITT, GEORGE DIBDIN. 1799-1855.
    Rookwood. Dicks, 1882 (2-act play
    based on the novel by *W. Harri-
    son Ainsworth, q.v.)
    Sweeney Todd, the Demon Barber of
    Fleet Street. Dicks, 1883 (2-
    act play.) Silent film: QTS,
    1928 (dir: Walter West). Sound
    film: King, 1936 (scw: Frederick
    Hayward, H. F. Maltby; dir:
    George King)

PLANT, FRED
    Tales and Sketches. Henderson, 1901
    ss, some mildly criminous

PLATER, ALAN (FREDEICK). 1935-
    Ref: CA.
    The Beiderbecke Affair. Methuen pb,
    1985 (Novelization of TV serial.)

*PLATT, KIN. Pseudonym: *Kirby Carr,
    q.v.

PLATTS, A. MONMOUTH. Pseudonym of
    *A(nthony) B(erkeley) Cox.
    Cicely Disappears. Long, 1927

*PLEYDELL, GEORGE
    *The Ware Case. Film: Silent film:
    Broadwest, 1917 (scw: J. Bertram
    Brown; dir: Walter West). Also:
    Film Manufacturing, 1928 (scw:
    Lydia Hayward; dir: H. Manning
    Haynes). Sound film: Ealing, 1938
    (scw: Roland Pertwee, Robert
    Stevenson, E. V. H. Emmett; dir:
    Stevenson)

*PLOMLEY, ROY. 1914-1985. Ref: CA.

PLUMMER, ROGER S., JR. Pseudonym:
    *Roger Sherman.

PLUNKETT, JOHN
    She'll Get Hers. Monarch, 1960
    <L.A.>

*POE, EDGAR A(LLAN). Ref also: TM.
    See also: *Tim J. Kelly.
    *The Prose Romances of Edgar A. Poe.
    Silent film (from ss "The Murders
    in the Rue Morgue"): Rosenberg,
    1914, as The Murders in the Rue
    Morgue (scw: Sol A. Rosenberg).
    Sound film (from same ss): Univer-
    sal, 1932, as The Murders in the
    Rue Morgue (scw: Tom Reed, Dale Van
    Every, John Huston; dir: Robert
    Florey). Also (based on same ss):
    Warner, 1953, as Phantom of the Rue
    Morgue (scw: Harold Medford, James
    R. Webb; dir: Roy Del Ruth). Also
    (based on same ss): AIP, 1971, as
    The Murders in the Rue Morgue (scw:
    Christopher Wicking, Henry Slesar;
    dir: Gordon Hessler)
    *Tales. Film (from "The Mystery of
    Marie Roget"): Universal, 1942, as
    The Mystery of Marie Roget
    (scw: Michael Jacoby; dir: Phil
    Rosen)

*POHL, FREDERIK
    The Cool War. Ballantine, 1982;
    Gollancz, 1981 <future>
    Demon in the Skull. DAW, 1984;
    Penguin, 1985
    *Edge of the City. (Novelization of
    film: MGM, 1957; scw: Robert Alan
    Aurthur; dir: Martin Ritt.)
    Gladiator-at-Law, with *C. M. Korn-
    bluth. Ballantine, 1955; Digit,
    1958 <future>

*POLLINI, FRANCIS
    *Pretty Maids All in a Row. Film:
    MGM, 1971 (scw: Gene Roddenberry;
    dir: Roger Vadim)

*POLLITZ, EDWARD A., JR.
    Empire State. Macmillan, 1983 <NYC>
    The Scorpion's Sting. Dell, 1983

*POLLOCK, CHANNING
    The Sign on the Door. French, 1924
    (3-act play.) Silent film: Tal-
    madge, 1921 (scw: Mary Murillo,
    Herbert Brenon; dir: Brenon).
    Sound film: Feature, 1929, as
    The Locked Door (scw: C. Gardner
    Sullivan; dir: George Fitzmaurice)

POLLOCK, J. C.
    Centrifuge. Crown, 1984; Severn,
    1985 <Can.>
    Crossfire. Crown, 1985 <Czech.>
    The Dennecker Code. GM, 1982
    Mission M.I.A. Crown, 1982

*POLLOCK, ROBERT
    *Loophole. Film: Walker, 1980 (scw:
    Jonathan Hales; dir: John Quested)

POLMAR, NORMAN. See: *Thomas B(enton)
    Allen.

*PONDER, PATRICIA. Pseudonym of
    *Patricia (Anne Ponder) Maxwell.

*PONTHIER, FRANCOIS (CHARLES)

POPE, DUDLEY (BERNARD EGERTON).
    1925-   . Ref: CA.
    Convoy. Secker, 1979 <1942>
    Decoy. Secker, 1983; Walker, 1985
    <WWII>

POPE, RUSSELL
    The Startex Assignment. Messenger,
    1984

*POPKIN, ZELDA. Ref: not in TC2.

*POPPLEWELL, JACK
    Blind Alley. French (London), 1956
    (3-act play.) Film: Alderdale,
    1958, as Tread Softly Stranger
    (scw: George Minter, Denis O'Dell;
    dir: Gordon Parry)
    *Busybody. Film: Laterna, 1969, as
    Mordskab (Busybody) (dir: Bent
    Christensen)
    *Dead Easy. (3-act play.)
    Dear Delinquent. Dramatists, 1958;
    Evans, 1958 (3-act play.)

*PORLOCK, MARTIN
    *Mystery in Kensington Gore. Film:
    Universal, 1942, as Nightmare
    (scw: Dwight Taylor; dir: Tim
    Whelan)
    *X v. Rex. Film: MGM, 1934, as The
    Mystery of Mr. X (scw: Philip
    MacDonald, Howard Emmett Rogers,
    Monckton Hoffe; dir: Edgar Selwyn).
    Also: MGM, 1952, as The Hour of
    Thirteen (scw: Leon Gordon, Howard
    Emmett Rogers; dir: Harold French)

PORTEOUS, (THOMAS) CLARK. 1911-
    South Wind Blows. Wyn, 1948

PORTER, ANNA
    Hidden Agenda. Irwin (Toronto), 1985;
    Dutton, 1986

*PORTER, JOYCE. Ref also: TM.

PORTER, R. W.
    Kiss and Kill. Hale, 1981

PORTUGALI, M.
    Khamsin. Futura, 1981

PORTUS, G. V. See: J. L. Rankin.

*PORTWINE, E(LIZABETH) T.
    *The Limping Wolf. delete: children's
    fiction

POSARD, COLEMAN
    Stranglehold. Pinnacle, 1981 <Calif.>

POSEY, CARL A(LFRED, JR.). 1933-
    Ref: CA. SC: Steven Borg, in at
    least those marked SB.
    Dead Issue. Hale, 1985
    Kiev Footprint. Dodd, 1983; Hale,
    1983 SB
    Prospero Drill. St. Martin's, 1985;
    Hale, 1984 SB

*POSNER, RICHARD. See also: Marie
    Castoire.
    *The Seven-Ups. (Novelization of film:
    TCF, 1973; scw: Albert Ruben,
    Alexander Jacobs; dir: Philip
    D'Antoni)

*POST, MELVILLE DAVISSON. Ref also:
    CA, TM.

POTTER, F(REDERICK) SCARLETT. 1834-
    Walter Gaydon. Low, 1894

*POTTER, JEREMY
    *Going West. <N.Z., Australia>

*POTTER, JERRY ALLEN. SC: Sam Tucker,
    in *A Talent for Dying, and in
    title marked ST below.
    If I Should Die Before I Wake.
    Popular Library, 1981 <S.F.> ST
    Needle. Texas Monthly Press, 1984
    <Tex.>

*POTTS, JEAN. Ref also: TM.
    *Death of a Stray Cat. Also published
    as: Dark Destination. Detective
    Book Club, 1955

*POURNELLE, JERRY. Pseudonym: *Wade
    Curtis, q.v.

POWELL, E(DWARD) ALEXANDER. 1879-
    Red Drums. Washburn, 1935

*POWELL, JOHN D.
    The Mungwe Affair. Hale, 1985 <Afr.>
    The Sacred Cave. Hale, 1983

POWELL, LARRY. See: Dick Stivers.

POWELL, MARGARET. 1907(?)-1984. Ref:
    CA.
    The Butler's Revenge. Joseph, 1984

*POWELL, TALMAGE. Pseudonym also: Anne
    Talmage, q.v. Ref: TC2, TM.

POWER, M. S. Born in Dublin; living in
    Eng.
    The Killing of Yesterday's Children.
    Chatto, 1985; Viking, 1986
    <Belfast>

POWERS, ELIZABETH. 1944-   . SC: Viera
    Kolarova, in both titles.
    The All That Glitters: The Case of
    the Ice-Cold Diamond. Doubleday,
    1981 <NYC>
    On Account of Murder. Avon, 1984
    <NYC>

POWERS, RON(ALD DEAN). 1941-   . Ref:
    CA.
    -Face Value. Delacorte, 1979; Arrow,
    1981

POYER, DAVID C. 1949-   . Ref: CA.
    The Shiloh Project. Avon, 1981
    <South>

*POYER, JOE
    Vengeance 10. Atheneum, 1980; Joseph,
    1981

*PRAGER, J. SIMON
    *The Newman Factor. <Wash. D.C.>

PRANTERA, AMANDA. Born and educated in
    Eng.; studied philosophy; living
    in Rome.
    Strange Loop. Cape, 1984; Dutton,
    1985 <church>

*PRATHER, RICHARD S(COTT). Ref also:
    TM.

*PRATT, AMBROSE
   First Person Paramount. Ward, 1908
   The Golden Kangaroo. NSW Bookstall, 1913 <Australia>
   *The Great "Push" Experiment. <Syd.>
   Three Years with Thunderbolt. Cassell, 1907 <Australia>
   Wolaroi's Cup. NSW Bookstall, 1922 <Australia>

PRATT, BRUCE W. See: J. L. Rankin.

PRATT, DENNIS. Birth name of *Quentin Crisp.

*PRATT, (MURRAY) FLETCHER. Ref: CA.

PRESCOTT, CASEY. Studied in Beirut for 7 years; now employed by an American consulting firm.
   Asset in Black. Arbor, 1985

*PRESNELL, FRANK G.
   *Send Another Coffin. Film: United Artists, 1940, as Slightly Honorable (scw: Ken Englund, John Hunter Lay, Robert Tallman; dir: Tay Garnett)

PRESSBURGER, EMERIC. 1902-   . Ref: CA.
   -Killing a Mouse on Sunday. Harcourt, 1961; Collins, 1961. Also published as: Behold a Pale Horse. Bantam, 1964; Fontana, 1964. Film: Columbia, 1964, as Behold a Pale Horse (scw: J. P. Miller; dir: Fred Zinnemann)

*PREST, THOMAS PECKETT. 1810-1859. See: *Tim J. Kelly.

PREUSS, PAUL
   Broken Symmetries. PB, 1984; Penguin, 1984

*PRICE, ANTHONY. Ref also: BM, TM; somewhat expanded: TC2. SC: Dr. David Audley, also in titles below.
   Gunner Kelly. Gollancz, 1983; Doubleday, 1984
   Here Be Monsters. Gollancz, 1985; Mysterious Press, 1986
   The Old Vengeful. Gollancz, 1982; Doubleday, 1983
   Sion Crossing. Gollancz, 1984; Mysterious Press, 1985
   Soldier No More. Gollancz, 1981; Doubleday, 1982 <Fr., 1957>

PRICE, DIANNE
   The Savage Spirits of Seahedge Manor. Zebra, 1981
   Shadowtide. Zebra, 1985

PRICE, E. HOFFMAN. Pseudonym: *Hamlin Daly.

*PRICE, EVADNE
   *Once a Crook. Film: TCF, 1941 (scw: Roger Burford; dir: Herbert Mason)
   *The Haunted Light. Film: Gaumont, 1934, as The Phantom Light (scw: Ralph Smart, Austin Melford; dir: Michael Powell)
   *Red for Danger. Film: Wilcox, 1938, as Blondes for Danger (scw: Gerald Elliott; dir: Jack Raymond)

PRICE, JOHN-ALLEN
   Doomsday Ship. Zebra, 1982 <ship, WWII>
   Operation Night Hawk. Zebra, 1985 <WWII>

*PRICE, RICHARD
   *Bloodbrothers. Film: Warner, 1978 (scw: Walter Newman; dir: Robert Mulligan)

*PRICHARD, (VERNON) HESKETH. See: *K(atherine O'Brien) Prichard.

*PRICHARD, K(ATHERINE O'BRIEN) and *(VERNON) HESKETH PRICHARD
   *The Chronicles of Don Q. Silent film: B&C, 1912, as The First Chronicles of Don Q (scw: Harold Brett; dir: H. O. Martinek)
   *Don Q's Love Story. Silent film: Elton, 1925, as Don Q, Son of Zorro (scw: Jack Cunningham; dir: Donald Crisp)

PRIEST, CHRISTOPHER. 1943-   . Ref: CA.
   -The Glamour. Cape, 1984; Doubleday, 1985

*PRIESTLEY, J(OHN) B(OYNTON). 1894-1984. See also: *Ruth Holland.
   *Benighted. Film: Universal, 1932, as The Old Dark House (scw: Benn W. Levy, R. C. Sherriff; dir: James Whale). Also: Hammer, 1963, as The Old Dark House (scw: Robert Dillon; dir: William Castle)
   *Dangerous Corner. Film: RKO, 1934 (scw: Anne Morrison Chapin, Madeleine Ruthven; dir: Phil Rosen)
   *An Inspector Calls. Film: Watergate, 1954 (scw: Desmond Davis; dir: Guy Hamilton)
   *Laburnum Grove. Film: ATP, 1936 (scw: Anthony Kimmins, Gordon Wellesley; dir: Carol Reed)

PROCTER, CHARLES
   Pools of the Past. Bale, 1922. Silent film: Stoll, 1924, as The Notorious Mrs. Carrick (dir: George Ridgwell)

*PROCTER, MAURICE. Ref also: TM.
   *Hell Is a City. Film: Hammer, 1959 (scw & dir: Val Guest)
   *No Proud Chivalry. Longmans, 1946 (date correction)
   *Rich Is the Treasure. Film: Gibraltar, 1954, as The Diamond; released in the U.S. as The Diamond Wizard (scw: John C. Higgins; dir: Montgomery Tully)

*PROKOSCH, FREDERIC
   *The Conspirators. Film: Warner, 1944 (scw: Vladimir Pozner, Leo Rosten; dir: Jean Negulesco)

*PRONZINI, BILL. Ref also: TM; expanded: TC2. Joint pseudonym with *Jeffrey M(iner) Wallmann: William Jeffrey, q.v. SC: "Nameless" private eye, also in titles marked PE.
   Bindlestiff. St. Martin's, 1983; Severn, 1984 PE <S.F.>
   Bones. St. Martin's, 1985 PE <S.F.>
   Casefile: The Best of the "Nameless Detective" Stories. St. Martin's, 1983 ss PE
   Cat's Paw. Waves, 1983 PE <S.F.>
   Double, with Marcia Muller, q.v. St. Martin's, 1984 PE (with Muller's SC Sharon McCone) <San Diego>
   Dragonfire. St. Martin's, 1982; Hale, 1983 PE <S.F.>
   The Eye, with *John Lutz, q.v. Mysterious Press, 1984 <NYC>
   The Gallows Land. Walker, 1983; Hale, 1984
   Graveyard Plots. St. Martin's, 1985 ss, including 3 about PE
   Hoodwink. St. Martin's, 1981; Hale, 1981 PE <S.F.>
   Masques. Arbor, 1981 <New Or.>
   Nightshades. St. Martin's, 1984; Severn, 1986 PE <Calif.>
   Quicksilver. St. Martin's, 1984; Severn, 1985 PE <S.F.>
   Quincannon. Walker, 1985 <S.F., 1893>
   Scattershot. St. Martin's, 1982; Hale, 1982 PE

*PROPPER, MILTON (MORRIS). Ref also: TM.

*PRYCE, LARRY. See: Clive Branson.

*PRYCE, RICHARD
   *The Quiet Mrs. Fleming. criminous

*PUCCETTI, ROLAND (PETER)
   *The Death of the Fuhrer. <Ger., WWII>

*PUDNEY, JOHN (SLEIGH)
   *The Net. Film: General Film, 1952; released in the U.S. as Project M7 (scw: William Fairchild; dir: Anthony Asquith

*PUGH, EDWIN (WILLIAM) and *CHARLES GLEIG
   *The Rogues' Paradise. <S. Pac.>

PULLEIN-THOMPSON, DENNIS. 1919-
   Pseudonym: Denis Cannan, q.v.

PURDY, JAMES (AMOS). 1923-   . Ref: CA.
   Cabot Wright Begins. Farrar, 1964; Secker, 1965

PURDY-GORDON, CAROLYN. See: Stuart Gordon.

PURTILL, RICHARD (L.). 1931-   Ref: CA.
   Murdercon. Doubleday, 1982 <San Diego>

*PUTNAM, FRANK
   *The Raid on the Mint. Street, 1902

*PUZO, MARIO. SC: Michael Corleone, in *The Godfather, and in new title below.
   *The Godfather. Film: Paramount, 1972 (scw: Mario Puzo, Francis Ford Coppola; dir: Coppola). Also: Paramount, 1974, as The Godfather, Part II (scw: Francis Ford Coppola, Mario Puzo; dir: Francis Ford Coppola)
   The Sicilian. Linden, 1984; Bantam (London), 1985

PYE, MICHAEL. 1946-
   Kingdom Come. PB, 1985

PYLE, A(LBERT) M.
   Trouble Making Toys. Walker, 1985 <Cin.>

PYLES, DANNY. Pseudonym: *Sterling Harkins.

PYNCHON, THOMAS. 1937-   . Ref: CA.
   "V". Lippincott, 1963; Cape, 1963

*Q, JOHN. See: *John Quirk.

QUAMMEN, DAVID. 1948-   . Ref: CA.
   The Zolta Configuration. Doubleday, 1983; Hale, 1984 <S.W.>

*QUARRY, NICK
   *The Don Is Dead. Film: Universal, 1973 (scw: Marvin H. Albert; dir: Richard Fleischer)

QUAYLE, ANTHONY. 1913-
   -Eight Hours from England. Heinemann, 1945; Doubleday, 1946 <Alb.>
   On Such a Night. Heinemann, 1947; Little, 1948 <Med. Is.>

*QUEEN, ELLERY. Ref also: TM.
   The Best of Ellery Queen. Beaufort, 1985 ss, all but one reassembled from previous collections
   *The Chinese Orange Mystery. Film: Republic, 1936, as The Mandarin Mystery (scw: John F. Larkin, Rex Taylor, Gertrude Orr, Cortland Fitzsimmons; dir: Ralph Staub)
   *The Devil to Pay; see *The Perfect Crime (in next entry)
   *The Door Between; see *Ellery Queen, Master Detective (in next entry)
   *The Dutch Shoe Mystery. Film (freely derived): Columbia, 1941, as Ellery Queen and the Murder Ring (scw: Eric Taylor, Gertrude Purcell; dir: James Hogan)
   *The Spanish Cape Mystery. Film: Republic, 1935 (scw: Albert DeMond; dir: Lewis D. Collins)
   *A Study in Terror. (Novelization of film: Compton, 1965; released in the U.S. as Fog; scw: Donald Ford, Derek Ford; dir: James Hill)
   Ten Days' Wonder. Film: Hemdale, 1971, as La Decade Prodigieuse (Ten Days' Wonder) (scw: Paul Gegauff, Paul Gardner, Eugene Archer; dir: Claude Chabrol)

*QUEEN, ELLERY. House name.
   *Ellery Queen, Master Detective. (Novelization of film, which was derived from the Queen novel *The Door Between: Columbia, 1940; scw: Eric Taylor; dir: Kurt Neumann)
   *The Penthouse Mystery. (Novelization of film: Columbia, 1941, as Ellery Queen's Penthouse Mystery; scw: Eric Taylor; dir: James Hogan)
   *The Perfect Crime. (Novelization of film, which was derived from the Queen novel *The Devil to Pay: Columbia, 1941, as Ellery Queen and the Perfect Crime; scw: Eric Taylor; dir: James Hogan)

*QUENEAU, RAYMOND
   *We Always Treat Women Too Well. (Translation of novel published in French in 1947.) <Dublin, 1916> Film: CIC, 1971, as On Est Toujours Trop Bon Avec Les Femmes

(One Is Always Too Good to Women) (scw: Marcel Julian, Michel Boisrond; dir: Boisrond)

*QUENTIN, PATRICK
 *Black Widow. Film: TCF, 1954 (scw & dir: Nunnally Johnson)
 *The Man in the Net. Film: United Artists, 1959 (scw: Reginald Rose; dir: Michael Curtiz)
 *Puzzle for Fiends. Film: Merton Park, 1958, as The Strange Awakening; released in the U.S. as Female Fiends (scw: J. McLaren Ross; dir: Montgomery Tully)
 *Puzzle for Puppets. Film: Republic, 1948, as Homicide for Three (scw: Bradbury Foote; dir: George Blair)
 *Shadow of Guilt. Film: Cyclops, 1960, as L'Homme a Femmes (Ladies' Man) (scw: Maurice Clavel, Alain Cavalier, Jacques Cornu; dir: Cornu)

*QUEST, ERICA
 Design for Murder. Doubleday, 1981
 *The October Cabaret. ... Hale, 1986

*QUEST, RODNEY
 *Countdown to Doomsday. <future>
 *The Fenton Affair. <future>

*QUICK, DOROTHY
 *The Cry in the Night. <Long Is.>

QUILL, MONICA. Pseudonym of *Ralph McInerny, q.v. SC: Sister Mary Teresa, in all titles.
 And Then There Was Nun. Vanguard, 1984 <Chi.>
 Let Us Prey. Vanguard, 1982 <Chi.>
 Not a Blessed Thing! Vanguard, 1981 <Chi.>
 Nun of the Above. Vanguard, 1985 <Chi.>

*QUILLER-COUCH, SIR ARTHUR T(HOMAS). Ref also: CA.

QUINN, ALISON
 The Satyr Ring. Harlequin, 1983 <Eng.>

*QUINN, JAKE. Pseudonym of *Jim C. Conaway.

QUINN, JOHN. Pseudonym of Dennis Rodriguez. SC: Rod Gavin (The Terminator), in all titles.
 Chameleon Kill. Pinnacle, 1984
 The Checkmate Kill. Pinnacle, 1985 (actually published?)
 Crystal Kill. Pinnacle, 1984 <L.A.>
 The Kill Squad. Pinnacle, 1983 <Ark.>
 Mercenary Kill. Pinnacle, 1982 <Cent. Am.>
 Silicon Valley Slaughter. Pinnacle, 1983 <Calif.>

QUINN, PATRICK EDWARD
 The Jewelled Belt. Robertson (Melb.), 1896 <Melb.>

*QUINN, SIMON
 *The Human Factor. (Novelization of film: Bryanston, 1975; scw: Tom Hunter, Peter Powell; dir: Edward Dmytryk.)

*QUINNELL, A. J.
 Blood Ties. Hodder, 1984
 The Mahdi. Macmillan (London), 1981; Morrow, 1982 <Mid. East>
 The Snap; see Snap Shot
 Snap Shot. Macmillan (London), 1982. U.S. title: The Snap. Morrow, 1983 <Iraq>

QUINTON, ANN
 Storm Islands. Piatkus, 1985

*QUIRK, JOHN
 *The Tournament. (title originally published under this byline, not as by *John Q)

*RABE, PETER. Ref also: TC2, TM.

*RACE, PHILIP. Pseudonym of Elmer M. Parsons.

*RACINA, THOM. Pseudonym: Lisa Wells, q.v.

*RADFORD, E(DWIN ISAAC) and M(ONA) A(GUSTA MANGAN) RADFORD
 *The Six Men. Film: Planet, 1951 (scw: Reed de Rouen, Michael Law, Richard Eastham; dir: Law)

*RADFORD, JOHN P. Pseudonym of William Bentley.

*RADFORD, M(ONA) A(GUSTA MANGAN). See: *E(dwin Isaac) Radford.

*RADLEY, SHEILA. Ref: TM. SC: Insp. Douglas Quantrill, also in titles below.
 Blood on the Happy Highway. Constable, 1983. U.S. title: The Quiet Road to Death. Scribner, 1984
 Fate Worse Than Death. Constable, 1985; Scribner, 1986
 The Quiet Road to Death; see Blood on the Happy Highway
 A Talent for Destruction. Constable, 1982; Scribner, 1982

*RADNOR, ALAN. Pseudonym of Richard Lewis, 1945- , q.v.
 Possessed. Macdonald, 1982. Reprinted as by Richard Lewis: Futura, 1983

RADVANYI, NETTY REILING. 1900-1983. Pseudonym: Anna Seghers, q.v.

*RAFFERTY, S. S. Ref: not in TC2.
 Cork of the Colonies; see *Fatal Flourishes
 Die Laughing and Other Murderous Shtick. International Polygonics, 1984 ss <NYC>
 *Fatal Flourishes. Also published as: Cork of the Colonies. International Polygonics, 1984

RAFTERY, ROGER. 1950-
 The Pink Triangle. Univ. of Queensland Press, 1981

*RAGOSTA, MILLIE J.
 *Witness to Treason. <Eng., 1200s>

RAIMES, H. P.
 Fate Accompli. Hale, 1984

*RAINE, WILLIAM MacLEOD
 The Big Town Round-Up. Houghton, 1920; Hodder, 1922. Silent film: Fox, 1921 (scw & dir: Lynn Reynolds)
 The Fighting Edge. Houghton, 1922; Hodder, 1923. Silent film: Warner, 1926 (scw: Edward T. Lowe, Jr., Jack Wagner; dir: Henry Lehrman)

RAINEY, RICH. SC: Alex Dartanian (The Protector), in all titles.
 Cult 45. Pinnacle, 1984 <Md.>
 The Dragon Slayings. Pinnacle, 1985
 Hit Parade. Pinnacle, 1983 <Vienna>
 Nightmare Network. Pinnacle, 1984
 The Porn Tapes. Pinnacle, 1983 <NYC>
 Venus Underground. Pinnacle, 1982 <NYC>

*RAISON, MILTON M(ICHAEL)
 *The Phantom of Forty-Second Street. Film: Producer's Releasing, 1945 (scw: Milton Raison; dir: Albert Herman)

*RALEIGH, CECIL. See: *Joseph Lyons, -1917.

*RALEIGH, H(ILARY) M(ASON)
 *Excess Baggage. Film: Real Art, 1933 (scw: H. Fowler Mear; dir: Redd Davis)

*RALSTON, GILBERT A(LEXANDER)
 *Ben. (Novelization of film: Cinerama, 1972; scw: Gilbert A. Ralston; dir: Phil Karlson.)

RAMM, CARL. SC: James Hawker, in all titles.
 Chicago Assault. Dell, 1984 <Chi.>
 Deadly in New York. Dell, 1984 <NYC>
 Detroit Combat. Dell, 1985 <Det.>
 Florida Firefight. Dell, 1985 <Fla.>
 Houston Attack. Dell, 1985 <Houston>
 L.A. Wars. Dell, 1984 <L.A.>
 Vegas Vengeance. Dell, 1985 <Las Veg.>

*RAMSEY, ERIC. Pseudonym of *David (James) Hagberg, q.v. Other pseudonyms: David Bannerman, q.v., Robert Pell. See also: *Nick Carter.

RAMSEY, LILA
 The Bestseller. PB, 1981

RAND, ANNE BINKLEY. Pseudonym: Anne Binkley, q.v.

*RAND, AYN
 *The Night of January 16. Film: Paramount, 1941 (scw: Delmar Daves, Robert Pirosh, Eve Greene; dir: William Clemens)

RAND, JAMES S. Pseudonym of Bernard George Attenborough. Ref: CA.
 The Stake. McLellan, 1959

*RAND, LOU. Pseudonym of Lou Rand Hogan.
 *The Gay Detective. Saber, 1961

*RANDALL, BOB. Pseudonym of Stanley B. Goldstein, 1937- . Ref: CA.
 The Calling. Simon, 1981; Severn, 1982 <NYC>
 *The Fan. Film: Paramount, 1981 (scw: Priscilla Chapman, John Hartwell; dir: Edward Bianchi)
 -The Next. Warner, 1981; Sphere, 1983

RANDALL, DIANE. Pseudonym of *W(illiam) E(dward) D(aniel) Ross. Other pseudonym: *Lydia Colby.
 Dragon Lover. Jove, 1981 <Tokyo>

*RANDALL, JOHN
 The Haunted Theatre. French, 1941 (1-act play.)
 I Want a Nurse. French, 1940 (3-act play.)
 *Reserve Two for Murder. French, 1940 (3-act play.)

*RANDISI, ROBERT J(OSEPH). 1951- . Ref: CA, TC2, TM. See also: *Nick Carter. Pseudonym: W. B. Longley, q.v. SC: Miles Jacoby, in all titles below.
 Eye in the Ring. Avon, 1982
 Full Contact. St. Martin's, 1984; Macmillan (London), 1986 <NYC>
 The Steinway Collection. Avon, 1983 <NYC>

RANK, CLIFTON. Pseudonym of Courtman Davies.
 Bury Him Gently. Hamilton Stafford, 1952
 Mind My Shroud. Hamilton Stafford, 1952
 Tigers on Tuesday. Hamilton Stafford, 1952

RANKIN, J. L., JANE CLUNIES ROSS, G. V. PORTUS, ALLAN CLUNIES ROSS, RUTH BEDFORD, BRUCE W. PRATT, M. BARNARD ELDERSHAW, W. J. DAKIN, WALTER MURDOCH, S. ELLIOTT NAPIER, C. H. BERTIE, E. MARIE IRVINE, LESLIE VICTOR, FRANCIS JACKSON, ETHEL TURNER and NOELLE BRENNAN. Dakin was a Professor of Zoology at the Univ. of Sydney; Eldershaw was the pseudonym of Flora Eldershaw and Marjorie Barnard; Murdoch was a professor of English, author and critic; Bertie was a librarian and historian; Irvine was a Professor of Economics at the Univ. of Sydney.
 Murder Pie. Angus, 1936 <Australia, acad.>

RANSOM, DANIEL. Pseudonym of Edward Gorman, 1942- , q.v.
 Daddy's Little Girl. Zebra, 1985

*RANSOME, STEPHEN
 *Hearses Don't Hurry. Film: TCF, 1942, as Who Is Hope Schuyler? (scw: Arnaud d'Usseau; dir: Thomas Z. Loring)

*RAPHAEL, RICK
 The President Must Die. Norton, 1981 <Wash. D.C., 1990s>

RASOF, HENRY. 1946- . Ref: CA. See: *Nick Carter.

*RATH, E. J.
 *Too Many Crooks. Silent film: Vitagraph, 1919 (scw: Edward J. Montagne; dir: Ralph Ince). Also: Famous Players, 1927 (scw: Rex Taylor; dir: Fred Newmeyer)

*RATH, VIRGINIA. See: Theo Durrant.

*RATHBONE, JULIAN. Ref also: TM. SC: Jan Argand, in *The Euro-Killers, and in titles marked JA below.
 Base Case. Joseph, 1981; Pantheon, 1981 JA
 Lying in State. Heinemann, 1985; Putnam, 1986 <Madrid, 1975>
 A Spy of the Old School. Joseph, 1982; Pantheon, 1983

Watching the Detectives. Joseph, 1983; Pantheon, 1984 JA
*RATHBONE, RICHARD A(DAMS)
  *Death in the Drawing Room. <Conn.>
*RATTRAY, SIMON
  *Queen in Danger. Film: Hammer, 1953, as Mantrap; released in the U.S. as Man in Hiding (scw: Paul Tabori, Terence Fisher; dir: Fisher)
*RAVEN, CHARLES
  *Underworld Nights. ... Sportshelf, 1957
*RAVEN, JAMES
  The Venice Ultimatum. Hale, 1982
*RAVEN, SIMON (ARTHUR NOEL)
  *Doctors Wear Scarlet. Film: Grafton, 1970; also released as Incense for the Damned, and as Bloodsuckers (scw: Julian More; dir: Michael Burrowes)
RAVIN, NEIL. 1947-   . Ref: CA.
  Seven North. Dutton, 1985 <Wash. D.C., hosp.>
*RAWSON, CLAYTON. Ref also: TM.
  *Death from a Top Hat. Film: MGM, 1939, as Miracles for Sale (scw: Harry Ruskin, Marion Parsonnet, James Edward Grant; dir: Tod Browning)
  *No Coffin for the Corpse. Film: TCF, 1942, as The Man Who Wouldn't Die (scw: Arnaud d'Usseau; dir: Herbert I. Leeds)
RAY, JOHN PHILIP. 1929-   . Pseudonym: *Peter Lovegrove.
RAYGOR, LARRY
  Catherine's Twins. Manor, 1979 <Berlin, post WWII>
RAYMOND, DEREK
  The Devil's Home on Leave. Alison, 1985
  He Died with His Eyes Open. Alison, 1984; Del Rey, 1987. Film: Swaine, 1985, as On Ne Meurt Que 2 Fois (He Died with His Eyes Open) (scw: Jacques Deray, Michel Audiard; dir: Deray)
*RAYMOND, ERNEST
  *For Them That Trespass. Film: ABPC, 1949 (scw: J. Lee Thompson, William Douglas Home; dir: Alberto Cavalcanti)
*RAYMOND, JOHN. Both titles are in the Dempsey and Makepeace series.
  Blind Eye. Futura, 1985
  Lucky Streak. Futura, 1985
*RAYMOND, RENE BRABAZON. 1906-1985.
  Pseudonym: *James Hadley Chase, q.v.
RAYNER, BARNABAS F.
  The Dumb Man of Manchester. Lacy, 1850 (2-act play.) Silent film: Haggar, 1908 (dir: William Haggar)
*RAYNER, CLAIRE (BERENICE)
  The Virus Man. Hutchinson, 1985
RAYNER, RICHARD. Ref: CA.
RAYNOR, MOLLY
  The Claw. English Theatre, 1951 (1-act play.)
  Something in the Attic. English Theatre, 1953 (1-act play.)
*REACH, JAMES. SC: Wing, in at least those marked W below; also (following *Brett Halliday): Mike Shayne, in the title marked MS below.
  *The Case of the Laughing Dwarf. W
  *Lunatics at Large. W
  Murder over Miami. French, 19?? (3-act play.) <Miami>
  *One Mad Night. W
  *We're All Guilty. (3-act play.)
READ, F. T.
  A Tramp's Wallet. Saxton, 1902 ss, one or two criminous
*READ, PIERS PAUL
  -The Villa Golitsyn. Alison, 1981; Harper, 1981 <Nice>
*READE, CHARLES
  *Foul Play. Silent film: Edison, 1911. Also: Eclectic, 1914, as The Ticket-of-Leave Man (scw: Theodore Wharton; dir: Louis Gasnier, Donald Mackenzie). Also: Master, 1920 (scw: W. C. Rowden)
  Hard Cash. Low, 1863; Fields, 1868. Silent film: Master, 1921 (scw: Walter Courtenay Rowden; dir: Edwin J. Collins)
  -It Is Never Too Late to Mend. Bentley, 1856; Ticknor, 1856. Play: Toulouse, 1940 <Australia> Silent film: Edison, 1913 (scw & dir: Charles M. Seay). Also: Martin's, 1917 (scw & dir: Dave Aylott)
*READY, STUART
  Cherry Brandy. Deane, 1957 (1-act play.)
  The Danger Line. Deane, 1961; Baker, 1961 (3-act play.)
  Escape Route. French (London), 1964 (1-act play.)
  Find the Girl. Deane, 1949 (3-act play.)
  Jackie. Deane, 1951 (1-act play.)
  The Legend of Raikes Cross. Deane, 1948 (1-act play.)
  Members of the Jury. French, 1937 (1-act play.)
  Mr. Hunter. French, 1946 (1-act play.)
  Mr. Pottinger. Deane, 1956; Baker, 1956 (3-act play.)
  The Seven Widows of Hempstead. Deane, 1961; Baker, 1961 (3-act play.)
  Sister Craven. Deane, 1952 (3-act play.)
  To Settle for Murder. Deane, 1953; Baker, 1958 (3-act play.)
REAKES, PAUL
  Bang, You're Dead. French, 1981 (Play.)
  Night Intruder. New Playwrights, 1980 (1-act play.)
REAMY, TOM. 1935-1977.
  San Diego Lightfoot Sue. Ace, 1983 ss, some criminous
REARDON, JAMES. 1917-
  The Sweet Life of Jimmy Riley. Wyndham, 1981
REAVES, J. MICHAEL
  Darkworld Detective. Bantam, 1982 <future>
  Hellstar, with Steve Perry, q.v. Berkley, 1984 <future>
*REDGRAVE, MICHAEL (SCUDAMORE)
  *The Aspern Papers. (3-act play.)
REED, BARRY C(LEMENT). 1927- Ref: CA.
  The Verdict. Simon, 1980; Granada, 1982. Film: TCF, 1982 (scw: David Mamet; dir: Sidney Lumet)
REED, GRAHAM. 1923-   . Ref: CA.
  The Grey Monk Walks. Deane, 1968 (Play.)
  When Thieves Fall Out. Deane, 1966 (Play.)
REED, HOWARD. 1885-   .
  Drums of Death. Dramatic, 1930 (3-act play.)
  The Feed Store Mystery. Dramatic, 1933 (1-act play.)
  The Good Bad Man. Banner, 1937 (3-act play.)
*REED, ISHMAEL. Ref: not in TC2.
*REED, J(AMES) D(ONALD)
  *Free Fall. Film: Polygram, 1981, as The Pursuit of D. B. Cooper (scw: Jeffrey Alan Fiskin; dir: Roger Spottiswoode)
*REED, MARK. Pseudonym of *Norman A. Daniels, q.v.
*REESE, JOHN (HENRY).   -1981.
  *The Looters. Film: Universal, 1973, as Charley Varrick (scw: Howard Rodman, Dean Riesner; dir: Don Siegel)
*REESE, (JOHN) TERENCE. Ref: CA.
*REEVE, ARTHUR B(ENJAMIN). Ref also: TM. John W. Grey is the uncredited author of *The Master Mystery and *The Mystery Mind. Film (based on Craig Kennedy stories): Oliver, 1919, as The Carter Case (scw: John W. Grey; dir: Donald MacKenzie)
  *The Exploits of Elaine. Silent film: Eclectic, 1915 (scw: Charles W. Goddard, George B. Seitz; dir: Louis Gasnier, Seitz)
  *The Master Mystery. (Novelization of film: Octagon, 1919; scw: Arthur B. Reeve, Charles A. Logue; dir: Burton King, E. Douglas Bingham.)
  *The Mystery Mind. (Novelization of film: Supreme, 1920; scw: Arthur B. Reeve, John W. Grey; dir: Fred W. Sittenham, William S. Davis.)
  *The Romance of Elaine. Film: Pathe, 1915 (scw: Bertram Millhauser, Charles W. Goddard, George B. Seitz; dir: Seitz)
*REEVE, CHRISTOPHER. Pseudonym of Anne Webb.
REEVES, FIONNUALA. 1943-   . Ref: CA.
  Deadly Inheritance. Avon, 1983 <Ire.>
*REEVES, JOHN. Ref: CA.
  Murder Before Matins. Doubleday, 1984; Hale, 1986 <Toronto>
  Murder with Muskets. Doubleday, 1985 <Toronto, theatre>
*REEVES, ROBERT. ca.1912-1945. Ref: TM.
REEVES, ROBERT (NICHOLAS). Born in Birmingham, Ala.; taught history and literature at Harvard; living in Boston.
  Doubting Thomas. Crown, 1985; Collins, 1986 <Boston, acad.>
REID, JAN. 1945-   . Ref: CA.
  Deer in Water. Texas Monthly, 1985 <Tex.>
*REILLY, HELEN. Ref also: TM.
*REINSMITH, RICHARD. SC: Ray Martin (The Bodyguard), also in all titles marked RM below.
  -A Body for Christmas. Leisure, 1984 RM
  -A Body in Paradise. Leisure, 1984 RM
  -The Model Body. Leisure, 1984 RM
  -Nobody's Perfect. Leisure, 1984 RM
  -The Savage Stars. Tower, 1981
  -Somebody to Kill. Leisure, 1983 RM
*REISS, BOB
  The Casco Deception. Little, 1983; Little (London), 1984 <Maine, WWII>
  Divine Assassin. Little, 1985
*REIZENSTEIN, ELMER L.
  *On Trial. Film: Silent film: Essanay, 1917 (scw & dir: James Young). Sound film: Warner, 1928 (scw: Robert Lord, Max Pollock; dir: Archie Mayo). Also: Warner, 1939 (scw: Don Ryan; dir: Terry Morse)
REJAUNIER, JEANNE. 1934-   . Ref: CA.
  Affair in Rome. Pinnacle, 1981 <Rome>
REMBO, KENT
  Visiting Hours. Pinnacle, 1982 (Novelization of film: Filmplan, 1982; scw: Brian Taggart; dir: Jean Claude Lord.)
RENA, SARAH MARY. 1941-   Pseudonym: Sally Rena, q.v.
RENA, SALLY. Pseudonym of Sarah Mary Rena, 1941-   . Ref: CA.
  Painless Death. Weidenfeld, 1981
*RENARD, MAURICE
  *The Hands of Orlac. Silent film: Pan-Film, 1924, as Orlacs Hande (The Hands of Orlac) (scw: Ludwig Nerz; dir: Robert Weine). Sound film: MGM, 1935; released in the U.S. as Mad Love (scw: Guy Endore, P. J. Wolfson, John I. Balderston; dir: Karl Freund). Also: Riviera, 1960, as Les Mains D'Orlac (The Hands of Orlac) (scw: Edmond T. Greville, John Baines, Donald Taylor; dir: Greville)
*RENAULD, RON. Pseudonym: Charles Heath, q.v. At least the title marked A is a novelization of the "A-Team" TV series.
  Backwoods Menace. Target, 1985
  Bullets, Bikinis and Bells. Target, 1985 A
  *Fade to Black. (Novelization of film:

American Cinema, 1980; scw & dir: Vernon Zimmerman.)

*RENDELL, RUTH. Ref also: CA, BM, TM; TC2 (revised). SC: Chief Inspector Wexford, also in titles marked W.
Death Notes; see Put On by Cunning
The Fever Tree and other stories of suspense. Hutchinson, 1982; Pantheon, 1983 ss
*A Judgement in Stone. Film: Rawifilm, 1986; released in the U.S. as The Housekeeper (scw: Elaine Waisglass; dir: Ousama Rawi)
The Killing Doll. Hutchinson, 1984; Pantheon, 1984
Master of the Moor. Hutchinson, 1982; Pantheon, 1982
A New Girl Friend and other stories. Hutchinson, 1985; Pantheon, 1986 ss
Put On by Cunning. Hutchinson, 1981. U.S. title: Death Notes. Pantheon, 1981 W
The Speaker of Mandarin. Hutchinson, 1983; Pantheon, 1983 W
The Tree of Hands. Hutchinson, 1984; Pantheon, 1985
An Unkindness of Ravens. Hutchinson, 1985; Pantheon, 1985 W

RESNICK, MIKE <MICHAEL DIAMOND RESNICK>. 1942- . Ref: CA.
Eros at Zenith. Phantasia, 1984 <future> ch: andrew jefferson crane

RESNICOW, HERBERT. Born in NYC; inventor and construction project manager; lives in N.Y. Ref: TM. SC: Alexander Gold, in those titles marked AG.
The Gold Deadline. St. Martin's, 1984; Hale, 1985 AG <NYC, theatre>
The Gold Frame. St. Martin's, 1985; Hale, 1986 AG <NYC>
The Gold Solution. St. Martin's, 1983; Hale, 1984 AG <NYC>
Murder Across and Down. Ballantine, 1985
The Seventh Crossword. Ballantine, 1985 <Vt., acad.>

RETCHKIN, NORMAN. Pseudonym: *Mike St. Clair, q.v.

*REVELL, LOUISA. Pseudonym of Ellen Hart Smith.

REVELL, NELLIE
-Spangles. Grosset, 1926 (Novelization of silent film: Universal, 1926; scw: Leah Baird; dir: Frank O'Connor.)

REVERE, JOHN D. SC: Justin Perry (The Assassin), in all titles.
The Assassin. Pinnacle, 1983 <Ger.>
Born to Kill. Pinnacle, 1984 <Jam.>
Death's Running Mate. Pinnacle, 1985
Stud Service. Pinnacle, 1985
Vatican Kill. Pinnacle, 1983 <Rome>

*REY, PIERRE
TNT. Charter, 1985

*REYMOND, HENRY
*Deadlier Than the Male. (Novelization of film: Santor, 1966; scw: Jimmy Sangster, David Osborn, Liz Charles-Williams; dir: Ralph Thomas.)

*REYNOLDS, MRS. BAILLIE
*Confession Corner. Silent film (from title ss): Stoll, 1925, as Confessions (scw: Lydia Hayward; dir: W. P. Kellino)
*The Notorious Miss Lisle. Silent film: First National, 1920 (scw & dir: James Young)

*REYNOLDS, DALLAS McCORD. 1917-1983. Pseudonym: *Mack Reynolds, q.v.

*REYNOLDS, FREDERIC MANSELL. 1800-1850.

*REYNOLDS, GEORGE WILLIAM MacARTHUR
Wagner the Werewolf. Dicks, 1848

*REYNOLDS, MACK. Pseudonym of Dallas McCord Reynolds, 1917-1983.
The Lagrangists. Pinnacle, 1983 <future>

REYNOLDS, PHILIP. 1916- .
When and If. Sloane, 1952. British title: It Happened Like This. Eyre, 1953 (Translation from the French.)

REYNOLDS, PHILIP THOMAS. 1912- .
"Cigarette." Raines, 1941 (1-act play.)

REYNOLDS, WILLIAM J. Senior editor and book columnist in TWA's magazine "Ambassador"; grew up in Omaha. Ref: TM.
The Nebraska Quotient. St. Martin's, 1984; Macmillan (London), 1986 <Omaha>

*RHEA, NICHOLAS
Constable Across the Moors. Hale, 1982
Constable Around the Village. Hale, 1981; St. Martin's, 1982
Constable by the Sea. Hale, 1985
Constable in the Dales. Hale, 1983

*RHODE, JOHN. Pseudonym of *Cecil John Charles Street, 1884-1964. Ref also: TM.
*The Murders in Praed Street. Film: WB-FN, 1936, as Twelve Good Men (scw: Sidney Gilliat, Frank Launder; dir: Ralph Ince)

*RHODES, RICHARD
Sons of Earth. Coward, 1981; Deutsch, 1981 <Mo.>

*RHODES, RUSSELL (LAWRENCE)
The Third Fury. Pinnacle, 1985
Tricycle. PB, 1983; Hamlyn, 1985 <acad.>

RHODES, VIVIAN. Ref: TM.
Groomed for Murder. Ballantine, 1984; Futura, 1984 <L.A.>

RIBEIRO, JOAO UBALDO. 1941- . Ref: CA.
Sergeant Getulio. Houghton, 1978 (Translation of "Sargento Getulio." Brazil, 1971.) <Brazil>

RICE, CRAIG. Ref also: CA, TM.
*Eight Faces at Three. Also published as: Murder Stops the Clock. Mystery Novel of the Month, 1941
*Having Wonderful Crime. Film: RKO, 1945 (scw: Howard J. Green, Stewart Sterling, Parke Levy; dir: A. Edward Sutherland)
*Home Sweet Homicide. Film: TCF, 1946 (scw: F. Hugh Herbert; dir: Lloyd Bacon)
*The Lucky Stiff. Film: United Artists, 1948 (scw & dir: Lewis R. Foster)
Murder Stops the Clock; see *Eight Faces at Three

RICH, VIRGINIA. 1914-1985. Ref: TM. SC: Eugenia Potter, in all titles.
The Baked-Bean Supper Murders. Dutton, 1983 <Maine>
The Cooking School Murders. Dutton, 1982 <Iowa>
The Nantucket Diet Murders. Delacorte, 1985

*RICHARDS, CURTIS
*Halloween. (Novelization of film: Falcon International, 1978; scw: John Carpenter, Debra Hill; dir: Carpenter.)

*RICHARDS, GUY
The Canaris Papers. Arrow, 1982

RICHARDS, JUDITH
Triple Indemnity. Arbor, 1982

*RICHARDS, TAD
The Brain of Agent Blue, with Steven L. Vorillas. Dell, 1984
The Virgel Directive. Popular Library, 1981 <late 1930s>

*RICHARDSON, FRANK
*-The Secret Kingdom. (Sherlock Holmes)

RICHARDSON, FRANKLIN DAVID. Grew up in Fla.; army veteran.
The Keepers of the Walls. Vantage, 1983

RICHARDSON, JAMES H(UGH). 1894- .
Spring Street. Times-Mirror, 1922 <L.A.>

RICHARDSON, ROBERT. 1940- . Journalist and editor living in Eng.
The Latimer Mercy. Gollancz, 1985; St. Martin's, 1986

*RICHBERG, DONALD (RANDALL). Ref: CA.

RICHMOND, DAVID. See: Bob Hall.

*RICHMOND, MARY
*Troubled Heritage. <N.Z.>

RICHMOND, ROALDUS FREDERICK. 1910- Pseudonym: Roe Richmond, q.v.

RICHMOND, ROE. Pseudonym of Roaldus Frederick Richmond, 1910- . Ref: CA.
Kelleway's Luck. Leisure, 1981

*RICKETT, FRANCES. 1921- . Ref: CA.
Stalked. Avon, 1983 <NYC>

*RICO, DON. 1913-1985. Pseudonym: *Donelle St. Michaels.

*RIDEAL, CHARLES F. See: *Maurice Moser.

RIDER, RICK
Dyed for Death. Belmont, 1980 <Iran>

*RIDGE, W(ILLIAM) PETT. 1857-1930.
*Mord Em'ly. Silent film: Welsh-Pearson, 1922 (scw: Eliot Stannard; dir: George Pearson)

*RIDGEWAR, PHILIP and *COLIN FRASER
*The Switch. (Novelization of film: RFD, 1963; scw: Philip Ridgeway, Colin Fraser; dir: Peter Maxwell.)

RIDGWAY, ATHELSTAN
The Phantom Drummer. Melrose, 1926
-The Secret Net. Melrose, 1924
-The Street of Shadows. Melrose, 1928

*RIDLEY, ARNOLD. 1896-1984. Ref: CA.
*The Ghost Train. <Maine> Silent film: Gainsborough, 1927 (dir: Geza M. Bolvary). Sound film: Gainsborough, 1931 (scw: Angus MacPhail, Lajos Biro; dir: Walter Forde). Also: City Production, 1933, in Hungarian (scw: Laszlo Bekeffy; dir: Lajos Lazar). Also: Gainsborough, 1941 (scw: Marriott Edgar, Val Guest, J. O. C. Orton; dir: Walter Forde). Also: Dansk-Svensk, 1976, as Spoegelsestoget (Ghost Train) (scw: Leif Panduro, Bent Christensen; dir: Christensen) <Maine>
*Recipe for Murder. Film: Real Art, 1934, as Blind Justice (scw: Vera Allinson; dir: Bernard Vorhaus)
Tabitha, with *Mary (Irene) Cathcart Borer. French (London), 1956 (3-act play.) Film: Eternal, 1966, as Who Killed the Cat? (scw: Maurice J. Wilson, Montgomery Tully; dir: Tully)
*The Wrecker. Film: Gainsborough, 1928 (scw: Angus MacPhail; dir: Geza M. Bolvary). Also: Columbia, 1933 (scw: Jo Swerling, Albert Roge II; dir: Roge). Also: Gaumont, 1936, as Seven Sinners, released in the U.S. as Doomed Cargo (scw: Frank Launder, Sidney Gilliat, L. DuGarde Peach, Austin Melford; dir: Albert de Courville)

*RIENITS, REX
*Assassin for Hire. Film: Merton, 1951 (scw: Rex Rienits; dir: Michael McCarthy)

RIFBJERG, KLAUS
Anna, I, Anna. Curbstone, 1982 (Translation of "Anna (jeg) Anna.")

*RIFE, ELLOUISE A.
*Broken Promise. <Wash.>

RIGDON, CHARLES. Pseudonym: *Antonia Scott.

*RIGG, JENNIFER. Pseudonym: *Genevieve Scott, q.v.

*RIGGS, JOHN R(AYMOND). 1945- . Ref: CA. SC: Garth Ryland, in both titles.
The Last Laugh. Dembner, 1984 <Wis.>
Let Sleeping Dogs Lie. Dembner, 1985 <Wis.>

*RIGSBY, HOWARD
*Lucinda. <Calif.>

RINALDI, NICHOLAS. 1934- . Ref: CA.
Bridge Fall Down. St. Martin's, 1985

*RINEHART, MARY ROBERTS. Ref also: CA, TM.
  *The Bat. Silent film: United Artists, 1926 (scw: Roland West, Julian Josephson; dir: West). Sound film: United Artists, 1930, as The Bat Whispers (scw & dir: Roland West). Also: Allied Artists, 1959 (scw & dir: Crane Wilbur)
  -The Breaking Point. Doran, 1922; Hodder, 1922. Silent film: Famous Players, 1924 (scw: Edfrid Bingham, Julie Herne; dir: Herbert Brenon)
  *The Circular Staircase. Silent film: Selig, 1915 (dir: Edward J. LeSaint)
  *Dangerous Days. Silent film: Eminent Authors, 1920 (scw: Charles Kenyon; dir: Reginald Barker)
  *Miss Pinkerton. Film: Warner, 1932 (scw: Niven Busch, Lillie Hayward; dir: Lloyd Bacon). Also: Warner, 1941, as The Nurse's Secret (scw: Anthony Coldeway; dir: Noel M. Smith)
  *The State vs. Elinor Norton. Film: TCF, 1935, as Elinor Norton; released in Britain as The Case of Elinor Norton (scw: Ross Franken, Philip Klein; dir: Hamilton MacFadden)

*RING, ADAM
  *Killers Play Rough. <NYC>

RINGGOLD, JACOB. Pseudonym: Rodissi, q.v.

*RIPPON, MARION (EDITH)
  *The Hand of Solange. ... Severn, 1985

*RITA
  "Half a Truth." Hutchinson, 1911. Silent film: Stoll, 1922 (scw: Leslie Howard Gordon; dir: Sinclair Hill)
  My Lord Conceit. Maxwell, 1884; Lovell, 1888. Silent film: Stoll, 1921 (scw & dir: F. Martin Thornton)
  *The Pointing Finger. Silent film: Stoll, 1922 (scw: Paul Rooff; dir: George Ridgwell). Sound film: Real Art, 1933 (scw: H. Fowler Mear; dir: George Pearson)

*RITCHIE, JACK. Ref also: CA, TM.
  *A New Leaf. Film (from title ss): Paramount, 1970, as A New Leaf (scw & dir: Elaine May)

RITTER, JOHN P.
  Chinatown Charlie, the Opium Fiend. Ogilvie, 19?? (Novelization of play by *Owen Davis.)

RIVERE, ALEC. Pseudonym of *Charles A(lexander) Nuetzel. Other pseudonym: John Davidson, q.v.
  -Wantons of Betrayal. N.A.C., 1964 <S. Pac.>

*RIVES, HALLIE ERMINIE
  Satan Sanderson. Bobbs, 1907

*ROBBE-GRILLET, ALAIN. Ref also: BM.
  The House of Assignation. Calder, 1970 (Translation of "La Maison de Rendez-Vous." Paris, 1965.)
  Recollections of the Golden Triangle. Calder, 1984 (Translation of "Souvenirs du Triangle d'Or.")

ROBBINS, HAROLD. Pseudonym of Harold Rubin, 1912- . Ref: CA.
  -Never Love a Stranger. Knopf, 1948; Hale, 1958. Film: Allied Artists, 1958 (scw: Harold Robbins, Richard Day; dir: Robert Stevens)
  Stiletto. Mayflower, 1969. Film: AVCO, 1969 (scw: A. J. Russell; dir: Bernard Kowalski)

*ROBBINS, TOD
  *The Unholy Three. Silent film: MGM, 1925 (scw: Waldemar Young; dir: Tod Browning). Sound film: MGM, 1930 (scw: Elliot Nugent; dir: Jack Conway)

ROBERSON, JENNIFER. 1953- . Ref: CA.
  Smoketree. Walker, 1985

ROBERT, LESLIE
  The Dipo Flight. Kimber, 1985

*ROBERTS, BEN. See: *Ivan Goff.

*ROBERTS, CARL ERIC BECHHOFER. See also: *George Goodchild.

Don Chicago. Heritage, 1933. Film: British National, 1945 (scw: Austin Melford; dir: Maclean Rogers)

ROBERTS, DENYS (TUDOR EMIL). 1923-
  Ref: CA.
  Smuggler's Circuit. Methuen, 1954. Film: British Lion, 1958, as Law and Disorder (scw: T. E. B. Clarke, Patrick Campbell, Vivienne Knight; dir: Charles Crichton)

ROBERTS, E. C.
  The Strange Case of the Megatherium Thefts. Cambridge University Press, 1945 (Sherlock Holmes)

ROBERTS, ERIC
  Murder by Arrangement. Deane, 1961 (1-act play.)

ROBERTS, GEORGE
  Lady Audley's Secret. Scott, 1863 (2-act play based on the novel by *M. E. Braddon, q.v.)

ROBERTS, HENRY HUNTER
  Occupational Hazards. Leisure, 1981

*ROBERTS, IRENE
  Sister on Leave. Hale, 1982

ROBERTS, JACK. 1952- . Both titles are novelizations of the "Street Hawk" TV series.
  Cons at Large. Target, 1985
  Street Hawk. Target, 1985

*ROBERTS, JANE <JANE ROBERTS BUTTS>. 1929-1984.

ROBERTS, JOHN MADDOX and ERIC KOTANI
  Act of God. Baen, 1985

*ROBERTS, LEE
  *Little Sister. (not Little Murder)

*ROBERTS, LILLIAN. Pseudonym of Ira Wallach.
  Rafferty and the Gold Dust Twins. (Novelization of film: Warner, 1975; scw: John Kaye; dir: Dick Richards.)

*ROBERTS, MARK K. SC: Stonewall (Soldier for Hire), in all titles.
  Commando Squad. Zebra, 1982 <El Salvador>
  Jakarta Coup. Zebra, 1983 <Djakarta>
  Pathet Vengeance. Zebra, 1983 <Far East>

*ROBERTS, MORLEY
  The Keeper of the Waters and other stories. Skeffington, 1898 ss, some criminous
  *The Prey of the Strongest. <Can.>

ROBERTS, NORA. Lives in western Md.
  Night Moves. Harlequin, 1985 <Md.>

ROBERTS, PATRICIA
  Tender Prey. Doubleday, 1983; Chatto, 1983 <NYC, 1930s>

ROBERTS, S(IDNEY) C(ASTLE). 1887- .
  Christmas Eve. Cambridge Univ. Press, 1936 (Sherlock Holmes)

*ROBERTS, SUZANNE. 1931- . Ref: CA.

*ROBERTS, WILLO DAVIS. Ref also: TC2, TM.
  The Annalise Experiment. Doubleday, 1985 <Calif.>
  *Dangerous Legacy. <Nev.>
  The Face at the Window. Raven, 1981; Hale, 1983
  *The Girl Who Wasn't There. <Maine>
  A Long Time to Hate. Avon, 1982 <Calif.>
  The Sniper. Doubleday, 1984 <Wash.>

ROBERTSON, A. K.
  The Zurich Syndicate. New Horizon, 1983

*ROBERTSON, ALEXANDER
  Detective Grime's Triumph. Street, 1902

*ROBERTSON, CHARLES. Born in Glasgow; living in Conn. since age 12; has B.A. from Univ. of Conn. and M.A. from Fairfield Univ.
  The Children. Bantam, 1982
  The Omega Deception. Bantam, 1984 <1943>
  Red Chameleon. Bantam, 1985 <Calif., Moscow>

*ROBERTSON, CONSTANCE PIERREPONT NOYES. 1897-1985.

ROBERTSON, KEITH. See: Hamilton Seymour.

ROBERTSON, LANIE
  Back County Crimes. French, 19?? (3-act play.) <South>

*ROBESON, KENNETH. SC: Doc Savage, also in all titles below. The series number is given in parenthesis.
  The Black, Black Witch. Bantam, 1981 <Fr., NYC> (108)
  Death Had Yellow Eyes. Bantam, 1982 <NYC> (110)
  Devils of the Deep. Bantam, 1984 <ship> (123)
  The Fiery Menace. Bantam, 1984 (122)
  The Goblins. Bantam, 1985 (125)
  The Golden Man. Bantam, 1984 (117)
  The Headless Man. Bantam, 1984 (124) <Cent. Am.>
  Jui San. Bantam, 1981 (107) <Jap.>
  The King of Terror. Bantam, 1984 (120)
  The Laugh of Death. Bantam, 1984 (119)
  *The Magic Island. (not The Magic Mountain, as given in CF.)
  *The Man of Bronze. Film: Warner, 1975 (scw: George Pal, Joe Morhaim; dir: Michael Anderson)
  The Man Who Fell Up. Bantam, 1982 (112)
  The Man Who Was Scared. Bantam, 1981 (104) <NYC>
  One-Eyed Mystic. Bantam, 1982 (111)
  Peril in the North. Bantam, 1984 (118)
  The Pharaoh's Ghost. Bantam, 1981 <Egypt> (101)
  Pirate Isle. Bantam, 1983 (115)
  The Screaming Man. Bantam, 1981 (106) <Manila>
  The Secret of the Su. Bantam, 1985 (126)
  The Shape of Terror. Bantam, 1982 <Czech.> (109)
  The Speaking Stone. Bantam, 1983 (116)
  The Talking Devil. Bantam, 1982 (113) <Mo.>
  The Ten Ton Snakes. Bantam, 1982 (114) <Braz.>
  They Died Twice. Bantam, 1981 (105) <Cent. Am.>
  The Three Wild Men. Bantam, 1984 (121)
  The Time Terror. Bantam, 1981 <Can.> (102)
  The Whisker of Hercules. Bantam, 1981 (103)

*ROBIN, LILIANE
  Chasm of Fear. Mystique, 1981 (Translation of "Malgre ta Trehison." Paris, 1959.)
  Dangerous Fascination. Mystique, 1981 (Translation of "Dangereuse Fascination." Paris, 1970.)
  Love's Captain. Mystique, 1981 (Translation of "Le Fille des Sables." Paris, 1979.)
  Search for Yesterday. Mystique, 1981 (Translation of "Perfidie." Paris, 1978.)

*ROBINETT, STEPHEN (ALLEN)
  *The Man Responsible. <2000s>

*ROBINS, DENISE (NAOMI). 1897-1985.
  The Triumph of the Rat. Allan, 1927

ROBINS, ELEANOR
  Tormenting Memories. Doubleday, 1983

ROBINSON, ABBY. 1947- . Ref: CA.
  The Dick and Jane. Delacorte, 1985 <NYC>

*ROBINSON, F(REDERICK) W(ILLIAM)
  *The Wrong That Was Done. criminous

*ROBINSON, FRANK M(ALCOLM)
  The Great Divide, with John Levin (1944- ; ref: CA). Rawson, 1982 <late 1980s>
  *The Power. Film: MGM, 1967 (scw: John Gay; dir: Byron Haskin)

ROBINSON, JANICE. 1937- .
  Deadly Inheritance. Hale, 1983
  Silent Killing. Hale, 1985

ROBINSON, JEFFREY
  Pietrov and Other Games. NEL, 1985

*ROBINSON, JIM
  *Together Brothers. (Novelization of film: TCF, 1974; scw: Jack De Witt, Joe Greene; dir: William A. Graham.)

*ROBINSON, LEWIS (GEORGE)
  *The General Goes Too Far. Film: ABFD, 1936, as The High Command (scw: Katherine Strueby, Walter Meade, Val Valentine; dir: Thorold Dickinson)

ROBINSON, PERCY. 1863- .
  The Crime of Margaret Foley. French, 1946 (Play.)
  To What Red Hell. Putnam, 1928 (Play.) Film: Strand, 1929 (scw: Leslie Hiscott; dir: Edwin Greenwood)
  The Whispering Gallery, with Terence De Marney. French, 1930 (3-act play.)

*ROBINSON, RICHARD
  *High Ballin'. (Novelization of film: American International, 1978; scw: Paul Edwards; dir: Peter Carter.)

*ROBINSON, SONDRA TILL. See: Susan Lee, 1944- .

ROBINSON, VINCE. Pseudonym of Michael Newton, 1951- . Other pseudonym: John Cannon, q.v. See also: *Don(ald Eugene) Pendleton.
  Death at Sea. Carousel, 1981
  Killer-Stalk. Carousel, 1982
  Terror at Boulder Dam. Carousel, 1981

*ROBY, MARY LINN
  *And Die Remembering. <Eng.>
  *Dig a Narrow Grave. <Eng.>

*ROCHE, ARTHUR SOMERS
  *The Case Against Mrs. Ames. Film: Paramount, 1936 (scw: Gene Towne, Graham Baker; dir: William A. Seiter)
  Come to My House. Century, 1927. Silent film: Fox, 1928 (scw: Marion Orth; dir: Alfred E. Green)
  *Find the Woman. Silent film: Cosmopolitan, 1922 (scw: Doty Hobart; dir: Tom Terriss)
  *Loot. Silent film: Universal, 1917, as The Gray Ghost (scw & dir: Stuart Paton). Also (?): Universal, 1919 (scw: Violet Clark; dir: William C. Dowlan)
  *Penthouse. Film: MGM, 1933; released in Britain as Crooks in Clover (scw: Frances Goodrich, Albert Hackett; dir: W. S. Van Dyke). Also: MGM, 1939, as Society Lawyer (scw: Frances Goodrich, Albert Hackett, Leon Gordon, Hugo Butler; dir: Edwin L. Marin)
  *The Pleasure Buyers. Silent film: Warner, 1925 (scw: Hope Loring, Louis D. Lighton; dir: Chester Withey)
  *Plunder. Silent film: Mayflower, 1922, as Living Lies (dir: Emile Chautard)
  *Shadow of Doubt. Film: MGM, 1935 (scw: Wells Root; dir: George B. Seitz)
  *The Star of Midnight. Film: RKO, 1935 (scw: Howard J. Green, Anthony Veiller, Edward Kaufman; dir: Stephen Roberts)

*ROCK, PHILIP
  *Dirty Harry. (Novelization of film: Warner, 1971; scw: Harry Julian Fink, R. M. Fink, Dean Riesner; dir: Don Siegel.)
  *Hickey and Boggs. (Novelization of film: United Artists, 1972; scw: Walter Hill; dir: Robert Culp.)
  *Tick...Tick...Tick. (Novelization of film: MGM, 1970; scw: James Lee Barrett; dir: Ralph Nelson.)

*RODDA, (PERCIVAL) CHARLES
  *Golden Corn. delete: not criminous

RODDY, LEE
  The Mystery of Aloha House. Chime, 1981

RODERICK, ROBERT. 1927- .
  The Greek Position. Wyndham, 1981; Sidgwick, 1981

RODERUS, FRANK. 1942- . Ref: CA.
  SC: Carl Heller, in all titles.
  The Coyote Crossing. Bantam, 1985
  The Dead Heat. Bantam, 1985
  <N. Mex.>
  The Oil Rig. Bantam, 1984 <Wyo.>
  The Rain Rustlers. Bantam, 1984 <Colo.>
  The Turn-Out Man. Bantam, 1984 <Reno>
  The Video Vandal. Bantam, 1984 <Colo.>

RODISSI. Pseudonym of Jacob Ringgold. Lord Jacquelin Burkney, the Whitechapel Terror. Anton, 1889

RODRIGUEZ, DENNIS. Pseudonym: John Quinn, q.v.

*ROEBURT, JOHN
  *Al Capone. (Novelization of film: Allied Artists, 1959; scw: Malvin Wald, Henry F. Greenberg; dir: Richard Wilson.)
  *The Unholy Wife. (Novelization of film: Universal, 1957; scw: Jonathan Latimer; dir: John Farrow.)

*ROFFEY, JACK
  *Hostile Witness. Film: Caralan, 1968 (scw: Jack Roffey; dir: Ray Milland)

ROGAN, DON
  Dames Take to Crime. Modern Fiction, 1950
  Gunmen Die Hard. Modern Fiction, 1951
  Unhappy Souls. Modern Fiction, 1950

ROGERS, CHUCK. See: Dick Stivers.

*ROGERS, GARET
  *Scandal in Eden. <S.F., ca.1930>

*ROGERS, J. TRUMBELL. See: *Marian J. Herrick.

*ROGERS, JAMES CASS
  *Foul Play. (Novelization of film: Paramount, 1978; scw & dir: Colin Higgins.)
  *Silver Streak. (Novelization of film: TCF, 1976; scw: Colin Higgins; dir: Arthur Hiller.)

*ROGERS, JOEL TOWNSLEY. 1896-1984. Ref also: TM.
  *The Red Right Hand. ... Panther, 1957

ROGERS, LANNY
  Crime Has No Friends. Spencer, 1951 <S.F.>

ROGERS, M. I. H.
  Horror in Hawaii. Mitre, 1944 <Haw.>

*ROGERS, MILTON
  *-Born Reckless. (Novelization of film: Warner, 1959; scw: Richard Landau; dir: Howard W. Koch.)

*ROGERS, SAMUEL (GREENE ARNOLD). Ref also: TM.
  *Don't Look Behind You! <Wis.>

*ROHMER, RICHARD (HEATH)
  Triad. Beaufort, 1982

*ROHMER, SAX. Ref also: CA, TM.
  *Daughter of Fu Manchu. Film: Paramount, 1931, as Daughter of the Dragon (scw: Lloyd Corrigan, Monte Katterjohn; dir: Corrigan)
  *The Devil Doctor. Film: Paramount, 1930, as The Return of Dr. Fu-Manchu (scw: Lloyd Corrigan; dir: Rowland V. Lee)
  *The Drums of Fu Manchu. Film: Republic, 1940 (scw: Franklyn Adreon, Morgan L. Cox, Ronald Davidson, Norman S. Hall, Barney A. Sarecky, Sol Shor; dir: William Witney, John English)
  *The Mask of Fu Manchu. Film: MGM, 1932 (scw: Irene Kuhn, Edgar Allan Woolf, John Willard; dir: Charles Brabin)
  *The Mystery of Dr. Fu-Manchu. Film: Paramount, 1929, as The Mysterious Dr. Fu Manchu (scw: Florence Ryerson, Lloyd Corrigan; dir: Rowland V. Lee)
  *Slaves of Sumuru. Film: Sumuru, 1967 (scw: Peter Welbeck; dir: Lindsay Shonteff)
  *The Yellow Claw. Silent film: Stoll, 1920 (scw: Gerard Fort Buckle; dir: Rene Plaissetty)

ROLAND, DONALD. Pseudonym: *Melissa Cordell.

*ROLFE, MARIO O(RLANDO)
  *The Band of Mystery. Street, 1902 (Magnet #259)
  *The Branded Hand. Street, 1903 (Magnet #303)
  *The Cross in the Dust. Street, 1904 (Magnet #325) (title correction)
  *An Eye for an Eye. Street, 1903 (Magnet #277)
  *The Man Who Knew. Street, 1903 (Magnet #269)
  *On the Stroke of Midnight. Street, 1903 (Magnet #293)
  *A Queen of Blackmailers. Street, 1904 (Magnet #347)
  *A Rascal's Nerve. Street, 1903 (Magnet #285)
  *A Secret Suspicion. Street, 1904 (Magnet #331)
  *A Transatlantic Puzzle. Street, 1903 (Magnet #311)
  *The Two Conspirators. Street, 1904 (Magnet #341)

*ROMAINE, DALLAS. Pseudonym of Norah Gibbs.

ROMANES, JULIAN
  Berlin Breakout. Allen, 1985; St. Martin's, 1985 <Berlin, 1948>
  -The Raid. Allen, 1983 <WWII>

*ROME, ANTHONY
  *The Lady in Cement. Film: TCF, 1968 (scw: Marvin H. Albert, Jack Guss; dir: Gordon Douglas)
  *Miami Mayhem. Film: TCF, 1967, as Tony Rome (scw: Richard L. Breen; dir: Gordon Douglas)

*RONALD, JAMES
  *Death Croons the Blues. Film: St. Margaret's, 1937 (scw: H. Fowler Mear; dir: David Macdonald)
  *Murder in the Family. Film: Fox British, 1938 (scw: David Evans; dir: Albert Parker)
  *They Can't Hang Me! Film: Universal, 1939, as The Witness Vanishes (scw: Robertson White; dir: Otis Garrett)
  *This Way Out. Film: Universal, 1945, as The Suspect (scw: Bertram Millhauser; dir: Robert Siodmak)

*RONNS, EDWARD
  *-But Not for Me. (Novelization of film: Paramount, 1959; scw: John Michael Hayes; dir: Walter Lang.)
  *The Glass Cage. Reprinted as by Aarons: Manor, 1973
  *The Lady Takes a Flier. (Novelization of film: Universal, 1958; scw: Danny Arnold; dir: Jack Arnold.)
  *Pickup Alley. (Novelization of film: studio?, 1957; scw: John Paxton.)

*RONSON, MARK. Pseudonym of Marc Alexander, 1929- . Other pseudonym: Marcus Aylward, q.v.

*ROOK, TONY
  The Labrador Trust. Hale, 1983

ROONEY, FRANK
  -The Heel of Spring. Vanguard, 1956; Bodley, 1957

*ROOS, AUDREY (KELLEY). Ref also: CA.
  *Speaking of Murder. (3-act play.) <N.Y.>

*ROOS, KELLEY. Ref also: TM.
  *The Blonde Died Dancing. Film: Kingsley, 1960, as Come Dance with Me (existence of film not confirmed)
  *The Frightened Stiff. Film: Columbia, 1942, as A Night to Remember (scw: Richard Flournoy, Jack Henley; dir: Richard Wallace)
  *Ghost of a Chance. Film: Scent of Mystery Productions, 1959, as Scent of Mystery (scw: William Roos; dir: Jack Cardiff)
  *If the Shroud Fits. Film: Columbia, 1943, as Dangerous Blondes (scw: Richard Flournoy, Jack Henley; dir: Leigh Jason)
  Murder on Martha's Vineyard. Walker, 1981; Hale, 1982 <Mass.>

ROOSEVELT, ELLIOTT. 1910- . Ref: CA. SC: Eleanor Roosevelt, in both titles.
  The Hyde Park Murder. St. Martin's, 1985; Weidenfeld, 1985 <N.Y., 1935>
  Murder and the First Lady. St. Martin's, 1984; Weidenfeld, 1984 <Wash. D.C., ca.1940>

R

*ROOSEVELT, FRANKLIN D(ELANO). Ref: CA.
  *The President's Mystery Story. Revised edition title: The President's Murder Plot. Film: Republic, 1936, as The President's Mystery (scw: Lester Cole, Nathaniel West; dir: Phil Rosen)

*ROOTE, MIKE
  *Badge 373. (Novelization of film: Paramount, 1973; scw: Pete Hamill; dir: Howard W. Koch.)
  *Born to Win. (Novelization of film: United Artists, 1971; scw: David Scott Milton; dir: Ivan Passer.)
  *CC and Company. (Novelization of film: AVCO, 1970; scw: Roger Smith; dir: Seymour Robbie.)
  *Enter the Dragon. (Novelization of film: Warner, 1973; scw: Michael Allin; dir: Robert Clouse.)
  *Prime Cut. (Novelization of film: Cinema Center, 1972; scw: Robert Dillon; dir: Michael Ritchie.)
  *Scorpio. (Novelization of film: United Artists, 1973; scw: David W. Rintels, Gerald Wilson; dir: Michael Winner.)

*ROPER, L(ESTER) V.
  The Reunion. Dell, 1981
  *Rage. (Novelization of film; see *Philip Friedman.)

*ROSCOE, MIKE. Ref: TM.

*ROSCOE, THEODORE
  *Only in New England. <1911>

*ROSE, EDWARD E(VERETT)
  *The Rear Car. Silent film: Goldwyn, 1923, as Red Lights (scw: Carey Wilson; dir: Clarence G. Badger). Sound film: MGM, 1934, as Murder in the Private Car (scw: Ralph Spence, Edgar Allan Woolf, Al Boasberg; dir: Harry Beaumont)

ROSE, REGINALD. 1920-   . Ref: CA.
  Twelve Angry Men. Dramatic, 1955; French (London), 1965 (3-act play.) Film: United Artists, 1957 (scw: Reginald Rose; dir: Sidney Lumet)

ROSE, RICHARD M.
  The Satyr Candidate. Exposition, 1979

ROSEN, DOROTHY. 1916-   . See: Sidney Rosen, 1916-

ROSEN, R(ICHARD) D(EAN). 1949-   . Lives in Boston area; writes and produces shows for public TV; his articles and essays have been widely published; author of two previous volumes of non-fiction. Ref: TM.
  Strike Three You're Dead. Walker, 1984 <R.I.>

ROSEN, SIDNEY, 1916-   , and DOROTHY ROSEN, 1916-   . Ref for both: CA.
  Death and Blintzes. Walker, 1985 <Boston, 1935>

ROSEN, VICTOR J. See: Terence Mix.

ROSENBERG, STEPHEN N(ICHOLAS). 1941-   . Ref: CA.
  The Brenda Maneuver. Newmarket, 1982 <NYC>

*ROSENBERGER, JOSEPH. Ref: TM. SC: Richard Camellion (The Death Merchant), also in all titles below.
  Afghanistan Crashout. Pinnacle, 1983 <Afghan.>
  Apocalypse U.S.A! Pinnacle, 1983
  The Atlantean Horror. Pinnacle, 1985 <Antarctic>
  Blood Bath. Pinnacle, 1981
  The Bulgarian Termination. Pinnacle, 1984
  The Burma Probe. Pinnacle, 1984 <Burma>
  *The Castro File. ... Corgi, 1982
  The Devil's Trashcan. Pinnacle, 1981 <Austria>
  *The Enigma Project. <Turk.>
  The Flight of the Phoenix. Pinnacle, 1982
  The Hellbomb Theft. Pinnacle, 1982
  The Inca File. Pinnacle, 1982
  Island of the Damned. Pinnacle, 1981
  The Judas Scrolls. Pinnacle, 1983
  *The Laser War. <Libya>
  The Methuselah Factor. Pinnacle,
   1984 <Ger.>
  Night of the Peacock. Pinnacle, 1982 <Yemen>
  Operation Skyhook. Pinnacle, 1981 <Indon.>
  The Pakistan Kill Ground. Pinnacle, 1985 <Pak.>
  The Psionics War. Pinnacle, 1982
  The Rim of Fire Conspiracy. Pinnacle, 1981
  The Roumanian Operation. Pinnacle, 1983
  The Silicon Valley Connection. Pinnacle, 1984 <Calif.>
  Slaughter in El Salvador. Pinnacle, 1983 <El Salvador>
  The Soul Search Project. Pinnacle, 1985
  *The Zembya Expedition. <ship, Arctic>

*ROSENBLUM, ROBERT (J.). Pseudonym: Robert Maxxe, q.v.

ROSENFELD, LULLA. 1914-   . Ref: CA.
  Death and the I Ching. Potter, 1981

*ROSMANITH, OLGA L. Pseudonym of Ferney Wood.

*ROSNER, JOSEPH
  Public Faces in Private Places. Delacorte, 1966

ROSS, ALLAN CLUNIES. See: J. L. Rankin.

*ROSS, ANGUS. SC: Marcus Aurelius Farrow, also in all titles below.
  A Bad April. Firecrest, 1984
  The Darlington Jaunt. Hale, 1983; Walker, 1984
  The Luxembourg Run. Firecrest, 1985
  The Manchester Connection; see *The Manchester Thing
  *The Manchester Thing. Reprinted as: The Manchester Connection. Severn, 1984
  The Menwith Tangle. Hale, 1982

*ROSS, CAMERON
  The Scaffold. Hale, 1981
  Villa Plot, Counterplot. Hale, 1981

*ROSS, CLARISSA
  The Dancing Years. Pinnacle, 1982 <ship, 1933>
  Satan Whispers. Leisure, 1981; Star, 1981
  *Voice from the Grave. <NYC>

*ROSS, DAN
  Moscow Maze. Leisure, 1983
  Murder Game. Playwrights, 1982 (Play.)
  *Out of the Night. <Can.>
  This Frightened Lady. Marginal, 1984 (Play.)

*ROSS, FRANK
  Goldship. Macmillan (London), 1981 (Probably by Colin Northway alone.)
  The Shining Day. Macmillan (London), 1981; Atheneum, 1981 <Eng., WWII> (by Michael Ewings alone)

ROSS, JANE CLUNIES. See: J. L. Rankin.

ROSS, JO ANN
  Risky Pleasure. Harlequin, 1985 <Calif.>

*ROSS, JOHN. Apparently pseudonym of Rudolph Clifford Jones, 1912-1987. Irish broadcaster and journalist.

*ROSS, JONATHAN. SC: Insp. George Rogers, also in all titles below.
  Burial Deferred. Constable, 1985; St. Martin's, 1986
  Dark Blue and Dangerous. Constable, 1981; Scribner, 1981
  Dead Eye. Constable, 1983; St. Martin's, 1984
  Death's Head. Constable, 1982; St. Martin's, 1983
  Dropped Dead. Constable, 1984; St. Martin's, 1985
  *A Rattling of Old Bones. ... Scribner, 1982

*ROSS, LEONARD Q.
  *The Dark Corner. Film: TCF, 1946 (scw: Jay Dratler, Bernard Schoenfeld; dir: Henry Hathaway)
  *Sleep My Love. criminous. Film: United Artists, 1948 (scw: St. Clair McKelway, Leo Rosten; dir: Douglas Sirk)

*ROSS, MARILYN
  *House of Dark Shadows. (Novelization of film: MGM, 1970; released in the U.S. as Dark Shadows; scw: Sam Hall, Gordon Russell; dir: Dan Curtiss.)

ROSS, MORGAN
  Any Number Can Die! Tower, 1981 <Calif.>

*ROSS, PAUL B.
  *Freebie and the Bean. (Novelization of film: Warner, 1974; scw: Robert Kaufman; dir: Richard Rush.)

ROSS, PHILIP. 1932-   . Pseudonym of writer and college professor who attended Amherst and Yale Drama School and who is writing a textbook on stage design.
  Blue Heron. Tor, 1985
  A Good Death. Dodd, 1983 <Switz.>
  The Kreuzeck Coordinates. Tor, 1985 <Austria>

*ROSS, REGINA
  The Face of Danger. Avon, 1982 <Czech.>

ROSS, ROBERT (BALDWIN). 1869-1918.
  Masques and Phases. Humphreys, 1909 ss, some criminous

*ROSS, SAM
  *He Ran All the Way. Film: United Artists, 1951 (scw: Guy Endore, Hugo Butler; dir: John Berry)
  *Ready for the Tiger. <L.A.>

*ROSS, W(ILLIAM) E(DWARD) D(ANIEL).
  Sometimes joint pseudonym with Orlando Joseph Rigoni: *Leslie Ames. Other pseudonyms: *Lydia Colby; Diane Randall, q.v.

ROSSEL, CAROL-LYNN
  Show Business Is Murder. Avon (U.K.), 1983

*ROSSI, BRUNO
  *Savage Slaughter. (by Paul Hofrichter)
  *Scarfaced Killer. (by Paul Hofrichter)
  *Triggerman. (by Russell Smith)

ROSSITER, ELIZABETH
  The Lemon Garden. Constable, 1983 <It.>

*ROSSITER, JOHN
  The Andropov Deception. Sherwood, 1984
  -Dark Flight. Eyre, 1981; Atheneum, 1981 <WWII>

*ROSSNER, ROBERT. Ref also: TM.
  *The End of Someone Else's Rainbow. Film: AAA/Revcon, 1985, as L'Homme aux Yeux d'Argent (The Man with Silver Eyes) (scw: Pierre Granier-Deferre, Guy-Patrick Sainderichin; dir: Granier-Deferre)

ROSSO, NICK
  Death Stalks My Lovely. Hamilton, 195?
  Some Are Born to Die. Hamilton, 195?

*ROSTAND, ROBERT
  Cross Currents. Pinnacle, 1985 <ship>
  *The Killer Elite. Film: United Artists, 1975 (scw: Marc Norman, Stirling Silliphant; dir: Sam Peckinpah)

*ROSTOV, MARA
  A Careless Feast. Putnam, 1985 <Vienna, WWII>

ROSZAK, THEODORE. 1933-   . Ref: CA.
  Dreamwatcher. Doubleday, 1985; Muller, 1985 <Calif.>

*ROTH, HOLLY. Ref also: TM.

*ROTHBLATT, HENRY B(ARNETT). 1916-1985. Ref: CA.

ROTHSTEIN, ALLAN. See: Bill Warren.

ROTSLER, WILLIAM. 1926-   . Ref: CA.
  Danger Maze. Wanderer, 1984; Target, 1985
  Defence Against Terror. Wanderer, 1983; Target, 1985
  Maui Mystery. Wanderer, 1983
  Vice Squad. Pinnacle, 1982 (Novelization of film: Embassy, 1982; scw: Sandy Howard, Kenneth Peters, Robert Vincent O'Neil; dir: Gary A. Sherman.) <L.A.>

*ROUDYBUSH, ALEXANDRA (BROWN)
  Blood Ties. Doubleday, 1981

*ROWE, ANNE
  *Deadly Intent. <NYC>

*ROWE, JOHN. Graduate of Australian military institution; intelligence officer in Viet Nam, later with intelligence agency in Wash. D.C.; writer since 1969.
  Long Live the King. Stein, 1984

ROWE, RON
  Bye-Bye Blackbird. New Horizon, 1982

*ROWLAND, HENRY C(OTTRELL)
  *The Closing Net. Silent film: Gold Rooster, 1915 (scw: George Brackett Seitz; dir: Edward Jose)
  *Duds. Silent film: Goldwyn, 1920 (scw: Harvey F. Thew; dir: Thomas R. Mills)
  *The Sultana. Silent film: Balboa, 1916.

ROWLEY, WALTER H. Born in Omaha; graduate of Grinnell College in journalism; jounalist, freelance writer, documentary writer-producer for TV, public relations consultant; in 1975 science editor for Office of University Communications, Colo. State Univ.
  Concerto for Murder. Carlton, 1975 <Colo.>

ROY, D. KINMOUNT
  -Linked Lives. Heath, 1913

ROYALE, JOHN
  The Nobbler. Long, 1952

*ROYCE, KENNETH. Ref also: TM. SC: Spider Scott, also in titles marked SS below.
  Channel Assault. Hodder, 1982; McGraw, 1982 <Chan. Is., 1942>
  The Crypto Man. Hodder, 1984; Stein, 1984 SS
  The Mosley Receipt. Hodder, 1985; Stein, 1985 SS
  The Stalin Account. Hodder, 1983
  10,000 Days. Hodder, 1981; McGraw, 1981 <1984, Mid. East>

*RUBEL, JAMES L(YON)
  -The Fraudulent Broad. Newstand, 1958; Digit, 1959

RUBEL, MARC. Screenwriter and contributing editor to Surfing Magazine.
  Flex. St. Martin's, 1983 <L.A., 1958>

RUBENS, BERNICE. 1923-   . Ref: CA.
  Mr. Wakefield's Crusade. H. Hamilton, 1985; Delacorte, 1985

*RUBIN, DANIEL N.
  *Riddle Me This! Film: Paramount, 1932, as Guilty As Hell; released in Britain as Guilty As Charged (scw: Arthur Kober, Frank Partos; dir: Erle Kenton). Also: Paramount, 1937, as Night Club Scandal (scw: Lillie Howard; dir: Ralph Murphy)

RUBIN, HAROLD. 1912-   . Pseudonym: Harold Robbins, q.v.

*RUCK, BERTA. 1878-1978.

RUFF, IVAN
  The Dark Red Star. Pluto, 1985 <Eng., 1990s>

RULE, ANN
  Possession. Norton, 1983. British title (?): Mind Games. Severn, 1984 <Wash.>

RUMANES, GEORGE N(ICHOLAS). 1925-   Ref: CA.
  The Man with the Black Worrybeads. Fields, 1973; Barrie, 1973

*RUNYON, DAMON. Ref also: CA.
  *A Slight Case of Murder, with Howard Lindsay. Film: Warner, 1938 (scw: Earl Baldwin, Joseph Shrank; dir: Lloyd Bacon). Also: Warner, 1952, as Stop, You're Killing Me (scw: James O'Hanlon; dir: Roy Del Ruth)

RUSH, MARK. Pseudonym: *Norman Conway, q.v.

RUSH, ROBERT
  -The Birthday Girl. Macdonald, 1983
  -The Birthday Treat. Futura, 1981

RUSHTON, WILLIAM
  The Day of the Grocer. Deutsch, 1971
  W. G. Grace's Last Case. Methuen, 1984

RUSSELL, A(RTHUR) J(AMES)
  -God's Prodigal. Laurie, 1922. Silent film: International Artists, 1923 (scw: Louis Stevens; dir: Bert Wynne, Edward Jose)

*RUSSELL, CHARLOTTE MURRAY
  *Hand Me a Crime. <Midwest>

*RUSSELL, FOX
  -The Honourable Bill. Arrowsmith, 1904

*RUSSELL, JACK GOLDEN. See: *George Clayton Johnson.

*RUSSELL, JOHN. Ref also: TM.
  *Far Wandering Men. Film (from title ss): Radio Pictures, 1930, as Girl of the Port (scw: Beulah Marie Dix; dir: Bert Glennon)
  *In Dark Places. Film (from ss): MGM, 1929, as The Pagan (scw: Dorothy Farnum; dir: W. S. Van Dyke)
  *The Red Mark, and other stories. Silent film (from title ss): Cruze, 1928 (scw: Julian Josephson; dir: James Cruze). Sound film (from ss "The Lost God"): Paramount, 1930, as The Sea God (scw & dir: George Abbott). Silent film (from ss "The Passion Vine"): Metro, 1923, as Where the Pavement Ends (scw & dir: Rex Ingram)

*RUSSELL, MARTIN (JAMES). Pseudonym: James Arney, q.v.
  All Part of the Service. Collins, 1982
  Backlash. Collins, 1981; Walker, 1983
  Censor. Collins, 1984
  *A Dangerous Place to Dwell. U.S. title: Unwelcome Audience. Walker, 1986
  The Darker Side of Death. Collins, 1985
  A Domestic Affair. Collins, 1984; Walker, 1985
  Prime Target. Collins, 1985
  Rainblast. Collins, 1982
  The Search for Sara. Collins, 1983; Walker, 1984
  Unwelcome Audience; see A Dangerous Place to Dwell

*RUSSELL, RAY. Ref: not in TC2.

*RUSSELL, RICHARD
  *Point of Reference. <Maine>
  *Reunion. <NYC>

*RUSSELL, W(ILLIAM)
  The Reminiscences of Jock Thirlstane, Yokel and Detective, at Musselburgh Races in Days Gone By. Adams, ca.1914 ss

*RUSSO, JOHN
  Day Care. PB, 1985
  *The Night of the Living Dead. (Novelization of film: Continental, 1974; scw: John A. Russo; dir: George A. Romero.)

*RUSSELL, W(ILLIAM) CLARK
  A Tale of Two Tunnels. Chapman, 1897. U.S. title: Captain Jackman. Buckles, 1899 <ship>

RUSTAN, JOHN
  The Attempted Murder of Peggy Sweetwater. French, 1983 (Play.)
  The Tangled Snarl, with Frank Semerano. French, 19?? (1-act play.) <L.A.>

*RUTHERFORD, DOUGLAS
  Porcupine Basin. Macmillan (London), 1982
  Stop at Nothing. Macmillan (London), 1983; Walker, 1983 <Rome>

*RUYLE, JOHN. SC: Turlock Loams, also in at least the titles marked TL.
  The Adventure of the Five Buffalo Chips. Pequod, 1975 TL
  *The Adventure of the Logophagous Client. Pequod, 1971
  *The Adventure of the Retired Weatherman. Pequod, 1972
  The Adventure of the Soledad Cyclist. Pequod, 1974 TL
  D Is for Duck. Pequod, 1981
  *His Last Vow. Pequod, 1973

RYAN, ALAN. 1940-   . Ref: CA.
  Dead White. Tor, 1983 <N.Y.>
  -The Kill. Tor, 1982

RYAN, CONALL
  Black Gravity. Ballantine, 1985 <Wyo.>

RYAN, DESMOND. 1893-1964. Ref: CA.
  Saint Eustace and the Albatross. Barker, 1935 ss, at least one criminous

RYAN, MARK. See: *Jonathan Craig.

*RYCK, FRANCIS
  *Undesirable Company. Film: Cinema National, 1975, as Le Secret (The Secret) (scw: Pascal Jardin; dir: Robert Enrico)
  *Woman Hunt. Film: Comacio, 1970, as Le Peau de Torpedo (Torpedo Skin) (scw: Jean Cau, Jean Delannoy; dir: Delannoy)

RYDZYNSKI, MARIE. Pseudonym: Marie Nicole, q.v.

RYER, J. C.
  -Georgie's Broads. Triumph, 1967

RYTON, ROYCE
  The Unvarnished Truth. French, 1978 (3-act play.)

SAAB, PETER. Pseudonym of "a bestselling author".
  The Sweetwater Point Motel. St. Martin's, 1981; Arlington, 1986 <N.C.>

SABATO, ERNESTO R. 1911-   .
  -The Outsider. Knopf, 1950 (Translation of "El Tunel." Buenos Aires, 1948.)

*SABER, ROBERT O.
  *City of Sin. Also published as by Milton K. Ozaki: Lancer, 1962

*SABERHAGEN, FRED (THOMAS)
  Earth Descended. Pinnacle, 1981 ss, one criminous

SADLER, ADAM
  Rogues. Ward, 1931

SADLER, BARRY
  Cry Havoc. Pinnacle, 1983 <Viet Nam>
  Nashville with a Bullet, with Billy Arr. Charter, 1981 <Nashville>

*SADLER, MARK. SC: Paul Shaw, also in title below.
  Touch of Death. Raven, 1981

*SADLIER, ANNA T(HERESA)
  The Lost Jewel of the Mortimers. Herder, 1904

*SAFFRON, ROBERT. ca.1918-1985.

SAFRONI-MIDDLETON, A(RNOLD)
  No Extradition. Ward, 1923 <S. Pac.>

*SAGER, GORDON
  *The Formula. <Venice>
  -Run, Sheep, Run. Vanguard, 1950 <W.I.>

SAGER, JEFFREY. See: Paul Jason.

SAGNIER, THIERRY J.
  The IFO Report. Avon, 1983

*SAGOLA, MARIO J. Pseudonym of *Henry Kane, q.v. Other pseudonym: Kenneth R. McKay, q.v.

SAHGAL, NAYANTARA (PANDIT). 1927-   Ref: CA.
  Plans for Departure. Norton, 1985; Heinemann, 1986 <India>

*ST. CLAIR, JEANANNE. Pseudonym of Kenneth L. Hassler.

*ST. CLAIR, LEONARD. 1916-1986.

ST. CLAIR, MAL(COLM), 1897-1952, and GEORGE O'HARA
  Side Street. Jacobsen, 1929 (Novelization of film: RKO, 1929; scw: Malcolm St. Clair, John Russell, George O'Hara; dir: St. Clair.)

S

S

*ST. CLAIR, MIKE. Pseudonym of Norman Retchkin.
  *Daddy's Gone A-Hunting. (Novelization of film: National General, 1969; scw: Larry Cohen, Lorenzo Semple, Jr.; dir: Mark Robson.)

*ST. DENNIS, MADELON
  *The Death Kiss. Film: Worldwide, 1933 (scw: Barry Barringer, Gordon Kahn; dir: Edward L. Marin)

ST. GEORGE, E. A.
  The King in Yellow. Spook, 1983 (Play.)

*ST. GEORGE, GEOFFREY. Pseudonym of Jeffrey Hart, an English professor.
  *The Proteus Pact. <WWII, Ger.>

ST. GERMAIN, GREGORY. All titles in WWII "Resistance" series.
  Magyar Massacre. Signet, 1982
  Night and Fog. Signet, 1982
  Road of Iron. Signet, 1983
  Shadows of Death. Signet, 1983 <Paris>
  Target: Sahara. Signet, 1983 <Afr., N.>

*ST. JAMES, BERNARD
  The Seven Dreamers. Doubleday, 1982 <Paris, 1800s>
  *The Witch. <Eng.>

*ST. JAMES, IAN
  The Balfour Conspiracy. Heinemann, 1981; Atheneum, 1981
  -The Killing Anniversary. Heinemann, 1984; Morrow, 1985 <Ire., 1916>
  Winner Harris. Heinemann, 1982

SAINT-JOHN, KRISTINE
  The Minigods. Black Sun, 1984

ST. LOUIS, ROBERT
  The Bushido Code. GM, 1981

*ST. MICHAELS, DONELLE. Pseudonym of *Don Rico, 1913-1985.

*ST. MOORE, ADAM. Pseudonym of Jacques Douyan.

ST. PIERRE, DENNIS
  The Marshal. Warner, 1981

*SALA, GEORGE AUGUSTUS (HENRY)
  -The Baddington Peerage. Skeet, 1860

*SALAS, FLOYD (FRANCIS). Ref: CA, TM.

SALE, DAVID
  Chiller. Sphere, 1983

*SALE, RICHARD (BERNARD). Ref also: TM.
  *Not Too Narrow--Not Too Deep. Film: MGM, 1940, as Strange Cargo (scw: Lawrence Hazard; dir: Frank Borzage)

SALEM, RICHARD
  New Blood. Signet, 1982; Futura, 1981 <W. Va.>

*SALINGER, PIERRE (EMILE GEORGE)
  The Dossier, with Leonard Gross. Doubleday, 1984; Deutsch, 1984

*SALISBURY, CAROLA (ISOBEL JULIEN)
  An Autumn in Araby. Century, 1983; Doubleday, 1983 <Egypt, 1869>

*SALTER, ELIZABETH (FULTON)
  *The Voice of the Peacock. <Australia>

*SALTUS, EDGAR (EVERTSON)
  *The Paliser Case. Silent film: Goldwyn, 1920 (scw: Edfrid Bingham; dir: William Parke)

*SAMSON, JOAN. Ref: TM.

*SANDBERG, BERENT
  *Brass Diamonds. ... Sphere, 1983
  The Chinese Spur. Signet, 1983; Sphere, 1985 <Far East>
  The Honeycomb Bid. Signet, 1981; Sphere, 1984

SANDERS, BUCK. House name. Those by Thomas Larry Adcock, 1947-   , q.v., are marked "by TA" below; those by Jeffrey Frentzen, 1956-   , are marked "by JF" (Ref: CA). SC: Ben Slayton (T-Man), in all titles.
  The Bayou Brigade. Warner, 1982 (by JF)
  A Clear and Present Danger. Warner, 1981 (by TA)
  Star of Egypt. Warner, 1981 (by JF)
  The Starshine Connection. Warner, 1982 <L.A.>
  Trail of the Twisted Cross. Warner, 1982 (by TA)

*SANDERS, GEORGE
  *Stranger at Home. Film: Hammer, 1954, as The Stranger Came Home; released in the U.S. as The Unholy Four (scw: Michael Carreras; dir: Terence Fisher)

*SANDERS, LAWRENCE. Ref also: TM; revised, expanded: TC2. SC: Edward X. Delaney, also in titles marked ED below.
  *The Anderson Tapes. Film: Columbia, 1971 (scw: Frank Pierson; dir: Sidney Lumet)
  -The Case of Lucy Bending. Putnam, 1982; NEL, 1983
  *The First Deadly Sin. Filmways, 1980 (scw: Mann Rubin; dir: Brian Hutton)
  The Fourth Deadly Sin. Putnam, 1985; NEL, 1985 ED <NYC>
  The Passion of Molly T. Putnam, 1984; NEL, 1985 <U.S., 1987>
  The Seduction of Peter S. Putnam, 1983; NEL, 1984 <NYC>
  The Third Deadly Sin. Putnam, 1981; Granada, 1981 ED <NYC>

*SANDERS, LEONARD
  Act of War. Simon, 1982 <NYC, WWII>

*SANDERSON, (RONALD) DOUGLAS. Ref also: TM.

SANDFORD, JANE. Pseudonym of Jane Cushman, NYC literary agent.
  In Safe Hands. GM, 1984; Collins, 1985

*SANDS, LESLIE
  *Intent to Murder. Film: Angel, 1951, as Another Man's Poison (scw: Val Guest; dir: Irving Rapper)
  *Something to Hide. English Theatre, 1959 (date correction)

*SANDS, MARTIN
  *The Jokers. (Novelization of film: Universal, 1967; scw: Dick Clement, Ian La Frenais; dir: Michael Winner.)
  *Maroc 7. (Novelization of film: Rank, 1967; scw: David Mercer; dir: Gerry O'Hara)

*SANFORD, HARRY. See: *Max Lamb.

*SANFORD, JOHN B. 1904-   .
  Seventy Times Seven. Knopf, 1939. Also published as: *Make My Bed in Hell.

*SANFORD, URSULA. Pseudonym of Alvaro Cardona-Hine.

*SANGSTER, JIMMY
  *The Terror of the Tongs. (Novelization of film: Hammer, 1960; scw: Jimmy Sangster; dir: Anthony Bushell.)

SAPERSTEIN, ALAN. Ref: CA.
  Camp. Ticknor, 1982; Houghton (London), 1984 <N.J.>

*SAPIR, RICHARD BEN. 1936-1987. Ref also: TC2. See also: *Warren B. Murphy.
  The Body. Doubleday, 1983; Allen, 1984 <Jerus.>
  *Bressio. ... Allen, 1986
  Spies. Doubleday, 1984; Allen, 1985 <R.I.>

SARALEGUI, JORGE
  -Last Rites. Charter, 1985 <S.F.>

SARDOU, VICTORIEN. 1831-1908.
  Diplomates. Denison, 1894 (4-act play, translated from the French.) Silent film: Davies, 1918, as The Burden of Proof (scw: Samuel M. Weller; dir: Julius Steger). Also: Famous Players, 1926, as Diplomacy (scw: Benjamin Glazer; dir: Marshall Neilan)

*SARTO, BEN
  *Disillusioned. Modern Fiction, 1952 (date correction)
  Donna with Green Eyes. Hermitage, 1948
  *Susie Comes to Soho. Hermitage, 1947

(date and publisher correction)
  Worth More Dead. Milestone, 1953

*SATCHELL, WILLIAM
  *The Greenstone Door. <N.Z.>
  The Land of the Lost. Methuen, 1902 <N.Z.>

*SATTERTHWAITE, WALTER
  The Aegean Affair. Dell, 1982

*SAUL, JOHN (RALSTON). Has Ph.D. from King's College, London; directed an investment firm in Paris; was assistant to the chairman of a national energy company.
  Baraka. Granada, 1983; Doubleday, 1985 <Afr., N.>

*SAUL, JOHN (W., III). 1942-   . Ref: CA. This is the author of *Punish the Sinners, and *Suffer the Children, incorrectly listed in CF as by above author.
  All Fall Down; see The God Project
  Brainchild. Bantam (U.S. & London), 1985
  *Comes the Blind Fury. ... Coronet, 1981 (byline correction)
  The God Project. Bantam hc, 1982. British title: All Fall Down. Corgi hc, 1983
  Nathaniel. Bantam, 1984; Corgi, 1984 <Neb.>
  -When the Wind Blows. Dell, 1981; Coronet, 1982

SAUNDERS, EARL
  The Investigation. Holloway, 1981 <Ala.>

SAUTER, ERIC. 1948-   . Ref: CA, TM. SC: Robert Lee Hunter, in all titles.
  Hunter. Avon, 1983 <N.J.>
  Hunter and the Ikon. Avon, 1984 <N.J.>
  Hunter and the Raven. Avon, 1984

*SAVA, GEORGE
  A Smile Through Tears. Hale, 1985

SAVAGE, ERNEST. 1918-   . Ref: CA, TC2.
  Two If by Sea. Scribner, 1982 <ship>

SAVAGE, JUANITA
  Bandit Love. Bles, 1931; Dial, 1931
  Golden Passion. Bles, 1929

*SAVAGE, MARY. Pseudonym of Mary Dresser.

*SAVAGE, RICHARD HENRY
  *My Official Wife. Silent film: Vitagraph, 1914 (scw: Marguerite Bertsch, Eugene Millin; dir: James Young). Sound film (?): Tobis-Rota, 1936, as Seine Offizielle Frau (His Official Wife) (scw: Rolf Meyer, T. Echtermeier, Thea von Harbou; dir: Erich Waschneck)

*SAVAGE, WALLACE
  *A Bait of Perjury. Droke House, 1970 (spelling correction)

SAVARIN, JULIAN JAY. Born in Dominica, moved to England at age 12; served in R.A.F.; toured England with rock band; author of science fiction novels. SC: Gordon Gallagher, in those titles marked GG.
  Gunship. Secker, 1985 <Tib.>
  Lynx. Secker, 1984; Walker, 1986
  Waterhole. Allison, 1982; St. Martin's, 1984 <Australia> GG
  Windshear. Allison, 1985 GG
  Wolfrun. Allison, 1984 GG

SAVILLE, ANDREW. SC: Bergerac, in both titles; see also: *Michael Hardwick.
  Bergerac Is Back. Severn, 1985 (Novelization of the TV series.)
  Crimes of the Season. Panther, 1985 (Novelization of the TV series.)

*SAX, ANDRE
  The Dancer Disappears. Charter, 1982; Firecrest, 1984

*SAXON, PETER
  *The Disoriented Man. Film: AIP, 1969, as Scream and Scream Again (scw: Christopher Wicking; dir: Gordon Hessler)

SAYERS, CHARLES E.
  The Jumping Double. Bookstall
  (Syd.), 1923   <Australia>
*SAYERS, DOROTHY L(EIGH). Ref also:
  TM. SC: Lord Peter Wimsey, also in
  new title below. Film (possibly
  based on unidentified novel):
  Phoenix, 1935, as The Silent
  Passenger (scw: Basil Mason; dir:
  Reginald Denham)
  The Abominable History of the Man
  with Copper Fingers. Inky Parrot,
  1982 PW ss
*Busman's Honeymoon. Film: MGM, 1940;
  released in the U.S. as Haunted
  Honeymoon (scw: Monckton Hoffe,
  Angus MacPhail, Harold Goldman;
  dir: Arthur B. Woods)

SAYLE, ALEXEI
  Train to Hell. Methuen, 1984

SCAIFE, ARTHUR HODGKIN. Pseudonym:
  Kim Bilir, q.v.

*SCANLON, NOEL
  *Quinn. <Mid. East>

SCANNELL, DAVID
  The Hood. Avon, 1984   <Calif.>

SCAPARRO, JACK
  Worst Enemies. Dell, 1983   <NYC>

SCARBERRY, ALMA SIOUX
  Dimpled Racketeer. Grosset, 1931
  <Phil.>

*SCARBOROUGH, CHUCK
  The Myrimidon Project, with William
  Murray. Coward, 1981; Piatkus,
  1981

*SCARBOROUGH, GEORGE
  *The Lure. Silent film: Shubert, 1914
  (scw & dir: Alice Blache)

*SCARPETTA, FRANK
  *Counterattack. <New Or.>
  *Die, Killer, Die. (by Russell Smith)
  *Kiss of Death.   <N. Mex.>
  *This Animal Must Die. (by Paul
  Hofrichter)

SCHAEFFER, SUSAN FROMBERG. 1941-
  Ref: CA.
  -The Madness of a Seduced Woman. Dut-
  ton, 1983; H. Hamilton, 1984

SCHEELE, MATT
  Art Boggs, Private Investigator.
  Exposition, 1981   comic strips

SCHENK, CRAIG. See: Bill Magee.

SCHENKAR, JOAN
  Cabin Fever. French, 1984 (Play.)

*SCHERF, MARGARET (LOUISE). Ref also:
  TM.
  *Always Murder a Friend. <Colo.>

SCHIDDEL, EDMUND. 1909-1982. Ref: CA.
  Bad Boy. Macmillan, 1982
  The Girl with the Golden Yo Yo.
  Manor, 1975

*SCHIFF, BARRY. See: *Hal Fishman.

*SCHISGALL, OSCAR. 1901-1984.

SCHLOSSSTEIN, STEVEN
  Kensei. Congdon, 1983; Severn, 1984
  <Jap., 1985>

SCHMIDT, DAN. Pseudonym: Dan
  Kellerman, q.v.

*SCHMITZ, JAMES H(ENRY)
  *The Telzey Toy. ... Hamlyn, 1983

SCHNEIDER, JOYCE ANNE. 1942-
  Ref: CA.
  Stryker's Children. Arbor, 1984
  <NYC>

SCHNEIDER, KURT
  Too Late for Tears. Gray, 195?
  Too Scared to Live. Gray, 195?

SCHOCK, T. A.   SC: Daniel Keel, in all
  titles.
  Deadpan. Leisure, 1981; Star, 1982
  Pratfall. Leisure, 1981
  Stopgap. Leisure, 1981

*SCHOLEFIELD, ALAN
  The King of the Golden Valley. H.
  Hamilton, 1985; St. Martin's, 1986
  <1939>

The Sea Cave. H. Hamilton, 1983;
  Congdon, 1984 <S. Afr., 1920s>
*Venom. Film: Aribage, 1981 (scw:
  Robert Carrington; dir: Piers
  Haggard)

SCHOR, AMY. 1954-   . Ref: CA.
  Line by Line. Marek, 1981 <NYC>

SCHORR, MARK. Born and raised in NYC;
  investigative reporter for NYC
  publications and later for an L.A.
  TV station; subsequently with
  "USA Today" in L.A. Ref: TM. SC:
  Red Diamond, in titles marked RD.
  Ace of Diamonds. St. Martin's, 1984
  <Las Veg.>   RD
  Bully! St. Martin's, 1985 <1903>
  Diamond Rock. St. Martin's, 1985   RD
  <L.A.>
  Red Diamond, Private Eye. St. Mar-
  tin's, 1983   RD

*SCHRADER, LEONARD
  *The Yakuza. (Novelization of film:
  Warner, 1975; scw: Paul Schrader;
  dir: Sydney Pollack.)

SCHREIBER, LOUIS A.
  Dangerous Games. Richardson, 1985

SCHULBERG, BUDD. 1914-   . Ref: CA.
  -Everything That Moves. Doubleday,
  1980; Robson, 1981
  Waterfront. Random, 1955; Bodley,
  1955. Reprinted as: On the Waterfront. Corgi, 1959. Screenplay:
  Southern Illinois Univ. Press,
  1980. Film: Columbia, 1954, as On
  the Waterfront (scw: Budd Schulberg; dir: Elia Kazan)

SCHUTZ, BENJAMIN M(ERRILL). 1949-
  Ref: CA. SC: Leo Haggerty, in
  both titles.
  All the Old Bargains. Bluejay, 1985
  <Wash. D.C>
  Embrace the Wolf. Bluejay, 1985
  <N.C.>

*SCHWARTZ, ALVIN
  *The Blowtop. <NYC>

*SCHWARZ, BRUNO
  *Dames Are Dynamite. Hamilton, 1952
  Halo for a Lady. Hamilton, 1952
  No Future for Miss Morrow. Hamilton,
  1952
  Ransom for Miss LeGrun. Hamilton,
  ca.1952 <NYC>

*SCIASCIA, LEONARDO
  The Day of the Owl; see *Mafia Ven-
  detta
  *Equal Danger. Film: PEA, 1975, as
  Cadaveri Eccellenti (Illustrious
  Corpses) (scw: Francesco Rosi,
  Tonino Guerra, Lino Jannuzzi; dir:
  Rosi)
  *Mafia Vendetta. Also published as:
  The Day of the Owl. Godine, 1984;
  Carcanet, 1984 <Sic.> Film: Panda
  Cinematografica, 1968, as Il Giorno
  Della Civetta (The Day of the Owl;
  Mafia) (scw: Daminao Damiani, Ugo
  Pirro; dir: Damiani)
  The Wine-Dark Sea. Carcanet, 1985
  ss, some criminous (Translation
  of "Il Mare Colore del Vino."
  Italy, 1982.)

SCOBER
  The Spirit House and other stories.
  Stockwell, 1926   ss, one or two
  criminous

*SCOPPETTONE, SANDRA. Pseudonym: Jack
  Early, q.v.

*SCORTIA, THOMAS N(ICHOLAS). 1926-1986.

*SCOTT, LADY A(IMEE BYNG HALL)
  *The Unknown Path. <Iraq>

*SCOTT, ANTONIA. Pseudonym of Charles
  Rigdon.

*SCOTT, BRUCE. SC: Supt. Steve
  MacLaren, in at least those marked
  SM.
  A Hell of a Spot. Hale, 1971
  The Prayer Mat. Hale, 1967 SM <Mal.>
  The Secret of the Elephant. Hale,
  1968 SM   <Mal.>

*SCOTT, CHRIS
  Hitler's Bomb. McClelland (Toronto),
  1983; Stein, 1985   <Ger., WWII>

*SCOTT, DANA. Pseudonym of Constance
  Pierrepont Noyes Robertson, 1897-
  1985.

*SCOTT, DEBORAH. Pseudonym of Deborah
  Snipes.

SCOTT, DON. SC: Raker, in both titles.
  Raker. Pinnacle, 1982
  Tijuana Traffic. Pinnacle, 1982

*SCOTT, DOUGLAS
  Chains. Secker (London & U.S.), 1984
  -Die for the Queen. Secker, 1981
  -Eagle's Blood. Secker, 1985
  The Hanged Man. Secker, 1983
  -In the Face of the Enemy. Secker,
  1982
  *Operation Artemis. <Greece>

SCOTT, ERIC CLEMENT
  The Fall of a Saint. Greening, 1910.
  Silent film: Gaumont-British,
  1920 (dir: W. P. Kellino)

*SCOTT, EVELYN. 1893-1963.

*SCOTT, G. FIRTH
  *The Rider of Waroona. <Australia>

*SCOTT, GENEVIEVE. Pseudonym of
  *Jennifer Rigg.
  *The Water Horse. <Scot.>

SCOTT, HARDIMAN. Formerly BBC politi-
  cal editor at Westminster.
  Blueprint for a Terrorist; see Deadly
  Nature
  Deadly Nature. Bodley, 1985. U.S.
  title: Blueprint for a Terrorist.
  Vanguard, 1986
  No Exit. Bodley, 1984; Vanguard, 1985
  <Moscow, future>
  Operation Ten. Bodley, 1982; Harper,
  1982

*SCOTT, J(AMES) M(AURICE). 1906-1986.

*SCOTT, JACK DENTON. Ref: CA. SC:
  Spargo, in *Spargo, and in title
  below.
  The Sea File. McGraw, 1981 <Cape Cod>

*SCOTT, JACK S. Ref also: TC2, TM. SC:
  Insp. Alf Rosher, also in titles
  below marked AR.
  All the Pretty People. Collins, 1983;
  St. Martin's, 1984 AR
  Corporal Smithers, Deceased. Gol-
  lancz, 1983; St. Martin's, 1983
  A Death in Irish Town. Collins, 1984;
  St. Martin's, 1985 AR
  A Distant View of Death. Collins,
  1981. U.S. title: The View from
  Deacon Hill. Ticknor, 1981 AR
  A Little Darling, Dead. Collins,
  1985; St. Martin's, 1986
  The Local Lads. Collins, 1982; Dut-
  ton, 1983 AR
  A Time of Fine Weather. Gollancz,
  1984; St. Martin's, 1985
  An Uprush of Mayhem. Collins, 1982;
  Ticknor, 1982 AR
  The View from Deacon Hill; see A
  Distant View of Death

*SCOTT, JEREMY. Pseudonym of Kay Dick,
  1915-   . Ref: CA.

*SCOTT, JUSTIN (BLAZER). Ref also: TM.
  The Auction. Granada, 1985 (U.S.
  title?)
  The Man Who Loved the Normandie; see
  The Normandie Triangle
  The Normandie Triangle. Arbor, 1981.
  British title: The Man Who Loved
  the Normandie. Granada, 1982
  <NYC, WWII>
  A Pride of Kings; see A Pride of
  Royals
  A Pride of Royals. Arbor, 1983. Bri-
  tish title: A Pride of Kings.
  Granada, 1984 <WWI>
  Rampage. Simon, 1985; Grafton, 1986
  <NYC>

*SCOTT, LEROY
  *Cordelia the Magnificent. Silent
  film: Zierler, 1923 (scw: Frank S.
  Beresford; dir: George Archainbaud)
  *Counsel for the Defense. Silent
  film: King, 1925 (scw: Arthur
  Hoerl; dir: Burton King)
  *A Daughter of Two Worlds. Silent
  film: First National, 1920 (scw:
  James Young, Edmund Goulding;
  dir: Lois Weber)
  *Mary Regan. Silent film: First Na-
  tional, 1919 (scw: Tom Geraghty;
  dir: Lois Weber,

*No. 13 Washington Square. Silent film: Universal, 1928, as 13 Washington Square (scw: Harry O. Hoyt; dir: Melville W. Brown)
*Partners of the Night. Silent film: Goldwyn, 1920 (scw: Charles E. Whittaker, Leroy Scott; dir: Paul Scardon)

*SCOTT, MANSFIELD
  *Behind Red Curtains. Silent film: Hampton, 1920, as One Hour Before Dawn (scw: Fred Myton, Fred Leon Smith; dir: Henry King)

*SCOTT, MARIANNE DE JAY. Pseudonym of Deborah Snipes.
  Drumbuie House. Lancer, 1972 <Scot.>

SCOTT, P. J.
  The Very Costly Escape. New Horizon, 1984

SCOTT, PETER GRAHAM. 1923-   Ref: CA.
  Dragonfire. Pinnacle, 1982
  A Feast of Vultures. Pinnacle, 1983

SCOTT, PETER T. Pseudonym: *George Werner.

*SCOTT, R(ONALD GUTHRIE) McNAIR. 1906-   Ref: CA.

*SCOTT, R(EGINALD) T(HOMAS) M(AITLAND). Ref: not in TC2.

*SCOTT, WILL
  *The Man. Film: BIP, 1931, as Creeping Shadows; released in the U.S. as The Limping Man (scw & dir: John Orton). Also: Welwyn, 1936, as The Limping Man (scw & dir: Walter Summers)

SCOTTI, R. A. Wrote catalog and promotion copy for Book of the Month Club.
  The Devil's Own. Fine, 1985 <Rome>
  The Kiss of Judas. Fine, 1984 <Rome>

*SEA-LION. Pseudonym of Geoffrey Martin Bennett, 1909-1983.

*SEAMAN, DONALD (PETER). Ref: CA. SC: Sydenham, also in *The Committee.
  Chase Royal. H. Hamilton, 1980; St. Martin's, 1982 <1867>
  The Wilderness of Mirrors. H. Hamilton, 1984; St. Martin's, 1985

*SEAMARK
  *Down River. Film: Gaumont, 1931 (scw: Ralph Gilbert Bettinson; dir: Peter Godfrey)

*SEARLS, HANK. Pseudonym: *Lee Costigan, q.v.
  -Firewind. Berkley, 1982; Sphere, 1982
  *Never Kill a Cop. delete

*SEARS, RUTH McCARTHY. Pseudonym: *Jane McCarthy.

SECOMBE, HARRY (DONALD). 1921-   Ref: CA.
  Welsh Fargo. Robson, 1981 <Wales>

SEE, JOHN WILLIAM
  The Lady Cries Murder. French, 1983 (Play.)

SEEBER, GERD CHRISTIAN. 1941-   Ref: CA.
  The Abduction. Secker, 1982; Holt, 1983 <It.>
  Patriots. Joseph, 1985
  The Proprietor. Methuen, 1983

*SEELEY, CLINTON
  *Storm Fear. Film: United Artists, 1955 (scw: Horton Foote; dir: Cornel Wilde)

SEELEY, ED
  -The Dollar Instinct. Digit, 1963
  Satan Takes a Hand. Digit, 1963

*SEELEY, MABEL (HODNEFIELD). Ref also: TM.

SEELY, NORMA. 1942-   Pseudonym: *Yvonne Norman.

SEGHERS, ANNA. Pseudonym of Netty Reiling Radvanyi, 1900-1983. Ref: CA.
  -The Seventh Cross. Little, 1942; H. Hamilton, 1943. (Translation of "Das Siebte Kreuz." Berlin, 1947.) Film: MGM, 1944 (scw: Helen Deutsch; dir: Fred Zinnemann)

*SELA, OWEN. Ref: TM.
  The Kremlin Control. Collins, 1984; Bantam, 1984 <Moscow>
  Triple Factor. Collins, 1982

SELBY, CHARLES. 1802(?)-1863.
  London by Night. Dick, 1886 (Play.) Silent film: Barker, 1913 (scw: Harry Engholm, Rowland Talbot; dir: Alexander Butler)

*SELIGSON, TOM
  Kidd. Dell, 1983 <NYC>

SELLAR, MAURICE
  The Front Man. Sphere, 1985; Zebra, 1986

*SELLERS, MICHAEL. 1941-   .
  Cache on the Rocks. Macmillan (London), 1982; Doubleday, 1983
  From Eternity to Here. Macmillan (London), 1981

SELVES, DAVID
  Quentin, a Spy. Book Guild, 1984

*SELWYN, FRANCIS. Pseudonym of Donald Thomas, 1935-   , q.v.
  *Sergeant Verity and the Swell Mob. Deutsch, 1981; Stein, 1981

SEMERANO, FRANK. See: John Rustan.

*SEMPRUN, JORGE. Ref: CA.
  *The Second Death of Roman Mercader. <Amst.>

SENTJURC, IGOR
  Prayer for an Assassin. Doubleday, 1959; Longmans, 1960 <Buda.> (Translation.)

*SERAFIN, DAVID. Pseudonym of Ian Michael, Oxford professor and medievalist. Ref: TM. SC: Insp. Luis Bernal, in *Saturday of Glory, and in titles below.
  The Body in Cadiz Bay. Collins, 1985; St. Martin's, 1985 <Sp.>
  Christmas Rising. Collins, 1982; St. Martin's, 1983 <Madrid>
  Madrid Underground. Collins, 1982; St. Martin's, 1984 <Madrid>
  *Saturday of Glory. ... St. Martin's, 1982 <Madrid>

*SERENY, GITTA. Pseudonym of Gitta Serenyi, 1923-

SERENYI, GITTA. 1923-   . Pseudonym: *Gitta Sereny.

*SERLING, ROBERT J(EROME)
  Air Force One Is Haunted. St. Martin's, 1985; Inner Circle, 1986 <Wash. D.C.>

*SETH, RONALD (SYDNEY). 1911-1985. Ref: CA.
  *Spy in the Nude. ... U.S. title: In the Nude. Day, 1962

SETON, ANYA. Ref: CA.
  -Dragonwyck. Houghton, 1944; Hodder, 1945 <NYC, 1840s> Film: TCF, 1946 (scw & dir: Joseph L. Mankiewicz)

*SETON, GRAHAM
  *The W Plan. Film: BIP, 1930 (scw: Victor Saville, Miles Malleson, Frank Launder; dir: Saville)

*SEWARD, JACK
  *The Frogman Assassination. Belmont, 1968 <Jap.>

*SEWARD, WILLIAM WARD
  *Skirts of the Dead Night. <Va.>

*SEWART, ALAN. 1928-   . Pseudonyms: Padder Nash, Alan Stewart Well, qq.v. Ref: CA.
  Close Your Eyes and Sleep, My Baby. Hale, 1981
  Dead Man Drifting. Hale, 1984
  Death Game--Five Players. Hale, 1982
  Drink! For Once Dead. Hale, 1983
  The Education of Quinton Quinn. Hale, 1984
  If I Should Die. Hale, 1983
  In That Rich Earth. Hale, 1981
  The Letter-Box Man. Hale, 1981
  A Multiplicity of Mrs. Browns. Hale, 1984
  My Hate Lies Bleeding. Hale, 1983
  Razor Jacques. Hale, 1985
  A Romp in Green Heat. Hale, 1981
  Smoker's Cough. Hale, 1983
  The Vengeful Flames. Hale, 1985

*SEYMOUR, (WILLIAM HERSCHEL KEAN) GERALD. Ref: TC2.
  Archangel. Collins, 1982; Dutton, 1982 <Russ.>
  Field of Blood. Collins, 1985; Norton, 1985 <Ire.>
  In Honor Bound. Collins, 1984; Norton, 1984 <Afghan.>

*SEYMOUR, H(ENRY)
  *Infernal Idol. Film: Harbour, 1973, as Craze (scw: Aben Kandel, Herman Cohen; dir: Freddie Francis)

SEYMOUR, HAMILTON and KEITH ROBERTSON
  The Golden Pin. Blackwood, 1884

SHAARA, MICHAEL (JOSEPH). 1929-   Ref: CA.
  The Herald. McGraw, 1982 <South>

*SHAFFER, ANTHONY (JOSHUA). Ref also: CA. See also: Robin Hardy.
  *Sleuth. Film: TCF, 1972 (scw: Anthony Shaffer; dir: Joseph L. Mankiewicz)
  Whodunnit. French, 1983 (Play.)

*SHAGAN, STEVE
  The Circle. Morrow, 1982; Sidgwick, 1983
  *City of Angels. Film: Paramount, 1975, as Hustle (scw: Steve Shagan; dir: Robert Aldrich)
  The Discovery. Morrow, 1984; Sidgwick, 1985 <Syr.>
  *The Formula. Film: MGM, 1980 (scw: Steve Shagan; dir: John G. Avildsen)

SHAHAR, DAVID. 1926-   . Ref: CA.
  His Majesty's Agent. Harcourt, 1980 <Isr.> (Translation of "Sokhen Hod Malkhuto." Israel, 1979.)

*SHAIRP, (ALEXANDER) MORDAUNT
  *The Crimson Blossoms. Film: B&D, 1933 (dir: Maclean Rogers). Also: Nettlefold, 1949, as Dark Secret (scw: A. R. Rawlinson, Moie Charles; dir: Maclean Rogers)

*SHALLITT, JOSEPH. Pseudonym: *Matt Brady.

SHAMIS, GIORA and DIANE
  A Crack in the House of God. Weidenfeld, 1983 <Mid. East>

SHANKMAN, SARAH. Magazine writer and editor; lived in S.F. for 12 years, then NYC.
  Impersonal Attractions. St. Martin's, 1985 <S.F.>

*SHANNON, BRAD
  Death Walks Softly. Scion, 1953 (by Victor J. Hanson)
  *Some Get It. (by Victor J. Hanson)
  *They Say I'm Bad. (by Victor J. Hanson)

*SHANNON, DELL. SC: Lt. Luis Mendoza, also in all titles below, set in L.A.
  Chaos of Crime. Morrow, 1985; Gollancz, 1986
  Destiny of Death. Morrow, 1984; Gollancz, 1985
  Exploit of Death. Morrow, 1983; Gollancz, 1984
  The Motive on Record. Morrow, 1982; Gollancz, 1982
  Murder Most Strange. Morrow, 1981; Gollancz, 1981

*SHANNON, DORIS. Pseudonym: E. X. Giroux, q.v.
  Family Money. St. Martin's, 1984; Severn, 1986 <NYC, 1914>
  Little Girls Lost. St. Martin's, 1981; Sphere, 1983 <Van.>
  The Punishment. St. Martin's, 1981; Sphere, 1982 <Maine>

SHANNON, JAMES
  Game of Soldiers. Sphere, 1985

*SHAPIRO, LIONEL (SEBASTIAN BERK)
  *The Sealed Verdict. Film: Paramount, 1948 (scw: Jonathan Latimer; dir: Lewis Allen)

*SHARKEY, JACK. Pseudonyms: Rick
    Abbot, Mike Johnson, qq.v.
    The Creature Creeps. French, 1977
        (3-act play.) <Rum.>
    Honestly, Now! French, 1981
        (3-act play.) <Fr.>
    Par for the Corpse. French, 1980
        (3-act play.) <N.Y.>
    Spinoff. French, 1974
        (3-act play.)

*SHARMAN, NICK. 1952-   .
    The Switch. NEL, 1984; Signet, 1984

*SHARP, ALAN
    *Night Moves. (Novelization of film:
        Warner, 1975; scw: Alan Sharp;
        dir: Arthur Penn.)

*SHARP, JACK
    *The Tell-Tale Tattoo. Street, 1903
        (Magnet #305)
    *The Wall Street Swindlers. Street,
        1903 (Magnet #301)

*SHARP, MARILYN. SC: Richard Owen, in
        *Sunflower, and in title marked
        RO below.
    Falseface. St. Martin's, 1984 RO
        <Mex.>
    Masterstroke. Marek, 1981; Severn,
        1982

SHARP, ROGER
    Quarmby. Hale, 1981

SHARPE, TOM. 1928-   . Ref: CA.
    Wilt on High. Secker, 1984; Random,
        1985 <acad.>

*SHATTUCK, RICHARD. Ref: TM.
    *The Wedding Guest Sat on a Stone.
        Film: Columbia, 1944, as The Ghost
        That Walks Alone (scw: Doris Shat-
        tuck, Clarence Upson Young; dir:
        Lew Landers)

*SHAW, BYNUM (GILLETTE)
    Days of Power, Nights of Fear. St.
        Martin's, 1980 <Wash. D.C., 1950s>

SHAW, FLOYD
    Devil's Daughter. Avon, 1954. Also
        published as: Park Avenue Girl.
        Avon, 1956

*SHAW, (COLIN) HOWARD. Ref: CA. SC:
        Insp. Barnaby, in *Killing No Mur-
        der, as by *Colin Howard, and in
        title below.
    Death of a Don. Hodder, 1982; Scrib-
        ner, 1981 <acad.>

*SHAW, IRWIN. 1913-1984.
    Acceptable Losses. Arbor, 1982; NEL,
        1983
    *The Gentle People. Film: Warner,
        1941, as Out of the Fog (scw:
        Robert Rossen, Jerry Wald, Richard
        Macaulay; dir: Anatole Litvak)
    *Nightwork. criminosi

SHAW, LINDA. 1938-   . Ref: CA.
    An Innocent Deception. PB, 1981
        <Switz.>

*SHAW, WILENE
    *Out for Kicks. <Las Veg.>

SHAW-TAYLOR, DOROTHY
    Thrill on the Underground. Leonard's,
        1953 (1-act play.)

SHEA, MICHAEL. 1946-   . Ref: CA.
    Pseudonym: *Michael Sinclair.
    Tomorrow's Men. Weidenfeld, 1982
        <Eng., future>

*SHEARING, JOSEPH. Ref also: CA.
    *Airing in a Closed Carriage. Film:
        Two Cities, 1948, as The Mark of
        Cain (scw: Francis Crowdy, Chris-
        tianna Brand, W. P. Lipscomb; dir:
        Brian Desmond Hurst)
    *Blanche Fury. Film: Cineguild, 1948
        (scw: Audrey Erskine Lindop,
        Cecil McGivern, Hugh Mills; dir:
        Marc Allegret)
    *For Her to See. Film: Paramount,
        1948, as So Evil My Love (scw:
        Leonard Spigelgass, Ronald Millar;
        dir: Lewis Allen)
    *Moss Rose. Film: TCF, 1947 (scw:
        Jules Furthman, Tom Read; dir:
        Gregory Ratoff)

SHEBAN, JOSEPH
    The Lost Diary. Exposition, 1953

*SHECKLEY, ROBERT
    *The Game of X. Film: Disney, 1981, as
        Condorman (scw: Marc Sturdivant,
        Glen Caron, Mickey Rose; dir:
        Charles Jarrott)
    *Live Gold. <Afr., N.>
    *The Tenth Victim. (Novelization of
        film: Embassy, 1965; scw: Elio
        Petri, Ennio Flaiano, Tonino
        Guerra; dir: Petri). Also (?):
        Swanic, 1983, as Le Prix du Danger
        (The Prize of Peril) (scw: Yves
        Boisset, Jean Curtelin; dir:
        Boisset)

*SHEDD, GEORGE C(LIFFORD)
    *In the Shadow of the Hills. Silent
        film: Meyberg, 1921, as Cold Steel
        (scw: Monte Katterjohn; dir:
        Sherwood MacDonald)

*SHEEHAN, PERLEY POORE
    *Three Sevens. Silent film: Vitagraph,
        1921 (scw: Calder Johnstone; dir:
        Chester Bennett)
    *The Whispering Chorus. Silent film:
        Artcraft, 1918 (scw: Jeanie
        MacPherson; dir: Cecil B. DeMille)

SHEFFIELD, CHARLES
    Erasmus Magister. Ace, 1982 <1700s>

*SHELBY, BRIT. Pseudonym of *James
        (Thomas) Grady, q.v.
    *The Great Pebble Affair. ... Coronet,
        1979, as by James Grady

*SHELDON, SIDNEY
    *Bloodline. Film: Paramount, 1979
        (scw: Laird Koenig; dir: Terence
        Young)
    If Tomorrow Comes. Morrow, 1985;
        Collins, 1985
    *The Naked Face. Film: Cannon, 1984
        (scw & dir: Bryan Forbes)
    *The Other Side of Midnight. Film:
        TCF, 1977 (scw: Herman Raucher,
        Daniel Taradash; dir: Charles
        Jarrott)
    *Rage of Angels. <NYC>

SHELDON, SUSANNA
    Susie's Girls. Leisure, 1975

*SHELDON, WALTER J. Ref also: TM.
    See also: George Kennedy. Pseudo-
        nym: *Shelly Walters.
    The Rites of Murder. St. Martin's,
        1984 <Wash. D.C.>

*SHELLEY, MARY. See also: Stephen
        Barrows, David Campton, Victor
        Gialanella, John Mattera, Alden
        Nowlan.
    *Frankenstein. Silent film: Edison,
        1910 (scw & dir: J. Searle Daw-
        ley). Also: Ocean Film, 1915, as
        Life Without Soul (scw: Jesse J.
        Goldburg; dir: Joseph W. Smiley).
        Sound film: Universal, 1931 (scw:
        Frances Edward Faragoh, John L.
        Balderston, Garrett Fort; dir:
        James Whale). Also: Hammer, 1957,
        as The Curse of Frankenstein (scw:
        Jimmy Sangster; dir: Terence
        Fisher). Also: Hammer, 1969
        as Frankenstein Must Be Destroyed
        (scw: Anthony Nelson Keys, Bert
        Batt; dir: Terence Fisher). Also:
        Hammer, 1970, as The Horror of
        Frankenstein (scw: Jimmy Sangster,
        Jeremy Burnham; dir: Sangster).
        Also: MCA, 1973, as Frankenstein:
        The True Story (scw: Christopher
        Isherwood, Don Bachardy; dir:
        Jack Smight). Also: Aspekt, 1977,
        as Victor Frankenstein (scw: Yvonne
        Floyd, Calvin Floyd; dir: Calvin
        Floyd). Also: Colgems, 1985, as
        The Bride (scw: Lloyd Fonvielle;
        dir: Frank Roddam)

SHELLEY, MIKE
    The Last Private Eye in Belfast.
        Domino, 1984
    Madame Eddie's Chamber of Horrors.
        Domino, 1984
    The Terror of Her Ways. Domino, 1984

*SHELLEY, SIDNEY (JOSEPH)
    *Bowmanville Break. Film: Brighton,
        1970, as The Mackenzie Break
        (scw: William Norton; dir: Lamont
        Johnson)

*SHELYNN, JACK
    Joker in a Stacked Deck. Hale, 1981

SHEM, SAMUEL. Pseudonym of a Boston
        psychiatrist.
    Fine. St. Martin's, 1985

SHEPARD, FERN. Pseudonym of Florence
        Stonebraker.
    Meter Maid. Arcadia, 1959

SHEPARD, KATHLEEN. Pseudonym.
    I Will Be Faithful. King, 1934.
        Film: TCF, 1936, as Human Cargo
        (scw: Jefferson Parker, Doris
        Malloy; dir: Allan Dwan)

*SHEPARD, SAM
    *Suicide in B-Flat. (3-act play.)

SHEPHERD, LISA
    The Ladies of Lambton Green. Hale,
        1984

*SHEPPARD, STEPHEN
    Monte Carlo. Summit, 1983; Secker,
        1983 <Fr., WWII>

*SHERBURNE, JAMES (ROBERT). Ref also:
        TM. SC: Paddy Moretti, in *Death's
        Pale Horse, and in titles below.
    Death's Clenched Fist. Houghton,
        1982; Houghton (London), 1983
        <NYC, 1890>
    Death's Gray Angel. Houghton, 1981
        <Kan., 1890>

*SHERIDAN, JUANITA. Ref: TM.

*SHERIDAN, LEE
    *The Pit and the Pendulum. (Noveliza-
        tion of film: American Interna-
        tional, 1961; scw: Richard
        Matheson; dir: Roger Corman.)

*SHERLOCK, JOHN
    The Amindra Gamble, with *David West-
        heimer. Coward, 1982 <ship, 1940>
    J. B.'s Daughter. McGraw, 1981;
        Allen, 1981
    *The Ordeal of Major Grigsby. Film:
        Cinerama, 1970, as The Last Grenade
        (scw: Kenneth Ware, James Mitchell,
        John Sherlock; dir: Gordon Flemyng)

*SHERMAN, DAN(IEL MICHAEL)
    *King Jaguar. ... Granada pb, 1983
    The Man Who Loved Mata Hari. Fine,
        1985 <WWII>
    The Prince of Berlin. Arbor, 1983;
        Severn, 1985 <Berlin>
    The White Mandarin. Arbor, 1982;
        Panther, 1984 <China>

*SHERMAN, JORY
    Gun for Hire. Major, 1978

*SHERMAN, ROGER. Pseudonym of Roger S.
        Plummer, Jr.

*SHERRIFF, R(OBERT) C(EDRIC)
    *Home at Seven. Film: British Lion,
        1952; released in the U.S. as
        Murder on Monday (scw: Anatole De
        Grunwald; dir: Ralph Richardson)

SHERROD, FLOYD
    The Secret Adventure of the Thor-
        oughbred Ghost. <Author>, 1972
        (Sherlock Holmes)

*SHERRY, EDNA
    *Sudden Fear. <NYC> Film: RKO, 1952
        (scw: Lenore Coffee, Robert Smith;
        dir: David Miller)

*SHERRY, GORDON
    *Black Limelight. Film: ABPC, 1938
        (scw: Dudley Leslie, Walter Sum-
        mers; dir: Paul L. Stein)

*SHERRY, JOHN (OLDEN). 1923-
        Ref: CA.

*SHERWOOD, JOHN (HERMAN MULSO). SC:
        Celia Grant = CG.
    A Botanist at Bay. Gollancz, 1985;
        Scribner, 1985 CG <N.Z.>
    Death at the BBC; see A Shot in the
        Arm
    Green Trigger Fingers. Gollancz,
        1984; Scribner, 1985 CG
    A Shot in the Arm. Gollancz, 1982.
        U.S. title: Death at the BBC.
        Scribner, 1983. Reprinted in the
        U.S. under British title: Inter-
        national Polygonics, 1985
        <Eng., 1937>

*SHERWOOD, ROBERT E(MMETT). 1876-
        1955. Ref: CA.
    The Petrified Forest. Scribner,
        1935 (3-act play.) <Ariz.> Film:

Warner, 1936 (scw: Charles Kenyon, Delmer Daves; dir: Archie L. Mayo). Also: Warner, 1945, as Escape in the Desert (scw: Thomas Job; dir: Edward A. Blatt)

*SHEW, E(DWARD) SPENCER
*Hands of the Ripper. (Novelization of film: Hammer, 1971; scw: L. W. Davidson; dir: Peter Sasdy.)

SHIAO, C. J. See: Dick Stivers.

*SHIEL, M(ATTHEW) P(HIPPS). Ref also: CA, TC2.

SHIELDS, DINAH. Born in Eng., has lived in Can. for many years.
Just Before Dawn. Harlequin, 1985 <Can.>

*SHIFFRIN, ABRAHAM B.
*Twilight Walk. <NYC>

*SHIMER, R(UTH) H. Ref: TM.

SHIRLEY, JOHN
The Brigade. Avon, 1981; Sphere, 1982

SHIVERS, LOUISE
Here to Get My Baby Out of Jail. Random, 1983; Collins, 1983 <South> Film: Atlantic, 1987, as Summer Heat (scw & dir: Michie Gleason)

SHLIAN, DEBORAH
Nursery. Charter, 1984

SHOBIN, DAVID
The Seeding. Linden, 1982; Pan, 1983 <Wash. D.C.>

*SHORT, (CHARLES) CHRISTOPHER (DUDLEY). Ref also: TM.

SHREVE, L(EVIN) G(ALE). 1910-
Ref: CA.
The Phoenix with Oily Feathers. Moore, 1980

SHROG, J. M. SC: Bernard McFoy, in both titles.
Hag Wood. Stockwell, 1936
White Circle. Stockwell, 1936

*SHRYACK, DENNIS. See: *Michael Butler.

*SHUBIN, SEYMOUR
The Captain. Stein, 1982
Holy Secrets. PB, 1984 <Phil.>

*SHULMAN, IRVING
 *The Amboy Dukes. Film: Universal International, 1949, as City Across the River (scw: Maxwell Shane, Dennis Cooper; dir: Shane)
 *Cry Tough. Film: United Artists, 1959 (scw: Harry Kleiner; dir: Paul Stanley)
 *The Notorious Landlady. (Novelization of film: Columbia, 1962; scw: Larry Gilbert, Richard Quine; dir: Quine.)
 *The Platinum High School. (Novelization of film: MGM, 1960; scw: Robert Smith; dir: Charles Haas.)

*SHUTE, NEVIL
Lonely Road. Cassell, 1932; Morrow, 1932. Film: ATP, 1936; released in the U.S. as Scotland Yard Commands (scw: James Flood, Gerard Fairlie, Anthony Kimmins; dir: Flood)

SIBBALD, GEORGE. 1943-
The Dodge Boys. French, 1977 (Play.) <Mich.>

SIDHWA, BAPSI N. 1938-   . Ref: CA.
The Crow Eaters. Cape, 1980; St. Martin's, 1981 <India, ca.1900>

SIEBERT, KATHY. See: Jon Franzen.

SILER, JACK
Triangles of Fire. Dell, 1984 <S.F.>

*SILLIPHANT, STIRLING (DALE). SC: John Locke = JL.
Bronze Bell. Ballantine, 1985 JL <Bali>
*The Slender Thread. (Novelization of film: Paramount, 1965; scw: Stirling Silliphant; dir: Sydney Pollack.)
Steel Tiger. Ballantine, 1983; Severn, 1986 JL <S. Pac.>

SILVER, VICTORIA. Ref: TM.
Death of a Harvard Freshman. Bantam, 1984 <acad., Mass.>

*SIMART, HELENA
Duel of Happiness. Mystique, 1981 (Translation of "Duel Pour le Bonheur." Paris, 1969.)
Till Proven Guilty. Mystique, 1981 (Translation of "Sa Derniere Chance." Paris, 1968.)

*SIMENON, GEORGES. Ref also: TM. Film (based on unidentified story): TCF, 1955, as Life in the Balance (scw: Robert Presnell, Jr., Leo Townsend; dir: Harry Horner).
*Act of Passion. Film: Cocinor, 1952, as Le Fruit Defendu (Forbidden Fruit) (scw: Jacques Companeez; dir: Henri Verneuil)
*A Battle of Nerves. Also published as: Maigret's War of Nerves. Harcourt, 1986. Film: A & T, 1948, as The Man on the Eifel Tower (scw: Harry Brown; dir: Burgess Meredith)
*Belle. Film: Lux, 1961, as La Mort de Belle (Death of a Beauty) (scw: Jean Anoulin; dir: Edouard Molinaro)
*The Bottom of the Bottle. Film: TCF, 1956; released in Britain as Beyond the River (scw: Sidney Boehm; dir: Henry Hathaway)
*The Brothers Rico. Film: Columbia, 1957 (scw: Lewis Meltzer, Ben Perry; dir: Phil Karlson)
*The Cat. Film: Valoria, 1971, as Le Chat (The Cat) (scw & dir: Pierre Granier-Deferre)
*Chit of a Girl. Published in the U.S. as: Justice. Harcourt, 1985. Film: Gordine, 1949, as La Marie du Port (scw: Louis Chavance, Marcel Carne; dir: Carne)
The Couple from Poitiers. H. Hamilton, 1985; Harcourt, 1986 (Translation of "Les Noces de Poitiers." Paris, 1960.)
*The Crossroads Murders. Film: Renoir, 1932, as La Nuit du Carrefour (The Night at the Crossroads) (dir: Jean Renoir)
*A Face for a Clue. Reprinted as: *Maigret and the Concarneau Murders. Film: Ord Halk, 1932, as Le Chien Jaune (The Yellow Dog) (dir: Jean Tarride)
*The Hatter's Ghosts. Film: Horizons, 1982, as Les Fantomes de Chapelier (The Hatter's Ghosts) (scw & dir: Claude Chabrol)
*In Case of Emergency. Film: Columbia, 1958, as En Cas de Malheur (In Case of Emergency; Love Is My Profession) (scw: Jean Aurenche, Pierre Bost; dir: Claude Autant-Lara)
Justice; see Chit of a Girl
*The Lodger. <Brus.> Film: Sara Films, 1982, as L'Etoile du Nord (The North Star) (scw: Pierre Granier-Deferre, Jean Aurenche, Michel Grisolia; dir: Granier-Deferre)
The Long Exile. H. Hamilton, 1983; Harcourt, 1982 (Translation of "Long Cours.")
*Magnet of Doom. Film: Spectacles Lumbroso, 1963, as L'Aine des Ferchaux (Magnet of Doom) (scw & dir: Jean-Pierre Melville)
*Maigret and the Gangsters. Reprinted in the U.S. under the British title: Harcourt, 1986. Film: Comacico, 1963, as Maigret Veit Rouge (Maigret Sees Red) (scw: Jacques Robert, Gilles Grangier; dir: Grangier)
*Maigret and the Hotel Majestic. Film: Domaines, 1945, as Les Caves du Majestic (Majestic Hotel Cellars) (scw: Charles Spaak; dir: Richard Pottier)
Maigret Bides His Time; see *The Patience of Maigret
*Maigret Has Doubts. ... Harcourt, 1982
*Maigret in Court. ... Harcourt, 1983
*Maigret Sets a Trap. Film: Intermondia, 1957, as Maigret Tend un Piege (Maigret Sets a Trap; also released as Inspector Maigret) (scw: R. M. Arlaud, Michael Audiard, Jean Delannoy; dir: Delannoy)
*Maigret's Pipe. (Translation of "La Pipe de Maigret." Paris, 1965)
*Maigret's Revolver. ... Harcourt, 1984

Maigret's War of Nerves; see *A Battle of Nerves
*The Man Who Watched the Trains Go By. Film: Stoss, 1953; released in the U.S. as Paris Express (scw & dir: Harold French)
*Mr. Hire's Engagement. Film: Filmsonor, 1946, as Panique (scw: Charles Spaak, Julien Duvivier; dir: Duvivier)
*Monsieur la Souris. Film: Distinguished Films, 1947, as Monsieur La Souris (Midnight in Paris) (scw: Walter Klee; dir: Georges Lecombe). Also: Triangle, 1950, as Midnight Episode (scw: Rita Barisse, Reeve Taylor, Paul Vincent Carroll, David Evans, William Templeton; dir: Gordon Parry)
*The Murderer. ... Harcourt, 1986
*Newhaven-Dieppe. Film: ABPC, 1947, as Temptation Harbour (scw: Rodney Ackland, Frederick Gotfurt, Victor Skutezky; dir: Lance Comfort)
*The Patience of Maigret. ... U.S. title: Maigret Bides His Time. Harcourt, 1985
*The Premier. Film: UFA, 1961, as Le President (The President) (scw: Michel Audiard; dir: Henri Verneuil)
The Reckoning. H. Hamilton, 1984; Harcourt, 1984 (Translation of "Le Bilan Maletras." Paris, 1948.)
*The Saint Fiacre Affair. Film: Cinedis, 1959, as Maigret et L'Affaire St. Fiacre (Maigret and the St. Fiacre Case) (scw: R. M. Arlaud, Michel Audiard, Jean Delannoy; dir: Delannoy)
*The Stain on the Snow. Film: Tellus, 1954, as La Neige Etait Sale (The Snow Was Black) (scw: Luis Saslavsky, Andre Tabet; dir: Saslavsky)
*The Stowaway. Film: Corona, 1958, as Le Passager Clandestin (scw: Maurice Auberge, Paul Andreota, Ralph Habib; dir: Habib)
*Strangers in the House. Film: Lopert, 1941, as Les Inconnus dan la Maison (Strangers in the House) (scw: Henri-George Clouzot; dir: Henri Decoin). Also: De Grunwald, 1967, as Stranger in the House (scw & dir: Pierre Rouve)
*The Survivors. ... Harcourt, 1985
*Three Beds in Manhattan. Film: Cocinor, 1965, as Trois Chambres a Manhattan (Three Rooms in Manhattan) (scw: Jacques Sigurd, Marcel Carne; dir: Carne)
*Ticket of Leave. Film: CFDC, 1971, as La Veuve Couderc (The Widow Couderc) (scw: Pascal Jardin, Pierre Granier-Deferre; dir: Granier-Deferre)
*The Train. Film: Fox-Lira, 1973, as Le Train (The Train) (scw: Pascal Jardin; dir: Pierre Granier-Deferre)
*The Trial of Bebe Donge. Film: UGC, 1952, as La Verite sur Bebe Donge (The Truth About Bebe Donge) (scw: Maurice Auberge; dir: Henry Decoin)
*Tropic Moon. Film: Corso, 1983, as Equateur (Equator) (scw & dir: Serge Gainsbourg)
*The Watchmaker of Everton. Film: Lira, 1974, as L'Horloger de Saint-Paul (The Watchmaker of Saint-Paul; The Clockmaker) (scw: Jean Aurenche, Pierre Bost; dir: Bertrand Tavernier)
*Young Cardinaud. Film: Rivers, 1956, as Le Sang a la Tete (The Blood to the Head) (scw: Michael Audiard, Gilles Grangier; dir: Grangier)

*SIMMEL, JOHANNES MARIO
*The Affair of Nina B. Film: Cinedis, 1961, as Affaire Nina B (The Affair Nina B) (scw: Roger Nimier, Robert Siodmak; dir: Siodmak)
*The Caesar Code. Film: Roxy, 1971, as Und Jimmy Ging zum Regenbogen (And Jimmy Went to the Rainbow's Foot) (scw: Manfred Purzer; dir: Alfred Vohrer)
*Cain '67. Film: Roxy, 1973, as Alle Menschen Werden Brueder (All People Will Be Brothers) (scw: Manfred Purzer; dir: Alfred Vohrer)
*Dear Fatherland. Film: Constantin, 1976, as Lieb Vaterland, Magst Ruhig Sein (Dear Fatherland, Be at Peace) (scw & dir: Roland Kirk)
*Love Is Just a Word. Film: Roxy, 1971, as Liebe Ist Nur ein Wort

(Love Is Only a Word) (scw: Manfred Purzer; dir: Alfred Vohrer)
No Man Is an Island. Popular Library, 1982
*The Traitor Blitz. Film: Roxy, 1972, as Der Stoff aus Dem die Traeume Sind (The Stuff That Dreams Are Made of) (scw: Manfred Purzer; dir: Alfred Vohrer)
*The Wind and the Rain. Film: Roxy, 1975, as Die Antwort Kennt Nur der Wind (Only the Wind Knows the Answer) (scw: Manfred Purzer; dir: Alfred Vohrer)

*SIMMONS, GEOFFREY
Murdock. Arbor, 1983 <2010, hosp.>

SIMMONS, JOHN
Cried the Piper. Dell, 1983
Lamplighter. GM, 1984 <Chi.>

*SIMMONS, MARY KAY
*The Girl with the Key. <NYC>

SIMMONS, RICHARD ALAN. See: Michael Lasker.

SIMON, HEATHER
Condorman. NEL pb, 1981

*SIMON, ROGER L(ICHTENBERG). Ref also: BM, TM. SC: Moses Wine, also in new title below.
*The Big Fix. Film: Universal, 1978 (scw: Roger L. Simon; dir: Jeremy Paul Kagan)
California Roll. Villard, 1985 <Calif.>

*SIMON, S. J. See: *Caryl Brahms.

SIMON, S(AMUEL) SYLVAN. 1910-   .
Murder at Mrs. Loring's. French, 19?? (1-act play.)

SIMONSEN, SIGURD JAY. 1891-   .
Below Third Street. Vantage, 1950 <Mpls., 1920s>

SIMPSON, ALAN (FRANCIS). See: *Ray(mond Percy) Galton.

*SIMPSON, DOROTHY. Ref: TC2. SC: Insp. Luke Thanet, in all titles below. Set: Eng.
Close Her Eyes. Joseph, 1984; Scribner, 1984
Last Seen Alive. Joseph, 1985; Scribner, 1985
The Night She Died. Joseph, 1981; Scribner, 1981
Puppet for a Corpse. Joseph, 1983; Scribner, 1983
Six Feet Under. Joseph, 1982; Scribner, 1982

*SIMPSON, HELEN (DE GUERRY). Ref also: CA; not in TC2. See also: *Clemence Dane.

*SIMPSON, HOWARD R(USSELL)
The Jumpmaster. Doubleday, 1984; Hale, 1985 <Mars.>

SIMPSON, JOHN. 1944-   .
A Fine and Private Place. Robson, 1982; St. Martin's, 1983 <Pol.>
Moscow Requiem. Robson, 1981; St. Martin's, 1981

SIMPSON, REGINALD and FRANK GREGORY
Living Dangerously. Cassell, 1934 (3-act play.) Film: BIP, 1936 (scw: Dudley Leslie, Marjorie Deans, Geoffrey Kerr; dir: Herbert Brenon)

*SIMPSON, RONALD. Pseudonym of Ronald Sugden Tilly.

*SIMS, GEORGE (FREDERICK ROBERT)
Coat of Arms. Macmillan (London), 1984
The Keys of Death. Macmillan (London), 1982
Who Is Cato? Macmillan (London), 1981

SIMSON, EVE. 1937-   . Ref: CA.
The Corona Affair. Icarus, 1983

SINBAD. Pseudonym of Aylward Edward Dingle, 1874-   .
Pipe All Hands! Harrap, 1935; Lippincott, 1935 ss, one criminous
Sailors Do Care. Harrap, 1936 ss, one criminous

SINCLAIR, CLIVE. 1948-   . SC: Joshua Smolinsky, in one ss in each volume below.
Bed Bugs. Allison, 1982 ss
Hearts of Gold. Allison, 1980 ss

SINCLAIR, CLOVER. Pseudonym of Dilys Gater, 1944-   . Ref: CA.
Lallie. Hale, 1983 <past>

*SINCLAIR, MAY
Tales Told by Simpson. Hutchinson, 1930; Macmillan, 1930 ss, at least one criminous

*SINCLAIR, MICHAEL
*How to Steal a Million. (Novelization of film: TCF, 1966; scw: Harry Kurnitz; dir: William Wyler.)

*SINCLAIR, MICHAEL. Pseudonym of Michael Shea, 1946-   , q.v.

*SINCLAIR, MURRAY. 1950-   . Ref: CA. SC: Ben Crandel, in *Tough Luck L.A., and in title below.
Only in L.A. A&W, 1982 <L.A.>

*SINCLAIR, OLGA (ELLEN WATERS)
*Hearts by the Tower. <Scot.>

SINCLAIR, UPTON (BEALL). 1878-1968. Ref: CA. SC: Lanny Budd, in all titles.
-Dragon Harvest. Viking, 1945; Laurie, 1945
-O Shepherd, Speak! Viking, 1949; Laurie, 1950
-One Clear Call. Viking, 1948; Laurie, 1949
-Presidential Agent. Viking, 1944; Laurie, 1944
-Presidential Mission. Viking, 1947; Laurie, 1948
-The Return of Lanny Budd. Viking, 1953
-A World to Win. Viking, 1946; Laurie, 1946

*SINGER, BART
*You're Wrong, Delaney. <Australia>

*SINGER, LOREN. Ref: TM.
*The Parallax View. Film: Paramount, 1974 (scw: David Giler, Lorenzo Semple, Jr.; dir: Alan J. Pakula)

SINGER, ROCHELLE. 1939-   . Pseudonym: Shelley Singer, q.v.

SINGER, SHELLEY. Pseudonym of Rochelle Singer, 1939-   . Ref: CA, TM. SC: Jake Samson, in both titles.
Free Draw. St. Martin's, 1984 <Calif.>
Samson's Deal. St. Martin's, 1983 <S.F.>

*SINGER, SALLY M.
Giver of Song. Warner, 1982

*SIODMAK, CURT. Ref: CA.
*Donovan's Brain. Film: Republic, 1944, as The Lady and the Monster; released in Britain as The Lady and the Doctor (scw: Dane Lussier, Frederick Kohner; dir: George Sherman). Also: United Artists, 1953 (scw & dir: Felix Feist). Also: Stross, 1962, as Vengeance (scw: Robert Stewart, Philip Mackie, John Kruse; dir: Freddie Francis)

SIRAUDIN, PAUL. 1813-1883. See: Eugene Moreau, 1806-1876.

SIRIS, PETER. 1944-   . Ref: CA.
The Peking Mandate. Putnam, 1983 <China>

*SJOWALL, MAJ and *PER WAHLOO. Ref also: TM.
*The Abominable Man. Film: AB Svensk, 1976, as Mannen Pa Taget (The Man on the Roof) (scw & dir: Bo Widerberg)
*The Laughing Policeman. Film: TCF, 1973; released in Britain as An Investigation of Murder (scw: Thomas Rickman; dir: Stuart Rosenberg)
*The Man Who Went Up in Smoke. Film: Libik, 1981, as Mannen Som Glick Upp i Roek (The Man Who Went Up in Smoke) (scw: Wolfgang Muelbauer; dir: Peter Bacso)

SKEDGELL, MARIAN (JAY). 1921-   .
Ref: CA.
Farm Boy. St. Martin's, 1985 <Conn.>

SKELTON, ALICE. Pseudonym: *Abigail Clements.

*SKIMIN, ROBERT (ELWAYNE). 1929-   .
Ref: CA. SC: Stonewall (Soldier for Hire), in all titles.
Bloodletting! Zebra, 1982
Libyan Warlord. Zebra, 1982 <Libya>
Trojan in Iran. Zebra, 1981
U.N. Sabotage. Zebra, 1981
Zulu Blood. Zebra, 1981

*SKINNER, AINSLIE. Pseudonym of *Paula Gosling, 1939-   , q.v.

SKINNER, MICHAEL. Pseudonym: *Alix De Marquand.

*SKINNER, MICHAEL. 1924-   .
When a Blonde Dies. Hale, 1983

*SKIRROW, DESMOND. Journalist. (corrected misprint)

*SKLAR, GEORGE. 1908-   .
Merry-Go-Round, with Eric Trent. (Brooklyn), 1932 (3-act play.) Film: Universal, 1932, as Afraid to Talk (scw: Tom Reed; dir: Edward L. Cahn)

*SKOTTOWE, B(RITIFFE) C(ONSTABLE). 1857-1925.

SLADE, MICHAEL. Joint pseudonym of Jay Clarke, John Banks, and Richard Covell, three Vancouver lawyers who specialize in the field of criminal insanity.
Headhunter. Allen, 1984; Morrow, 1985 <Van.>

*SLADEK, JOHN THOMAS. Ref: TM.
Book of Clues. Corgi, 1984

*SLATER, HUMPHREY
*The Conspirator. Film: MGM, 1949 (scw: Sally Benson, Gerard Fairlie; dir: Victor Saville)

*SLATER, IAN (DAVID)
Air Glow Red. Severn, 1982; Doubleday, 1981

SLATER, NIGEL. 1944-   . Ref: CA.
Mad Death. Granada pb, 1983

*SLAVITT, DAVID R(YTMAN). Pseudonym: *Henry Sutton.
Ringer. Dutton, 1982; Severn, 1983 <U.S., 1942>

*SLESAR, HENRY. Ref also: TM.
Acrostic Mysteries. Avon, 1985 puzzle ss
*A Bouquet of Clean Crimes and Neat Murders. ... Arrow, 1963

SLIGO, JOHN
The Concert Masters. Hodder, 1983

*SLIM, ICEBERG. Pseudonym of *Robert Beck.
Trick Baby. Holloway, 1968 <Chi.> Film: Universal, 1973 (scw: T. Raewyn, A. Neuberg, Larry Yust; dir: Yust)

SLOAN, CHRISTOPHER
-In Search of Eagles. Zebra, 1982
The Wings of Death. Zebra, 1983 <Fr., WWII>

SLOAN, MICHAEL
Underground. English Theatre, 1984 (Play.)

SLOANE, E. L.
Death on Delivery. Messenger, 1984
Prodigal Gun. Messenger, 1984

*SLOANE, WILLIAM (MILLIGAN)
*The Edge of Running Water. Film: Columbia, 1941, as The Devil Commands (scw: Robert D. Andrews, Milton Gunzberg; dir: Edward Dmytryk)

SLOTE, ALFRED. 1926-   . Member of English Dept. at Williams College.
Lazarus in Vienna. McGraw, 1956 <Vienna>

SLOVO, GILLIAN. 1952-   .
Morbid Symptoms. Pluto, 1984; Dembner, 1985

*SMALL, AUSTIN J.
   *The Man They Couldn't Arrest. Film:
      Gaumont British, 1933 (scw & dir:
      T. Hayes Hunter)

*SMART, HAWLEY
   *A Black Business. criminous

SMILEY, JANE (GRAVES). 1949-
      Ref: CA.
   Duplicate Keys. Knopf, 1984; Cape,
      1984 <NYC>

*SMITH, A(NTHONY) C(HARLES) H(OCKLEY).
      1935-   . Ref: CA.
   Extra Cover. Weidenfeld, 1981

SMITH, ALISON. 1932-   . Born in
      Boston suburb; raised 5 children
      and wrote 2 children's books; was
      newspaper columnist; living in
      R.I. Ref: TM.
   Someone Else's Grave. St. Martin's,
      1984 <Vt.>

*SMITH, CHARLES MERRILL.   -1985.
      Ref: CA, TM. SC: Reverend C. P.
      "Con" Randollph, also in title
      below.
   Reverend Randollph and the Unholy
      Bible. Putnam, 1983 <Chi.>

SMITH, CONRAD SUTTON
   Chain of Circumstances. Dramatists,
      1962 (3-act play.) <Paris>

SMITH, D(ENNIS) O. SC: Sherlock Holmes
      (following *A. Conan Doyle, q.v.),
      in all titles.
   The Adventure of the Christmas
      Visitor. Diogenes, 1985
   The Adventure of the Purple Hand.
      Diogenes, 1982
   The Adventure of the Unseen Tra-
      veler. Diogenes, 1983
   The Adventure of the Zodiac Plate.
      Diogenes, 1984
   The Secret of Shoreswood Hall.
      Diogenes, 1985

*SMITH, DAVID. Ref: TM. SC: Jim
      Stevens, in *The Leo Conversion,
      and in new title below.
   *The Leo Conversion. ... Hale, 1982
   Timbuktu. Dodd, 1983 <Afr.>

SMITH, DONALD
   Under Cover of Darkness. Leisure,
      1981; Star, 1981

SMITH, ELLEN HART. Pseudonym: *Louisa
      Revell.

SMITH, EVELYN E. Pseudonym: *Delphine
      Lyons.

SMITH, FRANCIS. Pseudonym: S. F. X.
      Dean, q.v.

*SMITH, FRANK E. 1919-1984. Pseudonym:
      *Jonathan Craig, q.v.

*SMITH, FREDERICK E(SCREET)
   *-633 Squadron. Film: Mirisch,
      1964 (scw: James Clavell, Howard
      Koch; dir: Walter E. Grauman)
   *Waterloo. delete: not criminous

*SMITH, FREDRIKA SHUMWAY. 1877-1968.
      Ref: CA.

SMITH, GEORGE H(ENRY). 1922-
      Pseudonym: Hal Stryker, q.v.
   The Second War of Worlds. Daw, 1978
      (Sherlock Holmes) <future>

*SMITH, GUY N(EWMAN)
   -Cannibal Cult. NEL pb, 1982
   *Satan's Snowdrop. ... PB, 1983
      <Switz.>

SMITH, HENRY T.
   Death in Small Corners. Hale, 1984

*SMITH, IAIN CRICHTON
   The Search. Gollancz, 1983

*SMITH, J. C. S. Pseudonym of Jane
      S. Smith, 1947-   . Ref: CA.
      SC: Quentin Jacoby, in *Jacoby's
      First Case, and in title below.
   Nightcap. Atheneum, 1984; Quartet,
      1985 <NYC>

SMITH, JANE S. 1947-   . Pseudonym:
      J. C. S. Smith, q.v.

*SMITH, JASPER
   Sledgehammer. Hamlyn, 1981

SMITH, JOAN
   The Devious Duchess. Crest, 1985
      <Eng., 1800s>
   Midnight Masquerade. Crest, 1985
      <Eng., 1800s>

SMITH, JOHN. 1943-   . Former RAF
      and charter pilot.
   Patterson's Volunteers. Century,
      1984; Norton, 1985
   Skytrap. Century, 1983; Norton, 1984

SMITH, JONATHAN
   Come Back. Joseph, 1983 <Czech.>

SMITH, JULIE. 1944-   . Ref: CA, TM.
      SC: Rebecca Schwartz = RS.
   Death Turns a Trick. Walker, 1982
      <S.F.> RS
   The Sourdough Wars. Walker, 1984
      <S.F.> RS
   True-Life Adventure. Mysterious
      Press, 1985 <S.F.>

*SMITH, KAY NOLTE. Ref also: TC2.
   Catching Fire. Coward, 1982 <NYC,
      theatre>
   Elegy for a Soprano. Villard, 1985;
      Severn, 1986 <NYC>
   Mindspell. Morrow, 1983

*SMITH, L. NEIL. SC: Win Bear, in
   *The Probability Broach, and in
      title marked WB below.
   Their Majesties' Bucketeers. Bal-
      lantine, 1981
   The Venus Belt. Ballantine, 1981;
      Futura, 1981 WB

SMITH, LEE. 1944-   . Ref: CA.
   Family Linen. Putnam, 1985

*SMITH, MARTIN CRUZ. Ref also: BM,
      TC2, TM.
   Gorky Park. Random, 1981; Collins,
      1981 <Moscow> Film: Orion, 1983
      (scw: Dennis Potter; dir: Michael
      Apted)
   *Nightwing. Film: Polyc, 1979 (scw:
      Steve Shagan, Bud Shrake, Martin
      Cruz Smith; dir: Arthur Hiller)

SMITH, MILBURN. Pseudonym: *Ellen
      Milburn.

*SMITH, NEVILLE
   *Gumshoe. (Novelization of film: Co-
      lumbia, 1971; scw: Neville Smith;
      dir: Stephen Frears.)

SMITH, PERRY MICHAEL. 1937-
   -Last Rites. Scribner, 1971

*SMITH, ROBERT ARTHUR
   *The Kramer Project. <Can.>

SMITH, RUSSELL. See: *Bruno Rossi,
      *Frank Scarpetta.

*SMITH, SHELLEY
   *The Ballad of the Running Man. Film:
      Peet, 1963, as The Running Man
      (scw: John Mortimer; dir: Carol
      Reed)

*SMITH, TERRENCE LORE
   *The Thief Who Came to Dinner. Film:
      Warner, 1973 (scw: Walter Hill;
      dir: Bud Yorkin)

SMITH, VERONICA
   Thunder Castle. Zebra, 1981

*SMITH, WILBUR (ADDISON)
   The Leopard Hunts in Darkness.
      Heinemann, 1984; Doubleday, 1984
      <Afr.>
   *The Train from Katanga. Film: MGM,
      1968, as The Dark of the Sun;
      released in Britain as The Mercen-
      aries (scw: Quentin Werty, Adrian
      Spies; dir: Jack Cardiff)

*SMITH, WILLIAM DALE. 1929-1986.

SMITH, WINCHELL, 1871-1933, and WILLIAM
      COLLIER, 1868-   .
   Going Crooked. French, 1926 (3-act
      play.) Silent film: Fox, 1926
      (scw: Keene Thompson, Albert Shelby
      Le Vino; dir: George Melford)

SMITHERS, JACK. SC: Richard Hannay,
      following *John Buchan; Bulldog
      Drummond, following *H. C. McNeile;
      and Bertram Pleydell, following
      *Dornford Yates.
   Combined Forces: Being the Latter-Day
      Adventures of Maj. Gen. Sir Richard
      Hannay, Captain Hugh (Bulldog)
      Drummond, and Berry & Co. Buchan,
      1983

*SMOKE, STEPHEN. See: Wade Barker.

SMULLYAN, RAYMOND. Mathematician,
      logician, university professor.
   The Chess Mysteries of Sherlock
      Holmes. Knopf, 1979; Hutchinson,
      1980 (Chess problems with a
      framing Sherlock Holmes narra-
      tive.)

*SMYTHE, FRANK S. 1900-1949.

*SNAITH, J(OHN) C(OLLIS)
   *-The Crime of Constable Kelly.
      Silent film: Stoll, 1925, as A
      Romance of Mayfair (dir: Thomas
      Bentley)

SNEAL, PATRICIA
   Is There Any Body There? ARC, 1984
      (Play.)

SNELGROVE, MICHAEL
   Hidden Meanings. French, 19??
      (1-act play.)

SNIPES, DEBORAH. Pseudonyms: *Deborah
      Scott, *Marianne De Jay Scott.

*SNOW, KATHLEEN. Ref also: TM.

*SNOWDEN, (JAMES) KEIGHLEY. 1860-1947.

SNYDER, GENE
   Tomb Seven. Charter, 1985 <Mex.>

SODERBERG, HJALMAR (EMIL FREDERIK).
      1869-1941.
   -Doctor Glas. Chatto, 1963; Little,
      1964 (Translation of "Doktor
      Glas." Stockholm, 1958.)

*SOHL, JERRY
   -Death Sleep. GM, 1983

SOHLAND, ALFRED
   Evidence Circumstantial. Vantage,
      1956 <Newark>

*SOLMSSEN, ARTHUR R. G.
   -Rittenhouse Square, Little, 1968;
      Hodder, 1969 <Phil.>

SOLSKI, WACLAW. Born in Poland.
   The Train Leaves at Midnight.
      Crown, 1951 <Pol.> (Translation
      of "Pociag Odchodzi o Polnocy.")

*SOMERS, PAUL
   *Beginner's Luck. Film: Merton Park,
      1959, as The Desperate Man (scw:
      James Eastwood; dir: Peter Max-
      well)

*SOMERVILLE-LARGE, PETER
   Hang Glider. Gollancz, 1985
   A Living Dog. Gollancz, 1981; Double-
      day, 1982

SOMMERS, BEVERLY
   Mistaken Identity. Harlequin, 1984

SONNY, ST. CLAIR
   The St. Lucian Affair. New Horizon,
      1982

SOREL, MARILYN MEESKE. Pseudonym:
      *Nina Lansdale.

SORRENTINO, GILBERT. 1929-   . Ref:
      CA.
   Odd Number. North Point, 1985

*SOUTAR, ANDREW
   *Back from the Dead. Silent film:
      Postman, 1925, as Back to Life
      (scw: Harry Chandlee; dir:
      Whitman Bennett)
   *A Beggar in Purple. Silent film:
      Pathe, 1920 (dir: Edgar Lewis)
   *Butterflies in the Rain. delete:
      not criminous
   *The Devil's Triangle. Film: TCF,
      1932, as Almost Married (scw:
      Wallace Smith; dir: William Cameron
      Menzies)
   *The Green Orchard. delete: not
      criminous
   *Hornet's Nest. delete: not criminous
   *In the Blood. Silent film: West,
      1923 (scw: J. Bertram Brown; dir:
      Walter West)
   *Other Men's Shoes. Silent film:
      Lewis, 1920 (scw: George Dubois
      Procter; dir: Edgar Lewis)
   *The Phantom in the House. Film:
      Trem Carr, 1929 (scw: Arthur

Hoerl; dir: Phil Rosen)
-Silent Thunder. Hutchinson, 1929.
 Film: World Wide, 1932, as The Man
 Called Back (scw: Robert Presnell;
 dir: Robert Florey)
*Snow in the Desert. delete: not
 criminous
*Worldly Goods. Film: Continental,
 1929 (scw: John Grey, Scott Little-
 ton; dir: Phil Rosen)

*SOUTHCOTT, AUDLEY. SC: Frank Marker,
 in *Cross That Palm When I Come
 to It, and in title by *Anthony
 Marriott.

*SOUVESTRE, PIERRE and *MARCEL ALLAIN
 *Fantomas. Silent film: Gaumont,
 1914. Also: Fox, 1921 (scw & dir:
 Edward Sedgwick). Sound film:
 Braunberger, 1934, in French
 (dir: Paul Fejos)

*SOUZA, ERNEST. Pseudonym of Evelyn
 Scott, 1893-1963.

SOWANDA, BODE
 Dangerous Games. Safari, 1983

*SPADE, DANNY
 Waterfront Rat. Scion, 1951

SPAIN, NICHOLAS
 Wine, Women & Bullets. Kozy, 1963

SPALDING, JOSEPH. Pseudonym of *Tom
 (Barnard) Taggart.
 Spider Island. French, 1942
 (3-act play.) <New Eng.>

*SPARK, MURIEL (SARAH)
 -The Driver's Seat. Macmillan (Lon-
 don), 1970; Knopf, 1970
 -The Mandelbaum Gate. Macmillan (Lon-
 don), 1965; Knopf, 1965
 -Memento Mori. Macmillan (London),
 1959; Lippincott, 1959
 The Only Problem. Bodley, 1984;
 Coward, 1984

*SPEARMAN, FRANK H(AMILTON)
 -Whispering Smith. Scribner, 1906;
 Hodder, 1916. Silent film: Metro-
 politan, 1926 (scw: Elliott J.
 Clawson, Will M. Ritchey; dir:
 George Melford). Sound film: Para-
 mount, 1948 (scw: Frank Butler,
 Karl Lamb; dir: Leslie Fenton)

SPENCE, DERMOT CHESSON
 Little Red Shoes. Williams, 1937
 ss, some criminous

SPENCE, MICHELE
 Rebekka Moon. Dell, 1983 <Midwest>

*SPENCE, RALPH
 *The Gorilla. Silent film: First Na-
 tional, 1927 (scw: Al Cohn, Henry
 McCarty; dir: Alfred Santell).
 Sound film: First National, 1930
 (scw: W. Harrison Orkow, Herman
 Ruby, Ralph Spence; dir: Bryan
 Foy). Also: Warner, 1937, as Sh!
 The Octopus (scw: George Bricker;
 dir: William McGann). Also: TCF,
 1939 (scw: Rian James, Sid Silvers;
 dir: Alan Dwan)

*SPENCE, WALL
 The Opening of a Door. Dramatic,
 1935 (1-act play.)
 *The Woman in Black. Silent film: AB,
 1916 (dir: Lawrence Marston)

SPENCER, FLOYD ALBERT. 1899-1978.
 Joint pseudonym with Paula Teresa
 Bayne Spencer, 1907-   : *Spencer
 Bayne, q.v.

*SPENCER, HANK
 *No Face for a Killer. Modern Fiction,
 1954 (date correction)

SPENCER, JOHN. 1944-   . SC: Charley
 Case, in both titles. Set: Calif.,
 1997.
 A Case for Charley. Fontana, 1984
 Charley Gets the Picture. Fontana,
 1985

SPENCER, PAULA TERESA BAYNE. 1907-   .
 Joint pseudonym with Floyd Albert
 Spencer, 1899-1978: *Spencer Bayne,
 q.v.

SPENCER, RICK. SC: Eric Ivorsen, in
 all titles.
 All That Glitters. Signet, 1983
 The Devil's Mirror. Signet, 1984
 Icebound. Signet, 1983

The Moneymaster. Signet, 1984
The Terror Merchant. Signet, 1984

*SPENCER, ROSS H(ARRISON). SC: Chance
 Purdue, also in title below marked
 CP.
 Echoes of Zero. St. Martin's, 1981
 <Ill.>
 The Missing Bishop. Mysterious Press,
 1985 <Chi., 1969>
 The Radish River Caper. Avon, 1981
 CP <Midwest>
 *The Reggis Arms Caper. (misprint
 correction)

*SPEWACK, BELLA COHEN and *SAMUEL
 SPEWACK, q.v.
 *The Solitaire Man. Film: MGM, 1933
 (scw: James Kavin McGuinness;
 dir: Jack Conway)

*SPEWACK, SAMUEL. See also: *Belle
 Cohen Spewack.
 *Murder in the Gilded Cage. Film:
 Columbia, 1931, as Secret Witness
 (scw: Samuel Spewack; dir: Thorn-
 ton Freeland)

*SPICER, BART. Ref also: TM.
 *The Adversary. <S.W.>

*SPICER, HENRY
 Bound to Please. Tinsley, 1867 ss,
 some criminous
 Brought to Book. Tinsley, 1870 ss,
 some criminous

SPICER, MICHAEL
 Final Act. Severn, 1981 <Eng., 2006>

SPIERING, FRANK. 1938-   Ref: CA.
 Berserker. Jove, 1981

*SPIKE, PAUL
 Last Rites. NAL, 1981; Granada, 1982
 <S.W.>

*SPILLANE, MICKEY. Ref also: TM. re-
 vised: TC2.
 *The Girl Hunters. Film: Colorama,
 1963 (scw: Mickey Spillane, Roy
 Rowland, Robert Fellows; dir:
 Rowland)
 *I, the Jury. Film: United Artists,
 1953 (scw & dir: Harry Essex).
 Also: American Cinema, 1982 (scw:
 Larry Cohen; dir: Richard T.
 Heffron)
 *Kiss Me, Deadly. Film: United Ar-
 tists, 1954 (scw: A. I. Bezzerides;
 dir: Robert Aldrich)
 *The Long Wait. Film: United Artists,
 1954 (scw: Alan Green, Lesser
 Samuels; dir: Victor Saville)
 *My Gun Is Quick. Film: United Ar-
 tists, 1957 (scw: Richard Powell,
 Richard Collins; dir: George A.
 White)
 Tomorrow I Die. Mysterious Press,
 1984 ss

SPIVEY, AMELIA JOSEPHINE. 1889-   .
 Michael. Dorrance, 1954 <Denver,
 1930s>

SPONDEE. Pseudonym.
 You're Far Too Young! Archer, 1932
 ss, criminous in part

SPONG, RICHARD. 1916-   .
 See If He Wins. Sloane, 1949
 <Paris, 1944>

SPRAGUE, GRETCHEN (BURNHAM). 1926-
 Ref: CA.
 Signpost to Terror. Dodd, 1967

*SPRIGG, C(HRISTOPHER) ST. JOHN. Ref:
 not in TC2.

SPRINGS, JOHN (B.), III
 Kansas. Holloway, 1984 <NYC>
 -Mink. Holloway, 1985

*SPRUILL, STEVEN G(REGORY). SC: Elias
 Kane, in *The Psychopath Plague,
 and in title marked EK below.
 The Genesis Shield. Tor, 1985
 The Imperator Plot. Doubleday, 1983
 <future> EK

STACEY, TOM <THOMAS CHARLES GERRARD>.
 1930-   . Ref: CA.
 The Worm in the Rose. Heinemann,
 1985; Stein, 1985 <Mid. East>

STACK, ANDY
 Lust Killer. Signet, 1983 <Oreg.>

*STACKELBERG, GENE
 *Double Agent. Film: Trio, 1966, as
 The Man Outside (scw: Samuel Gallu,
 Julian Bond, Roger Marshall; dir:
 Gallu)

*STACPOOLE, H(ENRY) DeVERE
 *The Cottage on the Fells. Probably
 = *The Man Without a Head, pub-
 lished as by *Tyler De Saix.

*STACTON, DAVID (DEREK). Pseudonyms:
 *Bud Clifton, *David West.
 -A Dancer in Darkness. Faber, 1960;
 Pantheon, 1962

*STADLEY, PAT (ANNA MAY GOUGH).
 1918-   . Ref: CA.

*STAGG, CLINTON H(OLLAND)
 *High Speed. Silent film: Hallmark,
 1920 (scw: John J. Glavey; dir:
 Charles Miller)

*STAHL, NORMAN
 The Buried Man, with Don Horan.
 McGraw, 1985

*STAHL, RAY
 *Death Stalks "The Wild Goose". (by
 William Maconachie)
 Murder Mayhem. Hamilton Stafford,
 1952 (by William Maconachie)
 *No Answer from a Corpse. (by *Harry
 Hossent)

STAHLMAN, J. I. See: Mary Crawford
 Fraser, 1851-1922.

STAINTON, AUDREY
 Sweet Rome. Holt, 1982; Allen, 1983
 <Rome>

*STALL, MIKE
 The Belshazzer Affair. Hale, 1981
 The Bormann Judgement. Hale, 1981
 Kill Hitler! Hale, 1981
 The Killing Mask. Hale, 1982
 The Wet Job. Hale, 1982

STANDER, SIEGFRIED. 1935-   . See:
 Christiaan (Neethling) Barnard,
 1922-

STANDISH, WALTER
 Blood for a Reckless Lady. Brown
 Watson, 1952
 Dames Are Welcome. Instructive Arts,
 1952
 Don't Sell Me Cheap. Brown Watson,
 1952
 Floosie Goes Astray. Brown Watson,
 1952
 Floosie on the Spot. Brown Watson,
 1952
 Floosie Passes By. Brown Watson,
 1952
 Floosie Takes a Fall. Brown Watson,
 1952
 I Like My Women Tough. Brown Watson,
 1950
 Just Like a Dame. Brown Watson, 1950
 No Time to Wait! Brown Watson, 1952
 Redheads Never Regret. Brown Watson,
 1952
 Softly--Softly. Brown Watson, 1952
 Street of Desire. Brown Watson, 1952
 Too Many Dames Spell Trouble. Brown
 Watson, ca.1952
 Without Virtue. Brown Watson, 1952
 Women That Are Lost. Instructional
 Arts, 1952

STANLEY, WILLIAM
 Cloud Nineteen. Walker, 1984 <WWII>

*STANFORD, ALFRED (BOLLER). 1900-1985.

STANFORD, TERRY. See: *Nat Karta.

*STANTON, KEN
 *Evil Cargo. <Carib.>
 *Sargasso Secret. <Carib.>
 *Whirlwind Beneath the Sea. <Ind. O.>

*STANWOOD, BROOKS. Joint pseudonym of
 Howard Kaminsky and Susan Stanwood
 Kaminsky, 1937-   . Ref for SSK:
 CA.
 The Seventh Child. Linden, 1981;
 Macdonald, 1982 <N.Y.>

*STANWOOD KAMINSKY, SUSAN. 1937-

STAPLES, REGINALD THOMAS. 1911-
 Pseudonym: Robert Tyler Stevens,
 q.v.

*STAPLETON, D.
  *The Crime, the Place, and the Girl. Arcadia, 1955 (date correction)

STARK, JACK ⟨JOHN H.⟩. 1914-   Ref: CA.
  -Killer Passion. Anchor, 1965

*STARK, RICHARD
  *The Hunter. Film: MGM, 1967, as Point Blank (scw: Alexander Jacobs, David Newhouse, Rafe Newhouse; dir: John Boorman)
  *The Jugger. Film: Pathe, 1967, as Made in U.S.A. (scw & dir: Jean-Luc Godard)
  *The Man with the Getaway Face. Reprinted in Eng. under the U.S. title: Allison, 1985
  *The Mourner. ⟨Wash. D.C.⟩
  *The Outfit. Film: MGM, 1973 (scw & dir: John Flynn)
  *The Score. Film: Ariane, 1967, as Mise a Sac (Pillaged) (scw: Claude Sautet, Alain Cavalier, Oscar Dancigers; dir: Cavalier)
  *The Seventh. Film: MGM, 1968, as The Split (scw: Robert Sabaroff; dir: Gordon Flemyng)
  *Slayground. Film: Thorn EMI, 1983, (scw: Trevor Preston; dir: Terry Bedford)

*STARKS, RICHARD. (Incorrectly given as Starko in early printings of CF.) 1947-   . Ref: CA.

*STARNES, RICHARD. Ref: CA.

STARR, BEN
  The Button. French, 19?? (3-act play.)

STARR, FRANK
  Tales of Mystery. Wren, 1983 ss

STARR, HELEN UPSHAW. Pseudonym: *Helen Upshaw.

*STARR, JIMMY
  *The Corpse Came C.O.D. Film: Columbia, 1947 (scw: George Bricker, Dwight Babcock; dir: Henry Levin)

STARR, LEONARD and STAN DRAKE. All titles are in Kelly Green series.
  The Blood Tapes. Dargaud, 1983
  The Million-Dollar Hit. Dargaud, 1983
  One-Two-Three Die. Dargaud, 1983

*STARR, RICHARD (HENRY)
  *Married to a Spy. criminous

*STARRETT, (CHARLES) VINCENT (EMERSON). Ref also: TM.
  *The Great Hotel Murder. Film: TCF, 1935 (scw: Arthur Kober; dir: Eugene Forde)

STASHOWER, DANIEL. Writer and magician living in Wash. D.C.
  The Adventures of the Ectoplasmic Man. Morrow, 1985 ⟨Eng., 1910⟩ (Sherlock Holmes)

STATHAM, S(HERARD) M(ONTAGU)
  Hephzibah. Stockwell, 1922

STATHAM, WALLACE
  Mystery of Mynd. New Horizon, 1981
  -Running from Me. New Horizon, 1979

STAVINGSON, ROBERT BATHOS
  The Stranger Case of Dr. Hide and Mr. Crushall. Bevington, 1886

*STAYTON, FRANK
  "The Joan Danvers." French (NYC), 1926; French (London), 1927. (Play.) Silent film: B&C, 1920, as A Gamble in Lives (scw & dir: George Ridgwell)
  *The Passionate Adventure. Silent film: Gainsborough, 1924 (scw: Alfred Hitchcock; dir: Graham Cutts)

STEAD, PHILIP JOHN. Ref: CA.

*STEEGMULLER, FRANCIS. Pseudonym: David Keith, q.v.

*STEEL, DAVE (byline correction)
  *Beauty Found a Grave. (title correction)
  *Lovely But Deadly. (title correction)
  *You'll Live to Talk. (title correction)

STEEL, DAVID
  Lips of Death. Consul, 1965

*STEEL, KURT. Ref also: TC2.
  *Murder Goes to College. Film: Paramount, 1937 (scw: Brian Marlow, Robert Wyler, Eddie Welch; dir: Charles Riesner). Also: Paramount, 1937, as Partners in Crime (scw: Garnett Weston; dir: Ralph Murphy)

STEEL, RAY
  Baby Face Gangster. Phoenix (London), 1953

STEELE, HELEN. Joint pseudonym with Jack Steele: *Jaclen Steele.

STEELE, JACK. Joint pseudonym with Helen Steele: *Jaclen Steele.

*STEELE, JACLEN. Joint pseudonym of Jack and Helen Steele.

*STEELE, TOM
  *Cunning Against Force. Street, 1903 (Magnet #313)

*STEELE, WILBUR DANIEL
  Tower of Sand and other stories. Harper, 1929 ss, some criminous
  Film (based on ss "Footfalls"): Fox, 1921, as Footfalls (dir: Charles J. Brabin)
  *The Way to Gold. Film: TCF, 1957, as The Way to the Gold (scw: Wendell Mayes; dir: Robert D. Webb)

*STEELEY, ROBERT DEREK. See also:
  *Nick Carter.
  *Hot Ice. ⟨NYC⟩

*STEEMAN, (STANISLAUS) ANDRE
  *Six Dead Men. Film: Fox British, 1935, as The Riverside Murder (scw: Selwyn Jepson, Leslie Landau; dir: Albert Parker)

*STEIN, AARON MARC. 1906-1985. Ref also: TM: somewhat revised: TC2. SC: Matt Erridge, also in at least those titles marked ME.
  A Body for Buddy. Doubleday, 1981; Hale, 1981
  The Bombing Run. Doubleday, 1983; Hale, 1983 ME ⟨Belg.⟩
  The Garbage Collector. Doubleday, 1984; Hale, 1986 ME ⟨Switz.⟩
  Hangman's Row. Doubleday, 1982; Hale, 1982 ME ⟨Amst.⟩

*STEIN, BENJAMIN (J.). Ref: CA.
  The Manhattan Gambit. Doubleday, 1983; Deutsch, 1984 ⟨1943⟩

STEIN, DUFFY
  Out in the Shadows. Dell, 1984

*STEIN, SOL. SC: George Thomassy, in all titles below.
  The Magician. Delacorte, 1971; Joseph, 1971
  Other People. Harcourt, 1979; Collins, 1979
  The Touch of Treason. St. Martin's, 1985; Macmillan (London), 1985

STEINER, SUSAN
  Murder on Her Mind. GM, 1985 ⟨L.A.⟩

STENSTROM, RUTH. Pseudonym: *Marion Babson, q.v.

*STEPHAN, LESLIE (BATES)
  Murder or Not. Hale, 1981

*STEPHENS, CASEY. Pseudonym of *Sharon (Blythe) Wagner, q.v.

*STEPHENS, EDWARD (CARL)
  *The Submariner. ⟨ship⟩

*STEPHENS, REED. Pseudonym of Stephen R. Donaldson. Ref: TM. SC: Mick "Brew" Axbrewder, in *The Man Who Killed His Brother, and in title below.
  The Man Who Risked His Partner. Ballantine, 1984; Fontana, 1985 ⟨S.W.⟩

STEPHENS, WALTER
  Lost. Last, 1871 (4-act play founded on *The Mystery of Edwin Drood, by *Charles Dickens, q.v.)

*STERLING, STEWART. Ref also: TC2.
  *The Big Ear. (not The Big Bear, as given incorrectly in first printings of CF)

*STERLING, THOMAS (L.)
  *The Evil of the Day. Film (partial source): United Artists, 1966, as The Honey Pot (scw & dir: Joseph L. Mankiewicz)

*STERN, PHILIP VAN DOREN. 1900-1984.
  *Love Is the One with Wings. Also published as: Manhunt. Berkley, 1955 ⟨Maine⟩

*STERN, RICHARD G(USTAV)
  *In Any Case. Reprinted as: The Chaleur Network. Second Chance, 1981; Sidgwick, 1981

*STERN, RICHARD MARTIN
  -The Big Bridge. Doubleday, 1982; Secker, 1983
  *The Tower. Film (from this and "The Glass Inferno," by Thomas M. Scortia and Frank M. Robinson): TCF, 1974, as The Towering Inferno (scw: Stirling Silliphant; dir: John Guillermin, Irwin Allen)

STEVENS, CARL. Pseudonym of *Raymond Obstfeld, 1952-   , q.v. Other pseudonym: Jason Frost, q.v. See also: *Don(ald Eugene) Pendleton. SC: Christian Daguerre, in both titles.
  The Centaur Conspiracy. Gold Eagle, 1983
  Ride of the Razorback. Gold Eagle, 1984

*STEVENS, CURTIS. Joint pseudonym of *Richard (Alan) Curtis, q.v., and Paul Stevens. Pseudonym of Curtis alone: Ray Lilly, q.v.
  *The Gravy Train Hit. ... Dell, 1974

STEVENS, GORDON. Producer/director of ITV in Eng.; former journalist in London and South America.
  Spider. Coronet, 1984; Popular Library, 1985 ⟨Lima⟩

STEVENS, GUS
  Six Days to Die. Tower, 1981; Star, 1982

STEVENS, JOAN M.
  This Game of Murder. Consolidated (Syd.), 1944

STEVENS, PAUL. Joint pseudonym with *Richard (Alan) Curtis, q.v.: *Curtis Stevens.

STEVENS, ROBERT TYLER. Pseudonym of Reginald Thomas Staples, 1911-   Ref: CA.
  -The Hostage. Severn, 1985
  Shadows in the Afternoon. Severn, 1983

STEVENS, SERITA DEBORAH. 1949-   Ref: CA.
  Before the Fourteenth. Dell, 1985; Grafton, 1986 (Novelization of the "Cagney and Lacey" TV series.)
  Bloodstone Inheritance. Zebra, 1985
  The Shrieking Shadow of Penporth Island. Zebra, 1983

*STEVENS, SHANE
  The Anvil Chorus. Delacorte, 1985; Deutsch, 1985 ⟨Paris, 1975⟩

*STEVENSON, ANNE
  Turkish Rondo. Piatkus, 1981; Morrow, 1981 ⟨Turk.⟩

*STEVENSON, BURTON E(GBERT)
  *Little Comrade. Silent film: World, 1917, as On Dangerous Ground (scw: Frances Marion; dir: Robert Thornby)
  *The Mystery of the Boule Cabinet. Silent film: Unity, 1916, as The Pursuing Vengeance (dir: Martin Sabine). Sound film (partially based on this): First National, 1930, as In the Next Room (scw: Harvey Gates, James A. Starr; dir: Eddie Cline). Also: Warner, 1941, as The Case of the Black Parrot (scw: Robert E. Kent; dir: Noel M. Smith)

*STEVENSON, FLORENCE
  The Moonlight Variations. Jove, 1981

STEVENSON, JANET and PHILIP
  Counterattack. Morris, 1942 (3-act play.) Film: Columbia, 1945; released in Britain as One Against Seven (scw: John Howard Lawson; dir: Zoltan Korda)

*STEVENSON, JOHN. See: *Nick Carter.

STEVENSON, PHILIP. See: Janet Stevenson.

STEVENSON, RICHARD. Pseudonym of Richard Lipez, 1938-   . Ref: CA. SC: Donald Strachey, in both titles.
 Death Trick. St. Martin's, 1981; Alyson, 1985
 On the Other Hand, Death. St. Martin's, 1984 <N.Y.>

*STEVENSON, ROBERT LOUIS. See also: Richard Abbott, Leonard H. Caddy.
*The Body Snatcher. Film: RKO, 1945 (scw: Philip MacDonald, Carlos Keith; dir: Robert Wise). Also: Triad, 1959, as The Flesh and the Fiends (scw: John Gilling, Leon Griffiths; dir: Gilling)
*The Merry Men and other tales and fables. ss, one criminous
*New Arabian Nights. Film (from ss "The Sire de Maletroit's Door"): Univeral International, 1951, as The Strange Door (scw: Jerry Sackheim; dir: Joseph Pevney). Silent film (from ss "The Pavilion on the Links"): Paramount, 1920, as The White Circle (scw: Jack Gilbert, Jules Furthman; dir: Maurice Tourneur)
*The Strange Case of Dr. Jekyll and Mr. Hyde. Silent film: Wrench, 1910, as The Duality of Man. Also: Imp, 1913, as Dr. Jekyll and Mr. Hyde (scw & dir: Herbert Brenon). Also: Lubin, 1915, as Horrible Hyde (scw: E. W. Sargent; dir: Howell Hansel?). Also: Famous Players, 1920, as Dr. Jekyll and Mr. Hyde (scw: Clara S. Beranger; dir: John S. Robertson). Also: Pioneer, 1920, as Dr. Jekyll and Mr. Hyde (scw & dir: George Edwardes Hall). Sound film: Paramount, 1931, as Dr. Jekyll and Mr. Hyde (scw: Samuel Hoffenstein, Percy Heath; dir: Rouben Mamoulian). Also: MGM, 1941, as Dr. Jekyll and Mr. Hyde (scw: John Lee Mahin; dir: Victor Fleming). Also: Universal, 1953, as Abbott and Costello Meet Dr. Jekyll and Mr. Hyde (scw: Lee Loeb, John Grant; dir: Charles Lamont). Also: Hammer, 1959, as The Ugly Duckling (scw: Sid Colin, Jack Davies; dir: Lance Comfort). Also: Hammer, 1960, as The Two Faces of Dr. Jekyll; released in the U.S. as House of Fright (scw: Wolf Mankowitz; dir: Terence Fisher). Also: Amicus, 1970, as I, Monster (scw: Milton Subotsky; dir: Stephen Weeks). Also: Hammer, 1971, as Doctor Jekyll and Sister Hyde (scw: Brian Clemens; dir: Roy Ward Baker). Also: Paramount, 1982, as Jekyll and Hyde... Together Again (scw: Monica Johnson, Harvey Miller, Jerry Belson, Michael Lesson; dir: Belson)
*The Suicide Club. Silent film: AB, 1909 (scw: Frank Woods; dir: D. W. Griffith). Also: B&C, 1914 (dir: Maurice Elvey). Sound film: MGM, 1936; released in the U.S. as Trouble For Two (scw: Manuel Seff, Edward E. Paramore, Jr.; dir: J. Walter Ruben). Also: Cinematografica Interamericana, 1946, as La Dama de la Muerte (The Lady of Death) (dir: Carlos Hugo Christensen)
*The Wrong Box. Film: Salamander, 1966 (scw: Larry Gelbart, Burt Shrevelove; dir: Bryan Forbes)

*STEVERMER, C. J.
 The Duke and the Veil. Charter, 1981

STEWARD, SAMUEL M(ORRIS). 1909-   Ref: CA.
 Murder Is Murder Is Murder. Alyson (U.S. and London), 1985 <Fr., 1937>

STEWART, DESMOND (STIRLING). 1924-1981. Ref: CA.
 Leopard in the Grass. Euphorion, 1951; Farrar, 1952

STEWART, DOUGLAS
 Cellars' Market. Collins, 1983

*STEWART, FRED MUSTARD
*The Mephisto Waltz. Film: TCF, 1971 (scw: Ben Maddow; dir: Paul Wendkos)

STEWART, GARY. Born in Salt Lake City and raised a Mormon; lives in Indiana; professor and Chairman of Theatre at Indiana State Univ.
 The Tenth Virgin. St. Martin's, 1983 <Salt Lake City>

*STEWART, IAN
 Deadline in Jakarta. Hamlyn, 1981
 An H-Bomb for Alice. Hamlyn, 1981

*STEWART, J(OHN) I(NNES) M(ACKINTOSH). Ref also: TM.
 An Open Prison. Gollancz, 1984; Norton, 1984

STEWART, JEFF
 -Boudoirs Are My Beat. Art Enterprises, 1962 <NYC>

*STEWART, KERRY
*The Concorde--Airport 1979. (Novelization of film: Universal, 1979; scw: Eric Roth; dir: David Lowell Rich.)

*STEWART, MARY (FLORENCE ELINOR)
*The Moon-Spinners. Film: Disney, 1964 (scw: Michael Dyne; dir: James Neilson)

*STEWART, MICHAEL. Author of the books for the Broadway musicals "Bye Bye Birdie," "Carnival," "Hello, Dolly!", and "George M!" Living in NYC and Canne.
*Belle. <Fr.>

STEWART, MICHAEL. 1945-   .
 Far Cry. Macmillan (London), 1984
 The Fifty-First. Arrow, 1983
 -Monkey-Shines. Macmillan (London), 1983; Random, 1984

*STEWART, RAMONA
 Desert Town. Morrow, 1946; Quality, 1949. Film: Paramount, 1947, as Desert Fury (scw: Robert Rossen, A. I. Bezzerides, Ramona Stewart; dir: Lewis Allen)
*The Possession of Joel Delany. Film: ITC, 1971 (scw: Matt Robinson, Grimes Grice; dir: Waris Hussein)

STEWART, RAYMOND M. 1910-   .
 The Passionate Sin. Comet, 1957

STINSON, JIM
 Double Exposure. Scribner, 1985 <L.A.>

STINSON, JOE <JOSEPH C.>
 Sudden Impact. Warner, 1983; NEL pb, 1984 (Novelization of film: Warner, 198; scw: Joseph C. Stinson; dir: Clint Eastwood.) (Dirty Harry Callahan)

*STIRLING, ELAINE K. Living in Toronto.
 Unsuspected Conduct. Harlequin, 1985 <Rio de J.>

*STIVENS, DAL(LAS GEORGE)
*The Wide Arch. <Syd.>

STIVERS, DICK. House name. See also: *Don(ald Eugene) Pendleton. SC: Able Team (Carl Lyons, Pol Blancanales, Gadgets Schwartz), in all titles.
 Amazon Slaughter. Gold Eagle, 1983; Mills, 1985 <Braz.> (by C. J. Shiao)
 Army of Devils. Gold Eagle, 1983 <L.A.> (by G. H. Frost)
 Cairo Countdown. Gold Eagle, 1983; Mills, 1985 <Cairo> (by Paul Hofrichter)
 Death Strike. Gold Eagle, 1985 <Guat.> (by G. H. Frost)
 Deathbites. Gold Eagle, 1984 <Ga.> (by Tom Arnett)
 Fire and Maneuver. Gold Eagle, 1985; Mills, 1985 <Colom.> (by G. H. Frost)
 Five Rings of Fire. Gold Eagle, 1984 <L.A.> (by Tom Arnett)
 The Hostaged Island. Gold Eagle, 1982; Mills, 1984 <Calif.> (by Norman Winski and L. R. Payne) <Calif.>
 Into the Maze. Gold Eagle, 1984 <Mex. City> (by G. H. Frost)
 Ironman. Gold Eagle, 1985; Mills, 1985 <Guat.> (by G. H. Frost)
 Justice by Fire. Gold Eagle, 1983 <Calif.> (by G. H. Frost)
 Kill School. Gold Eagle, 1983 <Honduras> (by G. H. Frost)
 Rain of Doom. Gold Eagle, 1985 <Mid. East> (by G. H. Frost)
 Royal Flush. Gold Eagle, 1984 <Eng.>
 Scorched Earth. Gold Eagle, 1984 <Mex.> (by G. H. Frost)
 Shot to Hell. Gold Eagle, 1985; Mills, 1986 <Belize> (by Chuck Rogers)
 Tech War. Gold Eagle, 1985; Mills, 1985 <Cey.> (by G. H. Frost)
 Texas Showdown. Gold Eagle, 1982; Mills, 1984 <Tex.> (by Larry Powell and L. R. Payne)
 They Came to Kill. Gold Eagle, 1984 (by G. H. Frost)
 Tower of Terror. Gold Eagle, 1982; Mills, 1983 (by L. R. Payne) <NYC>
 Warlord of Azatlan. Gold Eagle, 1983; Mills, 1985 <Guat.>

*STOCKBRIDGE, GRANT. SC: Richard Wentworth (The Spider), also in all titles below.
 Corpse Cargo. Dimedia, 1985 <train>
 The Prince of Evil. Dimedia, 1985 <NYC>
 Satan's Death Blast. Dimedia, 1984 <N.Y.>

*STOCKTON, FRANK R(ICHARD). Ref also: CA.

*STOCKWELL, GAIL. Pseudonym of Grace Stockwell.

STOCKWELL, GRACE. Pseudonym: *Gail Stockwell.

STOCKWELL, JOHN (ROBERT). 1937-   Ref: CA.
 In Search of Enemies. Norton, 1984
 Red Sunset. Morrow, 1982; Gollancz, 1982

*STOKER, BRAM. See also: Bob Hall, Stephen Hotchner, 1941-   *Tim J. Kelly, John Mattera, Anne Pearson. Ref: not in TC2.
*Dracula. Silent film (Germany): Prana, 1929, as Nosferatu (scw: Henrik Galeen; dir: Friedrich Wilhelm Murnau). Sound film: Universal, 1931 (scw: Garrett Fort; dir: Tod Browning). Also: Hammer, 1957; released in the U.S. as The Horror of Dracula (scw: Jimmy Sangster; dir: Terence Fisher). Also: Hammer, 1965, as Dracula, Prince of Darkness (scw: John Sansom, Anthony Hinds; dir: Terence Fisher). Also: Fenix, 1970, as El Conde Dracula (Count Dracula) (scw: Jess Franco, Peter Welbeck, Augusto Finochi; dir: Franco). Also: Latglen, 1974 (scw: Richard Matheson; dir: Dan Curtis). Also: Kodiak, 1979, as Dracula Sucks (scw: Darryl A. Marshak, David J. Kern; dir: Philip Marshak). Also (in part): Films Nautile, 1981, as Les Jeux de la Comtesse Dolingen de Gratz (The Games of the Countess Dolingen of Gratz) (scw & dir: Catherine Binet)
*Dracula's Guest. Film (from title ss): Universal, 1936, as Dracula's Daughter (scw: Garrett Fort; dir: Lambert Hillyer)
 The Gates of Life; see *The Man
*The Jewel of the Seven Stars. Film: Hammer, 1971, as Blood from the Mummy's Tomb (scw: Christopher Wicking; dir: Seth Holt, Michael Carreras). Also: Solofilm, 1980, as The Awakening (scw: Allan Scott, Chris Bryant, Clive Exton; dir: Mike Newell)
*The Man. U.S. title (abridged): The Gates of Life. Cupples, 1908

*STOKES, DONALD (HUBERT). 1913-1986. Ref: CA.

*STOKES, MANNING LEE. Pseudonym: March Marlowe, q.v.

*STONE, ANDREW L.
*Cry Terror. (Novelization of film: MGM, 1958; scw & dir: Andrew L. Stone.)
*The Decks Ran Red. (Novelization of film: MGM, 1958; scw: Andrew L. Stone, Virginia Stone; dir: Andrew L. Stone.)
*Julie. (Novelization of film: MGM, 1956; scw & dir: Andrew L. Stone.)

*STONE, AUSTIN
 Hangman's Harvest. Gifford, 1948

*STONE, EDDIE. Pseudonym of Carlton Hollander.

STONE, MARIE
    Little Murder. Olive, 1985

*STONE, PETER H(ESS)
    *Charade. (Novelization of film: Universal, 1964; scw: Peter Stone; dir: Stanley Donen.)

STONE, ROBERT (ANTHONY). 1937-
    Ref: CA.
    Dog Soldiers. Houghton, 1974; Secker, 1975. Film: United Artists, 1978, as Who'll Stop the Rain? (scw: Judith Roscoe, Robert Stone; dir: Karel Reisz)
    A Flag for Sunrise. Knopf, 1981; Secker, 1981 <Cent. Am.>

STONE, WILLIAM C. and H(ARRY) FOWLER MEAR
    Dangerous Love. Rich, 1933

*STONE, ZACHERY. Psseudonym of *Ken(neth Martin) Follett, q.v.
    *The Modigliani Scandal. ... Morrow, 1985, as by Ken Follett

STONEBRAKER, FLORENCE. Pseudonym: Fern Shepard, q.v.

STONEHOUSE, JOHN (THOMSON). 1925-
    Ref: CA. Pseudonym: *James Lund.
    The Baring Fault. Calder, 1985; Riverrun, 1986
    Ralph. Cape, 1982; Cape (U.S.), 1984 <Brus.>

*STOPPARD, TOM
    After Magritte. Faber, 1971 (1-act play.)
    Jumpers. Faber, 1972 (3-act play.)

*STORM, LESLIE
    *The Day's Mischief. Film: Two Cities, 1953, as Personal Affair (scw & dir: Anthony Pelissier)

*STORM, MICHAEL. Byline sometimes given as: Michael Storme. SC: Nick Cranley, also in titles below.
    Dame in My Bed. Archer, 1950; Kaywin, 1951 <Chi.>
    *Make Mine a Harlot. ... Kaywin 1952 <Chi.>

STORME, MICHAEL. Byline somtimes given this way for: *Michael Storm, q.v.

*STORY, JACK TREVOR
    *Live Now, Pay Later. Film: Regal, 1962 (scw: Jack Trevor Story; dir: Jay Lewis)
    Man Pinches Bottom. Allen, 1962
    *Mix Me a Person. Film: Wessex, 1962 (scw: Ian Dalrymple, Roy Kerridge; dir: Leslie Norman)
    *The Trouble with Harry. Film: Paramount, 1955 (scw: John Michael Hayes; dir: Alfred Hitchcock)

STORY, WILLIAM L.
    Cemeteries Are for Dying. Doubleday, 1982 <Boston>
    Domino Spell. Leisure, 1981

*STOUT, REX. Ref also: TM. SC: Nero Wolfe, also in title marked NW.
    Death Times Three. Bantam, 1985 (3 novelets.) NW
    *Fer-de-Lance. Film: Columbia, 1936, as Meet Nero Wolfe (scw: Howard J. Green, Bruce Manning, Joseph Anthony; dir: Herbert Biberman)
    *The League of Frightened Men. Film: Columbia, 1937 (scw: Eugene Solow, Guy Endore; dir: Alfred E. Green)
    *Too Many Cooks. (incorrectly given as Too Many Crooks in early printings of CF)

STOW, (JULIAN) RANDOLPH. 1935-
    Ref: CA.
    The Suburbs of Hell. Secker, 1984; Taplinger, 1984

*STRAKER, J(OHN) F(OSTER)
    Another Man's Poison. Hale, 1983
    A Choice of Victims. Hale, 1984
    *Hell Is Empty. Film: Dominion, 1967 (scw: John Ainsworth, Bernard Knowles, John Fowler; dir: Ainsworth, Knowles)

STRAKER, PHILIP
    Night Bait. Zebra, 1982

STRANGE, JOHN COTTAGE
    Coast of Echoes. Messenger, 1984

*STRANGE, JOHN STEPHEN. Ref also: TM.

STRATHAM, FRANCES PATTON
    From Love's Ashes. GM, 1984 <Atlanta, 1935>

STRATHERN, WILLIAM
    Don't Look for Me--I'm Dead. Hale, 1981

*STRATTON, CHRIS
    *Change of Mind. (Novelization of film: Sagittarus, 1969; scw: Seeleg Lester, Richard Wesson; dir: Kris Peterson.)
    *A Fine Pair. (Novelization of film: Cinema Center, 1969; scw: Francesco Maselli, Luisi Montagnana, Larry Gelbart, Virgil C. Leone; dir: Maselli.)
    *Underground. (Novelization of film: Levy-Gardner, 1970; scw: Ron Bishop, Andy Lewis; dir: Arthur Nadel.)

STRATTON, JEFF. Pseudonym of Leslie T. Barnard.
    Double Trouble. Hamilton Stafford, 1952
    Terror on the Railroad. Hamilton Stafford, 1952

*STRATTON, ROY (OLIN). 1910-1985.

*STRAUB, PETER (FRANCIS)
    *-Julia. Film: Fetter, 1976, as Full Circle (scw: Dave Humphries, Harry Bromley; dir: Richard Loncraine)

STRAUCH, KATINA PARTHEMOS. 1946-
    Pseudonym: Katina Alexis, q.v.

*STRAUSS, THEODORE
    *Moonrise. Film: Republic, 1949 (scw: Charles Haas; dir: Frank Borzage)

*STREET, BRADFORD. Pseudonym of *Al Hine.
    *For Pete's Sake. (Novelization of film: Rastar, 1974; scw: Stanley Shapiro, Maurice Richlin; dir: Peter Yates.)
    *The Glass Bottom Boat. (Novelization of film: MGM, 1966; scw: Everett Freeman; dir: Frank Tashlin.)
    *In Like Flint. (Novelization of film: TCF, 1967; scw: Hal Fimberg; dir: Gordon Douglas.)

*STREET, CECIL JOHN CHARLES. 1884-1964.

*STREIB, DAN(IEL T.). Ref: CA. Pseudonyms: *Frank Colter, *Mark Cruz. SC: Michael Hawk, also in titles marked MH; Steve Crown (Counter Force), in titles marked SC below.
    The Bloody Rose. GM, 1985 SC
    The Body Hunters. GM, 1984 SC
    California Shakedown. Jove, 1981; Sphere, 1983 MH <Calif.>
    The Cargo Gods. Jove, 1981 MH <S. Pac.>
    Counter Force. GM, 1983 SC <Russ.>
    The Death Riders. Jove, 1981 MH
    Death Shuttle. GM, 1983 SC
    Down Under and Dirty. Jove, 1981 MH <Australia>
    The Enemy Within. Jove, 1981 MH
    The Hawaiian Takeover. Jove, 1981 MH <Haw.>
    House of Silence. Powell, 1970 <Mex.>
    The Karate Killers. GM, 1983 SC <S.F.>
    The Mind Breakers. GM, 1984 SC
    The Seeds of Evil. Jove, 1981; Sphere, 1983 MH <Vienna>
    Terror for Sale. GM, 1984 SC <Can.>
    The Terror Merchants. Jove, 1981 MH
    Titan's Duel. GM, 1984 SC
    The Treasure Divers. Jove, 1981 MH
    The Trident Hijacking. GM, 1983 SC
    The Virgin Stealers. Jove, 1981 MH

STRIBLING, T(HOMAS) S(IGISMUND). Ref also: CA, TM.

*STRIEBER, WHITLEY
    Black Magic. Morrow, 1982; Granada pb, 1983
    *The Wolfen. Film: Orion, 1981 (scw: David Eyre, Michael Wadleigh; dir: Wadleigh)

STRIKER, RANDY. SC: MacMorgan, in all titles.
    Assassin's Shadow. Signet, 1981
    Cuban Death-Lift. Signet, 1981
    The Deadlier Sex. Signet, 1981
    The Deep Six. Signet, 1981
    Everglades Assault. Signet, 1982
    Grand Cayman Slam. Signet, 1982
    Key West Connection. Signet, 1981

*STRINGER, ARTHUR (JOHN ARBUTHNOTT)
    *Empty Hands. Silent film: Famous Players, 1924 (scw: Carey Wilson; dir: Victor Fleming)
    *The Gun-Runner. Silent film: Tiffany, 1929 (scw: J. F. Netteford; dir: Edgar Lewis)
    *The Hand of Peril. Silent film: Paragon, 1916 (scw & dir: Maurice Tourneur)
    *Manhandled. (Novelization of silent film: Paramount, 1924; scw: Frank Tuttle; dir: Allan Dwan.)
    *The Story Without a Name. (Novelization of silent film: Paramount, 1924; also released as Without Warning; scw: Arthur Stringer; dir: Irvin Willat.)

STRINGER, DAVID
    The Yesterday Man. Book Guild, 1985 <Fr., WWII>

*STRONG, MICHAEL
    Lamastre. Hale, 1984

STRONG, TERENCE
    Conflict of Lions. Hodder, 1985
    The Fifth Hostage. Coronet, 1983
    Whisper Who Dares. Coronet, 1982

STRONGMAN, MIKE
    -Death on Wheels. Currawong (Syd.), 1942
    Murder Market. Currawong (Syd.), 1942
    -Queen of the Night Clubs. Currawong (syd.), 1941

*STROTHER, ELSIE (FRANCES) W(ARMOTH WEITZEL)
    *Island of Terror. <P. Rico>

STRYKER, HAL. Pseudonym of George H(enry) Smith, 1922- , q.v.
    NYPD 2025. Pinnacle, 1985 <NYC, 2025>

*STUART, ANNE. Living in Vt.
    Catspaw. Harlequin, 1985 <S.F.>
    Tangled Lies. Harlequin, 1984

*STUART, ANTHONY. SC: Vladimir Gull, also in titles below.
    The London Affair. Arbor, 1981
    Russian Leave. Arbor, 1982

*STUART, DONALD
    *The Man Outside. Film: Real Art, 1933 (scw: H. Fowler Mear; dir: George A. Cooper)
    *The Shadow. Film: Real Art, 1933 (scw: H. Fowler Mear, Terence Egan; dir: George A. Cooper)

STUART, HARRY LEE. 1904- .
    -The Ginger Flower. North River, 1947 <Haw., 1900-1944>

*STUART, IAN
    *The Satan Bug. Film: United Artists, 1965 (scw: James Clavell, Edward Anhalt; dir: John Sturges)

*STUART, IAN. Ref also: TC2. SC: David Grierson, in at least those marked DG.
    End on the Rocks. Hale, 1981 DG
    The Garb of Truth. Hale, 1982; Doubleday, 1984 DG
    A Growing Concern. Hale, 1986; Doubleday, 1985 DG
    *Pictures in the Dark. ... Doubleday, 1986
    Thrilling--Sweet and Rotten. Hale, 1982

*STUART, SIDNEY
    *The Night Walker. (Novelization of film: Universal, 1964; scw: Robert Bloch; dir: William Castle.)
    *Young Dillinger. (Novelization of film: Allied Artists, 1965; scw: Arthur Hoerl, Don Zimbalist; dir: Terry O. Morse.)

*STUART, WILLIAM L(ISLE). Ref: TM.
    *Night Cry. Film: TCF, 1950, as Where the Sidewalk Ends (scw: Ben Hecht; dir: Otto Preminger)

STUBBINGTON, COLIN
   Blood Deep. Sphere, 1983
   -Blood Muster. Hale, 1985

*STURGEON, THEODORE (HAMILTON). 1918-1985.

STURROCK, DUDLEY
   Pixie at the Wheel. Hodder, 1923   ss

*STURROCK, JEREMY. SC: Jeremy Sturrock, also in all titles below.
   Captain Bolton's Corpse. Hale, 1982; Walker, 1982 <Eng., ca.1800>
   The Pangersbourne Murders. Hale, 1983; Walker, 1984 <Eng., ca.1800>
   Suicide Most Foul. Hale, 1981; Walker, 1981 <Belg., 1815>

*SUDAK, EUNICE
   *The Raven. (Novelization of film: American International, 1963; scw: Richard Matheson; dir: Roger Corman.)
   *Tales of Terror. (Novelization of film: American International, 1962; scw: Richard Matheson; dir: Roger Corman.)
   *X. (Novelization of film: American International, 1963; scw: Robert Dillon: dir: Roger Corman.)

*SUE, (MARIE JOSEPH) EUGENE
   *The Mysteries of Paris. Silent film: Bennett, 1922, as The Secrets of Paris (scw: Dorothy Farnum; dir: Kenneth Webb). Sound film: Franco-American, 1937, as Les Mysteres de Paris (The Mysteries of Paris) (scw & dir: Felix Ganders). Also: Unidex, 1962, as Les Mysteres de Paris (The Mysteries of Paris) (scw: Jean Halain, Pierre Foucault, Diego Fabbri; dir: Andre Hunnebelle)

SULITZER, PAUL LOUP. 1946-   .
   The Green King. Stuart, 1984; Granada, 1985 (Translation of "Le Roi Vert." Paris, 1983.)
   Money. Stuart, 1985 (Translation from the French.)

*SULLIVAN, VERNON. Ref: CA.

SUMMERS, JARON
   Safety Catch. Leisure, 1985

SUMNER, JILL
   Murder at the Mill. New Playwright's, 1981 (Play.)

*SUNAGEL, LOIS A(NN)
   *A Promise to Keep. Manor, 1979

SUNDELOF-ASBRAND, KARIN
   Bright Dummy. Baker, 1948 (3-act play.)
   Midnight Sun. Baker, 1948 (3-act play.)

*SUNDMAN, PER OLOF. Ref: CA.

*SUMMERTON, MARGARET.   -1979.
   Ref (revised, expanded): TC2.

*SUSSMAN, BARTH JULES
   The Crooked Cross. Signet, 1981 <Ger., WWII>

SUSSMAN, CORNELIA SILVER. 1914-   .
   Pseudonym: Cornelia Jessey, q.v.

SUSTER, GERALD
   The Handyman. Severn, 1985

SUTHERLAND, JOAN. Pseudonym of Joan Collings Kelly, 1890-   .
   In the Night. Mills, 1920 (Novelization of play by Cyril Harcourt.) Silent film (based on play): Granger, 1920 (scw: Frank Fowell; dir: Frankland A. Richardson)

*SUTTON, HENRY. Pseudonym of *David R(ytman) Slavitt.

*SUTTON, JEFFERSON (HOWARD). 1913-1979.

SUYKER, BETTY
   Death Scene. St. Martin's, 1981 <NYC, theatre>

SWANKLER, WALTER F.
   Skull's Light. Penn, 1930 (3-act play.)

*SWANN, FRANCIS. Pseudonym: *Jean Phillips.

*SWANTON, SCOTT. Ref: TM.

*SWARTHOUT, GLENDON (FRED). Ref also: TM.
   Cadbury's Coffin, with Kathryn Swarthout. Doubleday, 1982

SWAYBILL, ROGER E(LLIOTT). 1943-
   Ref: CA.
   Final Witness. Avon, 1983 <Wash. D.C.>

SWAYNE, HERBERT E.
   Caught in the Villain's Web. French, 1949 (3-act play.)
   The Curse of an Aching Heart. French, 1944 (3-act play.)

SWENSON, REX. See: Gar Wilson.

SWIFT, BRIAN. Pseudonym of William Cecil Knott, 1927-   . Ref: CA. SC: Mac Wingate, in all titles.
   Mission Code: Acropolis. Jove, 1982 <Greece> (by *Arthur Wise, q.v.)
   Mission Code: Granite Island. Jove, 1981 <Cors.>
   Mission Code: King's Pawn. Jove, 1981 <Balkans>
   Mission Code: Minotaur. Jove, 1981 <Crete>
   Mission Code: Scorpion. Jove, 1982
   Mission Code: Snow Queen. Jove, 1982 <Arctic, 1943>
   Mission Code: Springboard. Jove, 1982 <Warsaw>
   Mission Code: Survival. Jove, 1982 <It.>
   Mission Code: Symbol. Jove, 1981 <Afr., N.> (by *Arthur Wise, q.v.)
   Mission Code: Track and Destroy. Jove, 1982
   Mission Code: Volcano. Jove, 1982

SWIFT, GRAHAM. 1949-   . Ref: CA.
   Shuttlecock. Lane, 1981; Poseidon, 1985
   Waterland. Heinemann, 1983; Poseidon, 1984

SWIFT, REBECCA
   Project Norouz. Tower, 1982

SWIFT, STEVEN
   The Secret of Anna Katz. Piatkus, 1984

*SWITZER, ROBERT. Born in Canada, son of an itinerant dentist; author of novels and magazine ss.

SYDELL, ELEANOR
   Diplomatic Immunity. Lancer, 1966 <Cent. Am.>

SYKES, ERIC
   The Great Crime of Grapplewick. Macmillan (London), 1984

*SYLVAINE, VERNON
   *Warn That Man. Film: ABPC, 1943 (scw: Vernon Sylvaine, Lawrence Huntington; dir: Huntington)

*SYLVESTER, ROBERT (McPHIERSON)
   *The Big Boodle. Film: United Artists, 1957; released in Britain as A Night in Havana (scw: Jo Eisinger; dir: Richard Wilson)

*SYMONS, JULIAN (GUSTAVE). Ref also: TM.
   A Criminal Comedy; see The Criminal Comedy of the Contented Couple
   The Criminal Comedy of the Contented Couple. Macmillan (London), 1985. U.S. title: A Criminal Comedy. Viking, 1986 <Venice>
   The Detling Secret; see The Detling Murders
   The Detling Murders. Macmillan (London), 1982. U.S. title: The Detling Secret. Viking, 1983 <Eng., 1800s>
   How to Trap a Crook and 12 other mysteries. Davis, 1977   ss
   The Name of Annabel Lee. Macmillan (London), 1983; Viking, 1983
   *The Narrowing Circle. Film: Fortress, 1955 (scw: Doreen Montgomery; dir: Charles Saunders)
   The Tigers of Subtopia and other stories. Macmillan (London), 1982; Viking, 1983   ss

SYNGE, ALLEN
   Bowler, Batsman, Spy. Weidenfeld, 1985

SZANTO, GEORGE (H.). 1940-   . Ref: CA.
   Not Working. St. Martin's, 1982 <Wyo.>

SZILAGYE, ROBERT J. and STANLEY C. MONROE, q.v.
   Mediterranean Maneuver. Dell, 1984

SZULC, TAD. 1926-   . Ref: CA.
   Diplomatic Immunity. Simon, 1981; Heinemann, 1982 <S. Am.>

TABLER, JOSEPH
   Afghan Agent. Carousel, 1982
   Deadly Decoy. Carousel, 1982
   Escape from Poland. Carousel, 1982
   The Meteoric Affair. Carousel, 1982
   Undercover: El Salvador. Carousel, 1982 <El Salvador>

TABOR, MARGARET
   The Understudy. Severn, 1983

*TABORI, GEORGE
   -Original Sin. Houghton, 1947; Boardman, 1947 <Cairo>

*TABORI, PAUL
   Curtains for the Cobra. Progressive Press, ca.1949

*TACK, ALFRED
   *Death Takes a Dive. <ship>

TADRACK, MOSS. Pseudonym of Warren H. Caryl, 1920-   . Ref: CA.
   -Mistress of Evil. Brandon, 1966 <Wis.>

*TAFFRAIL
   *The Jade Lizard. <Med. Is.>

*TAGGART, TOM (BARNARD). Pseudonym: Joseph Spalding, q.v.

*TAKAGI, AKIMITSU. Ref: CA.

*TALBOT, HAKE. Ref also: TM.
   *Rim of the Pit. ... Stacey, 1972

TALLY, TED
   Coming Attractions. French, 1982 (3-act play.)

TALMAGE, ANNE. Pseudonym of *Talmage Powell.
   Dark Over Acadia. Lancer, 1971 <La.>

*TALMY, SHEL
   The Web. Dell, 1981

TAMMUZ, BENJAMIN. 1919-   . Ref: CA.
   Minotaur. NAL, 1981; Enigma, 1983 (Translation from the Hebrew.)

TANNER, JOHN. Pseudonym of *Jack Matcha, 1919-   . Other pseudonym: John Barclay, q.v.
   -Gambler's Girl. Athena, 1961
   The Killer Came Naked. Brandon, 1974

TAPPLY, WILLIAM G(EORGE). 1940-   .
   Ref: CA, TM. SC: Brady Coyne, in all titles.
   Death at Charity's Point. Scribner, 1984; Collins, 1985 <Boston, acad.>
   The Dutch Blue Error. Scribner, 1985; Collins, 1985 <Boston>
   Follow the Sharks. Scribner, 1985; Collins, 1985 <Boston>

*TARG, WILLIAM
   Secret Lives. Granada, 1983

*TARRANT, JOHN
   China Gold. Macdonald, 1982 <China>

TARVER, BEN. 1927-   . Ref: CA.
   The Murder of Auguste Dupin. Playwright Canada, 1982 (3-act play.)

*TAUBES, FRANK. 1924-   . Born in Vienna; came to U.S. at age 8; attended college in N.Y. and Ill., majoring in chemistry.
   *Run...Run...Run. <NYC>

TAYLOR, ANDREW (JOHN ROBERT). 1951-   .
   Ref: CA, TM. SC: William Dougal, in all titles. Set: Eng.
   Caroline Minuscule. Gollancz, 1982; Dodd, 1983
   Our Fathers' Lies. Gollancz, 1985; Dodd, 1985
   Waiting for the End of the World. Gollancz, 1984; Dodd, 1984

TAYLOR, ANTHONY
   Hour of the Scorpion. Jove, 1982

*TAYLOR, BERNARD
   *The Godsend. Film: Cannon, 1980 (scw: Olaf Pooley; dir: Gabrielle Beaumont)

The Kindness of Strangers. St. Martin's, 1985; Severn, 1986 <Eng.>
*TAYLOR, C(ONSTANCE) LINDSAY. Ref also: CA.

*TAYLOR, CHARLES D(OONAN)
Show of Force. Charter, 1982
The Sunset Patriots. Charter, 1983

TAYLOR, DOMINI. Pseudonym of *Roger Erskine Longrigg. Other pseudonyms: *Ivor Drummond; *Frank Parrish, q.v.
Gemini. H. Hamilton, 1984, Atheneum, 1985
Mother Love. H. Hamilton, 1983; Putnam, 1983

TAYLOR, DOUGLAS
Five in Judgment. Dramatists, 1956 (1-act play.) <Midwest>

TAYLOR, ELIZABETH ATWOOD. Born in San Antonio; educated at Bryn Mawr and Vassar; has worked as a film editor, TV news reporter, social worker, and art therapist; living in S.F. Ref: TM.
The Cable Car Murder. St. Martin's, 1982; Hale, 1983 <S.F.>

TAYLOR, FRED
Walking Shadows. St. Martin's, 1984; Bodley, 1986 <WWII>

*TAYLOR, H. BALDWIN
*The Triumvirate. (misprint correction)

TAYLOR, (KATHRINE) KRESSMANN
-Address Unknown. Simon, 1939; H. Hamilton, 1939. Film: Columbia, 1944 (scw: Kressmann Taylor, Herbert Dalmas; dir: William Cameron Menzies)

TAYLOR, L(AURIE) A(YLMA). 1939-   . Ref: CA. SC: J. J. Jamison, in titles marked JJ.
Deadly Objectives. Walker, 1984 JJ <Mpls.>
Footnote to Murder. Walker, 1983. British title: One for the Books. Hale, 1983 <Mpls.>
One for the Books; see Footnote to Murder
Only Half a Hoax. Walker, 1983; Hale, 1984 JJ <Mpls.>
Shed Light on Death. Walker, 1985 JJ <Minn.>

TAYLOR, MAY
Bird Watchers. Regency, 1982
The Bowling Green Murder. Regency, 1984

*TAYLOR, PHOEBE ATWOOD. Ref also: TM.

TAYLOR, ROBERT W. 1920-
Mimi. Pyramid, 1953

*TAYLOR, SAM S. Pseudonym: *Lehi Zane.

*TAYLOR, SAMUEL W(OOLEY). Ref also: TM.
*The Man with My Face. Film: United Artists, 1951 (scw: Samuel W. Taylor, T. J. McGowan, Edward J. Montagne; dir: Montagne)

*TAYLOR, TOM
"Still Waters Run Deep." Lacy, 1855; French, 1855 (3-act play.) Silent film: Ideal, 1916 (scw: Dane Stanton; dir: Fred Paul). Also: Barker, 1919, as The Thundercloud (dir: Alexander Butler)
*The Ticket-of-Leave Man. Silent film: AB, 1914 (dir: Travers Vale). Also: Barker, 1918 (dir: Bert Haldane). Sound film: King, 1937 (scw: H. F. Maltby, A. R. Rawlinson; dir: George King)

*TEILHET, DARWIN L. Ref: TM. See also: Theo Durrant.
The Fear Makers. Film: Pacemaker, 1958 (scw: Elliot West, Chris Appley; dir: Jacques Tournier)

TEIXEIRA, BERNARDO. 1926-   . Ref: CA.
Flowers for the Executioner. Avon, 1982; Avon (London), 1983 <Port.>

*TEMPLE, ROBIN
*Street Paved with Water. criminous

TEMPLETON, ALINE
Death Is My Neighbour. Hale, 1984

*TEMPLETON, CHARLES (B.)
*The Kidnapping of the President. Film: Sefel, 1980 (scw: Richard Murphy; dir: George Mendeluk)

*TENNANT, EMMA
Woman Beware Woman. Cape, 1983. U.S. title: The Half-Mother. Little, 1985 <Ire.>

*TERHUNE, ALFRED PAYSON. Ref: CA.

*TERMAN, DOUGLAS
Shell Game. Poseidon, 1985; Collins, 1985 <Cuba, 1962>

*TERRY, J(OSEPH) E(DWARD) HAROLD and *LECHMERE WORRALL
The Man Who Stayed at Home. Lacy, 1916; French, 1916 (3-act play.) Silent film: Hepworth, 1915 (dir: Cecil H. Hepworth). Also: Selznick, 1920 (scw & dir: George D. Baker)

TESICH, STEVE. 1943(?)-   . Ref: CA.
Passing Game. French, 1978 (2-act play.)

*TEY, JOSEPHINE. Ref also: CA, TM.
*Brat Farrar. Film: Hammer, 1950 (existence of film not confirmed)
*The Franchise Affair. Film: ABPC, 1950 (scw: Robert Hall, Lawrence Huntington; dir: Huntington)
*A Shilling for Candles. Film: Gaumont British, 1937, as Young and Innocent; released in the U.S. as The Girl Was Young (scw: Charles Bennett, Edwin Greenwood, Anthony Armstrong, Alma Reville, Gerald Savory; dir: Alfred Hitchcock)

*THAYER, JAMES STEWART
*The Stettin Secret. ... Arrow, 1983

*THAYER, (EMMA BEDINGTON) LEE. Ref also: TM.

*THAYER, TIFFANY (ELLSWORTH)
*The Illustrious Corpse. Film: Tiffany, 1932, as Strangers of the Evening (scw: Stuart Anthony, Warren B. Duff; dir: H. Bruce Humberstone)
-One Woman. Morrow, 1933; Long, 1939. Film: Paramount, 1949, as Chicago Deadline (scw: Warren Duff; dir: Lewis Allen)
Thirteen Women. Kendall, 1932. Film: RKO, 1932 (scw: Bartlett Cormack, Samuel Ornitz; dir: George Archainbaud)

*THEROUX, PAUL. SC: Spencer Monroe Savage, in titles below marked SS.
-The Consul's File. H. Hamilton, 1977; Houghton, 1977 ss SS
-The London Embassy. H. Hamilton, 1982; Houghton, 1983 ss SS
St. Jack. Bodley, 1973; Houghton, 1973

THIMBLETHORPE, JUNE SYLVIA. Pseudonym: Sylvia Thorpe, q.v.

*THOM, ROBERT
*Bloody Mama. (Novelization of film: AIP, 1969; scw: Robert Thom; dir: Roger Corman.)

*THOMAS, AUGUSTUS
Editha's Burglar. French, 1932 (1-act play.) Silent film: World, 1917, as The Burglar (scw: Virginia Tylor Hudson; dir: Harley Knoles). Also: Universal, 1924, as The Family Secret (scw: Lois Zellner; dir: William Seiter)
*The Witching Hour. Silent film: Frohman, 1916 (scw: Anthony Kelly; dir: George Irving). Also: Famous Players, 1921 (scw: Julia Crawford Ives; dir: William Desmond Taylor). Sound film: Paramount, 1934 (scw: Anthony Veiller; dir: Henry Hathaway)

*THOMAS, CRAIG (DAVID). Ref: CA. SC: Michael Grant, in *Firefox, and in title marked MG below.
The Bear's Tears. Joseph, 1985. U.S. title: Lion's Run. Bantam hc, 1985
*Firefox. Film: Warner, 1982 (scw: Alex Lasker, Wendell Willman; dir: Clint Eastwood)
Firefox Down. Joseph, 1983; Bantam hc, 1983 MG <Russ.>
Jade Tiger. Joseph, 1982; Viking, 1982

Lion's Run; see The Bear's Tears
Sea Leopard. Joseph, 1981; Viking, 1981

THOMAS, DONALD. 1935-   . Pseudonym: *Francis Selwyn, q.v.
Belladonna. Macmillan (London), 1984. U.S. title: Mad Hatter Summer. Viking, 1983 <Eng., 1880>
The Blindfold Game. Deutsch, 1981
The Day the Sun Rose Twice. Macmillan (London), 1985
Mad Hatter Summer; see Belladonna

THOMAS, DONALD (SERRELL)
Captain Wunder. Viking, 1981 <1907>

THOMAS, ERIC
Strip for Murder. Kozy, 1960

*THOMAS, FRANK
Sherlock Holmes and the Treasure Train. Pinnacle, 1985 (Sherlock Holmes)

*THOMAS, JACK W(ILLIAM)
Doing It. Bantam, 1981
Head On! Bantam, 1983

*THOMAS, LESLIE (JOHN)
*Dangerous Davies: The Last Detective. Film: ITC, 1980 (scw: Val Guest, Leslie Thomas; dir: Guest)

*THOMAS, MICHAEL M.
Hard Money. Viking, 1985; Hutchinson, 1985
Someone Else's Money. Wyndham, 1982; Hutchinson, 1982

*THOMAS, PAUL
*The Spy. Film: Seven Arts, 1966, as L'Espion (The Defector) (scw: Robert Guenette, Raoul Levy; dir: Levy)

*THOMAS, ROBERT
*Dead Ringer. (Novelization of film: Warner, 1964; scw: Albert Beich, Oscar Millard; dir: Paul Heinreid.)

*THOMAS, ROSS (ELMORE). Ref also: BM, TM; expanded: TC2.
Briarpatch. Simon, 1984; H. Hamilton, 1985 <S.W.>
*The Cold War Swap. Film: United Artists, 1969 (existence of film not confirmed)
*If You Can't Be Good. <Wash. D.C.>
Missionary Stew. Simon, 1983; H. Hamilton, 1984 <Cent. Am.>
The Mordida Man. Simon, 1981; H. Hamilton, 1981
*The Seersucker Whipsaw. <Afr.>
*Yellow-Dog Contract. <Wash. D.C.>

THOMAS, WARD. 1915-
-Stranger in the Land. Houghton, 1949; Secker, 1950 <New Eng.>

THOMPSON, CAROLINE. 1956-   . Ref: CA.
-First Born. Coward, 1983

*THOMPSON, ESTELLE
*The Lawyer and the Carpenter. <Australia>

*THOMPSON, (EU)GENE (ALLEN) SC: Dade Cooley, in *Murder Mystery, and in new title below.
*Lupe. <S.F.>
Nobody Cared for Kate. Random, 1983; Gollancz, 1983 <Fr.>

*THOMPSON, J. LEE
*Murder Without Crime. Film: Associated British, 1950 (scw & dir: J. Lee Thompson)

*THOMPSON, JIM. Ref: BM, TC2, TM.
*-Bad Boy.
*-Cropper's Cabin.
*The Getaway. Film: First Artists, 1972 (scw: Walter Hill; dir: Sam Peckinpah)
*The Grifters. ... Zomba, 1983 <L.A.>
*Heed the Thunder. delete: not criminous
*A Hell of a Woman. ... Banner, 1950s. Film: Gaumont, 1979, as Serie Noire (Thriller Story) (scw: Alain Corneau, Georges Perec; dir: Corneau)
*The Killer Inside Me. Film: Warner, 1976 (scw: Edward Mann, Robert Chamblee; dir: Burt Kennedy)
*-King Blood.
*Nothing More Than Murder. ... Airlift, 1985

*Now and on Earth. delete: not criminous
*Pop. 1280. ... Zomba, 1983 <South, late 1800s> Film: Les Films de la Tour, 1981, as Coup de Torchon (Clean Slate; Population 1280) (scw: Jean Aurenche, Bertrand Tavernier; dir: Tavernier)
*Recoil. ... Airlift, 1985
*-Roughneck.
*Savage Night. ... Airlift, 1986
*-South of Heaven.
*The Undefeated. delete: not criminous

THOMPSON, MARAVENE
-The Woman's Law. Stokes, 1914; Nash, 1914. Silent film: Arrow, 1916 (scw: Harvey Thew, Albert S. LeVino; dir: Lawrence McGill)

THOMPSON, MARCELLA. Joint pseudonym with Paula Thompson: Pamela Thompson, q.v.

THOMPSON, PAMELA. Joint pseudonym of Paula and Marcella Thompson.
Rainbow Ribbon. Harlequin, 1984 <Mo.>

THOMPSON, PAULA. Joint pseudonym with Marcella Thompson: Pamela Thompson, q.v.

*THOMPSON, STEVEN L(YNN). 1948-   Ref: CA. SC: Max Moss, in *Recovery, and in title marked MM below.
Bismarck Cross. Tor, 1985
Countdown to China. Warner, 1982 <China> MM

THOMPSON, THOMAS. 1934-1982. Ref: CA.
Celebrity. Doubleday, 1982; Lane, 1982 <Tex.>

*THOMSON, BASIL (HOME). Ref also: CA.

THOMSON, DAVID. 1941-   .
Suspects. Knopf, 1985; Secker, 1985

THOMSON, GEORGE MALCOLM. 1899-   Ref: CA.
Kronstadt 21. Secker, 1985

*THOMSON, JUNE. Ref also: TM; expanded: TC2. SC: Insp. Finch, also in all titles below (where he is called Insp. Rudd in U.S. editions).
A Dying Fall. Constable, 1985; Doubleday. 1986
Portrait of Lilith; see To Make a Killing
Shadow of a Doubt. Constable, 1981; Doubleday, 1982
Sound Evidence. Constable, 1984; Doubleday, 1985
To Make a Killing. Constable, 1982. U.S. title: Portrait of Lilith. Doubleday, 1983

THOMSON, NORMAN. Pseudonym: *Earl Norman, q.v.

*THOREAU, DAVID
-Dynasty of Power. Arbor, 1982 <S.F.>
The Satanic Condition. Arbor, 1981 <L.A.>

THORMAN, RICHARD. 1924-   . Ref: CA.
Buchman's Law. Norton, 1981

*THORN, RONALD SCOTT
*The Full Treatment. Film: Falcon, 1961; released in the U.S. as Stop Me Before I Kill (scw: Val Guest, Ronald Scott Thorn; dir: Guest)
*Upstairs and Downstairs. Film: Rank, 1959 (scw: Frank Harvey; dir: Ralph Thomas)

*THORNBURG, NEWTON
-Black Angus. Little, 1978; Heinemann, 1979 <Mo.>
*Cutter and Bone. Film: Gurian, 1981; released in Britain as Cutter's Way (scw: Jeffrey Alan Fiskin; dir: Ivan Passer)
Dreamland. Arbor, 1983; Sphere, 1986 <L.A.>

*THORNDYKE, (ARTHUR) RUSSELL
*Doctor Syn. Film: Gaumont British, 1937 (scw: Roger Burford, Michael Hogan; dir: Roy William Neill). Also: Disney, 1962, as Dr. Syn Alias the Scarecrow (scw: Robert Westerby; dir: James Neilson). Also: Universal, 1962, as Captain Clegg; released in the U.S. as Night Creatures (scw: Anthony Hinds, Barbara S. Harper; dir: Peter Graham Scott)

*THORNE, E(RNEST) P(OLLETT)
*The Black Sadhu. <India>
*Three Silent Men. Film: Butcher, 1940 (scw: Dudley Leslie, John Byrd; dir: Daniel Birt)

*THORNE, EMILY. Pseudonym of *Jeanne Judson.
Flight Hostess. Avalon, 1958 <New Or.>

*THORNE, GUY
*When It Was Dark. Silent film: Windsor, 1919 (scw: Kenelm Foss; dir: Arrigo Bocchi)

THORNTON, CHARLES
False Alibi. Brown, 1965 (1-act play.)

*THORP, RODERICK (MAYNE, JR.)
*The Detective. Film: TCF, 1968 (scw: Abby Mann; dir: Gordon Douglas)

*THORPE, SYLVIA. Pseudonym of June Sylvia Thimblethorpe. Ref: CA.

*THURLOW, DAVID
The Perfect Trap. Hale, 1984
Vinegar in the Spice. Hale, 1984

*THURMAN, STEVE
*"Mad Dog" Coll. (Novelization of film: Columbia, 1961; scw: Edward Schreiber; dir: Burt Balaban.)
*Night After Night. <ship>

*THURSTON, KATHERINE CECIL
*The Masquerader. Film: United Artists, 1933 (scw: Howard Estabrook, Moss Hart; dir: Richard Wallace)

THURSTON, ROBERT (DONALD). 1936-   Ref: CA. SC: Byron O'Toole ("Rugger"), in both titles.
For the Silvership. Avon, 1985 <Cent. Am.>
In Justice's Prison. Avon, 1985

*THYNNE, ALEXANDER
*The Carry-Cot. Film: Mallard, 1973, as Blue Blood (scw & dir: Andrew Sinclair)

*THYNNE, ROBERT
Irish Holidays; or, Studies Out of School. Long, 1898 ss, some criminous <Ire.>

TIBBLES, GEORGE
The Latest Mrs. Adams. French, 1979 (3-act play.) <Conn.>

*TICKELL, JERRARD
*Appointment with Venus. <Chan. Is.> Film: British Film, 1951; released in the U.S. as Island Rescue (scw: Nicholas Phipps; dir: Ralph Thomas)
*The Villa Mimosa. <Fr., WWII>

*TIDYMAN, ERNEST. 1928-1984.
Shaft. Film: MGM, 1971 (scw: John D. F. Black, Ernest Tidyman; dir: Gordon Parks)
*Shaft's Big Score. Film: MGM, 1972 (scw: Ernest Tidyman; dir: Gordon Parks)

TILLY, RONALD SUGDEN. Pseudonym: *Ronald Simpson.

TILSLEY, FRANK. 1904-
Thicker Than Water. Eyre, 1955

*TIMPERLEY, ROSEMARY (KENYON)
-Chidori's Room. Hale, 1983
Devil's Paradise. Hale, 1965 <Mor.>
-The Face in the Leaves. Hale, 1982
-Love and Death. Hale, 1985
Night Talk. Hale, 1982
-The Office Party--and After. Hale, 1984
-The Secret Dancer. Hale, 1984
The Spell of the Hanged Man. Hale, 1981 <Rome>
-That Year at the Office. Hale, 1981

*TINE, ROBERT. Pseudonym: Richard Harding, q.v.
-Broken Eagle. Pinnacle, 1985 <Russ.>
Built to Kill. Pinnacle, 1985
*State of Grace. ... Collins, 1982
Uneasy Lies the Head. Viking, 1982; Collins, 1983 <future, Eng.>
Who Killed Jock Ewing? Arrow, 1985

TINNISWOOD, PETER. 1936-   Ref: CA.
Shemerelda. Hodder, 1981

*TIPPETTE, GILES
*The Bank Robber. Film: United Artists, 1974, as The Spikes Gang (scw: Irving Ravetch, Harriet Frank, Jr.; dir: Richard Fleischer)
China Blue. Dell, 1984 <Cent. Am.>

TIPPIN, G. LEE
The Arab. Daring, 1985 <Mid. East>

*TITHERADGE, DION
*The Crooked Billet. Silent film (sound added later): Gainsborough, 1929 (scw: Angus MacPhail; dir: Adrian Brunel)

TOBEY, FRED S.
Never Hit a Lady. Bay Books, 1985 ss, mostly criminous

TOGAWA, MASAKO. 1933-   . Best-selling Japanese mystery writer, born in Tokyo.
The Lady Killer. Century, 1985; Dodd, 1986 <Tokyo>
The Master Key. Century, 1984; Dodd, 1985 <Tokyo>

*TOKSON, ELLIOT
Harem Games. Avon, 1984 <Istan., 1908>
When Dragons Dance. Avon, 1982 <Macao, 1900>

*TOMA, DAVID. 1933-   . Ref: CA.

*TOMS, BERNARD
*The Strange Affair. Film: Paramount, 1968 (scw: Stanley Mann; dir: David Greene)

TONE, TEONA. 1944-   . Ref: CA. SC: Kyra Keaton, in both titles.
Full Cry. GM, 1985 <Va., 1907>
Lady on the Line. GM, 1983 <U.S., 1899>

TOOMAY, PAT(RICK JAY). 1948-   Ref: CA.
On Any Given Sunday. Fine, 1984 <Wash. D.C.>

*TOOMBS, JANE JENKE
Heart of Winter. Walker, 1985 <Mich.>
Restless Obsession. Harlequin, 1984 <Can.>

TOOMBS, JOHN. 1927-   . Pseudonym: *Fortune Kent.

TOOMEY, COLLEEN
Bird of Prey. BBC, 1982 (Novelization of BBC TV series.)

TOPOL, EDWARD. See also: Fridrikh Neznansky.
Red Square, with Fridrikh Nezansky, q.v. Quartet (London & U.S.), 1983 <Moscow> (Translation of "Kraznaila Ploshchad.")
Submarine U-137. Quartet, 1983; Quartet (U.S.), 1984

*TOPOR, ROLAND
*The Tenant. Film: Marianne, 1976, as Le Locataire (The Tenant) (scw: Roman Polanski, Gerard Brach; dir: Polanski)

*TOPOR, TOM. SC: Kevin Fitzgerald, in *Bloodstar, and in title marked KF below.
Answers. Dramatists, 1973 (1-act play.)
Coda. Scribner, 1984 KF <NYC>

TOPPMAN, LAWRENCE. Joint pseudonym with Steven Garland: Lawrence Garland, q.v.

TORAL, JUDITH. Writer of ss living in Nevada.
Daddy's Gone A-Hunting. PB, 1983

*TORBETT, D.
*On Trial. Dodd, 1915; Readers Library, 1929

TORKELSON, LAYNE. Joint pseudonym with Marion Woolf and Margery Papich: Marion Margery Layne, q.v.

*TORRES, EDWIN. Ref: CA.

*TOURNEY, LEONARD. SC: Matthew Stock, in *The Player's Boy Is Dead, and in titles below.

Familiar Spirits. St. Martin's, 1985; Quartet, 1985 <Eng., ca.1600>
Low Treason. Dutton, 1983; Quartet, 1984 <Eng., ca.1600>

TOWNEND, W(ILLIAM). 1881-   .
Night's Black Agent. Rich, 1955 <ship>

*TOWNLEY, HOUGHTON
*The Bishop's Emeralds. Silent film: Virginia Pearson Photoplays, 1919 (scw: Frank S. Beresford; dir: John B. O'Brien)
*The Gay Lord Waring. Silent film: Bluebird, 1916 (scw: F. McGrew Willis; dir: Otis Turner)
*The Splendid Coward. Silent film: Harma, 1918 (dir: F. Martin Thornton)

TOWNSEND, GUY M. Has Ph.D. in British history from Tulane Univ.; law school graduate; editor and publisher of The Mystery Fancier, a fanzine; living in Indiana.
To Prove a Villain. Perseverence, 1985 <acad.>

*TRACY, DON(ALD FISKE). Ref also: TM. SC identified in CF by initials GS.
*Criss-Cross. <Balt.> Film: Universal International, 1949 (scw: Daniel Fuchs; dir: Robert Siodmak)

*TRACY, LOUIS
*Number Seventeen. Silent film: Fox, 1920 (scw & dir: George A. Beranger)
*One Wonderful Night. Silent film: Essanay, 1914 (dir: E. H. Calvert). Also (?): Universal, 1922 (dir: Stuart Paton)
*The Silent Barrier. Silent film: Gibraltar, 1920 (scw: Charles T. Dazey; dir: William Worthington)
*A Son of the Immortals. Silent film: Bluebird, 1916 (scw: Bertram Grassby; dir: Otis Turner)

TRACY, MARGARET. Joint pseudonym of Laurence and Andrew Klavin. Ref: TM.
Mrs. White. Dell, 1983

*TRAIL, ARMITAGE
*Scarface. Film: United Artists, 1932 (scw: Fred Pasley, W. R. Burnett, John Lee Mahin, Seton I. Miller, Ben Hecht; dir: Howard Hawks). Also: Universal, 1983 (scw: Oliver Stone; dir: Brian De Palma)
*The Thirteenth Guest. Film: Monogram, 1932 (scw: Francis Hyland, Arthur Hoerl; dir: Albert Ray). Also: Monogram, 1943, as Mystery of the Thirteenth Guest (scw: Charles Marlon, Tim Ryan; dir: William Beaudine)

*TRAIN, ARTHUR. Ref also: CA, TM.
*The Adventures of Ephraim Tutt. ss, reassembled from earlier collections
*The Blind Goddess. Silent film: Famous Players, 1926 (scw: Hope Loring, Louis D. Lighton, Gertrude Orr; dir: Victor Fleming)
*The Hermit of Turkey Hollow. <N.Y.>
Mr. Tutt at His Best. Scribner, 1961 ss, taken from earlier collections
*Mr. Tutt's Case Book. ss, reassembled from earlier collections
*Mortmain. Silent film: Vitagraph, 1915 (scw: Marguerite Bertsch; dir: Theodore Marston)
*Tut, Tut! Mr. Tutt. ss

*TRALINS, (STANLEY) ROBERT. 1926-
Pseudonym: Sean O'Shea, q.v.

*TRANTER, NIGEL
*Bridal Path.   delete, not criminous
*Cable from Kabul. <Afghan.>

*TRAVER, ROBERT
*Anatomy of a Murder. Film: Columbia, 1959 (scw: Wendell Mayes; dir: Otto Preminger)
*Laughing Whitefish. <Mich., 1800s>
People Versus Kirk. St. Martin's, 1981 <Mich.>

TRAVERS, BEN. 1886-1980. Ref: CA.
Plunder. Bickers, 1931 (3-act play.) Film: British and Dominions, 1930 (scw: W. P. Lipscomb; dir: Tom Walls)

TRAVIS, TRISTAN, JR. Pseudonym.
Lamia. Dutton, 1982; Deutsch, 1983 <Chi., 1968>

TRAYLOR, GENE
The Phantom of the Opera. Dramatic, 19?? (3-act play based on the novel by *Gaston Leroux.)

TRAYNOR, J. RICHARD
Death on the Viaduct. Mellifont, 1936

*TREAT, LAWRENCE. Ref also: TM.
Crime and Puzzlement. Godine, 1981; Dorling, 1982   24 crime puzzles
Crime and Puzzlement II. Godine, 1982   crime puzzles
*The Leather Man. <N.Y.>

TREHERNE, JOHN
The Trap. Cape, 1985; Beaufort, 1986

TRELL, MAX. 1900-   Ref: CA.
Lawyer Man. Macaulay, 1932. Film: Warner, 1932 (scw: Rian James, James Seymour; dir: William Dieterle)

TREMAINE, JENNIE. Pseudonym of Marion Chesney, 1936-   . Other pseudonym: M. C. Beaton, q.v.
Maggie. St. Martin's, 1984 <Glasgow, ca.1900>

TREMAYNE, PETER. Pseudonym of Peter Berresford Ellis, 1943-   . Ref: CA.
The Return of Raffles. Magnum, 1981 (Continuing the character created by *E. W. Hornung, q.v.)
Zombie! Sphere, 1981

TRENHAILE, JOHN (STEVENS). 1949-   .
Ref: CA. SC: General Povin, in all titles.
A Man Called Kyril; see Kyril
Kyril. Severn, 1981. U.S. title: A Man Called Kyril. Congdon, 1983
Nocturne for the General. Bodley, 1985; Congdon, 1985
A View from the Square. Bodley, 1983; Congdon, 1984

TRENT, ERIC. See: *George Sklar, 1908-

*TRENT, PAUL
*Bentley's Conscience. Silent film: Ideal, 1922 (scw & dir: Denison Clift)
*Red Mirage.   criminous
*When Greek Meets Greek. Silent film: West, 1922 (dir: Walter West)
*A Wife by Purchase. Silent film: Columbia, 1917, as God's Law and Man's (scw & dir: John H. Collins)

*TREVANIAN. Ref also: CA, TM; expanded: TC2. Some of the books actually by James T. Hashian, ca.1926-   ?
*The Eiger Sanction. Film: Universal, 1975 (scw: Hal Dresner, Warren B. Murphy, Rod Whitaker; dir: Clint Eastwood)
-The Summer of Katya. Crown, 1983; Granada, 1983 <Fr., 1914>

TREVERN, DOUGLAS and STEVE CONWAY
The Case Against Mrs. Dane. Deane, 1965; Baker, 1965 (Play.)

*TREVOR, ELLESTON. Ref also: TM.
*The Billboard Madonna. criminous
*The Burning Shore. <Mal.>
The Damocles Sword. Collins, 1981; Playboy, 1982 <Ger., ca.1941>
Deathwatch. Allen, 1985; Beaufort, 1984
*The Flight of the Phoenix. Film: TCF, 1965 (scw: Lukas Heller; dir: Robert Aldrich)
Miscellany. Swan, 1945 ss, some criminous
The Penthouse. Collins, 1983; Signet, 1983 <NYC>
*Second Chance. criminous
*The Shoot. <S. Pac.>
*The Theta Syndrome. <L.A.>
*Tiger Street. criminous

*TREVOR, GLEN. Pseudonym of James Hilton. Ref also: CA.

*TREVOR, JAMES. Pseudonym of *(Bertram) John Boland.

TREVOR, WILLIAM. Pseudonym of William Trevor Cox, 1928-   . Ref: CA.
Angels at the Ritz. Bodley, 1975; Viking, 1976   ss, some criminous

*TRIESCHMAN, CHARLES
*Two. (Novelization of film: Colmar, 1974; scw & dir: Charles Trieschman.)

*TREW, ANTHONY (FRANCIS)
Running Wild. Collins, 1982; St. Martin's, 1983 <ship>

TRIMBLE, BARBARA MARGARET. 1921-   .
Pseudonyms: Margaret Blake, *B. M. Gill, qq.v.

*TRINIAN, JOHN
*Any Number Can Win; see The Big Grab
The Big Grab. Pyramid, 1960. Also published as: *Any Number Can Win. Film: Cipra, 1963, as Melodie en Sous-Sol (Basement Melody; released in Britain as The Big Grab; released in the U.S. as Any Number Can Win) (scw: Albert Siminon, Michel Audiard, Henri Verneuil; dir: Verneuil)
Scratch a Thief. Ace, 1961. Also published as: Once a Thief. GM, 1965, as by Zekial Marko <S.F.> Film: MGM, 1965, as Once a Thief (scw: Zekial Marko; dir: Ralph Nelson)

*TRIPP, MILES (BARTON). SC: John Samson, also in at least the title marked JS.
A Charmed Death. Macmillan (London), 1984; St. Martin's, 1984
*Cruel Victim. ... St. Martin's, 1985
*The Eighth Passenger. delete: not criminous
Going Solo. Macmillan (London), 1981
One Lover Too Many. Macmillan (London), 1983
*A Quartet of Three. (misprint correction)
Some Predators Are Male. Macmillan (London), 1985; St. Martin's, 1986   JS

TROCCHI, ALEXANDER. 1925-1984. Ref: CA.
Young Adam. Calder, 1982; Riverrun, 1982 <Scot.>

TROTMAN, JACK H. Joint pseudonym with *Palma Harcourt, q.v.: John Penn, q.v.

TROTT, SUSAN. Ref also: TM.

TROW, M. J.
The Adventures of Inspector Lestrade. Macmillan (London), 1985. U.S. title: The Supreme Adventure of Inspector Lestrade. Stein, 1985 <Eng., 1891> (Sherlock Holmes)

*TROY, JONATHAN
*The Haunted Honeymoon. <Eng.>
*Web of Murder. (3-act play.) <West>

*TRUESDELL, JUNE
*Be Still, My Love. Film: Paramount, 1948, as The Accused (scw: Ketti Frings; dir: William Dieterle)

*TRUMAN, (MARY) MARGARET. Ref also: TM.
Murder at the FBI. Arbor, 1985 <Wash. D.C.>
Murder in the Smithsonian. Arbor, 1983; Chivers, 1984 <Wash. D.C.>
Murder in the Supreme Court. Arbor, 1982; Chivers, 1983 <Wash. D.C.>
Murder on Capitol Hill. Arbor, 1981; Sphere, 1982 <Wash. D.C.>
Murder on Embassy Row. Arbor, 1984; Chivers, 1985 <Wash. D.C.>

*TRUSS, (LESLIE) SELDON
*The Long Night. Film: Merton Park, 1958, as The Long Knife (scw: Ian Stuart Black; dir: Montgomery Tully)

*TRYON, THOMAS
-Lady. Knopf, 1974; Hodder, 1975
*The Other. Film: Rex-Benchmark, 1972 (scw: Thomas Tryon; dir: Robert Mulligan)

TUCKER, JAMES (ROSENBERG)
Ralph Rashleigh. Angus, 1952 <Australia>

*TUCKER, (ALLAN) JAMES
The King's Friends. Arrow, 1982

TUCKER, WILLIAM
Widow's Walk. Dell, 1983

*TUCKER, (ARTHUR) WILSON
Wild Talent. Rinehart, 1954; Joseph, 1955. Reprinted as: The Man from Tomorrow. Bantam, 1955 <future>

TULEJA, THADDEUS FRANCIS. 1944-
See: *Marshall Macao.

TULLY, JIM
-Beggars of Life. Boni, 1924; Chatto, 1925. Film (partial sound): Paramount, 1928 (scw: Benjamin Glazer, Jim Tully; dir: William A. Wellman)

TUNSTALL, BEATRICE
-The Shiny Night. Heinemann, 1931; Doubleday, 1931 <Eng., 1800s>

TUPPER, OSCAR
Jack the Knife. Elam, 1970 (1-act play.)

TURNBULL, PETER. 1950- . Born in Eng., recently a social worker. Ref: TM. SC: Insp. Fabian Donoghue, at least in those marked FD.
Big Money. Collins, 1984; St. Martin's, 1984 <Glasgow>
Dead Knock. Collins, 1982; St. Martin's, 1983 <Glasgow> FD
Deep and Crisp and Even. Collins, 1981; St. Martin's, 1982 FD <Glasgow>
Fair Friday. Collins, 1983; St. Martin's, 1983 FD <Glasgow>

TURNER, ETHEL. See: J. L. Rankin.

TURNER, HARVEY S. Pseudonym: *Sam Hill.

*TURNER, JAMES (ERNEST)
Condell. Cassell, 1961

*TURNEY, CATHERINE
*The Other One. Film: TCF, 1957, as Back from the Dead (scw: Catherine Turney; dir: Charles Marquis Warren)

TUTTIETT, MARY GLEED. -1923. Pseudonym: *Maxwell Gray.

*TWAIN, MARK
*A Double-Barrelled Detective Story. Film: Saloon Prod., 1965 (scw & dir: Adolfas Mekas)
*Tom Sawyer, Detective, and other stories. Film (from title ss): Paramount, 1939 (scw: Lewis Foster, Robert Yost, Stuart Anthony; dir: Louis King)

*TWEEDALE, VIOLET (CHAMBERS). 1862-1936. Ref: CA.

*TYLER, CHARLES W(ALLER). Born in N.H.; was railroad fireman, draftsman, steamfitter; traveled extensively; living in Calif. in 1929.

TYLER, PHILIPPA
The Lushington Mystery. Heath, 1919
-The Manaton Disaster. Heath, 1920
-A Quest for a Fortune. Arnold, 1924

TYLER, (JOHN) POYNTZ. 1907-1971. Ref: CA.
A Garden of Cucumbers. Random, 1960; Gollancz, 1961. Film: United Artists, 1967, as Fitzwilly; released in Britain as Fitzwilly Strikes Back (scw: Isobel Lennart; dir: Delbert Mann)

*TYLER, W. T. Pseudonym of Samuel J. Hamrick, Jr., 1929- . Ref: CA.
-The Ants of God. Dial, 1981; Collins, 1982
Rogue's March. Harper, 1982 <Belg. Cong., ca.1970>
The Shadow Cabinet. Harper, 1984 <Wash. D.C.>

*TYNAN, KATHERINE
The Moated Grange. Collins, 1925

*TYNAN, KATHLEEN
*Agatha. Film: Warner, 1979 (scw: Kathleen Tynan, Arthur Hopcraft; dir: Michael Apted)

*TYNER, PAUL
*Shoot It. Film: Levitt-Pickman, 1974, as Shoot It: Black, Shoot It: Blue (scw & dir: Dennis McGuire)

*TYRE, NEDRA. Ref also: TM.

*TYRER, WALTER
*Such Friends Are Dangerous. ... Garland, 1983

UHERNIK, NICK. Pseudonym: Jonathan Cain, q.v.

*UHNAK, DOROTHY. Ref also: TM; expanded: TC2.
False Witness. Simon, 1981; Hutchinson, 1982 <NYC>
Policewoman. Simon, 1964; Star, 1978
Victims. Simon, 1985; Century, 1986 <NYC>

*ULLMAN, ALLAN. Ref: CA.
*The Naked Spur. (Novelization of film: MGM, 1953; scw: Sam Rolfe, Harold Jack Bloom; dir: Anthony Mann.)

UNDERWOOD, MAVIS EILEEN. 1916-
Pseudonym: *Sarah Kilpatrick.

*UNDERWOOD, MICHAEL. Ref also: BM, TM. SC: Rosa Epton, in *Crime Upon Crime, *A Pinch of Snuff, and in at least those titles marked RE below; Nick Attwell, also in *Menaces, Menaces.
Death in Camera. Macmillan (London), 1984; St. Martin's, 1984 RE
Double Jeopardy. Macmillan (London), 1981; St. Martin's, 1981 RE
Goddess of Death. Macmillan (London), 1982; St. Martin's, 1982 RE
The Hand of Fate. Macmillan (London), 1981; St. Martin's, 1981
The Hidden Man. Macmillan (London), 1985; St. Martin's, 1985 RE
A Party to Murder. Macmillan (London), 1983; St. Martin's, 1984 RE

*UNEKIS, RICHARD
*The Chase. Film: TCF, 1974, as Dirty Mary, Crazy Larry (scw: Leigh Chapman, Antonio Santean; dir: John Hough)

*UNSWORTH, BARRY (FORSTER)
The Rage of the Vulture. Granada, 1982; Houghton, 1983 <Istan., 1908>
The Stone Virgin. H. Hamilton, 1985; Houghton, 1986 <Venice>

*UNSWORTH, MAIR. 1909- . Ref: CA.

UPCHURCH, BOYD. 1919- . Pseudonym: John Boyd, q.v.

*UPFIELD, ARTHUR W. Ref also: CA, TM.
*Bony and the Black Virgin. Reprinted as: The Torn Branch. Scribner pb, 1986
*A Royal Abduction. ... McMillan, 1984
The Torn Branch; see Bony and the Black Virgin

*UPSHAW, HELEN. Pseudonym of Helen Upshaw Starr.

*UPTON, ROBERT. Ref also: TM. SC: Amos McGuffin, in *Who'd Want to Kill Old George?, and in title below.
Fade Out. Viking, 1984

*UPWARD, ALLEN. Ref: CA.

*URIS, LEON (MARCUS)
The Angry Hills. Random, 1955; Wingate, 1956
*Topaz. Film: Universal International, 1969 (scw: Samuel Taylor; dir: Alfred Hitchcock)

*USHER, GRAY. See: *Duke Linton.

USTINOV, PETER (ALEXANDER). 1921-
Ref: CA.
Krumnagel. Heinemann, 1971; Little, 1971

UTERMAHLEN, BRIAN
The Hoffman File. Dell, 1983

*VACHA, ROBERT
Drop Dead in Dresden. Magread, 1983

*VACHELL, HORACE ANNESLEY
The Case of Lady Camber. Murray, 1916; French, 1916 (4-act play.) Silent film: Broadwest, 1920 (scw: Benedict James; dir: Walter West). Film: BIP, 1932, as Lord Camber's Ladies (scw: Benn W. Levy, Edwin Greenwood, Gilbert Wakefield; dir: Levy). Also: Nettlefold, 1948, as The Story of Shirley Yorke (scw: A. R. Rawlinson, Maclean Rogers, Kathleen Butler; dir: Rogers)
*Quinney's. Silent film: Samuelson, 1919 (scw: Roland Pertwee; dir: Rex Wilson). Also: Gaumont, 1927 (scw: John Longden; dir: Maurice Elvey)

VACHSS, ANDREW H(ENRY). 1942-
Ref: CA.
Flood. Fine, 1985; Collins, 1986 <NYC>

*VACZEK, LOUIS CHARLES. 1913-1983.

VAIL, CHRISTINA. Pseudonym of Linda Harvey.
Porcelain Dolls Don't Bleed. Laika, 1981 <Colo.>

*VAIL, LAURENCE. 1891-1968. Ref: BM, CA.

*VAIZEY, JOHN (ERNEST). 1929-1984.

VALCOUR, GARY F.
The Color of Greed. Avon, 1984

VALDEMI, MARIA. 1947- . Ref: CA.
A Vatican Affair. Pinnacle, 1982

*VALDEZ, PAUL. Pseudonym of *Alan Geoffrey Yates, 1923-1985. Other pseudonym: *Carter Brown, q.v.

*VALE, MARTIN
*The Two Mrs. Carrolls. Film: Warner, 1947 (scw: Thomas Job; dir: Peter Godfrey)

*VALENTINE, JO
*The Trouble with Thor. Reprinted as by Charlotte Armstrong: Berkley, 1971

*VALIN, JONATHAN (LOUIS). Ref also: CA, TM. SC: Harry Stoner, also in titles below.
Day of Wrath. Congdon, 1982; Collins, 1983 <Cin.>
Dead Letter. Dodd, 1981; Collins, 1982 <Cin.>
Natural Causes. Congdon, 1983; Collins, 1984 <Cin.>

*VALLANCE, DOUGLAS
*The Man in the Lubianka. <Moscow>

*VALLEY, MEL
*Magnum Force. (Novelization of film: Warner, 1973; scw: John Milius, Michael Cimino; dir: Ted Post.)

VALMONT, V(ICTOR)
The Prussian Spy. Washbourne, 1873

*VANARDY, VARICK
*Alias the Night Wind. Silent film: Fox, 1923 (scw: Robert N. Lee; dir: Joseph Franz)
*The Girl by the Roadside. Silent film: Bluebird, 1918 (scw: John C. Brownell; dir: Theodore Marston)

VAN ASH, CAY
Ten Years Beyond Baker Street. Harper, 1984; Futura, 1985 (Sherlock Holmes)

*VAN ATTA, WINFRED (LOWELL)
*Shock Treatment. Film: TCF, 1964 (scw: Sidney Boehm; dir: Denis Sanders)

VANCE, CHARLES G.
A Grave for a Russian. Avon, 1985 <Russ.>

*VANCE, ETHEL
*Escape. Film: MGM, 1940; reissued as When the Door Opened (scw: Arch Oboler, Marguerite Roberts; dir: Mervyn LeRoy)
*The Secret Thread. <N.Y.>

*VANCE, JACK. SC: Keith Gerson, also in title marked KG below.
The Book of Dreams. Daw, 1981; Coronet, 1982 KG
*The House on Lily Street. <S.F.>
*The Many Worlds of Magnus Ridolph. <future>
*To Live Forever. <future>

*VANCE, JOHN HOLBROOK. Ref also: TM.

*VANCE, LOUIS JOSEPH. Ref also: CA.
*Alias the Lone Wolf. Silent film: Columbia, 1927 (scw: Dorothy Howell, Edward H. Griffith; dir: Griffith)
*The Bandbox. Silent film: Hodkinson, 1919 (scw: Roy Somerville; dir: Roy William Neill)
*The Black Bag. Silent film: Universal, 1922 (scw: George Hively; dir: Stuart Paton)

*The Brass Bowl. Silent film: Edison, 1914. Also: Fox, 1924 (scw: Thomas Dixon, Jr.; dir: Jerome Storm). Also: Fox, 1929, as Masquerade (scw: Malcolm Stuart Boylan, F. H. Brennan; dir: Lumsden Hare)
*The Bronze Bell. Silent film: Ince, 1921 (scw: Del Andrews, Louis Stevens; dir: James W. Horne)
*Cynthia-of-the-Minute. Silent film: Artco, 1920 (dir: Perry Vekroff)
*The Dark Mirror. Silent film: Paramount, 1920 (scw: E. Magnus Ingleton; dir: Charles Giblyn)
 The Day of Days. Little, 1913; Richards, 1914. Silent film: Famous Players, 1914 (dir: Daniel Frohman)
*The Destroying Angel. Silent film: Edison, 1915 (scw & dir: Richard Ridgely). Also: Beck, 1923 (scw: Leah Baird; dir: W. S. Van Dyke)
*The False Faces. Silent film: Artcraft, 1919 (scw & dir: Irvin W. Willatt)
*The Lone Wolf. Silent film: Selznick, 1917 (scw: George Edwardes Hall; dir: Herbert Brenon). Also: McKeown, 1924 (scw & dir: S. E. V. Taylor). Sound film: Columbia, 1930, as The Last of the Lone Wolf (scw: James Whittaker, Dorothy Howell; dir: Richard Boleslavsky)
*The Lone Wolf Returns. Silent film: Columbia, 1926; also released as Return of the Lone Wolf (scw: J. Grubb Alexander; dir: Ralph Ince). Sound film: Columbia, 1936 (scw: Joseph Krumgold, Bruce Manning, Lionel Hauser; dir: Roy William Neill)
*No Man's Land. Silent film: Metro, 1918 (scw: Albert Shelby LeVino, Bert Lytell; dir: Will S. Davis)
*Nobody. Silent film: Rolfe, 1917, as The Outsider (scw: Charles A. Taylor; dir: William C. Dowlan)
*The Pool of Flame. Silent film: Red Feather, 1916 (scw: F. McGrew Willis; dir: Otis Turner)
*Sheep's Clothing. Silent film: Edison, 1914 (scw & dir: Charles M. Seay)

*VANCE, WILLIAM E. 1911-1986. Ref: CA.

*VANDERCOOK, JOHN W(OMACK)
 *Murder in Trinidad. Film: TCF, 1934 (scw: Seton I. Miller; dir: Louis King). Also: TCF, 1939, as Mr. Moto in Danger Island (scw: Peter Milne; dir: Herbert I. Leeds). Also: TCF, 1945, as The Caribbean Mystery (scw: Jack Andrews, Leonard Praskins; dir: Robert Webb)

*VAN DE WATER, FREDERIC F(RANKLYN). Ref: CA.

*VANDERGRIFF, AOLA
 *Sisters of Sorrow. <South>

*VAN DE WETERING, JANWILLEM. Ref also: BM, TM; revised, expanded: TC2. SC: Detectives Grijpstra and De Gier, also in titles marked G&D below.
 The Butterfly Hunter. Houghton, 1982; Severn, 1983
 Inspector Saito's Small Satori. Putnam, 1985 <Jap.>
 The Mind Murders. Houghton, 1981; Heinemann, 1981 G&D <Amst.>
 The Rattle-Rat. Pantheon, 1985; Gollancz, 1986 G&D <Amst.>
 The Streetbird. Putnam, 1983; Gollancz, 1984 G&D <Amst.>

*VAN DINE, S. S. Pseudonym of *Willard Huntington Wright. Ref also: CA, TM.
 *The Benson Murder Case. Film: Paramount, 1930 (scw: Bartlett Cormack; dir: Frank Tuttle)
 *The Bishop Murder Case. Film: MGM, 1930 (scw: Lenore J. Coffee; dir: Nick Grinde, David Burton)
 *The Canary Murder Case. Film: Paramount, 1929 (scw: Florence Ryerson, Albert Shelby LeVino; dir: Malcolm St. Clair)
 *The Casino Murder Case. Film: MGM, 1935 (scw: Florence Ryerson, Edgar Allen Woolf; dir: Edwin L. Marin)
 *The Dragon Murder Case. Film: Warner, 1934 (scw: F. Hugh Herbert, Robert Lee; dir: H. Bruce Humberstone)
 *The Garden Murder Case. Film: MGM, 1936 (scw: Bertram Millhauser; dir: Edwin L. Marin)
 *The Gracie Allen Murder Case. Film: Paramount, 1939 (scw: Nat Perrin; dir: Alfred E. Green)

*The Greene Murder Case. Film: Paramount, 1929 (scw: Louise Long; dir: Frank Tuttle). Also: Paramount, 1937, as Night of Mystery (scw: Frank Partos, Gladys Unger; dir: E. A. DuPont)
*The Kennel Murder Case. Film: Warner, 1933 (scw: Robert N. Lee, Peter Milne; dir: Michael Curtiz). Also: Warner, 1940, as Calling Philo Vance (scw: Tom Reed; dir: William Clemens)
*The Scarab Murder Case. Film: B&D, 1936 (scw: Selwyn Jepson; dir: Michael Hankinson)

*VANE, DEREK
 *Lady Varley. Silent film: F.X.B, 1923, as Modern Marriage (scw: Dorothy Farnum; dir: Lawrence C. Windom)

VAN EES, ERIK
 The Starfish Syndrome. Macdonald, 1982

*VAN GREENAWAY, PETER. Ref: CA, TC2. SC: Insp. Cherry, in *Doppelganger, and in *The Medusa Touch.
 "Cassandra" Bell. Gollancz, 1981
 Edgar Allan Who--? Gollancz, 1981 ss
 Graffiti. Gollancz, 1983
 The Lazarus Lie. Gollancz, 1982
 Manrissa Man. Gollancz, 1982
 *The Medusa Touch. Film: Elan, 1978 (scw: John Briley, Jack Gold; dir: Gold)

*VAN GULIK, ROBERT (HANS). Ref also: TM.
 The Given Day. McMillan, 1984 <Amst.>
 *The Haunted Monastery. ... Art Printing (Kuala Lampur), 1961
 *The Lacquer Screen. ... Art Printing (Kuala Lampur), 1962
 *The Red Pavilion. ... Art Printing (Kuala Lampur), 1961

VAN HASSEN, AMY. Pseudonym of *Domini Wiles, q.v.
 Menace. NEL, 1981

VAN LOAN, CHARLES E(MMETT). 1876-1919.
 Old Man Curry. Doran, 1917 ss, some criminous

VAN LOAN, H(ERBERT) H(ARTWELL). 1888-   .
 You Can't Beat the Law. Jacobsen, 1928 (Novelization of film: Trem Carr, 1928; scw: Arthur Hoerl; dir: Charles Hunt.)

*VAN LUSTBADER, ERIC. See: Lustbader, Eric Van.

VAN ORSDOL, PETER B.
 The Anarchy Plot. Leisure, 1982

*VAN RJNDT, PHILIPPE. This is author's real name. Pseudonym: Phillip Michaels, q.v.
 Last Message to Berlin. Putnam, 1984 <1940>
 Samaritan. Dial, 1983; Macdonald, 1983

*VAN VOGT, A(LFRED) E(LTON)
 The Violent Man. Farrar, 1962

VAN VORS, B. L. Living in Calif.
 The End of the River. Avon, 1983 <Cent. Am.>
 The Prince and the Sufi. Avon, 1985 <Mid. East>

VARDEMAN, ROBERT E. See: *Nick Carter.

*VARLEY, JOHN
 *The Barbie Murders and other stories. ... Futura, 1984. Also published as: Picnic on Nearside. Berkley, 1984

VASEL, MAJOR J. J. See: *Edwin D. Krell.

VASSILIKOS, VASSILIS. 1933-   Ref: CA.
 Z. Farrar, 1968; Macdonald, 1969 (Translation from the Greek.)

VAUGHAN, STUART
 The Royal Game. Dramatic, 1974 (3-act play.) <Eng., past>

*VAUGHN, JASON. Pseudonym of H. W. Barbour.

VEDER, BOB. 1940-   . Ref: CA.
 Playing with Fire. Linden, 1980 <N.Y.>

VEILLER, ANTHONY. 1903-1965.
 The Stranger. Hollywood Publications, 1946 (Novelization of film: International Pictures, 1946; scw: Anthony Veiller; dir: Orson Welles.)

*VEILLER, BAYARD
 *The Thirteenth Chair. Silent film: Acme, 1919 (scw & dir: Leonce Perret). Sound film: MGM, 1929 (scw: Elliott Clawson; dir: Tod Browning). Also: MGM, 1937 (scw: Marion Parsonnet; dir: George Seitz)
 *The Trial of Mary Dugan. Film: MGM, 1929 (scw: Bayard Veiller, Becky Gardiner; dir: Veiller). Also: Parufamet, 1931, as Mordprozess Mary Dugan (Trial of Mary Dugan) (scw: Becky Gardiner, Arthur Robison; dir: Robison). Also: MGM, 1941 (scw: Bayard Veiller; dir: Norman Z. McLeod)
 *Within the Law. Silent film: Vitagraph, 1917 (scw: Violet Mallory, Eugene Mullin; dir: William P. S. Earle). Also: Schenck, 1923 (scw: Frances Marion; dir: Frank Lloyd). Sound film: MGM, 1930, as Paid; released in Britain as Within the Law (scw: Charles MacArthur, Lucien Hubbard; dir: Sam Wood). Also: MGM, 1939 (scw: Charles Lederer, Edith Fitzgerald; dir: Gustav Machaty).

VENNER, NORMAN
 The Imperfect Imposter. Stokes, 1925; Heinemann, 1925. Silent film: Famous Players, 1925, as Irish Luck (scw: Tom J. Geraghty; dir: Victor Heerman)

*VENTERS, ARCHIE
 Blood on the Rocks. Hale, 1983
 Death Below Zero. Hale, 1981
 The Sicilian Connection. Hale, 1984

*VERALDI, ATTILIO
 *The Payoff. Film: Filmauro, 1978, as La Mazzetta (The Payoff) (scw: Dino Maiuri, Massima De Rita, Luciano De Crescenzo, Elvio Porta; dir: Sergio Corbucci)

VERITY, ELMA
 Across the Lawn. Deane, 1959; Baker, 1959 (1-act play.)
 Ladies in Danger, with Vera (Isabel) Allen. Deane, 1958; Baker, 1958 (3-act play.)

*VERNER, GERALD
 *Meet Mr. Callaghan. Film: Pinnacle, 1954 (scw: Brock Williams; dir: Charles Saunders)
 *The Show Must Go On. Film: Albany, 1952, as Tread Softly (scw: Gerald Verner; dir: David Macdonald)
 *The Whispering Woman. Film: Insignia, 1953, as Noose for a Lady (scw: Rex Rienits; dir: Wolf Rilla)

*VERNON, KAY R. Reporter, feature writer; romance novelist under the name Lesley Dixon.
 *The Phantom of Fonthill Park. <Eng., 1847>

VERY, PIERRE. 1900-1960
 In What Strange Land? Wingate, 1949 (Translation from the French.)

*VICAS, VICTOR and *VICTOR HAIM. Vicas is a film director.
 *The Impromptu Imposter. <Isr.>

*VICKERS, ROY. Ref also: TM. See also: Roger MacDougall. Film (from unidentified novel): Luckwell, 1961, as A Question of Suspense (scw: Lawrence Huntington; dir: Max Varnel).
 *Find the Innocent. ... U.S. title: The Girl Who Wouldn't Talk. Detective Book Club, 1959
 *The Girl in the News. Film: TCF, 1940 (scw: Sidney Gilliat, Frank Launder; dir: Carol Reed)
 The Girl Who Wouldn't Talk; see *Find the Innocent
 *I'll Never Tell. Film: Crusade, 1937, as False Evidence (scw & dir: Donovan Pedelty)

*Seven Chose Murder. Faber, 1959 (publisher correction)
*Terror of Tongues. Newnes, 1937 (publisher correction)
*The Unforbidden Sin. Film: Continental, 1929 (existence of film not confirmed)

VICTOR, LESLIE. See: J. L. Rankin.

VICTOR, SAM. Pseudonym of *Morris Hershman. SC: Talbot Lion, in both titles.
Cuban Inferno. Charter, 1981
White House Massacre. Charter, 1981

VILLARS, ELIZABETH. Pseudonym of Ellen Bette Feldman, 1941- . Ref: CA.
-The Normandie Affair. Doubleday, 1982; Chivers, 1983 <ship>

*VINCENT, RICHARD
*Portrait in Black. (Novelization of film; see *Ivan Goff.)

VINCENT, ROBERT
Blacklash. Carousel, 1980 <South>

*VINTER, MICHAEL
The Hemlock Option. Hale, 1983

*VIRMONNE, CLAUDETTE
The Broken Link. Mystique, 1982 (Translation of "Bois-Sauvage." Paris, 1957.)
A Cold Dawn. Mystique, 1982 (Translation of "Un Ange en Enfer." Paris, 1970.)
Dangerous Temptation. Mystique, 1981 (Translation of "La Sirene d'Aston Castle." Paris, 1975.)
Dark Side of Love. Mystique, 1981 (Translation of "Cet Amour d'Un." Paris, 1978.)
Lesson in Love. Mystique, 1981 (Translation of "Le Masque du Destin." Paris, 1971.)
Tender Conspiracy. Mystique, 1981 (Translation of "Le Secret du Lys Rouge." Paris, 1966.)
To Court Danger. Mystique, 1981 (Translation of "Qu'Importe a L'Amour." Paris, 1966.)
To Wed a Stranger. Mystique, 1981 (Translation of "La Porte d'Ebene." Paris, 1961.)
Under Cover of Night. Mystique, 1981 (Translation of "L'Homme des Ajoncs." Paris, 1956.)

VITU, AUGUSTE (CHARLES JOSEPH). 1823-1891.
The Strange Phantasy of Doctor Trintzius. Vizetelly, 1886 ss, some criminous

VIVIAN, CHARLES
The Cotswold Connection. Anchor, 1984

*VIVIAN, E(VELYN) CHARLES
Shooting Stars. Hurst, 1928 (Novelization of film: British International, 1928; scw: John Orton, Anthony Asquith; dir: A. V. Bramble, Asquith.)

VOLKOFF, VLADIMIR. 1932- . Ref: CA.
The Set-Up. Bodley, 1984; Arbor, 1985 <Paris> (Translation of "Le Montage." Paris, 1982.)
The Turn-Around. Bodley, 1981; Doubleday, 1981 <Paris> (Translation of "Le Retournement." Paris, 1979.)

*VON ELSNER, DON (BYRON). Ref also: TM.

*VON HARBOU, THEA
*The Spy. Silent film: (studio?), 1928, as Spione (The Spy) (scw: Thea Von Harbou; dir: Fritz Lang)

VON HOFFMAN, NICHOLAS. 1929-
Ref: CA.
Organized Crimes. Harper, 1984; Joseph, 1985 <Chi., 1929>

*VON RABE, BARONESS A. C. delete entry

VORILLAS, STEVEN. See: *Tad Richards.

*VOSPER, FRANK. 1899-1937.
*Love from a Stranger. Film: Trafalgar, 1937 (scw: Frances Marion; dir: Rowland V. Lee). Also: Renown, 1947; released in Britain as A Stranger Walked In (scw: Philip MacDonald; dir: Richard Whorf)

*Murder on the Second Floor. Film: WB-FN, 1932 (scw: Roland Pertwee, Challis Sanderson; dir: William McGann). Also: Warner, 1941, as Shadows on the Stairs (scw: Anthony Coldeway; dir: D. Ross Lederman)

*VREELAND, (WILLIAM CANTWELL) FRANK (THORPE)
*Dishonored. (Novelization of film: Paramount, 1931; scw: Daniel N. Rubin; dir: Josef Von Sternberg.)
*June 13. Film: Paramount, 1932, as *The Night of June 13 (scw: Agnes Brand Leahy, Brian Marlow, William Slavens McNutt; dir: Stephen Roberts)

*VULLIAMY, C(OLWYN) E(DWARD). Ref: not in TC2.
*Don Among the Dead Men. Film: Tower, 1964, as A Jolly Bad Fellow; released in the U.S. as They All Died Laughing (scw: Robert Hamer, Donald Taylor; dir: Don Chaffey)

WACHT, LEO
Mission to Warsaw. Brown, 1960 <WWII, Warsaw>

*WADDELL, E(LEANOR) LEE
*Murder at Drake's Anchorage. <also: acad.>

*WADDELL, MARTIN. Ref: CA.
*Come Back When I'm Sober. criminous
*Otley. Film: Open Road, 1968 (scw: Ian La Frenais, Dick Clement; dir: Clement)

*WADE, BOB. Ref: CA.
*Pop Goes the Queen. Also published as by Wade Miller: Unicorn Book Club, 1947

*WADE, GARRISON. Pseudonym of Wade Garrison Harding.

*WADE, HENRY. Ref also: CA, BM, TM. SC: Insp. Lott, in *The Dying Alderman, and in *The Hanging Captain.
*Mist on the Saltings. ... Perennial, 1985

WADSLEY, OLIVE
-Belonging. Cassell, 1920; Dodd, 1920. Silent film: Stoll, 1922 (scw: Leslie Howard Gordon; dir: F. Martin Thornton)

*WAGER, WALTER (HERMAN). Ref also: TM. SC: Alison Gordon, also in title marked AG.
The Assassin. Inner Circle, 1985 (U.S. title?)
*Blue Leader. <Burma>
Blue Murder. Arbor, 1981; Severn, 1984 AG
Designated Hitter. Arbor, 1982; Sphere, 1985
Otto's Boy. Macmillan, 1985; Futura, 1985 <NYC>
*Telefon. Film: MGM, 1977 (scw: Peter Hyams, Stirling Silliphant; dir: Don Siegel)
Viper Three. Film: Lorimar, 1977, as Twilight's Last Gleaming (scw: Ronald M. Cohen, Edward Huebsch; dir: Robert Aldrich)

*WAGNER, GEOFFREY (ATHELING)
*The Passionate Land. <Mex.>

*WAGNER, SHARON (BLYTHE). Pseudonym: *Casey Stephens.
*The Cove in Darkness. <Eng., ca.1700>

*WAHLOO, PER <PETER>. See also: *Maj Sjowall.
*The Assignment. Film: Nordisk Tonefilm, 1977 (scw: Lars Magnas Jansson, Ingemar Ejre, Mats Arehn; dir: Arehn)
*The Lorry. Film: Stockholm, 1978, as Black Sun (scw: Per Wahloo, Arne Mattson; dir: Mattson)
*Murder on the Thirty-First Floor. Film: Ziegler, 1982, as Kamikaze (in German) (scw: Robert Katz; dir: Wolf Gremm)

*WAINWRIGHT, JOHN (WILLIAM). Ref also: CA, TM. SC: Supt. Lennox, also in titles marked L; Supt. Blayde, in at least those titles marked B.
All on a Summer's Day. Macmillan (London), 1981; St. Martin's, 1982
All Through the Night. Macmillan (London), 1985; St. Martin's, 1985
Anatomy of a Riot. Macmillan (London), 1982
Blayde R.I.P. Macmillan (London), 1982; St. Martin's, 1982 B
*Brainwash. Film: Ariane, 1981, as Garde a Vue (The Inquisitor; The Grilling) (scw: Claude Miller, Jean Herman; dir: Miller)
Clouds of Guilt. Macmillan (London), 1985; St. Martin's, 1985
Cul-De-Sac. Macmillan (London), 1984; St. Martin's, 1984
*The Day of the Peppercorn Kill. L
The Distaff Factor. Macmillan (London), 1983
The Forest. Macmillan (London), 1984; St. Martin's, 1984
Heroes No More. Macmillan (London), 1983
The Ride. Macmillan (London), 1984; St. Martin's, 1984
Spiral Staircase. Macmillan (London), 1983; St. Martin's, 1983 L
The Tainted Man. Macmillan (London), 1980
Their Evil Ways. Macmillan (London), 1983; St. Martin's, 1983
An Urge for Justice. Macmillan (London), 1981; St. Martin's, 1982 B

*WAINWRIGHT, RICHARD ASHTON. Pseudonym of *Harrie I(rving) Hancock, 1868-1922, q.v.
Hunted Down. Street (Magnet #204), 1901
The Kidnapped Millionaire. Street (Magnet #237), 1902

*WAKEFIELD, H(ERBERT) RUSSELL. 1888-1964.

WAKEMAN, FREDERICK. 1909- .
-A Free Agent. Collins, 1983; Simon, 1963

*WALD, MALVIN (DANIEL)
*The Naked City. Screenplay of film: Universal, 1948 (scw: Malvin Wald, Albert Maltz; dir: Jules Dassin)

WALDEN, WILLIAM
Treasures on Earth. Dramatists, 1965 (3-act play.)

*WALDMAN, FRANK. See also: William Gleason.

*WALK, CHARLES EDWARD
*The Green Seal. Silent film: Bluebird, 1918, as The Girl in the Dark (scw: A. G. Kenyon; dir: Stuart Paton)

*WALKER, DAVID (ESDAILE)
*Diamonds for Moscow. Film: Universal, 1966, as A Man Could Get Killed (scw: Richard Breen, T. E. B. Clarke; dir: Ronald Neame)

*WALKER, DAVID (HARRY)
*The Storm and the Silence. <Scot.>

WALKER, DINSDALE
The Ess Club. Hodder, 1933

*WALKER, GERALD
*Cruising. Film: United Artists, 1980 (scw & dir: William Friedkin)

*WALKER, GERTRUDE
*The Suspect. <L.A.>

*WALKER, JERRY
*Mission Accomplished. <1950>

*WALKER, MARTIN
The Eastern Question. Panther, 1982

*WALKER, MAX
*The Last Escape. (Novelization of film: Oakmont, 1970; scw: Herman Hoffman; dir: Walter Grauman.)

*WALKER, PAUL
The Altar. PB, 1983 <N.J.>

*WALKER, PETER N(ORMAN). Pseudonym: Andrew Arncliffe, q.v. SC: Det. Sgt. Carnaby-King, also in at least the title marked C; Jock Patterson, in at least *Panda One Investigates, *Pando One on Duty, *Witchcraft for Panda One, and in title marked JP below.
Carnaby and the Campaigners. Hale, 1984 C
Robber in a Mole Trap. Hale, 1985
Seige for Panda One. Hale, 1981 JP
Teenage Cop. Hale, 1982

WALKER, ROBERT N.
  Brain Watch. Leisure, 1985 <Ill.>
WALKER, WALTER (HERBERT III).
  1949-   . Ref: CA.
  A Dime to Dance By. Harper, 1983
    <Boston>
  The Two Dude Defense. Harper, 1985
    <S.F.>
*WALLACE, ARTHUR. Pseudonym of Frank Armer.
  *Passion Pulls the Trigger. Also published as: Man Crazy. Falcon, 1951, as by James Clayford (house name)
WALLACE, DAVID RAINS. 1945-   . Ref: CA.
  The Turquoise Dragon. Sierra Club, 1985; Bodley, 1986   <Calif.>
WALLACE, EARL W. See: William Kelley, 1929-
*WALLACE, (RICHARD HORATO) EDGAR. Ref also: CA, TM. See also: *Robert (G.) Curtis, *Tim J. Kelly.
  Film (based on unidentified story): Merton Park, 1962, as Backfire! (scw: Robert Stewart; dir: Paul Almond). Also: Merton Park, 1962 (based on ss "The Best Laid Plans of a Man in Love"), as Candidate for Murder (scw: Lukas Heller; dir: David Villiers). Also: Merton Park, 1962, as Death Trap (scw: John Roddick; dir: John Moxey). Also (silent film): Davidson, 1924 (scw: Eliot Stannard; dir: Arthur Rooke). Also: Merton Park, 1964, as Downfall (scw: Robert Stewart; dir: John Moxey). Also: Merton Park, 1964, as Face of a Stranger (scw: John Sansom; dir: John Moxey). Also: Merton Park, 1963, as Incident at Midnight (scw: Arthur LaBern; dir: Norman Harrison). Also: Venture, 1933, as The Jewel (scw: Basil Mason; dir: Reginald Denham). Also: Twickenham, 1935, as The Lad (scw: Gerard Fairlie; dir: Henry Edwards). Also: Merton Park, 1962, as Locker 69 (scw: Richard Harris; dir: Norman Harrison). Also: Merton Park, 1964, as The Main Chance (scw: Richard Harris; dir: John Knight). Also: Gainsborough, 1931, as The Man They Could Not Arrest (scw: Arthur Wimperis, Angus MacPhail, T. Hayes Hunter; dir: Hunter). Also: Merton Park, 1964, as Never Mention Murder (scw: Robert Banks Stewart; dir: John Nelson Burton). Also: Merton Park, 1963, as On the Run (scw: Richard Harris; dir: Robert Tronson). Also: Merton Park, 1962, as Playback (scw: Robert Banks Stewart; dir: Quentin Lawrence). Also: Smith, 1936, as Prison Breaker (scw: Frank Witty; dir: Adrian Brunel). Also: Merton Park, 1963, as Return to Sender (scw: John Roddick; dir: Gordon Hales). Also: Merton Park, 1963, as The Set-Up (scw: Roger Marshall; dir: Gerard Glaister). Also: Merton Park, 1963 (based on ss "The Breaking Point"), as To Have and To Hold (scw: John Sansom; dir: Herbert Wise). Also: Merton Park, 1963, as The 20,000 Pound Kiss (scw: Philip Mackie; dir: John Moxey). Also (silent film): Universal, 1919, as Wanted at Headquarters (scw: Wallace Clifton; dir: Stuart Paton)
  *Angel Esquire. Silent film: Gaumont, 1919 (scw: George Pearson; dir: W. P. Kellino)
  *The Angel of Terror. Film: Merton Park, 1963, as Ricochet (scw: Roger Marshall; dir: John Moxey)
  *The Big Four. Film: Anglo-Amalgamated, 1964, as The Verdict (scw: Arthur LaBern; dir: David Eady)
  *The Black. Reprinted with two stories added: Digit, 1962
  *The Blue Hand. Small, 1923 (U.S. publisher correction)
  *Bones. Film (also based on *Lieutenant Bones). Gainsborough, 1938 (scw: Marriott Edgar, Val Guest, J. O. C. Orton; dir: Marcel Varnel).
  *The Brigand. ... Sutton, 1985
  *The Calendar. Film: Gaumont British, 1931; released in the U.S. as Bachelor's Folly (scw: Angus MacPhail, Robert Stevenson; dir: T. Hayes Hunter). Also: Gainsborough, 1948 (scw: Geoffrey Kerr; dir: Arthur Crabtree)
  *The Case of the Frightened Lady. Film: British Lion, 1932, as The Frightened Lady; released in the U.S. as Criminal at Large (scw: Angus MacPhail, Bryan Edgar Wallace; dir: T. Hayes Hunter)
  The Cheaters; see The Nine Bears
  *Chick. Silent film: British Lion, 1928 (scw: Eliot Stannard; dir: A. V. Bramble). Sound film: B&D, 1936 (scw: Irving Leroy, Daniel Wheddon, Gerard Fairlie, Cyril Gardner, D. B. Wyndham-Lewis; dir: Michael Hankinson)
  *The Clue of the New Pin. Silent film: British Lion, 1929 (scw: Kathleen Hayden; dir: Arthur Maude). Sound film: Merton Park, 1960 (scw: Philip Mackie; dir: Allan Davis)
  *The Clue of the Silver Key. Film: Merton Park, 1961 (scw: Philip Mackie; dir: Gerard Glaister)
  *The Clue of the Twisted Candle. Film: Merton Park, 1960 (scw: Philip Mackie; dir: Allan Davis)
  *The Crimson Circle. Silent film: Kinema, 1922 (scw: Patrick L. Mannock; dir: George Ridgwell). Also (partial sound): New Era, 1930 (scw: Howard Gaye; dir: Friedrich Zelnik). Sound film: Wainwright, 1936 (scw: Howard Irving Young; dir: Reginald Denham)
  *The Coat of Arms. Film (?): British Lion, 1931, as The Old Man (scw: Edgar Wallace; dir: Manning Haynes)
  *The Daffodil Mystery. Film: Omnia-Rialto, 1962, as The Devil's Daffodil (scw: Basil Dawson, Donald Taylor; dir: Akos Rathony)
  *The Dark Eyes of London. Film: Argyle, 1939; released in the U.S. as The Human Monster (scw: Patrick Kirwan, Walter Summers, John F. Argyle; dir: Summers). Also: Rialto, 1961, as Die Toten Augen von London (The Dead Eyes of London). Also: Rialto, 1968, as Der Gorilla von Soho (The Soho Gorilla) (scw: Freddy Gregor; dir: Alfred Vohrer).
  *A Debt Discharged. Film: Merton Park, 1961, as Man Detained (scw: Richard Harris; dir: Robert Tronson)
  *The Door with Seven Locks. Film: Rialto, 1940; released in the U.S. as Chamber of Horrors (scw: Norman Lee, Gilbert Gunn, John Argyle; dir: Lee)
  *The Double. Film: Merton Park, 1963 (scw: Lindsay Galloway, John Roddick; dir: Lionel Harris)
  *Down Under Donovan. Silent film: Stoll, 1922 (scw: Forbes Dawson; dir: Harry Lambart)
  *Educated Evans. Film: WB-FN, 1936 (scw: Frank Launder, Robert Edmunds; dir: William Beaudine)
  *Elegant Edward. Film: Merton Park, 1963, as The Rivals (scw: John Roddick; dir: Max Varnel)
  *The Face in the Night. Film: Independent Artists, 1960, as The Malpas Mystery (scw: Paul Tabori, Gordon Wellesley; dir: Sidney Hayers)
  *The Feathered Serpent. Film: Columbia, 1932, as The Menace (scw: Charles Logue, Roy Chanslor; dir: Roy William Neill). Also: GS Enterprises, 1934 (scw: Maclean Rogers, Kathleen Butler; dir: Rogers)
  *The Fellowship of the Frog. Small, 1923 (U.S. publisher correction) Film: Wilcox, 1937, as The Frog (scw: Ian Hay, Gerald Elliott; dir: Jack Raymond)
  *Flat 2. Film: Merton Park, 1962 (scw: Lindsay Galloway; dir: Alan Cooke)
  *The Flying Fifty-Five. Silent film: Stoll, 1924 (scw & dir: A. E. Coleby). Sound film: Admiral, 1939 (scw: Victor Greene, Vernon Clancey, Kenneth Horne; dir: Reginald Denham)
  *The Flying Squad. Silent film: British Lion, 1929 (scw: Kathleen Hayden; dir: Arthur Maude). Sound film: British Lion, 1932 (scw: Bryan Edgar Wallace; dir: F. W. Kraemer). Also: ABPC, 1940 (scw: Doreen Montgomery; dir: Herbert Brenon)
  *The Forger. Silent film: British Lion, 1928 (scw: Edgar Wallace; dir: G. B. Samuelson)
  *Forty-Eight Short Stories. Silent film (from ss "Fighting Snub Reilly"): Stoll, 1924, as Fighting Snub Reilly (dir: Andrew P. Wilson). Sound film (from ss "The Greek Poropulos"): Liberty, 1934, as Born to Gamble (scw: E. Morton Hough; dir: Phil Rosen)
  *The Four Just Men. Silent film: Stoll, 1921 (scw & dir: George Ridgwell). Sound film: Ealing, 1939; released in the U.S. as The Secret Four (scw: Angus MacPhail, Sergei Nolbandov, Roland Pertwee; dir: Walter Forde)
  *Four Square Jane. Film: Merton Park, 1961, as The Fourth Square (scw: James Eastwood; dir: Allan Davis)
  *The Frightened Lady. Film: Pennant 1940; released in Britain as The Case of the Frightened Lady (scw: Edward Dryhurst; dir: George King)
  *Good Evans! Film: WB-FN, 1938, as Thank Evans (scw: Austin Melford, John Dighton, John Meehan, Jr.; dir: Roy William Neill)
  *The Green Pack. Film: British Lion, 1934 (scw: John Hunter; dir: T. Hayes Hunter)
  *The Green Ribbon. Film: Merton Park, 1961, as Never Back Losers (scw: Lukas Heller; dir: Robert Tronson)
  *Green Rust. Silent film (?): Gaumont, 1919, as The Green Terror (scw: G. W. Gifford; dir: W. P. Kellino)
  *Grey Timothy. Silent film: Gaumont, 1919, as Pallard the Punter (scw: George Pearson; dir: J. L. V. Leigh)
  *The Gunner. Film: Merton Park, 1962, as Solo for Sparrow (scw: Roger Marshall; dir: Gordon Flemyng)
  *The India-Rubber Men. Film: Imperator, 1938, as The Return of the Frog (scw: Ian Hay, Gerald Elliott; dir: Maurice Elvey)
  *The Iron Grip. Readers Library, 1929 (date correction)
  *Jack o' Judgment. Film: Merton Park, 1962, as The Share Out (scw: Philip Mackie; dir: Gerard Glaister). Also: Merton Park, 1963, as Accidental Death (scw: Arthur LaBern; dir: Geoffrey Nethercott)
  *Kate Plus Ten. Film: Wainwright, 1938 (scw: Jack Hulbert, Jeffrey Dell; dir: Reginald Denham)
  *The Lone House Mystery. Film (from title story): Merton Park, 1961, as Attempt to Kill (scw: Richard Harris; dir: Royston Morley)
  *The Man at the Carlton. Film: Merton Park, 1961, as Man at the Carlton Tower (scw: Philip Mackie; dir: Robert Tronson)
  *The Man Who Bought London. Silent film: Windsor, 1916 (dir: F. Martin Thornton). Sound film: Merton Park, 1962, as Time to Remember (scw: Arthur LaBern; dir: Charles Jarrott)
  *The Man Who Changed His Name. Silent film: British Lion, 1928 (scw: Kathleen Hayden; dir: A. V. Bramble). Sound film: Real Art, 1934 (scw: H. Fowler Mear; dir: Henry Edwards)
  *The Man Who Knew. Film: Merton Park, 1960, as Partners in Crime (scw: Robert Stewart; dir: Peter Duffell)
  *The Man Who Was Nobody. Film: Merton Park, 1960 (scw: James Eastwood; dir: Montgomery Tully)
  *The Melody of Death. Silent film: Stoll, 1922 (scw: Leslie Howard Gordon; dir: F. Martin Thornton)
  *The Million Dollar Story. Film: Merton Park, 1963, as The Partner (scw: John Roddick; dir: Gerard Glaister)
  *The Mind of Mr. J. G. Reeder. Film: Grand National, 1939; released in the U.S. as The Mysterious Mr. Reeder (scw: Bryan Edgar Wallace, Marjorie Gaffney, Michael Hogan; dir: Jack Raymond). Also: Grand National, 1939, as The Missing People (scw: Lydia Hayward; dir: Jack Raymond)

*The Missing Million. Film: Signet, 1942 (scw: James Seymour; dir: Phil Brandon)
*More Educated Evans. Webster, 1926 (date correction)
*Nig Nog. ss, from *Forty-Eight Short Stories
*The Nine Bears. Also published as: The Cheaters. Digit, 1962. Film: British Lion, 1932, as The Other Man (dir: Manning Haynes)
*The Northing Tramp. Film: Gaumont British, 1936, as Strangers on a Honeymoon (scw: Sydney Gilliat, Bryan Edgar Wallace, Ralph Spence; dir: Albert de Courville)
*Number Six. Newnes, 1927 (date correction) Film: Merton Park, 1962 (scw: Philip Mackie; dir: Robert Tronson)
*On the Spot. Film: Paramount, 1938, as Dangerous to Know (scw: William R. Lipman, Horace McCoy; dir: Robert Florey)
*Red Aces. Silent film: British Lion, 1929 (scw & dir: Edgar Wallace)
*The Ringer. Silent film: British Lion, 1928 (scw: Mary Murillo, Edgar Wallace; dir: Arthur Maude). Sound film: Gainsborough, 1931 (scw: Angus MacPhail, Robert Stevenson; dir: Walter Forde). Also: Suedfilm, 1932, as Der Hexer (The Sorcerer) (scw: Knut Borris, G. Water; dir: Alfred Vohrer). Also: Ealing, 1938, as The Gaunt Stranger; released in the U.S. as The Phantom Strikes (scw: Sidney Gilliat; dir: Walter Forde). Also: London Films, 1952 (scw: Val Valentine, Lesley Storm; dir: Guy Hamilton)
*The River of Stars. Silent film: Stoll, 1921 (scw: Leslie Howard Gordon; dir: F. Martin Thornton)
*Room 13. Film: British National, 1938, as Mr. Reeder in Room 13; released in the U.S. as Mystery of Room 13 (scw: Doreen Montgomery, Victor Kendall, Elizabeth Meehan; dir: Norman Lee). Also: Rialto, 1964, as Zimmer 13 (Room 13) (scw: Quentin Philips; dir: Harald Reinl)
*Sanders of the River. Film: London, 1935 (scw: Lajos Biro, Jeffrey Dell, Arthur Wimperis; dir: Zoltan Korda). Also: Big Ben, 1963, as Death Drums Along the River (scw: Harry Alan Towers, Nicolas Roeg; dir: Lawrence Huntington). Also: Towers, 1964, as Coast of Skeletons (scw: Anthony Scott Veitch, Peter Welbeck; dir: Robert Lynn)
*Sergeant Dunn, C.I.D.; see Sergeant Sir Peter
*Sergeant Sir Peter. ... Also published as: Sergeant Dunn, C.I.D. Digit, 1962. Film (based on ss "The Death Watch"): RKO, 1933, as Before Dawn (scw: Marian Dix, Garrett Fort; dir: Irving Pichel)
*The Sinister Man. Film: Merton Park, 1961 (scw: Robert Stewart; dir: Clive Bonner)
"The Sooper" and others. Dent, 1984 ss, partly from earlier collections
*The Squeaker. Film: British Lion, 1930 (scw & dir: Edgar Wallace). Also: London, 1937; released in the U.S. as Murder on Diamond Row (scw: Bryan Edgar Wallace, Edward O. Berkman; dir: William K. Howard). Also: Rialto, 1965, as Der Hexer (The Squeaker) (scw: Herbert Reinecker; dir: Alfred Vohrer)
*The Steward. Film (from ss "The Ghost of John Holling"): Monogram, 1934, as The Ghost of John Holling (scw: Wellyn Totman; dir: William Nigh)
*The Terror. Reprinted with two additional stories: Digit, 1962. Film: Warner, 1928 (scw: Harvey Gates; dir: Roy del Ruth). Also: First National, 1934, as Return of the Terror (scw: Eugene Solow, Peter Milne; dir: Howard Bretherton). Also: ABPC, 1938 (scw: William Freshman; dir: Richard Bird)
*The Thief in the Night. Reprinted with 5 additional ss: Digit, 1962. Film: Merton Park, 1963, as Five to One (scw: Roger Marshall; dir: Gordon Flemyng)
*The Three Just Men. Hodder, 1925; Doubleday, 1929 (date corrections)

*The Three Oak Mystery. Film: Merton Park, 1960, as Marriage of Convenience (scw: Robert Stewart; dir: Clive Donner)
*The Traitor's Gate. Film: British International, 1930, as The Yellow Mask (scw: Val Valentine, Miles Malleson, George Arthurs, Walter C. Mycroft, W. David; dir: Harry Lachman). Also: Summit, 1964 (scw: John Sansom; dir: Freddie Francis)
*The Undisclosed Client. Film: Merton Park, 1964, as Who Was Maddox? (scw: Roger Marshall; dir: Geoffrey Nethercott)
*The Valley of Ghosts. Silent film: British Lion, 1928 (scw: Edgar Wallace; dir: G. B. Samuelson)
*We Shall See. Film: Merton Park, 1964 (scw: Donal Giltinan; dir: Quentin Lawrence)
*White Face. Film: Gainsborough, 1932 (scw: Angus MacPhail, Bryan Edgar Wallace; dir: T. Hayes Hunter)

*WALLACE, FRANCIS
Big Game. Little, 1936. Film: RKO, 1936 (scw: Irwin Shaw; dir: George Nicholl, Jr.)

*WALLACE, IRVING
The Almighty. Doubleday, 1982; Joseph, 1983 <NYC>

*WALLACE, JOHN. Pseudonyms: Aintree, *Gerald Grantham, qq.v.
*Invasion. Popular Publications (Melb.), 1937
Millionaire Gangster Again. Popular Publications (Melb.), 1942
*Vengeance of ?. Popular Publications (Melb.), 1937

WALLACE, MARILYN
A Case of Loyalties. St. Martin's, 1985 <S.F.>

WALLACE, PATRICIA
-The Children's Ward. Zebra, 1985
-The Taint. Zebra, 1982
Traces. Zebra, 1982

WALLACE, VERA. Living in Canada.
Call Sign: Death. Hale, 1983
Eyes Upon a Wet Grave. Hale, 1985 <Haw.>
The Knife. Hale, 1983

WALLACH, IRA. Pseudonym: *Lillian Roberts, q.v.

WALLBRIDGE, C(HARLES) S(EAFORTH)
Through a Glass Darkly. Stockwell, 1931 <Guyana>

WALLEN, VAN
Nowhere Fast. Heuer, 1945 (3-act play.)

*WALLER, LESLIE
Gameplan. Granada, 1983

*WALLING, R(OBERT) A(LFRED) J(OHN).
Ref also: TM; not in TC2.

*WALLIS, A(RTHUR) J(AMES) and *CHARLES F. BLAIR, JR.
*Thunder Above. Film: Rank, 1960, as Beyond the Curtain (scw: Compton Bennett, John Cresswell; dir: Bennett)

*WALLIS, J(AMES) H(AROLD)
*Once Off Guard. Film: RKO, 1944, as The Woman in the Window (scw: Nunnally Johnson; dir: Fritz Lang)

*WALLMANN, JEFFREY M(INER). Ref also: TM. Joint pseudonym with *Bill Pronzini, q.v.: William Jeffrey, q.v.

WALLS, J. C.
The Man in the Flypaper Hat. New Horizon, 1982

WALRAFEN, CONRAD KURT. Pseudonym: *Jean-Pierre Conty, q.v.

WALSH, BILL. 1933-
Barbs. Hale, 1984
Cheat. Hale, 1981
Live Bait. Hale, 1981
Tight Lines. Hale, 1984

*WALSH, J(AMES) M(ORGAN)
Freelance Spy. Collins, 1937

*WALSH, MAURICE
*Danger Under the Moon. <Ire.>
-The Hill Is Mine. Chambers, 1940; Stokes, 1940
-The Road to Nowhere. Chambers, 1934; Stokes, 1934

*WALSH, PERCY
*Chin-Chin-Chinaman. Film: Real Art, 1931; released in the U.S. as Boat from Shanghai (scw: Brock Williams, Guy Newall; dir: Newall)

WALSH, RAY. 1949- . Raised in Eng.; employed by a Norwegian oil company and living in Norway.
The Mycroft Memoranda. Deutsch, 1984; St. Martin's, 1985 <Eng., 1888> (Sherlock Holmes)

*WALSH, THOMAS (FRANCIS MORGAN). 1908-1984. Ref also: TM.
*The Night Watch. Film (from this and *Rafferty by *Bill S. Ballinger): Columbia, 1954, as Pushover (see Ballinger entry)
*Nightmare in Manhattan. Film: Paramount, 1950, as Union Station (scw: Sydney Boehm; dir: Rudolph Mate)

WALTER, EUGENE. 1874-1941.
Jealousy. French, 1932 (3-act play.)

*WALTERS, SHELLY. Pseudonym of *Walter J. Sheldon, q.v.

*WALTON, THOMAS
*The Sins of the Fathers. <Wales>

*WAMBAUGH, JOSEPH. Ref also: TM; revised, expanded): TC2.
*The Black Marble. Film: AVCO, 1980 (scw: Joseph Wambaugh; dir: Harold Becker)
*The Choirboys. Film: Lorimar, 1978 (scw: Christopher Knopf; dir: Robert Aldrich)
The Delta Star. Perigord, 1983; Macdonald, 1983 <L.A.>
The Glitter Dome. Perigord, 1981; Weidenfeld, 1981. Film: Thorn, 1984 (scw: Stanley Kallis; dir: Stuart Margolin)
Lines and Shadows. Morrow, 1984; Macdonald, 1984 (Novelized true crime.)
*The New Centurions. Film: Columbia, 1972; released in Britain as Los Angeles Precinct 45 (scw: Stirling Silliphant; dir: Richard Fleischer)
*The Onion Field. Film: AVCO, 1979 (scw: Joseph Wambaugh; dir: Harold Becker)
The Secrets of Harry Bright. Perigord, 1985; Joseph, 1986 <Calif.>

WARBASH, DENVER
Execution by Choice. Holloway, 1985

WARD, ALFRED C.
Sherlock Holmes Versus John Thorndyke and Reginald Fortune. Goldscheider, 1982 (SC: Sherlock Holmes, following *A. Conan Doyle q.v.; John Thorndyke, following *R. Austin Freeman, q.v.; Reginald Fortune, following *H. C. Bailey, q.v.)

*WARD, EDMUND
The Baltic Emerald. Eyre, 1981; St. Martin's, 1981

*WARD, ELIZABETH C(AMPBELL)
Coast Highway 1. Walker, 1983 <Calif.>

*WARD, WILLIAM
Jeff Clayton's Masked Foe. Westbrook, 1911

*WARDEN, FLORENCE
*The Baronet's Wife. criminous
*City and Suburban. criminous
*The Dazzling Miss Davison. Silent film: Mutual, 1917 (dir: Frank Powell)
*The House on the Marsh. Silent film: London, 1920 (dir: Fred Paul)
*The Matheson Money. criminous

*WARDEN, GERTRUDE
*The Severn Affair. criminous

*WARDEN, MIKE. SC: Hank Bradford, in *Dead Ringer, and in titles marked HB below.
Bitter Homicide. Carousel, 1980 HB

Model for Murder. Carousel, 198? HB
Wasps in the Woodpile. American Art,
1980 <Seattle>

WARDEN, PETER
A Consignment of Ore. Hale, 1983

*WARE, JUDITH
*The Faxon Secret. <Fla.>

WARGA, WAYNE. Former Life magazine
correspondent; head writer for TV
series "Entertainment Tonight";
book collector; living in L.A.
Hardcover. Arbor, 1985 <L.A.>

WARK, GEOFFREY
Alpine Treason. Hale, 1983
-Judgement Postponed. Hale, 1981
Recorded Verdict. Hale, 1983

*WARNER, DOUGLAS
*Death of a Snout. Film: Rank, 1963,
as The Informers; released in the
U.S. as Underworld Informers (scw:
Alun Falconer, Paul Durst; dir:
Ken Annakin)

*WARNER, MIGNON. SC: Mrs. Edwina
Charles, also in all titles below.
Death in Time. Doubleday, 1982
<Wales>
Devil's Knell. Hale, 1984; Double-
day, 1983
The Girl Who Was Clairvoyant. Hale,
1983; Doubleday, 1982
Illusion. Hale, 1985; Doubleday,
1984
Speak No Evil. Hale, 1986; Doubleday,
1985

WARNER, RALPH and TONI IHARA
Murder on the Air. Nolo, 1984 <S.F.>

*WARNER, WARREN
*The Experiences of a Barrister. Ano-
ther edition (containing 3 ss from
*The Experiences of a Barrister, 6
ss from *Confessions of an Attorney, and 2 other ss): The Experiences of a Barrister and other
tales. Chambers, 1884

WARREN, BILL and ALLAN ROTHSTEIN
Fandom Is a Way of Death. <Authors>,
1984 <L.A.>

WARREN, CHRISTOPHER. 1945-   Pseudonym.
The Allah Conspiracy. Beaufort, 1981

*WARREN, DOUG(LAS)
*Walking Tall. (Novelization of film:
Cinerama, 1973; scw: Mort Briskin;
dir: Phil Karlson.)

WARREN, FRANKLIN A(RTHUR). 1911-
Weather--Clearing. French, 1940
(3-act play.)

*WARREN, JOSEPH
*Revenge. (Novelization of film:
United Artists, 1928; scw: Finis
Fox; dir: Edwin Carewe.)

*WARREN, MARY DOUGLAS. See: *Jennifer
Ames.

*WARRINER, THURMAN. Ref also: TM.

*WARWICK, FRANCIS ALISTER. Pseudonym:
*Warwick Jardine.

*WARWICK, JAMES. ca.1894-1983. Ref: CA.
*Blind Alley. Film: Columbia, 1939
(scw: Philip MacDonald, Michael
Blankfort, Albert Duffy; dir:
Charles Vidor). Also: Columbia,
1948, as The Dark Past (scw: Malvin
Wald, Oscar Saul; dir: Rudolph
Maté)

*WASHBURN, MARK. SC: Sam Boggs, in
*The Armageddon Game and *The
Omega Threat.
Nightwind. Dell, 1982
*The Omega Threat. ... Sphere, 1982

*WASSERMAN, (CARL) JACOB
*The Maurizius Case. Film: France-
London, 1954, as L'Affaire Maurizius (The Maurizius Affair)
(scw & dir: Julien Duvivier)

WATERS, G. W.
Caught in a Corner; or, A Terrible
Adventure. Laird, 1887

*WATERS, THOMAS A.
The Probability Pad. Pyramid, 1970

*WATKINS, IVOR
Demon. Macdonald, 1983

WATKINS, MAURINE
Chicago. Knopf, 1927 (Play.)
Silent film: DeMille, 1927 (scw:
Lenore J. Coffee; dir: Frank
Urson)

*WATSON, CLARISSA. Ref also: TM. SC:
Persis Willum, also in title
below.
Runaway. Atheneum, 1985; Hale, 1986
<L.I., Fr.>

*WATSON, COLIN. 1920-1983. Ref also:
TM. SC: Insp. Purbright, also in
*Bump in the Night, and in title
below.
Whatever's Been Going on at Mumbles-
by? Methuen, 1982; Doubleday, 1983

WATSON, IAN. 1943-   . Ref: CA.
The Jonah Kit. Gollancz, 1975;
Scribner, 1976

*WATSON, JOHN
*The File of the Golden Goose.
(Novelization of film: United Ar-
tists, 1969; scw: John C. Higgins,
James B. Gordon; dir: Sam Wana-
maker.)

WATSON, MALCOLM and EDWARD LA SERRE
Sheerluck Jones. Schoffer, 1982
(Play.)

WATSON, PETER
The Nazi's Wife. Doubleday, 1985;
Grafton, 1986 <WWII, Ger.>

WATSON, WILLIAM. 1931-
The Knight on the Bridge. Chatto,
1982; Chatto (U.S.), 1983

*WAUGH, ALEC
Island in the Sun. Cassell, 1956;
Farrar, 1955 <W.I.> Film:
TCF, 1957 (scw: Alfred Hayes;
dir: Robert Rossen)
The Mule on the Minaret. Cassell,
1965; Farrar, 1966 <Mid. East>

*WAUGH, HILLARY (BALDWIN). Ref also:
TM. SC: Simon Kaye, in all new
titles below.
The Billy Cantrell Case. Raven,
1981; Gollancz, 1982
The Doria Rafe Case. Raven, 1981;
Gollancz, 1982
The Nerissa Claire Case. Gollancz,
1983
*Odds Run Out. <Conn.>
*Sleep Long, My Love. Film: Figaro,
1962, as Jigsaw (scw & dir:
Val Guest)
The Veronica Dean Case. Gollancz,
1984

WAY, JOHN H., M.D., and DAVID C.
MILLER
Dream Watch. Playboy, 1981 <hosp.>

*WAY, PETER (HOWARD). 1936-   . Ref:
CA.
Belshazzar's Feast. Gollancz, 1982;
Atheneum, 1982

*WAYDE, BERNARD. Pseudonym of Gerald
Carlton. Other pseudonym: *Lieut.
Carlton.
*An Anarchist's Oath. Street, 1904
An Anarchist's Pluck. Street, 1903
*The Belt of Diamonds. Street, 1903
*The Coiner's League. Street, 1903
*The Compact of Crime. Street, 1904
*The Crooked Inspector. Street, 1903
*The Custom House Fraud. Street, 1903
*The False Claim. Street, 1903
*The Golden Clew. Street, 1903
*A Government Trust. Street, 1902
*The Hand on the Window Sill. Street,
1903
*In the Secret Vault. Street, 1903
*The King of Anarchists. Street, 1904
*The Man from Texas. Street, 1903
*The Man Who Made Money. Street, 1903
*The Money Jugglers. Street, 1903
*The Privateer's Defiance. Street,
1903
*A Question of Policy. Street, 1904
*The Smuggler's Ally. Street, 1903
*The Tracker Tracked. Street, 1903
*The Treasury's Millions. Street, 1902
*The Untaxed Whiskey. Street, 1902

*WAYLAND, PATRICK. Ref: not in TC2.

*WEATHERBY, W(ILLIAM) J(OHN)
Goliath. Bantam, 1981

*WEATHERS, PHILIP
*Tell-Tale Murder. (3-act play.)

WEBB, ALEX. Pseudonym of *Allan Lyle-
Smythe. SC: Josh Dekker, in both
titles.
Blood Run. Pinnacle, 1985 <WWII,
Fr.>
Dekker's Demons. Pinnacle, 1985
<WWII, Fr.>

WEBB, ANNE. Pseudonym: *Christopher
Reeve.

*WEBB, JACK. Ref also: TM; revised,
expanded: TC2.

*WEBB, JEAN FRANCIS
*The Bride of Cairngorn. <Haw.>

WEBB, LLOYD
The Sealing. Corgi, 1982

WEBB, MARTHA G. <MARTHA ANNE GUICE WIN-
GATE>. 1943-   . Ref: CA. Pseudo-
nym: Lee Martin, q.v.
Darling Carey's Dead. Walker, 1984;
Hale, 1986 <Tex.>
A White Male Running. Walker, 1985
<Tex.>

WEBB, SHARON. 1936-   . Ref: CA.
The Adventures of Terra Tarkington.
Bantam, 1985 <future>

WEBB, THOMAS CHARLES PACKHAM. Pseudonym: *Tony Angelo.

WEBB, VICTORIA. Pseudonym of a teacher
and writer in northern Calif. who
has spent considerable time in
Peru.
A Little Lady Killing. Dial, 1982
<S.F., Peru>

WEBER, ROBERT
-The Pace That Thrills. Jacobsen,
1925 (Novelization of film: First
National, 1925; scw: Byron Morgan;
dir: Webster Campbell.)

WEBSTER, DAN
When Johnny the Cleaver Took Britain.
Macmillan (London), 1983

WEBSTER, ELIZABETH CHARLOTTE
Pot Holes. Chapman, 1928 <S. Afr.>

*WEBSTER, ERNEST
Cossack Hide-Out. Hale, 1981
Madonna of the Black Market. Hale,
1981
Million-Dollar Stand-In. Hale, 1983
Red Alert. Hale, 1982
The Venetian Spy-Glass. Hale, 1983
The Verratoli Inheritance. Hale, 1983
The Watchers. Hale, 1984

*WEBSTER, HENRY KITCHELL
*The Butterfly. Silent film: World,
1915 (scw: O. A. C. Lund)

*WEBSTER, (ALICE) JEAN (CHANDLER). Ref:
CA.

*WEBSTER, NOAH. See: *Robert MacLeod.

WEBSTER, PAUL
Kruger's Gold. Constable, 1984
<S. Afr.>

WEED, DUNSTAN
A Fate Worse Than Death. French, 1946
(3-act play.)

*WEIN, JACQUELINE
*Room Mate. (title correction)

WEINSTEIN, HOWARD and A. C. CRISPIN
East Coast Crisis. Pinnacle, 1984;
NEL pb, 1985 <NYC>

*WEINSTOCK, JACK and *WILLIE GILBERT
*Catch Me If You Can. (3-act play.)

WEISER, MELVIN
Within the Web. Dell, 1984

*WEISMAN, JOHN
Watchdogs. Viking, 1983 <Wash. D.C.,
1988>

*WEISMILLER, EDWARD (RONALD)
*The Serpent Sleeping. <Fr., WWII>

WEISSNER, CHARLES
A Feast of Vultures. Tower, 1981

WEITZ, JOHN
Friends in High Places. Macmillan,
1982

WEITZENKORN, LOUIS. 1893-1943.
  Five Star Final. French, 1931 (3-act play.) Film: Warner, 1931 (scw: Robert Lord, Byron Morgan; dir: Mervyn LeRoy). Also: Warner, 1936, as Two Against the World; released in Britain as The Case of Mrs. Pembroke (scw: Michel Jacoby; dir: William McGann)

WELDON, FAY. 1933-   . Ref: CA.
  The President's Child. Hodder, 1982; Doubleday, 1983

WELL, ALAN STEWART. Pseudonym of *Alan Sewart, 1928-   , q.v. Other pseudonym: Padder Nash, q.v.
  Candice Is Dead. Hale, 1984
  Epitaph for Poor Richard. Hale, 1982
  Mr. Crumblestone's Eden. Hale, 1980
  Where Lionel Lies. Hale, 1984

*WELLARD, JAMES (HOWARD)
  *Action of the Tiger. Film: Claridge, 1957 (scw: Robert Carson, Peter Myers; dir: Terence Young)

*WELLES, (GEORGE) ORSON. 1915-1985.
  *Mr. Arkadin. Film: Warner, 1955; released in Britain as Confidential Agent (scw & dir: Orson Welles)

*WELLES, PATRICIA
  *Angel in the Snow. (title correction)
  Members Only. Arbor, 1981 <Mich.>

*WELLMAN, MANLY WADE. 1903-1986.
  Lonely Vigils. Carcosa, 1981 ss of psychic detection
  The School of Darkness. Doubleday, 1985

*WELLS, CAROLYN. Ref also: CA, TM.
  *The Gold Bag. Silent film: Edison, 1913, as the Mystery of West Sedgwick.
  *The Mark of Cain. Silent film: Astra, 1917 (scw: Philip Bartholomae; dir: George Fitzmaurice)
  *Vicky Van. Silent film: Paramount, 1919; also released as The Woman Next Door (scw: Marion Fairfax; dir: Robert G. Vignola)
  *The White Alley. Silent film: Essanay, 1916.

WELLS, FAREMAN
  Christine in Murderland. Long, 1933
  Five Crooked Chairs. Mellifont, 1936

*WELLS, H(ERBERT) G(EORGE). Ref also: CA.

WELLS, LEE. Living near L.A.; works in advertising and TV production; author of ss.
  Night of the Running Man. St. Martin's, 1981

WELLS, LISA. Pseudonym of *Thom Racina.
  Magda. Ace, 1981

WELSH, KEN. 1941-   . Ref: CA.
  Dark Deeds. Methuen pb, 1982; Pinnacle, 1984
  Fear for the Hero! Eyre, 1981

WENDER, THEODORA
  Knight Must Fall. Avon, 1985 <Mass., acad.>

*WENTWORTH, PATRICIA. Ref also: TM. SC: Benbow Smith and Frank Garratt, in *Danger Calling, and in *Walk with Care.

WERLBERGER, HANS. 1906-   . Pseudonym: Hanes Kades, q.v.

WERLIN, MARK. See: Marvin Werlin.

WERLIN, MARVIN and MARK WERLIN
  The Face. GM, 1985

*WERNER, GEORGE. Pseudonym of Peter T. Scott.

WERNER, HERMA. 1926-   . Pseudonym: Eve Gladstone, q.v.

WERNER, PATRICIA (BARNES). Born in Okla.; living in NYC.
  If Truth Be Known. Harlequin, 1985 <Wash. D.C.>

*WERNICK, SAUL. Pseudonym: Robert Julian, q.v. See also: *Don(ald Eugene) Pendleton.

*WERRY, RICHARD R.
  Casket for a Lying Lady. Dodd, 1985; Macmillan (London), 1986 <Fla.>

*WESLEY, ELIZABETH. Pseudonym of *(Elizabeth) Adeline McElfresh.
  Sharon James, Free-Lance Photographer. Avalon, 1956

*WESLEY, ROBERT
  *The Rogue with a Past. Street, 1903 (Magnet #273)

*WEST, DAVID. Pseudonym of *David Derek Stacton.

*WEST, JOYCE (TARLTON). Ref: CA.
  Fatal Lady. Paul's Book Arcade, 1960

*WEST, JOHN B. Ref: TM.

*WEST, MORRIS
  *The Big Story. Film: Argo, 1964, as The Crooked Road (scw: J. Garrison, Don Chaffey; dir: Chaffey)
  *Daughter of Silence. <It.>
  *The Salamander. Film: ITC, 1983 (scw: Robert Katz; dir: Peter Zinner)

WEST, OWEN. Pseudonym of *Dean R(ay) Koontz, q.v. Other pseudonyms: Richard Paige, q.v.
  -The Funhouse. Jove, 1980; Sphere, 1981
  The Mask. Jove, 1981; Coronet, 1983
  The Pit. Jove, 1982 <L.A.>

WEST, PAMELA ELIZABETH. Joint pseudonym of two authors.
  Madeleine. St. Martin's, 1983 <Glasgow, 1857>

WEST, RICHARD F.
  Crystal Clear. Popular Library, 1981 <NYC>

WEST, ROLAND
  The Unknown Purple, with *Carlyle Moore. Johnston (Toronto), 1919 (4-act play.) Silent film: Truart, 1924 (dir: Roland West)

WEST, ROY W.
  Destroyer. Leisure, 1985 <Turk.>

WEST, STANLEY GORDON. 1932-
  Amos. Rawson, 1983 <Mont.>

*WESTALL, WILLIAM (BURY)
  *As a Man Sows. criminous

*WESTERBY, ROBERT
  The Small Voice. Methuen, 1940. Film: British Lion, 1948; released in the U.S. as Hideout (scw: Derek Neame, Julian Orde, George Barraud; dir: Fergus McDonnell)
  *Wide Boys Never Work. Film: Film Locations, 1956, as Soho Incident; released in the U.S. as Spin a Dark Web (scw: Ian Stuart Black; dir: Vernon Sewell)

*WESTHEIMER, DAVID. See: *John Sherlock.

*WESTLAKE, DONALD E(DWIN). Ref also: BM, TM. SC: John Dortmunder, also in title marked JD.
  *Bank Shot. Film: United Artists, 1974 (scw: Wendell Mayes; dir: Gower Champion)
  *The Busy Body. Film: Paramount, 1967 (scw: Ben Starr; dir: William Castle)
  *Cops and Robbers. Film: United Artists, 1973 (scw: Donald E. Westlake; dir: Aram Avakian)
  High Adventure. Mysterious Press, 1985 <Belize>
  *The Hot Rock. Film: TCF, 1972; released in Britain as How to Steal a Diamond in Four Uneasy Lessons (scw: William Goldman; dir: Peter Yates)
  *Jimmy the Kid. Film: Zephyr, 1982 (scw: Sam Bobrick; dir: Gary Nelson)
  Kahawa. Viking, 1982; Allison, 1985 <Uganda>
  Levine. Mysterious Press, 1984 <NYC> ss
  *Two Much! Film: Le Gueville, 1984, as Le Jumeau (The Twin) (scw: Yves Robert, Elizabeth Rappeneau, Boris Bergman; dir: Robert)
  Why Me? Viking, 1983; Futura, 1984 JD <NYC>

*WESTMINSTER, AYNN. Pseudonym of *Hester Mundis.

*WESTON, CAROLYN. Ref also: CA, TM.

*WESTON, GEORGE
  *Queen of the World. ... Hodder, 1924

WESTOVER, CLYDE C.
  The Dragon's Daughter. Neale, 1912. Silent film: Haworth, 1919, as The Tong Man (dir: William Worthington)

WESTWARD, ELTON
  No Answer. Brown Watson, 1954

*WETHERELL, JUNE
  The Dark Wing. Beagle, 1973 <Wash., 1871>

*WEVERKA, ROBERT
  *Murder by Decree. (Novelization of film: Ambassador, 1979; scw: John Hopkins; dir: Bob Clark.)
  *The Sting. (Novelization of film: Universal, 1973; scw: David S. Ward; dir: George Roy Hill.)

*WEXLEY, JOHN. 1907-1985. Ref: CA.
  *The Last Mile. Film: World Wide, 1932 (scw: Seton I. Miller; dir: Sam Bischoff). Also: United Artists, 1959 (scw: Milton Subotsky, Seton I. Miller; dir: Howard W. Koch)

WHALEN, STEVE
  Deep Water. Arlington, 1981

WHALLEY, PETER. 1946-   .
  Love and Murder. Macmillan (London), 1985
  The Mortician's Birthday Party. Macmillan (London), 1983
  Old Murders. Macmillan (London), 1984
  Post Mortem. Macmillan (London), 1982

WHEAT, CAROLYN. Has law degree from Univ. of Toledo; public defender with Legal Aid Society in Brooklyn. Ref: TM.
  Dead Man's Thoughts. St. Martin's, 1983 <NYC>

*WHEATLEY, DENNIS (YATES). Ref also: TM.
  *The Devil Rides Out. Bantam, ca.1968 (U.S. publisher correciton) Film: Hammer, 1968; released in the U.S. as The Devil's Bride (scw: Richard Matheson; dir: Terence Fisher).
  *The Eunich of Stamboul. Film: GFD, 1936, as The Secret of Stamboul; reissued as The Spy in White (scw: Richard Wainwright, Howard Irving Young, Noel Langley; dir: Andrew Marton)
  *The Forbidden Territory. Film: Progress, 1934 (scw: Dorothy Farnum, Alma Reville; dir: Phil Rosen)
  *The Ka of Gifford Hillary. Bantam, 1969 (U.S. publisher correciton)
  *Murder Off Miami. (Crimefile #1)
  *The Satanist. Bantam, 1967 (U.S. publisher correction)
  *To the Devil--a Daughter. Bantam, ca.1968 (U.S. publisher correction) Film: Hammer, 1975 (scw: Chris Wicking, John Peacock; dir: Peter Sykes)
  *Uncharted Seas. Film: Hammer, 1968, as The Lost Continent (scw: Michael Nash; dir: Michael Carreras)

*WHEELER, HUGH CALLINGHAM
  *We Have Always Lived in the Castle. <Vt.>

WHEELER, JOHN HARVEY, JR. 1918-
  See: Eugene (Leonard) Burdick, 1918-1965.

*WHEELER, PAUL
  *Ransom. (Novelization of film: Lion International, 1975; also released as The Terrorists; scw: Paul Wheeler; dir: Caspar Wrede.)

*WHELTON, PAUL. The questioned title correlations are correct: each paperback is an abridged reprint of the indicated hardcover.

*WHITE, ALAN. SC: Capt. Colson, in at least those titles marked C below.
  Black Alert. Granada, 1985
  The Long Day's Dying. <WWII> Film: Junction, 1968 (scw: Charles Wood; dir: Peter Collinson)
  *The Long Fuse. C <Fr., WWII>

WHITE, DANIEL
*The Long Midnight. C <Nor., WWII>
*The Long Night's Walk. (title correction) C <Holl., WWII)
*The Long Silence. C <Fr., WWII>
*The Long Watch. C <Fr., WWII>

WHITE, DANIEL
Southern Daughter. Avon, 1953 <Chi.>

*WHITE, ETHEL LINA. Ref also: CA; not in TC2.
*Midnight House. Film: Paramount, 1945, as The Unseen (scw: Hagar Wilde, Raymond Chandler; dir: Lewis Allen)
*Some Must Watch. Film: RKO, 1946, as The Spiral Staircase (scw: Mel Dinelli; dir: Robert Siodmak). Also: Raven, 1975, as The Spiral Staircase (scw: Allan Scott, Chris Bryant, Mel Dinelli; dir: Peter Collinson)
*The Wheel Spins. Film: Gaumont, 1938, as The Lady Vanishes (scw: Sydney Gilliat, Frank Launder; dir: Alfred Hitchcock). Also: Hammer, 1979, as The Lady Vanishes (scw: George Axelrod, Frank Launder, Sidney Gilliat; dir: Anthony Page)

*WHITE, FRED(ERICK) M(ERRICK)
*The Midnight Guest. Silent film (?): Universal, 1923 (dir: George Archainbaud)

*WHITE, GRACE MILLER. (Death date given wrongly; actual date not known.)
*From the Valley of the Missing. Silent film: Fox, 1915 (scw: Clara S. Beranger; dir: Frank Powell)
Her Mad Marriage. Ogilvie, 1905. (Novelization of a play called "A Mad Marriage" by Jean Barrymore.)
*Kidnapped for Revenge. delete
*New York by Night. delete
*Secrets of the Police. (Novelization of an unpublished play by *Owen Davis, q.v.)
-Two Little Sailor Boys. Ogilvie, 1904 (Novelization of an unpublished play.)
*The Warning Bell. Ogilvie, 1906 (Novelization of an unpublished play.)
-When Women Love. Ogilvie, 1904 (Novelization of an unpublished play.)

*WHITE, JON MANCHIP
Death by Dreaming. Apple-Wood, 1981
-The Last Grand Master. Countryman, 1985
*The Moscow Papers. <Greece>

*WHITE, LESLIE T(URNER)
*5,000 Trojan Horses. Film: Warner, 1943, as Northern Pursuit (scw: Frank Gruber, Alvah Bessie; dir: Raoul Walsh)
*Harness Bull. Film: United Artists, 1953, as Vice Squad; released in Britain as The Girl in Room 17 (scw: Lawrence Roman; dir: Arnold Laven)

*WHITE, LIONEL. Ref also: TM.
*The Big Caper. Film: United Artists, 1957 (scw: Martin Berkeley; dir: Robert Stevens)
*Clean Break. Film: United Artists, 1956, as The Killing (scw & dir: Stanley Kubrick)
*Coffin for a Hood. <Fla.>
*The Money Trap. Film: MGM, 1965 (scw: Walter Bernstein; dir: Burt Kennedy)
*Obsession. Film: Rome-Paris, 1965, as Pierrot Le Fou (Crazy Pete) (scw & dir: Jean-Luc Godard)
*The Ransomed Madonna. <NYC>
*The Snatchers. Film: Universal, 1969, as The Night of the Following Day (scw: Hubert Cornfield, Robert Phippeny; dir: Cornfield)

*WHITE, PALMER
*The Circle of confusion. criminous, and #2 in a series

*WHITE, PERCY
Cairo. Constable, 1914 <Egypt>

WHITE, STEVE. Pseudonym of Robert McGarvey, 1948- . Ref: CA. All titles in S-Com series.
The Battle in Botswana. Warner, 1982
The Fighting Irish. Warner, 1982
<Ire.>
The King of Kingston. Warner, 1982 <Jam.>
Sierra Death Dealers. Warner, 1982
Stars and Swastikas. Warner, 1981
Terror in Turin. Warner, 1981 <It.>

*WHITE, STEWART EDWARD
-The Gray Dawn. Doubleday, 1915; Hodder, 1915, as The Grey Dawn. <S.F., 1850s> Silent film: Hampton, 1922 (scw: E. Richard Schayer, Marie Jenney; dir: Eliot Howe, Jean Hersholt)

WHITE, STUART
Death Game. Methuen pb, 1982
Operation Raven. NEL, 1985; Beaufort, 1986 <Eng., 1940>

*WHITE, T(ERENCE) H(ANBURY)
*Darkness at Pemberley. (misprint correction)

WHITE, TERI. ca.1948- . Living in Cleveland suburb. Ref: TM.
Bleeding Hearts. Mysterious Press, 1984 <L.A.>
Triangle. Charter, 1982

*WHITECHURCH, VICTOR L(ORENZO). Ref: CA, TM; not in TC2.
*-The Canon in Residence.
-The Dean and Jecinora. Unwin, 1926; Duffield, 1926
Mixed Relations. Benn, 1928. U.S. title (in slightly revised form): *The Robbery at Rudwick House
*The Robbery at Rudwick House; see Mixed Relations

*WHITELAW, DAVID
*The Big Picture. Film: WB-FN, 1938, as It's in the Blood (scw: Reginald Purdell, John Dighton, J. O. C. Orton, Brock Williams, Basil Dillon; dir: Gene Gerrard)
*The Girl from the East. Silent film: Edison, 1916, as The Heart of the Hills (dir: Richard Ridgely)
*The Little Hour of Peter Wells. Silent film: Granger, 1920 (scw: Eliot Stannard; dir: B. E. Doxat-Pratt)
*The Roof. Film: Real Art, 1933 (scw: H. Fowler Mear; dir: George A. Cooper)

WHITESON, LEON. 1930- . Ref: CA.
White Snake. Beaufort, 1982 <Rhod., 1973>

WHITFIELD, MARTHA
The Bethnal Inheritance. Zebra, 1981

*WHITFIELD, RAOUL. Ref also: CA, TM; expanded: TC2.

WHITMAN, JOHN T. 1926- . CIA agent who participated in SALT II talks.
Geneva Accord. Crown, 1985. British title: The Killing Peace. Blond, 1985 <Geneva>

WHITMAN, STEPHEN FRENCH
Here's Luck. Appleton, 1931

WHITMORE, ELAINE. Member of biology dept. at Univ. of Texas.
D.E.A.D. Dembner, 1984 <future>

WHITMORE, KEN
The Turn of the Screw. French, 1983 (Play based on the novel by *Henry James, q.v.)

*WHITNEY, PHYLLIS A(YAME). Ref also: TM.
A Dream of Orchids. Doubleday, 1985; Hodder, 1985 <Fla.>
Emerald. Doubleday, 1983; Heinemann, 1983 <Calif.>
Rainsong. Doubleday, 1984; Heinemann, 1984 <L.I.>
Vermilion. Doubleday, 1981; Heinemann, 1982 <Ariz.>

WHITTEMORE, EDWARD
Nile Shadows. Holt, 1983 <Egypt, 1942>

*WHITTEN, LESLIE H(UNTER)
A Day Without Sunshine. Atheneum, 1985; Severn, 1986
A Killing Pace. Atheneum, 1983; Severn, 1985 <Phil., It.>
*Moon of the Wolf. Film: Filmways, 1972 (scw: Alvin Sapinsky; dir: Daniel Petrie)

*WHITTINGTON, HARRY (BENJAMIN). Ref also: TM.
*Desire in the Dust. Film: TCF, 1960 (scw: Charles Lang; dir: William F. Claxton)
*Nita's Place. delete: not criminous
Sinners Club. Carnival, 1954. Also published as: *Teenage Jungle
*Teenage Jungle; see Sinners Club
*Web of Murder. <Fla.>

*WIBBERLEY, LEONARD PATRICK O'CONNOR. 1915-1983.

*WICK, CARTER
Dark House, Dark Road. Raven, 1981 <L.A.>

*WICKES, MARTHA. Pseudonym of *Josephine Chase, 1883-1931.

*WIEGAND, WILLIAM (GEORGE). Ref: not in TC2.

*WIENER, WILLARD
*Four Boys and a Gun. Also published as: The Young Killers. Avon, 1957. Film: United Artists, 1957, as Four Boys and a Gun (scw: Philip Yordan, Leo Townsend; dir: William Berke)

WIGHT, AUDREY
The Cloister Cat. St. Paul, 1961

WIGHT, E. B.
Tangled Web. Stockwell, 1980

WILCE, B. N. F.
The Luke Martin Diamonds. New Horizon, 1983

*WILCOX, COLLIN. Ref also: TM. SC: Lt. Frank Hastings, also in titles marked FH below.
Spellbinder. GM, 1981
Stalking Horse. Random, 1982 FH <S.F.>
Victims. Mysterious Press, 1985; Hale, 1986 FH <S.F.>

WILCOX, EVELYN. Pseudonym: *Evelyn Dewar.

*WILDE, OSCAR (FINGAL O'FLAHERTIE WILLS)
*Lord Arthur Savile's Crime. Film (from title ss and others): Universal, 1943, as Flesh and Fantasy (scw: Ernest Pascal, Samuel Hoffenstein, Ellis St. Joseph; dir: Julien Duvivier)

*WILDE, PERCIVAL. Ref also: TM.

WILDEBLOOD, PETER. 1923- . Ref: CA.
West End People. Weidenfeld, 1958

*WILDEN, THEODORE
The Exchange. Collins, 1981. U.S. title: Exchange of Clowns. Little, 1981 <Berlin>

*WILDER, ROBERT (INGERSOLL)
*Fruit of the Poppy. Film: MGM, 1968, as Sol Madrid; released in Britain as The Heroin Gang (scw: David Karp; dir: Brian Hutton)
*Walk with Evil. <Fla.>

WILDERNESS, DAVID O. Pseudonym of Peter S. Brody, 1912- .
-Sinsation of a Sintury. Pageant, 1956 <Calif.>

*WILES, DOMINI. Pseudonym: Amy Van Hassen, q.v.
Pay-Off. Constable, 1982
X Factor. Constable, 1983 <L.I.>

*WILHELM, KATE
The Nevermore Affair. Doubleday, 1966
O, Susannah! Houghton, 1982; Houghton (London), 1983

WILHELM, LAMBERT
Abort Project K! Carousel, 1981

*WILKINSON, ELLEN (CICELY). 1891-1947. Ref also: BM.
*The Division Bell Mystery. ... Garland, 1976

WILKINSON, SANDRA D. Graduate of schools of nursing in Cin. and Univ. of Colo.; registered nurse; part-time administrator of large hospital near Boston.
Death on Call. Dodd, 1984 <hosp., New Eng.>

*WILLARD, JOHN. See also: Gerry Kingsley.
 *The Cat and the Canary. Jacobsen, 1927; Readers Library, 1927. Also published as: The Cat Creeps. Jacobsen, 1930 <N.Y.> Silent film: Universal, 1927 (scw: Alfred A. Cohn, Robert F. Hill, Walter Anthony; dir: Paul Leni). Sound film: Universal, 1930, as The Cat Creeps (scw: Gladys Lehman; dir: Rupert Julian). Also: Paramount, 1939 (scw: Walter De Leon, Lynn Starling; dir: Elliott Nugent). Also: Grenadier, 1981 (scw & dir: Radley Metzger)

*WILLARD, JOSHUA
 *The Thorne Theatre Mystery. Also published as: A Killer Back Stage. News Stand, 1950

*WILLEFORD, CHARLES (RAY III). SC: Sgt. Hoke Moseley, in both titles.
 Miami Blues. St. Martin's, 1984; Futura, 1985 <Miami>
 New Hope for the Dead. St. Martin's, 1985 <Miami>

*WILLETT, E(RNEST) NODALL
 *The Sitting Emperor. Gardner, 1930 (date correction)

*WILLETS, GILSON
 *The First Law. Silent film: Astra, 1918 (scw: Roy Somerville; dir: Lawrence McGill)

WILLIAMS, A. R.
 The Minutes. Fowler Wright, 1928
 ss, one criminous

*WILLIAMS, ALAN (EMLYN)
 *The Beria Papers. <Russ.>
 *Snake Water. <S. Am.> Film: Universal International, 1968, as The Pink Jungle (scw: Charles Williams; dir: Delbert Mann)
 *The Widow's War. <Carib.>

*WILLIAMS, BEN AMES
 -Evered. Dutton, 1921; Mills, 1921
 *Leave Her to Heaven. Film: TCF, 1945 (scw: Jo Swerling; dir: John M. Stahl)

WILLIAMS, BOB. Graduate of Univ. of Minn.; newspaper editor, theatre publicist, composer, lyricist; living near Mpls.
 Ozark Flats. Thueson, 1983 (Fictionalized true crime.) <Mpls., 1894>

WILLIAMS, BROCK
 The Earl of Chicago. Bobbs, 1937; Harrap, 1937. Film: MGM, 1939 (scw: Lesser Samuels; dir: Richard Thorpe)

WILLIAMS, CHARLES (WALTER STANSBY). 1886-1945.
 War in Heaven. Gollancz, 1930; Pellegrini, 1949

*WILLIAMS, CHARLES. Ref also: TM.
 *Aground. Film: CCFC, 1965, as L'Arme a Gauche (Arm at the Left) (scw: Charles Williams, Fouli Elia, Claude Sautet; dir: Sautet)
 *All the Way. Film: TCF, 1959, as The Third Voice (scw & dir: Hubert Cornfield)
 Confidentially Yours; see *The Long Saturday Night
 *The Diamond Bikini. Film: Oceanic-CCFC, 1971, as Fantasia Chez les Ploues (Fantasia Among the Squares) (scw & dir: Gerard Pires)
 Finally, Sunday!; see *The Long Saturday Night
 *The Long Saturday Night. Also published as: Finally, Sunday! Penguin, 1983. And as: Confidentially Yours. Penguin, 1986. Film: Films du Carrosse, 1983, as Vivement Dimanche (Let It Be Sunday) (scw: Francois Truffaut, Suzanne Schiffman, Jean Aurel; dir: Truffaut)
 *Nothing in the Way. Film: Omnia, 1963, as Peau de Banane (Banana Peel) (scw: Claude Sautet, Daniel Boulanger, Marcel Ophuls; dir: Ophuls)
 *The Sailcloth Shroud. Film: Centaur, 1975, as The Man Who Would Not Die (scw: George Chesbro, Stephen Taylor, Robert Arkless; dir: Arkless)

*The Wrong Venus. Film: Universal, 1967, as Don't Just Stand There (scw: Charles Williams; dir: Ron Winston)

WILLIAMS, D(AFDD) J(OHN)
 Tibesti Assignment. Hale, 1983

*WILLIAMS, DAVID. 1926-   . Ref: TC2, TM. SC: Mark Treasure, also in titles below.
 Advertise for Treasure. Collins, 1984; St. Martin's, 1984
 Copper, Gold and Treasure. Collins, 1982; St. Martin's, 1982
 Murder in Advent. Macmillan (London). 1985; St. Martin's, 1986
 Treasure Preserved. Collins, 1983; St. Martin's, 1983
 Wedding Treasure. Macmillan (London), 1985; St. Martin's, 1985

*WILLIAMS, ELIOT CRAWSHAY
 Strictly Confidential. Long, 1944
 ss, some criminous

*WILLIAMS, (GEORGE) EMLYN
 *Night Must Fall. Film: MGM, 1937 (scw: John Von Druten; dir: Richard Thorpe). Also: MGM, 1964 (scw: Clive Exton; dir: Karel Reisz)
 *Someone Waiting. Film: Harlequin, 1957, as Time Without Pity (scw: Ben Barzman; dir: Joseph Losey)

*WILLIAMS, ERIC
 *The Borders of Barbarism. <Balkans>
 *Dragoman Pass. <Rum.>

*WILLIAMS, F(RANK) C(HENHALLS)
 The Potter's Wheel. Hartley, 1931

*WILLIAMS, GORDON M(acLEAN). Ref: CA, TM.
 Pomeroy. Joseph, 1983; Arbor, 1982 <Eng., 1903>
 *The Siege of Trencher's Farm. Film: Cinerama, 1971, as Straw Dogs (scw: David Zelag Goodman, Sam Peckinpah; dir: Peckinpah)
 *They Used to Play on Grass. delete: not criminous

*WILLIAMS, HENRY
 *How to Murder Your Wife. (Novelization of film: United Artists, 1964; scw: George Axelrod; dir: Richard Quine.)

*WILLIAMS, LAWRENCE
 Images of Death. Hale, 1984
 The Murder Triangle. Hale, 1982

WILLIAMS, LOUIS
 Tropical Murder. Tower, 1981 <Venez.>

*WILLIAMS, MARGARET WETHERBY.   -1984.
 Pseudonym: *Margaret Erskine.

*WILLIAMS, MARY
 Merlake Towers. Kimber, 1984

*WILLIAMS, MOUNTFORD
 The Happy Chase. Heinemann, 1944

WILLIAMS, NEAL
 Blow Out. Bantam, 1981; Corgi, 1981 (Novelization of film: Filmways, 1981; scw & dir: Brian De Palma.)

*WILLIAMS, P(HILIP) C(LAXTON)
 *Hoyland Intervenes. 2 ss
 *Hoyland Steps Out. 3 ss

WILLIAMS, RAYMOND
 Loyalties. Chatto, 1985

WILLIAMS, ROGER. 1947-
 A-Train. Star, 1985

WILLIAMS, TIMOTHY. Born in London; has taught in universities in Eng. and Europe; living on French Riviera. SC: Commissario Trotti, in both titles.
 Converging Parallels. Gollancz, 1982. U.S. title: The Red Citroen. St. Martin's, 1983 <It.>
 The Metal Green Mercedes; see The Puppeteer
 The Puppeteer. Gollancz, 1985. U.S. title: The Metal Green Mercedes. St. Martin's, 1985 <It.>
 The Red Citroen; see Converging Parallels

*WILLIAMS, (GEORGE) VALENTINE. Ref also: CA.
 *The Crouching Beast. Film: Stafford, 1935 (dir: W. Victor Hanbury)
 *Fog. Film: Columbia, 1934 (scw: Ethel Hill, Dore Schary; dir: Albert Rogell)

*WILLIAMSON, A(LICE) M(URIEL LIVINGSTON). See also: C(harles) N(orris) Williamson. Possible pseudonym: *William Allison.
 *A Woman in Grey. Silent film: Serico, 1920 (scw: Walter Richard Hall; dir: James Vincent)
 *The Woman Who Dared. Silent film: California Motion Pictures, 1916 (scw: Leslie T. Peacock; dir: George E. Middleton)

*WILLIAMSON, AUDREY (MAY). 1913-1986. Ref: CA.

*WILLIAMSON, C(HARLES) N(ORRIS) and *A(LICE) M(URIEL LIVINGSTON) WILLIAMSON, q.v. Possible pseudonym: *William Allison.
 *The Demon. Silent film: Metro, 1918 (scw & dir: George D. Baker)
 *The Lion's Mouse. Silent film: Granger, 1922 (dir: Oscar Apfel)
 *Lord John in New York. criminous. Silent film: Gold Seal, 1915 (scw: Harvey Gates; dir: Edward J. LeSaint)
 *The Scarlet Runner. Silent film: Vitagraph, 1916 (scw: George H. Plympton; dir: Wallie Van, William P. S. Earle)
 *The Second Latchkey. Silent film: MacDonald, 1921, as My Lady's Latchkey (scw: Finis Fox; dir: Edwin Carewe)
 *The Shop Girl. Silent film: Vitagraph, 1916, as Winifred the Shop Girl (scw: George Plympton; dir: George D. Baker)

WILLIAMSON, DAVID
 The Removalists. Currency, 1972 (Play.) <Melb.> Film: Seven Keys, 1975 (scw: David Williamson; dir: Tom Jeffrey)

WILLIAMSON, JACK <JOHN WILLIAM>. 1908-   . See: *James (Edwin) Gunn.

WILLIAMSON, LESLIE
 The Crowded Cemetery. Hale, 1981
 Death of a Portrait. Hale, 1982

WILLIAMSON, MONCRIEFF. 1915-   . Ref: CA.
 Death in the Picture. Beaufort, 1982 <Eng.>

WILLIAMSON, STEPHEN. See: *Nick Carter.

WILLIE, ENNIS. Ref: TM.
 And Some Were Evil. Merit, 1964
 -The Work of the Devil. Merit, 1961

*WILLIS, MAUD
 *The Devil's Rain. (Novelization of film: Bryanston, 1975; scw: Gabe Essoe, James Ashton, Gerald Hopman; dir: Robert Fuest.)

*WILLIS, TED. Ref (expanded): TC2.
 *The Blue Lamp. Film: Ealing, 1950 (scw: T. E. B. Clarke, Alexander Mackendrick; dir: Basil Dearden)
 The Most Beautiful Girl in the World. Macmillan (London), 1982 <Carib.>

WILLOUGHBY, LEE DAVIS. House name.
 The Frontier Detective. Dell, 1984 <Colo., 1881>

*WILLS, (MAITLAND) CECIL M(ELVILLE). 1891-1966.
 *Defeat of a Detective. <Scot.>

*WILLS, THOMAS
 *Mine to Avenge. <Chi.>

*WILLS, W. G. and *MRS. GREEN
 *Whose Hand? ... Arrowsmith, 1886

*WILMOT, ROBERT PATRICK
 *Death Rides a Painted Horse. <Midwest> (setting correction)

WILSON, AUGUSTA JANE (EVANS). 1835-1909.
 At the Mercy of Tiberius. Dillingham, 1887; Low, 1887. Silent film: Samuelson, 1920; released in the U.S. as The Price of Silence (dir: Fred Leroy Granville)

WILSON, BARBARA (ELLEN). 1950-
Born in Calif., living in Seattle;
author of ss collections and an
earlier novel; work has appeared
in national literary and feminist
journals. Ref: TM.
Murder in the Collective. Women's
Press (U.S. & U.K.), 1984
<Seattle>

WILSON, BROWNLOW
The Devil's Staircase. Exposition,
1962 <N. Mex.>

*WILSON, COLIN (HENRY). Ref also: TM.
SC: Insp. Gregory Saltfleet, in
*The Schoolgirl Murder Case, and
in title below.
The Janus Murder Case. Granada, 1984

WILSON, D. B.
Betrayed. Holloway, 1984

*WILSON, DANA. Ref: TM.

WILSON, F. PAUL
The Keep. Morrow, 1981; NEL, 1982.
Film: Paramount, 1983 (scw & dir:
Michael Mann)

WILSON, GAR. House name. All titles
below are in the Phoenix Force
series.
Argentine Deadline. Gold Eagle, 1982;
Mills, 1984 (by *Robert Hoskins)
<Arg.>
Aswan Hellbox. Gold Eagle, 1983
<Egypt> (by Thomas P. Ramirez and
Rex Swenson)
Atlantic Scramble. Gold Eagle, 1982;
Mills, 1984 <ship> (by Thomas P.
Ramirez)
The Black Alchemists. Gold Eagle,
1984 (by William Fieldhouse)
Dragon's Kill. Gold Eagle, 1983
<Haw.> (by William Fieldhouse)
The Fury Bombs. Gold Eagle, 1983;
Mills, 1985 (by *Robert Hoskins)
Guerrilla Games. Gold Eagle, 1982;
Mills, 1984 (by *Dan J. Marlowe)
<Parag.>
Harvest Hell. Gold Eagle, 1984
<Greece> (by William Fieldhouse)
Korean Killground. Gold Eagle, 1984
<Kor.> (by Thomas P. Ramirez)
Night of the Thuggee. Gold Eagle,
1985; Mills, 1986 <India> (by
William Fieldhouse)
No Rules, No Referee. Gold Eagle,
1985 <Bahamas> (by William Field-
house)
Phoenix in Flames. Gold Eagle, 1984
<Istan.> (by William Fieldhouse)
Return to Armageddon. Gold Eagle,
1984 <Isr.> (by William Field-
house)
Sea of Savages. Gold Eagle, 1985;
Mills, 1985 <ship> (by William
Fieldhouse and Paul Glen Newman)
Tigers of Justice. Gold Eagle, 1983;
Mills, 1985 (by William Fieldhouse)
Tooth and Claw. Gold Eagle, 1985
(by William Fieldhouse)
Ultimate Terror. Gold Eagle, 1984
<Ger.> (by William Fieldhouse)
The Viper Factor. Gold Eagle, 1985
<Eng.> (by William Fieldhouse.)
Welcome to the Feast. Gold Eagle,
1985; Mills, 1985 <S.F.> (by
William Fieldhouse)
White Hell. Gold Eagle, 1983 (by
Thomas P. Ramirez) <Alaska>

WILSON, GUTHRIE
The Feared and the Fearless. Putnam,
1953; Hale, 1954 <N.Z.>

WILSON, HOWARD C. See: Evelyn V.
Adams.

*WILSON, JACQUELINE. Ref also: TC2.

WILSON, JOHN ROWAN. 1919-   .
-The Round Voyage. Doubleday, 1957;
Heinemann, 1957 <ship>

WILSON, MARY REILLY. Pseudonym: *Mary
McMullen, q.v.

*WILSON, MITCHELL A.
*None So Blind. Film: RKO, 1947, as
The Woman on the Beach (scw: Frank
Davis, Jean Renoir; dir: Renoir)

WILSON, RICK
The Amsterdam Silver. Harris, 1985

WILSON, ROBERT C(HARLES). 1951-   .
Icefire. Putnam, 1984; Futura, 1984
<hosp.>

*WILSON, STEVE. Same protagonist ap-
pears in two earlier titles and
the first listed below.
Dealer's Wheels. Macmillan (London),
1982; St. Martin's, TM.
13. Panther, 1985; St. Martin's, 1984
<La.>

WILSON, TOM. 1942-
A Criminal Act. Hale, 1984

*WILSTACH, JOHN
*Under Cover Man. Film: Paramount,
1932 (scw: Garrett Fort, Francis
Faragoh; dir: James Flood)

WILTSE, DAVID. 1940-   . Ref: CA.
The Assassin; see The Wedding Guest
The Fifth Angel. Macmillan, 1985;
Souvenir, 1985 <NYC>
The Serpent. Delacorte, 1983; Sou-
venir, 1984 <NYC>
The Wedding Guest. Delacorte, 1982;
Souvenir, 1982. Also published as:
The Assassin. Corgi, 1984 <Iran>

WILTSHIRE, DAVID. Pseudonym: *John
Bedford, q.v.

WILTZ, CHRIS(TINE). 1948-   . Ref: CA.
The Killing Circle. Macmillan, 1981;
Hale, 1982 <New Or.>

WINCH, ARDEN
Blood Money. BBC, 1981. U.S. title:
Blood Royal. Viking, 1982

WINDHAM, SUSANNAH
Missing. Leisure, 1984 <Ky.>

*WINER, ELIHU. 1914-   . Ref: CA.

*WINGATE, JOHN
*Seawaymen. <Far East>
Submarine. Weidenfeld, 1982; St.
Martin's, 1982

*WINGATE, WILLIAM
Crystal. Century, 1983; St. Martin's,
1983
*Shotgun. Film: Orion, 1987, as
Malone (scw: Christopher Frank;
dir: Harley Cokliss)

WINGFIELD, H. D.
Frost at Christmas. PaperJacks, 1985

*WINNINGTON, ALAN. 1910(?)-1983. Ref:
CA.

WINSKI, NORMAN. See also: Dick
Stivers. SC: Dick Spencer (The
Hitman), in all titles.
Chicago Deathwinds. Pinnacle, 1984
<Chi.>
L.A. Massacre. Pinnacle, 1984 <L.A.>
Nevada Nightmare. Pinnacle, 1984
<Nev.>

*WINSLOW, JOAN
*Griffin Towers. <Pa.>

*WINSLOW, PAULINE GLEN. Ref also: CA.
SC: Supt. Merlin Capricorn, also in
title marked MC below.
*The Counsellor Heart. Reprinted as:
Sister Death. Fontana, 1982
-I, Martha Adam. Arlington, 1982; St.
Martin's, 1984
Judgement Day. Arlington, 1984; St.
Martin's, 1986
The Kindness of Strangers. Arlington,
1983
The Rockefeller Gift. Collins, 1982;
St. Martin's, 1982   MC   <NYC>
Sister Death; see The Counsellor
Heart
The Windsor Plot. Arlington, 1981;
St. Martin's, 1985 <WWII>

*WINSOR, DIANA. SC: Tavy Martin, in
both titles.

*WINSTON, DAOMA
Family of Strangers. Piatkus, 1983
(U.S. title? copyright 1973)
*Flight of a Fallen Angel. <South>
The Hands of Death. Piatkus, 1982
(U.S. title? copyright 1972)
*The Long and Living Shadow. <Wash.
D.C.>
*The Love of Lucifer. ... Piatkus,
1986
The Mayeroni Myth. Lancer, 1971
<Fla.>
-Mira. Arbor, 1981; Macdonald, 1982
<Wash. D.C.>
*The Secrets of Cromwell Crossing. ...
Piatkus, 1984
*Shadow of an Unknown Woman. (misprint
correction)
*Sinister Stone. ... Piatkus, 1985
*The Trap. <L.I.>
-A Sweet Familiarity. Arbor, 1981;
Macdonald, 1983
*The Victim. ... Piatkus, 1985
A Visit After Dark. Piatkus, 1983
(U.S. title? copyright 1975)
Walk Around the Square. Piatkus, 1984
(U.S. title? copyright 1975)

*WINSTON, PETER. House name.
*The ABC Affair. (by *Paul Eiden)
*Assignment to Bahrein. (by *Paul
Eiden)
*The Glass Cipher. (by *Jim Bowser)

*WINTER, BEVIS. See: *Hyman Zore.

*WINTER, JOHN STRANGE
Beautiful Jim, of the Blankshire
Regiment. White, 1888; Lovell,
1888. Silent film: B&C, 1914 (scw:
Eliot Stannard; dir: Maurice
Elvey)
A Gay Little Woman. White, 1897
ss, criminous in small part
Grip. White, 1896; Stone, 1896. Si-
lent film: B&C, 1915 (scw: Eliot
Stannard; dir: Maurice Elvey)

WINTERS, J. C. Pseudonym of *Gilbert
B. Cross. Other pseudonym: Jon
Winters, q.v.
Berlin Fugue. Avon, 1985 <Berlin>

*WINTERS, JON. Pseudonym of *Gilbert
B. Cross. Other pseudonym: J. C.
Winters, q.v. SC: Anton Drakov, in
*The Drakov Memoranda, and in title
below.
The Catenary Exchange. Avon, 1983

WINTERS, MIKE. 1930-   . Ref: CA.
Miami, One Way. Weidenfeld, 1985
<Miami>

*WINWARD, (RICHARD) WALTER
The Ball Bearing Run. H. Hamilton,
1981. U.S. title (?): The Midas
Touch. Simon, 1984 <Ger., 1943>
The Canaris File; see The Canaris
Fragments
The Canaris Fragments. H. Hamilton,
1982; Morrow, 1983. Also published
as: The Canaris File. Jove, 1984
<Ger., 1945>
Circle of Deceit; see The Last and
Greatest Art
Cougar; see The Last and Greatest
Art
The Last and Greatest Art. H. Hamil-
ton, 1983. U.S. title: Circle of
Deceit. Charter, 1985. Also pub-
lished as: Cougar. Corgi, 1985
The Midas Touch; see The Ball Bearing
Run
-Rainbow Soldiers. H. Hamilton, 1985

*WISE, ARTHUR. 1923-ca.1982. Ref also:
CA. See also: Brian Swift.
Blood-Red Rose. Playboy, 1981 <NYC>
The Naughty Girls. Playboy, 1982
<Fr.>

WISE, DAVID
The Children's Game. St. Martin's,
1983
Spectrum. Viking, 1981; Lane, 1981
<1965>

*WISEMAN, THOMAS
Savage Day. Cape, 1981; Delacorte,
1981 <N. Mex., 1945>

*WITHERS, JULIA
*Caprice. (Novelization of film: TCF,
1967; scw: Jay Jayson, Frank
Tashlin; dir: Tashlin.)
*The Shuttered Room. (Novelization of
film: Seven Arts, 1967; scw: D. B.
Ledrov, Nathaniel Tanchuck; dir:
David Greene.)

WITTE, GLENNA FINLEY. 1925-
Pseudonym: *Glenna Finley, q.v.

*WITTMAN, GEORGE. Served in Military
Intelligence during Korean War;
head of firm which conducts
national security studies; political advisor to governments.

*WODEHOUSE, P(ELHAM) G(RENVILLE). Ref
also: TM.
*Piccadilly Jim. Silent film: Selz-
nick, 1920 (dir: Wesley Ruggles).
Sound film: MGM, 1936 (scw: Charles

Brackett, Edwin Knopf; dir: Robert Z. Leonard.
Wodehouse on Crime. Ticknor, 1981 ss

WOFFINGTON, BILL
Ghost Trap. SOS, 1985

*WOHL, BURTON
*The China Syndrome. (Novelization of film: Columbia, 1979; scw: Mike Gray, T. S. Cook; dir: James Bridges.)

WOLF, GARY K.
Who Censored Roger Rabbit? St. Martin's, 1981

WOLF, SIMON
Rape Squad. Manor, 1975

WOLFE, CARSON. Pseudonym of a Bronx criminal lawyer who lives in New Rochelle.
Murder at La Marimba. St. Martin's, 1984; Hale, 1985 <NYC>

WOLFE, ELIZABETH. Pseudonym of Paul Joseph Lederer, 1944-   . Ref: CA.
Ice Castles. Leisure, 1982 <Austria>

WOLFE, RON, 1945-   , and JOHN (STEVEN) WOOLEY, 1949-   . Ref for each: CA.
Old Fears. Watts, 1982 ss

*WOLFERT, IRA
*Tucker's People. Film: MGM, 1948, as Force of Evil (scw: Abraham Polonsky, Ira Wolfert; dir: Polonsky)

WOLFF, BENJAMIN. Living in L.A. SC: John Byron Hyde, in both titles.
Hyde and Seek. Avon, 1984 <L.A.>
Hyde in Deep Cover. Avon, 1985 <Bolivia>

WOLFF, MARITA M(ARTIN). 1918-   . Ref: CA.
Whistle Stop. Random, 1941. Film: United Artists, 1946 (scw: Philip Yordan; dir: Leonide Moguy)

WOLFSON, MURRAY, 1927-   , and VINCENT BURANELLI, 1919-   . Ref (both): CA.
In the Long Run We Are All Dead. St. Martin's pb, 1984 <Wash. D.C.>

*WOLK, GEORGE. Pseudonym: *Norman Gant, q.v.

WOLK, MICHAEL. Living in NYC.
The Big Picture. Signet, 1985 <NYC>

WOLLASTON, NICHOLAS. 1926-   .
Eclipse. Macmillan (London), 1974; Walker, 1974. Film: Celandine, 1977 (scw & dir: Simon Perry)

WOLMAN, DAVID
Little Boy Lost. Playboy, 1982 <N.Y.>

WOOD, ALLAN
The Weak Link. French, 1940 (3-act play.)

*WOOD, (SAMUEL) ANDREW
Hushabye Death. Hurst, 1950

*WOOD, BARBARA. Ref: CA.

*WOOD, BARI
Lightsource. NAL, 1984; Macdonald, 1985 <late 1980s>
The Tribe. NAL, 1981; NEL, 1981 <NYC>

*WOOD, CHRISTOPHER (HOVELLE)
-A Dove Against Death. Collins, 1983; Viking, 1983
*James Bond and Moonraker. (Novelization of film: United Artists, 1979, as Moonraker (scw: Christopher Wood; dir: Lewis Gilbert.)
*James Bond, the Spy Who Loved Me. (Novelization of film: United Artists, 1977, as The Spy Who Loved Me; scw: Christopher Wood, Richard Maibaum; dir: Lewis Gilbert.)
Kago. Collins, 1984; Holt, 1986 <New Guinea>
Taiwan. Joseph, 1981; Viking, 1982 <Formosa>

WOOD, FERNEY. Pseudonym: *Olga L. Rosmanith.

*WOOD, MRS. HENRY. See also: Brian J. Burton.
*The Channings. Silent film: Master, 1920 (scw: William J. Elliott; dir: Edwin J. Collins)
*East Lynne. Silent film: Harrison, 1902. Also: Selig, 1908. Also: Precision, 1910. Also: Thanhauser, 1912 (scw: Theodore Marston; dir: George Nicholls or Theodore Marston). Also: Barker, 1913 (scw: Harry Engholm; dir: Bert Haldane). Also: Brightonia, 1913 (dir: Arthur Charrington). Also: AB, 1915 (dir: Travers Vale). Also: Fox, 1916 (scw: Mary Murillo; dir: Bertram Bracken). Also: Master, 1922 (scw: W. C. Rowden; dir: H. B. Parkinson). Also: Fox, 1925 (scw: Lenore J. Coffee; dir: Emmett Flynn). Sound film: Liberty, 1930, as Ex-Flame (scw: George Draney; dir: Victor Halperin). Also: TCF, 1931 (scw: Bradley King, Tom Barry; dir: Frank Lloyd)

*WOOD, JAMES (ALEXANDER FRASER). 1918-1984. SC: James Fraser, also in *The Sealer.
*Fire Rock. <Arctic>

WOOD, TED. Born in Eng., came to Canada in 1953; spent 3 years on Toronto police force; worked for Toronto advertising agency; author of magazine articles, TV dramas, documentaries, and radio and stage plays; living on a farm north of Toronto. Ref: TM. SC: Reid Bennett, in all titles.
Dead in the Water. Scribner, 1983; Collins, 1984 <Can.>
Dead Centre; see Live Bait
The Killing Cold; see Murder on Ice
Live Bait. Scribner, 1985. British title (?): Dead Centre. Collins, 1985 <Toronto>
Murder on Ice. Scribner, 1984. British title: The Killing Cold. Collins, 1984 <Can.>

WOOD, WILLIAM P(RESTON). 1951-   . Ref: CA.
Rampage. St. Martin's, 1985 <Calif.>

WOODCOCK, CYRIL H.
The Serpent and the Slave. Stockwell, 1982

*WOODLEY, RICHARD
*Deadly Encounter. (Novelization of film: (studio?), 1979; scw: R. John Hugh.)
*It's Alive. (Novelization of film: Larco, 1977; scw & dir: Larry Cohen.)

*WOODROW, MRS. WILSON
-The Black Pearl. Appleton, 1912 <Ariz.> Silent film: Rayart, 1928 (scw: Arthur Hoerl; dir: Scott Pembroke)
*Burned Evidence. Film: Continental, 1929
*The Hornet's Nest. Silent film: Vitagraph, 1919 (scw: James Dayton; dir: James Young)
*The Second Chance. Silent film: First National, 1926, as Her Second Chance (scw: Eve Unsell; dir: Lambert Hillyer)

WOODRUM, LON (RILEY). 1901-   . Novelist, evangelist, minister in Evangelical United Brethren Church; resident of Okla.
Stumble Upon the Dark Mountains. Broadman, 1956 <Mo.>

WOODS, CLEE. 1893-   . Ref: CA.
Night Chant. Leisure, 1980 <N. Mex.>

WOODS, FREDRIC
Rundown. Hale, 1982
Shooting Star. Hale, 1984

*WOODS, SARA. Pseudonym of Sara Hutton Bowen-Judd, 1922-1985. Ref also: TM. SC: Antony Maitland, also in all titles below.
Away with Them to Prison. Macmillan (London), 1985; St. Martin's, 1985
The Bloody Book of Law. Macmillan (London), 1984; St. Martin's, 1984
Call Back Yesterday. Macmillan (London), 1983; St. Martin's, 1983
Cry Guilty. Macmillan (London), 1981; St. Martin's, 1981

Dearest Enemy. Macmillan (London), 1981; St. Martin's, 1982
Defy the Devil. Macmillan (London), 1984; St. Martin's, 1984
Enter a Gentlewoman. Macmillan (London), 1982; St. Masrtin's, 1982
The Lie Direct. Macmillan (London), 1983; St. Martin's, 1983
Most Grievous Murder. Macmillan (London), 1982; St. Martin's, 1982
Murder's Out of Tune. Macmillan (London), 1984; St. Martin's, 1984
An Obscure Grave. Macmillan (London), 1985; St. Martin's, 1985
Put Out the Light. Macmillan (London), 1985; St. Martin's, 1985
*This Little Measure. ... Avon, 1986
Villains by Necessity. Macmillan (London), 1982; St. Martin's, 1982
Where Should He Die? Macmillan (London), 1983; St. Martin's, 1983

*WOODS, STOCKTON
Game Bet. GM, 1981 <Conn.>
The Man Who Heard Too Much. GM, 1983

WOODS, STUART. 1938-   . Ref: CA.
Chiefs. Norton, 1981; Norton (U.K.), 1982 <Ga.>

*WOODTHORPE, R(ALPH) C(ARTER). Ref also: BM.

WOODWARD, W(ILLIAM) E. 1874-1950.
-Evelyn Prentice. Knopf, 1933; Cassell, 1933. Film: MGM, 1934 (scw: Lenore Coffee; dir: William K. Howard). Also: MGM, 1939, as Stronger Than Desire (scw: David Hertz, William Ludwig; dir: Leslie Fenton)

WOOLEY, JOHN (STEVEN). 1949-   . See: Ron Wolfe, 1945-

WOOLF, MARION. Joint pseudonym with Margery Papich and Layne Torkelson: Marion Margery Layne, q.v.

*WOOLFOLK, WILLIAM. 1917-   . Ref: CA. Pseudonym: *Winston Lyon, q.v.
The Adam Project. GM, 1984
The Sendai. Popular Library, 1981

*WOOLL, EDWARD
*Libel. Film: MGM, 1959 (scw: Anatole De Grunwald, Karl Tunberg; dir: Anthony Asquith)

*WOOLLCOTT, ALEXANDER (HUMPHRIES) and *GEORGE S(IMON) KAUFMAN
*The Dark Tower. Film: First National, 1934, as The Man with Two Faces (scw: Tom Reed, Niven Busch; dir: Archie Mayo). Also: Warner, 1943 (scw: Brock Williams, Reginald Purdell; dir: John Harlow)

*WOOLRICH, CORNELL (GEORGE HOPLEY). Ref also: TM.
*Black Alibi. Film: RKO, 1943, as The Leopard Man (scw: Ardel Wray, Edward Dein; dir: Jacques Tournier)
*The Black Angel. Film: Universal, 1946 (scw: Roy Chanslor; dir: Roy William Neill)
*The Black Curtain. ... Zomba, 1983. Film: Paramount, 1942, as Street of Chance (scw: Garrett Fort; dir: Jack Hively)
*The Black Path of Fear. Film: Columbia, 1946, as The Chase (scw: Philip Yordan; dir: Arthur Ripley)
Blind Date with Death. Carroll, 1985 ss
*The Bride Wore Black. Film: Films du Carosse, 1968, as Le Mariee Etait en Noire (The Bride Wore Black) (scw: Francois Truffaut, Jean-Louis Richard; dir: Truffaut)
*Manhattan Love Song. Film: Monogram, 1934 (scw: David Silverstein, Leonard Fields; dir: Fields)
*Nightmare. Film (from ss "Fear in the Night"): Paramount, 1947, as Fear in the Night (scw & dir: Maxwell Shane). Also (from ss): United Artists, 1956, as Nightmare (scw & dir: Maxwell Shane)
*Nightwebs. Film (from ss "The Corpse Next Door"): Kinesis, 1980, as Union City (scw & dir: Mark Reichert)
Vampire's Honeymoon. Carroll, 1985 4 novelets

*WOOTTON, (DeVERE) GARETH. 1937-   . Ref: CA.

*WORBOYS, ANNE(TTE ISOBEL)
  Run, Sara, Run. Severn, 1982; Scribner, 1981

*WORLEY, WILLIAM. See: Theo Durrant.

*WORMSER, RICHARD (EDWARD). Ref: TC2, TM.
  *Torn Curtain. (Novelization of film: Universal, 1966; scw: Brian Moore; dir: Alfred Hitchcock.)

*WORRALL, LECHMERE. See: *J(oseph) E(dward) Harold Terry.

WORRELL, JUDITH
  Sting of the Bee. Tower, 1982 <Maine>

*WORTS, GEORGE F(RANK)
  *The Phantom President. Film: Paramount, 1932 (scw: Walter De Leon, Harlan Thompson; dir: Norman Taurog)

*WREN, M. K. Ref also: TM. SC: Conan Flagg, in both titles below.
  Seasons of Death. Doubleday, 1981; Firecrest, 1984 <Ida.>
  Wake Up, Darlin' Corey. Doubleday, 1984; Chivers, 1985 <Oreg.>

WRIGHT, DERRICK
  The Denver Collection. Hale, 1983
  Scar. Hale, 1983

WRIGHT, ERIC. Teacher in Toronto; has written for magazines and TV. SC: Insp. Charlie Salter, in all titles.
  Death in the Old Country. Scribner, 1985; Collins, 1985 <Eng.>
  The Night the Gods Smiled. Scribner, 1983; Collins, 1983 <Toronto>
  Smoke Detector. Scribner, 1985; Collins, 1984 <Toronto>

*WRIGHT, GLOVER (GEOFFREY)
  The Hound of Heaven. Hutchinson, 1984; Arbor, 1986
  Whitefire. Hutchinson, 1983 <Arctic>

WRIGHT, L(AURALI) R. 1939- . Journalist living in Vancouver.
  The Suspect. Viking, 1985; Hale, 1986 <Can.>

*WRIGHT, LAURIE ROBESON
  *The Perfect Corpse. <Mass.>

*WRIGHT, RICHARD B(RUCE). Ref: CA.
  Tourists. Walker, 1984; Hale, 1985 <Mex.>

*WRIGHT, S(YDNEY) FOWLER
  -Prelude in Prague. Newnes, 1935. U.S. title: The War of 1938. Putnam, 1936 <1938>

*WRIGHT, WADE
  Death at Nostalgia Street. Hale, 1982
  The Girl from Yesterday. Hale, 1982
  It Leads to Murder. Hale, 1981

WRIGHT, WATKINS E(PPES). 1880(?)-1967.
  Creepy Crest. Eldridge, 1929 (Play.)
  The Ghost Walks. Eldridge, 1929 (3-act play.)
  Short of Murder. Eldridge, 1941 (1-act play.)

WRIGHT, WILBUR
  Carter's Castle. Century, 1983; St. Martin's, 1983 <Camb.>

WRIGHTSON, PEGGY
  -Thirteen Paint a Portrait. Ward, 1965

*WYLIE, PHILIP (GORDON). Ref also: TM.

*WYLLIE, JOHN (VECTIS CAREW). ref also: TM. SC: Dr. Quarshie, also in title below.
  The Long Dark Night of Baron Samedi. Doubleday, 1981; Hale, 1982

*WYND, OSWALD (MORRIS). Incorrectly given as Gavin (Morris) Wynd, in first printing of CF. Ref also: TM.

WYNNE, JOHN
  Crime Wave. Riverrun, 1982; Calder, 1982

*XANTIPPE
  *Death Catches Up with Mr. Kluck. Film: Universal, 1938, as Danger on the Air (scw: Betty Laidlow, Robert Lively; dir: Otis Garrett)

YAFFLE
  Pity the Poor Rich. Allen, 1946 ss, one a Sherlockian parody

*YARBOROUGH, CHARLOTTE
  *Murder on the Long Straight. <Australia, train>

*YARBRO, CHELSEA QUINN. Ref also: TM.

YARDE, JEANNE FRANCES TREASURE. 1925- . Pseudonym: Jeanne Montague, q.v.

*YARDLEY, HERBERT O(SBORN)
  Ciphergrams. Hutchinson, 1932 puzzle ss

YARIV, FRAN POKRAS
  The Hallowing. Jove, 1980
  Last Exit. Jove, 1981 <L.A.>

*YARROW, ARNOLD. Ref: CA.

*YATES, ALAN GEOFFREY. 1923-1985.
  Pseudonyms: *Carter Brown, q.v.; *Paul Valdez.

*YATES, DORNFORD. Ref also: CA, BM, TM. SC: Bertram Pleydell, also in title below.
  -And Berry Came Too. Ward, 1936; Putnam, 1935

*YATES, EDMUND (HODGSON)
  *Black Sheep. Silent film: AB, 1915 (dir: J. Farrell MacDonald)

*YELDHAM, PETER
  *But She Won't Lie Down. <Sp.>

YGLESIAS, HELEN. 1915- . Ref: CA.
  Sweetsir. Simon, 1981; Hodder, 1981 <New Eng.>

YONGDEN, LAMA (ALBERT ARTHUR). See: Alexandra David-Neel, 1868-1969.

*YORK, ANDREW
  The Combination. Severn, 1984; Doubleday, 1983
  *The Eliminator. Film: Amicus, 1967, as Danger Route (scw: Meade Roberts, Robert Stewart; dir: Seth Holt)

YORK, THOMAS (LEE). 1940- . Ref: CA.
  Trapper. Doubleday, 1981 <Can., 1931>

*YORKE, MARGARET. Ref also: TM.
  The China Doll. Hale, 1961
  Devil's Work. Hutchinson, 1982; St. Martin's, 1982
  Find Me a Villain. Hutchinson, 1983; St. Martin's, 1983
  The Hand of Death. Hutchinson, 1981; St. Martin's, 1981
  Intimate Kill. Hutchinson, 1985; St. Martin's, 1985
  *No Medals for the Major. no SC
  *Silent Witness. (not Silent Murder, as given in first printing of CF)
  The Smooth Face of Murder. Hutchinson, 1984; St. Martin's, 1984

*YOUD, (CHRISTOPHER) SAMUEL. Ref also: TM.

YOUNG, AXEL
  Blood Rubies. Avon (U.S. and London), 1982
  Wicked Stepmother. Avon, 1983 <Boston>

YOUNG, CHARLES LAWRENCE. 1839-1887.
  Jim the Penman. French, 1912 (4-act play.) Silent film: Famous Players (scw & dir: Hugh Ford). Also: First National, 1921 (scw: Dorothy Farnum; dir: Kenneth Webb)

*YOUNG, HOWARD IRVING
  Hawk Island. French, 1931 (3-act play.) Film: RKO, 1930, as Midnight Mystery (scw: Beulah Marie Dix; dir: George B. Seitz)
  *Not Herbert. Silent film: First National, 1927, as The Perfect Sap (dir: Howard Higgin)

*YOUNG, KENDAL
  *The Ravine. Film: Rank, 1971, as Assault (scw: John Kruse; dir: Sidney Hayers)

YOUNGER, JACK. Pseudonym of Russ Jones.

*YUILL, P. B. Ref also: BM.

YURICK, SOL. 1925- . Ref: CA.
  Fertig. Trident, 1966; Allen, 1966
  Richard A. Arbor, 1981; Methuen, 1982 <1962>
  -The Warriors. Holt, 1965; Allen, 1966. Film: Paramount, 1979 (scw: David Shaber, Walter Hill; dir: Hill)

ZACHARIA, IRWIN. SC: Irving Martin Reddy (The Protector) = IR; Landshark = L; Will Powers (Vendetta series) = WP.
  Brotherhood of Evil. Carousel, 1982 IR
  Landshark. Carousel, 1982 L
  The Murder Club. Carousel, 1982 WP
  Piranha, Piranha. Carousel, 1982 L
  Princess of Darkness. Carousel, 1982 IR
  Reddy or Not. Carousel, 1982 IR
  Vendetta. Carousel, 1982 WP

*ZACHARY, HUGH. Pseudonyms: Zach Hughes, Zachary Hughes, qq.v. SC: Tusk Smith, in *To Guard the Right, and in title marked TS below; Sheriff Jug Watson, in titles marked JW.
  Bloodrush. Leisure, 1981 JW <N.C.>
  Murder in White. Leisure, 1981 JW <N.C.>
  -One Day in Hell. Newstand, 1961 <Fla.>
  Top Level Death. Raven, 1981 TS <West>

*ZACKEL, FRED. Ref: TM.

ZAHN, TIMOTHY
  A Coming of Age. Bluejay, 1984 <future>

*ZANE, LEHI. Pseudonym of *Sam S. Taylor.

*ZANGWILL, ISRAEL. Ref also: TM.
  *The Big Bow Mystery. Film (with part sound): FBO, 1928, as The Perfect Crime (scw: William LeBaron; dir: Bert Glennon). Also: RKO, 1934, as The Crime Doctor (scw: Jane Murfin; dir: John Robertson). Also: Warner, 1946, as The Verdict (scw: Peter Milne; dir: Don Siegel)

*ZAREMBA, EVE. Ref: TM.

*ZARUBICA, MLADIN
  *Scutari. <Alb.>

ZEIGER, HENRY A. Pseudonym: *James Peterson, q.v.

ZERLIN, WALTER, JR. See: David McGillivray.

ZIMMERMAN, ERNEST O.
  The Blue Brotherhood. Leisure, 1981

ZIMMERMAN, ROBERT D(INGWALL). 1952- Graduate of Michigan State University; with U.S. Information Agency in Russia; then writer of children's mysteries under a pseudonym.
  The Cross and the Sickle. Zebra, 1984 <Russ.>

ZINDEL, PAUL. 1936- . Ref: CA.
  When Darkness Falls. Bantam hc, 1984 <L.A.>

ZIRAN, GOLAND
  The Counsellor. Arbor, 1982 <NYC>

*ZOCHERT, DONALD (PAUL, JR.). Ref also: TM. SC: Nick Caine, in *Another Weeping Woman, and in new title below.
  *Another Weeping Woman. ... Hale, 1983
  The Man of Glass. Holt, 1982; Hale, 1983

ZODROW, JOHN RESTER
  Vatican Gold. Dell, 1983

*ZORE, HYMAN. House name.
  *Blue Orchid. (by *Michael Barnes)
  *Cover That Corpse. (by *Victor J. Hanson)
  *It's a Sin. (by *Bevis Winter)
  *The Lady Is a Tramp. (by James Amesbury, q.v.)
  *Savage Siren. (by Scud Keddell)
  *Shadow of Sin. (by *Victor J. Hanson)
  *This Was a Woman. (by Scud Keddell)

*ZORRO
    Dr. Death and other terror tales.
        Corinth, 1966 ss

*ZUGSMITH, LEANNA. Ref: CA.

ZUMSTEG, M.
    -"And He Did Eat." Houghton & Scott-
        Snell, 1935

*ZUMWALT, EVA
    Mansion of Dark Mists. Leisure, 1981

Z

Title Index

Title Index

*ABC Affair. P. Winston
*ABC Murders. A. Christie
A4 Murder. P. A. Foxall
A-Haunting We Will Go. T. J. Kelly
"A" Is for Alibi. S. Grafton
AK-47 Firefight. J. Lansing
A-Team. C. Heath
A-Train. Roger Williams
*Abandoned Room. W. Camp
Abduction. G. C. Seeber
Abel/Baker/Charley. J. Maxim
Abominable History of the Man with Copper Fingers. D. L. Sayers
*Abominable Man. M. Sjowall
*Abomination. H. Janson
Abort Project K! L. Wilhelm
*About the Murder of the Circus Queen. A. Abbot
*About the Murder of the Clergyman's Mistress. A. Abbot
*About the Murder of the Night Club Lady. A. Abbot
Above All, Love. J. M. Greenleaf
*Above Suspicion. H. MacInnes
Abra Cadaver. J. Mattera
Absolute Proof. P. Kuttner
*Academic Murder. D. Fiske
Acceptable Loses. I. Shaw
Accidental Crimes. J. Hutton
Accidental Woman. R. Neely
*Account Rendered. P. Barrington
Accused. H. Janson
Ace of Diamonds. M. Schorr
Ace of Spades. J. C. Fraser
*Ace Up My Sleeve. J. H. Chase
*Aces High. W. Hughes
Acid Test. C. Lewis
Acquitaine Progression. R. Ludlum
*Across 110th. W. Ferris
*Across the Common. E. Berridge
Across the Lawn. E. Verity
*Across the Pacific. C. E. Blaney
*Across the World for a Wife. G. Boothby
Acrostic Mysteries. H. Slesar
Act of Darkness. F. King
Act of God. J. M. Roberts
Act of Love. J. R. Lansdale
*Act of Mercy. F. Clifford
*Act of Passion. G. Simenon
Act of Providence. J. P. Brennan
*Act of Violence. B. Heatter
Act of War. Leonard Sanders
*Action Man. J. Flynn
Action of the Tiger. G. Parker
*Action of the Tiger. J. Wellard
Active Measures. J. Morris
Ad for Murder. J. Penn
Adam Project. W. Woolfolk
Address Unknown. M. Hutton
Address Unknown. K. Taylor
Adlon Link. Z. Hughes
Adrenaline. J. Dillinger
Adria. R. Davis
*Advancement of Learning. Reginald Hill
Adventure of State. P. Cosgrave
Adventure of the Christmas Visitor. D. O. Smith
Adventure of the Clouded Crystal. T. J. Kelly
Adventure of the Copper Beeches. C. Fischer
Adventure of the Five Buffalo Chips. J. Ruyle
*Adventure of the Logophagous Client. J. Ruyle
Adventure of the Purple Hand. D. O. Smith
*Adventure of the Retired Weatherman. J. Ruyle
Adventure of the Soledad Cyclist. J. Ruyle
Adventure of the Speckled Band. T. J. Kelly
Adventure of the Unseen Traveler. D. O. Smith
Adventure of the Zodiac Plate. D. O. Smith
*Adventures of Captain Kettle. C. J. C. Hyne
*Adventures of Ephraim Tutt. A. Train
Adventures of Inspector Lestrade. M. J. Trow
*Adventures of Jimmy Dale. F. Packard
*Adventures of Miss Gregory. P. Gibbon
Adventures of Russell Howard. A. E. Jobson
*Adventures of Sherlock Holmes. A. C. Doyle
*Adventures of Sherlock Holmes' Smarter Brother. G. Pearlman
Adventures of Terra Tarkington. S. Webb
Adventures of the Ectoplasmic Man. D. Stashower
Adversary. G. Household
Adversary. A. M. Kabal
*Adversary. B. Spicer
Advertise for Treasure. D. Williams
Aegean Affair. W. Satterthwaite
*Affacombe Affair. E. Lemarchand

Affair at Barwold. L. Meynell
Affair in Rome. J. Rejaunier
*Affair of the Blood-Stained Egg-Cosy. James Anderson
Affair of the Mutilated Mink Coat. James Anderson
*Affair of the Nina B. J. M. Simmel
Affair of the Unprincipled Publisher. L. Garland
Affair on the Appian Way. M. Levey
Affaire Mysterieuse. G. Osmon
*Affairs of Paula. H. Janson
Afghan Agent. J. Tabler
Afghanistan Crashout. J. Rosenberger
Afghanistan Penetration. A. Kilgore
African Assignment. P. McAdam
After Dark. D. Boucicault
*After Dinner Story. W. Irish
After Eli. T. Kay
After Magritte. T. Stoppard
*After Midnight. M. Albrand
After Midnight. E. Fletcher-Allen
After-Shock. D. Howell
*After the Bride Takers. L. Carlton
*After the First Death. R. Cormier
*After the Funeral. A. Christie
After the Race. M. Elkoff
*After the Verdict. R. Hichens
Agatha. K. Tynan
Agatha Christie Hour. A. Christie
Agatha Christie Made Me Do It. E. Cope
Agatha's Friends. T. Hauser
*Age of Death. W. Marshall
*Agency. P. Gottlieb
*Agent of the Devil. H. Habe
Agent Out of Place. I. A. Greenfield
Agents of Sympathy. F. O'Neill
*Aground. C. Williams
*Agony Column. E. D. Biggers
Ah, Sweet Mystery. J. Kirkpatrick
Ainsley Case. B. Partridge
*Air Disaster. H. Innes
Air Force One Is Haunted. R. J. Serling
Air Glow Red. I. Slater
Air Tight Alibi. W. A. Hackett
*Airing in a Closed Carriage. J. Shearing
*Al Capone. J. Roeburt
Al Jazzar. Christopher Matthews
Alaska Deception. W. M. Brinton
Albanian Incident. S. Dodds
Albatross. E. Anthony
*Albatross. C. Armstrong
Alcatraz Break. S. Markham
Alchemist. K. Goddard
*Alden Case. R. Bridges
*Aleph Solution. S. Frankel
Alexandra, the Ambivalent. K. Kimbrough
Algarve Affair. Nick Carter
*Alias the Lone Wolf. L. J. Vance
Alias the Maestro. L. Mantz
*Alias the Night Wind. V. Vanardy
*Alibi. G. A. England
Alibi. R. Kroetsch
Alibi. M. Morton
*Alibi of Guilt. P. Daniels
*Alicia's Trump. J. Mathewson
Alien. L. P. Davies
Alien Trace. H. M. Major
All Fall Down. J. Saul
All Heaven in a Rage. M. Duffy
*All on a Summer's Day. J. Garden
All on a Summer's Day. J. Wainwright
All or Something. H. Brand
All Our Tomorrows. T. Allbeury
All Part of the Service. M. Russell
All That Glistens. M. Ashton
All That Glitters. M. Anthony
All That Glitters. Magali
All That Glitters. E. Powers
All That Glitters. R. Spencer
All the Old Bargains. B. M. Schutz
All the Pretty People. J. S. Scott
All the Virtues of the Dead. I. Cecil
*All the Way. C. Williams
*All the World to Nothing. W. Martyn
*All Through the Night. W. Masterson
All Through the Night. J. Wainwright
All Tramps Are Trouble. H. Janson
Allah Conspiracy. C. Warren
Allyson. J. Jenkins
Almighty. I. Wallace
Alpine Condo Cross Fire. M. G. Eberhart
Alpine Gambit. N. Cort
Alpine Treason. G. Wark
*Alster Case. R. Gillmore
Altar. P. Walker
Altar Boy. S. J. Cassidy
Alter Ego. M. Arrighi
Altered Egos. K. Girard
Always a Body to Trade. K. C. Constantine
*Always Murder a Friend. M. Scherf
Amateur. R. Littell
Amateur City. K. V. Forrest
*Amateur Cracksman. E. W. Hornung
*Amateur Gentleman. J. Farnol
*Amateur in Violence. M. Gilbert
*Amazing Dr. Clitterhouse. B. Lyndon
*Amazing Partnership. E. P. Oppenheim

*Amazing Quest of Mr. Ernest Bliss. E. Oppenheim
*Amazing Test Match Crime. A. Alington
Amazon Slaughter. D. Stivers
*Ambassador. S. Longstreet
Amberley Affair. P. Parrish
Ambler. F. Halliday
*Amboy Dukes. I. Shulman
Ambush on Blood River. D. Pendleton
*Ambushers. D. Hamilton
American Dream. N. Mailer
*American Marquis. Nicholas Carter
*American Prisoner. E. Phillpotts
American Quartet. W. Adler
American Reich. D. Muir
American Sextet. W. Adler
American Vengeance. J. Cutter
Aminda Gamble. J. Sherlock
Amok. G. Fox
Amok. H. Janson
Among the Water Lilies. C. M. Blake
*Amorous Captive. H. Janson
Amorous Leander. A. Hunter
Amos. S. G. West
Amsterdam Silver. R. Wilson
*Amzi, the Detective. Old Sleuth
Ana Mistral. S. Olson
Ana P. I. Magdalen
Anagram of Murder. S. Matthews
*Anarchist's Oath. B. Wayde
Anarchist's Pluck. B. Wayde
Anarchy Plot. P. B. Van Orsdol
*Anatomy of a Crime. J. F. Dinneen
*Anatomy of a Murder. R. Traver
Anatomy of a Riot. J. Wainwright
Ancestral Precipice. J. Ekstrom
And Berry Came Too. D. Yates
*And Die Remembering. M. L. Roby
"And He Did Eat." M. Zumsteg
*...And Justice for All. R. Grossbach
And Some Were Evil. E. Willie
And Then There Was Nun. M. Quill
And Then They Die. R. McCollum
*Anderson Tapes. Lawrence Sanders
Andropov Deception. J. Rossiter
Angel. C. Lucas
*Angel, Angel, Down We Go. W. Johnston
*Angel Astray. H. Janson
*Angel Came Down. M. Pereira
*Angel Dance. M. F. Beal
*Angel Esquire. E. Wallace
Angel Eyes. L. D. Estleman
Angel Face. S. Cohen
*Angel in the Snow. P. Welles
*Angel Loves Nobody. R. Miles
Angel of Death. A. Cohen
Angel of Light. B. W. Battin
Angel of Light. J. C. Oates
*Angel of Terror. E. Wallace
*Angel of the Bells. F. Du Boisgobey
Angel of the Chimes. F. Du Boisgobey
Angel of Vengeance. A. Cohen
*Angel of Vengeance. G. De Villiers
Angel of Zin. C. Irving
*Angel, Shoot to Kill. H. Janson
Angel Without Mercy. A. Cohen
Angela. S. Hanna
Angels Are So Few. E. Ellison
Angels at the Ritz. W. Trevor
Angel's Blood. V. B. Miller
Angels in Undress. M. Benney
Angels of Death. R. Peart
Angkor Massacre. L. Durand
Angry Hills. L. Uris
*Angry Silence. John Burke
Animal Factory. E. Bunker
*Animal-Lover's Book of Beastly Murders. P. Highsmith
Anna (I) Anna. K. Rifbjerg
*Anna the Adventuress. E. P. Oppenheim
Annalise Experiment. W. D. Roberts
Annihilators. D. Hamilton
Anodyne Necklace. M. Grimes
*Another Day, Another Stiff. M. Brett
Another Man's Poison. J. F. Straker
*Another Man's Shoes. V. Bridges
*Another Weeping Woman. D. Zochert
Answers. T. Topor
*Antiphonary. H. Aquin
Antwerp Appointment. J. Pattinson
Anvil Agreement. K. Begg
Anvil Chorus. S. Stevens
Any Four Women Could Rob the Bank of Italy. A. Cornelisen
*Any Man's Girl. B. Heatter
*Any Number Can Die. F. Carmichael
Any Number Can Die! Morgan Ross
*Any Number Can Play. E. H. Heth
*Any Number Can Win. J. Trinian
*Anything Might Happen. H. Balfour
Apartment Hotel. M. Morell
Aphrodite Cargo. A. Fullerton
Aphrodite Inheritance. M. J. Bird
Apocalypse U.S.A.! J. Rosenberger
Apple Crunch. F. V. Huber
Apple of Discord. M. Blake
Apple Spy in the Sky. M. Lovell
Apple to the Core. M. Lovell
*Apple Tree. D. Du Maurier
Appleby and Honeybath. M. Innes

A

*Appleby Talking. M. Innes
Appointment in Cairo. B. Kneale
Appointment in Haiphong. Nick Carter
Appointment in Kabul. D. Pendleton
*Appointment in Zahrein. Michael Barrett
Appointment with Danger. A. Hughes
*Appointment with Venus. J. Tickell
*April Shroud. Reginald Hill
April Snow. N. O'Donohoe
Aquarius Transfer. R. F. Joseph
Arab. G. L. Tippin
Arabian Assault. P. McAdam
Ararat. R. Houston
Arcade. R. Maxxe
Archangel. G. Seymour
Archangel 006. R. Hitchcock
*Archer Plus 20. H. Clevely
Archers of the Long Bow. A. Moore
Archibald the Great. C. B. Kelland
Archie. C. Morley
Argentine Deadline. G. Wilson
Argosy Project. J. A. G. Kitchener
*Argyle Case. H. Ford
Ariadne Clue. C. Clemeau
Ariel. J. Bickham
*Arizona Ambush. D. Pendleton
Ark. D. Daniel
Arlette. N. Freeling
*Arm of the Law. L. Carlton
*Armadale. W. Collins
Armageddon Conspiracy. J. Ahern
Armageddon Game. J. N. Frey
*Armageddon Game. M. Washburn
Armageddon Rag. G. R. R. Martin
Armageddon Run. R. Austin
Arms of Kali. W. B. Murphy
Army of Devils. D. Stiver
Arnold Robur. M. Combe
*Arrivederci, Baby! James Peterson
Arrow in the Dark. S. Allan
*Arsenal Stadium Mystery. L. Gribble
*Arsene Lupin. E. Jepson
*Arsenic and Old Lace. J. Kesselring
Arson. E. Fackler
*Arson Job. J. Moss
Art Boggs, Private Investigator. M. Scheele
Artemis Sanction. A. Aasheim
Artful Egg. J. McClure
*Aryan Onslaught. L. Derrick
As a Favor. S. Dunlap
*As a Man Sows. W. Westall
*As Good As Murdered. J. D. O'Hanlon
*As Strange a Maze. F. Leighton
As Tall As Pride. S. Kerr
As the Clock Strikes. E. Armstrong
Asgard Solution. J. Marino
*Ashenden. W. S. Maugham
*Ashes and Diamonds. J. Andrzeyevski
*Ashton Kirk. J. McIntyre
Asia Rip. G. Foy
Asian Affair. R. Holt
*Ask Agamemnon. Jenni Hall
Ask 'Beccles. C. Campion
Ask for Lois. J. Barclay
*Ask for Lois. J. Matcha
Ask the Cards a Question. M. Muller
Asking Price. J. B. Hilton
Aspern Papers. H. James
*Aspern Papers. M. Redgrave
*Asphalt Jungle. W. R. Burnett
Assassin! K. Blake
Assassin. J. D. Revere
Assassin. W. Wager
Assassin. D. Wiltse
Assassin Code. B. Mochan
Assassin Convention. Nick Carter
*Assassin for Hire. R. Rienits
*Assassination Bureau. J. London
Assassination Factor. L. Derrick
Assassins. E. Kazan
Assassin's Express. A. Kilgore
Assassin's Shadow. R. Striker
Assault. H. Mulisch
*Assault on a Queen. J. Finney
Assault on Agathon. A. Caillou
Assault with Intent. W. X. Kienzle
Asset in Black. C. Prescott
Assignment. L. Leamer
*Assignment. P. Wahloo
Assignment: Death Ship. W. B. Aarons
*Assignment in Brittany. H. MacInnes
Assignment in Venice. G. Ferrand
*Assignment: Murder. D. Hamilton
Assignment: Rio. Nick Carter
*Assignment--The Cairo Dancer. E. S. Aarons
*Assignment Tokyo. J. Dark
Assignment Unicorn. E. S. Aarons
Assisi Murders. T. Holme
*Assize of the Dying. E. Pargeter
Aswan Hellbox. G. Wilson
Aswan High. R. E. Harrington
*Asylum. W. Johnston
At Bay. P. Philips
At Break of Dawn. G. James
At Devil's Bridge. H. Marval
*At 9:45. O. Davis
*At One-Thirty. I. Ostrander

At Sword's Point. A. Norton
At the Hands of Another. Arthur Lyons
At the Mercy of Tiberius. A. J. Wilson
*At the Villa Rose. A. E. W. Mason
Atlantean Horror. J. Rosenberger
Atlantic Scramble. G. Wilson
Atom Bomb Angel. P. James
Atrocity. J. Ahern
Attack in the Desert. M. Home
Attempt. J. Dennison
Attempted Murder of Peggy Sweetwater. J. Rustan
Attorney Conspiracy. C. T. Cline
Auction. Alexander Cole
Auction. Justin Scott
*Auctioned. H. Janson
Audition for Murder. P. M. Carlson
*Audrey Rose. F. De Felitta
Aurora. S. Lowe
*Aurora Floyd. M. E. Braddon
*Austenburn Castle. Anonymous
*Authentic Death of Hendry Jones. C. Neider
*Author's Choice. M. Kantor
*Autobiography of a Blackguard. R. Paton
*Autopsy. J. R. Feegel
Autumn in Araby. C. Salisbury
Autumn Tiger. B. Langley
*Avalanche. G. Atherton
*Avalanche. K. Boyle
*Avalanche Express. C. Forbes
*Avenger. J. Goodwin
Avenging Angel. Rex Burns
*Avenging Nymph. H. Janson
Avenue of the Dead. E. Anthony
Avery's Knot. M. Cable
Away with Them to Prison. Sara Woods
*Axis. Clive Irving
"B" Is for Burglar. S. Grafton
Baby Blue Rip Off. M. A. Collins
Baby Doll Blues. L. Kent
*Baby, Don't Dare Squeal. H. Janson
Baby Face Gangster. R. Steel
Baby in the Icebox. J. M. Cain
Baby Killer. Jay Carroll
*Back Bay. W. Martin
Back County Crimes. L. Robertson
*Back from the Dead. A. Soutar
*Back Home. I. S. Cobb
Back of the North Wind. N. Freeling
Back of the Tiger. J. Gerson
Back Room in Somers Town. J. Malcolm
Back to Bandola. R. Castle
Back Toward Lisbon. Allison Cole
Backhoe Gothic. J. DeWeese
Backlash. A. Melville-Ross
Backlash. M. Russell
*Backlash of Infamy. H. Janson
*Backstage Mystery. O. R. Cohen
Backtrack. Joseph Hansen
Backwoods Menace. R. Renauld
Bad April. H. Ross
Bad Boy. E. Schiddel
*Bad Boy. J. Thompson
Bad Circle. J. N. Chance
Bad Company. L. Cody
*Bad Day at Black Rock. M. Niall
*Bad Girl. H. Janson
Bad Medicine. M. Borgenicht
Bad Name. J. J. Ellis
Bad Penny. H. Blackburn
Bad Room. C. C. Gilmore
*Bad Seed. M. Anderson
Bad Timing. O. De St. Jeor
Baddington Peerage. G. A. Sala
*Badge of Evil. W. Masterson
*Badge 373. M. Roote
Badlands. J. Frost
Bag o' Gold. N. Giltspar
*Bahama Crisis. D. Bagley
Bait of Perjury. W. Savage
Bait on the Hook. F. Parrish
Baja. Jack Jones
Baked-Bean Supper Murders. V. Rich
Baker Street Boys. B. N. Ball
Bakke's Night of Fame. J. McGrath
Baksheesh and Roses. C. Beardsley
Balance of Dangers. A. Forrest
Balance of Power. W. B. Murphy
Balance of Power. Jack Peterson
*Balaoo. G. Leroux
*Balcony. J. Genet
Balefire. K. Goddard
Balfour Conspiracy. I. St. James
Balinese Pearls. L. Lambert
Ball Bearing Run. W. Winward
Ballad of the Flim Flam Man. G. Owen
*Ballad of the Running Man. S. Smith
*Ballarat. E. Lambert
Balloon Affair. M. M. Layne
*Balloon Man. C. Armstrong
Baltic Emerald. E. Ward
Baltic Wolf. P. Allenby
Bamboo Bloodbath. P. Anthony
*Banana Men. M. Catto
*Band of Mystery. M. O. Rolfe
Bandaberry. L. Meynell
*Bandbox. L. J. Vance
*Bandersnatch. D. Lowden

Bandit Love. J. Savage
Bang Bang Beirut. R. Cooney
Bang, You're Death. P. Reakes
*Bank Note Plates. L. Carlton
*Bank Robber. G. Tippette
*Bank Shot. D. E. Westlake
Banker. D. Francis
*Banker's Millions. Warren Miller
*Banner for Pegasus. J. & E. Bonett
Banquets of the Black Widowers. I. Asimov
Banshee. M. Millar
Baraka. J. Saul
*Barbara, the Valiant. K. Kimbrough
*Barbie Murders. J. Varley
Barbs. B. Walsh
Bare Acquaintances. K. Berne
Baring Fault. J. Stonehouse
*Baronet's Wife. F. Warden
*Baroni. A. Harris
Barossa. J. Clive
Barrabas Run. J. Hild
Barracuda Run. S. Otfinoski
*Barradine Detects. E. Jepson
*Barton Mystery. W. Hackett
Base Case. J. Rathbone
*Basement Room. G. Greene
Basikasingo. J. Matthews
Baskerville Caper. F. Norman
*Bastard Brigade. P. Leslie
*Bat. M. R. Rinehart
Batman vs. the Fearsome Foursome. W. Lyon
*Battle for Inspector West. J. Creasey
Battle Group Peiper. J. Lucas
Battle in Botswana. Steve White
Battle of Jericho Street. F. Everton
*Battle of Nerves. G. Simenon
Bay City Burnout. R. Harding
Bay Psalm Book Murder. W. Harriss
Bayou Brigade. B. Sanders
Be Buried in the Rain. B. Michaels
*Be Still, My Love. J. Truesdell
*Beagle Scented Murder. F. Gruber
*Bear Island. A. MacLean
Bear's Tears. C. Thomas
Beast. A. Masters
*Beast Must Die. Nicholas Blake
Beast of the Baskervilles. T. J. Kelly
*Beast of the City. J. Lait
*Beast with Five Fingers. W. F. Harvey
Beastly Business. J. Blackburn
Beasts of Valhalla. G. Chesbro
Beat a Distant Drum. R. Emmett
*Beat the Devil. J. Helvick
*Beatrice Mystery. J. Johns
Beautiful Bait. L. Kent
*Beautiful Fugitive. Old Sleuth
Beautiful Jim of the Blankshire Regiment. J. S. Winter
Beauty and the Beast. E. McBain
*Beauty and the Heat. H. Janson
*Beauty Found a Grave. Dave Steel
Beauty Wins. Aintree
Beaver to Fox. D. Kartun
*Because of the Cats. N. Freeling
Because of the Night. J. Ellroy
Beckford Don. R. Haley
*Beckoning Hand. G. Allen
Beckoning Hands. M. M. Dreyer
*Becky. H. Janson
Bed Bugs. C. Sinclair
*Bedelia. V. Caspary
Bedroom in Hell. N. Daniels
Beekeeper. V. Andrews
Beer and Skittles. B. J. Morison
Beethoven Conspiracy. T. Hauser
*Beetle. Richard Marsh
Before I Die. H. Debrett
Before She Kills. Fredric Brown
*Before the Crossing. S. Jameson
*Before the Fact. F. Iles
Before the Fourteenth. S. D. Stevens
*Beggar in Purple. A. Soutar
Beggars of Life. J. Tully
*Beginner's Luck. P. Somers
*Behind Red Curtains. M. Scott
*Behind That Curtain. E. D. Biggers
Behind the Badge. B. Chandler
*Behind the Enemy. G. Marlowe
*Behind the Headlines. Robert Chapman
Beiderbecke Affair. A. Plater
Beirut Playback. D. Pendleton
Beirut Retaliation. J. Cutter
Bejeweled Death. M. Babson
Belchamber Scandal. F. Murray
*Belgravia. D. Linzee
Bella Donna. R. Hichens
Belladonna. D. Thomas
*Bellamy Trial. F. N. Hart
Bellarmine Jug. N. Hasluck
*Belle. G. Simenon
*Belle. Michael Stewart
Belle of the Bush. G. Darrell
Belonging. O. Wadsley
*Beloved Lady. B. Jefferis
*Beloved Traitor. H. Janson
*Below the Dead-Line. S. Campbell
Below Third Street. S. J. Simonsen
Belshazzar's Feast. P. Way

Title Index

Belshazzar Affair. M. Stall
*Belt of Diamonds. B. Wayde
*Ben. G. A. Ralston
*Ben Bradley's Puzzle. W. G. Forbes
*Ben Bradley's Weirdest Case. W. G. Forbes
Bend in the River. D. G. Deutsch
Beneath the Night Sky. A. M. Mountford
*Benighted. J. B. Priestley
Bennett's World. E. Lewis
*Benson Murder Case. S. S. Van Dine
Bentley's Conscience. P. Trent
*Beria Papers. A. Williams
Bergerac. M. Hardwick
Bergerac Is Back. A. Saville
Berlin Breakout. J. Romanes
Berlin Briefing. H. Janson
Berlin Fugue. J. C. Winters
Berlin Game. L. Deighton
*Berlin Memorandum. Adam Hall
Berlin Warning. N. Guild
Berserker. F. Spiering
Beset by Spies. J. Blyth
*Best Detective Stories of Cyril Hare. C. Hare
Best of Ellery Queen. E. Queen
Best of Randall Garrett. R. Garrett
*Best Stories of Peter Cheyney. P. Cheyney
Bestseller. L. Ramsey
Bethnel Green. M. Fisher
Bethnel Inheritance. M. Whitfield
Betrayed. D. B. Wilson
Betrayed by Death. P. Alding
*Better Angels. C. McCarry
Better Off Dead. M. McMullen
*Better Part of Valor. B. Heatter
Beware the Yellow Packard. L. Malloy
Bewitched. H. Janson
*Beyond a Reasonable Doubt. C. W. Grafton
Beyond Desire. C. Fayet
Beyond Murder. J. Buckley
Beyond Reason. A. Goetz
*Beyond Recall. D. Fletcher
Beyond the DMZ. J. Lansing
Beyond the Forest. S. Engstrand
Beyond the Mountain. W. Dieter
Beyond the Rim. G. K. Lovelady
*Beyond the Skyline. R. Hardinge
Beyond the Wicked. W. H. Bagbey
*Beyond This Place. A. J. Cronin
*Bicycle Detective. Old Sleuth
*Bicycle Jim. Old Sleuth
*Bid for Beauty. H. Janson
*Bid for Fortune. G. Boothby
Big Apple Money Is Rotten to the Core. J. M. Glazner
Big Bang. R. Goulart
Big Bear, Little Bear. D. Brierley
*Big Boodle. R. Sylvester
*Big Bounce. E. Leonard
*Big Bow Mystery. I. Zangwill
Big Boys. M. Ehrlich
Big Bridge. R. M. Stern
Big Byte. P. J. Ognibene
*Big Caper. L. White
*Big Clock. K. Fearing
Big Drop. P. Corris
*Big Ear. S. Sterling
Big Enchilada. L. A. Morse
Big Fake. M. Forbes
Big Fish. T. Perry
*Big Fix. R. L. Simon
*Big Four. E. Wallace
*Big Game. M. Brand
Big Game. F. Wallace
Big Goodnight. J. Gardiner
Big Grab. J. Trinian
*Big H. H. Janson
Big Hamburger. H. Helfer
*Big Heat. W. P. McGivern
*Big House. J. Lait
Big Knife. C. Odets
Big Lie. H. Janson
Big One. J. Cutter
*Big Picture. D. Whitelaw
Big Picture. M. Wolk
*Big Red Sun. D. Larany
Big Round Bed. H. Janson
Big Score. H. Barron
*Big Secret, Suzuki. J. Conty
*Big Sleep. R. Chandler
Big Steal. E. A. Beilke
*Big Stick-Up at Brink's! N. Behn
Big Stopper. H. Kantor
*Big Story. M. West
Big Town Round-Up. W. M. Raine
*Big Woman. M. Colton
Bikini Red North. T. Barling
Bilbao Looking Glass. C. MacLeod
Bill. John Burke
*Billboard Madonna. E. Trevor
Billingsgate Shoal. R. Boyer
*Billion Dollar Brain. L. Deighton
Billionaire. P. James
*Billy Binks, Hero. G. Boothby
Billy Cantrell Case. H. Waugh
Billy Irish. T. Babe
*Billy Rags. Ted Lewis

Billy's Army. N. Babcock
*Binary. J. Lange
*Bind. S. Ellin
Bindlestiff. B. Pronzini
Bird of Prey. C. Toomey
Bird Watchers. M. Taylor
*Birdcage. V. Canning
*Bird's Nest. S. Jackson
*Birds of Prey. G. Bronson-Howard
Birthday Girl. R. Rush
Birthday Treat. R. Rush
*Birthmark of Fear. M. Alexander
*Bishop Misbehaves. F. Jackson
*Bishop Murder Case. S. S. Van Dine
*Bishop's Emeralds. H. Townley
*Bishop's Move. L. Hiscott
Bishop's Room. K. Meyer
Bismarck Cross. S. L. Thompson
Bitch. Jackie Collins
Bitter Finish. L. J. Barnes
Bitter Heritage. D. Noel
Bitter Homicide. M. Warden
Bitter Lake. L. P. Bachmann
Bitter Path of Death. P. Audemars
*Bitter Springs. C. King
Bittersweet. S. Clausse
*Black. E. Wallace
Black Against the Mob. O. Fletcher
Black Alchemists. G. Wilson
Black Alert. A. White
*Black Alibi. C. Woolrich
Black Angel. D. Brandt
*Black Angel. C. Woolrich
Black Angels. S. Hobbs
Black Angus. N. Thornburg
*Black Arab. Operator 1384
*Black Bag. L. J. Vance
Black Berets. M. McCray
*Black Bird. A. Edwards
Black, Black Witch. K. Robeson
*Black Book. G. Bronson-Howard
Black Box. C. Kearey
*Black Box. E. P. Oppenheim
*Black Business. H. Smart
*Black Camel. E. D. Biggers
Black Candle. E. Harris
Black Christmas. T. Altman
*Black Coffee. A. Christie
Black Coral. N. Ferguson
Black Country Sketches. Amy Lyons
*Black Curtain. C. Woolrich
Black Deeds in Whitehorse. A. McDonald
*Black Doll. W. E. Hayes
Black Dwarf. M. Molloy
*Black Fire. L. Goldman
*Black Friday. D. Goodis
*Black Gang. H. C. McNeile
*Black Gangster. D. Goines
Black Glove. G. Miller
Black Godfather. O. Fletcher
Black Gold Briefing. P. Buck
Black Gold, Red Death. D. L. Lindsay
Black Gravity. C. Ryan
*Black Hand. Anonymous
Black Heart. E. V. Lustbader
Black Hotel. J. Laurance
Black House. P. Highsmith
*Black Inheritance. J. McEnery
Black Knight in Red Square. S. M. Kaminsky
*Black Limelight. G. Sherry
Black Magic. A. Goetz
Black Magic. W. Strieber
*Black Marble. J. Wambaugh
Black Maria. L. O. Johnson
Black Market Soldiers. A. J. Levatino
Black Narc. J. Feinman
*Black Orchid. J. Goodchild
Black Palm. M. McCray
*Black Path of Fear. C. Woolrich
Black Pearl. Mrs. W. Woodrow
*Black Pearl and The Vikings. P. O'Donnell
Black Phantoms. P. Cruger
Black Rainbow. B. Michaels
*Black Sadhu. E. P. Thorne
Black Seraphim. M. Gilbert
Black Shadow. J. W. Kneeshaw
*Black Sheep. E. Yates
*Black Spider. C. Dawe
*Black Sunday. T. Harris
Black Tide. H. Innes
Black Unicorns. C. Leach
Black Vendetta. D. Chesley
Black Wedding. P. Jenkins
Black Wednesday. B. Crowther
Black Widow. J. N. Chance
*Black Widow. P. Quentin
*Black Wings Has My Angel. E. Chaze
Black Yacht. J. Baxter
*Blackboard Jungle. E. Hunter
Blackhope Legend. G. Fraser
Blacklash. R. Vincent
*Blackmail. R. Alexander
*Blackmail. C. Bennett
Blackmail Incorporated. N. Harman
*Blackout. H. Aquin
*Blackshirt. B. Graeme
*Blair's Attic. J. C. Lincoln
Blanche Fury. E. Britton

*Blanche Fury. J. Shearing
*Blank Page. K. C. Constantine
*Blank Wall. E. S. Holding
Blast. T. Kenrick
Blayde R.I.P. J. Wainwright
*Blazing Launch Murder. R. Hardinge
*Bleak House. C. Dickens
Bleeding Hearts. T. White
Blind. J. Harvey
Blind Alley. J. Popplewell
*Blind Alley. J. Warwick
*Blind Date. Leigh Howard
Blind Date with Death. C. Woolrich
Blind Drop. J. Nicholas
Blind Eye. J. Raymond
Blind Goddess. P. Hastings
*Blind Goddess. A. Train
*Blind Man's Eyes. W. MacHarg
Blind Prophet. B. Davis
Blind Side. H. Klein
*Blind Terror. W. Hughes
*Blind Villain. E. Berckman
*Blindfold. L. Fletcher
Blindfold Game. D. Thomas
Blonde Avalanche. Carter Brown
Blonde, Cute and Wicked. D. Glinto
*Blonde Died Dancing. K. Roos
Blonde Dies First. J. Evans
*Blonde on the Spot. H. Janson
Blonde Vampire. D. Mooers
Blondy's Boy Friend. L. Homesley
Blood-Amber. A. Mackworth
Blood and Orchids. N. Katkov
*Blood Bath. H. Janson
Blood Bath. J. Rosenberger
Blood Deep. C. Stubbington
Blood Dues. D. Pendleton
Blood for a Reckless Lady. W. Standish
Blood for Blood. J. Gloag
Blood Fugue. S. Eskapa
Blood Games. C. Leach
*Blood Group O. D. Brierley
Blood Highway. R. Harding
Blood in the Ashes. W. W. Johnstone
Blood Island. P. McCurtin
Blood Ivory. A. McCoy
Blood Money. A. Fletcher
Blood Money. G. Middleton
Blood Money. A. Winch
Blood Mountain. W. Boyles
Blood Muster. C. Stubbington
Blood Oath. D. Morrell
Blood of Strangers. D. Hartman
Blood of the Czars. M. Kilian
Blood of the Eagle. F. Dickey
Blood of the Scimitar. Nick Carter
*Blood on Her Shoe. M. Field
Blood on the Branches. O. Crawford
Blood on the Happy Highway. S. Radley
Blood on the Moon. J. Ellroy
Blood on the Rocks. A. Venters
Blood on the Sand. C. Dekker
Blood Red Sky. A. Emmerton
*Blood Relatives. E. McBain
Blood Royal. A. Winch
Blood Rubies. A. Young
Blood Run. D. Kellerman
Blood Run. A. Webb
Blood Tango. R. Houston
Blood Tapes. L. Starr
Blood Ties. A. J. Quinnell
Blood Ties. A. Roudybush
Blood Tracks of the Bush. S. Newland
Blood Will Have Blood. L. J. Barnes
Bloodbath. P. McCurtin
*Bloodbrothers. R. Price
Bloodletting! R. Skimin
*Bloodline. Sidney Sheldon
Bloodmoon. R. Kalish
Bloodrose House. C. Crowe
Bloodrun. R. Kalish
Bloodrush. H. Zachary
Bloodsport. D. Pendleton
*Bloodstar. T. Topor
Bloodstone Inheritance. S. D. Stevens
Bloodtide. R. Kalish
Bloodtide. B. Knox
Bloody Book of Law. Sara Woods
Bloody Jack. T. J. Kelly
Bloody Kin. M. Maron
*Bloody Mama. R. Thom
Bloody Rose. D. Streib
Bloody Scandal. G. Milner
*Bloody Spur. C. Einstein
Blow Out. N. Williams
Blow Your House Down. P. Barker
*Blowtop. A. Schwartz
Blowtorch: O'Reilly. E. Agry
Blue Brotherhood. E. O. Zimmerman
*Blue City. K. Millar
*Blue Dahlia. R. Chandler
*Blue Envelope. S. Kerr
Blue-Eyed Shan. S. Becker
Blue Flame. J. Gilmore
*Blue Hand. E. Wallace
*Blue Harpsichord. D. Keith
Blue Haze. F. Nunn
Blue Heron. P. Ross
Blue Hurricane. J. Dyson

B

Blue Ice Affair. Nick Carter
*Blue Lamp. T. Willis
*Blue Leader. W. Wager
Blue Messiah. J. D. Horan
Blue Murder. W. Wager
*Blue Orchid. H. Zore
Bluebeard. M. Frisch
Bluebird Canyon. D. McCall
Bluegate Fields. A. Perry
Blueprint for a Terrorist. H. Scott
Blues for Charlie Darwin. N. Hentoff
*Blunderer. P. Highsmith
Blunt Darts. J. F. Healy
Blurred Reality. R. Lewis
*Boden's Boy. T. Gallon
*Bodies in a Bookshop. R. T. Campbell
Bodily Harm. M. Atwood
Body. R. B. Sapir
Body Count. E. Helm
Body for Buddy. A. M. Stein
Body for Christmas. R. Reinsmith
Body Hunters. D. Streib
Body in Cadiz Bay. D. Serafin
Body in Paradise. R. Reinsmith
*Body Snatcher. R. L. Stevenson
Body Was Missing. H. Brewis
Bodyguard. A. Mitchell
Bohemian Connection. S. Dunlap
*Boka Lives! H. Calvin
Bomb Scare. P. Chambers
Bomb Two. D. Henderson
*Bombay Mail. L. Blochman
Bombing Run. A. M. Stein
*Bombshell. M. Leblanc
Bombshell. Jennifer Phillips
*Bonaventure. C. Hastings
Bone Yard. D. Pendleton
Bones. B. Pronzini
*Bones. E. Wallace
Bonner Deception. D. Estey
*Bonnie and Clyde. B. Hirschfeld
*Bony and the Black Virgin. A. W. Upfield
Boocoo Death. J. Lansing
Boogey Man. B. W. Battin
Book of Clues. J. Sladek
Book of Dreams. J. Vance
Book of Numbers. R. D. Pharr
Book of the Dead. J. Blackburn
*Boomerang. W. H. Osborne
Boonie-Rat Body Burning. J. Cain
*Booty for a Babe. Carter Brown
Border Crossing. G. Blagowidow
Borderland of Hell. W. Barker
Borderland Studies. H. Pease
Borderline. J. T. Hospital
*Borders of Barbarism. Eric Williams
Bormann Judgement. M. Stall
*Born Reckless. M. Rogers
Born to Die. D. Glinto
Born to Kill. J. D. Revere
*Born to Win. M. Roote
*Borrowed Crime. W. Irish
Boss. J. Greaves
*Boss of Taroomba. E. W. Hornung
Bossa Nova Bed. E. Colby
Botanist at Bay. J. Sherwood
*Botany Bay. J. Lang
*Bottletop Affair. G. Cotler
Bottom Line. J. Chaloner
*Bottom of the Bottle. G. Simenon
*Bottom of the Well. F. U. Adams
Boudoirs Are My Beat. J. Stewart
Bound by Love. C. Lanigan
Bound to Please. H. Spicer
*Bound Together. H. Conway
Bouquet Garni. D. Clark
*Bouquet of Clean Crimes and Neat Murders. H. Slesar
*Boulevard Nights. D. Gram
Bounty Hunter. A. Fletcher
Bowler, Batsman, Spy. A. Synge
Bowling Green Murder. M. Taylor
*Bowmanville Break. S. Shelley
Box for One. P. Brook
Box of Tricks. S. Brett
Boy Detective. Anonymous
Boy from Nowhere. M. Hinxman
Boy Next Door. C. Loken
*Boy on a Dolphin. D. Divine
Boy on Platform One. V. Canning
*Boys from Brazil. I. Levin
Boys in the Island. C. J. Koch
Bradford's Trials. J. R. Beek
Bragg's Hunch. J. Lynch
Brain. R. Cook
Brain Dead. L. Brieno
Brain of Agent Blue. T. Richards
Brain Watch. R. N. Walker
Brainchild. A. Neiderman
Brainchild. J. Saul
Brainpicker. P. J. Helm
*Brainrack. K. Pedlar
*Brainwash. J. Wainwright
Brainz. R. Goulart
Braking Point. A. Neilson
*Brand Image. H. Janson
Brand T. H. Brand
*Branded. G. Biss
*Branded Hand. M. O. Rolfe

Brandon Papers. Q. Bell
Brandstetter and Others. Joseph Hansen
Brannigan's Lot. Barney Douglas
Brant Adams, the Emperor of Detectives. Old Sleuth
*Brass Bowl. L. J. Vance
*Brass Diamonds. B. Sandberg
Brass Faces. C. McEvoy
*Brass Knuckles. F. Gruber
Brass Knuckles. B. Mochan
*Brat Farrar. J. Tey
Bravo Romeo. R. Peters
*Brazen Seductress. H. Janson
Brea File. L. Charbonneau
*Bread and a Stone. A. Bessie
*Breadfruit Lotteries. R. Elman
*Break for a Lovely. H. Janson
Break In. D. Francis
*Break in the Circle. P. Loraine
Breakaway. F. Durbridge
*Breakheart Pass. A. MacLean
*Breaking Point. L. Meynell
Breaking Point. M. R. Rinehart
Breath of Spring. P. Coke
Brenda Maneuver. S. N. Rosenberg
*Bressio. R. Sapir
Briarpatch. R. Thomas
Brick Alley. D. Chacko
Brick Foxhole. R. Brooks
*Bridal Path. N. Tranter
Bride. G. Middleton
*Bride from Cairngorn. J. F. Webb
*Bride from the Bush. E. W. Hornung
*Bride of Donnybrook. L. Ames
*Bride Wore Black. C. Woolrich
*Bride Wore Weeds. H. Janson
*Bride's Bouquet. K. Gordon
Brides of Aberdar. C. Brand
Bridge at Branfield. J. E. Greene
Bridge Fall Down. N. Rinaldi
Brigade. J. Shirley
*Brigand. E. Wallace
Bright Dummy. K. Sundelof-Asbrand
Bright Sun, Dark Shadow. M. Blake
*Brighton Murder Trial. B. Hamilton
*Brighton Rock. G. Greene
Brilliant Kids. H. Lieberman
Bring Me Sorrow. H. Janson
Bring the Monkey. M. Franklin
Brink. N. J. Crisp
Brinkman. D. Meiring
Bristol Express Mystery. C. H. Ogilvie
Bristow's Wreck. A. Howlett
British Agent. H. B. Lockhart
British Cross. B. Granger
Broad Players. C. A. Harris
*Broads Don't Scare Easy. H. Janson
Broadway. P. Dunning
*Broadway Bab. J. McCulley
*Broadway Murders. E. J. Doherty
Brock. J. Bingham
Brock and the Defector. J. Bingham
Broken Eagle. R. Tine
Broken Fang. U. Key
Broken Idols. S. Flannery
Broken Image. V. Ebert
Broken Link. C. Virmonne
*Broken Promise. E. A. Rife
Broken Symmetries. P. Preuss
*Broker. M. A. Collins
Broker. H. Q. Masur
*Broker's Wife. M. A. Collins
Brond. F. Lindsay
Bronze Bell. S. Silliphant
*Bronze Bell. L. J. Vance
Brother Esau. D. Orgill
*Brother Orchid. L. Brady
*Brother Rat. N. Karta
*Brotherhood. L. J. Carlino
Brotherhood of Blood. L. Derrick
Brotherhood of Evil. I. Zacharia
*Brotherhood of Satan. L. Q. Jones
Brotherhood of the Rose. D. Morrell
Brotherly Love. W. Blankenship
Brothers in Blood. D. Pendleton
*Brothers in Law. H. Cecil
*Brothers Karamazov. F. M. Dostoevskii
Brothers Kresky. H. Bloomstein
*Brothers Rico. G. Simenon
Brought to Book. H. Spicer
Brown Satin Bomb. Anthea Goddard
Brown's Requiem. J. Ellroy
*Bruce Angelo, the City Detective. Old Sleuth
*Brute. G. Des Cars
*Brute. F. A. Kummer
*Bubble Moon. R. Bridges
Buchman's Law. R. Thorman
Buck Passes Flynn. G. McDonald
Buckingham Blowout. A. Kilgore
Budapest Run. Nick Carter
*Build My Gallows High. G. Homes
Built to Kill. R. Tine
Bulgarian Termination. J. Rosenberger
*Bulldog Drummond. H. C. McNeile
*Bulldog Drummond at Bay. H. C. McNeile
Bullet for Betty. C. Joyce
*Bullet for Pretty Boy. M. Avallone
Bullet-Proof Toga. L. Malloy
Bullets, Bikinis and Bells. R. Renauld

Bullion. J. Goldsmith
Bullion Run 101. B. McAllister
*Bulls of Ronda. E. P. Benson
*Bullshot Crummond. R. House
Bully! M. Schorr
*Bump in the Night. Colin Watson
*Bunny Lake Is Missing. E. Piper
*Burden of Proof. J. Barlow
*Burglar. D. Goodis
Burglar and the Girl. M. Boulton
Burglar Who Painted Like Mondrian. L. Block
Burglar Who Studied Spinoza. L. Block
Burial Deferred. J. Ross
Buried. D. Helfgott
Buried Crime. C. Elmore
Buried Man. N. Stahl
Burke Foundation. A. McCandless
Burma Probe. J. Rosenberger
*Burn. N. Gant
*Burn, Witch, Burn! A. Merritt
Burned Evidence. Mrs. W. Woodrow
Burning Bush. H. Herald
*Burning Court. J. D. Carr
*Burning Eye. V. Canning
*Burning Shore. E. Trevor
*Burning Sky. R. Faust
*Burnt Offerings. R. Marasco
Bury Him Gently. C. Rank
Bush Warfare. A. Kilgore
Bushido Code. R. St. Louis
*Bushigrams. G. Boothby
Business of Murder. R. Harris
Businessman. T. M. Disch
*Busman's Honeymoon. D. L. Sayers
Bust! S. McPhilemy
*Busy Body. D. E. Westlake
*Busybody. J. Popplewell
*But Not for Me. E. Ronns
*But She Won't Lie Down. P. Yeldham
"But Why Bump Off Barnaby?" R. Abbot
Butcher, Baker, Nightmare Maker. R. Natale
Butcher Block. M. Mandell
Butchers. P. Lovesey
Butcher's Boy. T. Perry
Butchers of Men. J. Hild
Butler Did It. T. J. Kelly
Butler Did It. W. Marks
Butler Did It. R. Pendark
Butler's Revenge. M. Powell
*Butterflies in the Rain. A. Soutar
*Butterfly. J. M. Cain
*Butterfly. H. K. Webster
Butterfly Hunter. J. Van De Wetering
Button. B. Starr
Button Zone. W. Greatorex
*Buyer Beware. J. Lutz
By Frequent Anguish. S. F. X. Dean
By Love Betrayed. M. Andrau
By Reason of Doubt. E. Godfrey
*By Snare of Love. A. W. Marchmont
Bye-Bye Blackbird. R. Rowe
*CC and Company. M. Roote
Cabin Fever. J. Schenkar
Cable Car Murder. E. A. Taylor
*Cable from Kabul. N. Tranter
Cabot Wright Begins. J. Purdy
*Cache. L. Damore
Cache on the Rocks. M. Sellers
Cachet. J. Ashford
Cactus. H. Janson
Cadbury's Coffin. G. Swarthout
Cadenza for Caruso. B. Paul
Caging the Raven. W. Heffernan
*Cain '67. J. M. Simmel
Cain's Chinese Puzzle. S. A. Key
Cain's Wife. O. G. Benson
*Cain's Woman. O. G. Benson
Cairo. Percy White
Cairo Countdown Crisis. D. Stivers
Calamityville Terror. W. Gleason
Calculated Risk. C. Joyce
*Calendar. E. Wallace
California Roll. R. L. Simon
California Shakedown. D. Streib
California Thriller. M. Byrd
Call Back Yesterday. Sara Woods
*Call for the Dead. J. Le Carre
Call in the Feds. G. Greer
*Call It Treason. G. Howe
*Call Mr. Fortune. H. C. Bailey
Call of Honor. D. Bannerman
Call of the East. M. Nyberg
Call on Kuprin. Jerome Lawrence
Call or Fold. W. Hughes
Call Sign--Death. V. Wallace
*Called Back. H. Conway
Calling. J. Jenkins
Calling. B. Randall
*Calling Bulldog Drummond. G. Fairlie
Calling Juliet Bravo. Mollie Hardwick
*Calling Mr. Callaghan. P. Cheyney
Cambodian Clash. D. Pendleton
*Came the Dawn. R. Bax
Cameo. W. Leeds
*Camera Clue. G. H. Coxe
Camp. A. Saperstein
*Campanile Murders. W. Chambers

Title Index

*Campbell's Kingdom. H. Innes
Can It Be True? C. Eedy
Canadian Killing Ground. A. Kilgore
Canaris File. W. Winward
Canaris Fragments. W. Winward
Canaris Papers. G. Richards
Canary. T. Cohan
*Canary Murder Case. S. S. Van Dine
Candice Is Dead. A. S. Well
*Candid Imposter. G. H. Coxe
*Candle for the Dead. H. Marlowe
*Candyleg. O. Demaris
Cannibal Cult. G. N. Smith
*Cannibal Heart. M. Millar
*Canon in Residence. V. L. Whitechurch
Canvas Prison. G. De Marco
*Cape Cod Caper. M. Arnold
*Caper of the Golden Bulls. W. P. McGivern
*Capital Crime. L. Ford
*Caprice. J. Withers
Capricorn and Cancer. G. Household
Captain. S. Shubin
Captain Applejack. W. Hackett
Captain Blood. J. Ahern
Captain Bolton's Corpse. J. Sturrock
Captain Confetti. F. J. Dee
Captain Jackman. W. C. Russell
Captain Justice. A. Forrest
*Captain Nash and the Wroth Inheritance. Ragan Butler
Captain Wunder. D. Thomas
Captive City. J. Appleby
Captive Heart. C. Jauniere
Car for Mr. Bradley. J. Pattinson
Caravaggio Obsession. O. Banks
*Caravan to Vaccares. A. MacLean
Cardinal and the Corpse. S. Blakesley
Care of Time. E. Ambler
*Career in C Major. J. M. Cain
*Careful, He Might Hear You. S. L. Elliott
*Careful Man. R. Deming
Careful with the Sharks. C. Phipps
Careless Feast. M. Rostov
Caretakers. T. King
Cargo Gods. D. Streib
Cargo of Tin. T. Henege
Caribbean Account. A. Furst
Caribbean Caper. H. Janson
Caribbean Coup. Nick Carter
Caribe. L. Maracotta
Carioca Fletch. G. McDonald
Carla. J. R. Marshall
Carlos Is Dead. N. Harman
Carnaby and the Campaigners. P. N. Walker
Carnival of Crime. Fredric Brown
Carol in the Dark. C. Jordan
*Carolina House. E. Kyle
Caroline Minuscule. Andrew Taylor
*Carpet from Bagdad. H. MacGrath
Carradice Chain. S. Hylton
Carriage Clock. V. Andrews
Carrington V.C. Dorothy Bennett
*Carrion Crows. Dorothy Bennett
*Carry-Cot. A. Thynne
Carson's Conspiracy. M. Innes
Carter's Castle. Wilbur Wright
Casablanca. J. J. Epstein
Casco Deception. B. Reiss
*Case Against Mrs. Ames. A. S. Roche
Case Against Mrs. Dane. D. Trevern
*Case File: FBI. Gordons
Case for Charley. J. Spenser
Case for the Cardinal. S. Blakesley
*Case in Nullity. E. Berckman
Case of Art Failure. F. Bream
*Case of Lady Camber. H. A. Vachell
Case of Loyalties. M. Wallace
Case of Lucy Bending. Lawrence Sanders
*Case of Need. J. Hudson
Case of the Alpha Murders. S. Blakesley
Case of the Angry Actress. E. V. Cunningham
Case of the Ashanti Gold. C. Mason
*Case of the Caretaker's Cat. E. S. Gardner
Case of the Chief Rabbi's Problem. V. Andrews
*Case of the Constant God. Rufus King
*Case of the Curious Bride. E. S. Gardner
Case of the Curious Moonstone. T. J. Kelly
Case of the Dancing Sandwiches. Fredric Brown
Case of the Dead Producer. V. MacClure
*Case of the Frightened Lady. E. Wallace
Case of the Happy Medium. C. Bush
Case of the Hardboiled Dicks. J. Blumenthal
*Case of the Headless Corpse. D. Allan
Case of the Hijacked Moon. T. B. Haughey
Case of the Hookbilled Kites. J. S. Borthwick
*Case of the Howling Dog. E. S. Gardner
Case of the Kidnapped Angel. E. V. Cunningham
*Case of the Laughing Dwarf. J. Reach
*Case of the Lucky Legs. E. S. Gardner
*Case of the Mischievous Doll. E. S. Gardner
Case of the Missing Bronte. R. Barnard
Case of the Murdered Mackenzie. E. V. Cunningham
Case of the Nameless Corpse. E. K. Goldthwaite
*Case of the Nameless Corpse. C. B. Kelland
*Case of the Petticoat Murder. J. Craig
Case of the Phantom Baseball. J. E. Lawrence
Case of the Revolutionist's Daughter. L. Feuer
Case of the Sliding Pool. E. V. Cunningham
*Case of the Stuttering Bishop. E. S. Gardner
*Case of the Velvet Claws. E. S. Gardner
*Case of the Weird Sisters. C. Armstrong
*Case with No Conclusion. L. Bruce
Casefile. B. Pronzini
*Casino Murder Case. S. S. Van Dine
*Casino Royale. I. Fleming
Casino Strip. H. Janson
*Casinopoly. H. Janson
Casket for a Lying Lady. R. R. Werry
"Cassandra" Bell. P. Van Greenaway
Cassandra Crossing. R. Katz
Castle at Jade Cove. H. B. Hicks
*Castle Minerva. V. Canning
Castle of the Sea. B. Dean
Castle Rock. C. G. Hart
*Castle Skull. J. D. Carr
*Castles Burning. Arthur Lyons
*Castro File. J. Rosenberger
Casual Affairs. L. O'Donnell
*Cat. G. Simenon
*Cat and Mouse. M. Halliday
*Cat and the Canary. G. Kingsley
*Cat and the Canary. J. Willard
Cat and the Mice. L. O. Mosley
Cat Chaser. E. Leonard
*Cat o'Nine Tails. P. J. Gillette
*Catacombs. Jay Bennett
Catacombs. J. Farris
*Catacombs of Death. Operator 1384
Catch a Falling Clown. S. M. Kaminsky
*Catch Me a Renegade. H. Janson
*Catch Me a Spy. G. Marton
*Catch Me If You Can. J. Weinstock
Catchee Chinaman. May Phillips
*Catching a Tartar. G. W. Appleton
Catching Fire. K. N. Smith
Catenary Exchange. J. Winters
Cathedral. N. De Mille
Catherine's Twins. L. Raygor
Cat's Eyes. Lee Jordan
Cat's Paw. H. Janson
*Cat's Paw. C. B. Kelland
Cat's Paw. B. Pronzini
Catskill Eagle. R. B. Parker
*Catspaw. W. H. Osborne
Catspaw. Anne Stuart
Catwalk Kill. J. Munro
Caught and Bowled. Anonymous
Caught in a Corner. G. W. Waters
Caught in the Villain's Web. H. E. Swayne
Cauldron of Hell. Nick Carter
*Caves of Night. John Christopher
Caves of Segada. A. Aikman
*Caves of Steel. I. Asimov
*Cecily. I. Holland
Cecily Disappears. A. M. Platts
Ceiling of Hell. W. B. Murphy
Celebrity. T. Thompson
*Celestial City. B. Orczy
*Cellar. R. Laymon
Cellars' Market. Douglas Stewart
Cemeteries Are for Dying. W. L. Story
Censor. M. Russell
Centaur Conspiracy. Carl Stevens
Centrifuge. J. C. Pollock
Cerberus Gambit. D. Houghton
Ceremony. R. B. Parker
Ceremony of Innocence. S. F. X. Dean
*Certain Blindness. R. Lewis
Chain of Circumstances. C. S. Smith
Chain of Violence. L. Egan
Chain Reaction. N. Guild
Chains. Douglas Scott
Chains of Gold. Margaret Lamb
Chainsaw Terror. Nick Blake
*Chair for Martin Rome. H. E. Helseth
Chairman. J. R. Kennedy
Chairman of the Board. J. Evans
Chaleur Network. R. G. Stern
*Chalk Garden. E. Bagnold
Challenge. H. C. McNeile
Challenge at Castle Gap. Ben Douglas
Chamber Music. A. Kopit
Chameleon. W. Diehl
Chameleon Corps. R. Goulart
Chameleon Kill. J. Quinn
Champagne and a Gardener. B. J. Morison
Champagne Bandits. P. A. Foxall
Chance. S. McAulay
*Chance Awakening. G. Markstein
Chance Encounter. J. Audrenn
*Change of Mind. C. Stratton
Channel Assault. K. Royce
*Channings. Mrs. H. Wood
*Chant of Jimmie Blacksmith. T. Keneally
Chaos of Crime. Dell Shannon
Charade. J. Mortimer
*Charade. P. H. Stone
Charge Is Murder. L. B. McMahon
Charisma. M. G. Coney
Charlatan. W. Hamilton
Charley Gets the Picture. J. Spenser
Charlie and the Iceman. J. Eller
Charlie Chan and the Curse of the Dragon Queen. M. Avallone
*Charlie Chan Carries On. E. D. Biggers
*Charlie Muffin. B. Freemantle
Charlie Muffin and the Russian Rose. B. Freemantle
Charmed Death. M. Tripp
Charters and Caldicott. S. Bingham
*Chase. K. R. Dwyer
*Chase. H. Foote
*Chase. J. Lermina
*Chase. R. Unekis
*Chase of the Golden Plate. J. Futrelle
Chase Royal. D. Seaman
Chasing the Dragon. S. Gall
Chasm of Fear. L. Robin
*Chautauqua. D. Keene
*Cheap Detective. R. Grossbach
Cheap Dream. R. Leigh
Cheap Shot. J. Cronley
Cheat. B. Walsh
*Cheating Cheaters. M. Marcin
Checkmate Kill. J. Quinn
Checkmate Mr. President. J. Gouriet
Checkpoint Charlie. B. Garfield
Checkpoint Orinoco. A. Ekert-Rotholz
Chelsea Ghost. A. Hunter
*Cheri-Bibi. G. Leroux
*Cheri-Bibi and Cecily. G. Leroux
*Cheri-Bibi, Mystery Man. G. Leroux
Cherry-Boy Body Bag. J. Cain
Cherry Brandy. S. Ready
Cheshire Cat's Eye. M. Muller
Chess Mysteries of Sherlock Holmes. R. Smullyan
Chessmaster. Nick Carter
Chessplayer. W. Pearson
*Chest of Opium. Mr. M--
Chiaroscuro. P. Clothier
Chicago. M. Watkins
Chicago Assault. C. Ramm
*Chicago Chick. H. Janson
Chicago Deathwinds. N. Winski
Chicago Jungle. M. Baroni
*Chick. E. Wallace
Chidori's Room. R. Timperley
Chief Tallon and the S.O.R. J. Ball
Chiefs. Stuart Woods
Child Player. W. Dobson
Child Sellers. W. Leeds
Children. C. Robertson
*Children Are Gone. A. Cavanagh
*Children Are Watching. P. L. Dixon
*Children of Light. H. L. Lawrence
Children of Tender Years. T. Allbeury
Children of the Night. M. Bingley
Children's Game. D. Wise
Children's Ward. P. Wallace
Children's Zoo. L. O'Donnell
Child's Play. D. Malouf
Child's Play. R. Marasco
Chill Winds of Ravenhall. M. Bishop
Chiller. D. Sale
Chimera. S. Gallagher
*Chin-Chin-Chinaman. P. Walsh
*Chin Chin, the Chinese Detective. A. W. Aiken
China Bloodhunt. A. Kilgore
China Blue. G. Tippette
China Doll. M. Yorke
China Gate. W. Arnold
China Gold. J. Tarrant
China Lovers. D. Bonavia
China Option. N. D. Milton
China Run. Eric Clark
*China Syndrome. B. Wohl
Chinatown Charlie, the Opium Fiend. J. P. Ritter
Chinese Bandit. S. Becker
Chinese Bungalow. M. Osmond
Chinese Burn. Eric Clark
Chinese Detective. M. Hardwick
Chinese Fairy Tales. A. M. Fielde
Chinese Girl. M. Hutton
Chinese Justice. S. Murray
Chinese Nights' Entertainment. A. M. Fielde
*Chinese Orange Mystery. E. Queen
*Chinese Parrot. E. D. Biggers
*Chinese Puzzle. M. Bower
Chinese Roulette. P. Kirk
Chinese Spur. B. Sandberg

*Chinese Ultimatum. R. Moore
*Chink in the Armour. M. B. Lowndes
*Chip on My Shoulder. E. North
*Chit of a Girl. G. Simenon
*Choice of Assassins. W. P. McGivern
Choice of Enemies. G. V. Higgins
Choice of Victims. J. F. Straker
*Choirboys. J. Wambaugh
Cholo. R. Houston
Choose Your Own Verdict. Hilary Landon
Chopper Command. E. Helm
Chosen People. B. Michelson
Chosen Prey. W. Brashler
Christine in Murderland. F. Wells
*Christmas at Candleshoe. M. Innes
Christmas Eve. S. C. Roberts
Christmas Kill. Nick Carter
Christmas Rising. D. Serafin
Chronicles of a Death Foretold. G. G. Marquez
Chronicles of Bustos Domecq. J. L. Borges
*Chronicles of Don Q. K. Prichard
*Chronicles of Golden Friars. J. S. Le Fanu
"Cigarette." P. T. Reynolds
Cinderella Spy. P. Daniels
Cinema Crook. Anonymous
Cinnamon Skin. J. D. MacDonald
*Cipher. A. Gordon
Ciphergrams. H. O. Yardley
Circle. S. Shagan
*Circle of Confusion. Palmer White
Circle of Death. P. A. Foxall
Circle of Deceit. W. Winward
*Circular Staircase. M. R. Rinehart
Cities of the Red Night. W. Burroughs
*City and Suburban. F. Warden
*City of Angels. S. Shagan
City of Blood. D. Hartman
City of Fading Light. J. Cleary
City of Glass. P. Auster
City of Masks. M. Browne
*City of Purple Dreams. Anonymous
*City of Sin. R. O. Saber
City of the Dead. L. Derrick
City Office Mystery. M. B. Giles
City Solitary. N. Freeling
Clairvoyant. H. Clement
Clandestine. J. Ellroy
Clans of the Alphane Moon. P. K. Dick
*Clash by Night. R. Croft-Cooke
Class Distinctions. T. Heald
Classical Death. A. Marsland
*Claudia's Pole. C. Dawe
Claverleigh Curse. S. Dubay
Claw. N. Lofts
Claw. M. Raynor
*Clean Break. L. White
Clear and Present Danger. B. Sanders
*Cleopatra Jones. R. Goulart
*Cleopatra Jones and the Casino of Gold. R. Goulart
*Cleveland Pipeline. D. Pendleton
*Climate for Conspiracy. P. Harcourt
*Climate of Courage. J. Cleary
Climax. N. Karta
*Climax. F. J. Lewis
Climax. E. Locke
Clinic. C. Johnson
*Clique of Gold. E. Gaboriau
Cloak-and-Doctor. F. E. Gibson
Cloak of Darkness. H. MacInnes
Clock Tower. J. Montague
*Clockwork Orange. A. Burgess
Cloister Cat. A. Wight
*Clone People. M. Johnson
*Close All Roads to Sospel. G. Bellairs
Close Her Eyes. D. Simpson
*Close to Death. J. Crowe
Close Your Eyes and Sleep, My Beauty. A. Sewart
*Closing Net. H. C. Rowland
*Cloud. R. Bridges
Cloud Nine. J. M. Cain
Cloud Nineteen. W. Stanley
Clouds of Guilt. J. Wainwright
Club Paradis Murders. C. McCormick
*Clubbable Woman. Reginald Hill
*Clue of the Missing Link. G. Evans
*Clue of the New Pin. E. Wallace
*Clue of the Silver Key. E. Wallace
*Clue of the Twisted Candle. E. Wallace
*Clue Sinister. C. Carnac
Clutch of Diamonds. W. Christopher
Clutterkill. G. Paulsen
Coast Highway 1. E. C. Ward
*Coast of Chance. E. Chamberlain
Coast of Echoes. J. C. Strange
Coast of Fear. C. Crane
Coat of Arms. G. Sims
*Coat of Arms. E. Wallace
Cobalt. N. Aldyne
*Cocaine. M. Olden
Cocaine Run. J. Ahern
*Coconut Wireless. F. Kauffman
Coda. T. Topor
Coda Alliance. M. Brady
Code Conquistador. W. P. Kennedy
Code Name Harlequin. B. Mitchell

Code Name: Love. M. Nicole
Code of Arms. L. Block
Code Zero: Shots Fired. J. Cain
Coffin Corner. S. Jason
*Coffin for a Cutie. S. Morelli
*Coffin for a Hood. L. White
Coffin for Clara. B. Diamond
Coffins Come in All Sizes. D. Benton
*Coffy. P. W. Fairman
*Coiner's League. B. Wayde
Cold Dawn. C. Virmonne
*Cold Dead Coed. H. Janson
Cold Dish. M. A. Collins
Cold Judgment. J. Fluke
Cold Light of Day. E. Page
Cold, Lone and Still. G. Mitchell
Cold River. W. Judson
*Cold Spell. J. Bruce
Cold Stove League. T. Boyle
Cold Vengeance. M. McCray
*Cold War. D. Brierley
*Cold War Swap. R. Thomas
Colder Than the Grave. R. Haigh
*Collected Stories of Ben Hecht. B. Hecht
*Collector. J. Fowles
Colleen Bawn. D. Boucicault
Collision. J. Gordon
Collusion. T. D. Irwin
Colombo Night. A. Philips
Colonel Jack. D. Defoe
Color Him Guilty. J. L. Hensley
Color of Greed. G. F. Valcour
Color of Green. L. Kaufman
*Color of Hate. J. L. Hensley
*Colorado Jim. G. Goodchild
Columbian Gold. J. Manrique
Columbo and the Samurai Sword. B. Magee
*Coma. R. Cook
Combination. A. York
Combined Forces. J. Smithers
Come Back. Jonathan Smith
Come Back, Alice Smythereene! N. J. McIver
*Come Back When I'm Sober. M. Waddell
Come Clean, Baby. B. Cagson
*Come Easy--Go Easy. J. H. Chase
Come, Follow Me. P. Michaels
Come Home, Toby Brown. J. Pattinson
Come-On. W. Chambers
*Come Quickly, Honey. H. Janson
Come the Night. Nick Blake
*Come to My House. A. S. Roche
*Comedians. G. Greene
*Comes the Blind Fury. J. Saul
Coming Attractions. T. Tally
Coming Down Again. J. Balaban
Coming of Age. T. Zahn
Command. A. Melville-Ross
*Command Strike. D. Pendleton
Commando Squad. M. K. Roberts
Commandos. E. Arnold
Commissar's Report. Martyn Burke
*Commissioner. R. Dougherty
Committed Agent. T. Gilchrist
*Committee. D. Seaman
Common People. A. E. Martin
Commune's Child. S. Ascani
Communicating Door. S. Allan
*Communicating Door. W. Camp
*Compact of Crime. B. Wayde
Company of Saints. E. Anthony
Company Secrets. A. Coburn
Compkill. G. Paulsen
Compleat Agent. W. Crisp
*Complete State of Death. J. Gardner
Comprador. D. R. Cudlip
*Compromising Positions. S. Isaacs
Compulsion. M. Levin
Compulsory Gangster. W. Darrell
Computer Criminals...It Began at the World's Fair. S. Fawcette
Concert Masters. J. Sligo
Concerto. R. Burlinson
Concerto for Murder. W. H. Rowley
Conclave. L. D. Klausner
*Concorde--Airport 1979. K. Stewart
Condell. J. Turner
Condemned. P. Kuttner
*Condemned. J. Pagano
Condensed Novels. B. Harte
Condo Kill. R. Barth
Condor. T. Luke
Condor. G. Masterton
Condorman. H. Simon
Conduct of Major Maxim. G. Lyall
*Cone of Silence. D. Beaty
*Coney Island Quickstep. G. Gipe
Confession. P. McAlan
*Confession Corner. Mrs. B. Reynolds
Confessional. J. Higgins
Confessions of a Crap Artist. P. K. Dick
Confessions of a Dangerous Mind. C. Barris
Confessions of a Fanatic. Anonymous
*Confessions of a Thug. Warren Miller
*Confessions of a Vagabond. C. Massie
*Confessions of an Attorney. W. Warner
*Confidence Man. L. Y. Erskine

*Confidential Agent. G. Greene
Confidentially Yours. C. Williams
*Conflict. H. Janson
Conflict of Interests. C. Egleton
Conflict of Lions. T. Strong
Confucius Enigma. Margaret Jones
*Connecting Rooms. W. Hughes
*Connie Burt. G. Boothby
Conquistadores. B. Langley
Cons at Large. Jack Roberts
*Consequence of Fear. T. Allbeury
Consignment of Ore. P. Warden
*Conspiracy. R. Baker
Conspiracy of Eagles. B. Davis
*Conspirator. H. Slater
*Conspirators. E. P. Oppenheim
*Conspirators. F. Prokosch
Constable Across the Moors. N. Rhea
Constable Around the Village. N. Rhea
Constable by the Sea. N. Rhea
Constable in the Dale. N. Rhea
Consul's File. P. Theroux
Conte's Run. A. Lassiter
*Contraband. H. Janson
*Contraband. C. B. Kelland
Contract! C. Dempster
Contract: White Lady. M. McCray
Control. W. Goldman
Convergence. J. Fuller
Converging Parallels. T. Williams
*Convict Has Escaped. J. Budd
*Convict 99. M. C. Leighton
Convivial Codfish. C. MacLeod
Convoy. D. Pope
Cooking School Murders. V. Rich
Cool Clear Death. T. Hallernan
Cool Repentance. Antonia Fraser
Cool Runnings. R. Hoyt
*Cool Sugar. H. Janson
*Cool Tom, the Sailor Boy Detective. Old Sleuth
Cool War. F. Pohl
Co-Op Kill. R. Barth
Cop. E. J. Morris
*Cop Hater. E. McBain
Cop Without a Shield. L. O'Donnell
Copenhagen Connection. Elizabeth Peters
Copper Crash. F. Danby
Copper, Gold and Treasure. D. Williams
Copperhead. W. Katz
Cops. T. C. Fox
*Cops and Robbers. D. E. Westlake
Copycat Killings. H. Pentecost
*Cordelia the Magnificent. L. Scott
Cork of the Colonies. S. S. Rafferty
Corona Affair. E. Simson
Coroner's Jury. E. Marsh
*Corporal Cameron. R. Connor
Corporal Smithers, Deceased. J. S. Scott
*Corpse by the River. H. Arre
*Corpse Came C.O.D. J. Starr
*Corpse Can't Walk. H. Long
Corpse Cargo. G. Stockbridge
*Corpse Diplomatique. D. Ames
Corpse in a Gilded Cage. R. Barnard
*Corpse in the Castle. E. Friend
Corpse Now Arriving. M. Hinxman
*Corpse of the Old School. J. Iams
Corpse on the Cruise. F. Bream
*Corpse to Cairo. M. O'Brine
Corpses Don't Kill. C. Benson
*Corpses in Enderby. G. Bellairs
Corpses in the Cellar. B. Latham
*Corridor of Death. L. Carlton
*Corridor of Mirrors. C. Massie
Corridors of Death. R. D. Edwards
Corridors of Guilt. J. B. Hilton
Corrigan. C. Blackwood
Corruption. H. Janson
Corsair. W. Green
Corsican. W. Heffernan
Cortez Letter. M. Gillette
Cossack Hideout. E. Webster
Cotswold Connection. C. Vivian
*Cottage on the Fells. H. D. Stacpoole
Cottages to Let. G. Kerr
*Cotton Comes to Harlem. C. Himes
*Couch. R. Bloch
Cougar. W. Winward
Coulter Conspiracy. K. Crowder
Council of Kings. D. Pendleton
*Counsel for the Defense. L. Scott
Counsellor. G. Ziran
*Counsellor Heart. P. G. Winslow
Countdown to China. S. L. Thompson
*Countdown to Doomsday. R. Quest
Counter-Clock World. P. K. Dick
*Counter-Feat. H. Janson
Counter Force. D. Streib
*Counterattack. F. Scarpetta
Counterattack. J. Stevenson
*Counterfeit Death. W. Bannister
*Counterfeit Gentleman. C. B. Kelland
Counterfeit Traitor. A. Klein
*Counterfeiter's Roguery. E. C. Derby
*Counterfeiter's Wake. L. Carlton
*Counterspy Express. A. S. Fleischman
Counterstrike. P. A. Foxall
Countess Dracula. N. Du Brock

Title Index

*Countess of Lowndes Square. E. F. Benson
Country Beyond. J. O. Curwood
Country Gothic. T. J. Kelly
County Court. R. Flanagan
Coup de Grass. P. Nash
Coup D'Etat. J. Harvey
Couple from Poitiers. G. Simenon
Courier. D. Kartun
*Courier Job. J. Pattinson
Courier of Lyons. E. Moreau
Courier to Danger. M. Blake
Courier's Fist. H. A. Eysman
Court-Martial. W. E. Butterworth
*Court of Crows. R. A. Knowlton
Court of the Stone Children. M. Bucci
*Courthouse. J. N. Iannuzzi
Courtney. J. Jenkins
Cousin Henrietta. E. Cave
Cousin Once Removed. G. Hammond
*Cove in Darkness. S. Wagner
Coven. J. M. Fox
*Covenant with Death. S. Becker
Cover Story. C. Forbes
*Cover That Corpse. H. Zore
Cover Zero. W. Hughes
Covering Fire. H. Janson
Cowboy Blues. S. Lewis
*Cowboy Detective. Old Sleuth
Coyote Connection. Nick Carter
Coyote Cried Twice. A. Bay
Coyote Crossing. F. Roderus
Cozumel. H. Hunt
Crack in the House of God. G. Shannon
*Crack in the Mirror. M. Haedrich
*Crackerjack. W. B. M. Ferguson
*Cracking of Spines. R. H. Lewis
Craftsmen in Crime. Tom Fallon
*Crazy Joe. M. Barone
*Creaking Chair. L. Meynell
Creative Kind of Killer. J. Early
Creature Creeps. J. Sharkey
Creatures in a Dream. I. S. Black
*Creep Shadow. A. Merritt
Creeper. P. Macaulay
Creepy Crest. W. E. Wright
Crescents of the Moon. J. Matthews
Crew of the Anaconda. A. G. McDonell
Crib. H. Friedman
Cried the Piper. J. Simmons
*Crime. G. Bernanos
*Crime and Punishment. F. M. Dostoevskii
Crime and Punishment Show. A. Hausvater
Crime and Puzzlement. L. Treat
Crime and Puzzlement II. L. Treat
Crime and the Crystal. E. Ferrars
*Crime at Blossoms. M. Shairp
Crime at the Cedars. A. Feist
Crime at the Club. W. Massey
Crime for Christmas. L. Egan
Crime Has No Friends. L. Rogers
Crime Minister. I. Barclay
*Crime of a Countess. Nicholas Carter
Crime of Constable Kelly. J. C. Snaith
Crime of Innocence. N. Garland
Crime of Margaret Foley. P. Robinson
*Crime of Silence. P. Carlon
*Crime of the Under-Seas. G. Boothby
*Crime on My Hands. C. G. Hodges
*Crime on My Hands. H. Janson
Crime on the Coast. Detection Club
*Crime Partners. A. C. Clark
Crime Story. J. R. Nash
*Crime, the Place, and the Girl. D. Stapleton
*Crime Unlimited. D. Hume
*Crime Upon Crime. M. Underwood
Crime Wave. J. Wynne
Crime Without Passion. R. Grayson
*Crimebeat Crisis. H. Janson
Crimes of the Season. A. Saville
Crimes Stalk the Fan World. F. L. Baldwin
Criminal Act. T. Wilson
Criminal Code. M. Flavin
Criminal Comedy. J. Symons
Criminal Comedy of the Contented Couple. J. Symons
Criminals. D. Kranes
*Crimson Circle. E. Wallace
Crimson City. A. Coldeway
Crimson Falcon. S. Hylton
Crimson Gardenia. R. Beach
*Crimson Glove. Warren Miller
Crimson Hairs. Anonymous
*Crimson Hairs. W. Graham
Criss-Cross. D. Tracy
Criss-Crossing. P. Magdalany
*Crocodile on the Sandbank. Elizabeth Peters
Crocus List. G. Lyall
Crone. B. Garnett
Cronus. W. L. DeAndrea
Crook Who Came Back. Anonymous
*Crooked Billet. D. Titherage
Crooked Courtship. G. E. Bollans
Crooked Cross. B. J. Sussman
Crooked Flight. B. Jackson
*Crooked Inspector. B. Wayde

Crooks for a Month. G. F. Mountford
*Cropper's Cabin. J. Thompson
Cross and the Sickle. R. D. Zimmerman
*Cross-Country. H. Kastle
Cross Currents. R. Rostand
*Cross in the Dust. M. O. Rolfe
*Cross That Palm When I Come to It. A. Southcott
Crossfire. J. C. Pollock
Crossing. J. Flanagan
Crossing in Berlin. F. Knebel
*Crossing of Clews. E. C. Derby
Crossover. W. Karlin
*Crossroads Murders. G. Simenon
*Crouching Beast. V. Williams
Crow Eaters. B. Sidhwa
Crowded Cemetery. L. Williamson
Crowning Design. L. Meacham
*Crowns Can Kill. H. Janson
Crozier Pharoahs. G. Mitchell
Crucible of Courage. H. Neban
Crucifer of Blood. P. Giovanni
Crucifixion Squad. P. Beere
Crude Kill. D. Pendleton
Cruel Betrayal. Coriola
Cruel Triumph. N. Pierlain
*Cruel Victim. M. Tripp
Cruise Breaker. A. Corbett
Cruise of a Deathtime. M. Babson
*Cruising. Gerald Walker
Crumplin! M. S. Gretton
Crunch. H. Janson
Crusade into Crime. R. W. Hunter
Cry Guilty. Sara Woods
Cry Havoc. D. Lowden
Cry Havoc. B. Sadler
Cry in the Night. M. H. Clark
*Cry in the Night. D. Quick
Cry of the Banshee. T. J. Kelly
*Cry Revenge. A. C. Clark
*Cry Terror. A. L. Stone
*Cry Tough. I. Shulman
Cry Wolf. K. Blake
*Cry Wolf. M. Carleton
Cryptic Clue. P. Conway
Crypto Man. K. Royce
Crystal. W. Wingate
Crystal Cat. V. Johnston
Crystal Clear. R. F. West
Crystal Destiny. C. Blair
Crystal Kill. J. Quinn
Cuban Confetti. S. Barlay
Cuban Deathlift. R. Striker
*Cuban Heel. B. Carson
*Cuban Heel. S. Harragan
Cuban Inferno. S. Victor
Cuban Passage. N. Lewis
*Cuckoos on the Hearth. P. Fennelly
Cul-de-Sac. J. Wainwright
Cult Counter Cult. L. Davies
Cult .45. R. Rainey
Cult of the Damned. S. Andrews
*Cunning Against Force. T. Steele
Cunning and the Haunted. R. Jessup
Cupboard. O. Ashdown
Cupid Turns Killer. H. Janson
Curse of an Aching Heart. H. E. Swayne
*Curse of Drink. C. E. Blaney
Curse of Magira. D. Bee
Curse of the Giant Hogweed. C. MacLeod
*Curse of the Island Pool. V. Coffman
Curse of the Montrolfes. R. O'Grady
Curse of the Nibelung. M. D'Agneau
Curse of the Pharoahs. Elizabeth Peters
*Curse of the Snake. G. Boothby
Cursed Inheritance. L. Loghry
*Curtain Fall. E. Dewhurst
Curtain of Night. D. Petri
Curtains. J. Gonzales
Curtains for the Cobra. P. Tabori
Curtains of Solomon. M. Osmond
*Curtis Wives. M. Alexander
Curves and Angles. J. Farrell
*Custom House Fraud. B. Wayde
Cut in Diamonds. R. MacLeod
Cut of the Ax. J. Jackson
*Cutie on Call. H. Janson
*Cutter and Bone. N. Thornburg
Cutthroat. J. Frost
Cutting Edge. L. Chance
Cyanide Kill. L. Kent
Cynara. R. Gore-Brown
Cynara. H. M. Harwood
*Cynthia-of-the-Minute. L. J. Vance
*Cypress Man. Jane Beynon
Czechmate. D. Brierley
D.E.A.D. E. Whitmore
D.E.A.T.H. Hunters. J. Ahern
D Is for Duck. J. Ruyle
Da Vinci. L. Perdue
*Daddy's Gone A-Hunting. M. St. Clair
Daddy's Gone A Hunting. J. Toral
Daddy's Little Girl. D. Ransom
*Daffodil Mystery. E. Wallace
Dagger. M. Mason
Dai-Sho. M. Olden
Daleth Effect. H. Harrison
Dam. R. Byrne
Dame Ain't Safe. L. O'Brien
Dame in My Bed. M. Storme

Dames Are Deadly. D. Glinto
*Dames Are Dynamite. B. Schwarz
Dames Are Welcome. W. Standish
Dames Can't Wait. S. Markham
Dames Die Hard. L. Kent
*Dames Don't Care. P. Cheyney
Dames Is My Undoing. M. Horgan
Dames Play Dumb. B. Barnato
Dames Spell Homicide. H. R. Oldham
Dames Take to Crime. D. Rogan
*Damned Innocents. R. Neely
Damocles Sword. E. Trevor
Dan Sanda. F. Abbot
Dan Turner, Hollywood Detective. R. L. Bellem
Dance Card. J. R. Feegel
Dance for a Diamond. C. Murphy
*Dance for Diplomats. P. Harcourt
*Dance Hall of the Dead. T. Hillerman
Dance in the Sun. D. Jacobson
*Dance of the Dwarfs. G. Household
Dancehall. B. F. Conners
Dancer and the King. C. E. Blaney
Dancer Disappears. A. Sax
Dancer in Darkness. D. Stacton
Dancer with One Leg. S. Dobyns
Dancer's Death. P. Davis
*Dancing Bear. J. Crumley
*Dancing Detective. W. Irish
*Dancing Druids. G. Mitchell
*Dancing Girl. G. Leroux
Dancing Men. D. Kyle
Dancing Years. Clarissa Ross
*Dandy in Aspic. D. Marlowe
Danger. D. Francis
*Danger Calling. P. Wentworth
Danger Doll. C. Dekker
Danger Draws a Wild Card. T. Lennox
Danger Line. S. Ready
Danger Maze. W. Rotsler
Danger on Target. D. G. Deutsch
*Danger on the Map. A. Aldous
Danger on the Right. L. Du G. Peach
Danger Signal. F. Peart
*Danger Under the Moon. M. Walsh
Dangerous Affair. A. Andre
Dangerous Afternoon. G. Anstruther
*Dangerous Business. E. Balmer
Dangerous Company. W. Massey
*Dangerous Corner. J. B. Priestley
*Dangerous Davies. L. Thomas
*Dangerous Days. M. R. Rinehart
Dangerous Edge. R. Daley
Dangerous Fascination. L. Robin
Dangerous Fragrance. L. Graham
*Dangerous Game. F. Duerrenmatt
Dangerous Games. L. Schreiber
Dangerous Games. B. Sowanda
Dangerous Glamour. M. Olden
*Dangerous Inheritance. I. L. Forrester
*Dangerous Legacy. W. D. Roberts
Dangerous Love. W. C. Stone
*Dangerous Place to Dwell. M. Russell
Dangerous Stranger. M. Martin
Dangerous Temptation. C. Virmonne
*Dare-Devil Conquest. B. Gray
*Daring Maddie. Old Sleuth
Dark Angel. S. Forestal
*Dark Backward. E. Lambert
Dark Blue and Dangerous. J. Ross
*Dark Corner. L. Q. Ross
*Dark Dame. W. Collison
Dark Deeds. K. Welsh
Dark Deeds at Swan's Place. T. J. Kelly
Dark Destination. J. Potts
*Dark Door. M. Collis
Dark Encounters. W. C. Dickinson
Dark Entry. B. Copper
*Dark Eyes of London. E. Wallace
*Dark Fantastic. M. Echard
Dark Fantastic. S. Ellin
Dark Flight. J. Rossiter
Dark Fountain. J. R. Nash
Dark Harbour. M. Browne
*Dark Hazard. W. R. Burnett
Dark House, Dark Road. C. Wick
Dark Is Mine. C. Bartholomew
Dark Journey Home. P. Hagan
*Dark Mirror. L. J. Vance
*Dark Mosaic. C. Brooker
Dark Over Acadia. A. Talmage
*Dark Page. S. Fuller
*Dark Passage. D. Goodis
Dark Persuasion. M. Andrau
Dark Place. A. J. Elkins
Dark Places. T. Altman
Dark Red Star. I. Ruff
Dark Runner. R. Ashe
Dark Secrets of the Manor. G. A. Bruce
Dark Side of Destiny. S. Morgan
Dark Side of Love. C. Virmonne
Dark Thirty. T. Kay
Dark Tower. A. Woollcott
*Dark Waters. F. Cockrell
Dark Wind. T. Hillerman
Dark Wing. J. Wetherell
Darker Side of Death. M. Russell
*Darker Than Amber. J. D. MacDonald
Darkest Hour. C. George
*Darkest Hour. W. P. McGivern

*Darkness at Pemberley. T. H. White
*Darkness I Leave You. N. W. Hooke
Darkworld Detective. J. M. Reaves
Darling Carey's Dead. M. G. Webb
*Darling Delinquent. H. Janson
*Darling Lili. H. Clement
Darlington Jaunt. A. Ross
Dartmouth Drop. P. Browne
Dartmouth Murders. C. Orr
Date with Death. W. B. Murphy
*Dateline Darlene. H. Janson
*Dateline Debbi. H. Janson
*Dateline Diane. H. Janson
Daughter of Darkness. H. P. Dunne
Daughter of Evil. P. Morton
*Daughter of Fu Manchu. S. Rohmer
*Daughter of Shame. H. Janson
*Daughter of Silence. M. West
*Daughter of Two Worlds. L. Scott
David's War. H. D. Kastle
Dawn and Vengeance. J. Keitges
Day Care. J. Russo
Day of Days. L. J. Vance
Day of Fate. T. A. R. Cheney
Day of Mourning. D. Pendleton
Day of Terror. S. Francis
*Day of the Arrow. P. Loraine
*Day of the Dolphin. R. Merle
Day of the Grocer. W. Rushton
*Day of the Jackal. F. Forsyth
Day of the Mahdi. Nick Carter
Day of the Moon. W. Jeffrey
Day of the Owl. L. Sciascia
*Day of the Peppercorn Kill. J. Wainwright
Day of Wrath. J. Valin
*Day the Fish Came Out. K. Cicellis
Day the Island Almost Sank. S. D. Frances
Day the Sun Rose Twice. D. Thomas
Day the Whores Came Out to Play Tennis. A. Kopit
*Day They Robbed the Bank of England. J. Brophy
Day They Stole the Queen Mary. T. Hughes
Day Without Sunshine. L. H. Whitten
Days Like These. N. Fountain
Day's Mischief. L. Storm
Days of Power, Nights of Fear. B. Shaw
Days of Wine and Murder. M. Glade
Dazzling Miss Davison. F. Warden
De Profundis. W. Gilbert
De Witt's War. H. Koning
Dead Are So Dumb. L. Cargill
Dead at 8 P.M. C. H. Ogilvie
Dead Bolt. R. Obstfeld
Dead Centre. T. Wood
*Dead Cert. D. Francis
*Dead Certainty. N. Gould
*Dead Certainty. H. Janson
Dead Collection. P. R. G. Birch
Dead Dog. C. Harris
*Dead Don't Care. J. Latimer
Dead Don't Scream. L. Gribble
Dead Drunk. P. Conway
*Dead Easy. J. Popplewell
Dead End. S. Kingsley
Dead End in Mayfair. L. Gribble
Dead Eye. J. Ross
Dead Fall. P. Kirk
Dead for a Ducat. L. Payne
*Dead Game. G. Hammond
Dead Girls. J. Ibarguengoitia
Dead Giveaway. S. Brett
Dead Ground. P. Kerrigan
Dead Heat. L. J. Barnes
Dead Heat. R. Obstfeld
Dead Heat. F. Roderus
*Dead Heat on a Merry-Go-Round. E. L. Heyman
Dead in Center Field. P. Engleman
Dead in the Water. T. Wood
Dead Issue. C. A. Posey
Dead Knock. P. Turnbull
Dead Letter. D. Clark
Dead Letter. W. B. Murphy
Dead Letter. J. Valin
Dead Letter Drop. P. James
Dead Loss. W. Massey
*Dead Man Blues. W. Irish
*Dead Man Calling. G. Black
Dead Man Drifting. A. Sewart
Dead Man Over All. Walter Allen
Dead Man Running. C. R. Lajeunesse
Dead Man Running. D. Pendleton
Dead Man's Handle. P. O'Donnell
Dead Man's Ransom. Ellis Peters
*Dead Man's Shoes. M. Innes
Dead Man's Tears. J. Newman
Dead Man's Thoughts. C. Wheat
Dead Matter. S. Frimmer
*Dead Men Tell No Tales. E. W. Hornung
*Dead Men's Money. J. S. Fletcher
Dead of Jericho. C. Dexter
Dead of Winter. F. Bramble
*Dead of Winter. C. Hale
Dead of Winter. J. Pattinson
*Dead on Course. M. Black
Dead on Cue. A. Morice

Dead on Time. A. Capelli
Dead Pigeon. L. Kantor
*Dead Pigeon on Beethoven Street. S. Fuller
*Dead Ringer. Arthur Lyons
Dead Ringer. R. Ormerod
*Dead Ringer. R. Thomas
Dead Ringer. M. Warden
Dead Romantic. S. Brett
Dead Run. J. Black
Dead Seed. W. C. Gault
Dead Sleep Lightly. J. D. Carr
Dead Spy, Dead Secret. W. E. Corfield
Dead Straight. A. Neilson
*Dead Take No Bows. Richard Burke
Dead to Rights. K. Davis
Dead 'Un Wins. Aintree
*Dead Weight. B. Lecomber
Dead Weight. T. Magnuson
Dead White. A. Ryan
*Dead Zone. Stephen King
Deadbolt. Jay Brandon
*Deadfall. D. Cory
*Deadfall. K. Laumer
Deadfall. L. Orde
Deadfall. T. A. Schock
Deadheads. Reginald Hill
Deadlier Sex. R. Striker
*Deadlier Than the Male. J. Gunn
*Deadlier Than the Male. H. Reymond
Deadliest Profession. W. Boyles
Deadliest Show in Town. M. McQuay
Deadline. J. Dunning
*Deadline. J. Eastwood
*Deadline at Dawn. W. Irish
Deadline in Jakarta. I. Stewart
Deadlines. C. Dunn
Deadlock. S. Paretsky
Deadly Birdman. P. Buck
Deadly Communion. O. Brookes
Deadly Connection. C. Cunningham
*Deadly Dames. M. Douglas
Deadly Decoy. J. Tabler
Deadly Dream. T. S. Drachman
*Deadly Duo. R. Jessup
*Deadly Encounter. R. Woodley
Deadly Games. F. Neznansky
Deadly Green. E. Harris
Deadly Horse-Race. H. Janson
Deadly in New York. C. Ramm
Deadly Inheritance. F. Reeves
Deadly Inheritance. Janice Robinson
*Deadly Intent. A. Rowe
*Deadly Interlude. M. O'Brine
Deadly Kisses. P. Berger
Deadly Legacy. Christina Blake
*Deadly Mission. H. Janson
Deadly Misunderstanding. C. Biddle
Deadly Nature. H. Scott
Deadly Objectives. L. A. Taylor
*Deadly Percheron. J. F. Bardin
Deadly Petard. R. Jeffries
Deadly Place to Stay. Josephine Bell
Deadly Record. N. W. Hooke
Deadly Reunion. J. Ekstrom
Deadly Reunion. R. Hayes
Deadly Reunion. M. McCray
Deadly Sickness. J. Penn
Deadly Silents. L. Killough
Deadly Snow. J. Decker
Deadly State of Mind. L. Hays
Deadly Streak. D. Enefer
Deadly Variations. P. Myers
*Deadly Witness. Old Spicer
Deadman's Game. R. Dennis
Deafman No Hear. D. Fulani
Deaken's War. B. Freemantle
*Dealer. M. A. Collins
Dealer of Death. D. Hartman
Dealer's Wheels. S. Wilson
*Dealing Out Death. W. T. Ballard
Dean and Jecinora. V. L. Whitechurch
Dear Delinquent. J. Popplewell
*Dear Fatherland. J. M. Simmel
*Dear John. Susan Lee
Dear Mr. Capote. G. Lish
Dear Murderer. S. L. Clowes
Dear Murderer. R. Parry-Ellis
*Dear Old Gentleman. G. Goodchild
Dear Pretender. A. R. Colver
Dearest Enemy. Sara Woods
Death Among Friends. C. Hare
Death and Blintzes. S. Rosen
Death and Lila Fell. M. J. Johnson
Death and the Good Life. R. Hugo
Death and the I Ching. L. Rosenfeld
Death and the Jack Shade. W. S. Brady
Death and the Mad Heroine. S. F. X. Dean
Death and the Pregnant Virgin. S. T. Haymon
Death and the Princess. R. Barnard
Death and the Single Girl. E. Lewis
*Death and the Sky Above. A. Garve
*Death at Broadcasting House. V. Gielgud
Death at Charity's Point. W. G. Tapply
Death at Nostalgia Street. Wade Wright
Death at St. Anselm's. I. Holland
*Death at St. Asprey's School. L. Bruce

Death at Sea. V. Robinson
*Death at Shinglestrand. P. Capon
Death at the BBC. J. Sherwood
Death at the Crossings. J. Nowak
Death at Yew Corner. R. Forrest
Death Audit. J. A. Howard
Death Beam. R. Moss
*Death Bed. S. Greenleaf
Death Below Zero. A. Venters
Death Beside the Sea. M. Babson
Death Beside the Seaside. M. Babson
Death by Arrangement. D. Alberts
Death by Dreaming. J. M. White
Death by Gaslight. M. Kurland
Death by My Destiny. N. H. Perrin
Death by Request. R. John
Death by Sheer Torture. R. Barnard
Death by Surprise. C. G. Hart
Death Called at Night. R. A. Bennett
*Death Came Uninvited. E. Backhouse
Death-Cap Dancers. G. Mitchell
Death Care. R. Haigh
*Death Catches Up with Mr. Kluck. Xantippe
Death Ceremony. James Melville
Death Chemist. J. N. Chance
Death Comes Home. J. Dekker
*Death Croons the Blues. J. Ronald
Death Cruise. J. Cannon
*Death Deal. B. E. Miller
Death Dealer. Nick Carter
Death Deals in Diamonds. Hal Murray
Death-Face, the Detective. Anonymous
Death for a Dancer. E. X. Giroux
Death for a Darling. E. X. Giroux
Death for Adonis. E. X. Giroux
Death for an Emerald. R. H. Lees
*Death Freak. H. Burkholz
*Death from a Top Hat. C. Rawson
Death Gambit. J. Dekker
Death Game. Stuart White
Death Game--Five Players. A. Sewart
Death Games. D. Pendleton
Death Goes to the Bahamas. K. Hess
Death Hand Play. Nick Carter
*Death Has Deep Roots. M. Gilbert
Death Importer. J. N. Chance
Death in a Deck Chair. K. K. Beck
Death in a High Latitude. J. R. L. Anderson
Death in a Tenured Position. A. Cross
Death in Autumn. M. Nabb
Death in Berlin. M. M. Kaye
Death in Blue Folders. M. Maron
Death in Camera. M. Underwood
*Death in Captivity. M. Gilbert
Death in China. W. D. Montalbano
Death in Cyprus. M. M. Kaye
Death in Donegal Bay. W. C. Gault
Death in Fashion. M. Babson
*Death in High Heels. C. Brand
Death in Ireland. P. Everett
Death in Irish Town. J. S. Scott
Death in Kenya. M. M. Kaye
*Death in Santiago. G. De Villiers
*Death in Seven Hours. S. Davis
*Death in Sheep's Clothing. S. Phillips
Death in Small Corners. H. T. Smith
Death in Springtime. M. Nabb
Death in the Air. D. Hartman
Death in the Andamans. M. M. Kaye
*Death in the City. J. R. L. Anderson
Death in the Cup. A. Hocking
*Death in the Deep South. W. Greene
Death in the Devil's Acre. A. Perry
*Death in the Doll's House. H. Lees
*Death in the Drawing Room. R. A. Rathbone
Death in the Faculty. A. Cross
*Death in the Greenhouse. J. R. L. Anderson
*Death in the Life Department. C. P. Cleary
Death in the Old Country. E. Wright
Death in the Picture. M. Williamson
Death in the Rain. F. Parrish
*Death in Tiger Valley. Reginald Campbell
Death in Time. M. Warner
Death in Yellow. S. Jason
Death in Zanzibar. M. M. Kaye
Death Is a Lonely Business. R. Bradbury
*Death Is Academic. A. MacKay
Death Is for Losers. W. Newton
*Death Is Forever. M. O'Callaghan
Death Is My Neighbour. A. Templeton
Death Is Relative. E. Phillips
*Death Is the Pay-Off. Simon Burke
Death Island. Nick Carter
*Death Kiss. M. St. Dennis
*Death Lifts the Latch. A. Gilbert
Death-Line. J. Mercer
*Death List. A. C. Clark
Death Lust. A. Kilgore
Death Machine Contract. M. McCray
*Death Mask of War. G. Marlowe
Death Masque. H. McLeave
Death Match. R. Glendinning
Death Merchants. S. Murray
Death Notes. R. Rendell

Title Index   Dodge Boys / 143

Death of a Burrowing Mole.   G. Mitchell
Death of a Butterfly.   M. Maron
*Death of a Citizen.   D. Hamilton
Death of a Crow.   U. Curtiss
Death of a Daimyo.   James Melville
Death of a Dancing Lady.   R. Harrison
Death of a Dissident.   S. M. Kaminsky
Death of a Don.   H. Shaw
Death of a Dreamer.   R. A. Bennett
Death of a Dutchman.   M. Nabb
*Death of a Fat God.   H. R. F. Keating
Death of a Friend.   R. Harris
Death of a Gossip.   M. C. Beaton
Death of a Harvard Freshman.   V. Silver
Death of a Hit-Man.   Frederick Davies
Death of a King.   P. C. Doherty
Death of a Minor Poet.   W. Krasner
Death of a Nymph.   D. Delman
Death of a Perfect Mother.   R. Barnard
Death of a Portrait.   L. Williamson
Death of a Shipowner.   T. Henege
*Death of a Snout.   D. Warner
*Death of a Stray Cat.   J. Potts
Death of a Terrorist.   J. Beeching
*Death of a Thin-Skinned Animal.   P. Alexander
Death of a Unicorn.   P. Dickinson
Death of a Voodoo Doll.   M. Arnold
Death of an Englishman.   M. Nabb
Death of an Honourable Member.   R. Harrison
Death of Descartes.   D. Bosworth
*Death of His Uncle.   C. H. B. Kitchin
Death of Lorenzo Jones.   B. Latham
Death of Men.   A. Massie
Death of Minor Character.   E. Ferrars
Death of Ruth.   E. Kata
Death of the Abbe Didier.   R. Grayson
*Death of the Fuhrer.   R. Puccetti
Death of the Party.   L. Cutter
Death on Call.   S. D. Wilkinson
Death on Delivery.   E. L. Sloane
*Death on the Borough Council.   J. Bell
Death on the Broadlands.   A. Hunter
*Death on the Diamond.   C. Fitzsimmons
Death on the Docks.   D. Hartman
Death on the Dragon's Tongue.   M. Arnold
Death on the Eno.   A. MacKay
Death on the Heath.   A. Hunter
*Death on the Nile.   A. Christie
Death on the River.   A. MacKay
*Death on the Set.   V. MacClure
Death on the Viaduct.   J. R. Traynor
Death on Wheels.   M. Strongman
Death on Widow's Walk.   L. Grant-Adamson
*Death Penalty.   A. Draper
Death Riders.   D. Streib
*Death Rides a Painted Horse.   R. P. Wilmot
Death Scene.   B. Suyker
*Death Set to Music.   M. Hebden
*Death Ship.   H. Edmonds
Death Shuttle.   D. Streib
Death Sleep.   J. Sohl
*Death Specialists.   G. Paulsen
Death Spiral.   Meredith Phillips
Death Squad.   P. McCurtin
Death Stalk.   R. Grayson
Death Stalks My Lovely.   N. Rosso
Death Stalks the Punjap.   M. A. Casberg
*Death Stalks "The Wild Goose."   R. Stahl
Death Star Affair.   Nick Carter
Death Strike.   D. Stivers
Death Swap.   M. Babson
*Death Takes a Dive.   A. Tack
Death Takes a Holiday.   Walter Ferris
Death Tide.   W. Norville
Death Times Three.   R. Stout
*Death to the Dancing Masters.   R. Harper
Death Trick.   R. Stevenson
Death Turns a Trick.   Julie Smith
Death Turns Right.   J. Mathewson
Death Under Par.   J. Law
Death Under the Lilacs.   R. Forrest
*Death Walked In.   B. Manktelow
*Death Walked in Berlin.   M. M. Kaye
*Death Walked in Cyprus.   M. M. Kaye
*Death Walked in Kashmir.   M. M. Kaye
Death Walks Softly.   B. Shannon
Death Warmed Up.   M. Babson
Death Wears a Bridal Veil.   K. M. Knight
*Death Wears a Petticoat.   H. Janson
*Death Wish.   B. Garfield
Death Wishes.   P. Loraine
Deathbites.   D. Stivers
Deathcalls.   R. Montana
Deathmate.   M. Caidin
Death's Angel.   W. B. Longley
Death's Bright Angel.   H. Davie-Martin
Death's Clenched Fist.   J. Sherburne
Death's Door.   W. Barker
Death's Gray Angel.   J. Sherburne
Death's Head.   J. Ross
Death's Little Sister.   J. Dekker
Death's Pale Horse.   J. Sherburne
Death's Running Mate.   J. D. Revere
*Deathsport.   W. Hughes
Deathstalk.   B. Clark

*Deathtrap.   I. Levin
Deathwatch.   J. Genet
Deathwatch.   R. Harrison
Deathwatch.   E. Trevor
*Debt Discharged.   E. Wallace
Debt of Honor.   A. Kennedy
Deceitful Death.   J. Penn
Decision.   A. Drury
*Decks Ran Red.   A. L. Stone
Declined with Thanks.   E. Mulliner
Decoy.   D. Pope
Decoy Hit.   Nick Carter
*Decoys.   R. Hoyt
*Deed of a Night.   Warren Miller
*Deeds of Dr. Deadcert.   J. Fleming
Deep and Crisp and Even.   P. Turnbull
*Deep Cover.   B. Garfield
Deep Cover Blastoff.   L. Derrick
*Deep End.   J. Hayes
Deep Kill.   J. Dugan
Deep Six.   C. Cussler
Deep Six.   R. Striker
*Deep Water.   P. Highsmith
Deep Water.   S. Whalen
Deepwater.   A. Finer
Deer in Water.   J. Reid
Deer Leap.   M. Grimes
*Defeat of a Detective.   C. Wills
*Defector.   E. Anthony
Defence Against Terror.   W. Rotsler
Defence of the Realm.   J. O. Easton
Defenders of the Law.   H. Del Ruth
*Definite Object.   J. Farnol
Defy the Devil.   Sara Woods
Dekker.   L. Cameron
Dekker's Demons.   A. Webb
Delaney.   Gilbert Morris
Delay on Turtle.   V. Canning
*Delicious Danger.   H. Janson
Deliverance.   J. Dickey
Delphi Betrayal.   L. Perdue
Delta Crossing.   J. Nazel
Delta Star.   J. Wambaugh
Demon.   I. Watkins
*Demon.   C. N. Williamson
Demon in the Skull.   F. Pohl
Demon Lover.   V. Holt
*Demon Tower.   V. Coffman
*Denis Dent.   E. W. Hornung
Dennecker Code.   J. C. Pollock
Dennison's War.   A. Lassiter
Denver Collection.   D. Wright
*Department K.   Hartley Howard
Depravity.   H. Janson
*Desert Fury.   H. Janson
Desert of the Damned.   B. McAllister
Desert Town.   R. Stewart
*Deserted Night.   T. B. Morris
*Design for Dupes.   H. Janson
*Design for Murder.   G. Baxt
Design for Murder.   E. Quest
Designated Hitter.   W. Wager
*Desire in the Dust.   H. Whittington
*Desire of the Eyes.   G. Allen
Desire to Kill.   A. Clarke
*Desmond Dare.   Old Sleuth
*Despair.   V. Nabokoff-Sirin
Despair and Die.   J. Midgley
*Desperate Chance.   Old Sleuth
*Desperate Game.   Old Spicer
*Desperate Hours.   J. Hayes
Desperate Love.   A. Andre
*Desperate Moment.   M. Albrand
*Desperate Search.   A. Maysee
*Destination Dames.   H. Janson
*Destination Death.   B. Bishop
Destiny of Death.   Dell Shannon
Destroyer.   R. W. West
*Destroying Angel.   L. J. Vance
Destroyers.   A. W. Miller
*Destructors.   M. Franklin
*Detective.   R. Thorp
Detective Grime's Triumph.   A. Robertson
*Detective Payne.   Old Sleuth
*Detective Payne's Shadow.   Old Sleuth
*Detective Story.   S. Kingsley
*Detective Thrash, the Trapper of Criminals.   Old Sleuth
*Detective Trio.   Old Sleuth
*Detective's Enigma.   Old Sleuth
Detling Murders.   J. Symons
Detling Secret.   J. Symons
Detonator.   W. Garys
Detonators.   D. Hamilton
*Detour.   M. M. Goldsmith
Detroit Combat.   C. Ramm
Deus Irae.   P. K. Dick
*Devil and the Deep.   H. Janson
Devil and the Dolce Vita.   T. Holme
*Devil Doctor.   S. Rohmer
Devil Dolls.   J. Nazel
*Devil Rides Out.   D. Wheatley
*Devil Stick.   F. Hume
*Devil Thumbs a Ride.   R. C. Du Soe
*Devil to Pay.   F. N. Greene
*Devil's Alternative.   F. Forsyth
*Devil's Chaplain.   G. Bronson-Howard
Devil's Child.   M. Bingley
Devil's Circus.   B. Christiansen
Devil's Claw.   D. Masters

Devil's Daughter.   P. Marsh
Devil's Daughter.   F. Shaw
Devil's Finger.   R. Emmett
*Devil's Highway.   H. Janson
Devil's Home on Leave.   D. Raymond
Devil's Knell.   M. Warner
Devil's Mirror.   R. Spencer
Devil's Novice.   Ellis Peters
Devils of the Deep.   K. Robeson
*Devil's Own.   P. Curtis
Devil's Own.   R. A. Scotti
Devil's Paintbrush.   M. Dibner
Devil's Paradise.   R. Timperley
Devil's Prison.   M. O'Donnell
Devil's Profession.   G. d. S. W. James
Devil's Rain.   M. Willis
Devil's Staircase.   B. Wilson
Devil's Trashcan.   J. Rosenberger
Devil's Triangle.   M. Macao
*Devil's Triangle.   A. Soutar
Devil's Work.   M. Yorke
Devious Duchess.   Jean Smith
*Devlin's Triangle.   B. Heatter
Dew of Slumber.   W. D. Browne
Dhow Patrol.   M. Gregg
Di Di Mau or Die.   J. Cain
*Dial "M" for Murder.   F. Knott
*Diamond Bikini.   C. Williams
Diamond Exchange.   T. Chastain
*Diamond Hitch.   A. Barker
*Diamond Master.   J. Futrelle
Diamond Rock.   M. Schorr
Diamonds.   T. Beattie
*Diamonds Are Forever.   I. Fleming
*Diamonds for Moscow.   David Walker
Diamonds of Despair.   R. Chester
Diana and Destiny.   C. Garvice
*Diana of the Islands.   B. Bolt
Diana's Destiny.   C. Garvice
Dick and Jane.   A. Robinson
*Dick, the Boy Detective.   Old Sleuth
Die a Little.   T. Kennedy
Die Again, Macready.   J. Livingston
*Die Fast, Die Happy.   M. Denning
Die for Love.   Elizabeth Peters
Die for the Queen.   Douglas Scott
*Die, Killer, Die.   F. Scarpetta
Die Laughing.   S. S. Rafferty
Die Like a Dog.   G. Moffat
*Died on a Rainy Sunday.   Joan Aiken
Different Drummer.   C. Egleton
Different Seasons.   Stephen King
*Dig a Narrow Grave.   M. L. Roby
*Dig Those Heels.   H. Janson
*Dillinger.   H. Clement
Dillinger.   H. Patterson
Dime to Dance By.   W. Walker
Diminished Responsibility.   J. Barnett
Dimpled Racketeer.   A. S. Scarberry
Din of Inequity.   M. Denning
*Dinah for Danger.   J. Bogar
Diner on the Other Track.   W. I. Frank
Dingane's War.   W. Charles
Dinky-Dau Death.   J. Cain
Dinner and Death.   W. R. Burnett
Diplomates.   V. Sardou
Diplomatic Immunity.   E. Sydell
Diplomatic Immunity.   T. Szulc
Dipo Flight.   L. Robert
Dirty Duck.   M. Grimes
*Dirty Harry.   P. Rock
Dirty War.   D. Pendleton
*Disappearance of Roger Tremayne.   B. Graeme
Discovery.   S. Shagan
Dish Ran Away.   H. Janson
*Dishonored.   F. Vreeland
*Dishonour Among Thieves.   E. C. R. Lorac
*Disillusioned.   B. Sarto
*Disoriented Man.   P. Saxon
Disposal Job.   E. Harris
Dissertation Upon Second Fiddles.   V. O'Sullivan
Distaff Factor.   J. Wainwright
Distant Stranger.   P. Harcourt
Distant View of Death.   J. S. Scott
Ditto List.   S. Greenleaf
*Dive into Death.   Clayton Matthews
Divine Assassin.   B. Reiss
*Division Bell Mystery.   E. Wilkinson
Doberman Wore Black.   Barbara Moore
*Doctor Artz.   R. Hichens
Doctor Austin's Guests.   W. Gilbert
*Dr. Cook's Garden.   I. Levin
Doctor Death and other terror tales.   Zorro
*Doctor Fix.   H. Janson
Doctor Glas.   H. Soderberg
*Doctor Mabuse, Master of Mystery.   N. Jacques
*Dr. Phibes.   W. Goldstein
*Dr. Phibes Rises Again.   W. Goldstein
*Doctor Rameau.   G. Ohnet
Doctor Sax.   J. Kerouac
*Doctor Syn.   R. Thorndyke
Doctor Was a Lady.   M. V. Heberden
*Doctor's Double.   N. Gould
*Doctors Wear Scarlet.   S. Raven
Dodge Boys.   G. Sibbald

*Dodge City Bombers.   L. Derrick
*Dodos Don't Duck.   M. O'Brine
*Dog Day Afternoon.   P. Mann
*Dog Detective and His Young Master.
   Lt. M. M. Murray
Dog in the Manger.   U. Curtiss
Dog Rock.   D. Foster
Dog Soldiers.   R. Stone
*Dogs of War.   F. Forsyth
Doing It.   J. W. Thomas
Doll.   F. Durbridge
*Doll Baby.   H. Janson
Dollar Instinct.   E. Seeley
Dolly and the Bird of Paradise.   D.
   Dunnett
*Dolly and the Starry Bird.   D. Dunnett
*Dolphin.   E. Lambert
Dolphin Shore.   P. Barstow
Domestic Affair.   M. Russell
Dominator.   J. Follett
*Domino Principle.   A. Kennedy
Domino Spell.   W. L. Story
Domino Vendetta.   A. Kennedy
*Don Among the Dead Men.   C. E. Vulliamy
Don Bueno.   Z. Ghose
Don Chicago.   C. E. B. Roberts
*Don Is Dead.   N. Quarry
*Don Q's Love Story.   K. Prichard
Dongola Script.   L. Johns
Donna with Green Eyes.   B. Sarto
Donnolly Murders.   W. Crichton
Donors.   L. A. Horvitz
*Donovan Affair.   O. Davis
*Donovan's Brain.   C. Siodmak
Don't Cry Now.   H. Janson
*Don't Dare Me, Sugar.   H. Janson
Don't Hold Your Breath.   W. Newton
Don't Just Die There.   H. Kane
Don't Kill Me Twice.   D. Bogard
*Don't Look Behind You.   S. Rogers
Don't Look for Me, I'm Dead.   W. Strathern
*Don't Mention My Name.   E. K. Goldthwaite
*Don't Mourn Me, Toots.   H. Janson
*Don't Scare Easy.   H. Janson
Don't Sell Me Cheap.   W. Standish
Don't Tell Daddy.   B. Petty
Don't Tell the Press.   H. Jobson
*Don't Tempt Me.   S. Coburn
Don't Walk Home.   B. Hastings
Dooming Eye.   P. Edler
Doomsday Disciples.   D. Pendleton
Doomsday Game.   R. E. Harrington
Doomsday Ship.   J. A. Price
Doomsday Spiral.   J. Land
Doone Walk.   D. Clark
Door to December.   R. Paige
*Door with Seven Locks.   E. Wallace
*Doors.   E. Hannon
Dope King.   H. J. S. Anderton
*Dope Runners.   G. Grantham
*Doppelganger.   P. Van Greenaway
Dora, the Beautiful Dishwasher.   N.
   Albert
Doria Rafe Case.   H. Waugh
Dorothy Parker Murder Case.   G. Baxt
*Dorrington Deed Box.   A. Morrison
Dossier.   P. Salinger
*Dossier 51.   G. Perrault
Double.   B. Pronzini
*Double.   E. Wallace
*Double Agent.   G. Stackelberg
*Double-Barrelled Detective Story.   M.
   Twain
Double-Blinded.   L. A. Horvitz
Double Cross.   M. Barak
*Double Cross Purposes.   R. A. Knox
Double Cross Squadron.   W. P. Evans
Double Crossfire.   D. Pendleton
Double Crossing.   E. Holzer
Double Dare.   E. Keyes
Double Door.   E. McFadden
Double Double.   F. M. Kelsall
Double Exposure.   F. W. Culver
Double Exposure.   J. Stimson
Double Fix.   C. Lawton
Double Griffin.   P. Blake
Double Image.   R. MacDougall
*Double Indemnity.   J. M. Cain
Double Jeopardy.   C. Forbes
Double Jeopardy.   M. Underwood
*Double Life.   G. Leroux
*Double Life of Mr. Alfred Burton.   E.
   P. Oppenheim
Double Man.   W. S. Cohen
Double Muscadine.   F. O. Gaither
*Double Negative.   D. Carkeet
Double or Nothing.   C. Dekker
Double Red.   D. Jordan
*Double Take.   D. Craig
Double Take.   G. Dowling
*Double Take.   R. Huggins
*Double Take.   H. Janson
Double Trouble.   E. Lewis
Double Trouble.   J. Stratton
Doublecross Dame.   B. Banato
Doubles.   V. Mikhanovsky
Doubting Castle.   R. Kavalier
Doubting Thomas.   R. Reeves

Down Among the Dead Men.   M. Hartland
Down East Murders.   J. S. Borthwick
Down for the Count.   S. M. Kaminsky
Down Home.   G. Mettler
*Down River.   Seamark
Down the Garden Path.   D. Cannell
*Down There.   D. Goodis
Down Under and Dirty.   D. Streib
*Down Under Donovan.   E. Wallace
*Down Yonder with Judge Priest.   I. S.
   Cobb
Downtown.   C. Borelli
*Downtown Doll.   H. Janson
Dowry of Death.   M. A. Casberg
Doyle's Disciples.   B. Leuci
*Dracula.   H. Deane
Dracula.   T. J. Kelly
Dracula.   J. Mattera
Dracula.   Anne Pearson
*Dracula.   B. Stoker
Dracula Murders.   P. Daniels
*Dracula's Guest.   B. Stoker
*Dragoman Pass.   Eric Williams
*Dragon.   Jack Bennett
Dragon Harvest.   U. Sinclair
Dragon Lover.   D. Randall
*Dragon Murder Case.   S. S. Van Dine
Dragon Rising.   W. Barker
Dragon Slayings.   R. Rainey
Dragon Strike.   P. G. Browne
Dragons Can Be Dangerous.   P. Chambers
*Dragon's Claw.   P. O'Donnell
Dragon's Daughter.   C. C. Westover
Dragon's Kill.   G. Wilson
Dragonwyck.   A. Seton
*Drakov Memorandum.   J. Winters
Dram of Evil.   D. J. Olson
*Dread and Water.   D. Clark
*Dreadful Summit.   S. Ellin
Dream-Boaters.   L. Frisch
Dream of Danger.   A. Nolder
Dream of Orchids.   P. A. Whitney
Dream Park.   L. Niven
Dream Watch.   H. Way
Dreamland.   N. Thornburg
Dreams of Glory.   T. Fleming
Dreamwatcher.   T. Roszak
*Dressed to Kill.   C. Black
Dressed to Kill.   M. Logan
Drink! For Once Dead.   A. Sewart
*Drip Dry Man.   E. Lambert
*Driven to Murder.   O. Chase
*Driver.   C. B. Phillips
Driver's Seat.   M. Spark
*Drop Dead.   M. Neville
Drop Dead in Dresden.   R. Vacha
Drop Dead, Sucker!   H. Janson
Dropped Dead.   J. Ross
*Drowning Pool.   J. R. Macdonald
Drug Farm.   P. A. Foxall
Drumbuie House.   M. D. Scott
Drums of Death.   H. Reed
Drums of Dombali.   E. Phillpotts
*Drums of Fu Manchu.   S. Rohmer
*Drums of Jeopardy.   H. MacGrath
*Dublin Nightmare.   P. Loraine
Dubrovnik Massacre.   Nick Carter
Ducetti Lair.   L. Hitchcock
Duchess.   L. L. Rogger
Duchess Intervenes.   M. B. Lowndes
Duchess Laura: Some Days of Her Life.
   M. B. Lowndes
Duckett's Condor.   Roy Burns
*Duds.   H. C. Rowland
Duel for Cannons.   D. Hartman
Duel in the Dark.   Anonymous
Duel of Happiness.   H. Simart
*Duet of Death.   H. Lawrence
*Duffy.   H. J. Brown, Jr.
*Duffy.   D. Kavanagh
Duke and the Veil.   C. J. Stevermer
Dumb Man of Manchester.   B. F. Rayner
Dumb Waiter.   H. Pinter
*Dummy.   H. J. O'Higgins
Dunn's Conundrum.   Stan Lee
*Dupe.   L. Cody
Duplicate.   A. Mather
Duplicate Keys.   J. Smiley
Durian Tree.   M. Keon
Dusty Ermine.   N. Grant
Dutch Blue Error.   W. G. Tapply
Dutch Shea, Jr.   J. G. Dunne
*Dutch Shoe Mystery.   E. Queen
Dwell in Danger.   R. Lewis
Dyed for Death.   W. Rider
*Dying Alderman.   H. Wade
Dying Breath.   J. Honeywood
Dying Fall.   J. Thomson
Dying, in Other Words.   M. Gee
Dying Space.   W. B. Murphy
Dying Trade.   P. Corris
Dynasty of Power.   D. Thoreau
*Each Dawn I Die.   J. Odlum
Eagle and Unicorn.   G. Brook-Shepherd
Eagle Down.   W. Mason
*Eagle Has Landed.   J. Higgins
Eagles.   L. Orde
Eagle's Blood.   Douglas Scott

*Eagle's Eye.   W. J. Flynn
Eagle's Nest.   J. Di Mona
*Earl Derr Biggers Tells Ten Stories.
   E. D. Biggers
Earl of Chicago.   Brock Williams
Early Autumn.   R. B. Parker
Earnshaw's Evidence.   P. Bowland
*Ears of the Jungle.   P. Boulle
Earth Descended.   F. Saberhagen
Earthfire North.   Nick Carter
Earthman's Burden.   P. Anderson
Earthrace.   T. Keene
East Coast Crisis.   H. Weinstein
East Lynne.   N. Albert
East Lynne.   B. J. Burton
*East Lynne.   Mrs. H. Wood
East of Everest.   B. Langley
*Easter Dinner.   D. Downes
Easter Egg Hunt.   G. Freeman
Eastern Question.   M. Walker
*Eastward in Eden.   D. Garth
Easy Access.   R. Flanders
Easy Come, Easy Go.   O. Davis
Easy Money.   S. Koperwas
Easy Pickings.   P. A. Cruzer
Echo.   K. Jupp
Echo Chamber.   R. Himmel
*Echo of Barbara.   Jonathan Burke
Echoes from the Past.   J. M. Backer
*Echoes of Celandine.   D. Marlowe
Echoes of Innocence.   Coriola
Echoes of War.   J. Dial
Echoes of Zero.   R. H. Spencer
Eclipse.   N. Wollaston
*Ecstasy.   H. Janson
*Eddie and the Cruisers.   P. F. Kluge
Eddie Macon's Run.   J. McLendon
Edgar Allan Who--?   P. Van Greenaway
*Edge of Darkness.   B. Clemens
*Edge of Doom.   L. Brady
*Edge of Panic.   H. Kane
*Edge of Running Water.   W. Sloane
*Edge of the City.   F. Pohl
Edge of the Deep.   A. Hutton
*Edge of the Tightrope.   J. H. Drew
Edged Weapons.   W. Goldman
Editha's Burglar.   A. Thomas
*Edith's Diary.   P. Highsmith
Educated Evans.   E. Wallace
Educating of Quinton Quinn.   A. Sewart
*Edwin of the Iron Shoes.   M. Muller
Eferding Diaries.   G. Brook-Shepherd
*Eiger Sanction.   Trevanian
Eight Black Horses.   E. McBain
*Eight Faces at Three.   C. Rice
Eight Hours from England.   A. Quayle
Eight Million Ways to Die.   L. Block
*813.   M. Leblanc
*Eighth Passenger.   M. Tripp
*Eighty Dollars to Stamford.   L.
   Fletcher
Einstein Plot.   B. Heatter
Einstein's Brain.   M. Olshaker
Eisenhower Deception.   C. Egleton
Elberg Collection.   A. Oliver
Eldorado Jane.   P. Bottome
*Eldorado Red.   D. Goines
*Elegant Edward.   E. Wallace
Elegy for a Soprano.   K. N. Smith
Elementary, Mr. Dear.   Philip King
Eleni.   N. Gage
*11 Harrowhouse.   G. A. Browne
Eleventh Hour.   C. N. Gattey
*Elfrida, the Red Rover's Daughter.
   N. Buntline
Elgar Variation.   M. Kenyon
*Eliminator.   A. York
Eliza's Galiardo.   J. Gollin
*Ellery Queen, Master Detective.   E.
   Queen
Elmer.   G. Menuhin
Elusive Exile.   M. Blake
*Elusive Isabel.   J. Futrelle
Elvis Murders.   A. Bourgeau
*Embassy.   S. Coulter
Embrace of the Butcher.   Anthony Burton
Embrace the Wolf.   B. M. Schutz
Emerald.   P. A. Whitney
Emerald Illusion.   R. Bass
Emerald Pool.   M. Andrau
Emily Dickinson Is Dead.   J. Langton
Emperor's Candlesticks.   B. Orczy
*Emperor's Snuff Box.   J. D. Carr
Empire State.   E. A. Pollitz, Jr.
Empty Beach.   P. Corris
*Empty Hands.   A. Stringer
*Empty Mail Bags.   E. C. Derby
Empty Silence.   B. Copper
*Emu's Head.   C. Dawe
Enchanted Isle.   J. M. Cain
Encounter.   C. Blackstock
Encounter Group.   W. B. Murphy
End Game.   M. Gilbert
*End of It All.   J. Danvers
*End of Someone Else's Rainbow.   R.
   Rossner
*End of the Affair.   G. Greene
End of the Game.   W. B. Murphy
End of the Line.   S. O'Cork
End of the River.   B. L. Van Vors

Title Index

End on the Rocks. I. Stuart
*End Play. R. Braddon
Endgame. James Mann
*Endless Night. A. Christie
Enemy of Man. H. Janson
Enemy Outpost. J. S. Childers
Enemy Within. D. Streib
*Enforcer. W. Morgan
*England Made Me. G. Greene
English Lady. W. Harrington
Englishman's Daughter. P. Evans
*Enigma. M. Barak
Enigma Variations. B. Murphy
Enormous Dwarf. R. Francis
Entangled. P. Jason
Enter a Gentlewoman. Sara Woods
Enter Pharoah Nussbaum. T. J. Kelly
*Enter Sir John. C. Dane
*Enter the Dragon. M. Roote
Entertaining Mrs. Sloane. J. Orton
Envy of the Stranger. C. Graham
Episode on an Autumn Evening. F. Duerrenmatt
*Epitaph for a Spy. E. Ambler
*Epitaph for Love. H. Clewes
Epitaph for Poor Richard. A. S. Well
*Equal Danger. L. Sciascia
Equal Opportunity. S. Dunlap
Erasmus Magister. C. Sheffield
Erika. J. McGovern
Erin. J. Jenkins
*Erminie. M. A. Fleming
*Ernest Maltravers. E. Bulwer-Lytton
Eros at Zenith. M. Resnik
Errant Sleuth. C. Joyce
Errant Target. C. Joyce
Errant Witness. C. Joyce
*Escalation. H. Janson
Escape. J. Galsworthy
*Escape. H. Janson
*Escape. E. Vance
Escape from New York. M. McQuay
Escape from Paris. C. G. Hart
Escape from Poland. J. Tabler
*Escape of the Notorious Sir William Heans. W. Hay
Escape Route. S. Ready
Escape the Night. R. N. Patterson
Escape the Past. P. Parrish
*Escape to Athena. P. Blake
Escape to Fear. R. Foley
*Espionage. G. Marlowe
Espionage Agent. D. Clift
Ess Club. Dinsdale Walker
*Establishment. R. Moore
Esther, Ruth and Jennifer. Jack Davies
Eternal Reich. J. M. Knopp
*Eugene Aram. E. Bulwer-Lytton
*Eunich of Stamboul. D. Wheatley
*Euro-Killers. J. Rathbone
Eva. I. Melchior
*Eve. J. H. Chase
*Eve, It's Extortion. Carter Brown
Evelyn Prentice. W. E. Woodward
*Even Jericho. W. Hall
Even My Foot's Asleep. L. Payne
Ever This Night. V. De Coursey
Evered. B. A. Williams
Everglades Assault. R. Striker
Everlasting. L. Bishop
Every Creature of God Is Good. A. Gould
*Every Little Crook and Nanny. E. Hunter
*Every Night About Half-Past Eight. L. J. Beeston
Every Second Thursday. E. Page
*Everything Is Thunder. J. L. Hardy
Everything That Moves. B. Schulberg
Evidence Circumstantial. A. Sohland
Evil Always Ends. J. P. Brennan
*Evil Cargo. K. Stanton
*Evil Come, Evil Go. W. Masterson
Evil in Waiting. Renate Chapman
Evil Mark. G. Miles
Evil Men Do. B. Kiely
*Evil of the Day. T. Sterling
Evil Ones. J. Mitchell
*Evil That Men Do. R. L. Hill
*Evil Under the Sun. A. Christie
*Ex-Duke. E. P. Oppenheim
*Ex-Pugilist Detective. Old Sleuth
Excellent Mystery. Ellis Peters
Excess Baggage. H. M. Raleigh
Exchange. T. Wilden
Exchange of Clowns. T. Wilden
*Exclusive. H. Janson
Exclusive Clue. J. Aeby
Execution by Choice. D. Warbash
Execution Exchange. Nick Carter
Execution of Necome Bowles. A. Mickle
*Executioners. J. D. MacDonald
Exercise in Terror. S. M. Kaminsky
Exeunt Murderers. A. Boucher
Exhibit. L. Hollander
Exile. P. Essex
Exile. Madison Jones
Exiled. S. Greene
Exiles. R. H. Davis

*Exit Actors, Dying. M. Arnold
Exit Lines. Reginald Hill
*Exit the Body. F. Carmichael
Exit Who? F. Carmichael
Exocet. J. Higgins
Exorcist. W. P. Blatty
*Exotic Seductress. H. Janson
*Expectant Nymph. H. Janson
Expendable Man. D. B. Hughes
Experiences of a Barrister. W. Warner
*Experiences of a Lady Detective. Anonymous
*Experiences of Loveday Brooke, Detective. C. L. Pirkis
Experiment. M. Carson
*Experiment at Proto. P. Oakes
*Experiment Perilous. M. Carpenter
Experiment with Death. E. Ferrars
*Expiation. E. P. Oppenheim
Exploit of Death. Dell Shannon
*Exploits of Elaine. A. B. Reeve
Exposure of the Land Swindlers. E. C. Hall
Exterminating Angels. P. Dunant
Extra Cover. A. C. Smith
Eye. B. Pronzini
*Eye for an Eye. M. O. Rolfe
Eye for Eye. A. Kilgore
Eye in the Ring. R. J. Randisi
Eye in the Sky. P. K. Dick
*Eye of the Beholder. M. Behm
Eye of the Eagle. G. V. Basile
Eye of the Fire. J. Hild
Eye of the Mind. L. Biederstadt
Eye-Witness. L. De Francquen
Eyes of Darkness. L. Nichols
*Eyes of Laura Mars. H. B. Gilmour
Eyes of Light. A. Moore
Eyes on Utopia Murders. B. D'Amato
*Eyes That Watch You. W. Irish
Eyes Upon a Wet Grave. V. Wallace
*Eyewitness. M. Hebden
Eyewitness. J. Minahan
FBI Girl. M. Marlowe
*F.E.U.D. H. Janson
Face. Marvin Werlin
Face at the Window. F. Parrish
Face at the Window. W. D. Roberts
*Face for a Clue. G. Simenon
Face in the Leaves. R. Timperley
*Face in the Night. E. Wallace
Face of Danger. Regina Ross
Face of Death. L. Grant-Adamson
Face of Fury. P. A. Foxall
*Face of Jalanath. R. Hardy
Face That Must Die. Ramsey Campbell
Face Value. R. Ormerod
Face Value. R. Powers
*Faces in the Dark. P. Boileau
Factory. J. Lynn
Fade Out. R. Upton
*Fade to Black. R. Renaud
Fagan. P. Gravesen
Fail-Safe. E. Burdick
*Faintley Speaking. G. Mitchell
Fair. V. Andrews
Fair Cops. C. N. Gattey
Fair Friday. P. Turnbull
Fair Game. G. Hammond
*Fair Kilmeny. V. Black
*Fairly Dangerous Thing. Reginald Hill
Faith. C. Barnard
Fala Factor. S. M. Kaminsky
Falcon for the Hawks. C. Egleton
Falcon Ring. M. F. Callan
Falklands Gambit. B. Langley
Fall from Grace. M. Borgenicht
Fall from Grace. L. Collins
Fall Guy. G. Abbott
Fall Guy. N. Harman
Fall of a Saint. E. C. Scott
Fall of the House of Heron. E. Phillpotts
Fall of the House of Usher. T. J. Kelly
Fall of the Russian Empire. D. James
Fallback. P. Niesewand
Fallen Angel. A. Cohen
Fallen Angel. P. Conway
*Fallen Angel. W. Ericson
*Fallen Angel. M. Holland
*Fallen Sparrow. D. Hughes
*Falling Angel. W. Hjortsberg
Falls the Shadow. E. Litvinoff
False Alibi. C. Thornton
False Claim. B. Wayde
False Colors. M. Borgenicht
*False Evidence. E. P. Oppenheim
*False Face. L. Edgley
False Faces. L. J. Vance
False Inspector Dew. P. Lovesey
False Prophets. S. Flannery
False Witness. D. Uhnak
Falseface. M. Sharp
Familiar Spirits. L. Tourney
Family Affair. M. G. Eberhart
Family Business. V. Patrick
Family Linen. L. Smith
Family Money. Doris Shannon
Family of Strangers. D. Winston
Family Passions. B. Aswad

Family Reunion. Joyce Harrington
*Family Skeleton. D. M. Disney
Family Skeletons. D. Hartman
Family Trade. James Carroll
Famine. G. Masterton
Famous Last Words. T. Findley
*Fan. B. Randall
*Fan Fare. H. Janson
Fandango Involvement. T. Mahon
Fandom Is a Way of Death. B. Warren
*Fanny. H. Janson
Fantastic Saint. L. Charteris
*Fantasy and Fugue. R. Fuller
Fantoccini. W. L. Gibson-Cowan
*Fantomas. P. Souvestre
Far Away Man. W. Marshall
Far Cry. M. Stewart
Far Horizon. B. Copper
*Far Place. B. Fuller
Far Side of Fear. B. Copper
*Far Wandering Men. J. Russell
Faraday's Flowers. T. Kenrick
Faraway Drums. J. Cleary
*Farewell, My Lovely. R. Chandler
*Farewell, Nikola. G. Boothby
Farewell Performance. E. P. Lehman
Farm Boy. M. Skedgell
Farmhouse by the Sea. Joyce Bell
Farndale Avenue Housing Estate Townswomen's Guild Dramatic Society Murder Mystery. D. McGillivray
*Fast Buck. H. Janson
*Fast Company. Marco Page
*Fast Man with a Dollar. R. Avery
Fast Track. C. A. Harris
Fastburn. D. Pendleton
Faster We Life. B. Brennan
Fat Cat Affair. K. Hagenbach
Fatal Attraction. Craig Jones
Fatal Beauty. J. Godey
Fatal Equilibrium. M. Jevons
Fatal Errand. J. Pattinson
Fatal Finish. M. D'Alton
Fatal Flourishes. S. S. Rafferty
Fatal Friend. B. Falkson
Fatal Lady. J. West
Fatal Obsession. S. Greenleaf
Fatal Odds. J. Halkin
*Fatal Request. A. L. Harris
Fatal Resemblance. Old Sleuth
Fatal Run. Ernest Clark
Fatal Shadow. G. Black
Fatal Shadows. E. S. Lockwood
Fate Accompli. H. P. Raimes
Fate of Mary Rose. C. Blackwood
Fate Worse Than Death. S. Radley
Fate Worse Than Death. D. Weed
*Fated Five. G. Biss
Fateful Summer. V. Johnston
Fault Tree. M. Friedman
Faust of the F.B.I. J. Mack
Faustian Pact. A. Beevor
Favilla. T. J. Corr
Favor. N. Guild
*Faxon Secret. J. Ware
*Fazackerley's Millions. F. Crisp
*Fear. T. Keneally
Fear for the Hero. K. Welsh
*Fear Fortune, Father. S. B. Hough
*Fear in a Handful of Dust. J. Ives
*Fear Is the Key. A. MacLean
Fear Itself. S. Kanfer
*Fear Makers. D. Teilhet
Fear No Evil. J. G. Davis
*Fear No More. L. Edgley
*Fear of Heights. V. Coffman
Feared and the Fearless. Guthrie Wilson
Feast of Vultures. P. G. Scott
Feast of Vultures. C. Weissner
*Feathered Serpent. E. Wallace
*Federal Bullets. G. F. Eliot
Feed Store Mystery. H. Reed
Feet of a Snake. B. Chubin
*Fell of Dark. Reginald Hill
Fellowship of Fear. A. J. Elkins
*Fellowship of the Frog. E. Wallace
Felony Report. E. Linington
Female Detective. C. H. Hazlewood
Female--Handle with Care. P. Chambers
*Fengriffin. D. Case
*Fennister Affair. Josephine Bell
Fenris Option. R. D. Jones
*Fenton Affair. R. Quest
*Fer-de-Lance. R. Stout
Ferret. G. Markstein
Fertig. S. Yurick
Festival. N. J. Crisp
Fete Fatale. R. Barnard
Fever. R. Cook
Fever Tree. R. Mason
Fever Tree. R. Rendell
Fiddle City. D. Kavanagh
Fiddle o' Dreams. A. Morrison
Fiddler's Green. E. K. Gann
Fidelio Affair. H. Green
Field of Blood. G. Seymour
Field of Night. R. W. Krepps
*Fields of Eden. M. T. Hinkemeyer
Fields of Heather. A. Hunter

Fieldwork. M. Danielle
Fiery Menace. K. Robeson
*Fifth Ace. D. Grant
Fifth Angel. D. Wiltse
Fifth Hostage. T. Strong
*5th of November. M. Franklin
Fifth Sally. D. Keyes
Fifth Wheel. B. Heron-Maxwell
*Fifty Candles. E. D. Biggers
Fifty-First. M. Stewart
Fifty Million Hijack. A. Cecil
*Fifty Roads to Town. F. Nebel
*Fifty-Two Pickup. E. Leonard
Fig Connection. J. Franzen
*Fight to a Finish. W. G. Forbes
*Fighting Against Millions. Nicholas Carter
*Fighting an Unknown Power. W. G. Forbes
Fighting Edge. W. M. Raine
*Fighting for a Fortune. Old Sleuth
*Fighting His Way. Old Sleuth
Fighting Irish. Steve White
*File No. 113. E. Gaboriau
*File of the Golden Goose. J. Watson
Files of Ms. Tree. M. A. Collins
*File on Devlin. C. Gaskin
*Filibuster's Warning. G. Jerome
*Filly Wore a Rod. H. Janson
Filthy Rich. K. Colquhoun
*Final Act. C. Hudson
Final Act. M. Spicer
*Final Count. H. C. McNeile
Final Cut. P. Chais
Final Doors. J. L. Hensley
Final Exam. G. Meyer
*Final Fair. M. Blair
Final Landscapes. K. Keller
*Final Night. R. Gaines
Final Safari. P. Ordway
Final Throw. M. Gilbert
Final Trace. B. R. Boylan
*Final Triumph. Old Sleuth
Final Witness. R. W. Swaybill
Finally, Sunday! C. Williams
Find Me a Villain. M. Yorke
Find the Girl. S. Ready
*Find the Innocent. R. Vickers
*Find the Woman. G. Burgess
*Find the Woman. A. S. Roche
Finders Weepers. M. Byrd
Fine. S. Shem
Fine and Private Place. J. Simpson
*Fine Pair. C. Stratton
*Finger to Her Lips. E. Berckman
Fire and Ice. R. Harding
Fire and Maneuver. D. Stivers
*Fire-Bomb Jack. Old Sleuth
Fire Down Below. N. Mastorakis
Fire Falcon. D. Hart-Davis
*Fire Flingers. W. J. Neidig
Fire Like the Sun. M. Bond
*Fire Rock. J. Wood
*Fireball. H. Janson
Firefly Gadroon. Jonathan Gash
*Firefox. C. Thomas
*Fireman Hot. C. J. C. Hyne
Fireman, Save My Child! N. Albert
Fireprint. G. Jenkins
Fires of Heaven. B. M. Miller
Fires of Paris. Zachary Hughes
*Firestarter. Stephen King
Firestorm. C. D. Peel
Firewind. H. Searls
Firing Squad. J. Barnett
First and Last Murder. R. Leigh
First Blood. D.Morrell
First Born. C. Thompson
*First Deadly Sin. Lawrence Sanders
First Directive. J. McNamara
*First Gravedigger. B. Paul
First Hit of the Season. J. Dentinger
*First Law. G. Willets
First Loyalty. R. Lourie
First Person Paramount. A. Pratt
*First Train to Babylon. M. Ehrlich
First You Have to Find Him. E. K. Goldthwaite
Fish Story. R. Hoyt
*Fit to Kill. H. C. Owen
*Five Against the House. J. Finney
Five Bright Stars. E. Lambert
Five Crooked Chairs. F. Wells
*Five Fragments. G. Dyer
Five in Judgment. Douglas Taylor
Five Little Rich Girls. C. Harrison
Five O'Clock Lightning. W. L. DeAndrea
Five Ports to Danger. V. Connolly
Five Rings of Fire. D. Stivers
Five Rivers to Death. M. A. Casberg
Five Star Final. L. Weitzenkorn
Five Tales. J. Galsworthy
*5000 Trojan Horses. L. T. White
Fix. A. Capelli
Fjord of Silent Men. P. L. Brown
Flag for Sunrise. R. Stone
Flair for Affairs. H. Brand
Flame from Persepolis. J. Griffin
Flaming Forest. J. O. Curwood
Flamingo. J. Gardner

Flanagan Boy. M. Catto
Flander's Folly. S. Christy
*Flash Casey, Detective. G. H. Coxe
*Flash of Green. J. D. MacDonald
Flashpoint. M. Duke
*Flashpoint. H. Janson
*Flashpoint. G. La Fountaine
*Flat 2. E. Wallace
Flaw in the System. R. B. Dominic
Flawless. B. Hirschfeld
*Flesh of the Orchid. J. H. Chase
Flesh Wounds. D. Pendleton
Fleshwound. F. W. Belland
*Fletch. G. McDonald
Fletch and the Man Who. G. McDonald
Fletch and the Widow Bradley. G. McDonald
Fletch Won. G. McDonald
Fletch's Moxie. G. McDonald
Flex. M. Rubel
Flight 800. D. Fulani
Flight from Fear. M. Blake
*Flight from Fear. H. Janson
Flight Hostess. E. Thorne
*Flight into Danger. J. Castle
Flight 902 Is Down! H. Fishman
Flight of a Dragon. L. R. Bobker
*Flight of a Fallen Angel. D. Winston
Flight of the Archangel. I. Holland
Flight of the Phoenix. J. Rosenberger
*Flight of the Phoenix. E. Trevor
Flight to the Sea. J. Pattinson
Flittermouse. D. Kartun
*Floating Dutchman. N. Bentley
Floating Fancies Among the Weird and Occult. C. H. Holmes
Floating on an Ice Cloud. N. Gulliver
Flood. A. H. Vachss
Floodgate. A. MacLean
*Floods of Fear. J. Hawkins
Floosie Goes Astray. W. Standish
Floosie on the Spot. W. Standish
Floosie Passes By. W. Standish
Floosie Takes a Fall. W. Standish
*Florentine Dagger. B. Hecht
Florida Burn. S. Grave
Florida Firefight. C. Ramm
Florida Is Closed Today. J. D. Hunter
*Flower of Desire. H. Janson
Flowers for the Executioner. B. Tebeira
Flowers from Berlin. N. Hynd
Fly Away Home. M. Percy
Fly Away, Jill. M. Byrd
Fly Away, Paul. V. Canning
Fly Paper. M. A. Collins
*Flying Fifty-Five. E. Wallace
*Flying Squad. E. Wallace
Flying to Nowhere. J. Fuller
Flynn's Inn. G. McDonald
*Fog. V. Williams
*Fog of a Killer. B. Graeme
*Poiling a Counterfeiter. E. C. Derby
*Follow, As the Night. P. McGerr
*Follow the Leader. J. Logue
*Follow the Little Pictures. A. Graham
Follow the Sharks. W. G. Tapply
Follower. H. Bromell
Follower. S. Gallagher
*Following Ann. K. R. G. Browne
Fool for Murder. M. Babson
*Fool Killer. H. Eustis
*Foolish Virgin Returns. N. Karta
Foolproof. P. Daniels
Fool's Blooding. P. Pike
Fool's Flight. W. B. Murphy
*Fool's Gold. D. Hitchens
Fool's Gold. W. B. Murphy
Fool's Mate. Ritchie Perry
Fool's Mercy. H. Allen
*Fool's Parade. D. Grubb
Footnote to Murder. L. A. Taylor
*Footsteps in the Dark. G. Heyer
*Footsteps in the Night. C. Fraser-Simpson
For Her C-h-e-ild's Sake. P. Loomis
*For Her to See. J. Shearing
For Love and Duty. E. Garth-Thornton
For Love of Audrey Rose. F. De Felitta
*For Love of Her. G. Boothby
*For Pete's Sake. B. Street
For Reasons of State. A. Beevor
For Special Services. J. Gardner
*For the Defense. F. Hume
For the Silverfish. R. Thurston
*For Them That Trespass. E. Raymond
*Forbidden Garden. U. Curtiss
Forbidden Love. C. May
Forbidden Places. M. Napier
*Forbidden Territory. D. Wheatley
*Force 10 from Navarone. A. MacLean
Forced Landing. T. H. Block
*Foreign Harry Complot. G. Hertz
Forest. J. Wainwright
Forest of Fear. A. G. Bennett
Foretelling. C. Crane
*Forger. E. Wallace
Forger's Wife. J. Lane
Forgotten Mission. G. Leodas
*Formula. G. Sager
*Formula. S. Shagan

Forsaking All Others. J. Breslin
Fort Apache, the Bronx. H. Gould
Fortress London. Z. Hughes
Fortunate Mistress. D. Defoe
*Fortune Is a Woman. Winston Graham
Fortunes and Misfortunes of the Famous Moll Flanders. D. Defoe
*48 Hours. H. Janson
*Forty-Eight Short Stories. E. Wallace
Forty-Minute War. J. Morris
*Forty Whacks. G. Homes
Foul Matter. J. Aiken
*Foul Play. C. Reade
*Foul Play. J. C. Rogers
Foul Shot. D. Hornig
Foul Up. Ritchie Perry
Found Money. G. A. Birmingham
*Founder Member. J. Gardner
*Four Boys and a Gun. W. Wiener
*Four Days' Wonder. A. A. Milne
*4.50 from Paddington. A. Christie
*Four Green Fish. E. Jepson
*Four Just Men. E. Wallace
*Four Men and a Prayer. D. Garth
Four Plays for Course Actors. M. Green
*Four Square Jane. E. Wallace
Four Walls. D. Burnet
Fourth Angel. R. Hunter
Fourth Arm. J. Brason
Fourth Deadly Sin. Lawrence Sanders
Fourth Down, Death. M. T. Hinkemeyer
Fourth Protocol. F. Forsyth
Fourth Shot. L. C. Balling
*Fourth Wall. A. A. Milne
Fowlhaven Werewolf. V. Andrews
Fox from His Lair. John Harris
Foxhole. K. Blake
Foxhole in Cairo. L. O. Mosley
*Fragment of Fear. J. Bingham
*Frails Can Be So Tough. H. Janson
Frame and Fortune. H. Janson
*Framed. H. Janson
France Security. S. Gandolfi
*Franchise Affair. J. Tey
Frankenstein. D. Campton
Frankenstein. V. Gialanella
*Frankenstein. T. J. Kelly
Frankenstein. J. Mattera
Frankenstein. A. Nowlan
*Frankenstein. Mary Shelley
Frankenstein. P. Webling
*Frantic. N. Calef
Fraternity of the Stone. D. Morrell
Fraudulent Broad. J. L. Rubel
*Fraulein. J. McGovern
Freak. M. Collins
Freak Show Murders. Fredric Brown
Fred in Situ. G. Hammond
Free Agent. F. Wakeman
Free Draw. S. Singer
*Free Fall. J. D. Reed
Free Fall in Crimson. J. D. MacDonald
Free Range Wife. M. Kenyon
*Freebie and the Bean. P. B. Ross
*Freedom Trap. D. Bagley
Freefall Factor. T. Geraghty
Freelance Spy. J. M. Walsh
Freemartin. D. K. Cohler
Freemason. J. P. Hart
Freeze-Frame. A. Hansl
*French Connection II. R. Moore
French Deal. W. Hughes
French Entrapment. N. Cort
*French Key. F. Gruber
French Ordinary Murder. R. Harrison
*Fresh Waters. R. W. Child
Friday Is a Killing Day. J. A. Howard
Friends. T. Hauser
*Friends. H. Herlin
Friends in High Places. J. Weitz
*Friends of Eddie Coyle. G. V. Higgins
*Frightened Child. D. Lyon
*Frightened Lady. E. Wallace
Frightened Stiff. K. Roos
Frisco Blues. G. De Marco
Frisco Rock. L. O'Brien
*Frogman Assassination. J. Seward
From a High Place. E. Mathis
*From Cuba with Love. Gordon Davis
*From Despair to Triumph. W. G. Forbes
From Eternity to Here. M. Sellers
From Hex to Hemlock. E. Harris
From Love's Ashes. F. P. Stratham
*From Now On. F. Packard
*From Russia with Love. I. Fleming
*From Satan, with Love. V. Coffman
From the Grave to the Cradle. C. Joyce
*From the Valley of the Missing. Grace M. White
*From This Dark Stairway. M. G. Eberhart
From Thunder Bay. A. Maling
From Violent Men. D. Curzon
Front Man. M. Sellar
Frontier Detective. L. D. Willoughby
Frost at Christmas. H. D. Wingfield
*Fruit of the Poppy. R. Wilder
Fugitive Feet. R. Burroughs
Fugitive Three. G. A. McPherson
*Fugitives. W. Hackett

Title Index

*Full Circle. H. Cecil
Full Contact. R. J. Randisi
Full Cry. T. Tone
*Full Treatment. R. S. Thorn
*Fun City. H. Barron
Funeral Games. J. Orton
*Funeral in Berlin. L. Deighton
Funeral of Gondolas. T. Holme
Funeral Sites. Jessica Mann
Funhouse. O. West
Funny Place to Hold a War. John Harris
*Fur-Bringers. H. Footner
Furioso. V. Lestienne
*Furious Old Women. L. Bruce
Furnished Room. L. Del Rivo
*Furtive Flame. H. Janson
*Fury. J. Farris
Fury Bombs. G. Wilson
*Fury on Sunday. R. Matheson
Fuse. T. Keene
*Fuzz. E. McBain
GG-2 Deception. C. R. Duggan
"G-Men." H. K. Long
*G-String Murders. G. R. Lee
*Gabriel Comes to 24. R. Braddon
Gabriel Set-Up. P. O'Donnell
Gabrielle's Way. A. Hunter
Gallegher. R. H. Davis
Gallows Land. B. Pronzini
*Gambit. K. Lane
Gamble with Hearts. A. Carlyle
Gamblers. C. Klein
*Gambler's Girl. J. Matcha
Gambler's Girl. J. Tanner
*Gambler's Syndicate. Nicholas Carter
Game. G. Hammond
*Game for Three Losers. E. Lustgarten
Game for Vultures. M. Hartmann
*Game of Liberty. E. P. Oppenheim
Game of Soldiers. J. Shannon
*Game of Terror. J. Messmann
*Game of X. R. Sheckley
Game, Set and Danger. A. Clarke
Gameplan. L. Waller
*Games. H. Ellson
*Games of Choice. M. Gee
Games to Keep the Dark Away. M. Muller
Gammon. S. Bosak
Gamov Factor. D. Bannerman
*Gang That Couldn't Shoot Straight. J. Breslin
Gangster Chronicles. M. Lasker
Gants. R. K. Abshire
Garb of Truth. I. Stuart
Garbage Collector. A. M. Stein
*Garden Murder Case. S. S. Van Dine
Garden of Cucumbers. P. Tyler
Garden of Malice. S. Kennedy
Garden of the Sun. Joyce Bell
*Gas. B. Hirschfeld
*Gas Light. P. Hamilton
*Gate of Sinners. Mrs. C. Kernahan
Gates of Doom. E. J. Jenkinson
Gates of Life. B. Stoker
Gateway. J. Jenkins
Gatherer. O. Brookes
*Gathering of Eagles. E. Lindall
Gathering of Ghosts. R. Lewis
Gathering Place. J. L. Breen
Gathering Storm. G. Glennon
*Gauntlet. M. Butler
*Gay Adventures. W. Hackett
Gay Detective. L. Rand
Gay Little Woman. J. S. Winter
*Gay Lord Waring. H. Townley
Gaynor's Passion. N. Garbo
Gaza Intercept. H. Hunt
*Gazebo. A. Coppel
Gemini. Domini Taylor
*Gemini Contenders. R. Ludlum
Gemini Man. S. Kelly
*Gemini Revenged. C. Hunt
Gemini Rising. J. S. Filbrun
*General Died at Dawn. C. G. Booth
*General Goes Too Far. L. Robinson
Generous Death. N. Pickard
Genesis Experiment. M. Carson
Geneva Accord. J. Whitman
Geneva Crisis. M. Golan
Geneva Touch. L. Hitchcock
Geneva Transfer. F. Geron
Genteel Little Murder. P. Daniels
Gentle Betrayal. L. Erickson
*Gentle People. I. Shaw
Gentleman's Fate. K. U. P.
Gently Between Tides. A. Hunter
Gently into Night. K. Coffaro
Geoffrey Hamlyn. H. Kingsley
*George and Georgina. E. Phillpotts
Georgie's Broads. J. C. Ryer
Georgina and Georgette. M. Hutton
Get Going Sister! D. Hudsen
*Get-Rich-Quick Wallingford. G. R. Chester
Get Smart. Mel Brooks
Get This Straight. C. Borelli
*Getaway. L. Charteris
*Getaway. J. Thompson
Getting a Way with Murder. R. McInerny

Getting Away with Murder. A. D. Burke
Getting Away with Murder. A. Morice
Ghost Breaker. C. W. Goddard
*Ghost in the Bank of England. Anonymous
Ghost Lover. D. M. Clausen
Ghost of a Chance. K. Roos
Ghost of an Idea. M. Challis
Ghost of Sherlock Holmes. L. Halliwell
Ghost of Staghorn. Auriel Douglas
Ghost of Veronica Gray. K. Eulo
Ghost on the Loose. A. M. Halff
Ghost Stories and Tales of Mystery. J. S. Le Fanu
*Ghost Train. A. Ridley
Ghost Trap. B. Woffington
Ghost Walks. W. E. Wright
Ghost Way. T. Hillerman
Ghostly Passenger. M. Crosby
*Ghosts Never Die. R. Heed
Ghost's Retreat. C. R. Averell
*Ghoul. F. King
*Giant Athlete. Old Sleuth
Giant Detective. Old Sleuth
*Giant Detective Among the Italian Brigands. Old Sleuth
Giant Killer. T. Hyman
*Gideon's Day. J. J. Marric
*Gideon's Force. W. V. Butler
Gideon's Law. W. V. Butler
Gideon's Way. W. V. Butler
Gift Horse. M. McMullen
Gift of Evil. E. K. Buzzelli
*Gift of Murder. G. Batson
*Gift Supreme. G. A. England
Gilded Canary. B. Latham
Gilded Frame. M. Ashton
Gillian's Chain. M. S. Craig
Ginger Flower. H. L. Stuart
Gipsy Queen's Vow. M. A. Fleming
Giri. M. Olden
Girl at Sea. A. Hunt
*Girl by the Roadside. V. Vanardy
*Girl Called Fathom. L. Forrester
Girl from Addis. T. Allbeury
Girl from Paris. J. Aiken
*Girl from the East. D. Whitelaw
Girl from Yesterday. Wade Wright
*Girl Hunters. M. Spillane
*Girl in Hand. H. Janson
*Girl in His House. H. MacGrath
*Girl in the Cage. B. Benson
Girl in the Dark. A. Hunt
*Girl in the News. R. Vickers
Girl Like Wigan. J. F. Leeming
*Girl, the Gold Watch, and Everything. J. D. MacDonald
Girl Who Was Clairvoyant. M. Warner
*Girl Who Wasn't There. W. D. Roberts
Girl Who Wouldn't Talk. R. Vickers
Girl with a Symphony in Her Fingers. M. G. Coney
Girl with the Bright Head. R. Leigh
Girl with the Golden Yo Yo. E. Schiddel
*Girl with the Green Eyes. M. Leblanc
*Girl with the Key. M. K. Simmons
*Girl with the Long Green Heart. L. Block
Girls in Bondage. P. Caval
Girls on the Row. P. Banks
Gironde Incident. M. Hughes
Give Me Liberty. J. Kent
Given Day. R. Van Gulik
Giver of Song. S. M. Singer
Glacier Run. P. Barstow
Gladiator-at-Law. F. Pohl
Glamour. C. Priest
*Glass Bottom Boat. B. Street
*Glass Cage. L. Ronns
*Glass Cell. P. Highsmith
*Glass Cipher. P. Winston
Glass Highway. L. D. Estleman
*Glass Key. D. Hammett
Glass Zoo. J. McNeish
*Glendower Legacy. T. Gifford
Glitter Dome. J. Wambaugh
*Glitterburn. H. Gould
Glitz. E. Leonard
Globe Probe. H. Janson
Glorious Morning, Comrade. M. Gee
Glory Hand. P. Boorstin
Glory Hole Murders. T. Fennelly
*Glory Thrown In. E. Lambert
Glowing Emeralds. F. I. Bennett
*Glyphs of Gold. P. Edwards
Go Die in Afghanistan. S. Jason
*Go to Thy Death Bed. S. Forbes
Go West, Inspector Ghote. H. R. F. Keating
*Go with a Jerk. H. Janson
Goblin Tree. R. Anzelon
Goblins. K. Robeson
God Project. J. Saul
God Squad Bod. M. Kenyon
*Goddess Game. H. Barron
Goddess of Death. M. Underwood
Goddess on the Gate. A. McKenna
*Godfather. M. Puzo
Godfires. W. Hoffman
Godplayer. R. Cook

*God's Clay. A. Askew
God's Pocket. P. Dexter
God's Prodigal. A. J. Russell
Gods, the Little Guys and the Police. H. Costantini
*Godsend. B. Taylor
Godwin Sideboard. J. Malcolm
Going Crooked. Winchell Smith
Going for the Gold. E. Lathen
*Going, Going, Gone. C. Hale
Going Solo. M. Tripp
*Going West. J. Potter
*Gold Bag. C. Wells
Gold Brick Cassie. D. G. Loth
Gold Coast. E. Leonard
*Gold Coast Nocturne. H. Nielsen
Gold Deadline. H. Resnicow
Gold Frame. H. Resnicow
Gold Hunters. J. O. Curwood
Gold Key. C. Payton
*Gold Maker's Secret. E. C. Derby
Gold Shield. M. Castoire
Gold Solution. H. Resnicow
Golden Ballast. A. Hodgson
Golden Bull. Nick Carter
*Golden Clew. B. Wayde
*Golden Corn. C. Rodda
Golden Creep. G. Bagby
Golden Earrings. Y. Foldes
Golden Express. D. Lambert
Golden Eyes. C. Gale
*Golden Gate. A. MacLean
Golden Heel. W. Neubauer
Golden Heron. H. Borrie
Golden Idol. H. J. S. Anderton
Golden Kangaroo. A. Pratt
*Golden Keel. D. Bagley
*Golden Kill. M. Olden
*Golden Land. B. L. Farjeon
Golden Lion and the Sun. Y. Hamizrachi
Golden Man. P. K. Dick
Golden Man. K. Robeson
Golden Master. W. B. Gibson
Golden Passage. J. Savage
Golden Pin. H. Seymour
*Golden Rain. D. Clark
*Golden Rendezvous. A. MacLean
Golden Sabre. J. Cleary
*Golden Salamander. V. Canning
Golden Snare. J. O. Curwood
*Golden Stag. B. Heatter
Golden Triangle. P. McCurtin
Golden Venture. J. S. Fletcher
*Goldfinger. I. Fleming
Goldilocks. Sheila Johnson
*Goldilocks. E. McBain
Goldship. F. Ross
Goliath. W. J. Weatherby
Gondola Scam. Jonathan Gash
Gone to Her Death. P. Audemars
Good Bad Man. H. Reed
Good Death. P. Ross
*Good Evans! E. Wallace
Good for One More Ride. W. I. Frank
*Good Guys Wear Black. M. Franklin
Good Old Stuff. J. D. MacDonald
Good Terrorist. D. Lessing
*Goodbye Charlie. M. H. Albert
Goodbye, Chicago. W. R. Burnett
Goodbye Goliath. E. Chaze
*Goodbye Piccadilly, Farewell Leicester Square. A. La Bern
Goodhues of Sinking Creek. W. R. Burnett
Goods. Arthur Douglas
Goosefoot. P. McGinley
*Gorilla. R. Spence
Gorky Park. M. C. Smith
Gotham Gore. S. Jason
Gourmet. J. Nisbet
Governess. E. Hervey
*Government Spy. L. Carlton
*Government Trust. B. Wayde
*Government's Man. E. C. Derby
Grace for the Dead. D. E. Fisher
*Gracie Allen Murder Case. S. S. Van Dine
Graffiti. P. Van Greenaway
*Grand Babylon Hotel. Arnold Bennett
Grand Cayman Slam. R. Striker
*Grand Central Murder. S. MacVeigh
*Grand Duke's Finances. F. Heller
Grand Jury. R. Liebman
*Grand National Night. D. Christie
Grandmaster. W. B. Murphy
*Grape Vine. H. Janson
Grass. P. Nash
Grass and Supergrass. P. Nash
Grass in Idleness. P. Nash
Grass Makes Hay. P. Nash
Grass Rain. E. Garrigues
Grass Widow. H. Janson
Grass Widow. R. McInerny
Grass's Fancy. P. Nash
Grave for a Russian. C. G. Vance
Grave Goods. Jessica Mann
Grave Without Flowers. M. McMullen
Grave Witness. P. Levi
Gravedigger. Joseph Hansen
Graves in Academe. S. Kennedy

G

Graveyard of My Own. R. Goulart
Graveyard Plots. B. Pronzini
Graveyard Shift. U. Curtiss
*Gravy Train Hit. Curtis Stevens
Gray Dawn. S. E. White
*Gray Mask. W. Camp
Gray Monk Walks. G. Reed
*Great Awakening. E. P. Oppenheim
Great Crime of Grapplewick. E. Sykes
Great Diamond Robbery. J. Minahan
*Great Dinosaur Robbery. D. Forrest
Great Divide. F. M. Robinson
*Great Enigma. Nicholas Carter
Great Fog and other weird tales. H. F. Heard
Great Free Enterprise Gambit. J. Barr
Great Gamble. Anonymous
*Great Gay Road. T. Gallon
*Great Gorme. C. Cairns
*Great Hotel Murder. V. Starrett
Great Hotel Robbery. J. Minahan
*Great Impersonation. E. P. Oppenheim
*Great K&A Train Robbery. P. L. Ford
Great Mine Mystery. F. Farrar
*Great Pebble Affair. M. Shelby
*Great Prince Shan. E. P. Oppenheim
*Great "Push" Experiment. A. Pratt
*Great Railway Mystery. Anonymous
*Great Train Robbery. M. Crichton
Greek Fire. J. Kirton
Greek Girl. Dorothea Bennett
Greek Position. R. Roderick
Greek Revival. F. Haring
Greek Summit. Nick Carter
Green Archer. T. J. Kelly
Green Bushes. O. Allan
Green Bushes. J. B. Buckstone
*Green Cloak. Y. Davis
Green Drift. J. Lymington
Green Fancy. G. B. McCutcheon
Green Fire. F. Jameson
*Green for Danger. C. Brand
Green Frontier. J. B. Hilton
*Green God. F. A. Kummer
Green Grow the Dollars. E. Lathen
Green Hell. P. McCurtin
*Green Ice. G. A. Browne
Green King. P. L. Sulitzer
*Green Lady. L. Ellis
*Green Orchard. A. Soutar
*Green Pack. E. Wallace
*Green Ribbon. E. Wallace
*Green Rust. E. Wallace
*Green Seal. C. E. Walk
*Green Shadow. J. E. Grant
Green Tea. J. S. Le Fanu
Green Trigger Fingers. J. Sherwood
*Greene Murder Case. S. S. Van Dine
*Greensea Island. V. Bridges
*Greenstone Door. W. Satchell
Greenstone Griffins. G. Mitchell
*Grell Mystery. F. Froest
Grey Beginning. B. Michaels
*Grey Timothy. E. Wallace
*Grif. B. L. Farjeon
*Griffin Towers. J. Winslow
*Grifters. J. Thompson
Grim Discovery. T. E. B. Clarke
Grip. J. S. Winter
*Grip of the Strangler. J. C. Cooper
Grizzly Trail. G. Moffat
Groomed for Murder. V. Rhodes
Ground Zero. R. Cox
Growing Concern. I. Stuart
Grub-and-Stakers Move a Mountain. A. Craig
Grub-and-Stakers Quilt a Bee. A. Craig
Grumpy. H. Hodges
Guardian Angel. A. Cohen
Guardians. R. Austin
Guardians of the Prince. Reginald Hill
Guerrilla Games. G. Wilson
Guilt with Honour. J. Ashford
*Guilty, But--. S. Kyle
*Guilty Bystander. Wade Miller
Guilty Conscience. H. O. Cooke
Guilty Conscience. R. Levinson
*Guilty Man. P. Coppee
Gulag War. J. Hild
Gulf Scenario. R. Bulliet
*Gumshoe. N. Smith
Gun for Hire. J. Sherman
*Gun for Sale. G. Greene
*Gun Moll for Hire. H. Janson
*Gun-Runner. A. Stringer
Gunmen Die Hard. D. Rogan
*Gunner. E. Wallace
Gunner Kelly. A. Price
Guns of Heaven. P. Hamill
*Guns of Navarone. A. MacLean
Gunship. J. J. Savarin
*Gunsmoke in Her Eyes. H. Janson
Gwen-Amyia. D. Le Litt
Gwen John Sculpture. J. Malcolm
H-Bomb for Alice. I. Stuart
Hadleigh Inheritance. A. Hunt
Hag Wood. J. Shrog
Hahnemann Sequela. H. King
Hailstone. T. Baxter
Hair of the Sleuthhound. J. L. Breen

Halcyon Way. M. McShane
*Half a Chance. F. S. Isham
"Half a Truth." Rita
Half-Mother. E. Tennant
*Halloween. C. Richards
Halloween II. J. Martin
Hallowing. F. Yariv
Halo for a Lady. B. Schwarz
*Hammer the Toff. J. Creasey
Hammered Gold. W. O. Johnson
*Hammerhead. J. Mayo
Hammerhead Reef. D. Pendleton
*Hammett. J. Gores
Hamptons. L. Harris
*Hand Me a Crime. C. M. Russell
Hand Me a Fig. J. H. Chase
Hand of Death. M. Yorke
Hand of Fate. M. Underwood
Hand of Glass. Jennie Melville
*Hand of Peril. A. Stringer
*Hand of Solange. M. Rippon
*Hand of the Spoiler. S. Paternoster
*Hand on the Window Sill. B. Wayde
Hands of a Stranger. R. Daley
Hands of Death. D. Winston
*Hands of Healing Murder. B. D'Amato
*Hands of Orlac. M. Renard
*Hands of the Ripper. E. S. Shew
Handyman. G. Suster
Hang Glider. P. Somerville-Large
Hang Loose. B. Copper
Hang Me in Hong Kong. E. Norman
Hang the Consequences. M. R. D. Meek
Hanged Man. Douglas Scott
*Hanging Captain. H. Wade
Hanging Doll Murder. R. Ormerod
Hanging On. D. R. Koontz
Hanging Tree. B. Knox
Hangman's Harvest. Austin Stone
Hangman's Row. A. M. Stein
*Hangover Murders. A. Hobhouse
*Hangover Square. P. Hamilton
Hanky Panky. L. Jarreau
Hanneman's War. T. Hauser
Hanoi Hellground. J. Lansing
*Hans, Who Goes There. F. Helitzer
*Happening. E. Curry
Happiest Ghost in Town. L. Malloy
Happy Are the Meek. A. Greeley
Happy Chase. Mountford Williams
Happy Man. E. C. Higgs
*Harassed Hero. E. Dudley
Hard Bargains. J. Grady
Hard-Boiled. R. DiChiara
Hard Cash. M. A. Collins
Hard Cash. C. Reade
Hard Contact. B. Copper
Hard Knocker's Luck. W. Murray
Hard Line. M. Z. Lewin
*Hard Man. L. Katcher
Hard Men. A. Kilgore
Hard Money. M. M. Thomas
Hard Rain. N. Hartley
Hard Trade. Arthur Lyons
Hard Way. J. Ahern
Hardball. D. Hornig
Hardcover. W. Warga
Hardman. D. Karp
Harem Games. E. Tokson
Harms Way. C. Aird
*Harness Bull. L. T. White
Harper's Folly. M. Aylward
Harper's Luck. M. Aylward
Harrier! D. MacKenzie
Harry and the Bikini Bandits. B. Heatter
Harsh Evidence. P. Fry
Hart to Hart. R. Bowdler
Harvest Hell. G. Wilson
*Hasty Wedding. M. G. Eberhart
Hatchet Men. D. Hartman
*Hate. H. Janson
Hate Is Thicker Than Blood. B. Latham
*Hate Ship. B. Graeme
*Hatter's Ghosts. G. Simenon
*Haunt of the "Queer" Makers. L. Carlton
*Haunted Honeymoon. J. Troy
*Haunted House. A. Bernede
*Haunted House. O. Davis
*Haunted Light. E. Price
*Haunted Monastery. R. Van Gulik
*Haunted Pajamas. F. P. Elliott
Haunted Theatre. J. Randall
Haunting at Lost Lake. E. Oliphant
*Haunting of Hill House. S. Jackson
Have a Nice Night. J. H. Chase
Have You Seen My Son? J. Olsen
*Having Wonderful Crime. C. Rice
Hawaiian Takeover. D. Streib
Hawk Island. H. I. Young
*Hawk of Rede. H. Harding
Hawk's Nest. W. Gunning
Hawksmoor. P. Ackroyd
Hawthorn Conspiracy. S. Hesla
*Hazard. R. Chanslor
He Died with His Eyes Open. D. Raymond
He Done Her Wrong. S. M. Kaminsky
*He Fell Down Dead. V. Perdue
*He Ran All the Way. S. Ross

*He Was Found in the Road. A. Armstrong
Head Case. L. Cody
Head of State. R. Hoyt
Head On! J. W. Thomas
Headcrash. W. H. Baker
*Headed for a Hearse. J. Latimer
Headhunter. M. Slade
Heading West. D. Betts
Headless Man. K. Robeson
Heads. D. Osborn
Heads You Lose. R. Gillespie
Healing Heart. Magali
Healthy Body. G. Linscott
Hear the Children Cry. R. J. Hendrickson
*Hearse. H. Clement
*Hearse of a Different Color. M. Constiner
*Hearses Don't Hurry. S. Ransome
Heart of Deception. C. Jauniere
*Heart of the Matter. G. Greene
Heart of the North. W. B. Mowery
Heart of Winter. J. J. Toombs
Heart Payments. G. J. Goldberg
*Heartache. H. Janson
Heartbeat. J. Jenkins
Heartland. D. Hagberg
Heartland. K. Heelan
Heartless Light. G. Green
*Hearts by the Tower. O. Sinclair
Hearts of Gold. C. Sinclair
Hearts of Gold and Hearts of Steel. H. Herman
Hearts of Stone. G. A. Larson
Heart's Revenge. C. Jauniere
Heat. W. Goldman
Heat. E. McBain
Heat from Another Sun. D. L. Lindsay
*Heat of the Sun. M. Birmingham
Heat of Winter. H. Hirt
*Heat's On. C. Himes
*Heberden's Seat. P. Clark
*Heed the Thunder. J. Thompson
Heel of Spring. F. Rooney
Heirloom. W. Haggard
Heirs of the Kingdom. K. Hudner
*Heisters. R. P. Jones
*Helga's Web. J. Cleary
Hell Bent for Heaven. S. O'Cork
Hell Brood. H. Janson
*Hell House. R. Matheson
*Hell Is a City. W. Ard
*Hell Is a City. M. Procter
*Hell Is Empty. J. F. Straker
Hell Is Forever. J. L. Gilmer
*Hell Is Sold out. M. Dekobra
Hell Let Loose. A. Carson
Hell Nest. M. Mandell
Hell of a Dame. H. Janson
*Hell of a Woman. J. Thompson
*Hell on Friday. W. Bogart
Hell on Wheels. A. Lassiter
Hellbinder. D. Pendleton
Hellbomb Theft. J. Rosenberger
Hellbound. S. Brandon
Hellcat. H. Janson
Hellcat. M. Logan
*Helldorado. H. Janson
*Hello Summer, Goodbye. M. G. Coney
Hellrider. D. Kellerman
*Hell's Angel. H. Janson
*Hell's Belles! R. Drayton
*Hell's Belles. H. Janson
Hell's Hostages. L. Derrick
*Hell's Our Destination. G. Brewer
Hellstar. J. M. Reaves
Help the Poor Struggler. M. Grimes
Hemlock Option. M. Vinter
*Henrietta Who. C. Aird
"Henry." M. A. Kay
Hephzibah. S. M. Stratham
Heptameron. H. Phillips
Her Fatal Beauty. W. Braun
Her Fatal Sin. M. E. Holmes
Her Mad Marriage. G. M. White
*Her Weapon Is Passion. H. Janson
Herald. M. Shaara
Hercule Poirot's Casebook. A. Christie
Here Be Monsters. A. Price
Here Comes Trouble. B. Channing
Here I Stay. B. Michaels
Here Lies Gloria Mundy. G. Mitchell
Here to Get My Baby Out of Jail. L. Shivers
Here Today. Z. Fairbairns
Here Today, Dead Tomorrow. E. Lewis
Here's Luck. S. F. Whitman
Heritage. P. Driscoll
Heritage. L. Orde
Heritage of Shadows. M. Brent
*Hermit of Turkey Hollow. A. Train
*Hero. P. Haining
Hero and the Terror. M. Blodgett
*Hero at Large. A. J. Carothers
Hero in His Time. A. A. Cohen
Heroes. D. Hagberg
Heroes No More. J. Wainwright
*Heroes of Yuca. Michael Barrett
Heroin Annie. P. Corris
*Hickey and Boggs. P. Rock

Title Index

Hidden. H. C. Armstrong
Hidden Agenda. A. Porter
*Hidden Chapel. L. Ames
Hidden Faces. P. May
Hidden Fires. Laura Jordan
*Hidden Flame. R. Dowling
Hidden Man. M. Underwood
Hidden Meanings. M. Snelgrove
Hidden Player. A. Noyes
Hidden River. R. Goertz
Hidden River. S. Jameson
Hidden Scar. J. R. Adamson
Hidden Spring. C. B. Kelland
*Hidden Target. H. MacInnes
Hide and Go Die. Nick Carter
Hide and Seek. L. Havard
Hide and Seek. L. Maracotta
*Hideaway. N. Content
*Hideaway. F. Nichols
Hideout. S. Markham
Hiding Places. R. Berliner
High Adventure. D. E. Westlake
*High Anxiety. R. H. Pilpel
*High Ballin'. Richard Robinson
*High Bright Sun. I. S. Black
*High Class Swindler. Old Spider
*High Commissioner. J. Cleary
High Crimes. W. Deverell
*High Game. P. Geddes
*High Hand. J. Futrelle
High Midnight. S. M. Kaminsky
*High Pavement. E. Bonett
*High Requiem. D. Cory
High Road. A. C. Martens
*High Road to China. J. Cleary
*High School Confidential. Morton Cooper
*High Sierra. W. R. Burnett
*High Speed. C. H. Stagg
High Spirits. J. Payn
High Stand. H. Innes
High Tide. A. F. Daniels
High Wall. A. R. Clark
*High Window. R. Chandler
*High Wray. K. Hughes
Highly Explosive Case. P. Chambers
*Hijacked. D. Harper
*Hilary. J. Jenkins
*Hilary's Terms. H. Janson
*Hill Is Mine. M. Walsh
*Hill of Ashes. L. Ames
*Hillman. E. P. Oppenheim
Hills of Homicide. L. L'Amour
Hindsight. P. Dickinson
*Hiroshima Reef. E. Lambert
His Best Girl. M. Bardon
*His Bones Are Coral. V. Canning
*His Father's Wife. D. Keene
*His First Offense. J. S. Clouston
*His Last Bow. A. C. Doyle
*His Last Vow. J. Ruyle
His Lordship's Arsenal. Christopher Moore
His Majesty's Agent. D. Shahar
*His Natural Life. W. Clarke
His One Talent. H. Bindloss
*His Robe of Honor. E. Dorrance
History and Remarkable Life of the Truly Honourable Col. Jacque. D. Defoe
*Hit and Run. J. H. Chase
Hit and Run. D. Klein
*Hit and Run. R. Marshall
Hit Girl. A. Johns
Hit Parade. R. Rainey
Hit Them Where It Hurts. J. H. Chase
Hitch-Hike Murders. M. Bryson
Hitler's Bomb. C. Scott
Hitler's Daughter. T. B. Benford
Hitler's Diaries. R. Hugo
Hobbema Prospect. J. B. Hilton
Hoffman File. B. Utermahlen
Hogan's Last Case. W. Charles
*Holcroft Covenant. R. Ludlum
*Hold Everything. D. Linton
Holding Pattern. Alistair Hamilton
*Holiday Express. J. J. Farjeon
Hollow Men. S. Flannery
*Hollow Triumph. M. Forbes
Hollow Vengeance. A. Morice
Hollywood Hell. D. Pendleton
Hollywood Wives. J. Collins
Hollywood Troubleshooter. W. T. Ballard
Holy Secrets. S. Shubin
*Holy Terror. L. Charteris
Home. D. Lippincott
*Home at Seven. R. C. Sherriff
Home Before Dark. E. Bassing
Home for the Heart. H. Goodwin
Home Sweet Home. R. J. Jensen
*Home Sweet Homicide. C. Rice
Homecoming. J. Pattinson
Homicide Sanitarium. Fredric Brown
Honestly, Now! J. Sharkey
Honey Drop That Weed. J. Kellan
*Honey for Me. H. Janson
Honey for the Bears. A. Burgess
Honey Seems Bitter. B. Kiely
*Honey, Take My Gun. H. Janson
Honeybuzzard. A. Carter
Honeycomb Bid. B. Sandberg

*Honeymoon Caper. J. Pattinson
*Honeymoon Killers. Paul Buck
Honor Bound. R. Harris
*Honorable Gentleman. A. Abdullah
*Honorary Consul. G. Greene
Honourable Bill. F. Russell
Honours Easy. R. Pertwee
Hood. D. Scannell
Hoodman's Bait. J. Bogar
Hoodoo Horror. S. Jason
*Hoods. H. Grey
*Hoods Take Over. O. Demaris
Hoodwink. B. Pronzini
Hoof. P. McCutchan
Hook. B. Copper
Hook. A. Page
Hooky Goes to Blazes. L. Meynell
Hooligans. W. Diehl
Hooray for Homicide. James Anderson
*Hopscotch. B. Garfield
*Hornet's Nest. B. Soutar
*Hornet's Nest. Mrs. W. Woodrow
Horror High. T. J. Kelly
Horror in Hawaii. M. I. H. Rogers
*Horses Head. E. Hunter
*Host of Extras. J. Leasor
*Hostage. C. Henry
Hostage. R. T. Stevens
*Hostage Tower. J. Denis
Hostaged Island. D. Stivers
*Hostages. S. Heym
*Hostile Witness. J. Roffey
Hot Car. L. Cameron
*Hot House. H. Janson
*Hot Ice. R. J. Casey
Hot Ice. L. Grex
*Hot Ice. R. D. Steeley
*Hot Line. J. Bruce
*Hot Line. H. Janson
Hot Money Can Cook Your Goose. J. M. Glazner
Hot Rain. C. Lewis
*Hot Rock. D. E. Westlake
*Hot Rod Gang Rumble. M. Dolinsky
Hot Time in Old Town. M. McQuay
*Hotsy, You'll Be Chilled. H. Janson
Hound of Heaven. G. Wright
*Hound of the Baskervilles. A. C. Doyle
Hounds of Spring. A. Lawman
Hour of the Assassins. A. Kaplan
Hour of the Clown. A. Aricha
Hour of the Dog. B. Mather
Hour of the Gaucho. B. Langley
*Hour of the Oxrun Dead. C. L. Grant
Hour of the Scorpion. Anthony Taylor
Hour of the Unicorn. J. Parish
*House. H. Lawrence
*House by the River. A. P. Herbert
House in Marsh Road. L. Meynell
House in the Hollow. E. Lockwood
*House of a Thousand Candles. M. Nicholson
House of Assignation. A. Robbe-Grillet
*House of Cards. S. Ellin
House of Cards. L. Garfield
House of Care. W. J. Burley
House of Crystal. H. Kades
*House of Dark Shadows. Marilyn Ross
*House of Dr. Edwardes. F. Beeding
*House of Evil. C. Lipman
House of Exile. J. E. Coyne
*House of Fear. W. Camp
*House of Fendon. R. Bridges
House of Gair. E. Linklater
House of Ghosts. W. B. Gibson
House of Glass. M. Marcin
House of Green Dragons. Rosa Hill
*House of Marney. J. Goodwin
House of Mist. M. L. Bombal
House of Montague. T. Lee
*House of Numbers. J. Finney
*House of Secrets. S. Horler
*House of Secrets. S. Noel
*House of Shade. M. M. Kaye
House of Shadows. A. Adams
House of Silence. D. Streib
*House of Strangers. Jennifer Hale
*House of the Arrow. A. E. W. Mason
*House of the Lost Court. D. T. De Savallo
House of the Roses. C. Baker
*House of the Seven Flies. V. Canning
*House of the Spaniard. A. Behrend
House of Thunder. L. Nichols
*House of Whipplestaff. E. F. Boyd
House of Whispering Aspens. A. Ainsley
*House of Whispers. W. Johnston
*House on Lily Street. J. Vance
House on Octavia Street. J. La Tourrette
House on Plymouth Street. U. Curtiss
*House on the Cliff. G. Batson
*House on the Marsh. F. Warden
*House Opposite. J. J. Farjeon
House That Jack Built. E. Dewhurst
*House Without a Key. E. D. Biggers
*House Without the Door. E. Daly
Housebound. W. Appel
Housekeeper's Daughter. D. H. Clarke
Houston Attack. C. Ramm

How German Is It. W. Abish
How Green Was My Apple. M. Lovell
*How to Murder Your Wife. H. Williams
*How to Steal a Million. Michael Sinclair
How to Trap a Crook. J. Symons
*Howling. G. Brandner
*Howling II. G. Brandner
Howling III. G. Brandner
*Hoyland Intervenes. P. C. Williams
*Hoyland Steps Out. P. C. Williams
Hub. R. Herring
Human Factor. E. S. Gardner
*Human Factor. G. Greene
*Human Factor. S. Quinn
Hundred and First. K. Cameron
*Hungry One. G. Brewer
*Hungry Sea. L. Ames
Hunt for Red October. T. Clancy
*Hunted. E. Leonard
Hunted Down. R. A. Wainwright
Hunted Woman. J. O. Curwood
Hunter. R. Busby
Hunter. Nick Carter
Hunter. J. Maudsley
Hunter. E. Sauter
*Hunter. R. Stark
Hunter and the Ikon. E. Sauter
Hunter and the Raven. E. Sauter
Hunter Equation. H. Gibbons
Hunter Squadron. R. Jackson
*Hunter's Moon. N. Benchley
Hunter's Orange. R. Lundeen
Hunting of Mr. Exe. J. N. Chance
*Hunting Party. J. Millard
Hunting Season. J. K. Mayo
*Huntingtower. J. Buchan
*Huntress. H. Footner
Hurricane Season. M. Friedman
Hurricane Squadron. R. Jackson
*Husband of the Corpse. M. Judd
Hush Money. M. A. Collins
Hush Little Baby. J. Miller
Hush, Winifred Is Dead. A. P. Johnson
Hushabye Death. A. Wood
Hyde and Seek. B. Wolff
Hyde in Deep Cover. B. Wolff
Hyde Park Murder. E. Roosevelt
Hydra. A. Heal
Hypocrite. W. Le Pretre
*I Am the Cat. R. Kutak
I Am Vidocq. V. McConnor
I, Anna. E. Lewin
I Cover the Waterfront. Max Miller
IFO Report. T. J. Sagnier
*I for Intrigue. H. Janson
I Give You Five Days. C. Curzon
*I Hate Actors. B. Hecht
I Hate Thee. M. Baroni
*I Killed the Count. A. Coppel
*I Like It Tough. J. A. Howard
I Like My Women Tough. W. Standish
*I Love You Again. O. R. Cohen
*I Married a Dead Man. W. Irish
I Met Murder. E. Ferrars
I Ring Doorbells. R. Birdwell
I, Said the Sparrow. M. Murphy
*I Saw Him Die. J. Drummond
*I Should Have Stayed Home. H. McCoy
I Speak for the Dead. J. J. Maloney
I Spy, You Die. Hosanna Brown
*I Start Counting. A. E. Lindop
*I Thank a Fool. A. E. Lindop
*I, the Jury. M. Spillane
*I Wake Up Screaming. S. Fisher
I Want a Nurse. J. Randall
I Want to Go to Moscow. M. Duffy
I Will Be Faithful. K. Shepard
I Will Kill. C. Borelli
I Wish He Would Not Die. J. Aldridge
*I Would Rather Stay Poor. J. H. Chase
*I Wouldn't Be in Your Shoes. W. Irish
Icarus Seal. C. Hyde
Icarus Threat. H. McLeave
Ice. E. McBain
Ice Castles. E. Wolfe
Ice Cathedral. G. Leonard
*Ice-Cold in Alex. C. Landon
Ice Cold Kill. D. Pendleton
Ice in Her Eyes. L. Como
Ice Pick. J. Baldwin
Ice Planet. P. Casciani
Ice Raid. R. Cox
*Ice Station Zebra. A. MacLean
Icebound. R. Spencer
Icebreaker. J. Gardner
Icefire. R. C. Wilson
Icekill. P. Lund
Icepick. A. Fletcher
Ideal Crime. J. Ashford
*If I Die Before I Wake. Sherwood King
If I Should Die. M. R. Henderson
If I Should Die. A. Sewart
If I Should Die Before I Wake. J. A. Potter
If It Weren't for Sex...I'd Have to Get a Job. James Burke
If Sherlock Holmes Were a Woman. T. J. Kelly
*If the Shroud Fits. K. Roos

If There Be Thorns. V. C. Andrews
If Tomorrow Comes. Sidney Sheldon
If Truth Be Known. P. Werner
If You Believe the Soldiers. A. Cordell
*If You Can't Be Good. R. Thomas
*If You Have Tears. J. Evans
Ikon. G. Masterton
I'll Be Wearing a White Carnation. J. Miller
*I'll Get You For This. J. H. Chase
*I'll Never Tell. R. Vickers
*I'll Say She Does. P. Cheyney
Illegal Entry. R. Hayes
Illusion. M. Warner
*Illustrious Corpse. T. Thayer
*Illustrious Prince. E. P. Oppenheim
Image of Evil. W. Beechcroft
*Image of the Beast. P. J. Farmer
Images of Death. Lawrence Williams
Immediate Action. R. Neebel
Immediate Release. W. Mathewson
Imp. A. Neiderman
Imperator Plot. S. G. Spruill
Imperfect Imposter. N. Venner
*Imperfect Lover. R. Gore-Brown
Imperial Express. J. Bellah
Impersonal Attractions. S. Shankman
*Imposter. H. McCloy
*Impromptu Imposter. V. Vicas
*In a Glass Darkly. J. S. Le Fanu
*In a Lonely Place. D. B. Hughes
In a Place Dark and Secret. J. Finch
In a Turkish Garden. A. B. Gwyn
In Any Case. R. G. Stern
In Calvert's Valley. M. P. Montague
*In Case of Emergency. G. Simenon
*In Cold Blood. T. Capote
*In Dark Places. J. Russell
In Dread of the Law. A. Adderley
*In Extremis. Mrs. Greenough
In for a Penny. D. Mardon
In for the Kill. D. Benfield
*In Full Cry. Richard Marsh
In Her Garden. J. Godden
*In His Grip. D. C. Murray
In Honour Bound. H. Seymour
In Justice's Prison. R. Thurston
*In League with the Counterfeiters. E. C. Derby
*In Like Flint. B. Street
*In My Father's Den. M. Gee
In Place of Reason. John Fraser
In Safe Hands. J. Capperton
In Safe Hands. J. Sandford
In Search of Eagles. C. Sloan
In Search of Enemies. J. Stockwell
In Shadows. T. Janeschutz
In Strict Confidence. B. M. Forester
*In Terror's Grasp. Warren Miller
In That Rich Earth. A. Sewart
In the Bishop's Carriage. M. Michelson
In the Bleak Midwinter. Jean Fraser
In the Blood. R. L. Duncan
*In the Blood. A. Soutar
*In the Dark. S. Horler
In the Days of My Youth. A. B. Edwards
In the Enemy Camp. R. L. Duncan
In the Face of the Enemy. Douglas Scott
*In the Fog. R. H. Davis
*In the Heat of the Night. J. Ball
In the Heat of the Summer. J. Katzenbach
In the Hollow of Her Hand. G. B. McCutcheon
In the House of Night. W. B. Huie
In the Long Run We Are All Dead. M. Wolfson
In the Next Room. R. E. Belmont
In the Night. J. Sutherland
In the Nude. R. Seth
*In the Secret Vault. B. Wayde
*In the Shadow. Old Spicer
In the Shadow of Death. G. Campbell
In the Shadow of Kings. N. Kelly
*In the Shadow of the Hills. G. C. Shedd
In the Shadow of the Wind. A. Hebert
*In the Wake of a Stranger. I. S. Black
In the Wink of an Eye. K. Cherry
In What Strange Land? P. Very
Inca File. J. Rosenberger
Inca Gold. N. Johnson
Inca Gold Hijack. L. Derrick
*Incendiary Blonde. K. Edgar
*Incense of Death. N. Deane
Incomer. G. Gaunt
Inconvenient Corpse. P. Daniels
Incredible Murder of Cardinal Tosca. A. Nowlan
Indecent Relations. K. R. McKay
Indemnity Only. S. Paretsky
*Independent Witness. H. Cecil
*India-Rubber Men. E. Wallace
Indian Wants the Bronx. I. Horovitz
Indigo. N. Carnac
*Inevitable Millionaires. E. P. Oppenheim
Inference of Guilt. H. Greene
Infernal Desire Machines of Doctor Hoffman. A. Carter

*Infernal Idol. H. Seymour
Infiltrator. M. Hughes
Infiltrator. H. Janson
Infiltrators. D. Hamilton
*Informer. L. O'Flaherty
Ingram Intervenes. A. Michaelis
Inheritor. M. Z. Bradley
Initiation. W. W. Johnstone
Inner Ring. M. Gagnon
*Innocence of Father Brown. G. K. Chesterton
Innocent. Josephine Bell
*Innocent Bystander. B. Frost
*Innocent Bystanders. J. Munro
Innocent Deception. L. Shaw
Innocent Madness. D. Hollyock
*Innocent Murderers. W. Johnston
*Inquest. M. Barringer
Inside Out. W. Hughes
Inside Out! G. Ludlow
*Inside the Lines. E. D. Biggers
Insider Out. C. Hudson
Inspector. J. De Hartog
*Inspector Calls. J. B. Priestley
*Inspector Henderson, the Central Office Detective. H. I. Hancock
Inspector Saito's Small Satori. J. Van De Wetering
*Intent to Kill. M. Bryan
*Intent to Murder. L. Sands
Intercept. N. Morrison
*Interference. R. Pertwee
Interrupted Wedding. L. T. Barnard
Interventions. P. Breslin
Intimate Kill. M. Yorke
Intimate Stranger. W. Lynch
*Into the Jaws of Death. W. G. Forbes
Into the Maze. D. Stivers
Intruder. T. Altman
Intruder. M. K. Lawrence
*Intruder in the Dust. W. Faulkner
*Invasion. H. Janson
*Invasion. J. Wallace
Invasion U.S.A. J. Frost
Investigation. E. Saunders
*Invisible Assassins. D. Pendleton
*Invisible Boarder. J. Davis
*Invisible Image. F. Chabrey
Invisible Line. V. C. Chadwick
*Invitation to a Murder. Rufus King
Invitation to Danger. D. Mai
*Ipcress File. L. Deighton
Iranian Hit. D. Pendleton
Irene, Good Night. D. R. Bensen
Iris, the Bewitched. K. Kimbrough
Irish Game. J. R. Lowell
Irish Holidays. R. Thynne
Irish Signorina. J. O'Faolain
*Iron Chalice. O. R. Cohen
*Iron Grip. E. Wallace
Iron Web. K. Crowder
Ironman. D. Stivers
*Ironsides Sees Red. V. Gunn
*Irralie's Bushranger. E. W. Hornung
Is There Any Body There? P. Sneal
Isaac Quartet. J. Charyn
Island Deathtrap. D. Pendleton
Island in the Sun. A. Waugh
Island Intrigue. P. McAdam
Island of Crimea. V. Aksyonov
Island of Fear. F. Bream
*Island of Intrigue. I. Ostrander
*Island of Terror. E. W. Strother
Island of the Damned. J. Rosenberger
Isobel. J. O. Curwood
*Israel Rank. R. Horniman
Istanbul Decision. Nick Carter
It. R. Hawkey
*It Always Rains on Sunday. A. La Bern
It Can't Be My Grave. S. F. X. Dean
It Is Never Too Late to Mend. C. Reade
It Leads to Murder. Wade Wright
It Never Comes Easy. W. Newton
*It Shouldn't Happen to a Dog. E. Lanham
*It Wasn't Me! I. Jefferies
*Italian Job. T. K. Martin
*It's a Sin. H. Zore
*It's Alive. R. Woodley
*It's Always Eve That Weeps. H. Janson
*It's Bedtime, Baby! H. Janson
It's Hard to Be a Russian Spy. A. Korotykov
It's Never Too Late to Mend. O. Harper
Ivory Slave. A. Hutton
*Ivory Snuffbox. A. Fredericks
J.B.'s Daughter. J. Sherlock
Jacintha. S. Hylton
*Jack and Gil. Old Sleuth
Jack and Susan in 1953. M. McDowell
Jack and the Beanstalk. E. McBain
*Jack Chanty. H. Footner
Jack Lane's Browning. D. Gethin
*Jack o'Judgment. E. Wallace
*Jack O'Lantern. G. Goodchild
*Jack Sheppard. W. H. Ainsworth
Jack Spot. J. B. Buckstone
*Jack Spot. H. Janson
Jack the Juggler's Ordeal. Old Sleuth
Jack the Knife. O. Tupper

*Jack the Ripper. S. James
Jack the Ripper. R. Pember
Jackal Helix. G. V. Basile
Jackey. A. J. Palmerio
Jackie. S. Ready
Jack's Mother. Anonymous
*Jack's Return Home. Ted Lewis
*Jacoby's First Case. J. C. S. Smith
Jacqui. P. Loughran
Jade Dragon. W. B. Gibson
*Jade Lizard. Taffrail
Jade Tiger. C. Thomas
Jail Bait. P. Chambers
Jakarta Coup. M. K. Roberts
*Jamaica Inn. D. Du Maurier
*James Bond and Moonraker. C. Wood
*James Bond, the Spy Who Loved Me. C. Wood
Jane. P. Bottome
*Jane with Green Eyes. H. Janson
Janell. J. Jenkins
Janitor. J. Minahan
*Janson, Go Home. H. Janson
Janus Murder Case. C. Wilson
Jassy. N. Lofts
Java Edge. J. E. Newton
Java Sea Mystery. F. Nunn
Jaws That Bite, the Claws That Catch. M. G. Coney
*Jazz Jungle. H. Janson
Jealousy. E. Walter
*Jeanne of the Marshes. E. P. Oppenheim
Jeff Clayton's Masked Foe. W. Ward
Jekyll and Hyde. L. H. Caddy
Jericho Rumble. C. Murphy
Jerry Abershaw. Anonymous
Jerusalem Conspiracy. I. McFarlane
Jerusalem Inn. M. Grimes
*Jewel of the Seven Stars. B. Stoker
Jewel Robbery. L. Fodor
Jeweled Eye. D. Clark
Jewelled Belt. P. E. Quinn
*Jews Without Jehovah. G. Kersh
Jian. E. V. Lustbader
*Jigsaw Man. Dorothea Bennett
Jihad. G. Clarkson
*Jim Hanvey, Detective. O. R. Cohen
Jim the Penman. C. L. Young
*Jimmy the Kid. D. E. Westlake
Jiu San. K. Robeson
"Joan Danvers." F. Stayton
*Joe Phoenix, Private Detective. A. W. Aiken
*Joe Phoenix, the Police Spy. A. W. Aiken
John Heriot's Wife. A. Askew
*John Needham's Double. J. Hatton
*Johnny Belinda. E. B. Harris
JoJo and the Private Eye. L. Malloy
Joker in a Stacked Deck. J. Shelynn
*Jokers. M. Sands
*Jolly Jess. Old Sleuth
Jonah. J. Herbert
Jonah Kit. I. Watson
Jones '38. D. Ogden
*Journey into Fear. E. Ambler
Journey of Fear. C. Jauniere
*Journey to Romance. L. Ames
Journey Toward Death. A. Aricha
*Journeying Boy. M. Innes
*Joy House. D. Keene
*Joyous Adventures of Aristide Pujol. W. J. Locke
Judas Code. D. Lambert
Judas Figures. A. E. Lindop
Judas Kiss. V. Holt
Judas Scrolls. J. Rosenberger
*Judge and His Hangman. F. Duerrenmatt
Judgement by Fire. T. Philo
Judgement Day. P. G. Winslow
*Judgement in Stone. R. Rendell
Judgement Postponed. G. Wark
Judge's Story. C. Morgan
*Jugger. R. Stark
Juggernaut. D. Bagley
*Juggernaut. A. Campbell
*Juggernaut. A. Hine
*Juice. S. Becker
Juice Town. D. Owen
*Julia. P. Straub
Julie. A. L. Stone
"Juliet." Anonymous
Juliet Bravo. Mollie Hardwick
July 7th. J. McCorkle
Jump for Glory. G. McDonnell
Jumpers. T. Stoppard
Jumpin' Jupiter. K. Gordon
Jumping Double. C. E. Sayers
Jumpmaster. H. R. Simpson
Jungle. M. Brett
Jungle Blitz. L. Derrick
*Junk Market. H. Janson
Junk on the Hill. J. Pikser
Juror. H. Jacobs
*Jury. G. Bullett
Juryman. F. Galbally
Just Another Day in Paradise. A. E. Maxwell
Just Before Dawn. D. Shields
Just Causes. M. McConnell

*Just Let Me Go. J. Cleary
Just Like a Dame. W. Standish
Justice. J. Galsworthy
Justice. G. Simenon
Justice by Fire. D. Stivers
*Justin Bayard. J. Cleary
*Juvenile Jungle. F. Counsel
KGB Directive. R. Cox
K605. C. Clarke
*Ka of Gifford Hillary. D. Wheatley
Kago. C. Wood
Kahawa. D. E. Westlake
*Kak-Abdullah Conspiracy. M. Macao
Kalahari. P. McCurtin
*Kaleidoscope. M. Avallone
Kali Death Cult. Nick Carter
Kamal. D. Arathorn
Kamchatka Incident. R. L. McKinney
Kansas. J. Springs III
Karate Killers. D. Streib
Karlyn. J. Jenkins
Karma. S. Dunlap
Karpov's Brain. W. G. Green
Katana. G. MacBeth
*Kate Plus Ten. E. Wallace
Katie. M. McDowell
Katie's Terror. D. E. Fisher
Kavalu Lion. J. Pattinson
Kay Assignation. H. Janson
Kazan. J. O. Curwood
Keep. F. P. Wilson
Keeper of the Waters. M. Roberts
Keepers of the Secret. Barnaby Conrad
Keepers of the Walls. F. D. Richardson
Keepsake. P. Huson
Kelleway's Luck. R. Richmond
*Kelly. E. Lambert
*Kennedy for the Defense. G. V. Higgins
*Kennel Murder Case. S. S. Van Dine
Kensei. S. Schlossstein
Kensington Gore. P. Fox
*Kenyatta's Escape. A. C. Clark
*Kenyatta's Last Hit. A. C. Clark
Kessler. J. Brason
Kew for Murder. C. Cruikshank
Key. R. Flanders
Key Largo. M. Anderson
*Key to Murder. Stewart Burke
*Key to Nicholas Street. S. Ellin
*Key to Yesterday. C. N. Buck
Key West Connection. R. Striker
*Key Witness. F. Kane
Keys of Death. G. Sims
Keys to Billy Tillo. E. Blau
Keystone. P. Lovesey
Khamsin. M. Portugali
*Kick-In. W. Mack
Kickback. A. Harrell
Kidd. T. Seligson
Kidnap. P. Bowland
Kidnap Hotel. S. Andrews
*Kidnapped for Revenge. G. M. White
Kidnapped Millionaire. R. A. Wainwright
*Kidnapping of the President. C. Templeton
Kiev Footprint. C. A. Posey
*Kilbourne Connection. G. D. Larsen
Kill. D. Heyes
Kill. A. Ryan
Kill and Tell. W. X. Kienzle
Kill Factor. R. Harper
Kill Fee. P. Baul
*Kill Her If You Can. H. Janson
*Kill Her with Passion. H. Janson
Kill Hitler. M. Stall
*Kill Kissinger. G. De Villiers
*Kill Me for Kicks. H. Janson
Kill Me Gently, Darling. B. Faith
Kill Me in Roppongi. E. Norman
Kill Me Quick. M. Mwangi
Kill Me Softly. E. King
Kill School. D. Stivers
Kill the Beloved. L. Kauffman
Kill the Bull! J. Breslin
*Kill This Man. H. Janson
Kill Your Darlings. M. A. Collins
Kill Zone. L. D. Estleman
Killbride Mystery. K. M. Harwell
Killed in the Act. W. L. DeAndrea
*Killed in the Ratings. W. L. DeAndrea
Killed on the Ice. W. L. DeAndrea
Killed with a Passion. W. L. DeAndrea
Killer. H. Janson
Killer Back Stage. J. Willard
*Killer Bait. D. Linton
Killer Budgies. M. Harding
Killer Came Naked. J. Tanner
Killer Cops. E. D. Krell
*Killer Elite. R. Rostand
*Killer Inside Me. J. Thompson
Killer Instinct. M. Mandell
*Killer Is Loose. G. Brewer
Killer Passion. J. Stark
Killer Patrol. G. Fennell
Killer Stalk. V. Robinson
Killer Virus. P. Kirk
Killer's Caress. C. Moran
*Killers Must Eat. M. O'Brine
*Killers Play Rough. A. Ring
Killer's Rights. N. Hamilton

Killing a Mouse on Sunday. E. Pressburger
Killing Anniversary. I. St. James
Killing Circle. C. Wiltz
Killing Cold. T. Wood
Killing Connection. D. Hartman
Killing Doll. R. Rendell
Killing Eyes. J. Miglis
*Killing Frost. M. Catto
Killing Frost. C. Leach
Killing Game. R. Faust
Killing in Antiques. B. Knox
Killing Mask. M. Stall
Killing Matter. P. Mallory
*Killing No Murder. H. Shaw
Killing of Quemada. M. Cronin
Killing of Yesterday's Children. M. S. Power
Killing Orders. S. Paretsky
Killing Pace. L. H. Whitten
Killing Peace. J. Whitman
Killing Time. J. T. Crawford
Killing Time. W. B. Murphy
Killing Trade. W. Boyles
Killing Trade. M. Judge
Killing Wonder. D. Bryant
*Kind Lady. E. Chodorov
*Kind of Justice. E. Lindall
Kind of Treason. G. MacBeth
Kindness of Dr. Avicenna. J. Pearson
Kindness of Strangers. B. Taylor
Kindness of Strangers. P. G. Winslow
King, Bishop, Knight. R. Emmett
*King Blood. J. Thompson
King Cobra. W. C. Mathews
*King Dan, the Factory Detective. G. W. Goode
King in Yellow. E. A. St. George
King Jaguar. D. Sherman
*King Murder. C. R. Jones
*King of Anarchists. B. Wayde
King of Kingston. Steve White
King of Terror. K. Robeson
King of the Golden Valley. A. Scholefield
*King of the Khyber Rifles. T. Mundy
King of the Mountain. A. Lassiter
King of the Roses. U. S. Andersen
Kingdom Come. M. Pye
*Kingdom of Johnny Cool. J. McPartland
*Kingfisher Scream. A. Fox
*King's Castle. L. Ames
King's Commissar. D. Kyle
King's Friends. J. Tucker
Kings in the Counting House. H. Mitgang
*King's Ransom. E. McBain
Kingsley, the Detective. Old Sleuth
Kingsley's Touch. J. Collee
Kingsroads Legacy. D. Kamm
Kiss a Stranger. G. Finley
Kiss and Kill. R. W. Porter
*Kiss Before Dying. I. Levin
*Kiss Me, Deadly. M. Spillane
Kiss Michelle Goodbye. Carter Brown
Kiss Mommy Goodbye. J. Fielding
*Kiss of Death. L. P. Bachmann
*Kiss of Death. E. Lipsky
*Kiss of Death. F. Scarpetta
Kiss of Judas. R. A. Scotti
Kiss of the Raven. J. Cox
Kiss on Each Cheek. D. De Simone
*Kiss the Blood Off My Hands. G. Butler
*Kiss Tomorrow Goodbye. H. McCoy
*Kitten with a Whip. Wade Miller
Kitten's Necklace. K. O'Neill
Kleber Flight. H. Koning
Klondike Kalamity. G. Peterson
*Klute. W. Johnston
Knife. V. Wallace
*Knife Is Dangerous. C. Jay
Knight Must Fall. T. Wender
Knight on the Bridge. W. Watson
Knight Rider. G. A. Larson
*Knight's Gambit. W. Faulkner
Knights of the Limits. B. Bayley
Knock on Any Door. M. Motley
*Knock-Out. H. C. McNeile
*Knock Three-One-Two. Fredric Brown
Knock Twice. H. J. Greenwald
Knocknagow. C. Kickham
Knotted Skein. C. A. Neggers
Known Homosexual. J. Colton
Knuckle. D. Hare
Kolwezi. Ritchie Perry
Konigsberg Assignment. D. Kydd
Korean Combat. R. Jackson
Korean Killground. G. Wilson
*Kosygin Is Coming. T. Ardies
*Kramer Project. R. A. Smith
Kremlin Conspiracy. H. Hunt
Kremlin Control. O. Sela
Kremlin Correction. J. Evans
Kremlin Directive. J. Midgley
Kremlin Kill. Nick Carter
*Kremlin Letter. N. Behn
Kreuzeck Coordinates. P. Ross
*Kronstadt. M. Pemberton
Kronstadt 21. G. M. Thomson
Kruger's Gold. P. Webster
Krumnagel. P. Ustinov

*Krush. H. Janson
L.A. Massacre. N. Winski
L.A. Wars. C. Ramm
*La Belle Laurine. B. Graeme
La Brava. E. Leonard
Labrador Trust. T. Rook
Laburnum Grove. T. Holland
*Laburnum Grove. J. B. Priestley
*Lackey and the Lady. T. Gallon
*Lacquer Screen. R. Van Gulik
*Lad of Mettle. N. Gould
Ladies in Danger. E. Verity
*Ladies in Retirement. E. Percy
*Ladies' Man. Rupert Hughes
Ladies of Lambton Green. L. Shepherd
Ladies of the Jury. J. F. Ballard
*Ladies Sleep Alone. L. Della
Lady. T. Tryon
*Lady and Her Doctor. E. Piper
*Lady Audley's Secret. M. E. Braddon
Lady Audley's Secret. B. J. Burton
Lady Cries Murder. J. W. See
Lady Dracula. T. J. Kelly
*Lady from Long Acre. V. Bridges
*Lady Has a Scar. H. Janson
*Lady in a Cage. R. Durand
*Lady in Cement. A. Rome
*Lady in Green. P. Cheyney
*Lady in the Car with Glasses and a Gun. S. Japrisot
*Lady in the Lake. R. Chandler
*Lady in the Morgue. J. Latimer
*Lady Is a Tramp. H. Zore
Lady Jade. L. O'Grady
*Lady Killer. W. M. Hardy
Lady Killer. M. Togawa
*Lady, Lady, I Did It! E. McBain
Lady Lawyer. T. Holloway
*Lady, Lie Low. H. Janson
Lady Middletower and the Red Dagger. J. K. Muir
*Lady, Mind That Corpse. H. Janson
Lady Mislaid. K. Horne
Lady of Stantonwyck. Maye Barrett
Lady of Storm House. E. Bond
*Lady of the Barge. W. W. Jacobs
*Lady on a Train. L. Charteris
Lady on the Line. T. Tone
Lady--Pass My Gat! J. Bogar
*Lady Saw Red. A. R. Long
Lady Sheba's Last Stunt. W. Caine
*Lady Takes a Flier. E. Ronns
*Lady, Toll That Bell. H. Janson
*Lady Varley. D. Vane
Lady Was Loaded. M. Horgan
Lady Who Never Was. P. Chambers
*Ladybirds Are In. H. Janson
*Ladycat. N. Greenwald
*Ladyfingers. J. Gregory
Ladykiller. L. O'Donnell
Lagrangists. Me. Reynolds
Laguna Heat. T. J. Parker
*Laidlaw. W. McIlvanney
Laird's Deed of Settlement. J. M. Kippen
*Lake Loot. H. Janson
Lake of the Diamond. J. Lee
Lallie. G. Sinclair
L'Amante Anglais. M. Duras
Lamastre. M. Strong
Lament for a Lover. H. Janson
Lamia. T. Travis
Lamplighter. J. Simmons
*Lancer Spy. M. McKenna
Land of Gold. M. A. Hammond
Land of the Lost. W. Satchell
Landfall in Sefton Carey. J. Escott
Landover Legacy. V. Holt
Landscape of the Body. J. Guare
Landshark. I. Zacharia
Lantern Lecture. A. Mars-Jones
Lapis. H. Hamman
Largely Luck. E. Harris
Laser Shuttle. P. Kirk
*Laser War. J. Rosenberger
Last Adventure. J. Fores
Last and Greatest Art. W. Winward
Last Assassin. D. Easterman
Last Battle. R. Jackson
Last Chance Country. G. Moffat
Last Crime. J. Domatilla
*Last Day in Limbo. P. O'Donnell
Last Days at St. Saturn's. E. Apffel
Last Days of America. P. Erdman
Last Deal. L. Gonzales
Last Ditch. R. Bradford
Last Drop. W. B. Murphy
*Last Escape. E. C. R. Lorac
*Last Escape. M. Walker
Last Exit. F. P. Yariev
*Last Express. B. Kendrick
Last Ferry from the Lido. B. Healey
Last Flight to Moscow. Nick Carter
*Last Frontier. A. MacLean
Last Gasp. T. Hoyle
Last Grand Master. J. M. White
Last Heroes of Merriott Manor. P. Pacotti
*Last Hour. C. Bennett
Last House Party. P. Dickinson

Last Innocent Man. P. M. Margolin
Last Judgement. R. Hugo
Last Judgment. A. Clarke
*Last Known Address. Joseph Harrington
*Last Lady. H. Janson
Last Laugh. J. R. Riggs
Last Leap. D. Enefer
Last Message to Berlin. P. Van Rjndt
*Last Mile. J. Wexley
*Last Mystery of Edgar Allan Poe. Manny Meyers
*Last Nazi. Max Lamb
Last of Days. M. Farhi
Last of Mrs. Cheyney. F. Lonsdale
Last of Mrs. Lonsdale. G. Fowler
*Last of Philip Banter. J. F. Bardin
*Last of Sheila. A. Edwards
Last of Sherlock Holmes. T. J. Kelly
Last of the Boatriders. D. MacKenzie
*Last Page. J. H. Chase
Last Patriot. J. N. Frey
Last Private Eye in Dublin. Mike Shelley
Last Respects. C. Aird
Last Reunion. V. Andrews
Last Rites. J. Saralegui
Last Rites. P. M. Smith
Last Rites. P. Spike
Last Samurai. Nick Carter
Last Scam. D. Harris
Last Seance. M. Lovell
Last Seen Alive. D. Simpson
Last Spring in Paris. H. Herlin
Last Starship from Earth. J. Boyd
Last Supper. C. McCarry
Last Survivor. R. Myers
Last Temptation. D. Mure
Last Throes. A. Lykiard
Last Touches. W. K. Clifford
*Last Trap. S. Gluck
*Last Voyage. A. Clarke
Last Walk Home. E. Page
Last White Man. F. D. Barber
Last Words of Dutch Schultz. W. Burroughs
*Late Boy Wonder. Angus Hall
Late Delivery. J. R. L. Anderson
*Late Edwina Black. W. Dinner
*Late Night Revel. H. Janson
*Later Than You Think. M. M. Kaye
Latest Mrs. Adams. G. Tibbles
Latimer Mercy. R. Richardson
Laugh of Death. K. Robeson
Laughing Man. M. Daniel
*Laughing Policeman. M. Sjowall
Laughing Whitefish. R. Traver
Laundryman. J. Evans
*Laura. V. Caspary
Laura, the Emperiled. K. Kimbrough
Laurie's Legacy. J. Aeby
Law and Order. G. F. Newman
Law-Breakers. P. Gibbs
Law Bringers. G. B. Lancaster
*Lawyer and the Carpenter. E. Thompson
Lawyer Man. K. Trell
Layers of Deceit. R. Jeffries
Layton Hall. M. Lemon
Lazarus in Vienna. A. Slote
Lazarus Lie. P. Van Greenaway
Leader and the Damned. C. Forbes
League of Death. H. J. S. Anderton
*League of Frightened Men. R. Stout
*League of Gentlemen. J. Boland
League of the Yellow Skull. H. J. S. Anderton
*League of Three. Old Sleuth
Leah Kleschna. C. M. S. McLellan
Leap in the Dark. W. Massey
*Leather Man. L. Treat
Leave a Message for Willie. M. Muller
*Leave Her to Heaven. B. A. Williams
*Leavenworth Case. A. K. Green
Legacy. D. Bagley
Legacy. J. A. Krentz
Legacy from Tenarife. R. MacLeod
*Legacy of a Spy. H. S. Maxfield
Legacy of Fear. K. T. Anders
Legacy of Fear. V. Coffman
Legend. N. Conde
Legend of Raikes Cross. S. Ready
Legend of the Slain Soldiers. M. Muller
Legion. W. P. Blatty
*Legion. R. Bridges
Lemon Garden. E. Rossiter
*Leo Conversion. David Smith
Leopard Hunts in Darkness. Wilbur Smith
Leopard in the Grass. Desmond Stewart
Leopard Lady. E. C. Carpenter
Leopold's Way. E. D. Hoch
Leper of Saint Giles. Ellis Peters
*Lepke. J. Pearl
Lesson in Love. C. Virmonne
Let No Man Write My Epitaph. W. Motley
Let Sleeping Dogs Lie. J. R. Riggs
Let the Dead Sleep On. B. Channing
Let Us Prey. M. Quill
Lethal Orders. J. Pattinson
Letitia, the Dreamer. K. Kimbrough
*Let's Kill Uncle. R. O'Grady
Let's Murder Marsha. M. Ferris

Let's Talk of Wills. S. J. Mason
Letter. W. S. Maugham
Letter-Box Man. A. Sewart
*Letty Lynton. M. B. Lowndes
Levantine. P. Delacorte
Level Five. D. Hart-Davis
Levine. D. E. Westlake
Liar's Dice. C. A. Charles
Libel. E. Wooll
Liberty Two. R. Lypsyte
Libya Connection. D. Pendleton
*Libyan Kill. W. O'Neill
Libyan Warlord. R. Skimin
License Renewed. J. Gardner
*Lie a Little, Die a Little. M. Brett
Lie Direct. Sara Woods
Lie Down with Lions. K. Follett
Life Adjuster. E. Cannon
Life and Adventures of Roxana. D. Defoe
Life and Death of Lilian Faulds. H. McLeave
*Life for Ruth. W. Drummond
Life of Colonel Jack. D. Defoe
Life of Her Own. M. Brandel
Life on the Bowery. T. J. Kelly
Life Penalty. J. Fielding
Life-Preserver. J. Pattinson
*Lifeline. P. Bottome
*Light of Day. E. Ambler
Light Thickens. N. Marsh
Light Through Glass. E. Lemarchand
Lighted Room. L. Cooper
Lightning. E. McBain
*Lightning May Strike Anywhere. M. Eldridge
Lights Are Warm and Coloured. W. Norfolk
Lightship. S. Lenz
Lightsource. Bari Wood
Like a Lamb to the Slaughter. L. Block
*Like Crazy. H. Janson
*Like Lethal. H. Janson
*Like Poison. H. Janson
Lilac Night. M. T. Hinkemeyer
*Lilies for My Lovely. H. Janson
Lily Henry. M. K. Cooper
*Limbo Line. V. Canning
*Limbo Lover. H. Janson
*Limehouse Nights. T. Burke
Limelight. T. Feely
Lime's Crisis. R. Bass
Limited Vision. R. Lewis
*Limping Wolf. E. T. Portwine
Lindsey. J. Jenkins
Line by Line. A. Schor
*Line of Succession. B. Garfield
*Line on Ginger. R. Maugham
Lines and Shadows. J. Wambaugh
Linked Lives. D. K. Roy
Linton Porcupine. R. Laidlaw
Linz Tatoo. N. Guild
Linz Testament. L. Perdue
*Lion and the Lamb. E. P. Oppenheim
*Lion and the Mouse. A. Hornblow
*Lions at the Kill. S. Kent
Lion's Fire. W. Barker
*Lion's Mouse. C. N. Williamson
Lion's Run. C. Thomas
Lion's Share. J. Man
Lion's Way. L. Orde
Lips of Death. David Steel
*Liquidator. J. Gardner
*Liquor Is Quicker. H. Janson
*List of Adrian Messenger. P. MacDonald
Listen for the Click. J. L. Breen
Listener. A. Blackwood
*Listener. T. Du Bois
*Listerdale Mystery. A. Christie
*Litany of Evil. R. Brennan
Little Boy Blue. E. Bunker
Little Boy Lost. L. Egan
Little Boy Lost. D. Wolman
Little Brother. J. McNeil
*Little Caesar. W. R. Burnett
Little Company. M. Elmblad
*Little Comrade. B. E. Stevenson
*Little Cowboy in New York. Old Sleuth
Little Darling, Dead. J. S. Scott
Little David. E. Chaze
Little Drummer Girl. J. Le Carre
*Little Giant. Old Sleuth
Little Girl in a Big City. J. K. McCurdy
*Little Girl Who Lives Down the Lane. L. Koenig
Little Girls Lost. Doris Shannon
*Little Hour of Peter Wells. D. Whitelaw
Little Lady Killing. J. Webb
Little Miss Christie. T. J. Kelly
Little Murder. M. Stone
Little Murders. J. Feiffer
Little Red Phone. H. Kane
Little Red Shoes. D. C. Spence
*Little Sister. R. Chandler
Little Sister. S. Gordon
Little Sister. L. Roberts
*Little Tales of Misogyny. P. Highsmith
Little Victims. R. Barnard
*Live and Let Die. I. Fleming

Live Bait. B. Walsh
Live Bait. T. Wood
*Live Gold. R. Sheckley
*Live Like a Hero. Angus Hall
*Live Now, Pay Later. J. T. Story
*Live Wire. J. Bruce
*Lives to Give. S. De Gramont
*Living and the Dead. P. Boileau
Living Clue. Anonymous
Living Dangerously. R. Simpson
Living Dog. P. Somerville-Large
Living Strong-Box. F. Mauzens
Liz Assignation. H. Janson
*Lizard's Tail. M. Brandel
Lizzie. E. Hunter
*Lizzie Borden of Fall River. T. Kelly
*Loaded Dice. E. H. Clark
Loaded Questions. P. Loraine
Loan Shark. J. W. O'Dell
Local Lads. J. S. Scott
Local Matter. J. M. Bennett
*Lock and the Key. F. Gruber
Locket for Tawi. J. Kinney
*Lodger. M. B. Lowndes
*Lodger. G. Simenon
Lola. Delacorta
*Lola Brought Her Wreath. H. Janson
Lombard Heiress. V. Coffman
London Affair. Anthony Stuart
*London After Midnight. M. Coolridge-Rask
London Belongs to Me. N. Collins
London by Night. C. Selby
London Calling North Pole. H. J. Giskes
London Crimes. C. Dickens
London Embassy. P. Theroux
London Fields. M. Milne
London Gun. B. Heatter
London Match. L. Deighton
London Merchant. G. Lillo
*Lone House Mystery. E. Wallace
*Lone Wolf. L. J. Vance
*Lone Wolf Returns. L. J. Vance
Lonely Margins. P. Kelly
Lonely Road. N. Shute
Lonely Sea. A. MacLean
Lonely Silver Rain. J. D. MacDonald
*Lonely Skier. H. Innes
Lonely Vigils. M. W. Wellman
*Lonely Way to Die. A. Bourgeau
Long After Midnight. R. Bradbury
*Long and Living Shadow. D. Winston
Long Arm. H. Janson
*Long Arm. E. P. Oppenheim
Long Dark Night of Baron Samedi. J. Wyllie
*Long Day's Dying. A. White
Long Death. D. Hartman
*Long Exile. G. Simenon
*Long Fuse. A. White
Long Good Friday. R. Claughton
*Long Goodbye. R. Chandler
Long Haul. A. I. Bezzerides
*Long Haul. M. Mills
Long Journey Home. M. Gilbert
Long Live the King. J. Rowe
Long Masquerade. M. Brent
*Long Memory. H. Clewes
*Long Midnight. A. White
*Long Night. S. Truss
*Long Night's Work. A. White
Long Rest. B. Copper
*Long Saturday Night. C. Williams
*Long Shadow. J. Cleary
Long Shadow. Anna Gilbert
Long Shot. W. Massey
Long Shot. P. Monette
Long Silence. J. R. Gould
*Long Silence. A. White
Long Time Dead. P. Chambers
Long Time to Hate. W. D. Roberts
*Long Wait. M. Spillane
*Long Watch. A. White
Long Way to Go. B. Deal
*Long Way to Shiloh. L. Davidson
*Long White Night. E. Lambert
Longest Pleasure. D. Clark
Longest Pleasure. C. Nicole
Look Out for Space. W. F. Nolan
Looking for a Kidnapper. C. I. Hammons
*Looking for Rachel Wallace. R. B. Parker
Looking for Sampson. J. N. Chance
Looking for Zoe. D. B. Dodson
*Looking Glass. V. Coffman
*Looking Glass War. J. Le Carre
Loom of Justice. E. Lothar
Loop of String. M. A. Kay
*Loophole. R. Pollock
Loose Connection. M. Brooks
*Loot. J. Orton
*Loot. A. S. Roche
*Looters. A. Conroy
*Looters. J. Reese
*Lord Arthur Savile's Crime. C. Cox
*Lord Arthur Savile's Crime. O. Wilde
*Lord Blackshirt. B. Graeme
Lord Darcy Investigates. R. Garrett

*Lord Edgware Dies. A. Christie
*Lord John in New York. C. N. Williamson
Lord Mullion's Secret. M. Innes
Lords of the Earth. W. B. Murphy
*Lorry. P. Wahloo
*Lose This Gun. H. Janson
*Loser Take All. G. Greene
*Loser Take All. J. J. Lamb
Losing Bet. M. Chernenok
Loss of Heart. R. McCrum
Loss of Patients. R. McInerny
Loss of the Culion. J. Ashford
Lost. L. Stephens
Lost American. B. Freemantle
Lost Diary. J. Sheban
*Lost Endeavor. G. Boothby
*Lost Gallows. J. D. Carr
Lost Heroes. A. Baldwin
Lost in Space and the Mortgage Due. T. J. Kelly
Lost Jewel of the Mortimers. A. T. Sadlier
*Lost Judge. C. R. Gull
*Lost Leader. E. P. Oppenheim
Lost Madonna. I. Holland
Lost Man's Lane. Anonymous
Lost Provinces. S. Glazier
Lost Road. R. H. Davis
Lottery. B. Duffield
*Loudwater Mystery. E. Jepson
*Louis Beretti. D. H. Clarke
Louisiana Firestorm. M. McCray
Lovable Stranger. A. Duffield
*Love and Bullets. J. Heddon
Love and Death. R. Timperley
Love and Murder. P. Whalley
Love and Terror. W. Herrick
Love and the Whirlwind. H. P. Lewis
Love and Treason. D. Osborn
Love Bade Me Welcome. J. Lodwick
Love Comes Flying. R. Eden
*Love from a Stranger. F. Vosper
Love Hunter. J. Hassler
*Love in Amsterdam. N. Freeling
Love-In and Lamentation. H. Janson
Love in Jeopardy. Magali
*Love Insurance. E. D. Biggers
Love Is a Racket. R. James
*Love Is Just a Word. J. M. Simmel
*Love Is the One with Wings. P. V. Stern
Love Is the Victim. John Lawrence
*Love Made Manifest. G. Boothby
Love Makers. H. Janson
*Love Me, Hurt Me. N. Karta
*Love Me to Death. F. Diamond
Love Murders. A. Goddard
*Love of Lucifer. D. Winston
Love Racket. B. K. Burns
*Love Rides the Rails. M. Cary
*Love Secretaries. H. Janson
*Love Talker. Elizabeth Peters
*Love Thing. H. Barron
Lovecraft's Book. R. A. Lupoff
Loveday Brooke. C. L. Pirkis
*Lovely But Deadly. Dave Steel
Lovely Day to Die. C. Fremlin
Lovely in Her Bones. S. McCrumb
*Lover. H. Janson
Lovers, Make Moan. G. Mitchell
Love's Captain. L. Robin
*Love's Lovely Counterfeit. J. M. Cain
Love's Lunatic. J. McCarter
Loving Brothers. L. Golding
Loving Elms. P. Cargill
*Low Company. H. Atkinson
Low Company. M. Benney
Low Company. D. Fuchs
Low Treason. L. Tourney
Loyal and Dedicated Servant. J. Griffiths
Loyalties. J. Galsworthy
Loyalties. Raymond Williams
Lubyanka. J. Burch
Luciano's Luck. J. Higgins
Lucifer Directive. J. Land
Lucifer Key. M. MacPherson
Lucifer's Weekend. W. B. Murphy
*Lucinda. H. Rigsby
Luck of the Irish. H. MacGrath
Lucky, Lucky Hudson and the 12th St. Gang. T. J. Kelly
*Lucky Stiff. C. Rice
Lucky Streak. J. Raymond
Lucy's Cottage. M. James
*Lugs O'Leary. A. Kimmons
Luke Martin Diamonds. B. N. F. Wilce
Lullaby of Murder. D. S. Davis
Luna. Delacorta
*Lunatic at Large. J. S. Clouston
*Lunatics at Large. J. Reach
*Lupe. G. Thompson
Lure. H. R. Hailey
*Lure. G. Scarborough
Lush Valley. P. Campbell
Lushington Mystery. Philippa Tyler
*Lust for Vengeance. H. Janson
Lust Killer. A. Stack
Luxembourg Run. A. Ross

Lychgate Hall. M. E. Francis
Lying in State. J. Rathbone
Lynx. J. J. Savarin
Lyssa. J. Jenkins
MacAlester. Ritchie Perry
McBain Brief. E. McBain
*McCabe. E. Naughton
McGarr and the Method of Descartes. B. Gill
McGarr and the P.M. of Belgrave Square. B. Gill
McGuffin. J. Bowen
*McQ. A. Edwards
*M. L. Falkner
Macao Massacre. Nick Carter
Macau. D. Carney
Mace! J. Grant
Mace's Luck. J. Grant
Machine. D. Hamill
*Macking Gangster. C. A. Harris
Mad Blood. D. Nemec
Mad Death. N. Slater
*"Mad Dog" Coll. S. Thurman
Mad Hatter Summer. D. Thomas
Mad Minute. J. Cain
Mad Virgins. V. B. Ibanez
*Mad with Much Heart. G. Butler
*Madam Tic-Tac. F. L. Cary
Madame Eddie's Chamber of Horros. Mike Shelley
*Madame X. M. Avallone
Madame X. J. W. MacConaughy
Made for TV. R. Breen
Madeleine. P. E. West
Madhouse on the Moors. F. Maule
Madman's Holiday. Fredric Brown
Madman's Will. J. Chance
Madness of a Seduced Woman. S. F. Schaeffer
Madness of the People. R. Cassilis
Madness on Madrona Drive. L. Flynn
Madonna of Avenue A. M. Canfield
Madonna of the Black Market. E. Webster
*Madonna of the Seven Moons. M. Lawrence
*Madonna of the Sleeping Cars. M. Dekobra
Madrid Underground. D. Serafin
Madrigal for Charlie Muffin. B. Freemantle
Maelstrom. M. J. Bird
Maelstrom. R. Haney
Maelstrom. H. Hunt
Mafia Diaries. J. R. Nash
*Mafia Vendetta. L. Sciascia
Magda. Lisa Wells
Maggie. J. Tremaine
Maggot. J. Fowles
Magic. W. Goldman
*Magic Dick, the Boy Detective. Old Sleuth
*Magic Island. K. Robeson
Magic Man. D. Bannerman
Magician. S. Stein
*Magnet of Doom. G. Simenon
Magnetic Fields. R. Loewinsohn
*Magnum for Schneider. J. Mitchell
*Magnum Force. M. Valley
Magnum P.I. R. Bowdler
Magwitch. M. Noonan
Magyar Massacre. G. St. Germain
Mahdi. A. J. Quinnell
Maid of the Mountain. J. Gregory
Maid of the Silver Sea. J. Oxenham
Maids and Deathwatch. J. Genet
*Maigret and the Concarneau Murders. G. Simenon
*Maigret and the Gangsters. G. Simenon
*Maigret and the Hotel Majestic. G. Simenon
Maigret Bides His Time. G. Simenon
*Maigret Has Doubts. G. Simenon
*Maigret in Court. G. Simenon
*Maigret Sets a Trap. G. Simenon
*Maigret's Pipe. G. Simenon
*Maigret's Revolver. G. Simenon
Maigret's War of Nerves. G. Simenon
*Mail Robber's Syndicate. E. C. Derby
*Main Attraction. S. Michaels
*Make Haste to Live. Gordons
Make Me Rich. P. Corris
*Make Mine a Harlot. M. Storm
*Make Mine Mink. H. Janson
*Make My Bed in Hell. J. B. Sanford
*Make Out with Murder. Chip Harrison
Make Them Pay. I. Ludlow
Makeover. M. Biederman
Makepeace Not War. J. C. Martindale
Malcolm. Old Sleuth
Malice Domestic. W. M. Hardy
Malice in Camera. L. Payne
Mall. S. Kahn
Mallory's Gambit. L. C. Balling
Malloy's Subway. R. W. Campbell
Malpractice. J. R. Feegel
Malta Victory. R. Jackson
*Maltese Falcon. D. Hammett
Maltese Vengeance. J. Cutter
Mamigon. J. Hashian
*Man. M. Dinelli

*Man. W. Scott
*Man. B. Stoker
*Man About a Dog. A. Coppel
*Man and His Money. F. S. Isham
*Man at Six. J. Celestin
*Man at the Carlton. E. Wallace
Man at the Wheel. M. Kenyon
Man Called Kyril. J. Trenhaile
Man Condemned. P. Alding
Man Crazy. A. Wallace
*Man Drowning. H. Kuttner
Man Eater of Jassapur. D. Hart-Davis
Man from Butler's. C. Landstone
Man from Internal Affairs. N. Hentoff
*Man from Kabul. G. De Villiers
*Man from Nowhere. V. Bridges
Man from St. Petersburg. K. Follett
*Man from Texas. B. Wayde
*Man from the Diner's Club. S. Baol
Man from White Hat. S. Jason
*Man in Charge. R. Jessup
*Man in Half Moon Street. B. Lyndon
Man in High Castle. P. K. Dick
*Man in Motley. T. Gallon
*Man in Stripes. L. Carlton
*Man in the Coach. E. C. Derby
Man in the Dark Suit. D. R. Caro
Man in the Flypaper Hat. J. C. Walls
Man in the Gray Flannel Shroud. F. Orenstein
Man in the Lane. T. Neild
*Man in the Lubianka. D. Vallance
*Man in the Mail. L. Carlton
Man in the Middle. M. Lewis
*Man in the Net. P. Quentin
Man in Wax. Anonymous
*Man Inside. M. E. Chaber
*Man Inside. N. S. Lincoln
*Man of a Hundred Masks. G. Leroux
*Man of Bronze. K. Robeson
Man of Glass. D. Zochert
Man of Gold. E. Hervey
Man of Mystery. Anonymous
*Man of Mystery. Old Sleuth
*Man on a Tightrope. N. Paterson
*Man on the Box. H. MacGrath
*Man on the Crag. G. Boothby
Man on the Landing. F. Jones
*Man Outside. D. Stuart
Man Pinches Bottom. J. T. Story
*Man Responsible. S. Robinett
*Man Running. S. Jepson
*Man They Couldn't Arrest. A. J. Small
*Man Trapper. Old Sleuth
*Man Who Bought London. E. Wallace
Man Who Broke the Bank at Monte Carlo. M. Butterworth
*Man Who Changed His Name. E. Wallace
Man Who Fell Up. K. Robeson
*Man Who Finally Died. John Burke
*Man Who Haunted Himself. Ralph Martin
Man Who Heard Too Much. Stockton Woods
*Man Who Killed. C. Farrere
*Man Who Killed His Brother. R. Stephens
*Man Who Knew. M. O. Rolfe
*Man Who Knew. E. Wallace
*Man Who Knew Too Much. R. Alexander
*Man Who Knew Too Much. G. K. Chesterton
Man Who Liked Slow Tomatoes. K. C. Constantine
*Man Who Liked to Look at Himself. K. C. Constantine
Man Who Limped. O. A. Kline
Man Who Lived at the Ritz. A. E. Hotchner
Man Who Loved Dirty Books. D. Guy
Man Who Loved Mata Hari. D. Sherman
Man Who Loved Normandie. Justin Scott
*Man Who Made Diamonds. Warren Miller
*Man Who Made Money. B. Wayde
Man Who Owned New York. J. J. Osborn, Jr.
*Man Who Ran Away. D. B. Dodson
Man Who Risked His Partner. R. Stephens
Man Who Rocked the Boat. W. J. Keating
Man Who Stayed at Home. J. E. H. Terry
Man Who Stole the Mona Lisa. Martin Page
Man Who Stole the Sun. G. Fraser
*Man Who Vanished. Old Sleuth
*Man Who Was Nobody. E. Wallace
Man Who Was Saturday. D. Lambert
Man Who Was Scared. K. Robeson
*Man Who Watched the Trains Go By. G. Simenon
*Man Who Went Up in Smoke. M. Sjowall
Man Who Won. C. T. Brady
*Man with a Gun. L. Carlton
Man with a Load of Mischief. M. Grimes
*Man with a Past. R. Patterson
*Man with Bogart's Face. A. J. Fenady
*Man with My Face. S. W. Taylor
Man with the Black Worrybeads. G. N. Rumanes
*Man with the Getaway Face. R. Stark
Man with the Glaring Eyes. A. Barclay
*Man with the Golden Gun. I. Fleming
*Man with the Magnetic Eyes. R. Daniel

*Man Within. G. Greene
Man You Sleep With. D. E. Fisher
Manaton Disaster. Philippa Tyler
*Manchurian Candidate. R. Condon
Mandelbaum Gate. M. Spark
Mandrake in Granada. J. Haythorne
Mandrake in the Monastery. J. Haythorne
Maneuvers. F. Neuman
Manfac. M. Caidin
*Manhandled. A. Stringer
Manhattan Gambit. B. Stein
Manhattan Gothic. M. Arrighi
*Manhattan Love Song. C. Woolrich
Manhattan Massacre. J. Grecco
Manhattan Revenge. J. Cutter
Manhunt. P. V. Stern
Manhunter. T. Harris
Manna Enzyme. R. Hoyt
Manrissa Man. P. Van Greenaway
Man's Illegal Life. K. Heller
Man's Storm. K. Heller
Mansion of Dark Mists. E. Zumwalt
*Mansion of Evil. J. Millard
*Manslaughter. A. D. Miller
Mantrap Manor. Anonymous
Manuscript Murders. R. H. Lewis
*Many Worlds of Magnus Ridolph. J. Vance
*Marathon Man. W. Goldman
*Marble Forest. T. Durrant
Marburg Virus. Stanley Johnson
*Marcel Levignet. E. Barron
Marco Polo, If You Can. W. F. Buckley, Jr.
Marge. K. Fitzgerald
*Margin for Error. C. Booth
*Margo. J. Jenkins
Margo's Reunion. J. Jenkins
Maria Canossa. S. Paretti
Maria Marten. Anonymous
Marigot Run. J. Ballem
*Mark. C. E. Israel
*Mark of Cain. S. A. Key
*Mark of Cain. C. Wells
*Mark of the Vulture. M. Macao
Mark Peterson's Daughter. M. Hutton
Marked for Destruction. J. Barnett
Marker Calls the Tune. A. Marriott
*Marnie. Winston Graham
*Maroc 7. M. Sands
Marrakesh One-Two. R. Grenier
*Marriage Lines. J. S. Fletcher
*Marriage of Esther. G. Boothby
Marriages of Mayfair. E. K. Chatterton
*Married to a Spy. R. Starr
Marry into Danger. C. Jauniere
Marseilles Connection. B. Peterson
Marshal. D. St. Pierre
Marvelous Boy. P. Corris
*Marvelous Escape. Old Sleuth
Mary Barton. E. Gaskell
*Mary Deare. H. Innes
*Mary Regan. L. Scott
Ma's Bar. P. Hallifax
*Masada Plan. Leonard Harris
*Mask. A. Hornblow
Mask. O. West
Mask of Abraham Morgenstern. D. Panger
Mask of Destiny. M. Andrau
*Mask of Dimitrios. E. Ambler
*Mask of Fu Manchu. S. Rohmer
Mask of Silence. S. McErlean
Mask of the Jaguar. J. North
Masks and Faces. C. Curzon
*Masque of the Red Death. Elsie Lee
*Masquerader. K. C. Thurston
Masques. B. Pronzini
Masques and Phases. Robert Ross
Mass. Jack Fuller
Massacre at Russian River. D. Hartman
*Master. M. Braly
Master and Maid. Frank Jones
Master Crime. J. Lyons
Master Key. W. Massey
Master Key. M. Togawa
*Master Mind. M. Dana
*Master Mind. H. Janson
*Master Mummer. E. P. Oppenheim
*Master Mystery. A. B. Reeve
*Master of Blue Mire. V. Coffman
Master of D.E.A.T.H. J. Ahern
*Master of Men. E. P. Oppenheim
*Master of Merripit. E. Phillpotts
Master of the Moor. R. Rendell
Master Plan. B. J. Freshman
*Master Stroke. E. C. Derby
Master Theron. C. Lawton
Master's Challenge. W. B. Murphy
Masters Connection. D. Chandler
Masterstroke. T. Heald
Masterstroke. M. Sharp
Masterworks of Crime and Mystery. A. C. Doyle
*Matheson Money. F. Warden
Matilda, My Darling. N. Krauth
Matilda Shouted Fire. J. Green
*Matrimony Most Murderous. L. Cargill
Matter of Conviction. E. Hunter
Matter of Honor. W. P. McGivern
*Matter of Thousands. Old Spicer

Matter of Time. G. Cook
Maui Mystery. W. Rotsler
*Maurizius Case. J. Wasserman
Maxwell's Train. C. Hyde
May Day in Magadan. A. Olcott
May Fair. M. Arlen
Mayan Connection. Nick Carter
Mayday from Malaga. R. MacLeod
Mayeroni Myth. D. Winston
*Mayfair Slayride. H. Janson
*Mayor's Wife. A. K. Green
Maze. A. H. Garnet
*Me--Gangster. C. F. Coe
Meagham. J. Jenkins
Mean Time. C. T. Leland
Measure of Fear. L. Demestichas
*Mechanic. L. J. Carlino
Medical Center Murders. L. Drake
*Medical Witness. R. Gordon
Mediterranean Maneuver. R. J. Szilagye
Medusa Complex. M. H. Albert
Medusa Syndrome. Ron Cutler
*Medusa Touch. P. Van Greenaway
Meet a Body. F. Launder
Meet Helga Rolfe. J. H. Chase
*Meet Mr. Callaghan. G. Verner
*Meet the Rev. G. Pedrick
*Meet the Tiger. L. Charteris
*Meg the Lady. T. Gallon
Megadeath Option. P. Buck
*Megstone Plot. A. Garve
Mekong Massacre. J. Lansing
Melancholy Virgin. A. Laine
Melody Man. H. J. Green
*Melody of Death. E. Wallace
Members of the Jury. S. Ready
Members Only. P. Welles
Memento Mori. M. Spark
*Memoirs of Sherlock Holmes. A. C. Doyle
Memory Boy. V. Canning
Memory Man. J. Griffiths
Memory of Murder. R. Bradbury
*Memory of Passion. G. Brewer
Memory's Dancer. S. W. Goss
Men in Arms. J. Crosby
Men in Her Death. A. Morice
Men Who Robbed the Bank of England. C. Branson
Men with Tangle. A. Ross
Men with the Guns. G. F. Newman
Men Without Women. E. Hemingway
Menace. A. Carson
*Menace. H. Janson
Menace. A. Van Hassen
*Menaces, Menaces. M. Underwood
Mendoza Manuscript. Nick Carter
Mendoza's Treasure. V. Daniels
Menu Cypher. R. Elman
*Mephisto Waltz. F. M. Stewart
*Mercenary. H. Barron
Mercenary Kill. J. Quinn
*Merchandise. R. Bridges
Merely Murder. G. Paxton
Meritocrats. W. Haggard
Merlake Towers. Mary Williams
Mermaids on the Golfcourse. P. Highsmith
Merry-Go-Round. G. Sklar
*Merry Men. R. L. Stevenson
Merry Murders at Montmarie. T. J. Kelly
Mesmerist's Secret. D. Dormer
Metal Green Mercedes. T. Williams
Meteoric Affair. J. Tabler
Meter Maid. F. Shepard
Methuselah Factor. J. Rosenberger
Metzger's Dog. T. Perry
Mexican Kill. D. Hartman
Mexican Stand-Off. M. Cronin
Mexico Set. L. Deighton
Miami Blues. C. Willeford
*Miami Mayhem. A. Rome
Miami, One Way. M. Winters
Michael. A. J. Spivey
Micro Kill. H. Janson
Microwave Factor. A. Fletcher
Midas. P. Kelaart
Midas Kill. P. Kirk
Midas Men. J. Evans
Midas Touch. W. Winward
Midnight Call. Gordon Morris
Midnight Ferry to Venice. B. Healey
*Midnight Guest. M. F. White
Midnight Gun. B. Mather
*Midnight House. E. L. White
Midnight Lace. W. Drummond
*Midnight Lady and the Mourning Man. D. Anthony
*Midnight Mail. H. Holt
Midnight Man. L. D. Estleman
Midnight Man. W. B. Murphy
Midnight Masquerade. Jean Smith
Midnight Patient. E. Hostovsky
Midnight Sun. K. Sundelof-Asbrand
*Midnight Vigil. Warren Miller
Midnight Waltz. J. Blake
Midnight Water. G. Norman
Midnight Whispers. P. Matthews
*Midsummer Mink. P. Coke
Midtown Aces. J. G. Bodyan

Might of a Wrongdoer. S. Brice
*Mike Dime. B. Fantoni
Miko. E. V. Lustbader
*Milady Took the Rap. H. Janson
*Mildred Pierce. J. M. Cain
Miller's Deal. A. Gooch
*Millijoy, the Determined. K. Kimbrough
*Million a Minute. H. Douglas
Million Cut. A. Heal
Million Dollar Babe. C. Borelli
Million Dollar Hit. L. Starr
Million Dollar Lift. R. E. Crighton
Million Dollar Massacre. W. Barker
*Million Dollar Mystery. H. MacGrath
Million Dollar Stand-In. E. Webster
*Million Dollar Story. E. Wallace
*Millionaire Baby. A. K. Green
Mills of God. E. Lothar
Milmorra House. Renata Chapman
Mimi. R. W. Taylor
*Mind Benders. J. Kennaway
Mind Breakers. D. Streib
Mind Games. A. Rule
Mind Murders. J. Van De Wetering
Mind My Shroud. C. Rank
*Mind of Mr. J. G. Reeder. E. Wallace
Mind over Murder. W. X. Kienzle
Mind Palace. S. R. Pieczenik
Mind Traders. J. M. Holly
Mindbend. R. Cook
Minder. A. Masters
Minder Back Again. A. Masters
Minder--Yet Again. A. Masters
Mindreader. C. T. Cline
Mindspell. K. N. Smith
*Mine Own Executioner. N. Balchin
*Mine to Avenge. T. Wills
Miner's Right. R. Boldrewood
Miniature Murder Mystery. P. Chambers
Minigods. K. Saint-John
*Ministry of Fear. G. Greene
Mink. J. Springs III
Minnie Swan. P. Baker
Minor Murder. R. Denham
Minotaur. J. Farris
Minotaur. B. Tammuz
*Minus One Corpse. J. Cleveland
Minutes. A. R. Williams
Minx Manx. L. Kent
Mira. D. Winston
Miracle Man. F. Packard
Miracle of Revenge. W. B. Longley
*Miriam Rozella. B. L. Farjeon
*Mirror Crack'd from Side to Side. A. Christie
Mirror Image. P. Conway
Mirror of Darkness. C. Gayet
Miscellany. E. Trevor
*Mischief. C. Armstrong
Mischief Makers. W. Haggard
Miser. L. Egan
Miser Is Murdered. A. Beaton
*Misfortunes of Mr. Teal. L. Charteris
*Miss Arnott's Marriage. Richard Marsh
Miss Astbury and Milordo. I. Northan
Miss Bede Is Staying. Anna Gilbert
*Miss Bracegirdle and others. S. Aumonier
Miss Brown. R. B. Brough
*Miss Callaghan Comes to Grief. J. H. Chase
Miss Deadly. C. Dekker
Miss Finney Kills Now and Then. A. Dempsey
Miss Marple. A. Christie
*Miss Pinkerton. M. R. Rinehart
*Miss Shumway Waves a Wand. J. H. Chase
*Missile Mob. H. Janson
Missing. S. Windham
Missing Airman. Anonymous
Missing and the Dead. J. Lynch
Missing Bishop. R. H. Spencer
Missing Bronte. R. Barnard
*Missing Bullet. Warren Miller
*Missing Million. E. Wallace
Missing Mr. Mosley. J. Greenwood
Missing Moon. H. Adams
Missing Person. N. Modiano
Missing Persons. C. T. Cline
Missing Persons. J. Olsen
Missing Woman. M. Lewin
*Mission Accomplished. J. Walker
Mission Code: Acropolis. B. Swift
Mission Code: Granite Island. B. Swift
Mission Code: King's Pawn. B. Swift
Mission Code: Minotaur. B. Swift
Mission Code: Scorpion. B. Swift
Mission Code: Snow Queen. B. Swift
Mission Code: Springboard. B. Swift
Mission Code: Survival. B. Swift
Mission Code: Symbol. B. Swift
Mission Code: Track and Destroy. B. Swift
Mission Code: Volcano. B. Swift
Mission M.I.A. J. C. Pollock
Mission to Warsaw. L. Wacht
*Mission to Siena. R. Marshall
*Mission to Venice. R. Marshall
Missionary Stew. R. Thomas
*Missioner. E. P. Oppenheim

Missouri Deathwatch. D. Pendleton
Mist in the Valley. D. Craig
*Mist on the Saltings. H. Wade
Mist over Morro Bay. C. G. Page
Mistaken Identity. B. Sommers
*Mr. Ace. H. Christy
*Mr. & Mrs. North. O. Davis
*Mr. Angel Comes Aboard. C. G. Booth
Mr. Apology. C. Black
*Mr. Arkadin. O. Welles
*Mr. Barnes of New York. A. C. Gunter
*Mr. Billingham, the Marquis and Madelon. E. P. Oppenheim
Mr. Calder and Mr. Behrens. M. Gilbert
Mr. Campion's Lady. M. Allingham
Mr. Crumblestone's Eden. A. S. Well
*Mr. Denning Drives North. A. Coppel
*Mr. Fortune Speaking. H. C. Bailey
Mr. Fothergill's Murder. P. O'Donnell
Mr. Fred. J. B. Hilton
*Mr. Grex of Monte Carlo. E. P. Oppenheim
Mr. Hamish Gleave. R. Llewellyn
*Mr. Hire's Engagement. G. Simenon
Mr. Hunter. S. Ready
Mr. Hyde. H. Arnott
*Mr. Justice Raffles. E. W. Hornung
*Mr. Lyndon at Liberty. V. Bridges
*Mr. Majestyk. E. Leonard
*Mr. Meeson's Will. H. R. Haggard
*Mister Midas. M. Catto
Mr. Pottinger. S. Ready
Mr. Sun. P. O'Donnell
Mr. Surie. O. K. Joshee
*Mister Target. W. Harrington
Mr. Tutt at His Best. A. Train
*Mr. Tutt's Case Book. A. Train
Mr. Wakefield's Crusade. B. Rubens
*Mr. Wingrave, Millionaire. E. P. Oppenheim
*Mr. Wu. L. J. Miln
Mister Yesterday. E. Chaze
*Mrs. Balfame. G. Atherton
*Mrs. Burlington. M. Isdale
Mrs. Christopher. E. Myers
Mrs. Craggs: Crimes Cleared Up. H. R. F. Keating
*Mistress Devon. V. Coffman
*Mrs. Erricker's Reputation. T. Cobb
Mrs. Keith's Crime. W. K. Clifford
*Mrs. McGinty's Dead. A. Christie
Mistress of Evil. M. Todrack
*Mistress of Fear. H. Janson
Mistress of Harrowgate. J. Laurie
Mistress of the Damned. J. Davidson
Mrs. Pollifax and the Hong Kong Buddha. D. Gilman
Mrs. Pollifax on the China Station. D. Gilman
Mrs. White. M. Tracy
*Mix Me a Person. J. T. Story
Mixed Relations. V. L. Whitechurch
Moated Grange. K. Tynan
Mobius Man. M. S. Karl
Mocking Bird. T. Browning
Model Body. R. Reinsmith
Model for Murder. M. Warden
*Model in Mayhem. H. Janson
*Modesty Blaise. P. O'Donnell
Modigliani Scandal. Z. Stone
Moll Flanders. D. Defoe
Moll for the Morgue. P. Costello
Molly. S. Gray
*Molly and the Confidence Man. S. Overholser
Molly and the Gold Baron. S. Overholser
*Molly Maguires. J. O'Neill
*Molly Maguires and the Detectives. A. Pinkerton
Moment in Time. J. Bedford
*Moment to Moment. A. Coppel
Monday Theory. D. Clark
Money. P. L. Sulitzer
Money Burn. T. Foster
*Money Jugglers. B. Wayde
Money Men. W. Haggard
Money Men and One-Shot Deal. G. Petievich
*Money Moon. J. Farnol
Money Plays. M. Beckner
*Money to Burn. R. W. Kauffman
*Money Trap. L. White
*Money with Menaces. P. Hamilton
Moneymaster. R. Spencer
Monimbo. A. De Borchgrave
Monitor Found in Orbit. M. G. Coney
Monkey-Shines. M. Stewart
Monopoly. Jonathan Evans
*Monsieur le Souris. G. Simenon
Monsieur Lecoq. E. Gaboriau
Monsieur Pamplemousse. M. Bond
Monsieur Pamplemousse and the Secret Mission. M. Bond
Monsieur Pamplemousse en Fete. M. Bond
Monster. G. Fraser
Montauk Fault. H. Mitgang
Monte Carlo. D. Daniels
Monte Carlo. S. Sheppard
Monterey. J. Lynch
Montmartre Murders. R. Grayson

Monza Protest. A. Neilson
Moon Country. G. Johnson
*Moon for Killers. G. Black
*Moon in the Gutter. D. Goodis
*Moon of the Wolf. L. H. Whitten
*Moon-Spinners. M. Stewart
Moondreamer. Z. Kamitses
Moondyne. J. B. O'Reilly
Moonlight and Murder. J. E. Davis
Moonlight Variations. F. Stevenson
Moonmist. G. Ferrand
*Moonrise. T. Strauss
*Moonshine Mountain. C. Glore
*Moonshine War. E. Leonard
*Moonshiner's Dupe. L. Carlton
*Moonstone. W. Collins
*Moorland Terror. H. Broadbridge
Moorland Tragedy. B. Orczy
Moose Murders. A. Bicknell
Moot Point. P. De Polnay
Morbid Symptoms. G. Slovo
*Mord Em'ly. W. P. Ridge
Mordida Man. R. Thomas
*More Educated Evans. E. Wallace
More Good Old Stuff. J. D. MacDonald
"More Things in Heaven..." W. Owen
*More to Be Pitied Than Scorned. C. E. Blaney
*Morgue Is Always Open. J. Odlum
*Morituri. W. J. Luddecke
Morning Walk. L. P. Davies
Moro. P. McCurtin
Morrison's Machine. J. S. Fletcher
*Mortal Coils. A. Huxley
*Mortal Storm. P. Bottome
Mortal Term. J. Penn
Mortician's Birthday Party. P. Whalley
*Mortmain. A. Train
Moscow Maze. D. Ross
*Moscow Papers. J. M. White
*Moscow Quadrille. T. Allbeury
Moscow Requiem. J. Simpson
Moscow Rules. R. Moss
*Moses Bottle. R. Mead
Mosley by Moonlight. J. Greenwood
Mosley Receipt. K. Royce
Mosley Went to Mow. J. Greenwood
Mosquito Squadron. R. Jackson
*Moss Rose. J. Shearing
*Mossbank Murder. H. Mills
Most Beautiful Girl in the World. T. Willis
Most Cunning Workmen. R. Lewis
*Most Deadly Game. E. Friend
Most Grievous Murder. Sara Woods
Most Likely Suspects. A. Bourgeau
Most Wanted. G. Bagby
Mother Love. Domini Taylor
Mother's Boys. R. Barnard
Motive on Record. Dell Shannon
*Motor City Blue. L. D. Estleman
Mount Eden. F. Marryat
Mountain of Fear. W. Barker
Mountain Rampage. D. Pendleton
Mountie on Trial. O. Olson
*Mourner. R. Stark
Mourning After. H. Q. Masur
*Mouse in the Mountain. N. Davis
*Mouse Who Wouldn't Play Ball. Anthony Gilbert
Moves on an Old Board. C. Hilton
Moving Finger. A. E. Meagher
Moving Picture Writes. P. Chambers
Moving Target. J. McClenaghan
*Moving Target. J. Macdonald
*Much in Evidence. H. Cecil
Mudland. M. Adams
*Mugger. E. McBain
Mule on the Minaret. A. Waugh
Multiplicity of Mrs. Browns. A. Sewart
Mumberley Inheritance. W. Graves
Mumbo-Jumbo. J. Barnard
Mummy Case. Elizabeth Peters
*Mumsy, Nanny, Sonny and Girly. B. Comport
Mungwe Affair. J. D. Powell
Munich 10. L. Orde
Murder. H. Adams
*Murder. H. Janson
Murder Across and Down. H. Resnicow
Murder After Tea Time. L. Cutter
Murder After the Fact. A. Ashforth
Murder After the Holidays. A. Arncliffe
*Murder Among Friends. B. Barry
Murder Among Friends. F. McConnell
*Murder and Gardenias. M. Neville
Murder and the First Lady. E. Roosevelt
Murder As the Curtain Rises. J. Philips
Murder at Bean and Beluga. D. Mayo
Murder at Bill's O'Jacks. J. Davenport
Murder at Buckingham Palace. T. E. B. Clarke
*Murder at Covent Garden. W. J. Makin
Murder at Dawn. L. O. Johnson
*Murder at Daybreak. G. A. Mayhew
*Murder at Drake's Anchorage. E. L. Waddell
*Murder at Glen Athol. N. Lippincott
Murder at La Marimba. C. Wolfe
*Murder at Maneuvers. R. Howes

Murder at Midday. F. Langhorn
Murder at Mrs. Loring's. S. S. Simon
Murder at Moose Jaw. T. Heald
Murder at Mt. Fuji. S. Natsuke
Murder at the Academy Awards. J. Hyams
Murder at the Big Store. D. Mayo
Murder at the Cheatin' Heart Motel. A. Bourgeau
*Murder at the Cookout. G. De Fraga
Murder at the F.B.I. M. Truman
Murder at the Howard Johnson's. R. Clark
*Murder at the Margin. M. Jevons
Murder at the Mill. J. Sumner
Murder at the 1984 Summer Games. S. Fawcette
Murder at the Red October. A. Olcott
Murder at Tomorrow. K. George
Murder Before Matins. J. Reeves
*Murder by an Aristocrat. M. G. Eberhart
Murder by Arrangement. E. Roberts
*Murder by Death. H. Keating
*Murder by Decree. R. Weverka
*Murder by Magic. A. R. Long
Murder by Membership Only. T. Hischak
Murder by Natural Causes. T. J. Kelly
Murder by Proxy. G. Ogan
Murder by the Book. D. Greenwood
*Murder by the Clock. Rufus King
*Murder Can't Stop. W. T. Ballard
Murder Circus. M. Litchfield
Murder Club. I. Zacharia
*Murder for a Wanton. W. Chambers
Murder for the Asking. D. Benfield
*Murder for the Million. Robert Chapman
*Murder, Four Miles High. R. A. Braun
Murder Game. D. Ross
*Murder-Go-Round. Jay Christopher
Murder Goes Mumming. A. Craig
*Murder Goes to College. K. Steel
Murder Has a Pretty Face. Jennie Melville
*Murder Has Your Number. H. Garner
Murder in Advent. D. Williams
Murder in Burgos. L. Foley
Murder in Cowboy Bronze. C. McCormick
Murder in Focus. R. Julian
Murder in High Places. H. Pentecost
Murder in Luxury. H. Pentecost
Murder in Mind. T. Feely
Murder in Mind. R. Fuller
Murder in Mind. H. Hartley
Murder in Mink. P. Costello
Murder in Paradise. J. Davey
Murder in Rehearsal. A. Goetz
*Murder in Style. D. Hoddinott
*Murder in the Bud. P. Bottome
Murder in the Central Committee. M. V. Montalban
Murder in the Collective. B. Wilson
Murder in the English Department. V. Miner
Murder in the Family. M. Brandel
Murder in the Family. D. Delman
*Murder in the Family. J. Ronald
*Murder in the Gilded Cage. S. Spewack
Murder in the Magnolias. T. J. Kelly
Murder in the Map Room. F. Bream
Murder in the Markets. A. McKee-Wright
*Murder in the Navy. R. Marsten
Murder in the Queen's Armes. A. J. Elkins
Murder in the Smithsonian. M. Truman
*Murder in the Stars. M. Halliday
Murder in the Supreme Court. M. Truman
*Murder in the Surgery. J. G. Edwards
Murder in the Title. S. Brett
*Murder in Trinidad. J. W. Vandercook
Murder in Vain. L. Mantell
Murder in White. H. Zachary
Murder, Inspector. M. Mangan
Murder Intended. A. Jagger
Murder Is a Pendulum. C. Joyce
Murder Is Academic. P. M. Carlson
*Murder Is Announced. L. Darbon
Murder Is Fun! C. Blankenship
Murder Is Its Own Reward. P. Chambers
Murder Is Murder Is Murder. S. M. Steward
*Murder Is My Business. B. Halliday
Murder Isn't Enough. D. Flynn
Murder Makes Tracks. G. Linscott
*Murder Man. W. Bogart
Murder Market. M. Strongman
*Murder Matinee. B. Carson
Murder Mayhem. R. Stahl
*Murder Mistaken. J. Green
Murder, Mr. Mosley. J. Greenwood
*Murder Moon. P. H. Dobbins
Murder Most Irregular. H. P. Jeffers
Murder Most Strange. Dell Shannon
*Murder Mystery. G. Thompson
Murder No Object. W. Massey
*Murder of a Fifth Columnist. L. Ford
Murder of a Moderate Man. J. Howlett
*Murder of a Mystery Writer. E. Heath
Murder of an Old-Time Movie Star. T. Kingsley-Smith
Murder of an Owl. G. Carr

*Murder of Ann Avery. H. Kuttner
Murder of Auguste Dupin. B. Tarver
Murder of Maria Marten. B. J. Burton
*Murder of Roger Ackroyd. A. Christie
*Murder of Sherlock Holmes. James Anderson
*Murder of Steven Kester. H. Ashbrook
*Murder Off Miami. D. Wheatley
Murder on Capitol Hill. M. Truman
Murder on Cue. J. Dentinger
Murder on Embassy Row. M. Truman
Murder on Her Mind. S. Steiner
Murder on High. G. Kennedy
*Murder on Ice. V. Gunn
Murder on Ice. T. Wood
Murder on Location. H. Engel
Murder on Location. G. Kennedy
Murder on Madison Avenue. F. Orenstein
Murder on Martha's Vineyard. K. Roos
Murder on Mike. H. P. Jeffers
*Murder on Mondays. C. Bush
Murder on Page Three. E. Griffiths
Murder on the Air. F. W. Warner
Murder on the Appalachian Trail. J. Carr
*Murder on the Blackboard. S. Palmer
Murder on the Hudson. D. Flynn
*Murder on the Long Straight. C. Yarborough
*Murder on the Orient Express. A. Christie
*Murder on the Second Floor. F. Vosper
*Murder on the Thirty-First Floor. P. Wahloo
*Murder on the Wild Side. J. Jacks
Murder or Not. L. Stephan
Murder Out of Wedlock. H. Pentecost
Murder Over Miami. J. Reach
Murder Pie. J. L. Rankin
Murder Play. B. J. Burton
*Murder Pool. E. Heath
Murder Post-Dated. A. Morice
Murder Round the Clock. H. Pentecost
Murder Sees the Light. H. Engel
Murder Stops the Clock. C. Rice
Murder Story. L. A. Knight
Murder Sweet and Sour. H. Pentecost
Murder Takes a Holiday. T. J. Kelly
Murder to Burn. L. Mantell
*Murder Town. L. Marshall
Murder Triangle. Lawrence Williams
Murder Unprompted. S. Brett
Murder Well Rehearsed. J. R. Carroll
*Murder Will Out. M. Leinster
Murder with Muskets. J. Reeves
*Murder with Pictures. G. H. Coxe
Murder Without Crime. J. L. Thompson
*Murder Without Weapon. Means Davis
Murdercon. R. Purtill
*Murderer. G. Simenon
*Murderer's Row. D. Hamilton
*Murder's a Swine. N. Lombard
*Murders in Praed Street. J. Rhode
Murder's Out of Tune. S. Woods
Murdock. G. Simmons
*Murray, the Detective. Old Sleuth
Muscle Beach Party. Elsie Lee
*Museum Piece No. 13. Rufus King
Music from Another Room. J. Kelly
Music Wars. G. Pape
Muskrat Ramble. L. Maddox
*Mutatis Mutandis. D. Campton
*Mute Witness. R. Pike
*Mutilator. B. Heatter
My Brow Is Wet. K. Leopold
*My Cousin Rachel. D. Du Maurier
*My Cousin Rachel. Diana Morgan
My Death Is a Mockery. D. G. Baber
*My Flesh Is Sweet. D. Keene
*My Gun Is Quick. M. Spillane
My Hate Lies Bleeding. A. Sewart
*My Indian Queen. G. Boothby
*My Lady's Garter. J. Futrelle
My Lord Conceit. Rita
*My Official Wife. R. H. Savage
*My Own Murderer. R. Hull
My Sister in This House. W. Kesselman
My Sister's Keeper. D. Merritt
My Sweet Andrina. V. C. Andrews
My Vision's Enemy. Robin Chapman
Mycroft Memorandum. R. Walsh
Myrimidon Project. C. Scarborough
*Mysteries and Miseries of New York. Old Sleuth
*Mysteries of Paris. E. Sue
Mysteries of Winterthurn. J. C. Oates
*Mysterious Miss Death. G. Evans
*Mysterious Mr. Garland. W. Martyn
*Mysterious Mr. Quin. A. Christie
Mysterious Murder of the Blonde Play-Girl. A. Abbot
Mystery and More Mystery. R. Arthur
*Mystery at Newton Ferry. L. Meynell
*Mystery at Spanish Hacienda. J. Gregory
Mystery at the Carrol Ranch. C. L. Kingsbury
*Mystery in Kensington Gore. M. Porlock
Mystery in Mdina. A. Hunt
*Mystery Man. Old Sleuth

*Mystery Mind. A. B. Reeve
*Mystery of a Hansom Cab. F. Hume
*Mystery of Alfred Doubt. W. Hay
Mystery of Aloha House. L. Roddy
Mystery of Cedar Valley. V. Henry
Mystery of Dr. Fu-Manchu. S. Rohmer
Mystery of Edwin Drood. C. Dickens
*Mystery of Enid Favell. J. N. Chance
*Mystery of Hunting's End. M. G. Eberhart
Mystery of Marlborough House. Anonymous
*Mystery of Mr. Bernard Brown. E. P. Oppenheim
Mystery of Mynd. W. Statham
*Mystery of One Night. Old Sleuth
*Mystery of Orcival. E. Gaboriau
Mystery of the Black Abbot. T. J. Kelly
*Mystery of the Black Dagger. P. Elliott
*Mystery of the Boule Cabinet. B. E. Stevenson
Mystery of the Boxing Contest. B. Hobson
Mystery of the Crooks' Contract. Anonymous
Mystery of the Ice-Cream Man. J. G. Brandon
*Mystery of the Louvre. A. Bernede
Mystery of the Priest's Parlour. G. Irons
*Mystery of the S.S. Timor. G. Grantham
Mystery of the Twisted Man. L. De Bechevet
*Mystery of the Yellow Room. G. Leroux
*Mystery Road. E. P. Oppenheim
*Mystery Stories. S. Ellin
Myth-ing Persons. R. Asprin
NYPD 2025. H. Stryker
Nailed. M. Litchfield
*Naked and the Lost. F. M. Davis
Naked Blade, Naked Gun. A. Kilgore
*Naked City. M. Wald
*Naked Face. Sidney Sheldon
*Naked Island. B. Heatter
*Naked Kiss. S. Fuller
Naked Liar. H. Adams
*Naked Runner. F. Clifford
*Naked Spur. A. Ullman
Name of Annabel Lee. J. Symons
Name of the Rose. U. Eco
Nameless. Ramsey Campbell
Nameless Corpse. C. B. Kelland
Names. D. De Lillo
Nana. Delacorta
*Nanny. E. Piper
Nantucket Diet Murders. V. Rich
Narrow Corner. B. Copper
Narrow Margin. R. Fleischer
*Narrowing Circle. J. Symons
Nashville with a Bullet. B. Sadler
Nasty Things. A. Lovegrove
Nathanial. J. Saul
*Natural Causes. H. Cecil
Natural Causes. J. Valin
Natural Enemy. J. Langton
Natural Victims. I. Eberstadt
Natural Weapon. G. Mitchelmore
Nature of the Beast. M. MacGowan
Naughty Girls. A. Wise
Nazi Hunter. M. Mandell
Nazi's Wife. P. Watson
Nearly Four. E. Coles
*Neat Little Corpse. M. Murray
Nebraska Quotient. W. J. Reynolds
Necessary End. Anthea Fraser
Necessity. B. Garfield
Need to Know. W. Haggard
Needle. J. A. Potter
Needle Track. P. Conway
*Nefarious Quest. H. Janson
*Negatives. P. Everett
*Negrohead. R. Bridges
*Neither the Sea Nor the Sand. G. Honeycombe
Nella. J. Godey
Nelson Touch. N. Grant
Nemarluck King of the Wilds. I. L. Idriess
Nemesis. J. Bedford
*Neon Madness. John Harvey
Nerissa Claire Case. H. Waugh
Nero's Luck. J. Kisner
Nerve Center. H. Janson
Nerve Endings. W. Martin
Nervous Affair. K. Wilhelm
*Net. J. Pudney
Neuromancer. W. Gibson
Neutron Nightmare. L. Derrick
Nevada Nightmare. N. Winski
*Never a Dull Moment. P. Cheyney
*Never Come Back. J. Mair
*Never-Fail Detective. H. Holmes
Never Forgive, Never Forget. J. Persico
Never Hit a Lady. F. S. Tobey
*Never Kill a Cop. L. Costigan
*Never Kill a Cop. H. Searls
Never Look Back. R. Pearson
Never Love a Stranger. H. Robbins
Nevermore. R. Boldrewood
Nevksy's Demon. D. Gat

Nevsky's Return. D. Gat
*New Arabian Nights. R. L. Stevenson
New Blood. R. Salem
*New Centurions. J. Wambaugh
New Friend. R. Eden
New Girl Friend. R. Rendell
New Hope for the Dead. C. Willeford
New Improved Murder. E. Gorman
*New Leaf. J. Ritchie
*New Othello. I. D. Hardy
New War. D. Pendleton
New Year Resolution. A. Cairns
*Newhaven-Dieppe. G. Simenon
*Newman Factor. J. S. Prager
News Girl. H. Brand
*News of Paul Temple. F. Durbridge
Newspaper Murders. Joe Gash
Next. B. Randall
*Next Man. M. Z. Lewin
Next of Kin. M. G. Eberhart
Next of Kin. W. B. Murphy
*Next-to-Last Train Ride. C. Dennis
Nhu Sting. E. Helm
Nice Day for a Murder. B. Adamson
Nice Knight for Murder. P. Daniels
Nice Sound Alibi. P. Lauben
*Nice Way to Die. H. Janson
*Nickel Ride. M. T. Kaufman
Nicole. J. H. Hull
*Nig-Nog. E. Wallace
*Night After Night. S. Thurman
Night and Fog. G. St. Germain
Night and Morning. E. Bulwer-Lytton
*Night and Morning. Old Sleuth
*Night and the City. G. Kersh
Night Bait. P. Straker
Night Before Christmas. L. Perelman
Night Call from a Distant Time Zone. H. Lieberman
Night Caller. B. Patrick
*Night Callers. F. Crisp
Night Chant. C. Woods
*Night-Comers. E. Ambler
*Night Cover. M. Z. Lewin
Night Cries. T. Krueger
*Night Cry. W. L. Stuart
*Night Darkens the Streets. A. La Bern
Night Ferry to Death. P. Moyes
Night Fishers of Antibes. C. Leopold
Night Has a Thousand Eyes. H. Astrup
*Night Has a Thousand Eyes. G. Hopley
*Night Has Eyes. A. Kennington
Night Hostess. P. Dunning
*Night in October. M. Callard
Night Intruder. P. Reakes
Night Is for Hunting. P. Barstow
Night Is My Undoing. D. Jackson
Night Mall Mystery. C. H. Ogilvie
Night Manhattan Burned. B. Jackson
Night Moves. N. Roberts
*Night Moves. A. Sharp
Night Music. L. Palmer
*Night Must Fall. W. Drummond
*Night Must Fall. Emlyn Williams
Night Nurse. D. Macy
Night of Error. D. Bagley
*Night of January 16. A. Rand
*Night of June 13. F. Vreeland
Night of Morningstar. P. O'Donnell
Night of the Falcon. J. Oxford
Night of the Fox. J. Lee
*Night of the Generals. H. H. Kirst
*Night of the Good Children. M. Carleton
*Night of the Hunter. D. Grubb
*Night of the Juggler. W. P. McGivern
*Night of the Living Dead. J. Russo
Night of the Peacock. J. Rosenberger
Night of the Phoenix. R. Austin
Night of the Ripper. R. Bloch
Night of the Running Man. Lee Wells
Night of the Thugee. G. Wilson
Night of the Tiger. M. Kistler
Night of the Warheads. Nick Carter
Night of the Wolf. C. Bryan
*Night of Wenceslas. L. Davidson
*Night on the Island. M. M. Kaye
*Night Operator. F. Packard
*Night Pieces. T. Burke
Night Probe! C. Cussler
Night Rituals. M. Jahn
Night She Died. D. Simpson
Night Sky. C. Francis
Night Talk. R. Timperley
Night the Gods Smiled. E. Wright
Night They Murdered Chelsea. M. Hinxman
*Night Walker. D. Hamilton
*Night Walker. S. Stuart
*Night Was Our Friend. M. Pertwee
*Night Watch. T. Walsh
Night Watcher. J. F. Murphy, Jr.
*Night Without Sleep. E. Moll
*Night Without Stars. Winston Graham
Nightbloom. H. Lieberman
*Nightcap. M. Marcin
Nightcap. J. C. S. Smith
*Nightcomers. M. Hastings
*Nightfall. D. Goodis
Nightflier. C. Fahy
Nightingale Trivet. R. Mead

Title Index

Nightlines. J. Lutz
*Nightmare. A. Blaisdell
*Nightmare. C. Woolrich
*Nightmare Alley. W. L. Gresham
Nightmare in Laos. J. Lansing
*Nightmare in Manhattan. T. Walsh
Nightmare Legacy. J. Corby
Nightmare Network. R. Rainey
Nightmare's Nest. K. O'Hara
Night's Black Agent. W. Townend
Nightscape. T. Chastain
Nightshades. B. Pronzini
*Nightwatch. L. Fletcher
*Nightwatchman. B. Hannah
*Nightwebs. C. Woolrich
Nightwind. M. Washburn
*Nightwing. M. C. Smith
Nightwork. Joseph Hansen
*Nightwork. I. Shaw
*Nihilist's Vengeance. E. C. Derby
Nile Green. D. Jordan
Nile Shadows. E. Whittemore
*Nimble Ike, the Detective. Old Sleuth
*Nine Bears. E. Wallace
*Nine Buck's Row. T. E. Huff
*Nine Days' Blunder. W. G. Elliott
Nine Girls. W. H. Pettitt
*Nine Lives Are Not Enough. J. Odlum
*Nine Times Nine. H. H. Holmes
1988. R. Lamm
1956. S. Marlowe
19 Purchase Street. G. A. Browne
*19 Red Roses. T. Nielsen
*Nineteen Stories. G. Greene
Ninety Nine. J. Ahern
*99 44/100% Dead. M. Franklin
*Ninja. E. V. Lustbader
Ninth Dragon. E. B. Cross
*Ninth Guest. O. Davis
Ninth Netsuke. James Melville
*Nita's Place. H. Whittington
No Answer. E. Westward
*No Answer from a Corpse. R. Stahl
*No Beasts So Fierce. E. Bunker
No City of Angels. N. Noye
No Clear Evidence. J. Heys
*No Coffin for the Corpse. C. Rawson
No Comebacks. F. Forsyth
No Condition is Permanent. D. Fulani
No Crime Like the Present. W. Gleason
No Cure for Death. M. A. Collins
*No Dame Wants to Die. M. Clinton
*No Down Payment. J. McPartland
*No Earth for Foxes. M. O'Brine
No Escape. J. Hayes
No Escape. S. Kemp
*No Exit. G. Goodchild
No Exit. H. Scott
No Extradition. A. Safroni-Middleton
*No Face for a Killer. H. Spencer
*No Face in the Mirror. H. McLeave (R. Copeland)
No Future for Miss Morrow. B. Schwarz
*No Hands on the Clock. G. Homes
No Lady in the House. L. Kallen
No Love for Miss Stent. W. Charles
No Man Is an Island. J. M. Simmel
No Man's Island. Jessica Mann
No Man's Land. Reginald Hill
*No Man's Land. L. J. Vance
*No Marks for Trying. S. Allan
*No Medals for the Major. M. Yorke
No Mother to Guide Her. A. Forsythe
*No Orchids for Miss Blandish. J. H. Chase
No Part in Your Death. N. Freeling
No Place to Be Somebody. C. Gordone
No Place to Hide. T. Allbeury
*No Pockets in a Shroud. H. McCoy
*No Quarter for a Star. D. Gray
*No Proud Chivalry. M. Procter
*No Regrets for Clara. H. Janson
No Rest for the Dying. J. Kelly
No Resting Place. I. Niall
No Rules, No Referee. G. Wilson
No Sanctuary. T. Harriott
No Stone. K. Blake
No Time to Wait! W. Standish
*No Vindication. Mrs. C. Kernahan
*No Way to Treat a Lady. H. Longbaugh
No Winding Sheet. G. Mitchell
Nobask. M. Creagh
Nobbler. J. Royale
Noble Enemy. C. Fox
Noble House. J. Clavell
*Nobody. L. J. Vance
Nobody Cared for Kate. G. Thompson
*Nobody Lives Forever. W. R. Burnett
Nobody Loves Me. E. Cannon
Nobody's Perfect. R. Reinsmith
Nobody's Supposed to Murder the Butler. J. N. Chance
Nocturnal. K. Eulo
Nocturne for the General. J. Trenhaile
Nomads of the North. J. O. Curwood
Nonconformist Parson. R. Horniman
None Should Look. R. Kingston
*None So Blind. M. A. Wilson
Noonday Devil. R. McInerny
Normandie Affair. E. Villiers

Normandie Triangle. Justin Scott
Normandy Code. Nick Carter
*North Star Crusade. W. Katz
Northern Exposure. M. Kilian
*Northing Tramp. E. Wallace
Northlight. Adam Hall
Norwegian Spring, 1940. S. Engstrand
Norwegian Typhoon. Nick Carter
*Norwich Victims. F. Beeding
Nose of Papa Hilaire. K. MacNichol
*Nose on My Face. L. Payne
Nostradamus Horoscope. Graham Lord
Not a Blessed Thing! M. Quill
Not a Stranger. J. R. Feegel
Not a Through Street. E. Larsen
*Not After Midnight. D. Du Maurier
*Not Comin' Home to You. P. Kavanagh
Not Dead, Only Resting. S. Brett
Not Exactly a Brahmin. S. Dunlay
*Not Exactly Ghosts. A. Caldecott
*Not Herbert. H. I. Young
Not My Thing. J. H. Chase
Not on the Agenda. N. Gilbert
*Not Safe to Be Free. J. H. Chase
*Not Too Narrow--Not Too Deep. R. Sale
Not Working. G. Szanto
*Nothing But the Night. J. Blackburn
*Nothing But the Truth. P. Orum
Nothing Ever Happens Here. A. McMaster
*Nothing in the Way. C. Williams
*Nothing Like Blood. L. Bruce
*Nothing More Than Murder. J. Thompson
Nothing New. Anonymous
Nothing to Do with the Case. E. Lemarchand
Nothing to Lose. R. Drayton
Notice of Death. J. Penn
*Notorious Landlady. I. Shulman
*Notorious Miss Lisle. Mrs. B. Reynolds
*Notorious Sophie Lang. F. I. Anderson
*November Man. B. Granger
*November Wind. P. Geddes
Novena for Murder. Sister C. A. O'Marie
*Now and On Earth. J. Thompson
Nowhere. T. Berger
Nowhere Fast. V. Wallen
*Nowhere to Go. D. MacKenzie
*No. 17. J. J. Farjeon
*Number Seventeen. L. Tracy
*Number Six. E. Wallace
*No. 13 Washington Square. L. Scott
Nun of the Above. M. Quill
*Nursemaid Who Disappeared. P. MacDonald
Nursery. D. Lippincott
Nursery. D. Shlian
Nyloned Avenger. H. Janson
*Nymph in the Night. H. Janson
*Nympho Named Silvia. H. Janson
Nymphs and Satires. R. Ferguson
OPEC Objective. M. Hammonds
O, Susannah! K. Wilhelm
*Oakdale Affair. E. R. Burroughs
*Obelists at Sea. C. D. King
Obscure Grave. Sara Woods
Obsession. H. Janson
*Obsession. L. White
Occupational Hazards. H. H. Roberts
*Ocean Road. Jack Bennett
*Ocean's 11. G. C. Johnson
Octavia's Hill. M. Dickson
*October Cabaret. J. Quest
*October Heat. G. De Marco
October Man. E. Britton
*Octopussy and The Living Daylights. I. Fleming
Octoroon. D. Boucicault
*Odd Man Out. F. L. Green
Odd Number. G. Sorrentino
*Odds Against Tomorrow. W. P. McGivern
Odds Are Murder. M. McQuay
*Odds Run out. H. Waugh
Odessa Beach. B. Leuci
*Odessa File. F. Forsyth
*Odor of Violets. B. Kendrick
Of Dope and Dervishes. L. Gainsborough
*Of Missing Persons. D. Goodis
Of Our Time. J. Gordon
Of Wilful Intent. Sheila Johnson
*Ofanu. G. Forve
*Off Duty. A. Coburn
*Off-Islanders. N. Benchley
Office Party. M. A. Gilbert
Office Party--and After. R. Timperley
*Officer 666. B. Currie
Official Secrets. J. Dell
Oh Shepherd, Speak! U. Sinclair
*Oil by Murder. J. Paul
Oil Pirates. L. O. Johnson
Oil Rig. F. Roderus
*Old Acquaintance. N. Guild
Old Country House. Anonymous
*Old Detective's Pupil. Nicholas Carter
Old Dick. L. A. Morse
Old-Fashioned Mystery. R. Fairleigh
Old Fears. R. Wolfe
Old Fox Deceiv'd. M. Grimes
*Old Ironsides Among the Italian Brigands. Old Sleuth
*Old Judge Priest. I. S. Cobb

*Old Lover's Ghost. L. Ford
Old Man Curry. C. E. Van Loan
*Old Man in the Corner. B. Orczy
Old Money. L. Fosburgh
Old Mortality, King of Detectives. Y. Baxter
Old Murders. P. Whalley
*Old Patch's Medley. M. Bowen
Old Scores to Settle. C. Heath
Old Vengeful. A. Price
*Oldest Confession. R. Condon
Oliver Twisted. T. J. Kelly
Omega Deception. C. Robertson
*Omega Operation. N. Conway
*Omega Threat. M. Washburn
Omelet Murder Case. T. J. Kelly
On Account of Murder. E. Powers
On Any Given Sunday. P. Toomey
On Course for Murder. P. A. Foxall
*On Her Majesty's Secret Service. I. Fleming
On Secret Air Service. L. L. T. Driggs
On Such a Night. A. Quayle
On Suspicion. David Fletcher
*On the Borderland. F. B. Austin
*On the Brink of Ruin. Old Spicer
*On the Double. Roger Fuller
On the Loose. E. V. Adams
*On the Night of the Fire. F. L. Green
On the Other Hand. R. Stevenson
*On the Spot. E. Wallace
On the Stroke of 12. J. LeBrandt
On the Third Day. M. Delahaye
On the Waterfront. B. Schulberg
*On the Yard. M. Braly
*On Trial. E. Reizenstein
*On Trial. D. Torbett
*Once a Crook. E. Price
Once a Mutt. W. B. Murphy
"Once a Prostitute." A. Hunter
Once a Spy. R. Airth
Once a Thief. J. Trinian
Once Dying, Twice Dead. R. Lewis
Once in Aleppo. D. R. Barton
*Once Off Guard. J. H. Wallis
Once There Was a Giant. K. Laumer
*Once Too Often. W. Chambers
Once Upon a Time in America. L. Hays
Once We Were Men. G. Nimse
One Against Time. H. Janson
*One Bright Summer Morning. J. H. Chase
*One Clear Call. F. N. Greene
One Clear Call. U. Sinclair
One Coffee With. M. Maron
One Damn Thing After Another. N. Freeling
One Day in Hell. H. Zachary
*One Deadly Summer. S. Japrisot
One Deathless Hour. R. Ormerod
One Dollar Death. R. Barth
*One Down. A. Bodelsen
One Easy Piece. D. Merritt
One Enchanted Summer. A. Brooks
One-Eyed Mystic. K. Robeson
One for the Books. L. A. Taylor
One for the Money. D. Belsky
One for the Money. E. Chaze
*One Jump Ahead. Robert Chapman
One Lover Too Many. M. Tripp
*One Mad Night. J. Reach
One-Man Army. J. Cutter
One Man in His Time. S. D. Frances
One Man's Justice. P. Alding
One Man's Reality. C. Cornwall
*One Man's Secret. S. Davis
*One More Time. M. Avallone
One Night in Winter. A. Massie
One Police Plaza. W. J. Caunitz
One-Shot War. B. O'Connor
One Step Ahead. R. Forest
*One Step from Murder. L. Meynell
*1001 Afternoons in New York. B. Hecht
One-Two-Three Die. L. Starr
One-Way Split. H. Janson
*One-Way Trail. R. Cullum
*One-Way Trip. R. Angel
One Woman. T. Thayer
*One Wonderful Night. L. Tracy
*Onion Field. J. Wambaugh
Only an Orphan Girl. H. Nelms
Only Good Apple in a Barrel of Spies. M. Lovell
*Only Good German. T. Allbeury
Only Half a Hoax. L. A. Taylor
Only in L.A. Murray Sinclair
*Only in New England. T. Roscoe
Only Men on Board. Cameron Blake
Only Problem. M. Spark
Only the Dead Know Brooklyn. T. Boyle
Only the Good Die. W. Barker
Only the Strong. M. Minehan
Only When I Larf. L. Deighton
Only When I Laugh. L. Deighton
Open and Shut Case. J. Mattera
Open Door. L. Meynell
Open House. W. Katz
Open Prison. J. I. M. Stewart
Open Secret. J. Leasor
Openers of the Gate. L. A. Beck
Opening of a Door. W. Spence

Opera House Murders. D. Hanna
Operation Aphrodite. J. Commmings
*Operation Artemis. Douglas Scott
Operation Atlantis. G. Ludi
Operation Black Sea. W. X. Davies
Operation Boudoir. S. O'Shea
Operation Choke Point. W. X. Davies
*Operation Cicero. L. C. Moyzisch
*Operation Cobra. A. Bodelsen
Operation: Death Ray. S. Cunningham
Operation Desert Sun. C. Heath
Operation Destruct. C. Nicole
Operation Diver. R. Jackson
Operation Emerald. D. McCartan
Operation Firedog. R. Jackson
Operation Heartbreak. A. D. Cooper
Operation Icicle. P. Buck
Operation Lila. M. H. Albert
Operation: McMurdo Sound. Nick Carter
Operation Manhunt. C. Nicole
Operation Midnight Climax. N. Bell
*Operation Missat. J. Dark
Operation Neptune. C. Nicole
Operation Night Hawk. J. A. Price
Operation North Africa. W. X. Davies
Operation Obliterate. H. Janson
Operation Parterre. G. Blagowidow
Operation Persian Gult. W. X. Davies
Operation Q-018. G. Ludi
Operation Raven. Stuart White
Operation Sharkbite. Nick Carter
Operation Skyhook. J. Rosenberger
Operation Smokescreen. M. Judge
Operation Susie. K. Blake
Operation Ten. H. Scott
*Operation Terror. Gordons
Operation Vendetta. Nick Carter
Operative. J. Covington
Opium. T. Cohan
Opium Hunter. A. Kilgore
Opium Strategem. H. Downes
Or All the Seas with Oysters. Avram Davidson
Or the Bambino Dies. P. Inchbald
Orange. J. Howlett
Orbit. T. H. Block
Orbiting Omega. D. Pendleton
Orchid Tree. V. Coffman
Orchids. T. H. Cook
*Ordeal. D. Collins
*Ordeal by Innocence. A. Christie
*Ordeal of Major Grigsby. J. Sherlock
*Orders to Kill. D. Downes
*Ordinary Lunacy. Jessica Anderson
Organized Crimes. N. Von Hoffman
Origin of a Vendetta. J. Ahern
Original Sin. G. Tabori
*Orion Line. N. Luard
Orion's Shroud. W. P. Cooke
O'Rourke Affair. J. Calder
Orphan Army. L. Derrick
*Oscar, the Detective. Old Sleuth
*Oshawa Project. F. Nolan
Oslo Intrigue. H. Astrup
Osprey Dilemma. Steve Hayes
*Osterman Weekend. R. Ludlum
Other. C. Carr
Other. P. Lindau
*Other. T. Tryon
*Other Anne Fletcher. S. Jaffe
Other David. C. Coker
Other Karen. V. Johnston
*Other Men's Shoes. A. Soutar
Other Men's Wives. W. Hackett
*Other One. C. Turney
Other People. M. Amis
Other People. S. Stein
*Other People's Money. E. Gaboriau
*Other Prison. F. Hume
*Other Romilly. E. P. Oppenheim
Other Shoe. M. McMullen
Other Side. D. Henstell
*Other Side of Midnight. Sidney Sheldon
Other Side of Silence. T. Allbeury
*Other Side of the Door. L. Chamberlain
*Otley. M. Waddell
Otto's Boy. W. Wager
Ouija. A. Laurance
Our Father's Lies. Anthony Taylor
Our Friends from Frolix 8. P. K. Dick
*Our Man Flint. J. Pearl
*Our Man in Havana. G. Greene
*Our Mother's House. J. Gloag
Ouster Conspiracy. Nick Carter
Out Are the Lights. R. Laymon
*Out by the River. L. Peters
*Out for Kicks. W. Shaw
Out in the Shadows. D. Stein
Out of Season. M. Lewin
Out of Sight--Out of Murder. F. Carmichael
Out of the Blackout. R. Barnard
Out of the Blue. J. McManus
Out of the Blue. J. Milne
*Out of the Dark. U. Curtiss
*Out of the Night. Dan Ross
*Out of the Storm. B. Braddon
Out of This World. A. Goetz
Out of Time. M. Lewin
Out to Win. R. Pertwee

Outback. A. Fletcher
Outback Ghosts. Nick Carter
Outbid. D. Hume
*Outcast. H. Janson
Outcasts. J. L. Hensley
Outer Edges. C. R. Jackson
*Outer Gate. O. R. Cohen
*Outfit. R. Stark
*Outlaw's Oath. E. C. Derby
Outrage. H. Denker
Outrageous Fortune. M. Elmblad
Outrageous Fortune. M. L. Machin
Outrider. R. Harding
Outside Man. R. N. Patterson
Outside the Law. T. Browning
Outsider. E. R. Sabato
*Outsiders. A. E. Martin
Overheard. S. Aumonier
Overload. C. Kearey
Owl. R. Forward
Oxford Blood. Antonia Fraser
Ozark Flats. Bob Williams
PK Factor. C. H. Martin
Pace That Thrills. R. Weber
*Pacific Cavalcade. V. Coffman
Pacific Clipper. R. Doyle
Pacific Interlude. L. Gentle
Pacific Vortex. C. Cussler
Pact of Love. Magali
Paddy's Puzzle. F. Kidman
Pagoda Tree. B. Mather
*Paid in Full. N. Cronin
*Paid in Full. J. Goodwin
Paige. J. Jenkins
Painless Death. S. Rena
*Painswick Line. H. Cecil
Paint the Town Red. H. Adams
Painted Castle. Jennie Melville
*Painted Woman. F. A. Kummer
Pakistan Kill Ground. J. Rosenberger
Palace Guard. C. MacLeod
*Palace of Chance. Old Spicer
*Pale Hand of Danger. M. Lynch
*Pale Horse. A. Christie
Palimpsest. M. E. Atkins
*Paliser Case. E. Saltus
*Palomino Blonde. T. Allbeury
Pals First. L. W. Dodd
Pam Slipped Up. Dirk Foster
*Pamela's Palace. A. J. Fitzgerald
Pamplona Affair. Nick Carter
Panda Bear Is Critical. F. Michaels
*Panda One Investigates. P. N. Walker
*Panda One on Duty. P. N. Walker
Pandora Plague. L. A. Matthias
Pandora Secret. A. Forrest
Pangersbourne Murders. J. Sturrock
*Pangolin. P. Driscoll
*Panic in Needle Park. J. Mills
"Panther". H. J. S. Anderton
Panther Throne. T. Murphy
Panther's Claw. A. Goetz
*Panther's Moon. V. Canning
Papa Legacy. J. R. Pici
Paper Boat. Palinuris
*Paper Chase. O. W. Bayer
*Paper Chase. R. Esser
Paper Chase. J. McNally
Paper Gun. H. Browne
Paper Orchid. A. La Bern
Papers of Tony Veitch. W. McIlvanney
Par for the Corpse. J. Sharkey
Parachutists. Ed Klein
*Paradine Case. R. Hichens
Paradine's Gauntlet. D. Pendleton
*Paradise Garden. G. F. Gibbs
Paradise in Flames. Joseph Brandon
Paradise Plot. E. Nahe
Paragon. R. Pertwee
Paragon Man. C. Garrison
Paragon Walk. A. Perry
*Parallax View. L. Singer
Paramilitary Plot. D. Pendleton
Parasite Person. C. Fremlin
*Paris Drop. A. Furst
Paris Kill. P. Kirk
Paris Puzzle. V. McConnor
Parisian Affair. Nick Carter
*Parisian Nights. R. Goyne
Park Avenue. W. V. Cole
Park Avenue Girl. F. Shaw
Park Is Mine. S. Peters
Parrot & Co. H. MacGrath
Parsifal Mosaic. R. Ludlum
Partisan Demolition. N. Cort
Partisans. A. MacLean
*Partners. W. Harrington
*Partners of the Night. L. Scott
*Party Girl. M. H. Albert
Party Killer. H. Pentecost
Party to Murder. M. Underwood
Passage. D. Fuller
Passage Through Midnight. U. Hall
*Passers-By. A. Partridge
Passing Game. S. Tesich
*Passing of Evil. M. McShane
*Passing of Mr. Quinn. G. R. McRae
Passion for Treason. R. Nicholson
Passion in the Peak. J. B. Hilton
Passion of Dracula. B. Hall

Passion of Molly T. Lawrence Sanders
*Passion Pact. H. Janson
*Passion Pulls the Trigger. A. Wallace
*Passionate Adventure. F. Stayton
*Passionate Land. G. Wagner
*Passionate Playmate. H. Janson
*Passionate Quest. E. P. Oppenheim
Passionate Sin. R. M. Stewart
Passionate Stranger. C. Gayet
*Passionate Waif. H. Janson
*Passport to Oblivion. J. Leasor
Passport to Peril. P. Buck
Passport to Peril. Anna C. Clarke
Passport to Peril. A. Hutton
*Passport to Treason. M. O'Brine
Past Murder Imperfect. B. Barton
Past, Present and Murder. H. Pentecost
Patch Unit. N. G. Bailey
Pathet Vengeance. M. K. Roberts
Patient in Cabin C. M. G. Eberhart
Patient in 4b. A. F. Daniels
*Patient in Room 18. M. G. Eberhart
Patricia Lancaster's Revenge. Beatrice Chase
*Patricia, the Beautiful. K. Kimbrough
Patriot Game. G. V. Higgins
Patriots. G. C. Seeber
Patrol of the Sun Dance Trail. R. Connors
*Patterned Rape. H. Janson
Patterns in the Dust. L. Grant-Adamson
Patterson's Volunteers. John Smith
*Paula. D. Kingery
Pauper Millionaire. A. Fryers
*Pawned. F. Packard
Pay Any Price. T. Allbeury
Pay-Off. D. Wiles
Paybacks. C. Britton
*Payment Deferred. J. Dell
*Payoff. A. Veraldi
*Payoff for Paula. J. Bogar
*Payroll. D. Bickerton
Peabody Experience. C. Carpenter
Peacock. S. Gibbons
Peacock Season. O. Bigelow
Peak of Frenzy. H. Brand
Pearlhanger. Jonathan Gash
Peeper. W. Brinkley
Peggy Paradine, House Agent. M. O'Nair
Pekin Target. Adam Hall
Peking Agent. J. D. Horan
Peking Mandate. P. Siris
Peking Target. Adam Hall
Pel and the Bombers. M. Hebden
*Pel and the Faceless Corpse. M. Hebden
Pel and the Pirates. M. Hebden
Pel and the Predators. M. Hebden
Pel and the Prowler. M. Hebden
Pel and the Staghound. M. Hebden
Pel Is Puzzled. M. Hebden
*Pel Under Pressure. M. Hebden
Pelican's Clock. R. Middlemiss
Penance for Jerry Kennedy. G. V. Higgins
*Penelope. E. V. Cunningham
*Penguin Pool Murder. S. Palmer
Penniless Millionaire. D. C. Murray
Penny Black. S. Moody
Penny Dreadful. S. Moody
Penny Ferry. R. Boyer
Penny Post. S. Moody
Pension for Death. R. H. Lewis
*Pentagon Case. V. J. Fox
*Penthouse. A. S. Roche
Penthouse. E. Trevor
*Penthouse Mystery. E. Queen
Penultimate Problem of Sherlock Holmes. J. Nassivera
*People Against Nancy Preston. J. A. Moroso
*People Against O'Hara. E. Lipsky
People in Glass Houses. E. Lewis
*People of Darkness. T. Hillerman
People vs. Kirk. R. Traver
People vs. Maxine Lowe. L. B. McMahon
People Who Knock on the Door. P. Highsmith
Perahera. Julia Leslie
*Pere Goriot. H. Balzac
Peregrine. W. Bayer
*Perfect Corpse. L. R. Wright
*Perfect Crime. E. Queen
Perfect End. W. Marshall
Perfect Fools. E. P. Green
Perfect Match. J. McGown
Perfect Poison. A. Campsie
Perfect Trap. D. Thurlow
*Perfectionist. L. Kauffman
Performance. D. Clark
*Perfume of the Lady in Black. G. Leroux
Perfumed Nemesis. H. Janson
Peril in the North. K. Robeson
*Perilous Passage. B. Nicolaysen
*Peripheral Spy. B. Peterson
Perish the Thought. J. Bonett
Perpetua. D. Calthrop
Persian Pride. H. Janson
Personal Justice. A. Hilborn
Perth Amboy Mystery. C. Clinch

Title Index

Peruvian Contracts. F. Fowlkes
Petals of Blood. Ngugi Wa Thiong'o
Petrified Forest. R. E. Sherwood
*Pew Group. A. Oliver
Phantom Drummer. A. Ridgway
*Phantom in the House. A. Soutar
*Phantom in the Wings. M. Elder
*Phantom Lady. W. Irish
*Phantom of Fonthill Park. K. R. Vernon
*Phantom of Forty-Second Street. M. M. Raison
*Phantom of the Opera. G. Leroux
Phantom of the Opera. G. Traylor
Phantom Plot. K. Kavanaugh
*Phantom President. G. F. Worts
Phantom Ship. Capt. Marryat
*Pharos the Egyptian. G. Boothby
*Philipp Steele of the Royal Northwest Mounted Police. J. O. Curwood
Philippa Sees It Through. D. Maule
*Phoenix. L. P. Bachmann
*Phoenix Formula. T. Leighton
Phoenix in Flames. G. Wilson
Phoenix Nest. M. Hermes
Phoenix Tree. J. Cleary
Phoenix with Oily Feathers. L. G. Shreve
*Phone for a Hearse. B. Carson
*Photo Finish. H. Mason
*Photocrimes. M. Horton
Physical Attraction. H. Janson
Piano Bird. L. Kallen
*Piano Box Mystery. Nicholas Carter
*Piccadilly Jim. P. G. Wodehouse
*Pickup Alley. E. Ronns
Picnic at Nearside. J. Varley
Picnic in November. E. Amshey
Picture on the Wall. J. B. Ellis
Pictures in the Dark. I. Stuart
*Pidgin Island. H. MacGrath
Piece of the Silence. J. Livingston
Pieces of Death. J. Lynch
*Pieces of Modesty. P. O'Donnell
Pier. R. Heppenstall
Pietrov and Other Games. Jeffrey Robinson
Pigeon Pie. N. Mitford
Pigeon's Blood. M. Pereira
Pigs Get Fat. W. B. Murphy
Pilgrim of Hate. Ellis Peters
*Pillory. B. Fleming
*Pinch of Snuff. M. Underwood
Pincher in Peace and War. C. M. Hincks
*Pink and the Brown. H. Atkinson
*Pink Panther. M. H. Albert
Pink Panther Strikes Again. W. Gleason
*Pink String and Sealing Wax. R. Pertwee
Pink Triangle. R. Raftery
*Pint of Murder. A. Craig
Pipe All Hands! Sinbad
Pipeline from Hell. D. Bannerman
Piper in the Street Today. B. Boswell
*Piper of Arristoun. B. Goldie
Pipes of Margaree. J. Aeby
*Pippin's Journal. R. O'Grady
Piranha, Piranha. I. Zacharia
Pirate Isle. K. Robeson
*Pirate's Retreat. L. Carlton
Pistolero. P. Kinsley
Pit. O. West
*Pit and the Pendulum. L. Sheridan
Pitch Dark. R. Adler
Pitchblende Quarry. A. Gordon
*Pitfall. J. J. Dratler
*Pity My Simplicity. C. Massie
Pity the Poor Rich. Yaffle
Pixie at the Wheel. D. Sturrock
Place for the Mighty. H. Denker
*Place in the Country. S. Gainham
Place of Little Birds. M. Home
Plagiarist. W. Myrtle
Plain Old Man. C. MacLeod
Plains of Fire. J. Hild
Plans for Departure. N. Sahgal
*Platinum Bullet. R. L. Graves
*Platinum High School. I. Shulman
*Play It Quiet. H. Janson
*Play Misty for Me. P. J. Gillette
*Play with Fire. E. Percy
Playback. R. Chandler
*Player and the Guest. G. F. Newman
*Player's Boy Is Dead. L. Tourney
*Playgirl. H. Janson
Playground of Death. J. B. Hilton
Playhouse. R. Levinson
Playing Catch-Up. A. B. Guthrie, Jr.
Playing Safe. E. Dewhurst
Playing with Fire. B. Veder
Playroom. M. Drayton
Please Communicate. M. Oldfield
*Pleasure Buyers. A. S. Roche
Pleasure Island. Nick Carter
Pleasuring of Rory Malone. C. Panati
*Pledge. F. Duerrenmatt
Pledge of Hatred. A. Andre
*Plotters of Peking. C. Dawe
Plowing Up a Snake. M. Drown
Plum Blossoms and Blue Incense. J. W. Bennett
Plum Thicket. J. Giles
Plumb. M. Gee
*Plunder. A. S. Roche
Plunder. B. Travers
*Plunder of the Sun. D. Dodge
Plundered Paradise. L. Derrick
*Plunderers. E. P. Oppenheim
Plutonium Factor. M. Bagley
*Poacher's Bag. D. Clark
Point of Honor. D. Gethin
*Point of Reference. Richard Russell
Point Team. J. B. Hadley
*Pointing Finger. Rita
*Poison. A. Askew
Poison. D. Linton
Poison in Putney. F. M. Long
*Poison Ivy. P. Cheyney
*Poison Pen. R. Llewellyn
*Poisoned Arrow. L. Carlton
*Poisoned Web. A. Clarke
Poker Game. F. Knebel
Pokerface. P. Corris
Policeman. Anonymous
Policeman's Lot. C. Bond
Policewoman. J. Uhnak
Pomeroy. G. M. Williams
*Pool of Flame. L. J. Vance
Pool Ticket. C. Baker
Pools of the Past. C. Procter
Poor Richard's Game. G. O'Toole
*Pop Goes the Queen. B. Wade
Pope Must Die. F. Norwood
*Pope of Greenwich Village. V. Patrick
*Pop. 1280. J. Thompson
Porcelain Dolls Don't Bleed. C. Vail
Porcupine Basin. D. Rutherford
Pork Butcher. D. Hughes
Porn Tapes. R. Rainey
*Port Afrique. B. V. Dryer
Port and a Star Boarder. B. J. Morison
*Port of Missing Men. N. Nicholson
Portland Murders. C. Larson
Portrait in Black. J. V. Frost
*Portrait in Black. I. Goff
Portrait in Black. Richard Vincent
Portrait in Fear. V. Henry
*Portrait in Smoke. B. Ballinger
*Portrait of a Mobster. H. Grey
*Portrait of Alison. F. Durbridge
Portrait of Lilith. J. Thomson
Position of Trust. R. Hart
Position of Ultimate Trust. W. Beechcroft
Possessed. A. Radnor
Possession. A. Rule
*Possession of Joel Delaney. R. Stewart
Post Mortem. P. Whalley
*Postman Always Rings Twice. J. M. Cain
Pot Holes. E. C. Webster
Potter's Wheel. F. C. Williams
Poverty Bay. E. W. Emerson
Powder Burn. W. D. Montalbano
*Power. F. M. Robinson
*Power. W. Harrington
Power and the Glory. D. Cannan
*Power and the Glory. G. Greene
*Power of a Villain. Warren Miller
Power of Nothingness. A. David-Neel
Powers. W. Bailey
*Practice to Deceive. G. Bradshaw
Prairie Fire. D. Pendleton
Pranks. D. Higman
Pratfall. T. A. Schock
Pray for Ricky Foster. J. Johnston
Prayer for an Assassin. I. Sentjurc
Prayer for Fair Weather. J. Broderick
Prayer for My Daughter. T. Babe
Prayer of a Chance. L. Leibee
Precinct 19. T. L. Adcock
Precinct #1: Siberia. T. Philbin
Precious Cargo. J. Pattinson
Precious Objects. D. G. Devon
Prediction. J. Hyde
Prelude in Prague. S. F. Wright
*Premature Burial. M. H. Danne
*Premier. G. Simenon
*Prescription: Murder. W. Link
*Presence in an Empty Room. V. Johnston
Present from Hugo. A. Paul
Present from Peking. D. Lampard
President Must Die. R. Raphael
*President Vanishes. Anonymous
Presidential Agent. U. Sinclair
Presidential Mission. U. Sinclair
President's Child. F. Weldon
President's Man. N. Guild
*President's Mystery Story. F. D. Roosevelt
Pressing Problems. V. Bird
Pressure Man. Zach Hughes
Pressure-Point. B. Copper
*Preston Jayne. Old Sleuth
Presumption of Guilt. J. Ashford
Presumption of Innocence. D. Pedneau
*Pretty Maids All in a Row. F. Pollini
Prey. C. T. Cline
Prey. G. Douglas
*Prey for a Newshawk. H. Janson
*Prey of the Falcon. R. Charles
*Prey of the Strongest. M. Roberts
Price of Heaven. S. Blackwelder
*Price of Protection. Warren Miller
Price of Silence. S. Barlay
Price of Silence. H. Pentecost
Pride of Kings. Justin Scott
Pride of Royals. Justin Scott
Priestly Murders. Joe Gash
Prima Donna at Large. B. Paul
*Prime Cut. M. Roote
Prime Suspect. R. D. Brown
Prime Target. J. MacAnthony
Prime Target. M. Russell
Prime Time Crime. W. Gleason
Prince and the Suti. B. L. Van Vors
Prince Buys the Manor. E. Huxley
Prince of Berlin. D. Sherman
Prince of Evil. G. Stockbridge
Prince of Malta. J. D. Buchanan
Princess Casamassina. H. James
Princess of Darkness. I. Zacharia
*Princess of Happy Chance. T. Gallon
Princess of New York. C. Hamilton
Princess of Steel. R. W. Kerr
Print-Out. R. Gillespie
*Prisoner. P. Boileau
Prisoner #3. D. McDaniel
*Prisoner of Fire. E. Cooper
Prisoner on the Dam. C. Coram
Prisoner on the Run. C. Coram
Prisoner's Wife. J. Holland
Prisonland. J. Frost
Private Life of Dr. Crippen. R. Gordon
Private Life of Dr. Watson. M. Hardwick
*Private Life of Sherlock Holmes. M. Hardwick
Private Memoirs and Confessions of a Justified Sinner. Anonymous
*Private Practice of Michael Shayne. B. Halliday
Private Screening. R. N. Patterson
*Privateer's Defiance. B. Wayde
*Privilege. John Burke
Prize Meets Murder. R. T. Edwards
*Prize of Gold. M. Catto
Prizzi's Honor. R. Condon
*Probability Broach. L. N. Smith
*Probability Factor. W. Kempley
Probability Pad. T. A. Waters
Problem in Prague. R. MacLeod
*Procane Chronicle. O. Bleeck
Process of Elimination. G. Baxt
Proctor Case. S. Blakesley
Prodigal. I. Osbourne
Prodigal Gun. E. L. Sloane
Productions of Time. J. Brunner
*Professional Guest. W. Garrett
Profit Motive. W. B. Murphy
Programmed for Danger. J. M. Favors
Programmed for Terror. B. W. Battin
Project Jael. A. Fletcher
Project Norouz. R. Swift
Prometheus Trap. V. Connolly
*Promise to Keep. L. A. Sunagel
Promises to Keep. H. Brett
Prompt for Murder. S. MacKellar
Proof. D. Francis
Property of a Lady. A. Oliver
Prophet Motive. Cleo Jones
Proprietor. G. C. Seeber
Props. J. B. Lynch
*Prose Romances of Edgar A. Poe. E. A. Poe
Prospero Drill. C. A. Posey
Protection of Democracy. P. Chesney
Protection Payoff. D. Glinto
Proteus Operation. J. P. Hogan
*Proteus Pact. G. St. George
Provence Puzzle. V. McConnor
Prussian Spy. V. Valmont
Psionics War. J. Rosenberger
*Psycho. R. Bloch
Psycho Soldiers. J. Cutter
Psycho II. R. Bloch
*Psychopath Plague. S. G. Spruill
*Public Enemy. K. Glasmon
Public Faces in Private Places. J. Rosner
*Public Murders. Joe Gash
Pungi Patrol. J. Lansing
*Punish the Sinners. J. Saul
Punishment. Doris Shannon
Puppet for a Corpse. D. Simpson
Puppet Master. Nick Carter
Puppet Master. A. McQuoid
*Puppet on a Chain. A. MacLean
Puppeteer. T. Williams
Pure As the Driven Snow. P. Loomis
Purple Mask. M. Lang
Purple Plant. A. Felton
*Pursuit. L. G. Blochman
Pursuit. H. Janson
Pursuit of Arms. G. Hammond
Pursuit of the Eagle. Nick Carter
Pursuit of the Owl. A. Howlett
*Pusher. E. McBain
Pushkin Shove. P. N. Gwynne
Put On by Cunning. R. Rendell
*Put on the Spot. J. Lait
Put Out the Light. Sara Woods

Putting the Boot In. D. Kavanagh
Puzzle for Experts. J. Nathanson
*Puzzle for Fiends. P. Quentin
*Puzzle for Puppets. P. Quentin
*Puzzle of the Pepper Tree. S. Palmer
*Puzzle of the Red Stallion. S. Palmer
*Puzzling Shadow. Old Sleuth
*Python Project. V. Canning
*Pyx. J. Buell
Q Factor. P. Kirk
Q-Man. Nick Carter
Quaking Terror. L. Derrick
*Qualified Adventurer. S. Jepson
Quality of the Informant. G. Petievich
Quality Parties. D. Clarins
*Qualtrough. Angus Hall
Quarmby. R. Sharp
Quarry. M. A. Collins
*Quarry. J. A. Moroso
Quarry's Cut. M. A. Collins
Quarry's Deal. M. A. Collins
Quarry's List. M. A. Collins
*Quartet of Three. M. Tripp
Queen Bee. E. Lee
*Queen in Danger. S. Rattray
*Queen of Blackmailers. M. O. Rolfe
Queen of Spades. J. C. Griffiths
Queen of Spades. H. H. Henderson
*Queen of the Black Hand. H. C. Davidson
Queen of the Night Clubs. M. Strongman
Queen of the Outlaw's Camp. O. Harper
*Queen of the World. G. Weston
*Queenie. W. F. Fauley
Queen's Crossing. B. Granger
Queen's Gate Reckoning. L. Perdue
Queen's Mate. T. Hughes
Queen's Messenger. W. R. Duncan
Quentin, a Spy. D. Selves
Quest for a Fortune. Philippa Tyler
Quest for Love. D. Faber
Quest of the Crimson Idol. H. J. S. Anderton
*Question of Evidence. Old Spicer
Question of Guilt. R. Gordon
Question of Judgment. T. Mix
Question of Law. M. Jon
Question of Murder. R. H. Lees
*Question of Policy. B. Wayde
Question of Quarry. G. Bagby
Question of Survival. E. Cannon
Quests of Simon Ark. E. D. Hoch
Quick Change. J. Cronley
Quicksilver. M. Gallagher
Quicksilver. B. Pronzini
*Quiet American. G. Greene
Quiet Assassin. T. Kirkwood
Quiet Dogs. J. Gardner
Quiet Earth. Craig Harrison
*Quiet Mrs. Fleming. R. Pryce
Quiet Murder and other stories. E. M. Bailey
*Quiet Place in the Country. H. Clement
Quiet Road to Death. S. Radley
Quiet Stranger. J. B. Hilton
*Quiet Waits the Grave. H. Janson
Quiller. Adam Hall
Quincannon. B. Pronzini
*Quinn. N. Scanlon
*Quinney's. H. A. Vachell
Quirinal Hall Affair. B. Hambly
*R.I.P. P. MacDonald
Rabbi's Spell. S. C. Cumberland
Race for the Golden Tide. Gordons
*Race of Death. Nick Carter
*Rachel, the Possessed. K. Kimbrough
*Racket. B. Cormack
Rackets and Dames. B. Barnato
Radiance. N. R. Nash
Radish River Caper. R. H. Spencer
*Rafferty. B. Ballinger
*Rafferty and the Gold Dust Twins. L. Roberts
*Raffles After Dark. B. Perowne
*Rag Bag Clan. R. Barth
*Rage. P. Friedman
*Rage. L. V. Roper
Rage in Heaven. J. Hilton
*Rage of Angels. S. Sheldon
Rage of Heaven. J. Eller
Rage of the Vulture. B. Unsworth
Ragged Plot. R. Barth
Raid. J. Romanes
*Raid on the Mint. F. Putnam
*Rain Before Seven. M. Brandel
Rain Lover. D. Burkey
Rain of Death. D. Stivers
Rain Rustlers. F. Roderus
*Rainbird Pattern. V. Canning
Rainblast. M. Russell
Rainbow in Hell. David Fletcher
Rainbow Ribbon. Pamela Thompson
Rainbow Soldiers. W. Winward
Rainbows End in Tears. David Fletcher
Rainsong. P. A. Whitney
Rainy City. E. W. Emerson
*Raise the Titanic! C. Cussler
Raker. Don Scott
Ralph. J. Stonehouse
Ralph Rashleigh. J. Tucker

Rambo: First Blood Part II. D. Morrell
Rampage. Justin Scott
Rampage. W. P. Wood
Rampage in Rio. L. Derrick
*Ramshackle House. H. Footner
Random Death. L. Egan
Rank Outsider. N. Gould
*Ransom. J. Messmann
*Ransom. P. Wheeler
Ransom for Miss Le Grun. B. Schwarz
Ransom Game. H. Engel
*Ransomed Madonna. L. White
Rap. E. Brawley
Rape One. F. Canavor
Rape Squad. S. Wolf
Rare and the Lovely. M. Blake
*Rascal's Nerve. M. O. Rolfe
*Rasp. P. MacDonald
Rat. P. Bottome
Rat Box. C. Clarke
Rat on Fire. G. V. Higgins
Rat Quotient. K. Hagenbach
Rat Race. J. Franklin
Ratcatcher. C. Dunne
Ratings Are Murder. R. R. Irvine
*Ratman's Notebooks. S. Gilbert
Rats' Alley. W. Garner
Rattle-Rat. J. Van De Wetering
*Rattling of Old Bones. J. Ross
*Rave for a Roughneck. H. Janson
Ravel of Waters. G. Jenkins
Raven. W. Kinsolving
Raven. M. Lundy
*Raven. E. Sudak
Raven's Longest Night. D. MacKenzie
Ravens of Rockhurst. M. Martin
Raven's Revenge. D. MacKenzie
Raven's Shadow. D. MacKenzie
Ravenshoe. H. Kingsley
Ravensley Touch. C. Heaven
*Ravine. K. Young
*Ravishing Idiot. C. Exbrayat
Razor Game. J. Grady
Razor Jacques. A. Sewart
Razorback. P. Brennan
Razzmatazz. J. Early
Ready, Aim, Die. P. Buck
*Ready for the Tiger. Sam Ross
Ready-Made Man. A. McMaster
Real Boyd. Carter Brown
*Real Endings. G. Duris
Realm Seven. T. Chiu
*Rear Car. E. E. Rose
Reason to Murder. R. A. Bennett
Reasonable Doubt. S. Barish
*Rebecca. D. Du Maurier
Rebekka Moon. M. Spence
*Recipe for a Crime. R. Denham
*Recipe for Murder. A. Ridley
*Reckoning. H. Atkinson
Reckoning. A. Fletcher
Reckoning. M. Logan
Reckoning. G. Simenon
*Recoil. J. L. Hardy
*Recoil. J. Thompson
Recollections of Geoffrey Hamlyn. H. Kingsley
Recollections of the Golden Triangle. A. Robbe-Grillet
Record of Sin. J. McGown
Recorded Verdict. G. Wark
*Recovery. S. L. Thompson
*Red Aces. E. Wallace
Red Alert. E. Webster
Red Arrows in the Night. D. A. Lord
Red Berets. T. Biracree
Red Chameleon. S. M. Kaminsky
Red Chameleon. C. Robertson
Red Citroen. T. Williams
Red Crystal. C. Francis
Red Dagger. H. Naybard
*Red Dancer of Moscow. H. L. Gates
Red Danube. B. Marshall
*Red Desert. H. Edmonds
Red Diamond. M. Schorr
Red Dove. D. Lambert
*Red Dragon. W. Curtis
Red Dragon. T. Harris
Red Drums. A. Powell
Red Eagle. J. Lucas
*Red for Danger. E. Price
Red for Terror. R. E. Crighton
Red Fox. A. Hyde
Red Gods. D. Lindquist
*Red-Haired Alibi. W. Collison
Red Hammer Down. J. Hild
*Red Harvest. D. Hammett
Red Heat. W. Katz
*Red Heroin. W. Curtis
Red Herrings. T. Heald
*Red House. G. A. Chamberlain
*Red House Mystery. Ruth Perry
Red Ice. M. J. Hutchinson
Red Key. C. Emery
Red-Light Victim. L. Kinsley
Red Man Contract. M. McCray
*Red Mark. J. Russell
*Red Mirage. P. Trent
Red Moon. W. B. Murphy
*Red Mouse. W. H. Osborne

Red Omega. J. Kruse
*Red Pavilion. R. Van Gulik
*Red Right Hand. J. T. Rogers
Red Rocking Bird. A. Marlowe
Red Rust of Death. P. Audemars
*Red Scarf. G. Brewer
Red Spy at Night. Robert King
Red Square. E. Topol
Red Sunset. J. Stockwell
Reddy or Not. I. Zacharia
*Redemption Factor. W. E. Chambers
*Redemption of Richard. M. Bryant
*Redhead. A. Andersch
Redheads Never Regret. W. Standish
Refrigerators. M. Fratti
*Reggis Arms Caper. R. H. Spencer
Regina v Rumpole. J. Mortimer
*Reincarnation of Peter Proud. M. Ehrlich
Relative Distance. R. Lewis
Religion. N. Conde
Reluctant Hostess. H. Janson
*Remains to Be Seen. H. Lindsay
Rembrandt File. O. Banks
Remedy. H. B. Drake
Remember to Kill Me. H. Pentecost
Remington Factor. R. Obstfeld
Reminiscences of a Raven. James Greenwood
Reminiscences of Jock Thirlstane. W. Russell
*Remittance Woman. A. Abdullah
Remo: The First Adventure. W. B. Murphy
*Remote Control. C. North
Removalists. D. Williamson
*Rendezvous with Death. J. Bentley
*Rendezvous with Fear. N. Davis
Renegade Agent. D. Pendleton
Renewable Virgin. B. Paul
*Repeat Performance. W. O'Farrell
Replay: Murder. J. Logue
*Report to the Commissioner. J. Mills
Reporter. K. Attiwill
Reprisal. I. Barclay
*Reprisal. A. Gordon
Reputation Dies. A. C. Ley
*Reputation for a Song. E. Grierson
*Requiem for a Redhead. L. Hardy
Requiem for a Spy. A. Giovannetti
*Reserve Two for Murder. J. Randall
Resort to Murder. W. Krasner
Respect. D. London
Rest in Pieces. R. McInerny
*Rest Is Silence. V. Coffman
Restless Obsession. J. J. Toombs
Resume for Murder. C. McCormick
Resurrection Day. D. Pendleton
Resurrection of Candy Sterling. R. W. Martin
Resurrection Row. A. Perry
Retreat. J. Mundis
Retreat for Death. Nick Carter
Retreat of Radiance. I. Moffitt
Retrieval. C. Dunne
Return. M. Fratti
*Return from the Ashes. H. Monteilhet
*Return of Bulldog Drummond. H. C. McNeile
Return of Dr. Sam: Johnson, Detector. L. De La Torre
Return of Lanny Budd. U. Sinclair
Return of Raffles. P. Tremayne
*Return of Sherlock Holmes. A. C. Doyle
*Return of the Maniac. M. Johnson
Return to Armageddon. G. Wilson
Return to Vietnam. D. Pendleton
Reunion. L. V. Roper
*Reunion. Richard Russell
*Reunion for Death. M. Meyers
Reunion on Gallows Hill. T. J. Kelly
Revelations. A. Lane
*Revelations of a Lady Detective. Anonymous
*Revelations of a Police Court Inspector. J. Jacobson
*Revenge. J. Warren
Revenge Game. G. Hammond
*Revenge of Annie Charlie. A. Fry
Revenge of the Master. J. Ahern
Revenge of the Robins Family. T. Chastain
Revengers. D. Hamilton
Reverend Randolph and the Unholy Bible. C. M. Smith
Revolt. H. Janson
*Reward. Michael Barrett
Reward Game. G. Hammond
Rich Die Young. C. G. Hart
*Rich Is the Treasure. M. Procter
Richard A. S. Yurick
Riches and Honor. T. Hyman
*Riddle Me This! D. N. Rubin
*Riddle of the Sands. E. Childers
Riddle of the Third Mile. C. Dexter
Riddle of the Veiled Song. C. B. MacDonald, Jr.
Ride. J. Wainwright
Ride a Pale Horse. H. MacInnes
*Ride a White Dolphin. A. Mayberry
Ride of the Razorback. Carl Stevens

Title Index

Ride the Golden Tiger. C. Fast
*Ride the Nightmare. R. Matheson
*Ride the Pink Horse. D. B. Hughes
Ride the Tiger. R. Emmett
*Rider of Waroona. G. F. Scott
Rig. R. Douglas
Rim of Fire Conspiracy. J. Rosenberger
*Rim of the Pit. H. Talbot
*Ring Around Rosy. Gordon Davis
Ringer. D. R. Slavitt
*Ringer. E. Wallace
Rings of Sand. T. McNab
Rio Contract. W. Newton
Riot. F. Elli
*Ripe for Rapture. H. Janson
Ripening. E. Clissant
*Ripley Underground. P. Highsmith
*Ripley's Game. P. Highsmith
Ripper. W. Dobson
*Rise and Fall of Legs Diamond. O. H. Gaylord
Rishi. L. Giroux, Jr.
*Rising of the Moon. G. Mitchell
Risky Pleasure. J. A. Ross
Rite of the Dragon. J. Gluckman
Rites of Murder. W. J. Sheldon
Rittenhouse Square. A. P. G. Solmssen
Ritual Fire Dance. L. Phillips
Ritual Murder. S. T. Haymon
River in the Sun. E. Beatty
River of Death. A. MacLean
River of Fire. G. J. Breckling
*River of Stars. E. Wallace
*River Pirate. C. F. Coe
River Raid. E. Helm
Rivermist. A. Harrell
River's End. J. O. Curwood
Rivers of Darkness. R. Hardy
Rivers of Flesh. J. Hild
Riviera Puzzle. V. McConnor
*Riviera Showdown. H. Janson
*Road House. W. Hackett
Road of Iron. G. St. Germain
Road to Ein Harod. A. Kenan
*Road to Murder. V. Gunn
Road to Nowhere. M. Walsh
Road to Paradise Island. V. Holt
*Road to the Coast. J. Harris
Roadshow. W. Marshall
Roast Eggs. D. Clark
Robak's Cross. J. L. Hensley
Robber in a Mole Trap. P. N. Walker
*Robbery at Rudwick House. V. L. Whitechurch
*Robbery Under Arms. R. Boldrewood
*Robin and the Seven Hoods. J. Pearl
Robots and Empire. I. Asimov
Robots of Dawn. I. Asimov
Rockabye. L. Koenig
Rockabye Baby. S. Gresham
Rockefeller Gift. P. G. Winslow
*Rocket to the Morgue. H. H. Holmes
*Rocksburg Railroad Murders. K. C. Constantine
Rockwell. P. McCurtin
*Rogue Cop. W. P. McGivern
*Rogue in Love. T. Gallon
Rogue Justice. G. Household
*Rogue Male. G. Household
Rogue of the Racecourse. Anonymous
*Rogue with a Past. R. Wesley
Rogues. A. Sadler
*Rogue's March. E. W. Hornung
Rogue's March. W. T. Tyler
*Rogue's Paradise. E. Pugh
Roker's Reef Affair. M. Cronin
Role of Honour. J. Gardner
Rollerball. P. McCutchan
Roman Enigma. W. F. Murphy
Roman Solution. W. Henley
*Romance in the First Degree. O. R. Cohen
*Romance of a Million Dollars. E. Dejeans
*Romance of a Spy. "E-7"
*Romance of Elaine. A. B. Reeve
Romanov Connection. W. M. Green
*Rome Express. R. Alexander
Romp in Green Heat. A. Sewart
Romula, the Dedicated. K. Kimbrough
Ronald the Fusilier. F. M. Peacock
*Roof. D. Whitelaw
Rooftops. Tom Lewis
*Rookwood. W. H. Ainsworth
Rookwood. G. D. Pitt
*Room in the Tower. E. F. Benson
*Room Mate. J. Wein
Room on Floor One. B. E. London
*Room 13. E. Wallace
*Rooney. C. Cookson
Rooney's Gold. I. Lambot
Root of All Evil. E. Ferrars
*Root of All Evil. J. S. Fletcher
*Rope. P. Hamilton
*Rope Began to Hang the Butcher. C. W. Grafton
Rose Exterminator. W. Carney
Rose for This Day's Madness. A. Longfellow
Rose Garden. K. Palka

Rose Tree. J. Broderick
*Rosebud. J. Hemingway
Rosemary for Remembrance. J. F. Martins
Rosemary King, Government Girl. T./Holloway
*Rosemary's Baby. I. Levin
Roses Are Dead. L. D. Estleman
Rostnikov's Corpse. S. M. Kaminsky
Rouge. H. McFall
Rough Justice. J. Oster
*Rough Shoot. G. Household
Rough Trade. A. Fowles
Roughcut. E. Gorman
*Roughneck. J. Thompson
Roumanian Circle. Lionel Black
Roumanian Operation. J. Rosenberger
Round Voyage. J. R. Wilson
Roxana. D. Defoe
*Roxy by Proxy. H. Janson
*Royal Abduction. A. W. Upfield
*Royal Affair. G. Boothby
Royal Flush. D. Stivers
Royal Game. S. Vaughan
*Royce of the Royal Mounted. A. Moore
Rubicon One. D. Jones
Rubout at the Onyx. H. P. Jeffers
Ruby of a Thousand Dreams. R. Daniel
Ruby Sweetwater and the Ringo Kid. S. Bart
Rugged Trail. H. L. Floyd
Ruins of Love. D. Mai
Rules of Engagement. B. Freemantle
Ruling Passion. S. Barlay
*Rumble on the Docks. F. Paley
Rumpelstiltskin. E. McBain
Rumpole and the Golden Thread. J. Mortimer
Rumpole for the Defence. J. Mortimer
*Rumpole of the Bailey. J. Mortimer
*Rumpole's Return. J. Mortimer
*Run for Lover. H. Janson
Run for Your Life. B. Abercrombie
Run from Nightmare. M. O'Callaghan
Run If You Can. J. Madison
*Run...Run...Run. F. Taubes
Run, Sara, Run. A. Worboys
Run, Sheep, Run. G. Sager
Run, Thief, Run. J. Manchester
Runaway. Old Sleuth
Runaway. Clarissa Watson
Rundown. F. Woods
Runner in the Street. J. Grady
*Running Duck. P. Gosling
*Running Fight. W. H. Osborne
Running Hot. D. Pendleton
Running Man. R. Bachman
Running Scared. H. Brand
*Running Scared. J. Burmeister
*Running Scared. G. McDonald
*Running Target. S. Frazee
*Running Water. A. E. W. Mason
Running Wild. A. Trew
Rupert Alison; or, Broken Lights. G. Forde
*Rush on the Ultimate. H. R. F. Keating
Russian Enigma. C. Egleton
*Russian Hide-and-Seek. K. Amis
Russian Leave. Anthony Stuart
Russian Professor. A. Gilchrist
Russian Spring. D. Jones
Russian Woman. T. Hyman
Ruthless Ones. L. Moody
Rutland Place. A. Perry
*Ryan's Rules. E. Leonard
*Rynox. P. MacDonald
S.O.S. W. W. Ellis
*S.P.Y.S. T. R. Joyce
*S--Portrait of a Spy. I. Adams
*Sable Lorcha. H. Hazeltine
Sabotage at Sea. W. R. D. McLaughlin
Sac Mau, Victor Charlie. J. Cain
Sacred Cave. J. D. Powell
Sacrife. R. P. Morrison
Sacrifice. G. Masterton
*Sadie, Don't Cry Now. H. Janson
Safekeeping. G. McDonald
Safety Catch. J. Summers
Sagomi Gambit. J. Evans
Saigon Commandos. J. Cain
Saigon Merchant. J. Pattinson
Saigon Slaughter. J. Lansing
*Sail a Crooked Ship. N. Benchley
*Sailcloth Shroud. C. Williams
*Sailor's Bride. G. Boothby
Sailors Do Care. Sinbad
Sailor's Leave. Brian Moore
*Sailor's Luck. B. Heatter
Saint Eustace and the Albatross. D. Ryan
*Saint Fiacre Affair. G. Simenon
Saint in London. L. Charteris
*Saint in New York. L. Charteris
Saint Jack. P. Theroux
St. Lucian Affair. S. Sonny
Saint Peter's Fair. Ellis Peters
*St. Peter's Finger. G. Mitchell
*St. Valentine's Day Massacre. B. O'Hara
Saint Valentine's Day Murders. R. D. Edwards

Sakkara. N. Barber
*Salamander. M. West
Salamandra Glass. A. W. Mykel
Sale of Lot 236. M. Delahaye
Saloon Bar. F. Harvey, Jr.
*Salt and Pepper. Alex Austin
Salted Almonds. F. Anstey
*Salute the Toff. J. Creasey
Salvage for the Saint. L. Charteris
*Salving of a Derelict. M. Drake
*Salzburg Connection. H. MacInnes
*Samantha. J. Carew
*Samantha. E. V. Cunningham
Samaritan. P. Van Rjndt
*Same Difference. H. Janson
Samson's Deal. S. Singer
San Andreas. A. MacLean
San Diego Lightfoot Sue. T. Reamy
San Juan Inferno. Nick Carter
San Quentin. J. Lynch
Sanction. W. W. Johnstone
*Sanctuary. W. Faulkner
Sanctuary Sparrow. Ellis Peters
Sand Trap. C. B. Cooney
*Sanders of the River. E. Wallace
Sandman. M. Gibson
Santa Claus Killer. A. H. Garnet
"Sapper": The Best Short Stories. H. C. McNeile
*Sapphire. E. G. Cousins
*Sarah Brown, Detective. K. F. Hill
Saratoga. D. Daniels
Saratoga Headhunter. S. Dobyns
*Saratoga Longshot. S. Dobyns
Saratoga Swimmer. S. Dobyns
*Sargasso Secret. K. Stanton
*Satan Bug. I. Stuart
Satan Sanderson. H. E. Rives
*Satan Stone. R. Hayes
Satan Takes a Hand. E. Seeley, Jr.
Satan Whispers. Clarissa Ross
Satanic Condition. D. Thoreau
Satanist. M. C. Fraser
*Satanist. D. Wheatley
Satan's Death Blast. G. Stockbridge
Satan's Master. J. Nazel
Satan's Messenger. P. Fox
*Satan's Snowdrop. G. N. Smith
Satan's Swarm. L. Derrick
Saturday of Glory. D. Serafin
Satyr Candidate. R. M. Rose
Satyr Ring. A. Quinn
Sauce for the Pigeon. G. Hammond
Sausalito. J. Lynch
Savage Day. T. Wiseman
*Savage Night. J. Thompson
Savage Place. R. B. Brown
*Savage Sequel. H. Janson
*Savage Siren. H. Zore
*Savage Sisters. Carter Brown
*Savage Slaughter. B. Rossi
Savage Spirits of Seahedge Manor. D. Price
Savannah Blue. W. Harrison
Savannah Swingsaw. D. Pendleton
Savannah Syndrome. John Davies
Save Johanna! F. P. Pascal
Save the Last Dance for Me. J. Miller
Saved by a Detective. Old Sleuth
*Say It with Candy. H. Janson
*Say No to Death. D. Cusack
Say No to Murder. N. Pickard
Sayonara, Sweet Amaryllis. James Melville
Scaffold. Cameron Ross
*Scallywag. G. Allen
Scalpel. I. Corn, Jr.
*Scalpel. H. McCoy
*Scandal in Eden. G. Rogers
*Scapegoat. D. Du Maurier
Scar. D. Wright
*Scarab Murder Case. S. S. Van Dine
Scarborough Fear. D. M. Cayer
Scarecrow. R. H. Morrieson
*Scarface. A. Trail
*Scarfaced Killer. B. Rossi
Scarlet Car. R. H. Davis
Scarlet Mansion. A. W. Eckert
*Scarlet Runners. C. N. Williamson
Scarlet Storm. M. De Moss
Scarlet Wreath. P. J. Carraher
*Scarred Man. B. Heatter
*Scattergood Baines. C. B. Kelland
Scattershot. B. Pronzini
*Scent from Heaven. H. Janson
*Scent of Danger. D. MacKenzie
Scent of Death. E. Page
Schism. B. Granger
School Days. Robert Hughes
School for Murder. R. Barnard
School for Slaughter. P. Buck
School of Darkness. M. W. Wellman
*School on 103rd Street. R. S. Jefferson
*Schoolgirl Murder Case. C. Wilson
Sci Fi. W. Marshall
*Scientists. E. Lipsky
Scimitar. P. Niesewand
*Scissors Cut Paper. G. Fairlie
Scissors, Paper, Stone. M. Boggs

S

Scoop. Detection Club
Scorched Earth. D. Stivers
*Score. R. Stark
*Scorpio. M. Roote
Scorpio Cipher. R. Hayes
*Scorpio Letters. V. Canning
Scorpion's Sting. E. A. Pollitz, Jr.
Scotch Murder. C. Cruikshank
Scottish Decision. A. Hunter
Scourge of the Steel Mask. R. J. Hogan
*Scratch a Thief. Z. Marko
Scratch a Thief. J. Trinian
Scratch Fever. M. A. Collins
Scream at the Sea. C. Murphy
Screaming Man. K. Robeson
*Screaming Mimi. Fredric Brown
*Scutari. M. Zarubica
Sea Cave. A. Scholefield
Sea-Change. P. Loraine
Sea-Crossed Fisherman. Y. Kemal
Sea File. J. D. Scott
Sea Leopard. C. Thomas
Sea of Savages. G. Wilson
*Sea Shall Not Have Them. John Harris
Sea Treasure. K. Bakker
*Sea Whispers. W. W. Jacobs
Seabird Nine. J. McVean
Seadrift House. C. Hamilton
Sealed and Despatched. F. Bream
*Sealed Orders. A. E. Carey
*Sealed Verdict. L. Shapiro
*Sealer. J. Wood
Sealing. L. Webb
Seance on a Wet Afternoon. M. McShane
Search. I. C. Smith
Search for Anderson. I. I. Magdalen
Search for Sara. M. Russell
Search for Simon. A. Hutton
Search for Yesterday. L. Robin
Season of Anguish. D. Noel
*Season of the Falcon. C. Darby
Season of the Strangler. Madison Jones
Seasons of Death. M. K. Wren
Seasons of Revenge. W. Paul
Seattle. J. Lynch
*Seawaymen. J. Wingate
*Second Bureau. C. R. Dumas
*Second Chance. E. Trevor
*Second Chance. Mrs. W. Woodrow
*Second Class Passenger. P. Gibbon
*Second Death of Roman Mercader. J. Semprun
Second Half. J. Greaves
*Second Latchkey. C. N. Williamson
Second Saladin. S. Hunter
*Second Sight. C. Bartholomew
Second Story Peggy. K. Kavanaugh
*Second String. H. Janson
Second Time Round. H. McLeave
Second War of Worlds. G. H. Smith
*Seconds. D. Ely
Secret Adventure of the Thornborough Ghost. F. Sherrod
*Secret Adversary. A. Christie
*Secret Agent. J. Conrad
Secret Below 103rd Street. R. S. Jefferson
Secret Ceremony. M. Denevi
*Secret Ceremony. W. Hughes
Secret Dancer. R. Timperley
Secret Generations. J. Gardner
Secret-Keeper. S. Eskapa
*Secret Kingdom. F. Richardson
Secret Lives. W. Targ
Secret Love. D. Noel
Secret Net. A. Ridgway
Secret of Anna Katz. S. Swift
Secret of Devil's Cave. Jennifer Hale
Secret of San Felipe. P. Buck
Secret of Shoreswood Hall. D. O. Smith
*Secret of Shower Tree. V. Coffman
Secret of the Elephant. B. Scott
*Secret of the Hills. W. Garrett
*Secret of the Moor. M. Gerard
Secret of the Pit. L. Meynell
*Secret of the Silver Car. W. Martyn
*Secret of the Snows. G. Chester
Secret of the Su. K. Robeson
Secret Past. A. Marmor
Secret Rage. C. Harris
*Secret Servant. G. Lyall
*Secret Service. W. Gillette
*Secret Service Operator 13. R. W. Chambers
*Secret Session. H. Janson
Secret Six. F. Marion
Secret Squadron. L. L. Driggs
*Secret Suspicion. M. O. Rolfe
*Secret Tent. E. Addyman
*Secret Thread. E. Vance
Secret Warriors. A. Baldwin
Secret Whispers. T. Allbeury
*Secretary of Frivolous Affairs. M. Futrelle
Secrets. B. Hastings
*Secrets of Cromwell Crossing. D. Winston
Secrets of Harry Bright. J. Wambaugh
Secrets of the Heart. J. Ashley
*Secrets of the Police. G. M. White

Sector 12. R. D. Bennett
Seduction in Berlin. W. Kotzwinkle
Seduction of Peter S. Lawrence Sanders
See How They Run. M. Litchfield
See If He Wins. R. Spong
See No Evil. G. McGill
See You Later, Alligator. W. F. Buckley, Jr.
Seeding. D. Shobin
*Seeds of Destruction. D. Nabarro
Seeds of Evil. D. Streib
Seeds of Yesterday. V. C. Andrews
*Seeing Life. E. P. Oppenheim
Seeing Red. R. Ormerod
Seek for Justice. R. Lewis
*Seersucker Whipsaw. R. Thomas
Seige for Panda One. P. N. Walker
Self-Destruct. Angus Hall
Seminar for Murder. B. M. Gill
*Send Another Coffin. F. G. Presnell
Send in the Lions. Eric Clark
Sendai. W. Woolfolk
Sense of Loyalty. J. Ashford
Senseless. J. D. Burtt
Sensuality. H. Janson
*Sentence for Sin. H. Janson
*Sentinel. J. Konvitz
Sequel to a Verdict. P. Dunning
*Serenade. J. M. Cain
Sergeant Dunn, C.I.D. E. Wallace
Sergeant Getulio. J. U. Ribeiro
Sergeant Horn's Murder Trap. J. O'Donoghue
Sergeant on Trial. I. Johnston
*Sergeant Sir Peter. E. Wallace
*Sergeant Verity and the Swell Mob. F. Selwyn
Serpent. D. Wiltse
Serpent and the Slave. C. H. Woodcock
*Serpent Sleeping. E. Weismiller
Serpent's Circle. P. Harpur
Serpent's Eye. W. Barker
Servants of Twilight. L. Nichols
Set a Thief. Martin Page
Set-Up. W. Newton
Set-Up. V. Volkoff
*Settled Out of Court. H. Cecil
*Seven Chose Murder. R. Vickers
*Seven Days in May. F. Knebel
*Seven Days to a Killing. C. Egleton
*711—Officer Needs Help. W. Masterson
*Seven Footprints to Satan. A. Merritt
*Seven Keys to Baldpate. E. D. Biggers
Seven Madmen. R. Arlt
Seven North. N. Ravin
*Seven-Per-Cent Solution. N. Meyer
Seven Silent Men. N. Behn
Seven Sleepers. J. Pattinson
Seven Sleepers. B. St. James
Seven Steps to Treason. M. Hartland
*Seven Thunders. R. Croft-Cooke
*Seven-Ups. P. Posner
*Seven Were Veiled. K. M. Knight
Seven Widows of Hempstead. S. Ready
Seven Wives for Dracula. T. J. Kelly
*Seventh. R. Stark
Seventh Child. B. Stanwood
Seventh Cross. A. Seghers
Seventh Crossword. H. Resnicow
Seventh Gate. D. Holliday
Seventh Hunch. W. H. Hamby
*Seventh Juror. P. Didelot
Seventh Man. G. Garden
Seventh Sacrament. Roland Cutler
Seventh Stone. W. B. Murphy
*77, Park Lane. W. Hackett
*70,000 Witness. C. Fitzsimmons
Seventy Times Seven. J. B. Sanford
Severed Wasp. M. L'Engle
*Severn Affair. G. Warden
*Sex Angle. H. Janson
Sex Cult Murders. J. Davidson
Sexton Blake at the Varsity. J. Andrews
*Sexy Vixen. H. Janson
*Shades of Gray. M. Denning
Shades Will Not Vanish. H. Fowler
Shadow. B. Garnett
Shadow. A. Melville-Ross
*Shadow. D. Stuart
Shadow Across the Sun. J. Ames
Shadow and the Golden Master. W. G. Gibson
Shadow Behind the Curtain. V. Johnston
Shadow Between. S. Hocking
*Shadow Beware. M. Grant
Shadow Cabinet. W. T. Tyler
Shadow Dance. A. Carter
Shadow in Pursuit. J. N. Chance
Shadow: Jade Dragon and House of Ghosts. W. B. Gibson
Shadow Kills. W. R. Philbrick
Shadow Line. L. Furman
Shadow Man. C. Barroll
Shadow Man. J. Lutz
Shadow of a Crime. C. K. Earl
*Shadow of a Doubt. H. Judd
Shadow of a Doubt. J. Thomson
Shadow of a Dream. R. Fernand
*Shadow of an Unknown Women. D. Winston
Shadow of Cain. V. T. Bugliosi

Shadow of Death. W. X. Keinzle
*Shadow of Doubt. A. S. Roche
*Shadow of Evil. C. Dawe
*Shadow of Guilt. Old Spicer
*Shadow of Guilt. P. Quentin
Shadow of Lies. D. E. McQuinn
*Shadow of My Brother. D. Grubb
Shadow of Shadows. T. Allbeury
*Shadow of Sin. H. Zore
Shadow of Terror. A. Goetz
Shadow of the Beast. G. F. Di Pego
Shadow of the Eagle. J. Hagar
Shadow of the Gestapo. W. Darrell
Shadow of the Moth. E. Hawkes
*Shadow of the Rope. E. W. Hornung
*Shadow on the House. M. Hansom
Shadow Over Beauclaire. S. Miles
Shadow Over the Island. J. Ames
Shadow President. S. Katz
*Shadow Syndicate. C. Hosken
Shadow Trade. A. Furst
*Shadowed to His Doom. Old Sleuth
Shadowplay. N. Hartley
Shadows from the Past. R. Neely
Shadows in the Afternoon. R. T. Stevens
Shadows of Cliffside. B. Lee
Shadows of Death. G. St. Germain
Shadows of Doubt. P. Harcourt
*Shadows of One Another. T. R. Cox
Shadows Under White Face. A. Heald
Shadowtide. D. Price
*Shadowy Thing. H. B. Drake
Shaft. P. Chevalier
*Shaft. E. Tidyman
Shaft's Big Score. E. Tidyman
Shaitan. M. Ehrlich
Shake Hands with the Devil. R. Conner
*Shakespeare Murders. N. Gordon
Shalom, My Love. H. Janson
Shame the Devil. P. Appleman
Shamrock Cohen and the Amorous Doppelganger. B. Buonocore
*Shamus. R. Giles
Shanghai Surprise. T. Kenrick
Shanghaied. F. Norris
Shannon. J. Jenkins
Shannon. M. Parnell
Shard at Bay. P. McCutchan
Shard Calls the Tune. P. McCutchan
Sharing. Sy Cook
*Sharky's Machine. W. Diehl
Sharon Jones, Free Lance Photographer. E. Wesley
Shattered Eye. B. Granger
Shattered Masks. D. G. Devon
*She Died Young. A. Kennington
*She Let Him Continue. S. Geller
*She Shall Have Murder. D. Ames
*She Sleeps to Conquer. H. Janson
*She Was a Lady. L. Charteris
She Wolf. H. Janson
Shed Light on Death. L. A. Taylor
*"Shed No Tears." D. Martin
*Sheep's Clothing. L. J. Vance
Sheer Torture. R. Barnard
Sheerluck Jones. M. Watson
Sheiks and Adders. M. Innes
Shelf Life. D. Clark
Shell Game. D. Terman
She'll Get Hers. J. Plunkett
Shemerelda. P. Tinniswood
Sheridan Road. H. T. Miller
Sheriff and the Branding Iron Murders. D. R. Meredith
Sheriff and the Panhandle Murders. D. R. Meredith
Sheriff of Bombay. H. R. F. Keating
*Sherlock Holmes. W. Gillette
Sherlock Holmes and a Theatrical Mystery. V. Andrews
Sherlock Holmes and the Curious Adventure of the Clockwork Prince. C. Haubold
Sherlock Holmes and the Treasure Train. F. Thomas
Sherlock Holmes and the Wood Green Empire Mystery. W. Lane
Sherlock Holmes at Elsinore. C. Muusmann
Sherlock Holmes at the 1902 Fifth Test. S. Shaw
Sherlock Holmes' First Case. T. J. Kelly
Sherlock Holmes Meets the Phantom. T. J. Kelly
Sherlock Holmes: My Life and Crimes. M. Hardwick
Sherlock Holmes Versus John Thorndyke and Reginald Fortune. A. C. Ward
She's Dynamite! J. Kellan
Shield and Sword. V. Kozhevnikov
*Shield for Murder. W. P. McGivern
*Shilling for Candles. J. Tey
Shiloh Project. D. C. Poyer
Shining Day. F. Ross
Shiny Night. B. Tunstall
Ship of Gold. T. B. Allen
Ship of Gold. J. Leasor
*Ship That Died of Shame. N. Monsarrat
Shirkers. C. M. S. McLellan

Shiwan Khan Returns. W. B. Gibson
*Shock Corridor. M. Avallone
Shock to the System. S. Brett
*Shock Treatment. W. Van Atta
Shock Value. K. Berne
Shock Value. W. B. Murphy
Shock Waves. D. Pendleton
Shoemaker. O. Harper
*Shoestring. P. Ableman
*Shoestring's Finest Hour. P. Ableman
*Shoot. D. Fairbairn
*Shoot. E. Trevor
*Shoot It. P. Tyner
Shoot-Out. B. Copper
Shoot to Kill. J. McCarter
Shooter. T. N. Murari
Shooting in the Dark. C. Hougan
Shooting Party. A. Chekhov
Shooting Star. D. Brierley
Shooting Star. F. Woods
Shooting Stars. N. Coleridge
Shooting Stars. E. C. Vivian
*Shop Girl. C. N. Williamson
Short Break in Venice. P. Inchbald
Short of Murder. W. E. Wright
Short Skirts. R. Eden
Short Stories. E. Bramah
Short Term. A. Baker
*Short-Term Wife. H. Janson
*Short Time to Live. R. Marshall
Short Walk to Death. R. A. Bennett
*Short Walk to the Stars. E. Lambert
Shortest Way to Hades. S. Caudwell
*Shot in the Arm. J. Sherwood
*Shot in the Dark. G. Fairlie
*Shot in the Dark. H. Kurnitz
Shot to Hell. J. Stivers
*Shotgun. W. Wingate
Show Business Is Murder. C. L. Ross
*Show Must Go On. G. Verner
Show of Force. C. D. Taylor
Shreiber. A. Boyarsky
*Shrewsdale Exit. J. Buell
Shrieking Shadow of Penporth Island. S. D. Stevens
Shroud. J. Coyne
Shroud for Aquarius. M. A. Collins
Shroud for Delilah. Anthea Fraser
Shrunken Heads. J. Kellerman
*Shulamite. A. Askew
*Shuttered Room. J. Withers
Shuttle People. G. Bishop
Shuttlecock. G. Swift
Siberian Alternative. A. Kilgore
Siberian Reservoir. I. Bush
Sicilian. M. Puzo
Sicilian Connection. A. Venters
*Sick Fox. P. Broderur
Sick of Shadows. S. McCrumb
Side Effects. Woody Allen
Side Effects. M. Palmer
Side Street. Malcolm St. Clair
*Siege of Trencher's Farm. G. M. Williams
Sierra Death Dealers. Steve White
Sight Unseen. B. Latham
Sign of Death. B. Merrell
*Sign of the Blue Dragon. J. Aeby
*Sign of the Dagger. H. O. Cooke
Sign of the Flying Fox. J. Grieg
*Sign of the Four. A. C. Doyle
Sign of the Four. J. Hershey
*Sign of the Ram. M. Ferguson
*Sign of the Rose. G. Beban
Sign of the Serpent. S. Hely
Sign on the Door. C. Pollock
*Signpost to Murder. M. Doyle
*Signpost to Murder. D. Folliott
Signs and Omens. B. M. Forester
Silence of Guilt. R. A. Bennett
*Silencers. D. Hamilton
*Silent Barrier. L. Tracy
*Silent Battle. G. F. Gibbs
*Silent House. John Brandon
Silent Informer. P. A. Foxall
Silent Killing. Janice Robinson
Silent Murder. C. Cunningham
Silent Ones. D. Ogilvie
Silent Place. R. C. Payne
Silent Reefs. D. Cottrell
*Silent Stranger. H. G. Harper
Silent Thunder. A. Soutar
Silent Witness. J. De Leon
*Silent Witness. M. Yorke
Silhouette in Scarlet. Elizabeth Peters
Silicon Valley Connection. J. Rosenberger
Silicon Valley Slaughter. J. Quinn
Silken Menace. H. Janson
*Silken Snare. H. Janson
*Silken Threads. G. Afterem
*Silver Bears. P. E. Erdman
Silver Bridge. H. P. Lewis
*Silver Bullet Gang. J. Miles
Silver Falcon. R. Anthony
Silver Guilt. L. Meynell
*Silver Jackass. C. K. Boston
*Silver King. H. A. Jones
*Silver Mistress. P. O'Donnell
Silver Spoon. C. B. Kelland

*Silver Streak. J. C. Rogers
Silver Threads. R. Flanders
Silver's City. M. Leitch
*Simon Lash, Private Detective. F. Gruber
Simple Truth. E. Hardwick
Sin in the South. D. Gallo
*Sin Is a Redhead. S. Harragan
Sin of Hagar. B. Mathers
Sin Pit. P. Meskil
*Sin Sniper. H. Garner
*Sin That Was His. F. Packard
*Sing a Song of Homicide. J. R. Langham
*Sing Sing Nights. H. S. Keeler
*Singapore. W. Bogart
Singer Not the Song. A. E. Lindop
*Single Clue. Old Sleuth
*Single Monstrous Act. K. Benton
*Sinister Errand. P. Cheyney
*Sinister Love. L. Ames
*Sinister Love. E. Wallace
*Sinister Lovely. N. Karta
Sinister Rapture. H. Janson
*Sinister Stone. D. Winston
*Sinister Widow Comes Back. R. Armstrong
Sinless Season. D. Galgut
*Sinner. D. Linton
Sinner's Club. H. Whittington
Sins of Commission. H. L. Klawans
*Sins of the Fathers. T. Walton
Sinsation of a Sintury. D. O. Wilderness
Sion Crossing. A. Price
*Sir, You Bastard. G. F. Newman
Sirens. E. V. Lustbader
Siren's Lure. Andrea Davidson
Siskiyou Two-Step. R. Hoyt
Sister Craven. S. Ready
Sister Death. P. G. Winslow
*Sister, Don't Hate Me. H. Janson
Sister on Leave. I. Roberts
*Sisterhood. B. Black
Sisterhood. M. Palmer
*Sisters of Sorrow. A. Vandergriff
Sitting Duck. C. Garrison
Sitting Ducks. M. R. D. Meek
*Sitting Emperor. E. N. Willett
*Sitting Target. L. Henderson
*Situation, Grave! H. Janson
Situation Tragedy. S. Brett
*Six Days of the Condor. J. Grady
Six Days to Die. Gus Stevens
*Six Dead Men. A. Steeman
Six Feet Under. D. Simpson
Six Letter Word for Death. P. Moyes
*Six Men. E. Radford
*Six Nights of Mystery. W. Irish
Six Problems for Don Isidro Parodi. J. L. Borges
666. J. Anson
*633 Squadron. F. E. Smith
16th of September Game. R. Houston
Skeleton in Search of a Cupboard. E. Ferrars
Skeletons in the Closet. E. Linington
Ski Lift to Love. Helen Murray
Skim. T. Henege
Skin Deep. W. Harrington
Skin Deep. W. B. Murphy
Skin Swindle. W. Barker
*Skirts Bring Me Sorrow. H. Janson
*Skirts of the Dead Night. W. W. Seward
Skorpion's Death. D. Brierley
Skulduggery. C. G. Hart
Skull Beneath the Skin. P. D. James
*Skull of the Marquis de Sade. R. Bloch
Skull's Light. W. F. Swankler
Sky Is Falling. W. B. Murphy
*Sky Steward. K. Attiwill
Sky Train. P. Cruger
Skyblazer. P. Allen
Skyhigh Betrayers. L. Derrick
Skyripper. D. Drake
Skyscraper. R. Byrne
Skyship. J. Brosnan
Skyshroud. T. Keene
Skysweep. D. Pendleton
Skytrap. John Smith
Slade's Marauders. S. Cade
*Slasher. M. A. Collins
Slate. N. Aldyne
Slate Secret. Roy Burns
*Slaughter. H. Clement
Slaughter in El Salvador. J. Rosenberger
Slaughter Run. A. Kilgore
Slaughter Street. A. Capelli
Slaughter Summit. M. Mandell
*Slaughter's Big Rip-Off. A. Kane
Slave of the Warmonger. A. Kilgore
Slaves for Seduction. H. Janson
*Slaves of Sumuru. S. Rohmer
*Slay-Ride for Cutie. H. Janson
*Slayground. R. Stark
Slease. L. A. Morse
Sledgehammer. Jasper Smith
*Sleep Long, My Love. H. Waugh
*Sleep, My Love. L. Q. Ross
*Sleep of Spies. P. Harcourt

Sleep on Death. A. Morice
*Sleeper Awakes. M. Hughes
*Sleepers East. F. Nebel
Sleepers of Erin. Jonathan Gash
Sleeping Beauty. L. L. Greene
*Sleeping Beauty Murders. L. O'Donnell
Sleeping Dog. D. Lochte
*Sin Is a Redhead. S. Harragan
Sleeping Spy. H. Burkholz
Sleeping Tiger. H. Jobson
*Sleeping Tiger. M. Moisewitsch
*Sleepless Eye. Warren Miller
Sleepwalker. D. Combs
Sleightly Murder. P. A. Kelly
*Slender Thread. S. Silliphant
*Sleuth. A. Shaffer
Slice of Life. J. Kisner
*Slight Case of Murder. D. Runyon
*Slightly Scarlet. P. Heath
*Sling and the Arrow. S. Engstrand
Slippy McGee. M. C. Oemler
Slow Burn. P. Cave
Slow Dancer. W. R. Philbrick
Slow Grave. W. R. Philbrick
Slow Twitch. R. Enders
*Slowly, Slowly in the Wind. P. Highsmith
*Slyboots. P. Flower
*Small Back Room. N. Balchin
Small But Deadly Wars. C. Heath
Small Masterpiece. T. Heald
Small Miracle. N. Krasna
Small Slain Body. P. Audemars
Small Town Big Shot. Dirk Foster
Small Voice. R. Westerby
Smart Dame. J. Grecco
*Smart Girls Don't Talk. H. Janson
Smile Through Tears. G. Sava
Smith and Son--Removers. M. Bentine
Smoke Detector. E. Wright
Smoked Out. W. B. Murphy
Smoker's Cough. A. Sewart
Smooth Face of Murder. M. Yorke
*Smuggler's Ally. B. Wayde
Smuggler's Circuit. D. Roberts
*Smuggler's Fate. E. C. Derby
*Snake Doctor. C. Garrison
*Snake Water. A. Williams
Snap. A. J. Quinnell
*Snap and Jerry. Old Sleuth
Snap Judgement. L. Denny
Snap Shot. A. J. Quinnell
Snare in the Dark. F. Parrish
Snares of the Enemy. Pauline King
Snark. W. L. DeAndrea
Snarleyow. Capt. Marryat
*Snatch. R. Airth
Snatch and Grab. Rex Grayson
*Snatchers. L. White
Sniper. W. D. Roberts
Snow. J. Levin
*Snow Fury. R. Holden
*Snow in the Desert. A. Soutar
Snow in Venice. Frederick Davies
Snow Job. R. Gallagher
Snow White and Rose Red. E. McBain
Snowbird Paradine. L. Clarke
*Snowman. N. Bognar
Snows of Craggmoor. S. Harte
Snowtrap. C. D. Peel
*So Dead, My Sweet. D. Linton
So Help Me Hannah. L. Malloy
So Little Cause for Caroline. E. Bercovici
So Long, See You Tomorrow. W. Maxwell
So Pitifully Slain. A. Evans
So Violent My Love. C. Hammond
Soap Opera Slaughters. M. Kaye
Soapy Murder Case. T. J. Kelly
*Social Buccaneer. F. S. Isham
Society of Nine. Nick Carter
*Society of the Spiders. R. Daniel
*Soft Cargo. H. Janson
*Soft Touch. J. D. MacDonald
Softener. M. Bolton
Softly--Softly. W. Standish
Softwar. T. Breton
Solar Menace. Nick Carter
Sold! N. Lyons
Sold for Slaughter. D. Pendleton
Soldier No More. A. Price
Soldier on the Other Side. P. Alexander
Soldier's Pay. C. Fuller
*Solitaire Man. B. C. Spewack
*Solitary Child. N. Bawden
Solitary Man. J. Evans
Solo for Several Players. B. Jefferis
Solo Run. H. Herlin
Somali Smashout. P. McCurtin
Some Are Born to Die. N. Rosso
Some Call It Love. R. James
Some Chose Hell. J. Hild
*Some Dame. N. Karta
*Some Get It. B. Shannon
*Some Kind of Hero. J. Kirkwood
*Some Look Better Dead. H. Janson
*Some Must Watch. E. L. White
Some Predators Are Male. M. Tripp
Some Rain Must Fall. W. A. Adler
Some Unaccountable Exploits of Sherlock Holmes. C. Fisher

*Somebody Killed Her Husband. C. B. Phillips
Somebody to Kill. R. Reinsmith
*Somebody's Done For. D. Goodis
Someday the Rabbi Will Leave. H. Kemelman
*Someone at the Door. D. Christie
Someone at the Door. C. Crane
Someone Else's Grave. A. Smith
Someone Else's Money. M. M. Thomas
Someone in the House. B. Michaels
*Someone Is Bleeding R. Matheson
*Someone Is Killing the Great Chefs of Europe. N. Lyons
*Someone Waiting. Emlyn Williams
Someone's Watching. A. Neiderman
Something Attempted. J. Brampton
Something Evil. C. Crane
Something for Nothing. K. Kilgore
*Something for the Birds. T. S. Drachman
Something in the Attic. M. Raynor
Something Missing. A. McColm
Something the Cat Dragged In. C. MacLeod
*Something to Hide. N. Monsarrat
*Something to Hide. L. Sands
Something Wicked. E. Ferrars
Sometimes They Bite. L. Block
Sometimes You Could Die. J. Mitchell
Somewhere in France. R. H. Davis
Somewhere in the Night. M. Borowsky
*Son of Desolation. M. Y. Halidom
Son of the Endless Night. J. Farris
*Son of the Father. R. Cullum
*Son of the Immortals. L. Tracy
*Song of Sixpence F. A. Kummer
Sons of Earth. R. Rhodes
*Sons of Satan. W. Lequeux
*Sookey. D. Newton
Soon She Must Die. A. Clarke
"Sooper" and others. E. Wallace
Sorority House. J. Park
*Sorry Wrong Number. J. Fletcher
Sorry You've Been Troubled. W. Hackett
Sort of Samurai. James Melville
Sort of Tragedy. P. Lauben
*Sort of Traitors. N. Balchin
Soul Search Project. J. Rosenberger
*Sound an Alarm. G. Holden
Sound Evidence. J. Thomson
Sound Like Laughter. D. Helwig
*Sound of Murder. W. Fairchild
Sound of Wings. S. Dunmore
Sourdough Wars. Julie Smith
*South by Java Head. A. MacLean
South Florida Book of the Dead. R. Merkin
*South of Heaven. J. Thompson
*South Sea Bubble. R. Pertwee
South Wind Blows. C. Porteous
Southern Daughter. D. White
Souvenir. D. A. Kaufelt
*Sovereign Solution. M. McNamara
Sow Death, Reap Death. H. Pentecost
Space for Hire. W. F. Nolan
Spandau Wager. M. Hammond
Spangles. N. Revell
*Spanish Cape Mystery. E. Queen
Spanish Gambit. S. Hunter
Spanish Jade. M. Hewlett
Spargo. J. D. Scott
Spawn. L. J. Key
Speak No Evil. J. Marton
Speak No Evil. M. Warner
Speaker of Mandarin. R. Rendell
Speakers in Silence. Ganpat
*Speaking of Murder. A. Roos
Speaking Stone. K. Robeson
Spearfield's Daughter. J. Cleary
Special Circumstances. B. Lysaght
*Special Collection. T. Allbeury
Special Drug Squad. I. Johnston
Special Flower. M. Gee
Special Guest. D. Elser
Special Occasion. C. Curzon
*Special Relationship. W. Clark
Speckled Band. T. J. Kelly
Spectre of Maralinga. M. Hughes
Spectrum. D. Wise
Speculations About Jakob. U. Johnson
Spell of the Hanged Man. R. Timperley
Spellbinder. C. Wilcox
*Spells of Evil. P. Boileau
Spence at Marlby Manor. M. Allen
*Sphinx. R. Cook
*Spider. F. Oursler
Spider. Gordon Stevens
Spider Island. J. Spalding
Spider's Eye. C. Fayet
*Spider's Web. A. Christie
*Spider's Web. R. W. Kauffman
Spies. R. B. Sapir
*Spike. A. De Borchgrave
*Spin the Glass Web. M. Ehrlich
Spinoff. J. Sharkey
Spiral of Death. D. Masters
Spiral Staircase. J. Wainwright
Spirals. W. Patrick
Spirit House. Scober

Splash of Red. Antonia Fraser
*Splendid Coward. H. Townley
*Splendid Crime. G. Goodchild
Splendid Hazard. H. MacGrath
*Splendid Outcasts. G. F. Gibbs
Split Images. E. Leonard
Split Second. M. R. D. Meek
*Spoil of the Desert. H. H. Hill
Spoils of War. W. B. Murphy
*Spook Who Sat by the Door. S. Greenlee
*Sport of Fate. Old Spicer
*Sporting Proposition. J. Aldridge
*Sports Freak. S. O'Cork
Spring 1940. S. Engstrand
Spring Street. J. R. Richardson
*Springboard. J. Fores
Sprung. H. Janson
*Spy. J. F. Cooper
*Spy. P. Thomas
*Spy. T. Von Harbou
Spy Fever. M. Hatfield
*Spy for Sale. L. Payne
*Spy Game. M. Lovell
*Spy in Black. J. S. Clouston
Spy in My Bed. H. Janson
*Spy in the Nude. R. Seth
*Spy in the Room. D. Clift
Spy in Winter. M. Hastings
Spy Next Door. L. Kessner
Spy of the Old School. J. Rathbone
Spy on the Run. M. Lovell
*Spy or Die. B. Graham
Spy Probe. K. Blake
*Spy Story. L. Deighton
Spy Who Came... L. Dawson
*Spy Who Came in from the Cold. J. Le Carre
Spy Who Got His Feet Wet. M. Lovell
*Spy with a Cold Nose. R. Galton
Spy with His Head in the Clouds. M. Lovell
Spycracker. G. Moxon
Spytrap. W. Crisp
Squad Room. T. J. Kelly
Squadron Scramble. R. Jackson
Square Circle. D. Carney
*Square Crooks. J. P. Judge
Square One. H. Janson
*Squeaker. E. Wallace
Squeal Man. M. Flusser
Squeeze Play. P. Benjamin
Stab in the Dark. L. Block
Stab in the Dark. Carter Brown
Stab in the Dark. C. Dekker
Stag Dinner Death. J. Penn
*Stain. F. Halsey
*Stain on the Snow. G. Simenon
Stainless Steel Rat for President. H. Harrison
Stainless Steel Rat Is Born. H. Harrison
Stake. J. S. Rand
Stalin Account. K. Royce
Stalked. F. Rickett
Stalker. L. Cody
Stalking Horse. J. Pattinson
Stalking Horse. D. Wilcox
Stalking Point. D. Kyle
*Stamboul Train. G. Greene
Stamp King. G. de Beauregard
Stand Proud. E. Kelton
Standing into Danger. D. Briggs
Star-Anchored, Star-Angered. S. H. Elgin
Star Bridge. J. Gunn
Star-Cluster Kill. L. Maddox
Star of Egypt. B. Sanders
*Star of Midnight. A. S. Roche
Star Spangled Crunch. R. Condon
Star Wormwood. C. Bok
Starfish Syndrome. E. Van Ees
Stars and Swastikas. Steve White
*Stars Give Warning. B. Conrad
Stars My Destination. A. Bester
Starshine Connection. B. Sanders
Startex Assignment. R. Pope
*Startling Discovery. Old Sleuth
State of Corruption. P. Geddes
State of Emergency. B. Jackson
State of Fear. M. Napier
*State of Grace. R. Tine
*State vs. Elinor Norton. M. R. Rinehart
Stately Homicide. S. T. Haymon
State's Evidence. S. Greenleaf
*Statesman's Game. J. Aldridge
Static. J. R. Lane
Steal Away. Ramona King
Steal the Sun. A. E. Maxwell
Steel Killer. R. Charles
*Steel Noose. A. Drake
Steel Tiger. S. Silliphant
Steinway Collection. R. J. Randisi
Stendal Raid. A. Dempsey
Step in the Right Direction. S. Frith
*Stepford Wives. I. Levin
Steps Going Down. Joseph Hansen
*Stettin Secret. J. S. Thayer
*Steward. E. Wallace
Stick. E. Leonard

Stickman. B. Fantoni
Stiletto. H. Robbins
Still Missing. B. Gutcheon
"Still Waters Run Deep." T. Taylor
Stillness at Sea. A. Aasheim
Stillwatch. M. H. Clark
*Sting. R. Weverka
*Sting of Death. Jessica Mann
Sting of the Bee. J. Worrell
Sting of the Scorpion. G. V. Basile
*Stingaree. E. W. Hornung
Stitch in Snow. A. McCaffrey
Stockholm Syndicate. C. Forbes
*Stolen Death. L. Grex
Stolen Idea. E. Godfrey
*Stolen Identity. Nicholas Carter
Stolen Jew. J. Neugeboren
*Stolen Jewels. Old Spicer
*Stolen Race. N. Gould
Stolen Stamps. J. B. Chittenden
*Stomping Ground. D. Hamill
Stone 588. G. A. Browne
Stone Killer. J. Midgley
*Stone Leopard. C. Forbes
*Stone Maiden. V. Johnston
Stone Virgin. B. Unsworth
Stony Man Doctrine. D. Pendleton
Stop at Nothing. D. Rutherford
Stop Press. A. McKee-Wright
*Stop Thief. Carlyle Moore
Stopgap. T. A. Schock
*Stopover: Tokyo. J. P. Marquand
*Stories from Scotland Yard. M. Moser
Stories Grave and Gray. Fred Davies
*Stories of Fear. J. McLaren
Stories of the Strange and Sinister. F. Baker
*Storm and the Silence. David Walker
*Storm Fear. C. Seeley
*Storm Island. K. Follett
Storm Islands. A. Quinton
Storm of Deception. A. Andre
Storms and Son. A. Caputi
Story of a Trust. A. G. Mears
Story of Henri Tod. W. F. Buckley, Jr.
*Story of Ivy. M. B. Lowndes
*Story Without a Name. A. Stringer
*Stowaway. G. Simenon
*Straight-Out Detective. Old Sleuth
Straight Through the Door. W. T. Hodge
Strained Relations. A. Cairns
*Stranded in Arcady. F. Lynde
Strands of War. J. A. Kemeny
Strange Adventure of Anelay Moreland. R. S. Gresson
*Strange Affair. P. Toms
Strange Alibi. L. T. White
*Strange Boarders. G. Bacon
*Strange Boarders of Palace Crescent. E. P. Oppenheim
*Strange Case of Cavendish. R. Parrish
*Strange Case of Dr. Jekyll and Mr. Hyde. R. L. Stevenson
*Strange Case of Mary Page. F. Lewis
*Strange Case of Mr. Pelham. A. Armstrong
Strange Case of the Megatherium Thefts. E. C. Roberts
Strange Daughter. L. De Wohl
Strange Destiny. S. Bray
Strange Destiny. H. Janson
*Strange Disappearance. A. K. Green
Strange Loop. A. Prantera
Strange Phantasy of Doctor Trintzius. A. Vitu
*Strange Ritual. H. Janson
Strange Secrets. V. Coffman
Strange Voyage. H. MacQueen
*Strange Witness. D. Keene
Stranger. A. Veiller
*Stranger Among Friends. E. Lindall
*Stranger at Christmas. A. MacVicar
*Stranger at Home. G. Sanders
Stranger at the Door. M. Blake
*Stranger Called the Blues. G. Cotler
Stranger Case of Dr. Hide and Mr. Crushall. R. B. Stavingson
*Stranger in Galah. Michael Barrett
Stranger in the Land. W. Thomas
*Stranger in Town. R. Bloomfield
*Stranger Is Watching. M. H. Clark
Stranger to Himself. J. Colton
*Strangers in the House. G. Simenon
*Strangers on a Train. P. Highsmith
Stranglehold. C. Posard
*Stranglers of Bombay. S. James
Strasbourg Connection. D. Hayward
Strathgallant. Laura Black
*Straw Man. D. M. Disney
Street Hawk. Jack Roberts
Street of Desire. W. Standish
Street of Shadows. A. Ridgway
*Street of the Lost. D. Goodis
*Street Paved with Water. Robin Temple
*Street Players. D. Goines
Streetbird. J. Van De Wetering
Strelsau Dimenson. J. Haythorne
Strictly Amateur. T. McCormack
Strictly Confidential. E. C. Williams
Strictly Wild. H. Brand

Title Index

Stride. J. Pattinson
Strike Force Ten. H. G. Konsalik
Strike Three You're Dead. R. D. Rosen
String of Chinese Peach Stones. W. A. Cornaby
Strip for Murder. E. Thomas
Strip Search. Rex Burns
*Strip Tease Angel. D. Linton
Striving with Gods. J. Bannister
*Stroke of a Knife. B. F. Mason
Stroke of Twelve. W. M. Berger
*Strong As Death. F. Adams
Strontium Code. Nick Carter
Struck Dumb. P. Conway
Stryker's Children. J. A. Schneider
Stud Service. J. D. Revere
Studies in Love and Terror. M. B. Lowndes
*Studio Murder Mystery. Edingtons
Studio Revels. N. W. Firth
*Study in Scarlet. A. C. Doyle
*Study in Terror. E. Queen
Stumble Upon the Dark Mountains. L. Woodrum
*Stunt Man. P. Brodeur
*Stuttering Death. L. Como
Styx. C. Hyde
Submarine. J. Wingate
Submarine U-137. E. Topol
*Submariner. E. Stephens
*Substitute Prisoner. M. Marcin
Substitute Victim. H. Pentecost
Suburbs of Hell. R. Stow
*Subway in the Sky. B. Birch
Subway Stalker. L. Cameron
*Such a Gorgeous Kid Like Me. H. Farrell
*Such Bitter Business. E. Ford
*Such Friends Are Dangerous. W. Tyrer
Such Good Neighbors. M. Bingley
Such Pretty Toys. S. F. X. Dean
Such Things Happen. W. Massey
Sucker for Dames. J. Grecco
Sudden Death. P. Brennan
Sudden Death. W. X. Kienzle
Sudden Death Finish. T. Halleran
*Sudden Fear. E. Sherry
Sudden Impact. J. C. Stinson
Sudden Madness. N. Garbo
Sudden Madness. R. Hayes
*Suddenly It's Sin. H. Janson
Suffer Little Children. Sheila Johnson
*Suffer the Children. J. Saul
*Sugar and Vice. H. Janson
Sugar for the Inspector. M. Kay
Sugar, You're Swell. J. Farrell
Sugartown. L. D. Estleman
*Suicide Club. R. L. Stevenson
*Suicide in B-Flat. S. Shepard
Suicide Most Foul. J. Sturrock
Suicide Murders. H. Engel
Suicide Plague. E. Nahe
Suicide's Grave. Anonymous
Suitable Case for Corruption. N. Lewis
Suitor. G. E. Hatvary
Sullivan's Revenge. J. Cutter
*Sultana. H. C. Rowland
*Sultry Avenger. H. Janson
Summer of Katya. Trevanian
Summitt. W. P. McGivern
Summon the Bright Water. G. Household
*Summons. A. E. W. Mason
Sun Blight. R. Holles
Sun Dogs. R. O. Butler
Sun Place. R. Connolly
Sunburst. F. Keast
Sunday Alibi. R. Lilly
*Sunday Woman. C. Fruttero
*Sunflower. M. Sharp
Sunset Gun. G. Bartram
Sunset Law. J. B. Hilton
Sunset Patriots. C. D. Taylor
Sunspot. D. Lowden
*Super Fly. P. Fenty
Supreme Adventure of Inspector Lestrade. M. J. Trow
Surfeit of Alibis. P. Lauben
Surprise Party. W. Katz
*Surprises of an Empty Hotel. A. C. Gunter
Surrender Value. J. B. Hilton
Surrogate. R. B. Parker
*Survivor. J. Herbert
*Survivor. T. Keneally
*Survivors. G. Simenon
Sus. B. Keefe
Susannah, Beware. T. E. Huff
*Susannah, the Righteous. K. Kimbrough
*Susie Comes to Soho. B. Sarto
Susie's Girls. Susanna Sheldon
*Suspect. Gertrude Walker
Suspect. L. R. Wright
Suspects. D. Thomson
*Suspense. B. Graeme
Suspense. H. Janson
*Suspense. I. Ostrander
Suspicions. P. Daniels
*Swag. E. Leonard
*Swan Dive. K. Korman
Swan Song. T. J. Binyon

Swan Song for Paolo. L. O'Brien
Sweeney Todd. R. Hull
Sweeney Todd. T. J. Kelly
Sweeney Todd the Barber. B. J. Burton
Sweeney Todd, the Demon Barber of Fleet Street. G. D. Pitt
Sweeny Todd, the Demon Barber of Fleet Street. C. G. Bond
Sweeper. G. Paulsen
Sweet and Deadly. C. Harris
Sweet Deals. B. Lysaght
Sweet Death, Kind Death. A. Cross
Sweet Eros, and Witness. T. McNally
Sweet Familiarity. D. Winston
Sweet Fury. H. Janson
Sweet Justice. J. Oster
Sweet Life of Jimmy Riley. J. Reardon
*Sweet Money Girl. B. Appel
Sweet Revenge. D. Beaird
Sweet Ride. W. Murray
Sweet Rome. A. Stainton
Sweet, Savage Death. O. Papazoglou
Sweet Short Grass. P. Inchbald
*Sweet Sister Seduced. S. B. Hough
*Sweet Talk. H. Janson
Sweetheart. A. Coburn
*Sweetheart, Here's Your Grave! H. Janson
*Sweetie, Hold Me Tight. H. Janson
Sweetsir. H. Yglesias
Sweetwater Point Motel. P. Saab
Swiss Abduction. M. Denning
Switch. W. Bayer
*Switch. P. Ridgeway
Switch. N. Sharman
Switchback City. J. R. Duncan
Sword of Allah. R. Elliott
*Sword of Fate. H. Herman
Sword of Mithras. C. Merlin
Sword to the Rescue. P. Curtis
*Sylvia. E. V. Cunningham
Synapse Function. M. J. Livingston
Syndicate of Crooks. Anonymous
Systems of Mr. M. R. Shurnas. D. Nemec
TNT. D. Masters
TNT. P. Rey
Tabernacle. T. H. Cook
Tabitha. A. Ridley
*Table. R. Curtis
*Table D'Hote. D. Clark
Table for Two. G. Hind
Taggart: Murder in Season. P. Cave
*Tailsting. H. Janson
Taint. P. Wallace
Tainted Man. J. Wainwright
Taiwan. C. Wood
Take It Easy. N. Perrelli
*Take My Life. Winston Graham
Take No Prisoners. J. Crosby
*Take One Ambassador. A. Broinowski
Take the Money and Run. L. Payne
*Take This--Sweetie. H. Janson
Take Two Blondes. H. Janson
Take What You Want. G. Nimse
Taken in Vein. J. Heys
Takeover. G. C. Edmondson
Takeover. J. Evans
Takers. J. Ahern
Taking Liberty. L. Dunning
*Taking of Pelham One Two Three. J. Godey
Taking of Satcon Station. B. Cohen
Talbot Odyssey. N. De Mille
Tale of Two Tunnels. W. C. Russell
Talent for Destruction. S. Radley
*Talent for Dying. J. A. Potter
Talent for Murder. J. Chodorov
Talent for Revenge. J. Cutter
*Talented Mr. Ripley. P. Highsmith
*Tales. E. A. Poe
Tales and Sketches. F. Plant
Tales for a Stormy Night. D. S. Davis
Tales from a Gilded Palace. Old Sleuth
*Tales of Adventurers. G. Household
Tales of Love and Mystery. J. Hogg
Tales of Mystery. F. Starr
Tales of Mystery and Suspense. A. Creese
Tales of Northumbria. H. Pease
Tales of Ordinary Madness. C. Bukowski
*Tales of Terror. E. Sudak
Tales of the Divining Rod. E. W. Beaven
Tales Told by Simpson. May Sinclair
Talk Show Murders. S. Allen
Talk with the Angels. D. Meiring
Talking Devil. K. Robeson
*Tall Headlines. A. E. Lindop
Talon. A. Melville-Ross
*Tamarind Seed. E. Anthony
*Tangled Evidence. P. C. De Crespigny
Tangled Lies. Anne Stuart
Tangled Skein. G. Mewburn
Tangled Snarl. J. Rustan
Tangled Web. E. B. Wright
Tantalus. I. Cullen
Tantalus. A. Hemingway
Tapping the Source. K. Nunn
Tara. M. Hutton
Target. S. Hunter
Target for Tragedy. J. Philips

Target Margaret Thatcher. J. Calder
*Target: Mike Shayne. B. Halliday
Target Norway. N. Cort
Target: Sahara. G. St. Germain
Target Tobruk. R. Jackson
Tarlov Cipher. Nick Carter
Tarotown. B. Jones
*Taste for Blood. R. Hayes
*Taste for Honey. H. F. Heard
Taste of Deception. E. Gladstone
Taste of Treachery. L. Denny
Taste of Treason. A. Maling
*Tatterly. T. Gallon
*Tattooed Wrist. Old Spicer
*Tavern. G. M. Cohan
Taxi to Dubrovnik. W. Cook
Tea with the Black Dragon. R. A. McAvoy
Tear of Kalee. H. E. Inman
*Tears of Autumn. C. McCarry
Tech War. D. Stivers
Technocrats. F. W. Horton, Jr.
Teenage Cop. P. N. Walker
*Teenage Jungle. H. Whittington
*Teeth of the Tiger. M. Leblanc
Teeth of the Wolf. A. Paris
Teheran Wipeout. D. Pendleton
*Telefon. W. Wager
Telephone Never Tells. M. Hinxman
*Tell-Tale Murder. P. Weathers
*Tell-Tale Tattoo. J. Sharp
*Telzey Toy. J. H. Schmitz
Tempest Squadron. R. Jackson
Temple Kent. D. G. Devon
*Temple of the Flaming God. D. T. Lindsay
*Temple Tower. H. C. McNeile
Temporary A.S.P. Smith. H. L. Jones
Temptation of Carlton Earle. S. M. During
*Temptation of Tavernake. E. P. Oppenheim
Temptation Sordid. W. Phelps
Ten-A-Penny People. J. Phelan
*Ten Days' Wonder. E. Queen
*Ten Little Niggers. A. Christie
*Ten Minute Alibi. A. Armstrong
Ten Percent of Trouble. C. Heath
Ten Plays. T. Eyen
*Ten Plus One. E. McBain
Ten--the Hard Way. K. Banks
*Ten Thousand Several Doors. M. Craig
*10:30 from Marseilles. S. Japrisot
*Ten-Thirty on a Summer Night. M. Duras
10,000 Days. K. Royce
Ten Ton Snakes. K. Robeson
*Ten Words of Poison. B. Perowne
Ten Years Beyond Baker Street. C. Van Ash
*Tenant. J. Gill
*Tenant. R. Topor
Tendencies. T. Cohrs
Tender Conspiracy. C. Virmonne
Tender Fate. Magali
Tender Loving Care. A. Neiderman
Tender Offers. P. Engel
Tender Prey. P. Roberts
Tengu. G. Masterton
Tennessee Smash. D. Pendleton
*Tension. H. Janson
Tenth Crusade. C. Hyde
Tenth Man. M. Greene
*Tenth Victim. R. Sheckley
Tenth Virgin. G. Stewart
*Term of Trial. J. Barlow
Terminal. C. Forbes
Terminal Transfer. Trevor Martin
Terminal Velocity. D. Pendleton
Terminate with Prejudice. T. Barling
Terminator. K. McKenney
Terrell in Trouble. S. Blakesley
Terrible Game. D. T. Morse
Terrible Tide. A. Craig
Terror. A. Machan
*Terror. E. Wallace
Terror at Boulder Dam. V. Robinson
Terror by Gaslight. T. J. Kelly
*Terror Comes Creeping. Carter Brown
Terror Contract. A. Kilgore
Terror Farm. B. Amis
Terror for Sale. D. Streib
Terror in the Sunlight. J. Hager
Terror in Turin. Steve White
Terror Merchant. R. Spencer
Terror Merchants. D. Streib
Terror of Her Ways. Mike Shelley
*Terror of the Tongs. J. Sangster
Terror of the Triads. S. O'Callaghan
*Terror of Tongues. R. Vickers
Terror on the Railroad. J. Stratton
Terror Train. J. N. Chance
Terrorist Conspiracy. R. Holloway
Terrorist Summit. D. Pendleton
Terrorist Torment. L. Derrick
Terrorist's Woman. J. Honeywood
Tesla Bequest. L. Perdue
*Test of Anarchy. E. C. Derby
Texas Showdown. D. Stivers
Texas Station. C. Leach
Texts of Dime. B. Nevitt
*Thank You, Mr. Moto. J. P. Marquand

*That Cold Day in the Park. R. Miles
That Eternal Triangle. M. Ashton
*That Man Bolt. P. Crowcraft
*That Royle Girl. E. Balmer
That Summer, That Fall, and Far Rockaway. F. Gilroy
That Woman. H. Moray
That Year at the Office. R. Timperley
Theft of the Persian Slipper. E. D. Hoch
Their Evil Ways. J. Wainwright
Their Majesties' Bucketeers. L. N. Smith
*Then Came Bronson. W. Johnston
Then There Was Murder. B. Parvin
Therapy for Murder. L. Munder
*There Ain't No Justice. J. Curtis
*There Is a Destiny... R. J. Burge
There Was a Little Girl. E. Dewhurst
*There Was an Old Man. E. Phillpotts
*There's Always a Price Tag. J. H. Chase
*There's Death in the Cup. A. Hocking
There's Nothing to Be Afraid Of. M. Muller
*These Tigers' Hearts. Jane Land
*Theseus Code. M. Hammond
*Theta Syndrome. E. Trevor
*They Called Him Death. D. Hume
*They Came by Night. B. Lyndon
They Came to Kill. D. Stivers
*They Can't Hang Me! J. Ronald
*They Cracked Her Glass Slipper. G. Butler
They Die Alone. H. Janson
They Died Twice. K. Robeson
*They Drive by Night. J. Curtis
*They Found Each Other. G. Fairlie
They Gave Him a Gun. W. J. Cowan
*They Say I'm Bad. B. Shannon
*They Shoot Horses, Don't They? H. McCoy
*They Used to Play on Grass. G. M. Williams
They Walk Alone. M. Catto
*They Walked in Fear. B. Amis
*They Won't Believe Me. G. McDonnell
*They're Going to Kill Me. K. M. Knight
Thick As Thieves. M. Nicole
Thicker Than Water. R. McInerny
Thicker Than Water. F. Tilsley
*Thief in the Night. E. Wallace
*Thief Who Came to Dinner. T. L. Smith
*Thieves Like Us. E. Anderson
*Thieves Market. A. I. Bezzerides
Thieves of Tumbutu. H. Greene
*Thin Line. E. Atiyah
*Thin Man. D. Hammett
Thin Woman. D. Cannell
Things Men Do. R. Marshall
Think Big, Think Dirty. W. Garner
*Think Fast, Mr. Moto. J. P. Marquand
*Think of a Number. A. Bodelsen
Thinner. R. Bachman
Thinner Than Water. E. Ferrars
Third Beast. P. Loughran
Third Blonde. M. S. Craig
*Third Bullet. J. D. Carr
Third Day. M. Delahaye
*Third Day. J. Hayes
Third Deadly Sin. Lawrence Sanders
*Third Degree. A. Hornblow
Third Fury. R. Rhodes
Third Grave. D. Case
*Third Man. G. Greene
Third One. R. Mead
*Third Party Risk. N. Bentley
Third Passenger. C. Crane
*Third Round. H. C. McNeile
*Third Time Unlucky. L. Meynell
13. S. Wilson
Thirteen for the Kill. P. Buck
Thirteen O'Clock. T. Clarke
Thirteen Paint a Portrait. P. Wrightson
Thirteen Sinners. A. Marmor
*Thirteen Trumpeters. L. Meynell
Thirteen Women. T. Thayer
*Thirteenth Chair. B. Veiller
*Thirteenth Guest. A. Trail
*Thirteenth Hour. S. Horler
13th Juror. H. I. Dodge
*Thirteenth Juror. F. T. Hill
*13th Man. M. T. Bloom
*Thirty Days Hath July. A. Brennan
30 for a Harry. R. Hoyt
*Thirty-Nine Steps. J. Buchan
*36 Hours. C. K. Hittleman
*This Animal Must Die. F. Scarpetta
*This Dame Dies Soon. H. Janson
This Frightened Lady. D. Ross
This Game of Murder. J. M. Stevens
*This Hood for Hire. H. Janson
This Is My Son. C. B. Kelland
This Is Your Death. D. Devine
*This Little Measure. Sara Woods
*This Man Is Dangerous. P. Cheyney
This Prize Is Dangerous. R. T. Edwards
*This Story of Yours. J. Hopkins
*This Sweet Sickness. P. Highsmith

This Time for Keeps. M. Baroni
This Was a Woman. Joan Morgan
*This Was a Woman. H. Zore
*This Way Out. J. Ronald
This Wicked Sex. H. Janson
*This Woman Is Death. H. Janson
This Year in Jerusalem. J. Gross
*Thomas Crown Affair. E. L. Heyman
Thomas Street Horror. R. Paul
*Thorne Theatre Mystery. J. Willard
Those Dark Eyes. E. M. Brez
*Thou Shouldst Be Living. J. Byrom
*Thousand Witnesses. G. Beardmore
Thread O' Scarlet. J. J. Bell
Threat. R. Jessup
Three and One Make Five. R. Jeffries
*Three Beds in Manhattan. G. Simenon
*Three Boy Detectives. Old Sleuth
Three Buccaneers. L. Lindsay
Three Cheers for the Good Guys. F. Dickens
*Three Dates with Death. V. Gunn
*Three Day Pass--to Kill. J. W. Burke
Three Days in Winter. J. Jenkins
*Three Faces East. A. P. Kelly
*Three Finger Marks. Old Spicer
Three for Passion. H. Evens
*Three Just Men. E. Wallace
*Three Keys. F. Ormand
Three Letters of Credit. K. Bilir
Three Live Ghosts. F. S. Isham
*Three Oak Mystery. E. Wallace
*Three of a Kind. J. M. Cain
*Three of a Kind. H. C. McNeile
Three Plays. J. Ashbery
Three Plays. J. Mortimer
Three Racketeers. A. Giancol
*Three Roads. K. Millar
*Three Roads to a Star. D. Garth
Three Rousing Cheers for the Rollo Boys. C. Ford
*Three Sevens. P. P. Sheehan
*Three Silent Men. E. P. Thorne
Three Wild Men. K. Robeson
Three with a Bullet. Arthur Lyons
*Three Witnesses. S. Fowler
Three Years with Thunderbolt. A. Pratt
*Thrill a Minute with Jack Albany. J. Godey
Thrill on the Underground. D. Shaw-Taylor
Thrilling--Sweet and Rotten. I. Stuart
Through a Glass Darkly. C. S. Wallbridge
*Through Another Gate. R. Bridges
"Through the Eyes of a Pig." H. Humphries
Through the Eyes of Evil. A. Blair
Through the Valley of Death. E. M. A. Allison
*Through the Wall. C. Moffett
Throwaway Man. P. Jarrett
*Thunder Above. A. J. Wallis
Thunder and Lightning Man. C. Cooper
Thunder at Dawn. J. Hoffenberg
*Thunder Castle. V. Smith
Thunder of Hell. R. Austin
*Thunder Over the Reefs. P. Minton
*Thunderball. I. Fleming
*Thunderbolt and Lightfoot. J. Millard
Thus Was Adonis Murdered. S. Caudwell
Thy Sting, Oh Death. J. K. Drummond
Tibesti Assignment. D. J. Williams
*Tick...Tick...Tick. P. Rock
*Ticket of Leave. G. Simenon
*Ticket-of-Leave Man. T. Taylor
Tickled to Death. S. Brett
Tidal Race. G. Foy
*Tidy Death. N. Lombard
*Tiger Among Us. L. Brackett
*Tiger by the Tail. J. H. Chase
*Tiger in the Smoke. M. Allingham
Tiger Life. S. Gainham
Tiger Lily. C. Emery
Tiger Rose. W. Mack
*Tiger Street. E. Trevor
Tiger, Tiger. A. Bester
Tiger War. D. Pendleton
Tigers of Justice. G. Wilson
Tigers of Subtopia. J. Symons
Tigers on Tuesday. C. Rank
Tight Lines. B. Walsh
Tight Squeeze. H. Enders
*Tightening of the Coils. Old Spicer
*Tightening String. A. Bridge
Tightrope. A. Melville-Ross
*Tigress. H. Janson
Tijuana Traffic. Don Scott
'Til Death You Do Pay. M. Davidson
Till Proven Guilty. H. Simart
*Timberjack. D. Cushman
Timbuktu. David Smith
*Time After Time. K. Alexander
Time After Time. J. Mattera
Time Bomb. J. N. Chance
Time for Frankie Coolin. B. Griffith
Time for Murder. J. Kirton
Time for Sherlock Holmes. D. Dvorkin
Time of Fine Weather. J. S. Scott
*Time of the Fire. M. Brandel

Time of the Hunter's Moon. V. Holt
Time Runs Out at the Democratic Convention. S. Fawcette
Time to Betray. D. Boggis
Time to Die. L. Johns
Time to Reap. M. T. Hinkemeyer
Time Too Soon. E. Lindall
Time Trial. W. B. Murphy
Times Have Changed. E. H. Davis
Timetable. A. Elon
*Timetable for the General. B. Frizell
Tin Angel. P. Pines
Tin Cop. F. C. Clinton
Tin Cravat. J. D. Hunter
Tinseltown Murders. J. Blumenthal
*Tiny Luttrell. E. W. Hornung
Tip on a Dead Crab. W. Murray
Tiptoe Boys. J. Follett
Titan's Duel. D. Streib
Titron Madness. J. Bedford
*To Be a Hero. J. McCague
*To Catch a King. H. Patterson
*To Catch a Thief. D. Dodge
To Court Danger. C. Virmonne
To Die in Beverly Hills. L. Petievich
*To Dusty Death. H. McCutcheon
*To Guard the Right. H. Zachary
To Have and to Have Not. E. Hemingway
To Hinder Their Coming. C. Drummond
To Kill a Mockingbird. H. Lee
To Live and Die in L.A. G. Petievich
*To Live Forever. J. Vance
To Love a Stranger. J. Howell
To Make a Killing. J. Thomson
To Play the Fox. M. S. Craig
To Prove a Villain. G. M. Townsend
*To Ride a Tiger. M. H. Cooper
To Settle for Murder. S. Ready
*To Shadow Our Love. L. Ames
*To Study a Long Silence. V. C. Clinton-Baddeley
*To the Devil--a Daughter. D. Wheatley
*To the Eagle's Nest. J. Di Mona
To Wed a Stranger. C. Virmonne
*To What Dread End. M. V. Heberden
To What Red Hell. P. Robinson
*Toff and the Stolen Tresses. J. Creasey
*Together Brothers. Jim Robinson
*Tom Gerrard. L. Becke
*Tom Rocket. A. Fonblanque
*Tom Sawyer, Detective. M. Twain
Tomb of Horror. E. Ellison
Tomb Seven. G. Snyder
*Tomboy. H. Ellison
Tombstone Cipher. I. Melchior
*Tomorrow and a Day. H. Janson
Tomorrow for the Roses. L. Grayson
Tomorrow I Die. M. Spillane
Tomorrow Is Too Late. J. Hayes
Tomorrow's Men. M. Shea
Tondeau of Chartres. G. Petrie
Tondo for Short. P. Inchbald
Tongues of Fire. P. Abrahams
Tony, the Bootblack. O. Harper
*Too Dangerous to Live. D. Hume
Too Hot to Handle. N. Johnson
*Too Late for Tears. R. Huggins
Too Late for Tears. K. Schneider
Too Late to Tell. J. Jenkins
*Too Many Cooks. R. Stout
*Too Many Crooks. E. J. Rath
Too Many Dames Spell Trouble. W. Standish
*Too Rich to Die. H. V. Dixon
Too Sane a Murder. L. Martin
Too Scared to Live. K. Schneider
Too Smart to Live. R. Callahan
*Too Soon to Die. H. Janson
Tooth and Claw. Gabrielle Lord
Tooth and Claw. G. Wilson
*Top Dog. F. Hume
Top Level Death. H. Zachary
*Top Ten. H. Janson
*Topaz. L. Uris
*Topless Tulip Caper. Chip Harrison
Toplin. M. McDowell
Torch. T. Biracree
Torment. H. Janson
*Torment for Trixie. H. Janson
*Torment Was a Woman. M. Carson
Tormenting Memories. E. Robins
Torn Branch. A. W. Upfield
*Torn Curtain. R. Wormser
*Torrid Temptress. H. Janson
Total Recall. W. B. Murphy
*Totem. D. Morrell
Touch a Wild Heart. V. Munn
Touch of Death. M. Sadler
Touch of Jade. A. Harrell
Touch of Terror. C. Bert
*Touch of the Child. T. Gallon
Touch of Treason. S. Stein
Touch of Violence. D. Forrest
Touche the Devil. J. Higgins
*Touch the Lion's Paw. D. Lambert
Tough Guys Don't Dance. N. Mailer
*Tough Luck L.A. Murray Sinclair
Tourists. R. B. Wright
*Tournament. J. Quirk

Title Index

*Tower. R. M. Stern
Tower of Blood. S. Andrews
Tower of Sand. W. D. Steele
Tower of Terror. D. Stivers
Tower of Treason. Z. Hughes
*Town of Masks. D. S. Davis
*Town Without Pity. M. Gregor
Trace. W. B. Murphy
Trace and 47 Miles of Rope. W. B. Murphy
Trace of Red. E. Hannibal
Traces. P. Wallace
*Tracked by a Pin. R. Hackstaff
*Tracker Tracked. B. Wayde
Trade. W. H. Hallahan
Traditional Murders. J. N. Chance
*Traffic in Souls. E. H. Ball
Tragedy at Tiverton. P. Raul
Tragedy of Errors. F. A. Munsey
*Tragic Mystery. Old Sleuth
Trail of Ashes. M. Babson
Trail of the Reaper. P. Fox
Trail of the Three Lean Men. N. Barclay
Trail of the Twisted Cross. B. Sanders
*Trail of the White Knight. B. Graeme
Trailersnatch. A. Harrell
*Train. G. Simenon
*Train from Katanga. Wilbur Smith
Train Leaves at Midnight. W. Solski
Train to Hell. A. Sayle
*Traitor Blitz. J. M. Simmel
*Traitor in London. F. Hume
*Traitor Spy. T. C. H. Jacobs
Traitor's Blood. Reginald Hill
*Traitor's Gate. E. Wallace
Tramp's Wallet. F. T. Read
Trance. D. Lambert
*Trans-Siberian Express. W. Adler
*Transatlantic Puzzle. M. O. Rolfe
Transfer. T. Palmer
Transparent Tree. R. Kelly
*Trap. J. Burke
*Trap. M. Foster
Trap. T. King
Trap. J. Treherne
*Trap. D. Winston
*Trap for Cinderella. S. Japrisot
Trap Line. W. D. Montalbano
Trapped. A. Capelli
Trapper. T. York
Trauma. R. Craig
Traveling Grave. L. P. Hartley
Traveling Lady. H. Foote
Traveling Man. P. James
Travellers in a Antique Land. D. Creed
*Travelling Executioner. B. Newman
*Travels with My Aunt. G. Greene
Treachery Game. J. Gerson
Treasure Divers. D. Streib
Treasure Preserved. D. Williams
Treasures of Darkness. C. Jessey
Treasures on Earth. W. Walden
*Treasury's Millions. B. Wayde
Tree of Death. M. Muller
Tree of Hands. R. Rendell
*Tremayne's Wife. C. Hunt
*Tremolo. E. Borneman
*Trent's Last Case. E. C. Bentley
Triad. R. Rohmer
Trial. A. Booth
*Trial. D. Mankiewicz
*Trial and Error. A. Berkeley
Trial by Fire. R. Austin
*Trial by Terror. P. Gallico
*Trial of Bebe Donge. G. Simenon
*Trial of Mary Dugan. B. Veiller
*Trial of Vivienne Ware. K. Ellis
*Trials of Rumpole. J. Mortimer
Triangle. A. Lassiter
Triangle. T. White
Triangles of Fire. J. Siler
Tribe. Bari Wood
Trick Baby. I. Slim
Trick of the Ga Bolga. P. McGinley
Trick of the Light. S. Faulks
Trick or Treat. C. Crane
*Tricks and Triumphs. Old Sleuth
Tricycle. R. Rhodes
Trident Hijacking. D. Streib
Trident Tragedy. S. C. Monroe
Trigger. A. Melville-Ross
Trigger Man. B. Copper
*Triggerman. B. Rossi
Trinity Factor. S. Flannery
Trio in Three Flats. E. Dewhurst
Triple Crown. J. L. Breen
Triple Factor. O. Sela
Triple Indemnity. J. Richards
*Triumph of Evil. P. Kavanagh
Triumph of the Rat. D. Robins
*Triumverate. H. B. Taylor
Trixie True, Teen Detective. K. Hamilton
Troika. C. Egleton
Trojan Hearse. C. Curzon
Trojan Horses. R. Emmett
Trojan in Iran. R. Skimin
Trojan Mule. J. Drummond
*Trooper O'Neill. G. Goodchild
Tropic Equations. D. Gordon

*Tropic Moon. G. Simenon
Tropical Murder. S. Murray
Tropical Murder. Louis Williams
Trotsky's Run. R. Hoyt
Trouble at Aquitaine. N. Livingston
*Trouble at Wrekin Farm. J. Bell
Trouble Crossing the Pyrenees. G. D. Larsen
Trouble for Tallon. J. Ball
Trouble in Bugland. W. Kotzwinkle
Trouble in Muristan. J. Marlowe
*Trouble in Thor. J. Valentine
Trouble Making Toys. A. M. Pyle
*Trouble Man. J. D. F. Black
*Trouble with Harry. J. T. Story
*Troubled Heritage. M. Richmond
Troubled Waters. P. H. Fine
Troubled Waters. E. Lemarchand
Troy Dossier. Manny Meyers
True Bride. T. Altman
*True Confessions. J. G. Dunne
True Crime. M. A. Collins
True Detective. M. A. Collins
*True Detective Stories. M. Moser
True-Life Adventure. Julie Smith
True or False. M. Borgenicht
*Trunk Crime. E. Percy
Trust Doesn't Rust. G. A. Larson
Truthful Lady. J. S. Clouston
Tsurane Enterprise. M. Cronin
*Tucker's People. I. Wolfert
Tularemia Gambit. S. Perry
Tulku. Stephen Hayes
Tumbledown Farm. J. Muir
*Turf Conspiracy. N. Gould
Turkish Rondo. A. Stevenson
Turn-Around. V. Volkoff
Turn for the Nurse. R. Abbot
*Turn Killer. B. Lecomber
Turn Loose the Dragon. G. Chesbro
*Turn of the Screw. H. James
Turn of Traitors. P. Harcourt
Turn-Out Man. F. Roderus
Turn the Key Softly. J. Brophy
Turner's Wife. N. Garbo
Turnpike. G. E. Evans
Turquoise Dragon. D. R. Wallace
Tuscany Terror. D. Pendleton
*Tut, Tut! Mr. Tutt. A. Train
Tuxedo Park. B. Copper
Twelfth Juror. B. M. Gill
Twelfth Night of Ramadan. K. J. Peel
Twelfth of April. R. Doliner
Twelfth Power of Evil. J. Morgulas
Twelve Angry Men. R. Rose
12:15 A.M.: I'm Blasted. M. Horgan
Twelve Hours to Kill. R. M. Stern
*Twentieth Day of January. T. Allbeury
*Twenty Plus Two. F. Gruber
*Twenty Thousand Thieves. E. Lambert
Twice Burned. R. Gettel
Twice Shy. D. Francis
*Twice Told Tales. N. Hawthorne
Twilight. L. Nichols
Twilight of Honor. A. Dewlin
Twilight Tigress. H. Janson
*Twilight Walk. A. B. Shiffrin
Twin Bridges Murder. A. Harrell
Twin Detectives. K. F. Hill
*Twin Ventriloquists. Old Sleuth
*Twist for Two. H. Janson
*Twist of Sand. G. Jenkins
*Twist of Yarn. E. Lookabee
Twisted Tree. P. Harcourt
Two. J. D. MacDonald
*Two. C. Trieschman
Two Bottles of Relish. E. Darby
*Two Conspirators. M. O. Rolfe
Two Crimes. J. Ibarguengoitia
Two Dude Defense. W. Walker
Two Equals One. P. Dagmar
*Two Faces of January. P. Highsmith
*Two for the Price of One. T. Kenrick
*Two Hours to Doom. P. Bryant
Two If by Sea. E. Savage
Two Little Sailor Boys. G. M. White
*Two Living and One Dead. S. Christiansen
*Two Minute Warning. G. La Fountaine
*Two Mrs. Carrolls. M. Vale
Two Mrs. Grenvilles. D. Dunne
Two Mrs. Hemingways. W. Massey
*Two Much! D. E. Westlake
*Two O'Clock Courage. E. Burgess
Two Small Bodies. N. Bell
Two Steps from Three East. W. B. Murphy
*Two Thousand Maniacs. H. G. Lewis
Two Thyrdes. B. Denham
Two Women and Their Man. Mervyn Jones
Tyro. J. Milne
U.N. Sabotage. R. Skimin
Ubik. P. K. Dick
Ultimate Deterrent. H. Janson
Ultimate Game. R. Glendinning
Ultimate Good Luck. R. Ford
Ultimate Issue. G. Markstein
Ultimate Judge. A. Howlett
Ultimate Terror. G. Wilson
*Uncharted Seas. D. Wheatley

Uncivil Seasons. M. Malone
*Unclaimed Daughter. Anonymous
Uncle Harry. T. Job
*Uncle Silas. J. S. Le Fanu
Uncollected Stories. A. C. Doyle
*Uncommon Danger. E. Ambler
*Uncommon Market. H. Janson
*Uncover Agent. H. Janson
*Undefeated. J. Thompson
*Under Cover. R. C. Megrue
*Under Cover Man. J. Wilstach
Under Cover of Darkness. Donald Smith
Under Cover of Night. C. Virmonne
Under Etna. L. Cook
Under Jekyll's Hyde. T. J. Kelly
Under the Freeze. G. Bartram
*Under Western Eyes. J. Conrad
*Undercover Cat. Gordons
Undercover: El Salvador. J. Tabler
Undercurrent. B. Jefferis
*Underground. J. S. Dutton, Jr.
Underground. M. Sloan
*Underground. C. Stratton
Underground City. H. L. Humes
*Underground Connection. P. Niesewand
Understudy. M. Tabor
*Underworld Nights. C. Raven
*Undesirable Company. F. Ryck
*Undisclosed Client. E. Wallace
Undying Monster. J. D. Kerruish
*Uneasy Freehold. D. Macardle
Uneasy Lies the Head. R. Tine
*Uneasy Terms. P. Cheyney
*Unexpected Corpse. E. L. Cushing
Unexpected Developments. R. B. Dominic
*Unexpected Guest. A. Christie
*Unexpected Mrs. Pollifax. D. Gilman
*Unfair Exchange. M. Babson
*Unforbidden Sin. R. Vickers
Unforgiven. P. J. MacDonald
*Unfortunate Rogue. Warren Miller
Unhanged Man. A. Hunter
Unhappy Souls. D. Rogan
Unholy Alliance. B. Crowther
*Unholy Child. C. Breslin
Unholy Communion. Richard Hughes
Unholy Moses. P. Degrave
Unholy Mourning. D. Lippincott
*Unholy Three. T. Robbins
*Unholy Wife. J. Roeburt
Unhung Man. A. Hunter
*Uninvited. F. A. Chittenden
Uninvited. T. J. Kelly
Uninvited Guest. B. Kennedy
Union Club Mysteries. I. Asimov
Unkindness of Ravens. R. Rendell
Unknown Conan Doyle. A. C. Doyle
*Unknown Path. Lady A. Scott
Unknown People. R. West
Unmasking a King. O. Newman
Unofficial Executor. H. F. Moulton
Unpleasant Profession of Jonathan Hoag. R. A. Heinlein
Unraveled Skeins. G. Gow
*Unravelled Knots. B. Orczy
Unripe Gold. G. Jenkins
Unseemly End. R. Jeffries
*Unseen Assassin. H. Janson
Unseen Way. D. Newing
*Unsuitable Job for a Woman. P. D. James
*Unsuspected. C. Armstrong
Unsuspected Conduct. E. K. Stirling
Untamed. H. Janson
*Untaxed Whiskey. B. Wayde
Until Death Do Us Part. M. McMullen
Until Proven Guilty. J. A. Jance
Untold Sherlock Holmes. W. E. Dudley
*Untouchable Juli. J. Aldridge
Untouchables. K. Blake
Unvarnished Truth. R. Ryton
Unveiled. M. A. Dickens
Unwelcome Audience. M. Russell
Up for Grabs. John Harris
Up Will Go Parliament. G. Jones
Up with Your hands. G. Jones
Upon Some Midnights Clear. K. C. Constantine
Upperdown. Stephen Cook
Uprush of Mayhem. J. S. Scott
Upside Downside. R. Goulart
*Upstairs and Downstairs. R. S. Thorn
Urban Prey. P. Beere
Urge for Justice. J. Wainwright
Urgent Conference. N. Forde
"V." T. Pynchon
*V for Vitality. H. Janson
V-3. I. Melchior
*Vagabond Vamp. H. Janson
Vail. T. Hoyle
Vain Citadel. B. S. Morgan
*Valdez Is Coming. E. Leonard
Valediction. R. B. Parker
Valiant. H. Hall
Valkyrie Project. M. Kilian
*Valley of Fear. A. C. Doyle
*Valley of Ghosts. E. Wallace
Valley of Silent Men. J. O. Curwood
Valley of the Fox. J. Hone

Vampire's Honeymoon. C. Woolrich
*Vampires of the China Coast. Bok
*Van, the Government Detective. Old Sleuth
Vanderleigh Legacy. B. Caldwell
*Vanished. F. Knebel
*Vanishing Corpse. Anthony Gilbert
Vanishing Holes Murder. P. Chambers
*Vanishing Point. V. Canning
Vanishing Vector. J. P. Evans
*Vanity Row. W. R. Burnett
Variable Man. P. K. Dick
Variations on a Theme. D. E. Fisher
*Variety. R. Connell
*Variety Jack. Old Sleuth
Varkaus Conspiracy. J. Dalmas
Vatican Affairs. M. Valdemi
Vatican Gold. J. R. Zodrow
Vatican Kill. J. D. Revere
Vatican Rip. Jonathan Gash
Vectors. T. Krueger
Vegas Legacy. O. Demaris
Vegas Vengeance. C. Ramm
Veiled Threat. J. Jenkins
*Velvet Ape. D. C. Holmes
*Velvet Black. R. W. Child
*Velvet Fleece. L. Eby
Velvet Shadows of Justin Wood. A. Haley
*Velvet Well. J. Gearon
Vendetta. J. Cutter
Vendetta. J. D. Humphreys
Vendetta. I. Zacharia
*Venetian Affair. H. MacInnes
*Venetian Bird. V. Canning
Venetian Spy. E. Webster
Vengeance. H. Janson
Vengeance Army. A. Kilgore
Vengeance Game. S. Grave
Vengeance Is His. W. Barker
Vengeance Mountain. J. Cutter
Vengeance, My Love. E. G. Fulton
*Vengeance of ?. J. Wallace
Vengeance 10. J. Poyer
Vengeance Trail. W. B. Mowery
Vengeful Flames. A. Sewart
Venice Ultimatum. J. Raven
*Venom. A. Scholefield
Venom Squadron. R. Jackson
*Ventriloquist Detectives. Old Sleuth
Venus Belt. L. N. Smith
*Venus Makes Three. H. Janson
Venus Shoe. C. A. Neggers
Venus Underground. R. Rainey
Verdict. B. Reed
Verdict of the Heart. C. Garvice
Verdugo Affair. B. Hirschfeld
*Vermilion. N. Aldyne
Vermilion. P. A. Whitney
Verona Passamezzo. J. Gollin
Veronica Dean Case. H. Waugh
Verratoli Inheritance. E. Webster
Very British Coup. C. Mullin
Very Costly Escape. P. J. Scott
Very Good Hater. M. Challis
Very Good Hater. Reginald Hill
Very Great Grandson of Sherlock Holmes. B. Majeski
Very Old Money. S. Ellin
Very Private Enterprise. E. Ironside
*Veterans. E. Lambert
Vet's Daughter. B. Comyns
Vicar Done It. F. Bream
Vicar Investigates. F. Bream
Vicar's Roses. J. L. Breen
Vice Squad. W. Rotsler
Vicious Circle. D. Clark
*Vicky Van. C. Wells
*Victim. W. Drummond
Victim. M. Fratti
*Victim. D. Winston
Victim of Love. J. Delutry
Victims. D. Uhnak
Victims. C. Wilcox
*Victoria's House. F. Carmichael
Vida. Delacorta
Video Vandal. F. Roderus
Vienna Blood. L. Payne
*Viennese Love. H. Bettauer
Viennese Snuffbox. H. Drury
View from Deacon Hill. J. S. Scott
View from the Square. J. Trenhaile
View to Ransom. J. Arney
Viking Summer. C. A. Brady
*Villa Caprice. I. Alexander
Villa Golitsyn. P. P. Read
*Villa Mimosa. J. Tickell
Villa Plot, Counterplot. Cameron Ross
Village Detective. V. Lipatov
Villain and the Virgin. J. H. Chase
*Villains. C. Keppel
Villains by Necessity. Sara Woods
Villon of the Piece. H. Janson
Vinegar in the Spice. D. Thurlow
Violent Man. A. E. Van Vogt
Violent Past. E. Berridge
*Violent Saturday. W. L. Heath
Violent Streets. D. Pendleton
Viper Factor. G. Wilson
Viper Squad. J. B. Hadley
Viper Three. W. Wager

Virgel Detective. T. Richards
Virgin and Martyr. A. Greeley
*Virgin Cay. B. Heatter
Virgin in the Ice. Ellis Peters
Virgin on the Rocks. M. Butterworth
Virgin Stealers. D. Streib
Virtue Triumphant. P. Norris
Virus Man. C. Rayner
Visions of Terror. W. Katz
Visit. F. Duerrenmatt
Visit After Dark. D. Winston
*Visit from a Broad. H. Janson
Visiting Hours. K. Rembo
Voice. C. Connolly
*Voice from the Grave. Clarissa Ross
Voice in the Dark. R. Dyar
Voice in the Fog. H. MacGrath
Voice in the Night. V. Johnston
Voice of Armageddon. D. Lippincott
Voice of the Clown. B. B. Canary
Voice of the Past. M. Leek
*Voice of the Peacock. E. Salter
*Voice on the Wire. E. H. Ball
Voice Outside. K. Grimwood
Voices in the House. P. S. Buck
Voices in the Wind. E. Anthony
Volunteers for Danger. R. T. Bickers
*Voodoo Violence. H. Janson
Vortex. J. Land
Vortex Assignment. A. Handley
Vulcan Academy Murders. J. Lorrah
Vulcan Rising. A. Aasheim
*Vulnerable. D. Collins
Vulture's Vengeance. D. Pendleton
W. G. Grace's Last Case. W. Rushton
*W.I.L. One to Curtis. P. Loraine
*W Plan. G. Seton
*Wages of Fear. G. Arnaud
Wagner the Wehrwolf. G. W. M. Reynolds
Waif's Paradise. Howard Hall
*Wait Until Dark. F. Knott
Waiting Darkness. M. Bingley
*Waiting for a Tiger. B. Healey
Waiting for the End of the World. M. S. Bell
Waiting for the End of the World. Andrew Taylor
Wake in Darkness. D. E. McQuinn
*Wake in Fright. K. Cook
Wake Up and Die. C. Grey
Wake Up, Darlin' Corey. M. K. Wren
Waldorf. J. Goldman
*Walk a Wicked Mile. R. P. Hansen
Walk a Winter Beach. Sandy Johnson
Walk Around the Square. D. Winston
Walk in the Dark. C. Phillips
Walk Softly and Beware. M. Blake
*Walk with Care. P. Wentworth
*Walk with Evil. R. Wilder
Walking Shadow. B. J. Appleton
Walking Shadows. F. Taylor
*Walking Stick. Winston Graham
*Walking Tall. D. Warren
Walking Tall: Part 2. W. Carey
*Walking Trip. H. Buckmaster
*Wall Street Haul. Nicholas Carter
*Wall Street Swindlers. J. Sharp
Wallington Case. M. Jon
*Walls Came Tumbling Down. J. Eisinger
Walls Have Eyes. Ganpat
Walter Graydon. F. S. Potter
Waltz into Darkness. W. Irish
Wanted on Holiday. F. Jefkins
Wanton Wench. J. Craig
Wantons of Betrayal. A. Rivere
War Chest. P. A. Foxall
War in Heaven. C. Williams
War Machine. W. Marshall
War of Dreams. A. Carter
War of 1938. S. F. Wright
War Toys. Hampton Howard
War Without Frontiers. A. Osmond
*Ware Case. G. Pleydell
Warfield Syndrome. H. Denker
Warhead. F. R. Baker
Warlord. J. Frost
Warlord of Azatlan. D. Stivers
*Warlord's Hill. G. Fox
*Warn That Man. V. Sylvaine
*Warning Bell. G. M. White
Warning Wings. R. Adam
Warriors. S. Yurick
Wartime. A. Mitchell
Washed in the Blood. C. H. Flynn
Washington Square Ensemble. M. S. Bell
Wasps in the Woodpile. M. Warden
Waste Remains. J. Cook
Wasting Assets. T. Palmer
Watch the Birdie. Ramsey Campbell
Watchdogs. J. Weisman
Watcher. J. R. Janes
Watcher. C. MacLean
Watcher Within. W. Appel
Watchers. E. Webster
Watching the Detectives. J. Rathbone
*Watchmaker of Everton. G. Simenon
Watchman. D. G. Finlay
*Water Horse. G. Scott
Watercress File. A. Gilchrist
Waterfront. J. Brophy

*Waterfront. F. Findley
Waterfront Rat. D. Spade
Waterhole. J. J. Savarin
Waterland. G. Swift
*Waterloo. F. E. Smith
*Waterman. E. Lambert
Watson's Apology. B. Bainbridge
Wavecrest. B. Knox
Wavelengths. D. M. Klein
Wax Model. C. Dekker
*Way of the Strong. R. Cullum
*Way Out. B. Graeme
*Way Out Wanton. H. Janson
*Way the Cookie Crumbles. J. H. Chase
Way to Get Dead. W. Newton
*Way to Gold. W. D. Steele
Way to Santiago. A. Calder-Marshall
Ways of Darkness. J. Hayes
*Ways of Death. H. C. Owen
*Ways of the Hour. J. F. Cooper
Wayward Seeds of Grass. P. Nash
*We Always Treat Women Too Well. R. Queneau
We Are Not Alone. J. Hilton
*We Have Always Lived in the Castle. H. C. Wheeler
*We Must Kill Toni. I. S. Black
*We Shall See. E. Wallace
We the Bereaved. A. Clarke
*We the Condemned. N. Karta
Weak Link. Allan Wood
Weather--Clearing. F. A. Warren
Web. A. Capelli
Web. S. Talmy
Web of Intrigue. E. Lamartine
*Web of Murder. J. Troy
*Web of Murder. H. Whittington
Web of Terror. J. Cannon
Wedding Guest. D. Wiltse
*Wedding Guest Sat on a Stone. R. Shattuck
Wedding Treasure. D. Williams
*Week-Ends with Henry. H. Holland
Week of the Scorpion. B. Healey
*Weekend at Thrackley. A. Melville
Weekend for Murder. M. Babson
*Weird Sea Mystery. Old Sleuth
Weird Tales of Terror and Detection. H. F. Heard
Weird Transformation. M. Y. Halidom
*Weird Wedlock. R. M. Gilchrist
Welcome to the Feast. G. Wilson
Welcome to the Torture Chamber. Mastero Storyteller
Well, After All... F. F. Moore
We'll Share a Double Funeral. J. H. Chase
Well-Wisher. P. Carder
Welsh Fargo. H. Secombe
*We're All Guilty. J. Reach
Werewolf. P. McCutchan
*Werewolf of Paris. G. Endore
West End People. P. Wildeblood
West Point Detective. Old Sleuth
Wet Job. M. Stall
*Wettermark. E. Chaze
Wharf Girl. W. Manners
*What Beckoning Ghost. D. G. Browne
*What Changed Charley Farthing. M. Hebden
*What Ever Happened to Baby Jane? H. Farrell
What Happened Then? L. T. Bradley
What Nigel Knew. E. Field
What Then Is Love. E. Loring
Whatever's Been Going on at Mumblesby? Colin Watson
*What's Bred in the Bone. G. Allen
What's Bred in the Bone. R. Davies
What's Left of Fred. W. Maner
*What's the Matter with Helen? R. Deming
Wheel of Fortune. S. Howatch
*Wheel Spins. E. L. White
Wheel Turns. E. Lemarchand
When a Blonde Dies. M. Skinner
When and If. P. Reynolds
*When Dames Get Tough. H. Janson
When Darkness Falls. P. Zindel
When Dragons Dance. E. Tokson
*When Eight Bells Toll. A. MacLean
When Elephants Forget. W. B. Murphy
When Fish Begin to Smell. H. M. Cooper
*When Greek Meets Greek. P. Trent
When I Was Otherwise. S. Benatar
*When It Was Dark. G. Thorne
When Johnny the Cleaver Took Britain. D. Webster
*When Last Seen... M. J. Herrick
When the Bough Breaks. J. Kellerman
When the Dark Man Calls. S. M. Kaminsky
When the Death Penalty Came Back. G. J. Cadbury
When the Sky Falls. M. Ashton
When the Wind Blows. J. Saul
When Thieves Fall Out. G. Reed
When Trouble Beckons. M. McQuay
When We Ran. K. Leopold
When Women Love. G. M. White
When You Comin' Back, Range Rider. C.

Title Index

Heath
*Where Are the Children? M. H. Clark
Where East Is East. T. Browning
*Where Is Mary Bostwick? R. Foley
Where Lionel Lies. A. S. Well
Where Should He Die? Sara Woods
Where the Rail Runs Now. F. F. Moore
Where There's a Will. E. Phillips
Which Side Gave In? J. Hitchins
*While the Patient Slept. M. G. Eberhart
*Whip Hand. V. Canning
*Whiplash. H. Janson
Whirlpool. A. Howlett
*Whirlpool. V. Morton
*Whirlwind Beneath the Sea. K. Stanton
Whisker of Hercules. K. Robeson
Whisky Murders. R. Grayson
*Whisper Her Name. H. Hunt
Whisper in the Night. J. Aiken
Whisper of Treason. Hartshorne
Whisper Who Dares. T. Strong
*Whispering Chorus. P. P. Sheehan
*Whispering Death. D. Carney
Whispering Gallery. R. H. Francis
Whispering Gallery. P. Robinson
Whispering Smith. F. H. Spearman
Whispering Walls. E. Brennan
*Whispering Window. C. Fitzsimmons
*Whispering Windows. T. Burke
*Whispering Wires. H. Leverage
Whispering Woman. V. Verner
Whistle Blower. John Hale
Whistle Stop. M. M. Wolff
*Whistling in the Dark. L. Gross
*White Alley. C. Wells
White Circle. J. Shrog
*White Cockatoo. M. G. Eberhart
White Death. Nick Carter
White Eagles Over Serbia. L. Durrell
*White Face. E. Wallace
White Hell. G. Wilson
White House Massacre. S. Victor
White House Murder Case. J. Feiffer
*White Lie. W. Lequeux
*White Lie Assignment. P. Driscoll
White Male Running. M. G. Webb
White Mandarin. D. Sherman
*White Man's Justice: Black Man's Grief. D. Goines
White Meat. P. Corris
*White Mice. R. H. Davis
*White Moll. F. Packard
White Plague. F. Herbert
*White Rook. J. B. Harris-Burland
White Sheep of the Family. L. du G. Peach
White Snake. L. Whiteson
*White South. H. Innes
White Wash. L. Ludlow
Whitefire. G. Wright
Who Censored Roger Rabbit? G. K. Wolf
Who Dare to Live. R. Lucas
Who Guards a Prince. Reginald Hill
Who Is Cato? G. Sims
Who Killed Farraby? C. H. Ogilvie
Who Killed Jock Ewing? R. Tine
Who Killed Robin Cock. B. McDermott
Who Shall Win? J. A. Loughman
*Who Was He? P. Little
*Who Was That Lady I Saw You With? N. Krasna
Who'd Hire Brett? J. Brett
*Who'd Want to Kill Old George? R. Upton
Whodunnit. A. C. Martens
Whodunnit. A. Shaffer
Whoever I Am. E. Dewhurst
Whole Truth. P. Mackie
*Whom God Hath Joined. F. Hume
*Whoreson. D. Goines
*Who's Sorry Now. D. Linton
*Whose Hand? W. G. Wills
*Whose Little Girl Are You? D. Craig
*Whose Wife. C. H. Bullivant
Whosoever Shall Offend... F. M. Crawford
Why Kill Arthur Potter? R. Harrison
Why Me? D. E. Westlake
*Why Should Sylvia? H. Janson
*Wicked. A. Applin
*Wicked Designs. L. O'Donnell
Wicked Flee. A. Hocking
Wicked, Loving Murder. O. Papazoglou
Wicked Stepmother. A. Young
Wicked Widow. Carter Brown
*Wicked Woman. Anne Austin
*Wicker Man. Robin Hardy
*Wide Arch. D. Stivens
*Wide Boys Never Work. R. Westerby
Widening Gyre. R. B. Parker
*Widow and the Cavalier. R. Armstrong
Widow, Weep for Me. Marc Miller
*Widow with the Pink Gloves. M. Dekobra
Widows. L. La Plante
Widow's Beads. C. Joyce
Widows II. L. La Plante
Widow's Walk. A. Coburn
Widow's Walk. T. J. Kelly
Widow's Walk. W. Tucker
*Widow's War. A. Williams
*Wife by Purchase. P. Trent
Wife Found Slain. C. Crane
*Wife of the Red-Haired Man. B. S. Ballinger
*Wife Whom God Forgot. C. H. Bullivant
*Wilby Conspiracy. P. Driscoll
Wild About Harry. P. Pickering
Wild Card. P. A. Foxall
Wild Geese. D. Carney
Wild Geese II. D. Carney
*Wild Girl. H. Janson
*Wild Grapes. B. Jefferis
*Wild Party. J. McPartland
Wild Ride. W. Boyles
Wild Talent. W. Tucker
Wildcliffe Bird. C. Heaven
Wilderness of Mirrors. D. Seaman
Will of Her Own. D. M. Day
*Will-Power. H. Janson
Will to Kill. J. Penn
Wilt on High. T. Sharpe
Wind in the Rain. J. M. Simmel
Windfall. D. Bagley
*Winding Stair. A. E. W. Mason
*Windows. H. B. Gilmour
Winds of Pentecost. R. Chester
Winds of Terror. P. Hagan
Windshear. J. J. Savarin
Windsor Plot. P. G. Winslow
Wine Dark Sea. L. Sciascia
Wine of Life. L. Egan
Wine, Women and Bullets. N. Spain
Winged Dancer. C. Grae
Wings of Death. C. Sloan
Winifred Power. Anonymous
Winner Harris. I. St. James
*Winning a Princess. Old Sleuth
Winning Side. P. Corris
Winning Streak. A. Grisman
*Winston Affair. H. Fast
Winter and the Widowmakers. B. Gaston
Winter and the Wild Rover. B. Gaston
Winter Chill. J. Fluke
Winter Evening Tales Collected Among the Cottagers in the South of England. J. Hogg
*Winter Kills. R. Condon
Winter Nights. N. Drake
Winter Roses. L. Hagen
Winter Touch. C. Eqleton
*Winter Wears a Shroud. Robert Chapman
Wired. H. Hellerstein
Wireman. B. S. Mosiman
*Wisdom of Father Brown. G. K. Chesterton
Wise Child. S. Gray
*Wisteria Cottage. R. M. Coates
*Witch. B. St. James
*Witch Tree. L. B. Long
Witch Who Wouldn't Hang. T. J. Kelly
*Witchcraft for Panda One. P. N. Walker
Witching. C. John
*Witching Hour. A. Thomas
With Flowers That Fell. M. R. D. Meek
With Intent to Kill. H. Pentecost
With Murder in Mind. F. Bream
With Penalty and Interest. D. Mardon
*Within the Labyrinth. N. Lewis
*Within the Law. B. Veiller
Within the Web. M. Weiser
Without Armour. J. Hilton
Without Fear. M. Judge
Without Mercy. Leonard Jordan
Without Ransom. R. Bliss
Without Virtue. W. Standish
Witness. W. Kelley
*Witness for the Defense. A. E. W. Mason
*Witness for the Prosecution. A. Christie
*Witness to Treason. M. J. Ragosta
*Witnesses. A. Holden
Wodehouse on Crime. P. G. Wodehouse
Wolaroi's Cup. A. Pratt
Wolf Hunters. J. O. Curwood
Wolf in Sheep's Clothing. V. Bird
Wolf-Lure. A. Castle
Wolf Trap. F. Nolan
*Wolfen. W. Strieber
Wolfnight. N. Freeling
Wolfrun. J. J. Savarin
Wolves at the Door. T. King
*Wolves of New York. A. W. Aiken
Wolves of Summer. J. Nazel
Woman at Dead Oaks. J. Kirkpatrick
Woman at Point Zero. N. El Saadawi
*Woman Ayisha. T. Mundy
Woman Beware Woman. E. Tennant
Woman Called Omega. H. Green
Woman Called Scylla. D. Gurr
*Woman Hunt. F. Ryck
*Woman in Black. W. Spence
*Woman in Grey. A. M. Williamson
*Woman in Purple Pajamas. W. Kent
*Woman in Red. S. Campbell
*Woman in Red. Anthony Gilbert
Woman in Red. P. Gosling
Woman in the Case. C. Fitch
Woman in the Window. D. Clarins
*Woman in White. W. Collins
Woman of Cairo. N. Barber
Woman of Consequence. S. Gottlieb
*Woman of Mystery. M. Leblanc
*Woman of Mystery. G. Ohnet
*Woman of Straw. C. Arley
*Woman of the Iron Bracelets. F. Barrett
Woman They Sent to Fight. D. Boggis
Woman Trap. A. Capelli
Woman Trap. H. Janson
Woman Vanishes. C. Crane
*Woman Who Dared. A. M. Williamson
*Woman Who Was. P. Boileau
Woman Who Went Away. F. Haring
*Woman Wins. C. H. Bullivant
*Woman's Hand. Nicholas Carter
Woman's Law. M. Thompson
*Women Hate Till Death. H. Janson
Women That Are Lost. W. Standish
Women Without Men. R. Marr
Woodchuck Jerry, the Country Detective. Old Sleuth
Wooden Kimono. J. Floyd
Word of a Gentleman. P. Niesewand
Word of Honor. N. De Mille
Words Can Kill. K. Davis
*Words for Murder Perhaps. E. Candy
Work of the Devil. E. Willie
World Bewitched. J. M. Graham
*World in My Pocket. J. H. Chase
World to Win. U. Sinclair
*Worldly Goods. A. Soutar
*World's Finger. T. W. Hanshew
*World's Great Snare. E. P. Oppenheim
Worlds Made of Fire. M. Childress
Worm in the Rose. T. Stacey
Worse Than a Crime. Anne Burton
Worst Enemies. J. Scaparro
Worth More Dead. B. Sarto
*Wounded and the Slain. D. Goodis
Wrack and Rune. C. MacLeod
*Wrath of God. J. Graham
Wreath for a Ragman. B. Parvin
*Wreath for a Redhead. Brian Moore
*Wreath of Cherry Blossoms. C. Leader
*Wrecker. A. Ridley
*Wrecking Crew. D. Hamilton
*Write Me a Murder. F. Knott
Wroclaw Dracula. M. Murdoch
Wrong Box. G. Napier
*Wrong Box. R. L. Stevenson
*Wrong Case. J. Crumley
Wrong Target. W. Kaye
*Wrong That Was Done. F. W. Robinson
Wrong Turn. D. Harper
*Wrong Venus. C. Williams
Wyatt. D. Gethin
Wyatt and the Moresby Legacy. D. Gethin
Wyatt's Orphan. D. Gethin
Wycliffe and the Beales. W. J. Burley
Wycliffe and the Four Jacks. W. J. Burley
*Wycliffe and the Scapegoat. W. J. Burley
Wycliffe's Wild-Goose Chase. W. J. Burley
*Wyss Pursuit. Adam Hamilton
*X. E. Sudak
X Factor. D. Wiles
XPD. L. Deighton
X v. Rex. M. Porlock
Xanadu Program. R. Carroll
Xanadu Talisman. P. O'Donnell
*Yakuza. L. Schrader
*Yang Meridian. J. Leasor
Yankee Doodle Detective. A. La Croix
*Yankee Rue, the Ex-Pugilist Detective. Old Sleuth
*Year of Living Dangerously. C. J. Koch
Year of the Dragon. R. Daley
Year of the Gun. M. Mewshaw
*Year of the Tiger. L. Chang
Yearbook Killer. T. Philbin
Yellow Angel. M. A. Gilbert
*Yellow Claw. S. Rohmer
Yellow Claws. H. J. S. Anderton
*Yellow-Dog Contract. R. Thomas
*Yellow Dove. G. F. Gibbs
*Yellow Mask. W. Collins
*Yellow Men and Gold. Gouverneur Morris
Yellow Rain. P. McCurtin
Yellow Ticket. V. Morton
*Yellow Typhoon. H. MacGrath
*Yellow Violet. F. Crane
Yesterday Man. D. Stringer
*Yield to the Night. J. Henry
*Yonder Grow the Daisies. W. Lipman
You Can Go Feet First. W. Newton
*You Can Help Me. M. Birmingham
You Can't Beat the Law. H. H. Van Loan
You Can't Kill a Dead Man. D. Pranger
*You Can_t See Round Corners. J. Cleary
You Die, Du Man! J. Cain
*You Have Yourself a Deal. J. H. Chase
You Only Die Once. B. Copper
*You Only Live Twice. I. Fleming
*You, Pay Your Money. M. Cronin
*You Stand Accused. D. Hughston

You, the Jury. A. C. Martens
You'd Better Believe It. B. James
You'll Be All Right. K. Blake
*You'll Like My Mother. N. A. Hintze
*You'll Live to Talk. Dave Steel
*You'll Never Get Me. S. Morelli
Young Adam. A. Trocchi
*Young and Wild. Morton Cooper
Young Blood. K. Alexis
*Young Cardinaud. G. Simenon
*Young Dillinger. S. Stuart
*Young Don't Cry. R. Jessup
*Young Eve and Old Adam. T. Gallon
Young Fair God. H. Fleetwood
Young Killers. W. Wiener
Young Lady from Paris. J. Aiken
Young Sherlock Holmes. A. Arnold
*Young Wolves. H. Janson
*Your Deal, My Lovely. P. Cheyney
Your Eyelids Are Growing Heavy. B. Paul
*You're Best Alone. P. Curtis
You're Far Too Young! Spondee
*You're Hired; You're Dead. K. Carr
*You're Wrong, Delaney. B. Singer
Yukon Target. Nick Carter
Z. V. Vassilikos
Zaharoff Commission. A. Jute
Zaibatsu. John Brown
*Zembya Expedition. J. Rosenberger
Zepplin. R. Florence
Zero Hour Strike Force. Nick Carter
*Zero Takes All. H. Janson
Zigzag. M. Kenyon
*Zofloya. C. Dacre
Zoharoff Commission. A. Jute
Zolta Configuration. D. Quammen
Zombie. T. J. Kelly
Zombie! P. Tremayne
Zone of Violence. D. Dunham
Zones of Silence. W. Garner
Zooman and the Sign. C. Fuller
Zukovka Experiment. N. Gottlieb
Zulu Blood. R. Skimin
Zurich Numbers. B. Granger
Zurich Syndicate. A. K. Robertson

Settings Index

Settings Index

ABYSSINIA. See: Ethiopia.

ACADEMIA (Acad. School settings at all levels)
Apffel, E. R. Last Days at St. Saturn's
Barnard, R. Little Victims
Bourgeau, A. Most Likely Suspect
Brown, R. D. Prime Suspect
Byrom, J. Thou Shouldst Be Living
Carlson, P. M. Audition for Murder
  Murder Is Academic
Clark, D. Golden Rain
Clemeau, C. Ariadne Clue
Cook, S. Upperdown
Cross, A. Sweet Death, Kind Death
Dean, S. F. X. By Frequent Anguish
Delman, D. Death of a Nymph
Dickinson, P. Hindsight
Eulo, E. Y. Ice Orchids
Fox, P. Kensington Gore
Garnet, A. H. Maze
Hannah, B. Nightwatchman
Heald, T. Masterstroke
Janeschutz, T. In Shadows
Jevons, M. Fatal Equilibrium
Jordan, C. Carol in the Dark
Kelly, N. In the Shadow of King's
Kenney, S. Graves in Academe
King, P. Snares of the Enemy
Lemarchand, E. Light Through Glass
McCormick, C. Resume for Murder
Marasco, R. Child's Play
Miner, V. Murder in the English Department
Murphy, B. Enigma Variations
Murphy, W. B. Dead Letter
Nowak, J. Death at the Crossings
O'Marie, C. A. Novena for Murder
Park, J. Sorority House
Penn, J. Mortal Term
Rankin, J. L. Murder Pie
Reeves, R. Doubting Thomas
Resnicow, H. Seventh Crossword
Rhodes, R. Tricycle
Sharpe, T. Wilt on High
Shaw, H. Death of a Don
Silver, V. Death of a Harvard Freshman
Tapply, W. G. Death at Charity's Point
Townsend, G. M. To Prove a Villain
Waddell, E. L. Murder at Drake's Anchorage
Wender, T. Knight Must Fall

AFGHANISTAN (Afghan.)
De Villiers, G. Man from Kabul
Follett, K. Lie Down with Lions
Griffiths, J. C. Queen of Spades
Hamman, H. Lapis
Innes, H. Black Tide
Jason, S. Go Die in Afghanistan
McCurtin, P. Yellow Rain
Niesewand, P. Scimitar
Pendleton, D. Appointment in Kabul
Rosenberger, J. Afghanistan Crashout
Seymour, G. In Honour Bound
Trantor, N. Cable from Kabul

AFRICA (Afr. See also: Africa, East; Africa, North; Africa, West; individual countries)
Amesbury, J. E. Sporting Chance
Barber, F. D. Last White Man
Bee, D. Our Fatal Shadows
Buck, P. Passport to Peril
Calvin, H. Boka Lives!
Cory, D. High Requiem
Essex, P. Exile
Fuller, B. Far Place
Greene, H. Thieves of Timbutu
Hardinge, R. Beyond the Skyline
Harrison, W. Savannah Blue
Hild, J. Barrabas Run
Kearey, C. both titles
Keene, T. Earthrace
Kilgore, A. Bush Warfare
McAllister, B. Bullion Run 101
McCoy, A. Blood Ivory
McCurtin, P. Kalahari
Murphy, C. Dance for a Diamond
Ordway, P. Final Safari
Pendleton, D. Terrorist Summit
Powell, J. D. Mungwe Affair
Smith, David. Timbuktu
Smith, Wilbur. Leopard Hunts in Darkness
Thomas, R. Seesucker Whipsaw

AFRICA, EAST (Afr., E. See also: Africa; Africa, North; Africa, West; individual countries)
Bennett, J. Ocean Road
Canning, V. Burning Eye

AFRICA, NORTH (Afr., N. See also: Africa; Africa, East; Africa,
 West; individual countries)
Brierley, D. Skorpion's Death
O'Neill, F. Agents of Sympathy
St. Germain, G. Target: Sahara
Saul, J. Baraka
Sheckley, R. Live Gold
Swift, B. Mission Code: Symbol

AFRICA, WEST (Afr., W. See also: Africa; Africa, East; Africa, North; individual countries)
Bagley, D. Juggernaut
Harcourt, P. Twisted Tree
Henege, T. Skim

AIRCRAFT (air)
Kennedy, G. Murder on High
Pendleton, D. Vulture's Vengeance

ALABAMA (Ala. See also: South)
Chaze, E. three titles
Feegel, J. R. Not a Stranger
Greene, F. N. One Clear Call
Hagan, P. Winds of Terror
Jones, M. Season of the Strangler
Patterson, R. N. Outside Man
Saunders, E. Investigation

ALASKA
Butler, R. O. Sun Dogs
Hall, W. Even Jericho
Pendleton, D. White Hell

ALBANIA (Alb. See also: Balkans)
Napier, M. Forbidden Places
O'Brine, M. Crambo
Quayle, A. Eight Hours from England
Zarubica, M. Scutari

ALBUQUERQUE (Albuq. See also: New Mexico; Sante Fe; Southwest)
(no additional entries)

ALGERIA (See also: Algiers; Africa; Africa, North)
Driscoll, P. Heritage

ALGIERS (See also: Algeria; Africa; Africa, North)
Hertz, G. Foreign Harry Complot

AMSTERDAM (Amst. See also: Holland)
Guild, N. Favor
Hougan, C. Shooting in the Dark
Semprun, J. Second Death of Roman Mercader
Stein, A. M. Hangman's Row
Van de Wetering, J. three titles
Van Gulik, R. Given Day

ANDORRA
(no additional entries)

ANGOLA (See also: Africa)
(no additional entries)

ANTARCTIC (See also: Arctic)
Carter, Nick. Operation: McMurdo Sound
  White Death
Keneally, T. Survivor
Rosenberger, J. Antlantean Horror

ANTWERP (See also: Brussels; Belgium)
(no additional entries)

ARABIA. See: Saudi Arabia.

ARCTIC (See also: Antarctic)
McVean, J. Seabird Nine
Rosenberger, J. Zembya Expedition
Swift, B. Mission Code: Snow Queen
Wood, J. Fire Rock
Wright, G. Whitefire

ARGENTINA (Arg. See also: Buenos Aires; South America)
Boothby, G. Across the World for a Wife
Constantini, H. Gods, the Little Guys and the Police
Houston, R. Blood Tango
Langley, B. Conquistadores
Wilson, G. Argentine Deadline

ARIZONA (Ariz. See also: Phoenix; Tucson; Southwest)
Backer, J. M. Echoes from the Past
Conde, N. Legend
D'Amato, B. Eyes on Utopia Murders
Harper, R. Kill Factor
Heath, C. When You Comin' Back, Range Rider
Jessey, C. Treasures of Darkness
Johnston, V. Voice in the Night
Kelland, C. B. Archibald the Great
  This Is My Son
McCormick, G. Last Chance Country
Neban, H. Crucible of Courage
Pendleton, D. Orbiting Omega
Sherwood, R. E. Petrified Forest
Whitney, P. A. Vermilion
Woodrow, W. Black Pearl

ARKANSAS (Ark. See also: South)
Giles, J. Plum Thicket
Herring, R. Hub
Morris, G. Delaney
Quinn, J. Kill Squad

ATHENS (See also: Greece; Balkans; Crete; Macedonia)
De Lillo, D. Names

ATLANTA (See also: Georgia; South)
Feegel, J. R. Dance Card
Lee, E. Queen Bee
Stratham, F. P. From Love's Ashes

AUSTRALIA (See also: Melbourne; Sydney; Solomon Islands; Tasmania)
Adams, F. Strong As Death
Adamson, B. Nice Day for a Murder
Aldous, A. Danger on the Map
Aldridge, J. Sporting Proposition
  Untouchable Juli
Atkinson, H. three titles
Backhouse, E. Death Came Uninvited
Barrett, M. Stranger in Galah
Beck, L. Tom Gerrard
Boldrewood, R. Miner's Right
  Nevermore
Boothby, G. five titles
Bradden, R. Gabriel Comes to 24
  Out of the Storm
Brennan, P. Razorback
Bridges, R. Alden Case
  Cloud
Carlon, P. Crime of Silence
Carter, Nick. Outback Ghosts
Cleary, J. Long Shadow
Clive, J. Barossa
Cook, K. Wake in Fright
Corris, P. Marvelous Boy
  White Meat
Dawe, C. Emu's Head
De Fraga, G. Murder at the Cookout
Denham, R. Minor Murder
Doyle, R. M. both titles
Elliott, P. Mystery of the Black Dagger
Elliott, S. L. Careful, He Might Hear You
Farjeon, B. L. Golden Land
  Grif
Foster, D. Dog Rock
Gould, N. three titles
Hay, W. Mystery of Alfred Doubt
Hill, H. H. Spoil of the Desert
Hornung, E. W. four titles
Idriess, I. L. Nemarluk, King of the Wilds
James, B. Loser Pays
Jay, C. Knife Is Dangerous
Jefferis, B. Solo for Several Players
  Wild Grapes
Keneally, T. Chant of Jimmie Blacksmith
  Fear
Kimmins, A. Lugs O'Leary
Krauth, N. Matilda, My Darling
Lambert, E. three titles
Lang, J. Forger's Wife
Leopold, K. My Brow Is Wet
Lindall, E. Gathering of Eagles
Lord, G. Tooth and Claw
McCarter, J. Love's Lunatic
Martin, A. E. Common People
Meagher, A. E. Moving Finger
Michaelis, A. Intrepid Intervenes
Noonan, M. Magwitch
North, E. Chip on My Shoulder
O'Reilly, J. B. Moondyne
Peel, C. D. Snowtrap
Potter, J. Going West
Pratt, A. three titles
Rankin, J. L. Murder Pie
Salter, E. Voice of the Peacock
Savarin, J. Waterhole
Sayers, C. E. Jumping Double

Settings Index

174 / Austria

Scott, G. F. Rider of Waroona
Singer, B. You're Wrong, Delaney
Streib, D. Down Under and Dirty
Thompson, E. Lawyer and the Carpenter
Tucker, J. Ralph Rashleigh
Yarborough, C. Murder on the Long Straight

AUSTRIA (See also: Vienna)
Bottom, P. Lifeline
Canning, V. Whip Hand
Gainham, S. Place in the Country
Rosenberger, J. Devil's Trashcan
Ross, P. Kreuzeck Coordinates
Wolfe, E. Ice Castles

AZORES
(no additional entries)

BAGHDAD (See also: Middle East; Mesopotamia)
(no additional entries)

BAHAMAS (See also: Nassau; West Indies; Caribbean)
Connolly, R. Sun Place
Graves, R. L. Platinum Bullet
Heatter, B. Naked Island
Hess, K. Death Goes to the Bahamas
Wilson, G. No Rules, No Referee

BALI (See also: Indonesia; Borneo; Djakarta; Java; New Guinea; Sumatra)
Silliphant, S. Bronze Bell

BALKANS (See also: Albania; Bulgaria; Greece; Rumania; Macedonia; Turkey; Yugoslavia)
Peters, L. Out by the River
Swift, B. Mission Code: King's Pawn
Williams, Eric. Borders of Barbarism

BALTIMORE (Balt. See also: Maryland)
Berliner, R. Hiding Places
Cain, J. M. Enchanted Isle
Grady, J. Razor Game
Harris, C. A. Macking Gangster
Tracy, D. Criss-Cross

BANGKOK (See also: Thailand; Far East)
Kalish, R. Bloodrun
Noye, N. No City of Angels

BARBADOS (See also: West Indies; Caribbean)
Phillpotts, E. George and Georgina

BEIRUT (See also: Lebanon; Middle East)
Creed, D. Travellers in a Antique Land
Cutter, J. Beirut Retaliation
Pendleton, D. Beirut Playback

BELFAST (See also: Ireland; Dublin)
Holland, J. Prisoner's Wife
Power, M. S. Killing of Yesterday's Children

BELGIAN CONGO (Bel. Cong. See also: Africa)
Pendleton, D. Ambush on Blood River
Tyler, W. T. Rogue's March

BELGIUM (Belg. See also: Antwerp; Brussels)
Stein, A. M. Bombing Run
Sturrock, J. Suicide Most Foul

BELGRADE (See also: Yugoslavia; Balkans; Macedonia)
(no additional entries)

BELIZE (See also: South America)
Stivers, D. Shot to Hell
Westlake, D. E. High Adventure

BERLIN (East and West. See also: Germany; Frankfurt; Hamburg; Munich)
Balling, L. C. Mallory's Gambit

Buckley, W. F., Jr. Story of Henri Tod
Cleary, J. City of Fading Light
Emmett, R. Beat a Distant Drum
Gainham, S. Tiger, Life
Hughes, Z. Adlon Link
Kirkwood, T. Quiet Assassin
Knebel, F. Crossing in Berlin
Kotzwinkle, W. Seduction in Berlin
McQuoid, A. Puppet Master
Raygor, L. Catherine's Twins
Romanes, J. Berlin Breakout
Sherman, D. Prince of Berlin
Wilden, T. Exchange
Winters, J. C. Berlin Fugue

BERMUDA
Ames, J. Shadow Across the Sun
Leighton, F. As Strange a Maze

BOLIVIA (See also: South America)
Derrick, L. City of the Dead
Wolff, B. Hyde in Deep Cover

BOMBAY (See also: India; Calcutta; New Delhi)
Joshee, O. K. Mr. Surie
Keating, H. R. F. Sheriff of Bombay

BORNEO (See also: Indonesia; Malaysia; Bali; Djakarta; Java; New Guinea; Sumatra)
(no additional entries)

BOSTON (See also: Massachusetts; Cape Cod; New England)
Aldyne, N. Slate
Barnes, L. J. Dead Heat
Boyer, R. Billingsgate Shoal
Bryson, M. Hitch-Hike Murders
Coburn, A. Sweetheart
Dobyns, S. Dancer with One Leg
Gilmore, J. Blue Flame
Giroux, L., Jr. Rishi
Gutcheon, B. Still Missing
Hancock, H. I. Inspector Henderson
Hartman, D. Family Skeletons
Heatter, B. Golden Stag
Higgins, G. V. four titles
Kelly, S. Gemini Man
Kimbrough, K. Susannah, the Righteous
Kinsley, L. Red-Light Victim
MacLeod, C. Palace Guard
McNeil, J. Little Brother
Murray, Lt. M. M. Dog Detective and His Young Master
Palmer, M. both titles
Parker, R. B. Ceremony Valediction
Philbrick, W. R. Shadow Kills
Reeves, R. Doubting Thomas
Rosen, S. Death and Blintzes
Story, W. Cemeteries Are for Dying
Tapply, W. G. all three titles
Walker, W. Dime to Dance By
Young, A. Wicked Stepmother

BRAZIL (See also: Rio de Janeiro; South America)
Ghose, Z. Don Bueno
McDonald, G. Carioca Fletch
MacLean, A. River of Death
Ribeiro, J. U. Sergeant Getulio
Robeson, K. Ten Ton Snakes
Stivers, D. Amazon Slaughter

BRITISH GUIANA. See: Guyana.

BRITISH HONDURAS. See: Belize.

BRUSSELS (Brus. See also: Antwerp; Belgium)
May, P. Hidden Faces
Simenon, G. Lodger
Stonehouse, J. Ralph

BUCHAREST (Buch. See also: Rumania; Balkans)
(no additional entries)

BUDAPEST (Buda. See also: Hungary)
Sentjurc, I. Prayer for an Assassin

BUENOS AIRES (Buen. A. See also: Argentina; South America)
(no additional entries)

BULGARIA (Bulg. See also: Balkans; Macedonia)
Carter, Nick. Pursuit of the Eagle

BURMA (See also: Far East)
Becker, S. Blue-Eyed Shan
Kilgore, A. Opium Eater
Nimse, G. Take What You Want
Rosenberger, J. Burma Probe
Wager, W. Blue Leader

CAIRO (See also: Egypt; Africa, North)
Kneale, B. Appointment in Cairo
Mosley, L. O. Cat and the Mice
Stivers, D. Cairo Countdown
Tabori, G. Original Sin

CALCUTTA (See also: Bombay; New Delhi; India)
(no additional entries)

CALIFORNIA (Calif. See also: Los Angeles; San Diego; San Francisco; West)
Abercrombie, B. Run for Your Life
Alexander, M. Birthmark of Fear
Altman, T. Intruder
Andrews, V. C. If There Be Thorns
Anzelon, R. Goblin Tree
Barnes, L. J. Bitter Finish
Bercovici, E. So Little Cause for Caroline
Berne, K. Bare Acquaintances Shock Value
Bradbury, R. Death Is a Lonely Business
Breen, J. L. Listen for the Click
Browne, W. D. Dew of Slumber
Bryant, D. Killing Wonder
Buckley, J. Beyond Murder
Byrne, R. Dam
Cleveland, J. Minus One Corpse
Craig, M. S. Ten Thousand Several Doors To Play the Fox
Crighton, R. E. Million Dollar Lift
Cunningham, C. Silent Murder
Davidson, J. Sex Cult Murders
Davis, K. Words Can Kill
Derrick, L. Brotherhood of Blood Skyhigh Betrayers
Dixon, H. V. Too Rich to Die
Drew, J. H. Edge of the Tightrope
Drummond, J. K. Thy Sting, Oh Death
Dunlap, S. Bohemian Connection Equal Opportunity Death
Fine, P. H. Troubled Waters
Fletcher, D. Beyond Recall
Frost, J. Warlord
Frost, J. V. Portrait in Black
Garfield, B. Necessity
Gault, W. C. both titles
Goddard, K. Alchemist
Grafton, S. both titles
Greenleaf, S. State's Evidence
Gregory, J. Maid of the Mountain
Hale, Jennifer. Secret of Devil's Cave
Hammonds, M. OPEC Objective
Hansen, J. Steps Going Down
Harding, R. Bay City Burnout
Harriss, W. Bay Psalm Book Murder
Hartman, D. Massacre at Russian River
Henderson, M. R. If I Should Die
Hicks, H. B. Castle at Jade Cove
Howard, J. A. Death Audit
Hughston, D. You Stand Accused
Johnson, C. Clinic
Johnson, G. Moon Country
Kaminsky, S. M. Catch a Falling Clown
Koontz, D. R. Phantoms
Krentz, J. A. Legacy
Levine, R. M. Bad Blood
Levinson, R. Playhouse
Lewis, E. Death and the Single Girl Here Today, Dead Tomorrow
Lynch, J. four titles
Lyons, A. At the Hands of Another
McNamara, J. D. First Directive
Maxwell, A. E. Just Another Day in Paradise
Miles, J. Silver Bullet Gang
Millar, M. Banshee Cannibal Heart
Muller, M. Legend of the Slain Soldiers Tree of Death
Murray, W. Hard Knocker's Luck Tip on a Dead Crab
Nash, J. R. Dark Fountain
Nichols, L. Twilight
Nunn, K. Tapping the Source
Owen, D. Juice Town
Page, C. G. Mist over Morro Bay
Pendleton, D. Skysweeper
Petievich, G. Quality of the Informant
Phillips, M. Death Spiral
Posard, C. Stranglehold
Pronzini, B. Nightshades

Quinn, J. Silicon Valley Slaughter
Rigsby, H. Lucinda
Roberts, W. D. Annalise Experiment
     Long Time to Hate
Robertson, C. Red Chameleon
Rosenberger, J. Silicon Valley
     Connection
Ross, J. A. Risky Pleasure
Ross, Morgan. Any Number Can Die!
Roszak, T. Dreamwatcher
Scannell, D. Hood
Simon, R. L. California Roll
Singer, S. Free Draw
Spencer, J. both titles
Stivers, D. Hostaged Island
     Justice by Fire
Streib, D. California Shakedown
Wallace, D. R. Turquoise Dragon
Wambaugh, J. Secrets of Harry Bright
Ward, E. C. Coast Highway 1
Whitney, P. A. Emerald
Wilderness, D. O. Sinsation of a
     Sintury
Wood, W. P. Rampage

     CAMBODIA (Camb. See also: Far
          East)
Hild, J. Rivers of Flesh
Pendleton, D. Cambodian Clash
Wright, W. Cater's Castle

     CANADA (Can. See also: Montreal;
          Ottawa; Toronto; Winnipeg;
          Vancouver)
Aeby, J. Pipes of Margaree
Bennett, R. D. Sector 12
Burke, J. If It Weren't for Sex...I'd
     Have to Get a Job
Chadwick, V. C. Invisible Line
Childers, J. A. Enemy Outpost
Connor, R. Patrol of the Sun Dance
     Trail
Craig, A. all titles
Derrick, L. Deep Cover Blast-Off
Dutton, J. S., Jr. Underground
Engel, H. all 4 titles
Estey, D. Bonner Deception
Footner, H. Fur Bringers
     Jack Chanty
Fry, P. Harsh Evidence
Heald, T. Murder at Moose Jaw
Helwig, D. Sound Like Laughter
Hyde, C. Icarus Seal
Innes, H. High Stand
Janes, J. R. Watcher
Kilgore, A. Canadian Killing Ground
Lamb, J. J. Losers Take All
Lovelady, G. K. Beyond the Rim
McDonald, A. Black Deeds in Whitehorse
Maling, A. From Thunder Bay
Mowery, W. B. Vengeance Trail
Olson, O. N. Mountie on Trial
Paul, J. Oil by Murder
Peterson, G. Klondike Kalamity
Pollock, J. C. Centrifuge
Roberts, M. Prey of the Strongest
Robeson, K. Time Terror
Ross, D. Out of the Night
Shields, D. Just Before Dawn
Smith, R. A. Kramer Project
Streib, D. Terror for Sale
Toombs, J. J. Restless Obsession
Wood, T. Dead in the Water
     Murder on Ice
Wright, L. R. Suspect
York, T. Trapper

     CANARY ISLANDS (Can. Is. See
          also: Spain; Madrid;
          Majorca)
MacLeod, R. Legacy from Tenerife

     CAPE COD (See also: Boston;
          Massachusetts; New England)
Aldyne, N. Cobalt
Boyer, R. Billingsgate Shoal
Damore, L. Cache
Diamond, F. Love Me to Death
Foy, G. Asia Rip
Mead, R. Nightingale Trivet
Scott, J. D. Sea File

     CAPE TOWN (See also: South Africa;
          Johannesburg; Transvaal)
(no additional entries)

     CARACAS (See also: Venezuela;
          South America)
(no additional entries)

     CARIBBEAN (Carib. See also: West
          Indies; individual West Indies
          countries)

Atwood, M. Bodily Harm
Ballem, J. Marigot Run
Buchanan, J. Prince of Malta
Cade, S. Slade's Marauders
Cairns, C. Great Gorme
Carter, Nick. Caribbean Coup
Chesbro, G. Turn Loose the Dragon
Cutter, J. Big One
Daniels, V. Mendoza's Treasure
Davey, J. Murder in Paradise
Dodson, D. B. Man Who Ran Away
Ferguson, N. Black Coral
Heatter, B. Devlin's Triangle
Hutton, A. Edge of the Deep
Levin, J. Snow
McCray, M. Black Palm
Mountford, A. M. Beneath the Night Sky
Stanton, K. Evil Cargo
     Sargasso Secret
Williams, A. Widow's War
Willis, T. Most Beautiful Girl in the
     World

     CASABLANCA (Casa. See also:
          Morocco; Africa, North;
          Tangier)
(no additional entries)

     CENTRAL AMERICA (Cent. Am. See
          also: individual countries)
Ahern, J. Cocaine Run
Breckling, G. J. River of Fire
Carter, Nick. Mayan Connection
Charles, C. A. Liar's Dice
Crosby, J. Take No Prisoners
Fennell, J. Killer Patrol
Holmes, D. C. Velvet Ape
McCray, M. Death Machine Contract
Pendleton, D. New War
Quinn, J. Mercenary Kill
Robeson, K. Headless Man
     They Died Twice
Stone, R. Flag for Sunrise
Sydell, E. Diplomatic Immunity
Thomas, R. Missionary Stew
Thurston, R. For the Silverfish
Tippette, G. China Blue
Van Vors, B. L. End of the River

     CEYLON (Cey.)
Hild, J. Butchers of Eden
Leslie, J. Perahera
Stivers, D. Tech War

     CHANNEL ISLANDS (Chan. Is. See
          also: England)
Royce, K. Channel Assault
Tickell, J. Appointment with Venus

     CHARLESTON (See also: West Vir-
          ginia; South Carolina; South)
Fleming, T. F. Dreams of Glory

     CHICAGO (Chi. See also: Illinois;
          Midwest)
Benson, C. Corpses Don't Kill
Burnett, W. R. Goodbye, Chicago
Carroll, J. Baby Killer
Collins, M. A. three titles
Craig, M. S. Gillian's Chain
     Third Blonde
Derrick, L. Inca Gold Hijack
Eckert, A. W. Scarlet Mansion
Fox, T. C. Cops
Gash, Joe. both titles
Gettel, R. Twice Burned
Greeley, A. Happy Are the Meek
Griffith, B. Time for Frankie Coolin
Heed, R. Ghosts Never Die
Janson, H. Chicago Chick
     Nice Way to Die
Jenkins, J. twelve titles
Kaminsky, S. M. When the Dark Man Calls
Kantor, H. Big Stopper
King, Ramona. Steal Away
Kisner, J. Slice of Life
Klawans, H. L. Sins of Commission
McConnell, F. D. Murder Among Friends
McGivern, W. P. Matter of Honor
McManus, J. Out of the Blue
Nash, J. R. Crime Story
Paretsky, S. all three titles
Paulsen, G. Clutterkill
Quill, M. all four titles
Ramm, C. Chicago Assault
Simmons, J. Lamplighter
Slim, I. Trick Baby
Smith, C. M. Reverend Randollph and the
     Unholy Bible
Spencer, R. H. Missing Bishop
Storm, M. Dame in My Bed
Von Hoffman, N. Organized Crimes
White, D. Southern Daughter
Wills, T. Mine to Avenge

Winski, N. Chicago Deathwinds

     CHILE (See also: South America)
Breslin, P. Interventions
De Villiers, G. Death in Santiago

     CHINA (See also: Peking; Shanghai;
          Formosa; Hong Kong; Mongolia;
          Far East)
Aldridge, J. Statesman's Game
Becker, S. Chinese Bandit
Bonavia, D. China Lovers
Dawe, C. Plotters of Peking
Gilman, D. Mrs. Pollifax on the China
     Station
Hutton, M. Chinese Girl
Kilgore, A. China Bloodhunt
M--, Mr. Chest of Opium
Milton, N. D. China Option
Montalbano, W. D. Death in China
O'Grady, L. Lady Jane
Pendleton, D. Fastburn
Sherman, D. White Mandarin
Siris, P. Peking Mandate
Tarrant, J. China Gold
Thompson, S. L. Countdown to China

     CHURCH
Harpur, P. Serpent's Circle
Holland, I. Death at St. Anselm's
L'Engle, M. Severed Wasp
Prantera, A. Strange Loop

     CINCINNATI (Cin. See also: Ohio;
          Cleveland; Columbus; Midwest)
Pyle, A. M. Trouble Making Toys
Valin, J. all three titles

     CLEVELAND (Cleve. See also: Ohio;
          Cincinnati; Columbus; Midwest)
Bolton, R. L. Sleep with the Angels

     COLOMBIA (Colom. See also: South
          America)
Graves, R. L. Platinum Bullet
Manrique, J. Colombian Gold
Stivers, D. Fire and Maneuver

     COLORADO (Colo. See also: Denver;
          West)
Burns, R. Avenging Angel
Chance, L. Cutting Edge
Forest, R. One Step Ahead
Howard, J. A. I Like It Tough
Moore, B. Doberman Wore Black
Overholser, S. Molly and the Gold Baron
Pendleton, D. Mountain Rampage
Roderus, F. Rain Rustlers
     Video Vandal
Rowley, W. H. Concerto for Murder
Scherf, M. Always Murder a Friend
Vail, C. Porcelain Dolls Don't Bleed
Willoughby, L. D. Frontier Detective

     COLUMBUS (See also: Ohio; Cincin-
          nati; Cleveland; Midwest)
(no additional entries)

     CONGO. See: Belgian Congo.

     CONNECTICUT (Conn. See also: New
          England)
Avery, R. Fast Man with a Dollar
Bachman, R. Thinner
Brandel, M. Murder in the Family
Carpenter, C. Peabody Experiment
Curtiss, U. Death of a Crow
Forrest, R. both titles
Glendinning, R. Ultimate Game
Goulart, R. Graveyard of My Own
Grant, C. Hour of the Oxrun Dead
Greene, J. E. Bridge at Branfield
Harrington, W. Skin Deep
Homesley, L. Blondy's Boy Friend
Iams, J. Corpse of the Old School
Johnston, V. Crystal Cat
Kahn, S. Mall
Kirkpatrick, J. Woman at Dead Oaks
Lamb, M. Chains of Gold
Mardon, D. With Penalty and Interest
Mix, T. Question of Judgement
Pentecost, H. three titles
Philips, J. both titles
Rathbone, R. A. Death in the Drawing
     Room
Skedgell, M. Farm Boy
Tibbles, G. Latest Mrs. Adams
Waugh, H. Odds Run Out
Woods, S. Game Bet

C

COPENHAGEN (Copen. See also: Denmark; Greenland; Scandinavia)
Peters, E. Copenhagen Connection

CORSICA (Cors. See also: France; Marseilles; Nice; Paris; Mediterranean Island)
Buck, P. School for Slaughter
Swift, B. Mission Code: Granite Island

COSTA RICA (See also: Central America)
Goldman, J. A. Waldorf

CRETE (See also: Greece; Athens; Mediterranean Island)
Hammond, M. Theseus Code
Swift, B. Mission Code: Minotaur

CUBA (See also: Havana; West Indies; Caribbean)
Boothby, G. Across the World for a Wife
Buckley, W. F., Jr. See You Later, Alligator
Catto, M. Banana Men
Hild, J. Eye of the Fire
Hunt, H. Whisper Her Name
Lewis, N. Cuban Passage
Terman, D. Shell Game

CYPRUS (See also: Mediterranean Island)
Bird, M. J. Aphrodite Inheritance

CZECHOSLOVAKIA (Czech. See also: Prague)
Blackstock, C. Encounter
Carter, Nick. Dubrovnik Massacre
Littell, R. Amateur
Pollock, J. C. Crossfire
Robeson, K. Shape of Terror
Ross, Regina. Face of Danger
Smith, Jonathan. Come Back

DALLAS (See also: Texas; Houston; San Antonio; Southwest)
Abshire, R. K. Gants

DAMASCUS (See also: Syria; Middle East)
(no additional entries)

DELAWARE (Dela. See also: South)
(no additional entries)

DENMARK (Den. See also: Copenhagen; Greenland; Scandinavia)
(no additional entries)

DENVER (See also: Colorado; West)
Battin, B. W. Boogey Man
Burns, R. Strip Search
McCaffrey, A. Stitch in Snow
Spivey, A. J. Michael

DETROIT (Det. See also: Michigan; Midwest)
Caval, P. Girls in Bondage
Clark, A. C. Crime Partners Death List
Estleman, L. D. all six titles
Garnet, A. H. Santa Claus Killer
Kienzle, W. X. all five titles
Ramm, C. Detroit Combat

DISTRICT OF COLUMBIA. See: Washington D.C.

DJAKARTA (See also: Indonesia; Bali; Borneo; Java; New Guinea; Sumatra)
Roberts, M. K. Jakarta Coup

DOMINICAN REPUBLIC (Dom. Rep. See also: West Indies; Caribbean)
(no additional entries)

DUBLIN (Dub. See also: Ireland; Belfast)
Cleary, C. P. Death in the Life Department
Connolly, C. Voice
Lawton, C. Double Fix
Lovell, M. Spy Who Got His Feet Wet

McGinley, P. Goosefoot
Queneau, R. We Always Treat Women Too Well

DUTCH WEST INDIES. See: Indonesia.

DUTCH GUIANA. See: Surinam.

ECUADOR (Ecua. See also: South America)
Keitges, J. Dawn and Vengeance

EDINBURGH (Edin. See also: Scotland; Glasgow; Hebrides)
(no additional entries)

EGYPT (See also: Cairo; Africa, North)
Aldridge, J. I Wish He Would Not Die
Barber, N. Women of Cairo
Ellison, E. Tomb of Horror
Garth, D. Eastward in Eden
Harrington, R. E. Aswan High
Jordan, D. Nile Green
Kabal, A. M. Adversary
Mastero Storyteller. Welcome to the Torture Chamber
Peters, E. Curse of the Pharaohs Mummy Case
Robeson, K. Pharaoh's Ghost
Salisbury, C. Autumn in Araby
White, P. Cairo
Whittemore, E. Nile Shadows
Wilson, G. Aswan Hellbox

EL SALVADOR (See also: Central America)
Roberts, M. K. Commando Squad
Rosenberger, J. Slaughter in El Salvador

ENGLAND (Eng. Here is a selection of books with English settings by non-British authors. See also: next entry; Channel Islands; Isle of Man)
Allison, E. M. A. Through the Valley of Death
Batson, G. Gift of Murder
Bennett, J. M. Local Matter
Blair, A. Through the Eyes of Evil
Bloch, R. Night of the Ripper
Brookes, O. Gatherer
Byrd, M. Fly Away, Jill
Coffman, V. Master of Blue Mire
Cutter, L. all titles
Dean, S. F. X. Ceremony of Innocence It Can't Be My Grave
DeAndrea, W. L. Snark
Doherty, P. C. Death of a King
Domatilla, J. Last Crime
Elkins, A. J. Murder in the Queen's Armes
Elmblad, M. Outrageous Fortune
Giroux, E. X. all three titles
Grimes, M. all seven titles
Hanshew, T. W. World's Finger
Haughey, T. B. Case of the Hijacked Moon
Hawkes, E. Shadow of the Moth
Heller, K. both titles
Hodgson, A. Golden Ballast
Hughes, Z. Fortress London
Jeffers, H. Murder Most Irregular
Kelly, N. In the Shadow of King's
Kenney, S. Garden of Malice
Kilgore, A. Buckingham Blowout
Knott, F. Write Me a Murder
Kurland, M. Death by Gaslight
Linzee, D. Belgravia
McErlean, S. Mask of Silence
McMullen, M. Grave Without Flowers
Matthias, L. A. Pandora Plague
Merrell, B. Sign of Death
Michaels, B. Black Rainbow
Olden, M. Golden Kill
Orde, L. Eagles Heritage
Quinn, A. Satyr Ring
Roby, M. L. both titles
St. James, B. Witch
Stashower, D. Adventures of the Ectoplasmic Man
Stivers, D. Royal Flush
Taylor, B. Kindness of Strangers
Tine, R. Uneasy Lies the Head
Tourney, L. both titles
Troy, J. Haunted Honeymoon
Vaughan, R. Royal Game
Vernon, K. R. Phantom of Fonthill Park
Williamson, M. Death in the Picture
Wilson, G. Viper Factor
Wright, E. Death in the Old Country

ENGLAND (Eng. Here is a representative listing of British authors who principally use English settings. See also: previous entry; Channel Islands; Isle of Man)
Allbeury, T.
Cody, L.
Cohen, A.
Greenwood, J.
Harrison, R.
Haymon, S. T.
Hervey, E.
Jon, M.
Malcolm, J.
Penn, J.
Radley, S.
Rhea, N.
Simpson, D.
Taylor, A.

ETHIOPIA (Ethio. See also: Africa, North)
Allbeury, T. Girl from Addis
McCurtin, P. Somali Smashout

FAR EAST (See also: individual countries)
Arnold, W. China Gate
Balaban, J. B. Coming Down Again
Black, G. Moon for Killers
Boulle, P. Ears of the Jungle
Downes, H. Opium Strategem
Goodchild, G. Black Orchid
Hall, Adam. Pekin Target
Hamilton, A. Wyss Pursuit
Hardy, R. Face of Jalanath
Heffernan, W. Corsican
Lustbader, E. V. Black Heart
Mather, B. Midnight Gun
Moffitt, I. Retreat of Radiance
Newton, J. E. Java Edge
Nunn, F. Blue Haze
Roberts, M. K. Pathet Vengeance
Sandberg, B. Chinese Spur
Wingate, J. Seawayman

FINLAND (Fin. See also: Helsinki; Scandinavia)
Gardner, J. Icebreaker

FLORENCE (See also: Italy; Milan; Naples; Rome; Sardinia; Sicily; Venice)
Coker, C. Other David
Michaels, B. Grey Beginning
Nabb, M. all four titles

FLORIDA (Fla. See also: Jacksonville; Miami; Tampa; South)
Beatty, E. River in the Sun
Becker, S. Juice
Beechcroft, W. Position of Ulimate Trust
Brewer, G. Hungry One Red Scarf
Cline, C. T., Jr. Missing Persons
Conty, J.-P. Big Secret, Suzuki
Conway, N. Omega Operation
Feegel, J. R. Autopsy
Flanders, R. Silver Threads
Friedman, M. Hurricane Season
Granger, B. Schism
Greth, L. Nightmare!
Hagan, P. Dark Journey Home
Halleran, T. both titles
Hayes, J. No Escape
Heatter, B. Scarred Man
Hilton, J. B. Sunset Law
Hunter, J. D. Florida Is Closed Today
Kallen, L. Piano Bird
Kennedy, B. Uninvited Guest
Koperwas, S. Easy Money
Leonard, E. Split Images Stick
Lippincott, D. Home
McBain, E. four titles
MacDonald, J. D. Free Fall in Crimson Lonely Silver Rain
Merkin, R. South Florida Book of the Dead
Neely, E. J. Chateau Laurens
Norman, G. Midnight Water
Pendleton, D. Hammerhead Reef Paramilitary Plot
Ramm, C. Florida Firefight
Ware, J. Faxon Secret
Werry, R. R. Casket for a Lying Lady
White, L. Coffin for a Hood
Whitney, P. A. Dream of Orchids
Whittington, H. Web of Murder
Wilder, R. Walk with Evil
Winston, D. Mayeroni Myth

Zachary, H. One Day in Hell

FORMOSA (See also: Far East; China)
Wood, C. Taiwan

FRANCE (Fr. Monaco is included here. See also: Marseilles; Nice; Paris; Corsica)
Aiken, Joan. Foul Matter
Albert, M. H. Operation Lila
Ames, D. Corpse Diplomatique
Anthony, E. Voices on the Wind
Arnold, M. Death on the Dragon's Tongue
Beardmore, G. Thousand Witnesses
Bond, M. three titles
Brason, J. Fourth Arm
Brooker, C. Dark Mosaic
Burge, R. J. There Is a Destiny
Butterworth, J. M. Man Who Broke the Bank at Monte Carlo
Canning, V. Boy on Platform One
Castle, A. Wolf-Lure
Cort, N. French Entrapment
Crane, C. Coast of Fear
Cutter, J. Talent for Revenge
Daley, R. Dangerous Edge
Daniels, D. Monte Carlo
Dawe, C. Black Spider
De Gramont, S. Lives to Give
Delacorta. Lola
E-7. Romance of a Spy
Fairlie, G. They Found Each Other
Forrest, A. Captain Justice
Freeling, N. all five new titles
Glazier, S. Lost Provinces
Graeme, B. La Belle Laurine
Granger, B. Shattered Eye
Greene, G. Tenth Man
Heatter, B. Mutilator
Hebden, M. six titles
Hebert, A. In the Shadow of the Wind
Hertz, G. Foreign Harry Complot
Hiscott, L. Bishop's Move
Hughes, D. Pork Butcher
Humes, H. L. Underground City
Kartun, D. Courier
King, Robert. Red Spy at Night
Koontz, D. R. Hanging On
Leslie, P. Bastard Brigard
Lestienne, V. Furioso
Linscott, G. Healthy Body
Loraine, P. Death Wishes
McConnor, V. Riviera Puzzle
Marlowe, A. Red Rocking Bird
Marsland, A. Classic Death
Moray, H. That Woman
Morrell, D. Blood Oath
Mykel, A. W. Salamandra Glass
Nicolaysen, B. Perilous Passage
Peart, R. Angels of Death
Pendleton, D. Paradine's Gauntlet
    Running Hot
Perry, R. Fool's Mate
Resnick, M. Eros at Zenith
Robeson, K. Black, Black Witch
Sanders, Lawrence. Passion of Molly T
Sharkey, J. Honestly, Now!
Sheppard, S. Monte Carlo
Sloan, C. Wings of Death
Steward, S. M. Murder Is Murder Is Murder
Stewart, Michael. Belle
Stringer, D. Yesterday Man
Thompson, G. Nobody Cared for Kate
Tickell, J. Villa Mimosa
Trevanian. Summer of Katya
Watson, Clarissa. Runaway
Webb, A. both titles
Weismiller, E. Serpent Sleeping
White, A. three titles
Wise, A. Naughty Girls

FRANKFURT (Frank. See also: Germany; Berlin; Hamburg; Munich)
(no additional entries)

FRENCH ANTILLES (Fr. Ant. See also: West Indies; Caribbean)
(no additional entries)

FUTURE (Here listed are books explicitly set at a time later than that of writing. See also: Past)
Abrahams, P. Tongues of Fire
Allbeury, T. All Our Tomorrows
Amis, K. Russian Hide-and-Seek
Asimov, I. Robots and Empire
    Robots of Dawn
Austin, R. all five titles
Bachman, R. Running Man
Basile, G. V. three titles
Bass, R. Lime's Crisis
Bayley, B. J. Knights of the Limits
Bishop, G. Shuttle People
Boyd, J. Last Starship from Earth
Burdick, E. Fail-Safe
Caro, D. R. Man in the Dark Suit
Cassilis, R. Madness of the People
Clark, E. Send in the Lions
Clark, W. Special Relationship
Cohen, B. Taking of Satcon Station
Cole, W. V. Park Avenue
Cooper, E. Prisoner of Fire
Cordell, A. If You Believe the Soldiers
Cudlip, D. R. Comprader
Cussler, C. Deep Six
    Night Probe!
Dalmas, J. Varkaus Conspiracy
Delahaye, M. Third Day
Domatilla, J. Last Crime
Edmondson, G. C. Takeover
Elgin, S. H. Star-Anchored, Star Angered
Evans, J. Midas Men
Filbrun, J. S. Gemini Rising
Forsyth, F. Devil's Alternative
    Fourth Protocol
Franklin, J. Rat Race
Freed, D. China Card
Gibson, William. Neuromancer
Goddard, K. Balefire
Goulart, R. three titles
Gunn, J. Star Bridge
Haining, P. Hero
Hamilton, B. Brighton Murder Trial
Harding, R. all four titles
Harrington, R. E. Aswan High
Harris, L. Masada Plan
Harrison, H. Stainless Steel Rat for President
    Stainless Steel Rat Is Born
Holly, J. H. Mind Traders
Hoyle, T. Vail
Hudner, K. Heirs of the Kingdom
Hyman, T. Giant Killer
James, D. Fall of the Russian Empire
Janson, H. Unseen Assassin
Jenkins, J. Fireprint
Johnson, W. O. Hammered Gold
Jones, D. Rubicon One
Kelly, T. J. Lost in Space and the Mortgage Due
Kilian, M. Northern Exposure
Lamm, R. 1988
Laumer, K. Once There Was a Giant
Lee, S. Dunn's Conundrum
Lowe, S. Aurora
McKinney, R. L. Kamchatka Incident
McQuay, M. four titles
Major, H. M. Alien Trace
Milton, N. D. China Option
Mitchell, A. Bodyguard
Morris, J. both titles
Mullin, C. Very British Coup
Niven, L. Dream Park
Nolan, W. F. Look Out for Space
Pohl, F. Cool War
    Gladiator-at-Law
Quest, R. both titles
Raphael, R. President Must Die
Reaves, J. M. both titles
Reynolds, M. Lagrangists
Robinett, S. Man Responsible
Robinson, F. M. Great Divide
Royce, K. 10,000 Days
Ruff, I. Dark Red Star
Schlosstein, S. Kensei
Scott, H. No Exit
Shea, M. Tomorrow's Men
Simmons, G. Murdock
Smith, G. H. Second War of Worlds
Spencer, J. both titles
Spicer, M. Final Act
Spruill, S. G. Imperator Plot
Stryker, H. NYPD 2025
Tine, R. Uneasy Lies the Head
Tucker, W. Wild Talent
Vance, J. Many Worlds of Magnus Ridolph
    To Live Forever
Webb, S. Adventures of Terra Tarkington
Weisman, J. Watchdogs
Whitmore, E. D.E.A.D.
Wood, Bari. Lightsource
Wright, S. F. Prelude in Prague
Zahn, T. Coming of Age

GENEVA (See also: Switzerland; Zurich)
Eskapa, S. Secret-Keeper
Golan, M. Geneva Crisis
Whitman, J. T. Geneva Accord

GEORGIA (Ga. See also: Atlanta; South)
Cline, C. T., Jr. Prey
Derrick, L. Dixie Death Squad
Diehl, W. Hooligans
Feegel, J. R. Malpractice
Jessup, R. Cunning and the Haunted
Kay, T. After Eli
    Dark Thirty
Kimbrough, K. Barbara, the Valiant
    Millijoy, the Determined
McCrumb, S. Sick of Shadows
Mettler, G. Down Home
Pendleton, D. Savannah Swingsaw
Stivers, D. Deathbites
Woods, Stuart. Chiefs

GERMANY (Ger. Both East and West Germany are included here. See also: Frankfurt; Hamburg; Munich; Berlin)
Allbeury, T. Only Good German
    Special Collection
Berckman, E. Finger to Her Lips
Brodeur, P. Sick Fox
Butterworth, W. E. Court-Martial
Carney, D. Square Circle
Cook, T. H. Orchids
Cort, N. Alpine Gambit
Dial, J. Echoes of War
Dunne, C. Retrieval
Elkins, A. J. Fellowship of Fear
Esser, R. Paper Chase
Evans, W. P. Double Cross Squadron
Forbes, C. Leader and the Damned
Hallahan, W. H. Trade
Hardy, J. L. Recoil
Harrington, W. English Lady
Hart-Davis, D. Level Five
Helitzer, F. Hans, Who Goes There?
Herlin, H. Friends
    Solo Run
Hunter, J. D. Tin Cravat
Jute, A. Zaharoff Commission
Kemeny, J. A. Strands of War
Knopp, J. M. Eternal Reich
Kozhevnikov, V. Shield and Sword
Lucas, R. Who Dares to Live
Melchior, I. Eva
    V-3
Neuman, F. Maneuvers
Newman, B. Traveling Executioner
Nicholson, G. Passion for Treason
Nolan, F. Wolf Trap
Palmer, L. Night Music
Paris, A. Teeth of the Wolf
Parish, J. Hour of the Unicorn
Pendleton, D. Bloodsport
Peters, R. Bravo Romeo
Puccetti, R. Death of the Fuhrer
Revere, J. D. Assassin
Rosenberger, J. Methuselah Factor
St. George, G. Proteus Pact
Scott, C. Hilter's Bomb
Sussman, B. J. Crooked Cross
Trevor, E. Damocles Sword
Watson, P. Nazi's Wife
Wilson, G. Ultimate Terror
Winward, W. Ball Bearing Run
    Canaris Fragments

GIBRALTAR (Gib.)
(no additional entries)

GLASGOW (See also: Scotland; Edinburgh; Hebrides)
Knox, B. Hanging Tree
McIlvanney, W. Papers of Tony Veitch
Tremaine, J. Maggie
Turnbull, P. all four titles
West, P. E. Madeleine

GREECE (See also: Athens; Balkans; Crete; Macedonia)
Emmett, R. Trojan Horses
Gage, N. Eleni
Harvey, J. Coup D'Etat
Kirton, J. Greek Fire
O'Donnell, P. Dead Man's Handle
Scott, Douglas. Operation Artemis
Swift, B. Mission Code: Acropolis
White, J. M. Moscow Papers
Wilson, D. Harvest Hell

GREENLAND (Green. See also: Denmark; Copenhagen; Scandinavia)
(no additional entries)

GUATEMALA (Guat. See also: Central America)
Murphy, W. B. Time Trial
O'Donnell, P. Last Day in Limbo
Stivers, D. three titles

GUIANA (See also: Guyana; Surinam; South America)
(no additional entries)

GUYANA (See also: Guiana; Surinam; South America)

Adams, M. Mudland
Davies, W. X. Operation Choke Point
Hesla, S. Hawthorn Conspiracy
Wallbridge, C. S. Through a Glass Darkly

    HAITI (See also: West Indies; Caribbean)
Buck, P. Deadly Birdman
Hayes, R. Illegal Entry

    HAMBURG (Hamb. See also: Germany; Berlin; Frankfurt; Munich)
(no additional entries)

    HANOI (See also: Viet Nam; Saigon; Far East)
(no additional entries)

    HAVANA (See also: Cuba; West Indies; Caribbean)
Colton, M. Big Woman
Goldman, L. Black Fire
Green, E. P. Perfect Fools
Harragan, S. Cuban Heel

    HAWAII (Haw. Principally Honolulu settings)
Barroll, C. Shadow Man
Coffman, V. Orchid Tree
Glendinning, R. Death Match
Katkov, N. Blood and Orchids
McCurtin, P. Bloodbath
Rogers, M. I. H. Horror in Hawaii
Streib, D. Hawaiian Takeover
Stuart, H. L. Ginger Flower
Wallace, V. Eyes Upon a Wet Grave
Webb, J. F. Bride of Cairngorn
Wilson, G. Dragon's Kill

    HEBRIDES (See also: Scotland; Edinburgh; Glasgow)
Grayson, R. Death Stalk

    HELSINKI (See also: Finland; Scandinavia)
Granger, B. British Cross

    HISTORICAL SETTINGS. See: Past.

    HOLLAND (Holl. See also: Amsterdam)
Brierley, D. Blood Group O
Koning, H. De Witt's War
Lawman, A. Hounds of Spring
MacLean, A. Floodgate
Norton, A. At Sword's Point
White, A. Long Night's Walk

    HONDURAS (See also: Central America)
Stivers, D. Kill School

    HONG KONG (H. Kong. See also: China; Shanghai; Peking; Formosa; Far East)
Bennett, J. Dragon
Bobker, L. R. Flight of a Dragon
Clavell, J. Noble House
Cohan, T. Opium
Coquhoun, K. Filthy Rich
Driscoll, P. Pangolin
Gilman, D. Mrs. Pollifax and the Hong Kong Buddha
Hartland, M. Down Among the Dead Men
Hutton, A. Ivory Slave
Key, S. A. Cain's Chinese Puzzle
Lustbader, E. V. Jian
Marshall, W. five titles
Mather, B. Hour of the Dog
Norman, E. Hang Me in Hong Kong
Pereira, M. Pigeon's Blood

    HONOLULU. See: Hawaii.

    HOSPITAL (Hosp.)
Bachmann, L. Bitter Lake
Berliner, R. Hiding Places
Carroll, J. Baby Killer
Carson, M. Experiment
Collee, J. Kingsley's Touch
Craig, R. Trauma
Hastings, C. Bonaventure
Klawans, H. L. Sins of Commission
Mix, T. Question of Judgement
Munder, L. Therapy for Murder
Palmer, M. Sisterhood
Ravin, N. Seven North
Simmons, G. Murdock

Way, J. H. Dream Watch
Wilkinson, S. D. Death on Call
Wilson, R. C. Icefire

    HOUSTON (See also: Texas; Dallas; San Antonio; Southwest)
Furman, L. Shadow Line
Hilborn, A. Personal Justice
Lansdale, J. R. Act of Love
Lindsey, D. L. Cold Mind
    Heat from Another Sun
Mosiman, B. S. Wireman
Ramm, C. Houston Attack

    HUNGARY (Hung. See also: Budapest)
Graeme, B. Trail of the White Knight
Klein, E. Parachutists

    ICELAND (Ice.)
Decker, J. Death Gambit
Kilian, M. Valkyrie Project

    IDAHO (Ida. See also: West)
Ahern, J. D.E.A.T.H. Hunters
Burroughs, R. Fugitive Feet
Dobbins, P. H. Murder Moon
Pendleton, D. Brothers in Blood
Wren, M. K. Seasons of Death

    ILLINOIS (Ill. See also: Chicago; Midwest)
Burkey, D. Rain Lover
Jenkins, R. four titles
McInerny, R. four titles
Maxwell, So Long, See You Tomorrow
Spencer, R. H. Echoes of Zero
Walker, R. N. Brain Watch

    INDIA (See also: Bombay; Calcutta; New Delhi; Indian Ocean)
Aylward, M. Harper's Luck
Carnac, N. Indigo
Casberg, M. A. Dowry of Death
    Five Rivers to Death
Cleary, J. Faraway Drums
Friedman, M. Fault Tree
Ganpat. Speakers in Silence
Hart-Davis, D. Man-Eaters of Jassapur
Hirt, H. Heat of Winter
Ironside, E. Very Private Enterprise
Jenkinson, E. J. Gates of Doom
King, F. Act of Darkness
Sahgal, N. Plans for Departure
Sidhwa, B. N. Crow Eaters
Thorne, E. P. Black Sadhu
Wilson, G. Night of the Thuggee

    INDIAN OCEAN (Ind. O. See also: India; Bombay; Calcutta; Ceylon; New Delhi)
O'Brine, M. Dodos Don't Duck
Stanton, K. Whirlwind Beneath the Sea

    INDIANA (Ind. See also: Indianapolis; Midwest)
Appleman, P. Shame the Devil
Decker, J. Death Comes Home
Hensley, J. L. all three titles
Lewin, M. Z. Missing Woman

    INDIANAPOLIS (See also: Indiana; Midwest)
Lewin, M. Z. Hard Line
    Out of Season

    INDONESIA (Indon. See also: Djakarta; Bali; Borneo; Java; New Guinea; Sumatra)
Duncan, R. L. In the Enemy Camp
Koch, C. J. Year of Living Dangerously
Rosenberger, J. Operation Skyhook

    IOWA (Ia. See also: Midwest)
Collins, M. A. four titles
Greenleaf, S. Fatal Obsession
Parrish, P. Escape the Past
Rich, V. Cooking School Murders

    IRAN (See also: Iraq; Teheran; Middle East)
Chubin, B. Feet of a Snake
Easterman, D. Last Assassin
Hamizrachi, Y. Golden Lion and the Sun
Hayes, R. Scorpio Cipher
Hild, J. Plains of Fire
Rider, R. Dyed for Death
Wiltse, D. Wedding Guest

    IRAQ (See also: Iran; Terehan; Middle East)
Quinnell, A. J. Snap Shot
Scott, A. Unknown Path

    IRELAND (Ire. Both Ireland and Northern Ireland included here. See also: Belfast; Dublin)
Allan, O. Green Bushes
Brennan, E. Whispering Walls
Everett, P. Death in Ireland
Gill, B. both titles
Hely, S. Sign of the Serpent
Higgins, J. Confessional
Hollyock, D. Innocent Madness
Innes, M. Journeying Boy
Kickham, C. Knocknagow
Lowell, J. R. Irish Game
McCartan, D. Operation Emerald
McCurtin, P. Green Hell
McGinley, P. Trick of the Ga Bolga
McNamara, M. M. Sovereign Solution
Reeves, F. Deadly Inheritance
St. James, I. Killing Anniversary
Seymour, G. Field of Blood
Tennant, E. Woman Beware Woman
Thynne, R. Irish Holidays
Walsh, M. Danger Under the Moon
White, S. Fighting Irish

    ISLE OF MAN (See also: England; Channel Islands)
(no additional entries)

    ISRAEL (Isr. See also: Jerusalem; Tel Aviv; Middle East)
Kenan, A. Road to Ein Harod
Lane, A. Revelations
McFarlane, I. Jerusalem Conspiracy
Operator 1384. Black Arab
Pendleton, D. Hellbinder
Shahar, D. His Majesty's Agent
Vicas, V. Impromptu Imposter
Wilson, G. Return to Armageddon

    ISTANBUL (Istan. See also: Turkey; Middle East; Balkans)
Arrighi, M. Turkish White
Tokson, E. Harem Games
Unsworth, B. Rage of the Vulture
Wilson, G. Phoenix in Flames

    ITALY (It. See also: Florence; Milan; Naples; Rome; Sardinia; Sicily; Venice)
Bagley, D. Golden Keel
Clewes, H. Epitaph for Love
Coffman, V. Demon Lover
Cornelisen, A. Any Four Women Could Rob the Bank of Italy
Crighton, R. E. Red for Terror
Dacre, C. Zofloya
Davidson, A. Siren's Lure
Dickens, F. Three Cheers for the Good Guys
Fraser, J. In Place of Reason
Fraser, M. C. Satanist
Godey, J. Fatal Beauty
Hitchcock, L. Ducetti Heir
Holland, I. Lost Madonna
Inchbald, P. Or the Bambino Dies
Johns, D. Beatrice Mystery
Linscott, G. Murder Makes Tracks
Meynell, L. Thirteen Trumpeters
O'Brine, M. No Earth for Foxes
Pendleton, D. Tuscany Terror
Rossiter, E. Lemon Garden
Seeber, G. C. Abduction
Swift, B. Mission Code: Survival
West, M. Daughter of Silence
White, S. Terror in Turin
Whitten, L. Killing Pace
Williams, T. both titles

    JACKSONVILLE (Jack. See also: Florida; Miami; Tampa; South)
(no additional titles)

    JAKARTA. See: Djakarta.

    JAMAICA (Jam. See also: West Indies; Caribbean)
Revere, J. D. Born to Kill
White, S. King of Kingston

    JAPAN (Jap. See also: Tokyo; Far East)
Black, G. Dead Man Calling

Settings Index

Broinowski, A. Take One Ambassador
Carter, Nick. Christmas Kill
Cleary, J. Phoenix Tree
Forve, G. Ofanu
Hayes, S. K. Tulku
Leader, C. Wreath of Cherry Blossoms
Melville, P. all five titles
Natsuki, S. Murder at Mt. Fuji
Norman, E. Kill Me in Roppongi
Olden, M. Dai-Sho
Pendleton, D. Invisible Assassins
Robeson, K. Jui San
Schlossstein, S. Kensei
Seward, J. Frogman Assassination
Van de Wetering, J. Inspector Saito's Small Satori

JAVA (See also: Indonesia; Bali; Borneo; Djakarta; New Guinea; Sumatra)
Crisp, F. Fazackerley's Millions

JERUSALEM (Jerus. See also: Israel; Tel Aviv; Middle East)
Gross, J. This Year in Jerusalem
Sapir, R. Body

JOHANNESBURG (Johan. See also: South Africa; Cape Town; Transvaal)
(no additional entries)

KANSAS (Kan. See also: Midwest)
Derrick, L. Dodge City Bombers
Flanders, R. Easy Access
Pendleton, D. Prairie Fire
Sherburne, J. Death's Gray Angel

KANSAS CITY (Kan. City. See also: Missouri; St. Louis; Midwest)
Battin, B. W. Programmed for Terror
DeCoursey, V. Enter This Night
Maloney, J. J. I Speak for the Dead

KENTUCKY (Ky. See also: Louisville; South)
Anderson, U. S. King of the Roses
Grafton, C. W. Beyond a Reasonable Doubt
Rope Began to Hang the Butcher
Lauben, P. Nice Sound Alibi
Surfeit of Alibis
Windham, S. Missing

KENYA (See also: Africa, East)
Bagley, D. Legacy
Windfall
Barstow, P. Night Is for Hunting
Garrigues, E. Grass Rain
Hutton, A. Passport to Peril
Mwangi, M. Kill Me Quick
Ngugi Wa Thiong'o. Petals of Blood

KOREA (Kor. Both North and South Korea included here. See also: Far East)
Davis, F. M. Naked and the Lost
Wilson, G. Korean Killground

KUWAIT (Kuw. See also: Middle East)
De Villiers, G. Kill Kissinger

LAOS (See also: Far East)
Meiring, D. Brinkman

LAS VEGAS (Las Veg. See also: Nevada; Reno; West)
Ahern, J. Hard Way
Beckner, M. Money Plays
Clark, A. C. Kenyatta's Last Hit
Demaris, O. Vegas Legacy
Goldman, W. Heat
Murphy, W. B. Trace and 47 Miles of Rope
Two Steps from Three East
Nichols, L. Eyes of Darkness
Pendleton, D. Bone Yard
Perry, T. Butcher's Boy
Ramm, C. Vegas Vengeance
Schorr, M. Ace of Diamonds
Shaw, W. Out for Kicks

LEBANON (Leb. See also: Beirut; Middle East)
(no additional entries)

LEIPZIG (Leip. See also: Germany)
(no additional entries)

LIBYA (See also: Africa, North)
Emmett, R. Devil's Finger
Home, M. Place of Little Birds
Lewis, N. Suitable Case for Corruption
Pendleton, D. Libya Connection
Rosenberger, J. Laser War
Skimin, R. Libyan Warlord

LIMA (See also: Peru; South America)
Houston, R. Cholo
Stevens, G. Spider

LISBON (See also: Portugal; Madeira)
Delman, D. Murder in the Family
Lambert, D. Judas Code

LITHUANIA (Lith.)
(no additional entries)

LONG ISLAND (L. I. See also: New York; New York City; Rochester)
Bigelow, O. Peacock Season
Crane, C. Someone at the Door
Early, J. Razzamatazz
Flusser, M. Squeal Man
Goldthwaite, E. K. First You Have to Find Him
Harris, L. Hamptons
Hinkemeyer, M. T. Lilac Night
Johnson, S. Walk a Winter Beach
Johnston, V. Fateful Summer
Kutak, R. I Am the Cat
Leonard, G. Ice Cathedral
Maxxe, R. Arcade
Nazel, J. Delta Crossing
Pentecost, H. Sow Death, Reap Death
Philbin, T. Yearbook Killer
Quick, D. Cry in the Night
Watson, Clarissa. Runaway
Whitney, P. A. Rainsong
Wiles, D. X Factor
Winston, D. Trap

LOS ANGELES (L.A. See also: California; San Diego; San Francisco; West)
Alexander, M. Curtis Wives
Aricha, A. Journey Toward Death
Bellem, R. L. Dan Turner, Hollywood Detective
Berger, O. Deadly Kisses
Beynon, J. Cypress Man
Blumenthal, J. Tinseltown Murders
Bogar, J. Payoff for Paula
Boston, C. K. Silver Jackass
Boyles, J. Wild Ride
Braudy, S. Who Killed Sal Mineo?
Breen, J. L. Gathering Place
Brett, J. Who'd Hire John Brett?
Bugliosi, V. T. Shadow of Cain
Bunker, E. Little Boy Blue
Cameron, L. Hot Car
Carr, K. You're Hired; You're Dead
Chais, P. Final Cut
Clark, A. C. Cry Revenge
Cunningham, E. C. all Masuto titles
Delacorta. Vida
De Marco, G. Canvas Prison
Dillinger, J. Adrenaline
Eden, R. Short Skirts
Egan, L. all titles
Eldridge, M. Lightning May Strike Anywhere
Ellroy, J. all four titles
Enders, R. Tight Squeeze
Fawcette, S. Murder at the 1984 Summer Games
Flynn, C. H. Washed in the Blood
Forrest, K. V. Amateur City
Forward, R. L. Owl
Frank, W. I. Good for One More Ride
Goddard, K. Balefire
Goldberg, G. J. Heart Payments
Grant, J. Mace!
Green, G. Heartless Light
Greenleaf, S. Ditto List
Hamilton, N. Killer's Rights
Hansen, J. Backtrack
Gravedigger
Heath, C. three titles
Heath, E. Murder Pool
Heyes, D. Kill
Horgan, M. Dames Is My Undoing
Hyams, J. Murder at the Academy Awards
Irvine, R. R. Ratings Are Murder
Johnson, M. Clone People
Johnson, W. O. Hammered Gold
Kaminsky, S. M. four titles

Keating, H. R. F. Go West, Inspector Ghote
Kellerman, J. When the Bough Breaks
Lewis, S. Cowboy Blues
Linington, E. both titles
Lochte, D. Sleeping Dog
Lovesey, P. Keystone
Ludlow, I. all three titles
Lyons, A. Hard Trade
Lysaght, B. both titles
McCoy, H. I Should Have Stayed Home
McDonald, G. Fletch Won
Fletch's Moxie
Magee, B. Columbo and the Samurai Sword
Mandell, M. Killer Instinct
Masterton, G. Tengu
Miller, G. Black Glove
Miller, V. B. Angel's Blood
Morse, L. A. all three titles
Murphy, W. B. Smoked Out
Nash, N. R. Radiance
Nathanson, J. Puzzle for Experts
Nazel, J. Devil Dolls
Paige, R. Door to December
Panger, D. Mask of Abraham Morgenstern
Parker, B. Savage Place
Parker, T. J. Laguna Heat
Pendleton, D. Hollywood Hell
Perry, T. Big Fish
Metzger's Dog
Petievich, G. three titles
Plunkett, J. She'll Get Hers
Quinn, J. Crystal Kill
Ramm, C. L. A. Wars
Rhodes, V. Groomed for Murder
Richardson, J. H. Spring Street
Ross, S. Ready for the Tiger
Rotsler, W. Vice Squad
Rubel, M. Flex
Rustan, J. Tangled Snarl
Sanders, B. Starshine Connection
Schorr, M. Diamond Rock
Shannon, Dell. all five titles
Sinclair, M. Only in L.A.
Steiner, S. Murder on Her Mind
Stinson, J. Double Exposure
Stivers, R. Army of Devils
Five Rings of Fire
Thompson, J. Grifters
Thoreau, D. Satanic Condition
Thornburg, N. Dreamland
Trevor, E. Theta Syndrome
Walker, G. Suspect
Wambaugh, J. Delta Star
Warga, W. Hardcover
Warren, B. Fandom Is a Way of Death
West, O. Pit
White, T. Bleeding Hearts
Wick, C. Dark House, Dark Road
Winski, N. L. A. Massacre
Wolff, B. Hyde and Seek
Yariv, F. P. Last Exit
Zindel, P. When Darkness Falls

LOUISIANA (La. See also: New Orleans; South)
Blake, J. Midnight Waltz
Fuller, C. Soldier's Play
Grimwood, K. Voice Outside
Harris, C. Sweet and Deadly
McCray, M. Louisiana Firestorm
Mitchelmore, N. Natural Weapon
Talmage, A. Dark Over Acadia

LOUISVILLE (See also: Kentucky; South)
(no additional entries)

MACAO (See also: China; Far East; Shanghai; Peking; Formosa)
Carney, D. Macau
Tokson, E. When Dragons Dance

MACEDONIA (Maced. See also: Balkans; Bulgaria; Greece; Yugoslavia)
(no additional entries)

MADEIRA (See also: Portugal; Lisbon)
(no additional entries)

MADISON (See also: Wisconsin; Midwest)
(no additional entries)

MADRID (See also: Spain; Canary Islands; Majorca)
Rathbone, J. Lying in State
Serafin, D. three titles

MAINE (See also: New England)

Anderson, J. Hooray for Homicide
    Murder of Sherlock Holmes
Boorstin, P. Glory Hand
Borthwick, J. S. Down East Murders
Clark, B. Deathstalk
Dickson, M. Octavia's Hill
Fennelly, P. Cuckoos on the Hearth
Gould, J. R. Long Silence
Hermes, M. Phoenix Nest
Johnston, V. Other Karen
Kalish, R. Bloodtide
Kenney, S. Graves in Academe
Kimbrough, K. Rachel, the Possessed
Morison, B. J. all three titles
Parker, R. B. Early Autumn
Pendleton, D. Island Deathtrap
Philbrick, W. R. Slow Dancer
Reiss, B. Casco Deception
Rich, V. Baked-Bean Supper Murders
Roberts, W. D. Girl Who Wasn't There
Russell, R. Point of Reference
Shannon, Doris. Punishment
Stern, P. V. D. Love Is the One with
    Wings
Worrell, J. Sting of the Bee

         MAJORCA (Maj. See also: Spain;
            Madrid; Canary Islands)
Hild, J. Red Hammer Down
Jeffries, R. all four titles
O'Brine, M. Passport for Treason

MALAYA. See: Malaysia.

         MALAYSIA. (Mal. Malaya included
            here. See also: Far East)
Collis, M. Dark Door
Kauffman, F. Coconut Wireless
Keon, M. Durian Tree
Scott, B. Prayer Mat
    Secret of the Elephants
Trevor, E. Burning Shore

         MALI (See also: Africa, West)
(no additional entries)

         MALLORCA. See: Majorca.

         MALTA (See also: Mediterranean Island)
Cutter, J. Maltese Vengeance

         MANILA (See also: Philippines;
            Far East)
McQuinn, D. E. Wake in Darkness
Robeson, K. Screaming Man

         MARSEILLES (Mars. See also:
            France; Nice; Paris; Corsica)
Simpson, H. R. Jumpmaster

         MARYLAND (Md. See also: Baltimore)
Beechcroft, W. Image of Evil
Finch, P. In a Place Dark and Secret
Lippincott, D. Nursery
Michaels, B. Here I Stay
Pendleton, D. Iranian Hit
Rainey, R. Cult .45
Roberts, N. Night Moves

         MASSACHUSETTS (Mass. See also:
            Boston; Cape Cod; New England)
Batson, G. Strange Boarders
Boyer, R. Penny Ferry
Carew, J. Samantha
Cassidy, S. J. Altar Boy
Cormier, R. After the First Death
Coyne, J. E. House of Exile
Curtiss, U. Dog in the Manger
Ehrlich, M. Big Boys
Goode, G. W. King Dan, the Factory
    Detective
Healy, J. M. Blunt Darts
Kalish, R. Bloodmoon
Kemelman, H. Someday the Rabbi Will
    Leave
Langton, J. both titles
Lincoln, J. C. Blair's Attic
Lynch, M. Pale Hand of Danger
MacLeod, C. five titles
Mailer, N. Tough Guys Don't Dance
Patrick, W. Spirals
Pickard, N. both titles
Roos, K. Murder on Martha's Vineyard
Silver, V. Death of a Harvard Freshman
Wender, T. Knight Must Fall
Wright, L. R. Perfect Corpse

MEDICAL SETTINGS. See: Hospital.

         MEDITERRANEAN ISLAND. (Med. Is.
            See also: Corsica; Crete;
            Cyprus; Majorca; Sardinia;
            Sicily)
Canning, V. Python Project
Quayle, A. On Such a Night
Taffrail. Jade Lizard

         MELBOURNE (Melb. See also: Australia; Sydney; Solomon Islands; Tasmania)
Galbally, F. Juryman
Koch, C. J. Boys in the Island
Quinn, P. E. Jewelled Belt
Williamson, D. Removalists

         MEMPHIS (See also: Tennessee;
            Nashville; South)
(no additional entries)

         MESOPOTAMIA (Mesop. See also:
            Turkey; Middle East)
(no additional entries)

         MEXICO (Mex. See also: Mexico
            City)
Ahern, J. Master of D.E.A.T.H.
Bannister, W. Counterfeit Death
Bellah, J. Imperial Express
Calder-Marshall, A. Way to Santiago
Carter, Nick. Golden Bull
Cutter, J. Vengeance Mountain
Denham, R. Recipe for a Crime
Denning, M. Die Fast, Die Happy
Edwards, P. Glyphs of Gold
Fleetwood, H. Young Fair God
Ford, R. Ultimate Good Luck
Harris, D. Last Scam
Hartman, D. Mexico Kill
Heath, C. A-Team
Hunt, H. Maelstrom
Ibarguengoitia, J. both titles
Karl, M. S. Mobius Man
Kelly, J. Music from Another Room
Kennedy, G. Murder on Location
Lindop, A. E. Judas Figures
    Singer Not the Song
Lindsey, D. L. Black Gold, Red Death
Mathews, W. C. King Cobra
Patterson, H. Dillinger
Sharp, M. Falseface
Snyder, G. Tomb Seven
Stivers, D. Scorched Earth
Streib, D. House of Silence
Wagner, G. Passionate Land
Wright, R. B. Tourists

         MEXICO CITY (Mex. City. See also:
            Mexico)
Stivers, D. Into the Maze

         MIAMI (See also: Florida; Jacksonville; Tampa; South)
Chandler, B. Behind the Badge
De Borchgrave, A. Monimbo
Grave, S. both titles
Leonard, E. Cat Chaser
    La Brava
Montalbano, W. D. Powder Burn
Palmer, T. Transfer
Reach, J. Murder Over Miami
Willeford, C. both titles
Winters, M. Miami, One Way

         MICHIGAN (Mich. See also:
            Detroit; Midwest)
Beek, J. R. Bradford's Trials
Brennan, A. Thirty Days Hath July
Davis, D. S. Town of Masks
Dreyer, M. M. Beckoning Hands
Garnet, A. H. Maze
Howes, R. Murder at Maneuvers
Leonard, E. Big Bounce
Lippincott, D. Unholy Mourning
Martin, C. H. PK Factor
Mayhew, G. A. Murder at Daybreak
Patch, D. E. L. all titles
Sibbald, G. Dodge Boys
Toombs, J. J. Heart of Winter
Traver, R. Laughing Whitefish
    People vs. Kirk
Welles, P. Members Only

         MICRONESIA
(no additional entries)

         MIDDLE EAST (Mid. East. See also:
            individual countries)

Bachmann, L. Bitter Lake
Buck, P. Black Gold Briefing
Carter, Nick. Day of the Mahdi
Cox, R. Ground Zero
Delacorte, P. Levantine
Delahaye, M. Third Day
Derrick, L. Hell's Hostages
Edmonds, H. Red Desert
Emmett, R. King, Bishop, Knight
Farhi, M. Last of Days
Fulton, E. G. Vengeance, My Love
Graham, B. Spy or Die
Heath, C. Operation Desert Sun
Jones, D. Rubicon One
McAdam, P. Arabian Assault
Marchmont, A. W. By Snare of Love
Meiring, D. Talk with the Angels
O'Brine, M. Dagger Before Me
Osmond, M. Curtains of Solomon
Paul, A. Present from Hugo
Pereira, M. Angel Came Down
Quinnell, A. J. Mahdi
Royce, K. 10,000 Days
Scanlon, N. Quinn
Shamis, G. Crack in the House of God
Stacey, T. Worm in the Rose
Stivers, D. Rain of Doom
Tippin, G. L. Arab
Van Vors, B. L. Prince and the Sufi
Waugh, A. Mule on the Minaret

MIDDLE WEST. See: Midwest.

         MIDWAY ISLAND (Midway Is.)
(no additional entries)

         MIDWEST (See also: the twelve
            individual states)
Cox, T. R. Shadows of One Another
Echard, M. Dark Fantastic
Fackler, E. Arson
Flanders, R. Key
Heelan, K. Heartland
Marlowe, M. F.B.I. Girl
Nowak, J. Death at the Crossings
Russell, C. M. Hand Me a Crime
Spence, M. Rebekka Moon
Spencer, R. H. Radish River Caper
Taylor, D. Five in Judgment
Wilmot, R. P. Death Rides a Painted
    Horse

         MILAN (See also: Italy; Florence;
            Naples; Rome; Sardinia;
            Sicily; Venice)
(no additional entries)

         MILWAUKEE (Milw. See also: Wisconsin; Madison; Midwest)
(no additional entries)

         MINNEAPOLIS (Mpls. See also:
            Minnesota; Midwest)
Breslin, C. Unholy Child
Simonsen, S. J. Below Third Street
Taylor, L. A. three titles
Williams, Bob. Ozark Flats

         MINNESOTA (Minn. See also:
            Minneapolis; Midwest)
Adams, H. Murder
Boardman, N. S. Wine of Violence
Clark, M. H. Cry in the Night
Fluke, J. Winter Chill
Hinkemeyer, M. T. Fourth Down
    Time to Reap
Pendleton, D. Violent Streets
Taylor, L. A. Shed Light on Death

         MISSISSIPPI (Miss. See also:
            South)
Bakker, K. Sea Treasure
Hannah, B. Nightwatchman

         MISSOURI (Mo. See also: Kansas
            City; St. Louis; Midwest)
Behn, N. Seven Silent Men
Krasner, W. both titles
Rhodes, R. Sons of Earth
Robeson, K. Talking Devil
Thompson, P. Rainbow Ribbon
Thornburg, N. Black Angus
Woodrum, L. Stumble Upon the Dark
    Mountains

         MONACO. See: France.

         MONGOLIA (See also: China;
            Russia)
(no additional entries)

MONTANA (Mont. See also: West)
Ashley, J. Secrets of the Heart
Guthrie, A. B., Jr. Playing Catch-Up
Hugo, R. Death and the Good Life
Lassiter, A. King of the Mountain
Moffat, G. Grizzly Trail
West, S. G. Amos

MONTE CARLO. See: France.

MONTREAL (Montr. See also: Canada; Ottawa; Toronto; Vancouver; Winnipeg)
Moore, B. Wreath for a Redhead
Newman, J. Dead Man's Tears
Phillips, E. Death Is Relative

MOROCCO (Mor. See also: Casablanca; Tangier; Africa, North)
Garth, D. Three Roads to a Star
Grenier, R. Marrakesh One-Two
Timperley, R. Devil's Paradise

MOSCOW (See also: Russia; Mongolia)
Bannerman, D. Gamov Factor
Binyon, T. J. Swan Song
Burch, J. Lubyanka
Charles, R. Steel Killer
Evans, P. Englishman's Daughter
Freemantle, B. Rules of Engagement
Green, G. Karpov's Brain
Hunt, H. Kremlin Conspiracy
Jones, D. Russian Spring
Kaminsky, S. M. three titles
Moss, R. Moscow Rules
Neznansky, F. Deadly Games
Olcott, A. Murder at the Red October
Pape, G. Music Wars
Pearson, W. Chessplayer
Pieczenik, S. R. Mind Palace
Robertson, C. Red Chameleon
Scott, H. No Exit
Sela, O. Kremlin Control
Smith, M. C. Gorky Park
Topol, E. Red Square
Vallance, D. Man in the Lubianka

MOZAMBIQUE (Mozam. See also: Africa, East)
Hardy, R. Rivers of Darkness

MUNICH (See also: Germany; Berlin; Frankfurt; Hamburg)
Orde, L. Munich 10

NAMIBIA. See: South West Africa.

NAPLES (See also: Italy; Florence; Milan; Rome; Sardinia; Sicily; Venice)
(no additional entries)

NASHVILLE (Nashv. See also: Tennessee; Memphis; South)
Sadler, B. Nashville with a Bullet

NASSAU (See also: Bahamas; West Indies; Caribbean)
(no additional entries)

NEBRASKA (Neb. See also: Omaha; Midwest)
Lane, J. R. Static
Saul, J. Nathaniel

NEPAL
Hauser, T. Hanneman's War
Mason, R. Fever Tree

NETHERLANDS. See: Holland.

NEVADA (Nev. See also: Las Vegas; Reno; West)
Clark, A. C. Kenyatta's Escape
Hagen, L. Winter Roses
McCray, M. Red Man Contract
Roberts, W. D. Dangerous Legacy
Winski, N. Nevada Nightmare

NEW DELHI (See also: India; Bombay; Calcutta)
(no additional entries)

NEW ENGLAND (New Eng. See also: the six individual states)
Altman, T. Black Christmas
Babson, M. Trail of Ashes
Benchley, N. Hunter's Moon
Carleton, M. Night of the Good Children
Coburn, A. Widow's Walk
Cook, R. Fever
Corby, J. Nightmare Legacy
Cross, A. Sweet Death, Kind Death
Dean, S. F. X. By Frequent Anguish
 Death and the Mad Heroine
Julian, R. Murder in Focus
Keene, D. His Father's Wife
Murphy, W. B. Dead Letter
Pentecost, H. Party Killer
Spalding, J. Spider Island
Thomas, W. Stranger in the Land
Wilkinson, S. D. Death on Call
Yglesias, H. Sweetsir

NEW GUINEA (See also: Indonesia; Djakarta; Bali; Borneo; Java; Sumatra)
Boothby, G. Crime of the Under-Seas
Lambert, E. Veterans
Lindall, E. Time Too Soon
Wood, C. Kago

NEW HAMPSHIRE (N.H. See also: New England)
Brett, H. Promises to Keep
Drown, M. Plowing Up a Snake
Heatter, B. Act of Violence
Holden, R. Snow Fury

NEW JERSEY (N.J. See also: Newark)
Ballard, F. Ladies of the Jury
Caldwell, B. Vanderleigh Legacy
Clinch, C. Perth Amboy Mystery
Drayton, R. Hell's Belles
Engleman, P. Dead in Center Field
Fox, G. Warlord's Hill
Gilmore, C. C. Bad Room
Kilgore, K. Something for Nothing
Leonard, E. Glitz
Murphy, W. B. Trace
Pikser, J. Junk on the Hill
Saperstein, A. Camp
Sauter, E. Hunter
 Hunter and the Ikon
Walker, P. Altar

NEW MEXICO (N. Mex. See also: Albuquerque; Sante Fe; Southwest)
Dean, S. F. X. Such Pretty Toys
Hillerman, T. Dark Wind
 Ghost Way
Johnston, V. Shadow Behind the Curtain
Kazan, E. Assassins
Layne, M. M. Balloon Affair
McMullen, M. Gift Horse
Maxwell, A. E. Steal the Sun
Murphy, W. B. Date with Death
Roderus, F. Dead Heat
Scarpetta, F. Kiss of Death
Wilson, Brownlow. Devil's Staircase
Wiseman, T. Savage Day
Woods, C. Night Chant

NEW ORLEANS (New Or. See also: Louisiana; South)
Arnold, M. Death of a Voodoo Doll
Boyles, W. Killing Trade
Fawcette, S. Computer Criminals
Fennelly, T. Glory Hole Murders
Lee, T. House of Montague
Pronzini, B. Masques
Scarpetta, F. Counterattack
Thorne, E. Flight Hostess
Wiltz, C. Killing Circle

NEW YORK CITY (NYC. See also: New York; Long Island; Rochester)
Adcock, T. L. Precinct 19
Altman, T. Dark Places
Andrews, S. all three titles
Arrighi, M. Alter Ego
 Manhattan Gothic
Asimov, I. Caves of Steel
Auster, P. City of Glass
Bagby, G. Most Wanted
Baker, C. Pool Ticket .025
Ballinger, B. Wife of the Red-Headed Man
Bardon, J. F. Deadly Percheron
Barry, B. Murder Among Friends
Bart, S. Ruby Sweetwater and the Ringo Kid
Barth, R. three titles
Batson, G. Design for Murder
Baxt, G. Dorothy Parker Murder Case

Bayer, W. Peregrine
 Switch
Bell, M. S. Waiting for the End of the World
 Washington Square Ensemble
Belsky, D. One for the Money
Benjamin, P. Squeeze Play
Biracree, T. Red Berets
 Torch
Black, C. Apology
Black, J. Dead Run
Blackwelder, S. Price of Heaven
Blake, R. Double Griffin
Blau, E. Keys to Billy Trillo
Block, L. four titles
Blumenthal, J. Case of the Hardboiled Dicks
Borgenicht, M. Fall from Grace
 False Colors
Boyle, T. Only the Dead Know Brooklyn
Breslin, J. Gang That Couldn't Shoot Straight
 Kill That Bull!
Brez, E. M. Those Dark Eyes
Bromell, H. Follower
Byrne, R. Skyscraper
Campbell, R. W. Malloy's Subway
Canavor, F. Rape One
Caputi, A. Storms and Son
Castoire, M. Gold Shield
Caunitz, W. One Police Plaza
Chambers, W. E. Redemption Factor
Chastain, T. Diamond Exchange
 Nightscape
Clarins, D. Woman in the Window
Cleary, J. Spearfield's Daughter
Coffaro, K. Gently into Night
Cohen, O. R. Romance in the First Degree
Cohen, S. Angel Face
Cohler, D. K. Freemartin
Cole, W. V. Park Avenue
Conde, N. Religion
Condon, R. Prizzi's Honor
Cook, R. Brain
Cook, S. Sharing
Crane, C. Wife Found Slain
Cronley, J. Cheap Shot
Cutter, J. Manhattan Revenge
 Vendetta
Daley, R. Hands of a Stranger
 Year of the Dragon
D'Alton, M. Fatal Finish
Davis, D. S. Lullaby of Murder
Davis, J. G. Fear No Evil
Davis, P. Dancer's Death
DeAndrea, W. L. three titles
DeGrave, P. Unholy Moses
De Mille, N. Cathedral
Dentinger, J. both titles
Devon, D. G. Shattered Mask
 Temple Kent
Dodson, D. B. Looking for Zoe
Drake, A. Steel Noose
Drake, L. Medical Center Murders
Drummond, June. Trojan Mule
Du Bois, T. Listener
Duris, G. Real Endings
Eberhart, M. G. Family Affair
 Next of Kin
Eller, J. both titles
Ellin, S. Dark Fantastic
 Very Old Money
Eulo, K. Nocturnal
Field, E. What Nigel Knew
Fisher, D. Katie's Terror
Flynn, D. both titles
Forester, B. M. In Strict Confidence
Foy, G. Asia Rip
Frankel, S. Aleph Solution
Frimmer, S. Dead Matter
Frost, B. Innocent Bystander
Furst, A. Shadow Trade
Gallagher, M. Quicksilver
Garys, W. Detonator
Gillespie, R. Print-Out
Gipe, G. Coney Island Quickstep
Gladstone, E. Taste of Deception
Glazner, J. M. Big Apple Money Is Rotten to the Core
Godey, J. Nella
Gollin, J. Eliza's Galiardo
Gordon, K. Jumpin' Jupiter
Gould, H. Fort Apache, the Bronx
Graham, Whidden. Crimson Hairs
Grecco, J. Manhattan Massacre
Guare, J. Landscape of the Body
Halliday, F. Ambler
Hamill, D. Machine
Hamill, P. Guns of Heaven
Hammond, G. So Violent My Love
Harper, O. It's Never Too Late to Mend
Harragan, S. Sin Is a Redhead
Harrington, W. Mister Target
Harris, R. Honor Bound
Hatvary, G. E. Suiter
Hauser, T. Agatha's Friends
 Beethoven Conspiracy
Hayes, J. Deep End
Hays, L. Once Upon a Time in America

Hentoff, N. both titles
Herrick, M. J. When Last Seen...
Holland, I. Death at St. Anselm's
Hollander, L. Exhibit
Horovitz, I. Indian Wants the Bronx
Hoyt, R. Cool Runnings
Huber, F. V. Apple Crunch
Hunter, E. Horse's Head
Iannuzzi, J. Courthouse
Jacobs, H. Juror
Jahn, M. Night Rituals
Jason, P. Entangled
Jeffers, H. P. Murder on Mike
    Rubout at the Onyx
Jessup, R. Threat
Johnston, J. Pray for Ricky Foster
Kane, H. Edge of Panic
Karp, D. Hardman
Katz, W. Open House
    Surprise Party
Kenrick, T. Blast
Keyes, E. Double Dare
Knott, F. Wait Until Dark
Koenig, L. Rockabye
Larsen, E. Not a Through Street
Latham, B. Corpses in the Cellar
    Gilded Canary
L'Engle, M. Severed Wasp
Leuci, B. both titles
Lewis, T. Rooftops
Lieberman, H. Nightbloom
Link, W. Prescription: Murder
Lipsky, E. People Against O'Hara
Livingston, J. both titles
Lourie, R. First Loyalty
Lustbader, E. V. Ninja
McCormack, T. Strictly Amateur
McDonald, G. Safekeeping
McDowell, M. Katie
McInerny, R. Noonday Devil
McIver, N. J. Come Back, Alice
    Smythereene!
McMullen, M. Until Death Do Us Part
Manchester, J. Run, Thief, Run!
Maracotta, L. Hide-and-Seek
Mardon, D. In for a Penny
Marmor, A. both titles
Maron, M. three titles
Marsh, P. Devil's Daughter
Mason, C. Case of the Ashanti Gold
Masur, H. Q. Mourning After
Matheson, R. Fury on Sunday
Mathewson, J. Death Turns Right
Maxim, J. Abel/Baker/Charley
Mayo, D. Murder at the Big Store
Meyers, M. Reunion for Death
Michaels, P. Come, Follow Me
Miller, B. E. Death Deal
Miller, J. I'll Be Wearing a White
    Carnation
    Save the Last Dance for Me
Minahan, J. all three titles
Mochan, B. Brass Knuckles
Moran, C. Killer's Caress
Murphy, W. B. Remo: The First
    Adventure
    When Elephants Forget
Neely, R. Shadows from the Past
Nemec, D. Mad Blood
Newman, G. F. Men with the Guns
Newman, O. Unmasking a King
Nicole, M. Code Name: Love
O'Cork, S. Hell Bent for Heaven
O'Dell, J. W. Loan Shark
O'Donnell, L. three titles
Olden, M. Giri
Orenstein, F. both titles
Osborn, J. J. Man Who Owned New York
Oster, J. Sweet Justice
Ostrander, I. At One-Thirty
Paley, F. Rumble on the Docks
Panati, C. Pleasuring of Rory Malone
Papazoglou, O. both titles
Patrick, V. Family Business
Patterson, R. N. Escape the Night
Paul, B. three titles
Paul, R. Thomas Street Horror
Pendleton, D. Shock Waves
Pentecost, H. seven titles
Peters, E. Die for Love
Peters, S. Park Is Mine
Philbin, T. Precinct #1: Siberia
Pines, P. Tin Angel
Piper, E. Bunny Lake Is Missing
Pollitz, E. A. Empire State
Powers, E. both titles
Pronzini, B. Eye
Rafferty, S. S. Die Laughing
Rainey, R. Porn Tapes
    Venus Underground
Ramm, C. Deadly in New York
Randall, B. Fan
Randisi, R. J. Full Contact
    Steinway Collection
Resnicow, H. three titles
Rickett, F. Stalked
Ring, A. Killers Play Tough
Roberts, P. Tender Prey
Robeson, K. three titles
Robinson, A. Dick and Jane

Rosenberg, S. N. Brenda Maneuver
Ross, C. Voice from the Grave
Rowe, A. Deadly Intent
Russell, R. Reunion
Sanders, Lawrence. three titles
Sanders, Leonard. Act of War
Scaparro, J. Worst Enemies
Schneider, J. A. Stryker's Children
Schor, A. Line by Line
Schwartz, A. Blowtop
Schwarz, B. Ransom for Miss LeGrun
Scott, J. Normandie Triangle
    Rampage
Seligson, T. Kidd
Seton, A. Dragonwyck
Shannon, Doris. Family Money
Sheldon, S. Rage of Angels
Sherburne, J. Death's Clenched Fist
Sherry, E. Sudden Fear
Shiffrin, A. B. Twilight Walk
Simmons, M. K. Girl with the Key
Smiley, J. Duplicate Keys
Smith, J. C. S. Nightcap
Smith, K. N. Catching Fire
    Elegy for a Soprano
Springs, J. Kansas
Steeley, R. D. Hot Ice
Stewart, J. Boudoirs Are My Beat
Stivers, D. Tower of Terror
Stockbridge, G. Prince of Evil
Stryker, H. NYPD 2025
Suyker, B. Death Scene
Taubes, F. Run...Run...Run
Topor, T. Coda
Trevor, E. Penthouse
Uhnak, D. False Witness
    Victims
Vachss, A. H. Flood
Wager, W. Otto's Boy
Wallace, I. Almighty
Weinstein, H. East Coast Crisis
West, R. F. Crystal Clear
Westlake, D. E. Levine
    Why Me?
Wheat, C. Dead Man's Thoughts
White, L. Ransomed Madonna
Wiltse, D. Fifth Angel
    Serpent
Winslow, P. G. Rockefeller Gift
Wise, A. Blood-Red Rose
Wolfe, C. Murder at la Marimba
Wolk, M. Big Picture
Ziran, G. Counsellor

NEW YORK State (N.Y. See also:
    Long Island; New York City;
    Rochester)
Block, L. Girl with the Long Green
    Heart
Borgenicht, M. True or False
Carlson, P. M. Audition for Murder
    Murder Is Academic
Connors, B. F. Dancehall
Cooper, J. F. Ways of the Hour
Crane, C. four titles
Cutler, R. Medusa Syndrome
Cutter, J. Psycho Soldiers
Daniels, D. Saratoga
DeAndrea, W. L. Killed with a Passion
Delman, D. Death of a Nymph
Dobyns, S. Saratoga Headhunter
    Saratoga Swimmer
Drachman, T. S. Something for the Birds
Fisher, D. Variations on a Theme
Gordon, K. Bride's Bouquet
Haring, F. Greek Revival
Hart, F. N. Bellamy Trial
Hastings, W. Don't Walk Home Alone
Heald, A. Shadows Under White Face
Holland, I. Flight of the Archangel
Johnson, A. P. Hush, Winifred Is Dead
Kessner, L. Spy Next Door
King, H. Hahnemann Sequela
Lathen, E. Going for the Gold
Lipsky, E. Scientists
Mills, H. Mossbank Murder
Neiderman, A. Brainchild
    Someone's Watching
Oates, J. C. Mysteries of Winterthurn
O'Cork, S. End of the Line
O'Donnell, L. Sleeping Beauty Murders
Partridge, B. Ainsley Case
Paul, R. Tragedy at Tiverton
Piper, E. Lady and Her Doctor
Roos, A. Speaking of Murder
Roosevelt, E. Hyde Park Murder
Ryan, A. Dead White
Sharkey, J. Par for the Corpse
Stanwood, B. Seventh Child
Stevenson, R. On the Other Hand
Stockbridge, G. Satan's Death Blast
Train, A. Hermit of Turkey Hollow
Treat, L. Leather Man
Vance, E. Secret Thread
Veder, B. Playing with Fire
Willard, J. Cat and the Canary
Wolman, D. Little Boy Lost
Wood, B. Tribe

NEW ZEALAND (N.Z.)
Calder, J. O'Rourke Affair
Crawford, J. T. Killing Time
Gee, M. all five titles
McClenaghan, J. Moving Target
Mantell, L. both titles
Potter, J. Going West
Richmond, M. Troubled Heritage
Satchell, W. both titles
Sherwood, M. Botanist at Bay
Wilson, Guthrie. Feared and the
    Fearless

NEWARK (See also: New Jersey)
Sohland, A. Evidence Circumstantial

NICARAGUA (Nic. See also: Central
    America)
Elman, R. Menu Cypher

NICE (See also: France;
    Marseilles; Paris; Corsica)
Read, P. P. Villa Golitsyn

NIGERIA (Nig. See also: Africa,
    West)
(no additional entries)

NORTH CAROLINA (N.C. See also:
    South)
Cooney, C. B. Sand Trap
Knowlton, R. A. Court of Crows
MacKay, A. Death on the Eno
Malone, M. Uncivil Seasons
Maron, M. Bloody Kin
Saab, P. Sweetwater Point Motel
Schutz, B. M. Embrace the Wolf
Zachary, H. Bloodrush
    Murder in White

NORTH DAKOTA (N. Dak. See also:
    Midwest)
(no additional entries)

NORTHWEST (N.W. See also: Oregon;
    Washington)
Cutter, J. Sullivan's Revenge
Davis, K. Dead to Rights
Olsen, J. Missing Persons

NORWAY (Nor. See also: Oslo;
    Scandinavia)
Engstrand, S. Spring 1940
White, A. Long Midnight

OCEAN. See: Ship.

OHIO (See also: Cincinnati;
    Cleveland; Columbus; Midwest)
Falkner, L. M
Gilbert, M. A. Office Party
Hale, C. Going, Going, Gone
Harrington, W. Power

OKLAHOMA (Okla. See also: Okla-
    homa City; Southwest)
(no additional entries)

OKLAHOMA CITY (Okla. City. See
    also: Oklahoma; Southwest)
(no additional entries)

OMAHA (See also: Nebraska;
    Midwest)
Moss, J. Arson Job
Reynolds, W. J. Nebraska Quotient

OPERA. See: Theatre.

OREGON (Oreg. See also: Portland;
    Northwest)
Goodwin, H. Home for the Heart
Hoyt, R. Manna Enzyme
    Siskiyou Two-Step
Munn, V. Touch a Wild Heart
Pendleton, D. Council of Kings
Stack, A. Lust Killer
Wren, M. K. Wake Up, Darlin' Corey

ORIENT. See: Far East; individual
    countries.

Settings Index

OSLO (See also: Norway; Scandinavia)
Henege, T. Death of a Shipowner

OTTAWA (See also: Canada; Montreal; Toronto; Vancouver; Winnipeg)
Adams, I. S--Portrait of a Spy
Kilian, M. Northern Exposure

PAKISTAN (Pak.)
Lewis, R. H. Where Agents Fear to Tread
Rosenberger, J. Pakistan Kill Ground

PALESTINE. See: Israel.

PANAMA (Pan. See also: Central America)
Conrad, B. Stars Give Warning

PARAGUAY (Parag. See also: South America)
Masters, D. Spiral of Death
Pendleton, D. Guerrilla Games
Pickering, P. Wild About Harry

PARIS (See also: France; Nice; Marseilles)
Anders, K. T. Legacy of Fear
Bass, R. Emerald Illusion
Butterworth, M. Virgin on the Rocks
Carter, Nick. Parisian Affair
Christopher, J. Murder-Go-Round
Cutter, J. American Vengeance
Delacorta. Diva
  Nana
Eberstadt, I. Natural Victims
Fick, C. Disturbance in Paris
Hart, C. G. Escape from Paris
Herrick, M. J. When Last Seen...
Holt, V. Demon Lover
Hotchner, A. E. Man Who Lived at the Ritz
Howard, H. War Toys
Hughes, C. Fires of Paris
Kartun, D. Beaver to Fox
Kaufelt, D. A. Souvenir
Lodwick, J. Love Bade Me Welcome
McConnor, V. I Am Vidocq
  Paris Puzzle
Page, M. Set a Thief
Peterson, B. Peripheral Spy
St. Germain, G. Shadows of Death
St. James, B. Seven Dreamers
Smith, C. S. Chain of Circumstances
Sponq, R. See If He Wins
Stevens, S. Anvil Chorus
Volkoff, V. both titles

PAST (Here listed are books explicitly set at a time distinctly earlier than the time of writing. Year and place of setting are given where identified. See also: Future)
Adams, H. Murder (1930s, Minn.)
  Naked Liar (1930s, S. Dak.)
  Paint the Town Red (1930s, S. Dak.)
Aiken, Joan. Young Lady from Paris (ca. 1850)
Albert, M. H. Operation Lila (1942, Fr.)
Allison, E. M. A. Through the Valley of Death (1379, Eng.)
Anderson, J. Affair of the Mutilated Mink Coat (1930s, Eng.)
Anonymous. Mystery of Marlborough House (ca.1800)
Anthony, E. Voices on the Wind (WWII, Fr.)
Arnold, W. China Gate (1960s-1970s, Far East)
Bainbridge, B. Watson's Apology (1871, London)
Baldwin, A. Last Heroes (WWII)
  Secret Warriors (WWII)
Balling, L. C. Fourth Shot (1963)
Barber, N. Women of Cairo (1940s, Egypt)
Barlay, S. Cuban Confetti (1962)
Bart, S. Ruby Sweetwater and the Ringo Kid (1901, NYC)
Bass, R. Emerald Illusion (1944, Paris)
Baxt, G. Dorothy Parker Murder Case (1920s, NYC)
Beck, K. K. Death in a Deck Chair (1927, ship)
Behn, N. Seven Silent Men (1971, Mo.)
Bellah, J. Imperial Express (1937, Mex.)
Bennett, J. M. Local Matter (1914, Eng.)
Berckman, E. Finger to Her Lips (1700s, Ger.)
Binyon, T. J. Swan Song (1970s, Moscow)
Black, Laura. Strathgallant (1863, Eng.)
Blake, J. Midnight Waltz (ca.1850, La.)
Blake, P. Double Griffin (1944, NYC)
Bloch, R. Night of the Ripper (1888, Eng.)
Block, L. Code of Arms (1940)
Blyth, J. Beset by Spies (1904)
Bok, C. Star Wormwood (1931, U.S.)
Bond, C. Sweeney Todd, the Demon Barber of Fleet Street (early 1800s, London)
Borrie, H. Golden Heron (1930s)
Bowen, M. Old Patch's Medley (1690-1795, London)
Boyarsky, A. Shreiber (1945-6, Pol.)
Bradbury, R. Death Is a Lonely Business (1950, Calif.)
Brason, J. Fourth Arm (WWII, Fr.)
Brent, M. Heritage of Shadows (1890s, Eng.)
Bridges, R. Bubble Moon (1700s)
Brierley, D. Big Bear, Little Bear (1948, Berlin)
Briggs, D. Standing into Danger (1960s)
Britton, C. Paybacks (1971, San Diego)
Buckley, W. F., Jr. Marco Polo, If You Can (1959)
  See You Later, Alligator (1962, Cuba)
  Story of Henri Tod (1961, Berlin)
Burch, J. Lubyanka (1978, Moscow)
Burnett, W. R. Goodbye, Chicago (1928, Chi.)
Burroughs, W. Fugitive Feet (1944, Ida.)
Burton, B. J. Murder of Maria Marten (1827, Eng.)
Butterworth, M. Virgin on the Rocks (1933, Paris)
Cable, M. Avery's Knot (1832, R.I.)
Campbell, G. In the Shadow of Death (1790)
Campbell, P. Lush Valley (1890s)
Carmichael, F. Any Number Can Die (1920s)
  Victoria's House (ca.1900)
Carnac, N. Indigo (1857, India)
Chacko, D. Brick Alley (1960, Pa.)
Clarke, J. Last Voyage (1939, Eng.)
Clarke, T. E. B. Murder at Buckingham Palace (1935, Eng.)
Cleary, J. City of Fading Light (1939, Berlin)
  Faraway Drums (1911, India)
  Golden Sabre (early 1900s, Russ.)
  Phoenix Tree (1945, Jap.)
Coffman, V. Demon Tower (1808, It.)
  Master of Blue Mire (1814, Eng.)
  Orchid Tree (1930s, Haw.)
Collins, L. Fall from Grace (WWII)
Collins, M. A. No Cure for Death (1974, Ia.)
  True Crime (1934, Chi.)
  True Detective (1920s, Chi.)
Cooper, L. U. Lighted Room (1600s, Eng.)
Cooper, M. H. When Fish Begin to Smell (1951, London)
Cort, N. all titles (WWII)
Crichton, W. Donnelly Murders (1800s, U.S.)
Crowder, K. Iron Web (WWII, S. Afr.)
Dacre, C. Zofloya (1400s, It.)
Daley, R. Dangerous Edge (1952, Fr.)
Daniels, D. Monte Carlo (ca.1900, Fr.)
  Saratoga (1880s, N.Y.)
Darby, C. Season of the Falcon (1774, Eng.)
Davenport, J. Murder at Bill's O'Jacks (1832, Eng.)
DeAndrea, W. L. Five O'Clock Lightning (1953, NYC)
De Gramont, S. Lives to Give (WWII, Fr.)
De Marco, G. Canvas Prison (1949, L.A.)
Devine, D. This Is Your Death (1962, Eng.)
Dial, J. Echoes of War (WWII, Ger.)
Dobyns, S. Dancer with One Leg (1970s, Boston)
Doherty, P. C. Death of a King (1344, Eng.)
Doliner, R. Twelfth of April (1920-58)
Douglas, Ben. Challenge at Castle Gap (1912, Tex.)
Driscoll, P. Heritage (1945-62, Algeria)
Drown, M. Plowing Up a Snake (1956, N.H.)
E-7. Romance of a Spy (WWII, Fr.)
Echard, M. Dark Fantastic (1870s, Midwest)
Eckert, A. W. Scarlet Mansion (1800s, Chi.)
Eco, U. Name of the Rose (1327, It.)
Egleton, C. Russian Enigma (1962)
  Winter Touch (1956, Eng.)

Past / 183

Ellroy, J. Clandestine (1951, L.A.)
Elon, A. Timetable (1944)
Engleman, P. Dead in Center Field (1961, N.J.)
Evans, A. So Pitifully Slain (1500s, Eng.)
Fairlie, G. They Found Each Other (WWII, Fr.)
Ferrand, G. Moonmist (1840, Eng.)
Feuer, L. Case of the Revolutionist's Daughter (1881, Eng.)
Findley, T. Famous Last Words (WWII)
Flannery, S. Trinity Factor (WWII)
Fleming, T. F. Dreams of Glory (1780, Charleston)
Flynn, C. H. Washed in the Blood (1938, L.A.)
Follett, K. Man from St. Petersburg (1914, Eng.)
Forbes, C. Leader and the Damned (WWII, Ger.)
Ford, E. Such Bitter Business (1800s, Eng.)
Forrest, A. Balance of Dangers (ca.1804)
  Captain Justice (1804, Fr.)
  Pandora Secret (1804, Eng.)
Fowles, J. Maggot (1700s)
Fox, G. Warlord's Hill (1940s, N.J.)
Francis, C. Night Sky (1935-45)
Frank, W. I. Good for One More Ride (early 1900s, L.A.)
Friedman, M. Hurricane Season (1950s, Fla.)
Frizell, B. Timetable for the General (WWII)
Fuller, C. Soldier's Play (1944, La.)
Gainham, S. Place in the Country (1946, Austria)
Gaither, F. O. Double Muscadine (1850s, South)
Gardner, J. Flamingo (1930s, Shanghai)
  Secret Generations (1909-35, Eng.)
Giancol, A. Three Racketeers (1920s)
Gilbert, A. Miss Bede Is Staying (1800s, Eng.)
Gipe, G. Coney Island Quickstep (1891, NYC)
Glazier, S. Lost Provinces (1907-11, Fr.)
Goldberg, G. J. Heart Payments (1966, L.A.)
Gordon, R. Medical witness (1936, Eng.)
  Private Life of Dr. Crippin (1909, Eng.)
Graeme, B. Trail of the White Knight (1919, Hung.)
Grafton, C. W. Rope Began to Hang the Butcher (1941, Ky.)
Graves, W. Mumberley Inheritance (1900, Eng.)
Grayson, R. Crime Without Passion (ca.1900, Paris)
  Death of the Abbe Didier (ca.1900, Paris)
  Montmartre Murders (ca.1900, Paris)
Green, W. M. Romanov Connection (ca.1920, Russ.)
Greene, D. Tenth Man (1945, Fr.)
Gretton, M. S. Crumplin! (1491, Eng.)
Guild, N. Berlin Warning (1941)
  Chain Reaction (1944)
Hall, B. Passion of Dracula (1911, Eng.)
Hambly, B. Quirinal Hill Affair (116, Rome)
Hamilton, P. Gas Light (1800s, Eng.)
Hammond, M. Theseus Code (1943, 1978, Crete)
Hammond, M. A. Land of Gold (1800s, S.F.)
Hardwick, Michael. Private Life of Dr. Watson
Harrington, W. English Lady (1931-WWII, Ger.)
Harris, J. Fox from His Lair (WWII)
Harrison, R. all four titles (1890s, Eng.)
Hart, C. G. Escape from Paris (1940, Paris)
Hartland, M. Down Among the Dead Men (1970s, H. Kong)
Hatfield, M. Spy Fever
Haubold, C. Sherlock Holmes and the Curious Adventure of the Clockwork Prince (1899, London)
Hawkes, E. Shadow of the Moth (1917, London)
Hays, L. Once Upon a Time in America (1933-68, NYC)
Heatter, B. Einstein Plot (1941)
  London Gun (WWII)
Hebert, A. In the Shadow of the Wind (1936, Fr.)
Heller, K. Man's Illegal Life (1722, London)
  Man's Storm (1703, London)
Hely, S. Sign of the Serpent (1700s, Ire.)

184 / Past Settings Index

P

Herlin, H. Solo Run (ca.1975, Ger.)
Hervey, E. Governess (1870, Eng.)
    Man of Gold (1874, Eng.)
Heyes, D. Kill (1938, L.A.)
Hicks, H. B. Castle at Jade Cove (1884, Calif.)
Hilton, J. Knight Without Armour (ca.1915, Russ.)
Hirt, H. Heat of Winter (1952, India)
Hogan, J. P. Proteus Operation (1939)
Hollyock, D. Innocent Madness (1838, Ire.)
Holt, V. Demon Lover (1800s, Paris)
    Road to Paradise (1800s, Eng.)
    Time of the Hunter's Moon (1800s, Eng.)
Hotchner, A. E. Man Who Lived at the Ritz (1940, Paris)
Hughes, T. J. Queen's Mate (1943, ship)
Humes, H. L. Underground City (WWII, Fr.)
Hunter, E. Lizzie (1890s, U.S.)
Hunter, J. D. Tin Cravat (1945, Ger.)
Hunter, S. Spanish Gambit (1930s, Sp.)
Hylton, S. Carradice Chain (WWI, Eng.)
    Crimson Falcon (ca.1900, Vienna)
Hynd, N. Flowers from Berlin (1939, U.S.)
Irving, C. Angel of Zin (1943, Pol.)
    Axis (1936-40)
Jameson, F. Green Fire (1968, S. Am.)
Jameson, S. Before the Crossing (1939, Eng.)
Jarrett, P. Throwaway Man (1943)
Jefferis, B. Beloved Lady (1400s, Eng.)
Jeffers, H. P. Murder on Mike (1939, NYC)
    Rubout at the Onyx (1935, NYC)
Johnston, V. Fateful Summer (1910, L.I.)
Jones, F. Master and Maid (1915, Toronto)
Jones, M. Season of the Strangler (1969, Ala.)
Jones, R. D. Fenris Option (WWII)
Jordan, L. Hidden Fires (ca.1900, Tex.)
Jute, A. Zaharoff Commission (WWII, Ger.)
Kaminsky, S. M. Catch a Falling Clown (ca.1942, Calif.)
    Down for the Count (1942, L.A.)
    Fala Factor (ca.1942, L.A.)
    He Done Her Wrong (ca.1942, L.A.)
    High Midnight (1942, L.A.)
Kantor, H. Big Stopper (1920s, Chi.)
Kartun, D. Courier (1940, Fr.)
Katkov, N. Blood and Orchids (1930, Haw.)
Kaufelt, D. A. Souvenir (1942, Paris)
Kavaler, R. Doubting Castle (late 1800s)
Kay, T. After Eli (1800s, Ga.)
Kelly, T. J. Terror by Gaslight (1800s, Phil.)
Kelton, E. Stand Proud (ca.1905, Tex.)
Kemeny, J. A. Strands of War (WWII, Ger.)
Kenrick, T. Faraday's Flowers (1940, Shanghai)
Keppel, C. Villains (1744, Eng.)
Kimbrough, K. Barbara, the Valient (1859, Ga.)
    Millijoy, the Determined (1858, Ga.)
    Patricia, the Beautiful (1787, Va.)
    Rachel, the Possessed (1798, Maine)
    Susannah, the Righteous (1807, Boston)
King, F. Act of Darkness (1930s, India)
King, Ramona. Steal Away (1930s, Chi.)
Kingsley-Smith, T. Murder of an Old-Time Movie Star (1930s, L.A.)
Kisner, J. Slice of Life (1915, Chi.)
Klein, E. Parachutists (1944, Hung.)
Koning, H. De Witt's War (1941, Holl.)
Konsalik, H. G. Strike Force Ten (1945, Russ.)
Koontz, D. R. Hanging On (WWII, Fr.)
Kozhevnikov, V. Shield and Sword (WWII, Ger.)
Krauth, N. Matilda, My Darling (1890s, Australia)
Kriz, J. Karsten's Flats (1938, Tex.)
Kruse, J. Red Omega (1951)
Kurland, M. Death by Gaslight (ca.1890, Eng.)
Kyle, D. King's Commissar (1918, Russ.)
    Stalking Point (WWII)
Laidlaw, R. Linton Porcupine (1500s, Eng.)
Laine, A. Melancholy Virgin (1800s, Eng.)
Lambert, D. Golden Express (1940, train)
    Judas Code (1941, Lisbon)
Land, Jane. These Tiger's Hearts (1860s, Vienna)
Lanigan, C. Bound by Love (1914)
Latham, B. Gilded Canary (1930s, NYC)
La Tourrette, J. House on Octavia Street (1899, S.F.)
Lawman, A. Hounds of Hell (1940, Holl.)
Lee, J. Lake of the Diamond (WWII)
Leighton, T. Phoenix Formula (WWII)
Leslie, P. Bastard Brigate (WWII, Fr.)
Lestienne, V. Furioso (WWII, Fr.)
Levey, M. Affair on the Appian Way (ancient Rome)
Lewis, N. Cuban Passage (1959, Cuba)
Ley, A. C. Reputation Dies (1816, London)
Lofts, N. Jassy (1800s, Eng.)
Lovesey, P. False Inspector Dew (1921, ship)
    Keystone (1915, L.A.)
Lowell, J. R. Irish Game (1939, Ire.)
Lucas, R. Who Dare to Live (WWII, Ger.)
Lupoff, R. Lovecraft's Book (1927)
MacBeth, G. Kind of Treason (ca.1940, Sing.)
McCarry, C. Tears of August (1963)
McConnor, V. I Am Vidocq (1823, Paris)
McDonald, G. Safekeeping (1940s, NYC)
McDowell, M. Jack and Susan in 1953 (1953)
    Katie (1871, NYC)
MacLean, A. Partisans (1943, Yugos.)
    San Andreas (WWII, ship)
McQuay, M. Escape from New York (1976)
Man, J. Lion's Share (1976)
Markstein, G. Ultimate Issue (1961)
Marlowe, S. 1956 (1956)
Massie, A. Death of Men (1978, Rome)
Masterton, G. Condor (WWII)
    Ikon (1962)
Mather, B. Hour of the Dog (1941, H. Kong)
Matthias, L. A. Pandora Plague (1902, Eng.)
Maxwell, A. E. Steal the Sun (1945, N. Mex.)
Maxwell, W. So Long, See You Tomorrow (1920s, Ill.)
Meiring, D. Brinkman (1960, Laos)
Melchior, I. Eva (WWII, Ger.)
Merritt, R. My Sister's Keeper (1960s)
Michaels, B. Black Rainbow (1855, Va.)
Miles, G. Evil Mark (1820s, Eng.)
Montague, J. Clock Tower (1900, Eng.)
Moray, H. That Woman (ca.1790, Fr.)
Morgulas, J. Twelfth Power of Evil
Morison, B. J. Beer and Skittles (1972, Maine)
Murray, F. Belchamber Scandal (1860s, Eng.)
Nash, J. R. Dark Fountain (1927, Calif.)
Neely, R. Shadows from the Past (1942, NYC)
Neuman, F. Maneuvers (1962, Ger.)
Nicholson, R. Passion for Treason (WWII, Ger.)
Nicolaysen, B. Perilous Passage (WWII, Ger.)
Nolan, F. Wolf Trap (WWII, Ger.)
Noonan, M. Magwitch (ca.1850, Australia)
Oates, J. C. Mysteries of Winterthurn (1800s, N.Y.)
Page, M. Set a Thief (1911, Paris)
Paretti, S. Maria Canossa (1943, Rome)
Paris, A. Teeth of the Wolf (1945, Ger.)
Partridge, B. Ainsley Case (1885, N.Y.)
Patterson, H. Dillinger (1934, Mex.)
Paul, B. Credenza for Caruso (1910, NYC)
    Prima Donna at Large (1915, NYC)
Paul, R. Thomas Street Horror (1836, NYC)
    Tragedy at Tiverton (1832, N.Y.)
Peart, R. Angels of Death (1942, Fr.)
Pember, R. Jack the Ripper (1888, London)
Perry, A. all five titles (1880s, Eng.)
Peters, Elizabeth. Curse of the Pharaohs (ca.1900, Egypt)
    Mummy Case (late 1800s, Egypt)
Peters, Ellis. all eight titles (1100s, Eng.)
Peterson, G. Klondike Kalamity (1888, Can.)
Pope, D. Convoy (1942)
    Decoy (WWII)
Price, A. Soldier No More (1957, Fr.)
Price, J.-A. Doomsday Ship (WWII, ship)
    Operation Night Hawk (WWII)
Pronzini, B. Quincannon (1893, S.F.)
Puccetti, R. Death of the Fuhrer (WWII, Ger.)
Queneau, R. We Always Treat Women Too Well (1916, Dub.)
Ragosta, M. J. Witness to Treason (1200s, Eng.)
Rathbone, J. Lying in State (1975, Madrid)
Raygor, L. Catherine's Twins (post-WWII, Berlin)
Reiss, B. Casco Deception (WWII, Maine)
Richards, T. Virgel Directive (late 1930s)
Roberts, P. Tender Prey (1930s, NYC)
Robertson, C. Omega Deception (1943)
Rogers, G. Scandal in Eden (ca.1930, S.F.)
Romanes, J. Berlin Breakout (1948, WWII)
    Raid (WWII)
Roosevelt, E. Hyde Park Murder (1935, N.Y.)
    Murder and the First Lady (ca.1940, Wash. D.C.)
Roscoe, T. Only in New England (1911)
Rosen, S. Death and Blintzes (1935, Boston)
Ross, C. Dancing Years (1933, ship)
Ross, F. Shining Day (WWII, Eng.)
Rossiter, J. Dark Flight (WWII)
Rostov, M. Careless Feast (WWII, Vienna)
Royce, K. Channel Assault (1942, Chan. Is.)
Rubel, M. Flex (1958, L.A.)
St. George, G. Proteus Pact (WWII, Ger.)
St. James, B. Seven Dreamers (1800s, Paris)
St. James, I. Killing Anniversary (1916, Ire.)
Salisbury, C. Autumn in Araby (1869, Egypt)
Sanders, Leonard. Act of War (WWII, NYC)
Scholefield, A. King of the Golden Valley (1939)
    Sea Cave (1920s, S. Afr.)
Schorr, M. Bully! (1903, U.S.)
Scott, C. Hitler's Bomb (WWII, Ger.)
Scott, J. Normandie Triangle (WWII, NYC)
    Pride of Royals (WWI)
Seaman, D. Chase Royal (1867)
Seton, A. Dragonwyck (1840s, NYC)
Shannon, Doris. Family Money (1914, NYC)
Shaw, B. Days of Power, Nights of Fear (1950s, Wash. D.C.)
Sheffield, C. Erasmus Magister (1700s)
Sheppard, S. Monte Carlo (WWII, Fr.)
Sherburne, J. Death's Clenched Fist (1890, NYC)
    Death's Gray Angel (1890, Kan.)
Sherlock, J. Amindra Gamble (1940, ship)
Sherman, D. Man Who Loved Mati Hari (WWII)
Sherwood, J. Shot in the Arm (1937, Eng.)
Sidhwa, B. N. Crow Eaters (ca.1900, India)
Simonsen, S. J. Below Third Street (1920s, Mpls.)
Sinclair, C. Lallie
Slavitt, D. R. Ringer (1942, U.S.)
Sloan, C. Wings of Death (WWII, Fr.)
Smith, Joan. both titles (1800s, Eng.)
Spencer, R. H. Missing Bishop (1969, Chi.)
Spivey, A. J. Michael (1930s, Denver)
Spong, R. See If He Wins (1944, Paris)
Stanley, W. Cloud Nineteen (1944)
Stashower, D. Adventures of the Ecto-plasmic Man (1910, Eng.)
Stein, B. Manhattan Gambit (1943)
Stevens, S. Anvil Chorus (1975, Paris)
Steward, S. M. Murder Is Murder Is Murder (1937, Fr.)
Stratham, F. P. From Love's Ashes (1935, Atlanta)
Stringer, D. Yesterday Man (WWII, Fr.)
Stuart, H. L. Ginger Flower (1900-44, Haw.)
Sturrock, J. Captain Bolton's Corpse (ca.1800, Eng.)
    Pangersbourne Murders (ca.1800, Eng.)
    Suicide Most Foul (1815, Belg.)
Sussman, B. J. Crooked Cross (WWII, Ger.)
Swift, B. Mission Code: Snow Queen (1943, Arctic)
Symons, J. Detling Murders (1800s, Eng.)
Taylor, F. Walking Shadows (WWII)
Terman, D. Shell Game (1962, Cuba)
Thomas, C. Belladonna (1880, Eng.)
    Mad Hatter Summer (1800s, Eng.)
Thomas, D. Captain Wunder (1907)
Thompson, J. Pop. 1280 (late 1800s, South)
Tickell, J. Villa Mimosa (WWII, Fr.)
Tokson, E. Harem Games (1908, Istan.)
    When Dragons Dance (1900, Macao)
Tone, T. Full Cry (1907, Va.)
    Lady on the Line (1899, U.S.)
Tourney, L. both titles (ca.1600, Eng.)
Traver, R. Laughing Whitefish (1800s, Mich.)
Travis, T., Jr. Lamia (1968, Chi.)

Tremaine, J. Maggie (ca.1900, Glasgow)
Trevanian. Summer of Katya (1914, Fr.)
Trevor, E. Damocles Sword (ca.1941, Ger.)
Trow, M. J. Adventures of Inspector Lestrade (1891, Eng.)
Tunstall, B. Shiny Night (1800s, Eng.)
Tyler, W. T. Rogue's March (ca.1970, Belg. Congo)
Unsworth, B. Rage of the Vulture (1908, Istan.)
Van Rjndt, P. Last Message to Berlin (1940)
Vaughan, S. Royal Game (Eng.)
Vernon, K. R. Phantom of Fonthill Park (1847, Eng.)
Von Hoffman, N. Organized Crimes (1929, Chi.)
Wacht, L. Mission to Warsaw (WWII, Warsaw)
Wagner, S. Cove in Darkness (ca.1700, Eng.)
Walker, T. Mission Accomplished (1950)
Walsh, R. Mycroft Memoranda (1888, Eng.)
Watson, P. Nazi's Wife (WWII, Ger.)
Webb, A. both titles (WWII, Fr.)
Weismiller, E. Serpent Sleeping (WWII, Fr.)
West, P. E. Madeleine (1857, Glasgow)
Wetherell, J. Dark Wing (1871, Wash.)
White, A. all six titles (WWII)
White, S. Operation Raven (1940, Eng.)
White, S. E. Gray Dawn (1850s, S.F.)
Whiteson, L. White Snake (1973, Rhod.)
Whittemore, E. Nile Shadows (1942, Egypt)
Williams, Bob. Ozark Flats (1894, Mpls.)
Williams, G. M. Pomeroy (1903, Eng.)
Willoughby, L. D. Frontier Detective (1881, Colo.)
Winslow, P. G. Windsor Plot (WWII)
Winward, W. Ball Bearing Run (1943, Ger.)
  Canaris Fragments (1945, Ger.)
Wise, D. Spectrum (1965)
Wiseman, T. Savage Day (1945, N. Mex.)
York, T. Trapper (1931, Can.)
Yurick, S. Richard A (1962)

PEKING (See also: China; Shanghai; Formosa; Hong Kong; Far East; Mongolia)
Clark, E. Chinese Burn
Jones, Margaret. Confucius Enigma
Larany, D. Big Red Sun

PENNSYLVANIA (Pa. See also: Philadelphia; Pittsburgh)
Aswad, B. Family Passions
Chacko, D. Brick Alley
Constantine, K. C. all titles
Duncan, R. L. In the Blood
John, C. Witching
Kelley, P. A. Sleightly Murder
McCormick, C. Resume for Murder
Michaels, B. Someone in the House
Millard, J. Mansion of Evil
Murphy, W. B. Lucifer's Weekend
O'Donnell, L. Cop Without a Shield
Pendleton, D. Flesh Wounds
Winslow, J. Griffin Towers

PERSIA. See: Iran.

PERU (See also: South America)
Helfgott, D. Buried
Leamer, L. Assignment
Murphy, W. B. Master's Challenge
Webb, V. Little Lady Killing

PHILADELPHIA (Phil. See also: Pennsylvania; Pittsburgh)
Berckman, E. Blind Villain
Dexter, P. God's Pocket
Fuller, C. Zooman and the Sign
Kelly, T. J. Terror by Gaslight
Liebman, R. Grand Jury
Scarberry, A. S. Dimpled Racketeer
Shubin, S. Holy Secrets
Solmssen, A. R. G. Rittenhouse Square
Whitten, L. Killing Pace

PHILIPPINES (Philip. See also: Manila; Far East)
Fox, G. Amok
McCurtin, P. Moro

PHOENIX (See also: Arizona; Tucson; Southwest)
Altman, T. True Bride
Kelland, C. B. Counterfeit Gentleman

PITTSBURGH (Pitt. See also: Pennsylvania; Philadelphia)
Gat, N. Nevsky's Return

POLAND (Pol. See also: Warsaw)
Hagar, J. Shadow of the Eagle
Irving, C. Angel of Zin
Simpson, J. Fine and Private Place

PORTLAND (See also: Oregon; Northwest)
Larson, C. Portland Murders
Margolin, P. M. Last Innocent Man

PORTUGAL (Port. See also: Lisbon; Madeira)
Bosak, S. Gammon
Boyle, T. Cold Stove League
Canning, V. Birdcage
MacKenzie, D. Raven's Longest Night
Teixeira, B. Flowers for the Executioner

PORTUGUESE EAST AFRICA. See: Mozambique.

PORTUGUESE WEST AFRICA. See: Angola.

PRAGUE (See also: Czechoslovakia)
MacLeod, R. Problem in Prague

PUERTO RICO (P. Rico. See also: San Juan; West Indies; Caribbean)
Carter, Nick. San Juan Inferno
Strother, E. W. Island of Terror

RAILWAY. See: Train.

RELIGIOUS SETTINGS. See: Church.

RENO (See also: Nevada; Las Vegas; West)
Arre, H. Corpse by the River
Denning, M. Din of Inequity
Roderus, F. Turn-Out Man

RHODE ISLAND (R.I. See also: New England)
Cable, M. Avery's Knot
Rosen, R. D. Strike Three You're Dead
Sapir, R. Spies

RHODESIA (Rhod. See also: Africa)
Whiteson, L. White Snake

RICHMOND (See also: Virginia; South)
(no additional entries)

RIO DE JANEIRO (Rio de J. See also: Brazil; South America)
Carter, Nick. Assignment: Rio
Colby, E. Bossa Nova Bed
Derrick, L. Rampage in Rio
Stirling, E. K. Unsuspected Conduct

ROCHESTER (Roch. See also: New York; Long Island; New York City)
(no additional entries)

ROMANIA. See: Rumania.

ROME (See also: Italy; Florence; Milan; Naples; Sardinia; Sicily; Venice)
Banks, O. Caravaggio Obsession
Gash, Jonathan. Vatican Rip
Geddes, P. State of Corruption
Hambly, B. Quirinal Hill Affair
Levey, M. Affair on the Appian Way
Longstreet, S. Ambassador
Massie, A. Death of Men
Mewshaw, M. Year of the Gun
Meyer, K. Bishop's Room
Murphy, W. F. Roman Enigma
Norwood, F. Pope Must Die
Paretti, S. Maria Canossa
Pearson, J. Kindness of Dr. Avicenna
Rejaunier, J. Affair in Rome
Revere, J. D. Vatican Kill
Rutherford, D. Stop at Nothing

Scotti, R. A. both titles
Stainton, A. Sweet Rome
Timperley, R. Spell of the Hanged Man

RUMANIA (Rum. See also: Bucharest; Balkans)
Rosenberger, J. Roumanian Question
Sharkey, J. Creature Creeps
Williams, Eric. Dragoman Pass

RUSSIA (Russ. See also: Moscow; Mongolia)
Ahern, J. Captain Blood
  Origin of a Vendetta
Aksyonov, V. Island of Crimea
Albeury, T. Consequence of Fear
  Moscow Quadrille
Bannerman, D. Pipeline from Hell
Buck, P. Operation Icicle
Burgess, A. Honey for the Bears
Chernenok, M. Losing Bet
Cleary, J. Golden Sabre
Evans, J. Midas Men
Hall, Adam. Northlight
Hild, J. Gulag War
Hoyt, R. Head of State
James, D. Fall of the Russian Empire
Kilian, M. Blood of the Czars
Konsalik, H. G. Strike Force Ten
Korotyukov, A. It's Hard to Be a Russian Spy
Kyle, D. King's Commissar
Lambert, D. Man Who Was Saturday
Lipatov, V. Village Detective
McEnery, P. Black Inheritance
McKinney, R. L. Kamchatka Incident
Niesewand, P. Fallback
Olcott, A. May Day in Magadan
Pendleton, D. Ice Cold Kill
  Terminal Velocity
Seymour, G. Archangel
Streib, D. Counter Force
Thomas, C. Firefox Down
Tine, R. Broken Eagle
Vance, C. G. Grave for a Russian
Williams, A. Beria Papers
Zimmerman, R. D. Cross and the Sickle

SAIGON (See also: Viet Nam; Hanoi; Far East)
Cain, J. three titles

ST. LOUIS (See also: Missouri; Kansas City; Midwest)
Krell, E. D. Killer Cops
Lutz, J. Nightlines
Meskil, P. Sin Pit
Pendleton, D. Missouri Deathwatch

SALT LAKE CITY (See also: Utah; West)
Cook, T. H. Tabernacle
Stewart, G. Tenth Virgin

SAN ANTONIO (See also: Texas; Dallas; Houston; Southwest)
(no additional entries)

SAN DIEGO (See also: California; Los Angeles; San Francisco; West)
Carney, W. Rose Exterminator
Higgs, E. C. Happy Man
Lange, J. Binary
Mathews, W. C. King Cobra
Pendleton, D. Resurrection Day
Pronzini, B. Double
Purtill, R. Murdercon

SAN FRANCISCO (S.F. See also: California; Los Angeles; San Diego; West)
Barish, S. Reasonable Doubt
Beal, M. F. Angel Dance
Biederman, M. Makeover
Brooks, A. One Enchanted Summer
Bucci, M. Court of the Stone Children
Byrd, M. California Thriller
  Finders Weepers
Chang, L. Year of the Tiger
Combs, D. Sleepwalker
Corris, P. Big Drop
  Heroin Annie
Curzon, D. From Violent Men
De Marco, G. Frisco Blues
Denning, M. Shades of Gray
Dunlap, S. As a Favor
  Not Exactly a Brahmin
Fawcette, S. Time Runs Out at the Democratic Convention
Gilmer, J. L. Hell Is Forever
Hammond, M. A. Land of Gold
Hartman, D. four titles

Hellerstein, H. Wired
Kuttner, P. Absolute Proof
Lipman, C. House of Evil
Lynch, J. Bragg's Hunch
MacAvoy, R. A. Tea with the Black Dragon
Mandell, M. Butcher Block
Miner, V. Murder in the English Department
Minton, P. Thunder over the Reefs
Muller, M. five titles
Murphy, W. B. Pigs Get Fat
Nisbet, J. Gourmet
O'Marie, C. A. Novena for Murder
Pendleton, D. Doomsday Disciples
Potter, J. A. If I Should Die Before I Wake
Pronzini, B. seven titles
Rogers, G. Scandal in Eden
Rogers, L. Crime Has No Friends
Saralegui, J. Last Rites
Shankman, S. Impersonal Attractions
Siler, J. Triangles of Fire
Singer, S. Samson's Deal
Smith, Julie. all three titles
Streib, D. Karate Killers
Stuart, A. Catspaw
Taylor, E. A. Cable Car Murder
Thompson, G. Lupe
Thoreau, D. Dynasty of Power
Trinian, J. Scratch a Thief
Vance, J. House on Lily Street
Walker, W. Two Dude Defense
Wallace, M. Case of Loyalties
Warner, R. Murder on the Air
Webb, V. Little Lady Killing
White, S. E. Gray Dawn
Wilcox, C. Stalking Horse
    Victims
Wilson, G. Welcome to the Feast

SAN JUAN (See also: Puerto Rico; West Indies; Caribbean)
(no additional entries)

SANTE FE (See also: New Mexico; Albuquerque; Southwest)
(no additional entries)

SARDINIA (Sard. See also: Italy; Florence; Milan; Naples; Rome; Sicily; Venice)
(no additional entries)

SAUDI ARABIA (Saud. Arab. See also: Middle East)
Peel, K. J. Twelfth Night of Ramadan

SCANDINAVIA (Scand. See also: individual countries)
Forbes, C. Cover Story

SCHOOL. See: Academia.

SCOTLAND (Scot. See also: Edinburgh; Glasgow; Hebrides)
Beaton, M. C. Death of a Gossip
Collee, J. Kingsley's Touch
Goldie, B. Piper of Arristoun
Goodchild, G. Dear Old Gentleman
Graham, A. Follow the Little Pictures!
Grayson, R. Whisky Murders
Hammond, G. six titles
Hart-Davis, D. Fire Falcon
Hunter, A. Gabrielle's Way
Knox, B. Bloodtide
    Wavecrest
Law, J. Death Under Par
Linklater, E. House of Gair
Meek, M. R. D. Split Second
Ogilvie, E. Silent Ones
Scott, G. Water Horse
Scott, M. D. J. Drumbuie House
Sinclair, O. Hearts by the Tower
Trocchi, A. Young Adam
Walker, D. Storm and the Silence
Wills, C. Defeat of a Detective

SEA. See: Ship.

SEATTLE (See also: Washington; Northwest)
Elmblad, M. Little Company
Emerson, E. W. both titles
Hoyt, R. Fish Story
    30 for a Harry
Jance, J. A. Until Proven Guilty
McQuinn, D. E. Shadow of Lies
Warden, M. Wasps in the Woodpile
Wilson, B. Murder in the Collective

SENEGAL (Sen. See also: Africa, West)
(no additional entries)

SHANGHAI (See also: China; Peking; Formosa; Hong Kong; Far East; Mongolia)
Gardner, J. Flamingo
Kenrick, T. Faraday's Flowers

SHIP
Babson, M. Cruise of a Deathtime
Beck, K. K. Death in a Deck Chair
Bell, Josephine. Fennister Affair
Blake, C. Deadly Legacy
Block, T. H. Forced Landing
Boothby, G. Bid for Fortune
Bream, F. Corpse on the Cruise
Cannon, J. Web of Terror
Clancy, T. Hunt for Red October
Collins, D. Vulnerable
Connolly, V. Five Ports to Danger
Cussler, C. Pacific Vortex
Deverell, W. High Crimes
Eberhart, M. G. Patient in Cabin C
Edmonds, H. Death Ship
Finer, A. Deepwater
Granger, B. Queen's Crossing
Gregg, M. Dhow Patrol
Harris, J. Road to the Coast
Hughes, T. J. Queen's Mate
Innes, H. Black Tide
Lovesey, P. False Inspector Dew
Lowden, D. Bandersnatch
MacLean, A. San Andreas
Norris, F. Shanghaied
O'Brine, M. Corpse to Cairo
Pattinson, J. Precious Cargo
Pendleton, D. Crude Kill
Price, J.-A. Doomsday Ship
Rosenberger, J. Zembya Expedition
Ross, C. Dancing Years
Rostand, R. Cross Currents
Russell, W. C. Tale of Two Tunnels
Savage, E. Two If by Sea
Sherlock, J. Amindra Gamble
Stephens, E. Submariner
Tack, A. Death Takes a Dive
Thurman, S. Night After Night
Townend, W. Night's Black Agent
Trew, A. Running Wild
Villars, E. Normandie Affair
Wilson, G. Atlantic Scramble
    Sea of Savages
Wilson, J. R. Round Voyage

SIAM. See: Thailand.

SICILY (Sic. See also: Italy; Florence; Milan; Naples; Rome; Sardinia; Venice)
Sciascia, L. Mafia Vendetta

SIERRA LEONE (See also: Africa, West)
Harris, J. Funny Place to Hold a War

SINGAPORE (Sing. See also: Far East)
MacBeth, G. Kind of Treason
Pereira, M. Pigeon's Blood

SOLOMON ISLANDS (Sol. Is. See also: Australia; South Pacific)
(no additional entries)

SOUTH (See also: the 14 individual states)
Boggs, M. Scissors, Paper, Stone
Clemeau, C. Ariadne Clue
Deal, B. Long Way to Go
Gaither, F. O. Double Muscadine
Gallo, D. Sin in the South
Garland, N. Crime of Innocence
Garrison, C. Paragon Man
Grubb, D. Shadow of My Brother
Harrington, J. Family Reunion
Harris, C. Secret Rage
Kelly, T. J. Murder in the Magnolias
Lermina, J. Chase
Logue, J. Replay: Murder
McCorkle, J. July 7th
Poyer, D. C. Shiloh Project
Robertson, L. Back County Crimes
Shaara, M. Herald
Shivers, L. Here to Get My Baby Out of Jail
Thompson, J. Pop. 1280
Vandergriff, A. Sisters of Sorrow
Vincent, R. Blacklash
Winston, D. Flight of a Fallen Angel

SOUTH AFRICA (S. Afr. See also: Cape Town; Johannesburg; Transvaal)
Crowder, K. Iron Web
Davis, B. Conspiracy of Eagles
Drummond, J. I Saw Him Die
Ebersohn, W. Divide the Night
Eskapa, S. Blood Fugue
Galgut, D. Sinless Season
Hayes, R. Satan Stone
Hild, J. Some Chose Hell
Hume, F. Traitor in London
Jacobson, D. Dance of the Sun
Jason, S. Man from White Hat
McClure, J. Artful Egg
Scholefield, A. Sea Cave
Webster, E. C. Pot Holes
Webster, P. Kruger's Gold

SOUTH AMERICA (S. Am. See also: individual countries)
Carter, A. Infernal Desire Machines of Doctor Hoffman
Carter, Nick. Death Hand Play
Grae, C. Winged Dancer
Hamilton, D. Annihilators
Jameson, F. Green Fire
Kaplan, A. Hour of the Assassins
Messmann, J. Ransom!
Neebel, R. Immediate Action
Szulc, T. Diplomatic Immunity
Williams, A. Snake Water

SOUTH CAROLINA (S.C. See also: Charleston; South)
Long, L. B. Witch Tree

SOUTH DAKOTA (S. Dak. See also: Midwest)
Adams, H. Naked Liar
    Paint the Town Red
Jordan, C. Carol in the Dark

SOUTH PACIFIC (S. Pac. See also: individual islands or countries)
Bannerman, D. Call of Honor
Carter, Nick. Death Island
Kinney, J. Locket for Tawi
McLaren, J. Stories of Fear
Pugh, E. Rogues' Paradise
Rivere, A. Wantons of Betrayal
Safroni-Middleton, A. No Extradition
Silliphant, S. Steel Tiger
Streib, D. Cargo Gods
Trevor, E. Shoot

SOUTH WEST AFRICA (S. W. Africa)
(no additional entries)

SOUTHWEST (S.W. See also: 4 individual states)
Keene, D. My Flesh Is Sweet
Kingsbury, C. L. Mystery of the Carroll Ranch
Leland, C. T. Mean Time
Quammen, D. Zolta Configuration
Spicer, B. Adversary
Spike, P. Last Rites
Stephens, Reed. Man Who Risked His Life
Thomas, R. Briarpatch

SOVIET UNION. See: Russia.

SPAIN (Sp. See also: Madrid; Canary Islands; Majorca)
Allen, S. No Marks for Trying
Benson, E. P. Bulls of Ronda
Davidson, H. C. Queen of the Black Hand
Gosling, P. Woman in Red
Halidom, M. Y. Son of Desolation
Hunter, S. Spanish Gambit
Lamb, M. Last Nazi
Lovell, M. Apple Spy in the Sky
MacLeod, R. Mayday from Malaga
Mason, A. E. W. Summons
Montalban, M. V. Murder in the Central Committee
Serafin, D. Body in Cadiz Bay
Yeldham, P. But She Won't Lie Down

SRI LANKA. See: Ceylon.

STOCKHOLM (Stock. See also: Sweden; Scandinavia)
(no additional entries)

SUDAN (See also: Africa)
(no additional entries)

Settings Index

SUMATRA (Sum. See also: Indonesia; Djakarta; Bali; Borneo; Java; New Guinea)
(no additional entries)

SURINAM (Suri. See also: South America)
(no additional entries)

SWEDEN (Swed. See also: Stockholm: Scandinavia)
Covington, J. Operative
Peters, E. Silhouette in Scarlet

SWITZERLAND (Switz. See also: Geneva; Zurich)
Baker, P. Minnie Swan
Barstow, P. Glacier Run
Burkholz, H. Mulligan's Seed
Denning, M. Swiss Abduction
Duerrenmatt, F. Dangerous Game
Erdman, P. E. Last Days of America
Forbes, C. Terminal
Gaskin, C. File on Devlin
Gialanella, V. Frankenstein
Kelaart, P. Midas
Kelly, T. J. Frankenstein
Kelso, J. Ghost Skier
Ross, P. Good Death
Shaw, L. Innocent Deception
Smith, G. N. Satan_s Snowdrop
Stein, A. M. Garbage Collector

SYDNEY (Syd. See also: Australia; Melbourne; Solomon Islands; Tasmania)
Anderson, Jessica. Ordinary Lunacy
Cleary, J. three titles
Corris, P. five titles
Jefferis, B. Undercurrent
Neville, M. Drop Dead
  Murder and Gardenias
Pratt, A. Great "Push" Experiment
Stivens, D. Wide Arch

SYRIA (Syr. See also: Damascus; Middle East)
Barton, D. R. Once in Aleppa
Shagan, S. Discovery

TAHITI (See also: South Pacific)
McCormick, C. Club Paradis Murders

TAIWAN. See: Formosa.

TAMPA (See also: Florida; Jacksonville; Miami; South)
(no additional entries)

TANGANYIKA (Tang. See also: Tanzania; Africa; Zanzibar)
(no additional entries)

TANGIER (See also: Morocco; Casablanca; Africa, North)
O'Brine, M. Deadly Interlude

TANZANIA (Tanz. See also: Tanganyika; Zanzibar; Africa)
(no additional entries)

TASMANIA (Tas. See also: Australia; Sydney; Melbourne; Solomon Islands)
Bridges, R. Negrohead
Hay, W. Escape of the Notorious Sir William Heans
Koch, C. J. Boys in the Island

TEHERAN (See also: Iran; Iraq; Middle East)
Pendleton, D. Teheran Wipeout

TEL AVIV (See also: Israel; Jerusalem; Middle East)
Litvinoff, E. Falls the Shadow

TENNESSEE (Tenn. See also: Memphis; Nashville; South)
Borgeau, A. Elvis Murders
  Murder at the Cheatin' Heart Motel
Constiner, M. Hearse of a Different Color

McGivern, W. P. Summitt

TEXAS (Tex. See also: Dallas; Houston; San Antonio; Southwest)
Bay, A. Coyote Cried Twice
Bird, S. M. Do Evil Cheerfully
Borthwick, J. S. Case of the Hook-Billed Kites
Brandon, J. Deadbolt
Dewlin, A. Twilight of Honor
Douglas, B. Challenge at Castle Gap
Gardner, J. For Special Services
Harrington, W. Partners
Jordan, L. Hidden Fires
Kellerman, D. both titles
Kelton, E. Stand Proud
Kingery, D. Paula
Kriz, J. Karsten's Flats
Leach, C. Blood Games
McCollom, R. And Then They Die
McDonald, G. Buck Passes Flynn
Martin, L. Too Sane a Murder
Mathis, E. From a High Place
Meredith, D. R. both titles
Potter, J. A. Needle
Reid, J. Deer in Water
Stivers, D. Texas Showdown
Thompson, T. Celebrity
Webb, M. G. both titles

THAILAND (Thai. See also: Bangkok; Far East)
Decker, J. Deadly Snow
Duncan, W. R. Queen's Messenger
Emmett, R. Ride the Tiger
Pendleton, D. Tiger War

THEATRE
Brett, S. Murder in the Title
  Murder Unprompted
Dentinger, J. First Hit of the Season
  Murder on Cue
Elder, M. Phantom in the Wings
Gray, D. No Quarter for a Star
Hanna, D. Opera House Murders
Long, A. M. Lady Saw Red
Marsh, N. Light Thickens
Miller, J. Save the Last Dance for Me
Morice, A. Sleep of Death
Paul, B. Cadenza for Caruso
  Prima Donna at Large
Reeves, J. Murder with Muskets
Resnicow, H. Gold Deadline
Smith, K. N. Catching Fire
Suyker, B. Death Scene

TIBET (Tib.)
Cotler, G. Stranger Called the Blues
Langley, B. East of Everest
Savarin, J. Gunship

TOKYO (See also: Japan; Far East)
Lustbader, E. V. Miko
Randall, D. Dragon Lover
Togawa, M. both titles

TORONTO (See also: Canada; Montreal; Ottawa; Vancouver; Winnipeg)
Cushing, E. L. Unexpected Corpse
Jones, F. Master and Maid
Reeves, J. both titles
Wood, T. Live Bait
Wright, E. Night the Gods Smiled
  Smoke Detector

TRAIN
Hyde, C. Maxwell's Train
Karlin, W. Crossover
Lambert, D. Golden Express
Stockbridge, G. Corpse Cargo
Yarborough, C. Murder on the Long Straight

TRANSVAAL (Trans. See also: South Africa; Cape Town; Johannesburg)
(no additional entries)

TRINIDAD (Trin. See also: West Indies; Caribbean)
(no additional entries)

TUCSON (See also: Arizona; Phoenix; Southwest)
Garfield, B. Deep Cover

TUNISIA (Tun. See also: Africa, North)
Operator 1384. Catacombs of Death

TURKEY (Turk. See also: Istanbul; Middle East; Balkans)
Daniel, D. Ark
Kemal, Y. Sea-Crossed Fisherman
Pendleton, D. Double Crossfire
Rosenberger, J. Enigma Project
Stevenson, A. Turkish Rondo
West, R. W. Destroyer

UGANDA (See also: Africa)
Westlake, D. E. Kahawa

UNITED STATES (U.S. Here is a selection of titles by non-U.S. authors which use non-specific U.S. settings. See also: each of the 50 states; Washington D.C.; Puerto Rico; Virgin Islands)
Allbeury, T. Pay Any Price
  Twentieth Day of January
Bogar, J. Dinah for Danger
Byrom, J. Thou Shouldst Be Living

UNIVERSITY. See: Academia.

URUGUAY (Urug. See also: South America)
De Villiers, G. Angel of Vengeance

U.S.S.R. See: Russia.

UTAH (See also: Salt Lake City; West)
Derrick, L. Aryan Onslaught
Jones, C. Prophet Motive
Keller, K. Final Landscapes

VANCOUVER (Van. See also: Canada; Montreal; Ottawa; Toronto; Winnipeg)
Moore, C. His Lordship's Arsenal
Shannon, Doris. Little Girls Lost
Slade, M. Headhunter

VENEZUELA (Venez. See also: Caracas; South America)
Ekert-Rotholz, A. Checkpoint Orinoco
Paulsen, G. Death Specialists
Williams, L. Tropical Murder

VENICE (See also: Italy; Florence; Milan; Naples; Rome; Sardinia; Sicily)
Boothby, G. Farewell, Nicola
Caudwell, S. Thus Was Adonis Murdered
Gash, Jonathan. Gondola Scam
Healey, B. Last Ferry from the Lido
Holme, T. all three titles
Inchbald, P. three titles
Maybury, A. Ride a White Dolphin
Sager, G. Formula
Symons, J. Criminal Comedy of the Contented Couple
Unsworth, B. Stone Virgin

VERMONT (Vt. See also: New England)
Babe, T. Billy Irish
Carmichael, F. Exit the Body
  Exit Who?
Hayes, J. Ways of Darkness
Hughes, R. Unholy Communion
Judd, M. Husband of the Corpse
Levin, I. Dr. Cook's Garden
Loomis, P. Pure As the Driven Snow
Resnicow, H. Seventh Crossword
Smith, A. Someone Else's Grave
Wheeler, H. C. We Have Always Lived in the Castle

VIENNA (See also: Austria)
Crisp, W. Spytrap
Eden, M. Gilt-Edged Traitor
Hylton, S. Crimson Falcon
Land, Jane. These Tiger's Hearts
Payne, L. Vienna Blood
Rainey, R. Hit Parade
Rostov, M. Careless Feast
Slote, A. Lazarus in Vienna
Streib, D. Seeds of Evil

VIET NAM (See also: Hanoi; Saigon; Far East)

188 / Virgin Islands

Cain, J. Dinky-Dau Death
Cross, E. B. Ninth Dragon
Derrick, L. Jungle Blitz
Helm, E. all four titles
Lassiter, A. Triangle
McCray, M. Deadly Reunion
McCurtin, P. Golden Triangle
Pendleton, D. Dirty War
    Return to Vietnam
Sadler, B. Cry Havoc

    VIRGIN ISLANDS (Vir. Is.)
(no additional entries)

    VIRGINIA (Va. See also: Richmond; South)
Andrews, V. C. Seeds of Yesterday
Carr, J. Murder on the Appalachian Trail
Flannagan, R. Country Court
Hoffman, W. Godfires
Hornig, D. both titles
Kimbrough, K. Patricia, the Beautiful
McCrumb, S. Lovely in Her Bones
Michaels, B. Be Buried in the Rain
Pendleton, D. Day of Mourning
Seward, W. W. Skirts of the Dead Night
Tone, T. Full Cry

    WALES
Christie, A. Unexpected Guest
Craig, D. Double Take
Finley, G. Kiss a Stranger
Jones, Mervyn. Two Women and Their Man
MacLeod, C. Curse of the Giant Hogweed
Moffat, G. Die Like a Dog
Ormerod, R. Seeing Red
Payne, L. Take the Money and Run
Secombe, H. Welsh Fargo
Walton, W. Sins of the Fathers
Warner, M. Death in Time

    WARSAW (See also: Poland)
Swift, B. Mission Code: Springboard
Wacht, L. Mission to Warsaw

    WASHINGTON D.C. (Wash. D.C.)
Adler, W. American Quartet
    American Sextet
Anthony, E. Avenue of the Dead
Banks, C. Girls on the Row
Baxter, T. Hailstone
Benford, T. B. Hitler's Daughter
Blatty, W. P. Legion
Clark, M. H. Stillwatch
Cohen, W. S. Double Man
Decker, J. Death's Little Sister
Denker, H. Place for the Mighty
    Warfield Syndrome
Dominic, R. B. Unexpected Developments
Drury, A. Decision
Evans, J. P. Vanishing Vector
Feiffer, J. White House Murder Case
Fox, V. J. Pentagon Case
Garfield, B. Line of Succession
Grady, J. Hard Bargains
    Runner in the Street
Guild, N. President's Men
Heffernan, W. Caging of the Raven
Henley, W. Roman Solution
Horton, F. W., Jr. Technocrats
Hudson, C. Insider Out
Hyman, T. Russian Woman
Kennedy, A. Debt of Honor
Knebel, F. Vanished
Lambert, D. Trance
Lee, S. Dunn's Conundrum
Martin, M. Ravens of Rockhurst
Munder, L. Therapy for Murder
O'Connor, B. One-Shot War
Osborn, D. Love and Treason
Pearson, W. Chessplayer
Pendleton, D. Dead Man Running
Peterson, J. Balance of Power
Prager, J. S. Newman Factor
Raphael, R. President Must Die
Ravin, N. Seven North
Roosevelt, E. Murder and the First Lady
Schutz, B. M. All the Old Bargains
Serling, R. Air Force One Is Haunted
Sheldon, W. J. Rites of Murder
Shobin, D. Seeding
Stark, R. Mourner
Swaybill, R. E. Final Witness
Thomas, R. If You Can't Be Good
    Yellow-Dog Contract
Toomay, P. On Any Given Sunday
Truman, M. all five titles
Tyler, W. T. Shadow Cabinet
Weisman, J. Watchdogs
Werner, P. If Truth Be Known
Winston, D. Long and Living Shadow
    Mira
Wolfson, M. In the Long Run We Are All Dead

    WASHINGTON state (Wash. See also: Seattle; Northwest)
Ball, J. Chief Tallon and the S.O.R.
Campbell, P. Lush Valley
Elkins, A. J. Dark Place
Higman, D. Pranks
Rife, E. A. Broken Promise
Roberts, W. D. Sniper
Rule, A. Possession
Wetherell, J. Dark Wing

    WEST (See also: individual states)
Blair, C. Crystal Destiny
Henderson, H. H. Queen of Spades
Jackson, D. Cut of the Ax
Troy, J. Web of Murder

    WEST INDIES (W.I. See also: individual countries; Caribbean)
Bennett, D. Carrion Crows
Lecomber, B. Dead Weight
    Turn Killer
Mathewson, W. Immediate Release
Sager, G. Run, Sheep, Run
Waugh, A. Island in the Sun
Zachary, H. Top Level Death

    WEST VIRGINIA (W. Va. See also: Charleston; South)
Nicole, M. Thick As Thieves
Pedneau, D. Presumption of Innocence
Salem, R. New Blood

    WINNIPEG (See also: Canada; Montreal; Ottawa; Toronto; Vancouver)
(no additional entries)

    WISCONSIN (Wis. See also: Madison; Milwaukee; Midwest)
Bloomfield, R. Stranger in Town
Edgley, L. False Face
Loken, C. Boy Next Door
Machin, M. L. Outrageous Fortune
Riggs, J. R. both titles
Rogers, S. Don't Look Behind You!
Tadrack, M. Mistress of Evil

    WYOMING (Wyo. See also: West)
Roderus, F. Oil Rig
Ryan, C. Black Gravity
Szanto, G. Not Working

    YEMEN (Yem. See also: Middle East)
Rosenberger, J. Night of the Peacock

    YUGOSLAVIA (Yugos. See also: Belgrade; Balkans; Macedonia)
Cook, W. Taxi to Dubrovnik
Durrell, L. White Eagles over Serbia
Karlin, W. Crossover
MacLean, A. Partisans

    ZAIRE. See: Belgian Congo.

    ZAMBIA (See also: Africa)
(no additional entries)

    ZANZIBAR (Zanz. See also: Tanzania; Tanganyika; Africa)
(no additional entries)

    ZIMBABWE. See: Rhodesia.

    ZURICH (See also: Switzerland; Geneva)
(no additional entries)

Series Index

A-Team; C. Heath,
    R. Renauld
Abbot, Sgt. Bill; J. Penn
*Abbott, Pat and Jean; F. Crane
Able Team; D. Stivers
Adams, Charlie; R. Boyer
Alba; Delacorta
*Allyn, Supt. Roderick; N. Marsh
*Alvarez, Insp.; R. Jeffries
American Avenger; R. Emmett
Amiss, Robert; R. D. Edwards
Anders, Jonathan; C. Nicole
Anderson, Lou (Shifty); W. Murray
Angel Eyes; W. B. Longley
Antigua Players; J. Gollin
*Appleby, John; M. Innes
*Aragon, Tom; M. Millar
Argand, Jan; J. Rathbone
*Aristo Autos; J. Leasor
*Ark, Simon; E. D. Hoch
Armiston, Oliver; F. I. Anderson
Armitage, Stephen; H. McLeave
*Arrow, Sgt. Steve; L. Mantell
*Asch, Jacob; A. Lyons
Assassin, The; J. D. Revere
*Attwell, Nick; M. Underwood
*Audley, Dr. David; A. Price
Avenger, American; R. Emmett
Axbrewder, Mick; R. Stephens
Baldwin, T. T.; S. OCork
*Baley, Elijah; I. Asimov
*Balzac, Mario; K. C. Constantine
*Bannion, Burns; E. Norman
Barnaby, Insp.; H. Shaw
*Barnes, John; R. Ottolengui
Barrabas, Nile; J. Hild
Barradine, Lord; E. Jepson
*Bascombe, Carver; K. Davis
Basnet, Andrew; E. Ferrars
Bates, Norman; R. Bloch
*Battle, Supt.; A. Christie
Baum, Alfred; D. Kartun
Bear, Win; L. N. Smith
*Beaumont, Insp. Henry; M. E. Atkins
Bellman; W. L. DeAndrea
Benham, John; M. Home
*Bennett, Fred; E. Lewis
Bennett, Reid; T. Wood
Berets, Black; M. McCray
Bergerac; Michael Hardwick,
    A. Saville
Bernal, Insp. Luis; D. Serafin
Binton, Margaret; R. Barth
*Birge, Sam; W. Krasner
*Birkett, Insp. Sam; L. Payne
Birney, Joe; J. Livingston
Birnkov, Anton; M. Chernenok
Black Berets; M. McCray
Black Eagles; J. Lansing
Black, Thomas; E. W. Emerson
*Black Widowers; I. Asimov
*Blair, Major Peter; J. R. L. Anderson
*Blaise, Modesty; P. O'Donnell
*Blake, Sexton; J. Andrews,
    J. G. Brandon,
    G. Chester
Blancanales, Pol; D. Stivers
Blayde, Supt.; J. Wainwright
*Bliss, Vicki; Elizabeth Peters
*Blixen, Nils-Frederik; C. Larson
*Bodyguard, The; R. Reinsmith
Boggs, Sam; M. Washburn
*Bognor, Simon; T. Heald
*Bolan, Mack; D. Pendleton
Boles, Orson; E. Chaze
*Bond, James; J. Gardner
Bonner; R. Harding
*Boone, Jefferson; J. Messmann
*Bordelon, Johnny; G. Organ
Borg, Steven; C. A. Posey
Borges, Insp.; J. Bonett
Borgneff, Vasily; H. Burkholz
Bounty Hunter; W. Boyles
Boxer Unit; N. Cort
*Boyd, Danny; C. Brown
Bradford, Hank; M. Warden
*Bradley, Mrs. Adela Beatrice Lestrange;
    G. Mitchell
Bradshaw, Charlie; S. Dobyns
Bragg, Sgt. Joseph; R. Harrison
Bragg, Peter; J. Lynch
Brain, Colonel; H. Cecil
Brand, Hilary; H. Brand
*Brandstetter, Dave; J. Hansen
Brent, Mike; G. Fennell
Brock, Supt. "Badger"; J. Bingham
Brogan, Jerry; J. L. Breen
*Brunt, Insp. Thomas; J. B. Hilton
Budd, Lanny; U. Sinclair
*Burford, Archie; V. MacClure
Burlane, James; R. Hoyt
Burroughs, Julian; W. B. Murphy
*Butcher, The; S. Jason
Butler; P. Kirk
CAT; S. Andrews
*Cadfael; Ellis Peters
Cain; S. A. Key
Cain, Jenny; N. Picard

Caine, Nick; D. Zochert
Calder, Keith; G. Hammond
*Callaghan, Slim; P. Cheyney
*Callahan, Brock; W. C. Gault
Callahan, Dirty Harry; D. Hartman,
    J. Stinson
*Camellion, Richard; J. Rosenberger
Cameron, Sgt./Corp.; R. Connor
*Capricorn, Supt. Merlin; P. G. Winslow
Carmichael, Agnes; Anthea Cohen
Carnaby-King, Det. Sgt.; P. N. Walker
*Carrick, Webb; B. Knox
Carter, Insp Neil; E. Dewhurst
*Carter, Nick; Nick Carter
Caruso, Enrico; B. Paul
Carvalho, Pepe; M. V. Montalban
Case, Charlie; J. Spencer
Casey, Dr. Peter; R. Mead
Cassidy, Horatio; J. Crosby
*Castang, Henri; N. Freeling
*Chambrun, Pierre; H. Pentecost
*Chan, Charlie; M. Avallone
*Chan, David; C. Leader
Chaney, Ace; C. Garrison
*Charles, Mrs. Edwina; M. Warner
*Charleston, Sheriff Chick; A. B.
    Guthrie
Chase, Nick; N. Cort
Chee, Jim; T. Hillerman
Cherry, Insp.; P. Van Greenaway
Cheyney, Colonel Allen; P. Cosgrave
*Christopher, Bob; R. R. Irvine
*Christopher, Paul; C. McCarry
Clay, Capt. Homer; P. Lauben
Cobb, Matt; W. L. DeAndrea
Cody; D. Brierley
Coll, Matthew; R. H. Lewis
*Collin, Mr.; F. Heller
Colson, Capt.; A. White
*Columbo; L. Hays
    B. Magee
Cooley, Dade; G. Thompson
Cooperman, Benny; H. Engel
Corleone, Michael; M. Puzo
Corti, Insp. Franco; P. Inchbald
Countdown WWIII; W. X. Davies
Counter Force; D. Streib
Coyne, Brady; T. Tapply
Craggs, Mrs.; H. R. F. Keating
*Craig, Peter; K. Benton
Crandel, Ben; Murray Sinclair
*Cranley, Nick; M. Storm
*Cranston, Lamont; W. Gibson
*Crichton, Tessa; A. Morice
Crime Minister, The; I. Barclay
Crisis Aversion Team; S. Andrews
*Crow, Insp. John; Roy Lewis
*Crowder, George; H. Pentecost
Crown, Steve; D. Streib
Cuddy, John Francis; J. F. Healy
Daguerre, Christian; C. Stevens
*Dalziel, Supt. Andrew; Reginald Hill
Damiot, Insp.; V. McConnor
*Daniels, Charmian; Jennie Melville
Darblay, Insp. Jean; Mollie Hardwick
*Darcy, Lord; R. Garrett
Dartanian, Alex; R. Rainey
Dartley, Richard; I. Barclay
Dean, Marc; P. Buck
Deane, Sarah; J. S. Borthwick
Death Merchant, The; J. Rosenberger
*De Gier, Detective; J. Van de Wetering
DeGraaf, Dr. Garrett; B. D'Amato
Dekker, Carl; D. Dekker
Dekker, Josh; A. Webb
*Delaney, Edward X.; Lawrence Sanders
Dempsey; J. Raymond
Dennison; A. Lassiter
Denson, John; R. Hoyt
*d'Espinal, Harcourt; B. Healey
*Destroyer, The; W. B. Murphy
Devereaux; B. Granger
Deveril, Peter; H. Innes
Devlin, Liam; J. Higgins
*Devlin, Timothy; B. Heatter
Diamond, Red; M. Schorr
Digger, The; W. B. Murphy
*Di Griz, Slippery Jim; H. Harrison
Dime, Mike; B. Fantoni
Dobbs, Insp. Ronald; Christina Blake
*Dollanganger, Chris and Cathy; V. C.
    Andrews
Donoghue, Insp. Fabian; P. Turnbull
*Dortmunder, John; D. E. Westlake
Dougal, William; Andrew Taylor
*Dowling, Father Roger; R. McInerny
Drakov, Anton; J. Winters
Driscoll, Clifford; W. L. DeAndrea
*Drummond, Bulldog; H. C. McNeile
Duffy, Nick; D. Kavanagh
*Durell, Sam; E. S. Aarons,
    W. B. Aarons
Eagles, Black; J. Lansing
*87th Precinct; E. McBain
Eisenberg, Aaron; P. Chase
*Ellison, Charlotte; A. Perry
Emerson, Amelia Peabody; Elizabeth
    Peters
Epton, Rosa; M. Underwood
*Erridge, Matt; A. M. Stein

*Executioner, The; D. Pendleton
Eyes, Angel; W. B. Longley
*Falkenstein, Jesse; L. Egan
*Fang, Wu; R. Daniel
*Fansler, Kate; A. Cross
*Faraday, Mike; B. Copper
*Farrow, Marcus Aurelius; A. Ross
*Feiffer, Insp. Harry; W. Marshall
Fender, Ludovic; P. Geddes
*Fenner, Jack; G. H. Coxe
*Finch, Insp.; J. Thomson
Fitzgerald, Ed; D. Flynn
Fitzgerald, Fiona; W. Adler
Fitzgerald, Kevin; T. Topor
*Flagg, Conan; M. K. Wren
*Fletch; G. McDonald
*Fletcher, Irwin M.; G. McDonald
Fletcher, Jessica; J. Anderson
*Flynn, Francis Xavier; G. McDonald
Flynn, Terry; Joe Gash
Force; J. Decker
Force, Counter; D. Streib
Force, Phoenix; G. Wilson
Forsythe, Robert; E. X. Giroux
*Fortune, Dan; M. Collins
*Fortune, Reggie; A. C. Ward
Franklin, Ev; F. Orenstein
*Fraser, James; J. Wood
*Frederickson, Robert; G. Chesbro
*Freer, Virginia; E. Ferrars
French, Alan; J. Gollin
*Frost, Hank; A. Kilgore
*Fusil, Insp.; P. Alding
*G-8; R. J. Hogan
Gallagher, Gordon; J. J. Savarin
Garratt, Frank; P. Wentworth
Garrett, Henry; G. D. Larsen
*Gaunt, Jonathan; R. MacLeod
*Gautier, Insp.; R. Grayson
Gavin, Rod; John Quinn
*Gently, Supt.; A. Hunter
Gerard, Phillip; J. Dentinger
Gerber, Mack; E. Helm
*Gerson, Keith; J. Vance
*Ghote, Insp. Ganesh; H. R. F. Keating
*Gideon, Commander George; W. V. Butler
*Glendower, Tobias; M. Arnold
Gold, Alexander; H. Resnicow
Gold, Lt. Ronnie; G. Paulsen
*Gordon, Alison; W. Wager
Gordon, Ellie; K. Berne
Gordon, Yudel; W. Ebersohn
Gorodish, Serge; Delacorta
Gould, Harry; R. Obstfeld
Gould, Skipper; R. Kalish
Graham, Davina; E. Anthony
Grant, Celia; J. Sherwood
Grant, Michael; C. Thomas
Grass; P. Nash
Gray; D. Cory
Gray, Cordelia; P. D. James
Green, Kelly; L. Starr
Green, Noah; N. Hentoff
*Greenfield, C. B.; L. Kallen
Gregory, Miss; P. Gibbon
Grey, Jennifer; J. Jenkins
Grierson, David; I. Stuart
*Grijpstra, Detective; J. Van de
    Wetering
*Grogan, Insp.; M. Neville
Guardians; R. Austin
Guarnaccia, Marshall; M. Nabb
*Guinness, Ray; N. Guild
*Gull, Vladimir; Anthony Stuart
Haggerty, Leo; B. M. Schutz
Haig, Tubby; Anonymous
Haller, Mike; M. Byrd
Hammond, Crane; F. Carmichael
*Handyman; J. Messmann
*Hannay, Richard; J. Smithers
Harald, Lt. Sigrid; M. Maron
*Hardin, Mark; L. Derrick
Hardy, Cliff; P. Corris
Harmon, Prof. Robert; R. Elman
Harper; M. Aylward
Harry, Dirty; D. Hartman,
    J. Stinson
Haskell, Vejay; S. Dunlap
*Hastings, Lt. Frank; C. Wilcox
Hatcher, Amos; O. Banks
Hawk, Michael; D. Streib
Hawk, Street; J. Roberts
Hawker, James; C. Ramm
Hawthorne, Nimue; G. Linscott
Haydon, Stuart; D. L. Lindsey
*Hayes, Julie; D. S. Davis
*Hedley, Paul; B. Healey
*Heffernan, Hooky; L. Meynell
Heller, Carl; F. Roderus
Heller, Jesse; D. Kellerman
Heller, Nate; M. A. Collins
*Helm, Matt; D. Hamilton
Hitman, The; N. Winski
Hockney, Robert; A. De Borchgrave
*Holmes, Sherlock; V. Andrews,
    A. Arnold,
    D. R. Bensen,
    J. S. Clouston,
    M. D'Agneau,
    W. E. Dudley,

D. Dvorkin,
L. Feuer,
C. Fischer,
C. Fisher,
G. Frow,
L. Garland,
P. Giovanni,
L. Halliwell,
C. Haubold,
J. Hershey,
T. J. Kelly,
M. Kurland,
W. Lane,
L. A. Matthias,
C. Muusmann,
J. Nassivera,
A. Nowlan,
F. Richardson,
E. C. Roberts,
S. C. Roberts,
F. Sherrod,
D. O. Smith,
G. H. Smith,
R. Smullyan,
D. Stashower,
F. Thomas,
M. J. Trow,
C. Van Ash,
R. Walsh,
A. C. Ward
*Honeybath, Charles; M. Innes
Hook, The; B. Latham
Hope, Matthew; E. McBain
Hopkins, Sgt. Lloyd; J. Ellroy
*Horowitz, Lt. Jacob; D. Delman
Howard, Roz; S. Kenney
Hunter, Bounty; W. Boyles
Hunter, Nazi; M. Mandell
Hunter, Robert Lee; E. Sauter
Hunter, Sam; L. A. Morse
Hyde, John Byron; B. Wolff
Ingelram, Raymond; G. Household
Ivorsen, Eric; R. Spencer
Jacoby, Miles; R. J. Randisi
Jacoby, Quentin; J. C. S. Smith
Jaeger, Curt; M. Mandell
Jamison, J. J.; L. A. Taylor
*Janson, Hank; H. Janson
*Johnson, Johnson; D. Halliday
*Johnson, Dr. Sam; L. De La Torre
*Jordan, Scott; H. Q. Masur
Journey, Jack; J. R. Nash
Jurnet, Insp. Ben; S. T. Haymon
Jury, Insp. Richard; M. Grimes
Justice, Capt. John Valcourt; A. Forrest
Kale, Stephen; M. Jon
Kane, Elias; S. G. Spruill
*Kane, Sugar; L. Marshall
*Kauffman, Insp. Max; T. Chastain
Kaye, Simon; H. Waugh
Keaton, Kyra; T. Tone
Keel, Daniel; T. A. Schock
*Keene, Franklyn; H. Long
*Kelling, Sarah; C. MacLeod
*Kelly, Homer; J. Langton
*Kelly, Joe; R. Avery
Kelly, Prof. Neil; S. F. X. Dean
Kelsey, Insp.; E. Page
Kemp, Lennox; M. R. D. Meek
Kendall, William; P. Chase
Kennedy, George; G. Kennedy
Kennedy, Jerry; G. V. Higgins
Kent, Temple; D. G. Devon
*Kenworthy, Supt. Simon; J. B. Hilton
Keogh, Father; A. E. Lindop
*Kerr, Constable; P. Alding
Kinderman, Lt. Bill; W. P. Blatty
*Kirby, Jacqueline; Elizabeth Peters
Kirlin, Claude "Snake"; A. Bourgeau
Knight Rider; G. A. Larson
Knight, Sam; D. K. Cohler
*Koesler, Father Bob; W. X. Kienzle
Kolarova, Viera; E. Powers
Kovacks, Riley; G. De Marco
*Kramer, Lt.; J. McClure
*Kruger, Herbie; J. Gardner
Kuvakin, Ivan; A. Olcott
Laidlaw, Insp. Jack; W. McIlvanney
*Laird, Andrew; R. MacLeod
Land, Hannah; A. MacKay
Landon, Arnold; Roy Lewis
Landshark; I. Zacharia
Lee, Anna; L. Cody
*Leffing, Lucius; J. P. Brennan
*Lennox, Supt.; J. Wainwright
*Levin, Roger; A. Furst
Lewis, Butch; D. Klein
*Lewker, Abercrombie; G. Carr
Linkum, Sam; H. Mitgang
Linnett, Birdie; J. Linscott
Lion, Talbot; S. Victor
*Loams, Turlock; J. Ruyle
*Locke, Jeremy; M. Challis
Locke, John; S. Silliphant
Lockwood, Bill; B. Latham
Long, Michael; G. A. Larson
*Lord, Michael; C. D. King
Lott, Insp.; H. Wade
*Lovejoy; Jonathan Gash
Lovelace, Clarisse; N. Aldyne

Lowell, Dr.; A. Merritt
Lyons, Carl; D. Stivers
MacCardle, Cam; T. Halleran
McCone, Sharon; M. Muller
McFoy, Bernard; J. M. Shrog
*McGarr, Insp.; B. Gill
*McGee, Travis; J. D. MacDonald
McGuffin, Amos; R. Upton
McKenna, Patience Campbell; O. Papazoglou
McKenzie, Alex; J. S. Borthwick
MacLaren, Supt. Steve; B. Scott
*Maclean, Dr. Gregor; H. McLeave
MacMorgan, Harry; R. Striker
MacNeil, Harry; H. P. Jeffers
*MacTavish, Alonzo; P. Cheyney
McVeigh, Mike; R. Emmett
Mace; J. Grant
Macklin, Brett; I. Ludlow
Macklin, Peter; L. D. Estleman
*Maddox, Ivor; E. Linington
*Magellan, Philip; A. Fletcher
Magic Man, The; D. Bannerman
Mahoney, John; S. Flannery
*Maitland, Antony; S. Woods
Makepeace; J. Raymond
*Mallet, Dan; F. Parrish
*Mallin, David; R. Ormerod
Mallory; M. A. Collins
Man, George; K. Heller
Man, Magic, The; D. Bannerman
Mancuso, Eddie; R. Burkholz
Mandrake; J. Haythorne
Marker, Frank; A. Marriott
  A. Southcott
*Marlow, Peter; J. Hone
*Marple, Jane; A. Christie
*Marryat, Stephen; M. Leek
Marshall, John; M. Denning
Martin, Ray; R. Reinsmith
Martin, Tavy; Diana Winsor
Master, Ninja, The; W. Barker
*Masters, Insp./Supt. George; D. Clark
*Masuto, Sgt. Masao; E. V. Cunningham
Matthews, Sheriff Charles Timothy;
  D. R. Meredith
Maxim, Major Harry; G. Lyall
*Mendoza, Luis; Dell Shannon
Mercenary, The; P. Buck
Mercenary, The; A. Kilgore
*Merchant, Death, The; J. Rosenberger
Miami Vice; S. Grave
Millhone, Kinsey; S. Grafton
Milodragovitch, Milo; J. Crumley
Minder; A. Masters
Minister, Crime; I. Barclay
*Mitchell, Scott; J. Harvey
*Mitchell, Insp. Steven; Josephine Bell
*Mongo; G. Chesbro
Monk, Osbert; A. Craig
Moon, Martin; L. Malloy
Moore, John; J. Logue
Moretti, Paddy; J. Sherburne
*Morse, Insp.; C. Dexter
Morton, Constable James; R. Harrison
Moseley, Sgt. Hoke; C. Willford
Mosley, Insp.; J. Greenwood
Moss, Max; S. L. Thompson
*Moss, Phil; B. Knox
Mott, Sgt. Angus; C. Curzon
*Muffin, Charlie; B. Freemantle
Mulcahaney, Norah; L. O'Donnell
"Murder, She Wrote"; J. Anderson
*Murdoch, Bruce; N. Deane
*N, Mrs.; D. S. Davis
Nairn, David; M. Hartland
*Nameless; B. Pronzini
Narayan, Capt. Prem; M. A. Casberg
Nazi Hunter; M. Mandell
Nevers, Billy; J. M. Glazner
Nevsky, Yuri; D. Gat
Newman, Bob; C. Forbes
*Nicolson, Supt. Mark; R. Charles
Ninja Master, The; W. Barker
*Nolan, Frank; M. A. Collins
Nudger, Al; J. Lutz
*Oakes, Blackford; W. F. Buckley, Jr.
Oliver, Mrs. Ariadne; A. Christie
Oliver, Gideon; A. J. Elkins
Oliverez, Elena; M. Muller
O'Malley, Ben; B. Lysaght
O'Meara, Donald Briggs; D. Bannerman
O'Roarke, Jocelyn; J. Dentinger
*Otani, Supt.; James Melville
O'Toole, Byron; R. Thurston
Outrider; R. Harding
Owen, Richard; D. Sharp
Owens, Molly; S. Overholser
Pamplemousse, Monsieur; M. Bond
*Paris, Charles; S. Brett
Patterson, Jock; P. N. Walker
Peckover, Insp. Harry; M. Kenyon
*Pel, Insp. Clovis; M. Hebden
*Penetrator, The; L. Derrick
Peroni, Insp. Achille; T. Holme
Perry, Justin; J. D. Revere
*Peters, Anna; J. Law
*Peters, Toby; S. M. Kaminsky
*Phenwick Women; K. Kimbrough
*Philis; R. Perry

Phoenix Force; G. Wilson
Pig, Lord; N. Lombard
*Pinaud, Monsieur; P. Audemars
*Pinch, Dearborn V.; E. P. Green
*Pine, Paul; H. Browne
*Pink, Melinda; G. Moffat
*Piper, Peter; A. R. Long
*Pitt, Dirk; C. Cussler
*Pitt, Insp. Thomas; A. Perry
*Pleydell, Bertram; J. Smithers,
  D. Yates
Point Team; J. B. Hadley
*Poirot, Hercule; A. Christie
*Pollard, Insp. Tom; E. Lemarchand
*Pollifax, Mrs. Emily; D. Gilman
Porter, Appleton; M. Lovell
*Potter, Brock; A. Maling
Potter, Eugenia; V. Rich
Povin, General; J. Trenhaile
Powder, Lt. Leroy; M. Z. Lewin
Powers, Will; I. Zacharia
*Preston, Mark; P. Chambers
*"Professionals"; K. Blake
Protector, The; R. Rainey
Protector, The; I. Zacharia
*Purbright, Insp.; Colin Watson
*Purdue, Chance; R. H. Spencer
*Quantrill, Insp. Douglas; S. Radley
*Quarshie, Dr.; J. Wyllie
*Quayle, Hilary; M. Kaye
*Quiller; Adam Hall
*Quist, Julian; H. Pentecost
*Raffles, A. J.; P. Tremayne
*Rainey, Jim; P. McCurtin
Raker; D. Scott
*Randolph, Rev. C. P.; C. M. Smith
Rankin, James; J. Grady
*Rason, Insp. J.; S. Kyle
*Raven, John; D. MacKenzie
*Raven, Richard; J. Griffin
Rawlings, "Little John"; J. Minahan
Rayne, Brigadier; P. Coke
Reddy, Irving Martin; I. Zacharia
Renwick, Roger; H. MacInnes
Resistance; G. St. Germain
*Rhodenbarr, Bernie; L. Block
Rhys, Insp. Madoc; A. Craig
Rider, Knight; G. A. Larson
*Robak, Donald; J. L. Hensley
Robins family; T. Chastain
Rogers, Insp. George; Jonathan Ross
*Rolfe, Zach; J. J. Lamb
Roosevelt, Eleanor; E. Roosevelt
Rope, Charlie; J. Eller
*Rosher, Insp. Alf; J. S. Scott
Rostnikov, Insp. Porfiry; S. M. Kaminsky
*Rudd, Insp.; J. Thomson
Rugger; R. Thurston
*Rumpole; J. Mortimer
*Russell, Col. Charles; W. Haggard
Ryan, Monsignor John Blackwood; A.
  Greeley
Ryan, Maggie; P. M. Carlson
Ryder, William (Tiny); W. Boyles
Ryland, Garth; J. R. Riggs
S-Com; Steve White
SOB's; J. Hild
*Safford, Ben; R. B. Dominic
Saigon Commandos; J. Cain
*Saint, The; L. Charteris
St. James, Kiel; E. Chaze
Salis, Jo; W. O. Greener
Salter, Insp. Charlie; E. Wright
Saltfleet, Insp. Gregory; Colin Wilson
*Samson, Albert; M. Z. Lewin
Samson, Bernard; L. Deighton
Samson, Jake; S. Singer
*Samson, John; M. Tripp
Sand, Robert; M. Olden
*Savage, Doc; K. Robeson
*Savage, Marc; M. Eden
Savage, Mark; L. Payne
Savage, Spencer Monroe; P. Theroux
*Schmidt, Insp; G. Bagby
Schwartz, Gadgets; D. Stivers
Schwartz, Rebecca; Julie Smith
Scorpion Squad; E. Helm
*Scott, Spider; K. Royce
*Scudamore, Laura; R. Armstrong
*Scudder, Matthew; L. Block
*Shadow, The; W. Gibson
*Shandy, Prof. Peter; C. MacLeod
*Shard, Simon; P. McCutchan
*Shaw, Commander Esmonde; P. McCutchan
*Shaw, Paul; M. Sadler
*Shayne, Michael; J. Reach
Sherriff, Michael; P. McAdam
Shield, The; P. McAdam
Shore, Jemima; Antonia Fraser
*Sidel, Isaac; J. Charyn
*Silk, Steve; J. B. O'Sullivan
Simmons, Ralph; R. Gillespie
Simpson, Tim; J. Malcolm
Sinclair, Steve; J. Decker
Slade, Mac; J. Blumenthal
Slayton, Ben; B. Sanders
*Sloan, Insp. C. S.; C. Aird
*Small, Rabbi David; H. Kemelman
Smith, Benbow; P. Wentworth
Smith, Jill; S. Dunlap

*Smith, Supt. Owen; J. Barnett
Smith, Tusk; H. Zachary
Smolinsky, Joshua; C. Sinclair
Soldier for Hire; M. K. Roberts,
    R. Skimin
Space; W. F. Nolan
Spargo; J. D. Scott
Sparrow; C. Murphy
Spearman, Henry; M. Jevons
Specialist, The; J. Cutter
*Spence, Supt. Ben; M. Allen
*Spence, Margo Franklin; J. Jenkins
*Spence, Philip; J. Jenkins
Spencer, Dick; N. Winski
*Spenser; R. B. Parker
*Spider, The; G. Stockbridge
Sprague, Michael; L. J. Barnes
*Spring, Penelope; M. Arnold
Stafford family; B. Mather
*Stevens, Insp.; B. Graeme
Stevens, Jim; D. Smith
Stock, Matthew; L. Tourney
*Stone, J. Rockingham; R. Armstrong
*Stoner, Harry; J. Valin
Stonewall; M. K. Roberts,
    R. Skimin
Strachey, Donald; R. Stevenson
Street Hawk, The; J. Roberts
*Striker, Jason; P. Anthony
Stryker, Sgt. Mark; J. Cain
*Sturrock, Jeremy; J. Sturrock
*Styles, Peter; J. Philips
Sullivan, Jack; J. Cutter
Swain, Matthew; M. McQuay
Swift, Loren; D. Hornig
*Sydenham; D. Seaman
T-Man; B. Sanders
TNT; D. Masters
Tallon, Jack; J. Ball
Tamar, Hilary; S. Caudwell
*Tanner, John Marshall; S. Greenleaf
Team, Able; D. Stivers
Team Three; C. Cunningham
*Templar, Simon; L. Charteris
Teresa, Sister Mary; M. Quill
Terminator, The; John Quinn
Tewkesbury, Mr.; H. Cecil
*Thane, Colin; B. Knox
Thanet, Insp. Luke; D. Simpson
*Thatcher, John Putnam; E. Lathen
Thomas, Lizzie; A. Oliver
Thomassy, George; S. Stein
*Thorndyke, John; A. C. Ward
Thorne, Insp. George; J. Penn
Three, Team; C. Cunningham
Thyrde, Derek; B. Denham
*Tibbett, Henry and Emmy; P. Moyes
Tibbett, John; L. Payne
Track, Dan; J. Ahern
Tracy, Devlin; W. B. Murphy
*Travers, Ludovic; C. Bush
*Treasure, Mark; David Williams
Tree, Ms.; M. A. Collins
Trelawney; A. Melville-Ross
Trenton, Richard; A. Burton
Trethowan, Insp. Perry; R. Barnard
Trotti, Commissario; T. Williams
Tucker, Roy; A. Kennedy
Tucker, Sam; J. A. Potter
Tweed; C. Forbes
Twin, Anthony Nicholas; D. Masters
Unwin, Harriet; E. Hervey
*Usher, Ambrose; J. Davey
Valentine, Dan; N. Aldyne
*Van Der Valk, Arlette; N. Freeling
*Van Dusen, Prof. Augustus S. F. X.;
    J. Futrelle
*Varallo, Vic; L. Egan
*Velvet, Nick; E. D. Hoch
Vendetta; I. Zacharia
Vice, Miami; S. Grave
Vigilante, The; I. Ludlow
Von Helsing, Alicia; J. Mathewson
*Wager, Gabriel; Rex Burns
*Walker, Amos; L. D. Estleman
Wallace, Brett; W. Barker
Waltz, John; C. McCormick
Wanawake, Penny; S. Moody
Ward, Eric; Roy Lewis
Warlord, The; J. Frost
Warshawski, V. I.; S. Paretsky
Watson, Sheriff Jug; H. Zachary
Weatherley, Kate; M. Birmingham
Webb, Chief Insp.; Anthea Fraser
Webber, Insp. John; A. Oliver
*Wentworth, Lyon; R. Forrest
*Wentworth, Richard; G. Stockbridge
West, Delilah; M. O'Callaghan
*Weston, Geoffrey; T. B. Haughey
*Wexford, Chief Insp.; R. Rendell
*Wheeler, Al; Carter Brown
Whippletree, Sheriff Emil; M. T.
    Hinkemeyer
*Widowers, Black; I. Asimov
Widows; L. La Plante
Wilcox, Carl; H. Adams
Wilkins, Insp.; J. Anderson
*Williams, Remo; W. B. Murphy
*Willis, George; W. Hughes
*Willum, Persis; Clarissa Watson

Wilson, Cyrus; A. H. Garnet
*Wimsey, Lord Peter; D. L. Sayers
*Wine, Moses; R. L. Simon
Wing; J. Reach
Wingate, Mac; Brian Swift
Winter, Charles; C. Egleton
Winterbottom, Lettie; L. Cutter
Winterstone, Lord; N. Lombard
*Wintringham, Dr. David; Josephine Bell
*Wolfe, Nero; R. Stout
Worthington, Elizabeth Lamb; B. J.
    Morison
Wren, Russel; T. Berger
Wyatt; D. Gethin
*Wycliffe, Supt. Charles; W. J. Burley
Yeadings, Supt. Mike; C. Curzon
Yeoman; R. Jackson
Zevich, F. T.; A. Bourgeau
*Zondi, Sgt.; J. McClure

Movie Title Index

Abbey Grange. A. C. Doyle; Return of Sherlock Holmes
Abbott and Costello Meet Dr. Jekyll and Mr. Hyde. R. L. Stevenson; Strange Case of Dr. Jekyll and Mr. Hyde
Abominable Dr. Phibes. W. Goldstein; Dr. Phibes
Above Suspicion. H. MacInnes
Accidental Death. E. Wallace; Jack o' Judgment
Accomplice. F. Gruber; Simon Lash, Private Detective
Account Rendered. P. Barrington
Accused. J. Truesdell; Be Still, My Love
Accused of Murder. W. R. Burnett; Vanity Row
Ace of Spades. J. C. Fraser
Ace Up Your Sleeve. J. H. Chase; Ace Up My Sleeve
Across 110th. W. Ferris
Across the Bridge. G. Greene; Nineteen Stories
Across the Pacific. C. E. Blaney
Act of Aggression. J. Buell; Shrewsdale Exit
Act of Mercy. F. Clifford
Act of Murder. E. Lothar; Mills of God
Action Man. J. Flynn
Action of the Tiger. J. Wellard
Address Unknown. K. Taylor
Adventure, Inc. A. Christie; Secret Adversary
Adventures in Diplomacy. J. Futrelle; Elusive Isabel
Adventures of Captain Kettle. C. J. C. Hyne
Adventures of Sherlock Holmes. W. Gillette; Sherlock Holmes
Adventures of Sherlock Holmes' Smarter Brother. G. Pearlman
Affair Nina B. J. M. Simmel; Affair of Nina B
Affair of Three Nations. J. McIntyre
Afraid to Talk. G. Sklar; Merry-Go-Round
After Dark. D. Boucicault
After Midnight. M. Albrand
After the Verdict. R. Hichens
Against All Odds. G. Homes; Build My Gallows High
Agatha. K. Tynan
Age of Indiscretion. T. D. Irwin; Collusion
Agency. P. Gottlieb
Agent 8 3/4. L. Davidson; Night of Wenceslas
Agony Column. E. D. Biggers
Al Capone. J. Roeburt
Alias Ladyfingers. J. Gregory; Ladyfingers
Alias the Lone Wolf. L. J. Vance
Alias the Night Wind. V. Vanardy
Alibi. G. A. England
Alibi. M. Morton
All People Will Be Brothers. J. M. Simmel; Cain '67
All the Winners. A. Applin; Wicked
All the World to Nothing. W. Martyn
Almost Married. A. Soutar; Devil's Triangle
Alphabet Murders. A. Christie; ABC Murders
Alster Case. R. Gillmore
Amateur. R. Littell
Amateur Gentleman. J. Farnol
Amazing Dr. Clitterhouse. B. Lyndon
Amazing Partnership. E. P. Oppenheim
Amazing Quest of Mr. Ernest Bliss. E. P. Oppenheim
Ambassador. E. Leonard; Fifty-Two Pickup
Ambushers. D. Hamilton
American Dream. N. Mailer
American Friend. P. Highsmith; Ripley's Game
American Prisoner. E. Phillpotts
Amorous Adventures of Moll Flanders. D. Defoe; Fortunes and Misfortunes of the Famous Moll Flanders
Amsterdam Affair. N. Freeling; Love in Amsterdam
Anatomy of a Murder. R. Traver
And Hope to Die. D. Goodis; Black Friday
And Jimmy Went to the Rainbow's Foot. J. M. Simmel; Caesar Code
And Justice for All. R. Grossbach
And Now the Screaming Starts. D. Case; Fengriffin
And Then There Were None. A. Christie; Ten Little Niggers
Anderson Tapes. Lawrence Sanders
Angel, Angel, Down We Go. W. Johnston
Angel Esquire. E. Wallace
Angel Heart. W. Hjortsberg; Falling Angel
Angel Street. P. Hamilton; Gas Light
Angry Silence. John Burke
Anna the Adventuress. E. P. Oppenheim

Another Man's Poison. L. Sands; Intent to Murder
Another Man's Shoes. V. Bridges
Any Number Can Play. E. H. Heth
Any Number Can Win. J. Trinian
Anything Might Happen. H. Balfour
Appointment with Venus. J. Tickell
Arabesque. Alex Gordon
Ardent Room. J. D. Carr; Burning Court
Argyle Case. H. Ford
Arm at the Left. C. Williams; Aground
Armadale. W. Collins
Armageddon. D. Lippincott; Voice of Armageddon
Arrest Bulldog Drummond. H. C. McNeile; Final Count
Arrivederci, Baby! R. Deming; Careful Man
Arsenal Stadium Mystery. L. Gribble
Arsene Lupin. E. Jepson
Arsene Lupin. M. Leblanc (headnote)
Arsenic and Old Lace. J. Kesselring
Ashes and Diamonds. J. Andrzeyevski
Aspern. H. James; Aspern Papers
Asphalt Jungle. W. R. Burnett
Assassin. V. Canning; Venetian Bird
Assassin for Hire. R. Rienits
Assassination Bureau. J. London
Assault. K. Young; Ravine
Assault on a Queen. J. Finney
Assault on Agathon. A. Caillou
Assignment. P. Wahloo
Assignment in Brittany. H. MacInnes
Assignment K. H. Howard; Department K
Assignment--Paris. P. Gallico; Trial by Terror
Asylum. W. Johnston
At Bay. P. Phillips
At the Mercy of Tiberius. A. J. Wilson
At the Villa Rose. A. E. W. Mason
Attempt to Kill. E. Wallace; Lone House Mystery
Attention, the Kids Are Watching. P. L. Dixon; Children Are Watching
Audrey Rose. F. De Felitta
Avalanche. G. Atherton
Avalanche. K. Boyle
Avalanche Express. C. Forbes
Avenger. J. Goodwin
Awakening. B. Stoker; Jewel of the Seven Stars
Baby, Take a Bow. J. P. Judge; Square Crooks
Baby, the Rain Must Fall. H. Foote; Traveling Lady
Bachelor's Folly. E. Wallace; Calendar
Back from the Dead. C. Turney; Other One
Back to Life. A. Soutar; Back from the Dead
Backfire! E. Wallace (headnote)
Background to Danger. E. Ambler; Uncommon Danger
Bad Blonde. M. Catto; Flanagan Boy
Bad Company. J. Lait; Put on the Spot
Bad Day at Black Rock. M. Niall
Bad for Each Other. H. McCoy; Scalpel
Bad Seed. M. Anderson
Badge 373. M. Roote
Badlanders. W. R. Burnett; Asphalt Jungle
Balcony. J. Genet
Banana Peel. C. Williams; Nothing in the Way
Band of Outsiders. D. Hitchens; Fools' Gold
Bandbox. L. J. Vance
Bank Shot. D. E. Westlake
Banker's Double. S. Campbell; Below the Dead-Line
Barbarous Street. D. Goodis; Street of the Lost
Barnes Murder Case. E. P. Oppenheim; Conspirators
Barton Mystery. W. Hackett
Basement Melody. J. Trinian; Big Grab
Bat. M. R. Rinehart
Bat Whispers. M. R. Rinehart; Bat
Batman. W. Lyon
Bear Island. A. MacLean
Beast from Marseilles. R. Croft-Cooke; Seven Thunders
Beast of the City. J. Lait
Beast with Five Fingers. W. F. Harvey
Beat the Devil. J. Helvick
Beautiful Jim, of the Blankshire Regiment. J. S. Winter
Because of the Cats. N. Freeling
Bedelia. V. Caspary
Bedroom Window. A. Holden; Witnesses
Beetle. R. Marsh
Before Dawn. E. Wallace; Sergeant Sir Peter
Before I Die. H. Debrett
Beggar in Purple. A. Soutar
Beggars of Life. J. Tully
Behind Masks. E. P. Oppenheim; Jeanne of the Marshes
Behind That Curtain. E. D. Biggers
Behind the Headlines. R. Chapman

Behind the Mask. E. P. Oppenheim; Jeanne of the Marshes
Behold a Pale Horse. E. Pressburger; Killing a Mouse on Sunday
Behold This Woman. E. P. Oppenheim; Hillman
Bella Donna. R. Hichens
Bellamy Trial. F. N. Hart
Belonging. O. Wadsley
Ben. G. A. Ralston
Benson Murder Case. S. S. Van Dine
Bentley's Conscience. P. Trent
Beryl Coronet. A. C. Doyle; Adventures of Sherlock Holmes
Beware, My Lovely. M. Dinelli; Man
Beyond the Curtain. A. J. Wallis; Thunder Above
Beyond the Forest. S. Engstrand
Beyond the Limit. G. Greene; Honorary Consul
Beyond the River. G. Simenon; Bottom of the Bottle
Beyond This Place. A. J. Cronin
Bid for Fortune. G. Boothby
Big Boodle. R. Sylvester
Big Bounce. E. Leonard
Big Caper. L. White
Big Chance. P. Barrington (headnote)
Big Clock. K. Fearing
Big Fix. R. L. Simon
Big Gamble. O. R. Cohen; Iron Chalice
Big Game. F. Wallace
Big Grab. J. Trinian
Big Heat. W. P. McGivern
Big House. J. Lait
Big Knife. C. Odets
Big Night. S. Ellin; Dreadful Summit
Big Operator. R. Airth; Snatch
Big Sleep. R. Chandler
Big-Town Round-Up. W. M. Raine
Billion Dollar Brain. L. Deighton
Birds. D. Du Maurier; Apple Tree
Birds of Prey. G. Bronson-Howard
Birds of Prey. A. A. Milne; Fourth Wall
Bishop Misbehaves. F. Jackson
Bishop Murder Case. S. S. Van Dine
Bishop's Misadventures. F. Jackson; Bishop Misbehaves
Bitch. Jackie Collins
Bitter Springs. C. King
Bizarre, Bizarre. J. S. Clouston; His First Offense
Black Angel. C. Woolrich
Black Bag. L. J. Vance
Black Bird. T. Browning; Mocking Bird
Black Bird. A. Edwards
Black Box. E. P. Oppenheim
Black Camel. E. D. Biggers
Black Coffee. A. Christie
Black Doll. W. E. Hayes
Black Eye. J. Jacks; Murder on the Wild Side
Black Glove. E. Borneman; Tremolo
Black Limelight. G. Sherry
Black Marble. J. Wambaugh
Black Mask. B. Graeme; Blackshirt
Black Pearl. W. Woodrow
Black Peter. A. C. Doyle; Return of Sherlock Holmes
Black Secret. R. W. Chambers; In Secret
Black Sheep. E. Yates
Black Spider. C. Dawe
Black Sun. P. Wahloo; Lorry
Black Sunday. T. Harris
Black Watch. T. Mundy; King of the Khyber Rifles
Black Widow. P. Quentin
Black Windmill. C. Egleton; Seven Days to a Killing
Blackboard Jungle. E. Hunter
Blackguard. R. Paton; Autobiography of a Blackguard
Blackmail. C. Bennett
Blackmailed. E. Myers; Mrs. Christopher
Blackout. M. Gilbert; Death in Captivity
Blackout. H. Nielsen; Gold Coast Nocturne
Blade Runner. P. K. Dick; Do Androids Dream of Electric Sheep?
Blanche Fury. J. Shearing
Bleak House. C. Dickens
Blind Adventure. E. D. Biggers; Agony Column
Blind Alley. J. Warwick
Blind Date. L. Howard
Blind Goddess. P. Hastings
Blind Goddess. A. Train
Blind Justice. A. Ridley; Recipe for Murder
Blind Man's Eyes. W. MacHarg
Blind Terror. W. Hughes
Blindfold. L. Fletcher
Blonde from Peking. J. H. Chase; You Have Yourself a Deal
Blonde Ice. W. Chambers; Once Too Often
Blonde Like That! J. H. Chase; Miss Shumway Waves a Wand
Blonde Sinner. J. Henry; Yield to the Night

B

Blonde Vampire. D. Mooers
Blondes for Danger. E. Price; Red for Danger
Blood and Roses. J. S. Le Fanu; In a Glass Darkly
Blood Beast from Outer Space. F. Crisp; Night Callers
Blood Brothers. R. Price
Blood from the Mummy's Tomb. B. Stoker; Jewel of the Seven Stars
Blood Money. C. H. Bullivant
Blood on My hands. G. Butler; Kiss the Blood Off My Hands
Blood Relatives. E. Hunter
Blood Spattered Bride. J. S. Le Fanu; In a Glass Darkly
Blood to the Head. G. Simenon; Young Cardinaud
Bloodline. S. Sheldon
Bloodlust. R. Connell; Variety
Bloodsuckers. S. Raven; Doctors Wear Scarlet
Bloody Mama. R. Thom
Blow Out. N. Williams
Blue City. K. Millar
Blue Coronet. A. C. Doyle; Adventures of Sherlock Holmes
Blue Dahlia. R. Chandler
Blue Envelope Mystery. S. Kerr; Blue Envelope
Blue Lamp. T. Willis
Boat from Shanghai. P. Walsh; Chin-Chin-Chinaman
Body Snatcher. R. L. Stevenson
Bombay Mail. L. G. Blochman
Bombsight Stolen. G. Kerr; Cottages to Let
Bonaventure. C. Hastings
Bones. E. Wallace
Bonnie and Clyde. B. Hirschfeld
Book of Numbers. R. D. Pharr
Boomerang. W. H. Osborne
Born Reckless. D. H. Clarke; Louis Beretti
Born Reckless. M. Rogers
Born to Gamble. E. Wallace; Forty-Eight Short Stories
Born to Kill. J. Gunn; Deadlier Than the Male
Born to Win. M. Roote
Boscombe Valley Mystery. A. C. Doyle; Adventures of Sherlock Holmes
Bottom of the Bottle. G. Simenon
Bottom of the Well. F. U. Adams
Boulevard Nights. D. Gram
Boy Cried Murder. W. Irish; Dead Man Blues
Boy on a Dolphin. D. Divine
Boys from Brazil. I. Levin
Branded. G. Biss
Brandy for the Parson. G. Household; Tales of Adventurers
Brasher Doubloon. R. Chandler; High Window
Brass Bowl. L. J. Vance
Brass Bullet. F. R. Adams; Pleasure Island
Brass Target. F. Nolan; Oshawa Project
Brat Farrar. J. Tey
Break in the Circle. P. Loraine
Breakheart Pass. A. MacLean
Breaking Point. E. Hemingway; To Have and Have Not
Breaking Point. L. Meynell
Breaking Point. M. R. Rinehart
Breakup. C. Armstrong; Balloon Man
Breath of Scandal. E. Balmer
Breathless Moment. M. Bryant; Redemption of Richard
Bride. S. Olivier
Bride. M. Shelley; Frankenstein
Bride of the Lake. D. Boucicault; Colleen Bawn
Bride Wore Black. C. Woolrich
Brighton Rock. G. Greene
Brink's Job. N. Behn; Big Stick-Up at Brink's!
British Agent. H. B. Lockhart
British Intelligence. A. P. Kelly; Three Faces East
Broad Daylight. P. Highsmith; Talented Mr. Ripley
Broadway. P. Dunning
Broken Blossoms. T. Burke; Limehouse Nights
Bronze Bell. L. J. Vance
Brooding Eyes. J. Goodwin; Paid in Full
Brother Orchid. L. Brady
Brotherhood. L. J. Carlino
Brotherhood. E. Wallace; Educated Evans
Brotherhood of Satan. L. Q. Jones
Brothers in Law. H. Cecil
Brothers Karamazov. F. M. Dostoevskii
Brothers Rico. G. Simenon
Bruce-Partington Plans. A. C. Doyle; His Last Bow
Brute. F. A. Kummer
Build My Gallows High. G. Homes
Bulldog Drummond. H. C. McNeile
Bulldog Drummond at Bay. H. C. McNeile

Bulldog Drummond Comes Back. H. C. McNeile; Female of the Species
Bulldog Drummond in Africa. H. C. McNeile; Challenge
Bulldog Drummond Strikes Back. H. C. McNeile; Knock-Out
Bulldog Drummond's Peril. H. C. McNeile; Third Round
Bulldog Drummond's Revenge. H. C. McNeile; Return of Bulldog Drummond
Bulldog Drummond's Secret Police. H. C. McNeile; Temple Tower
Bulldog Drummond's Third Round. H. C. McNeile; Third Round
Bulldog Sees It Through. G. Fairlie; Scissors Cut Paper
Bullet for Pretty Boy. M. Avallone
Bullitt. R. Pike; Mute Witness
Bullshot. R. House; Bullshot Crummond
Bunny Lake Is Missing. E. Piper
Burden of Proof. V. Sardou; Diplomates
Burglar. L. Block (headnote)
Burglar. A. Thomas; Editha's Burglar
Burglar and the Girl. M. Boulton
Burglars. D. Goodis; Burglar
Buried Treasure. F. B. Austin; On the Borderland
Burn. N. Gant
Burned Evidence. W. Woodrow
Burnt Offerings. R. Marasco
Busman's Honeymoon. D. L. Sayers
Busy Body. D. E. Westlake
Busybody. J. Popplewell
But Not for Me. E. Ronns
Butcher, Baker, Nightmare Maker. R. Natale
Butterfly. J. M. Cain
Butterfly. H. K. Webster
Butterfly on the Shoulder. J. Gearon; Velvet Well
CC and Company. M. Roote
Cairo. W. R. Burnett; Asphalt Jungle
Calendar. E. Wallace
Call Harry Crown. M. Franklin
Callan. J. Mitchell; Magnum for Schneider
Called Back. H. Conway
Calling Bulldog Drummond. G. Fairlie
Calling Philo Vance. S. S. Van Dine; Kennel Murder Case
Calvert's Valley. M. P. Montagu; In Calvert's Valley
Cameron of the Bottle. R. Connor; Corporal Cameron
Campbell's Kingdom. H. Innes
Canary Murder Case. S. S. Van Dine
Candidate for Murder. E. Wallace (headnote)
Candles at Nine. A. Gilbert; Mouse Who Wouldn't Play Ball
Candleshoe. M. Innes; Christmas at Candleshoe
Cape Fear. J. D. MacDonald; Executioners
Caper of the Golden Bulls. W. P. McGivern
Caprice. J. Withers
Captain Applejack. W. Hackett
Captain Carey, U.S.A. M. Albrand; After Midnight
Captain Clegg. R. Thorndyke; Dr. Syn
Captive City. J. Appleby
Caravan to Vaccares. A. MacLean
Cardboard Box. A. C. Doyle; His Last Bow
Careful, He Might Hear You. S. L. Elliott
Carey Treatment. J. Hudson; Case of Need
Caribbean Mystery. J. W. Vandercook; Murder in Trinidad
Carnival of Thieves. W. P. McGivern; Caper of the Golden Bulls
Carpet from Bagdad. H. MacGrath
Carrington, V.C. D. Christie
Carry-Cot. A. Thynne
Carter Case. A. B. Reeve (headnote)
Casablanca. J. J. Epstein
Case Against Mrs. Ames. A. S. Roche
Case of Elinor Norton. M. R. Rinehart; State vs. Elinor Norton
Case of Identity. A. C. Doyle; Adventures of Sherlock Holmes
Case of Jonathan Drew. M. B. Lowndes; Lodger
Case of Lady Camber. H. A. Vachell
Case of Mrs. Pembroke. L. Weitzenkorn; Five Star Final
Case of the Black Cat. E. S. Gardner; Case of the Caretaker's Cat
Case of the Black Parrot. B. E. Stevenson; Mystery of the Boule Cabinet
Case of the Curious Bride. E. S. Gardner
Case of the Frightened Lady. E. Wallace; Frightened Lady
Case of the Howling Dog. E. S. Gardner
Case of the Lucky Stiff. E. S. Gardner
Case of the Missing Blonde. J. Latimer; Lady in the Morgue

Case of the Stuttering Bishop. E. S. Gardner
Case of the Vanished Bonds. S. Campbell; Below the Dead-Line
Case of the Velvet Claws. E. S. Gardner
Casino Murder Case. S. S. Van Dine
Casino Royale. I. Fleming
Cassandra Crossing. R. Katz
Cast a Dark Shadow. J. Green; Murder Mistaken
Castle of Crimes. A. E. W. Mason; House of the Arrow
Cat. G. Simenon
Cat and Mouse. M. Halliday
Cat and the Canary. J. Willard
Cat Creeps. J. Willard; Cat and the Canary
Cat o' Nine Tails. P. J. Gillette
Catacombs. Jay Bennett
Catamount Killing. J. H. Chase; I Would Rather Stay Poor
Catch Me a Spy. G. Marton
Cat's Paw. C. B. Kelland
Catspaw. W. H. Osborne
Caves of Night. J. Christopher
Celestial City. B. Orczy
Chairman. J. R. Kennedy
Chalk Garden. E. Bagnold
Challenge. H. C. McNeile
Chamber of Horrors. E. Wallace; Door with Seven Locks
Chance Meeting. L. Howard; Blind Date
Change of Mind. C. Stratton
Channings. H. Wood
Chant of Jimmie Blacksmith. T. Keneally
Charade. P. H. Stone
Charge Is Murder. A. Dewlen; Twilight of Honor
Charles Augustus Milverton. A. C. Doyle; Return of Sherlock Holmes
Charley Varrick. J. Reese; Looters
Charlie Chan and the Curse of the Dragon Queen. M. Avallone
Charlie Chan Carries On. E. D. Biggers
Charlie Chan's Courage. E. D. Biggers; Chinese Parrot
Charlie Chan's Greatest Case. E. D. Biggers; House Without a Key
Charlie Chan's Murder Cruise. E. D. Biggers; Charlie Chan Carries On
Charlie Muffin. B. Freemantle; Charlie Muffin
Chase. H. Foote
Chase. C. Woolrich; Black Path of Fear
Cheap Detective. R. Grossbach
Cheating Cheaters. M. Marcin
Cheerful Fraud. K. R. G. Browne; Following Ann
Cheri-Bibi. G. Leroux
Chicago. M. Watkins
Chicago Deadline. T. Thayer; One Woman
Chick. E. Wallace
Children of the Corn. Stephen King; Different Seasons
Child's Play. R. Marasco
Chin-Chin-Chinaman. P. Walsh
China Syndrome. B. Wohl
Chinese Bungalow. M. Osmond
Chinese Den. M. Osmond; Chinese Bungalow
Chinese Parrot. E. D. Biggers
Chinese Puzzle. P. Bower
Choice of Assassins. W. P. McGivern
Choirboys. J. Wambaugh
Cinema Murder. E. P. Oppenheim; Other Romilly
Circular Staircase. M. R. Rinehart
Circus Queen Murder. A. Abbot; About the Murder of the Circus Queen
City Across the River. I. Shulman; Amboy Dukes
City After Midnight. J. D. Carr; Emperor's Snuff Box
City of Purple Dreams. Anonymous
City of Silent Men. J. Moroso; Quarry
Clairvoyant. H. Clement
Clash by Night. R. Croft-Cooke
Clayton Treasure Mystery. N. Gordon; Shakespeare Murders
Clean Slate. J. Thompson; Pop. 1280
Cleopatra Jones. R. Goulart
Cleopatra Jones and the Casino of Gold. R. Goulart
Climax. F. J. Lewis
Cloak and Dagger. W. Irish; Dead Man Blues
Clockmaker. G. Simenon; Watchmaker of Everton
Clockwork Orange. A. Burgess
Closing Net. H. C. Rowland
Clue of the New Pin. E. Wallace
Clue of the Silver Key. E. Wallace
Clue of the Twisted Candle. E. Wallace
Coast of Chance. E. Chamberlain
Coast of Skeletons. E. Wallace; Sanders of the River
Cobra. P. Gosling; Running Duck
Code Name: Emerald. R. Bass; Emerald Illusion
Code of Scotland Yard. E. Percy; Play with Fire

Coffy. P. W. Fairman
Cold River. W. Judson
Cold Steel. G. C. Shedd; In the Shadow of the Hills
Collector. J. Fowles
Colleen Bawn. D. Boucicault
Colorado Pluck. G. Goodchild; Colorado Jim
Colorado Territory. W. R. Burnett; High Sierra
Coma. R. Cook
Come Back, Charleston Blue. C. Himes; Heat's On
Come Dance with Me. K. Roos; Blonde Died Dancing
Come-On. W. Chambers
Come to My House. A. S. Roche
Comedians. G. Greene
Compromising Positions. S. Isaacs
Compulsion. M. Levin
Concorde--Airport 1979. K. Stewart
Condemned to Death. G. Goodchild; Jack O'Lantern
Condemned to Life. W. Drummond
Condorman. R. Sheckley; Game of X
Cone of Silence. D. Beaty
Confessions. B. Reynolds; Confession Corner
Confidence Man. L. Y. Erskine
Confidential Agent. G. Greene
Confidential Agent. O. Welles; Mr. Arkadin
Conflict. C. B. Kelland
Conspiracy. R. Baker
Conspirator. H. Slater
Conspirators. E. P. Oppenheim
Conspirators. F. Prokosch
Contraband. C. B. Kelland
Convict 99. M. C. Leighton
Convicted. M. Flavin; Criminal Code
Convicted. W. Irish; Six Nights of Mystery
Cool Breeze. W. R. Burnett; Asphalt Jungle
Cop Hater. E. Hunter
Copper Beeches. A. C. Doyle; Adventures of Sherlock Holmes
Cops and Robbers. D. E. Westlake
Cops' Sunday. A. Coburn; Off Duty
Cordelia the Magnificent. L. Scott
Corpse Came C.O.D. J. Starr
Corridor of Mirrors. C. Massie
Corsair. W. Green
Cottage to Let. G. Kerr; Cottages to Let
Cotton Comes to Harlem. C. Himes
Couch. R. Bloch
Counsel for the Defense. L. Scott
Count Dracula. B. Stoker; Dracula
Counterattack. J. Stevenson
Counterfeit Traitor. A. Klein
Country Beyond. J. O. Curwood
Court Marshall. A. Christie; Carrington, V.C.
Covenant with Death. S. Becker
Crack in the Mirror. M. Haedrich
Crack-Up. Fredric Brown; Madman's Holiday
Crackerjack. W. B. M. Ferguson
Crash. F. Packard; Night Operator
Craze. H. Seymour; Infernal Idol
Crazy Joe. M. Barone
Crazy Pete. L. White
Creeping Shadow. W. Scott; Man
Crime. G. Bernanos
Crime and Passion. J. H. Chase; Ace Up My Sleeve
Crime and Punishment. F. M. Dostoevskii
Crime and Punishment USA. F. M. Dostoevskii; Crime and Punishment
Crime at Blossoms. M. Shairp
Crime by Night. G. Homes; Forty Whacks
Crime Doctor. I. Zangwill; Big Bow Mystery
Crime Unlimited. D. Hume
Crime Without Passion. B. Hecht; Collected Stories of Ben Hecht
Crimes at the Dark House. W. Collins; Woman in White
Criminal Code. M. Flavin
Criminal Within. N. Lippincott; Murder at Glen Athol
Criminals at Large. E. Wallace; Case of the Frightened Lady
Crimson Circle. D. Tracy
Crimson City. A. Coldeway
Crimson Gardenia. R. Beach
Crooked Billet. D. Titheradge
Crooked Man. A. C. Doyle; Memoirs of Sherlock Holmes
Crooked Road. M. West; Big Story
Crooks in Clover. M. A. S. Roche
Cross-Country. H. D. Kastle
Cross Currents. W. G. Elliott; Nine Days' Blunder
Cross Up. J. Mair
Crossfire. R. Brooks; Brick Foxhole
Crosstrap. J. N. Chance (headnote)
Crouching Beast. V. Williams
Crown v. Stevens. L. Meynell; Third Time Unlucky

Cruising. G. Walker
Cry in the Night. W. Masterson; All Through the Night
Cry of the City. H. E. Helseth; Chair for Martin Rome
Cry Terror. A. L. Stone
Cry Tough. I. Shulman
Cry Uncle. M. Brett; Lie a Little, Die a Little
Curly Top. T. Burke; Whispering Windows
Curse of Drink. C. E. Blaney
Curse of Frankenstein. M. Shelley; Frankenstein
Curse of the Werewolf. G. Endore; Werewolf of Paris
Curtain at Eight. O. R. Cohen; Back-stage Mystery
Cutter and Bone. N. Thornburg
Cutter's Way. N. Thornburg; Cutter and Bone
Cynara. R. Gore-Brown; Imperfect Lover
Cynthia-by-the-Minute. L. J. Vance
Daddy's Gone A-Hunting. Mike St. Clair
Dames Get Along. P. Cheyney; Dames Don't Care
Damned. H. L. Lawrence; Children of the Light
Dancer and the King. C. E. Blaney
Dancing Men. A. C. Doyle; Return of Sherlock Holmes
Dandy in Aspic. D. Marlowe
Danger on the Air. Xantippe; Death Catches Up with Mr. Kluck
Danger Route. A. York; Eliminator
Danger Signal. P. Bottome; Murder in the Bud
Danger Within. M. Gilbert; Death in Captivity
Dangerous Afternoon. G. Anstruther
Dangerous Blondes. K. Roos; If the Shroud Fits
Dangerous Corner. J. B. Priestley
Dangerous Crossing. J. D. Carr; Dead Sleep Lightly
Dangerous Davies. L. Thomas
Dangerous Days. M. R. Rinehart
Dangerous Lies. E. P. Oppenheim (headnote)
Dangerous Partners. O. W. Bayer; Paper Chase
Dangerous to Know. E. Wallace; On the Spot
Dare-Devil Conquest. B. Gray
Dark Corner. L. Q. Ross
Dark Eyes of London. E. Wallace
Dark Hazard. W. R. Burnett
Dark Hour. S. Gluck; Last Trap
Dark Mirror. L. J. Vance
Dark of the Sun. Wilbur Smith; Train from Katanga
Dark Page. S. Fuller
Dark Passage. D. Goodis
Dark Past. J. Warwick; Blind Alley
Dark Secret. M. Shairp; Crime at Blossoms
Dark Shadows. Marilyn Ross; House of Dark Shadows
Dark Stairway. M. Eberhart; From This Dark Stairway
Dark Tower. A. Woollcott
Dark Waters. F. Cockrell
Darker Than Amber. J. D. MacDonald
Darling Lili. H. Clement
Daughter of Darkness. M. Catto; They Walk Alone
Daughter of the Dragon. S. Rohmer; Daughter of Fu Manchu
Daughter of Two Worlds. L. Scott
Day of Days. L. J. Vance
Day of the Dolphin. R. Merle
Day of the Jackal. F. Forsyth
Day of the Owl. L. Sciascia; Mafia Vendetta
Day the Fish Came Out. K. Cicellis
Day They Robbed the Bank of England. J. Brophy
Dazzling Miss Davison. F. Warden
Dead Certainty. N. Gould
Dead End. S. Kingsley
Dead Eyes of London. E. Wallace; Dark Eyes of London
Dead Heat on a Merry-Go-Round. E. L. Heyman
Dead Men Are Dangerous. H. C. Armstrong; Hidden
Dead Men Tell No Tales. F. Beeding; Norwich Victims
Dead Men Tell No Tales. E. W. Hornung
Dead of Night. E. F. Benson; Room in the Tower
Dead on a Rainy Sunday. Joan Aiken
Dead on Course. M. Black
Dead Pigeon on Beethoven Street. S. Fuller
Dead Ringer. R. Thomas
Dead Secret. W. Collins
Dead Zone. Stephen King
Deadfall. D. Cory
Deadlier Than the Male. H. Reymond
Deadline. J. Eastwood

Deadline at Dawn. W. Irish
Deadline U.S.A. J. Eastwood; Deadline
Deadly Affair. J. Le Carre; Call for the Dead
Deadly Bees. H. F. Heard; Taste of Honey
Deadly Circuit. M. Behm; Eye of the Beholder
Deadly Duo. R. Jessup
Deadly Encounter. R. Woodley
Deadly Game. N. Bentley; Third Party Risk
Deadly Is the Female. M. Kantor; Author's Choice
Deadly Record. N. W. Hooke
Deadly Trap. A. Cavanagh; Children Are Gone
Dear Fatherland, Be at Peace. J. M. Simmel; Dear Fatherland
Dear Murderer. S. L. Clowes
Death at a Broadcast. V. Gielgud; Death at Broadcasting House
Death at Broadcasting House. V. Gielgud
Death Croons the Blues. J. Ronald
Death Drums Along the River. E. Wallace; Sanders of the River
Death Goes to School. S. Davis; Death in Seven Hours
Death in High Heels. C. Brand
Death Kiss. M. St. Dennis
Death of a Beauty. G. Simenon; Belle
Death of a Champion. F. Gruber; Brass Knuckles
Death on the Diamond. C. Fitzsimmons
Death on the Nile. A. Christie
Death on the Set. V. MacClure
Death Takes a Holiday. W. Ferris
Death Trap. E. Wallace (headnote)
Death Wish. B. Garfield
Deathsport. W. Hughes
Deathtrap. I. Levin
Decision Before Dawn. G. Howe; Call It Treason
Decks Ran Red. A. L. Stone
Deep Water. P. Highsmith
Defector. P. Thomas; Spy
Defenders of the Law. H. Del Ruth
Definite Object. J. Farnol
Delavine Affair. Robert Chapman; Winter Wears a Shroud
Deliverance. J. Dickey
Demon. C. N. Williamson
Descent into Hell. D. Goodis; Wounded and the Slain
Desert Attack. C. Landon; Ice-Cold in Alex
Desert Fury. R. Stewart; Desert Town
Design for Murder. E. Percy; Trunk Crime
Desire in the Dust. H. Whittington
Despair. V. Nabokoff-Sirin
Desperate Hours. J. Hayes
Desperate Man. P. Somers; Beginner's Luck
Desperate Men. M. Halliday; Cat and Mouse
Desperate Moment. M. Albrand
Desperate Search. A. Mayse
Destroying Angel. L. J. Vance
Destructors. M. Franklin
Detective. G. K. Chesterton; Innocence of Father Brown
Detective. L. J. Vance
Detective Story. S. Kingsley
Detour. M. M. Goldsmith
Devil Commands. W. Sloane; Edge of Running Water
Devil-Doll. A. Merritt; Burn, Witch, Burn!
Devil Makes Three. L. P. Bachmann; Kiss of Death
Devil Rides Out. D. Wheatley
Devil Thumbs a Ride. R. C. Du Soe
Devil to Pay. F. N. Greene
Devil's Agent. H. Habe; Agent of the Devil
Devil's Bride. D. Wheatley; Devil Rides Out
Devil's Chaplain. G. Bronson-Howard
Devil's Circus. B. Christiansen
Devil's Daffodil. E. Wallace; Daffodil Mystery
Devil's Foot. A. C. Doyle; His Last Bow
Devil's Own. P. Curtis
Devil's Profession. G. de St. W. James
Devil's Rain. M. Willis
Diabolique. P. Boileau; Woman Who Was
Dial "M" for Murder. F. Knott
Dial 999. B. Graeme; Way Out
Diamond. M. Procter; Rich Is the Treasure
Diamond Man. E. Wallace (headnote)
Diamond Wizard. M. Procter; Rich Is the Treasure
Diamonds Are Forever. I. Fleming
Diana and Destiny. C. Garvice
Dick Turpin. W. H. Ainsworth; Rookwood
Dick Turpin's Ride to York. W. H. Ainsworth; Rookwood

D

Dickson's Diamonds. S. Campbell; Below the Dead-Line
Die! Die! My Darling. A. Blaisdell; Nightmare
Dillinger. H. Clement
Diplomacy. V. Sardou; Diplomates
Diplomatic Courier. P. Cheyney; Sinister Errand
Dirty Harry. P. Rock
Dirty Mary, Crazy Larry. R. Unekis; Chase
Dirty Tricks. T. Gifford; Glendower Legacy
Disappearance. D. Marlowe; Echoes of Celandine
Disappearance of the Judge. C. R. Gull; Lost Judge
Dishonored. F. Vreeland
Diva. Delacorta
Do You Know This Voice? E. Berckman
Dock Brief. J. Mortimer
Dr. Jekyll and Mr. Hyde. R. L. Stevenson; Strange Case of Dr. Jekyll and Mr. Hyde
Doctor Jekyll and Sister Hyde. R. L. Stevenson; Strange Case of Dr. Jekyll and Mr. Hyde
Dr. Mabuse, Gambler. N. Jacques
Doctor No. I. Fleming
Doctor Phibes Rises Again. W. Goldstein
Doctor Rameau. G. Ohnet
Dr. Strangelove. P. Bryant; Two Hours to Doom
Dr. Syn. R. Thorndyke
Dr. Syn Alias the Scarecrow. R. Thorndyke; Dr. Syn
Doctors Wear Scarlet. S. Raven
Dog Day Afternoon. P. Mann
Dogs of War. F. Forsyth
Domino Killings. A. Kennedy; Domino Principle
Domino Principle. A. Kennedy
Don Chicago. C. E. B. Roberts
Don Is Dead. N. Quarry
Don Q, Son of Zorro. K. Prichard; Don Q's Love Story
Donovan Affair. O. Davis
Donovan's Brain. C. Siodmak
Don't Bother to Knock. C. Armstrong; Mischief
Don't Just Stand There. C. Williams; Wrong Venus
Don't Look Now. D. Du Maurier; Not After Midnight
Doomed Cargo. A. Ridley; Wrecker
Door with Seven Locks. E. Wallace
Dossier 51. G. Perrault
Double. E. Wallace
Double-Barrelled Detective Story. M. Twain
Double Confession. J. Garden; All on a Summer's Day
Double Cross Roads. W. Lipman; Yonder Grow the Daisies
Double Door. E. McFadden
Double Identity. J. O. Curwood; River's End
Double Indemnity. J. M. Cain
Double Life of Mr. Alfred Burton. E. P. Oppenheim
Double Man. H. S. Maxfield; Legacy of a Spy
Double Negative. K. Millar; Three Roads
Double Tour. S. Ellin; Key to Nicholas Street
Down Under. Seamark
Down Three Dark Streets. Gordons; Case File: FBI
Down Under Donovan. E. Wallace
Downfall. E. Wallace (headnote)
Dracula. H. Deane
Dracula. B. Stoker
Dracula, Prince of Darkness. B. Stoker; Dracula
Dracula Sucks. B. Stoker; Dracula
Dracula's Daughter. B. Stoker; Dracula's Guest
Dragon Murder Case. S. S. Van Dine
Dragonwyck. A. Seton
Dream Street. T. Burke; Limehouse Nights
Dressed to Kill. C. Black
Dressed to Kill. R. Burke; Dead Take No Bows
Driver. C. B. Phillips
Drop Dead. R. Deming; Careful Man
Drowning Pool. J. R. Macdonald
Drums of Fu Manchu. S. Rohmer
Drums of Jeopardy. H. MacGrath
Duality of Man. R. L. Stevenson; Strange Case of Dr. Jekyll and Mr. Hyde
Dublin Nightmare. P. Loraine
Duds. H. C. Rowland
Duffy. H. J. Brown, Jr.
Dulcimer Street. N. Collins; London Belongs to Me
Dumb Man of Manchester. B. F. Rayner
Dummy. H. J. O'Higgins

Dust in the Sun. J. Cleary; Justin Bayard
Dusty Ermine. N. Grant
Dying Detective. A. C. Doyle; His Last Bow
Dynamite Man from Glory Jail. D. Grubb; Fool's Parade
Each Dawn I Die. J. Odlum
Eagle Has Landed. J. Higgins
Eagle's Eye. W. J. Flynn
Earl of Chicago. Brock Williams
East Lynne. H. Wood
Easy Come, Easy Go. O. Davis
Easy Pickings. P. Cruger
Echo of Barbara. Jonathan Burke
Eclipse. N. Wollaston
Eddie and the Cruisers. P. F. Kluge
Eddie Macon's Run. J. McLendon
Edge of Doom. L. Brady
Edge of Fury. R. M. Coates; Wisteria Cottage
Edge of the City. F. Pohl
Edith's Diary. P. Highsmith
Educated Evans. E. Wallace
Eiger Sanction. Trevanian
Eight Million Ways to Die. L. Block
813. M. Leblanc
Eleni. N. Gage
Elevator to the Gallows. N. Calef; Frantic
11 Harrowhouse. G. A. Browne
Eleventh Commandment. B. Fleming; Pillory
Elinor Norton. M. R. Rinehart; State vs. Elinor Norton
Ellery Queen and the Murder Ring. E. Queen; Dutch Shoe Mystery
Ellery Queen and the Perfect Crime. E. Queen; Perfect Crime
Ellery Queen, Master Detective. E. Queen
Ellery Queen's Penthouse Mystery. E. Queen; Penthouse Mystery
Elusive Isabel. J. Futrelle
Embassy. S. Coulter
Emperor's Candlesticks. B. Orczy
Empty Beach. P. Corris
Empty Hands. A. Stringer
Empty House. A. C. Doyle; Return of Sherlock Holmes
End of the Affair. G. Greene
End of the Game. F. Duerrenmatt; Judge and His Hangman
End of the Road. E. Bulwer-Lytton; Ernest Maltravers
End Play. R. Braddon
Endless Night. A. Christie
Enemies of the Public. K. Glasmon; Public Enemy
Enemy Agent. A. P. Kelly; Three Faces East
Enemy to Society. G. Bronson-Howard
Enforcer. W. Morgan
Engineer's Thumb. A. C. Doyle; Adventures of Sherlock Holmes
England Made Me. G. Greene
Enigma. M. Barak
Enough Rope. P. Highsmith; Blunderer
Enter Arsene Lupin. M. Leblanc; Girl with the Green Eyes
Enter the Dragon. M. Roote
Entertaining Mr. Sloane. J. Orton
Equator. G. Simenon; Tropic Moon
Ernest Maltravers. E. Bulwer-Lytton
Escape. J. Galsworthy
Escape. E. Vance
Escape by Night. R. Croft-Cooke; Clash by Night
Escape from New York. M. McQuay
Escape from Zahrein. M. Barrett; Appointment in Zahrein
Escape in the Desert. R. Sherwood; Petrified Forest
Escape to Athena. P. Blake
Eternal Struggle. G. B. Lancaster; Law Bringers
Eugene Aram. E. Bulwer-Lytton
Eve. J. H. Chase; Eve
Evelyn Prentice. W. E. Woodward
Every Little Crook and Nanny. E. Hunter
Everybody Does It. J. M. Cain; Career in C Major
Everything Is Thunder. J. L. Hardy
Evil That Men Do. R. L. Hill
Evil Under the Sun. A. Christie
Evil Women Do. E. Gaboriau; Clique of Gold
Ex-Flame. H. Wood; East Lynne
Excess Baggage. H. M. Raleigh
Exiles. R. H. Davis
Exorcist. W. P. Blatty
Experiment in Terror. Gordons; Operation Terror
Experiment Perilous. M. Carpenter
Expiation. E. P. Oppenheim
Exploits of Elaine. A. B. Reeve
Eye of the Devil. P. Loraine; Day of the Arrow
Eye of the Needle. K. Follett; Storm Island

Eyes in the Night. B. Kendrick; Odor of Violets
Eyes of Laura Mars. H. B. Gilmour
Eyewitness. M. Hebden
Eyewitness. J. Minahan
Face in the Night. B. Graeme; Suspense
Face of a Stranger. E. Wallace (headnote)
Face the Music. E. Borneman; Tremolo
Faces in the Dark. P. Boileau
Fade to Black. R. Renaud
Fail-Safe. E. Burdick
Falcon Takes Over. R. Chandler; Farewell, My Lovely
Fall Guy. G. Abbott
Fall of a Saint. E. C. Scott
Fallen Angel. M. Holland
Fallen Idol. G. Greene; Basement Room
Fallen Sparrow. D. B. Hughes
False Evidence. E. P. Oppenheim
False Evidence. R. Vickers; I'll Never Tell
False Faces. L. J. Vance
Family Doctor. J. Fleming; Deeds of Dr. Deadcert
Family Plot. V. Canning; Rainbird Pattern
Family Secret. A. Thomas; Editha's Burglar
Fan. B. Randall
Fanatic. A. Blaisdell; Nightmare
Fantasia Among the Squares. C. Williams; Diamond Bikini
Fantasist. P. McGinley; Goosefoot
Fantomas. P. Souvestre
Farewell, My Lovely. R. Chandler
Fast Company. M. Page
Fast Walking. E. Brawley; Rap
Fatal Night. E. K. Chatterton; Marriages of Mayfair
Fatal Night. M. Arlen; May Fair
Father Brown. G. K. Chesterton; Innocence of Father Brown
Father Brown, Detective. G. K. Chesterton
Fathom. L. Forrester; Girl Called Fathom
Fear. F. M. Dostoevskii; Crime and Punishment
Fear in the Night. W. Irish; I Wouldn't Be in Your Shoes
Fear in the Night. C. Woolrich; Nightmare
Fear Is the Key. A. MacLean
Fear Makers. D. L. Teilhet
Fear No More. L. Edgley
Feathered Serpent. E. Wallace
Federal Bullets. G. F. Eliot
Female Fiends. P. Quentin; Puzzle for Fiends
ffoulkes. J. Davies; Esther, Ruth and Jennifer
Fiend Who Walked the West. E. Lipsky; Kiss of Death
Fiends. P. Boileau; Woman Who Was
5th of November. M. Franklin
Fifty Candles. E. D. Biggers
51 File. G. Perrault; Dossier 51
Fifty Roads to Town. F. Nebel
Fifty-Two Pickup. E. Leonard
Fighting Edge. W. M. Raine
Fighting Snub Reilly. E. Wallace; Forty-Eight Short Stories
File of the Golden Goose. J. Watson
File 113. E. Gaboriau; File No. 113
Final Exam. G. Meyer
Final Problem. A. C. Doyle; Memoirs of Sherlock Holmes
Find the Woman. A. S. Roche
Finders Keepers. C. Dennis; Next-to-Last Train Ride
Fine Pair. C. Stratton
Fire Flingers. W. J. Neidig
Firefox. C. Thomas
Firestarter. Stephen King
First and the Last. J. Galsworthy; Five Tales
First Blood. D. Morrell
First Chronicles of Don Q. K. Prichard; Chronicles of Don Q
First Comes Courage. E. Arnold; Commandos
First Deadly Sin. Lawrence Sanders
First Great Train Robbery. M. Crichton; Great Train Robbery
First Law. G. Willets
Fitzwilly. Poyntz Tyler; Garden of Cucumbers
Fitzwilly Strikes Back. Poyntz Tyler; Garden of Cucumbers
Five Against the House. J. Finney
Five Ashore for Singapore. J. Bruce; Cold Spell
Five Fingers. L. C. Moyzisch; Operation Cicero
Five Star Final. L. Weitzenkorn
Five Steps to Danger. D. Hamilton; Assignment: Murder
Five to One. E. Wallace; Thief in the Night

Flaming Forest. J. O. Curwood
Flanagan Boy. M. Catto
Flash of Green. J. D. MacDonald
Flashpoint. G. La Fountaine
Flat 2. E. Wallace
Flesh and Fantasy. O. Wilde; Lord Arthur Savile's Crime
Flesh and the Fiends. R. L. Stevenson; Body Snatcher
Flesh of the Orchid. J. H. Chase
Fleshburn. J. Ives; Fear in a Handful of Dust
Fletch. G. McDonald
Flight from Destiny. A. Berkeley; Trial and Error
Flight of the Phoenix. E. Trevor
Flim Flam Man. G. Owen
Floating Dutchman. N. Bentley
Floods of Fear. J. Hawkins
Floor Above. E. P. Oppenheim (headnote)
Florentine Dagger. B. Hecht
Flying Fifty-Five. E. Wallace
Flying Squad. E. Wallace
Fog. E. Queen; Study in Terror
Fog. V. Williams
Fog Over Frisco. G. Dyer; Five Fragments
Follow That Horse. H. Mason; Photo Finish
Folly of Desire. A. Askew; Shulamite
Fool Killer. H. Eustis
Foolish Monte Carlo. C. Dawe; Black Spider
Fool's Parade. D. Grubb
Footfalls. W. D. Steele
Footsteps in the Fog. W. W. Jacobs; Sea Whispers
Footsteps in the Night. C. Fraser-Simpson
For Pete's Sake. B. Street
For the Term of His Natural Life. M. Clarke; His Natural Life
For Them That Trespass. E. Raymond
Forbidden Fruit. G. Simenon; Act of Passion
Forbidden Territory. D. Wheatley
Force of Evil. I. Wolfert; Tucker's People
Force 10 from Navarone. A. MacLean
Forger. E. Wallace
Forgotten Faces. R. W. Child; Velvet Black
Formula. S. Shagan
Fort Apache, the Bronx. H. Gould
Fortune Is a Woman. Winston Graham
Forty Naughty Girls. S. Palmer (headnote)
Foul Play. C. Reade
Foul Play. J. C. Rogers
Four Boys and a Gun. W. Wiener
Four Dark Hours. G. Greene (headnote)
Four Days' Wonder. A. A. Milne
Four Hours to Kill. N. Krasna; Small Miracle
Four Just Men. E. Wallace
Four Men and a Prayer. D. Garth
Four Walls. D. Burnet
Fourth Protocol. F. Forsyth
Fourth Square. E. Wallace; Four Square Jane
Foxhole in Cairo. L. O. Mosley; Cat and the Mice
Fragment of Fear. J. Bingham
Franchise Affair. J. Tey
Frankenstein. M. Shelley
Frankenstein Must Be Destroyed. M. Shelley; Frankenstein
Frankenstein: The True Story. M. Shelley; Frankenstein
Fraulein. J. McGovern
Freebie and the Bean. P. B. Ross
French Connection II. R. Moore
French Key. F. Gruber
Frenzy. A. La Bern; Goodbye Piccadilly, Farewell Leicester Square
Friends of Eddie Coyle. G. V. Higgins
Frightened Bride. A. E. Lindop; Tall Headlines
Frightened Lady. E. Wallace
Frightened Lady. E. Wallace; Case of the Frightened Lady
Frog. E. Wallace; Fellowship of the Frog
From Now On. F. Packard
From Russia with Love. I. Fleming
From the Boys. R. Matheson; Ride the Nightmare
From the Valley of the Missing. G. M. White
Front Page Story. R. Gaines; Final Night
Fugitive. F. L. Green; On the Night of the Fire
Fugitive. G. Greene; Power and the Glory
Fugitives. R. H. Davis; Exiles
Full Treatment. R. S. Thorn
Funeral in Berlin. L. Deighton
Fury. J. Farris
Fury at Furnace Creek. D. Garth; Four Men and a Prayer

Fuzz. E. Hunter
"G" Men. H. K. Long
Gables Mystery. J. Celestin; Man at Six
Gambit. K. Lane
Gamble in Lives. F. Stayton; Joan Danvers
Gamble with Hearts. A. Carlyle
Gamblers. C. Klein
Game for Three Losers. E. Lustgarten
Game for Vultures. M. Hartmann
Game of Death. R. Connell; Variety
Game of Liberty. E. P. Oppenheim
Games. H. Ellson
Games of the Countess Dolingen of Gratz. B. Stoker; Dracula
Gang That Couldn't Shoot Straight. J. Breslin
Gang War. O. Demaris; Hoods Take Over
Gang War. F. L. Green; Odd Man Out
Gangster. D. Fuchs; Low Company
Garden Murder Case. S. S. Van Dine
Gas. B. Hirschfeld
Gas Light. P. Hamilton
Gaunt Stranger. E. Wallace; Ringer
Gauntlet. M. Butler
Gay Adventure. W. Hackett
Gay Lord Waring. H. Townley
Gazebo. A. Coppel
Gemini Contenders. R. Ludlum
General Died at Dawn. C. G. Booth
Gentleman After Dark. R. W. Child; Velvet Black
Gentleman Burglar. M. Leblanc (headnote)
Gentleman's Fate. K. U. P.
George Barnwell, the London Apprentice. G. Lillo; London Merchant
Get Carter. T. Lewis; Jack's Return Home
Get-Rich-Quick-Wallingford. G. R. Chester
Getaway. J. Thompson
Ghost Breakers. C. W. Goddard
Ghost of John Holling. E. Wallace; Steward
Ghost That Walks Alone. R. Shattuck; Wedding Guest Sat on a Stone
Ghost Train. A. Ridley
Ghoul. Frank King
Gideon of Scotland Yard. J. J. Marric; Gideon's Day
Gideon's Day. J. J. Marric
Gift Supreme. G. A. England
Girl by the Roadside. V. Vanardy
Girl from Mandalay. R. Campbell; Death in Tiger Valley
Girl Hunters. M. Spillane
Girl in Room 17. L. T. White; Harness Bull
Girl in His House. H. MacGrath
Girl in the Dark. C. E. Walk; Green Seal
Girl in the Headlines. L. Payne; Nose on My Face
Girl in the News. R. Vickers
Girl in the Web. G. Bonner; Miss Maitland, Private Secretary
Girl in the Woods. O. Crawford; Blood on the Branches
Girl of the Port. J. Russell; Far Wandering Men
Girl Was Young. J. Tey; Shilling for Candles
Girl Who Dared. Medora Field; Blood on Her Shoe
Glass Bottom Boat. B. Street
Glass Cage. A. E. Martin; Outsiders
Glass Cell. P. Highsmith
Glass Key. D. Hammett
Glass Tomb. A. E. Martin; Outsiders
Glass Web. M. Ehrlich; Spin the Glass Web
Glitter Dome. J. Wambaugh
Gloria Scott. A. C. Doyle; Memoirs of Sherlock Holmes
Godfather. M. Puzo
Godfather, Part II. M. Puzo; Godfather
God's Clay. A. Askew
God's Law and Man's. P. Trent; Wife by Purchase
God's Prodigal. A. J. Russell
Godsend. B. Taylor
Going Crooked. Winchell Smith
Golden Earrings. Y. Foldes
Golden Gate. A. MacLean
Golden Pince-Nez. A. C. Doyle; Return of Sherlock Holmes
Golden Rendezvous. A. MacLean
Golden Salamander. V. Canning
Golden Snare. J. O. Curwood
Golden Web. E. P. Oppenheim; Plunderers
Goldfinger. I. Fleming
Good Girls Beware. J. H. Chase; Miss Callaghan Comes to Grief
Good Guys Wear Black. M. Franklin
Good Time Girl. A. La Bern; Night Darkens the Streets
Goodbye Charlie. M. H. Albert
Goodbye Gemini. J. Hall; Ask Agamemnon

Gooseflesh. J. H. Chase; Come Easy--Go Easy
Gorilla. R. Spence
Gorky Park. M. C. Smith
Gracie Allen Murder Case. S. S. Van Dine
Grand Babylon Hotel. A. Bennett
Grand Central Murder. S. MacVeigh
Grand National Night. D. Christie
Grandeur and Decadence of a Small-Time Filmmaker. J. H. Chase (headnote)
Grandfather Smallweed. C. Dickens; Bleak House
Grasp of Greed. H. R. Haggard; Mr. Meeson's Will
Grasshopper. M. McShane; Passing of Evil
Gray Dawn. S. E. White
Gray Ghost. A. S. Roche; Loot
Gray Mask. W. Camp
Great Armored Car Swindle. L. Meynell; Breaking Point
Great Hospital Mystery. M. Eberhart (headnote)
Great Hotel Murder. V. Starrett
Great Impersonation. E. P. Oppenheim
Great K&A Train Robbery. P. L. Ford
Great Prince Shan. E. P. Oppenheim
Greater Than a Crown. V. Bridges; Lady from Long Acre
Greek Interpreter. A. C. Doyle; Memoirs of Sherlock Holmes
Green Cloak. Y. Davis
Green Cockatoo. G. Greene (headnote)
Green Eyes. H. Ashbrook; Murder of Steven Kester
Green for Danger. C. Brand
Green God. F. A. Kummer
Green Ice. G. A. Browne
Green Man. F. Launder; Meet a Body
Green Pack. E. Wallace
Green Scarf. G. Des Cars; Brute
Green Terror. E. Wallace; Green Rust
Greene Murder Case. S. S. Van Dine
Grell Mystery. F. Froest
Grilling. J. Wainwright; Brainwash
Grip. J. S. Winter
Grip of Fear. Gordons; Operation Terror
Grip of the Strangler. J. C. Cooper
Grissom Gang. J. H. Chase; No Orchids for Miss Blandish
Groundstar Conspiracy. L. Davies; Alien
Grumpy. H. Hodges
Guilt Is My Shadow. P. Curtis; You're Best Alone
Guilty? M. Gilbert; Death Has Deep Roots
Guilty. W. Irish; Dancing Detective
Guilty As Charged. D. N. Rubin; Riddle Me This!
Guilty As Hell. D. N. Rubin; Riddle Me This!
Guilty Bystander. Wade Miller
Guilty Man. F. Coppee
Gumshoe. N. Smith
Gun Crazy. M. Kantor; Author's Choice
Gun Moll. P. Cheyney; Poison Ivy
Gun-Runner. A. Stringer
Gun Runners. E. Hemingway; To Have and Have Not
Guns of Darkness. F. Clifford; Act of Mercy
Guns of Navarone. A. MacLean
Gypsy and the Gentleman. N. W. Hooke; Darkness I Leave You
Half a Chance. F. S. Isham
Half a Truth. Rita
Half Million Bribe. W. H. Osborne; Red Mouse
Halloween. C. Richards
Halloween II. J. Martin
Hammer the Toff. J. Creasey
Hammerhead. J. Mayo
Hammett. J. Gores
Hammond Mystery. J. D. Kerruish; Undying Monster
Hand. M. Brandel; Lizard's Tail
Hand of Peril. A. Stringer
Hands of Orlac. M. Renard
Hands of the Ripper. E. S. Shew
Hanged Man. D. B. Hughes; Expendable Man
Hangover Square. P. Hamilton
Hanky Panky. L. Jarreau
Happening. E. Curry
Happy Thieves. R. Condon; Oldest Confession
Hard Cash. C. Reade
Hard Man. L. Katcher
Hard Traveling. A. Bessie; Bread and a Stone
Harper. J. Macdonald; Moving Target
Harrassed Hero. E. Dudley
Hate. W. Camp; Communicating Door
Hate Ship. B. Graeme
Hatter's Ghost. G. Simenon
Haunted Bell. J. Futrelle; Diamond Master
Haunted Honeymoon. D. L. Sayers; Busman's Honeymoon

Haunted House. O. Davis
Haunted Pajamas. F. P. Elliott
Haunted Strangler. J. C. Cooper
Haunting. S. Jackson; Haunting of Hill House
Haunting Shadows. M. Nicholson; House of a Thousand Candles
Having Wonderful Crime. C. Rice
Hawk's Nest. W. Gunning
Hazard. R. Chanslor
He Died with His Eyes Open. D. Raymond
He Ran All the Way. S. Ross
Heads or Tails. A. Harris; Baroni
Hearse. H. Clement
Heart and Soul. R. Horniman; Nonconformist Parson
Heart of the Hills. D. Whitelaw; Girl from the East
Heart of the Matter. G. Greene
Heart of the North. W. B. Mowery
Heart Trump for OSS 117 in Tokyo. J. Bruce; Hot Line
Heat. W. Goldman
Heatwave. K. Hughes; High Wray
Heliotrope. R. W. Child; Velvet Black
Hell Below Zero. H. Innes; White South
Hell Is a City. M. Procter
Hell Is Empty. J. F. Straker
Hell Is Sold Out. M. Dekobra
Hell on Frisco Bay. W. P. McGivern; Darkest Hour
Hennessy. M. Franklin
Her Bitter Lesson. M. E. Braddon; Aurora Floyd
Her Fatal Sin. M. E. Holmes
Her Second Chance. W. Woodrow; Second Chance
Hero at Large. A. J. Carothers
Heroin Gang. R. Wilder; Fruit of the Poppy
Hickey and Boggs. P. Rock
Hidden Hand. Rufus King; Invitation to a Murder
Hidden Homicide. P. Capon; Death at Shinglestrand
Hidden Room. A. Coppel
Hidden Spring. C. B. Kelland
Hideout. R. Westerby; Small Voice
Hideout in the Alps. N. Grant; Dusty Ermine
High and Low. E. Hunter; King's Ransom
High Anxiety. R. H. Pilpel
High Ballin'. Richard Robinson
High Bright Sun. I. S. Black
High Command. L. Robinson; General Goes Too Far
High Commissioner. J. Cleary
High Hand. J. Futrelle
High Road to China. J. Cleary
High School Confidential. Morton Cooper
High Sierra. W. R. Burnett
High Speed. C. H. Stagg
High Wall. A. R. Clark
High Window. R. Chandler
Highest Bidder. M. Foster; Trap
Highways by Night. C. B. Kelland; Silver Spoon
His Lordship. N. Grant; Nelson Touch
His Official Wife. R. H. Savage; My Official Wife
His Robe of Honor. E. Dorrance
His Wife's Friend. J. B. Harris-Burland; White Rook
His Wife's Husband. A. K. Green; Mayor's Wife
Hit and Run. L. Fletcher; Eighty Dollars to Stamford
Hit and Run. R. Marshall
Hit Man. T. Lewis; Jack's Return Home
Hitler's Gold. W. Hughes; Inside Out
Holcroft Covenant. R. Ludlum
Hold-Up. J. Cronley; Quick Change
Hollow Triumph. M. Forbes
Home at Seven. R. C. Sherriff
Home Before Dark. E. Bassing
Home Sweet Homicide. C. Rice
Homicide for Three. P. Quentin; Puzzle for Puppets
Honey Pot. T. Sterling; Evil of the Day
Honeymoon Adventure. C. Fraser-Simpson; Footsteps in the Night
Honeymoon Killers. Paul Buck
Honor First. G. F. Gibbs; Splendid Outcast
Honorary Consul. G. Greene
Honours Easy. R. Pertwee
Hoodlum's Son. J. Flynn; Action Man
Hopscotch. B. Garfield
Horizontal Lieutenant. G. Cotler; Bottletop Affair
Hornet's Nest. W. Woodrow
Horrible Hyde. R. L. Stevenson; Strange Case of Dr. Jekyll and Mr. Hyde
Horror of Dracula. B. Stoker; Dracula
Horror of Frankenstein. M. Shelley; Frankenstein
Hostage. C. Henry
Hostages. S. Heym
Hostile Witness. J. Roffey
Hot Enough for June. L. Davidson; Night of Wenceslas
Hot Ice. A. Melville; Week-End at Thrackley
Hot Rock. D. E. Westlake
Hot Rod Rumble. M. Dolinsky
Hot Spot. S. Fisher; I Wake Up Screaming
Hotel Reserve. E. Ambler; Epitaph for a Spy
Hound of the Baskervilles. A. C. Doyle
Hounds of Zaroff. R. Connell; Variety
Hour of Thirteen. M. Porlock; X v. Rex
House Across the Lake. K. Hughes; High Wray
House by the River. A. P. Herbert
House in Marsh Road. L. Meynell
House of a Thousand Candles. M. Nicholson
House of Cards. S. Ellin
House of Dark Shadows. Marilyn Ross
House of Fate. J. E. Grant; Green Shadow
House of Fear. W. Camp
House of Fear. A. C. Doyle; Adventures of Sherlock Holmes
House of Fright. R. L. Stevenson; Strange Case of Dr. Jekyll and Mr. Hyde
House of Glass. M. Marcin
House of Intrigue. H. J. Giskes; London Calling North Pole
House of Marney. J. Goodwin
House of Menace. E. Chodorov; Kind Lady
House of Mystery. A. E. W. Mason; At the Villa Rose
House of Numbers. J. Finney
House of Peril. M. B. Lowndes; Chink in the Armour
House of Secrets. S. Horler
House of Secrets. S. Noel
House of Silence. E. Barron; Marcel Levignet
House of the Arrow. A. E. W. Mason
House of the Long Shadows. E. D. Biggers; Seven Keys to Baldpate
House of the Lost Court. D. T. De Savallo
House of the Seven Hawks. V. Canning; House of the Seven Flies
House of the Spaniard. A. Behrend
House of Whispers. W. Johnston
House on Telegraph Hill. D. Lyon; Frightened Child
House on the Marsh. F. Warden
House Opposite. J. J. Farjeon
Housekeeper. R. Rendell; Judgement in Stone
Housekeeper's Daughter. D. H. Clarke
How Sir Andrew Lost His Vote. R. H. Davis; In the Fog
How to Murder Your Wife. H. Williams
How to Steal a Diamond in Four Uneasy Lessons. D. E. Westlake; Hot Rock
How to Steal a Million. M. Sinclair
How Women Love. I. L. Forrester; Dangerous Inheritance
Howling. G. Brandner
Howling II. G. Brandner
Human Cargo. K. Shepard
Human Factor. G. Greene
Human Factor. S. Quinn
Human Monster. E. Wallace; Dark Eyes of London
Hunted Woman. J. O. Curwood
Hunting Party. J. Millard
Huntingtower. J. Buchan
Huntress. H. Footner
Hustle. S. Shagan; City of Angels
Hutch Stirs 'Em Up. H. Harding; Hawk of Rede
I Became a Criminal. J. Budd; Convict Has Escaped
I Cover the Waterfront. Max Miller
I Died a Thousand Times. W. R. Burnett; High Sierra
I Hate Actors. B. Hecht
I Killed the Count. A. Coppel
I Love Trouble. R. Huggins; Double Take
I Love You Again. O. R. Cohen
I Married a Dead Man. W. Irish
I, Monster. R. L. Stevenson; Strange Case of Dr. Jekyll and Mr. Hyde
I Ring Doorbells. R. Birdwell
I Saw What You Did. U. Curtiss; Out of the Dark
I Start Counting. A. E. Lindop
I Thank a Fool. A. E. Lindop
I, the Jury. M. Spillane
I Wake Up Screaming. S. Fisher
I Walk the Line. Madison Jones; Exile
I Wouldn't Be in Your Shoes. W. Irish
Ice-Cold in Alex. C. Landon
Ice Station Zebra. A. MacLean
Icy Breasts. R. Matheson; Someone Is Bleeding
I'll Get You for This. J. H. Chase
Illustrious Corpses. L. Sciascia; Equal Danger
Illustrious Prince. E. P. Oppenheim
In a Lonely Place. D. B. Hughes
In Case of Emergency. G. Simenon
In Cold Blood. T. Capote
In Defiance of the Law. J. O. Curwood; Isobel
In Full Cry. R. Marsh
In His Grip. D. C. Murray
In Like Flint. B. Street
In the Balance. E. P. Oppenheim; Hillman
In the Blood. A. Soutar
In the Hands of the Spoilers. S. Paternoster; Hand of the Spoiler
In the Heat of the Night. J. Ball
In the Hollow of Her Hand. G. B. McCutcheon; Hollow of Her Hand
In the Next Room. E. R. Belmont
In the Next Room. B. E. Stevenson; Mystery of the Boule Cabinet
In the Night. J. Sutherland
In the Wake of a Stranger. I. S. Black
Incense for the Damned. S. Raven; Doctors Wear Scarlet
Incident at Midnight. E. Wallace (headnote)
Informer. L. O'Flaherty
Informers. D. Warner; Death of a Snout
Inheritance. J. S. Le Fanu; Uncle Silas
Innocent Bystander. J. Munro
Innocents. H. James; Turn of the Screw
Innocents with Dirty Hands. R. Neely; Damned Innocents
Inquest. M. Barringer
Inquisitor. J. Wainwright; Brainwash
Inside Out. J. Bernard
Inside Out. W. Hughes
Inside the Lines. E. D. Biggers
Inspector. J. De Hartog
Inspector Calls. J. B. Priestley
Inspector Hornleigh on Holiday. L. Grex; Stolen Death
Inspector Maigret. G. Simenon; Maigret Sets a Trap
Intent to Kill. M. Bryan
Interference. R. Pertwee
Interlude. J. M. Cain; Serenade
Intruder. R. Maugham; Line on Ginger
Intruder in the Dust. W. Faulkner
Invasion U.S.A. J. Frost
Investigation of Murder. M. Sjowall; Laughing Policeman
Invincible Six. M. Barrett; Heroes of Yuca
Ipcress File. L. Deighton
Irish Luck. N. Venner; Imperfect Imposter
Island in the Sun. A. Waugh
Island of Intrigue. I. Ostrander
Island Rescue. J. Tickell; Appointment with Venus
Isobel. J. O. Curwood
It Always Rains on Sunday. A. La Bern
It Happens in Broad Daylight. F. Duerrenmatt; Pledge
It Is Never Too Late to Mend. C. Reade
It Only Happens to the Living. R. Marshall; Things Men Do
It Shouldn't Happen to a Dog. E. Lanham
It Started in Tokyo. F. Gruber; Twenty Plus Two
Italian Job. T. K. Martin
It's Alive. R. Woodley
It's in the Blood. D. Whitelaw; Big Picture
Ivory Snuff Box. A. Fredericks
Ivy. M. B. Lowndes; Story of Ivy
Jack Chanty. H. Footner
Jack Sheppard. W. H. Ainsworth
Jack Sheppard. J. B. Buckstone
Jack the Ripper. S. James
Jamaica Inn. D. Du Maurier
Jamaica Run. M. Murray; Neat Little Corpse
Jassy. N. Lofts
Jeanne of the Marshes. E. P. Oppenheim
Jekyll and Hyde...Together Again. R. L. Stevenson; Strange Case of Dr. Jekyll and Mr. Hyde
Jewel. E. Wallace (headnote)
Jewel Robbery. L. Fodor
Jigsaw. W. Ericson; Fallen Angel
Jigsaw. H. Waugh; Sleep Long, My Love
Jigsaw Man. Dorothea Bennett
Jim Hanvey, Detective. O. R. Cohen
Jim the Penman. C. L. Young
Jimmy Dale, Alias "The Grey Seal." F. Packard; Adventures of Jimmie Dale
Jimmy the Kid. D. E. Westlake
Jo, the Crossing Sweeper. C. Dickens; Bleak House
John Heriot's Wife. A. Askew
John Needham's Double. J. Hatton
Johnny Angel. C. G. Booth; Mr. Angel Comes Aboard
Johnny Cool. J. McPartland; Kingdom of Johnny Cool
Johnny on the Spot. M. Cronin; Paid in Full
Jokers. M. Sands
Jolly Bad Fellow. C. E. Vulliamy; Don Among the Dead Men

Journey into Fear. E. Ambler
Joy House. D. Keene
Joyless Street. H. Bettauer; Viennese Love
Joyous Adventures of Aristide Pujol. W. J. Locke
Judge Priest. I. S. Cobb; Down Yonder with Judge Priest
Judgement in Stone. R. Rendell
Jugger. R. Stark
Juggernaut. A. Campbell
Juggernaut. A. Hine
Julia. P. Straub
Julie. A. L. Stone
Jump for Glory. G. McDonell
Just Before Nightfall. E. Atiyah; Thin Line
Justice. J. Galsworthy
Juvenile Jungle. F. Counsel
Kaleidoscope. M. Avallone
Kamikaze. P. Wahloo; Murder on the Thirty-First Floor
Kate Plus Ten. E. Wallace
Kazan. J. O. Curwood
Keep. F. P. Wilson
Keep Talking, Baby. D. Keene; Strange Witness
Kennel Murder Case. S. S. Van Dine
Key Largo. M. Anderson
Key to Yesterday. C. N. Buck
Key Witness. F. Kane
Kick-In. W. Mack
Kidnapping of the President. C. Templeton
Kill the Referee. A. Draper; Death Penalty
Killer. Nicholas Blake; Beast Must Die
Killer Elite. R. Rostand
Killer Inside Me. J. Thompson
Killer Walks. G. Glennon; Gathering Storm
Killers. E. Hemingway
Killing. L. White; Clean Break
Kind Hearts and Coronets. R. Horniman; Israel Rank
Kind Lady. E. Chodorov
King Murder. C. R. Jones
King of the Khyber Rifles. T. Mundy
Kiss Before Dying. I. Levin
Kiss Me Deadly. M. Spillane
Kiss of Death. E. Lipsky
Kiss the Blood Off My Hands. C. Butler
Kiss Tomorrow Goodbye. H. McCoy
Kitten with a Whip. Wade Miller
Klute. W. Johnston
Knight Without Armor. J. Hilton
Knock on Any Door. W. Motley
Knocknagow. C. Kickham
Kremlin Letter. N. Behn
Kronstadt. P. Pemberton
Laburnam Grove. J. B. Priestley
Lackey and the Lady. T. Gallon
Lacquered Box. A. Christie; Black Coffee
Lad. E. Wallace (headnote)
Ladies Club. B. Black; Sisterhood
Ladies in Retirement. E. Percy
Ladies' Man. R. Hughes
Ladies' Man. P. Quentin; Shadow of Guilt
Ladies of the Jury. F. Ballard
Lady and the Monster. C. Siodmak; Donovan's Brain
Lady Audley's Secret. M. E. Braddon
Lady Frances Carfex. A. C. Doyle; His Last Bow
Lady from Long Acre. V. Bridges
Lady from Shanghai. Sherwood King; If I Die Before I Wake
Lady Ice. M. Braly; Master
Lady in a Cage. R. Durand
Lady in Cement. A. Rome
Lady in the Car with Glasses and a Gun. S. Japrisot
Lady in the Lake. R. Chandler
Lady in the Morgue. J. Latimer
Lady Mislaid. A. Hornblow
Lady of Burlesque. G. R. Lee; G-String Murders
Lady of Death. R. L. Stevenson; Suicide Club
Lady on a Train. L. Charteris
Lady Takes a Flier. E. Ronns
Lady Vanishes. E. L. White; Wheel Spins
Ladyfingers. J. Gregory
Lancer Spy. M. McKenna
Laramie Trail. J. Gregory; Mystery at Spanish Hacienda
Larceny. L. Eby; Velvet Fleece
Larceny, Inc. L. Perelman; Night Before Christmas
Last Bow. A. C. Doyle; His Last Bow
Last Embrace. M. T. Bloom; 13th Man
Last Escape. M. Walker
Last Express. B. Kendrick
Last Grenade. J. Sherlock; Ordeal of Major Grigsby
Last Hour. C. Bennett
Last Journey. J. J. Farjeon; Holiday Express

Last Known Address. J. Harrington
Last Man to Hang. G. Bullett; Jury
Last Mile. J. Wexley
Last of Mrs. Cheyney. F. Lonsdale
Last of Philip Banter. J. F. Bardin
Last of Sheila. A. Edwards
Last of the Lone Wolf. L. J. Vance; Lone Wolf
Last Page. J. H. Chase
Last Shot You Hear. W. Fairchild; Sound of Murder
Last Turning. J. M. Cain; Postman Always Rings Twice
Last Warning. W. Camp; House of Fear
Last Warning. J. Latimer; Dead Don't Care
Late Edwina Black. W. Dinner
Laughing Policeman. M. Sjowall
Laura. V. Caspary
Law and Disorder. D. Roberts
Law and the Lady. F. Lonsdale
Law and the Woman. C. Fitch
Lawyer Man. M. Trell
League of Frightened Men. R. Stout
League of Gentlemen. J. Boland
Leah Kleschna. C. M. S. McLellan
Leave Her to Heaven. B. A. Williams
Leavenworth Case. A. K. Green
Legend of Hell House. R. Matheson; Hell House
Legend of the Lawman. W. Carey
Leopard Lady. E. C. Carpenter
Leopard Man. C. Woolrich; Black Alibi
Lepke. J. Pearl
Let 'Er Go Gallegher. R. H. Davis; Gallegher
Let It Be Sunday. C. Williams; Long Saturday Night
Let No Man Write My Epitaph. W. Motley
Let the Beast Die. Nicholas Blake; Beast Must Die
Let's Kill Uncle. R. O'Grady
Letter. W. S. Maugham
Letters to an Unknown Lover. P. Boileau; Prisoner
Letty Lynton. M. B. Lowndes
Libel. E. Wooll
Life for Ruth. W. Drummond
Life for Sale. S. Horler; In the Dark
Life Goes On. W. Hackett; Sorry You've Been Troubled
Life in the Balance. G. Simenon (headnote)
Life Without Soul. M. Shelley; Frankenstein
Lightning Strikes Twice. M. Echard; Dark Fantastic
Lights and Shadows. P. Dunning; Night Hostess
Lily of Kilarney. D. Boucicault; Colleen Bawn
Limbo Line. V. Canning
Limping Man. W. Scott; Man
Lion and the Lamb. E. P. Oppenheim
Lion and the Mouse. A. Hornblow
Lion Man. R. Parrish; Strange Case of Cavendish
Lion's Mouse. C. N. Williamson
Liquidator. J. Gardner
Lisa. J. De Hartog; Inspector
List of Adrian Messenger. P. MacDonald
Little Caesar. W. R. Burnett
Little Drummer Girl. J. Le Carre
Little Girl in a Big City. J. K. McCurdy
Little Girl Who Lives Down the Lane. L. Koenig
Little Hour of Peter Wells. D. Whitelaw
Little Murders. J. Feiffer
Little Virtuous. R. Marshall; Short Time to Live
Live and Let Die. I. Fleming
Live Now, Pay Later. J. T. Story
Live Today for Tomorrow. E. Lothar; Mills of God
Living Dangerously. R. Simpson
Living Lies. A. S. Roche; Plunder
Lizzie. S. Jackson; Bird's Nest
Loaded Dice. E. H. Clark
Locked Door. C. Pollock; Sign on the Door
Locker 69. E. Wallace (headnote)
Lodger. M. B. Lowndes
London After Midnight. M. Coolridge-Rask
London Belongs to Me. N. Collins
London by Night. C. Selby
Lone Wolf. L. J. Vance
Lone Wolf Returns. L. J. Vance
Lonely Hearts. E. Hunter; Lady, Lady, I Did It!
Lonely Road. N. Shute
Long Arm of Mannister. E. P. Oppenheim; Long Arm
Long Day's Dying. A. White
Long Goodbye. R. Chandler
Long Haul. M. Mills
Long Knife. S. Truss; Long Night
Long Memory. H. Clewes
Long Wait. M. Spillane

Longest Night. C. Fitzsimmons; Whispering Window
Look Out, Girls. J. H. Chase; Miss Callaghan Comes to Grief
Looking Glass War. J. Le Carre
Loophole. R. Pollock
Loot. J. Orton
Loot. A. S. Roche
Lord Camber's Ladies. H. A. Vachell; Case of Lady Camber
Lord Edgware Dies. A. Christie
Lord John in New York. C. N. Williamson
Los Angeles Precinct 45. J. Wambaugh; New Centurions
Loser Takes All. G. Greene
Lost Continent. D. Wheatley; Uncharted Seas
Lost Illusion. G. Greene; Basement Room
Lost Leader. E. P. Oppenheim
Lost Man. F. L. Green
Lost Moment. H. James; Aspern Papers
Loudwater Mystery. E. Jepson
Louis Beretti. D. H. Clarke
Love and Bullets. J. Heddon
Love and the Whirlwind. H. P. Lewis
Love Cage. D. Keene; Joy House
Love from a Stranger. F. Vosper
Love Insurance. E. D. Biggers
Love Is a Racket. R. James
Love Is My Profession. G. Simenon; In Case of Emergency
Love Is Only a Word. J. M. Simmel; Love Is Just a Word
Love Letters. C. Massie; Pity My Simplicity
Love Letters of a Star. Rufus King; Case of the Constant God
Love on the Spot. H. C. McNeile; Three of a Kind
Love Racket. B. K. Burns; Jury Woman
Love Under Fire. W. Hackett; Fugitives
Love Without Question. W. Camp; Abandoned Room
Love's Boomerang. D. C. Calthrop; Perpetua
Loves of Colleen Bawn. D. Boucicault; Colleen Bawn
Loyalties. J. Galsworthy
Luck of the Irish. H. MacGrath
Lucky Nick Cain. J. H. Chase; I'll Get You for This
Lucky Stiff. C. Rice
Lunatic at Large. J. S. Clouston
Lure. G. Scarborough
Lure of the Swamp. G. Brewer; Hell's Our Destination
Lyons Mail. E. Moreau; Courier of Lyons
McCabe and Mrs. Miller. E. Naughton; McCabe
McGuffin. J. Bowen
McGuire Go Home! I. S. Black; High Bright Sun
Mackenzie Break. S. Shelley; Bowmanville Break
Mackintosh Man. D. Bagley; Freedom Trap
McQ. A. Edwards
Macabre. T. Durant; Marble Forest
Machine Gun McCain. O. Demaris; Candyleg
"Mad Dog" Coll. S. Thurman
Mad Love. M. Renard
Mad Room. E. Percy; Ladies in Retirement
Mad Whirl. R. W. Child; Fresh Waters
Madame X. J. W. MacConaughy
Madhouse. Angus Hall; Qualtrough
Madigan. R. Dougherty; Commissioner
Madonna of Avenue A. M. Canfield
Madonna of the Seven Moons. M. Lawrence
Madonna of the Sleeping Cars. M. Dekobra
Mafia. L. Sciascia; Mafia Vendetta
Magic. W. Goldman
Magnet of Doom. G. Simenon
Magnum Force. M. Valley
Maid of the Silver Sea. J. Oxenham
Maids. J. Genet
Maigret and the St. Fiacre Case. G. Simenon; Saint Fiacre Affair
Maigret Sees Red. G. Simenon; Maigret and the Gangsters
Maigret Sets a Trap. G. Simenon
Main Attraction. S. Michaels
Main Chance. E. Wallace (headnote)
Maisie. W. Collison; Dark Dame
Majestic Hotel Cellars. G. Simenon; Maigret and the Hotel Majestic
Make Haste to Live. Gordons
Make Mine Mink. P. Coke; Breath of Spring
Malaga. D. MacKenzie
Malone. W. Wingate; Shotgun
Malpas Mystery. E. Wallace; Face in the Night
Maltese Falcon. D. Hammett
Man and His Money. F. S. Isham
Man at Six. J. Celestin
Man at the Carlton Tower. E. Wallace; Man at the Carlton
Man Behind the Mask. J. Futrelle; Chase of the Golden Plate

Man Called Back. A. Soutar; Silent Thunder
Man Could Get Killed. D. Walker; Diamonds for Moscow
Man Detained. E. Wallace; Debt Discharged
Man from Headquarters. G. Bronson-Howard; Black Book
Man from Marrakech. R. P. Jones; Heisters
Man from the Diner's Club. S. Baol
Man Hunt. G. Household; Rogue Male
Man in Half Moon Street. B. Lyndon
Man in Hiding. S. Rattray; Queen in Danger
Man in Motley. T. Gallon
Man in the Attic. M. B. Lowndes; Lodger
Man in the Middle. H. Fast; Winston Affair
Man in the Net. P. Quentin
Man in the Raincoat. J. H. Chase; Tiger by the Tail
Man in the Road. A. Armstrong; He Was Found in the Road
Man in the Shadow. S. Davis; One Man's Secret
Man in the Vault. F. Gruber; Lock and the Key
Man Inside. M. E. Chaber
Man Inside. N. S. Lincoln
Man of Affairs. N. Grant; Nelson Touch
Man of Bronze. K. Robeson
Man on a Tightrope. N. Paterson
Man on the Box. H. MacGrath
Man on the Eifel Tower. G. Simenon; Battle of Nerves
Man on the Roof. M. Sjowall; Abominable Man
Man Outside. G. Stackelberg; Double Agent
Man Outside. D. Stuart
Man They Could Not Arrest. E. Wallace (headnote)
Man They Couldn't Arrest. A. J. Small
Man-Trap. J. D. MacDonald; Soft Touch
Man Who Bought London. E. Wallace
Man Who Changed His Name. E. Wallace
Man Who Could Cheat Death. B. Lyndon; Man in Half Moon Street
Man Who Disappeared. A. C. Doyle; Adventures of Sherlock Holmes
Man Who Finally Died. John Burke
Man Who Haunted Himself. A. Armstrong; Strange Case of Mr. Pelham
Man Who Knew Too Much. R. Alexander
Man Who Knew Too Much. G. K. Chesterton
Man Who Murdered. C. Farrere; Man Who Killed
Man Who Stayed at Home. J. E. H. Terry
Man Who Vanished. S. Campbell; Below the Dead-Line
Man Who Was Nobody. E. Wallace
Man Who Watched the Trains Go By. G. Simenon
Man Who Went Up in Smoke. M. Sjowall
Man Who Won. C. T. Brady
Man Who Would Not Die. C. Williams; Sailcloth Shroud
Man Who Wouldn't Die. C. Rawson; No Coffin for a Corpse
Man Who Wouldn't Talk. H. Hall; Valiant
Man with a Cloak. J. D. Carr; Third Bullet
Man with Bogart's Face. A. J. Fenady
Man with My Face. S. W. Taylor
Man with 100 Faces. W. B. M. Ferguson; Crackerjack
Man with the Deadly Lens. C. McCarry; Better Angels
Man with the Golden Gun. I. Fleming
Man with the Magnetic Eyes. R. Daniel
Man with the Silver Eyes. R. Rossner; End of Someone Else's Rainbow
Man with the Twisted Lip. A. C. Doyle; Adventures of Sherlock Holmes
Man with Two Faces. A. Woolcott; Dark Tower
Man Within. G. Greene
Man Without a Face. A. Budrys; Who?
Manbait. J. H. Chase; Last Page
Manchurian Candidate. R. Condon
Mandarin Mystery. E. Queen; Chinese Orange Mystery
Manhandled. A. Stringer
Manhattan. J. Farnol; Definite Object
Manhattan Knight. G. Burgess; Find the Woman
Manhattan Love Song. C. Woolrich
Maniac. M. Brandel; Time of the Fire
Manslaughter. A. D. Miller
Mantrap. S. Rattray; Queen in Danger
Marathon Man. W. Goldman
Margin for Error. C. Booth
Maria Marten. Anonymous
Marie du Port. G. Simenon; Chit of a Girl
Mark. C. E. Israel
Mark of Cain. J. Shearing; Airing in a Closed Carriage

Mark of Cain. C. Wells
Mark of the Vampire. M. Coolridge-Rask; London After Midnight
Mark of the Whistler. W. Irish; Borrowed Crime
Marlowe. R. Chandler; Little Sister
Marnie. Winston Graham
Maroc. M. Sands
Marriage Lines. J. S. Fletcher
Marriage of Convenience. E. Wallace; Three Oak Mystery
Mary Regan. L. Scott
Mask. A. Hornblow
Mask of Dimitrios. E. Ambler
Mask of Fu Manchu. S. Rohmer
Masque of the Red Death. Elsie Lee
Masquerade. V. Canning; Castle Minerva
Masquerade. L. J. Vance; Brass Bowl
Masquerader. K. C. Thurston
Master Mind. M. Dana
Master Mind. A. B. Reeve
Master Mummer. E. P. Oppenheim
Master of Men. E. P. Oppenheim
Master of Merripit. E. Phillpotts
Maurizius Affair. J. Wasserman; Maurizius Case
Maxwell Archer, Detective. H. Clevely; Archer Plus 20
Mazarin Stone. A. C. Doyle; Adventures of Sherlock Holmes
Me--Gangster. C. F. Coe
Mean Season. J. Katzenbach; In the Heat of the Summer
Mechanic. L. J. Carlino
Medusa Touch. P. Van Greenaway
Meet Maxwell Archer. H. Clevely; Archer Plus 20
Meet Mr. Callaghan. G. Verner
Meet Nero Wolfe. R. Stout; Fer-de-Lance
Meet Simon Cherry. G. Pedrick; Meet the Rev
Meg the Lady. T. Gallon
Melody Man. H. J. Green
Melody of Death. E. Wallace
Men of Zanzibar. R. H. Davis; Lost Road
Menace. P. MacDonald; R.I.P
Menace. E. Wallace; Feathered Serpent
Menace in the Night. B. Graeme; Suspense
Mephisto Waltz. F. M. Stewart
Mercenaries. Wilbur Smith; Train from Katanga
Michael Shayne, Private Detective. B. Halliday; Private Practice of Michael Shayne
Midnight Episode. G. Simenon; Monsieur la Souris
Midnight Guest. F. M. White
Midnight in Paris. G. Simenon; Monsieur la Souris
Midnight Lace. J. Green; Matilda Shouted Fire
Midnight Life. R. W. Kauffman; Spider's Web
Midnight Man. D. Anthony; The Midnight Lady and the Mourning Man
Midnight Mystery. H. I. Young
Mildred Pierce. J. M. Cain
Million a Minute. H. Douglas
Million Dollar Manhunt. L. Hardy; Requiem for a Redhead
Million Dollar Mystery. H. MacGrath
Millionaire. E. D. Biggers; Earl Derr Biggers Tells Ten Stories
Millionaire Baby. A. K. Green
Millionaires. E. P. Oppenheim; Inevitable Millionaires
Mind Benders. J. Kennaway
Mind of Mr. J. G. Reeder. E. Wallace
Mine Own Executioner. N. Balchin
Ministry of Fear. G. Greene
Miracle Man. F. Packard
Miracles for Sale. C. Rawson; Death from a Top Hat
Mirage. W. Ericson; Fallen Angel
Miriam Rozella. B. L. Farjeon
Mirror Crack'd. A. Christie; Mirror Crack'd from Side to Side
Miss Bracegirdle Does Her Duty. S. Aumonier; Miss Bracegirdle and others
Miss Pinkerton. M. R. Rinehart
Missing Million. E. Wallace
Missing People. E. Wallace; Mind of Mr. J. G. Reeder
Missing Rembrandt. A. C. Doyle; Return of Sherlock Holmes
Missing Ten Days. B. Graeme; Disappearance of Roger Tremayne
Missing Three-Quarter. A. C. Doyle; Return of Sherlock Holmes
Missioner. E. P. Oppenheim
Mississippi Mermaid. W. Irish; Waltz into Darkness
Mist in the Valley. Dorin Craig
Mr. Ace. H. Christy
Mr. & Mrs. North. O. Davis
Mr. Arkadin. O. Welles
Mr. Barnes of New York. A. C. Gunter
Mr. Denning Drives North. A. Coppel

Mister Flow. G. Leroux; Man of a Hundred Masks
Mr. Grex of Monte Carlo. E. P. Oppenheim
Mr. Justice Raffles. E. W. Hornung
Mr. Lyndon at Liberty. V. Bridges
Mr. Majestyk. E. Leonard
Mr. Moses. M. Catto; Mister Midas
Mr. Moto in Danger Island. J. W. Vandercook; Murder in Trinidad
Mr. Potter of Texas. A. C. Gunter
Mr. Reeder in Room 13. E. Wallace; Room 13
Mr. Wu. L. J. Miln
Mrs. Balfame. G. Atherton
Mrs. Erricker's Reputation. T. Cobb
Mrs. Pollifax, Spy. D. Gilman; Unexpected Mrs. Pollifax
Mrs. Pym of Scotland Yard. N. Morland (headnote)
Mix Me a Person. J. T. Story
Mob. F. Findley; Waterfront
Model Murder Case. L. Payne; Nose on My Face
Modern Marriage. D. Vane; Lady Varley
Modesty Blaise. P. O'Donnell
Molly Maguires. J. O'Neill
Moment of Danger. D. MacKenzie
Moment to Moment. A. Coppel
Money Moon. J. Farnol
Money to Burn. R. W. Kauffman
Money Trap. L. White
Monkey's Paw. W. W. Jacobs; Lady of the Barge
Monsieur la Souris. G. Simenon
Monsieur Lecoq. E. Gaboriau
Monte Carlo Nights. E. P. Oppenheim; Mr. Billingham, the Marquis and Madelon
Moon in the Gutter. D. Goodis
Moon of the Wolf. L. H. Whitten
Moon-Spinners. Mary Stewart
Moonraker. C. Wood
Moonrise. T. Strauss
Moonshine Mountain. C. Glore
Moonshine War. E. Leonard
Moonstone. W. Collins
Moral Sinner. C. M. S. McLellan; Leah Kleschna
Mord Em'ly. W. P. Ridge
More Deadly Than the Male. P. Chevalier
More to Be Pitied Than Scorned. C. E. Blaney
Moriarty. W. Gillette; Sherlock Holmes
Morituri. W. J. Luddecke
Mortal Storm. P. Bottome
Mortmain. A. Train
Moss Rose. J. Shearing
Most Dangerous Game. R. Connell; Variety
Most Dangerous Man in the World. J. R. Kennedy; Chairman
Most Dangerous Sin. F. M. Dostoevskii; Crime and Punishment
Mountain Music. M. Kantor; Author's Choice
Moving Target. J. Macdonald
Mugger. E. Hunter
Mumsy, Nanny, Sonny and Girly. B. Comport
Murder. C. Dane; Enter Sir John
Murder at Covent Garden. W. J. Makin
Murder at Glen Athol. N. Lippincott
Murder at Site Three. W. H. Baker; Crime Is My Business
Murder at the Baskervilles. A. C. Doyle; Memoirs of Sherlock Holmes
Murder at the Gallop. A. Christie; After the Funeral
Murder by an Aristocrat. M. Eberhart
Murder by Death. H. Keating
Murder by Decree. H. Weverka
Murder by Proxy. H. Nielsen; Gold Coast Nocturne
Murder by the Clock. Rufus King
Murder Goes to College. K. Steel
Murder in the Central Committee. M. V. Montalban
Murder in the Family. J. Ronald
Murder in the Private Car. E. E. Rose; Rear Car
Murder in Thornton Square. P. Hamilton; Gas Light
Murder in Trinidad. J. W. Vandercook
Murder Is My Business. B. Halliday
Murder Most Foul. A. Christie; Mrs. McGinty's Dead
Murder, My Sweet. R. Chandler; Farewell, My Lovely
Murder, My Sweet Matilda. J. Green; Matilda Shouted Fire
Murder of Dr. Harrigan. M. Eberhart; From This Dark Stairway
Murder on a Bridal Path. S. Palmer; Puzzle of the Red Stallion
Murder on a Honeymoon. S. Palmer; Puzzle of the Pepper Tree
Murder on Diamond Row. E. Wallace; Squeaker
Murder on Monday. R. C. Sherriff; Home at Seven

Murder on the Blackboard. S. Palmer
Murder on the Bridge. F. Duerrenmatt; Judge and His Hangman
Murder on the Campus. W. Chambers; Campanile Murders
Murder on the Orient Express. A. Christie
Murder on the Roof. E. J. Doherty; Broadway Murders
Murder on the Second Floor. F. Vosper
Murder Reported. Robert Chapman; Murder for the Millions
Murder, She Said. A. Christie; 4.50 from Paddington
Murder Will Out. M. Leinster
Murder with Pictures. G. H. Coxe
Murder Without Crime. J. L. Thompson
Murderer. F. M. Dostoevskii; Brothers Karamazov
Murderer. P. Highsmith; Blunderer
Murderer's Row. D. Hamilton
Murders in the Rue Morgue. E. A. Poe; Prose Romances of Edgar A. Poe
Muscle Beach Party. Elsie Lee
Musgrave Ritual. A. C. Doyle; Memoirs of Sherlock Holmes
Muss 'Em Up. J. E. Grant; Green Shadow
Mutiny. B. Bolt; Diana of the Islands
My Cousin Rachel. D. Du Maurier
My Death Is a Mockery. D. G. Baber
My Gun Is Quick. M. Spillane
My Lady's Garter. J. Futrelle
My Lady's Latchkey. C. N. Williamson; Second Latchkey
My Lord Conceit. Rita
My Lover, My Son. E. Grierson; Reputation for a Song
My Name Is Julia Ross. A. Gilbert; Woman in Red
My Official Wife. R. H. Savage
My Sister and I. E. Bonett; High Pavement
Mysteries of Paris. E. Sue
Mysterious Dr. Fu Manchu. S. Rohmer; Mystery of Dr. Fu-Manchu
Mysterious Mr. Reeder. E. Wallace; Mind of Mr. J. G. Reeder
Mysterious Mr. Wong. H. S. Keeler; Sing Sing Nights
Mystery at the Villa Rose. A. E. W. Mason; At the Villa Rose
Mystery Girl. G. B. McCutcheon; Green Fancy
Mystery House. M. Eberhart; Mystery of Hunting's End
Mystery Mind. A. B. Reeve
Mystery of a Hansom Cab. F. Hume
Mystery of Boscombe Vale. A. C. Doyle; Adventures of Sherlock Holmes
Mystery of Edwin Drood. C. Dickens
Mystery of Marie Roget. E. A. Poe; Tales
Mystery of Mr. Bernard Brown. E. P. Oppenheim
Mystery of Mr. X. M. Porlock; X v. Rex
Mystery of Orcival. E. Gaboriau
Mystery of Room 13. E. Wallace; Room 13
Mystery of the Thirteenth Guest. A. Trail; Thirteenth Guest
Mystery of the Villa Rose. A. E. W. Mason; At the Villa Rose
Mystery of the White Room. J. G. Edwards; Murder in the Surgery
Mystery of the Yellow Room. G. Leroux
Mystery of West Sedgwick. C. Wells; Gold Bag
Mystery Road. E. P. Oppenheim
Naked City. M. Wald
Naked Edge. M. Ehrlich; First Train to Babylon
Naked Face. S. Sheldon
Naked Kiss. S. Fuller
Naked Runner. F. Clifford
Naked Spur. A. Ullman
Name of the Rose. U. Eco
Nanny. E. Piper
Narrowing Circle. J. Symons
Naval Treaty. A. C. Doyle; Memoirs of Sherlock Holmes
Negatives. P. Everett
Neither the Sea Nor the Sand. G. Honeycombe
Net. J. Pudley
Nets of Destiny. M. Drake; Salving of a Derelict
Never a Dull Moment. J. Godey; Thrill a Minute with Jack Albany
Never Let Me Go. R. Bax; Came the Dawn
Never Look Back. E. Wallace; Green Ribbon
Never Love a Stranger. H. Robbins
Never Mention Murder. E. Wallace (headnote)
Never Say Never Again. I. Fleming; Thunderball
New Adventures of J. Rufus Wallingford. G. R. Chester; Get-Rich-Quick-Wallingford
New Centurions. J. Wambaugh
New Leaf. J. Ritchie
New York. B. Chambers

Next Man. M. Z. Lewin
Nickel Ride. M. T. Kaufman
Night and Morning. E. Bulwer-Lytton
Night and the City. G. Kersh
Night at the Crossroads. G. Simenon; Crossroads Murders
Night Caller. F. Crisp; Night Callers
Night Club Lady. A. Abbot; About the Murder of the Night Club Lady
Night Club Scandal. D. N. Rubin; Riddle Me This!
Night-Comers. E. Ambler
Night Creatures. R. Thorndyke; Dr. Syn
Night Has a Thousand Eyes. G. Hopley
Night Has Eyes. A. Kennington
Night in Havana. R. Sylvester; Big Boodle
Night in New Orleans. J. R. Langham; Sing a Song of Homicide
Night Invader. J. Bentley; Rendezvous with Death
Night Journey. J. Phelan; Ten-a-Penny People
Night Moves. A. Sharp
Night Must Fall. Emlyn Williams
Night Nurse. D. Macy
Night of January 16. A. Rand
Night of June 13. F. Vreeland
Night of Mystery. S. S. Van Dine; Greene Murder Case
Night of the Following Day. L. White; Snatchers
Night of the Generals. H. H. Kirst
Night of the Hunter. D. Grubb
Night of the Juggler. W. P. McGivern
Night of the Living Dead. J. Russo
Night to Remember. K. Roos; Frightened Stiff
Night Walker. S. Stuart
Night Was Our Friend. M. Pertwee
Night Watch. L. Fletcher
Night Without Sleep. E. Moll
Night Without Stars. Winston Graham
Nightcomers. Michael Hastings
Nightfall. D. Goodis
Nightmare. M. Porlock; Mystery in Kensington Gore
Nightmare. C. Woolrich
Nightmare Alley. W. L. Gresham
Nightmare Honeymoon. L. Block (headnote)
Nightwing. M. C. Smith
Nine Forty-Five. O. Davis; At 9:45
Nine Girls. W. H. Pettit
Nine Lives Are Not Enough. J. Odlum
19 Red Roses. T. Nielsen
99 and 44/100% Dead. M. Franklin; 99 44/100% Dead
Ninth Guest. O. Davis
No Down Payment. J. McPartland
No Escape. G. Goodchild
No Hands on the Clock. G. Homes
No Man of Her Own. W. Irish; I Married a Dead Man
No Man's Land. L. J. Vance
No Orchids for Miss Blandish. J. H. Chase
No Place Like Homicide. Frank King; Ghoul
No Pockets in a Shroud. H. McCoy
No Resting Place. I. Niall
No Road Back. F. L. Cary; Madam Tic-Tac
No Way Back. T. Burke; Limehouse Nights
No Way to Treat a Lady. H. Longbaugh
Noble Bachelor. A. C. Doyle; Adventures of Sherlock Holmes
Nobody Lives Forever. W. R. Burnett
Nobody Runs Forever. J. Cleary; High Commissioner
Nobody's Perfekt. T. Kenrick; Two for the Price of One
Nomads of the North. J. O. Curwood
Non-Conformist Parson. R. Horniman
Non-Stop New York. K. Attiwill; Sky Steward
Noose for a Lady. G. Verner; Whispering Woman
Norman Conquest. B. Gray; Dare-Devil Conquest
North Sea Hijack. J. Davies; Esther, Ruth and Jennifer
North Star. G. Simenon; Lodger
Northern Pursuit. L. T. White; 5,000 Trojan Horses
Norwood Builder. A. C. Doyle; Return of Sherlock Holmes
Nosferatu. B. Stoker; Dracula
Not Guilty. H. MacGrath; Parrot & Co.
Nothing But the Best. S. Ellin; Mystery Stories
Nothing But the Night. J. Blackburn
Nothing But the Truth. P. Orum
Notorious Landlady. I. Shulman
Notorious Miss Lisle. B. Reynolds
Notorious Mrs. Carrick. C. Procter; Pools of the Past
Notorious Sophie Lang. F. I. Anderson
Nowhere to Go. D. MacKenzie
Number 17. J. J. Farjeon
Number Seventeen. L. Tracy
Number Six. E. Wallace

Nursemaid Who Disappeared. P. MacDonald
Nurse's Secret. M. R. Rinehart; Miss Pinkerton
OSS 117--Mission for a Killer. J. Bruce; Live Wire
Oakdale Affair. E. R. Burroughs
Obsessed. W. Dinner; Late Edwina Black
Obsession. J. M. Cain; Serenade
Obsession. A. Coppel; Man About a Dog
Obsession. W. Irish; Dead Man Blues
Ocean's 11. G. C. Johnson
October Man. E. Britton
Octopussy. I. Fleming
Octoroon. D. Boucicault
Odd Man Out. F. L. Green
Odds Against Tomorrow. W. P. McGivern
Odessa File. F. Forsyth
Offence. J. Hopkins; This Story of Yours
Officer 666. B. Currie
Old Dark House. J. P. Priestley; Benighted
Old Man. E. Wallace; Coat of Arms
On a Nice Summer Day. J. H. Chase; One Bright Summer Morning
On Dangerous Ground. G. Butler; Mad with Much Heart
On Dangerous Ground. B. E. Stevenson; Little Comrade
On Friday at Eleven. J. H. Chase; World in My Pocket
On Her Majesty's Secret Service. I. Fleming
On the Double. Roger Fuller
On the Night of the Fire. F. L. Green
On the Run. E. Wallace (headnote)
On the Waterfront. B. Schulberg; Waterfront
On the Yard. M. Braly
On Thin Ice. A. R. Colver; Dear Pretender
On Trial. E. L. Reizenstein
Once a Crook. E. Price
Once a Thief. J. Trinian
Once Upon a Time in America. H. Grey; Hoods
Once You Kiss a Stranger. P. Highsmith; Strangers on a Train
One Against Seven. J. Stevenson; Counterattack
One Born Every Minute. G. Owen
One Deadly Summer. S. Japrisot
One-Eyed Jacks. C. Neider; Authentic Death of Hendry Jones
One Hour Before Dawn. M. Scott; Behind Red Curtains
One Is Always Too Good to Women. R. Queneau; We Always Treat Women Too Well
One Jump Ahead. Robert Chapman
One More Time. M. Avallone
One Night in the Tropics. E. D. Biggers; Love Insurance
One of Our Dinosaurs Is Missing. D. Forrest; Great Dinosaur Robbery
One of Those Things. A. Bodelsen; One Down
One Step to Eternity. P. McGerr; Follow, As the Night
One Way Ticket. H. E. Helseth; Chair for Martin Rome
One Wonderful Night. L. Tracy
Onion Field. J. Wambaugh
Only Saps Work. O. Davis; Easy Come, Easy Go
Only the Wind Knows the Answer. J. M. Simmel; Wind and the Rain
Only When I Larf. L. Deighton
Operation Cobra. A. Bodelsen
Operation Undercover. J. Mills; Report to the Commissioner
Operator 13. R. W. Chambers; Secret Service Operator 13
Ordeal by Innocence. A. Christie
Order of Death. H. Fleetwood
Orders to Kill. D. Downes
Orient Express. G. Greene; Stamboul Train
Osterman Weekend. R. Ludlum
Other. T. Tryon
Other Man. E. Wallace; Nine Bears
Other Men's Shoes. A. Soutar
Other People's Money. E. Gaboriau
Other Person. F. Hume
Other Side of Midnight. S. Sheldon
Other Side of the Door. L. Chamberlain
Otley. M. Waddell
Our Man Flint. J. Pearl
Our Man in Havana. G. Greene
Our Mother's House. J. Gloag
Out of the Clouds. J. Fores; Springboard
Out of the Fog. B. Graeme; Fog for a Killer
Out of the Fog. I. Shaw; Gentle People
Out of the Past. G. Homes; Build My Gallows High
Out of the Shadow. E. W. Hornung; Shadow of the Rope
Outback. K. Cook; Wake in Fright

Outer Gate. O. R. Cohen
Outfit. R. Stark
Outside the Law. T. Browning
Outsider. L. J. Vance; Nobody
Over My Dead Body. J. D. O'Hanlon; As Good As Murdered
PT Raiders. N. Monsarrat; Ship That Died of Shame
Pace That Thrills. R. Weber
Pagan. J. Russell; In Dark Places
Pagan Love. A. Abdullah; Honorable Gentleman
Paid. B. Veiller; Within the Law
Paliser Case. E. Saltus
Pallard the Punter. E. Wallace; Grey Timothy
Pals First. L. W. Dodd
Panic in Needle Park. J. Mills
Panique. G. Simenon; Mr. Hire's Engagement
Panther's Moon. V. Canning
Paper Orchid. A. La Bern
Parachute Jumper. R. James; Some Call It Love
Paradine Case. R. Hichens
Paradise Garden. G. F. Gibbs
Parallax View. L. Singer
Paris at Midnight. H. Balzac; Le Pere Goriot
Paris Express. G. Simenon; Man Who Watched the Trains Go By
Parisian Nights. R. Goyne
Partner. E. Wallace; Million Dollar Story
Partners in Crime. K. Steel; Murder Goes to College
Partners in Crime. E. Wallace; Man Who Knew
Partners of the Night. L. Scott
Party Girl. E. Balmer; Dangerous Business
Party Girl. M. H. Albert
Passage. B. Nicolaysen; Perilous Passage
Passage from Hong Kong. E. D. Biggers; Agony Column
Passager Clandestin. G. Simenon; Stowaway
Passengers. K. R. Dwyer; Chase
Passing of Mr. Quin. A. Christie; Mysterious Mr. Quin
Passionate Adventure. F. Stayton
Passionate Quest. E. P. Oppenheim
Passport to Treason. M. O'Brine
Patient in Room 18. M. Eberhart
Patient Vanishes. D. Hume; They Called Him Death
Paul Temple's Triumph. F. Durbridge; News of Paul Temple
Pawned. F. Packard
Payment Deferred. J. Dell
Payoff. A. Veraldi
Payroll. D. Bickerton
Pearl of Death. A. C. Doyle; Return of Sherlock Holmes
Peeper. K. Laumer; Deadfall
Penelope. E. V. Cunningham
Penguin Pool Murder. S. Palmer
Penguin Pool Mystery. S. Palmer; Penguin Pool Murder
Penitentiary. M. Flavin; Criminal Code
Penniless Millionaire. D. C. Murray
Penthouse. A. S. Roche
People Against O'Hara. E. Lipsky
People vs. Nancy Preston. J. Moroso; People Against Nancy Preston
Perfect Alibi. A. A. Milne; Fourth Wall
Perfect Crime. I. Zangwill; Big Bow Mystery
Perfect Sap. H. I. Young; Not Herbert
Perfume of the Lady in Black. G. Leroux
Permission to Kill. P. Loraine; W.I.L. One to Curtis
Perpetua. D. C. Calthrop
Personal Affair. L. Storm; Day's Mischief
Petrified Forest. R. Sherwood
Phantom Buccaneer. V. Bridges; Another Man's Shoes
Phantom Fiend. M. B. Lowndes; Lodger
Phantom in the House. A. Soutar
Phantom Lady. W. Irish
Phantom Light. E. Price; Haunted Light
Phantom of Forty-Second Street. M. M. Raison
Phantom of Paris. G. Leroux; Cheri-Bibi and Cecily
Phantom of the Opera. G. Leroux
Phantom of the Rue Morgue. E. A. Poe; Prose Romances of Edgar A. Poe
Phantom President. G. F. Worts
Phantom Strikes. E. Wallace; Ringer
Piccadilly Jim. P. G. Wodehouse
Pickup Alley. E. Ronns
Pidgin Island. H. MacGrath
Pigeon That Took Rome. D. Downes; Easter Dinner
Pilgrims of the Night. A. Partridge; Passers-By

Pillaged. R. Stark; Score
Pink Jungle. A. Williams; Snake Water
Pink Panther. M. H. Albert
Pink String and Sealing Wax. R. Pertwee
Pit and the Pendulum. L. Sheridan
Pit of Darkness. H. McCutcheon; To Dusty Death
Pitfall. J. J. Dratler
Place to Go. M. Fisher; Bethnel Green
Platinum High School. I. Shulman
Play Misty for Me. P. J. Gillette
Playback. E. Wallace (headnote)
Pleasure Buyers. A. S. Roche
Plot Thickens. S. Palmer (headnote)
Plunder. B. Travers
Plunder of the Sun. D. Dodge
Point Blank. R. Stark; Hunter
Pointing Finger. M. R. Rinehart
Poison. A. Askew
Poison Pen. R. Llewellyn
Pool of Flame. L. J. Vance
Pope of Greenwich Village. V. Patrick
Population 1280. J. Thompson; Pop. 1280
Port Afrique. B. V. Dryer
Port of Missing Men. M. Nicholson
Portrait in Black. I. Goff
Portrait of a Mobster. H. Grey
Portrait of Alison. F. Durbridge
Possession of Joel Delaney. R. Stewart
Postman Always Rings Twice. J. M. Cain
Postmark for Danger. F. Durbridge; Portrait of Alison
Power. F. M. Robinson
Power and the Glory. G. Greene
Praying Mantis. H. Monteilhet; Preying Mantises
Premature Burial. M. H. Danne
President. G. Simenon; Premier
President Vanishes. Anonymous
President's Mystery. F. D. Roosevelt; President's Mystery Story
Pretty Maids All in a Row. F. Pollini
Pretty Poison. S. Geller; She Let Him Continue
Prey. C. Aird; Henrietta Who
Price of Silence. L. Meynell; One Step from Murder
Price of Silence. A. J. Wilson; At the Mercy of Tiberius
Prime Cut. M. Roote
Prince of Tempters. E. P. Oppenheim; Ex-Duke
Princess of New York. C. Hamilton
Priory School. A. C. Doyle; Return of Sherlock Holmes
Prison Breaker. E. Wallace (headnote)
Private Lessons. D. Greenberg; Philly
Private Life of Sherlock Holmes. M. Hardwick
Privilege. John Burke
Prize of Gold. M. Catto
Prizzi's Honor. R. Condon
Professional. P. Alexander; Death of a Thin-Skinned Animal
Professional Guest. W. Garrett
Project M7. J. Pudney; Net
Psycho. R. Bloch
Public Defender. G. Goodchild; Splendid Crime
Public Enemy. K. Glasmon
Public Prosecutor's Speech. A. D. Miller; Manslaughter
Puppet on a Chain. A. MacLean
Purple Noon. P. Highsmith; Talented Mr. Ripley
Pursuing Vengeance. B. E. Stevenson; Mystery of the Boule Cabinet
Pursuit. L. G. Blochman
Pursuit of D. B. Cooper. J. D. Reed
Pushover. B. Ballinger; Rafferty
Pyx. J. Buell
Qualified Adventurer. S. Jepson
Quarry. J. Moroso
Queenie. W. F. Fauley
Question of Suspense. R. Vickers (headnote)
Quiet American. G. Greene
Quiet Place in the Country. H. Clement
Quiller Memorandum. Adam Hall; Berlin Memorandum
Quinney's. H. A. Vachell
Race Gang. G. Greene (headnote)
Racket. B. Cormack
Rafferty and the Gold Dust Twins. L. Roberts
Raffles. E. W. Hornung; Amateur Cracksman
Raffles, the Amateur Cracksman. E. W. Hornung; Amateur Cracksman
Rage. P. Friedman
Rage in Heaven. J. Hilton
Raging Tide. E. Gann; Fiddler's Green
Raise the Titanic! C. Cussler
Rambo: First Blood II. D. Morrell
Ramshackle House. H. Footner
Rank Outsider. N. Gould
Ransom. P. Wheeler
Rape. N. Freeling; Because of the Cats
Rasp. P. MacDonald
Rat. P. Bottome

Rats. J. Herbert
Raven. E. Sudak
Ravishing Idiot. C. Exbrayat
Razorback. P. Brennan
Razumov. J. Conrad; Under Western Eyes
Rear Window. W. Irish; After-Dinner Story
Rebecca. D. Du Maurier
Reckless Age. E. D. Biggers; Love Insurance
Reckless Moment. E. S. Holding; Blank Wall
Red Aces. E. Wallace
Red Barn Crime. Anonymous; Maria Marten
Red Circle. A. C. Doyle; His Last Bow
Red Dance. H. L. Gates; Red Dancer of Moscow
Red Danube. B. Marshall; Vespers in Vienna
Red Dice. O. R. Cohen; Iron Chalice
Red Feather. V. Bridges; Man from Nowhere
Red Glove. D. Grant; Fifth Ace
Red-Haired Alibi. W. Collison
Red-Headed League. A. C. Doyle; Adventures of Sherlock Holmes
Red House. G. A. Chamberlain
Red Ibis. Fredric Brown; Knock Three-One-Two
Red Lights. E. E. Rose; Rear Car
Red Mark. J. Russell
Redhead. A. Andersch
Reflection of Fear. S. Forbes; Go to Thy Death Bed
Reigate Squires. A. C. Doyle; Reigate Puzzle
Reincarnation of Peter Proud. M. Ehrlich
Remains to Be Seen. H. Lindsay
Remember Last Night? A. Hobhouse; Hangover Murders
Remember That Face! F. Findley; Waterfront
Remittance Woman. A. Abdullah
Remo: The First Adventure. W. Murphy
Remote Control. C. North
Removalists. D. Williamson
Repeat Performance. W. O'Farrell
Report to the Commissioner. J. Mills
Reporter. K. Attiwill
Reprisal. Arthur Gordon
Resident Patient. A. C. Doyle; Memoirs of Sherlock Holmes
Return from the Ashes. H. Monteilhet
Return of Bulldog Drummond. H. C. McNeile
Return of Dr. Fu Manchu. S. Rohmer; Devil Doctor
Return of Sherlock Holmes. A. C. Doyle; His Last Bow
Return of Sophie Lang. F. I. Anderson; Notorious Sophie Lang
Return of the Frog. E. Wallace; India-Rubber Men
Return of the Lone Wolf. L. J. Vance; Lone Wolf Returns
Return of the Terror. E. Wallace; Terror
Return of the Whistler. W. Irish; Eyes That Watch You
Return to Sender. E. Wallace (headnote)
Reunion. K. Leopold; When We Ran
Revenge. J. Warren
Revenge Squad. L. Fletcher; Eighty Dollars to Stamford
Reward. M. Barrett
Ricochet. E. Wallace; Angel of Terror
Riddle of the Sands. E. Childers
Ride a Wild Pony. J. Aldridge; Sporting Proposition
Ride the Pink Horse. D. B. Hughes
Rigged. J. H. Chase; Hit and Run
Right to Love. C. Farrere
Ringer. E. Wallace
Riot. F. Elli
Rise and Fall of Legs Diamond. O. H. Gaylord
Rise Up, Spy. G. Markstein; Chance Awakening
Risk. N. Balchin; Sort of Traitors
Rivals. E. Wallace; Elegant Edward
River of Stars. E. Wallace
River Pirate. C. F. Coe
River's End. J. O. Curwood
Riverside Murder. A. Steeman; Six Dead Men
Road House. W. Hackett
Road to Fortune. H. Broadbridge; Moorland Terror
Roadhouse Murder. M. Level (headnote)
Roadhouse Nights. D. Hammett; Red Harvest
Robbery Under Arms. R. Boldrewood
Robin and the Seven Hoods. J. Pearl
Rogue Cop. W. P. McGivern
Rogue in Love. T. Gallon
Romance and Riches. E. P. Oppenheim; Amazing Quest of Mr. Ernest Bliss
Romance of a Million Dollars. E. Dejeans

Romance of Elaine. A. B. Reeve
Romance of Mayfair. J. C. Snaith; Crime of Constable Kelly
Rome Express. R. Alexander
Roof. D. Whitelaw
Room 13. E. Wallace
Rooney. C. Cookson
Root of All Evil. J. S. Fletcher
Rope. P. Hamilton
Rope for Killing. P. McGerr; Follow, As the Night
Rosebud. J. Hemingway
Rosemary's Baby. I. Levin
Rough Company. D. Hamilton; Night Walker
Rough Cut. D. Lambert; Touch the Lion's Paw
Rough Shoot. G. Household
Rumble on the Docks. F. Paley
Run for the Sun. R. Connell; Variety
Running Fight. W. H. Osborne
Running Man. S. Smith; Ballad of the Running Man
Running Scared. G. McDonald
Running Target. S. Frazee
Running Water. A. E. W. Mason
Running Wild. B. Benson; Girl in the Cage
Russian Roulette. T. Ardies; Kosygin Is Coming
Russians Are Coming, The Russians Are Coming. N. Benchley; Off-Islanders
Ruth of the Rockies. J. McCulley; Broadway Bab
Rx Murder. J. Fleming; Deeds of Dr. Deadcert
Rynox. P. MacDonald
S.O.S. W. W. Ellis
S*P*Y*S. T. R. Joyce
Sable Lorcha. P. Hazeltine
Sabotage. J. Conrad; Secret Agent
Saboteur. W. J. Luddecke; Morituri
Sail a Crooked Ship. N. Benchley
Saint in London. L. Charteris; Holy Terror
Saint in New York. L. Charteris
Saint in Palm Springs. L. Charteris (headnote)
St. Ives. O. Bleeck; Procane Chronicle
Saint Meets the Tiger. L. Charteris; Meet the Tiger
Saint Strikes Back. L. Charteris; She Was a Lady
St. Valentine's Day Massacre. B. O'Hara
Saint's Double. L. Charteris (headnote)
Saint's Vacation. L. Charteris; Getaway
Salamander. M. West
Saloon Bar. F. Harvey
Salt and Pepper. A. Austin
Salute the Toff. J. Creasey
Salzburg Connection. H. MacInnes
Sanctuary. W. Faulkner
Sanders of the River. E. Wallace
Sapphire. E. G. Cousins
Satan Bug. I. Stuart
Satan Met a Lady. D. Hammett; Maltese Falcon
Scallywag. G. Allen
Scandal in Bohemia. A. C. Doyle; Adventures of Sherlock Holmes
Scandal Sheet. S. Fuller; Dark Page
Scapegoat. D. Du Maurier
Scar. M. Forbes; Hollow Triumph
Scar. E. Gaboriau (headnote)
Scarab Murder Case. S. S. Van Dine
Scarecrow. R. H. Morrieson
Scared Stiff. C. W. Goddard; Ghost Breakers
Scarface. A. Trail
Scarlet Car. R. H. Davis
Scarlet Claw. A. C. Doyle; Hound of the Baskervilles
Scarlet Runner. C. N. Williamson
Scarlet Weekend. W. Kent; Woman in Purple Pajamas
Scattergood Baines. C. B. Kelland
Scent of Mystery. K. Roos; Ghost of a Chance
Scobie Malone. J. Cleary; Helga's Web
Scorpio. M. Roote
Scorpio Letters. V. Canning
Scotland Yard Commands. N. Shute; Lonely Road
Scream and Scream Again. P. Saxon; Disoriented Man
Scream in the Dark. J. Odlum; Morgue Is Always Open
Screaming Mimi. Fredric Brown
Sea God. J. Russell
Sea Shall Not Have Them. J. Harris
Sealed Verdict. L. Shapiro
Second Bureau. C. R. Dumas
Second Floor Mystery. E. D. Biggers; Agony Column
Second Stain. A. C. Doyle; Return of Sherlock Holmes
Seconds. D. Ely
Secret. F. Ryck
Secret Agent. W. S. Maugham; Ashenden
Secret Beyond the Door. Rufus King; Museum Piece No. 13

Secret Ceremony. M. Denevi
Secret Document-Vienna. M. Dekobra; Widow with the Pink Gloves
Secret Four. E. Wallace; Four Just Men
Secret of Deep Harbor. Max Miller; I Cover the Waterfront
Secret of Stamboul. D. Wheatley; Eunich of Stamboul
Secret of the Hills. W. Garrett
Secret of the Moor. M. Gerard
Secret of the Purple Reef. D. Cottrell; Silent Reefs
Secret Service. W. Gillette
Secret Six. F. Marion
Secret Tent. E. Addyman
Secret Ways. A. MacLean; Last Frontier
Secret Witness. S. Spewack; Murder in the Gilded Cage
Secretary of Frivolous Affairs. M. Futrelle
Secrets of Paris. E. Sue; Mysteries of Paris
Secrets of the Night. M. Marcin; Nightcap
See No Evil. W. Hughes; Blind Terror
See Venice and Die. R. Marshall; Mission to Venice
See You in Hell, Darling. N. Mailer; American Dream
Sentinel. J. Konvitz
Serenade. J. M. Cain
Set-Up. E. Wallace (headnote)
Seven Days in May. F. Knebel
Seven Footprints to Satan. A. Merritt
Seven Keys to Baldpate. E. D. Biggers
Seven-Per-Cent Solution. N. Meyer
Seven Sinners. A. Ridley; Wrecker
Seven Thieves. S. Kent; Lions at the Kill
Seven Thunders. R. Croft-Cooke
Seven-Ups. R. Posner
Seventh Cross. A. Seghers
Seventh Juror. F. Didelot
77, Park Lane. W. Hackett
77 Rue Chalgrin. W. Hackett; 77, Park Lane
70,000 Witnesses. C. Fitzsimmons
Sh! The Octopus. R. Spence; Gorilla
Shadow. D. Stuart
Shadow Between. S. Hocking
Shadow Man. L. Meynell; Creaking Chair
Shadow of a Woman. V. Perdue; He Fell Down Dead
Shadow of Doubt. A. S. Roche
Shadow of Evil. C. Dawe
Shadow of Fear. H. Debrett; Before I Die
Shadow of the Law. J. Moroso; Quarry
Shadow on the Wall. J. B. Ellis; Picture on the Wall
Shadow on the Wall. H. Lees; Death in the Doll's House
Shadows on the Stairs. F. Vosper; Murder on the Second Floor
Shaft. E. Tidyman
Shaft's Big Score. E. Tidyman
Shake Hands with the Devil. R. Conner
Shamus. R. Giles
Shanghai Surprise. T. Kenrick; Faraday's Flowers
Share Out. E. Wallace; Jack o' Lantern
Shark. V. Canning; His Bones Are Coral
Sharky's Machine. W. Diehl
She Made Her Bed. J. M. Cain; Baby in the Icebox
She Played with Fire. Winston Graham; Fortune Is a Woman
She Shall Have Murder. D. Ames
She Wolves. P. Boileau; Prisoner
Shed No Tears. D. Martin
Sheep's Clothing. L. J. Vance
She'll Have to Go. I. S. Black; We Must Kill Toni
Sherlock Holmes. W. Gillette
Sherlock Holmes and the Secret Weapon. A. C. Doyle; Return of Sherlock Holmes
Sherlock Holmes and the Voice of Terror. A. C. Doyle; His Last Bow
Sherlock Holmes Faces Death. A. C. Doyle; Memoirs of Sherlock Holmes
Sherlock Holmes's Fatal Hour. A. C. Doyle; Memoirs of Sherlock Holmes
Shield for Murder. W. P. McGivern
Ship from Shanghai. D. Collins; Ordeal
Ship That Died of Shame. N. Monsarrat
Shock Corridor. M. Avallone
Shock Treatment. W. Van Atta
Shoot. D. Fairbairn
Shoot First. G. Household; Rough Shoot
Shoot It: Black, Shoot It: Blue. P. Tyner; Shoot It
Shoot the Pianist. D. Goodis; Down There
Shooting Stars. E. C. Vivian
Shop at Sly Corner. E. Percy; Play with Fire
Short Cut to Hell. G. Greene; Gun for Sale
Shot in the Dark. G. Fairlie

Shot in the Dark. H. Kurnitz
Shot in the Dark. C. Orr; Dartmouth Murders
Shulamite. A. Askew
Shuttered Room. J. Withers
Side Street. M. St. Clair
Sign of the Four. A. C. Doyle
Sign of the Ram. M. Ferguson
Sign on the Door. C. Pollock
Signpost to Murder. M. Doyle
Silencers. D. Hamilton
Silent Barrier. L. Tracy
Silent Battle. G. F. Gibbs
Silent Dust. R. Pertwee; Paragon
Silent House. J. G. Brandon
Silent Master. E. P. Oppenheim; Seeing Life
Silent Partner. A. Bodelsen; Think of a Number
Silent Witness. J. De Leon
Silver Bears. P. E. Erdman
Silver Blaze. A. C. Doyle; Memoirs of Sherlock Holmes
Silver Bridge. H. P. Lewis
Silver Car. W. Martyn; Secret of the Silver Car
Silver King. H. A. Jones
Silver Streak. J. C. Rogers
Sin That Was His. F. Packard
Sing Sing Nights. H. S. Keeler
Singapore. W. Bogart
Sinister Man. E. Wallace
Sinner Take All. W. Chambers; Murder for a Wanton
Sisters of Eve. E. P. Oppenheim; Temptation of Tavernake
Sitting Pretty. L. Henderson
Six Bridges to Cross. J. F. Dinneen; Anatomy of a Crime
Six Men. E. Radford
Six Napoleons. A. C. Doyle; Return of Sherlock Holmes
633 Squadron. F. E. Smith
Skull. R. Bloch; Skull of the Marquis de Sade
Skyjacked. D. Harper; Hijacked
Slaughter. H. Clement
Slaughter's Big Rip-Off. A. Kane
Slave Market. F. A. Kummer; Painted Woman
Slaves of Sumuru. S. Rohmer
Slayground. R. Stark
Sleep My Love. L. Q. Ross
Sleepers East. F. Nebel
Sleepers West. F. Nebel; Sleepers East
Sleeping Car Murders. S. Japrisot; 10:30 from Marseilles
Sleeping Car to Trieste. R. Alexander; Rome Express
Sleeping Cardinal. A. C. Doyle; Memoirs of Sherlock Holmes
Sleeping Memory. E. P. Oppenheim; Great Awakening
Sleeping Tiger. M. Moisewitsch
Slender Thread. S. Silliphant
Sleuth. A. Shaffer
Slight Case of Murder. D. Runyon
Slightly Honorable. F. G. Presnell; Send Another Coffin
Slightly Scarlet. J. M. Cain; Love's Lovely Counterfeit
Slightly Scarlet. P. Heath
Slippy McGee. M. C. Oemler
Small Back Room. N. Balchin
Small Voice. R. Westerby
Smugglers. G. Greene; Man Within
Snow Was Black. G. Simenon; Stain on the Snow
Snowbound. H. Innes; Lonely Skier
So Evil My Love. J. Shearing; For Her to See
Social Buccaneer. F. S. Isham
Society Lawyer. A. S. Roche; Penthouse
Soho Gorilla. E. Wallace; Dark Eyes of London
Soho Incident. R. Westerby; Wide Boys Never Work
Sol Madrid. R. Wilder; Fruit of the Poppy
Soldier's Story. C. Fuller; Soldier's Play
Solitaire Man. B. C. Spewack
Solitary Child. N. Bawden
Solitary Cyclist. A. C. Doyle; Return of Sherlock Holmes
Solo for Sparrow. E. Wallace; Gunner
Some Kind of Hero. J. Kirkwood
Somebody Killed Her Husband. C. B. Phillips
Someone at the Door. D. Christie
Something to Hide. N. Monsarrat
Somewhere in France. R. H. Davis
Son of His Father. R. Cullum
Son of the Immortals. L. Tracy
Song of Sixpence. F. A. Kummer
Sons of Satan. W. LeQueux
Sonya and the Madman. F. M. Dostoevskii; Crime and Punishment
Sophie Lang Goes West. F. I. Anderson; Notorious Sophie Lang

Sorcerer. G. Arnaud; Wages of Fear
Sorcerer. E. Wallace; Ringer
Sorcery. P. Boileau; Spells of Evil
Sorry Wrong Number. L. Fletcher
Sorry You've Been Troubled. W. Hackett
Sound of the Fury. J. Pagano; Condemned
South Sea Bubble. R. Pertwee
Spangles. N. Revell
Spaniard's Curse. E. Pargeter; Assize of the Dying
Spanish Cape Mystery. E. Queen
Spanish Jade. M. Hewlett
Speckled Band. A. C. Doyle; Adventures of Sherlock Holmes
Spellbound. F. Beeding; House of Dr. Edwardes
Sphinx. R. Cook
Spider. H. Holt; Midnight Mail
Spider. F. Oursler
Spider's Web. A. Christie
Spies. E. Hostovsky; Midnight Patient
Spies of the Air. J. Dell; Official Secret
Spikes Gang. G. Tippette
Spin a Dark Web. R. Westerby; Wide Boys Never Work
Spiral Staircase. E. L. White
Splendid Coward. H. Townley
Splendid Hazard. H. MacGrath
Split. R. Stark; Seventh
Spook Who Sat by the Door. S. Greenlee
Spy. J. F. Cooper
Spy. T. von Harbou
Spy Hunt. V. Canning; Panther's Moon
Spy in Black. J. S. Clouston
Spy in the Sky. A. S. Fleischman; Counterspy Express
Spy in White. D. Wheatley; Eunich of Stamboul
Spy Ship. G. Dyer; Five Fragments
Spy 13. R. W. Chambers; Secret Service Operator 13
Spy Who Came in from the Cold. J. Le Carre
Spy Who Loved Me. C. Wood; James Bond, the Spy Who Loved Me
Spy with a Cold Nose. R. Galton
Square Crooks. J. P. Judge
Squeaker. E. Wallace
Squeeze. David Craig; Whose Little Girl Are You?
Stage Fright. S. Jepson; Man Running
Star of Midnight. A. S. Roche
Star Reporter. W. Martyn; Mysterious Mr. Garland
Steele of the Royal Mounted. J. O. Curwood; Philipp Steele of the Royal Northwest Mounted Police
Stella. D. M. Disney; Family Skeleton
Stepford Wives. I. Levin
Stew in the Caribbean. A. Conroy; Looters
Stick. E. Leonard
Stiletto. H. Robbins
Still Waters Run Deep. T. Taylor
Sting. R. Weverka
Stingaree. E. W. Hornung
Stock-Broker's Clerk. A. C. Doyle; Memoirs of Sherlock Holmes
Stolen Papers. A. C. Doyle; Memoirs of Sherlock Holmes
Stone Cold Dead. H. Garner; Sin Sniper
Stone Killer. J. Gardner; Complete State of Death
Stone Leopard. C. Forbes
Stop Me Before I Kill. R. S. Thorn; Full Treatment
Stop Thief! Carlyle Moore
Stop, You're Killing Me. D. Runyon; Slight Case of Murder
Stopover: Tokyo. J. P. Marquand
Storm Fear. C. Seeley
Story of Shirley Yorke. H. A. Vachell; Case of Lady Camber
Story of Temple Drake. W. Faulkner; Sanctuary
Story Without a Name. A. Stringer
Straight Is the Way. D. Burnet; Four Walls
Straight Time. E. Bunker; No Beast So Fierce
Stranded in Arcady. F. Lynde
Strange Adventures of David Gray. J. S. Le Fanu; In a Glass Darkly
Strange Affair. B. Toms
Strange Affair of Uncle Harry. T. Job; Uncle Harry
Strange Awakening. P. Quentin; Puzzle for Fiends
Strange Boarders. E. P. Oppenheim; Strange Boarders at Palace Crescent
Strange Cargo. R. Sale; Not Too Narrow--Not Too Deep
Strange Case of Mary Page. F. Lewis
Strange Disappearance. A. K. Green
Strange Door. R. L. Stevenson; New Arabian Nights
Strange Intruder. H. Fowler; Shades Will Not Vanish

Stranger. J. Galsworthy; Five Tales
Stranger. A. Veiller
Stranger Came Home. G. Sanders
Stranger in the House. G. Simenon; Strangers in the House
Stranger in Town. F. A. Chittenden; Uninvited
Stranger Is Watching. M. H. Clark
Stranger Walked In. F. Vosper; Love from a Stranger
Strangers in the House. G. Simenon
Strangers of the Evening. T. Thayer; Illustrious Corpse
Strangers on a Honeymoon. E. Wallace; Northing Tramp
Strangers on a Train. P. Highsmith
Stranglers of Bombay. S. James
Straw Dogs. G. M. Williams; Siege of Trencher's Farm
Straw Man. D. M. Disney
Street of Chance. C. Woolrich; Black Curtain
Street of Shadows. L. Meynell; Creaking Chair
Street Without Joy. H. Bettauer; Viennese Love
Striptease Lady. G. R. Lee; G-String Murders
Stronger Than Desire. W. E. Woodward; Evelyn Prentice
Stronger Than Fear. L. Brady; Edge of Doom
Studio Murder Mystery. Edingtons
Study in Scarlet. A. C. Doyle
Study in Terror. E. Queen
Stuff That Dreams Are Made Of. J. M. Simmel; Traitor Blitz
Stunt Man. P. Brodeur
Subway in the Sky. B. Birch
Such a Lovely Kid Like Me. H. Farrell; Such a Gorgeous Kid Like Me
Sudden Fear. E. Sherry
Sudden Impact. J. C. Stinson
Sudden Terror. M. Hebden; Eyewitness
Suicide Club. R. L. Stevenson
Sultana. H. C. Rowland
Summer Heat. L. Shivers; Here to Get My Baby Out of Jail
Summer Storm. A. Chekhov; Shooting Party
Sun Shines Bright. I. S. Cobb; Old Judge Priest
Sun-Up. M. Marcin; Substitute Prisoner
Sunburn. S. Ellin; Bind
Sunday Woman. C. Fruttero
Super Fly. P. Fenty
Surgeon's Knife. A. Hocking; Wicked Flee
Surprises of an Empty Hotel. A. C. Gunter
Survivor. J. Herbert
Suspect. N. Balchin; Sort of Traitors
Suspect. J. Ronald; This Way Out
Suspense. I. Ostrander
Suspicion. F. Iles; Before the Fact
Sweeney Todd, the Demon Barber of Fleet Street. G. D. Pitt
Sweet Ride. W. Murray
Sweethearts and Wives. W. Hackett; Other Men's Wives
Swinging Pearl Mystery. S. Palmer (headnote)
Switch. P. Ridgeway
Sword of Fate. H. Herman
Sylvia. E. V. Cunningham
Tabitha. A. Ridley
Take. G. F. Newman; Sir, You Bastard
Take My Life. Winston Graham
Taking of Pelham One Two Three. J. Godey
Tales of Terror. E. Sudak
Talk About a Stranger. C. Armstrong; Albatross
Tall Headlines. A. E. Lindop
Tamarind Seed. E. Anthony
Tangled Evidence. P. C. De Crespigny
Tangled Hearts. C. H. Bullivant; Wife Whom God Forgot
Tangled Lives. W. Collins; Woman in White
Target. S. Hunter
Taste of Excitement. B. Healey; Waiting for a Tiger
Tatterly. T. Gallon
Teeth of the Tiger. M. Leblanc
Telefon. W. Wager
Tell Him I Love Him. P. Highsmith; This Sweet Sickness
Temple Tower. H. C. McNeile
Temptation. R. Hichens; Bella Donna
Temptation Harbour. G. Simenon; Newhaven-Dieppe
Temptation of Carlton Earle. S. M. During
Temptress. A. Campbell; Juggernaut
Ten Days in Paris. B. Graeme; Disappearance of Roger Tremayne
Ten Days' Wonder. E. Queen
Ten Little Indians. A. Christie; Ten Little Niggers

Ten Minute Alibi. A. Armstrong
Ten Seconds to Hell. L. P. Bachmann; Phoenix
Ten Thirty P.M. Summer. M. Duras; Ten-Thirty on a Summer Night
Tenant. R. Topor
Tenth Victim. R. Sheckley
Term of Trial. J. Barlow
Terrible Game. D. T. Moore
Terror. E. Wallace
Terror House. A. Kennington; Night Has Eyes
Terror of the Tongs. J. Sangster
Terrorists. P. Wheeler; Ransom
Test of Honor. E. P. Oppenheim; Mr. Wingrave, Millionaire
Thank Evans. E. Wallace; Good Evans!
Thank You, Mr. Moto. J. P. Marquand
That Cold Day in the Park. R. Miles
That Darn Cat. Gordons; Undercover Cat
That Man Bolt. P. Crowcraft
That Royle Girl. E. Balmer
That Was George. R. P. Jones; Heisters
That Way with Women. E. D. Biggers; Earl Derr Biggers Tells Ten Stories
That Woman Opposite. J. D. Carr; Emperor's Snuff Box
Then Came Bronson. W. Johnston
There Ain't No Justice. J. Curtis
These Are the Damned. H. L. Lawrence; Children of Light
They All Died Laughing. C. E. Vulliamy; Don Among the Dead Men
They Came by Night. B. Lyndon
They Drive by Night. A. I. Bezzerides; Long Haul
They Drive by Night. J. Curtis
They Gave Him a Gun. W. J. Cowen
They Live by Night. E. Anderson; Thieves Like Us
They Made Me a Fugitive. J. Budd; Convict Has Escaped
They Met in the Dark. A. Gilbert; Vanishing Corpse
They Shoot Horses, Don't They. H. McCoy
They Won't Believe Me. G. McDonell
They Won't Forget. W. Greene; Death in the Deep South
Thief Who Came to Dinner. T. L. Smith
Thieves' Highway. A. I. Bezzerides; Thieves Market
Thieves Like Us. E. Anderson
Thin Man. D. Hammett
Think Fast, Mr. Moto. J. P. Marquand
Think of a Number. A. Bodelsen
Third Clue. N. Gordon; Shakespeare Murders
Third Day. J. Hayes
Third Degree. A. Hornblow
Third Man. G. Greene
Third Party Risk. N. Bentley
Third Time Lucky. G. Butler; They Cracked Her Glass Slipper
Third Visitor. G. Anstruther
Third Voice. C. Williams; All the Way
13 Washington Square. L. Scott; No. 13 Washington Square
13 West Street. L. Brackett; Tiger Among Us
Thirteen Women. T. Thayer
Thirteenth Chair. B. Veiller
Thirteenth Guest. A. Trail
Thirteenth Hour. S. Horler
Thirteenth Juror. F. T. Hill
Thirty-Nine Steps. J. Buchan
36 Hours. C. K. Hittleman
This Gun for Hire. G. Greene; Gun for Sale
This Man Is Dangerous. P. Cheyney
This Man Is Dangerous. D. Hume; They Called Him Death
This Was a Woman. Joan Morgan
Thomas Crown Affair. E. L. Heyman
Thor Bridge. A. C. Doyle; Adventures of Sherlock Holmes
Thou Shalt Not Steal. E. Gaboriau; File No. 113
Thread o' Scarlet. J. J. Bell
Three Days of the Condor. J. Grady; Six Days of the Condor
Three Faces East. A. P. Kelly
Three in a Cellar. Angus Hall; Late Boy Wonder
Three Keys. F. Ormond
Three Live Ghosts. F. S. Isham
Three Rooms in Manhattan. G. Simenon; Three Beds in Manhattan
Three Sevens. P. P. Sheehan
Three Silent Men. E. P. Thorne
Three Students. A. C. Doyle; Return of Sherlock Holmes
Three Weird Sisters. C. Armstrong; Case of the Weird Sisters
Three Witnesses. S. Fowler
Three's a Crowd. M. Eberhart; Hasty Wedding
Thriller Story. J. Thompson; Hell of a Woman
Through Fire and Water. V. Bridges; Greensea Island

Through the Wall. C. Moffett
Thunder on the Hill. C. Hastings; Bonaventure
Thunderball. I. Fleming
Thunderbolt and Lightfoot. J. Millard
Thundercloud. T. Taylor; Still Waters Run Deep
Tick...Tick...Tick. P. Rock
Ticket-of-Leave Man. C. Reade; Foul Play
Ticket of Leave Man. T. Taylor
Tiger by the Tail. J. Mair; Never Come Back
Tiger in the Smoke. M. Allingham
Tiger of San Pedro. A. C. Doyle; His Last Bow
Tiger Rose. W. Mack
Tiger's Coat. E. Dejeans
Tigers Don't Cry. J. Burmeister; Running Scared
Tight Spot. L. Kantor; Dead Pigeon
Timberjack. D. Cushman
Time After Time. K. Alexander
Time to Die. M. Cleri; Six Graves to Munich
Time to Kill. R. Chandler; High Window
Time to Remember. E. Wallace; Man Who Bought London
Time Without Pity. Emlyn Williams; Someone Waiting
Times Have Changed. E. Davis
To Catch a King. H. Patterson
To Catch a Thief. D. Dodge
To Have and Have Not. E. Hemingway
To Have and To Hold. E. Wallace (headnote)
To Kill a Mockingbird. H. Lee
To Live and Die in L.A. G. Petievich
To the Devil--a Daughter. D. Wheatley
To the Public Danger. P. Hamilton; Money with Menaces
To What Red Hell. P. Robinson
Together Brothers. Jim Robinson
Tom Sawyer, Detective. M. Twain
Tomorrow. W. Faulkner; Knight's Gambit
Tong Man. C. C. Westover; Dragon's Daughter
Tony Rome. A. Rome; Miami Mayhem
Too Dangerous to Live. D. Hume
Too Many Chefs. N. Lyon; Someone Is Killing the Great Chefs of Europe
Too Many Crooks. E. J. Rath
Too Small My Friend. J. H. Chase; Way the Cookie Crumbles
Too Late for Tears. R. Huggins
Top Dog. F. Hume
Topaz. L. Uris
Topkapi. E. Ambler. Light of Day
Torn Curtain. R. Wormser
Torpedo Skin. F. Ryck; Woman Hunt
Torso Murder Mystery. T. C. H. Jacobs; Traitor Spy
Touch of Evil. W. Masterson; Badge of Evil
Touch of Larceny. A. Garve; Megstone Plot
Touch of the Child. T. Gallon
Towering Inferno. R. M. Stern; Tower
Town Without Pity. M. Gregor
Traffic in Souls. E. H. Ball
Trail of the Yukon. J. O. Curwood; Gold Hunters
Train. G. Simenon
Traitor Spy. T. C. H. Jacobs
Traitor's Gate. E. Wallace
Trans-Siberian Express. W. Adler
Trap. John Burke
Trap for Cinderella. S. Japrisot
Trapeze. M. Catto; Killing Frost
Travels with My Aunt. G. Greene
Tread Softly. G. Verner; Show Must Go On
Tread Softly Stranger. J. Popplewell; Blind Alley
Trent's Last Case. E. C. Bentley
Trial. D. M. Mankiewicz
Trial and Error. J. Mortimer
Trial of Madame X. J. W. MacConaughy; Madame X
Trial of Mary Dugan. B. Veiller
Trial of Vivienne Ware. K. Ellis
Trick Baby. I. Slim
Triple Deception. S. Noel; House of Secrets
Triumph of Sherlock Holmes. A. C. Doyle; Valley of Fear
Trooper O'Neill. G. Goodchild
Trouble for Two. R. L. Stevenson; Suicide Club
Trouble in the Sky. D. Beaty; Cone of Silence
Trouble Man. J. D. F. Black
Trouble with Girls. D. Keene; Chautauqua
Trouble with Harry. J. T. Story
True Confessions. J. G. Dunne
True Story of the Lyons Mail. E. Moreau; Courier of Lyons
Trunk Crime. E. Percy
Trust Your Wife. G. Abbott; Fall Guy

Truth About Bebe Donge. G. Simenon; Trial of Bebe Donge
Try and Get Me. J. Pagano; Condemned
Turf Conspiracy. N. Gould
Turn of the Screw. H. James
Turn the Key Softly. J. Brophy
Twelve Angry Men. R. Rose
Twelve Good Men. J. Rhode; Murders in Praed Street
21 Days. J. Galsworthy; Five Tales
21 Days Together. J. Galsworthy; Five Tales
Twenty Plus Two. F. Gruber
20,000 Pound Kiss. E. Wallace (headnote)
23 Paces to Baker Street. P. MacDonald; Nursemaid Who Disappeared
Twice Told Tales. N. Hawthorne
Twilight of Honor. A. Dewlen
Twilight's Last Gleaming. W. Wager; Viper Three
Twin. D. E. Westlake; Two Much!
Twin Pawns. W. Collins; Woman in White
Twist of Sand. G. Jenkins
Twisted Road. E. Anderson; Thieves Like Us
Two. C. Trieschmann
Two Against the World. L. Weitzenkorn; Five Star Final
Two Faces of Dr. Jekyll. R. L. Stevenson; Strange Case of Dr. Jekyll and Mr. Hyde
Two Faces of January. P. Highsmith
Two in the Dark. G. Burgess; Two O'Clock Courage
Two-Letter Alibi. A. Garve; Death and the Sky Above
Two Living and One Dead. S. Christiansen
Two Minute Warning. G. La Fountaine
Two Mrs. Carrolls. M. Vale
Two O'Clock Courage. G. Burgess
Two-Soul Woman. G. Burgess; White Cat
Two Thousand Maniacs. H. G. Lewis
U-Boat 29. J. S. Clouston; Spy in Black
Ugly Duckling. R. L. Stevenson; Strange Case of Dr. Jekyll and Mr. Hyde
Uncle Harry. T. Job
Uncle Silas. J. S. Le Fanu
Under Cover. R. C. Megrue
Under Cover Man. J. Wilstach
Under Suspicion. E. P. Oppenheim; Game of Liberty
Under the Lash. A. Askew; Shulamite
Under Western Eyes. J. Conrad
Underground. C. Stratton
Undertaker Parlor Computer. W. Kempley; Probability Factor
Underworld Informers. D. Warner; Death of a Snout
Undying Monster. J. D. Kerruish
Uneasy Terms. P. Cheyney
Unfaithful. W. S. Maugham; Letter
Unforbidden Sin. R. Vickers
Unholy Four. G. Sanders; Stranger at Home
Unholy Three. T. Robbins
Unholy Wife. J. Roeburt
Uninvited. D. Macardle; Uneasy Freehold
Union City. C. Woolrich; Nightwebs
Union Station. T. Walsh; Nightmare in Manhattan
Unknown Blonde. T. D. Irwin; Collusion
Unknown Purple. R. West
Unseen. E. L. White; Midnight House
Unsewing Machine. G. Brewer; Killer Is Loose
Unstoppable Man. M. Gilbert; Amateur in Violence
Unsuitable Job for a Woman. P. D. James
Unsuspected. C. Armstrong
Untamable. G. Burgess; White Cat
Up in the Cellar. Angus Hall; Late Boy Wonder
Upstairs and Downstairs. R. S. Thorn
Uptight. L. O'Flaherty; Informer
Valdez Is Coming. E. Leonard
Valiant. H. Hall
Valley of Fear. A. C. Doyle
Valley of Ghosts. E. Wallace
Valley of Silent Men. J. O. Curwood
Vendetta. A. C. Gunter
Venetian Affair. H. MacInnes
Venetian Bird. V. Canning
Vengeance. C. Siodmak; Donovan's Brain
Venom. A. Scholefield
Verdict. B. C. Reed
Verdict. E. Wallace; Big Four
Verdict. I. Zangwill; Big Bow Mystery
Verdict of the Heart. C. Garvice
Vertigo. P. Boileau; Living and the Dead
Vice Squad. W. Rotsler
Vice Squad. L. T. White; Harness Bull
Vicious Circle. H. Herald; Burning Bush
Vicki. S. Fisher; I Wake Up Screaming
Vicky Van. C. Wells
Victim. W. Drummond
Victor Frankenstein. M. Shelley; Frankenstein

Villain. J. Barlow; Burden of Proof
Violent Enemy. H. Marlowe; Candle for the Dead
Violent Saturday. W. L. Heath
Visit. F. Duerrenmatt
Visiting Hours. K. Rembo
Voice in the Dark. R. E. Dyar
Voice in the Fog. H. MacGrath
Voice on the Wire. E. H. Ball
W Plan. G. Seton
Wages of Fear. G. Arnaud
Wait Until Dark. F. Knott
Waiting Room for the Other Side. R. Marshall; Mission to Siena
Walking Stick. Winston Graham
Walking Tall. D. Warren
Walking Tall: Part 2. W. Carey
Walls Came Tumbling Down. J. Eisinger
Wanted at Headquarters. E. Wallace (headnote)
Ware Case. G. Pleydell
Warn That Man. V. Sylvaine
Warning Shot. W. Masterson; 711--Officer Needs Help
Warriors. S. Yurick
Waste-Land. H. Ellison; Tomboy
Watchmaker of Saint-Paul. G. Simenon; Watchmaker of Everton
Waterfront. J. Brophy
Waterfront Woman. J. Brophy; Waterfront
Way of the Strong. R. Cullum
Way Out. B. Graeme
Way to the Gold. W. D. Steele; Way to Gold
We Are Not Alone. J. Hilton
We Shall See. E. Wallace
Web of Evidence. A. J. Cronin; Beyond This Place
Web of Passion. S. Ellin; Key to Nicholas Street
Weekend of Shadows. H. Atkinson; Reckoning
We're on the Jury. F. Ballard; Ladies of the Jury
West 11. L. Del Rivo; Furnished Room
Westland Case. J. Latimer; Headed for a Hearse
What a Carve Up! Frank King; Ghoul
What a Girl! P. Cheyney; I'll Say She Does
What Became of Jack and Jill? L. Moody; Ruthless Ones
What Changed Charley Farthing. M. Hebden
What Happened Then? L. T. Bradley
Whatever Happened to Aunt Alice? U. Curtiss; Forbidden Garden
Whatever Happened to Baby Jane? H. Farrell
What's Bred...Comes Out in the Flesh. G. Allen; What's Bred in the Bone
What's the Matter with Helen? R. Deming
When Eight Bells Toll. A. MacLean
When Greek Meets Greek. P. Trent
When It Was Dark. G. Thorne
When the Door Opened. E. Vance; Escape
When Thief Meets Thief. G. McDonell; Jump for Glory
When Tomorrow Comes. J. M. Cain; Serenade
Where Are the Children? M. H. Clark
Where Eagles Dare. A. MacLean
Where East Is East. T. Browning
Where the Pavement Ends. J. Russell; Red Mark
Where the Sidewalk Ends. W. L. Stuart; Night Cry
Where the Spies Are. J. Leasor; Passport to Oblivion
While the City Sleeps. C. Einstein; Bloody Spur
While the Patient Slept. M. Eberhart
Whirlpool. L. P. Bachmann; Lorelei
Whirlpool. G. Endore; Methinks the Lady--
Whirlpool. V. Morton
Whispering Chorus. P. P. Sheehan
Whispering Smith. F. H. Spearman
Whispering Wires. H. Leverage
Whistle Blower. John Hale
Whistle Stop. M. M. Wolff
Whistling in the Dark. L. Gross
White Alley. C. Wells
White Circle. R. L. Stevenson; New Arabian Nights
White Cockatoo. M. Eberhart
White Face. E. Wallace
White Lie. W. LeQueux
White Mice. R. H. Davis
White Moll. F. Packard
Who? A. Budrys
Who Dares Wins. J. Follett; Tiptoe Boys
Who Is Guilty? A. Coppel; I Killed the Count
Who Is Hope Schuyler? S. Ransome; Hearses Don't Hurry
Who Is Killing the Great Chefs of Europe? N. Lyons; Someone Is Killing the Great Chefs of Europe

Who Killed Aunt Maggie? Medora Field
Who Killed John Savage? P. MacDonald; Rynox
Who Killed the Cat? A. Ridley; Tabitha
Who Was Maddox? E. Wallace; Undisclosed Client
Who Was That Lady? N. Krasna; Who Was That Lady I Saw You With?
Whole Truth. P. Mackie
Who'll Stop the Rain? R. Stone; Dog Soldiers
Whose Wife? C. H. Bullivant
Whosoever Shall Offend... F. M. Crawford
Wicked As They Come. B. Ballinger; Portrait in Smoke
Wicked Wife. D. Christie; Grand National Night
Wicked Woman. A. Austin
Wicker Man. R. Hardy
Wickham Mystery. J. McNally; Paper Chase
Widow Couderc. G. Simenon; Ticket of Leave
Wife, Husband and Friend. J. M. Cain; Career in C Major
Wife Whom God Forgot. C. H. Bullivant
Wilby Conspiracy. P. Driscoll
Wild Geese. D. Carney
Wild Geese II. D. Carney; Square Circle
Wild Party. J. McPartland
Willard. S. Gilbert; Ratman's Notebooks
Winding Stair. A. E. W. Mason
Window. W. Irish; Dead Man Blues
Windows. H. B. Gilmour
Wine, Women and Horses. W. R. Burnett; Dark Hazard
Wings of Danger. M. Black; Dead on Course
Winifred, the Shop Girl. C. N. Williamson; Shop Girl
Winter Kills. R. Condon
Wiser Sex. C. Fitch; Woman in the Case
Witches. P. Curtis; Devil's Own
Witching Hour. A. Thomas
With All Hands. J. Gunn; Deadlier Than the Male
Within the Law. B. Veiller
Without a Trace. B. Gutcheon; Still Missing
Without Apparent Motive. E. Hunter; Ten Plus One
Without Regret. R. Pertwee; Interference
Without Warning. A. Stringer; Story Without a Name
Witness. H. Judd; Shadow of a Doubt
Witness. W. Kelley
Witness for the Defense. A. E. W. Mason
Witness for the Prosecution. A. Christie
Witness Vanishes. J. Ronald; They Can't Hang Me!
Wizard. G. Leroux; Balaoo
Wolf Hunters. J. O. Curwood
Wolfen. W. Strieber
Woman Alone. J. Conrad; Secret Agent
Woman in Grey. A. M. Williamson
Woman in the Case. C. Fitch
Woman in the Window. J. H. Wallis; Once Off Guard
Woman Is a Stranger. J. H. Chase; Not Safe to Be Free
Woman Next Door. C. Wells; Vicky Van
Woman of Mystery. G. Ohnet
Woman of Straw. C. Arley
Woman of the Iron Bracelets. F. Barrett
Woman on the Beach. M. A. Wilson; None So Blind
Woman Racket. P. Dunning; Night Hostess
Woman Who Came Back. C. M. S. McLellan; Leah Kleschna
Woman Who Dared. A. M. Williamson
Woman Who Wouldn't Die. Jay Bennett; Catacombs
Woman Wins. C. H. Bullivant
Woman's Law. Maravene Thompson
Woman's Vengeance. A. Huxley; Mortal Coils
World in My Pocket. J. H. Chase
Worldly Goods. A. Soutar
World's Great Snare. E. P. Oppenheim
Wrath of God. J. Graham
Wreck of the Mary Deare. H. Innes; Mary Deare
Wrecker. A. Ridley
Wrecking Crew. D. Hamilton
Wrong Box. R. L. Stevenson
Wrong Is Right. C. McCarry; Better Angels
X. E. Sudak
Yakuza. L. Schrader
Year of the Dragon. R. Daley
Yellow Canary. W. Masterson; Evil Come, Evil Go
Yellow Claw. S. Rohmer
Yellow Dog. G. Simenon; Face for a Clue
Yellow Dove. G. F. Gibbs
Yellow Face. A. C. Doyle; Memoirs of Sherlock Holmes

Yellow Mask. E. Wallace; Traitor's Gate
Yellow Men and Gold. Gouverneur Morris
Yellow Passport. V. Morton; Yellow Ticket
Yellow Ticket. V. Morton
Yellow Typhoon. H. MacGrath
Yield to the Night. J. Henry
Yosemite Trail. R. Cullum; One-Way Trail
You Can't Beat the Law. H. H. Van Loan
You Can't Escape. A. Kennington; She Died Young
You Can't See Round Corners. J. Cleary
You Do It, Cutie. P. Cheyney; Your Deal, My Lovely
You Only Live Twice. I. Fleming
You Pay Your Money. M. Cronin
You'll Like My Mother. N. A. Hintze
Young and Innocent. J. Tey; Shilling for Candles
Young and Wild. Morton Cooper
Young Dillinger. S. Stuart
Young Don't Cry. R. Jessup
Young Eve and Old Adam. T. Gallon
Young Girls Reward. J. H. Chase; Miss Callaghan Comes to Grief
Young Savages. E. Hunter; Matter of Conviction
Young Scarface. G. Greene; Brighton Rock
Young Sherlock Holmes. A. Arnold
Zero Hour! J. Castle; Flight into Danger

Screenwriters Index

Abbott, George
 Manslaughter. A. D. Miller
 Sea God. J. Russell; Red Mark
Accursi, Claude
 Sorcery. P. Boileau; Spells of Evil
Ackland, Rodney
 No. 17. J. J. Farjeon
 Temptation Harbour. G. Simenon; Newhaven-Dieppe
Adams, Frank R.
 She Made Her Bed. J. M. Cain; Baby in the Icebox
Adamson, Ewart
 Dark Hour. S. Gluck; Last Trap
 Inside the Lines. E. D. Biggers
Adreon, Franklyn
 Drums of Fu Manchu. S. Rohmer
Agee, James
 Night of the Hunter. D. Grubb
Agi
 Sunday Woman. C. Fruttero
Ainsworth, John
 Hell Is Empty. J. F. Straker
Alexander, Gilbert
 Hunting Party. J. Millard
Albert, Marvin H.
 Don Is Dead. N. Quarry
 Lady in Cement. A. Rome
 Twist of Sand. G. Jenkins
Aldrich, Robert
 Chinese Parrot. E. D. Biggers
 Ten Seconds to Hell. L. P. Bachmann; Phoenix
Alexander, J. Grubb
 Gamblers. C. Klein
 Haunted Bell. J. Futrelle; Diamond Master
 Lone Wolf Returns. L. J. Vance
 Murder Will out. M. Leinster
 Not Guilty. H. MacGrath; Parrot & Co.
 Voice on the Wire. E. H. Ball
Alicata, Mario
 Obsession. J. M. Cain; Serenade
Allen, Janis
 Double Negative. K. Millar; Three Roads
Allen, Jay Presson
 Deathtrap. I. Levin
 Marnie. Winston Graham
 Travels with My Aunt. G. Greene
Allin, Michael
 Enter the Dragon. M. Roote
Allinson, Vera
 Bella Donna. R. Hichens
 Blind Justice. A. Ridley; Recipe for Murder
 Ten Minute Alibi. A. Armstrong
Altman, Robert
 McCabe and Mrs. Miller. E. Naughton; McCabe
 Thieves Like Us. E. Anderson
Amann, Pelham Leigh
 Cross Currents. W. G. Elliott; Nine Days' Blunder
Amateau, Rod
 Wilby Conspiracy. P. Driscoll
Ambler, Eric
 October Man. E. Britton
 Rough Shoot. G. Household
 Wreck of the Mary Deare. H. Innes; Mary Deare
Ambrose, David
 Survivor. J. Herbert
Anderson, Doris
 Grumpy. H. Hodges
 Sophie Lang Goes West. F. I. Anderson; Notorious Sophie Lang
 Without Regret. R. Pertwee; Interference
Anderson, Maxwell
 Death Takes a Holiday. Walter Ferris
Andreota, Paul
 Passager Clandestin. G. Simenon; Stowaway
Andrews, Del
 Bronze Bell. L. J. Vance
Andrews, Jack
 Caribbean Mystery. J. W. Vandercook; Murder in Trinidad
 Subway in the Sky. B. Birch
Andrews, Robert D.
 Devil Commands. W. Sloan; Edge of Running Water
 Longest Night. C. Fitzsimmons; Whispering Window
Anhalt, Edna
 Bulldog Drummond Strikes Back. H. C. McNeile; Knock-Out
Anhalt, Edward
 Bulldog Drummond Strikes Back. H. C. McNeile; Knock-Out
 Escape to Athena. P. Blake
 Green Ice. G. A. Browne
 Holcroft Covenant. R. Ludlum
 Satan Bug. I. Stuart
 Young Savages. E. Hunter; Matter of Conviction
Anouilh, Jean
 Trap for Cinderella. S. Japrisot
Anoulin, Jean

Death of a Beauty. G. Simenon; Belle
Anstruther, Gerald
 Third Visitor. G. Anstruther
Anthony, Joseph
 Crime and Punishment. F. M. Dostoevskii
 Meet Nero Wolfe. R. Stout; Fer-de-Lance
Anthony, Stuart
 Strangers of the Evening. T. Thayer; Illustrious Corpse
 Tom Sawyer, Detective. M. Twain
Anthony, Walter
 Cat and the Canary. J. Willard
Apply, Chris
 Fear Makers. D. L. Teilhet
Apstein, Theodore
 Whatever Happened to Aunt Alice? U. Curtiss; Forbidden Garden
Aranda, Vicente
 Blood Spattered Bride. J. S. Le Fanu; In a Glass Darkly
 Murder in the Central Committee. M. V. Montalban
Arcady, Alexandre
 Hold-Up. J. Cronley; Quick Change
Arcalli, Franco
 Once Upon a Time in America. H. Grey; Hoods
Archer, Eugene
 Ten Days' Wonder. E. Queen
Archibald, William
 Innocents. H. James; Turn of the Screw
Ardies, Tom
 Russian Roulette. T. Ardies; Kosygin Is Coming
Arehn, Mats
 Assignment. P. Wahloo
Argento, Dario
 Cat o' Nine Tails. P. J. Gillette
Argyle, John
 Dark Eyes of London. E. Wallace
 Door with Seven Locks. E. Wallace
 Night Has Eyes. A. Kennington
 This Man Is Dangerous. D. Hume; They Called Him Death
 Traitor Spy. T. C. H. Jacobs
Arkless, Robert
 Man Who Would Not Die. C. Williams; Sailcloth Shroud
Arlaud, R. M.
 Maigret and the St. Fiacre Case. G. Simenon; Saint Fiacre Affair
Arliss, Leslie
 Night Has Eyes. A. Kennington
 Road House. W. Hackett
 Saint Meets the Tiger. L. Charteris; Meet the Tiger
 Too Dangerous to Live. D. Hume
Arlorio, Giorgio
 Burn. N. Gant
Armitage, George
 Hit Man. T. Lewis; Jack's Return Home
Armitage, Graham
 Gas. B. Hirschfeld
Armstrong, Anthony
 Young and Innocent. J. Tey; Shilling for Candles
Arnold, Danny
 Lady Takes a Flier. E. Ronns
Arthurs, George
 Yellow Mask. E. Wallace; Traitor's Gate
Ashton, James
 Devil's Rain. M. Willis
Asquith, Anthony
 Shooting Stars. E. C. Vivian
Asquith, Mary
 Lady Audley's Secret. M. E. Braddon
Atkinson, Frank
 Third Clue. N. Gordon; Shakespeare Murders
Atlas, Leopold
 Mystery of Edwin Drood. C. Dickens
Atteberry, Duke
 Mountain Music. M. Kantor; Author's Choice
Auberge, Maurice
 Passager Clandestin. G. Simenon; Stowaway
 Truth About Bebe Donge. G. Simenon; Trial of Bebe Donge
Audiard, Jacques
 Deadly Circuit. M. Behm; Eye of the Beholder
Audiard, Michel
 Any Number Can Win. J. Trinian
 Big Operation. R. Airth; Snatch
 Blood to the Head. G. Simenon; Young Cardinaud
 Deadly Circuit. M. Behm; Eye of the Beholder
 He Died with His Eyes Open. D. Raymond
 Heads or Tails. A. Harris; Baroni
 Little Virtuous. R. Marshall; Short Time to Live
 Maigret and the St. Fiacre Case. G. Simenon; Saint Fiacre Affair

Maigret Sets a Trap. G. Simenon
 On a Nice Summer Day. J. H. Chase; One Bright Summer Morning
 President. G. Simenon; Premier
 Professional. P. Alexander; Death of a Thin-Skinned Animal
 Rise Up, Spy. G. Markstein; Chance Awakening
Auerbach, George
 Bishop Misbehaves. F. Jackson
Aurel, Jean
 Hit and Run. R. Marshall
 Let It Be Sunday. C. Williams; Long Saturday Night
Aurenche, Jean
 Clockmaker. G. Simenon; Watchmaker of Everton
 In Case of Emergency. G. Simenon
 Murderer. P. Highsmith; Blunderer
 North Star. G. Simenon; Lodger
 Population 1280. J. Thompson; Pop. 1280
Aurthur, Robert Alan
 Edge of the City. F. Pohl
 Lost Man. F. L. Green; Odd Man Out
Austin, Ronald
 Happening. E. Curry
Avery, Stephen Morehouse
 Woman in White. W. Collins
Axelrod, David
 Charlie Chan and the Curse of the Dragon Queen. M. Avallone
Axelrod, George
 Holcroft Covenant. R. Ludlum
 How to Murder Your Wife. H. Williams
 Lady Vanishes. E. L. White; Wheel Spins
 Manchurian Candidate. R. Condon
Axelrod, Jonathan
 Every Little Crook and Nanny. E. Hunter
Aylott, Dave
 It Is Never Too Late to Mend. C. Reade
Ayme, Marcel
 Crime and Punishment. F. M. Dostoevskii
Babcock, Dwight
 Corpse Came C.O.D. J. Starr
Bachardy, Don
 Frankenstein: The True Story. M. Shelley; Frankenstein
Bachmann, Lawrence P.
 Lorelei. L. P. Bachmann
Baedekerl, Klaus
 Glass Cell. P. Highsmith
Bailey, John
 Riddle of the Sands. E. Childers
Baines, John
 Dead of Night. E. F. Benson; Room in the Tower
 Hands of Orlac. M. Renard
 Seven Thunders. R. Croft-Cooke
Baird, Leah
 Destroying Angel. L. J. Vance
 Spangles. N. Revell
Baird, Philip
 Game for Vultures. M. Hartmann
Baker, C. Graham/Graham
 Case Against Mrs. Ames. A. S. Roche
 Danger Signal. P. Bottome; Murder in the Bud
 Shadow of a Woman. V. Perdue; He Fell Down Dead
 Third Degree. A. Hornblow
Baker, George D.
 Buried Treasure. F. B. Austin; On the Borderland
 Demon. C. N. Williamson
 Heliotrope. R. W. Child; Velvet Black
 Man Who Stayed Home. J. E. H. Terry
Baker, Herbert
 Ambushers. D. Hamilton
 Hammerhead. J. Mayo
 Murderer's Row. D. Hamilton
 Scared Stiff. C. W. Goddard; Ghost Breakers
Baker, Melville
 Above Suspicion. H. MacInnes
Balchin, Nigel
 Mine Own Executioner. N. Balchin
 Suspect. N. Balchin; Sort of Traitors
 23 Paces to Baker Street. P. MacDonald; Nursemaid Who Disappeared
Balderston, John
 Amazing Quest of Mr. Ernest Bliss. E. P. Oppenheim
 Frankenstein. M. Shelley
 Gas Light. P. Hamilton
 Hands of Orlac. M. Renard
 Mystery of Edwin Drood. C. Dickens
Baldwin, Earl
 Slight Case of Murder. D. Runyon
Balling, Erik
 One of Those Things. A. Bodelsen; One Down
Balshofer, Fred J.
 Haunted Pajamas. F. P. Elliott
 Hidden Spring. C. B. Kelland
 Paradise Garden. G. F. Gibbs

Pidgin Island. H. MacGrath
Bardawill, Georges
  On a Nice Summer day. J. H. Chase; One Bright Summer Morning
Barisse, Rita
  Midnight Episode. G. Simenon; Monsieur la Souris
Barjaval, Rene
  Gooseflesh. J. H. Chase; Come Easy--Go Easy
  Man in the Raincoat. J. H. Chase; Tiger by the Tail
Barnett, Charles
  Amazing Partnership. E. P. Oppenheim
  Beryl Coronet. A. C. Doyle; Adventures of Sherlock Holmes
  Priory School. A. C. Doyle; Return of Sherlock Holmes
Barnwell, John
  Five Against the House. J. Finney
Barnwell, Peggy
  Mrs. Pym of Scotland Yard. N. Morland (headnote)
Baron, Alexander
  Robbery Under Arms. R. Boldrewood
Barraud, George
  Small Voice. R. Westerby
Barrett, James Lee
  Fool's Parade. D. Grubb
  Tick...Tick...Tick. P. Rock
Barringer, Barry
  Death Kiss. M. St. Dennis
Barringer, Michael
  Black Mask. B. Graeme; Blackshirt
  Death on the Set. V. MacClure
  Inquest. M. Barringer
  Murder at Covent Gardens. W. J. Makin
  Third Clue. N. Gordon; Shakespeare Murders
  Three Witnesses. S. Fowler
Barry, Tom
  East Lynn. H. Wood
  Valiant. H. Hall
Bartholomae, Philip
  Mark of Cain. C. Wells
  Stranded in Arcady. F. Lynde
Bartlett, Basil
  They Met in the Dark. Anthony Gilbert; Vanishing Corpse
Bartlett, Hall
  Zero Hour! J. Castle; Flight into Danger
Bartlett, Randolph
  White Mice. R. H. Davis
Bartlett, Sy
  Murder of Dr. Harrigan. M. G. Eberhart; From This Dark Stairway
Barzman, Ben
  Blind Date. L. Howard
  Time Without Pity. E. Williams; Someone Waiting
Bass, Ronald
  Code Name: Emerald. R. Bass; Emerald Illusion
Bassing, Eileen
  Home Before Dark. E. Bassing
Bassing, Robert
  Home Before Dark. E. Bassing
Bast, William
  Hammerhead. J. Mayo
Batt, Bart
  Frankenstein Must Be Destroyed. M. Shelley; Frankenstein
Baxt, George
  Payroll. D. Bickerton
Beaumont, Charles
  Masque of the Red Death. Elsie Lee
  Mr. Moses. M. Catto; Mister Midas
  Premature Burial. M. H. Danne
Beckerman, Barry
  St. Ives. O. Bleeck; Procane Chronicle
  Shamus. R. Giles
Bee, Richard
  Haunted House. O. Davis
  Seven Footprints to Satan. A. Merritt
Behat, Gilles
  Barbarous Street. D. Goodis; Street of the Lost
Behm, Marc
  Blonde from Peking. J. H. Chase; You Have Yourself a Deal
Beich, Albert
  Dead Ringer. R. Thomas
Beineix, Jean-Jacques
  Diva. Delacorta
  Moon in the Gutter. D. Goodis
Bekeffy, Laszlo
  Ghost Train. A. Ridley
Belden, Charles
  Shot in the Dark. C. Orr; Dartmouth Murders
Bell, Monta
  After Midnight. E. Fletcher-Allen
  Bellamy Trial. F. N. Hart
Beloin, Edmund
  Lady on a Train. L. Charteris
Belson, Jerry
  Grasshopper. M. McShane; Passing of Evil

Jekyll and Hyde...Together Again. R. L. Stevenson; Strange Case of Dr. Jekyll and Mr. Hyde
Benchley, Robert
  Murder on a Honeymoon. S. Palmer; Puzzle of the Pepper Tree
Bengal, Ben
  Crack-Up. F. Brown; Madman's Holiday
Bennett, Charles
  Blackmail. C. Bennett
  Ivy. M. B. Lowndes; Story of Ivy
  Kind Lady. E. Chodorov
  Man Who Knew Too Much. R. Alexander
  Sabotage. J. Conrad; Secret Agent
  Secret Agent. W. S. Maugham; Ashenden
  Sign of the Ram. M. Ferguson
  Thirty-Nine Steps. J. Buchan
  Young and Innocent. J. Tey; Shilling for Candles
Bennett, Compton
  Beyond the Curtain. A. J. Wallis; Thunder Above
  That Woman Opposite. J. D. Carr; Emperor's Snuff Box
Bennison, Andrew
  Wizard. G. Leroux; Balaoo
Benson, Sally
  Conspirator. H. Slater
  No Man of Her Own. W. Irish; I Married a Dead Man
  Signpost to Murder. M. Doyle
Bentley, Robert
  Shanghai Surprise. T. Kenrick; Faraday's Flowers
Bentley, Thomas
  Lackey and the Lady. T. Gallon
Benton, Robert
  Bonnie and Clyde. B. Hirschfeld
Benvenuti, Leonardo
  Once Upon a Time in America. H. Grey; Hoods
Beranger, Clara
  Dr. Jekyll and Mr. Hyde. R. L. Stevenson; Strange Case of Dr. Jekyll and Mr. Hyde
  From the Valley of the Missing. G. M. White
  Grumpy. H. Hodges
  Man on the Box. H. MacGrath
  Master Mind. M. Dana
  Number Seventeen. L. Tracy
  Painted Woman. F. A. Kummer
Beraud, Luc
  Tell Him I Love Him. P. Highsmith; This Sweet Sickness
Bercovici, Eric
  Captive City. J. Appleby
Bercovici, Leonardo
  Kiss the Blood Off My Hands. G. Butler
  Lost Moment. H. James; Aspern Papers
Beresford, Frank S.
  Bishop's Emeralds. H. Townley
  Cordelia the Magnificent. L. Scott
Berg, Dick
  Shoot. D. Fairbairn
Bergere, Ouida
  Avalanche. G. Atherton
  Bella Donna. R. Hichens
  Kick-In. W. Mack
  Right to Love. C. Farrere; Man Who Killed
  Witness for the Defence. A. E. W. Mason
Bergman, Andrew
  Fletch. G. McDonald
Bergman, Boris
  Twin. D. E. Westlake; Two Much!
Berk, Howard
  Target. S. Hunter
Berkeley, Martin
  Big Caper. L. White
Berkeley, Reginald
  77 Park Lane. W. Hackett
Berkman, Edward O.
  Four Dark Hours. G. Greene (headnote)
  Squeaker. E. Wallace
Berkman, Ted
  Short Cut to Hell. G. Greene; Gun for Sale
Berland, Jacques
  Gun Moll. P. Cheyney; Poison Ivy
  This Man Is Dangerous. P. Cheyney
Bern, Paul
  Great Deception. G. F. Gibbs; Yellow Dove
  Prince of Tempters. E. P. Oppenheim; Ex-Duke
Bernard, Judd
  Destructors. M. Franklin
  Inside Out. W. Hughes
Bernstein, Walter
  Fail-Safe. E. Burdick
  Molly Maguires. J. O'Neill
  Money Trap. L. White
Bertsch, Marguerite
  Mortmain. A. Train
  My Official Wife. R. H. Savage
  Through the Wall. C. Moffett
Bessie, Alvah

Northern Pursuit. L. T. White; 5,000 Trojan Horses
Bessie, Dan
  Hard Traveling. A. Bessie; Bread and a Stone
Bettinson, Ralph Gilbert
  Down River. Seamark
  Reporter. K. Attiwill
  Thread o' Scarlet. J. J. Bell
  Traitor Spy. T. C. H. Jacobs
Bezzerides, A. I.
  Desert Fury. R. Stewart; Desert Town
  Kiss Me, Deadly. M. Spillane
  On Dangerous Ground. G. Butler; Mad with Much Heart
  Thieves' Highway. A. I. Bezzerides; Thieves Market
Binet, Catherine
  Games of the Countess Dolingen of Gratz. B. Stoker; Dracula
Bingham, Elfrid A.
  Breaking point. M. R. Rinehart
  Paliser Case. E. Saltus
Binyon, Claude
  Stella. D. M. Disney; Family Skeleton
Bird, John
  Embassy. S. Coulter
Birkin, Andrew
  Name of the Rose. U. Eco
Biro, Lajos
  Ghost Train. A. Ridley
  Haunted House. O. Davis
  Knight Without Armour. J. Hilton
  Sanders of the River. E. Wallace
Birt, Daniel
  Third Party Risk. N. Bentley
Birt, Louise
  Three Weird Sisters. C. Armstrong; Case of the Weird Sisters
Bishop, Ron
  Underground. C. Stratton
Blache, Alice
  Lure. G. Scarborough
Black, Ian Stuart
  High Bright Sun. I. S. Black
  Long Knife. S. Truss; Long Night
  Soho Incident. R. Westerby; Wide Boys Never Work
Black, John D. F.
  Shaft. E. Tidyman
  Trouble Man. J. D. F. Black
Blackmore, Peter
  Make Mine Mink. P. Coke; Breath of Spring
Blackton, J. Stuart
  Passionate Quest. E. P. Oppenheim
Blair, Charles
  Return from the Ashes. H. Monteilhet
Blake, Oliver
  Scarlet Weekend. W. Kent; Woman in Purple Pajamas
Blankfort, Michael
  Act of Murder. E. Lothar; Mills of God
  Blind Alley. J. Warwick
Blatchford, Frederick
  Mr. Wu. L. J. Miln
Blatty, William Peter
  Exorcist. W. P. Blatty
  Man from the Diner's Club. S. Baol
  Shot in the Dark. H. Kurnitz
Blau, Raphael
  Short Cut to Hell. G. Greene; Gun for Sale
Blees, Robert
  Dr. Phibes Rises Again. W. Goldstein
  Glass Web. M. Ehrlich; Spin the Glass Web
  High School Confidential. Morton Cooper
  Screaming Mimi. F. Brown
  Slightly Scarlet. J. M. Cain; Love's Lovely Counterfeit
Bleich, Bill
  Hearse. H. Clement
Blizzard, Helen
  Beetle. R. Marsh
  Perpetua. D. C. Calthrop
Bloch, Robert
  Asylum. W. Johnston
  Couch. R. Bloch
  Deadly Bees. H. F. Heard; Taste of Honey
  Night Walker. S. Stuart
Blochman, Lawrence G.
  Bombay Mail. L. G. Blochman
Block, Ralph
  Dark Hazard. W. R. Burnett
Blondin, Antoine
  Obsession. W. Irish; Dead Man Blues
Bloom, Harry Jack
  Naked Spur. A. Ullman
  You Only Live Twice. I. Fleming
Bloom, Jeffrey
  11 Harrowhouse. G. A. Browne
Bluestone, George
  Walking Stick. Winston Graham
Blum, Edwin
  Sherlock Holmes. W. Gillette
Boam, Jeffrey

Dead Zone. Stephen King
Straight Time. E. Bunker; No Beast So Fierce
Boasberg, Al
Murder in the Private Car. E. E. Rose; Rear Car
Bobrick, Sam
Jimmy the Kid. D. E. Westlake
Bock, Edward
Return of the Whistler. W. Irish; Eyes That Watch You
Bodelsen, Anders
One of Those Things. A. Bodelsen; One Down
Boehm, Endre
Girl from Mandalay. R. Campbell; Death in Tiger Valley
House of a Thousand Candles. M. Nicholson
Boehm, Sydney
Big Heat. W. P. McGivern
Bottom of the Bottle. G. Simenon
Hell on Frisco Bay. W. P. McGivern; Darkest Hour
High Wall. A. R. Clark
Rogue Cop. W. P. McGivern
Seven Thieves. S. Kent; Lions at the Kill
Shock Treatment. W. Van Atta
Six Bridges to Cross. J. F. Dinneen; Anatomy of a Crime
Sylvia. E. V. Cunningham
Union Station. T. Walsh; Nightmare in Manhattan
Violent Saturday. W. L. Heath
Bognor, Norman
Privilege. John Burke
Boileau, Pierre
Letters to an Unknown Lover. P. Boileau; Prisoner
She Wolves. P. Boileau; Prisoner
Boisrond, Michel
One Is Always Too Good to Women. R. Queneau; We Always Treat Women Too Well
Boisset, Yves
Prize of Peril. R. Sheckley; Tenth Victim
Rise Up, Spy. G. Markstein; Chance Awakening
Boland, Bridget
Gas Light. P. Hamilton
Spies of the Air. J. Dell
Bolton, Guy
Yellow Ticket. V. Morton
Bolton, Muriel Roy
My Name Is Julia Ross. Anthony Gilbert; Woman in Red
Bond, Julian
Man Outside. G. Stackelberg; Double Agent
Whistle Blower. John Hale
Bonicelli, Vittorio
Crime. G. Bernanos
Bonner, James P.
Carey Treatment. J. Hudson; Case of Need
House of Cards. S. Ellin
Booth, Charles G.
Fury at Furnace Creek. D. Garth; Four Men and a Prayer
Booth, James
Sunburn. S. Ellin; Bind
Booth, John Hunter
Valiant. H. Hall
Borderie, Bernard
Dames Get Along. P. Cheyney; Dames Don't Care
Gun Moll. P. Cheyney; Poison Ivy
What a Girl! P. Cheyney; I'll Say She Does
You Do It, Cutie. P. Cheyney; Your Deal, My Lovely
Boretz, Alvin
Brass Target. F. Nolan; Oshawa Project
Boris, Robert
Some Kind of Hero. J. Kirkwood
Borneman, Ernest
Face the Music. E. Borneman; Tremolo
Borris, Knut
Sorcerer. E. Wallace; Ringer
Bost, Pierre
Clockmaker. G. Simenon; Watchmaker of Everton
In Case of Emergency. G. Simenon
Murderer. P. Highsmith; Blunderer
Boteler, Wade
Seven Keys to Baldpate. E. D. Biggers
Boucicault, Dion
Octoroon. D. Boucicault
Boudard, Alphonse
Action Man. J. Flynn
Boulanger, Daniel
Banana Peel. C. Williams; Nothing in the Way
Boulting, Roy
Brothers in Law. H. Cecil
Suspect. N. Balchin; Sort of Traitors
Bourguignon, Serge

Reward. M. Barrett
Boussinot, Roger
Keep Talking, Baby. D. Keene; Strange Witness
Bower, Pamela Wilcox
Trent's Last Case. E. C. Bentley
Bowers, William
Assignment--Paris. P. Gallico; Trial by Terror
Convicted. M. Flavin; Criminal Code
Five Against the House. J. Finney
Larceny. L. Eby; Velvet Fleece
Mob. F. Findley; Waterfront
Tight Spot. L. Kantor; Dead Pigeon
Box, Muriel
Blind Goddess. P. Hastings
Dear Murderer. S. L. Clowes
Good Time Girl. A. La Bern; Night Darkens the Streets
Man Within. G. Greene
Box, Sydney
Blind Goddess. P. Hastings
Dear Murderer. S. L. Clowes
Good Time Girl. A. La Bern; Night Darkens the Streets
Man Within. G. Greene
Boylan, Malcolm Stuart
Masquerade. L. J. Vance; Brass Bowl
Brach, Gerard
Name of the Rose. U. Eco
Tenant. R. Topor
Bracken, Bertram
Mask. A. Hornblow
Brackett, Charles
Piccadilly Jim. P. G. Wodehouse
Without Regret. R. Pertwee; Interference
Brackett, Leigh
Big Sleep. R. Chandler
Long Goodbye. R. Chandler
Brady, Earl
Brother Orchid. L. Brady
Brady, Jasper E.
Surprises of an Empty Hotel. A. C. Gunter
Braly, Malcolm
On the Yard. M. Braly
Brand, Christianna
Mark of Cain. J. Shearing; Airing in a Closed Carriage
Brandel, Marc
Captive City. J. Appleby
Brandner, Gary
Howling II. G. Brandner
Brandt, Joe
Lion Man. R. Parrish; Strange Case of Cavendish
Brazee, A. Laurie
Outer Gate. O. R. Cohen
Breen, Richard L.
Man Could Get Killed. D. Walker; Diamonds for Moscow
Stopover: Tokyo. J. P. Marquand
Tony Rome. A. Rome; Miami Mayhem
Brennan, F. H.
Masquerade. L. J. Vance; Brass Bowl
Brenner, Alfred
Key Witness. F. Kane
Brenon, Herbert
Dr. Jekyll and Mr. Hyde. R. L. Stevenson; Strange Case of Dr. Jekyll and Mr. Hyde
Sign on the Door. C. Pollock
Brent, Romney
Rat. P. Bottome
Breslow, Lou
Sleepers West. F. Nebel; Sleepers East
Brett, Harold
First Chronicles of Don Q. K. Prichard; Chronicles of Don Q
Bricker, George
Corpse Came C.O.D. J. Starr
Mark of the Whistler. W. Irish; Borrowed Crime
Sh! The Octopus. R. Spence; Gorilla
Bridie, James
Stage Fright. S. Jepson; Man Running
Bright, John
Broadway. P. Dunning
Public Enemy. K. Glasmon
Sherlock Holmes and the Voice of Terror. A. C. Doyle; His Last Bow
Briley, John
Enigma. M. Barak
Hammerhead. J. Mayo
Medusa Touch. P. Van Greenaway
Walking Tall. D. Warren
Broadbridge, Hugh
Road to Fortune. H. Broadbridge; Moorland Terror
Brodney, Oscar
Bonaventure. C. Hastings
Brooke, Ralph
Bloodlust. R. Connell; Variety
Brooks, George
Double Cross Roads. W. Lipman; Yonder Grow the Daisies
Brooks, Jeremy

Our Mother's House. J. Gloag
Brooks, Mel
High Anxiety. R. H. Pilpel
Brooks, Richard
Any Number Can Play. E. H. Heth
Blackboard Jungle. E. Hunter
Brothers Karamazov. F. M. Dostoevskii
Deadline. J. Eastwood
In Cold Blood. T. Capote
Key Largo. M. Anderson
Wrong Is Right. C. McCarry; Better Angels
Brophy, John
Turn the Key Softly. J. Brophy
Waterfront. J. Brophy
Brown, Earl
Sherlock Holmes. W. Gillette
Brown, George H.
Desperate Moment. M. Albrand
Brown, Harry
Fiend Who Walked the West. E. Lipsky; Kiss of Death
Kiss Tomorrow Goodbye. H. McCoy
Man on the Eifel Tower. G. Simenon; Battle of Nerves
Ocean's 11. G. C. Johnson
Brown, Harry Joe, Jr.
Duffy. H. J. Brown, Jr.
Brown, J. Bertram
In the Blood. A. Soutar
Ware Case. G. Pleydell
Brown, Karl
Federal Bullets. G. F. Eliot
Browne, Howard
Portrait of a Mobster. H. Grey
St. Valentine's Day Massacre. B. O'Hara
Brownell, John C.
Girl by the Roadside. V. Vanardy
Browning, Tod
Devil-Doll. A. Merritt; Burn, Witch, Burn!
London After Midnight. M. Coolridge-Rask
Outside the Law. T. Browning
Bruce, George
Gentleman After Dark. R. W. Child; Velvet Mask
Brule, Claude
Blood and Roses. J. S. Le Fanu; In a Glass Darkly
Brunel, Adrian
Cross Currents. W. G. Elliott; Nine Days' Blunder
Bruner, James
Invasion U.S.A. J. Frost
Bryan, Peter
Hound of the Baskervilles. A. C. Doyle
Bryant, Chris
Awakening. B. Stoker; Jewel of the Seven Stars
Spiral Staircase. E. L. White; Some Must Watch
Buchanan, James D.
Happening. E. Curry
Buchman, Harold
Sleeping Tiger. M. Moisewitsch
Buchman, Sidney
Deadly Trap. A. Cavanagh; Children Are Gone
Mark. C. E. Israel
Buckingham, Thomas
Bad Company. J. Lait; Put on the Spot
Buckle, Gerard Fort
Yellow Claw. S. Rohmer
Buckley, Harold
Black Doll. W. E. Hayes
Buckner, Robert
Confidential Agent. G. Greene
House of Secrets. S. Noel
Prize of Gold. M. Catto
Buffington, Adele
Midnight Life. R. W. Kauffman; Spider's Web
Moonstone. W. Collins
Bull, Donald
Arsenal Stadium Mystery. L. Gribble
Bullett, Gerald
Last Man to Hang. G. Bullett; Jury
Bullock, Walter
Repeat Performance. W. O'Farrell
Bunker, Edward
Straight Time. E. Bunker; No Beast So Fierce
Burford, Roger
Doctor Syn. R. Thorndyke
Once a Crook. E. Price
Burlock, William Elliot
Madame X. J. W. MacConaughy
Burnett, W. R.
Accused of Murder. W. R. Burnett; Vanity Row
Background to Danger. E. Ambler; Uncommon Danger
High Sierra. W. R. Burnett
I Died a Thousand Times. W. R. Burnett; High Sierra
Nobody Lives Forever. W. R. Burnett

Racket. B. Cormack
Scarface. A. Trail
This Gun for Hire. G. Greene; Gun for Sale
Burnham, Jeremy
Horror of Frankenstein. M. Shelly; Frankenstein
Burnham, Julie
Fatal Hour. E. Chatterton; Marriages of Mayfair
Burns, Francis
Rough Cut. D. Lambert; Touch the Lion's Paw
Burns, Stan
Charlie Chan and the Curse of the Dragon Queen. M. Avallone
Burton, William A.
Easy Pickings. P. Cruger
Busch, Niven
Man with Two Faces. A. Woollcott; Dark Tower
Miss Pinkerton. M. R. Rinehart
Postman Always Rings Twice. J. M. Cain
Butler, David
Bear Island. A. MacLean
Butler, Frank
Golden Earrings. Y. Foldes
Hostages. S. Heym
Remote Control. C. North
Whispering Smith. F. N. Spearman
Butler, Gerald
Fatal Night. M. Arlen; May Fair
Third Time Lucky. G. Butler; They Cracked Her Glass Slipper
Butler, Hugo
Eva. J. H. Chase; Eve
He Ran All the Way. S. Ross
Society Lawyer. A. S. Roche; Penthouse
Butler, Kathleen
Feathered Serpent. E. Wallace
Story of Shirley Yorke. H. A. Vachell; Case of Lady Camber
Temptress. A. Campbell; Juggernaut
Butler, Michael
Flashpoint. G. La Fountaine
Gauntlet. M. Butler
Byrd, Jack
Man Behind the Mask. J. Futrelle; Chase of the Golden Plate
Byrne, Jack
End of the Road. E. Bulwer-Lytton; Ernest Maltravers
Byron-Webber, R.
Barton Mystery. W. Hackett
Woman Wins. C. H. Bullivant
Byrum, John
Sphinx. R. Cook
Cacoyannis, Michael
Day the Fish Came Out. K. Cicellis
Cady, Jerry
Great Hospital Mystery. M. G. Eberhart (headnote)
Saint in Palm Springs. L. Charteris (headnote)
Caesar, Arthur
Three Faces East. A. P. Kelly
Caillou, Alan
Assault on Agathon. A. Caillou
Callahan, George
I'll Get You for This. J. H. Chase
Cameron, James
Rambo: First Blood Part II. D. Morrell
Camiller, Edgar J.
Definite Object. J. Farnol
Campbell, Colin
In Defiance of the Law. J. O. Curwood; Isobel
Campbell, Keith
Snowbound. H. Innes; Lonely Skier
Campbell, Patrick
Girl in the Headlines. L. Payne; Nose on My Face
Law and Disorder. D. Roberts; Smuggler's Circuit
Campbell, R. Wright
Masque of the Red Death. Elsie Lee
Campbell, Scott
Dickson's Diamonds. S. Campbell; Below the Dead-Line
Campion, Cyril
Juggernaut. A. Campbell
Campion, John
Zero Hour! J. Castle; Flight into Danger
Canaway, Bill
Ipcress File. L. Deighton
Canfield, Mark
Crack in the Mirror. M. Haedrich
Cannan, Denis
Amorous Adventures of Moll Flanders. D. Defoe; Fortunes and Misfortunes of the Famous Moll Flanders
Canning, Victor
Golden Salamander. V. Canning
Venetian Bird. V. Canning
Capote, Truman
Beat the Devil. J. Helvick

Innocents. H. James; Turn of the Screw
Carewe, Edwin
Across the Pacific. C. E. Blaney
Dancer and the King. C. E. Blaney
Isobel. J. O. Curwood
Carlino, Lewis John
Brotherhood. L. J. Carlino
Crazy Joe. M. Barone
Mechanic. L. J. Carlino
Reflection of Fear. S. Forbes; Go to Thy Death Bed
Seconds. D. Ely
Carne, Marcel
Marie du Port. G. Simenon; Chit of a Girl
Three Rooms in Manhattan. G. Simenon; Three Beds in Manhattan
Waste-Land. H. Ellison; Tomboy
Carnes, Charles Robert
Terrible Game. D. T. Moore
Caron, Glen
Condorman. R. Sheckley; Game of X
Carothers, A. J.
Hero at Large. A. J. Carothers
Never a Dull Moment. J. Godey; Thrill a Minute with Jack Albany
Carpenter, John
Eyes of Laura Mars. H. B. Gilmour
Halloween. C. Richards
Carreras, Michael
Stranger Came Home. G. Sanders; Stranger at Home
Carriere, Jean-Claude
Butterfly on the Shoulder. J. Gearon; Velvet Well
Flesh of the Orchid. J. H. Chase
Carrington, Jane-Howard
Kaleidoscope. M. Avallone
Wait Until Dark. F. Knott
Carrington, Robert
Fear Is the Key. A. MacLean
Kaleidoscope. M. Avallone
Venom. A. Scholefield
Wait Until Dark. F. Knott
Carroll, Paul Vincent
Midnight Episode. G. Simenon; Monsieur a Souris
Carruth, Milton
Love Letters of a Star. Rufus King; Case of the Constant God
Carson, Robert
Action of the Tiger. J. Wellard
Carstairs, John Paddy
Footsteps in the Night. C. Fraser-Simpson
Love on the Spot. H. C. McNeile; Three of a Kind
Cartier, Rudolph
Corridors of Mirrors. C. Massie
Carton, Brian
Taste of Excitement. B. Healey; Waiting for a Tiger
Caspary, Vera
Belinda. V. Caspary
Cataldo, Gaspare
Brothers Karamazov. F. M. Dostoevskii
Catto, Max
Daughter of Darkness. M. Catto; They Walk Alone
Cau, Jean
Torpedo Skin. F. Ryck; Woman Hunt
Cavalier, Alain
Ladies' Man. P. Quentin; Shadow of Guilt
Pillaged. R. Stark; Score
Cavanagh, James P.
Murder at the Gallop. A. Christie; After the Funeral
Cayatte, Andre
Trap for Cinderella. S. Japrisot
Chabrol, Claude
Blood Relatives. E. McBain
Breakup. C. Armstrong; Balloon Man
Hatter's Ghosts. G. Simenon
Innocents with Dirty Hands. R. Neely; Damned Innocents
Just Before Nightfall. E. Atiyah; Thin Line
Let the Beast Die. Nicholas Blake; Beast Must Die
Chaffey, Don
Crooked Road. M. West; Big Story
Chambers, Whitman
Come-On. W. Chambers
Shadow of a Woman. V. Perdue; He Fell Down Dead
Chamblee, Robert
Killer Inside Me. J. Thompson
Chandler, Harry
Back to Life. A. Soutar; Back from the Dead
Chandler, Raymond
Blue Dahlia. R. Chandler
Double Indemnity. J. M. Cain
Strangers on a Train. P. Highsmith
Unseen. E. L. White; Midnight House
Chanslor, Roy
Black Angel. C. Woolrich

Hazard. R. Chanslor
House of Fear. A. C. Doyle; Adventures of Sherlock Holmes
Menace. E. Wallace; Feathered Serpent
Murder by an Aristocrat. M. G. Eberhart
Wine, Women and Horses. W. R. Burnett; Dark Hazard
Chapin, Anne Morrison
Dangerous Corner. J. B. Priestley
Chapin, Frederic
Argyle Case. H. Ford
Chapman, Leigh
Dirty Mary, Crazy Harry. R. Unekis; Chase
Chapman, Michael
Next Man. M. Z. Lewin
Chapman, Priscilla
Fan. B. Randall
Chapman, Robin
Force 10 from Navarone. A. MacLean
Chappell, Connery
Nursemaid Who Disappeared. P. MacDonald
Too Dangerous to Live. D. Hume
Charles, Moie
Bedelia. V. Caspary
Dark Secret. M. Shairp; Crime at Blossoms
Hell Is Sold Out. M. Dekobra
Charles-Williams, Liz
Deadlier Than the Male. H. Reymond
Charteris, Leslie
Saint's Vacation. L. Charteris; Getaway
Chautard, Emile
Mystery of the Yellow Room. G. Leroux
Chavance, Louis
Marie du Port. G. Simenon; Chit of a Girl
Cheney, J. Benton
Laramie Trail. J. Gregory; Mystery at Spanish Hacienda
Chereau, Patrice
Flesh of the Orchid. J. H. Chase
Chesbro, George
Man Who Would Not Die. C. Williams; Sailcloth Shroud
Chester, George Randolph
Dead Men Tell No Tales. E. W. Hornung
Scarlet Car. R. H. Davis
Chester, Lilian
Dead Men Tell No Tales. E. W. Hornung
Cheyney, Peter
Uneasy Terms. P. Cheyney
Chodorov, Edward
Kind Lady. E. Chodorov
Chodorov, Jerry
Case of the Lucky Legs. E. S. Gardner
Christensen, Bent
Ghost Train. A. Ridley
Christiansen, Benjamin
Devil's Circus. B. Christiansen
Christie, Campbell
Grand National Night. D. Christie
Jassy. N. Lofts
Christie, Dorothy
Grand National Night. D. Christie
Jassy. N. Lofts
Cimber, Matt
Butterfly. J. M. Cain
Time to Die. M. Cleri; Six Graves to Munich
Cimino, Michael
Magnum Force. M. Valley
Thunderbolt and Lightfoot. J. Millard
Year of the Dragon. R. Daley
Clancey, Vernon
Dead Men Are Dangerous. H. C. Armstrong; Hidden
Flying Fifty-Five. E. Wallace
Clapp, Chester B.
Sable Lorcha. H. Hazeltine
Clark, Ron
High Anxiety. R. H. Pilpel
Clark, Violet
Loot. A. S. Roche
Love Without Question. W. Camp; Abandoned Room
Clarke, T. E. B.
Blue Lamp. T. Willis
Dead of Night. E. F. Benson; Room in the Tower
Gideon's Day. J. J. Marric
Law and Disorder. D. Roberts; Smuggler's Circuit
Man Could Get Killed. D. Walker; Diamonds for Moscow
Claus, Hugo
Because of the Cats. N. Freeling
Clavel, Maurice
Ladies' Man. P. Quentin; Shadow of Guilt
Clavell, James
Satan Bug. I. Stuart
633 Squadron. F. E. Smith
Clawson, Elliott
Evil Women Do. E. Gaboriau; Clique of Gold
Jack Chanty. H. Footner

Let 'Er Go Gallegher. R. H. Davis; Gallegher
Phantom of the Opera. G. Leroux
Thirteenth Chair. B. Veiller
Whispering Smith. F. H. Spearman
Clay, Melvin
　Spook Who Sat by the Door. S. Greenlee
Clemens, Brian
　Blind Terror. W. Hughes
　Doctor Jekyll and Sister Hyde. R. L. Stevenson; Strange Case of Dr. Jekyll and Mr. Hyde
Clemens, Harold
　Lady Ice. M. Braly; Master
Clement, Dick
　Catch Me a Spy. G. Marton
　Jokers. M. Sands
　Otley. M. Waddell
　Villain. J. Barlow; Burden of Proof
Clement, Rene
　Broad Daylight. P. Highsmith; Talented Mr. Ripley
　Joy House. D. Keene
Clevely, Hugh
　Meet Maxwell Archer. H. Clevely; Archer Plus 20
Clewes, Howard
　Day They Robbed the Bank of England. J. Brophy
Clifford, William M.
　Man from Nowhere. V. Bridges
Clift, Denison
　Bentley's Conscience. P. Trent
　Out to Win. R. Pertwee
Clifton, Elmer
　Two-Soul Woman. G. Burgess; White Cat
Clifton, Wallace
　Wanted at Headquarters. E. Wallace (headnote)
Clork, Harry
　Remember Last Night? A. Hobhouse; Hangover Murders
　Whistling in the Dark. L. Gross
Clouzot, Henri-Georges
　Diabolique. P. Boileau; Woman Who Was
　Spies. E. Hostovsky; Midnight Patient
　Strangers in the House. G. Simenon
　Wages of Fear. G. Arnaud
Clowes, St. John L.
　No Orchids for Miss Blandish. J. H. Chase
Cockrell, Marian
　Dark Waters. F. Cockrell
Coe, Charles Francis
　Me--Gangster. C. F. Coe
Coen, Franklin
　Interlude. J. M. Cain; Serenade
　Take. G. F. Newman; Sir, You Bastard
　We're on the Jury. F. Ballard; Ladies of the Jury
Coffee, Lenore J.
　Age of Indiscretion. T. D. Irwin; Collusion
　Arsene Lupin. M. Leblanc; Girl with the Green Eyes
　Beyond the Forest. S. Engstrand
　Bishop Murder Case. S. S. Van Dine
　Chicago. M. Watkins
　East Lynne. H. Wood
　End of the Affair. G. Greene
　Evelyn Prentice. W. E. Woodward
　Footsteps in the Fog. W. W. Jacobs; Sea Whispers
　Ladyfingers. J. Gregory
　Lightning Strikes Twice. M. Echard; Dark Fantastic
　Sudden Fear. E. Sherry
Cohan, George M.
　Seven Keys to Baldpate. E. D. Biggers
Cohen, Herman
　Craze. H. Seymour; Infernal Idol
Cohen, Larry
　Daddy's Gone A-Hunting. Mike St. Clair
　I, the Jury. M. Spillane
　It's Alive. R. Woodley
Cohen, Lawrence J.
　S*p*y*S. T. R. Joyce
Cohen, Ronald M.
　Twilight's Last Gleaming. W. Wager; Viper Three
Cohn, Alfred A.
　Cat and the Canary. J. Willard
　Gorilla. R. Spence
　Last Warning. W. Camp; House of Fear
Cohn, Bruce
　Good Guys Wear Black. M. Franklin
Coldeway, Anthony
　Crimson City. A. Coldeway
　Hidden Hand. Rufus King; Invitation to a Murder
　Nurse's Secret. M. R. Rinehart; Miss Pinkerton
　Scream in the Night. J. Odlum; Morgue Is Always Open
　Shadows on the Stairs. F. Vosper; Murder on the Second Floor
Cole, Lester
　Charlie Chan's Greatest Case. E. D. Biggers; House Without a Key
　High Wall. A. R. Clark
　Hostages. S. Heym
　President's Mystery. F. D. Roosevelt; President's Mystery Story
　Sleepers East. F. Nebel
Coleby, A. E.
　Flying Fifty-Five. E. Wallace
　Great Prince Shan. E. P. Oppenheim
Coleman, Patricia
　Above Suspicion. H. MacInnes
Coletti, Duilio
　House of Intrigue. H. J. Giskes; London Calling North Pole
Colin, Sid
　Ugly Duckling. R. L. Stevenson; Strange Case of Dr. Jekyll and Mr. Hyde
Collins, Edwin J.
　Eugene Aram. E. Bulwer-Lytton
Collins, John H.
　Wife by Purchase. P. Trent
Collins, Richard
　Badlanders. W. R. Burnett; Asphalt Jungle
Columbus, Chris
　Young Sherlock Holmes. A. Arnold
Comfort, Lance
　Pit of Darkness. H. McCutcheon; To Dusty Death
Commandini, Adele
　Country Beyond. J. O. Curwood
　Danger Signal. P. Bottome; Murder in the Bud
Companeez, Jacques
　Forbidden Fruit. G. Simenon; Act of Passion
Comport, Brian
　Mumsy, Nanny, Sonny and Girly. B. Comport
Condon, Frank
　City of Silent Men. J. A. Moroso; Quarry
Condon, Richard
　Prizzi's Honor. R. Condon
Connors, Barry
　Black Camel. E. D. Biggers
　Charlie Chan Carries On. E. D. Biggers
　Spider. F. Oursler
　Trial of Vivienne Ware. K. Ellis
Connors, Kathleen
　Fatal Night. M. Arlen; May Fair
Conselman, William
　Fifty Roads to Town. F. Nebel
　Great Hospital Mystery. M. G. Eberhart (headnote)
Considine, Mildred
　Jimmy Dale, Alias "The Grey Seal". F. Packard; Adventures of Jimmie Dale
Constance, Marian
　Behold the Woman. E. P. Oppenheim; Hillman
　Passionate Quest. E. P. Oppenheim
Cook, Peter
　Hound of the Baskervilles. A. C. Doyle
Cook, T. S.
　China Syndrome. B. Wohl
Cook, Virginia
　"Shed No Tears." D. Martin
Cook, Whitfield
　Stage Fright. S. Jepson; Man Running
Coolidge, Karl L.
　Lion Man. R. Parrish; Strange Case of Cavendish
Coon, Gene L.
　Killers. E. Hemingway; Men Without Women
Cooney, Ray
　What a Carve Up! F. King; Ghoul
Cooper, Courtney Riley
　Eagle's Eye. W. J. Flynn
Cooper, Dennis
　City Across the River. I. Shulman; Amboy Dukes
　Fear. F. M. Dostoevskii; Crime and Punishment
Cooper, Olive
　Jim Hanvey, Detective. O. R. Cohen
Cooper, Willis
　Thank You, Mr. Moto. J. P. Marquand
Coppel, Alec
　Hell Below Zero. H. Innes; White South
　I Killed the Count. A. Coppel
　Mr. Denning Drives North. A. Coppel
　Moment to Moment. A. Coppel
　Obsession. A. Coppel; Man About a Dog
　Vertigo. P. Boileau; Living and the Dead
Coppola, Francis Ford
　Godfather. M. Puzo
　Godfather, Part II. M. Puzo; Godfather
Cormack, Bartlett
　Benson Murder Case. S. S. Van Dine
　Kick-In. W. Mack
　Racket. B. Cormack
　Thirteen Women. T. Thayer
Corneau, Alain
　Thriller Story. J. Thompson; Hell of a Woman
Cornelius, Henry
　It Always Rains on Sunday. A. La Bern
Cornfield, Hubert
　Night of the Following Day. L. White; Snatchers
　Third Voice. C. Williams; All the Way
Cornu, Jacques
　Ladies' Man. P. Quentin; Shadow of Guilt
Corrigan, Lloyd
　Daughter of the Dragon. S. Rohmer; Daughter of Fu Manchu
　Mysterious Dr. Fu Manchu. S. Rohmer; Mystery of Dr. Fu Manchu
　Return of Dr. Fu Manchu. S. Rohmer; Devil Doctor
Cory, Desmond
　England Made Me. G. Greene
Cosmatos, George Pan
　Cassandra Crossing. R. Katz
Cosmos, Jean
　It Only Happens to the Living. R. Marshall; Things Men Do
Cotten, Joseph
　Hotel Reserve. E. Ambler; Journey into Fear
Couffer, Jack C.
　Running Target. S. Frazee
Court, Joanne
　Cairo. W. R. Burnett; Asphalt Jungle
Courtney, Syd
　Man Behind the Mask. J. Futrelle; Chase of the Golden Plate
Cox, Morgan L.
　Drums of Fu Manchu. S. Rohmer
Cox, Vivian A.
　Deadly Record. N. W. Hooke
Crawford, Oliver
　Girl in the Woods. O. Crawford; Blood on the Branches
Creelman, James Ashmore
　Most Dangerous Game. R. Connell; Variety
　Red Dance. H. L. Gates; Red Dancer of Moscow
Cresswell, John
　Beyond the Curtain. A. J. Wallis; Thunder Above
　Cast a Dark Shadow. J. Green; Murder Mistaken
　Port Afrique. B. V. Dryer
　Yield to the Night. J. Henry
Crichton, Charles
　Floods of Fear. J. Hawkins
Crichton, Michael
　Coma. R. Cook
　First Great Train Robbery. M. Crichton; Great Train Robbery
Croise, Hugh
　Affair at the Novelty Theatre. B. Orczy; Old Man in the Corner
　Brighton Mystery. B. Orczy; Old Man in the Corner
　Hocussing of Cigarette. B. Orczy; Old Man in the Corner
　Kensington Mystery. B. Orczy; Old Man in the Corner
　Mystery of Brudenell Court. B. Orczy; Old Man in the Corner
　Mystery of Dogstooth Cliff. B. Orczy; Old Man in the Corner
　Mystery of the Khaki Tunic. B. Orczy; Old Man in the Corner
　Northern Mystery. B. Orczy; Old Man in the Corner
　Regent's Park Mystery. B. Orczy; Old Man in the Corner
　Tragedy of Barnsdale Manor. B. Orczy; Old Man in the Corner
　York Mystery. B. Orczy; Old Man in the Corner
Crouse, Russell
　Mountain Music. M. Kantor; Author's Choice
Crowdy, Francis
　Mark of Cain. J. Shearing; Airing in a Closed Carriage
Crowther, John
　Evil That Men Do. R. L. Hill
Cullen, Robert J.
　Woman in White. W. Collins
Cummings, Irving
　Country Beyond. J. O. Curwood
Cunard, Grace
　Study in Scarlet. A. C. Doyle
Cunningham, Jack
　Contraband. C. B. Kelland
　Devil to Pay. F. N. Greene
　Don Q, Son of Zorro. K. Prichard; Don Q's Love Story
　Double Door. E. McFadden
　Ghost Breakers. C. W. Goddard
　House of Whispers. W. Johnston
　Tiger's Coat. E. Dejeans
Curtelin, Jean
　Prize of Peril. R. Sheckley; Tenth Victim

Curtin, Valerie
  And Justice for All. R. Grossbach
Curtis, James
  Ten Days in Paris. B. Graeme; Disappearance of Roger Tremayne
  There Ain't No Justice. J. Curtis
Curtiss, Jean-Louis
  Woman Is a Stranger. J. H. Chase; Not Safe to Be Free
Curwood, James Oliver
  Golden Snare. J. O. Curwood
  Nomads of the North. J. O. Curwood
Cushing, Tom
  Yellow Ticket. V. Morton
Cutts, Graham
  Rat. P. Bottome
Dabadie, Jean-Louis
  Descent into Hell. D. Goodis; Wounded and the Slain
  Such a Lovely Kid Like Me. H. Farrell; Such a Gorgeous Kid Like Me
Dahl, Roald
  You Only Live Twice. I. Fleming
Dalmas, Herbert
  Address Unknown. K. Taylor
Dalrymple, Ian
  Heart of the Matter. G. Greene
  Mix Me a Person. J. T. Story
Daly, John
  Sunburn. S. Ellin; Bind
Damiani, Damiano
  Day of the Owl. L. Sciascia; Mafia Vendetta
Dancigers, Oscar
  Pillaged. R. Stark; Score
Dane, Clemence
  Amateur Gentleman. J. Farnol
Danischewsky, Monja
  Bitter Springs. C. King
  Mr. Moses. M. Catto; Mister Midas
  Topkapi. E. Ambler; Light of Day
Darling, W. Scott
  813. M. Leblanc
  Great Impersonation. E. P. Oppenheim
  Sherlock Holmes and the Secret Weapon. A. C. Doyle; Return of Sherlock Holmes
  Spider. F. Oursler
  Trent's Last Case. E. C. Bentley
  Wolf Hunters. J. O. Curwood
Dassin, Jules
  10:30 P.M. Summer. M. Duras; Ten-Thirty on a Summer Night
  Uptight. L. O'Flaherty; Informer
Davenport, John
  Hotel Reserve. E. Ambler; Epitaph for a Spy
Daves, Delmar
  Dark Passage. D. Goodis
  Night of February 16. A. Rand
  Petrified Forest. R. E. Sherwood
  Red House. G. A. Chamberlain
David, W.
  Yellow Mask. E. Wallace; Traitor's Gate
Davidson, Arlene
  Eddie and the Cruisers. P. F. Kluge
Davidson, L. W.
  Hands of the Ripper. E. S. Shew
Davidson, Martin
  Eddie and the Cruisers. P. F. Kluge
Davidson, Ronald
  Drums of Fu Manchu. S. Rohmer
Davies, Jack
  Gambit. K. Lane
  North Sea Hijack. J. Davies
  Someone at the Door. D. Christie
  Ugly Duckling. R. L. Stevenson; Strange Case of Dr. Jekyll and Mr. Hyde
Davies, Rosemary
  Neither the Sea Nor the Sand. G. Honeycombe
Davis, Desmond
  Inspector Calls. J. B. Priestley
Davis, Frank
  Woman on the Beach. M. A. Wilson; None So Blind
Davis, Jerry
  Devil Makes Three. L. P. Bachmann; Kiss of Death
  Kind Lady. E. Chodorov
Davis, Luther
  Across 110th. Wally Ferris
  Lady in a Cage. R. Durand
Davis, Ossie
  Cotton Comes to Harlem. C. Himes
Davis, Owen
  Green Cloak. Y. Davis
Davis, Stratford
  Man in the Shadow. S. Davis; One Man's Secret
Davis, Will S.
  Doctor Rameau. G. Ohnet
Dawley, J. Searle
  Frankenstein. M. Shelley
Dawn
  For the Term of His Natural Life. M. Clarke; His Natural Life
Dawson, Basil

Dawson, Forbes
  Down Under Donovan. E. Wallace
Day, Richard
  Never Love a Stranger. H. Robbins
Dayton, James
  Called Back. H. Conway
  Hornet's Nest. W. Woodrow
  Spy. J. F. Cooper
Dazey, Charles T.
  Silent Barrier. L. Tracy
Dean, Basil
  Birds of Prey. A. A. Milne; Fourth Wall
  Escape. J. Galsworthy
  Return of Sherlock Holmes. A. C. Doyle; His Last Bow
Deans, Marjorie
  Living Dangerously. R. Simpson
  Someone at the Door. D. Christie
Dearden, Basil
  Man Who Haunted Himself. A. Armstrong; Strange Case of Mr. Pelham
  Ship That Died of Shame. N. Monsarrat
De Baroncelli, Jacques
  Rope for a Killing. P. McGerr; Follow, As the Night
De Bernardi, Piero
  Once Upon a Time in America. H. Grey; Hoods
Decoin, Henri
  Rope for a Killing. P. McGerr; Follow, As the Night
  Sorcery. P. Boileau; Spells of Evil
De Concini, Ennio
  House of Intrigue. H. J. Giskes; London Calling North Pole
  Order of Death. H. Fleetwood
De Crescenzo, Luciano
  Payoff. A. Veraldi
Dee, Ruby
  Uptight. L. O'Flaherty; Informer
De Felitta, Frank
  Audrey Rose. F. De Felitta
Degas, Brian
  My Lover, My Son. E. Grierson; Reputation for a Song
De Grunwald, Anatole
  Cottage to Let. G. Kerr; Cottages to Let
  Home at Seven. R. C. Sherriff
  Libel. E. Wooll
  They Met in the Dark. Anthony Gilbert; Vanishing Corpse
Dehn, Paul
  Deadly Affair. J. Le Carre; Call for the Dead
  Fragment of Fear. J. Bingham
  Goldfinger. I. Fleming
  Murder on the Orient Express. A. Christie
  Night of the Generals. H. H. Kirst
  Orders to Kill. D. Downes
  Spy Who Came in from the Cold. J. Le Carre
Dein, Edward
  Leopard Man. C. Woolrich; Black Alibi
De La Huerta, Alvarid
  Last of Philip Banter. J. F. Bardin
de la Iglesia, Eloy
  Turn of the Screw. H. James
Delannoy, Jean
  Action Man. J. Flynn
  Maigret and the St. Fiacre Case. G. Simenon; Saint Fiacre Affair
  Maigret Sets a Trap. G. Simenon
  Obsession. W. Irish; Dead Man Blues
  Torpedo Skin. F. Ryck; Woman Hunt
De Laurentis, Robert
  Green Ice. G. A. Browne
Delay, Florence
  Deep Water. P. Highsmith
De Leon, Walter
  Big Gamble. O. R. Cohen; Iron Chalice
  Cat and the Canary. J. Willard
  Ghost Breakers. C. W. Goddard
  Phantom President. G. F. Worts
Dell, Jeffrey
  Brothers in Law. H. Cecil
  Cone of Silence. D. Beaty
  Kate Plus Ten. E. Wallace
  Saint's Vacation. L. Charteris; Getaway
  Sanders of the River. E. Wallace
  Suspect. N. Balchin; Sort of Traitors
Del Ruth, Hampton
  Defenders of the Law. H. Del Ruth
DeLuca, Rudy
  High Anxiety. R. H. Pilpel
De Marney, Derrick
  No Way Back. T. Burke; Limehouse Nights
De Mille, Cecil B.
  Ghost Breakers. C. W. Goddard
De Mond, Albert
  Leavenworth Case. A. K. Green
  Spanish Cape Mystery. E. Queen
Denham, Reginald

Called Back. H. Conway
  Ladies in Retirement. E. Percy
Denker, Henry
  Twilight of Honor. A. Dewlin
Dennis, Charles
  Double Negative. K. Millar; Three Roads
  Finders Keepers. C. Dennis; Next-to-Last Train Ride
De Palma, Brian
  Blow Out. N. Williams
  Dressed to Kill. Campbell Black
Deray, Jacques
  He Died with His Eyes Open. D. Raymond
  Man from Marrakech. R. P. Jones; Heisters
  On a Nice Summer Day. J. H. Chase; One Bright Summer Morning
De Rita, Massima
  Payoff. A. Veraldi
De Roche, Everett
  Razorback. P. Brennan
De Rouen, Reed
  Six Men. E. Radford
De Santis, Giuseppi
  Obsession. J. M. Cain; Serenade
Deutsch, Helen
  Golden Earrings. Y. Foldes
  Seventh Cross. A. Seghers
Deville, Michel
  Deep Water. P. Highsmith
  Dossier 51. G. Perrault
De Vore, Gary
  Dogs of War. F. Forsyth
Dewhurst, George W.
  Lunatic at Large. J. S. Clouston
  Mist in the Valley. Dorin Craig
  Shadow Between. S. Hocking
Dewhurst, Keith
  Empty Beach. P. Corris
DeWitt, Jack
  Rumble on the Docks. F. Paley
  Together Brothers. Jim Robinson
DeWolf, Karen
  Nine Girls. W. H. Pettitt
Diamond, I. A. L.
  Private Life of Sherlock Holmes. Michael Hardwick
Dickey, Basil
  Sun-Up. M. Marcin; Substitute Prisoner
Dickey, James
  Deliverance. J. Dickey
Dickins, Stafford
  Dead Men Tell No Tales. F. Beeding; Norwich Victims
Dickinson, Thorold
  Arsenal Stadium Mystery. L. Gribble
Didion, Joan
  Panic in Needle Park. J. Mills
  True Confessions. J. G. Dunne
Dighton, John
  Brandy for the Parson. G. Household; Tales of Adventurers
  It's in the Blood. D. Whitelaw; Big Picture
  Kind Hearts and Coronets. R. Horniman; Israel Rank
  Saloon Bar. F. Harvey
  Thank Evans. E. Wallace; Good Evans!
Dillon, Basil
  Dark Stairway. M. G. Eberhart; From This Dark Stairway
  It's in the Blood. D. Whitelaw; Big Picture
  Who Killed John Savage? P. MacDonald; Rynox
Dillon, Laurie
  French Connection II. R. Moore
Dillon, Robert A.
  French Connection II. R. Moore
  Key to Yesterday. C. N. Buck
  Muscle Beach Party. Elsie Lee
  99 and 44/100% Dead. M. Franklin
  Old Dark House. J. B. Priestley; Benighted
  Prime Cut. M. Roote
  Three Keys. F. Ormond
  X. E. Sudak
Dinelli, Mel
  Beware, My Lovely. M. Dinelli; Man
  House by the River. A. P. Herbert
  Lizzie. S. Jackson; Bird's Nest
  Spiral Staircase. E. L. White; Some Must Watch
  Window. W. Irish; Dead Man Blues
Di Pego, Gerald
  Sharky's Machine. W. Diehl
Dix, Beulah Marie
  Conspiracy. R. Baker
  Girl of the Port. J. Russell; Far Wandering Men
  Leopard Lady. E. C. Carpenter
  Midnight Mystery. H. I. Young; Hawk Island
  Secret Service. W. Gillette
  Woman Who Came Back. C. M. S. McLellan; Leah Kleschna
Dix, Marion

Before Dawn. E. Wallace; Sergeant Sir Peter
Everything Is Thunder. J. L. Hardy
Ladies of the Jury. F. Ballard
Dixon, Thomas, Jr.
 Brass Bowl. L. J. Vance
Dolinsky, Meyer
 Hot Rod Rumble. M. Dolinsky; Hot Rod Gang Rumble
Doniger, Walter
 Desperate Search. A. Mayse
Doran, James
 Ipcress File. L. Deighton
Dortort, David
 Cry in the Night. W. Masterson; All Through the Night
Doty, Douglas
 Silent Witness. J. De Leon
Douglas, Gordon
 Housekeeper's Daughter. D. H. Clarke
Douglas, Warren
 Come-On. W. Chambers
 Strange Intruder. H. Fowler; Shades Will Not Vanish
Downing, Rupert
 Footsteps in the Night. C. Fraser-Simpson
 Ghoul. F. King
Doxat-Pratt, B. E.
 Bulldog Drummond. H. C. McNeile
 John Heriot's Wife. A. Askew
Doyle, Laird
 British Agent. H. B. Lockhart
Doyle, Ray
 Madonna of Avenue A. M. Canfield
Dozier, Robert
 Big Bounce. E. Leonard
Drake, Oliver
 Trail of the Yukon. J. O. Curwood; Gold Hunters
Drake, Ronald
 Killer Walks. G. Glennon; Gathering Storm
Drake, William
 Sherlock Holmes. W. Gillette
Draney, George
 East Lynne. H. Wood
 Party Girl. E. Balmer; Dangerous Business
Dratler, Jay
 Laura. V. Caspary
Dresner, Hal
 Eiger Sanction. Trevanian
Dreux, Jacques
 Kill the Referee. A. Draper; Death Penalty
Dreyer, Carl Theodore
 Strange Adventure of Donald Gray. J. S. Le Fanu; In a Glass Darkly
Dryhurst, Edward
 Clayton Treasure Mystery. N. Gordon; Shakespeare Murders
 Crimes at the Dark House. W. Collins; Woman in White
 Frightened Lady. E. Wallace
 House of the Arrow. A. E. W. Mason
 Night Invader. J. Bentley; Rendezvous with Death
 Stranger in Town. F. A. Chittenden; Uninvited
 This Man Is Dangerous. D. Hume; They Called Him Death
Dudley, Ernest
 Guilty? M. Gilbert; Death Has Deep Roots
Duerrenmatt, Friedrich
 It Happens in Broad Daylight. F. Duerrenmatt; Pledge
Duey, Helen
 Blue Envelope Mystery. S. Kerr; Blue Envelope
Duff, Warren
 Chicago Deadline. T. Thayer; One Woman
 Each Dawn I Die. J. Odlum
 Experiment Perilous. M. Carpenter
 Fallen Sparrow. D. B. Hughes
 Make Haste to Live. Gordons
 Strangers of the Evening. T. Thayer; Illustrious Corpse
Duffell, Peter
 England Made Me. G. Greene
Duffy, Albert
 Blind Alley. J. Warwick
Duffy, Gerald C.
 Mr. Barnes of New York. A. C. Gunter
 Officer 666. B. Currie
Dunbar, Robert
 Solitary Child. N. Bawden
Dunne, John Gregory
 Panic in Needle Park. J. Mills
 True Confessions. J. G. Dunne
Dunne, Philip
 Blindfold. L. Fletcher
 Escape. J. Galsworthy
 Lancer Spy. M. McKenna
Duras, Marguerite
 10:30 P.M. Summer. M. Duras; Ten-Thirty on a Summer Night
Durst, Paul

Informers. D. Warner; Death of a Snout
d'Usseau, Arnaud
 Man Who Wouldn't Die. C. Rawson; No Coffin for the Corpse
 Who Is Hope Schuyler? S. Ransome; Hearses Don't Hurry
Duvivier, Julien
 Ardent Room. J. D. Carr; Burning Court
 Gooseflesh. J. H. Chase; Come Easy-- Go Easy
 Man in the Raincoat. J. H. Chase; Tiger by the Tail
 Maurizius Affair. J. Wasserman; Maurizius Case
 Panique. G. Simenon; Mr. Hire's Engagement
Dyab, Mahmoud
 Sonya and the Madman. F. M. Dostoevskii; Crime and Punishment
Dyne, Michael
 Moon-Spinners. Mary Stewart
D'Yvre, Louis
 Mystery of the Villa Rose. A. E. W. Mason; At the Villa Rose
Eastham, Richard
 Six Men. E. Radford
Eastwood, James
 Desperate Man. P. Somers; Beginner's Luck
 Fourth Square. E. Wallace; Four Square Jane
 Man Who Was Nobody. E. Wallace
Ebeling, Fran Lewis
 Ladies Club. Betty Black; Sisterhood
Eberhart, Mignon G.
 Murder by an Aristocrat. M. G. Eberhart
Echtermeier, T.
 His Official Wife. R. H. Savage; My Official Wife
Edgar, Marriott
 Bones. E. Wallace
 Ghost Train. A. Ridley
Edmunds, Robert
 Educated Evans. E. Wallace
Edwards, Blake
 Darling Lili. H. Clement
 Pink Panther. M. H. Albert
 Shot in the Dark. H. Kurnitz
 Tamarind Seed. E. Anthony
Edwards, Edgar
 Convicted. W. Irish; Six Nights of Mystery
Edwards, Paul
 High Ballin'. Richard Robinson
Edwin, Walter
 Master Mummer. E. P. Oppenheim
Egan, Terence
 Shadow. D. Stuart
Eger, J. C.
 Rope for a Killing. P. McGerr; Follow, As the Night
Eglee, Charles
 Rats. J. Herbert
Ehrlich, Max
 Reincarnation of Peter Proud. M. Erhlich
Eisinger, Jo
 Big Boodle. R. Sylvester
 House of the Seven Hawks. V. Canning; House of the Seven Flies
 Jigsaw Man. Dorothea Bennett
 Night and the City. G. Kersh
 Scorpio Letters. V. Canning
 Spider. F. Oursler
Ejre, Ingemar
 Assignment. P. Wahloo
Elder, John
 Curse of the Werewolf. G. Endore; Werewolf of Paris
 Phantom of the Opera. G. Leroux
Eldridge, John
 Out of the Clouds. J. Fores; Springboard
Elia, Fouli
 Arm at the Left. C. Williams; Aground
Elles, Fred
 Mrs. Pym of Scotland Yard. N. Morland (headnote)
Ellin, Stanley
 Big Night. S. Ellin; Dreadful Summit
Elliott, F. P.
 Pals First. L. W. Dodd
Elliott, Gerald
 Blondes for Danger. E. Price; Red for Danger
 Frog. E. Wallace; Fellowship of the Frog
 Return of the Frog. E. Wallace; India-Rubber Men
Elliott, William J.
 Bleak House. C. Dickens
 Case of Identity. A. C. Doyle; Adventures of Sherlock Holmes
 Channings. H. Wood
 Copper Beeches. A. C. Doyle; Adventures of Sherlock Holmes
 Devil's Foot. A. C. Doyle; His Last Bow
 Dying Detective. A. C. Doyle; His Last Bow
 Empty House. A. C. Doyle; Return of Sherlock Holmes
 Hound of the Baskervilles. A. C. Doyle
 Lost Leader. E. P. Oppenheim
 Man with the Twisted Lip. A. C. Doyle; Adventures of Sherlock Holmes
 Noble Bachelor. A. C. Doyle; Adventures of Sherlock Holmes
 Red-Headed League. A. C. Doyle; Adventures of Sherlock Holmes
 Resident Patient. A. C. Doyle; Memoirs of Sherlock Holmes
 Scandal in Bohemia. A. C. Doyle; Adventures of Sherlock Holmes
 Solitary Cyclist. A. C. Doyle; Return of Sherlock Holmes
 Tiger of San Pedro. A. C. Doyle; His Last Bow
 Yellow Face. A. C. Doyle; Memoirs of Sherlock Holmes
Ellis, Andersen
 Mortal Storm. P. Bottome
Ellis, Robert
 Man Who Wouldn't Talk. H. Hall; Valiant
Elman, Irving
 Accomplice. F. Gruber; Simon Lash, Private Detective
 Challenge. H. C. McNeile
Elmes, Guy
 Across the Bridge. G. Greene; Nineteen Stories
 Captive City. J. Appleby
 Flanagan Boy. M. Catto
Elvey, Maurice
 Last Man to Hang. G. Bullett; Jury
 Maria Marten. Anonymous
 Sign of the Four. A. C. Doyle
Emmett, E. V. H.
 Sabotage. J. Conrad; Secret Agent
 Ware Case. G. Pleydell
Enders, Robert
 Maids. J. Genet
Endore, Guy
 Devil-Doll. A. Merritt; Burn, Witch, Burn!
 Hands of Orlac. M. Renard
 He Ran All the Way. S. Ross
 League of Frightened Men. R. Stout
 Mark of the Vampire. M. Coolridge-Rask; London After Midnight
 Vicious Circle. H. Herald; Burning Bush
Engholm, Harry
 East Lynne. H. Wood
 London by Night. C. Selby
 Study in Scarlet. A. C. Doyle
 True Story of the Lyons Mail. E. Moreau; Courier of Lyons
 Valley of Fear. A. C. Doyle
England, Paul
 Trial of Madame X. J. W. MacConaughy; Madame X
Englund, Ken
 Slightly Honorable. F. G. Presnell; Send Another Coffin
Enrico, Robert
 Heads or Tails. A. Harris; Baroni
Enright, Don
 Hit and Run. L. Fletcher; Eighty Dollars to Stamford
Epstein, Julius J.
 Arsenic and Old Lace. J. Kesselring
 Casablanca. J. J. Epstein
 Return from the Ashes. H. Monteilhet
Epstein, Philip G.
 Arsenic and Old Lace. J. Kesselring
 Casablanca. J. J. Epstein
Essex, Harry
 I, the Jury. M. Spillane
Essoe, Gabe
 Devil's Rain. M. Willis
Estabrook, Howard
 Double Cross Roads. W. Lipman; Yonder Grow the Daisies
 Forgotten Faces. R. W. Child; Velvet Black
 Masquerader. K. C. Thurston
 Slightly Scarlet. P. Heath
Estridge, Robin
 Boy Cried Murder. W. Irish; Dead Man Blues
 Campbell's Kingdom. H. Innes
 Escape from Zahrein. M. Barrett; Appointment in Zahrein
 Eye of the Devil. P. Loraine; Day of the Arrow
 Permission to Kill. P. Loraine; W.I.L. One to Curtis
Ettinger, Edward
 Man Who Wouldn't Talk. H. Hall; Valiant
Ettlinger, Don
 Guilty Bystander. Wade Miller
Evans, David
 Late Edwina Black. W. Dinner

Midnight Episode. G. Simenon;
  Monsieur la Souris
Murder in the Family. J. Ronald
Snowbound. H. Innes; Lonely Skier
Strange Intruder. H. Fowler; Shades
  Will Not Vanish
Third Visitor. G. Anstruther
Three Weird Sisters. C. Armstrong;
  Case of the Weird Sisters
Everett, Peter
  Negatives. P. Everett
Exton, Clive
  Awakening. B. Stoker; Jewel of the
    Seven Stars
  Entertaining Mr. Sloane. J. Orton
  Night Must Fall. E. Williams
  Place to Go. M. Fisher; Bethnel Green
  Running Scared. G. McDonald
Eyre, David
  Wolfen. W. Streiber
Fabbri, Diego
  Mysteries of Paris. E. Sue
Fabian, Maximilian
  Thirteenth Hour. S. Horler
Fabre, Maurice
  On a Nice Summer Day. J. H. Chase;
    One Bright Summer Morning
Faenza, Robert
  Order of Death. H. Fleetwood
Fairchild, William
  Embassy. S. Coulter
  Front Page Story. R. Gaines; Final
    Night
  Net. J. Pudney
Fairfax, Marion
  Love Insurance. E. D. Biggers
  Mr. Grex of Monte Carlo. E. P. Oppen-
    heim
  Mystery Girl. G. B. McCutcheon; Green
    Fancy
  River's End. J. O. Curwood
  Sherlock Holmes. W. Gillette
  Vicky Van. C. Wells
Fairlie, Gerard
  Ace of Spades. J. C. Fraser
  Calling Bulldog Drummond. G. Fairlie
  Chick. E. Wallace
  Conspirator. H. Slater
  Lad. E. Wallace (headnote)
  Lonely Road. N. Shute
Falconer, Alun
  Informers. D. Warner; Death of a
    Snout
  Unstoppable Man. M. Gilbert; Amateur
    in Violence
Fancher, Hampton
  Blade Runner. P. K. Dick; Do Androids
    Dream of Electric Sheep?
Faragoh, Francis Edward
  Frankenstein. M. Shelley
  Little Caesar. W. R. Burnett
  Under Cover Man. J. Wilstach
Farjeon, J. Jefferson
  Rasp. P. MacDonald
  Rynox. P. MacDonald
Farnum, Dorothy
  Forbidden Territory. D. Wheatley
  His Wife's Husband. A. K. Green;
    Mayor's Wife
  How Women Love. I. L. Forrester;
    Dangerous Inheritance
  Jim the Penman. C. L. Young
  Modern Marriage. D. Vane; Lady Varley
  Pagan. J. Russell; In Dark Places
  Secrets of Paris. E. Sue; Mysteries
    of Paris
Farnum, George
  How Women Love. I. L. Forrester;
    Dangerous Inheritance
Farrell, Henry
  What's the Matter with Helen? R.
    Deming
Farris, John
  Fury. J. Farris
Faulkner, William
  Big Sleep. R. Chandler
  To Have and Have Not. E. Hemingway
Faye, Randall
  Maria Marten. Anonymous
Feiffer, Jules
  Little Murders. J. Feiffer
Feist, Felix
  Devil Thumbs a Ride. R. C. Du Soe
  Donovan's Brain. C. Siodmak
Fellows, Robert
  Girl Hunters. M. Spillane
Fenady, Andrew J.
  Man with Bogart's Face. A. J. Fenady
Fennell, Albert
  Park Plaza 605. B. Gray; Dare-Devil
    Conquest
Fenton, Frank
  Falcon Takes Over. R. Chandler;
    Farewell, My Lovely
  Highways by Night. C. B. Kelland;
    Silver Spoon
  Man with a Cloak. J. D. Carr; Third
    Bullet
  Saint in London. L. Charteris; Holy
    Terror

Fenty, Philip
  Super Fly. P. Fenty
Ferrini, Franco
  Once Upon a Time in America. H. Grey;
    Hoods
Ferris, Walter
  Four Men and a Prayer. D. Garth
Field, Leonard
  Unknown Blonde. T. D. Irwin;
    Collusion
Fields, Leonard
  Manhattan Love Song. C. Woolrich
Figurovski, Nikolai
  Crime and Punishment. F. M. Dostoev-
    skii
Finberg, Hal
  In Like Flint. B. Street
  Our Man Flint. J. Pearl
Finch, Scott
  Whispering Death. D. Carney
Fine, Morton
  Fool Killer. H. Eustis
  Next Man. M. Z. Lewin
Fink, Harry Julian
  Dirty Harry. P. Rock
Fink, R. M.
  Dirty Harry. P. Rock
Finklehoff, Fred
  Mr. Ace. H. Christy
Finochi, Augusto
  Count Dracula. B. Stoker; Dracula
Fisher, George
  Delavine Affair. R. Chapman; Winter
    Wears a Shroud
Fisher, Steve
  I Wouldn't Be in Your Shoes. W. Irish
  Johnny Angel. C. G. Booth; Mr. Angel
    Comes Aboard
Fisher, Terence
  Mantrap. S. Rattray; Queen in Danger
Fiskin, Jeffrey Alan
  Cutter and Bone. N. Thornburg
  Pursuit of D. B. Cooper. J. D. Reed;
    Free Fall
Fitts, Margaret
  Talk About a Stranger. C. Armstrong;
    Albatross
Fitzgerald, Edith
  Within the Law. B. Veiller
Fitzsimmons, Cortland
  Death of a Champion. F. Gruber; Brass
    Knuckles
  Mandarin Mystery. E. Queen; Chinese
    Orange Mystery
Flaiano, Ennio
  Tenth Victim. R. Sheckley
Fleetwood, Hugh
  Order of Death. H. Fleetwood
Fleming, Brandon
  Dangerous Afternoon. G. Anstruther
  Eleventh Commandment. B. Fleming;
    Pillory
Fletcher, Lucille
  Sorry Wrong Number. L. Fletcher
Flicker, Theodore J.
  Three in a Cellar. Angus Hall; Late
    Boy Wonder
Flippen, Ruth Brooks
  Sail a Crooked Ship. N. Benchley
Flood, James
  Lonely Road. N. Shute
Florey, Robert
  Study in Scarlet. A. C. Doyle
Flournoy, Richard
  Dangerous Blondes. K. Roos; If the
    Shroud Fits
  Night to Remember. K. Roos;
    Frightened Stiff
Floyd, Calvin
  Victor Frankenstein. M. Shelley;
    Frankenstein
Floyd, Yvonne
  Victor Frankenstein. M. Shelley;
    Frankenstein
Flynn, John
  Outfit. R. Stark
Fonvielle, Lloyd
  Bride. M. Shelley; Frankenstein
Foote, Bradbury
  Homicide for Three. P. Quentin;
    Puzzle for Puppets
Foote, Horton
  Baby, the Rain Must Fall. H. Foote;
    Traveling Lady
  Storm Fear. C. Seeley
  To Kill a Mockingbird. H. Lee
  Tomorrow. W. Faulkner; Knight's
    Gambit
Forbes, Bryan
  Angry Silence. John Burke
  Danger Within. M. Gilbert; Death in
    Captivity
  Deadfall. D. Cory
  High Bright Sun. I. S. Black
  Hopscotch. B. Garfield
  House of Secrets. S. Noel
  League of Gentlemen. J. Boland
  Naked Face. S. Sheldon
  Seance on a Wet Afternoon. M. McShane
Ford, Derek

Study in Terror. E. Queen
Ford, Donald
  Study in Terror. E. Queen
Ford, Hugh
  Bella Donna. R. Hichens
  Jim the Penman. C. L. Young
  Seven Keys to Baldpate. E. D. Biggers
Foreman, Carl
  Force 10 from Navarone. A. MacLean
  Guns of Navarone. A. MacLean
  Sleeping Tiger. M. Moisewitsch
Forest, Joseph
  Caravan to Vaccares. A. MacLean
Forlani, Remo
  Choice of Assassins. W. P. McGivern
Forsyth, Frederick
  Fourth Protocol. F. Forsyth
Fort, Garrett
  Before Dawn. E. Wallace; Sergeant Sir
    Peter
  Devil-Doll. A. Merritt; Burn, Witch,
    Burn!
  Dracula. B. Stoker
  Dracula's Daughter. B. Stoker;
    Dracula's Guest
  Frankenstein. M. Shelley
  Ladies in Retirement. E. Percy
  Letter. W. S. Maugham
  Return of Sherlock Holmes. A. C.
    Doyle; His Last Bow
  Roadhouse Nights. D. Hammett; Red
    Harvest
  70,000 Witnesses. C. Fitzsimmons
  Street of Chance. C. Woolrich; Black
    Curtain
  Under Cover Man. J. Wilstach
Foss, Kenelm
  Arsene Lupin. E. Jepson
  Double Life of Mr. Alfred Burton. E.
    P. Oppenheim
  House of Peril. M. B. Lowndes; Chink
    in the Armour
  Shulamite. A. Askew
  Top Dog. F. Hume
  When It Was Dark. G. Thorne
  Whosoever Shall Offend. F. M. Craw-
    ford
Foster, Lewis R.
  Jamaica Run. M. Murray; Neat Little
    Corpse
  Love Letters of a Star. Rufus King;
    Case of the Constant God
  Lucky Stiff. C. Rice
  Tom Sawyer, Detective. M. Twain
Foster, Norman
  Thank You, Mr. Moto. J. P. Marquand
  Think Fast, Mr. Moto. J. P. Marquand
Foucard, Pierre
  Stew in the Caribbean. A. Conroy;
    Looters
Foucaud, Pierre
  Heart Trump for OSS 117 in Tokyo. J.
    Bruce; Hot Line
  OSS 117--Mission for a Killer. J.
    Bruce; Live Wire
Foucault, Pierre
  Mysteries of Paris. E. Sue
Fourastie, Philippe
  Choice of Assassins. W. P. McGivern
Fowell, Frank
  In Full Cry. R. Marsh
  In the Night. J. Sutherland
  Penniless Millionaire. D. C. Murray
Fowler, Gene
  Love Under Fire. W. Hackett;
    Fugitives
  Roadhouse Murder. M. Level (headnote)
Fowler, John
  Hell Is Empty. J. F. Straker
Fox, Finis
  Bride. S. Olivier
  My Lady's Latchkey. C. N. Williamson;
    Second Latchkey
  Revenge. J. Warren
  Way of the Strong. R. Cullum
Fox, Paul Hervey
  Dusty Ermine. N. Grant
Fox, Stephen
  All the World to Nothing. W. Martyn
Foxwell, Ivan
  Guilt Is My Shadow. P. Curtis; You're
    Best Alone
  Touch of Larceny. A. Garve; Megstone
    Plot
Fraenkel, Heinrich
  Juggernaut. A. Campbell
Francis, Allen
  Moorland Tragedy. B. Orczy;
    Unravelled Knots
Francke, Caroline
  Wiser Sex. C. Fitch; Woman in the
    Case
Franco, Jesus
  Count Dracula. B. Stoker; Dracula
Frank, Charles
  Late Edwina Black. W. Dinner
Frank, Christopher
  Attention, the Kids Are Watching. P.
    L. Dixon; Children Are Watching
  Deep Water. P. Highsmith

Malone. W. Wingate; Shotgun
Frank, Harriet, Jr.
 Spikes Gang. G. Tippette; Bank Robber
Franken, Ross
 Elinor Norton. M. R. Rinehart; State vs. Elinor Norton
Franklin, Howard
 Name of the Rose. U. Eco
Fraser, Colin
 Switch. P. Ridgeway
Fraser, George MacDonald
 Force 10 from Navarone. A. MacLean
 Octopussy. I. Fleming
Freedman, Fred
 S*P*Y*S. T. R. Joyce
Freeman, Denis
 Across the Bridge. G. Greene; Nineteen Stories
Freeman, Everett
 Glass Bottom Boat. B. Street
 Larceny, Inc. L. Perelman; Night Before Christmas
Freeman, Gillian
 That Cold Day in the Park. R. Miles
French, Harold
 Jump for Glory. G. McDonell
 Man Who Watched the Trains Go By. G. Simenon
Freshman, William
 Poison Pen. R. Llewellyn
 Terror. E. Wallace
Friedkin, David
 Fool Killer. H. Eustis
Friedkin, William
 Cruising. G. Walker
 To Live and Die in L.A. G. Petievich
Friedman, Philip
 Rage. P. Friedman
Frings, Ketti
 Accused. J. Truesdell; Be Still, My Love
Froeschel, George
 Mortal Storm. P. Bottome
 Never Let Me Go. R. Bax; Came the Dawn
Fuccini, Gianni
 Obsession. J. M. Cain; Serenade
Fuchs, Daniel
 Criss-Cross. D. Tracy
 Gangster. D. Fuchs; Low Company
 Hollow Triumph. M. Forbes
 Interlude. J. M. Cain; Serenade
Fuest, Robert
 Dr. Phibes Rises Again. W. Goldstein
Fuller, Charles
 Soldier's Story. C. Fuller; Soldier's Play
Fuller, Samuel
 Dead Pigeon on Beethoven Street. S. Fuller
 Naked Kiss. S. Fuller
 Shark. V. Canning; His Bones Are Coral
 Shock Corridor. M. Avallone
Fulton, Maude
 Captain Applejack. W. Hackett
 Maltese Falcon. D. Hammett
Furthman, Charles
 Broadway. P. Dunning
Furthman, Jules
 Big Sleep. R. Chandler
 Calvert's Valley. M. P. Montagu; In Calvert's Valley
 Colorado Jim. G. Goodchild
 Moss Rose. J. Shearing
 Nightmare Alley. W. L. Gresham
 To Have and Have Not. E. Hemingway
 Yellow Ticket. V. Morton
Gabrielson, Frank
 It Shouldn't Happen to a Dog. E. Lanham
Gaffney, Marjorie
 Mind of Mr. J. G. Reeder. E. Wallace
 Rat. P. Bottome
Gage, Beth
 Fleshburn. J. Ives; Fear in a Handful of Dust
Gage, George
 Fleshburn. J. Ives; Fear in a Handful of Dust
Gainsbourg, Serge
 Equator. G. Simenon; Tropic Moon
Galeen, Henrik
 Nosferatu. B. Stoker; Dracula
Galloway, Lindsay
 Double. E. Wallace
 Flat 2. E. Wallace
 Two Living and One Dead. S. Christiansen
Gallu, Samuel
 Man Outside. G. Stackelberg; Double Agent
Galton, Ray
 Loot. J. Orton
 Spy with a Cold Nose. R. Galton
Gamet, Kenneth
 Blonde Ice. W. Chambers; Once Too Often
 Case of the Stuttering Bishop. E. S. Gardner

Ganders, Felix
 Mysteries of Paris. E. Sue
Gangelin, Paul
 Black Mask. B. Graeme; Blackshirt
 Nursemaid Who Disappeared. P. MacDonald
 Too Dangerous to Live. D. Hume
Gann, Ernest K.
 Raging Tide. E. K. Gann; Fiddler's Green
Gardiner, Becky
 Square Crooks. J. P. Judge
 Stingaree. E. W. Hornung
 Trial of Mary Dugan. B. Veiller
Gardner, April
 Chick. E. Wallace
Gardner, Paul
 Ten Days' Wonder. E. Queen
Garfield, Brian
 Hopscotch. B. Garfield
Garnett, Tay
 Bad Company. J. Lait; Put on the Spot
Garrett, Oliver H. P.
 Forgotten Faces. R. W. Child; Velvet Black
 Night Nurse. D. Macy
 Story of Temple Drake. W. Faulkner; Sanctuary
 Three Faces East. A. P. Kelly
Garrison, J.
 Crooked Road. M. West; Big Story
Garson, Henry
 Reckless Moment. E. S. Holding; Blank Wall
Gates, Harvey
 Breathless Moment. M. Bryant; Redemption of Richard
 In the Next Room. B. E. Stevenson; Mystery of the Boule Cabinet
 Lord John in New York. C. N. Williamson
 Terror. E. Wallace
Gates, Tudor
 My Lover, My Son. E. Grierson; Reputation for a Song
Gaunthier, Gene
 After Dark. D. Boucicault
 Colleen Bawn. D. Boucicault
Gavras, Costa
 Sleeping Car Murders. S. Japrisot; 10:30 from Marseilles
Gay, John
 Fifth of November. M. Franklin
 Happy Thieves. R. Condon; Oldest Confession
 No Way to Treat a Lady. H. Longbaugh
 Power. F. M. Robinson
Gaye, Howard
 Crimson Circle. E. Wallace
Gegauff, Paul
 Broad Daylight. P. Highsmith; Talented Mr. Ripley
 Let the Beast Die. Nicholas Blake; Beast Must Die
 Ten Days' Wonder. E. Queen
 Web of Passion. S. Ellin; Key to Nicholas Street
Geissendoerfer, Hans W.
 Edith's Diary. P. Highsmith
 Glass Cell. P. Highsmith
Gelbart, Larry
 Fine Pair. C. Stratton
 Wrong Box. R. L. Stevenson
Geller, Bruce
 Sail a Crooked Ship. N. Benchley
Gelsey, Erwin S.
 Jewel Robbery. L. Fodor
 Muss 'Em Up. J. E. Grant; Green Shadow
Gendron, Pierre
 Brooding Eyes. J. Goodwin; Paid in Full
Gentilomo, Giacomo
 Brothers Karamazov. F. M. Dostoevskii
George, Peter
 Dr. Strangelove. P. Bryant; Two Hours to Doom
George, William
 Lure of the Swamp. G. Brewer; Hell's Our Destination
Geraghty, Tom
 Irish Luck. N. Venner; Imperfect Imposter
 Mary Regan. L. Scott
Geromini, Jerome
 Diabolique. P. Boileau; Woman Who Was
Gessner, Nicolas
 Blonde from Peking. J. H. Chase; You Have Yourself a Deal
Gidding, Nelson
 Haunting. S. Jackson; Haunting of Hill House
 Inspector. J. De Hartog
Gifford, Camille
 Dirty Tricks. T. Gifford; Glendower Legacy
Gifford, G. W.
 Green Terror. E. Wallace; Green Rust
Gifford, Thomas
 Dirty Tricks. T. Gifford; Glendower Legacy
Gilbert, Edwin
 Larceny, Inc. L. Perelman; Night Before Christmas
Gilbert, Jack
 White Circle. R. L. Stevenson; New Arabian Nights
Gilbert, Larry
 Notorious Landlady. I. Shulman
Gilbert, Lewis
 Sea Shall Not Have Them. J. Harris
Giler, David
 Black Bird. A. Edwards
 Parallax View. L. Singer
Gilliat, Sidney
 Endless Night. A. Christie
 Fortune Is a Woman. Winston Graham
 Gaunt Stranger. E. Wallace; Ringer
 Girl in the News. R. Vickers
 Green for Danger. R. Brand
 Green Man. F. Launder; Meet a Body
 Inspector Hornleigh on Holiday. L. Grex; Stolen Death
 Jamaica Inn. D. Du Maurier
 Lady Vanishes. E. L. White; Wheel Spins
 London Belongs to Me. N. Collins
 Rome Express. R. Alexander
 Seven Sinners. A. Ridley; Wrecker
 Strange Boarders. E. P. Oppenheim; Strange Boarders of Palace Crescent
 Strangers on a Honeymoon. E. Wallace; Northing Tramp
 They Came by Night. B. Lyndon
 Twelve Good Men. J. Rhode; Murders in Praed Street
Gilling, John
 Dead on Course. Mansell Black
 Flesh and the Fiends. R. L. Stevenson; Body Snatchers
 Guilt Is My Shadow. P. Curtis; You're Best Alone
 Man Inside. M. E. Chaber
 Tiger by the Tail. J. Mair; Never Come Back
Giltinan, Donal
 We Shall See. E. Wallace
Giovanni, Jose
 Last Known Address. J. Harrington
 Man from Marrakech. R. P. Jones; Heisters
 One Way Ticket. H. E. Helseth; Chair for Martin Rome
Girard, Bernard
 Dead Heat on a Merry-Go-Round. E. L. Heyman
 Mad Room. E. Percy; Ladies in Retirement
Girod, Francis
 Descent into Hell. D. Goodis; Wounded and the Slain
Gittens, Wyndham
 Greater Than a Crown. V. Bridges; Lady from Long Acre
Glasmon, Kubec
 Glass Key. D. Hammett
 Public Enemy. K. Glasmon
Glavey, John J.
 High Speed. C. H. Stagg
Glazer, Benjamin
 Beggars of Life. J. Tully
 Diplomacy. V. Sardou; Diplomates
Gleason, Michie
 Summer Heat. L. Shivers; Here to Get My Baby Out of Jail
Glenville, Peter
 Term of Trial. J. Barlow
Glore, Charles
 Moonshine Mountain. C. Glore
Godard, Alain
 Name of the Rose. U. Eco
Godard, Jean-Luc
 Band of Outsiders. D. Hitchens; Fool's Gold
 Crazy Pete. L. White; Obsession
 Grandeur and Decadence of a Small-Time Filmmaker. J. H. Chase (headnote)
 Made in U.S.A. R. Stark; Jugger
Goddard, Charles W.
 Exploits of Elaine. A. B. Reeve
 Romance of Elaine. A. B. Reeve
Goff, Ivan
 King of the Khyber Rifles. T. Mundy
 Midnight Lace. J. Green; Matilda Shouted Fire
 Portrait in Black. I. Goff
 Serenade. J. M. Cain
 Shake Hands with the Devil. R. Conner
Goff, John
 Butterfly. J. M. Cain
 Rigged. J. H. Chase; Hit and Run
 Time to Die. M. Cleri; Six Graves to Munich
Gold, Jack
 Medusa Touch. P. Van Greenaway
Goldbeck, Willis
 Murder on the Blackboard. S. Palmer
 Penguin Pool Murder. S. Palmer
Goldberg, Heinz

Man Who Murdered. C. Farrere; Man Who Killed
Goldburg, Jesse J.
  Life Without Soul. M. Shelley; Frankenstein
Goldman, Harold
  Busman's Honeymoon. D. L. Sayers
  Emperor's Candlesticks. B. Orczy
Goldman, William
  Heat. W. Goldman
  Magic. W. Goldman
  Marathon Man. W. Goldman
  Masquerade. V. Canning; Castle Minerva
  Moving Target. J. Macdonald
  Stepford Wives. I. Levin
Goldsmith, George
  Children of the Corn. Stephen King
Goldsmith, Isadore
  Bedelia. V. Caspary
Goldsmith, Martin
  Detour. M. M. Goldsmith
Goldstein, William
  Abominable Dr. Phibes. W. Goldstein; Dr. Phibes
Golkoetxea, Gonzalo
  Turn of the Screw. H. James
Goodis, David
  Burglar. D. Goodis
  Unfaithful. W. S. Maugham; Letter
Goodman, David Zelag
  Eyes of Laura Mars. H. B. Gilmour
  Farewell, My Lovely. R. Chandler
  Stranglers of Bombay. S. James
  Straw Dogs. G. M. Williams; Siege of Trencher's Farm
Goodrich, Frances
  Penthouse. A. S. Roche
  Society Lawyer. A. S. Roche; Penthouse
  Thin Man. D. Hammett
Goodrich, John F.
  Love Racket. B. K. Burns; Jury Woman
Goodwins, Fred
  Chinese Puzzle. M. Bower
Gordon, James B.
  File of the Golden Goose. J. Watson
Gordon, Leon
  Bishop Misbehaves. F. Jackson
  Hour of Thirteen. M. Porlock; X v. Rex
  Last of Mrs. Cheyney. F. Lonsdale
  Society Lawyer. A. S. Roche; Penthouse
Gordon, Leslie Howard
  Belonging. O. Wadsley
  Dick Turpin's Ride to York. W. H. Ainsworth; Rookwood
  "Half a Truth." Rita
  Melody of Death. E. Wallace
  River of Stars. E. Wallace
Gordons
  Down Three Dark Streets. Gordons; Case File: FBI
  Experiment in Terror. Gordons; Operation Terror
  That Darn Cat. Gordons; Undercover Cat
Gore, Ivan Patrick
  George Barnwell, the London Apprentice. G. Lillo; London Merchant
Goslar, Juergen
  Whispering Death. D. Carney
Gotfurt, Frederick
  Lady Mislaid. K. Horne
  Temptation Harbour. G. Simenon; Newhaven-Dieppe
Gottlieb, Alex
  Mystery of the White Room. J. G. Edwards; Murder in the Surgery
Goulard, Didier
  On a Nice Summer Day. J. H. Chase; One Bright Summer Morning
Gould, Heywood
  Boys from Brazil. I. Levin
  Fort Apache, the Bronx. H. Gould
Gould, John
  Who? A. Budrys
Goulding, Edmund
  Daughter of Two Worlds. L. Scott
  Sin That Was His. F. Packard
  Tiger Rose. W. Mack
Gow, James
  Murder on a Bridle Path. S. Palmer; Puzzle of the Red Stallion
Graham, Michael
  Aspern. H. James; Aspern Papers
Graham, Ronny
  Finders Keepers. C. Dennis; Next-to-Last Train Ride
Graham, Winston
  Night Without Stars. Winston Graham
  Take My Life. Winston Graham
Grangier, Gilles
  Blood to the Head. G. Simenon; Young Cardinaud
  Maigret Sees Red. G. Simenon; Maigret and the Gangsters
Granier-Deferre, Pierre

Cat. G. Simenon
Man with the Silver Eyes. R. Rossner; End of Someone Else's Rainbow
North Star. G. Simenon; Lodger
Widow Couderc. G. Simenon; Ticket of Leave
Grant, Frances E.
  Sword of Fate. H. Herman
Grant, James Edward
  Miracles for Sale. C. Rawson; Death from a Top Hat
Grant, John
  Abbott and Costello Meet Dr. Jekyll and Mr. Hyde. R. L. Stevenson; Strange Case of Dr. Jekyll and Mr. Hyde
Grassby, Bertram
  Son of the Immortals. L. Tracy
Gray, Mike
  China Syndrome. B. Wohl
Gray, William
  Cross-Country. H. D. Kastle
Grayson, Charles
  One Night in the Tropics. E. D. Biggers; Love Insurance
Grayson, Godfrey
  Meet Simon Cherry. G. Pedrick; Meet the Rev
Greatorex, Wilfred
  High Commissioner. J. Cleary
Green, Alan
  Long Wait. M. Spillane
Green, F. L.
  Odd Man Out. F. L. Green
Green, Guy
  Portrait of Alison. F. Durbridge
Green, Howard J.
  Donovan Affair. O. Davis
  Having Wonderful Crime. C. Rice
  Meet Nero Wolfe. R. Stout; Fer-de-Lance
  Melody Man. H. J. Green
  Star of Midnight. A. S. Roche
Green, Janet
  Gypsy and the Gentleman. N. W. Hooke; Darkness I Leave You
  Life for Ruth. W. Drummond
  Sapphire. E. G. Cousins
  Victim. W. Drummond
Green, Walon
  Brink's Job. N. Behn; Big Stick-Up at Brink's!
  Wages of Fear. G. Arnaud
Greenberg, Dan
  Private Lessons. D. Greenberg; Philly
Greenberg, Henry F.
  Al Capone. J. Roeburt
Greenberg, Stanley R.
  Skyjacked. D. Harper; Hijacked
Greene, Eve
  Born to Kill. J. Gunn; Deadlier Than the Male
  Great Impersonation. E. P. Oppenheim
  Night of January 16. A. Rand
  Operator 13. R. W. Chambers; Secret Service Operator 13
Greene, Graham
  Brighton Rock. G. Greene
  Comedians. G. Greene
  Fallen Idol. G. Greene; Basement Room and other stories
  First and the Last. J. Galsworthy; Five Tales
  Loser Takes All. G. Greene
  Our Man in Havana. G. Greene
  Third Man. G. Greene
Greene, Joe
  Together Brothers. Jim Robinson
Greene, Victor M.
  Flying Fifty-Five. E. Wallace
  Spider. H. Holt; Midnight Mail
Greenlee, Sam
  Spook Who Sat by the Door. S. Greenlee
Greenwood, Edward
  Man Who Knew Too Much. R. Alexander
  Young and Innocent. J. Tey; Shilling for Candles
Greenwood, Edwin
  Lord Camber's Ladies. H. A. Vachell; Case of Lady Camber
Gregor, Freddy
  Soho Gorilla. E. Wallace; Dark Eyes of London
Greifer, Lewis
  Man Who Finally Died. John Burke
Grendel, Frederic
  Diabolique. P. Boileau; Woman Who Was
Greville, Edmond T.
  Hands of Orlac. M. Renard
Grey, Clifford
  Rome Express. R. Alexander
Grey, John W.
  Carter Case. A. B. Reeve (headnote)
  Forty Naughty Girls. S. Palmer (headnote)
  Mystery Mind. A. B. Reeve
  Worldly Goods. A. Soutar
Grice, Grimes
  Possession of Joel Delaney. R.

Stewart
Griffin, Frank
  Seven Keys to Baldpate. E. D. Biggers
Griffith, D. W.
  Broken Blossoms. T. Burke; Limehouse Nights
Griffith, Edward H.
  Alias the Lone Wolf. L. J. Vance
Griffiths, Leon
  Flesh and the Fiends. R. L. Stevenson; Body Snatchers
  Grissom Gang. J. H. Chase; No Orchids for Miss Blandish
  Squeeze. David Craig; Whose Little Girl Are You?
Grimberg, Jean-Claude
  Too Small, My Friend. J. H. Chase; Way the Cookie Crumbles
Grisolia, Michel
  North Star. G. Simenon; Lodger
Grodin, Charles
  11 Harrowhouse. G. A. Browne
Groome, Mrs. Sydney
  Mystery of Mr. Bernard Brown. E. P. Oppenheim
Gruber, Frank
  Accomplice. F. Gruber; Simon Lash, Private Detective
  Bulldog Drummond at Bay. H. C. McNeile
  Challenge. H. C. McNeile
  French Key. F. Gruber
  Johnny Angel. C. G. Booth; Mr. Angel Comes Aboard
  Mask of Dimitrios. E. Ambler
  Northern Pursuit. L. T. White; 5,000 Trojan Horses
  Twenty Plus Two. F. Gruber
Gruskin, Jerry
  Slippy McGee. M. C. Oemler
Guenette, Robert
  Defector. P. Thomas; Spy
Guerney, Claud
  Green for Danger. C. Brand
Guerra, Tonino
  Butterfly on the Shoulder. J. Gearon; Velvet Well
  Illustrious Corpses. L. Sciascia; Equal Danger
  Tenth Victim. R. Sheckley
Guest, Val
  Another Man's Poison. L. Sands; Intent to Murder
  Assignment K. H. Howard; Department K
  Bones. E. Wallace
  Break in the Circle. P. Loraine
  Dangerous Davies. L. Thomas
  Full Treatment. R. S. Thorn
  Ghost Train. A. Ridley
  Hell Is a City. M. Procter
  Jigsaw. H. Waugh; Sleep Long, My Love
  Paper Orchid. A. La Bern
  Where the Spies Are. J. Leasor; Passport to Oblivion
Gundrey, V. Gareth
  Hound of the Baskervilles. A. C. Doyle
Gunn, Gilbert
  Door with Seven Locks. E. Wallace
Gunn, James
  Lady of Burlesque. G. R. Lee; G-String Murders
  Unfaithful. W. S. Maugham; Letter
Gunzberg, Milton
  Devil Commands. W. Sloane; Edge of Running Water
Gurney, Robert
  Edge of Fury. R. M. Coates; Wisteria Cottage
Gurr, Jill
  Rigged. J. H. Chase; Hit and Run
Guss, Jack
  Lady in Cement. A. Rome
Gutcheon, Beth
  Without a Trace. B. Gutcheon; Still Missing
Haas, Charles
  Moonrise. T. Strauss
Haas, Willy
  Joyless Street. H. Bettauer; Viennese Love
Habib, Ralph
  Passager Clandestin. G. Simenon; Stowaway
Hachuel, Herve
  Last of Philip Banter. J. F. Bardin
Hackett, Albert
  Penthouse. A. S. Roche
  Society Lawyer. A. S. Roche; Penthouse
  Thin Man. D. Hammett
Haggard, Mark
  Black Eye. J. Jacks; Murder on the Wild Side
Hailey, Arthur
  Zero Hour! J. Castle; Flight into Danger
Haines, William Wister
  Racket. B. Cormack
Halain, Jean

Mysteries of Paris. E. Sue
OSS 117--Mission for a Killer. J.
 Bruce; Live Wire
Hales, Jonathan
 Loophole. R. Pollock
 Mirror Crack'd. A. Christie; Mirror
 Crack'd from Side to Side
Hall, Conrad
 Running Target. S. Frazee
Hall, Franklyn
 Boomerang. W. H. Osborne
Hall, George Edwardes
 Dr. Jekyll and Mr. Hyde. R. L.
 Stevenson; Strange Case of Dr.
 Jekyll and Mr. Hyde
 Lone Wolf. L. J. Vance
Hall, Jenni
 My Lover, My Son. E. Grierson;
 Reputation for a Song
Hall, Norman S.
 Drums of Fu Manchu. S. Rohmer
 Slippy McGee. M. C. Oemler
Hall, Robert
 Franchise Affair. J. Tey
 You Can't Escape. A. Kennington; She
 Died Young
Hall, Sam
 House of Dark Shadows. Marilyn Ross
Hall, Walter Richard
 Woman in Grey. A. M. Williamson
Hall, Willis
 Man in the Middle. H. Fast; Winston
 Affair
 West 11. L. Del Rivo; Furnished Room
Hallett, Helen
 Three Live Ghosts. F. S. Isham
Halperin, Victor
 Party Girl. E. Balmer; Dangerous
 Business
Halsey, Forrest
 New York. B. Chambers
 Sweethearts and Wives. W. Hackett;
 Other Men's Wives
Hamer, Robert
 Father Brown. G. K. Chesterton;
 Innocence of Father Brown
 It Always Rains on Sunday. A. La Bern
 Jolly Bad Fellow. C. E. Vulliamy;
 Don Among the Dead Men
 Kind Hearts and Coronets. R. Horni-
 man; Israel Rank
 Long Memory. H. Clewes
 Pink String and Sealing Wax. R. Per-
 twee
 Scapegoat. D. Du Maurier
Hamill, Pete
 Badge 373. M. Roote
Hamilton, Guy
 Touch of Larceny. A. Garve; Megstone
 Plot
Hampton, Christopher
 Honorary Consul. G. Greene
Hanemann, H. W.
 House of a Thousand Shadows. M.
 Nicholson
Hankinson, Michael
 Dusty Ermine. N. Grant
 Ten Minute Alibi. A. Armstrong
Hanna, Mark
 Slaughter. H. Clement
Hannah, Dorothy
 High Window. R. Chandler
Hanson, Curtis
 Bedroom Window. A. Holden; Witnesses
 Silent Partner. A. Bodelsen; Think of
 a Number
Harareet, Haya
 Our Mother's House. J. Gloag
Hardy, Robin
 Fantasist. P. McGinley; Goosefoot
Harlow, John
 Candles at Nine. Anthony Gilbert;
 Mouse Who Wouldn't Play Ball
Harmon, David P.
 Reprisal. Arthur Gordon
Harper, Barbara S.
 Account Rendered. P. Barrington
 Captain Clegg. R. Thorndyke; Dr. Syn
Harris, James B.
 Fast-Walking. E. Brawley; Rap
Harris, Owen
 Deadly Duo. R. Jessup
 Secret of Deep Harbor. Max Miller;
 I Cover the Waterfront
Harris, Richard
 Attempt to Kill. E. Wallace; Lone
 House Mystery
 I Start Counting. A. E. Lindop
 Lady in the Car with Glasses and a
 Gun. S. Japrisot
 Locker 69. E. Wallace (headnote)
 Main Chance. E. Wallace (headnote)
 Man Detained. E. Wallace; Debt Dis-
 charged
 On the Run. E. Wallace (headnote)
Harris, Vernon
 Sea Shall Not Have Them. J. Harris
Harrison, Joan
 Dark Waters. F. Cockrell
 Jamaica Inn. D. Du Maurier
 Rebecca. D. Du Maurier
 Suspicion. F. Iles; Before the Fact
Hart, Moss
 Masquerader. K. C. Thurston
Hartford, David M.
 Golden Snare. J. O. Curwood
 Nomads of the North. J. O. Curwood
Hartley, Graham
 Reunion. K. Leopold; When We Ran
Hartmann, Edmund L.
 Last Express. B. Kendrick
 Last Warning. J. Latimer; Dead Don't Care
 Scarlet Claw. A. C. Doyle; Hound of
 the Baskervilles
 Sherlock Holmes and the Secret Weapon.
 A. C. Doyle; Return of Sherlock
 Holmes
Hartwell, John
 Fan. B. Randall
Harvey, Frank
 Brothers in Law. H. Cecil
 Danger Within. M. Gilbert; Death in
 Captivity
 Long Memory. H. Clewes
 On Friday at Eleven. J. H. Chase;
 World in My Pocket
 Thirty-Nine Steps. J. Buchan
 Upstairs and Downstairs. R. S. Thorn
Harwood, Johanna
 Doctor No. I. Fleming
Harwood, Ronald
 Arrivederci, Baby! R. Deming; Careful
 Man
 Eyewitness. M. Hebden
Hassett, Ray
 Green Ice. G. A. Browne
Hastings, Michael
 Nightcomers. M. Hastings
Hatton, Frederick
 Curlytop. T. Burke; Whispering
 Windows
 Mad Whirl. R. W. Child; Fresh Waters
Hawks, J. G.
 Eternal Struggle. G. B. Lancaster;
 Law Bringers
Hay, Ian
 Frog. E. Wallace; Fellowship of the
 Frog
 Man Behind the Mask. J. Futrelle;
 Chase of the Golden Plate
 Return of the Frog. E. Wallace;
 India-Rubber Men
 Sabotage. J. Conrad; Secret Agent
 Secret Agent. W. S. Maugham; Ashenden
 Thirty-Nine Steps. J. Buchan
Hayden, Kathleen
 Clue of the New Pin. E. Wallace
 Flying Squad. E. Wallace
 Man Who Changed His Name. E. Wallace
Hayes, Alfred
 Double Man. H. S. Maxfield; Legacy of
 a Spy
 Island in the Sun. A. Waugh
Hayes, John Michael
 But Not for Me. E. Ronns
 Chalk Garden. E. Bagnold
 Rear Window. W. Irish; After-Dinner
 Story
 To Catch a Thief. D. Dodge
 Trouble with Harry. J. T. Story
Hayes, Joseph
 Desperate Hours. J. Hayes
Hayles, Kenneth
 Passport to Treason. M. O'Brine
Haynes, Stanley
 Man Behind the Mask. J. Futrelle;
 Chase of the Golden Plate
Hayward, Frederick
 Crimes at the Dark House. W. Collins;
 Woman in White
 Sweeney Todd, the Demon Barber of
 Fleet Street. G. D. Pitt
Hayward, Lillie
 Amateur Gentleman. J. Farnol
 Margin for Error. C. Booth
 Miss Pinkerton. M. R. Rinehart
 Undying Monster. J. D. Kerruish
 White Cockatoo. M. G. Eberhart
Hayward, Lydia
 Confessions. B. Reynolds; Confession
 Corner
 Missing People. E. Wallace; Mind of
 Mr. J. G. Reeder
 Monkey's Paw. W. W. Jacobs; Lady of
 the Barge
 Ware Case. G. Pleydell
Hazard, Lawrence
 Strange Cargo. R. Sale; Not Too
 Narrow--Not Too Deep
Hazlewood, Jean
 Secret Ways. A. MacLean; Last
 Frontier
Healy, Gerard
 No Resting Place. I. Niall
Heath, Michael
 Scarecrow. R. H. Morrieson
Heath, Percy
 Dr. Jekyll and Mr. Hyde. R. L.
 Stevenson; Strange Case of Dr.
 Jekyll and Mr. Hyde
 Huntress. H. Footner
 Only Saps Work. O. Davis; Easy Come,
 Easy Go
 Slightly Scarlet. P. Heath
Hecht, Ben
 Crime Without Passion. B. Hecht;
 Collected Stories of Ben Hecht
 Kiss of Death. E. Lipsky
 Ride the Pink Horse. D. B. Hughes
 Scarface. A. Trail
 Spellbound. F. Beeding; House of Dr.
 Edwardes
 Where the Sidewalk Ends. W. L.
 Stuart; Night Cry
 Whirlpool. G. Endore; Methinks the
 Lady--
Hedley, Thomas, Jr.
 Double Negative. K. Millar; Three
 Roads
Heifetz, Louis
 Defenders of the Law. H. Del Ruth
Heins, Jo
 Play Misty for Me. P. J. Gillette
 You'll Like My Mother. N. A. Hintze
Heller, Lukas
 Blue City. K. Millar
 Candidate for Murder. E. Wallace
 (headnote)
 Flight of the Phoenix. E. Trevor
 Hot Enough for June. L. Davidson;
 Night of Wenceslas
 Never Back Losers. E. Wallace; Green
 Ribbon
 What Ever Happened to Baby Jane? H.
 Farrell
Hellman, Lillian
 Chase. H. Foote
 Dead End. S. Kingsley
Hemmings, David
 Running Scared. G. McDonald
Henley, Jack
 Dangerous Blondes. K. Roos; If the
 Shroud Fits
 Night to Remember. K. Roos;
 Frightened Stiff
Henry, Buck
 Day of the Dolphin. R. Merle
Henry, David Lee
 Eight Million Ways to Die. L. Block
 Evil That Men Do. R. L. Hill
Henry, Joan
 Yield to the Night. J. Henry
Herald, Heinz
 Vicious Circle. H. Herald; Burning
 Bush
Herbert, F. Hugh
 Case of the Black Cat. E. S. Gardner;
 Case of the Caretaker's Cat
 Dragon Murder Case. S. S. Van Dine
 Home Sweet Homicide. C. Rice
 Murder on the Roof. E. J. Doherty;
 Broadway Murders
Herkomer, S. H.
 Temptation of Carlton Earle. S. M.
 During
Herman, Jean
 Inquisitor. J. Wainwright; Brainwash
Herne, Julie
 Breaking Point. M. R. Rinehart
Hertz, David
 Stranger Than Desire. W. E. Woodward;
 Evelyn Prentice
Hervey, Harry
 Wiser Sex. C. Fitch; Woman in the
 Case
Heyes, Douglas
 Ice Station Zebra. A. MacLean
 Kitten with a Whip. Wade Miller
Hidaka, Masaya
 Lonely Hearts. E. McBain; Lady, Lady,
 I Did It!
Higgins, Colin
 Foul Play. J. C. Rogers
 Silver Streak. J. C. Rogers
Higgins, John C.
 Diamond. M. Procter; Rich Is the
 Treasure
 File of the Golden Goose. J. Watson
 Shield for Murder. W. P. McGivern
Hill, Carpenter
 Halloween II. J. Martin
Hill, Debra
 Halloween. C. Richards
Hill, Ethel
 Fog. V. Williams
Hill, Gladys
 Kremlin Letter. N. Behn
Hill, Jack
 Coffy. P. W. Fairman
Hill, Robert F.
 Cat and the Canary. J. Willard
Hill, Sinclair
 At the Villa Rose. A. E. W. Mason
 Conspirators. E. P. Oppenheim
 Expiation. E. P. Oppenheim
 Qualified Adventurer. S. Jepson
Hill, Walter
 Blue City. K. Millar
 Driver. C. B. Phillips
 Drowning Pool. J. R. Macdonald

Getaway. J. Thompson
Hickey and Boggs. P. Rock
Mackintosh Man. D. Bagley; Freedom Trap
Thief Who Came to Dinner. T. L. Smith
Warriors. S. Yurick
Hilton, James
  We Are Not Alone. J. Hilton
Hilton, Tony
  What a Carve Up! F. King; Ghoul
Hinds, Anthony
  Captain Clegg. R. Thornyke; Dr. Syn
  Dracula, Prince of Darkness. B. Stoker; Dracula
Hines, Leonard
  Ghoul. F. King
Hisaita, Eijiro
  High and Low. E. McBain; King's Ransom
Hiscott, Leslie S.
  Missing Rembrandt. A. C. Doyle; Return of Sherlock Holmes
  Passing of Mr. Quin. A. Christie; Mysterious Mr. Quin
  To What Red Hell. P. Robinson
Hitchcock, Alfred
  Blackguard. R. Paton; Autobiography of a Blackguard
  Blackmail. C. Bennett
  Case of Jonathan Drew. M. B. Lowndes; Lodger
  Murder. C. Dane; Enter Sir John
  No. 17. J. J. Farjeon
  Passionate Adventure. F. Stayton
Hively, George
  Black Bag. L. J. Vance
Hobart, Doty
  Find the Woman. A. S. Roche
  Under Cover. R. C. Megrue
Hodges, Mike
  Get Carter. T. Lewis; Jack's Return Home
Hoerl, Arthur
  Black Pearl. W. Woodrow
  Counsel for the Defense. L. Scott
  Devil's Chaplain. G. Bronson-Howard
  Drums of Jeopardy. H. MacGrath
  Man from Headquarters. G. Bronson-Howard; Black Book
  Phantom in the House. A. Soutar
  Romance of a Million Dollars. E. Dejeans
  Sisters of Eve. E. P. Oppenheim; Tempting of Tavernake
  Thirteenth Chair. A. Trail
  You Can't Beat the Law. H. H. Van Loan
  Young Dillinger. S. Stuart
Hoffe, Monkton
  Busman's Honeymoon. D. L. Sayers
  Emperor's Candlestick. B. Orczy
  Hate Ship. B. Graeme
  Last of Mrs. Cheyney. F. Lonsdale
  Mystery of Mr. X. M. Porlock; X v. Rex
Hoffenstein, Samuel
  Dr. Jekyll and Mr. Hyde. R. L. Stevenson; Strange Case of Dr. Jekyll and Mr. Hyde
  Flesh and Fantasy. O. Wilde; Lord Arthur Savile's Crime
  Laura. V. Caspary
  Phantom of the Opera. G. Leroux
Hoffman, Herman
  Last Escape. M. Walker
Hoffman, Hugh
  Untamable. G. Burgess; White Cat
Hoffs, Tamar
  Lepke. J. Pearl
Hogan, Michael
  Doctor Syn. R. Thorndyke
  Mind of Mr. J. G. Reeder. E. Wallace
  They Came by Night. B. Lyndon
Holland, Tom
  Cloak and Dagger. W. Irish; Dead Man Blues
Holloway, Jean
  Madame X. J. C. MacConaughy
Holmes, Ben
  Saint's Double. L. Charteris (headnote)
Holmes, Brown
  Avenger. J. Goodwin
  Case of the Lucky Legs. E. S. Gardner
  Dark Hazard. W. R. Burnett
  Florentine Dagger. B. Hecht
  Maltese Falcon. D. Hammett
  Satan Met a Lady. D. Hammett; Maltese Falcon
  "Shed No Tears." D. Martin
  While the Patient Slept. M. G. Eberhart
Holt, Andrew
  Avalanche. K. Boyle
Holt, Seth
  Nowhere to Go. D. MacKenzie
Home, William Douglas
  Follow That Horse. H. Mason; Photo Finish
  For Them That Trespass. E. Raymond

Sleeping Car to Trieste. R. Alexander; Rome Express
Homes, Geoffrey
  Build My Gallows High. G. Homes
Honeycombe, Gordon
  Neither the Sea Nor the Sand. G. Honeycombe
Hopcraft, Arthur
  Agatha. K. Tynan
Hopkins, John
  Holcroft Covenant. R. Ludlum
  Murder by Decree. R. Weverka
  Offense. J. Hopkins; This Story of Yours
  Thunderball. I. Fleming
Hopman, Gerald
  Devil's Rain. M. Willis
Horkheimer, H. M.
  Arsene Lupin. M. Leblanc (headnote)
Horman, Arthur T.
  Juvenile Jungle. F. Counsel
  Young and Wild. Morton Cooper
Horne, James W.
  Stingaree. E. W. Hornung
Horne, Kenneth
  Flying Fifty-Five. E. Wallace
  Spider. H. Holt; Midnight Mail
Hough, E. Morton
  Born to Gamble. E. Wallace; Forty-Eight Short Stories
House, Ron
  Bullshot. R. House; Bullshot Crummond
Houser, Lionel
  Lone Wolf Returns. L. J. Vance
Houston, Norman
  Game of Death. R. Connell; Variety
  Monte Carlo Nights. E. P. Oppenheim; Mr. Billingham, the Marquis and Madelon
Hovey, Carl
  Orient Express. G. Greene; Stamboul Train
Howard, Clifford
  Other Side of the Door. L. Chamberlain
Howard, Cy
  Every Little Crook and Nanny. E. Hunter
Howard, Eldon
  Spider's Web. A. Christie
Howard, Lillie
  Night Club Scandal. D. N. Rubin; Riddle Me This!
Howard, Matthew
  Groundstar Conspiracy. L. Davies; Alien
Howard, Sandy
  Vice Squad. W. Rotsler
Howard, Sidney
  Bulldog Drummond. H. C. McNeile
  Raffles. E. W. Hornung; Amateur Cracksman
Howard, Walter K.
  Trooper O'Neill. G. Goodchild
Howatt, Nina
  Mysterious Mr. Wong. H. S. Keeler; Sing Sing Nights
Howell, Dorothy
  Alias the Lone Wolf. L. J. Vance
  Birds of Prey. G. Bronson-Howard
  Donovan Affair. O. Davis
  Last of the Lone Wolf. L. J. Vance; Lone Wolf
Howell, Maude T.
  His Lordship. N. Grant; Nelson Touch
Howells, Jack
  Front Page Story. R. Gaines; Final Night
Hoyt, Harry O.
  Curse of Drink. C. E. Blaney
  Half Million Bribe. W. H. Osborne; Red Mouse
  13 Washington Square. L. Scott; No. 13 Washington Square
  Wizard. G. Leroux; Balaoo
Hubbard, Lucien
  Gamblers. C. Klein
  Maltese Falcon. D. Hammett
  Outside the Law. T. Browning
  Within the Law. B. Veiller
Hudis, Norman
  Face in the Night. B. Graeme; Suspense
  Passport to Treason. M. O'Brine
  Stranger in Town. F. A. Chittenden; Uninvited
Hudson, Virginia Tylor
  Burglar. A. Thomas; Editha's Burglar
Huggins, Roy
  I Love Trouble. R. Huggins; Double Take
  Pushover. B. Ballinger; Rafferty
  Too Late for Tears. R. Huggins
Hugh, R. John
  Deadly Encounter. R. Woodley
Hughes, Brian
  Nothing But the Night. J. Blackburn
Hughes, Eric
  Against All Odds. G. Homes; Build My Gallows High

Raise the Titanic! C. Cussler
Hughes, Harry
  Dead Men Are Dangerous. H. C. Armstrong; Hidden
  House of Marney. J. Goodwin
  Man at Six. J. Celestin
  Rogue in Love. T. Gallon
  Shadow of Evil. C. Dawe
Hughes, Ken
  Arrivederci, Baby! R. Deming; Careful Man
  House Across the Way. K. Hughes; High Wray
  Long Haul. M. Mills
  Portrait of Alison. F. Durbridge
  Wicked As They Come. B. Ballinger; Portrait in Smoke
Hughes, Llewellyn
  Temple Tower. H. C. McNeile
Hulbert, Jack
  Kate Plus Ten. E. Wallace
Hull, George C.
  Conflict. C. B. Kelland
Hume, Cyril
  They Gave Him a Gun. W. J. Cowen
Hume, Edward
  Reflection of Fear. S. Forbes; Go to Thy Death Bed
  Two Minute Warning. G. La Fountaine
Hume, Kenneth
  Hot Ice. A. Melville; Week-End at Thrackley
Humphrey, William J.
  Black Spider. C. Dawe
Humphries, Dave
  Julia. P. Straub
Hunabelle, Andre
  OSS 117--Mission for a Killer. J. Bruce; Live Wire
Hunter, Evan
  Birds. D. Du Maurier; Apple Tree
  Fuzz. E. McBain
Hunter, John
  Carrington, V.C. D. Christie
  Cross-Country. H. D. Kastle
  Green Pack. E. Wallace
  Intruder. R. Maugham; Line on Ginger
Hunter, N. C.
  Poison Pen. R. Llewellyn
Hunter, T. Hayes
  Man They Could Not Arrest. E. Wallace (headnote)
  Man They Couldn't Arrest. A. J. Small
Hunter, Tom
  Human Factor. S. Quinn
Huntington, Laurence
  Deadly Record. N. W. Hooke
  Franchise Affair. J. Tey
  I Killed the Count. A. Coppel
  Question of Suspense. R. Vickers (headnote)
  Warn That Man. V. Sylvaine
Hurdalek, Georg
  Town Without Pity. M. Gregor
Hurst, Brian Desmond
  On the Night of the Fire. F. L. Green
Husson, Albert
  Sorcery. P. Boileau; Spells of Evil
Huston, Jimmy
  Final Exam. G. Meyer
Huston, John
  Amazing Dr. Clitterhouse. B. Lyndon
  Asphalt Jungle. W. R. Burnett
  Beat the Devil. J. Helvick
  High Sierra. W. R. Burnett
  Key Largo. M. Anderson
  Kremlin Letter. N. Behn
  Maltese Falcon. D. Hammett
  Murders in the Rue Morgue. E. A. Poe; Prose Romances of Edgar A. Poe
Huxley, Aldous
  Woman's Vengeance. A. Huxley; Mortal Coils
Hyams, Peter
  Telefon. W. Wager
Hyde, Kenneth
  Spaniard's Curse. E. Pargeter; Assize of the Dying
Hyland, Dick Irving
  I Ring Doorbells. R. Birdwell
Hyland, Francis
  Thirteenth Chair. A. Trail
Hynd, Noel
  Agency. P. Gottlieb
Ichikawa, Kon
  Lonely Hearts. E. McBain; Lady, Lady, I Did It!
Ince, Ralph
  Argyle Case. H. Ford
Ingleton, E. Magnus
  Dark Mirror. L. J. Vance
  Ivory Snuff Box. A. Fredericks
  Moonstone. W. Collins
  Secret of the Hills. W. Garrett
Ingram, Rex
  Where the Pavement Ends. J. Russell; Red Mark
Innes, Hammond
  Campbell's Kingdom. H. Innes

Isaacs, Susan
 Compromising Positions. S. Isaacs
Isherwood, Christopher
 Frankenstein: The True Story. M. Shelley; Frankenstein
 Rage in Heaven. J. Hilton
Ivers, Julia Crawford
 Witching Hour. A. Thomas
Jack, Max
 Ambassador. E. Leonard; Fifty-Two Pickup
Jackson, Felix
 Broadway. P. Dunning
Jackson, Fred
 Exiles. R. H. Davis
Jackson, Joseph
 Second Floor Mystery. E. D. Biggers; Agony Column
Jacobs, Alexander
 French Connection II. R. Moore
 Point Blank. R. Stark; Hunter
 Seven-Ups. R. Posner
 Sitting Target. L. Henderson
Jacobson, Leigh
 Cheerful Fraud. K. R. G. Browne; Following Ann
Jacoby, George
 Vendetta. A. C. Gunter; Mr. Barnes of New York
Jacoby, Hans
 It Happens in Broad Daylight. F. Duerrenmatt; Pledge
Jacoby, Michel
 Mystery of Marie Roget. E. A. Poe; Tales
 Two Against the World. L. Weitzenkorn; Five Star Final
 Undying Monster. J. D. Kerruish
Jacquot, Benoit
 With All Hands. J. Gunn; Deadlier Than the Male
James, Benedict
 Case of Lady Camber. H. A. Vachell
 In Full Cry. R. Marsh
 Lyons Mail. E. Moreau; Courier of Lyons
 Other Person. F. Hume
James, Donald
 Limbo Line. V. Canning
James, Edward
 Over My Dead Body. J. D. O'Hanlon; As Good As Murdered
James, Rian
 Gorilla. R. Spence
 Housekeeper's Daughter. D. H. Clarke
 Lawyer Man. M. Trell
Jannuzzi, Lino
 Illustrious Corpses. L. Sciascia; Equal Danger
Jansson, Lars Magnas
 Assignment. P. Wahloo
Japrisot, Sebastien
 And Hope to Die. D. Goodis; Black Friday
 One Deadly Summer. S. Japrisot
 Sleeping Car Murders. S. Japrisot; 10:30 from Marseilles
 Trap for Cinderella. S. Japrisot
Jardin, Pascal
 Joy House. D. Keene
 Secret. F. Ryck; Undesirable Company
 Train. G. Simenon
 Widow Couderc. G. Simenon; Ticket of Leave
Jayson, Jay
 Caprice. J. Withers
Jeanson, Henri
 Mister Flow. G. Leroux; Man of a Hundred Masks
Jefferson, L. V.
 Yellow Men and Gold. Gouverneur Morris
Jenkins, Michael
 Careful, He Might Hear You. S. L. Elliott
Jenny, Marie
 Gray Dawn. S. E. White
Jepson, Selwyn
 Riverside Murder. A. Steeman; Six Dead Men
 Scarab Murder Case. S. S. Van Dine
Jeronimi, Jerome
 Spies. E. Hostovsky; Midnight Patient
Jessua, Alain
 Armageddon. D. Lippincott; Voice of Armageddon
Jessup, Richard
 Young Don't Cry. R. Jessup
Jevne, Jack
 I Cover the Waterfront. Max Miller
Job, Thomas
 Escape in the Desert. R. E. Sherwood; Petrified Forest
 Two Mrs. Carrolls. M. Vale
John, Graham
 Monkey's Paw. W. W. Jacobs; Lady of the Barge
Johnson, Adrian
 Thou Shalt Not Steal. E. Gaboriau; File No. 113

Johnson, Charles
 Slaughter's Big Rip-Off. A. Kane
 That Man Bolt. P. Crowcraft
Johnson, Monica
 Jekyll and Hyde...Together Again. R. L. Stevenson; Strange Case of Dr. Jekyll and Mr. Hyde
Johnson, Nunnally
 Black Widow. P. Quentin
 Bulldog Drummond Strikes Back. H. C. McNeile; Knock-Out
 Everybody Does It. J. M. Cain; Career in C Major
 My Cousin Rachel. D. Du Maurier
 Woman in the Window. J. H. Wallis; Once Off Guard
Johnstone, Adrian
 Money Moon. J. Farnol
 Wife Whom God Forgot. C. H. Bullivant
Johnstone, Calder
 Three Sevens. P. P. Sheehan
Jones, Charles Reed
 King Murder. C. R. Jones
Jones, Evan
 Damned. H. L. Lawrence; Children of Light
 Eva. J. H. Chase; Eve
 Funeral in Berlin. L. Deighton
 Modesty Blaise. P. O'Donnell
 Night Watch. L. Fletcher
 Outback. K. Cook; Wake in Fright
Josephson, Julian
 Bat. M. R. Rinehart
 Millionaire. E. D. Biggers; Earl Derr Biggers Tells Ten Stories
 Red Mark. J. Russell
Julian, Marcel
 Heads or Tails. A. Harris; Baroni
 One Is Always Too Good to Women. R. Queneau; We Always Treat Women Too Well
Julien, Max
 Cleopatra Jones. R. Goulart
Juttke, Herbert
 Hound of the Baskervilles. A. C. Doyle
Kaeutner, Helmut
 Redhead. A. Andersch
Kahn, Gordon
 Death Kiss. M. St. Dennis
 Two O'Clock Courage. G. Burgess
Kahn, Harry
 Man Who Murdered. C. Farrere; Man Who Killed
Kalfon, Pierre
 Five Ashore for Singapore. J. Bruce; Cold Spell
Kallis, Stanley
 Glitterdome. J. Wambaugh
Kandel, Aben
 Craze. H. Seymour; Infernal Idol
 They Won't Forget. W. Greene; Death in the Deep South
Kane, Henry
 Cop Hater. E. McBain
 Mugger. E. McBain
Kanen, Jeff
 Eddie Macon's Run. J. McLendon
Kantor, MacKinlay
 Deadly Is the Female. M. Kantor; Author's Choice
Karp, David
 Sol Madrid. R. Wilder; Fruit of the Poppy
Kastle, Leonard
 Honeymoon Killers. Paul Buck
Katcha, Vahe
 Burglars. D. Goodis; Burglar
Katcher, Leo
 Hard Man. L. Katcher
Katkov, Norman
 Once You Kiss a Stranger. P. Highsmith; Strangers on a Train
Katterhorn, Monty
 Yellow Typhoon. H. MacGrath
Katterjohn, Monte
 Cold Steel. G. C. Shedd; In the Shadow of the Hills
 Daughter of the Dragon. S. Rohmer; Daughter of Fu Manchu
 Eternal Struggle. G. B. Lancaster; Law Bringers
 Great Impersonation. E. P. Oppenheim
 Inside the Lines. E. D. Biggers
 Party Girl. E. Balmer; Dangerous Business
 Three Faces East. A. P. Kelly
Katz, Lee
 British Intelligence. A. P. Kelly; Three Faces East
 Heart of the North. W. B. Mowery
Katz, Robert
 Cassandra Crossing. R. Katz
 Kamikaze. P. Wahloo; Murder on the Thirty-First Floor
 Salamander. M. West
Kaufman, Charles
 Saint in New York. L. Charteris
Kaufman, Edward
 Star of Midnight. A. S. Roche
Kaufman, Millard

Bad Day at Black Rock. M. Niall
 Deadly Is the Female. M. Kantor; Author's Choice
Kaufman, Robert
 Freebie and the Bean. P. B. Ross
Kaurismaki, Aki
 Crime and Punishment. F. M. Dostoevskii
Kaus, Gina
 Red Danube. B. Marshall; Vespers in Vienna
Kaye, John
 Rafferty and the Gold Dust Twins. L. Roberts
Kearney, Gene
 Games. H. Ellson
Keefe, Barrie
 Long Good Friday. R. Claughton
Keene, Ralph
 Double Confession. J. Garden; All on a Summer's Day
Keindorff, Eberhard
 Waiting Room for the Other Side. R. Marshall; Mission to Siena
Keith, Carlos
 Body Snatcher. R. L. Stevenson
Keller, Sheldon
 Cleopatra Jones. R. Goulart
Kelley, William
 Witness. W. Kelley
Kellino, Roy
 Guilt is My Shadow. P. Curtis; You're Best Alone
Kelly, Anthony P.
 Raffles. E. W. Hornung; Amateur Cracksman
 Witching Hour. A. Thomas
 Woman in the Case. C. Fitch
Kendall, Victor
 Dead Men Are Dangerous. H. C. Armstrong; Hidden
 Dick Turpin. W. H. Ainsworth; Rookwood
 Man at Six. J. Celestin
 Mr. Reeder in Room 13. E. Wallace; Room 13
Kennaway, James
 Mind Benders. J. Kennaway
Kennedy, Adam
 Domino Principle. A. Kennedy
 Raise the Titanic! C. Cussler
Kennedy, Burt
 Man in the Vault. F. Gruber; Lock and the Key
Kennedy, Margaret
 Take My Life. Winston Graham
Kenrick, Tony
 Nobody's Perfekt. T. Kenrick; Two for the Price of One
Kent, Robert E.
 Case of the Black Parrot. B. E. Stevenson; Mystery of the Boule Cabinet
 Spy Ship. G. Dyer; Five Fragments
 Twice Told Tales. N. Hawthorne
 Two O'Clock Courage. G. Burgess
Kenyon, A. G.
 Girl in the Dark. C. E. Walk; Green Seal
Kenyon, Charles
 Crash. F. Packard; Night Operator
 Dangerous Days. M. R. Rinehart
 Man in Half Moon Street. B. Lyndon
 Night Nurse. D. Macy
 Petrified Forest. R. E. Sherwood
 River's End. J. O. Curwood
 Stop Thief! Carlyle Moore
Kern, David J.
 Dracula Sucks. B. Stoker; Dracula
Kerr, Geoffrey
 Calendar. E. Wallace
 Jassy. N. Lofts
 Living Dangerously. R. Simpson
Kerridge, Roy
 Mix Me a Person. J. T. Story
Kessel, Joseph
 Night of the Generals. H. H. Kirst
Kessler, Henry S.
 Five Steps to Danger. D. Hamilton; Assignment: Murder
Keys, Anthony Nelson
 Frankenstein Must Be Destroyed. M. Shelley; Frankenstein
Kibbee, Roland
 Amorous Adventures of Moll Flanders. D. Defoe; Fortunes and Misfortunes of the Famous Moll Flanders
 Midnight Man. D. Anthony; Midnight Lady and the Mourning Man
 Valdez Is Coming. E. Leonard
Kikushima, Ryuzo
 High and Low. E. McBain; King's Ransom
Killens, John O.
 Odds Against Tomorrow. W. P. McGivern
Kimmins, Anthony
 Laburnum Grove. J. B. Priestley
 Lonely Road. N. Shute
King, Bradley
 East Lynne. H. Wood
 Mystery of Edwin Drood. C. Dickens

King, Frank
  Ghoul. F. King
Kingsbridge, John
  Shark. V. Canning; His Bones Are Coral
Kirk, Roland
  Dear Fatherland, Be at Peace. J. M. Simmel; Dear Fatherland
Kirkwood, James
  Some Kind of Hero. J. Kirkwood
Kirwan, Patrick
  Bulldog Drummond at Bay. H. C. McNeile
  Dark Eyes of London. E. Wallace
  Desperate Moment. M. Albrand
  On the Night of the Fire. F. L. Green
  Rooney. C. Cookson
Kjaerulff-Schmidt, Palle
  Think of a Number. A. Bodelsen
Klane, Robert
  Every Little Crook and Nanny. E. Hunter
Klaren, G. C.
  Hound of the Baskervilles. A. C. Doyle
Klauber, Marcel
  Girl in the Woods. O. Crawford; Blood on the Branches
Klee, Walter
  Midnight in Paris. G. Simenon; Monsieur la Souris
Klein, Philip
  Baby, Take a Bow. J. P. Judge; Square Crooks
  Black Camel. E. D. Biggers
  Charlie Chan Carries On. E. D. Biggers
  Elinor Norton. M. R. Rinehart; State vs Elinor Norton
  Spider. F. Oursler
  Trial of Vivienne Ware. K. Ellis
Kleiner, Harry
  Bullitt. R. Pike; Mute Witness
  Cry Tough. I. Shulman
  Fallen Angel. M. Holland
Kleinman, Dan
  Rage. P. Friedman
Kneale, Nigel
  Devil's Own. P. Curtis
Knight, Vivienne
  Floods of Fear. J. Hawkins
  Girl in the Headlines. L. Payne; Nose on My Face
  Law and Disorder. D. Roberts; Smuggler's Circuit
Knoblock, Edward
  Amateur Gentleman. J. Farjeon
Knopf, Christopher
  Choirboys. J. Wambaugh
Knopf, Edwin
  Piccadilly Jim. P. G. Wodehouse
Knott, Frederick
  Dial "M" for Murder. F. Knott
  Last Page. J. H. Chase
Knowles, Bernard
  Hell Is Empty. J. F. Straker
  Park Plaza 605. B. Gray; Dare-Devil Conquest
Kober, Arthur
  Great Hotel Murder. V. Starrett
  Guilty As Hell. D. N. Rubin; Riddle Me This!
Koch, Howard
  Casablanca. J. J. Epstein
  Letter. W. S. Maugham
  633 Squadron. F. E. Smith
Koenig, Laird
  Bloodline. S. Sheldon
  Little Girl Who Lives Down the Lane. L. Koenig
Koestveld, Graeme
  Robbery Under Arms. R. Boldrewood
Kogan, Ephraim
  Faces in the Dark. P. Boileau
Kohn, John
  Collector. J. Fowles
  Shanghai Surprise. T. Kenrick; Faraday's Flowers
Kohner, Frederick
  Lady and the Monster. C. Siodmak; Donovan's Brain
Konvitz, Jeffrey
  Sentinel. J. Konvitz
Kosterlitz, Herman
  Man Who Murdered. C. Farrere; Man Who Killed
Kozoll, Michael
  First Blood. D. Morrell
Krafft, John W.
  Murder at Glen Athol. N. Lippincott
Kraly, Hans
  Last of Mrs. Cheyney. F. Lonsdale
Krasna, Norman
  Four Hours to Kill. N. Krasna
  Who Was That Lady? N. Krasna; Who Was That Lady I Saw You With?
Krawczyk, Gerard
  I Hate Actors. B. Hecht
Kreitsek, Howard B.
  Walking Tall: Part 2. W. Carey

Krims, Milton
  We Are Not Alone. J. Hilton
Krohnke, Erich
  Ten Little Indians. A. Christie; Ten Little Niggers
Krumgold, Joseph
  Jim Hanvey, Detective. O. R. Cohen
  Lone Wolf Returns. L. J. Vance
Kruse, John
  Assault. K. Young; Ravine
  Echo of Barbara. Jonathan Burke
  Vengeance. C. Siodmak; Donovan's Brain
Kubrick, Stanley
  Clockwork Orange. A. Burgess
  Dr. Strangelove. P. Bryant; Two Hours to Doom
  Killing. L. White; Clean Break
Kuhn, Irene
  Mask of Fu Manchu. S. Rohmer
Kulijanov, Lev
  Crime and Punishment. F. M. Dostoevskii
Kurnitz, Harry
  Goodbye Charlie. M. H. Albert
  How to Steal a Million. M. Sinclair
  I Love You Again. O. R. Cohen
  Witness for the Prosecution. A. Christie
Kurosawa, Akira
  High and Low. E. McBain; King's Ransom
La Bern, Arthur
  Accidental Death. E. Wallace; Jack o' Judgment
  Incident at Midnight. E. Wallace (headnote)
  Time to Remember. E. Wallace; Man Who Bought London
  Verdict. E. Wallace; Big Four
Labro, Philippe
  Without Apparent Motive. E. McBain; Ten Plus One
La Frenais, Ian
  Catch Me a Spy. G. Marton
  Jokers. M. Sands
  Otley. M. Waddell
  Villain. J. Barlow; Burden of Proof
Laidlow, Betty
  Danger on the Air. Xantippe; Death Catches Up with Mr. Kluck
Lamb, Karl
  Pitfall. J. J. Dratler
  Whispering Smith. F. H. Spearman
Lambert, Peter
  Breaking Point. L. Meynell
Lamothe, Julian L.
  His Robe of Honor. E. Dorrance
Lampell, Millard
  Blind Date. L. Howard
Landau, Leslie
  Riverside Murder. A. Steeman; Six Dead Men
Landau, Richard
  Born Reckless. M. Rogers
  Flanagan Boy. M. Catto
  Glass Cage. A. E. Martin
  Murder by Proxy. H. Nielsen; Gold Coast Nocturne
Landon, Christopher
  Ice-Cold in Alex. C. Landon
Landon, Joseph
  Johnny Cool. J. McPartland; Kingdom of Johnny Cool
  Rise and Fall of Legs Diamond. O. H. Gaylord
Lane, Richard
  You Can't See Round Corners. J. Cleary
Lang, Charles
  Desire in the Dust. H. Whittington
Lang, Phil
  Third Degree. A. Hornblow
Langley, Lee
  Interlude. J. M. Cain; Serenade
Langley, Noel
  Secret of Stamboul. D. Wheatley; Eunuch of Stamboul
  They Made Me a Fugitive. J. Budd; Convict Has Escaped
Laning, Robert
  Hostage. C. Henry
Lanoe, H.
  Man from Marrakech. R. P. Jones; Heisters
Larey, Pierre
  It Only Happens to the Living. R. Marshall; Things Men Do
Larkin, John Francis
  Mandarin Mystery. E. Queen; Chinese Orange Mystery
  Some Call It Love. R. James
Laroche, Pierre
  Seventh Juror. F. Didelot
Lasker, Alex
  Firefox. C. Thomas
Lasko, Leo
  Vendetta. A. C. Gunter; Mr. Barnes of New York
Lasky, Jesse, Jr.

Ace Up Your Sleeve. J. H. Chase; Ace Up My Sleeve
  Secret Agent. W. S. Maugham; Ashenden
Latimer, Jonathan
  Big Clock. K. Fearing
  Glass Key. D. Hammett
  Night Has a Thousand Eyes. G. Hopley
  Night in New Orleans. J. R. Langham; Sing a Song of Homicide
  Plunder of the Sun. D. Dodge
  Sealed Verdict. L. Shapiro
  They Won't Believe Me. G. McDonell
  Unholy Wife. J. Roeburt
  Whole Truth. P. Mackie
Lau, Wesley
  Lepke. J. Pearl
Laudenbach, Roland
  Obsession. W. Irish; Dead Man Blues
Launder, Frank
  Black Mask. B. Graeme; Blackshirt
  Educated Evans. E. Wallace
  Fortune Is a Woman. Winston Graham
  Girl in the News. R. Vickers
  Green Man. F. Launder; Meet a Body
  Inspector Hornleigh on Holiday. L. Grex; Stolen Death
  Seven Sinners. A. Ridley; Wrecker
  They Came by Night. B. Lyndon
  Twelve Good Men. J. Rhode; Murders in Praed Street
  W Plan. G. Seton
Lauren, S. K.
  Crime and Punishment. F. M. Dostoevskii
  Mr. & Mrs. North. O. Davis
Laurent, Davis
  I Married a Dead Man. W. Irish
Laurent, Patrick
  I Married a Dead Man. W. Irish
Laurents, Arthur
  Rope. P. Hamilton
Lautner, Georges
  Icy Breasts. R. Matheson; Someone Is Bleeding
Lavon, Arthur
  Mask. A. Hornblow
Law, John
  Casino Royale. I. Fleming
Law, Michael
  Six Men. E. Radford
Lawson, John Howard
  One Against Seven. J. Stevenson; Counterattack
  Ship from Shanghai. D. Collins; Ordeal
Lay, John Hunter
  Slightly Honorable. F. G. Presnell; Send Another Coffin
Leahy, Agnes Brand
  Night of June 13. F. Vreeland
Leasor, James
  Where the Spies Are. J. Leasor; Passport to Oblivion
LeBaron, William
  Perfect Crime. I. Zangwill; Big Bow Mystery
Lebrun, Marcel
  Stew in the Caribbean. A. Conroy; Looters
Lederer, Charles
  I Love You Again. O. R. Cohen
  Kiss of Death. E. Lipsky
  Mountain Music. M. Kantor; Author's Choice
  Ocean's 11. G. C. Johnson
  Ride the Pink Horse. D. B. Hughes
  Within the Law. B. Veiller
Ledrov, D. B.
  Shuttered Room. J. Withers
Lee, Connie
  Nine Girls. W. H. Pettitt
Lee, Leonard
  Glass Web. M. Ehrlich; Spin the Glass Web
  Panther's Moon. V. Canning
  Sinner Take All. W. Chambers; Murder for a Wanton
Lee, Norman
  Door with Seven Locks. E. Wallace
  Monkey's Paw. W. W. Jacobs; Lady of the Barge
Lee, Robert N.
  Alias the Night Wind. V. Vanardy
  Dragon Murder Case. S. S. Van Dine
  Fog Over Frisco. G. Dyer; Five Fragments
  Hunted Woman. J. O. Curwood
  Kennel Murder Case. S. S. Van Dine
  70,000 Witnesses. C. Fitzsimmons
  While the Patient Slept. M. G. Eberhart
Leeds, Charles A.
  No Road Back. F. L. Cary; Madam Tic-Tac
Le Frane, Guy
  Keep Talking, Baby. D. Keene; Strange Witness
Legrand, Andre
  Secret Document--Vienna. M. Dekobra; Widow with the Pink Gloves

Lehman, Ernest
 Black Sunday. T. Harris
 Family Plot. V. Canning; Rainbird Pattern
Lehman, Gladys
 Cat Creeps. J. Willard; Cat and the Canary
 Death Takes a Holiday. Walter Ferris
 Double Door. E. McFadden
Leigh, Rowland
 Summer Storm. A. Chekhov; Shooting Party
Leitzbach, Adeline
 House of Secrets. S. Horler
Lennart, Isobel
 Fitzwilly. Poyntz Tyler; Garden of Cucumbers
Lennon, Thomas
 Murder on a Bridle Path. S. Palmer; Puzzle of the Red Stallion
Lenzmann, Jacques
 Without Apparent Motive. E. McBain
Leonard, Elmore
 Fifty-Two Pickup. E. Leonard
 Mr. Majestyk. E. Leonard
 Moonshine War. E. Leonard
 Stick. E. Leonard
Leonard, Hugh
 Interlude. J. M. Cain; Serenade
Leone, Sergio
 Once Upon a Time in America. H. Grey; Hoods
Leone, Virgil C.
 Fine Pair. C. Stratton
Leroy, Irving
 Chick. E. Wallace
Leroy, Serge
 Attention, the Kids Are Watching. P. L. Dixon; Children Are Watching Passengers. K. R. Dwyer; Chase
Le Saint, Edward J.
 Men of Zanzibar. R. H. Davis; Man of Zanzibar
Leslie, Dudley
 Black Limelight. G. Sherry
 Living Dangerously. R. Simpson
 Three Silent Men. E. P. Thorne
Lesslie, Colin
 No Resting Place. I. Niall
Lesson, Michael
 Jekyll and Hyde...Together Again. R. L. Stevenson; Strange Case of Dr. Jekyll and Mr. Hyde
Lester, Seeleg
 Change of Mind. C. Stratton
Levant, Oscar
 Orient Express. G. Greene; Stamboul Train
Levien, Sonya
 Behind That Curtain. E. D. Biggers
 Four Men and a Prayer. D. Garth
LeVino, Albert Shelby
 Canary Murder Case. S. S. Van Dine
 Going Crooked. Winchell Smith
 Island of Intrigue. I. Ostrander
 Law and the Woman. C. Fitch; Woman in the Case
 No Man's Land. L. J. Vance
 Sleeping Memory. E. P. Oppenheim; Great Awakening
 Woman Racket. P. Dunning; Night Hostess
 Woman's Law. Maravene Thompson
Levinson, Barry
 And Justice for All. R. Grossbach
 High Anxiety. R. H. Pilpel
Levison, Ken
 Madhouse. Angus Hall; Qualtrough
Levitt, Saul
 Covenant with Death. S. Becker
Levy, Benn W.
 Blackmail. C. Bennett
 Hate Ship. B. Graeme
 Informer. L. O'Flaherty
 Lord Camber's Ladies. H. A. Vachell; Case of Lady Camber
Levy, Melvin
 First Comes Courage. E. Arnold; Commandos
Levy, Parke
 Having Wonderful Crime. C. Rice
Levy, Raoul
 Defector. P. Thomas; Spy
Lewis, Andy
 Klute. W. Johnston
 Underground. C. Stratton
Lewis, D. B. Wyndham
 Gay Adventure. W. Hackett
 Man Who Knew Too Much. R. Alexander
Lewis, Dave
 Klute. W. Johnston
Lewis, Eugene B.
 Haunting Shadows. M. Nicholson; House of a Thousand Shadows
Lewis, Frederick
 Strange Case of Mary Page. F. Lewis
Lewis, Hershell G.
 Two Thousand Maniacs. H. G. Lewis
Lewis, Jay
 Front Page Story. R. Gaines; Final Night

Lighton, Louis D.
 Blind Goddess. A. Train
 Pleasure Buyers. A. S. Roche
Lindop, Audrey Erskine
 Blanche Fury. J. Shearing
 Tall Headlines. A. E. Lindop
Ling, Eugene
 Dark Page. S. Fuller
 It Shouldn't Happen to a Dog. E. Lanham
Lipman, William R.
 Dangerous to Know. E. Wallace; On the Spot
Lipscomb, W. P.
 Bitter Springs. C. King
 Loyalties. J. Galsworthy
 Mark of Cain. J. Shearing; Airing in a Closed Carriage
 Plunder. B. Travers
 Robbery Under Arms. R. Boldrewood
 Sign of the Four. A. C. Doyle
 Speckled Band. A. C. Doyle; Adventures of Sherlock Holmes
Littell, Robert
 Amateur. R. Littell
Littleton, Scott
 Worldly Goods. A. Soutar
Lively, Robert
 Danger on the Air. Xantippe; Death Catches Up with Mr. Kluck
Llovet, Enrique
 Ten Little Indians. A. Christie; Ten Little Niggers
Lloyd, Frank
 Madame X. J. W. MacConaughy
Lochte, Richard S.
 Escape to Athena. P. Blake
Loeb, Joseph, III.
 Burglar. L. Block (headnote)
Loeb, Lee
 Abbott and Costello Meet Dr. Jekyll and Mr. Hyde. R. L. Stevenson; Strange Case of Dr. Jekyll and Mr. Hyde
 Seven Keys to Baldpate. E. D. Biggers
Logan, Helen
 Man Who Wouldn't Talk. H. Hall; Valiant
Logue, Charles A.
 Cheating Cheaters. M. Marcin
 Man on the Box. H. MacGrath
 Master Mystery. A. B. Reeve
 Menace. E. Wallace; Feathered Serpent
 Sing Sing Nights. H. S. Keeler
Lonegan, Lloyd F.
 Million Dollar Mystery. H. MacGrath
Lonergan, Lloyd
 Highest Bidder. M. Foster; Trap
 My Lady's Garter. J. Futrelle
 Woman in White. W. Collins
Long, Louise
 Greene Murder Case. S. S. Van Dine
Long, Reginald
 Spider. H. Holt; Midnight Mail
Longden, John
 Quinney's. H. A. Vachell
Longstreet, Stephen
 Uncle Harry. T. Job
Lord, Robert
 Five Star Final. L. Weitzenkorn
 On Trial. E. L. Reizenstein
Loring, Hope
 Blind Goddess. A. Train
 Interference. R. Pertwee
 Pleasure Buyers. A. S. Roche
 Red Glove. D. Grant; Fifth Ace
Losey, Joseph
 Big Night. S. Ellin; Dreadful Summit
Lovett, Josephine
 Corsair. W. Green
 Perpetua. D. C. Calthrop
 Spanish Jade. M. Hewlett
Lowe, Edward T.
 Agony Column. E. D. Biggers
 Broadway. P. Dunning
 Bulldog Drummond Comes Back. H. C. McNeile; Female of the Species
 Bulldog Drummond's Revenge. H. C. McNeile; Return of Bulldog Drummond
 Curtain at Eight. O. R. Cohen; Backstage Mystery
 Fighting Back. W. M. Raine
 Red-Haired Alibi. W. Collison
 Scattergood Baines. C. B. Kelland
 Sherlock Holmes and the Secret Weapon. A. C. Doyle; Return of Sherlock Holmes
Lowe, Sherman L.
 Mystery House. M. G. Eberhart; Mystery of Hunting's End
Lowry, Roger
 Negatives. P. Everett
Luckwell, Bill
 Hidden Homicide. P. Capon; Death at Shinglestrand
Lucoque, H. Lisle
 Tatterly. T. Gallon
Ludwig, William
 Shadow on the Wall. H. Lees; Death in the Doll's House

Stronger Than Desire. W. E. Woodward; Evelyn Prentice
Lund, O. A. C.
 Butterfly. H. K. Webster
Lussier, Dane
 Lady and the Monster. C. Siodmak; Donovan's Brain
 Three's a Crowd. M. G. Eberhart; Hasty Wedding
Lustig, H. G.
 Under Western Eyes. J. Conrad
Lynch, John
 Valley of Silent Men. J. O. Curwood
Lyndon, Barre
 Hangover Square. P. Hamilton
 Lodger. M. B. Lowndes
 Man in the Attic. M. B. Lowndes; Lodger
 Night Has a Thousand Eyes. G. Hopley
Lytell, Bert
 No Man's Land. L. J. Vance
MacArthur, Charles
 Crime Without Passion. B. Hecht; Collected Stories of Ben Hecht
 New Adventures of Get-Rich-Quick Wallingford. G. R. Chester; Get-Rich-Quick Wallingford
 Within the Law. B. Veiller
Macaulay, Richard
 Born to Kill. J. Gunn; Deadlier Than the Male
 Out of the Fog. I. Shaw; Gentle People
 They Drive by Night. A. I. Bezzerides; Long Haul
McCall, Mary, Jr.
 Maisie. W. Collison; Dark Dame
McCarty, Henry
 Gorilla. R. Spence
 Shadow on the Wall. J. B. Ellis; Picture on the Wall
MacClure, Victor
 They Met in the Dark. Anthony Gilbert; Vanishing Corpse
McCormick, John
 Life for Ruth. W. Drummond
 Victim. W. Drummond
McCoy, Horace
 Bad for Each Other. H. McCoy; Scalpel
 Dangerous to Know. E. Wallace; On the Spot
McCracken, Esther
 Poison Pen. R. Llewellyn
Macdonald, Norman
 Loudwater Mystery. E. Jepson
MacDonald, Philip
 Blind Alley. J. Warwick
 Body Snatcher. R. L. Stevenson
 Love from a Stranger. F. Vosper
 Mystery of Mr. X. M. Porlock; X v. Rex
MacDougall, Ranald
 Breaking Point. E. Hemingway; To Have and Have Not
 Mildred Pierce. J. M. Cain
 Unsuspected. C. Armstrong
MacDougall, Roger
 Touch of Larceny. A. Garve; Megstone Plot
McGivern, Cecil
 Blanche Fury. J. Shearing
McGivern, William P.
 I Saw What You Did. U. Curtiss; Out of the Dark
 Wrecking Crew. D. Hamilton
McGowan, T. J.
 Man with My Face. S. W. Taylor
McGrath, John
 Billion Dollar Brain. L. Deighton
McGrath, William
 70,000 Witnesses. C. Fitzsimmons
McGuinness, James Kavin
 Solitaire Man. B. C. Spewack
McGuire, Dennis
 Shoot It: Black, Shoot It: Blue. P. Tyner; Shoot It
MacGunigle, Robert
 Whistling in the Dark. L. Gross
McIntosh, Blanche
 Anna the Adventuress. E. P. Oppenheim
 Mr. Justice Raffles. E. W. Hornung
 Mrs. Erricker's Reputation. T. Cobb
 Touch of the Child. T. Gallon
MacKay, Elizabeth
 Unsuitable Job for a Woman. P. D. James
McKelway, St. Clair
 Sleep My Love. L. Q. Ross
Mackendrick, Alexander
 Blue Lamp. T. Willis
Mackie, Philip
 Clue of the New Pin. E. Wallace
 Clue of the Silver Key. E. Wallace
 Clue of the Twisted Candle. E. Wallace
 Man at the Carlton Tower. E. Wallace; Man at the Carlton
 Number Six. E. Wallace
 Praying Mantis. H. Monteilhet; Preying Mantises

Share Out. E. Wallace; Jack o'Judgment
20,000 Pound Kiss. E. Wallace (headnote)
Vengeance. C. Siodmak; Donovan's Brain
Mackinnon, Allan
  Behind the Headlines. R. Chapman
  She Shall Have Murder. D. Ames
  Sleeping Car to Trieste. R. Alexander; Rome Express
McKnight, C. A. [Rosalind Russell]
  Mrs. Pollifax, Spy. D. Gilman; Unexpected Mrs. Pollifax
MacLean, Alistair
  Breakheart Pass. A. MacLean
  Puppet on a Chain. A. MacLean
  When Eight Bells Toll. A. MacLean
  Where Eagles Dare. A. MacLean
McNamara, Walter
  Traffic in Souls. E. H. Ball
McNutt, Patterson
  Gentleman After Dark. R. W. Child; Velvet Black
  Return of Sophie Lang. F. I. Anderson; Notorious Sophie Lang
McNutt, William Slavens
  Night of June 13. F. Vreeland
McPartland, John
  Wild Party. J. McPartland
MacPhail, Angus
  Busman's Honeymoon. D. L. Sayers
  Calendar. E. Wallace
  Crooked Billet. D. Titherage
  Dead of Night. E. F. Benson; Room in the Tower
  Four Just Men. E. Wallace
  Frightened Lady. E. Wallace; Case of the Frightened Lady
  Ghost Train. A. Ridley
  It Always Rains on Sunday. A. La Bern
  Man They Could Not Arrest. E. Wallace (headnote)
  Ringer. E. Wallace
  Saloon Bar. F. Harvey
  South Sea Bubble. R. Pertwee
  White Face. E. Wallace
  Wrecker. A. Ridley
MacPherson, Jeanie
  Manslaughter. A. D. Miller
  Red Dice. O. R. Cohen; Iron Chalice
  Whispering Chorus. P. P. Sheehan
Macrae, Arthur
  Dusty Ermine. N. Grant
  Silver Blaze. A. C. Doyle; Memoirs of Sherlock Holmes
MacRauch, Earl
  Stranger Is Watching. M. H. Clark
Maas, Ernest
  Country Beyond. J. O. Curwood
Mack, Willard
  Madame X. J. W. MacConaughy
Maddow, Ben
  Asphalt Jungle. W. R. Burnett
  Balcony. J. Genet
  Chairman. J. R. Kennedy
  Intruder in the Dust. W. Faulkner
  Mephisto Waltz. F. M. Stewart
Maddox, Diana
  Amateur. R. Littell
Magnier, Claude
  Gazebo. A. Coppel
Mahin, John Lee
  Bad Seed. M. Anderson
  Beast of the City. J. Lait
  Dr. Jekyll and Mr. Hyde. R. L. Stevenson; Strange Case of Dr. Jekyll and Mr. Hyde
  Moment to Moment. A. Coppel
  Scarface. A. Trail
Maibaum, Richard
  Day They Robbed the Bank of England. J. Brophy
  Diamonds Are Forever. I. Fleming
  Doctor No. I. Fleming
  From Russia with Love. I. Fleming
  Goldfinger. I. Fleming
  Hell Below Zero. H. Innes; White South
  Man Inside. M. E. Chaber
  Man with the Golden Gun. I. Fleming
  Octopussy. I. Fleming
  On Her Majesty's Secret Service. I. Fleming
  Spy Who Loved Me. C. Wood; James Bond, the Spy Who Loved Me
  They Gave Him a Gun. W. J. Cowen
  Thunderball. I. Fleming
Maigne, Charles
  In the Hollow of Her Hand. G. B. McCutcheon; Hollow of Her Hand
Mainwaring, Daniel
  Catacombs. Jay Bennett
  Gun Runners. E. Hemingway; To Have and Have Not
Maiuri, Dino
  Payoff. A. Veraldi
Malins, Geoffrey H.
  Abbey Grange. A. C. Doyle; Return of Sherlock Holmes
  Black Peter. A. C. Doyle; Return of Sherlock Holmes
  Blue Carbuncle. A. C. Doyle; Adventures of Sherlock Holmes
  Boscombe Valley Mystery. A. C. Doyle; Adventures of Sherlock Holmes
  Bruce-Partington Plans. A. C. Doyle; His Last Bow
  Cardboard Box. A. C. Doyle; His Last Bow
  Charles Augustus Milverton. A. C. Doyle; Return of Sherlock Holmes
  Crooked Man. A. C. Doyle; Memoirs of Sherlock Holmes
  Dancing Men. A. C. Doyle; Return of Sherlock Holmes
  Engineer's Thumb. A. C. Doyle; Adventures of Sherlock Holmes
  Final Problem. A. C. Doyle; Memoirs of Sherlock Holmes
  Gloria Scott. A. C. Doyle; Memoirs of Sherlock Holmes
  Golden Pince-Nez. A. C. Doyle; Return of Sherlock Holmes
  Greek Interpreter. A. C. Doyle; Memoirs of Sherlock Holmes
  His Last Bow. A. C. Doyle
  Lady Frances Carfax. A. C. Doyle; His Last Bow
  Mazarin Stone. A. C. Doyle; Casebook of Sherlock Holmes
  Missing Three-Quarter. A. C. Doyle; Return of Sherlock Holmes
  Musgrave Ritual. A. C. Doyle; Memoirs of Sherlock Holmes
  Naval Treaty. A. C. Doyle; Memoirs of Sherlock Holmes
  Norwood Builder. A. C. Doyle; Return of Sherlock Holmes
  Red Circle. A. C. Doyle; His Last Bow
  Reigate Squires. A. C. Doyle; Memoirs of Sherlock Holmes
  Second Stain. A. C. Doyle; Return of Sherlock Holmes
  Silver Blaze. A. C. Doyle; Memoirs of Sherlock Holmes
  Six Napoleons. A. C. Doyle; Return of Sherlock Holmes
  Speckled Band. A. C. Doyle; Adventures of Sherlock Holmes
  Stock-Broker's Clerk. A. C. Doyle; Memoirs of Sherlock Holmes
  Thor Bridge. A. C. Doyle; Casebook of Sherlock Holmes
  Three Students. A. C. Doyle; Return of Sherlock Holmes
Malko, George
  Dogs of War. F. Forsyth
Malle, Louis
  Elevator to the Gallows. N. Calef; Frantic
Malleson, Miles
  Rat. P. Bottome
  They Met in the Dark. Anthony Gilbert; Vanishing Corpse
  W Plan. G. Seton
  Yellow Mask. E. Wallace; Traitor's Gate
Mallory, Violet
  Within the Law. B. Veiller
Malloy, Doris
  Human Cargo. K. Shepard; I Will Be Faithful
  Remember Last Night. A. Hobhouse; Hangover Murders
Malmberg, Bertil
  Crime and Punishment. F. M. Dostoevskii
Malone, Joel
  Crime by Night. G. Homes; Forty Whacks
Maltby, H. F.
  Crimes at the Dark House. W. Collins; Woman in White
  Sweeney Todd, the Demon Barber of Fleet Street. G. D. Pitt
  Ticket-of-Leave Man. T. Taylor
Maltz, Albert
  Naked City. M. Wald
  This Gun for Hire. G. Greene; Gun for Sale
Mamet, David
  Postman Always Rings Twice. J. M. Cain
  Verdict. B. C. Reed
Manchete, Jean-Patrick
  Undertaker Parlor Computer. W. Kempley; Probability Factor
Mandel, Loring
  Little Drummer Girl. J. Le Carre
Mander, Miles
  Lodger. M. B. Lowndes
Mankiewicz, Don M.
  House of Numbers. J. Finney
  Trial. D. M. Mankiewicz
Mankiewicz, Herman J.
  Dummy. H. J. O'Higgins
  Ladies' Man. R. Hughes
Mankiewicz, Joseph L.
  Dragonwyck. A. Seton
  Honey Pot. T. Sterling; Evil of the Day
  Only Saps Work. O. Davis; Easy Come, Easy Go
  Quiet American. G. Greene
  Slightly Scarlet. P. Heath
Mankiewicz, Tom
  Cassandra Crossing. R. Katz
  Diamonds Are Forever. I. Fleming
  Eagle Has Landed. J. Higgins
  Live and Let Die. I. Fleming
  Man with the Golden Gun. I. Fleming
  Sweet Ride. W. Murray
Mankowitz, Wolf
  Assassination Bureau. J. London
  Casino Royale. I. Fleming
  House of Fright. R. L. Stevenson; Strange Case of Dr. Jekyll and Mr. Hyde
  Where the Spies Are. J. Leasor; Passport to Oblivion
Mann, Abby
  Detective. R. Thorp
  Report to the Commissioner. J. Mills
Mann, Edward
  Killer Inside Me. J. Thompson
Mann, Michael
  Keep. F. P. Wilson
  Manhunter. T. Harris; Red Dragon
Mann, Stanley
  Collector. J. Fowles
  Eye of the Needle. K. Follett; Storm Island
  Firestarter. Stephen King
  Mark. C. E. Israel
  Naked Runner. F. Clifford
  Russian Roulette. T. Ardies; Kosygin Is Coming
  Strange Affair. B. Toms
  Woman of Straw. C. Arley
Mannheimer, Albert
  Whistling in the Dark. L. Gross
Manning, Bruce
  Lone Wolf Returns. L. J. Vance
  Meet Nero Wolfe. R. Stout; Fer-de-Lance
Mannock, Patrick L.
  Abbey Grange. A. C. Doyle; Return of Sherlock Holmes
  Black Peter. A. C. Doyle; Return of Sherlock Holmes
  Blue Carbuncle. A. C. Doyle; Adventures of Sherlock Holmes
  Boscombe Valley Mystery. A. C. Doyle; Adventures of Sherlock Holmes
  Bruce-Partington Plans. A. C. Doyle; His Last Bow
  Cardboard Box. A. C. Doyle; His Last Bow
  Charles Augustus Milverton. A. C. Doyle; Return of Sherlock Holmes
  Crimson Circle. E. Wallace
  Crooked Man. A. C. Doyle; Memoirs of Sherlock Holmes
  Dancing Men. A. C. Doyle; Return of Sherlock Holmes
  Dead Certainty. N. Gould
  Engineer's Thumb. A. C. Doyle; Adventures of Sherlock Holmes
  Final Problem. A. C. Doyle; Memoirs of Sherlock Holmes
  Gloria Scott. A. C. Doyle; Memoirs of Sherlock Holmes
  Golden Pince-Nez. A. C. Doyle; Return of Sherlock Holmes
  Greek Interpreter. A. C. Doyle; Memoirs of Sherlock Holmes
  His Last Bow. A. C. Doyle
  Lady Frances Carfax. A. C. Doyle; His Last Bow
  Mazarin Stone. A. C. Doyle; Casebook of Sherlock Holmes
  Missing Three-Quarter. A. C. Doyle; Return of Sherlock Holmes
  Musgrave Ritual. A. C. Doyle; Memoirs of Sherlock Holmes
  Naval Treaty. A. C. Doyle; Memoirs of Sherlock Holmes
  Norwood Builder. A. C. Doyle; Return of Sherlock Holmes
  Rank Outsider. N. Gould
  Red Circle. A. C. Doyle; His Last Bow
  Reigate Squires. A. C. Doyle; Memoirs of Sherlock Holmes
  Second Stain. A. C. Doyle; Return of Sherlock Holmes
  Silver Blaze. A. C. Doyle; Memoirs of Sherlock Holmes
  Six Napoleons. A. C. Doyle; Return of Sherlock Holmes
  Speckled Band. A. C. Doyle; Adventures of Sherlock Holmes
  Stock-Broker's Clerk. A. C. Doyle; Memoirs of Sherlock Holmes
  Thor Bridge. A. C. Doyle; Casebook of Sherlock Holmes
  Three Students. A. C. Doyle; Return of Sherlock Holmes
  Trent's Last Case. E. C. Bentley

Mantle, Burns
　Silver King. H. A. Jones
Marceau, Felecien
　Blonde Like That. J. H. Chase; Miss Shumway Waves a Wand
Marchant, William
　My Lover, My Son. E. Grierson; Reputation for a Song
Marcin, Max
　Shadow of the Law. J. A. Moroso; Quarry
Marcus, Larry/Lawrence B.
　Covenant with Death. S. Becker
　Stunt Man. P. Brodeur
Margolin, Arnold
　Russian Roulette. T. Ardies; Kosygin Is Coming
Margolis, Herbert F.
　Larceny. L. Eby; Velvet Fleece
Marion, Frances
　Big House. J. Lait
　Cinema Murder. E. P. Oppenheim; Other Romilly
　Cynara. R. Gore-Brown; Imperfect Lover
　Knight Without Armour. J. Hilton
　Le Pere Goriot. H. Balzac
　Love from a Stranger. F. Vosper
　On Dangerous Ground. B. E. Stevenson; Little Comrade
　Secret Six. F. Marion
　Within the Law. B. Veiller
Marion, George, Jr.
　Fifty Roads to Town. F. Nebel
Marko, Zekial
　Once a Thief. J. Trinian; Scratch a Thief
Markson, Ben
　Case of the Howling Dog. E. S. Gardner
　Case of the Lucky Legs. E. S. Gardner
　White Cockatoo. M. G. Eberhart
Markstein, George
　Odessa File. F. Forsyth
Marlon, Charles
　Mystery of the Thirteenth Guest. A. Trail; Thirteenth Guest
Marlow, Brian
　Forgotten Faces. R. W. Child; Velvet Black
　Murder Goes to College. K. Steel
　Night of June 13. F. Vreeland
　Return of Sophie Lang. F. I. Anderson; Notorious Sophie Lang
　Sophie Lang Goes West. F. I. Anderson; Notorious Sophie Lang
Marlowe, Derek
　Dandy in Aspic. D. Marlowe
Marmorstein, Malcolm
　S*P*Y*S. T. R. Joyce
Marriott, Anthony
　Deadly Bees. H. F. Heard; Taste of Honey
Marsh, Terence
　Finders Keepers. C. Dennis; Next-to-Last Train Ride
Marshak, Darryl A.
　Dracula Sucks. B. Stoker; Dracula
Marshall, Garry
　Grasshopper. M. McShane; Passing of Evil
Marshall, Roger
　And Now the Screaming Starts. D. Case; Fengriffin
　Five to One. E. Wallace; Thief in the Night
　Game for Three Losers. E. Lustgarten
　Man Outside. G. Stackelberg; Double Agent
　Ricochet. E. Wallace; Angel of Terror
　Set-Up. E. Wallace (headnote)
　Solo for Sparrow. E. Wallace; Gunner
　Two-Letter Alibi. A. Garve; Death and the Sky Above
　What Became of Jack and Jill? L. Moody; Ruthless Ones
　Who Was Maddox? E. Wallace; Undisclosed Client
Marston, Theodore
　Aurora Floyd. M. E. Braddon
　East Lynne. H. Wood
Martin, A. Z.
　Mad Room. E. Percy; Ladies in Retirement
Martin, Claude
　Blood and Roses. J. S. Le Fanu; In a Glass Darkly
Martin, Jim
　Black Eye. J. Jacks; Murder on the Wild Side
Martin, Paul
　Orient Express. G. Greene; Stamboul Train
Martin, Troy Kennedy
　Italian Job. T. K. Martin
Marton, Pierre
　Arabesque. Alex Gordon; Cipher
Martyn, Wyndham
　Silver Car. W. Martyn; Secret of the Silver Car

Maselli, Francesco
　Fine Pair. C. Stratton
Mason, Basil
　Candles at Nine. Anthony Gilbert; Mouse Who Wouldn't Play Ball
　Crackerjack. W. B. M. Ferguson
　Death at Broadcasting House. V. Gielgud
　House of the Spaniard. A. Behrend
　Jewel. E. Wallace (headnote)
Mason, Howard
　Follow That Horse. H. Mason; Photo Finish
Mason, Paul
　Ladies Club. Betty Black; Sisterhood
Masson, Rene
　Diabolique. P. Boileau; Woman Who Was
Masters, Ian
　Osterman Weekend. R. Ludlum
Matalon, Eddy
　Too Small, My Friend. J. H. Chase; Way the Cookie Crumbles
Mather, Berkley
　Doctor No. I. Fleming
Matheson, Richard
　Devil Rides out. D. Wheatley
　Die! Die! My Darling. A. Blaisdell; Nightmare
　Dracula. B. Stoker
　Legend of Hell House. R. Matheson; Hell House
　Pit and the Pendulum. L. Sheridan
　Raven. E. Sudak
　Tales of Terror. E. Sudak
Mathis, June
　Blind Man's Eyes. W. MacHarg
　Hate. W. Camp; Communicating Door
　Island of Intrigue. I. Ostrander
　Way of the Strong. R. Cullum
Mattson, Arne
　Black Sun. P. Wahloo; Lorry
Mauchette, Jean-Patrick
　Act of Aggression. J. Buell; Shrewsdale Exit
Maugham, Robin
　Intruder. R. Maugham; Line on Ginger
May, Elaine
　New Leaf. J. Ritchie
Mayer, Edwin Justus
　Phantom of Paris. G. Leroux; Cheri-Bibi and Cecily
Mayersberg, Paul
　Disappearance. D. Marlowe; Echoes of Celandine
Mayes, Wendell
　Anatomy of a Murder. R. Traver
　Bank Shot. D. E. Westlake
　Death Wish. B. Garfield
　Love and Bullets. J. Heddon
　Way to the Gold. W. D. Steele; Way to Gold
Mayfield, Julian
　Uptight. L. O'Flaherty; Informer
Maylam, Tony
　Riddle of the Sands. E. Childers
Meade, Walter
　Brandy for the Parson. G. Household; Tales of Adventurers
　High Command. L. Robinson; General Goes Too Far
Mear, H(arry) Fowler
　Alibi. M. Morton
　Anything Might Happen. H. Balfour
　Bella Donna. R. Hichens
　Black Coffee. A. Christie
　Chinese Puzzle. M. Bower
　Condemned to Death. G. Goodchild; Jack O'Lantern
　Death Croons the Blues. J. Ronald
　Dusty Ermine. N. Grant
　Excess Baggage. H. M. Raleigh
　Juggernaut. A. Campbell
　Last Hour. C. Bennett
　Last Journey. J. J. Farjeon; Holiday Express
　Lily of Kilarney. D. Boucicault; Colleen Bawn
　Lord Edgware Dies. A. Christie
　Lyons Mail. ℑ. Moreau; Courier of Lyons
　Man Outside. D. Stuart
　Man Who Changed His Name. E. Wallace
　Murder at Covent Garden. W. J. Makin
　Pointing Finger. Rita
　Professional Guest. W. Garrett
　Roof. D. Whitelaw
　Shadow. D. Stuart
　Shot in the Dark. G. Fairlie
　Silent House. J. G. Brandon
　Silver Blaze. A. C. Doyle
　Tangled Evidence. P. C. De Crespigny
　Valley of Fear. A. C. Doyle
Meckert, Jean
　Look Out, Girls. J. H. Chase; Miss Callaghan Comes to Grief
Medford, Harold
　Phantom of the Rue Morgue. E. A. Poe; Prose Romances of Edgar A. Poe
Medioli, Enrico
　Once Upon a Time in America. H. Grey; Hoods

Medoff, Mark
　Good Guys Wear Black. M. Franklin
Medwin, Michael
　My Sister and I. E. Bonett; High Pavement
Meehan, Elizabeth
　Mr. Reeder in Room 13. E. Wallace; Room 13
Meehan, John, Jr.
　Jump for Glory. G. McDonell
　Letty Lynton. M. B. Lowndes
　Madame X. J. C. MacConaughy
　Phantom of Paris. G. Leroux; Cheri-Bibi and Cecily
　Ten Days in Paris. B. Graeme; Disappearance of Roger Tremayne
　Thank Evans. E. Wallace; Good Evans!
Mekas, Adolfas
　Double-Barrelled Detective Story. M. Twain
Melford, Austin
　Don Chicago. C. E. B. Roberts
　Phantom Light. E. Price; Haunted Light
　Road House. W. Hackett
　Seven Sinners. A. Ridley; Wrecker
　Thank Evans. E. Wallace; Good Evans!
Melson, John
　Love and Bullets. J. Heddon
Meltzer, Lewis
　Brothers Rico. G. Simenon
　First Comes Courage. E. Arnold; Commandos
　High School Confidential. Morton Cooper
Melville, Jean-Pierre
　Magnet of Doom. G. Simenon
Mendeluk, George
　Stone Cold Dead. H. Garner; Sin Sniper
Menger, W. H.
　Blindfold. L. Fletcher
Mercer, David
　Maroc 7. M. Sands
Meredyth, Bess
　Great Hospital Mystery. M. G. Eberhart (headnote)
　Phantom of Paris. G. Leroux; Cheri-Bibi and Cecily
　Strangers of the Night. W. Hackett; Captain Applejack
Merivale, Bernard
　Condemned to Death. G. Goodchild; Jack O'Lantern
Merwin, Bannister
　Rogue in Love. T. Gallon
　Turf Conspiracy. N. Gould
Mesnier, Paul
　Cheri-Bibi. G. Leroux
Metzger, Radley
　Cat and the Canary. J. Willard
Meyer, Nicholas
　Seven-Per-Cent Solution. N. Meyer
　Time After Time. K. Alexander
Meyer, Rolf
　His Official Wife. R. H. Savage; My Official Wife
Michaels, Sidney
　Key Witness. F. Kane
Michel, Bernard T.
　Five Ashore for Singapore. J. Bruce; Cold Spell
Mida, Massimo
　House of Intrigue. H. J. Giskes; London Calling North Pole
Miles, Christopher
　Maids. J. Genet
Milius, John
　Dillinger. H. Clement
　Magnum Force. M. Valley
Millar, Ronald
　Never Let Me Go. R. Bax; Came the Dawn
　So Evil My Love. J. Shearing; For Her to See
Millard, Oscar
　Dead Ringer. R. Thomas
　Reward. M. Barrett
　Salzburg Connection. H. MacInnes
Miller, Albert G.
　Spider's Web. A. Christie
Miller, Alice D. G.
　Four Walls. D. Burnet
Miller, Claude
　Inquisitor. J. Wainwright; Brainwash
　Tell Him I Love Him. P. Highsmith; This Sweet Sickness
Miller, Francis
　Inquest. M. Barringer
　Trunk Crime. E. Percy
Miller, Frank
　Bleak House. C. Dickens
　False Evidence. E. P. Oppenheim
　Joyous Adventures of Aristide Pujol. W. J. Locke
Miller, Harvey
　Jekyll and Hyde...Together Again. R. L. Stevenson; Strange Case of Dr. Jekyll and Mr. Hyde

Miller, Irene
  Jo, the Crossing Sweeper. C. Dickens; Bleak House
Miller, J. Clarkson
  Moral Sinner. C. M. S. McLellan; Leah Kleschna
Miller, J. P.
  Behold a Pale Horse. E. Pressburger; Killing a Mouse on Sunday
  Young Savages. E. Hunter; Matter of Conviction
Miller, Max
  I Cover the Waterfront. Max Miller
Miller, Seton I.
  Charlie Chan's Courage. E. D. Biggers; Chinese Parrot
  Convicted. M. Flavin; Criminal Code
  Criminal Code. M. Flavin
  "G" Men. H. K. Long
  Last Mile. J. Wexley
  Ministry of Fear. G. Greene
  Murder in Trinidad. J. W. Vandercook
  Murder on a Honeymoon. S. Palmer; Puzzle of the Pepper Tree
  Penitentiary. M. Flavin; Criminal Code
  Scarface. A. Trail
  Singapore. W. Bogart
  Two in the Dark. G. Burgess; Two O'Clock Courage
Miller, Sigmund
  Wicked As They Come. B. Ballinger; Portrait in Smoke
Miller, Victor
  Stranger Is Watching. M. H. Clark
Millhauser, Bertram
  Black Secret. R. W. Chambers; In Secret
  Enter Arsene Lupin. M. Leblanc; Girl with the Green Eyes
  Garden Murder Case. S. S. Van Dine
  Pearl of Death. A. C. Doyle; Return of Sherlock Holmes
  River's End. J. O. Curwood
  Romance of Elaine. A. B. Reeve
  Sherlock Holmes. W. Gillette
  Sherlock Holmes and the Spider Woman. A. C. Doyle; Study in Scarlet
  Sherlock Holmes Faces Death. A. C. Doyle; Memoirs of Sherlock Holmes
  Suspect. J. Ronald; This Way Out
Millin, Eugene
  My Official Wife. R. H. Savage
Mills, Hugh
  Blackmailed. E. Myers; Mrs. Christopher
  Blanche Fury. J. Shearing
Milne, A. A.
  Birds of Prey. A. A. Milne; Fourth Wall
Milne, Peter
  House of Fear. W. Camp
  Kennel Murder Case. S. S. Van Dine
  Mr. Moto in Danger Island. J. W. Vandercook; Murder in Trinidad
  Murder of Dr. Harrigan. M. G. Eberhart; From This Dark Stairway
  Return of the Terror. E. Wallace; Terror
  Verdict. I. Zangwill; Big Bow Mystery
Milton, David Scott
  Born to Win. M. Roote
Minter, George
  Tread Softly, Stranger. J. Popplewell; Blind Alley
Mintz, Sam
  Cheerful Fraud. K. R. G. Browne; Following Ann
  Only Saps Work. O. Davis; Easy Come, Easy Go
Mitchell, James
  Callan. J. Mitchell; Magnum for Schneider
  Innocent Bystander. J. Munro
  Last Grenade. J. Sherlock; Ordeal of Major Grigsby
Mitchell, Julian
  Arabesque. Alex Gordon; Cipher
Mithois, Marcel
  Heart Trump for OSS 117 in Tokyo. J. Bruce; Hot Line
Mocky, Jean-Pierre
  Kill the Referee. A. Draper; Death Penalty
  No Pockets in a Shroud. H. McCoy
  Red Ibis. F. Brown; Knock Three-One-Two
  Unsewing Machine. G. Brewer; Killer Is Loose
Moessinger, David
  Caper of the Golden Bulls. W. P. McGivern
Moffat, Ivan
  Black Sunday. T. Harris
  Boy on a Dolphin. D. Divine
Moffitt, John C.
  Mountain Music. M. Kantor; Author's Choice
  Murder with Pictures. G. H. Coxe
Molinaro, Edouard
  Ravishing Idiot. C. Exbrayat

Moll, Elick
  House on Telegraph Hill. D. Lyon; Frightened Child
  Night Without Sleep. E. Moll
Monash, Paul
  Friends of Eddie Coyle. G. V. Kennedy
  Gun Runners. E. Hemingway; To Have and Have Not
Monks, John, Jr.
  Knock on Any Door. W. Motley
  People Against O'Hara. E. Lipsky
Montagnana, Luisi
  Fine Pair. C. Stratton
Montagne, Edward J.
  Man with My Face. S. W. Taylor
  Secrets of the Night. M. Marcin; Nightcap
  Too Many Crooks. E. J. Rath
Montagu, Ivor
  Last Man to Hang. G. Bullett; Jury
Montgomery, Doreen
  At the Villa Rose. A. E. W. Mason
  Bulldog Sees It Through. G. Fairlie; Scissors Cut Paper
  Dead Men Tell No Tales. F. Beeding; Norwich Victims
  Flying Squad. E. Wallace
  House of the Arrow. A. E. W. Mason
  Mr. Reeder in Room 13. E. Wallace; Room 13
  Murder Reported. R. Chapman; Murder for the Million
  Narrowing Circle. J. Symons
  One Jump Ahead. R. Chapman
  Poison Pen. R. Llewellyn
  You Can't Escape. A. Kennington; She Died Young
Montgomery, James
  Ghost Breakers. C. W. Goddard
Moore, Brian
  Torn Curtain. R. Wormser
Moore, Dudley
  Hound of the Baskervilles. A. C. Doyle
Moore, Victoria
  Little Girl in a Big City. J. K. McCurdy
More, Julian
  Catamount Killings. J. H. Chase; I Would Rather Stay Poor
  Doctors Wear Scarlet. S. Raven
More, Sheila
  Catamount Killings. J. H. Chase; I Would Rather Stay Poor
Morgan, Byron
  Five Star Final. L. Weitzenkorn
  Pace That Thrills. R. Weber
Morgan, Diana
  Pink String and Sealing Wax. R. Pertwee
Morgan, Guy
  Front Page Story. R. Gaines; Final Night
  Hell Is Sold Out. M. Dekobra
  Man in the Road. A. Armstrong; He Was Found in the Road
Morgan, Sidney
  Bid for Fortune. G. Boothby
  Bulldog Drummond's Third Round. H. C. McNeile; Third Round
  Miriam Rozella. B. L. Farjeon
  What's Bred...Comes Out in the Flesh. G. Allen; What's Bred in the Bone
  Woman of the Iron Bracelets. F. Barrett
Morhaim, Joe
  Man of Bronze. K. Robeson
Morheim, Louis
  Hunting Party. J. Millard
  Larceny. L. Eby; Velvet Fleece
  Rumble on the Docks. F. Paley
Morland, Nigel
  Mrs. Pym of Scotland Yard. N. Morland (headnote)
Morphett, Tony
  Robbery Under Arms. R. Boldrewood
Morrison, Greg
  Madhouse. Angus Hall; Qualtrough
Morrison, T. J.
  To the Public Danger. P. Hamilton; Money with Menaces
Morrissey, Paul
  Hound of the Baskervilles. A. C. Doyle
Mortimer, John
  Act of Mercy. F. Clifford
  Bunny Lake Is Missing. E. Piper
  Innocents. H. James; Turn of the Screw
  Running Man. S. Smith; Ballad of the Running Man
Mortimer, Penelope
  Bunny Lake Is Missing. E. Piper
Moses, Andrew
  Green Eyes. H. Ashbrook; Murder of Steven Kester
  Murder on the Campus. W. Chambers; Campanile Murders
Mosley, Leonard
  Foxhole in Cairo. L. Mosley; Cat and the Mice

Moury, Alain
  No Pockets in a Shroud. H. McCoy
Moussy, Marcel
  Shoot the Pianist. D. Goodis; Down There
Muelbauer, Wolfgang
  Man Who Went Up in Smoke. M. Sjowall
Mulhauser, James
  Love Letters of a Star. Rufus King; Case of the Constant God
Muller, Robert
  Woman of Straw. C. Arley
Mullin, Eugene
  Mr. Barnes of New York. A. C. Gunter
  Within the Law. B. Veiller
Murfin, Jane
  Crime Doctor. I. Zangwill; Big Bow Mystery
  Seven Keys to Baldpate. E. D. Biggers
Murillo, Mary
  East Lynne. H. Wood
  Ringer. E. Wallace
  Sign on the Door. C. Pollock
  Tangled Lives. W. Collins; Woman in White
Murphy, Dennis
  Eye of the Devil. P. Loraine; Day of the Arrow
Murphy, Richard
  Compulsion. M. Levin
  Cry of the City. H. E. Helseth; Chair for Martin Rome
  Kidnapping of the President. C. Templeton
Murphy, Warren B.
  Eiger Sanction. Trevanian
Mycroft, Walter C.
  Murder. C. Dane; Enter Sir John
  Yellow Mask. E. Wallace; Traitor's Gate
Myers, Henry
  Father Brown, Detective. G. K. Chesterton; Wisdom of Father Brown
  Murder by the Clock. Rufus King
Myers, Peter
  Action of the Tiger. J. Wellard
  Half a Chance. F. S. Isham
  Murder Is My Business. B. Halliday
  One Hour Before Dawn. M. Scott; Behind Red Curtains
  Social Buccaneer. F. S. Isham
Myton, Kennedy
  Parisian Nights. R. Goyne
Nakano, Desmond
  Boulevard Nights. D. Gram
Narcejac, Thomas
  Letters to an Unknown Lover. P. Boileau; Prisoner
  She Wolves. P. Boileau; Prisoner
Nash, J. E.
  Madame X. J. W. MacConaughy
  Under the Lash. A. Askew; Shulamite
Nash, Michael
  Lost Continent. D. Wheatley; Uncharted Seas
Natkin, Rick
  Night of the Juggler. W. P. McGivern
Natteford, J. Francis
  File 113. E. Gaboriau; File No. 113
  Gun-Runner. A. Stringer
Neame, Derek
  Small Voice. R. Westerby
Neame, Ronald
  Golden Salamander. V. Canning
Nebenzal, Harold
  Wilby Conspiracy. P. Driscoll
Neill, Roy William
  Scarlet Claw. A. C. Doyle; Hound of the Baskervilles
Nelson, Ralph
  Wrath of God. J. Graham
Nerz, Ludwig
  Hands of Orlac. M. Renard
Neuberger, A.
  Trick Baby. I. Slim
Neuman, E. Jack
  Venetian Affair. H. MacInnes
Newall, Guy
  Chin-Chin-Chinaman. P. Walsh
  Maid of the Silver Sea. J. Oxenham
Newhouse, David
  Point Blank. R. Stark; Hunter
Newhouse, Rafe
  Point Blank. R. Stark; Hunter
Newman, David
  Bonnie and Clyde. B. Hirschfeld
Newman, Walter
  Bloodbrothers. R. Price
  Crime and Punishment USA. F. M. Dostoevskii; Crime and Punishment
Niblo, Fred, Jr.
  Convicted. M. Flavin; Criminal Code
  Criminal Code. M. Flavin
  Nine Lives Are Not Enough. J. Odlum
  Passage from Hong Kong. E. D. Biggers; Agony Column
  Penitentiary. M. Flavin; Criminal Code
Nichols, Dudley

Lehman, Ernest
  Black Sunday. T. Harris
  Family Plot. V. Canning; Rainbird Pattern
Lehman, Gladys
  Cat Creeps. J. Willard; Cat and the Canary
  Death Takes a Holiday. Walter Ferris
  Double Door. E. McFadden
Leigh, Rowland
  Summer Storm. A. Chekhov; Shooting Party
Leitzbach, Adeline
  House of Secrets. S. Horler
Lennart, Isobel
  Fitzwilly. Poyntz Tyler; Garden of Cucumbers
Lennon, Thomas
  Murder on a Bridle Path. S. Palmer; Puzzle of the Red Stallion
Lenzmann, Jacques
  Without Apparent Motive. E. McBain
Leonard, Elmore
  Fifty-Two Pickup. E. Leonard
  Mr. Majestyk. E. Leonard
  Moonshine War. E. Leonard
  Stick. E. Leonard
Leonard, Hugh
  Interlude. J. M. Cain; Serenade
Leone, Sergio
  Once Upon a Time in America. H. Grey; Hoods
Leone, Virgil C.
  Fine Pair. C. Stratton
Leroy, Irving
  Chick. E. Wallace
Leroy, Serge
  Attention, the Kids Are Watching. P. L. Dixon; Children Are Watching Passengers. K. R. Dwyer; Chase
Le Saint, Edward J.
  Men of Zanzibar. R. H. Davis; Man of Zanzibar
Leslie, Dudley
  Black Limelight. G. Sherry
  Living Dangerously. R. Simpson
  Three Silent Men. E. P. Thorne
Lesslie, Colin
  No Resting Place. I. Niall
Lesson, Michael
  Jekyll and Hyde...Together Again. R. L. Stevenson; Strange Case of Dr. Jekyll and Mr. Hyde
Lester, Seeleg
  Change of Mind. C. Stratton
Levant, Oscar
  Orient Express. G. Greene; Stamboul Train
Levien, Sonya
  Behind That Curtain. E. D. Biggers
  Four Men and a Prayer. D. Garth
LeVino, Albert Shelby
  Canary Murder Case. S. S. Van Dine
  Going Crooked. Winchell Smith
  Island of Intrigue. I. Ostrander
  Law and the Woman. C. Fitch; Woman in the Case
  No Man's Land. L. J. Vance
  Sleeping Memory. E. P. Oppenheim; Great Awakening
  Woman Racket. P. Dunning; Night Hostess
  Woman's Law. Maravene Thompson
Levinson, Barry
  And Justice for All. R. Grossbach
  High Anxiety. R. H. Pilpel
Levison, Ken
  Madhouse. Angus Hall; Qualtrough
Levitt, Saul
  Covenant with Death. S. Becker
Levy, Benn W.
  Blackmail. C. Bennett
  Hate Ship. B. Graeme
  Informer. L. O'Flaherty
  Lord Camber's Ladies. H. A. Vachell; Case of Lady Camber
Levy, Melvin
  First Comes Courage. E. Arnold; Commandos
Levy, Parke
  Having Wonderful Crime. C. Rice
Levy, Raoul
  Defector. P. Thomas; Spy
Lewis, Andy
  Klute. W. Johnston
  Underground. C. Stratton
Lewis, D. B. Wyndham
  Gay Adventure. W. Hackett
  Man Who Knew Too Much. R. Alexander
Lewis, Dave
  Klute. W. Johnston
Lewis, Eugene B.
  Haunting Shadows. M. Nicholson; House of a Thousand Shadows
Lewis, Frederick
  Strange Case of Mary Page. F. Lewis
Lewis, Hershell G.
  Two Thousand Maniacs. H. G. Lewis
Lewis, Jay
  Front Page Story. R. Gaines; Final Night

Lighton, Louis D.
  Blind Goddess. A. Train
  Pleasure Buyers. A. S. Roche
Lindop, Audrey Erskine
  Blanche Fury. J. Shearing
  Tall Headlines. A. E. Lindop
Ling, Eugene
  Dark Page. S. Fuller
  It Shouldn't Happen to a Dog. E. Lanham
Lipman, William R.
  Dangerous to Know. E. Wallace; On the Spot
Lipscomb, W. P.
  Bitter Springs. C. King
  Loyalties. J. Galsworthy
  Mark of Cain. J. Shearing; Airing in a Closed Carriage
  Plunder. B. Travers
  Robbery Under Arms. R. Boldrewood
  Sign of the Four. A. C. Doyle
  Speckled Band. A. C. Doyle; Adventures of Sherlock Holmes
Littell, Robert
  Amateur. R. Littell
Littleton, Scott
  Worldly Goods. A. Soutar
Lively, Robert
  Danger on the Air. Xantippe; Death Catches Up with Mr. Kluck
Llovet, Enrique
  Ten Little Indians. A. Christie; Ten Little Niggers
Lloyd, Frank
  Madame X. J. W. MacConaughy
Lochte, Richard S.
  Escape to Athena. P. Blake
Loeb, Joseph, III
  Burglar. L. Block (headnote)
Loeb, Lee
  Abbott and Costello Meet Dr. Jekyll and Mr. Hyde. R. L. Stevenson; Strange Case of Dr. Jekyll and Mr. Hyde
  Seven Keys to Baldpate. E. D. Biggers
Logan, Helen
  Man Who Wouldn't Talk. H. Hall; Valiant
Logue, Charles A.
  Cheating Cheaters. M. Marcin
  Man on the Box. H. MacGrath
  Master Mystery. A. B. Reeve
  Menace. E. Wallace; Feathered Serpent
  Sing Sing Nights. H. S. Keeler
Lonegan, Lloyd F.
  Million Dollar Mystery. H. MacGrath
Lonergan, Lloyd
  Highest Bidder. M. Foster; Trap
  My Lady's Garter. J. Futrelle
  Woman in White. W. Collins
Long, Louise
  Greene Murder Case. S. S. Van Dine
Long, Reginald
  Spider. H. Holt; Midnight Mail
Longden, John
  Quinney's. H. A. Vachell
Longstreet, Stephen
  Uncle Harry. T. Job
Lord, Robert
  Five Star Final. L. Weitzenkorn
  On Trial. E. L. Reizenstein
Loring, Hope
  Blind Goddess. A. Train
  Interference. R. Pertwee
  Pleasure Buyers. A. S. Roche
  Red Glove. D. Grant; Fifth Ace
Losey, Joseph
  Big Night. S. Ellin; Dreadful Summit
Lovett, Josephine
  Corsair. W. Green
  Perpetua. D. C. Calthrop
  Spanish Jade. M. Hewlett
Lowe, Edward T.
  Agony Column. E. D. Biggers
  Broadway. P. Dunning
  Bulldog Drummond Comes Back. H. C. McNeile; Female of the Species
  Bulldog Drummond's Revenge. H. C. McNeile; Return of Bulldog Drummond
  Curtain at Eight. O. R. Cohen; Backstage Mystery
  Fighting Back. W. M. Raine
  Red-Haired Alibi. W. Collison
  Scattergood Baines. C. B. Kelland
  Sherlock Holmes and the Secret Weapon. A. C. Doyle; Return of Sherlock Holmes
Lowe, Sherman L.
  Mystery House. M. G. Eberhart; Mystery of Hunting's End
Lowry, Roger
  Negatives. P. Everett
Luckwell, Bill
  Hidden Homicide. P. Capon; Death at Shinglestrand
Lucoque, H. Lisle
  Tatterly. T. Gallon
Ludwig, William
  Shadow on the Wall. H. Lees; Death in the Doll's House

Stronger Than Desire. W. E. Woodward; Evelyn Prentice
Lund, O. A. C.
  Butterfly. H. K. Webster
Lussier, Dane
  Lady and the Monster. C. Siodmak; Donovan's Brain
  Three's a Crowd. M. G. Eberhart; Hasty Wedding
Lustig, H. G.
  Under Western Eyes. J. Conrad
Lynch, John
  Valley of Silent Men. J. O. Curwood
Lyndon, Barre
  Hangover Square. P. Hamilton
  Lodger. M. B. Lowndes
  Man in the Attic. M. B. Lowndes; Lodger
  Night Has a Thousand Eyes. G. Hopley
Lytell, Bert
  No Man's Land. L. J. Vance
MacArthur, Charles
  Crime Without Passion. B. Hecht; Collected Stories of Ben Hecht
  New Adventures of Get-Rich-Quick Wallingford. G. R. Chester; Get-Rich-Quick Wallingford
  Within the Law. B. Veiller
Macaulay, Richard
  Born to Kill. J. Gunn; Deadlier Than the Male
  Out of the Fog. I. Shaw; Gentle People
  They Drive by Night. A. I. Bezzerides; Long Haul
McCall, Mary, Jr.
  Maisie. W. Collison; Dark Dame
McCarty, Henry
  Gorilla. R. Spence
  Shadow on the Wall. J. B. Ellis; Picture on the Wall
MacClure, Victor
  They Met in the Dark. Anthony Gilbert; Vanishing Corpse
McCormick, John
  Life for Ruth. W. Drummond
  Victim. W. Drummond
McCoy, Horace
  Bad for Each Other. H. McCoy; Scalpel
  Dangerous to Know. E. Wallace; On the Spot
McCracken, Esther
  Poison Pen. R. Llewellyn
Macdonald, Norman
  Loudwater Mystery. E. Jepson
MacDonald, Philip
  Blind Alley. J. Warwick
  Body Snatcher. R. L. Stevenson
  Love from a Stranger. F. Vosper
  Mystery of Mr. X. M. Porlock; X v. Rex
MacDougall, Ranald
  Breaking Point. E. Hemingway; To Have and Have Not
  Mildred Pierce. J. M. Cain
  Unsuspected. C. Armstrong
MacDougall, Roger
  Touch of Larceny. A. Garve; Megstone Plot
McGivern, Cecil
  Blanche Fury. J. Shearing
McGivern, William P.
  I Saw What You Did. U. Curtiss; Out of the Dark
  Wrecking Crew. D. Hamilton
McGowan, T. J.
  Man with My Face. S. W. Taylor
McGrath, John
  Billion Dollar Brain. L. Deighton
McGrath, William
  70,000 Witnesses. C. Fitzsimmons
McGuinness, James Kavin
  Solitaire Man. B. C. Spewack
McGuire, Dennis
  Shoot It: Black, Shoot It: Blue. P. Tyner; Shoot It
MacGunigle, Robert
  Whistling in the Dark. L. Gross
McIntosh, Blanche
  Anna the Adventuress. E. P. Oppenheim
  Mr. Justice Raffles. E. W. Hornung
  Mrs. Erricker's Reputation. T. Cobb
  Touch of the Child. T. Gallon
MacKay, Elizabeth
  Unsuitable Job for a Woman. P. D. James
McKelway, St. Clair
  Sleep My Love. L. Q. Ross
Mackendrick, Alexander
  Blue Lamp. T. Willis
Mackie, Philip
  Clue of the New Pin. E. Wallace
  Clue of the Silver Key. E. Wallace
  Clue of the Twisted Candle. E. Wallace
  Man at the Carlton Tower. E. Wallace; Man at the Carlton
  Number Six. E. Wallace
  Praying Mantis. H. Monteilhet; Preying Mantises

Share Out. E. Wallace; Jack o'Judgment
20,000 Pound Kiss. E. Wallace (headnote)
Vengeance. C. Siodmak; Donovan's Brain

Mackinnon, Allan
Behind the Headlines. R. Chapman
She Shall Have Murder. D. Ames
Sleeping Car to Trieste. R. Alexander; Rome Express

McKnight, C. A. [Rosalind Russell]
Mrs. Pollifax, Spy. D. Gilman; Unexpected Mrs. Pollifax

MacLean, Alistair
Breakheart Pass. A. MacLean
Puppet on a Chain. A. MacLean
When Eight Bells Toll. A. MacLean
Where Eagles Dare. A. MacLean

McNamara, Walter
Traffic in Souls. E. H. Ball

McNutt, Patterson
Gentleman After Dark. R. W. Child; Velvet Black
Return of Sophie Lang. F. I. Anderson; Notorious Sophie Lang

McNutt, William Slavens
Night of June 13. F. Vreeland

McPartland, John
Wild Party. J. McPartland

MacPhail, Angus
Busman's Honeymoon. D. L. Sayers
Calendar. E. Wallace
Crooked Billet. D. Titherage
Dead of Night. E. F. Benson; Room in the Tower
Four Just Men. E. Wallace
Frightened Lady. E. Wallace; Case of the Frightened Lady
Ghost Train. A. Ridley
It Always Rains on Sunday. A. La Bern
Man They Could Not Arrest. E. Wallace (headnote)
Ringer. E. Wallace
Saloon Bar. F. Harvey
South Sea Bubble. R. Pertwee
White Face. E. Wallace
Wrecker. A. Ridley

MacPherson, Jeanie
Manslaughter. A. D. Miller
Red Dice. O. R. Cohen; Iron Chalice
Whispering Chorus. P. P. Sheehan

Macrae, Arthur
Dusty Ermine. N. Grant
Silver Blaze. A. C. Doyle; Memoirs of Sherlock Holmes

MacRauch, Earl
Stranger Is Watching. M. H. Clark

Maas, Ernest
Country Beyond. J. O. Curwood

Mack, Willard
Madame X. J. W. MacConaughy

Maddow, Ben
Asphalt Jungle. W. R. Burnett
Balcony. J. Genet
Chairman. J. R. Kennedy
Intruder in the Dust. W. Faulkner
Mephisto Waltz. F. M. Stewart

Maddox, Diana
Amateur. R. Littell

Magnier, Claude
Gazebo. A. Coppel

Mahin, John Lee
Bad Seed. M. Anderson
Beast of the City. J. Lait
Dr. Jekyll and Mr. Hyde. R. L. Stevenson; Strange Case of Dr. Jekyll and Mr. Hyde
Moment to Moment. A. Coppel
Scarface. A. Trail

Maibaum, Richard
Day They Robbed the Bank of England. J. Brophy
Diamonds Are Forever. I. Fleming
Doctor No. I. Fleming
From Russia with Love. I. Fleming
Goldfinger. I. Fleming
Hell Below Zero. H. Innes; White South
Man Inside. M. E. Chaber
Man with the Golden Gun. I. Fleming
Octopussy. I. Fleming
On Her Majesty's Secret Service. I. Fleming
Spy Who Loved Me. C. Wood; James Bond, the Spy Who Loved Me
They Gave Him a Gun. W. J. Cowen
Thunderball. I. Fleming

Maigne, Charles
In the Hollow of Her Hand. G. B. McCutcheon; Hollow of Her Hand

Mainwaring, Daniel
Catacombs. Jay Bennett
Gun Runners. E. Hemingway; To Have and Have Not

Maiuri, Dino
Payoff. A. Veraldi

Malins, Geoffrey H.
Abbey Grange. A. C. Doyle; Return of Sherlock Holmes
Black Peter. A. C. Doyle; Return of Sherlock Holmes
Blue Carbuncle. A. C. Doyle; Adventures of Sherlock Holmes
Boscombe Valley Mystery. A. C. Doyle; Adventures of Sherlock Holmes
Bruce-Partington Plans. A. C. Doyle; His Last Bow
Cardboard Box. A. C. Doyle; His Last Bow
Charles Augustus Milverton. A. C. Doyle; Return of Sherlock Holmes
Crooked Man. A. C. Doyle; Memoirs of Sherlock Holmes
Dancing Men. A. C. Doyle; Return of Sherlock Holmes
Engineer's Thumb. A. C. Doyle; Adventures of Sherlock Holmes
Final Problem. A. C. Doyle; Memoirs of Sherlock Holmes
Gloria Scott. A. C. Doyle; Memoirs of Sherlock Holmes
Golden Pince-Nez. A. C. Doyle; Return of Sherlock Holmes
Greek Interpreter. A. C. Doyle; Memoirs of Sherlock Holmes
His Last Bow. A. C. Doyle
Lady Frances Carfax. A. C. Doyle; His Last Bow
Mazarin Stone. A. C. Doyle; Casebook of Sherlock Holmes
Missing Three-Quarter. A. C. Doyle; Return of Sherlock Holmes
Musgrave Ritual. A. C. Doyle; Memoirs of Sherlock Holmes
Naval Treaty. A. C. Doyle; Memoirs of Sherlock Holmes
Norwood Builder. A. C. Doyle; Return of Sherlock Holmes
Red Circle. A. C. Doyle; His Last Bow
Reigate Squires. A. C. Doyle; Memoirs of Sherlock Holmes
Second Stain. A. C. Doyle; Return of Sherlock Holmes
Silver Blaze. A. C. Doyle; Memoirs of Sherlock Holmes
Six Napoleons. A. C. Doyle; Return of Sherlock Holmes
Speckled Band. A. C. Doyle; Adventures of Sherlock Holmes
Stock-Broker's Clerk. A. C. Doyle; Memoirs of Sherlock Holmes
Thor Bridge. A. C. Doyle; Casebook of Sherlock Holmes
Three Students. A. C. Doyle; Return of Sherlock Holmes

Malko, George
Dogs of War. F. Forsyth

Malle, Louis
Elevator to the Gallows. N. Calef; Frantic

Malleson, Miles
Rat. P. Bottome
They Met in the Dark. Anthony Gilbert; Vanishing Corpse
W Plan. G. Seton
Yellow Mask. E. Wallace; Traitor's Gate

Mallory, Violet
Within the Law. B. Veiller

Malloy, Doris
Human Cargo. K. Shepard; I Will Be Faithful
Remember Last Night. A. Hobhouse; Hangover Murders

Malmberg, Bertil
Crime and Punishment. F. M. Dostoevskii

Malone, Joel
Crime by Night. G. Homes; Forty Whacks

Maltby, H. F.
Crimes at the Dark House. W. Collins; Woman in White
Sweeney Todd, the Demon Barber of Fleet Street. G. D. Pitt
Ticket-of-Leave Man. T. Taylor

Maltz, Albert
Naked City. M. Wald
This Gun for Hire. G. Greene; Gun for Sale

Mamet, David
Postman Always Rings Twice. J. M. Cain
Verdict. B. C. Reed

Manchette, Jean-Patrick
Undertaker Parlor Computer. W. Kempley; Probability Factor

Mandel, Loring
Little Drummer Girl. J. Le Carre

Mander, Miles
Lodger. M. B. Lowndes

Mankiewicz, Don M.
House of Numbers. J. Finney
Trial. D. M. Mankiewicz

Mankiewicz, Herman J.
Dummy. H. J. O'Higgins
Ladies' Man. R. Hughes

Mankiewicz, Joseph L.
Dragonwyck. A. Seton

Honey Pot. T. Sterling; Evil of the Day
Only Saps Work. O. Davis; Easy Come, Easy Go
Quiet American. G. Greene
Slightly Scarlet. P. Heath

Mankiewicz, Tom
Cassandra Crossing. R. Katz
Diamonds Are Forever. I. Fleming
Eagle Has Landed. J. Higgins
Live and Let Die. I. Fleming
Man with the Golden Gun. I. Fleming
Sweet Ride. W. Murray

Mankowitz, Wolf
Assassination Bureau. J. London
Casino Royale. I. Fleming
House of Fright. R. L. Stevenson; Strange Case of Dr. Jekyll and Mr. Hyde
Where the Spies Are. J. Leasor; Passport to Oblivion

Mann, Abby
Detective. R. Thorp
Report to the Commissioner. J. Mills

Mann, Edward
Killer Inside Me. J. Thompson

Mann, Michael
Keep. F. P. Wilson
Manhunter. T. Harris; Red Dragon

Mann, Stanley
Collector. J. Fowles
Eye of the Needle. K. Follett; Storm Island
Firestarter. Stephen King
Mark. C. E. Israel
Naked Runner. F. Clifford
Russian Roulette. T. Ardies; Kosygin Is Coming
Strange Affair. B. Toms
Woman of Straw. C. Arley

Mannheimer, Albert
Whistling in the Dark. L. Gross

Manning, Bruce
Lone Wolf Returns. L. J. Vance
Meet Nero Wolfe. R. Stout; Fer-de-Lance

Mannock, Patrick L.
Abbey Grange. A. C. Doyle; Return of Sherlock Holmes
Black Peter. A. C. Doyle; Return of Sherlock Holmes
Blue Carbuncle. A. C. Doyle; Adventures of Sherlock Holmes
Boscombe Valley Mystery. A. C. Doyle; Adventures of Sherlock Holmes
Bruce-Partington Plans. A. C. Doyle; His Last Bow
Cardboard Box. A. C. Doyle; His Last Bow
Charles Augustus Milverton. A. C. Doyle; Return of Sherlock Holmes
Crimson Circle. E. Wallace
Crooked Man. A. C. Doyle; Memoirs of Sherlock Holmes
Dancing Men. A. C. Doyle; Return of Sherlock Holmes
Dead Certainty. N. Gould
Engineer's Thumb. A. C. Doyle; Adventures of Sherlock Holmes
Final Problem. A. C. Doyle; Memoirs of Sherlock Holmes
Gloria Scott. A. C. Doyle; Memoirs of Sherlock Holmes
Golden Pince-Nez. A. C. Doyle; Return of Sherlock Holmes
Greek Interpreter. A. C. Doyle; Memoirs of Sherlock Holmes
His Last Bow. A. C. Doyle
Lady Frances Carfax. A. C. Doyle; His Last Bow
Mazarin Stone. A. C. Doyle; Casebook of Sherlock Holmes
Missing Three-Quarter. A. C. Doyle; Return of Sherlock Holmes
Musgrave Ritual. A. C. Doyle; Memoirs of Sherlock Holmes
Naval Treaty. A. C. Doyle; Memoirs of Sherlock Holmes
Norwood Builder. A. C. Doyle; Return of Sherlock Holmes
Rank Outsider. N. Gould
Red Circle. A. C. Doyle; His Last Bow
Reigate Squires. A. C. Doyle; Memoirs of Sherlock Holmes
Second Stain. A. C. Doyle; Return of Sherlock Holmes
Silver Blaze. A. C. Doyle; Memoirs of Sherlock Holmes
Six Napoleons. A. C. Doyle; Return of Sherlock Holmes
Speckled Band. A. C. Doyle; Adventures of Sherlock Holmes
Stock-Broker's Clerk. A. C. Doyle; Memoirs of Sherlock Holmes
Thor Bridge. A. C. Doyle; Casebook of Sherlock Holmes
Three Students. A. C. Doyle; Return of Sherlock Holmes
Trent's Last Case. E. C. Bentley

Mantle, Burns
 Silver King. H. A. Jones
Marceau, Felecien
 Blonde Like That. J. H. Chase; Miss Shumway Waves a Wand
Marchant, William
 My Lover, My Son. E. Grierson; Reputation for a Song
Marcin, Max
 Shadow of the Law. J. A. Moroso; Quarry
Marcus, Larry/Lawrence B.
 Covenant with Death. S. Becker
 Stunt Man. P. Brodeur
Margolin, Arnold
 Russian Roulette. T. Ardies; Kosygin Is Coming
Margolis, Herbert F.
 Larceny. L. Eby; Velvet Fleece
Marion, Frances
 Big House. J. Lait
 Cinema Murder. E. P. Oppenheim; Other Romilly
 Cynara. R. Gore-Brown; Imperfect Lover
 Knight Without Armour. J. Hilton
 Le Pere Goriot. H. Balzac
 Love from a Stranger. F. Vosper
 On Dangerous Ground. B. E. Stevenson; Little Comrade
 Secret Six. F. Marion
 Within the Law. B. Veiller
Marion, George, Jr.
 Fifty Roads to Town. F. Nebel
Marko, Zekial
 Once a Thief. J. Trinian; Scratch a Thief
Markson, Ben
 Case of the Howling Dog. E. S. Gardner
 Case of the Lucky Legs. E. S. Gardner
 White Cockatoo. M. G. Eberhart
Markstein, George
 Odessa File. F. Forsyth
Marlon, Charles
 Mystery of the Thirteenth Guest. A. Trail; Thirteenth Guest
Marlow, Brian
 Forgotten Faces. R. W. Child; Velvet Black
 Murder Goes to College. K. Steel
 Night of June 13. F. Vreeland
 Return of Sophie Lang. F. I. Anderson; Notorious Sophie Lang
 Sophie Lang Goes West. F. I. Anderson; Notorious Sophie Lang
Marlowe, Derek
 Dandy in Aspic. D. Marlowe
Marmorstein, Malcolm
 S*P*Y*S. T. R. Joyce
Marriott, Anthony
 Deadly Bees. H. F. Heard; Taste of Honey
Marsh, Terence
 Finders Keepers. C. Dennis; Next-to-Last Train Ride
Marshak, Darryl A.
 Dracula Sucks. B. Stoker; Dracula
Marshall, Garry
 Grasshopper. M. McShane; Passing of Evil
Marshall, Roger
 And Now the Screaming Starts. D. Case; Fengriffin
 Five to One. E. Wallace; Thief in the Night
 Game for Three Losers. E. Lustgarten
 Man Outside. G. Stackelberg; Double Agent
 Ricochet. E. Wallace; Angel of Terror
 Set-Up. E. Wallace (headnote)
 Solo for Sparrow. E. Wallace; Gunner
 Two-Letter Alibi. A. Garve; Death and the Sky Above
 What Became of Jack and Jill? L. Moody; Ruthless Ones
 Who Was Maddox? E. Wallace; Undisclosed Client
Marston, Theodore
 Aurora Floyd. M. E. Braddon
 East Lynne. H. Wood
Martin, A. Z.
 Mad Room. E. Percy; Ladies in Retirement
Martin, Claude
 Blood and Roses. J. S. Le Fanu; In a Glass Darkly
Martin, Jim
 Black Eye. J. Jacks; Murder on the Wild Side
Martin, Paul
 Orient Express. G. Greene; Stamboul Train
Martin, Troy Kennedy
 Italian Job. T. K. Martin
Marton, Pierre
 Arabesque. Alex Gordon; Cipher
Martyn, Wyndham
 Silver Car. W. Martyn; Secret of the Silver Car

Maselli, Francesco
 Fine Pair. C. Stratton
Mason, Basil
 Candles at Nine. Anthony Gilbert; Mouse Who Wouldn't Play Ball
 Crackerjack. W. B. M. Ferguson
 Death at Broadcasting House. V. Gielgud
 House of the Spaniard. A. Behrend
 Jewel. E. Wallace (headnote)
Mason, Howard
 Follow That Horse. H. Mason; Photo Finish
Mason, Paul
 Ladies Club. Betty Black; Sisterhood
Masson, Rene
 Diabolique. P. Boileau; Woman Who Was
Masters, Ian
 Osterman Weekend. R. Ludlum
Matalon, Eddy
 Too Small, My Friend. J. H. Chase; Way the Cookie Crumbles
Mather, Berkley
 Doctor No. I. Fleming
Matheson, Richard
 Devil Rides out. D. Wheatley
 Die! Die! My Darling. A. Blaisdell; Nightmare
 Dracula. B. Stoker
 Legend of Hell House. R. Matheson; Hell House
 Pit and the Pendulum. L. Sheridan
 Raven. E. Sudak
 Tales of Terror. E. Sudak
Mathis, June
 Blind Man's Eyes. W. MacHarg
 Hate. W. Camp; Communicating Door
 Island of Intrigue. I. Ostrander
 Way of the Strong. R. Cullum
Mattson, Arne
 Black Sun. P. Wahloo; Lorry
Mauchette, Jean-Patrick
 Act of Aggression. J. Buell; Shrewsdale Exit
Maugham, Robin
 Intruder. R. Maugham; Line on Ginger
May, Elaine
 New Leaf. J. Ritchie
Mayer, Edwin Justus
 Phantom of Paris. G. Leroux; Cheri-Bibi and Cecily
Mayersberg, Paul
 Disappearance. D. Marlowe; Echoes of Celandine
Mayes, Wendell
 Anatomy of a Murder. R. Traver
 Bank Shot. D. E. Westlake
 Death Wish. B. Garfield
 Love and Bullets. J. Heddon
 Way to the Gold. W. D. Steele; Way to Gold
Mayfield, Julian
 Uptight. L. O'Flaherty; Informer
Maylam, Tony
 Riddle of the Sands. E. Childers
Meade, Walter
 Brandy for the Parson. G. Household; Tales of Adventurers
 High Command. L. Robinson; General Goes Too Far
Mear, H(arry) Fowler
 Alibi. M. Morton
 Anything Might Happen. H. Balfour
 Bella Donna. R. Hichens
 Black Coffee. A. Christie
 Chinese Puzzle. M. Bower
 Condemned to Death. G. Goodchild; Jack O'Lantern
 Death Croons the Blues. J. Ronald
 Dusty Ermine. N. Grant
 Excess Baggage. H. M. Raleigh
 Juggernaut. A. Campbell
 Last Hour. C. Bennett
 Last Journey. J. J. Farjeon; Holiday Express
 Lily of Kilarney. D. Boucicault; Colleen Bawn
 Lord Edgware Dies. A. Christie
 Lyons Mail. 2. Moreau; Courier of Lyons
 Man Outside. D. Stuart
 Man Who Changed His Name. E. Wallace
 Murder at Covent Garden. W. J. Makin
 Pointing Finger. Rita
 Professional Guest. W. Garrett
 Roof. D. Whitelaw
 Shadow. D. Stuart
 Shot in the Dark. G. Fairlie
 Silent House. J. G. Brandon
 Silver Blaze. A. C. Doyle
 Tangled Evidence. P. C. De Crespigny
 Valley of Fear. A. C. Doyle
Meckert, Jean
 Look Out, Girls. J. H. Chase; Miss Callaghan Comes to Grief
Medford, Harold
 Phantom of the Rue Morgue. E. A. Poe; Prose Romances of Edgar A. Poe
Medioli, Enrico
 Once Upon a Time in America. H. Grey; Hoods

Medoff, Mark
 Good Guys Wear Black. M. Franklin
Medwin, Michael
 My Sister and I. E. Bonett; High Pavement
Meehan, Elizabeth
 Mr. Reeder in Room 13. E. Wallace; Room 13
Meehan, John, Jr.
 Jump for Glory. G. McDonell
 Letty Lynton. M. B. Lowndes
 Madame X. J. C. MacConaughy
 Phantom of Paris. G. Leroux; Cheri-Bibi and Cecily
 Ten Days in Paris. B. Graeme; Disappearance of Roger Tremayne
 Thank Evans. E. Wallace; Good Evans!
Mekas, Adolfas
 Double-Barrelled Detective Story. M. Twain
Melford, Austin
 Don Chicago. C. E. B. Roberts
 Phantom Light. E. Price; Haunted Light
 Road House. W. Hackett
 Seven Sinners. A. Ridley; Wrecker
 Thank Evans. E. Wallace; Good Evans!
Melson, John
 Love and Bullets. J. Heddon
Meltzer, Lewis
 Brothers Rico. G. Simenon
 First Comes Courage. E. Arnold; Commandos
 High School Confidential. Morton Cooper
Melville, Jean-Pierre
 Magnet of Doom. G. Simenon
Mendeluk, George
 Stone Cold Dead. H. Garner; Sin Sniper
Menger, W. H.
 Blindfold. L. Fletcher
Mercer, David
 Maroc 7. M. Sands
Meredyth, Bess
 Great Hospital Mystery. M. G. Eberhart (headnote)
 Phantom of Paris. G. Leroux; Cheri-Bibi and Cecily
 Strangers of the Night. W. Hackett; Captain Applejack
Merivale, Bernard
 Condemned to Death. G. Goodchild; Jack O'Lantern
Merwin, Bannister
 Rogue in Love. T. Gallon
 Turf Conspiracy. N. Gould
Mesnier, Paul
 Cheri-Bibi. G. Leroux
Metzger, Radley
 Cat and the Canary. J. Willard
Meyer, Nicholas
 Seven-Per-Cent Solution. N. Meyer
 Time After Time. K. Alexander
Meyer, Rolf
 His Official Wife. R. H. Savage; My Official Wife
Michaels, Sidney
 Key Witness. F. Kane
Michel, Bernard T.
 Five Ashore for Singapore. J. Bruce; Cold Spell
Mida, Massimo
 House of Intrigue. H. J. Giskes; London Calling North Pole
Miles, Christopher
 Maids. J. Genet
Milius, John
 Dillinger. H. Clement
 Magnum Force. M. Valley
Millar, Ronald
 Never Let Me Go. R. Bax; Came the Dawn
 So Evil My Love. J. Shearing; For Her to See
Millard, Oscar
 Dead Ringer. R. Thomas
 Reward. M. Barrett
 Salzburg Connection. H. MacInnes
Miller, Albert G.
 Spider's Web. A. Christie
Miller, Alice D. G.
 Four Walls. D. Burnet
Miller, Claude
 Inquisitor. J. Wainwright; Brainwash
 Tell Him I Love Him. P. Highsmith; This Sweet Sickness
Miller, Francis
 Inquest. M. Barringer
 Trunk Crime. E. Percy
Miller, Frank
 Bleak House. C. Dickens
 False Evidence. E. P. Oppenheim
 Joyous Adventures of Aristide Pujol. W. J. Locke
Miller, Harvey
 Jekyll and Hyde...Together Again. R. L. Stevenson; Strange Case of Dr. Jekyll and Mr. Hyde

Miller, Irene
　Jo, the Crossing Sweeper. C. Dickens; Bleak House
Miller, J. Clarkson
　Moral Sinner. C. M. S. McLellan; Leah Kleschna
Miller, J. P.
　Behold a Pale Horse. E. Pressburger; Killing a Mouse on Sunday
　Young Savages. E. Hunter; Matter of Conviction
Miller, Max
　I Cover the Waterfront. Max Miller
Miller, Seton I.
　Charlie Chan's Courage. E. D. Biggers; Chinese Parrot
　Convicted. M. Flavin; Criminal Code
　Criminal Code. M. Flavin
　"G" Men. H. K. Long
　Last Mile. J. Wexley
　Ministry of Fear. G. Greene
　Murder in Trinidad. J. W. Vandercook
　Murder on a Honeymoon. S. Palmer; Puzzle of the Pepper Tree
　Penitentiary. M. Flavin; Criminal Code
　Scarface. A. Trail
　Singapore. W. Bogart
　Two in the Dark. G. Burgess; Two O'Clock Courage
Miller, Sigmund
　Wicked As They Come. B. Ballinger; Portrait in Smoke
Miller, Victor
　Stranger Is Watching. M. H. Clark
Millhauser, Bertram
　Black Secret. R. W. Chambers; In Secret
　Enter Arsene Lupin. M. Leblanc; Girl with the Green Eyes
　Garden Murder Case. S. S. Van Dine
　Pearl of Death. A. C. Doyle; Return of Sherlock Holmes
　River's End. J. O. Curwood
　Romance of Elaine. A. B. Reeve
　Sherlock Holmes. W. Gillette
　Sherlock Holmes and the Spider Woman. A. C. Doyle; Study in Scarlet
　Sherlock Holmes Faces Death. A. C. Doyle; Memoirs of Sherlock Holmes
　Suspect. J. Ronald; This Way Out
Millin, Eugene
　My Official Wife. R. H. Savage
Mills, Hugh
　Blackmailed. E. Myers; Mrs. Christopher
　Blanche Fury. J. Shearing
Milne, A. A.
　Birds of Prey. A. A. Milne; Fourth Wall
Milne, Peter
　House of Fear. W. Camp
　Kennel Murder Case. S. S. Van Dine
　Mr. Moto in Danger Island. J. W. Vandercook; Murder in Trinidad
　Murder of Dr. Harrigan. M. G. Eberhart; From This Dark Stairway
　Return of the Terror. E. Wallace; Terror
　Verdict. I. Zangwill; Big Bow Mystery
Milton, David Scott
　Born to Win. M. Roote
Minter, George
　Tread Softly, Stranger. J. Popplewell; Blind Alley
Mintz, Sam
　Cheerful Fraud. K. R. G. Browne; Following Ann
　Only Saps Work. O. Davis; Easy Come, Easy Go
Mitchell, James
　Callan. J. Mitchell; Magnum for Schneider
　Innocent Bystander. J. Munro
　Last Grenade. J. Sherlock; Ordeal of Major Grigsby
Mitchell, Julian
　Arabesque. Alex Gordon; Cipher
Mithois, Marcel
　Heart Trump for OSS 117 in Tokyo. J. Bruce; Hot Line
Mocky, Jean-Pierre
　Kill the Referee. A. Draper; Death Penalty
　No Pockets in a Shroud. H. McCoy
　Red Ibis. F. Brown; Knock Three-One-Two
　Unsewing Machine. G. Brewer; Killer Is Loose
Moessinger, David
　Caper of the Golden Bulls. W. P. McGivern
Moffat, Ivan
　Black Sunday. T. Harris
　Boy on a Dolphin. D. Divine
Moffitt, John C.
　Mountain Music. M. Kantor; Author's Choice
　Murder with Pictures. G. H. Coxe
Molinaro, Edouard
　Ravishing Idiot. C. Exbrayat

Moll, Elick
　House on Telegraph Hill. D. Lyon; Frightened Child
　Night Without Sleep. E. Moll
Monash, Paul
　Friends of Eddie Coyle. G. V. Kennedy
　Gun Runners. E. Hemingway; To Have and Have Not
Monks, John, Jr.
　Knock on Any Door. W. Motley
　People Against O'Hara. E. Lipsky
Montagnana, Luisi
　Fine Pair. C. Stratton
Montagne, Edward J.
　Man with My Face. S. W. Taylor
　Secrets of the Night. M. Marcin; Nightcap
　Too Many Crooks. E. J. Rath
Montagu, Ivor
　Last Man to Hang. G. Bullett; Jury
Montgomery, Doreen
　At the Villa Rose. A. E. W. Mason
　Bulldog Sees It Through. G. Fairlie; Scissors Cut Paper
　Dead Men Tell No Tales. F. Beeding; Norwich Victims
　Flying Squad. E. Wallace
　House of the Arrow. A. E. W. Mason
　Mr. Reeder in Room 13. E. Wallace; Room 13
　Murder Reported. R. Chapman; Murder for the Million
　Narrowing Circle. J. Symons
　One Jump Ahead. R. Chapman
　Poison Pen. R. Llewellyn
　You Can't Escape. A. Kennington; She Died Young
Montgomery, James
　Ghost Breakers. C. W. Goddard
Moore, Brian
　Torn Curtain. R. Wormser
Moore, Dudley
　Hound of the Baskervilles. A. C. Doyle
Moore, Victoria
　Little Girl in a Big City. J. K. McCurdy
More, Julian
　Catamount Killings. J. H. Chase; I Would Rather Stay Poor
　Doctors Wear Scarlet. S. Raven
More, Sheila
　Catamount Killings. J. H. Chase; I Would Rather Stay Poor
Morgan, Byron
　Five Star Final. L. Weitzenkorn
　Pace That Thrills. R. Weber
Morgan, Diana
　Pink String and Sealing Wax. R. Pertwee
Morgan, Guy
　Front Page Story. R. Gaines; Final Night
　Hell Is Sold Out. M. Dekobra
　Man in the Road. A. Armstrong; He Was Found in the Road
Morgan, Sidney
　Bid for Fortune. G. Boothby
　Bulldog Drummond's Third Round. H. C. McNeile; Third Round
　Miriam Rozella. B. L. Farjeon
　What's Bred...Comes Out in the Flesh. G. Allen; What's Bred in the Bone
　Woman of the Iron Bracelets. F. Barrett
Morhaim, Joe
　Man of Bronze. K. Robeson
Morheim, Louis
　Hunting Party. J. Millard
　Larceny. L. Eby; Velvet Fleece
　Rumble on the Docks. F. Paley
Morland, Nigel
　Mrs. Pym of Scotland Yard. N. Morland (headnote)
Morphett, Tony
　Robbery Under Arms. R. Boldrewood
Morrison, Greg
　Madhouse. Angus Hall; Qualtrough
Morrison, T. J.
　To the Public Danger. P. Hamilton; Money with Menaces
Morrissey, Paul
　Hound of the Baskervilles. A. C. Doyle
Mortimer, John
　Act of Mercy. F. Clifford
　Bunny Lake Is Missing. E. Piper
　Innocents. H. James; Turn of the Screw
　Running Man. S. Smith; Ballad of the Running Man
Mortimer, Penelope
　Bunny Lake Is Missing. E. Piper
Moses, Andrew
　Green Eyes. H. Ashbrook; Murder of Steven Kester
　Murder on the Campus. W. Chambers; Campanile Murders
Mosley, Leonard
　Foxhole in Cairo. L. Mosley; Cat and the Mice

Moury, Alain
　No Pockets in a Shroud. H. McCoy
Moussy, Marcel
　Shoot the Pianist. D. Goodis; Down There
Muelbauer, Wolfgang
　Man Who Went Up in Smoke. M. Sjowall
Mulhauser, James
　Love Letters of a Star. Rufus King; Case of the Constant God
Muller, Robert
　Woman of Straw. C. Arley
Mullin, Eugene
　Mr. Barnes of New York. A. C. Gunter
　Within the Law. B. Veiller
Murfin, Jane
　Crime Doctor. I. Zangwill; Big Bow Mystery
　Seven Keys to Baldpate. E. D. Biggers
Murillo, Mary
　East Lynne. H. Wood
　Ringer. E. Wallace
　Sign on the Door. C. Pollock
　Tangled Lives. W. Collins; Woman in White
Murphy, Dennis
　Eye of the Devil. P. Loraine; Day of the Arrow
Murphy, Richard
　Compulsion. M. Levin
　Cry of the City. H. E. Helseth; Chair for Martin Rome
　Kidnapping of the President. C. Templeton
Murphy, Warren B.
　Eiger Sanction. Trevanian
Mycroft, Walter C.
　Murder. C. Dane; Enter Sir John
　Yellow Mask. E. Wallace; Traitor's Gate
Myers, Henry
　Father Brown, Detective. G. K. Chesterton; Wisdom of Father Brown
　Murder by the Clock. Rufus King
Myers, Peter
　Action of the Tiger. J. Wellard
Myton, Fred
　Half a Chance. F. S. Isham
　Murder Is My Business. B. Halliday
　One Hour Before Dawn. M. Scott; Behind Red Curtains
　Social Buccaneer. F. S. Isham
Myton, Kennedy
　Parisian Nights. R. Goyne
Nakano, Desmond
　Boulevard Nights. D. Gram
Narcejac, Thomas
　Letters to an Unknown Lover. P. Boileau; Prisoner
　She Wolves. P. Boileau; Prisoner
Nash, J. E.
　Madame X. J. W. MacConaughy
　Under the Lash. A. Askew; Shulamite
Nash, Michael
　Lost Continent. D. Wheatley; Uncharted Seas
Natkin, Rick
　Night of the Juggler. W. P. McGivern
Natteford, J. Francis
　File 113. E. Gaboriau; File No. 113
　Gun-Runner. A. Stringer
Neame, Derek
　Small Voice. R. Westerby
Neame, Ronald
　Golden Salamander. V. Canning
Nebenzal, Harold
　Wilby Conspiracy. P. Driscoll
Neill, Roy William
　Scarlet Claw. A. C. Doyle; Hound of the Baskervilles
Nelson, Ralph
　Wrath of God. J. Graham
Nerz, Ludwig
　Hands of Orlac. M. Renard
Neuberg, A.
　Trick Baby. I. Slim
Neuman, E. Jack
　Venetian Affair. H. MacInnes
Newall, Guy
　Chin-Chin-Chinaman. P. Walsh
　Maid of the Silver Sea. J. Oxenham
Newhouse, David
　Point Blank. R. Stark; Hunter
Newhouse, Rafe
　Point Blank. R. Stark; Hunter
Newman, David
　Bonnie and Clyde. B. Hirschfeld
Newman, Walter
　Bloodbrothers. R. Price
　Crime and Punishment USA. F. M. Dostoevskii; Crime and Punishment
Niblo, Fred, Jr.
　Convicted. M. Flavin; Criminal Code
　Criminal Code. M. Flavin
　Nine Lives Are Not Enough. J. Odlum
　Passage from Hong Kong. E. D. Biggers; Agony Column
　Penitentiary. M. Flavin; Criminal Code
Nichols, Dudley

Fugitive. G. Greene; Power and the Glory
Informer. L. O'Flaherty
Judge Priest. I. S. Cobb; Down Yonder with Judge Priest
Louis Beretti. D. H. Clarke
Man Hunt. G. Household; Rogue Male
Run for the Sun. R. Connell; Variety
Ten Little Indians. A. Christie; Ten Little Niggers
Ten Little Niggers. A. Christie

Nicolaysen, Bruce
  Passage. B. Nicolaysen; Perilous Passage
Nimier, Roger
  Affair of Nina B. J. M. Simmel
  Elevator to the Gallows. N. Calef; Frantic
Nobles, William
  Scarlet Weekend. W. Kent; Woman in Purple Pajamas
Nolan, William F.
  Burnt Offerings. R. Marasco
Nolbandov, Sergei
  Amateur Gentleman. J. Farnol
  Four Just Men. E. Wallace
  There Ain't No Justice. J. Curtis
Norman, Marc
  Killer Elite. R. Rostand
Norris, Chuck
  Invasion U.S.A. J. Frost
North, Edmund H.
  Colorado Territory. W. R. Burnett; High Sierra
  Murder on a Bridle Path. S. Palmer; Puzzle of the Red Stallion
North, Marion
  Sing Sing Nights. H. S. Keeler
Norton, Eleanor Elias
  Dirty Tricks. T. Gifford; Glendower Legacy
Norton, William
  Hunting Party. J. Millard
  Mackenzie Break. S. Shelly; Bowmanville Break
Norton, William, Sr.
  Dirty Tricks. T. Gifford; Glendower Legacy
  Night of the Juggler. W. P. McGivern
Novello, Ivor
  Lodger. M. B. Lowndes
Noy, Wilfred
  Marriage Lines. J. S. Fletcher
Nugent, Elliott
  Unholy Three. T. Robbins
  Whistling in the Dark. L. Gross
Nunez, Victor
  Flash of Green. J. D. MacDonald
Oaksey, John
  Dead Cert. D. Francis
Oboler, Arch
  Escape. E. Vance
O'Brien, Liam
  Diplomatic Courier. P. Cheyney; Sinister Errand
O'Brien, Robert
  Lady on a Train. L. Charteris
O'Brine, Manning
  Murder at Site Three. W. H. Baker; Crime Is My Business
O'Connolly, Jim
  Night Caller. F. Crisp; Night Callers
O'Connor, Manning
  Dressed to Kill. R. Burke; Dead Take No Bows
  Michael Shayne, Private Detective. B. Halliday; Private Practice of Michael Shayne
O'Connor, Mary
  Dangerous Lies. E. P. Oppenheim (headnote)
  Mystery Road. E. P. Oppenheim
Odell, David
  Cry Uncle. M. Brett; Lie a Little, Die a Little
O'Dell, Denis
  Tread Softly, Stranger. J. Popplewell; Blind Alley
Odets, Clifford
  Deadline at Dawn. W. Irish
  General Died at Dawn. C. G. Booth
O'Donohoe, James T.
  Hawk's Nest. W. Gunning
Offner, Mortimer
  Saint in New York. L. Charteris
O'Flaherty, Dennis
  Hammett. J. Gores
Oguni, Hideo
  High and Low. E. McBain; King's Ransom
O'Hanlon, James
  Slight Case of Murder. D. Runyon
O'Hara, George
  Side Street. M. St. Clair
O'Hara, Gerry
  Bitch. Jackie Collins
O'Hara, Mary
  Love Racket. B. K. Burns; Jury Woman
Oliver, Stephen
  Sunburn. S. Ellin; Bind

O'Neil, Robert Vincent
  Vice Squad. W. Rotsler
Ophuls, Marcel
  Banana Peel. C. Williams; Nothing in the Way
Oppenheimer, George
  I Love You Again. O. R. Cohen
Orde, Julian
  Small Voice. R. Westerby
Orkow, W. Harrison
  Gorilla. R. Spence
Ormonde, Czenzi
  Strangers on a Train. P. Highsmith
Ornitz, Samuel
  Thirteen Women. T. Thayer
Orr, Gertrude
  Blind Goddess. A. Train
  Mandarin Mystery. E. Queen; Chinese Orange Mystery
Orrom, Michael
  No Resting Place. I. Niall
Orth, Marion
  Charlie Chan's Greatest Case. E. D. Biggers; House Without a Key
  Come to My House. A. S. Roche
  People vs. Nancy Preston. J. A. Moroso; People Against Nancy Preston
Orton, J. O. C.
  Bones. E. Wallace
  Cottage to Let. G. Kerr; Cottages to Let
  Ghost Train. A. Ridley
  It's in the Blood. D. Whitelaw; Big Picture
  Non-Stop New York. K. Attiwill; Sky Steward
Orton, Joe
  Celestial City. B. Orczy
Orton, John
  Everything Is Thunder. J. L. Hardy
  Limping Man. W. Scott; Man
  Shooting Stars. E. C. Vivian
Osborn, David
  Deadlier Than the Male. H. Reymond
  Moment of Danger. D. MacKenzie; Scent of Danger
  Murder, She Said. A. Christie; 4.50 from Paddington
  Trap. John Burke
O'Shaughnessy, Alfred
  Brandy for the Parson. G. Household; Tales of Adventurers
Osiecki, Stefan
  No Way Back. T. Burke; Limehouse Nights
Ostrer, Bertram
  Park Plaza 605. B. Gray; Dare-Devil Conquest
Oswald, Richard
  Hound of the Baskervilles. A. C. Doyle
Oya, Ikuko
  Lonely Hearts. E. McBain; Lady, Lady, I Did It!
Packard, Frank L.
  Pawned. F. L. Packard
Pagano, Jo
  Try and Get Me. J. Pagano; Condemned
Page, Marco
  Fast Company. Marco Page
Pal, George
  Man of Bronze. K. Robeson
Pala, Giogio
  Brothers Karamazov. F. M. Dostoevskii
Palmer, Stuart
  Arrest Bulldog Drummond. H. C. McNeile; Final Count
  Bulldog Drummond's Peril. H. C. McNeile; Third Round
  Death of a Champion. F. Gruber; Brass Knuckles
  Who Killed Aunt Maggie? Medora Field
Panduro, Leif
  Ghost Train. A. Ridley
Paramore, Edward E., Jr.
  Baby, Take a Bow. J. P. Judge; Square Crooks
  Trouble for Two. R. L. Stevenson; Suicide Club
Park, Ida May
  Grasp of Greed. H. R. Haggard; Mr. Meeson's Will
Parker, Alan
  Angel Heart. W. Hjortsberg; Falling Angel
Parker, Jefferson
  Human Cargo. K. Shepard; I Will Be Faithful
Parker, William
  Scarlet Car. R. H. Davis
Parrish, James
  Bulldog Drummond at Bay. H. C. McNeile
Parsonnet, Marion
  Dangerous Partners. O. W. Bayer; Paper Chase
  Miracles for Sale. C. Rawson; Death from a Top Hat
  Thirteenth Chair. B. Veiller
Partos, Frank

Guilty As Hell. D. N. Rubin; Riddle Me This!
House on Telegraph Hill. D. Lyon; Frightened Child
Night of Mystery. S. S. Van Dine; Greene Murder Case
Night Without Sleep. E. Moll
Port Afrique. B. V. Dryer
Pascal, Ernest
  Flesh and Fantasy. O. Wilde; Lord Arthur Savile's Crime
  Hound of the Baskervilles. A. C. Doyle
  Interference. R. Pertwee
  Love Under Fire. W. Hackett; Fugitives
Pasley, Fred
  Scarface. A. Trail
Paton, Stuart
  Loot. A. S. Roche
Patrick, John
  Main Attraction. S. Michaels
Patrick, Vincent
  Pope of Greenwich Village. V. Patrick
Patton, N. F.
  Knocknagow. C. Kickham
Paxton, John
  Crack-Up. F. Brown; Madman's Holiday
  Crossfire. R. Brooks; Brick Foxhole
  Farewell, My Lovely. R. Chandler
  Pickup Alley. E. Ronns
  Prize of Gold. M. Catto
Peach, L. Du Garde
  Dusty Ermine. N. Grant
  Ghoul. F. King
  His Lordship. N. Grant; Nelson Touch
  Seven Sinners. A. Ridley; Wrecker
Peacock, John
  To the Devil--a Daughter. D. Wheatley
Peacock, Leslie T.
  Woman Who Dared. A. M. Williamson
Pearson, George
  Angel Esquire. E. Wallace
  Pollard the Punter. E. Wallace; Grey Timothy
Peckinpah, Sam
  Straw Dogs. G. M. Williams; Siege of Trencher's Farm
Pedelty, Donovan
  I'll Never Tell. R. Vickers
Pedrick, Gale
  Meet Simon Cherry. G. Pedrick; Meet the Rev
Pelissier, Anthony
  Personal Affair. L. Storm; Day's Mischief
  Tiger in the Smoke. M. Allingham
Pemberton, Max
  Kronstadt. M. Pemberton
Pentti, Pauli
  Crime and Punishment. F. M. Dostoevskii
People, David
  Blade Runner. P. K. Dick; Do Androids Dream of Electric Sheep?
Perec, Georges
  Thriller Story. J. Thompson; Hell of a Woman
Perkins, Anthony
  Last of Sheila. A. Edwards
Perl, Arnold
  Cotton Comes to Harlem. C. Himes
Perrault, Giles
  Dossier 51. G. Perrault
Perret, Leonce
  Silent Master. E. P. Oppenheim; Seeing Life
  Thirteen Chairs. B. Veiller
  Twin Pawns. W. Collins; Woman in White
Perrin, Nat
  Gracie Allen Murder Case. S. S. Van Dine
Perry, Ben
  Brothers Rico. G. Simenon
Perry, Charles
  Each Dawn I Die. J. Odlum
Perry, Eleanor
  Lady in the Car with Glasses and a Gun. S. Japrisot
Perry, Simon
  Eclipse. N. Wollaston
Pertwee, Michael
  Crackerjack. W. B. M. Ferguson
  Make Mine Mink. P. Coke; Breath of Spring
  Night Was Our Friend. M. Pertwee
  One More Time. M. Avallone
  Salt and Pepper. Alex Austin
  Silent Dust. R. Pertwee; Paragon
Pertwee, Roland
  Four Just Men. E. Wallace
  Ghoul. F. King
  Madonna of the Seven Moons. M. Lawrence
  Murder on the Second Floor. F. Vosper
  Night Invader. J. Bentley; Rendezvous with Death
  Non-Stop New York. K. Attiwill; Sky Steward

Quinney's. H. A. Vachell
Spy in Black. J. S. Clouston
They Came by Night. B. Lyndon
Ware Case. G. Pleydell
Peters, Kenneth
　Vice Squad. W. Rotsler
Petersen, Don
　Target. S. Hunter
Petievich, Gerald
　To Live and Die in L.A. G. Petievich
Petit, Christopher
　Unsuitable Job for a Woman. P. D. James
Petri, Elio
　Quiet Place in the Country. H. Clement
　Tenth Victim. R. Sheckley
Petticlerc, Denne Bart
　Then Came Bronson. W. Johnston
Pettitt, Wilfrid H.
　Walls Came Tumbling Down. J. Eisinger
Peyser, Arnold
　Trouble with Girls. D. Keene; Chautauqua
Peyser, Lois
　Trouble with Girls. D. Keene; Chautauqua
Phelan, Jim
　Night Journey. J. Phelan; Ten-a-Penny People
Philips, Quentin
　Room 13. E. Wallace
Phippeny, Robert
　Night of the Following Day. L. White; Snatchers
Phipps, Nicholas
　Appointment with Venus. J. Tickell
Piedmont, Leon
　Mean Season. J. Katzenbach; In the Heat of Summer
Pierson, Arthur
　Footsteps in the Fog. W. W. Jacobs; Sea Whispers
Pierson, Frank R.
　Anderson Tapes. Lawrence Sanders
　Dog Day Afternoon. P. Mann
　Happening. E. Curry
　Looking Glass War. J. Le Carre
Pieters, Vivian
　Prey. C. Aird; Henrietta Who
Pietrangeli
　Obsession. J. M. Cain; Serenade
Pigott, William
　Lion Man. R. Parrish; Strange Case of Cavendish
Pilcher, Jay
　Steele of the Royal Mounted. J. O. Curwood; Philip Steele of the Royal Northwest Mounted Police
Pinoteau, Claude
　Big Operator. R. Airth; Snatch
Pinter, Harold
　Quiller Memorandum. Adam Hall; Berlin Memorandum
Pires, Gerard
　Act of Aggression. J. Buell; Shrewsdale Exit
　Fantasia Among the Squares. C. Williams; Diamond Bikini
　Undertaker Parlor Computer. W. Kempley; Probability Factor
Piriev, Ivan
　Brothers Karamazov. F. M. Dostoevskii
Pirosh, Robert
　Night of January 16. A. Rand
Pirro, Ugo
　Day of the Owl. L. Sciascia; Mafia Vendetta
Plympton, George H.
　Alibi. G. A. England
　Blind Adventure. E. D. Biggers; Agony Column
　Scarlet Runner. C. N. Williamson
　Winifred the Shop Girl. C. N. Williamson; Shop Girl
Poe, James
　Big Knife. C. Odets
　Dark Page. S. Fuller
　Riot. F. Elli
　Sanctuary. W. Faulkner
　They Shoot Horses, Don't They? H. McCoy
Pogostin, Lee
　High Road to China. J. Cleary
　Nightmare Honeymoon. L. Block (headnote)
Pogue, Charles
　Hound of the Baskervilles. A. C. Doyle
　Sign of the Four. A. C. Doyle
Poland, Joseph Franklin
　Honor First. G. F. Gibbs; Splendid Outcast
Polanski, Roman
　Rosemary's Baby. I. Levin
　Tenant. R. Topor
Pollock, Barry
　Cool Breeze. W. R. Burnett; Asphalt Jungle
Pollock, Max
　On Trial. E. L. Reizenstein

Polonsky, Abraham
　Avalanche Express. C. Forbes
　Force of Evil. I. Wolfert; Tucker's People
　Golden Earrings. Y. Foldes
　Madigan. R. Dougherty; Commissioner
Pooley, Olaf
　Godsend. B. Taylor
Porta, Elvio
　Payoff. A. Veraldi
Porter, Edward S.
　Gentleman Burglar. M. Leblanc (headnote)
Potter, Dennis
　Gorky Park. M. C. Smith
Potter, Paul
　Arsene Lupin. E. Jepson
Powell, A. Van Buren
　Blue Envelope Mystery. S. Kerr; Blue Envelope
Powell, Frank
　Mrs. Balfame. G. Atherton
Powell, Michael
　77, Park Lane. W. Hackett
　Small Back Room. N. Balchin
Powell, Peter
　Human Factor. S. Quinn
Powell, Richard
　My Gun Is Quick. M. Spillane
Pozner, Vladimir
　Conspirators. F. Prokosch
Praskins, Leonard
　Caribbean Mystery. J. W. Vandercook; Murder in Trinidad
　Gentleman's Fate. K. U. P.
Preminger, Erik Lee
　Rosebud. J. Hemingway
Presnell, Robert, Jr.
　Let No Man Write My Epitaph. W. Motley
　Life in the Balance. G. Simenon (headnote)
　Man in the Attic. M. B. Lowndes; Lodger
　Third Day. J. Hayes
　13 West Street. L. Brackett; Tiger Among Us
Presnell, Robert R., Sr.
　Guilty. W. Irish; Dancing Detective
　Man Called Back. A. Soutar; Silent Thunder
Pressburger, Emeric
　Small Back Room. N. Balchin
　Spy in Black. J. S. Clouston
Preston, Trevor
　Slayground. R. Stark
Prevert, Jacques
　Bizarre, Bizarre. J. S. Clouston; His First Offense
Price, Stanley
　Arabesque. Alex Gordon; Cipher
　Golden Rendezvous. A. MacLean
Priestley, J. B.
　Jamaica Inn. D. Du Maurier
Printzlau, Olga
　John Needham's Double. J. Hatton
　Pals First. L. W. Dodd
Prochnik, Leon
　Child's Play. R. Marasco
Proctor, George Dubois
　Other Men's Shoes. A. Soutar
Purcell, Gertrude
　Ellery Queen and the Murder Ring. E. Queen; Dutch Shoe Mystery
　One Night in the Tropics. E. D. Biggers; Love Insurance
Purdell, Reginald
　Dark Tower. A. Woollcott
　It's in the Blood. D. Whitelaw; Big Picture
　Love on the Spot. H. C. McNeile; Three of a Kind
Pursall, David
　Alphabet Murders. A. Christie; ABC Murders
　Murder at the Gallop. A. Christie; After the Funeral
　Murder Most Foul. A. Christie; Mrs. McGinty's Dead
　Murder, She Said. A. Christie; 4.50 from Paddington
　What Changed Charley Farthing? M. Hebden
Purzer, Manfred
　All People Will Be Brothers. J. M. Simmel; Cain '67
　And Jimmy Went to the Rainbow's Foot. J. M. Simmel; Caesar Code
　Love Is Only a Word. J. M. Simmel; Love Is Just a Word
　Only the Wind Knows the Answer. J. M. Simmel; Wind and the Rain
　Stuff That Dreams Are Made Of. J. M. Simmel; Traitor Blitz
Puzo, Mario
　Godfather. M. Puzo
　Godfather, Part II. M. Puzo; Godfather
Quine, Richard
　Notorious Landlady. I. Shulman

Rackin, Martin
　Hell on Frisco Bay. W. P. McGivern; Darkest Hour
Rader, George
　Mr. Potter of Texas. A. C. Gunter
Raewyn, T.
　Trick Baby. I. Slim
Raine, Norman Reilly
　Each Dawn I Die. J. Odlum
Raison, Milton
　Phantom of Forty-Second Street. M. M. Raison
Ralston, Gilbert A.
　Ben. G. A. Ralston
　Willard. S. Gilbert; Ratman's Notebooks
Rameau, Hans Gulder
　Rat. P. Bottome
Rand, Ayn
　Love Letters. C. Massie; Pity My Simplicity
Rank, Christopher
　Passengers. K. R. Dwyer; Chase
Rapf, Maurice
　They Gave Him a Gun. W. J. Cowen
Raphael, Frederic
　Nothing But the Best. S. Ellin; Mystery Stories
Raphaelson, Samson
　Last of Mrs. Cheyney. F. Lonsdale
　Suspicion. F. Iles; Before the Fact
Rappeneau, Elizabeth
　Twin. D. E. Westlake; Two Much!
Raskin, Harry
　Postman Always Rings Twice. J. M. Cain
Rattigan, Terence
　Brighton Rock. G. Greene
Raucher, Herman
　Other Side of Midnight. S. Sheldon
Rauh, Stanley
　Dressed to Kill. R. Burke; Dead Take No Bows
　Michael Shayne, Private Detective. B. Halliday; Private Practice of Michael Shayne
　Sleepers West. F. Nebel; Sleepers East
Ravetch, Irving
　Spikes Gang. G. Tippette; Bank Robber
Rawlinson, A. R.
　Chinese Bungalow. M. Osmond
　Crackerjack. W. B. M. Ferguson
　Dark Secret. M. Shairp; Crime at Blossoms
　Gas Light. P. Hamilton
　Man Who Knew Too Much. R. Alexander
　Meet Simon Cherry. G. Pedrick; Meet the Rev
　My Sister and I. E. Bonett; High Pavement
　News of Paul Temple. F. Durbridge
　Someone at the Door. D. Christie
　Spies of the Air. J. Dell
　Story of Shirley Yorke. H. A. Vachell; Case of Lady Camber
　Strange Boarders. E. P. Oppenheim; Strange Boarders of Palace Crescent
　Ticket-of-Leave Man. T. Taylor
Rayfiel, David
　Three Days of the Condor. J. Grady; Six Days of the Condor
　Valdez Is Coming. E. Leonard
Read, Jan
　Grip of the Strangler. J. C. Cooper
　Secret Tent. E. Addyman
Read, Tom
　Moss Rose. J. Shearing
Rebot, Saddy
　Too Small, My Friend. J. H. Chase; Way the Cookie Crumbles
Reed, Katharine
　Girl in His House. H. MacGrath
Reed, Tom
　Bombay Mail. L. G. Blochman
　Calling Philo Vance. S. S. Van Dine; Kennel Murder Case
　Case of the Curious Bride. E. S. Gardner
　Case of the Velvet Claws. E. S. Gardner
　Florentine Dagger. B. Hecht
　Last Warning. W. Camp; House of Fear
　Murders in the Rue Morgue. E. A. Poe; Prose Romances of Edgar A. Poe
Rees, Joan
　My Sister and I. E. Bonett; High Pavement
Reeve, Arthur B.
　Master Mystery. A. B. Reeve
　Mystery Mind. A. B. Reeve
Reichert, Mark
　Union City. C. Woolrich; Nightwebs
Reid, Alastair
　Something to Hide. N. Monsarrat
Reid, Arthur
　To the Public Danger. P. Hamilton; Money with Menaces
Reid, Dorothy

Reinecker, Herbert
  Squeaker. E. Wallace
Reinhardt, Betty
  Laura. V. Caspary
Reinhardt, John
  River Pirate. C. F. Coe
Reinhardt, Silvia
  Town Without Pity. M. Gregor
Reinits, Rex
  Out of the Clouds. J. Fores; Springboard
Reisch, Walter
  Gas Light. P. Hamilton
  Stopover: Tokyo. J. P. Marquand
Reisman, Del
  Take. G. F. Newman; Sir, You Bastard
Relph, Michael
  Assassination Bureau. J. London
  Man Who Haunted Himself. A. Armstrong; He Was Found in the Road
  Masquerade. V. Canning; Castle Minerva
  Out of the Clouds. J. Fores; Springboard
  Place to Go. M. Fisher; Bethnel Green
  Ship That Died of Shame. N. Monsarrat
  Woman of Straw. C. Arley
Renoir, Jean
  Woman on the Beach. M. A. Wilson; None So Blind
Reville, Alma
  After the Verdict. R. Hichens
  Murder. C. Dane; Enter Sir John
  No. 17. J. J. Farjeon
  Sabotage. J. Conrad; Secret Agent
  Secret Agent. W. S. Maugham; Ashenden
  South Sea Bubble. H. Pertwee
  Stage Fright. S. Jepson; Man Running
  Suspicion. F. Iles; Before the Fact
  Thirty-Nine Steps. J. Buchan
  Young and Innocent. J. Tey; Shilling for Candles
Rey, Henri-Francois
  Waste-Land. H. Ellison; Tomboy
Reynolds, Lynn
  Big-Town Round-Up. W. M. Raine
Richard, Jean-Louis
  Bride Wore Black. C. Woolrich
Richards, Silvia
  Secret Beyond the Door. Rufus King; Museum Piece No. 13
Richardson, Tony
  Dead Cert. D. Francis
Richert, William
  Winter Kills. R. Condon
Richlin, Maurice
  For Pete's Sake. B. Street
  Pink Panther. M. H. Albert
Richter, W. D.
  Dracula. H. Deane
  Peeper. K. Laumer; Deadfall
Ricketts, Thomas
  Secretary of Frivolous Affairs. M. Futrelle
Rickman, Thomas
  Laughing Policeman. M. Sjowall
Ridgely, Richard
  Destroying Angel. L. J. Vance
  Eugene Aram. E. Bulwer-Lytton
Ridgeway, Philip
  Switch. P. Ridgeway
Ridgwell, George
  Four Just Men. E. Wallace
  Joan Danvers. F. Stayton
  Lily of Kilarney. D. Boucicault; Colleen Bawn
Ridley, Roy
  Bedelia. V. Caspary
Rienits, Rex
  Assassin for Hire. R. Rienits
  Noose for a Lady. G. Verner; Whispering Woman
Riesner, Dean
  Charley Varrick. J. Reese; Looters
  Dirty Harry. P. Rock
  Enforcer. W. Morgan
  Play Misty for Me. P. J. Gillette
Rigby, Gordon
  Tiger Rose. W. Mack
Rigby, L. G.
  Whispering Wires. H. Leverage
Riggs, Lynn
  Sherlock Holmes and the Voice of Terror. A. C. Doyle; His Last Bow
Rintels, David W.
  Scorpio. M. Roote
Riskin, Robert
  Night Club Lady. A. Abbot; About the Murder of the Night Club Lady
Ritchey, Will M.
  Arsene Lupin. M. Leblanc (headnote)
  Whispering Smith. F. H. Spearman
Rivkin, Allen
  Cheating Cheaters. M. Marcin
  Love Under Fire. W. Hackett; Fugitives
  Timberjack. D. Cushman
Roach, Janet
  Prizzi's Honor. R. Condon

Robbins, Harold
  Never Love a Stranger. H. Robbins
  Pusher. E. McBain
Robert, Jacques
  Blonde Like That. J. H. Chase; Miss Shumway Waves a Wand
  Maigret Sees Red. G. Simenon; Maigret and the Gangsters
  See Venice and Die. R. Marshall; Mission to Venice
  Seventh Juror. F. Didelot
Robert, Yves
  Twin. D. E. Westlake; Two Much!
Roberts, Ben
  King of the Khyber Rifles. T. Mundy
  Midnight Lace. J. Green; Matilda Shouted Fire
  Portrait in Black. I. Goff
  Serenade. J. M. Cain
  Shake Hands with the Devil. R. Conner
Roberts, Marguerite
  Escape. E. Vance
  Forgotten Faces. R. W. Child; Velvet Black
Roberts, Meade
  Danger Route. A. York; Eliminator
Robinson, Casey
  Diplomatic Courier. P. Cheyney; Sinister Errand
  Scobie Malone. J. Cleary; Helga's Web
  She Made Her Bed. J. M. Cain; Baby in the Icebox
  While the City Sleeps. C. Einstein; Bloody Spur
Robinson, Matt
  Possession of Joel Delaney. R. Stewart
Robison, Arthur
  Trial of Mary Dugan. B. Veiller
Robson, Michael
  Thirty-Nine Steps. J. Buchan
Roddenberry, Gene
  Pretty Maids All in a Row. F. Pollini
Roddick, John
  Death Trap. E. Wallace (headnote)
  Double. E. Wallace
  Partner. E. Wallace; Million Dollar Story
  Return to Sender. E. Wallace (headnote)
  Rivals. E. Wallace; Elegant Edward
Rodgers, Mark
  Let's Kill Uncle. R. O'Grady
Rodman, Howard
  Charley Varrick. J. Reese; Looters
Roeg, Nicolas
  Death Drums Along the River. E. Wallace; Sanders of the River
Roffey, Jack
  Hostile Witness. J. Roffey
Roge, Albert, II
  Wrecker. A. Ridley
Rogers, Howard Emmett
  Assignment in Brittany. H. MacInnes
  Calling Bulldog Drummond. G. Fairlie
  Eyes in the Night. B. Kendrick; Odor of Violets
  Hour of Thirteen. M. Porlock; X v. Rex
  Mystery of Mr. X. M. Porlock; X v. Rex
Rogers, P. Maclean
  Feathered Serpent. E. Wallace
  God's Clay. A. Askew
  Johnny on the Spot. M. Cronin; Paid in Full
  Story of Shirley Yorke. H. A. Vachell; Case of Lady Camber
  You Pay Your Money. M. Cronin
Roland, Sandra Weintraub
  High Road to China. J. Cleary
Rolfe, Sam
  Naked Spur. A. Ullman
Roli, Mino
  Machine Gun McCain. O. Demaris; Candyleg
Roman, Lawrence
  Kiss Before Dying. I. Levin
  McQ. A. Edwards
  Vice Squad. L. T. White; Harness Bull
Romney, Edana
  Corridor of Mirrors. C. Massie
Rooff, Paul
  Branded. G. Biss
  In His Grip. D. C. Murray
  Missioner. E. P. Oppenheim
  Pointing Finger. Rita
Rooke, Arthur
  God's Clay. A. Askew
Roos, William
  Scent of Mystery. K. Roos; Ghost of a Chance
Root, Lynn
  Falcon Takes Over. R. Chandler; Farewell, My Lovely
  Highways by Night. C. B. Kelland; Silver Spoon
  Saint in London. L. Charteris; Holy Terror
Root, Wells

I Cover the Waterfront. Max Miller
  Pursuit. L. G. Blochman
  Secret of Deep Harbor. Max Miller; I Cover the Waterfront
  Shadow of Doubt. A. S. Roche
Roscoe, Judith
  Who'll Stop the Rain? R. Stone; Dog Soldiers
Rose, Jack
  On the Double. Roger Fuller
Rose, Mickey
  Condorman. R. Sheckley; Game of X
Rose, Reginald
  Man in the Net. P. Quentin
  Somebody Killed Her Husband. C. B. Phillips
  Twelve Angry Men. R. Rose
  Who Dares Wins. J. Follett; Tiptoe Boys
  Wild Geese. D. Carney
  Wild Geese II. D. Carney; Square Circle
Rose, William
  Flim Flam Man. G. Owen; Ballad of the Flim Flam Man
  I'll Get You for This. J. H. Chase
  Russians Are Coming, The Russians Are Coming. N. Benchley; Off-Islanders
Rosenbaum, Henry
  Bullet for Pretty Boy. M. Avallone
  Hanky Panky. L. Jarreau
Rosenberg, Sol A.
  Murders in the Rue Morgue. E. A. Poe; Prose Romances of Edgar A. Poe
Rosi, Francesco
  Illustrious Corpses. L. Sciascia; Equal Danger
Ross, J. McLaren
  Strange Awakening. P. Quentin; Puzzle for Fiends
Ross, Kenneth
  Black Sunday. T. Harris
  Day of the Jackal. F. Forsyth
  Odessa File. F. Forsyth
Rossen, Robert
  Desert Fury. R. Stewart; Desert Town
  Out of the Fog. I. Shaw; Gentle People
Rossi, J. B.
  Trap for Cinderella. S. Japrisot
Rosten, Leo
  Conspirators. F. Prokosch
  Sleep My Love. L. Q. Ross
Roth, Eric
  Concorde--Airport 1979. K. Stewart
  Nickel Ride. M. T. Kaufman
Rotha, Paul
  Cat and Mouse. M. Halliday
  Lodger. M. B. Lowndes
  No Resting Place. I. Niall
Rouse, Russell
  House of Numbers. J. Finney
Rouve, Pierre
  Dock Brief. J. Mortimer; Three Plays
  Stranger in the House. G. Simenon; Strangers in the House
Rowden, Walter Courtenay
  East Lynne. H. Wood
  Foul Play. C. Reade
  Hard Cash. C. Reade
  Scallywag. G. Allen
Rowland, Roy
  Girl Hunters. M. Spillane
Ruben, Albert
  Seven-Ups. R. Posner
Ruben, J. Walter
  Roadhouse Murder. M. Level (headnote)
Rubin, Daniel N.
  Dishonored. F. Vreeland
Rubin, Mann
  American Dream. N. Mailer
  First Deadly Sin. Lawrence Sanders
  Warning Shot. W. Masterson; 711--Officer Needs Help
Ruby, Herman
  Gorilla. R. Spence
Ruellan, Andre
  Red Ibis. F. Brown; Knock Three-One-Two
Ruric, Peter
  Grand Central Murder. S. MacVeigh
Ruskin, Harry
  Miracles for Sale. C. Rawson; Death from a Top Hat
Russell, A. J.
  Stiletto. H. Robbins
Russell, Gordon
  House of Dark Shadows. Marilyn Ross
Russell, John
  Side Street. M. St. Clair
Russell, Ray
  Premature Burial. M. H. Danne
Russell, William
  Time to Die. M. Cleri; Six Graves to Munich
Russo, John A.
  Night of the Living Dead. J. Russo
Ruthven, Madeleine
  Dangerous Corner. J. B. Priestley
Ruys, Ton
  Prey. C. Aird; Henrietta Who

Ryan, Don
  Case of the Stuttering Bishop. E. S. Gardner
  On Trial. E. L. Reizenstein
Ryan, Tim
  Mystery of the Thirteenth Guest. A. Trail; Thirteenth Guest
Ryerson, Florence
  Canary Murder Case. S. S. Van Dine
  Casino Murder Case. S. S. Van Dine
  Drums of Jeopardy. H. MacGrath
  Easy Come, Easy Go. O. Davis
  Mysterious Dr. Fu Manchu. S. Rohmer; Mystery of Dr. Fu Manchu
  Wicked Woman. Anne Austin
Sabaroff, Roberts
  Split. R. Stark; Seventh
Sackheim, Jerry
  Strange Door. R. L. Stevenson; New Arabian Nights
Sackheim, William
  First Blood. D. Morrell
Sainderichin, Guy-Patrick
  Man with the Silver Eyes. R. Rossner; End of Someone Else's Rainbow
St. Clair, Malcolm
  Side Street. M. St. Clair
St. George, George
  Orders to Kill. D. Downes
Saint-Hamont, Daniel
  Hold Up. J. Cronley; Quick Change
St. Joseph, Ellis
  Flesh and Fantasy. O. Wilde; Lord Arthur Savile's Crime
Salkow, Sidney
  Murder with Pictures. G. H. Coxe
Salmon, John
  Only When I Larf. L. Deighton
Salt, Waldo
  Gang That Couldn't Shoot Straight. J. Breslin
Samuel, Yvon
  Keep Talking, Baby. D. Keene; Strange Witness
Samuels, Lesser
  Earl of Chicago. Brock Williams
  Long Wait. M. Spillane
Sanderson, Challis
  Murder on the Second Floor. F. Vosper
Sandler, Barry
  Mirror Crack'd. A. Christie; Mirror Crack'd from Side to Side
Sangster, Jimmy
  Curse of Frankenstein. M. Shelley; Frankenstein
  Deadlier Than the Male. H. Reymond
  Intent to Kill. M. Bryan
  Jack the Ripper. S. James
  Man Who Could Cheat Death. B. Lyndon; Amazing Dr. Clitterhouse
  Maniac. M. Brandel; Time of the Fire
  Nanny. E. Piper
  Terror of the Tongs. J. Sangster
Sansom, John
  Dracula, Prince of Darkness. B. Stoker; Dracula
  Face of a Stranger. E. Wallace (headnote)
  To Have and To Hold. E. Wallace (headnote)
  Traitor's Gate. E. Wallace
Santean, Antonio
  Dirty Mary, Crazy Larry. R. Unekis; Chase
Santoni, Joel
  Dead on a Rainy Sunday. Joan Aiken
Sapinsley, Alvin
  Moon of the Wolf. L. H. Whitten
Sarecky, Barney A.
  Drums of Fu Manchu. S. Rohmer
Sargent, Alvin
  Gambit. K. Lane
  I Walk the Line. Madison Jones; Exile
  Straight Time. E. Bunker; No Beast So Fierce
Sargent, E. W.
  Horrible Hyde. R. L. Stevenson; Strange Case of Dr. Jekyll and Mr. Hyde
  Lion and the Mouse. A. Hornblow
Sarns, Robert
  Howling II. G. Brandner
Saslavsky, Luis
  She Wolves. P. Boileau; Prisoner
  Snow Was Black. G. Simenon; Stain on the Snow
Sastre, Angel
  Turn of the Screw. H. James
Saul, Oscar
  Dark Past. J. Warwick; Blind Alley
  Silencers. D. Hamilton
Sautet, Claude
  Arm at the Left. C. Williams; Aground
  Banana Peel. C. Williams; Nothing in the Way
  Little Virtuous. R. Marshall; Short Time to Live
  Pillaged. R. Stark; Score
Sauvajon, Marc-Gilbert
  What a Girl! P. Cheyney; I'll Say She Does
  You Do It, Cutie. P. Cheyney; Your Deal, My Lovely
Saville, Victor
  W Plan. G. Seton
Savory, Gerald
  Young and Innocent. J. Tey; Shilling for Candles
Sayers, Michael
  Casino Royale. I. Fleming
Sayles, John
  Howling. G. Brandner
Scarpelli
  Sunday Woman. C. Fruttero
Schary, Dore
  Fog. V. Williams
Schayer, E. Richard
  Gray Dawn. S. E. White
Schell, Maximilian
  Murder on the Bridge. F. Duerrenmatt; Judge and His Hangman
Schepsi, Fred
  Chant of Jimmie Blacksmith. T. Keneally
Schiffman, Suzanne
  Let It Be Sunday. C. Williams; Long Saturday Night
Schlitt, Robert
  Pyx. J. Buell
Schneck, Stephen
  Inside Out. W. Hughes
Schnee, Charles
  They Live by Night. E. Anderson; Thieves Like Us
Schnee, Thelma
  Father Brown. G. K. Chesterton; Innocence of Father Brown
Schnitzer, Gerald
  Scream in the Dark. J. Odlum; Morgue Is Always Open
Schoenfeld, Bernard C.
  Dark Cover. L. Q. Ross
  Down Three Dark Streets. Gordons; Case File: FBI
  Phantom Lady. W. Irish
  Straight Is the Way. D. Burnet; Four Walls
Schofield, Paul
  That Royle Girl. E. Balmer
Schrader, Paul
  Yakuza. L. Schrader
Schreiber, Edward
  "Mad Dog" Coll. S. Thurman
Schubert, Bernard
  Kind Lady. E. Chodorov
  Mark of the Vampire. M. Coolridge-Rask; London After Midnight
  Public Defender. G. Goodchild; Splendid Crime
  Secret Service. W. Gillette
Schulberg, Budd
  On the Waterfront. B. Schulberg; Waterfront
Schwartz, David R.
  Robin and the Seven Hoods. J. Pearl
Schweig, Bontche
  Come Back, Charleston Blue. C. Himes; Heat's On
Scobie, Brian
  Unsuitable Job for a Woman. P. D. James
Scola, Kathryn
  Glass Key. D. Hammett
Scoponi, Giuseppi
  House of Intrigue. H. J. Giskes; London Calling North Pole
Scott, Allan
  Awakening. B. Stoker; Jewel of the Seven Stars
  Don't Look Now. D. Du Maurier; Not After Midnight
  Spiral Staircase. E. L. White; Some Must Watch
Scott, Leroy
  Partners of the Night. L. Scott
Scott, Peter Graham
  Big Chance. P. Barrington (headnote)
Scully, Mary Alice
  Brooding Eyes. J. Goodwin; Paid in Full
Seabourne, A.
  77 Rue Chalgrin. W. Hackett; 77, Park Lane
Sears, Zelda
  Operator 13. R. W. Chambers; Secret Service Operator 13
  Wicked Woman. Anne Austin
Seaton, George
  Counterfeit Traitor. A. Klein
  36 Hours. C. K. Hittleman
Seay, Charles M.
  It Is Never Too Late to Mend. C. Reade
  Sheep's Clothing. L. J. Vance
Seddon, Jack
  Alphabet Murders. A. Christie; ABC Murders
  Murder at the Gallop. A. Christie; After the Funeral
  Murder Most Foul. A. Christie; Mrs. McGinty's Dead
  Murder, She Said. A. Christie; 4.50 to Paddington
  What Changed Charley Farthing? M. Hebden
Sedgwick, Edward
  Fantomas. P. Souvestre
Seff, Manuel
  Trouble for Two. R. L. Stevenson; Suicide Club
Seiter, William A.
  Cheerful Fraud. K. R. G. Browne; Following Ann
Seitz, George Brackett
  Closing Net. H. C. Rowland
  Exploits of Elaine. A. B. Reeve
  Romance of Elaine. A. B. Reeve
Sellers, Arlene
  Murder on the Bridge. F. Duerrenmatt; Judge and His Hangman
Selznick, David O.
  Paradine Case. R. Hichens
Semple, Lorenzo, Jr.
  Batman. W. Lyon
  Daddy's Gone A-Hunting. Mike St. Clair
  Drowning Pool. J. R. Macdonald
  Fathom. L. Forrester; Girl Called Fathom
  Never Say Never Again. I. Fleming; Thunderball
  Parallax View. L. Singer
  Pretty Poison. S. Geller; She Let Him Continue
  Three Days of the Condor. J. Grady; Six Days of the Condor
Serling, Rod
  Assault on a Queen. J. Finney
  Seven Days in May. F. Knebel
  Yellow Canary. W. Masterson; Evil Come, Evil Go
Setbon, Philippe
  Dead on a Rainy Sunday. Joan Aiken
Sewell, Vernon
  Floating Dutchman. N. Bentley
Seymour, James
  Lawyer Man. M. Trell
  Missing Million. E. Wallace
  Saint Meets the Tiger. L. Charteris; Meet the Tiger
  They Met in the Dark. Anthony Gilbert; Vanishing Corpse
Shaber, David
  Last Embrace. M. T. Bloom; 13th Man
  Warriors. S. Yurick
Shaffer, Anthony
  Death on the Nile. A. Christie
  Evil Under the Sun. A. Christie
  Frenzy. A. La Bern; Goodbye Piccadilly, Farewell Leicester Square
  Sleuth. A. Shaffer
  Wicker Man. R. Hardy
Shagan, Steve
  Formula. S. Shagan
  Hustle. S. Shagan; City of Angels
  Nightwing. M. C. Smith
Shane, Maxwell
  City Across the River. I. Shulman; Amboy Dukes
  Fear in the Night. W. Irish; I Wouldn't Be in Your Shoes
  Fear in the Night. C. Woolrich; Nightmare
  Nightmare. C. Woolrich
  No Hands on the Clock. G. Homes
Shapiro, Stanley
  For Pete's Sake. B. Street
Sharman, Maisie
  Death Goes to School. S. Davis; Death in Seven Hours
  Night Journey. J. Phelan; Ten-a-Penny People
  Reporter. K. Attiwill
Sharp, Alan
  Night Moves. A. Sharp
  Osterman Weekend. R. Ludlum
Sharp, Don
  Bear Island. A. MacLean
  Puppet on a Chain. A. MacLean
  Taste of Excitement. B. Healey; Waiting for a Tiger
Shattuck, Doris
  Ghost That Walks Alone. R. Shattuck; Wedding Guest Sat on a Stone
Shaughnessy, Alfred
  Follow That Horse. H. Mason; Photo Finish
Shavelson, Melville
  On the Double. R. Fuller
  Pigeon That Took Rome. D. Downes; Easter Dinner
Shaw, David
  Man Inside. M. E. Chaber
Shaw, Irwin
  Big Game. F. Wallace
Shearman, Alan
  Bullshot. R. House; Bullshot Crummond
Sheekman, Arthur
  Hazard. R. Chanslor

Sheldon, E. Lloyd
  White Moll. F. Packard
Sheldon, H. S.
  Sherlock Holmes. W. Gillette
Sheldon, Sidney
  Remains to Be Seen. H. Lindsay
Sherdeman, Ted
  Dark Page. S. Fuller
Sherie, Fenn
  Silver King. H. A. Jones
Sherlock, John
  Last Grenade. J. Sherlock; Ordeal of Major Grigsby
Sherman, John
  Face in the Night. B. Graeme; Suspense
Sherman, Joseph
  Death on the Diamond. C. Fitzsimmons
Sherman, Richard
  Four Men and a Prayer. D. Garth
Sherman, Tedd
  Ten Seconds to Hell. L. P. Bachmann; Phoenix
Sherman, Vincent
  Heart of the North. W. B. Mowery
Sherriff, R. C.
  Odd Man Out. F. L. Green
  Old Dark House. J. B. Priestley; Benighted
Sherwood, Robert E.
  Man on a Tightrope. N. Paterson
  Rebecca. D. Du Maurier
Shevelove, Burt
  Wrong Box. R. L. Stevenson
Shields, Tim
  Last Shot You Hear. W. Fairchild; Sound of Murder
Sholder, Jack
  Where Are the Children? M. H. Clark
Shor, Sol
  Drums of Fu Manchu. S. Rohmer
Shrake, Bud
  Nightwing. M. C. Smith
Shrank, Joseph
  Slight Case of Murder. D. Runyon
Shrock, Raymond L.
  Another Man's Shoes. V. Bridges
  Breathless Moment. M. Bryant; Redemption of Richard
  Elusive Isabel. J. Futrelle
  Man Inside. N. S. Lincoln
  Millionaires. E. P. Oppenheim; Inevitable Millionaires
  Phantom of the Opera. G. Leroux
  Strange Disappearance. A. K. Green
Shryack, Dennis
  Flashpoint. G. La Fountaine
  Gauntlet. M. Butler
Sibelius, Johanna
  Waiting Room for the Other Side. R. Marshall; Mission to Siena
Siegel, Barry
  Windows. G. Simenon
Sieveking, Lance
  Third Clue. N. Gordon; Shakespeare Murders
Sigurd, Jacques
  Three Rooms in Manhattan. G. Simenon; Three Beds in Manhattan
Silliphant, Stirling
  Enforcer. W. Morgan
  Five Against the House. J. Finney
  In the Heat of the Night. J. Ball
  Killer Elite. R. Rostand
  Marlowe. R. Chandler; Little Sister
  New Centurians. J. Wambaugh
  Nightfall. D. Goodis
  Slender Thread. S. Silliphant
  Telefon. W. Wager
  Towering Inferno. R. M. Stern; Tower
Silver, Pat
  Ace Up Your Sleeve. J. H. Chase; Ace Up My Sleeve
Silvernail, Clarke
  Behind That Curtain. E. D. Biggers
Silvers, Sid
  Gorilla. R. Spence
Silverstein, David
  Manhattan Love Song. C. Woolrich
  Unknown Blonde. T. D. Irwin; Collusion
Siminon, Albert
  Any Number Can Win. J. Trinian
Simmons, Anthony
  Green Ice. G. A. Browne
Simmons, Michael L.
  Scattergood Baines. C. B. Kelland
Simmons, Richard Alan
  Juggernaut. A. Hine
  Shield for Murder. W. P. McGivern
Simon, Neil
  Cheap Detective. R. Grossbach
  Murder by Death. H. Keating
Simon, Roger L.
  Big Fix. R. L. Simon
Simoun, Henri
  Madigan. R. Dougherty; Commissioner
Simpson, Alan
  Loot. J. Orton
  Spy with a Cold Nose. R. Galton

Simpson, Helen
  Sabotage. J. Conrad; Secret Agent
Sinclair, Andrew
  Blue Blood. A. Thynne; Carry-Cot
Sinclair, Roy
  Dream Street. T. Burke; Limehouse Nights
Siodmak, Kurt/Curt
  Beast with Five Fingers. W. F. Harvey
  Climax. F. J. Lewis
  Non-Stop New York. K. Attiwill; Sky Steward
Siodmak, Robert
  Affair of Nina B. J. M. Simmel
Sisson, Rosemary Anne
  Candleshoe. M. Innes; Christmas at Candleshoe
  Ride a Wild Pony. J. Aldridge; Sporting Proposition
Skutezky, Victor
  Temptation Harbour. G. Simenon; Newhaven-Dieppe
Slesar, Henry
  Murders in the Rue Morgue. E. A. Poe; Prose Romances of Edgar A. Poe
Sloane, Paul H.
  Confidence Man. L. Y. Erskine
  Manhattan. J. Farnol; Definite Object
  Manhattan Knight. G. Burgess; Find the Woman
Sloman, Edward
  Pilgrims of the Night. A. Partridge; Passers-By
Smart, Ralph
  Crime Unlimited. D. Hume
  Phantom Light. E. Price; Haunted Light
Smith, Fred Leon
  One Hour Before Midnight. M. Scott; Behind Red Curtains
Smith, Hamilton
  Scar. E. Gaboriau; File No. 113
Smith, Howard Ellis
  Think Fast, Mr. Moto. J. P. Marquand
Smith, James Bell
  Golden Web. E. P. Oppenheim; Plunderers
Smith, James R.
  Money to Burn. R. W. Kauffman
Smith, Martin Cruz
  Nightwing. M. C. Smith
Smith, Murray
  Bear Island. A. MacLean
Smith, Neville
  Gumshoe. N. Smith
Smith, R. Cecil
  His Wife's Friend. J. B. Harris-Burland; White Rook
Smith, Robert
  Platinum High School. I. Shulman
  Sudden Fear. E. Sherry
Smith, Roger
  CC and Company. M. Roote
Smith, Wallace
  Almost Married. A. Soutar; Devil's Triangle
  Bulldog Drummond. H. C. McNeile
  Seven Keys to Baldpate. E. D. Biggers
Soderberg, Robert W.
  Reckless Moment. E. S. Holding; Blank Wall
Solinas, Franco
  Burn. N. Gant
Solow, Eugene
  Fog Over Frisco. G. Dyer; Five Fragments
  League of Frightened Men. R. Stout
  Patient in Room 18. M. G. Eberhart
  Return of the Terror. E. Wallace; Terror
  While the Patient Slept. M. G. Eberhart
Solt, Andrew
  Bonaventure. C. Hastings
  In a Lonely Place. D. B. Hughes
  Whirlpool. G. Endore; Methinks the Lady--
Somerville, Roy
  Bandbox. L. J. Vance
  First Law. G. Willets
  Teeth of the Tiger. M. Leblanc
Sondheim, Stephen
  Last of Sheila. A. Edwards
Sonego, Rodolfo
  Witness. H. Judd; Shadow of a Doubt
Soskin, Paul
  Waterfront. J. Brophy
Soutar, John
  Last Journey. J. J. Farjeon; Holiday Express
Southern, Terry
  Dr. Strangelove. P. Bryant; Two Hours to Doom
Spaak, Charles
  Ardent Room. J. D. Carr; Burning Court
  Crime and Punishment. F. M. Dostoevskii
  Last Turning. J. M. Cain; Postman Always Rings Twice

Majestic Hotel Cellars. G. Simenon; Maigret and the Hotel Majestic
  Panique. G. Simenon; Mr. Hire's Engagement
Spence, Ralph
  Death on the Diamond. C. Fitzsimmons
  Gorilla. R. Spence
  Lunatic at Large. J. S. Clouston
  Murder in the Private Car. E. E. Rose; Rear Car
  Strangers on a Honeymoon. E. Wallace; Northing Tramp
Spencer, Ray
  Crack-Up. F. Brown; Madman's Holiday
Spencer, Richard V.
  Paradise Garden. G. F. Gibbs
  Pidgin Island. H. MacGrath
Spewack, Samuel
  Secret Witness. S. Spewack; Murder in the Gilded Cage
Spiegel, Larry
  Book of Numbers. R. D. Pharr
Spies, Adrian
  Dark of the Sun. W. Smith; Train from Katanga
  Scorpio Letters. V. Canning
Spigelgass, Leonard
  Law and the Lady. F. Lonsdale; Last of Mrs. Cheyney
  So Evil My Love. J. Shearing; For Her to See
Spillane, Mickey
  Girl Hunters. M. Spillane
Squiers, Lucita
  Gamble with Hearts. A. Carlyle
Squire, Anthony
  Intruder. R. Maugham; Line on Ginger
Stallings, Laurence
  Sun Shines Bright. I. S. Cobb; Old Judge Priest
Stallone, Sylvester
  Cobra. P. Gosling; Running Duck
  First Blood. D. Morrell
  Rambo: First Blood Part II. D. Morrell
Stannard, Eliot
  American Prisoner. E. Phillpotts
  Beautiful Jim, of the Blankshire Regiment. J. S. Winter
  Case of Jonathan Drew. M. B. Lowndes; Lodger
  Chick. E. Wallace
  Colleen Bawn. D. Boucicault
  Diamond Man. E. Wallace (headnote)
  Ernest Maltravers. E. Bulwer-Lytton
  Grip. J. S. Winter
  Hate Ship. B. Graeme
  Hutch Stirs 'Em Up. H. Hancock; Hawk of Rede
  Justice. J. Galsworthy
  Lady Audley's Secret. M. E. Braddon
  Little Hour of Peter Wells. D. Whitelaw
  Mord Em'ly. W. P. Ridge
  Mystery of a Hansom Cab. F. Hume
  Nets of Destiny. M. Drake; Salving of a Derelict
  Nonconformist Parson. R. Horniman
  Silver Bridge. H. P. Lewis
  Through Fire and Water. V. Bridges; Greensea Island
Stanton, Dane
  Still Waters Run Deep. T. Taylor
Starling, Lynn
  Cat and the Canary. J. Willard
  Climax. F. J. Lewis
  Cynara. R. Gore-Brown; Imperfect Lover
  President Vanishes. Anonymous
Starr, Ben
  Busy Body. D. E. Westlake
  Our Man Flint. J. Pearl
Starr, James A.
  In the Next Room. E. R. Belmont
  In the Next Room. B. E. Stevenson; Mystery of the Boule Cabinet
Statter, Arthur F.
  Voice in the Dark. R. E. Dyar
Steck, H. Tipton
  Phantom Buccaneer. V. Bridges; Another Man's Shoes
Stefano, Joseph
  Naked Edge. M. Ehrlich; First Train to Babylon
  Psycho. R. Bloch
Steppling, John
  Fifty-Two Pickup. E. Leonard
Sterling, Stewart
  Having Wonderful Crime. C. Rice
Stevens, Louis
  Bronze Bell. L. J. Vance
  Easy Pickings. P. Cruger
  God's Prodigal. A. J. Russell
Stevenson, Robert
  Calendar. E. Wallace
  Ringer. E. Wallace
  Ware Case. G. Pleydell
Stewart, Donald Ogden
  Moment of Danger. D. MacKenzie; Scent of Danger

Stewart, Ramona
   Desert Fury. R. Stewart; Desert Town
Stewart, Robert
   Backfire! E. Wallace (headnote)
   Danger Route. A. York; Eliminator
   Downfall. E. Wallace (headnote)
   Marriage of Convenience. E. Wallace; Three Oak Mystery
   Never Mention Murder. E. Wallace (headnote)
   Partners in Crime. E. Wallace; Man Who Knew
   Playback. E. Wallace (headnote)
   Sinister Man. E. Wallace
   Vengeance. C. Siodmak; Donovan's Brain
Stinson, Joseph C.
   Stick. E. Leonard
   Sudden Impact. J. C. Stinson
Stock, Ralph
   Rome Express. R. Alexander
Stolpe, Sven
   Crime and Punishment. F. M. Dostoevskii
Stone, Andrew L.
   Cry Terror. A. L. Stone
   Decks Ran Red. A. L. Stone
   Julie. A. L. Stone
Stone, John
   Black Watch. T. Mundy; King of the Khyber Rifles
   Fugitives. R. H. Davis; Exiles
   Great K&A Train Robbery. P. L. Ford
Stone, Oliver
   Eight Million Ways to Die. L. Bloch
   Hand. M. Brandel; Lizard's Tail
   Scarface. A. Trail
   Year of the Dragon. R. Daley
Stone, Peter
   Charade. P. H. Stone
   Mirage. W. Ericson; Fallen Angel
   Silver Bears. P. E. Erdman
   Taking of Pelham One Two Three. J. Godey
   Who Is Killing the Great Chefs of Europe? N. Lyons; Someone Is Killing the Great Chefs of Europe
Stone, Robert
   Who'll Stop the Rain? R. Stone; Dog Soldiers
Stone, Virginia
   Decks Ran Red. A. L. Stone
Stoppard, Tom
   Despair. V. Nabokoff-Sirin
   Human Factor. G. Greene
Storch, Wolfgang
   Two Faces of January. P. Highsmith
Storm, Lesley
   Fallen Idol. G. Greene; Basement Room and other stories
   Golden Salamander. V. Canning
   Heart of the Matter. G. Greene
   Ringer. E. Wallace
Story, Jack Trevor
   Live Now, Pay Later. J. T. Story
Streeter, Coolidge
   Ramshackle House. H. Footner
Stringer, Arthur
   Story Without a Name. A. Stringer
Strucby, Katherine
   High Command. L. Robinson; General Goes Too Far
   Meet Maxwell Archer. H. Clevely; Archer Plus 20
   Shop at Sly Corner. E. Percy; Play with Fire
Strumwasser, Jack
   Times Have Changed. E. Davis
   Yosemite Trail. R. Cullum; One-Way Trail
Strutton, Bill
   Assignment K. H. Howard; Department K
Stuart, Alexander
   Ordeal by Innocence. A. Christie
Stuart, Katherine
   Jeanne of the Marshes. E. P. Oppenheim
Stuart, Kathryn
   Cheating Cheaters. M. Marcin
Sturdivant, Marc
   Condorman. R. Sheckley; Game of X
Stuyvesant, Eve
   Leavenworth Case. A. K. Green
Subotsky, Milton
   Last Mile. J. Wexley
   I, Monster. R. L. Stevenson; Strange Case of Dr. Jekyll and Mr. Hyde
   Skull. R. Bloch; Skull of the Marquis de Sade
Sullivan, C. Gardner
   Boomerang. W. H. Osborne
   Father Brown, Detective. G. K. Chesterton; Wisdom of Father Brown
   Locked Door. C. Pollock; Sign on the Door
   Three Faces East. A. P. Kelly
Sullivan, Fred G.
   Cold River. W. Judson
Summers, Walter
   Black Limelight. G. Sherry

Dark Eyes of London. E. Wallace
Dead Men Tell No Tales. F. Beeding; Norwich Victims
House Opposite. J. J. Farjeon
Limping Man. W. Scott; Man
Return of Bulldog Drummond. H. C. McNeile; Black Gang
Traitor Spy. T. C. H. Jacobs
What Happened Then? L. T. Bradley
Sutherland, Sidney
   Leavenworth Case. A. K. Green
Swerling, Jo
   Behind the Mask. E. P. Oppenheim; Jeanne of the Marshes
   Circus Queen Murder. A. Abbot; About the Murder of the Circus Queen
   Leave Her to Heaven. B. A. Williams
   Wrecker. A. Ridley
Swift, David
   Candleshoe. M. Innes; Christmas at Candleshoe
Sydeny, R.
   Blood Relatives. E. McBain
Sylvaine, Vernon
   Warn That Man. V. Sylvaine
Tabet, Andre
   Ravishing Idiot. C. Exbrayat
   Snow Was Black. G. Simenon; Stain on the Snow
Tabet, Georges
   Ravishing Idiot. C. Exbrayat
Tabori, George
   Secret Ceremony. M. Denevi
Tabori, Paul
   Malpas Mystery. E. Wallace; Face in the Night
   Mantrap. S. Rattray; Queen in Danger
Taggart, Brian
   Visiting Hours. K. Rembo
Talbot, Rowland
   London by Night. C. Selby
Tallman, Robert
   Slightly Honorable. F. G. Presnell; Send Another Coffin
Tanchuck, Nathaniel
   Shuttered Room. J. Withers
Taradash, Daniel
   Don't Bother to Knock. C. Armstrong; Mischief
   Knock on Any Door. W. Motley
   Morituri. W. J. Luddecke
   Other Side of Midnight. S. Sheldon
Tarkington, Booth
   Millionaire. E. D. Biggers; Earl Derr Biggers Tells Ten Stories
Tarloff, Frank
   Double Man. H. S. Maxfield; Legacy of a Spy
   Once You Kiss a Stranger. P. Highsmith; Strangers on a Train
Tarshis, Harold
   Fast Company. Marco Page
Tashlin, Frank
   Caprice. J. Withers
Tavernier, Bertrand
   Population 1280. J. Thompson; Pop. 1280
Taylor, Charles A.
   Outsider. L. J. Vance; Nobody
Taylor, David
   Hanky Panky. L. Jarreau
Taylor, Donald
   Devil's Daffodil. E. Wallace; Daffodil Mystery
   Foxhole in Cairo. L. O. Mosley; Cat and the Mice
   Hands of Orlac. M. Renard
   Jolly Bad Fellow. C. E. Vulliamy; Don Among the Dead Men
   Straw Man. D. M. Disney
Taylor, Dwight
   Boy on a Dolphin. D. Divine
   I Wake Up Screaming. S. Fisher
   Nightmare. M. Porlock; Mystery in Kensington Gore
   Vicki. S. Fisher; I Wake Up Screaming
   When Tomorrow Comes. J. M. Cain; Serenade
Taylor, Eric
   Ellery Queen and the Murder Ring. E. Queen; Dutch Shoe Mystery
   Ellery Queen and the Perfect Crime. E. Queen; Perfect Crime
   Ellery Queen, Master Detective. E. Queen
   Ellery Queen's Penthouse Mystery. E. Queen; Penthouse Mystery
   Lady in the Morgue. J. Latimer
   Phantom of the Opera. G. Leroux
Taylor, Kenneth
   Beyond This Place. A. J. Cronin
Taylor, Kressmann
   Address Unknown. K. Taylor
Taylor, Matt
   Lion and the Lamb. E. P. Oppenheim
Taylor, Reeve
   Midnight Episode. G. Simenon; Monsieur la Souris
Taylor, Rex
   Cheerful Fraud. K. R. G. Browne;

Following Ann
Mandarin Mystery. E. Queen; Chinese Orange Mystery
Reckless Age. E. D. Biggers; Love Insurance
Too Many Crooks. E. J. Rath
Taylor, S. E. V.
   Lone Wolf. L. J. Vance
Taylor, Samuel W.
   Cat's Paw. C. B. Kelland
   Gambler. C. Klein
   Man with My Face. S. W. Taylor
   Topaz. L. Uris
   Vertigo. P. Boileau; Living and the Dead
Taylor, Stephen
   Man Who Would Not Die. C. Williams; Sailcloth Shroud
Taylor, Valerie
   Take My Life. Winston Graham
Templeton, William
   Double Confession. J. Garden; All on a Summer's Day
   Fallen Idol. G. Greene; Basement Room and other stories
   Midnight Episode. G. Simenon; Monsieur la Souris
Tennant, William
   Cleopatra Jones and the Casino of Gold. R. Goulart
Tennyson, Pen
   There Ain't No Justice. J. Curtis
Terrett, Courtney
   Love Is a Racket. R. James
Terriss, Tom
   Lion and the Mouse. A. Hornblow
   Mystery of Edwin Drood. C. Dickens
Terwilliger, George W.
   Gamblers. C. Klein
Tesich, Steve
   Eleni. N. Gage
   Eyewitness. J. Minahan
Tewkesbury, Joan
   Thieves Like Us. E. Anderson
Thew, Harvey
   Argyle Case. H. Ford
   Cheerful Fraud. K. R. G. Browne; Following Ann
   Death on the Diamond. C. Fitzsimmons
   Duds. H. C. Rowland
   Four Days' Wonder. A. A. Milne
   Operator 13. R. W. Chambers; Secret Service Operator 13
   Public Enemy. K. Glasmon
   Raffles, the Amateur Cracksman. E. W. Hornung; Amateur Cracksman
   Tiger Rose. W. Mack
   Woman's Law. Maravene Thompson
Thoeren, Robert
   Act of Murder. E. Lothar; Mills of God
   Captain Carey, U.S.A. M. Albrand; After Midnight
   Rage in Heaven. J. Hilton
   Singapore. W. Bogart
   Temptation. R. Hichens; Bella Donna
Thom, Robert
   Angel, Angel, Down We Go. W. Johnston
   Bloody Mama. R. Thom
Thomas, Dylan
   Three Weird Sisters. C. Armstrong; Case of the Weird Sisters
Thomas, Leslie
   Dangerous Davies. L. Thomas
Thomas, Michael
   McGuffin. J. Bowen
Thomas, Ross
   Hammett. J. Gores
Thompson, Garfield
   Arsene Lupin. E. Jepson
   In the Balance. E. P. Oppenheim; Hillman
Thompson, Harlan
   Phantom President. G. F. Worts
Thompson, J. Lee
   For Them That Trespass. E. Raymond
   Ice-Cold in Alex. C. Landon
   Murder Without Crime. J. L. Thompson
Thompson, Keene
   Going Crooked. Winchell Smith
Thompson, Marian
   Shake Hands with the Devil. R. Conner
Thompson, Robert E.
   They Shoot Horses, Don't They? H. McCoy
Thorn, Ronald Scott
   Full Treatment. R. S. Thorn
Thornton, F. Martin
   My Lord Conceit. Rita
Tidyman, Ernest
   Report to the Commissioner. J. Mills
   Shaft's Big Score. E. Tidyman
Tolnay, Akos
   Second Bureau. C. R. Dumas
Tombragel, Maurice
   Return of the Whistler. W. Irish; Eyes That Watch You
Totheroh, Dan
   Remember Last Night? A. Hobhouse; Hangover Murders

Totman, Wellyn
 Girl from Mandalay. R. Campbell
 Steward. E. Wallace
Tourneur, Maurice
 Hand of Peril. A. Stringer
Towers, Harry Alan
 Death Drums Along the River. E. Wallace; Sanders of the River
Towne, Gene
 Case Against Mrs. Ames. A. S. Roche
Townley, Jack
 Plot Thickens. S. Palmer (headnote)
Townsend, Leo
 Dangerous Crossing. J. D. Carr; Dead Sleep Lightly
 Four Boys and a Gun. W. Wiener
 Fraulein. J. McGovern
 Life in the Balance. G. Simenon (headnote)
 Running Wild. B. Benson; Girl in the Cage
 That Way with Women. E. D. Biggers; Earl Derr Biggers Tells Ten Stories
Toy, Barbara
 Monkey's Paw. W. W. Jacobs; Lady of the Barge
Travers, Ben
 Inheritance. J. S. Le Fanu; Uncle Silas
Trell, Max
 Hell Below Zero. H. Innes; White South
 Last Man to Hang. G. Bullett; Jury
Trieschman, Charles
 Two. C. Trieschman
Trivers, Barry
 Flight from Destiny. A. Berkeley; Trial and Error
 River's End. J. O. Curwood
Trosper, Guy
 Eyes in the Night. B. Kendrick; Odor of Violets
 One-Eyed Jacks. C. Neider; Authentic Death of Hendry Jones
 Spy Who Came in from the Cold. J. Le Carre
Trotti, Lamar
 Country Beyond. J. O. Curwood
 Judge Priest. I. S. Cobb; Down Yonder with Judge Priest
Truffaut, Francois
 Bride Wore Black. C. Woolrich
 Let It Be Sunday. C. Williams; Long Saturday Night
 Mississippi Mermaid. W. Irish; Waltz into Darkness
 Shoot the Pianist. D. Goodis; Down There
 Such a Lovely Kid Like Me. H. Farrell; Such a Gorgeous Kid Like Me
Trustman, Alan R.
 Bullitt. R. Pike; Mute Witness
 Lady Ice. M. Braly; Master
 Next Man. M. Z. Lewin
 Thomas Crown Affair. E. L. Heyman
Tryon, Thomas
 Other. T. Tryon
Tuchock, Wanda
 Letty Lynton. M. B. Lowndes
Tucker, George Loane
 Folly of Desire. A. Askew; Shulamite
 Miracle Man. F. Packard
 Traffic in Souls. E. H. Ball
Tudor, F. C. S.
 Devil's Profession. G. de S. W. James
Tully, Jim
 Beggars of Life. J. Tully
Tully, John
 Faces in the Dark. P. Boileau
 In the Wake of a Stranger. I. S. Black
Tully, Montgomery
 Clash by Night. R. Croft-Cooke
 Dial 999. B. Graeme; Way Out
 No Road Back. F. L. Cary; Madam Tic-Tac
 Out of the Fog. B. Graeme; Fog for a Killer
 Who Killed the Cat? A. Ridley; Tabitha
Tunberg, Karl
 I Thank a Fool. A. E. Lindop
 Law and the Lady. F. Lonsdale; Last of Mrs. Cheyney
 Libel. E. Wooll
Turnbull, Hector
 Voice in the Fog. H. MacGrath
Turnbull, Margaret
 House of Silence. E. Barron; Marcel Levignet
 Princess of New York. C. Hamilton
Turner, John Hastings
 Ghoul. F. King
Turney, Catherine
 Back from the Dead. C. Turney; Other One
 Cry Wolf. M. Carleton
 No Man of Her Own. W. Irish; I Married a Dead Man
Turner, Otis

Black Box. E. P. Oppenheim
 Spy. J. F. Cooper
Tuttle, Frank W.
 Manhandled. A. Stringer
 Manhattan. J. Farnol; Definite Object
 Studio Murder Mystery. Edingtons
Twist, Derek
 Family Doctor. J. Fleming
 Non-Stop New York. K. Attiwill; Sky Steward
 They Drive by Night. J. Curtis
Twist, John
 Colorado Territory. W. R. Burnett; High Sierra
 Saint Strikes Back. L. Charteris; She Was a Lady
 Serenade. J. M. Cain
Twyford, Cyril
 House of the Arrow. A. E. W. Mason
 Missing Rembrandt. A. C. Doyle; Return of Sherlock Holmes
 Mystery at the Villa Rose. A. E. W. Mason; At the Villa Rose
 Sleeping Cardinal. A. C. Doyle; Memoirs of Sherlock Holmes
 Valley of Fear. A. C. Doyle
Tynan, Kathleen
 Agatha. K. Tynan
Tynan, Kenneth
 Nowhere to Go. D. MacKenzie
Unger, Gladys
 Cheating Cheaters. M. Marcin
 Mystery of Edwin Drood. C. Dickens
 Night of Mystery. S. S. Van Dine; Greene Murder Case
Unsell, Eve
 Breath of Scandal. E. Balmer
 Dummy. H. J. O'Higgins
 Her Second Chance. W. Woodrow; Second Chance
 Shadow of the Rope. E. W. Hornung
 Suspense. I. Ostrander
 Test of Honor. E. P. Oppenheim; Mr. Wingrave, Millionaire
 Whirlpool. V. Morton
Uris, Michael H.
 Four Days' Wonder. A. A. Milne
Vadim, Roger
 Blackmailed. E. Myers; Mrs. Christopher
 Blood and Roses. J. S. Le Fanu; In a Glass Darkly
Vadja, Ernest
 Payment Deferred. J. Dell
Vailland, Roger
 Blood and Roses. J. S. Le Fanu; In a Glass Darkly
Vajda, Ladislav
 It Happens in Broad Daylight. F. Duerrenmatt; Pledge
Valentine, Val
 Fortune Is a Woman. Winston Graham
 High Command. L. Robinson; General Goes Too Far
 Ringer. E. Wallace
 This Was a Woman. J. Morgan
 Yellow Mask. E. Wallace; Traitor's Gate
Vance, Leigh
 Black Windmill. C. Egleton; Seven Days to a Killing
Van Druten, John
 Gas Light. P. Hamilton
 Raffles. E. W. Hornung; Amateur Cracksman
Van Every, Dale
 Murders in the Rue Morgue. E. A. Poe; Prose Romances of Edgar A. Poe
Van Hamme, Jean
 Diva. Delacorta
Vanlo, Rolfe E.
 Informer. L. O'Flaherty
Van Lusil, Jan
 Traitor Spy. T. C. H. Jacobs
Vautrin, Jean
 Barbarous Street. D. Goodis; Street of the Lost
Veber, Francis
 Hold-Up. J. Cronley; Quick Change
Vecchietti, Alberto
 Brothers Karamazov. F. M. Dostoevskii
Veiller, Anthony
 Assignment in Brittany. H. MacInnes
 Killers. E. Hemingway; Men Without Women
 List of Adrian Messenger. P. MacDonald
 Notorious Sophie Lang. F. I. Anderson
 R.I.P. P. MacDonald
 Seven Keys to Baldpate. E. D. Biggers
 Star of Midnight. A. S. Roche
 Stranger. A. Veiller
 Witching Hour. A. Thomas
Veiller, Bayard
 Arsene Lupin. M. Leblanc; Girl with the Green Eyes
 Trial of Mary Dugan. B. Veiller
Veillot, Claude
 Rise Up, Spy. G. Markstein; Chance Awakening

Veitch, Anthony Scott
 Coast of Skeletons. E. Wallace; Sanders of the River
Verner, Gerald
 Tread Softly. G. Verner; Show Must Go On
Verneuil, Henri
 Any Number Can Win. J. Trinian
Vernon, Richard
 Street of Shadows. L. Meynell; Creaking Chair
Versini, Andre
 See Venice and Die. R. Marshall; Mission to Venice
Vianey, Michel
 Cops' Sunday. A. Coburn; Off Duty
Victor, Herbert
 Bedelia. V. Caspary
Vidal, Gore
 Scapegoat. D. Du Maurier
Viertel, Peter
 Decision Before Dawn. G. Howe; Call It Treason
Vilfrid, Jacques
 Blonde from Peking. J. H. Chase; You Have Yourself a Deal
 Dames Get Along. P. Cheyney; Dames Don't Care
 Gazebo. A. Coppel
Vincenzoni, Luciano
 Quiet Place in the Country. H. Clement
Visconti, Luchino
 Obsession. J. M. Cain; Serenade
Vittes, Louis
 Gang War. O. Demaris; Hoods Take Over
Von Druten, John
 Night Must Fall. E. Williams
von Harbou, Thea
 Dr. Mabuse, Gambler. N. Jacques; Dr. Mabuse, Master of Mystery
 His Official Wife. R. H. Savage; My Official Wife
 Spy. T. von Harbou
von Stackelberg, Carla
 Hound of the Baskervilles. A. C. Doyle
Von Stroheim, Erich
 Devil-Doll. A. Merritt; Burn, Witch, Burn!
Vosper, Frank
 Rome Express. R. Alexander
Wadleigh, Michael
 Wolfen. W. Streiber
Wagner, Jack
 Fighting Edge. W. M. Raine
Wahloo, Per
 Black Sun. P. Wahloo; Lorry
Wainwright, Richard
 Secret of Stamboul. D. Wheatley; Eunich of Stamboul
Waisglass, Elaine
 Judgement in Stone. R. Rendell
Wajda, Andrzej
 Ashes and Diamonds. J. Andrzeyevski
Wakefield, Gilbert
 Lord Camber's Ladies. H. A. Vachell; Case of Lady Camber
Wald, Jerry
 Out of the Fog. I. Shaw; Gentle People
 They Drive by Night. A. Bezzerides; Long Haul
Wald, Malvin
 Al Capone. J. Roeburt
 Dark Past. J. Warwick; Blind Alley
 Naked City. M. Wald
Wallace, Bryan Edgar
 Flying Squad. E. Wallace
 Frightened Lady. E. Wallace; Case of the Frightened Lady
 Mind of Mr. J. G. Reeder. E. Wallace
 Squealer. E. Wallace
 Strangers on a Honeymoon. E. Wallace; Northing Tramp
 White Face. E. Wallace
Wallace, Earl W.
 Witness. W. Kelley
Wallace, Edgar
 Hound of the Baskervilles. A. C. Doyle
 Old Man. E. Wallace; Coat of Arms
 Ringer. E. Wallace
 Squeaker. E. Wallace
 Valley of Ghosts. E. Wallace
Wallace, Irving
 Bad for Each Other. H. McCoy; Scalpel
Walsh, Bill
 One of Our Dinosaurs Is Missing. D. Forrest; Great Dinosaur Robbery
 That Darn Cat. Gordons; Undercover Cat
Walsh, Raoul
 From Now On. F. Packard
Wambaugh, Joseph
 Black Marble. J. Wambaugh
 Onion Field. J. Wambaugh
Ward, Albert
 Poison. A. Askew

W

Ward, David S.
  Sting. R. Weverka
Ward, Edmund
  Amsterdam Affair. N. Freeling; Love in Amsterdam
  Goodbye Gemini. J. Hall; Ask Agamemnon
  Violent Enemy. H. Marlowe; Candle for the Dead
Ward, Luci
  Murder by an Aristocrat. M. G. Eberhart
Ware, Kenneth
  Last Grenade. J. Sherlock; Ordeal of Major Grigsby
Warren, Carol
  Honorable Gentleman. A. Abdullah
Water, G.
  Sorcerer. E. Wallace; Ringer
Waterhouse, John
  She'll Have to Go. I. S. Black; We Must Kill Toni
Waterhouse, Keith
  Man in the Middle. H. Fast; Winston Affair
  West 11. L. Del Rivo; Furnished Room
Waters, Ed
  Caper of the Golden Bulls. W. P. McGivern
  Darker Than Amber. J. D. MacDonald
  Man-Trap. J. D. MacDonald; Soft Touch
Webb, James R.
  Cape Fear. J. D. MacDonald; Executioners
  Phantom of the Rue Morgue. E. A. Poe; Prose Romances of Edgar A. Poe
  Trapeze. M. Catto; Killing Frost
Webb, Millard
  Tiger Rose. W. Mack
Webster, Henry Kitchell
  Green Cloak. Y. Davis
Weil, Richard
  Crime by Night. G. Homes; Forty Whacks
Weinstein, Marvin R.
  Running Target. S. Frazee
Weisman, Matthew
  Burglar. L. Block (headnote)
Welbeck, Peter
  Coast of Skeletons. E. Wallace; Sanders of the River
  Count Dracula. B. Stoker; Dracula
  Slaves of Sumuru. S. Rohmer
Welch, Eddie
  Murder Goes to College. K. Steel
Welch, William
  Brotherhood of Satan. L. Q. Jones
Weller, Samuel M.
  Burden of Proof. V. Sardou; Diplomates
Welles, Orson
  Journey into Fear. E. Ambler
  Lady from Shanghai. Sherwood King; If I Die Before I Wake
  Mr. Arkadin. O. Welles
  Touch of Evil. W. Masterson; Badge of Evil
Wellesley, George
  Chinese Bungalow. M. Osmond
Wellesley, Gordon
  Green Scarf. G. Des Cars; Brute
  Laburnum Grove. J. B. Priestley
  Malpas Mystery. E. Wallace; Face in the Night
  Peterville Diamond. L. Fodor; Jewel Robbery
Wells, George
  Gazebo. A. Coppel
  Horizontal Lieutenant. G. Cotler; Bottletop Affair
  Party Girl. M. H. Albert
  Penelope. E. V. Cunningham
Wenders, Wim
  American Friend. P. Highsmith; Ripley's Game
Werty, Quentin
  Dark of the Sun. W. Smith; Train from Katanga
  Jigsaw. W. Ericson; Fallen Angel
  That Man Bolt. P. Crowcraft
Wesson, Richard
  Change of Mind. C. Stratton
West, Claudine
  Last of Mrs. Cheyney. F. Lonsdale
  Mortal Storm. P. Bottome
West, Elliot
  Fear Makers. D. L. Teilhet
West, Nathanial
  President's Mystery. F. D. Roosevelt; President's Mystery Story
West, Roland
  Bat. M. R. Rinehart
  Bat Whispers. M. E. Rinehart; Bat
Westerby, Robert
  Break in the Circle. P. Loraine
  Cone of Silence. D. Beaty
  Devil's Agent. H. Habe; Agent of the Devil
  Dr. Syn Alias the Scarecrow. R. Thorndyke; Dr. Syn

My Sister and I. E. Bonett; High Pavement
Surgeon's Knife. A. Hocking; Wicked Flee
Wicked As They Come. B. Ballinger; Portrait in Smoke
Westlake, Donald E.
  Cops and Robbers. D. E. Westlake
Westlake, Dorothy
  Hound of the Baskervilles. A. C. Doyle
Weston, Garnett
  American Prisoner. E. Phillpotts
  Blackmail. C. Bennett
  Bulldog Drummond in Africa. H. C. McNeile; Challenge
  Bulldog Drummond's Secret Police. H. C. McNeile; Temple Tower
  Ninth Guest. O. Davis
  Partners in Crime. K. Steel; Murder Goes to College
Wexley, John
  Amazing Dr. Clitterhouse. B. Lyndon
Wharton, Theodore
  Ticket-of-Leave Man. C. Reade; Foul Play
Wheddon, Daniel
  Chick. E. Wallace
Wheeler, Hugh
  Travels with My Aunt. G. Greene
Wheeler, Paul
  Caravan to Vaccares. A. MacLean
  Puppet on a Chain. A. MacLean
  Ransom. P. Wheeler
Wheeler, Rene
  Look Out, Girls. J. H. Chase; Miss Callaghan Comes to Grief
Whelan, Tim
  Fall Guy. G. Abbott
Whitaker, Rod
  Eiger Sanction. Trevanian
White, Dizz
  Bullshot. R. House; Bullshot Crummond
White, Robb
  Macabre. T. Durrant; Marble Forest
White, Robertson
  Charlie Chan's Murder Cruise. E. D. Biggers; Charlie Chan Carries On
  Lady in the Morgue. J. Latimer
  Mystery House. M. G. Eberhart; Mystery of Hunting's End
  Patient in Room 18. M. G. Eberhart
  Westland Case. J. Latimer; Headed for a Hearse
  Witness Vanishes. J. Ronald
Whiting, John
  Ship That Died of Shame. N. Monsarrat
Whiton, James
  Abominable Dr. Phibes. W. Goldstein; Dr. Phibes
Whittaker, Charles E.
  House of Glass. M. Marcin
  Huntingtower. J. Buchan
  Partners of the Night. L. Scott
Whittaker, James
  Last of the Lone Wolf. L. J. Vance; Lone Wolf
Wicking, Christopher
  Blood from the Mummy's Tomb. B. Stoker; Jewel of the Seven Stars
  Murders in the Rue Morgue. E. A. Poe; Prose Romances of Edgar A. Poe
  Scream and Scream Again. P. Saxon; Disoriented Man
  To the Devil--a Daughter. D. Wheatley
Widerberg, Bo
  Man on the Roof. M. Sjowall
Wiene, Robert
  Raskolnikov. F. M. Dostoevskii; Crime and Punishment
Wilbur, Crane
  Bat. M. R. Rinehart
Wilcox, Herbert
  Woman in White. W. Collins
Wilde, Hagar
  Unseen. E. L. White; Midnight House
Wilder, Billy
  Double Indemnity. J. M. Cain
  Private Life of Sherlock Holmes. Michael Hardwick
  Witness for the Prosecution. A. Christie
Wilder, Gene
  Adventures of Sherlock Holmes' Smarter Brother. G. Pearlman
Wilder, Myles
  Spy in the Sky. A. S. Fleischman; Counterspy Express
Wilhelm, H.
  Under Western Eyes. J. Conrad
Wilhelm, Wolfgang
  Saint Meets the Tiger. L. Charteris; Meet the Tiger
Willard, John
  Mask of Fu Manchu. S. Rohmer
Willat, Irvin W.
  False Faces. L. J. Vance
  Yelloe Men and Gold. Gouverneur Morris
Willets, Gilson

City of Purple Dreams. Anonymous
House of a Thousand Candles. M. Nicholson
Loaded Dice. E. H. Clark
Millionaire Baby. A. K. Green
Quarry. J. A. Moroso
Williams, Bob
  Accused of Murder. W. R. Burnett; Vanity Row
Williams, Brock
  Black Coffee. A. Christie
  Chin-Chin-Chinaman. P. Walsh
  Condemned to Death. G. Goodchild; Jack O'Lantern
  Crime Unlimited. D. Hume
  Crown v. Stevens. L. Meynell; Third Time Unlucky
  Dark Stairway. M. G. Eberhart; From This Dark Stairway
  Dark Tower. A. Woolcott
  Harassed Hero. E. Dudley
  It's in the Blood. D. Whitelaw; Big Picture
  Madonna of the Seven Moons. M. Lawrence
  Meet Mr. Callaghan. G. Verner
  Night Invader. J. Bentley; Rendezvous with Death
  Nine Forty-Five. O. Davis; At 9:45
  Peterville Diamond. L. Fodor; Jewel Robbery
  Root of All Evil. J. S. Fletcher
Williams, Charles
  Arm at the Left. C. Williams; Aground
  Don't Just Stand There. C. Williams; Wrong Venus
  Joy House. D. Keene
  Pink Jungle. A. Williams; Snake Water
Williams, Don
  Slaughter. H. Clement
Williams, Emlyn
  Broken Blossoms. T. Burke; Limehouse Nights
  Dead Men Tell No Tales. F. Beeding; Norwich Victims
  Man Who Knew Too Much. R. Alexander
Williams, J. B.
  Chinese Bungalow. M. Osmond
  London Belongs to Me. N. Collins
Williamson, David
  Removalists. D. Williamson
Williamson, Tony
  Night Watch. L. Fletcher
Willingham, Calder
  One-Eyed Jacks. C. Neider; Authentic Death of Hendry Jones
  Thieves Like Us. E. Anderson
Willis, F. McGrew
  Big Gamble. O. R. Cohen; Iron Chalice
  Gay Lord Waring. H. Townley
  Pool of Flame. L. J. Vance
  Silent Battle. G. F. Gibbs
Willis, Ted
  Good Time Girl. A. La Bern; Night Darkens the Streets
Willman, Wendell
  Firefox. C. Thomas
Willshrei, Karl Heinz
  Two Faces of January. P. Highsmith
Wilson, Carey
  Arsene Lupin. M. Leblanc; Girl with the Green Eyes
  Empty Hands. A. Stringer
  President Vanishes. Anonymous
  Red Lights. E. E. Rose; Rear Car
Wilson, Gerald
  Scorpio. M. Roote
  Stone Killer. J. Gardner; Complete State of Death
Wilson, Hugh
  Burglar. L. Block (headnote)
Wilson, Maurice J.
  Clash by Night. R. Croft-Cooke
  Guilty? M. Gilbert; Death Has Deep Roots
  Price of Silence. L. Meynell; One Step from Murder
  Who Killed the Cat? A. Ridley; Tabitha
Wilson, Michael
  Five Fingers. L. C. Moyzisch; Operation Cicero
Wilson, Michael G.
  Octopussy. I. Fleming
Wimperis, Arthur
  Calling Bulldog Drummond. G. Fairlie
  Four Dark Hours. G. Greene (headnote)
  Knight Without Armour. J. Hilton
  Man They Could Not Arrest. E. Wallace (headnote)
  Red Danube. B. Marshall; Vespers in Vienna
  Sanders of the River. E. Wallace
Wincelberg, Shimon
  From the Boys. R. Matheson; Ride the Nightmare
Wing, William E.
  Breathless Moment. M. Bryant; Redemption of Richard
Winkless, Terence H.

Howling. G. Brandner
Winner, Michael
  Big Sleep. R. Chandler
  Sentinel. J. Konvitz
Winslow, Dicky
  East Lynne. H. Wood
  Maria Marten. Anonymous
Winter, Keith
  Above Suspicion. H. MacInnes
  Uncle Harry. T. Job
Winterton, Paul
  Touch of Larceny. A. Garve; Megstone Plot
Wise, Walter
  Sinner Take All. W. Chambers; Murder for a Wanton
Witting, Clifford
  Park Plaza 605. B. Gray; Dare-Devil Conquest
Witty, Frank
  Prison Breakers. E. Wallace (headnote)
Wohl, Burton
  Third Day. J. Hayes
Wolf, David M.
  Next Man. M. Z. Lewin
Wolfert, Ira
  Force of Evil. I. Wolfert
Wolfson, P. J.
  Hands of Orlac. M. Renard
Wood, Charles
  Long Day's Dying. A. White
Wood, Christopher
  Moonraker. C. Wood; James Bond and Moonraker
  Remo. W. B. Murphy
  Spy Who Loved Me. C. Wood; James Bond, the Spy Who Loved Me
Wood, Frank
  Great Impersonation. E. P. Oppenheim
Wood, Kinchen
  Eugene Aram. E. Bulwer-Lytton
  Running Water. A. E. W. Mason
Woodlock, Graham
  Scobie Malone. J. Cleary; Helga's Web
Woods, Frank
  Suicide Club. R. L. Stevenson
Woods, Walter
  Brass Bullet. F. R. Adams; Pleasure Island
Woolf, Edgar Allan
  Casino Murder Case. S. S. Van Dine
  Mask of Fu Manchu. S. Rohmer
  Murder in the Private Car. E. E. Rose; Rear Car
Worth, Cedric
  President Vanishes. Anonymous
Wray, Ardel
  Leopard Man. C. Woolrich; Black Alibi
Wrestler, Philip
  Crosstrap. J. N. Chase (headnote)
Wright, William H.
  Assignment in Brittany. H. MacInnes
Wyler, Robert
  Detective Story. S. Kingsley
  Murder Goes to College. K. Steel
  Sophie Lang Goes West. F. I. Anderson; Notorious Sophie Lang
Wyndham-Lewis, D. B.
  Chick. E. Wallace
Wynn, Tracy Keenan
  Drowning Pool. J. R. Macdonald
Yablonsky, Harold
  Secret of the Purple Reef. D. Cottrell; Silent Reefs
Yeldham, Peter
  Liquidator. J. Gardner
  Ten Little Indians. A. Christie; Ten Little Niggers
  Weekend of Shadows. H. Atkinson; Reckoning
Yordan, Philip
  Chase. C. Woolrich; Black Path of Fear
  Detective Story. S. Kingsley
  Edge of Doom. L. Brady
  Fiend Who Walked the West. E. Lipsky; Kiss of Death
  Four Boys and a Gun. W. Wiener
  No Down Payment. J. McPartland
  Whistle Stop. M. M. Wolff
Yost, Dorothy
  Murder on a Bridle Path. S. Palmer; Puzzle of the Red Stallion
  Queenie. W. F. Fauley
Yost, Robert M.
  Forgotten Faces. R. W. Child; Velvet Black
  Tom Sawyer, Detective. M. Twain
Young, Clarence Upson
  Ghost That Walks Alone. R. Shattuck; Wedding Guest Sat on a Stone
  Plot Thickens. S. Palmer (headnote)
  Time to Kill. R. Chandler; High Window
Young, Howard Irving
  Crimson Circle. E. Wallace
  Million a Minute. H. Douglas
  Secret of Stamboul. D. Wheatley; Eunich of Stamboul

Young, James
  Daughter of Two Worlds. L. Scott
  Notorious Miss Lisle. B. Reynolds
  On Trial. E. L. Reizenstein
Young, Terence
  Heart Trump for OSS 117 in Tokyo. J. Bruce; Hot Line
  On the Night of the Fire. F. L. Green
Young, Tony
  Hidden Homicide. P. Capon; Death at Shinglestrand
Young, Waldemar
  Black Bird. T. Browning; Mocking Bird
  Fire Flingers. W. J. Neidig
  Flaming Forest. J. O. Curwood
  Girl in the Web. G. Bonner; Miss Maitland, Private Secretary
  London After Midnight. M. Coolridge-Rask
  Miracle Man. F. Packard
  Unholy Three. T. Robbins
  Where East Is East. T. Browning
Yust, Larry
  Trick Baby. I. Slim
Zanuck, Darryl Francis
  Across the Pacific. C. E. Blaney
  On Thin Ice. A. R. Colver; Dear Pretender
Zeisler, Alfred
  Fear. F. M. Dostoevskii; Crime and Punishment
Zellner, Lois
  Family Secret. A. Thomas; Editha's Burglar
Ziffren, Lester
  Charlie Chan's Murder Cruise. E. D. Biggers; Charlie Chan Carries On
  Man Who Wouldn't Talk. H. Hall; Valiant
Zimbalist, Don
  Young Dillinger. S. Stuart
Zimmer, Bernard
  Second Bureau. C. R. Dumas
Zimmerman, Vernon
  Fade to Black. R. Renaud
Zoty, Douglas
  Red Dice. O. R. Cohen; Iron Chalice
Zuckerman, George
  Panther's Moon. V. Canning

Directors Index

Directors Index

Abbott, George
  Manslaughter. A. D. Miller
  Sea God. J. Russell; Red Mark
Adolfi, John G.
  Man Inside. N. S. Lincoln
  Millionaire. E. D. Biggers; Earl Derr Biggers Tells Ten Stories
Ainsworth, John
  Hell Is Empty. J. F. Straker
Aldrich, Robert
  Big Knife. C. Odets
  Choirboys. J. Wambaugh
  Flight of the Phoenix. E. Trevor
  Grissom Gang. J. H. Chase; No Orchids for Miss Blandish
  Hustle. S. Shagan; City of Angels
  Kiss Me, Deadly. M. Spillane
  Ten Seconds to Hell. L. P. Bachmann; Phoenix
  Twilight's Last Gleaming. W. Wager; Viper Three
  Whatever Happened to Baby Jane? H. Farrell
Allegret, Marc
  Blackmailed. E. Myers; Mrs. Christopher
  Blanche Fury. J. Shearing
Allegret, Yves
  Look Out Girls. J. H. Chase; Miss Callaghan Comes to Grief
Allen, A. K. [Real name: Janet Greek]
  Ladies Club. B. Black; Sisterhood
Allen, Irving
  Avalanche. K. Boyle
Allen, Irwin
  Towering Inferno. R. M. Stern; Tower
Allen, Lewis
  Chicago Deadline. T. Thayer; One Woman
  Desert Fury. Ramona Stewart; Desert Town
  Sealed Verdict. L. Shapiro
  So Evil My Love. J. Shearing; For Her to See
  Uninvited. D. Macardle; Uneasy Freehold
  Unseen. E. L. White; Midnight House
  Whirlpool. L. P. Bachmann; Lorelei
Almond, Paul
  Backfire! E. Wallace (headnote)
Altman, Robert
  Long Goodbye. R. Chandler
  McCabe and Mrs. Miller. E. Naughton; McCabe
  That Cold Day in the Park. R. Miles
  Thieves Like Us. E. Anderson
Anderson, Michael
  Hell Is Sold Out. M. Dekobra
  House of the Arrow. A. E. W. Mason
  Man of Bronze. K. Roberson
  Naked Edge. M. Ehrlich; First Train to Babylon
  Night Was Our Friend. M. Pertwee
  Quiller Memorandum. Adam Hall; Berlin Memorandum
  Shake Hands with the Devil. R. Conner
  Waterfront. J. Brophy
  Wreck of the Mary Deare. H. Innes; Mary Deare
Annakin, Ken
  Across the Bridge. G. Greene; Nineteen Stories
  Double Confession. J. Garden; All on a Summer's Day
  Informers. D. Warner; Death of a Snout
  Loser Takes All. G. Greene
Annaud, Jean-Jacques
  Name of the Rose. U. Eco
Anthony, Joseph
  Captive City. J. Appleby
  Tomorrow. W. Faulkner; Knight's Gambit
Apfel, Oscar
  Bulldog Drummond. H. C. McNeile
  Half a Chance. F. S. Isham
  Lion's Mouse. C. N. Williamson
  Man on the Box. H. MacGrath
  Master Mind. M. Dana
  Oakdale Affair. E. R. Burroughs
Apted, Michael
  Agatha. K. Tynan
  Gorky Park. M. C. Smith
  Squeeze. David Craig; Whose Little Girl Are You?
Aranda, Vicente
  Blood Spattered Bride. J. S. Le Fanu; In a Glass Darkly
  Murder in the Central Committee. M. V. Montalban
Arcady, Alexandre
  Hold-Up. J. Cronley; Quick Change
Archainbaud, George A.
  Cordelia the Magnificent. L. Scott
  Easy Pickings. P. Cruger
  Midnight Guest. F. M. White
  Murder on the Blackboard. S. Palmer
  Penguin Pool Murder. S. Palmer
  Return of Sophie Lang. E. Anderson; Notorious Sophie Lang

Thirteen Women. T. Thayer
Arehn, Mats
  Assignment. P. Wahloo
Argento, Dario
  Cat o' Nine Tails. P. J. Gillette
Arkin, Alan
  Little Murders. J. Feiffer
Arkless, Robert
  Man Who Would Not Die. C. Williams; Sailcloth Shroud
Arkush, Allan
  Deathsport. W. Hughes
Arliss, Leslie
  Night Has Eyes. A. Kennington
Armitage, George
  Hit Man. Ted Lewis; Jack's Return Home
Arnett, James
  Mackintosh Man. D. Bagley; Freedom Trap
Arnold, Jack
  Black Eye. J. Jacks; Murder on the Wild Side
  Glass Web. M. Ehrlich; Spin the Glass Web
  High School Confidential. Morton Cooper
  Lady Takes a Flier. E. Ronns
Artaud, E.
  Dancer and the King. C. E. Blaney
Arzner, Dorothy
  First Comes Courage. E. Arnold; Commandos
Ashby, Hal
  Eight Million Ways to Die. L. Block
Asher, Robert
  Make Mine Mink. P. Coke; Breath of Spring
  She'll Have to Go. I. S. Black; We Must Kill Toni
Asher, William
  Johnny Cool. J. McPartland; Kingdom of Johnny Cool
  Muscle Beach Party. Elsie Lee
Asquith, Anthony
  Act of Mercy. F. Clifford
  Carrington, V.C. D. Christie
  Cottage to Let. G. Kerr; Cottages to Let
  Libel. E. Wooll
  Net. J. Pudney
  Orders to Kill. D. Downes
  Shooting Stars. E. C. Vivian
  Two Living and One Dead. S. Christiansen
Attenborough, Richard
  Magic. W. Goldman
Aurthur, Robert Alan
  Lost Man. F. L. Green; Odd Man Out
Autant-Lara, Claude
  In Case of Emergency. G. Simenon
  Murderer. P. Highsmith; Blunderer
Avakian, Aram
  Cops and Robbers. D. E. Westlake
  11 Harrowhouse. G. A. Browne
Avildsen, John G.
  Cry Uncle. Michael Brett; Lie a Little, Die a Little
  Formula. S. Shagan
Aylott, Dave
  It Is Never Too Late to Mend. C. Reade
Bacon, Lloyd
  Brother Orchid. L. Brady
  Home Sweet Homicide. C. Rice
  Larceny, Inc. L. Perelman; Night Before Christmas
  Miss Pinkerton. M. R. Rinehart
  Slight Case of Murder. D. Runyon
Bacso, Peter
  Man Who Went Up in Smoke. M. Sjowall
Badger, Clarence
  Murder Will Out. M. Leinster
  Red Lights. E. E. Rose; Rear Car
  Sweethearts and Wives. W. Hackett; Other Men's Wives
Badham, John
  Dracula. H. Deane
Baggott, King
  Raffles, the Amateur Cracksman. E. W. Hornung; Amateur Cracksman
Bailey, Oliver D.
  Sun-Up. M. Marcin; Substitute Prisoner
Bain, Bill
  What Became of Jack and Jill? L. Moody; Ruthless Ones
Baker, George D.
  Buried Treasure. F. B. Austin; On the Borderland
  Cinema Murder. E. P. Oppenheim; Other Romilly
  Demon. C. N. Williamson
  Heliotrope. R. W. Child; Velvet Black
  Man Who Stayed Home. J. E. H. Terry
  Sleeping Memory. E. P. Oppenheim; Great Awakening
  Winifred the Shop Girl. C. N. Williamson; Shop Girl
Baker, Robert S.

Jack the Ripper. S. James
Passport to Treason. M. O'Brine
Baker, Roy Ward
  And Now the Screaming Starts. D. Case; Fengriffin
  Asylum. W. Johnston
  Doctor Jekyll and Sister Hyde. R. L. Stevenson; Strange Case of Dr. Jekyll and Mr. Hyde
  Don't Bother to Knock. C. Armstrong; Mischief
  Night Without Sleep. E. Moll
  October Man. E. Britton
  Paper Orchid. A. La Bern
  Tiger in the Smoke. M. Allingham
Balaban, Burt
  "Mad Dog" Coll. S. Thurman
Balin, Hugo
  Pagan Love. A. Abdullah; Honorable Gentleman
Ball, Chuck
  Cleopatra Jones and the Casino of Gold. R. Goulart
Balling, Anders
  One of Those Things. A. Bodelsen; One Down
Balshofer, Fred J.
  Haunted Pajamas. F. P. Elliott
  Paradise Garden. G. F. Gibbs
  Pidgin Island. H. MacGrath
Barker, Reginald
  Crimson Gardenia. R. Beach
  Dangerous Day. M. R. Rinehart
  Eternal Struggle. G. B. Lancaster; Law Bringers
  Flaming Forest. J. O. Curwood
  Moonstone. W. Collins
  Seven Keys to Baldpate. E. D. Biggers
Barnes, Arthur W.
  China Bungalow. M. Osmond
Barringer, Michael
  Murder at Covent Garden. W. J. Makin
Barrymore, Lionel
  Madame X. J. W. MacConaughy
Barsha, Leon
  Convicted. W. Irish; Six Nights of Mystery
Bartlett, Hall
  Zero Hour! J. Castle; Flight into Danger
Barton, Charles T.
  Murder with Pictures. G. H. Coxe
Bary, Leon
  In the Hands of the Spoilers. S. Paternoster; In the Hands of the Spoiler
Beaudine, William
  Educated Evans. E. Wallace
  Fugitives. R. H. Davis; Exiles
  Mystery of the Thirteenth Guest. A. Trail
Beaumont, Gabrielle
  Godsend. B. Taylor
Beaumont, Harry
  Man and His Money. F. S. Isham
  Murder in the Private Car. E. E. Rose; Rear Car
  Officer 666. B. Currie
  Stop Thief! Carlyle Moore
Becker, Harold
  Black Marble. J. Wambaugh
  Onion Field. J. Wambaugh
Becker, Jean
  One Deadly Summer. S. Japrisot
Bedford, Terry
  Slayground. R. Stark
Beebe, Forde
  Enter Arsene Lupin. M. Leblanc; Girl with the Green Eyes
Behat, Gilles
  Barbarous Street. D. Goodis; Street of the Lost
Beineix, Jean-Jacques
  Diva. Delacorta
  Moon in the Gutter. D. Goodis
Bell, Monta
  After Midnight. E. Fletcher-Allen
  Bellamy Trial. F. N. Hart
Bellamy, Earl
  Walking Tall: Part 2. W. Carey
Belson, Jerry
  Jekyll and Hyde...Together Again. R. L. Stevenson; Strange Case of Dr. Jekyll and Mr. Hyde
Benedek, Laslo
  Assault on Agathon. A. Caillou
  Moment of Danger. D. MacKenzie; Scent of Danger
Bennett, Chester
  Secret of the Hills. W. Garrett
  Three Sevens. P. P. Sheehan
Bennett, Compton
  Beyond the Curtain. A. J. Wallis; Thunder Above
  Desperate Moment. M. Albrand
  That Woman Opposite. J. D. Carr; Emperor's Snuff Box
Bennett, Whitman
  Back to Life. A. Soutar; Back from the Dead

Bentley, Thomas
  American Prisoner. E. Phillpotts
  Lackey and the Lady. T. Gallon
  Romance of Mayfair. J. C. Snaith; Crime of Constable Kelly
  Silver Blaze. A. C. Doyle; Memoirs of Sherlock Holmes
  Through Fire and Water. V. Bridges; Greensea Island
Beranger, George A(ndre)
  Manhattan Knight. G. Burgess; Find the Woman
  Number Seventeen. L. Tracy
Berke, William
  Cop Hater. E. McBain
  Four Boys and a Gun. W. Wiener
  Mugger. E. McBain
Bernhard, Jack
  Blonde Ice. W. Chambers; Once Too Often
Bernhardt, Curtis/Kurt
  High Wall. A. R. Clark
  Man Who Murdered. C. Farrere; Man Who Killed
Berry, John
  He Ran All the Way. S. Ross
Berthelet, Arthur
  Sherlock Holmes. W. Gillette
Bessie, Dan
  Hard Traveling. A. Bessie; Bread and a Stone
Bianchi, Edward
  Fan. B. Randall
Biberman, Abner
  Running Wild. B. Benson; Girl in the Cage
Biberman, Herbert J.
  Meet Nero Wolfe. R. Stout; Fer-de-Lance
Billington, Kevin
  Interlude. J. M. Cain; Serenade
Billon, Pierre
  Second Bureau. C. R. Dumas
Binet, Catherine
  Games of the Countess Dolingen of Gratz. B. Stoker; Dracula
Bingham, E. Douglas
  Master Mystery. A. B. Reeve
Binyon, Claude
  Stella. D. M. Disney; Family Skeleton
Bird, Richard
  Terror. E. Wallace
Birdwell, Russell J.
  Come-On. W. Chambers
Birt, Daniel
  She Shall Have Murder. D. Ames
  Third Party Risk. N. Bentley
  Three Silent Men. E. P. Thorne
  Three Weird Sisters. C. Armstrong; Case of the Weird Sisters
Bischoff, Sam
  Last Mile. J. Wexley
Bishop, Terry
  Unstoppable Man. M. Gilbert; Amateur in Violence
Blache, Alice
  Lure. G. Scarborough
Blache, Herbert
  Loaded Dice. E. H. Clark
  Secrets of the Night. M. Marcin; Nightcap
  Untamable. G. Burgess; White Cat
Black, Noel
  Pretty Poison. S. Geller; She Let Him Continue
Blackton, J. Stuart
  Behold This Woman. E. P. Oppenheim; Hillman
  Passionate Quest. E. P. Oppenheim
Blair, George
  Homicide for Three. P. Quenton; Puzzle for Puppets
Blatt, Edward A.
  Escape in the Desert. R. Sherwood; Petrified Forest
Bloomfield, George
  Double Negative. K. Millar; Three Roads
Bocchi, Arrigo
  Top Dog. F. Hume
  When It Was Dark. G. Thorne
  Whosoever Shall Offend... F. M. Crawford
Boetticher, Budd/Oscar
  Rise and Fall of Legs Diamond. O. H. Gaylord
  Wolf Hunters. J. O. Curwood
Bogart, Paul
  Marlowe. R. Chandler; Little Sister
Boisrond, Michel
  Heart Trump for OSS 117 in Tokyo. J. Bruce; Hot Line
  One Is Always Too Good to Women. R. Queneau; We Always Treat Women Too Well
Boisset, Yves
  Prize of Peril. R. Sheckley; Tenth Victim
  Rise Up, Spy. G. Markstein; Chance Awakening

Boleslavksy [Boleslawski], Richard
  Last of Mrs. Cheyney. F. Lonsdale
  Last of the Lone Wolf. L. J. Vance; Lone Wolf
  Operator 13. R. W. Chambers; Secret Service Operator 13
Bolvary, Geza M.
  Ghost Train. A. Ridley
  No. 17. J. J. Farjeon
  Wrecker. A. Ridley
Bonerz, Peter
  Nobody's Perfekt. T. Kenrick; Two for the Price of One
Bonner, Clive
  Sinister Man. E. Wallace
Boorman, John
  Deliverance. J. Dickey
  Point Blank. R. Stark; Hunter
Borderie, Bernard
  Dames Get Along. P. Cheyney; Dames Don't Care
  Gun Moll. P. Cheyney; Poison Ivy
  Hit and Run. R. Marshall
  What a Girl! P. Cheyney; I'll Say She Does
  You Do It, Cutie. P. Cheyney; Your Deal, My Lovely
Borsos, Philip
  Mean Season. J. Katzenbach; In the Heat of Summer
Borzage, Frank
  Get-Rich-Quick-Wallingford. G. R. Chester
  Moonrise. T. Strauss
  Mortal Storm. P. Bottome
  Strange Cargo. R. Sale; Not Too Narrow--Not Too Deep
  Valley of Silent Men. J. O. Curwood
Boulting, John
  Brighton Rock. G. Greene
Boulting, Roy
  Brothers in Law. H. Cecil
  Inquest. M. Barringer
  Run for the Sun. R. Connell; Variety
  Suspect. N. Balchin; Sort of Traitors
  Trunk Crime. E. Percy
Bourguignon, Serge
  Reward. M. Barrett
Bowers, George
  Hearse. H. Clement
Box, Muriel
  Subway in the Sky. B. Birch
Brabin, Charles J.
  Beast of the City. J. Lait
  Footfalls. W. D. Steele; Tower of Sand
  House of the Lost Court. D. T. De Savallo
  Mask of Fu Manchu. S. Rohmer
  Ship from Shanghai. D. Collins; Ordeal
  Wicked Woman. A. Austin
Bracken, Bertram
  Boomerang. W. H. Osborne
  East Lynn. H. Wood
  Kazan. J. O. Curwood
  Long Arm of Mannister. E. P. Oppenheim; Long Arm
  Mask. A. Hornblow
Bradley, David
  Talk About a Stranger. C. Armstrong; Albatross
Brahm, John/Hans
  Broken Blossoms. T. Burke; Limehouse Nights
  Hangover Square. P. Hamilton
  High Window. R. Chandler
  Lodger. M. B. Lowndes
  Penitentiary. M. Flavin; Criminal Code
  Singapore. W. Bogart
  Undying Monster. J. D. Kerruish
Bramble, A. V.
  Chick. E. Wallace
  Man Who Changed His Name. E. Wallace
  Nonconformist Parson. R. Horniman
  Shooting Stars. E. C. Vivian
Brando, Marlon
  One-Eyed Jacks. C. Neider; Authentic Death of Hendry Jones
Brandon, Phil
  Missing Million. E. Wallace
Braverman, Charles
  Hit and Run. L. Fletcher; Eighty Dollars to Stamford
Breakston, George
  Boy Cried Murder. W. Irish; Dead Man Blues
Brecher, Irving S.
  Sail a Crooked Ship. N. Benchley
Breen, Richard L.
  Stopover: Tokyo. J. P. Marquand
Brenon, Herbert
  Breaking Point. M. R. Rinehart
  Dr. Jekyll and Mr. Hyde. R. L. Stevenson; Strange Case of Dr. Jekyll and Mr. Hyde
  Flying Squad. E. Wallace
  Honours Easy. R. Pertwee
  Living Dangerously. R. Simpson

Lone Wolf. L. J. Vance
  Sign on the Door. C. Pollock
  Someone at the Door. D. Christie
Bresnard, Jacques
  Stew in the Caribbean. A. Conroy; Looters
Bretherton, Howard
  Argyle Case. H. Ford
  Girl from Mandalay. R. Campbell; Death in Tiger Valley
  Return of the Terror. E. Wallace; Terror
Bridges, James
  China Syndrome. B. Wohl
Bromley, Harry
  Full Circle. P. Straub; Julia
Bromly, Alan
  Follow That Hearse. H. Mason; Photo Finish
Brooke, Ralph
  Bloodlust. R. Connell; Variety
Brooks, Mel
  High Anxiety. R. H. Pilpel
Brooks, Richard
  Blackboard Jungle. E. Hunter
  Brothers Karamazov. F. M. Dostoevskii
  Deadline. J. Eastwood
  In Cold Blood. T. Capote
  Wrong Is Right. C. McCarry; Better Angels
Brouett, Albert
  Rogue in Love. T. Gallon
Brown, Clarence
  Intruder in the Dust. W. Faulkner
  Letty Lynton. M. B. Lowndes
Brown, Karl
  Federal Bullets. G. F. Eliot
Brown, Melville W.
  13 Washington Square. L. Scott; No. 13 Washington Square
Browning, Tod
  Black Bird. T. Browning; Mocking Bird
  Devil-Doll. A. Merritt; Burn, Witch, Burn!
  Dracula. B. Stoker
  London After Midnight. M. Coolridge-Rask
  Mark of the Vampire. M. Coolridge-Rask; London After Midnight
  Miracles for Sale. C. Rawson; Death from a Top Hat
  Outside the Law. T. Browning
  Unholy Three. T. Robbins
  Where East Is East. T. Browning
Brunel, Adrian
  Crooked Billet. D. Titheradge
  Cross Currents. W. G. Elliott; Nine Days' Blunder
  Prison Breaker. E. Wallace (headnote)
Bruun, Einar J.
  In Full Cry. R. Marsh
  Penniless Millionaire. D. C. Murray
Buchanan, Larry
  Bullet for Pretty Boy. M. Avallone
Buchowetzki, Dimitri
  Public Prosecutor's Speech. A. D. Miller; Manslaughter
Buckland, Warwick
  After Dark. D. Boucicault
Buckland, Wilfred
  Man on the Box. H. MacGrath
Bucknell, Robert
  More Deadly Than the Male. P. Chevalier
Bucksey, Colin
  McGuffin. J. Bowen
Burnley, Fred
  Neither the Sea Nor the Sand. G. Honeycombe
Burnside, R. H.
  Manhattan. J. Farnol; Definite Object
Burrowes, Michael
  Doctors Wear Scarlet. S. Raven
Burstall, Tim
  End Play. R. Braddon
Burton, David
  Bishop Murder Case. S. S. Van Dine
  Man Who Wouldn't Talk. H. Hall; Valiant
Burton, John Nelson
  Never Mention Murder. E. Wallace (headnote)
Bushell, Anthony
  Terror of the Tongs. J. Sangster
Butler, Alexander
  Beetle. R. Marsh
  Disappearance of the Judge. C. R. Gull; Lost Judge
  Jo, the Crossing Sweeper. C. Dickens; Bleak House
  London by Night. C. Selby
  Thundercloud. T. Taylor; Still Waters Run Deep
  Valley of Fear. A. C. Doyle
Butler, Robert
  Night of the Juggler. W. P. McGivern
Buzzell, Edward
  Fast Company. M. Page
Cabanne, Christy
  Conspiracy. R. Baker

Directors Index

Red-Haired Alibi. W. Collison
Scattergood Baines. C. B. Kelland
Westland Case. J. Latimer; Headed for a Hearse
Cacoyannis, Michael
  Day the Fish Came Out. K. Cicellis
Cagney, James
  Short Cut to Hell. G. Greene; Gun for Sale
Cahill, David
  You Can't See Round Corners. J. Cleary
Cahn, Edward L.
  Dangerous Partners. O. W. Bayer; Paper Chase
  Secret of Deep Harbor. Max Miller; I Cover the Waterfront
Cairns, Dallas
  Silver Bridge. H. P. Lewis
Calvert, C(harles) C.
  Branded. G. Biss
  In His Grip. D. C. Murray
Calvert, E(lisha) H(elm)
  One Wonderful Night. L. Tracy
Camiller, Edgar J.
  Definite Object. J. Farnol
Campbell, Colin
  Carpet from Bagdad. H. MacGrath
  City of Purple Dreams. Anonymous
  In Defiance of the Law. J. O. Curwood; Isobel
Campbell, Webster
  Pace That Thrills. R. Weber
Canutt, Yakima
  Flim Flam Man. G. Owen; Ballad of the Flim Flam Man
Capra, Frank R.
  Arsenic and Old Lace. J. Kesselring
  Donovan Affair. O. Davis
Cardiff, Jack
  Beyond This Place. A. J. Cronin
  Dark of the Sun. Wilbur Smith; Train from Katanga
  Intent to Kill. M. Bryan
  Liquidator. J. Gardner
  Scent of Mystery. K. Roos; Ghost of a Chance
Carewe, Edwin
  Across the Pacific. C. E. Blaney
  Isobel. J. O. Curwood
  My Lady's Latchkey. C. N. Williamson; Second Latchkey
  Pals First. L. W. Dodd
  Revenge. J. Warren
  Way of the Strong. R. Cullum
Carne, Marcel
  Bizarre, Bizarre. J. S. Clouston; His First Offense
  Marie du Port. G. Simenon; Chit of a Girl
  Three Rooms in Manhattan. G. Simenon; Three Beds in Manhattan
  Waste-Land. H. Ellison; Tomboy
Carpenter, John
  Halloween. C. Richards
Carreras, Michael
  Blood from the Mummy's Tomb. R. L. Stevenson; Jewel of the Seven Stars
  Lost Continent. D. Wheatley; Uncharted Seas
  Maniac. M. Brandel; Time of the Fire
Carruth, Milton
  Love Letters of a Star. Rufus King; Case of the Constant God
Carstairs, John Paddy
  Devil's Agent. H. Habe; Agent of the Devil
  Meet Maxwell Archer. H. Clevely; Archer Plus 20
  Saint in London. L. Charteris; Holy Terror
  Sleeping Car to Trieste. R. Alexander; Rome Express
Carter, Peter
  High Ballin'. Richard Robinson
Castle, William
  Busy Body. D. E. Westlake
  I Saw What You Did. U. Curtiss; Out of the Dark
  Let's Kill Uncle. R. O'Grady
  Macabre. T. Durrant; Marble Forest
  Mark of the Whistler. W. Irish; Borrowed Crime
  Night Walker. S. Stuart
  Old Dark House. J. B. Priestley; Benighted
Cavalcanti, Alberto
  For Them That Trespass. E. Raymond
  They Made Me a Fugitive. J. Budd; Convict Has Escaped
Cavalier, Alain
  Pillaged. R. Stark; Score
Cayette, Andre
  Trap for Cinderella. S. Japrisot
Chabrol, Claude
  Blood Relatives. E. McBain
  Breakup. C. Armstrong; Balloon Man
  Dirty Hands. R. Neely; Damned Innocents
  Hatter's Ghosts. G. Simenon
  Just Before Nightfall. E. Atiyah; Thin Line
  Let the Beast Die. N. Blake; Beast Must Die
  Ten Days' Wonder. E. Queen
  Web of Passion. S. Ellin; Key to Nicholas Street
Chaffey, Don
  Crooked Road. M. West; Big Story
  Danger Within. M. Gilbert; Death in Captivity
  Jolly Bad Fellow. C. E. Vulliamy; Don Among the Dead Men
  Ride a Wild Pony. J. Aldridge; Sporting Proposition
  Secret Tent. E. Addyman
  Twist of Sand. G. Jenkins
Champion, Gower
  Bank Shot. D. E. Westlake
Charrington, Arthur
  East Lynne. H. Wood
Chautard, Emile
  House of Glass. M. Marcin
  Living Lies. A. S. Roche; Plunder
  Mystery of the Yellow Room. G. Leroux
  Out of the Shadow. E. W. Hornung; Shadow of the Rope
Chenal, Pierre
  Crime and Punishment. F. M. Dostoevskii
  Last Turning. J. M. Cain; Postman Always Rings Twice
  Section des Disparus. D. Goodis; Of Missing Persons
Chereau, Patrice
  Flesh of the Orchid. J. H. Chase
Christiansen, Benjamin
  Devil's Circus. B. Christiansen
  Haunted House. O. Davis
  Hawk's Nest. W. Gunning
  Seven Footprints to Satan. A. Merritt
Christensen, Bent
  Busybody. J. Popplewell
  Ghost Train. A. Ridley
Christensen, Carlos Hugo
  Lady of Death. R. L. Stevenson; Suicide Club
Cimber, Matt
  Butterfly. J. M. Cain
  Time to Die. M. Cleri; Six Graves to Munich
Cimino, Michael
  Thunderbolt and Lightfoot. J. Millard
  Year of the Dragon. R. Daley
Clair, Rene
  Ten Little Niggers. A. Christie
Clark, Bob
  Murder by Decree. R. Weverka
Clark, Jim/James B.
  Madhouse. Angus Hall; Qualtrough
Clarkson, Stephen
  Death Goes to School. S. Davis; Death in Seven Hours
Claxton, William F.
  Desire in the Dust. H. Whittington
Clayton, Jack
  Innocents. H. James; Turn of the Screw
  Our Mother's House. J. Gloag
Clemens, William B.
  Calling Philo Vance. S. S. Van Dine; Kennel Murder Case
  Case of the Stuttering Bishop. E. S. Gardner
  Case of the Velvet Claws. E. S. Gardner
  Crime by Night. G. Homes; Forty Whacks
  Night in New Orleans. J. R. Langham; Sing a Song of Homicide
  Night of January 16. A. Rand
Clement, Dick
  Bullshot Crummond. R. House
  Catch Me a Spy. G. Marton
  Otley. M. Waddell
Clement, Rene
  And Hope to Die. D. Goodis; Black Friday
  Broad Daylight. P. Highsmith; Talented Mr. Ripley
  Deadly Trap. A. Cavanagh
  Love Cage. D. Keene; Joy House
Clements, Roy S.
  Tiger's Coat. E. Dejeans
Clift, Denison
  Bentley's Conscience. P. Trent
  Out to Win. R. Pertwee
Clifton, Elmer
  Let 'Er Go Gallegher. R. H. Davis; Gallegher
  Two-Soul Woman. G. Burgess; White Cat
Cline, Edward F.
  Crash. F. Packard; Night Operator
  Forty Naughty Girls. S. Palmer (headnote)
  In the Next Room. E. R. Belmont
  In the Next Room. E. Stevenson; Mystery of the Boule Cabinet
Clouse, Robert
  Enter the Dragon. M. Roote
  Rats. J. Herbert
  Terrible Game. D. T. Moore
Clouzot, Henri-Georges
  Diabolique. P. Boileau; Woman Who Was Spies. E. Hostovsky; Midnight Patient
  Wages of Fear. G. Arnaud
Clowes, St. John L.
  No Orchids for Miss Blandish. J. H. Chase
Clurman, Harold
  Deadline at Dawn. W. Irish
Cohen, Larry
  It's Alive. R. Woodley
Cokliss, Harley
  Malone. W. Wingate; Shotgun
Coleby, A. E.
  Flying Fifty-Five. E. Wallace
  Great Prince Shan. E. P. Oppenheim
Coletti, Duilio
  House of Intrigue. H. J. Giskes; London Calling North Pole
Colla, Richard A.
  Fuzz. E. McBain
Collins, Edwin J.
  Channings. H. Wood
  Eugene Aram. E. Bulwer-Lytton
  Gamble with Hearts. A. Carlyle
  Hard Cash. C. Reade
Collins, John H.
  God's Law and Man's. P. Trent; Wife by Purchase
Collins, Lewis D.
  Leavenworth Case. A. K. Green
  Sing Sing Nights. H. S. Keeler
  Spanish Cape Mystery. E. Queen
Collinson, Peter
  Innocent Bystanders. J. Munro
  Italian Job. T. K. Martin
  Long Day's Dying. A. White
  Spiral Staircase. E. L. White; Some Must Watch
  Ten Little Indians. A. Christie; Ten Little Niggers
Colmes, Walter
  Accomplice. F. Gruber; Simon Lash, Private Detective
  French Key. F. Gruber
Comfort, Lance
  Bedelia. V. Caspary
  Breaking Point. L. Meynell
  Daughter of Darkness. M. Catto; They Walk Alone
  Face in the Night. B. Graeme; Suspense
  Hotel Reserve. E. Ambler; Epitaph for a Spy
  Man in the Road. A. Armstrong; He Was Found in the Road
  Pit of Darkness. H. McCutcheon; To Dusty Death
  Silent Dust. R. Pertwee; Paragon
  Temptation Harbour. G. Simenon; Newhaven-Dieppe
  Ugly Duckling. R. L. Stevenson; Strange Case of Dr. Jekyll and Mr. Hyde
Connolly, Bobby
  Patient in Room 18. M. G. Eberhart
Conway, Jack
  Another Man's Shoes. V. Bridges
  Arsene Lupin. M. Leblanc; Girl with the Green Eyes
  Assignment in Brittany. H. MacInnes
  Haunted Woman. J. O. Curwood
  Silent Battle. G. F. Gibbs
  Solitaire Man. B. C. Spewack
  Unholy Three. T. Robbins
Cooke, Alan
  Flat 2. E. Wallace
Cooper, George A.
  Anything Might Happen. H. Balfour
  Eleventh Commandment. B. Fleming; Pillory
  Man Outside. Donald Stuart
  Sexton Blake and the Bearded Doctor. R. Hardinge; Blazing Launch Murder
  Shadow. Donald Stuart
  Tangled Evidence. P. C. De Crespigny
Cooper, Stuart
  Disappearance. D. Marlowe; Echoes of Celandine
Coppola, Francis Ford
  Godfather. M. Puzo
  Godfather Part II. M. Puzo; Godfather
Corbucci, Sergio
  Payoff. A. Veraldi
Corman, Roger
  Bloody Mama. R. Thom
  Gas. B. Hirschfeld
  Masque of the Red Death. Elsie Lee
  Pit and the Pendulum. L. Sheridan
  Premature Burial. M. H. Danne
  Raven. E. Sudak
  St. Valentine's Day Massacre. B. O'Hara
  Tales of Terror. E. Sudak
  X. E. Sudak
Corneau, Alain
  Thriller Story. J. Thompson; Hell of a Woman

Cornfield, Hubert
  Lure of the Swamp. G. Brewer; Hell's Our Destination
  Night of the Following Day. L. White; Snatchers
  Third Voice. C. Williams; All the Way
Cornu, Jacques
  Ladies' Man. P. Quentin; Shadow of Guilt
Corrigan, Lloyd
  Daughter of the Dragon. S. Rohmer; Daughter of Fu Manchu
  Murder on a Honeymoon. S. Palmer; Puzzle of the Pepper Tree
Cosmatos, George Pan
  Cassandra Crossing. R. Katz
  Cobra. P. Gosling; Running Duck
  Escape to Athena. P. Blake
  Rambo: First Blood Part II. D. Morrell
Costello, Maurice
  Mr. Barnes of New York. A. C. Gunter
Crabtree, Arthur
  Calendar. E. Wallace
  Dear Murderer. S. J. Clowes
  Madonna of the Seven Moons. M. Lawrence
Craft, William James
  Birds of Prey. G. Bronson-Howard
Crane, Frank H.
  Gray Mask. W. Camp
  Hutch Stirs 'Em Up. H. Harding; Hawk of Rede
  Moonstone. W. Collins
  Scar. E. Gaboriau (headnote)
  Stranded in Arcady. F. Lynde
Crichton, Charles
  Floods of Fear. J. Hawkins
  Law and Disorder. D. Roberts; Smuggler's Circuit
Crichton, Michael
  Coma. R. Cook
  Great Train Robbery. M. Crichton
Crisp, Donald
  Don Q, Son of Zorro. K. Prichard; Don Q's Love Story
  House of Silence. E. Barron; Marcel Levignet
  Love Insurance. E. D. Biggers
  Princess of New York. C. Hamilton
Croise, Hugh
  Affair at the Novelty Theatre. B. Orczy; Old Man in the Corner
  Brighton Mystery. B. Orczy; Old Man in the Corner
  Burglar and the Girl. M. Boulton
  Grandfather Smallweed. C. Dickens; Bleak House
  Hocussing of Cigarette. B. Orczy; Old Man in the Corner
  Kensington Mystery. B. Orczy; Old Man in the Corner
  Mystery of Brudenell Court. B. Orczy; Old Man in the Corner
  Mystery of Dogstooth Cliff. B. Orczy; Old Man in the Corner
  Mystery of the Khaki Tunic. B. Orczy; Old Man in the Corner
  Northern Mystery. B. Orczy; Old Man in the Corner
  Regent's Park Mystery. B. Orczy; Old Man in the Corner
  Tragedy of Barnsdale Manor. B. Orczy; Old Man in the Corner
  Tremarne Case. B. Orczy; Old Man in the Corner
  York Mystery. B. Orczy; Old Man in the Corner
Crombie, Donald
  Robbery Under Arms. R. Boldrewood
Cromwell, John
  Racket. B. Cormack
Cronenberg, David
  Dead Zone. Stephen King
Crosland, Alan
  Case of the Howling Dog. E. S. Gardner
  Contraband. C. B. Kelland
  Great Impersonation. E. P. Oppenheim
  Whirlpool. V. Morton
  White Cockatoo. M. G. Eberhart
Crowley, William X.
  Trail of the Yukon. J. O. Curwood; Gold Hunters
Crump, Owen
  Couch. R. Bloch
Cruze, James
  I Cover the Waterfront. Max Miller
  Red Mark. J. Russell
Cukor, George
  Gas Light. P. Hamilton
  Grumpy. H. Hodges
  Travels with My Aunt. G. Greene
Culp, Robert
  Hickey and Boggs. P. Rock
Cummings, Irving
  Behind That Curtain. E. D. Biggers
  Country Beyond. J. O. Curwood
  Night Club Lady. A. Abbot; About the Murder of the Night Club Lady

Cunningham, Sean S.
  Stranger Is Watching. M. H. Clark
Curtis, Dan
  Burnt Offerings. R. Marasco
  Dracula. B. Stoker
  House of Dark Shadows. Marilyn Ross
Curtiz, Michael
  Breaking Point. E. Hemingway; To Have and Have Not
  British Agent. H. B. Lockhart
  Casablanca. J. J. Epstein
  Case of the Curious Bride. E. S. Gardner
  Gamblers. C. Klein
  Kennel Murder Case. S. S. Van Dine
  Madonna of Avenue A. M. Canfield
  Man in the Net. P. Quentin
  Mildred Pierce. J. M. Cain
  River's End. J. O. Curwood
  Third Degree. A. Hornblow
  Unsuspected. C. Armstrong
Cutry, C. M.
  Rigged. J. H. Chase; Hit and Run
Cutts, Graham
  Blackguard. R. Paton; Autobiography of a Blackguard
  God's Clay. A. Askew
  Love on the Spot. H. C. McNeile; Three of a Kind
  Passionate Adventure. F. Stayton
  Rat. P. Bottome
  Sign of the Four. A. C. Doyle
Daley, William Robert
  End of the Road. E. Bulwer-Lytton; Ernest Maltravers
Daly, Arnold
  Affair of Three Nations. J. McIntyre (headnote)
Damiami, Damiano
  Day of the Owl. L. Sciascia; Mafia Vendetta
Dante, Joe
  Howling. G. Brandner
D'Antoni, Philip
  Seven-Ups. R. Posner
Dassin, Jules
  Naked City. M. Wald
  Night and the City. G. Kersh
  10:30 P.M. Summer. M. Duras; Ten-Thirty on a Summer Night
  Thieves' Highway. A. I. Bezzerides; Thieves Market
  Topkapi. E. Ambler; Light of Day
  Uptight. L. O'Flaherty; Informer
Daves, Delmer
  Badlanders. W. R. Burnett; Asphalt Jungle
  Dark Passage. D. Goodis
  Never Let Me Go. R. Bax; Came the Dawn
  Red House. G. A. Chamberlain
David, Charles
  Lady on a Train. L. Charteris
Davidson, Martin
  Eddie and the Cruisers. P. F. Kluge
  Hero at Large. A. J. Carothers
Davis, Allan
  Clue of the New Pin. E. Wallace
  Clue of the Twisted Candle. E. Wallace
  Fourth Square. E. Wallace; Four Square Jane
Davis, Desmond
  Ordeal by Innocence. A. Christie
  Sign of the Four. A. C. Doyle
Davis, Ossie
  Cotton Comes to Harlem. C. Himes
Davis, Redd
  Excess Baggage. H. M. Raleigh
Davis, Robin
  I Married a Dead Man. W. Irish
Davis, Will S.
  Doctor Rameau. G. Ohnet
  Mystery Mind. A. B. Reeve
  No Man's Land. L. J. Vance
Dawley, J. Searle
  Frankenstein. M. Shelley
  Leah Kleschna. C. M. S. McLellan
Dawn, Norman
  For the Term of His Natural Life. M. Clarke; His Natural Life
Day, Ernest
  Green Ice. G. A. Browne
Day, Robert
  Green Man. F. Launder; Meet a Body
  Grip of the Strangler. J. C. Cooper
  Man with Bogart's Face. A. J. Fenady
Dean, Basil
  Birds of Prey. A. A. Milne; Fourth Wall
  Escape. J. Galsworthy
  First and the Last. J. Galsworthy; Five Tales
  Loyalties. J. Galsworthy
  Return of Sherlock Holmes. A. C. Doyle; His Last Bow
Dean, Ralph
  Song of Sixpence. F. A. Kummer
Dearden, Basil
  Assassination Bureau. J. London

  Blue Lamp. T. Willis
  Dead of Night. E. F. Benson; Room in the Tower
  League of Gentlemen. J. Boland
  Life for Ruth. W. Drummond
  Man Who Haunted Himself. A. Armstrong; Strange Case of Mr. Pelham
  Masquerade. V. Canning; Castle Minerva
  Mind Benders. J. Kennaway
  Only When I Larf. L. Deighton
  Out of the Clouds. J. Fores; Springboard
  Place to Go. M. Fisher; Bethnel Green
  Sapphire. E. G. Cousins
  Ship That Died of Shame. N. Monsarrat
  Victim. W. Drummond
  Woman of Straw. C. Arley
Decoin, Henri
  Rope for Killing. P. McGerr; Follow, As the Night
  Sorcery. P. Boileau; Spells of Evil
  Strangers in the House. G. Simenon
  Truth About Bebe Donge. G. Simenon; Trial of Bebe Donge
de Cordova, Frederick
  That Way with Women. E. D. Biggers; Earl Derr Biggers Tells Ten Stories
de Courville, Albert
  Crackerjack. W. B. M. Ferguson
  Seven Sinners. A. Ridley; Wrecker
  77, Park Lane. W. Hackett
  77 Rue Chalgrin. W. Hackett; 77, Park Lane
  Strangers on a Honeymoon. E. Wallace; Northing Tramp
De Grasse, Joseph
  Grasp of Greed. H. R. Haggard; Mr. Meeson's Will
  His Wife's Friend. J. B. Harris-Burland; White Rook
  Scarlet Car. R. H. Davis
de Grigorio, Eduardo
  Aspern. H. James; Aspern Papers
de la Iglesia, Eloy
  Turn of the Screw. H. James
Delannoy, Jean
  Action Man. J. Flynn
  Maigret and the St. Fiacre Case. G. Simenon; Saint Fiacre Affair
  Maigret Sets a Trap. G. Simenon
  Obsession. W. Irish; Dead Man Blues
  Torpedo Skin. F. Ryck; Woman Hunt
De Limur, Jean
  Letter. W. S. Maugham
del Ruth, Roy
  Across the Pacific. C. E. Blaney
  Agony Column. E. D. Biggers
  Bulldog Drummond Strikes Back. H. C. McNeile; Knock-Out
  Maltese Falcon. D. Hammett
  Phantom of the Rue Morgue. E. A. Poe; Prose Romances of Edgar A. Poe
  Second Floor Mystery. E. D. Biggers; Agony Column
  Stop, You're Killing Me. D. Runyon; Slight Case of Murder
  Terror. E. Wallace
  Three Faces East. A. P. Kelly
De Mille, Cecil B.
  Man on the Box. H. MacGrath
  Manslaughter. A. D. Miller
  Whispering Chorus. P. P. Sheehan
De Mille, William C.
  Grumpy. H. Hodges
  Mystery Girl. G. B. McCutcheon; Green Fancy
Demme, Jonathan
  Last Embrace. M. T. Bloom; 13th Man
Denham, Reginald
  Crimson Circle. E. Wallace
  Death at Broadcasting House. V. Gielgud
  Flying Fifty-Five. E. Wallace
  House of the Spaniard. A. Behrend
  Jewel. E. Wallace (headnote)
  Kate Plus Ten. E. Wallace
Denton, Jack
  Ernest Maltravers. E. Bulwer-Lytton
  Lady Audley's Secret. M. E. Braddon
De Palma, Brian
  Blow Out. N. Williams
  Dressed to Kill. Campbell Black
  Fury. J. Farris
  Scarface. A. Trail
Deray, Jacques
  Butterfly on the Shoulder. J. Gearon; Velvet Well
  He Died with His Eyes Open. D. Raymond
  Man from Marrakech. R. P. Jones; Heisters
  On a Nice Summer Day. J. H. Chase; One Bright Summer Morning
de Toth, Andre
  Dark Waters. F. Cockrell
  Pitfall. J. J. Dratler
Deville, Michel
  Deep Water. P. Highsmith

Directors Index

Dossier 51. G. Perrault
Dewhurst, George
  Dead Certainty. N. Gould
  Shadow Between. S. Hocking
Dewsbury, Ralph
  Man in Motley. T. Gallon
Dickinson, Thorold
  Arsenal Stadium Mystery. L. Gribble
  Gas Light. P. Hamilton
  High Command. L. Robinson; General Goes Too Far
Dieterle, William
  Accused. J. Truesdell; Be Still, My Love
  Fog Over Frisco. G. Dyer; Five Fragments
  Jewel Robbery. L. Fodor
  Lawyer Man. M. Trell
  Love Letters. C. Massie; Pity My Simplicity
  Satan Met a Lady. D. Hammett; Maltese Falcon
Dillon, Edward
  Bride. S. Olivier
Dillon, Jack/John Francis
  Behind the Mask. E. P. Oppenheim; Jeanne of the Marshes
  Calvert's Valley. M. P. Montagu; In Calvert's Valley
Dixon, Ivan
  Spook Who Sat by the Door. S. Greenlee
Dmytryk, Edward
  Crossfire. R. Brooks; Brick Foxhole
  Devil Commands. W. Sloane; Edge of Running Water
  End of the Matter. G. Greene
  Farewell, My Lovely. R. Chandler
  Human Factor. S. Quinn
  Mirage. W. Ericson; Fallen Angel
  Obsession. A. Coppel; Man About a Dog
Donahue, Jack
  Assault on a Queen. J. Finney
Donen, Stanley
  Arabesque. Alex Gordon; Cipher
  Charade. P. H. Stone
Donner, Clive
  Charlie Chan and the Curse of the Dragon Queen. M. Avallone
  Marriage of Convenience. E. Wallace; Three Oak Mystery
  Nothing But the Best. S. Ellin; Mystery Stories
Donner, Richard
  Salt and Pepper. A. Austin
Doughton, Russell S., Jr.
  Hostage. C. Henry
Douglas, Gordon
  Detective. R. Thorp
  Fiend Who Walked the West. E. Lipsky; Kiss of Death
  In Like Flint. B. Street
  Kiss Tomorrow Goodbye. H. McCoy
  Lady in Cement. A. Rome
  Robin and the Seven Hoods. J. Pearl
  Slaughter's Big Rip-Off. A. Kane
  Sylvia. E. V. Cunningham
  Tony Rome. A. Rome; Miami Mayhem
Dowlan, William C.
  Loot. A. S. Roche
  Outsider. L. J. Vance; Nobody
Doxat-Pratt, B. E.
  John Heriot's Wife. A. Askew
  Little Hour of Peter Wells. D. Whitelaw
  Other Person. F. Hume
Drake, Ronald
  Killer Walks. G. Glennon; Gathering Storm
Drew, S. Rankin
  Hunted Woman. J. O. Curwood
Dreyer, Carl Theodore
  Strange Adventure of David Gray. J. S. Le Fanu; In a Glass Darkly
Duffell, Peter (John)
  England Made Me. G. Greene
  Inside Out. W. Hughes
  Letters to an Unknown Lover. P. Boileau; Prisoner
  Partners in Crime. E. Wallace; Man Who Knew
Duke, Daryl
  Silent Partner. A. Bodelsen; Think of a Number
Dunlap, Scott R.
  Midnight Life. R. W. Kauffman; Spider's Web
  Trooper O'Neill. G. Goodchild
Dunne, Phillip
  Blindfold. L. Fletcher
  Inspector. J. De Hartog
Dupont, E(wald) A(ndre)
  Bishop Misbehaves. F. Jackson
  Night of Mystery. S. S. Van Dine; Greene Murder Case
Durning, Bernard J.
  Yosemite Trail. R. Cullum; One-Way Trail
Duvivier, Julien
  Ardent Room. J. D. Carr; Burning Court
  Flesh and Fantasy. O. Wilde; Lord Arthur Savile's Crime
  Gooseflesh. J. H. Chase; Come Easy--Go Easy
  Man in the Raincoat. J. H. Chase; Tiger by the Tail
  Maurizius Affair. J. Wasserman; Maurizius Case
  Panique. G. Simenon; Mr. Hire's Engagement
Dwan, Allan
  Cheating Cheaters. M. Marcin
  Conspiracy. R. Baker
  Gorilla. R. Spence
  Human Cargo. K. Shepard; I Will Be Faithful
  Luck of the Irish. H. MacGrath
  Manhandled. A. Stringer
  Slightly Scarlet. J. M. Cain; Love's Lovely Counterfeit
  Splendid Hazard. H. MacGrath
Eades, Wilfred
  You Can't Escape. A. Kennington
Eady, David
  Faces in the Dark. P. Boileau
  In the Wake of a Stranger. I. S. Black
  Verdict. E. Wallace; Big Four
Eagle, Oscar
  Coast of Chance. E. Chamberlain
Earle, William P. S.
  Scarlet Runner. C. N. Williamson
  Within the Law. B. Veiller
Eason, B. Reeves
  Shadow on the Wall. J. B. Ellis; Picture on the Wall
  Spy Ship. G. Dyer; Five Fragments
Eastwood, Clint
  Eiger Sanction. Trevanian
  Firefox. C. Thomas
  Gauntlet. M. Butler
  Sudden Impact. J. C. Stinson
Edwards, Blake
  Carey Treatment. J. Hudson; Case of Need
  Darling Lili. H. Clement
  Experiment in Terror. Gordons; Operation Terror
  Pink Panther. M. H. Albert
  Shot in the Dark. H. Kurnitz
  Tamarind Seed. E. Anthony
Edwards, Henry
  Amazing Quest of Mr. Ernest Bliss. E. P. Oppenheim
  Juggernaut. A. Campbell
  Lad. E. Wallace (headnote)
  Lord Edgware Dies. A. Christie
  Lunatic at Large. J. S. Clouston
  Man Who Changed His Name. E. Wallace
Edwards, J. Gordon
  Tangled Lives. W. Collins; Woman in White
Edwards, Roland G.
  Drums of Jeopardy. H. MacGrath
Edwin, Walter
  Master Mummer. E. P. Oppenheim
Eldridge, John
  Brandy for the Parson. G. Household; Tales of Adventurers
Elles, Fred
  Mrs. Pym of Scotland Yard. N. Morland (headnote)
Elvey, Maurice
  Amateur Gentleman. J. Farnol
  At the Villa Rose. A. E. W. Mason
  Beautiful Jim, of the Blankshire Regiment. J. S. Winter
  Beryl Coronet. A. C. Doyle; Adventures of Sherlock Holmes
  Bleak House. C. Dickens
  Case of Identity. A. C. Doyle; Adventures of Sherlock Holmes
  Copper Beeches. A. C. Doyle; Adventures of Sherlock Holmes
  Curly Top. T. Burke; Whispering Windows
  Devil's Foot. A. C. Doyle; His Last Bow
  Dick Turpin's Ride to York. W. H. Ainsworth; Rookwood
  Dying Detective. A. C. Doyle; His Last Bow
  Empty House. A. C. Doyle; Return of Sherlock Holmes
  Footsteps in the Night. C. Fraser-Simpson
  Grip. J. S. Winter
  Harrassed Hero. E. Dudley
  Hound of the Baskervilles. A. C. Doyle
  Justice. J. Galsworthy
  Late Edwina Black. W. Dinner
  Lily of Killarney. D. Boucicault; Colleen Bawn
  Lodger. M. B. Lowndes
  Man with the Twisted Lip. A. C. Doyle; Adventures of Sherlock Holmes
  Maria Marten. Anonymous
  Meg the Lady. T. Gallon
  Mr. Wu. L. J. Milne
  Noble Bachelor. A. C. Doyle; Adventures of Sherlock Holmes
  Priory School. A. C. Doyle; Return of Sherlock Holmes
  Quinney's. H. A. Vachell
  Red-Headed League. A. C. Doyle; Adventures of Sherlock Holmes
  Resident Patient. A. C. Doyle; Memoirs of Sherlock Holmes
  Return of the Frog. E. Wallace; India-Rubber Men
  Road House. W. Hackett
  Running Water. A. E. W. Mason
  Scandal in Bohemia. A. C. Doyle; Adventures of Sherlock Holmes
  Sign of the Four. A. C. Doyle
  Solitary Cyclist. A. C. Doyle; Return of Sherlock Holmes
  Spider. H. Holt; Midnight Mail
  Suicide Club. R. L. Stevenson
  Third Visitor. G. Anstruther
  Tiger of San Pedro. A. C. Doyle; His Last Bow
  Who Killed John Savage? P. MacDonald; Rynox
  Yellow Face. A. C. Doyle; Memoirs of Sherlock Holmes
Endfield, Cyril
  Try and Get Me. J. Pagano; Condemned
  Trial of Madame X. J. W. MacConaughy; Madame X
England, Paul
  Drums of Fu Manchu. S. Rohmer
English, John
  Laramie Trail. J. Gregory; Mystery at Spanish Hacienda
Englund, George
  Signpost to Murder. M. Doyle
Enrico, Robert
  Heads or Tails. A. Harris; Baroni Secret. F. Ryck; Undesirable Company
Enright, Ray
  River's End. J. O. Curwood
  While the Patient Slept. M. G. Eberhart
Essex, Harry
  I, the Jury. M. Spillane
Faenza, Robert
  Order of Death. H. Fleetwood
Fargo, James
  Enforcer. W. Morgan
  Game for Vultures. M. Hartmann
Farnum, Marshall
  Lady Audley's Secret. M. E. Braddon
Farrow, John
  Big Clock. K. Fearing
  Night Has a Thousand Eyes. G. Hopley
  Plunder of the Sun. D. Dodge
  Saint Strikes Back. L. Charteris; She Was a Lady
  Unholy Wife. J. Roeburt
Fassbinder, Rainer Werner
  Despair. V. Nabokoff-Sirin
Faustman, Lhampe
  Crime and Punishment. F. M. Dostoevskii
Feist, Felix E.
  Devil Thumbs a Ride. R. C. Du Soe
  Donovan's Brain. C. Siodmak
Fejos, Paul
  Broadway. P. Dunning
  Fantomas. P. Souvestre
Fenton, Leslie
  Saint's Vacation. L. Charteris; Getaway
  Stronger Than Desire. W. E. Woodward; Evelyn Prentice
  Whispering Smith. F. H. Spearman
Feyder, Jacques
  Knight Without Armour. J. Hilton
Fields, Leonard
  Manhattan Love Song. C. Woolrich
Figman, Max
  Jack Chanty. H. Footner
Fisher, Terence
  Blackout. H. Nielsen; Gold Coast Nocturne
  Curse of Frankenstein. M. Shelley; Frankenstein
  Curse of the Werewolf. G. Endore; Werewolf of Paris
  Dead on Course. M. Black
  Devil Rides Out. D. Wheatley
  Dracula. B. Stoker
  Dracula, Prince of Darkness. B. Stoker; Dracula
  Face the Music. E. Borneman; Tremolo
  Frankenstein Must Be Destroyed. M. Shelley; Frankenstein
  Hound of the Baskervilles. A. C. Doyle
  House of Fright. R. L. Stevenson; Strange Case of Dr. Jekyll and Mr. Hyde
  Last Man to Hang. G. Bullett; Jury
  Last Page. J. H. Chase
  Man Who Could Cheat Death. B. Lyndon; Amazing Dr. Clitterhouse
  Mantrap. S. Rattray; Queen in Danger

Phantom of the Opera. G. Leroux
Stranger Came Home. G. Sanders; Stranger at Home
Stranglers of Bombay. S. James
To the Public Danger. P. Hamilton
Fitzmaurice, George
  At Bay. P. Phillips
  Avalanche. G. Atherton
  Bella Donna. R. Hichens
  Emperor's Candlesticks. B. Orczy
  Kick-In. W. Mack
  Locked Door. C. Pollock; Sign on the Door
  Mark of Cain. C. Wells
  Raffles. E. W. Hornung; Amateur Cracksman
  Right to Love. C. Farrere; Man Who Killed
  Stop Thief! Carlyle Moore
  Tiger Rose. W. Mack
  Witness for the Defense. A. E. W. Mason
Fleischer, Richard
  Blind Terror. W. Hughes
  Compulsion. M. Levin
  Crack in the Mirror. M. Haedrich
  Don Is Dead. N. Quarry
  Mr. Majestyk. E. Leonard
  New Centurions. J. Wambaugh
  Spikes Gang. G. Tippette; Bank Robber
  Violent Saturday. W. L. Heath
Fleming, Victor
  Blind Goddess. A. Train
  Dr. Jekyll and Mr. Hyde. R. L. Stevenson
  Empty Hands. A. Stringer
Flemyng, Gordon
  Five to One. E. Wallace; Thief in the Night
  Last Grenade. J. Sherlock; Ordeal of Major Grigsby
  Solo for Sparrow. E. Wallace; Gunner
  Split. R. Stark; Seventh
Flicker, Theodore J.
  Three in a Cellar. Angus Hall; Late Boy Wonder
Flood, James
  Lonely Road. N. Shute
  Times Have Changed. E. Davis
  Under Cover Man. J. Wilstach
Florey, Robert
  Beast with Five Fingers. W. F. Harvey
  Danger Signal. P. Bottome; Murder in the Bud
  Dangerous to Know. E. Wallace; On the Spot
  Death of a Champion. F. Gruber; Brass Knuckles
  Florentine Dagger. B. Hecht
  Man Called Back. A. Soutar; Silent Thunder
  Mountain Music. M. Kantor; Author's Choice
  Murders in the Rue Morgue. E. A. Poe; Prose Romances of Edgar A. Poe
Floyd, Calvin
  Victor Frankenstein. M. Shelley; Frankenstein
Flynn, Emmett J.
  East Lynne. H. Wood
Flynn, John
  Outfit. R. Stark
Forbes, Bryan
  Deadfall. D. Cory
  Naked Face. S. Sheldon
  Seance on a Wet Afternoon. M. McShane
  Stepford Wives. I. Levin
  Wrong Box. R. L. Stevenson
Ford, Francis
  Study in Scarlet. A. C. Doyle
Ford, Hugh
  Jim the Penman. C. L. Young
  Secret Service. W. Gillette
  Seven Keys to Baldpate. E. D. Biggers
  Slave Market. F. A. Kummer; Painted Woman
  Woman in the Case. C. Fitch
Ford, John
  Black Watch. T. Mundy; King of the Khyber Rifles
  Four Men and a Prayer. D. Garth
  Fugitive. G. Greene; Power and the Glory
  Gideon's Day. J. J. Marric
  Informer. L. O'Flaherty
  Judge Priest. I. S. Cobb; Down Yonder with Judge Priest
  Louis Beretti. D. H. Clarke
  Sun Shines Bright. I. S. Cobb; Old Judge Priest
Forde, Eugene
  Charlie Chan's Murder Cruise. E. D. Biggers; Charlie Chan Carries On
  Country Beyond. J. O. Curwood
  Dressed to Kill. R. Burke; Dead Take No Bows
  Great Hotel Murder. V. Starrett
  Michael Shayne, Private Eye. B. Halliday; Private Practice of Michael Shayne
  Sleepers West. F. Nebel; Sleepers East
Forde, Walter
  Condemned to Death. G. Goodchild; Jack O'Lantern
  Four Just Men. E. Wallace
  Gaunt Stranger. E. Wallace; Ringer
  Ghost Train. A. Ridley
  Inspector Hornleigh on Holiday. L. Grex; Stolen Death
  Last Hour. C. Bennett
  Peterville Diamond. L. Fodor; Jewel Robbery
  Ringer. E. Wallace
  Rome Express. R. Alexander
  Saloon Bar. F. Harvey
  Silent House. J. G. Brandon
Forman, Tom
  City of Silent Men. J. A. Moroso; Quarry
  People vs. Nancy Preston. J. A. Moroso; People Against Nancy Preston
Foss, Kenelm
  House of Peril. M. B. Lowndes; Chink in the Armour
Foster, Lewis R.
  Jamaica Run. M. Murray; Neat Little Corpse
  Love Letters of a Star. Rufus King; Case of the Constant God
  Lucky Stiff. C. Rice
Foster, Norman
  Journey into Fear. E. Ambler
  Kiss the Blood Off My Hands. G. Butler
  Thank You, Mr. Moto. J. P. Marquand
  Think Fast, Mr. Moto. J. P. Marquand
Fourastie, Philippe
  Choice of Assassins. W. P. McGivern
Fowler, Gene, Jr.
  Gang War. O. Demaris; Hoods Take Over
Foy, Bryan
  Gorilla. R. Spence
Fraker, William A.
  Reflection of Fear. S. Forbes; Go to Thy Death Bed
Francis, Freddie
  Craze. H. Seymour; Infernal Idol
  Deadly Bees. H. F. Heard; Taste of Honey
  Mumsy, Nanny, Sonny and Girlie. B. Comport
  Skull. R. Bloch; Skull of the Marquis de Sade
  Traitor's Gate. E. Wallace
  Vengeance. C. Siodmak; Donovan's Brain
Franco, Jesus
  Count Dracula. B. Stoker; Dracula
Frank, Charles
  Uncle Silas. J. S. Le Fanu
Frankel, Cyril
  Permission to Kill. P. Loraine; W.I.L. One to Curtis
  Witches. P. Curtis; Devil's Own
Frankenheimer, John
  Black Sunday. T. Harris
  Fifty-Two Pickup. E. Leonard
  French Connection II. R. Moore
  Holcroft Covenant. R. Ludlum
  I Walk the Line. Madison Jones; Exile
  Manchurian Candidate. R. Condon
  99 and 44/100% Dead. M. Franklin; 99 44/100% Dead
  Seconds. D. Ely
  Seven Days in May. F. Knebel
  Young Savages. E. Hunter; Matter of Conviction
Franklin, Chester M.
  File 113. E. Gaboriau; File No. 113
  Thirteenth Hour. S. Horler
Franklin, Richard
  Cloak and Dagger. W. Irish; Dead Man Blues
Franklin, Sidney A.
  Last of Mrs. Cheyney. F. Lonsdale
  Not Guilty. H. MacGrath; Parrot & Co.
  Tiger Rose. W. Mack
Franz, Joseph
  Alias the Night Wind. V. Vanardy
Frears, Stephen
  Gumshoe. N. Smith
Freeland, Thornton
  Amateur Gentleman. J. Farnol
  Secret Witness. S. Spewack; Murder in the Gilded Cage
  Three Live Ghosts. F. S. Isham
Fregonese, Hugo
  Man in the Attic. M. B. Lowndes; Lodger
  Seven Thunders. R. Croft-Cooke
French, Harold
  Blind Goddess. P. Hastings
  Dead Men Are Dangerous. H. C. Armstrong; Hidden
  Hour of Thirteen. M. Porlock; X v. Rex
  House of the Arrow. A. E. W. Mason
Man Who Watched the Trains Go By. G. Simenon
Frend, Charles
  Cone of Silence. D. Beaty
Freund, Karl
  Hands of Orlac. M. Renard
Friedkin, William
  Brink's Job. N. Behn; Big Stick-Up at Brink's!
  Cruising. G. Walker
  Exorcist. W. P. Blatty
  To Live and Die in L.A. G. Petievich
  Wages of Fear. G. Arnaud
Frohman, Daniel
  Day of Days. L. J. Vance
Fuest, Robert
  Abominable Dr. Phibes. W. Goldstein; Dr. Phibes
  Devil's Rain. M. Willis
  Dr. Phibes Rises Again. W. Goldstein
Fuller, Samuel
  Dead Pigeon on Beethoven Street. S. Fuller
  Naked Kiss. S. Fuller
  Shark. V. Canning; His Bones Are Coral
  Shock Corridor. M. Avallone
Furie, Sidney J.
  Ipcress File. L. Deighton
  Naked Runner. F. Clifford
Furthman, Jules
  Colorado Pluck. G. Goodchild; Colorado Jim
Gabel, Martin
  Lost Moment. H. James; Aspern Papers
Gage, George
  Fleshburn. J. Ives; Fear in a Handful of Dust
Gaillord, Robert
  Mr. Barnes of New York. A. C. Gunter
Gainsbourg, Serge
  Equateur. G. Simenon; Tropic Moon
Gainville, Rene
  Woman Is a Stranger. J. H. Chase; Not Safe to Be Free
Galeen, Henrik
  After the Verdict. R. Hichens
Gallagher, Donald
  Temple Tower. H. C. McNeile
Gallu, Samuel
  Double Agent. G. Stackelberg
  Limbo Line. V. Canning
Ganders, Felix
  Mysteries of Paris. E. Sue
Gardner, Cyril
  Grumpy. H. Hodges
  Only Saps Work. O. Davis; Easy Come, Easy Go
Garnett, Tay
  Bad Company. J. Lait; Put on the Spot
  Postman Always Rings Twice. J. M. Cain
  Slightly Honorable. F. G. Presnell; Send Another Coffin
Garrett, Otis
  Black Doll. W. E. Hayes
  Danger on the Air. Xantippe; Death Catches Up with Mr. Kluck
  Lady in the Morgue. J. Latimer
  Last Express. B. Kendrick
  Mystery of the White Room. J. G. Edwards; Murder in the Surgery
  Witness Vanishes. J. Ronald; They Can't Hang Me!
Garrick, Richard
  Armadale. W. Collins
  Rank Outsider. N. Gould
  Trent's Last Case. E. C. Bentley
Gasnier, Louis
  Breath of Scandal. E. Balmer
  Exploits of Elaine. A. B. Reeve
  Shadow of the Law. J. A. Moroso; Quarry
  Slightly Scarlet. P. Heath
  Ticket-of-Leave Man. C. Reade; Foul Play
Gavras, Costa
  Sleeping Car Murders. S. Japrisot; 10:30 from Marseilles
Geissendoerfer, Hans C.
  Edith's Diary. P. Highsmith
  Glass Cell. P. Highsmith
Gentilomo, Giacomo
  Brothers Karamazov. F. M. Dostoevskii
Geraghty, Tom J.
  Perpetua. D. C. Calthrop
  Spanish Jade. M. Hewlett
Gerrard, Gene
  It's in the Blood. D. Whitelaw; Big Picture
Gessner, Nicolas
  Blonde from Peking. J. H. Chase; You Have Yourself a Deal
  Little Girl Who Lives Down the Lane. L. Koenig
Giblyn, Charles
  Dark Mirror. L. J. Vance
  Leavenworth Case. A. K. Green
  Somewhere in France. R. H. Davis
Gibson, Alan

Goodbye Gemini. J. Hall; Ask Agamemnon
Gilbert, Arthur
 Convict 99. M. C. Leighton
 Mystery of Edwin Drood. C. Dickens
Gilbert, Lewis
 Cast a Dark Shadow. J. Green; Murder Mistaken
 Moonraker. C. Wood; James Bond and Moonraker
 Sea Shall Not Have Them. J. Harris
 Spy Who Loved Me. C. Wood; James Bond, the Spy Who Loved Me
 You Only Live Twice. I. Fleming
Giler, David
 Black Bird. A. Edwards
Gilliat, Sidney
 Endless Night. A. Christie
 Fortune Is a Woman. Winston Graham
 Green for Danger. C. Brand
 London Belongs to Me. N. Collins
Gilling, John
 Flesh and the Fiends. R. L. Stevenson; Body Snatcher
 Man Inside. M. E. Chaber
 Night Caller. F. Crisp; Night Callers
 Tiger by the Tail. J. Mair; Never Come Back
Giovanni, Jose
 Last Known Address. J. Harrington
 One Way Ticket. H. E. Helseth; Chair for Martin Rome
Girard, Bernard
 Dead Heat on a Merry-Go-Round. E. L. Heyman
 Mad Room. E. Percy; Ladies in Retirement
Girault, Jean
 Gazebo. A. Coppel
Girod, Francis
 Descent into Hell. D. Goodis; Wounded and the Slain
Gist, Robert
 American Dream. N. Mailer
Glaister, Gerard
 Clue of the Silver Key. E. Wallace
 Partner. E. Wallace; Million Dollar Story
 Set-Up. E. Wallace (headnote)
 Share Out. E. Wallace; Jack o' Judgment
Gleason, Michie
 Summer Heat. L. Shivers; Here to Get My Baby Out of Jail
Glen, John
 Octopussy. I. Fleming; Octopussy and The Living Daylights
Glennon, Burt
 Girl of the Port. J. Russell; Far Wandering Men
 Perfect Crime. I. Zangwill; Big Bow Mystery
Glenville, Peter
 Comedians. G. Greene
 Term of Trial. J. Barlow
Godard, Jean-Luc
 Band of Outsiders. D. Hitchens; Fool's Gold
 Crazy Pete. L. White; Obsession
 Grandeur and Decadence of a Small-Time Filmmaker. J. H. Chase (headnote)
 Made in U.S.A. R. Stark; Jugger
Goddard, Jim
 Shanghai Surprise. T. Kenrick; Faraday's Flowers
Godfrey, Peter
 Cry Wolf. M. Carleton
 Down River. Seamark
 Highways by Night. C. B. Kelland; Silver Spoon
 Thread O'Scarlet. J. J. Bell
 Two Mrs. Carrolls. M. Vale
 Woman in White. W. Collins
Golan, Menahem
 Lepke. J. Pearl
Gold, Jack
 Medusa Touch. P. Van Greenaway
 Praying Mantis. H. Monteilhet; Praying Mantises
 Who? A. Budrys
Goldstone, James
 Gang That Couldn't Shoot Straight. J. Breslin
 Jigsaw. W. Ericson; Fallen Angel
Gonzalez, Servando
 Fool Killer. H. Eustis
Goodwins, Fred
 Blood Money. C. H. Bullivant
 Chinese Puzzle. M. Bower
Gordon, Michael
 Act of Murder. E. Lothar; Mills of God
 Portrait in Black. I. Goff
Goslar, Juergen
 Whispering Death. D. Carney
Goulding, Edmund
 Everybody Does It. J. M. Cain; Career in C Major
 Nightmare Alley. W. L. Gresham
 We Are Not Alone. J. Hilton

Graham, William A.
 Then Came Bronson. W. Johnston
 Together Brothers. Jim Robinson
Grandon, Francis E.
 Dummy. H. J. O'Higgins
Grangier, Gilles
 Blood to the Head. G. Simenon; Young Cardinaud
 Maigret Sees Red. G. Simenon; Maigret and the Gangsters
Granier-Deferre, Pierre
 Cat. G. Simenon
 Man with the Silver Eyes. R. Rossner; End of Someone Else's Rainbow
 North Star. G. Simenon; Lodger
 Train. G. Simenon
 Widow Couderc. G. Simenon; Ticket of Leave
Grant, Frances E.
 Sword of Fate. H. Herman
Granville, Fred Leroy
 At the Mercy of Tiberius. A. J. Wilson
Grauman, Walter E.
 Lady in a Cage. R. Durand
 Last Escape. M. Walker
 633 Squadron. F. E. Smith
Grayson, Godfrey
 Meet Simon Cherry. G. Pedrick; Meet the Rev
 Spider's Web. A. Christie
Green, Alfred E.
 Come to My House. A. S. Roche
 Dark Hazard. W. R. Burnett
 Gracie Allen Murder Case. S. S. Van Dine
 League of Frightened Men. R. Stout
 Parachute Jumper. R. James; Some Call It Love
Green, Guy
 Angry Silence. John Burke
 House of Secrets. S. Noel
 Mark. C. E. Israel
 Portrait of Allison. F. Durbridge
Greene, David
 I Start Counting. A. E. Lindop
 Shuttered Room. J. Withers
 Strange Affair. B. Toms
Greene, Max
 Hotel Reserve. E. Ambler; Epitaph for a Spy
Greenwood, Edwin
 Miss Bracegirdle Does Her Duty. S. Aumonier; Miss Bracegirdle and Others
 To What Red Hell. P. Robinson
Gremm, Wolf
 Kamikaze. P. Wahloo; Murder on the Thirty-First Floor
Greville, Edmond T.
 Guilty? M. Gilbert; Death Has Deep Roots
 Hands of Orlac. M. Renard
Grey, Richard M.
 Man with the Twisted Lip. A. C. Doyle; Adventures of Sherlock Holmes
Gries, Tom
 Breakheart Pass. A. MacLean
 Girl in the Woods. O. Crawford; Blood on the Branches
 Lady Ice. M. Braly; Master
Griffith, D. W.
 Broken Blossoms. T. Burke; Limehouse Nights
 Dream Street. T. Burke; Limehouse Nights
 Suicide Club. R. L. Stevenson
 That Royle Girl. E. Balmer
Griffith, Edward H.
 Alias the Lone Wolf. L. J. Vance
 White Mice. R. H. Davis
Grimes, Lee
 Miss Bracegirdle Does Her Duty. S. Aumonier; Miss Bracegirdle and Others
Grinde, Nick
 Bishop Murder Case. S. S. Van Dine
 Remote Control. C. North
Grosbard, Ula
 Straight Time. E. Bunker; No Beast So Fierce
 True Confessions. J. G. Dunne
Guest, Val
 Assignment K. Hartley Howard; Department K
 Break in the Circle. P. Loraine
 Casino Royale. I. Fleming
 Dangerous Davies. L. Thomas
 Full Treatment. R. S. Thorn
 Hell Is a City. M. Procter
 Jigsaw. H. Waugh; Sleep Long, My Love
 Where the Spies Are. J. Leasor; Passport to Oblivion
Guillermin, John
 Day They Robbed the Bank of England. J. Brophy
 Death on the Nile. A. Christie
 House of Cards. S. Ellin
 Skyjacked. D. Harper; Hijacked
 Towering Inferno. R. M. Stern; Tower

Whole Truth. P. Mackie
Gundry, V. Gareth
 Hound of the Baskervilles. A. C. Doyle
Haas, Charles
 Platinum High School. I. Shulman
Haas, Hugo
 Lizzie. S. Jackson; Bird's Nest
Habib, Ralph
 Passager Clandestin. G. Simenon; Stowaway
Hachuel, Herve
 Last of Philip Banter. J. F. Bardin
Hackford, Taylor
 Against All Odds. G. Homes; Build My Gallows High
Hadden, George
 Charlie Chan's Courage. E. D. Biggers; Chinese Parrot
Hagen, Julius
 Passing of Mr. Quin. A. Christie; Mysterious Mr. Quin
Haggar, William
 Dumb Man of Manchester. B. F. Rayner
Haggard, Piers
 Venom. A. Scholefield
Haguet, Andrew
 Secret Document--Vienna. M. Dekobra; Widow with the Pink Gloves
Haines, Ronald
 Man with the Magnetic Eyes. R. Daniel
Haldane, Bert
 East Lynne. H. Wood
 Ticket-of-Leave Man. T. Taylor
Hales, Gordon
 Return to Sender. E. Wallace (headnote)
Hall, George Edwardes
 Dr. Jekyll and Mr. Hyde. R. L. Stevenson; Strange Case of Dr. Jekyll and Mr. Hyde
Halperin, Victor
 Ex-Flame. H. Wood; East Lynne
 Party Girl. E. Balmer; Dangerous Business
Hamer, Robert
 Father Brown. G. K. Chesterton; Innocence of Father Brown
 It Always Rains on Sunday. A. La Bern
 Kind Hearts and Coronets. R. Horniman; Israel Rank
 Long Memory. H. Clewes
 Pink String and Sealing Wax. R. Pertwee
 Scapegoat. D. Du Maurier
Hamilton, Guy
 Diamonds Are Forever. I. Fleming
 Evil Under the Sun. A. Christie
 Force 10 from Navarone. A. MacLean
 Funeral in Berlin. L. Deighton
 Goldfinger. I. Fleming
 Inspector Calls. J. B. Priestley
 Intruder. R. Maugham; Line on Ginger
 Live and Let Die. I. Fleming
 Man in the Middle. H. Fast; Winston Affair
 Man with the Golden Gun. I. Fleming
 Mirror Crack'd. A. Christie; Mirror Crack'd from Side to Side
 Remo: The First Adventure. W. B. Murphy
 Ringer. E. Wallace
 Touch of Larceny. A. Garve; Megstone Plot
Hamilton, William
 Murder on the Bridle Path. S. Palmer; Puzzle of the Red Stallion
 Seven Keys to Baldpate. E. D. Biggers
Hanbury, W. Victor
 Crouching Beast. V. Williams
 Dick Turpin. W. H. Ainsworth; Rookwood
 Hotel Reserve. E. Ambler; Epitaph for a Spy
 Second Bureau. C. R. Dumas
Hankey, Anthony
 Too Dangerous to Live. D. Hume
Hankinson, Michael
 Chick. E. Wallace
 Scarab Murder Case. S. S. Van Dine
Hannam, Ken
 Robbery Under Arms. R. Boldrewood
Hansel, Howell
 Horrible Hyde. R. L. Stevenson; Strange Case of Dr. Jekyll and Mr. Hyde
 Million Dollar Mystery. H. MacGrath
Hanson, Curtis
 Bedroom Window. A. Holden; Witnesses
Hardy, Robin
 Wicker Man. R. Hardy
Hare, Lumsden
 Masquerade. L. J. Vance; Brass Bowl
Harlow, John
 Candles at Nine. Anthony Gilbert; Mouse Who Wouldn't Play Ball
 Dark Tower. A. Woollcott
 Reporter. K. Attiwill
Harrington, Curtis
 Games. H. Ellson

What's the Matter with Helen? R. Deming
Harris, Jack
 Called Back. H. Conway
Harris, James B.
 Fast-Walking. E. Brawley; Rap
Harris, Lionel
 Double. E. Wallace
Harrison, Norman
 Incident at Midnight. E. Wallace (headnote)
 Locker 69. E. Wallace (headnote)
Hart, Harvey
 Pyx. J. Buell
 Shoot. D. Fairbairn
 Sweet Ride. W. Murray
Hartford, David M.
 Golden Snare. J. O. Curwood
 Inside the Lines. E. D. Biggers
 Nomads of the North. J. O. Curwood
Hartford-Davis, Robert
 Crosstrap. J. H. Chase (headnote)
 Take. G. F. Newman; Sir, You Bastard
Harvey, Laurence
 Dandy in Aspic. D. Marlowe
Haskin, Byron
 Power. F. M. Robinson
 Too Late for Tears. R. Huggins
Hathaway, Henry
 Bottom of the Bottle. G. Simenon
 Dark Corner. L. Q. Ross
 Diplomatic Courier. P. Cheyney; Sinister Errand
 Kiss of Death. E. Lipsky
 Seven Thieves. S. Kent; Lions at the Kill
 23 Paces to Baker Street. P. MacDonald; Nursemaid Who Disappeared
 Witching Hour. A. Thomas
Hawks, Howard
 Big Sleep. R. Chandler
 Scarface. A. Trail
 To Have and Have Not. E. Hemingway
 Trent's Last Case. E. C. Bentley
Hawks, William
 Criminal Code. M. Flavin
Haydon, J. Charles
 Alster Case. R. Gillmore
 Phantom Buccaneer. V. Bridges; Another Man's Shoes
 Strange Case of Mary Page. F. Lewis
Hayers, Sidney
 Assault. K. Young; Ravine
 Echo of Barbara. John Burke
 Malpas Mystery. E. Wallace; Face in the Night
 Payroll. D. Bickerton
 Trap. John Burke
 What Changed Charley Farthing. M. Hebden
Haynes, H. Manning
 Clayton Treasure Mystery. N. Gordon; Shakespeare Murders
 Monkey's Paw. W. W. Jacobs; Lady of the Barge
 Old Man. E. Wallace; Coat of Arms
 Other Man. E. Wallace; Nine Bears
 Ware Case. G. Pleydell
Hecht, Ben
 Crime Without Passion. B. Hecht; Collected Stories of Ben Hecht
Heerman, Victor
 Confidence Man. L. Y. Erskine
 Imperfect Imposter. N. Venner
Hoffron, Richard T.
 I, the Jury. M. Spillane
Heffron, T. N.
 House of a Thousand Candles. M. Nicholson
Heinreid, Paul
 Dead Ringer. R. Thomas
Heisler, Stuart
 Glass Key. D. Hammett
 I Died a Thousand Times. W. R. Burnett; High Sierra
Hemmings, David
 Running Scared. G. McDonald
 Survivor. J. Herbert
Henabery, Joseph
 Stranger. J. Galsworthy; Five Tales
Henley, Hobart
 Captain Applejack. W. Hackett
 Roadhouse Nights. D. Hammett; Red Harvest
 Sin That Was His. F. Packard
 Unknown Blonde. T. D. Irwin; Collusion
Hepworth, Cecil M(ilton)
 Anna the Adventuress. E. P. Oppenheim
 House of Marney. J. Goodwin
 Man Who Stayed at Home. J. E. H. Terry
 Mist in the Valley. Dorin Craig
 Mrs. Erricker's Reputation. T. Cobb
 Touch of the Child. T. Gallon
Herman, Albert
 Phantom of Forty-Second Street. M. M. Raison
Hersholt, Jean
 Gray Dawn. S. E. White

Hervil, Renee
 Mystery of the Villa Rose. A. E. W. Mason; At the Villa Rose
Hessler, Gordon
 Catacombs. Jay Bennett
 Embassy. S. Coulter
 Last Shot You Hear. W. Fairchild; Sound of Murder
 Murders in the Rue Morgue. E. A. Poe; Prose Romances of Edgar A. Poe
 Scream and Scream Again. P. Saxon; Disoriented Man
Heyes, Douglas
 Kitten with a Whip. Wade Miller
Hickox, Douglas
 Entertaining Mr. Sloane. J. Orton
 Hound of the Baskervilles. A. C. Doyle
 Sitting Target. L. Henderson
Higgin, Howard
 Great Deception. G. F. Gibbs; Yellow Dove
 Perfect Sap. H. I. Young; Not Herbert
Higgins, Colin
 Foul Play. J. C. Rogers
Hill, George
 Big House. J. Lait
 Secret Six. F. Marion
Hill, George Roy
 Little Drummer Girl. J. Le Carre
 Sting. R. Weverka
Hill, Jack
 Coffy. P. W. Fairman
Hill, James
 Study in Terror. E. Queen
Hill, Robert F.
 Breathless Moment. M. Bryant; Redemption of Richard
Hill, Sinclair
 China Bungalow. M. Osmond
 Conspirators. E. P. Oppenheim
 Expiation. E. P. Oppenheim
 Gay Adventure. W. Hackett
 Half a Truth. Rita
 Mystery of Mr. Bernard Brown. E. P. Oppenheim
 Qualified Adventurer. S. Jepson
Hill, Walter
 Driver. C. B. Phillips
 Warriors. S. Yurok
Hiller, Arthur
 Nightwing. M. C. Smith
 Penelope. E. V. Cunningham
 Silver Streak. J. C. Rogers
Hillyer, Lambert
 Dracula's Daughter. B. Stoker; Dracula's Guest
 Her Second Chance. W. Woodrow; Second Chance
Hiscott, Leslie
 Alibi. M. Morton
 Black Coffee. A Christie
 Death on the Set. V. MacClure
 House of the Arrow. A. E. W. Mason
 Missing Rembrandt. A. C. Doyle; Return of Sherlock Holmes
 Murder at Covent Garden. W. J. Makin
 Mystery at the Villa Rose. A. E. W. Mason; At the Villa Rose
 S.O.S. W. W. Ellis
 Sleeping Cardinal. A. C. Doyle; Memoirs of Sherlock Holmes
 Three Witnesses. S. Fowler
 Triumph of Sherlock Holmes. A. C. Doyle; Valley of Fear
Hitchcock, Alfred
 Birds. D. Du Maurier; Apple Tree
 Blackmail. C. Bennett
 Dial "M" for Murder. F. Knott
 Family Plot. V. Canning; Rainbird Pattern
 Frenzy. A. La Bern; Goodbye Piccadilly, Farewell Leicester Square
 Jamaica Inn. D. Du Maurier
 Lady Vanishes. E. L. White; Wheel Spins
 Lodger. M. B. Lowndes
 Man Who Knew Too Much. R. Alexander
 Marnie. Winston Graham
 Murder. C. Dane; Enter Sir John
 Paradine Case. R. Hichens
 Psycho. R. Bloch
 Rear Window. W. Irish; After-Dinner Story
 Rebecca. D. Du Maurier
 Rope. P. Hamilton
 Sabotage. J. Conrad; Secret Agent
 Secret Agent. W. S. Maugham; Ashenden
 Spellbound. F. Beeding; House of Dr. Edwardes
 Stage Fright. S. Jepson; Man Running
 Strangers on a Train. P. Highsmith
 Suspicion. F. Iles; Before the Fact
 Thirty-Nine Steps. J. Buchan
 To Catch a Thief. D. Dodge
 Topaz. L. Uris
 Torn Curtain. R. Wormser
 Trouble with Harry. J. T. Story
 Vertigo. P. Boileau; Living and the Dead

Young and Innocent. J. Tey; Shilling for Candles
Hively, Jack
 Saint in Palm Springs. L. Charteris (headnote)
 Saint's Double Trouble. L. Charteris (headnote)
 Street of Chance. C. Woolrich; Black Curtain
Hodges, Mike
 Get Carter. Ted Lewis; Jack's Return Home
Hogan, James
 Arrest Bulldog Drummond. H. C. McNeile; Final Count
 Bulldog Drummond's Peril. H. C. McNeile; Third Round
 Bulldog Drummond's Secret Police. H. C. McNeile; Temple Tower
 Ellery Queen and the Murder Ring. E. Queen; Dutch Shoe Mystery
 Ellery Queen's Penthouse Mystery. E. Queen; Penthouse Mystery
 Perfect Crime. E. Queen
Holmes, Ben
 Plot Thickens. S. Palmer (headnote)
 Saint in New York. L. Charteris
 We're on the Jury. F. Ballard; Ladies of the Jury
Holt, Seth
 Blood from the Mummy's Tomb. B. Stoker; Jewel of the Seven Stars
 Danger Route. A. York; Eliminator
 Nanny. E. Piper
 Nowhere to Go. D. MacKenzie
Hopper, E. Mason
 Curtain at Eight. O. R. Cohen; Backstage Mystery
 Hidden Spring. C. B. Kelland
 Paris at Midnight. H. Balzac; Le Pere Goriot
Horne, James W.
 Bronze Bell. L. J. Vance
Horner, Harry
 Beware, My Lovely. M. Dinelli; Man
 Life in the Balance. G. Simenon (headnote)
 Vicki. S. Fisher; I Wake Up Screaming
 Wild Party. J. McPartland
Hough, John
 Dirty Mary, Crazy Larry. R. Unekis; Chase
 Brass Target. F. Nolan; Oshawa Project
 Eyewitness. M. Hebden
 Legend of Hell House. R. Matheson; Hell House
Hough, R. L.
 Silent Witness. J. De Leon
Howard, Cy
 Every Little Crook and Nanny. E. Hunter
Howard, William K.
 Evelyn Prentice. W. E. Woodward
 Red Dice. O. R. Cohen; Iron Chalice
 River Pirate. C. F. Coe
 Sherlock Holmes. W. Gillette
 Squeaker. E. Wallace
 Trial of Vivienne Ware. K. Ellis
 Valiant. H. Hall
Howe, Eliot
 Gray Dawn. S. E. White
Hoyt, Harry O.
 Curse of Drink. C. E. Blaney
 Love Racket. B. K. Burns; Jury Woman
Hughes, Harry
 Gables Mystery. J. Celestin; Man at Six
 Man at Six. J. Celestin
Hughes, Ken
 Arrivederci, Baby! R. Deming; Careful Man
 Casino Royale. I. Fleming
 House Across the Way. K. Hughes; High Wray
 Long Haul. M. Mills
 Wicked As They Come. B. Ballinger; Portrait in Smoke
Hugon, Andre
 Street Without Joy. H. Bettauer; Viennese Love
Humberstone, H. Bruce
 Dragon Murder Case. S. S. Van Dine
 Fury at Furnace Creek. D. Garth; Four Men and a Prayer
 I Wake Up Screaming. S. Fisher
 Strangers of the Evening. T. Thayer; Illustrious Corpse
Hume, Kenneth
 Hot Ice. A. Melville; Week-End at Thrackley
Humphrey, William J.
 Black Spider. C. Dawe
 Foolish Monte Carlo. C. Dawe; Black Spider
 Wife Whom God Forgot. C. H. Bullivant
Hunabelle, Andre
 OSS 117--Mission for a Killer. J. Bruce; Live Wire
Hunnebelle, Andre

Mysteries of Paris. E. Sue
Hunt, Charles
　You Can't Beat the Law. H. H. Van Loan
Hunt, Peter
　On Her Majesty's Secret Service. I. Fleming
　Wild Geese II. D. Carney; Square Circle
Hunter, T. Hayes
　Calendar. E. Wallace
　Frightened Lady. E. Wallace; Case of the Frightened Lady
　Ghoul. F. King
　Green Pack. E. Wallace
　Man They Could Not Arrest. E. Wallace (headnote)
　Man They Couldn't Arrest. A. J. Small
　Silver King. H. A. Jones
　South Sea Bubble. R. Pertwee
　White Face. E. Wallace
Huntington, Lawrence
　Deadly Record. N. W. Hooke
　Death Drums Along the River. E. Wallace; Sanders of the River
　Franchise Affair. J. Tey
　This Man Is Dangerous. D. Hume; They Called Him Death
　Warn That Man. V. Sylvaine
Hurst, Brian Desmond
　Mark of Cain. J. Shearing; Airing in a Closed Carriage
　On the Night of the Fire. F. L. Green
Hussein, Waris
　Possession of Joel Delaney. Ramona Stewart
Huston, John
　Asphalt Jungle. W. R. Burnett
　Beat the Devil. J. Helvick
　Casino Royale. I. Fleming
　Final Exam. G. Meyer
　Key Largo. M. Anderson
　Kremlin Letter. N. Behn
　List of Adrian Messenger. P. MacDonald
　Mackintosh Man. D. Bagley; Freedom Trap
　Maltese Falcon. D. Hammett
　Prizzi's Honor. R. Condon
Huth, Harold
　Bulldog Sees It Through. G. Fairlie; Scissors Cut Paper
　My Sister and I. E. Bonett; High Pavement
Hutton, Brian G.
　First Deadly Sin. Lawrence Sanders
　High Road to China. J. Cleary
　Night Watch. L. Fletcher
　Sol Madrid. R. Wilder; Fruit of the Poppy
　Where Eagles Dare. A. MacLean
Hyams, Peter
　Peeper. K. Laumer; Deadfall
Ichikawa, Kon
　Lonely Hearts. E. McBain; Lady, Lady, I Did It!
Ince, John
　Beloved Adventurer. E. C. Hall
　Blind Man's Eyes. W. MacHarg
Ince, Ralph
　Argyle Case. H. Ford
　Black Mask. B. Graeme; Blackshirt
　Crime Unlimited. D. Hume
　Lone Wolf Returns. L. J. Vance
　Moral Sinner. C. M. S. McLellan; Leah Kleschna
　Too Many Crooks. E. J. Rath
　Twelve Good Men. J. Rhode; Murders in Praed Street
Ince, Thomas H.
　Boomerang. W. H. Osborne
Ingraham, Lloyd
　Sable Lorcha. H. Hazeltine
Ingram, Rex
　His Robe of Honor. E. Dorrance
　Where the Pavement Ends. J. Russell; Red God
Irvin, John
　Dogs of War. F. Forsyth
Irving, George
　Raffles. E. W. Hornung; Amateur Cracksman
　Silver King. H. A. Jones
Jabely, Jean
　Blonde Like That! J. H. Chase; Miss Shumway Waves a Wand
Jackson, Patrick
　Shadow on the Wall. H. Lees; Death in the Doll's House
　What a Carve Up! F. King; Ghoul
Jacoby, George
　Vendetta. A. C. Gunter; Mr. Barnes of New York
Jacquot, Benoit
　With All Hands. J. Gunn; Deadlier Than the Male
Jaffe, Stanley R.
　Without a Trace. B. Gutcheon; Still Missing
Jameson, Jerry
　Raise the Titanic! C. Cussler
Jarrott, Charles
　Amateur. R. Littell
　Condorman. R. Sheckley; Game of X
　Other Side of Midnight. S. Sheldon
　Time to Remember. E. Wallace; Man Who Bought London
Jason, Leigh
　Dangerous Blondes. K. Roos; If the Shroud Fits
　Nine Girls. W. H. Pettitt
Jeffrey, Tom
　Removalists. D. Williamson
　Weekend of Shadows. H. Atkinson; Reckoning
Jessua, Alain
　Armageddon. D. Lippincott; Voice of Armageddon
Jewison, Norman
　...And Justice for All. R. Grossbach
　In the Heat of the Night. J. Ball
　Russians Are Coming, The Russians Are Coming. N. Benchley; Off-Islanders
　Soldier's Story. C. Fuller; Soldier's Play
　Thomas Crown Affair. E. L. Heyman
Johnson, Lamont
　Covenant with Death. S. Becker
　Groundstar Conspiracy. L. P. Davies; Alien
　Mackenzie Break. S. Shelley; Bowmanville Break
　Somebody Killed Her Husband. C. B. Phillips
　You'll Like My Mother. N. Hintze
Johnson, Nunnally
　Black Widow. P. Quentin
Jones, Edgar
　Enemy to Society. G. Bronson-Howard
　Half Million Bribe. W. H. Osborne; Red Mouse
Jones, F. Richard
　Bulldog Drummond. H. C. McNeile
Jose, Edward
　Closing Net. H. C. Rowland
　God's Prodigal. A. J. Russell
　Yellow Typhoon. H. MacGrath
Julian, Rupert
　Cat Creeps. J. Willard; Cat and the Canary
　Evil Women Do. E. Gaboriau; Clique of Gold
　Fire Flingers. W. J. Neidig
　Leopard Lady. E. C. Carpenter
　Phantom of the Opera. G. Leroux
　Three Faces East. A. P. Kelly
Kaczender, George
　Agency. P. Gottlieb
Kaeutner, Helmut
　Redhead. A. Andersch
Kagan, Jeremy Paul
　Big Fix. R. L. Simon
Kane, Joe
　Accused of Murder. W. R. Burnett; Vanity Row
　Timberjack. D. Cushman
Kanen, Jeff
　Eddie Macon's Run. J. McLendon
Karger, Maxwell
　Hate. W. Camp; Communicating Door
Karlson, Phil
　Ben. G. A. Ralston
　Brothers Rico. G. Simenon
　Dark Page. S. Fuller
　Five Against the House. J. Finney
　Key Witness. F. Kane
　Secret Wars. A. MacLean; Last Frontier
　Silencers. D. Hamilton
　Tight Spot. L. Kantor; Dead Pigeon
　Walking Tall. D. Warren
　Wrecking Crew. D. Hamilton
Kastle, Leonard
　Honeymoon Killers. Paul Buck
Katselas, Milton
　Report to the Commissioner. J. Mills
Katzin, Lee H.
　Salzburg Connection. H. MacInnes
　Whatever Happened to Aunt Alice? U. Curtiss; Forbidden Garden
Kaufman, Joseph
　World's Great Snare. E. P. Oppenheim
Kaurismaki, Aki
　Crime and Punishment. F. M. Dostoevskii
Kazan, Elia
　Man on a Tightrope. N. Paterson
　On the Waterfront. B. Schulberg; Waterfront
Keighley, William
　Each Dawn I Die. J. Odlum
　"G" Men. H. K. Long
Kellino, Roy
　Guilt Is My Shadow. P. Curtis; You're Best Alone
Kellino, W. P.
　Angel Esquire. E. Wallace
　Colleen Bawn. D. Boucicault
　Confessions. B. Reynolds; Confession Corner
Fall of a Saint. E. C. Scott
　Green Terror. E. Wallace; Green Rust
Kelly, A.
　Woman Racket. P. Dunning; Night Hostess
Kelly, Albert
　Slippy McGee. M. C. Oemler
Kemm, Jean
　Lacquered Box. A. Christie; Black Coffee
Kemplen, Ralph
　Spaniard's Curse. E. Pargeter; Assize of the Dying
Kennedy, Burt
　Killer Inside Me. J. Thompson
　Money Trap. L. White
Kenton, Erle
　Guilty As Hell. D. N. Rubin; Riddle Me This!
Kershner, Irvin
　Eyes of Laura Mars. H. B. Gilmour
　Flim Flam Man. G. Owen; Ballad of the Flim Flam Man
　Never Say Never Again. I. Fleming; Thunderball
　S*P*Y*S. T. R. Joyce
Kessler, Henry S.
　Five Steps to Danger. D. Hamilton; Assignment: Murder
Kibbee, Roland
　Midnight Man. D. Anthony; Midnight Lady and the Mourning Man
Kiersch, Fritz
　Children of the Corn. Stephen King; Different Seasons
Killy, Edward
　Murder on a Bridle Path. S. Palmer; Puzzle of the Red Stallion
　Seven Keys to Baldpate. E. D. Biggers
Kimmins, Anthony
　Mine Own Executioner. N. Balchin
　Mr. Denning Drives North. A. Coppel
King, Burton
　Counsel for the Defense. L. Scott
　Little Girl in a Big City. J. K. McCurdy
　Master Mystery. A. B. Reeve
King, George
　China Bungalow. M. Osmond
　Crimes at the Dark House. W. Collins; Woman in White
　Frightened Lady. E. Wallace
　Maria Marten. Anonymous
　Nine Forty-Five. O. Davis
　Professional Guest. W. Garrett
　Shop at Sly Corner. E. Percy; Play with Fire
　Sweeney Todd, the Demon Barber of Fleet Street. G. D. Pitt
　Ticket-of-Leave Man. T. Taylor
King, Henry
　All the World to Nothing. W. Martyn
　Haunting Shadows. M. Nicholson; House of a Thousand Candles
　King of the Khyber Rifles. T. Mundy
　One Hour Before Dawn. M. Scott; Behind Red Curtains
King, Louis
　Bulldog Drummond Comes Back. H. C. McNeile; Female of the Species
　Bulldog Drummond in Africa. H. C. McNeile; Challenge
　Bulldog Drummond's Revenge. H. C. McNeile; Return of Bulldog Drummond
　Murder in Trinidad. J. W. Vandercook
　Tom Sawyer, Detective. M. Twain
　Wine, Women and Horses. W. R. Burnett; Dark Hazard
Kirk, Roland
　Dear Fatherland, Be at Peace. J. M. Simmel; Dear Fatherland
Kirkland, Hardee
　Aurora Floyd. M. E. Braddon
Kirkwood, James
　Floor Above. E. P. Oppenheim (headnote)
Kjaerulff-Schmidt, Palle
　Think of a Number. A. Bodelsen
Knight, John
　Main Chance. E. Wallace (headnote)
Knoles, Harley
　Burglar. A. Thomas; Edith's Burglar
Knopf, Edwin H.
　Law and the Lady. F. Lonsdale; Last of Mrs. Cheyney
　Only Saps Work. O. Davis; Easy Come, Easy Go
Knowles, Bernard
　Hell Is Empty. J. F. Straker
　Jassy. N. Lofts
　Man Within. G. Greene
　Park Plaza 605. B. Gray; Dare-Devil Conquest
Koch, Howard W.
　Badge 373. M. Roote
　Born Reckless. M. Rogers
　Last Mile. J. Wexley
Korber, Serge
　Little Virtuous. R. Marshall; Short Time to Live

Korda, Zoltan
 Counterattack. J. Stevenson
 Sanders of the River. E. Wallace
 Woman's Vengeance. A. Huxley; Mortal Coils
Koster, Henry
 Fraulein. J. McGovern
 My Cousin Rachel. D. Du Maurier
Kotcheff, Ted
 First Blood. D. Morrell
 Outback. K. Cook; Wake in Fright
 Who Is Killing the Great Chefs of Europe. N. Lyons; Someone Is Killing the Great Chefs of Europe
Kowalski, Bernard
 Stiletto. H. Robbins
Kraemer, F. W.
 Flying Squad. E. Wallace
Kramer, Stanley
 Domino Principle. A. Kennedy
Krawozyk, Gerard
 I Hate Actors. B. Hecht
Kubrick, Stanley
 Clockwork Orange. A. Burgess
 Dr. Strangelove. P. Bryant; Two Hours to Doom
 Killing. L. White; Clean Break
Kulijanov, Lev
 Crime and Punishment. F. M. Dostoevskii
Kulik, Buzz
 Riot. F. Elli
 Shamus. R. Giles
 Warning Shot. W. Masterson; 711--Officer Needs Help
 Yellow Canary. W. Masterson; Evil Come, Evil Go
Kurosawa, Akira
 High and Low. E. McBain; King's Ransom
Labro, Philippe
 Without Apparent Motive. E. McBain; Ten Plus One
Lachman, Harry
 Baby, Take a Bow. J. P. Judge; Square Crooks
 They Came by Night. B. Lyndon
 Yellow Mask. E. Wallace; Traitor's Gate
Laemmle, Edward
 Cheating Cheaters. M. Marcin
 Thirteenth Juror. F. T. Hill
Lamac, Karl/Karel
 Hound of the Baskervilles. A. C. Doyle
 They Met in the Dark. Anthony Gilbert; Vanishing Corpse
Lambert, Harry
 Down Under Donovan. E. Wallace
Lamont, Charles
 Abbott and Costello Meet Dr. Jekyll and Mr. Hyde. R. L. Stevenson; Strange Case of Dr. Jekyll and Mr. Hyde
 Dark Hour. S. Gluck; Last Trap
 Shot in the Dark. C. Orr; Dartmouth Murders
Lampin, Georges
 Crime and Punishment. F. M. Dostoevskii
Lancaster, Burt
 Midnight Man. D. Anthony; Midnight Lady and the Mourning Man
Landers, Lew
 Ghost That Walks Alone. R. Shattuck; Wedding Guest Sat on a Stone
 Seven Keys to Baldpate. E. D. Biggers
Lanfield, Sidney
 Hound of the Baskervilles. A. C. Doyle
Lang, Fritz
 Big Heat. W. P. McGivern
 Dr. Mabuse, Gambler. N. Jacques; Dr. Mabuse, Master of Mystery
 House by the River. A. P. Herbert
 Man Hunt. G. Household; Rogue Male
 Ministry of Fear. G. Greene
 Secret Beyond the Door. Rufus King; Museum Piece No. 13
 Spy. T. Von Harbau
 While the City Sleeps. C. Einstein; Bloody Spur
 Woman in the Window. J. H. Wallis; Once Off Guard
Lang, Walter
 But Not for Me. E. Ronns
 Golden Web. E. P. Oppenheim
 Money to Burn. R. W. Kauffman
Langman, Chris
 Reunion. M. Anderson
Langton, Simon
 Whistle Blower. J. Hale
Laughton, Charles
 Night of the Hunter. D. Grubb
Lautner, Georges
 Icy Breasts. R. Matheson; Someone Is Bleeding
 Professional. P. Alexander; Death of a Thin-Skinned Animal
 Seventh Juror. F. Didelot

Laven, Arnold
 Down Three Dark Streets. Gordons; Case File: FBI
 Vice Squad. L. T. White; Harness Bull
Law, Michael
 Six Men. E. Radford
Lawrence, Edmund
 House of Secrets. S. Horler
Lawrence, Quentin
 Man Who Finally Died. John Burke
 Playback. E. Wallace (headnote)
 We Shall See. E. Wallace
Lazar, Lajos
 Ghost Train. A. Ridley
Lazarus, Ashley
 Golden Rendezvous. A. MacLean
Leacock, Philip
 Let No Man Write My Epitaph. W. Motley
 13 West Street. L. Brackett; Tiger Among Us
Lean, David
 Take My Life. Winston Graham
Leborg, Reginald
 Deadly Duo. R. Jessup
 Flanagan. M. Catto
Lecombe, Georges
 Midnight in Paris. G. Simenon; Monsieur la Souris
Lederman, D. Ross
 Passage from Hong Kong. E. D. Biggers; Agony Column
 Return of the Whistler. W. Irish; Eyes That Watch You
 Shadows on the Stairs. F. Vosper; Murder on the Second Floor
Lee, Jack
 Robbery Under Arms. R. Boldrewood
 Turn the Key Softly. J. Brophy
Lee, Norman
 Bulldog Drummond at Bay. H. C. McNeile
 Door with Seven Locks. E. Wallace
 Mr. Reeder in Room 13. E. Wallace; Room 13
 Monkey's Paw. W. W. Jacobs; Lady of the Barge
 No Exit. G. Goodchild
Lee, Rowland V.
 Love from a Stranger. F. Vosper
 Man of Zanzibar. R. H. Davis; Lost Road
 Mysterious Dr. Fu Manchu. S. Rohmer; Mystery of Dr. Fu-Manchu
 Return of Dr. Fu Manchu. S. Rohmer; Devil Doctor
 Sign of the Four. A. C. Doyle
Leeds, Herbert I.
 It Shouldn't Happen to a Dog. E. Lanham
 Man Who Wouldn't Die. C. Rawson; No Coffin for the Corpse
 Mr. Moto in Danger Island. J. W. Vandercook; Murder in Trinidad
 Time to Kill. R. Chandler; High Window
Le Frane, Guy
 Keep Talking, Baby. D. Keene; Strange Witness
Lehrman, Henry
 Fighting Edge. W. M. Raine
Leigh, J. L. V.
 Pallard the Punter. E. Wallace; Grey Timothy
Leisen, Mitchell
 Captain Carey, U.S.A. M. Albrand; After Midnight
 Death Takes a Holiday. W. Ferris
 Four Hours to Kill. N. Krasna; Small Miracle
 Golden Earrings. Y. Foldes
 No Man of Her Own. W. Irish; I Married a Dead Man
Leni, Paul
 Cat and the Canary. J. Willard
 Chinese Parrot. E. D. Biggers
 Last Warning. W. Camp; House of Fear
Leonard, Robert Z.
 Piccadilly Jim. P. G. Wodehouse
Leone, Sergio
 Once Upon a Time in America. H. Grey; Hoods
Lerner, Joseph
 Guilty Bystander. Wade Miller
Lerner, Peter
 Edge of Fury. R. M. Coates; Wisteria Cottage
LeRoy, Mervyn
 Any Number Can Play. E. H. Heth
 Bad Seed. M. Anderson
 Escape. E. Vance
 Five Star Final. L. Weitzenkorn
 Gentleman's Fate. K. U. P.
 Home Before Dark. E. Bassing
 Little Caesar. W. R. Burnett
 Moment to Moment. A. Coppel
 They Won't Forget. W. Greene; Death in the Deep South
Leroy, Serge
 Attention, the Kids Are Watching. P.

L. Dixon; Children Are Watching Passengers. K. R. Dwyer; Chase
Le Saint, Edward J.
 Brooding Eyes. J. Goodwin; Paid in Full
 Circular Staircase. M. R. Rinehart
 Lord John in New York. C. N. Williamson
 More to Be Pitied Than Scorned. C. E. Blaney
 Three Keys. F. Ormond
Lessey, George A.
 Eagle's Eye. W. J. Flynn
 Strange Disappearance. A. K. Green
Lester, Mark L.
 Firestarter. Stephen King
Lester, Richard
 Finders Keepers. C. Dennis; Next-to-Last Train Ride
 Juggernaut. A. Hine
Levering, Joseph
 Defenders of the Law. H. Del Ruth
Levin, Henry
 Ambushers. D. Hamilton
 Convicted. M. Flavin; Criminal Code
 Corpse Came C.O.D. J. Starr
 Murderer's Row. D. Hamilton
 That Man Bolt. P. Crowcraft
Levinson, Barry
 Young Sherlock Holmes. A. Arnold
Levy, Benn W.
 Lord Camber's Ladies. H. A. Vachell; Case of Lady Camber
Levy, Raoul
 Defector. P. Thomas; Spy
Lewis, Edgar
 Beggar in Purple. A. Soutar
 Gun-Runner. A. Stringer
 Other Men's Shoes. A. Soutar
Lewis, Jay
 Live Now, Pay Later. J. T. Story
Lewis, Jerry
 One More Time. M. Avallone
Lewis, Joseph H.
 Deadly Is the Female. M. Kantor; Author's Choice
 Desperate Search. A. Mayse
 My Name Is Julia Ross. Anthony Gilbert; Woman in Red
L'Herbier, Marcel
 Mystery of the Yellow Room. G. Leroux
 Perfume of the Lady in Black. G. Leroux
Litvak, Anatole
 Amazing Dr. Clitterhouse. B. Lyndon
 Decision Before Dawn. G. Howe; Call It Treason
 Lady in the Car with Glasses and a Gun. S. Japrisot
 Night of the Generals. H. H. Kirst
 Out of the Fog. I. Shaw; Gentle People
 Sorry Wrong Number. L. Fletcher
Lizzani, Carlo
 Crazy Joe. M. Barone
Lloyd, Frank
 East Lynn. H. Wood
 Madame X. J. W. MacConaughy
 Voice in the Dark. R. E. Dyar
 Within the Law. B. Veiller
Lombardo, Lou
 Russian Roulette. T. Ardies; Kosygin Is Coming
Loncraine, Richard
 Julia. P. Straub
Lord, Jean Claude
 Visiting Hours. K. Rembo
Loring, Thomas Z.
 Who Is Hope Schuyler? S. Ransome; Hearses Don't Hurry
Losey, Joseph
 Big Night. S. Ellin; Dreadful Summit
 Blind Date. Leigh Howard
 Damned. H. L. Lawrence; Children of Light
 Eva. J. H. Chase; Eve
 Gypsy and the Gentleman. N. W. Hooke; Darkness I Leave You
 Modesty Blaise. P. O'Donnell
 Secret Ceremony. M. Denevi
 Sleeping Tiger. M. Moisewitsch
 Time Without Pity. E. Williams; Someone Waiting
Lubin, Arthur
 Footsteps in the Fog. W. W. Jacobs; Sea Whispers
 House of a Thousand Candles. M. Nicholson
 Phantom of the Opera. G. Leroux
 Who Killed Aunt Maggie? M. Field
Lucoque, H. Lisle
 Tatterly. T. Gallon
Lumet, Sidney
 Anderson Tapes. Lawrence Sanders
 Child's Play. R. Marasco
 Deadly Affair. J. Le Carre; Call for the Dead
 Deathtrap. I. Levin
 Dog Day Afternoon. P. Mann
 Fail-Safe. E. Burdick

Murder on the Orient Express. A. Christie
Offense. J. Hopkins; This Story of Yours
Twelve Angry Men. R. Rose
Verdict. B. C. Reed
Lynch, Paul
Cross-Country. H. D. Kastle
Lynn, Robert
Coast of Skeletons. E. Wallace; Sanders of the River
Two-Letter Alibi. A. Garve; Death and the Sky Above
MacArthur, Charles
Crime Without Reason. B. Hecht; Collected Stories of Ben Hecht
McCarthy, Michael
Assassin for Hire. R. Rienits
Macdonald, David
Dead Men Tell No Tales. F. Beeding; Norwich Victims
Death Croons the Blues. J. Ronald
Good Time Girl. A. La Bern; Night Darkens the Street
Lady Mislaid. K. Horne
Snowbound. H. Innes; Lonely Skier
Spies of the Air. J. Dell; Official Secret
Tread Softly. G. Verner; Show Must Go On
McDonald, Frank
Bulldog Drummond Strikes Back. H. C. McNeile; Knock-Out
Murder by an Aristocrat. M. G. Eberhart
Murder of Dr. Harrington. M. G. Eberhart; From This Dark Stairway
No Hands on the Clock. G. Homes
MacDonald, J. Farrell
Black Sheep. E. Yates
Mystery of Orcival. E. Gaboriau
Macdonald, Norman
Loudwater Mystery. E. Jepson
MacDonald, Sherwood
Cold Steel. G. C. Shedd; In the Shadow of the Hills
McDonnell, Fergus
Small Voice. R. Westerby
McEveety, Bernard
Brotherhood of Satan. L. Q. Jones
MacFadden, Hamilton
Black Camel. E. D. Biggers
Charlie Chan Carries On. E. D. Biggers
Charlie Chan's Greatest Case. E. D. Biggers; House Without a Key
Elinor Norton. M. R. Rinehart; State vs. Elinor Norton
McGann, William
Case of the Black Cat. E. S. Gardner; Case of the Caretaker's Cat
Murder on the Second Floor. F. Vosper
Sh! The Octopus. R. Spence; Gorilla
Two Against the World. L. Weitzenkorn; Five Star Final
McGill, Lawrence
Crime and Punishment. F. M. Dostoevskii
First Law. G. Willets
Woman's Law. M. Thompson
McGowan, J. P.
Red Glove. D. Grant; Fifth Ace
McGrath, Joe
Casino Royale. I. Fleming
McGuire, Dennis
Shoot It: Black, Shoot It: Blue. P. Tyner; Shoot It
MacKenna, Kenneth
Sleepers East. F. Nebel
Spider. F. Oursler
Mackenzie, Donald
Carter Case. A. B. Reeve (headnote)
Ticket-of-Leave Man. C. Reade; Foul Play
Mackenzie, John
Fourth Protocol. F. Forsyth
Honorary Consul. G. Greene
Long Good Friday. R. Claughton
McLaglen, Andrew V.
Fool's Parade. D. Grubb
Man in the Vault. F. Gruber; Lock and the Key
North Sea Hijack. J. Davies; Esther, Ruth and Jennifer
Wild Geese. D. Carney
McLeod, Norman Z.
Miracle Man. F. Packard
Trial of Mary Dugan. B. Veiller
McNaught, Bob
Grand National Night. D. Christie
Macrae, Duncan
Love and the Whirlwind. H. P. Lewis
MacRae, Henry
Cameron of the Mounted. R. Connor; Corporal Cameron
Machaty, Gustav
Within the Law. B. Veiller
Maigne, Charles
In the Hollow of Her Hand. G. B. McCutcheon; Hollow of Her Hand

Malins, Geoffrey H.
All the Winners. A. Applin; Wicked
Golden Web. E. P. Oppenheim; Plunderers
Greek Interpreter. A. C. Doyle; Memoirs of Sherlock Holmes
Malle, Louis
Elevator to the Gallows. N. Calef; Frantic
Malmuth, Bruce
Where Are the Children? M. H. Clark
Mamoulian, Rouben
Dr. Jekyll and Mr. Hyde. R. L. Stevenson; Strange Case of Dr. Jekyll and Mr. Hyde
Mankiewicz, Joseph L.
Dragonwyck. A. Seton
Escape. J. Galsworthy
Honey Pot. T. Sterling; Evil of the Day
Operation Cicero. L. C. Moyzisch
Quiet American. G. Greene
Sleuth. A. Shaffer
Mann, Anthony
Dandy in Aspic. D. Marlowe
Naked Spur. A. Ullman
Serenade. J. M. Cain
Two O'Clock Courage. G. Burgess
Mann, Daniel
Our Man Flint. J. Pearl
Willard. S. Gilbert; Ratman's Notebooks
Mann, Delbert
Fitzwilly. Poyntz Tyler; Garden of Cucumbers
Pink Jungle. A. Williams; Snake Water
Mann, Michael
Keep. F. P. Wilson
Manhunter. T. Harris; Red Dragon
Manning, Michelle
Blue City. K. Millar
March, Alex
Big Bounce. E. Leonard
Margolin, Stuart
Glitter Dome. J. Wambaugh
Marin, Edwin L.
Avenger. J. Goodwin
Bombay Mail. L. G. Blochman
Casino Murder Case. S. S. Van Dine
Death Kiss. M. St. Dennis
Garden Murder Case. S. S. Van Dine
Gentleman After Dark. R. W. Child; Velvet Black
Johnny Angel. C. G. Booth; Mr. Angel Comes Aboard
Maisie. W. Collison; Dark Dame
Mr. Ace. H. Christy
Pursuit. L. G. Blochman
Society Lawyer. A. S. Roche; Penthouse
Study in Scarlet. A. C. Doyle
Marion, George F.
Madame X. J. W. MacConaughy
Markham, Mansfield
Return of Raffles. E. W. Hornung (headnote)
Markle, Fletcher
Man with a Cloak. J. D. Carr; Third Bullet
Marquand, Richard
Eye of the Needle. K. Follett; Storm Island
Marshak, Philip
Dracula Sucks. B. Stoker; Dracula
Marshall, George E.
Blue Dahlia. R. Chandler
Gazebo. A. Coppel
Happy Thieves. R. Condon; Oldest Confession
Hazard. R. Chanslor
Lady from Long Acre. V. Bridges
Love Under Fire. W. Hackett; Fugitives
Ruth of the Rockies. J. McCulley; Broadway Bab
Marston, Lawrence
East Lynne. H. Wood
Girl by the Roadside. V. Vanardy
Millionaire Baby. A. K. Green
Mortmain. A. Train
Quarry. J. A. Moroso
Woman in Black. W. Spence
Marston, Theodore
Aurora Floyd. M. E. Braddon
Surprises of an Empty Hotel. A. C. Gunter
Martin, Paul
Orient Express. G. Greene; Stamboul Train
Martinek, H. O.
First Chronicle of Don Q. K. Prichard; Chronicles of Don Q
Martinson, Leslie H.
Batman. W. Lyon
Fathom. L. Forrester; Girl Called Fathom
Hot Rod Rumble. M. Dolinsky; Hot Rod Gang Rumble
Mrs. Pollifax, Spy. D. Gilman; Unex-

pected Mrs. Pollifax
Marton, Andrew
Devil Makes Three. L. P. Bachmann; Kiss of Death
Secret of Stamboul. D. Wheatley; Eunich of Stamboul
Maselli, Francesco
Fine Pair. C. Stratton
Mason, Herbert
His Lordship. N. Grant; Nelson Touch
Night Invader. J. Bentley; Rendezvous with Death
Once a Crook. E. Price
Strange Boarders. E. P. Oppenheim; Strange Boarders of Palace Crescent
Matalan, Eddy
Too Small, My Friend. J. H. Chase; Way the Cookie Crumbles
Mate, Rudolph
Dark Past. J. Warwick; Blind Alley
Port Afrique. B. V. Dryer
Union Station. T. Walsh; Nightmare in Manhattan
Mathot, Leon
Cheri-Bibi. G. Leroux
Mattson, Arne
Black Snow. P. Wahloo; Lorry
Maude, Arthur
Clue of the New Pin. E. Wallace
Flying Squad. E. Wallace
Lyons Mail. E. Moreau; Courier of Lyons
Ringer. E. Wallace
Maxwell, Peter
Desperate Man. P. Somers; Beginner's Luck
Switch. P. Ridgeway
May, Elaine
New Leaf. J. Ritchie
May, Joe
House of Fear. W. Camp
Maylam, Tony
Riddle of the Sands. E. Childers
Mayo, Archie L.
Case of the Lucky Legs. E. S. Gardner
Crimson City. A. Coldeway
Man with Two Faces. A. Woollcott; Dark Tower
On Trial. E. L. Reizenstein
Petrified Forest. R. E. Sherwood
Medak, Peter
Negatives. P. Everett
Medford, Don
Hunting Party. J. Millard
Meinert, Rudolf
Hound of the Baskervilles. A. C. Doyle
Mekas, Adolfas
Double-Barrelled Detective Story. M. Twain
Melford, George
Going Crooked. Winchell Smith
Great Impersonation. E. P. Oppenheim
Scarlet Weekend. W. Kent; Woman in Purple Pajamas
Whispering Smith. F. H. Spearman
Melville, Jean-Pierre
Magnet of Doom. G. Simenon
Mendeluk, George
Kidnapping of the President. C. Templeton
Stone Cold Dead. H. Garner; Sin Sniper
Mendez, Lothar
Interference. R. Pertwee
Ladies' Man. Rupert Hughes
Payment Deferred. J. Dell
Prince of Tempters. E. P. Oppenheim; Ex-Duke
Walls Came Tumbling Down. J. Eisinger
Menzies, William Cameron
Address Unknown. K. Taylor
Almost Married. A. Soutar; Devil's Triangle
Four Dark Hours. G. Greene (headnote)
Spider. F. Oursler
Mercanton, Louis
Letter. W. S. Maugham
Meredith, Burgess
Man on the Eifel Tower. G. Simenon; Battle of Nerves
Merwin, Bannister
Rogue in Love. T. Gallon
Metzger, Radley
Cat and the Canary. J. Willard
Meyer, Nicholas
Time After Time. K. Alexander
Michel, Bernard T.
Five Ashore for Singapore. J. Bruce; Cold Spell
Middleton, George E.
Woman Who Dared. A. M. Williamson
Miles, Christopher
Maids. J. Genet
Milestone, Lewis
General Died at Dawn. C. G. Booth
Ocean's 11. G. C. Johnson
Racket. B. Cormack
Milford, Gene
Pusher. E. McBain

Milius, John
  Dillinger. H. Clement
Milland, Ray
  Hostile Witness. J. Roffey
Millarde, Harry
  White Moll. F. Packard
Miller, Ashley
  Affair of Three Nations. J. McIntyre (headnote)
Miller, Charles
  High Speed. C. H. Stagg
Miller, Claude
  Deadly Circuit. M. Behm; Eye of the Beholder
  Inquisitor. J. Wainwright; Brainwash
  Tell Him I Love Him. P. Highsmith; This Sweet Sickness
Miller, David
  Hammerhead. J. Mayo
  Midnight Lace. J. Green; Matilda Shouted Fire
  Sudden Fear. E. Sherry
Miller, Frank
  Joyous Adventures of Aristide Pujol. W. J. Locke
Mills, Tom/Thomas R.
  Duds. H. C. Rowland
  Girl in His House. H. MacGrath
Milton, Meyrick
  Adventures of Captain Kettle. C. J. C. Hyne
Milton, Robert
  Bella Donna. R. Hichens
  Dummy. H. J. O'Higgins
Minnelli, Vincente
  Goodbye Charlie. M. H. Albert
Mitchell, Howard M.
  Queenie. W. F. Fauley
Mitchell, Oswald
  Night Journey. J. Phelan; Ten-a-Penny People
  Temptress. A. Campbell; Juggernaut
Mocky, Jean-Pierre
  Kill the Referee. A. Draper; Death Penalty
  No Pockets in a Shroud. H. McCoy
  Red Ibis. Fredric Brown; Knock Three-One-Two
  Unsewing Machine. D. Keene; Killer Is Loose
  Witness. H. Judd; Shadow of a Doubt
Moguy, Leonide
  Whistle Stop. M. M. Wolff
Molinaro, Edouard
  Death of a Beauty. G. Simenon; Belle Ravishing Idiot. C. Exbrayat
Montagne, Edward
  Man with My Face. S. W. Taylor
Montaldo, Giuliano
  Machine Gun McCain. O. Demaris; Candyleg
Montgomery, Robert
  Lady in the Lake. R. Chandler
  Ride the Pink Horse. D. B. Hughes
Moore, Robert
  Cheap Detective. R. Grossbach
  Murder by Death. H. Keating
Mora, Philippe
  Howling II. G. Brandner
Morgan, Sidney
  Bulldog Drummond's Third Round. H. C. McNeile; Third Round
  Miriam Rozella. B. L. Farjeon
  What's Bred...Comes Out in the Flesh. G. Allen; What's Bred in the Bone
  Woman of the Iron Bracelets. F. Barrett
Morley, Royston
  Attempt to Kill. E. Wallace; Lone House Mystery
Morrissey, Paul
  Hound of the Baskervilles. A. C. Doyle
Morse, Terry O.
  British Intelligence. A. P. Kelly; Three Faces East
  On Trial. E. L. Reizenstein
  Young Dillinger. S. Stuart
Mortimer, Edmund
  Exiles. R. H. Davis
Mostafa, Hossam El Dine
  Sonya and the Madman. F. M. Dostoevskii; Crime and Punishment
Moxey, John
  Angel of Terror. E. Wallace
  Death Trap. E. Wallace (headnote)
  Downfall. E. Wallace (headnote)
  Face of a Stranger. E. Wallace (headnote)
  Foxhole in Cairo. L. O. Mosley; Cat and the Mice
  20,000 Pound Kiss. E. Wallace (headnote)
Mulcahy, Russell
  Razorback. P. Brennan
Mulligan, Robert
  Baby, the Rain Must Fall. H. Foote; Traveling Lady
  Bloodbrothers. R. Price
  Nickel Ride. M. T. Kaufman
  Other. T. Tryon
  To Kill a Mockingbird. H. Lee
Murnau, Friedrich Wilhelm
  Nosferatu. B. Stoker; Dracula
Murphy, Ralph
  Man in Half Moon Street. B. Lyndon
  Menace. P. MacDonald; R.I.P.
  Night Club Scandal. D. N. Rubin; Riddle Me This!
  Notorious Sophie Lang. F. I. Anderson
  Partners in Crime. K. Steel; Murder Goes to College
  70,000 Witnesses. C. Fitzsimmons
  She Made Her Bed. J. M. Cain; Baby in the Icebox
Myerson, Alan
  Private Lessons. D. Greenberg; Philly
Nadel, Arthur
  Underground. C. Stratton
Narizzano, Silvio
  Die! Die! My Darling. A. Blaisdell; Nightmare
  Loot. J. Orton
Nash, Percy
  Jack Sheppard. J. B. Buckstone
Neame, Ronald
  Chalk Garden. E. Bagnold
  Escape from Zahrein. M. Barrett; Appointment in Zahrein
  Gambit. K. Lane
  Golden Salamander. V. Canning
  Hopscotch. B. Garfield
  Mr. Moses. M. Catto; Mister Midas
  Odessa File. F. Forsyth
Negulesco, Jean
  Boy on a Dolphin. D. Divine
  Conspirators. F. Prokosch
  Mask of Dimitrios. E. Ambler
  Nobody Lives Forever. W. R. Burnett
Neilan, Marshall
  Diplomacy. V. Sardou; Diplomates
  River's End. J. O. Curwood
Neill, Roy William
  Bandbox. L. J. Vance
  Black Angel. C. Woolrich
  Circus Queen Murder. A. Abbot; About the Murder of the Circus Queen
  Doctor Syn. R. Thorndyke
  Greater Than a Crown. V. Bridges; Lady from Long Acre
  House of Fear. A. C. Doyle; Adventures of Sherlock Holmes
  Lone Wolf Returns. L. J. Vance
  Menace. E. Wallace; Feathered Serpent
  Ninth Guest. O. Davis
  Pearl of Death. A. C. Doyle; Return of Sherlock Holmes
  Scarlet Claw. A. C. Doyle; Hound of the Baskervilles
  Sherlock Holmes and the Secret Weapon. A. C. Doyle; Return of Sherlock Holmes
  Sherlock Holmes and the Spider Woman. A. C. Doyle; Study in Scarlet
  Sherlock Holmes Faces Death. A. C. Doyle; Memoirs of Sherlock Holmes
  Thank Evans. E. Wallace; Good Evans!
Neill, William
  Melody Man. H. J. Green
Neilson, James
  Dr. Syn Alias the Scarecrow. R. Thorndyke; Dr. Syn
  Moon-Spinners. Mary Stewart
Nelson, Gary
  Jimmy the Kid. D. E. Westlake
Nelson, Ralph
  Once a Thief. J. Trinian; Scratch a Thief
  Tick...Tick...Tick. P. Rock
  Wilby Conspiracy. P. Driscoll
  Wrath of God. J. Graham
Nethercott, Geoffrey
  Accidental Death. E. Wallace; Jack o' Judgment
  Who Was Maddox? E. Wallace; Undisclosed Client
Neumann, Kurt
  Ellery Queen, Master Detective. E. Queen
Newall, Guy
  Chinese Puzzle. M. Bower
  Maid of the Silver Sea. J. Oxenham
Newell, Mike
  Awakening. B. Stoker; Jewel of the Seven Stars
Newfield, Sam
  Murder Is My Business. B. Halliday
Newland, John
  My Lover, My Son. E. Grierson; Reputation for a Song
Newman, Joseph M.
  Dangerous Crossing. J. D. Carr; Dead Sleep Lightly
  Lucky Nick Cain. J. H. Chase; I'll Get You for This
  Twenty Plus Two. F. Gruber
Newmeyer, Fred
  Lunatic at Large. J. S. Clouston
  Seven Keys to Baldpate. E. D. Biggers
  Too Many Crooks. E. J. Rath
Niblo, Fred
  Big Gamble. O. R. Cohen; Iron Chalice
  Strangers of the Night. W. Hackett; Captain Applejack
Nicholl, George, Jr.
  Big Game. F. Wallace
Nicholls, George
  East Lynne. H. Wood
Nichols, Mike
  Day of the Dolphin. R. Merle
Nigh, William
  Four Walls. D. Burnet
  Ghost of John Holling. E. Wallace; Steward
  Monte Carlo Nights. E. P. Oppenheim; Mr. Billingham, the Marquis and Madelon
Nixon, Ivan
  Trouble Man. J. D. F. Black
Noble, John W.
  I Wouldn't Be in Your Shoes. W. Irish
  Million a Minute. H. Douglas
  Mysterious Mr. Wong. H. S. Keeler; Sing Sing Nights
  Thou Shalt Not Steal. E. Gaboriau; File No. 113
Nocita, Salvatore
  Crime. G. Bernanos
Norman, Leslie
  Mix Me a Person. J. T. Story
  Too Dangerous to Live. D. Hume
North, Wilfred
  Blue Envelope Mystery. S. Kerr; Blue Envelope
Northcote, Sidney
  Monkey's Paw. W. W. Jacobs; Lady of the Barge
Noy, Wilfred
  Marriage Lines. J. S. Fletcher
  Master of Men. E. P. Oppenheim
  Master of Merripit. E. Phillpotts
  Night and Morning. E. Bulwer-Lytton
  Temptation of Carlton Earle. S. M. During
  Verdict of the Heart. C. Garvice
Nugent, Elliott
  Cat and the Canary. J. Willard
  Whistling in the Dark. L. Gross
Nunez, Victor
  Flash of Green. J. D. MacDonald
Ober, Robert
  Woman Racket. P. Dunning; Night Hostess
O'Brien, Edmund
  Man-Trap. J. D. MacDonald; Soft Touch
  Shield for Murder. W. P. McGivern
O'Brien, John B.
  Bishop's Emeralds. H. Townley
O'Connor, Frank
  Spangles. N. Revell
O'Donovan, Fred
  Knocknagow. C. Kickham
Oernbak, Henning
  Nothing But the Truth. P. Orum
O'Ferrall, George More
  Green Scarf. G. Des Cars; Brute Heart of the Matter. G. Greene
O'Hara, Gerry
  Amsterdam Affair. N. Freeling; Love in Amsterdam
  Bitch. Jackie Collins
  Game for Three Losers. E. Lustgarten
  Maroc 7. M. Sands
Ohlsson, Terry
  Scobie Malone. J. Cleary; Helga's Web
Olcott, Sidney
  After Dark. D. Boucicault
  Amateur Gentleman. J. Farnol
  Colleen Bawn. D. Boucicault
O'Neil, Barry
  Gamblers. C. Klein
  Lion and the Mouse. A. Hornblow
  Third Degree. A. Hornblow
Ophuls, Marcel
  Banana Peel. C. Williams; Nothing in the Way
Opuls, Max
  Reckless Moment. E. S. Holding; Blank Wall
Orton, Joe
  Celestial City. B. Orczy
Orton, John
  Creeping Shadows. W. Scott; Man
Osiecki, Stefan
  No Way Back. T. Burke; Limehouse Nights
Oswald, Gerd
  Kiss Before Dying. I. Levin
  Screaming Mimi. Fredric Brown
Oswald, Richard
  Hound of the Baskervilles. A. C. Doyle
Otto, Henry
  Haunted Bell. J. Futrelle; Diamond Master
  Island of Intrigue. I. Ostrander
  Man from Nowhere. V. Bridges
Pabst, G. L.
  *Joyless Street. H. Bettauer; Viennese Love

Page, Anthony
　Lady Vanishes. E. L. White; Wheel Spins
Pagliero, Marcello
　Cheri-Bibi. G. Leroux
Pakula, Alan J.
　Klute. W. Johnston
　Parallax View. L. Singer
Paris, Jerry
　Grasshopper. M. McShane; Passing of Evil
　Never a Dull Moment. J. Godey; Thrill a Minute with Jack Albany
Parke, William
　Other People's Money. E. Gaboriau
　Paliser Case. E. Saltus
　Yellow Ticket. V. Morton
Parker, Alan
　Angel Heart. W. Hjortsberg; Falling Angel
Parker, Albert
　Murder in the Family. J. Ronald
　Riverside Murder. A. Steeman; Six Dead Men
　Sherlock Holmes. W. Gillette
　Third Clue. N. Gordon; Shakespeare Murders
Parkinson, H. B.
　Bleak House. C. Dickens
　East Lynne. H. Wood
Parks, Gordon, Jr.
　Shaft. E. Tidyman
　Shaft's Big Score. E. Tidyman
　Super Fly. P. Fenty
Parrish, Robert
　Assignment--Paris. P. Gallico; Trial by Terror
　Casino Royale. I. Fleming
　Destructors. M. Franklin
　Duffy. H. J. Brown, Jr.
　Mob. F. Findley; Waterfront
　Rough Shoot. G. Household
Parry, Gordon
　Front Page Story. R. Gaines; Final Night
　Midnight Episode. G. Simenon; Monsieur la Souris
　Surgeon's Knife. A. Hocking; Wicked Flee
　Third Time Lucky. G. Butler; They Cracked Her Glass Slipper
　Tread Softly Stranger. J. Popplewell; Blind Alley
Passer, Ivan
　Ace Up Your Sleeve. J. H. Chase; Ace Up My Sleeve
　Born to Win. M. Roote
　Cutter and Bone. N. Thornburg
　Silver Bears. P. E. Erdman
Paton, Stuart
　Black Bag. L. J. Vance
　Conflict. C. B. Kelland
　Elusive Isabel. J. Futrelle
　Girl in the Dark. C. E. Walk; Green Seal
　One Wonderful Night. L. Tracy
　Scarlet Car. R. H. Davis
　Voice on the Wire. E. H. Ball
　Wanted at Headquarters. E. Wallace (headnote)
　Wolf Hunters. J. O. Curwood
Paul, Fred
　House on the Marsh. F. Warden
　Lyons Mail. E. Moreau; Courier of Lyons
　Money Moon. J. Farnol
　Mord Em'ly. W. P. Ridge
　Still Waters Run Deep. T. Taylor
Pearce, A. Leslie
　Fall Guy. G. Abbott
Pearson, George
　Ace of Spades. J. C. Fraser
　Huntingtower. J. Buchan
　Pointing Finger. Rita
　Shot in the Dark. G. Fairlie
　Study in Scarlet. A. C. Doyle
　True Story of the Lyons Mail. E. Moreau; Courier of Lyons
Peckinpah, Sam
　Getaway. J. Thompson
　Killer Elite. R. Rostand
　Osterman Weekend. R. Ludlum
　Straw Dogs. G. M. Williams; Siege of Trencher's Farm
Pedelty, Donovan
　False Evidence. R. Vickers; I'll Never Tell
Peerce, Larry
　Two Minute Warning. G. La Fountaine
Pelissier, Anthony
　Night Without Stars. Winston Graham
　Personal Affair. L. Storm; Day's Mischief
Pembroke, Scott
　Black Pearl. W. Woodrow
　Sisters of Eve. E. P. Oppenheim; Temptation of Tavernake
Penn, Arthur
　Bonnie and Clyde. B. Hirschfeld
　Chase. H. Foote

Night Moves. A. Sharp
　Target. S. Hunter
Perier, Etienne
　When Eight Bells Toll. A. MacLean
Perret, Leonce
　Silent Master. E. P. Oppenheim; Seeing Life
　Thirteenth Chair. B. Veiller
　Twin Pawns. W. Collins; Woman in White
Perry, Frank
　Compromising Positions. S. Isaacs
Perry, Simon
　Eclipse. N. Wollaston
Peterson, Kris
　Change of Mind. C. Stratton
Petit, Christopher
　Unsuitable Job for a Woman. P. D. James
Petri, Elio
　Quiet Place in the Country. H. Clement
　Tenth Victim. R. Sheckley
Petrie, Daniel
　Fort Apache, the Bronx. H. Gould
　Main Attraction. S. Michaels
　Moon of the Wolf. L. Whitten
　Spy with a Cold Nose. R. Galton
Pevney, Joseph
　Portrait of a Mobster. H. Grey
　Six Bridges to Cross. J. F. Dinneen; Anatomy of a Crime
　Strange Door. R. L. Stevenson; New Arabian Nights
Physioc, Wray
　Blonde Vampire. D. Mooers
Pichel, Irving
　Before Dawn. E. Wallace; Sergeant Sir Peter
　Most Dangerous Game. R. Connell; Variety
　Temptation. R. Hichens; Bella Donna
　They Won't Believe Me. G. McDonell
Pierce, Douglas
　Delavine Affair. R. Chapman; Winter Wears a Shroud
Pierson, Frank R.
　Looking Glass War. J. Le Carre
Pieters, Vivian
　Prey. C. Aird; Henrietta Who
Pilsbury, Sam
　Scarecrow. R. H. Morrieson
Pinoteau, Claude
　Big Operation. R. Airth; Snatch
Pires, Gerard
　Act of Aggression. J. Buell; Shrewsdale Exit
　Fantasia Among the Squares. C. Williams; Diamond Bikini
　Undertaker Parlor Computer. W. Kempley; Probability Factor
Piriev, Ivan
　Brothers Karamazov. F. M. Dostoevskii
Plaissetty, Rene
　Yellow Claw. S. Rohmer
Plumb, Hay
　George Barnwell, the London Apprentice. G. Lillo; London Merchant
Poitier, Sidney
　Hanky Panky. L. Jarreau
Polanski, Roman
　Rosemary's Baby. I. Levin
　Tenant. R. Topor
Pollack, Barry
　Cool Breeze. W. R. Burnett; Asphalt Jungle
Pollack, Sydney
　Slender Threat. S. Silliphant
　They Shoot Horses, Don't They? H. McCoy
　Three Days of the Condor. J. Grady; Six Days of the Condor
　Yakuza. L. Schrader
Pollard, Harry
　Reckless Age. E. D. Biggers; Love Insurance
Pollock, George
　Murder at the Gallop. A. Christie; After the Funeral
　Murder, She Said. A. Christie; 4.50 from Paddington
　Rooney. C. Cookson
　Stranger in Town. F. A. Chittenden; Uninvited
　Ten Little Indians. A. Christie; Ten Little Niggers
Polonsky, Abraham
　Force of Evil. I. Wolfert; Tucker's People
Pomeroy, John
　Dublin Nightmare. P. Loraine
Pomeroy, Roy J.
　Inside the Lines. E. D. Biggers
　Interference. R. Pertwee
Pontecorvo, Gillo
　Burn. N. Gant
Porter, Edwin S.
　Bella Donna. R. Hichens
　Gentleman Burglar. M. Leblanc (headnote)

Post, Ted
　Good Guys Wear Black. M. Franklin
　Magnum Force. M. Valley
Pottier, Richard
　Majestic Hotel Cellars. G. Simenon; Maigret and the Hotel Majestic
Powell, Frank
　Dazzling Miss Davison. F. Warden
　From the Valley of the Missing. G. M. White
　Mrs. Balfame. G. Atherton
　Stain. F. Halsey
Powell, Michael
　Crown v. Stevens. L. Meynell; Third Time Unlucky
　Man Behind the Mask. J. Futrelle; Chase of the Golden Plate
　Phantom Light. E. Price; Haunted Light
　Rasp. P. MacDonald
　Rynox. P. MacDonald
　Small Back Room. N. Balchin
　Spy in Black. J. S. Clouston
Powell, Paul
　Dangerous Lies. E. P. Oppenheim (headnote)
　Mystery Road. E. P. Oppenheim
Preminger, Otto
　Anatomy of a Murder. R. Traver
　Bunny Lake Is Missing. E. Piper
　Fallen Angel. M. Holland
　Human Factor. G. Greene
　Laura. V. Caspary
　Margin for Error. C. Booth
　Rosebud. J. Hemingway
　Where the Sidewalk Ends. W. L. Stuart; Night Cry
　Whirlpool. G. Endore; Methinks the Lady--
Pressburger, Emeric
　Small Back Room. N. Balchin
Pressman, Michael
　Boulevard Nights. D. Gram
　Some Kind of Hero. J. Kirkwood
Quested, John
　Loophole. R. Pollock
Quine, Richard
　Moonshine War. E. Leonard
　Notorious Landlady. I. Shulman
　Pushover. B. Ballinger; Rafferty
Quiribet, Gaston
　Mr. Justice Raffles. E. W. Hornung
Rademakers, Fons
　Because of the Cats. N. Freeling
Rafelson, Bob
　Postman Always Rings Twice. J. M. Cain
Rakoff, Alvin
　Dirty Tricks. T. Gifford; Glendower Legacy
　World in My Pocket. J. H. Chase
Rapper, Irving
　Another Man's Poison. L. Sands; Intent to Murder
　Bad for Each Other. H. McCoy; Scalpel
　Strange Intruder. H. Fowler; Shades Will Not Vanish
Rathony, Akos
　Devil's Daffodil. E. Wallace; Daffodil Mystery
Ratoff, Gregory
　Lancer Spy. M. McKenna
　Moss Rose. J. Shearing
　Wife, Husband and Friend. J. M. Cain; Career in C Major
Rawi, Onsama
　Judgement in Stone. R. Rendell
Rawlins, John
　Great Impersonation. E. P. Oppenheim
　Sherlock Holmes and the Voice of Terror. A. C. Doyle; His Last Bow
Ray, Albert
　Thirteenth Guest. A. Trail
　Whispering Wires. H. Leverage
Ray, Nicholas
　In a Lonely Place. D. B. Hughes
　Knock on Any Door. W. Motley
　On Dangerous Ground. G. Butler; Mad with Much Heart
　Party Girl. M. H. Albert
　They Live by Night. E. Anderson; Thieves Like Us
Raymaker, Herman
　Millionaires. E. P. Oppenheim; Inevitable Millionaires
Raymond, Jack
　Blondes for Danger. E. Price; Red for Danger
　Frog. E. Wallace; Fellowship of the Frog
　Mind of Mr. J. G. Reeder. E. Wallace
　Missing People. E. Wallace; Mind of Mr. J. G. Reeder
　Rat. P. Bottome
　Sorry You've Been Troubled. W. Hackett
　Speckled Band. A. C. Doyle; Adventures of Sherlock Holmes
Readon, James
　Shadow of Evil. C. Dawe

R

Reed, Carol
  Fallen Idol. G. Greene; Basement Room
  Girl in the News. R. Vickers
  Laburnum Grove. J. B. Priestley
  Odd Man Out. F. L. Green
  Our Man in Havana. G. Greene
  Running Man. S. Smith; Ballad of the Running Man
  Third Man. G. Greene
  Trapeze. M. Catto; Killing Frost

Reed, Luther
  New York. B. Chambers

Reeve, Geoffrey
  Caravan to Vaccares. A. MacLean
  Puppet on a Chain. A. MacLean

Reicher, Frank
  Jeanne of the Marshes. E. P. Oppenheim
  Mr. Grex of Monte Carlo. E. P. Oppenheim
  Suspense. I. Ostrander
  Voice in the Fog. H. MacGrath

Reichert, Mark
  Union City. C. Woolrich; Nightwebs

Reid, Alastair
  Something to Hide. N. Monsarrat

Reinhardt, Gottfried
  Town Without Pity. M. Gregor

Reinhardt, John
  Guilty. W. Irish; Dancing Detective

Reinl, Harald
  Room 13. E. Wallace

Reis, Irving
  Crack-Up. Fredric Brown; Madman's Holiday
  Falcon Takes Over. R. Chandler; Farewell, My Lovely

Reisner, Charles
  Man on the Box. H. MacGrath

Reisz, Karel
  Night Must Fall. E. Williams
  Who'll Stop the Rain? R. Stone; Dog Soldiers

Renoir, Jean
  Night at the Crossroads. G. Simenon; Crossroads Murder
  Woman on the Beach. M. A. Wilson; None So Blind

Reynolds, Burt
  Sharky's Machine. W. Diehl
  Stick. E. Leonard

Reynolds, Lynn
  Big Town Round-Up. W. M. Raine
  Huntress. H. Footner

Rich, David Lowell
  Concorde--Airport 1979. K. Stewart
  Madame X. J. W. MacConaughy
  That Man Bolt. P. Crowcraft

Richards, Dick
  Farewell, My Lovely. R. Chandler
  Rafferty and the Gold Dust Twins. L. Roberts

Richards, R. M.
  Heat. W. Goldman

Richardson, Frankland A.
  In the Night. J. Sutherland

Richardson, Ralph
  Home at Seven. R. C. Sherriff

Richardson, Tony
  Dead Cert. D. Francis
  Sanctuary. W. Faulkner

Richert, William
  Winter Kills. R. Condon

Ricketts, Thomas
  Other Side of the Door. L. Chamberlain
  Secretary of Frivolous Affairs. M. Futrelle

Ridgely, Richard
  Destroying Angel. L. J. Vance
  Eugene Aram. E. Bulwer-Lytton
  Heart of the Hills. D. Whitelaw; Girl from the East

Ridgwell, George
  Abbey Grange. A. C. Doyle; Return of Sherlock Holmes
  Amazing Partnership. E. P. Oppenheim
  Black Peter. A. C. Doyle; Return of Sherlock Holmes
  Blue Carbuncle. A. C. Doyle; Adventures of Sherlock Holmes
  Boscombe Valley Mystery. A. C. Doyle; Adventures of Sherlock Holmes
  Bruce-Partington Plans. A. C. Doyle; His Last Bow
  Cardboard Box. A. C. Doyle; His Last Bow
  Charles Augustus Milverton. A. C. Doyle; Return of Sherlock Holmes
  Crimson Circle. E. Wallace
  Crooked Man. A. C. Doyle; Memoirs of Sherlock Holmes
  Dancing Men. A. C. Doyle; Return of Sherlock Holmes
  Engineer's Thumb. A. C. Doyle; Adventures of Sherlock Holmes
  Final Problem. A. C. Doyle; Memoirs of Sherlock Holmes
  Four Just Men. E. Wallace
  Gamble in Lives. F. Stayton; Joan Danvers
  Gloria Scott. A. C. Doyle; Memoirs of Sherlock Holmes
  Golden Pince-Nez. A. C. Doyle; Return of Sherlock Holmes
  Lady Frances Carfax. A. C. Doyle; His Last Bow
  Last Bow. A. C. Doyle; His Last Bow
  Lily of Killarney. D. Boucicault; Colleen Bawn
  Lost Leader. E. P. Oppenheim
  Mazarin Stone. A. C. Doyle; Casebook of Sherlock Holmes
  Missing Three-Quarter. A. C. Doyle; Return of Sherlock Holmes
  Missioner. E. P. Oppenheim
  Musgrave Ritual. A. C. Doyle; Memoirs of Sherlock Holmes
  Naval Treaty. A. C. Doyle; Memoirs of Sherlock Holmes
  Norwood Builder. A. C. Doyle; Return of Sherlock Holmes
  Notorious Mrs. Carrick. C. Procter; Pools of the Past
  Pointing Finger. Rita
  Red Circle. A. C. Doyle; His Last Bow
  Reigate Squires. A. C. Doyle; Memoirs of Sherlock Holmes
  Second Stain. A. C. Doyle; Return of Sherlock Holmes
  Silver Blaze. A. C. Doyle; Memoirs of Sherlock Holmes
  Six Napoleons. A. C. Doyle; Return of Sherlock Holmes
  Speckled Band. A. C. Doyle; Adventures of Sherlock Holmes
  Stock-Broker's Clerk. A. C. Doyle; Memoirs of Sherlock Holmes
  Thor Bridge. A. C. Doyle; Casebook of Sherlock Holmes
  Three Students. A. C. Doyle; Return of Sherlock Holmes

Riesner, Charles
  Murder Goes to College. K. Steel
  Sophie Lang Goes West. E. Anderson; Notorious Sophie Lang

Rilla, Wolf
  Cairo. W. R. Burnett; Asphalt Jungle
  Noose for a Lady. G. Verner; Whispering Woman

Ripley, Arthur
  Chase. C. Woolrich; Black Path of Fear

Ritchie, Michael
  Fletch. G. McDonald
  Prime Cut. M. Roote

Ritt, Martin
  Brotherhood. L. J. Carlino
  Edge of the City. F. Pohl
  Molly Maguires. J. O'Neill
  No Down Payment. J. McPartland
  Spy Who Came in from the Cold. J. Le Carre

Roach, Hal
  Housekeeper's Daughter. D. H. Clarke

Robbie, Seymour
  CC and Company. M. Roote

Roberts, Harry
  Barton Mystery. W. Hackett

Roberts, Stephen
  Night of June 13. F. Vreeland
  Star of Midnight. A. S. Roche
  Story of Temple Drake. W. Faulkner; Sanctuary

Roberts, Yves
  Twin. D. E. Westlake; Two Much!

Robertson, John S.
  Bottom of the Well. F. U. Adams
  Crime Doctor. I. Zangwill; Big Bow Mystery
  Dr. Jekyll and Mr. Hyde. R. L. Stevenson; Strange Case of Dr. Jekyll and Mr. Hyde
  Perpetua. D. C. Calthrop
  Phantom of Paris. G. Leroux; Cheri-Bibi and Cecily
  Test of Honor. E. P. Oppenheim; Mr. Wingrave, Millionaire

Robinson, Arthur
  Informer. L. O'Flaherty

Robison, Arthur
  Trial of Mary Dugan. B. Veiller

Robson, Mark
  Avalanche Express. C. Forbes
  Daddy's Gone A-Hunting. Mike St. Clair
  Edge of Doom. L. Brady
  Hell Below Zero. H. Innes; White South
  Prize of Gold. M. Catto
  Trial. D. M. Mankiewicz

Roddam, Frank
  Bride. M. Shelley; Frankenstein

Roeg, Nicholas
  Don't Look Now. D. Du Maurier; Not After Midnight
  Nightmare Honeymoon. L. Block (headnote)

Roge, Albert, II
  Wrecker. A. Ridley

Rogell, Al
  Before I Die. H. Debrett
  Fog. V. Williams
  Last Warning. J. Latimer; Dead Don't Care

Rogers, Maclean
  Crime at Blossoms. M. Shairp
  Dark Secret. M. Shairp; Crime at Blossoms
  Don Chicago. C. E. B. Roberts
  Feathered Serpent. E. Wallace
  Hammer the Toff. J. Creasey
  Johnny on the Spot. M. Cronin; Paid in Full
  Paul Temple's Triumph. F. Durbridge; News of Paul Temple
  Salute the Toff. J. Creasey
  Story of Shirley Yorke. H. A. Vachell; Case of Lady Camber
  You Pay Your Money. M. Cronin

Rolfe, B. A.
  Love Without Question. W. Camp; Abandoned Room

Romero, George A.
  Night of the Living Dead. J. Russo

Rooke, Arthur
  Diamond Man. E. Wallace (headnote)
  Double Life of Mr. Alfred Burton. E. P. Oppenheim
  Eugene Aram. E. Bulwer-Lytton
  God's Clay. A. Askew
  Nets of Destiny. M. Drake; Salving of a Derelict

Rosen, Phil
  Born to Gamble. E. Wallace; Forty-Eight Short Stories
  Dangerous Corner. J. B. Priestley
  Forbidden Territory. D. Wheatley
  Jim Hanvey, Detective. O. R. Cohen
  Mystery of Marie Roget. E. A. Poe; Tales
  Phantom in the House. A. Soutar
  President's Mystery. F. D. Roosevelt; President's Mystery Story
  Worldly Goods. A. Soutar

Rosenberg, Stuart
  Drowning Pool. J. R. Macdonald
  Laughing Policeman. M. Sjowall
  Love and Bullets. J. Heddon
  Pope of Greenwich Village. V. Patrick

Rosenthal, Rick
  Halloween II. J. Martin

Rosi, Francesco
  Illustrious Corpse. L. Sciascia; Equal Danger

Rosmer, Milton
  Everything Is Thunder. J. L. Hardy

Ross, Herbert
  Last of Sheila. A. Edwards
  Seven-Per-Cent Solution. N. Meyer

Rossen, Richard
  Island in the Sun. A. Waugh
  Wizard. G. Leroux; Balaoo

Rotha, Paul
  Cat and Mouse. M. Halliday
  No Resting Place. I. Niall

Rouse, Russell
  Caper of the Golden Bulls. W. P. McGivern
  House of Numbers. J. Finney

Rouve, Pierre
  Stranger in the House. G. Simenon; Strangers in the House

Rowland, Roy
  Girl Hunters. M. Spillane
  Rogue Cop. W. P. McGivern

Ruben, J. Walter
  Public Defender. G. Goodchild; Splendid Crime
  Roadhouse Murder. M. Level (headnote)
  Secret Service. W. Gillette
  Suicide Club. R. L. Stevenson

Ruggles, Wesley H.
  Agony Column. C. B. Biggers
  Monkey's Paw. W. W. Jacobs; Lady of the Barge
  Piccadilly Jim. P. G. Wodehouse
  Remittance Woman. A. Abdullah

Rush, Richard
  Freebie and the Bean. P. B. Ross
  Stunt Man. P. Brodeur

Russell, Albert
  Lion Man. R. Parrish; Strange Case of Cavendish

Russell, Ken
  Billion Dollar Brain. L. Deighton

Sabine, Martin
  Pursuing Vengeance. B. E. Stevenson; Mystery of the Boule Cabinet

Sacha, Jean
  This Man Is Dangerous. P. Cheyney

Sagal, Boris
  Twilight of Honor. A. Dewlin

St. Clair, Malcolm
  Canary Murder Case. S. S. Van Dine
  Over My Dead Body. J. D. O'Hanlon; As Good As Murdered
  Remote Control. C. North
  Side Street. Mal St. Clair
  Thin Ice. A. R. Colver; Dear Pretender

St. Jacques, Raymond
 Book of Numbers. R. D. Pharr
Salkow, Sidney
 Bulldog Drummond at Bay. H. C. McNeile
 Four Days' Wonder. A. A. Milne
 Twice Told Tales. N. Hawthorne
Samuelson, G. B.
 Convict 99. M. C. Leighton
 Forger. E. Wallace
 Inquest. M. Barringer
 Valley of Ghosts. E. Wallace
 Wickham Mystery. J. McNally; Paper Chase
Sanders, Denis
 Crime and Punishment USA. F. M. Dostoevskii; Crime and Punishment
 Shock Treatment. W. Van Atta
Sanderson, Challis
 Scallywag. G. Allen
Sanger, Jonathan
 Code Name: Emerald. R. Bass; Emerald Illusion
Sangster, Jimmy
 Horror of Frankenstein. M. Shelley; Frankenstein
Santell, Al
 Gorilla. R. Spence
 Parisian Nights. R. Goyne
Santley, Joseph
 Shadow of a Woman. V. Perdue; He Fell Down Dead
Santoni, Joel
 Died on a Rainy Sunday. Joan Aiken
Sarafian, Richard C.
 Next Man. M. Z. Lewin
 Sunburn. S. Ellin; Bind
Sargent, Joseph
 Taking of Pelham One Two Three. J. Godey
Sasdy, Peter
 Hands of the Ripper. E. S. Shew
 Nothing But the Night. J. Blackburn
Saslavsky, Luis
 She Wolves. P. Boileau; Prisoner
 Snow Was Black. G. Simenon; Stain on the Snow
Sauer, Fred
 Adventure, Inc. A. Christie; Secret Adversary
Saunders, Charles
 Behind the Headlines. R. Chapman
 Dangerous Afternoon. G. Anstruther
 Meet Mr. Callaghan. G. Verner
 Murder Reported. R. Chapman; Murder for the Million
 Narrowing Circle. J. Symons
 One Jump Ahead. R. Chapman
Sautet, Claude
 Arm at the Left. C. Williams; Aground
Saville, Victor
 Calling Bulldog Drummond. G. Fairlie
 Conspirator. H. Slater
 Long Wait. M. Spillane
 W Plan. G. Seton
Saytor, Tony
 It Only Happens to the Living. R. Marshall; Things Men Do
Scaffner, Franklin
 Sphinx. R. Cook
Scardon, Paul
 Alibi. G. A. England
 Arsene Lupin. E. Jepson
 Gamblers. C. Klein
 Green God. F. A. Kummer
 Grell Mystery. F. Froest
 In the Balance. E. P. Oppenheim; Hillman
 Man Who Won. C. T. Brady
 Partners of the Night. L. Scott
Schaffner, Franklin J.
 Boys from Brazil. I. Levin
 Double Man. H. S. Maxfield; Legacy of a Spy
Schatzberg, Jerry
 Panic in Needle Park. James Mills
Schell, Maximilian
 Murder on the Bridge. F. Duerrenmatt; Judge and His Hangman
Schepsi, Fred
 Chant of Jimmie Blacksmith. T. Keneally
Schertzinger, Victor
 Forgotten Faces. R. W. Child; Velvet Black
 Mr. Barnes of New York. A. C. Gunter
 Son of His Father. R. Cullum
Schlesinger, John
 Marathon Man. W. Goldman
Schroedsack, Ernest B.
 Most Dangerous Game. R. Connell; Variety
Schultz, Carl
 Careful, He Might Hear You. S. L. Elliott
Scott, George C.
 Rage. P. Friedman
Scott, Peter Graham
 Account Rendered. P. Barrington
 Big Chance. P. Barrington (headnote)
 Captain Clegg. R. Thorndyke; Dr. Syn

Scott, Ridley
 Blade Runner. P. K. Dick; Do Androids Dream of Electric Sheep?
Searle, Francis
 Murder at Site Three. W. H. Baker; Crime Is My Business
 Someone at the Door. D. Christie
Sears, Fred F.
 Rumble on the Docks. F. Paley
Seaton, George
 Counterfeit Traitor. A. Klein
 36 Hours. C. K. Hittleman
Seay, Charles M.
 It Is Never Too Late to Mend. C. Reade
 Sheep's Clothing. L. J. Vance
Sedgwick, Edward
 Death on the Diamond. C. Fitzsimmons
 Fantomas. P. Souvestre
 Father Brown, Detective. G. K. Chesterton; Wisdom of Father Brown
Seiler, Lewis
 Great K&A Train Robbery. P. L. Ford
 Heart of the North. W. B. Mowery
 Square Crooks. J. P. Judge
Seiter, William A.
 Broadway. P. Dunning
 Case Against Mrs. Ames. A. S. Roche
 Cheerful Fraud. K. R. G. Browne; Following Ann
 Love Racket. B. K. Burns; Jury Woman
 Mad Whirl. R. W. Child; Fresh Waters
 Make Haste to Live. Gordons
 Witching Hour. A. Thomas
Seitz, George B.
 Drums of Jeopardy. H. MacGrath
 Exploits of Elaine. A. B. Reeve
 In Secret. R. W. Chambers
 Kind Lady. E. Chodorov
 Lion and the Lamb. E. P. Oppenheim
 Midnight Mystery. H. I. Young; Hawk Island
 Murder on the Roof. E. J. Doherty; Broadway Murders
 Romance of Elaine. A. B. Reeve
 Shadow of Doubt. A. S. Roche
 Thirteenth Chair. B. Veiller
Sekely, Steve
 Hollow Triumph. M. Forbes
Selander, Lesley
 Three's a Crowd. M. G. Eberhart; Hasty Wedding
Sellers, Ollie L.
 Gift Supreme. G. A. England
Selwyn, Edgar
 Mystery of Mr. X. M. Porlock; X v. Rex
Sewell, Vernon
 Floating Dutchman. N. Bentley
 Soho Incident. R. Westerby; Wide Boys Never Work
 Uneasy Terms. P. Cheyney
Shane, Maxwell
 City Across the River. I. Shulman; Amboy Dukes
 Fear in the Night. W. Irish; I Wouldn't Be in Your Shoes
 Fear in the Night. C. Woolrich; Nightmare
 Nightmare. C. Woolrich
Sharp, Don
 Bear Island. A. MacLean
 Callan. J. Mitchell
 Fifth of November. M. Franklin
 Puppet on a Chain. A. MacLean
 Taste of Excitement. B. Healey; Waiting for a Tiger
 Thirty-Nine Steps. J. Buchan
 Violent Enemy. H. Marlowe; Candle for the Dead
Sharp, Ian
 Who Dares Wins. J. Follett; Tiptoe Boys
Shavelson, Melville
 On the Double. Roger Fuller
 Pigeon That Took Rome. D. Downes; Easter Dinner
Shaw, Harold
 False Evidence. E. P. Oppenheim
 Love and the Whirlwind. H. P. Lewis
 Mr. Lyndon at Liberty. V. Bridges
Shear, Barry
 Across 110th. W. Ferris
Sherin, Edwin
 Valdez Is Coming. E. Leonard
Sherman, Gary A.
 Vice Squad. W. Rotsler
Sherman, George
 Hard Man. L. Katcher
 Lady and the Monster. C. Siodmak; Donovan's Brain
 Larceny. L. Eby; Velvet Fleece
 Panther's Moon. V. Canning
 Raging Tide. E. K. Gann; Fiddler's Green
 Reprisal. Arthur Gordon
 Scream in the Dark. J. Odlum; Morgue Is Always Open
Sherman, Lowell
 Ladies of the Jury. F. Ballard

Sherman, Vincent
 Flight from Destiny. A. Berkeley; Trial and Error
 Unfaithful. W. S. Maugham; Letter
Shonteff, Lindsay
 Slaves of Sumuru. S. Rohmer
 Spy Story. L. Deighton
Shumlin, Herman
 Confidential Agent. G. Greene
Sidney, George
 Red Danube. B. Marshall; Vespers in Vienna
 Who Was That Lady? N. Krasna; Who Was That Lady I Saw You With?
Sidney, Scott
 813. M. Leblanc
Siegel, Don
 Black Windmill. C. Egleton; Seven Days to a Killing
 Charley Varrick. J. Reese; Looters
 Dirty Harry. P. Rock
 Gun Runners. E. Hemingway; To Have and Have Not
 Killers. E. Hemingway; Men Without Women
 Madigan. R. Dougherty; Commissioner
 Play Misty for Me. P. J. Gillette
 Rough Cut. D. Lambert; Touch the Lion's Paw
 Telefon. W. Wager
 Verdict. I. Zangwill; Big Bow Mystery
Silver, Raphael D.
 On the Yard. M. Braly
Silverstein, Elliot
 Happening. E. Curry
 Nightmare Honeymoon. L. Block (headnote)
Simon, S. Sylvan
 Grand Central Murder. S. MacVeigh
 I Love Trouble. R. Huggins; Double Take
 Whistling in the Dark. L. Gross
Sinclair, Andrew
 Blue Blood. A. Thynne; Carry-Cot
Sinclair, Robert B.
 Mr. & Mrs. North. O. Davis
 Rage in Heaven. J. Hilton
Siodmak, Robert
 Affair Nina B. J. M. Simmel; Affair of Nina B
 Criss-Cross. D. Tracy
 Cry of the City. H. E. Helseth; Chair for Martin Rome
 Killers. E. Hemingway; Men Without Women
 Mister Flow. G. Leroux; Man of a Hundred Masks
 Phantom Lady. W. Irish
 Spiral Staircase. E. L. White; Some Must Watch
 Strange Affair of Uncle Harry. T. Job; Uncle Harry
 Suspect. J. Ronald; This Way Out
Sirk, Douglas
 Bonaventure. C. Hastings
 Interlude. J. M. Cain; Serenade
 Sleep My Love. L. Q. Ross
 Summer Storm. A. Chekhov; Shooting Party
Sittenham, Fred W.
 Mystery Mind. A. B. Reeve
Sloan, Paul
 Straight Is the Way. D. Burnet; Four Walls
Sloman, Edward
 Murder by the Clock. Rufus King
 Pilgrims of the Night. A. Partridge; Passers-By
Smalley, Phillips
 John Needham's Double. J. Hatton
Smart, Ralph
 Bitter Springs. C. King
Smight, Jack
 Frankenstein: The True Story. M. Shelley; Frankenstein
 Kaleidoscope. M. Avallone
 Moving Target. J. Macdonald
 No Way to Treat a Lady. H. Longbaugh
 Third Day. J. Hayes
Smiley, Joseph W.
 Beloved Adventurer. E. C. Hall
 Life Without Soul. M. Shelley; Frankenstein
Smith, David
 Silver Car. W. Martyn; Secret of the Silver Car
 Steele of the Royal Mounted. J. O. Curwood; Philipp Steele of the Royal Northwest Mounted Police
Smith, Noel M.
 Case of the Black Parrot. B. E. Stevenson; Mystery of the Boule Cabinet
 Mystery House. M. G. Eberhart; Mystery of Hunting's End
 Nurse's Secret. M. R. Rinehart; Miss Pinkerton
Solem, Ola
 Operation Cobra. A. Bodelsen
Sparr, Robert

Once You Kiss a Stranger. P. Highsmith; Strangers on a Train
Spottiswoode, Roger
 Pursuit of D. B. Cooper. J. D. Reed; Free Fall
Squire, Anthony
 11 Harrowhouse. G. A. Browne
Stahl, John M.
 Leave Her to Heaven. B. A. Williams
 When Tomorrow Comes. J. M. Cain; Serenade
Stanlaws, Penrhyn
 Woman in the Case. C. Fitch
Stanley, Paul
 Cry Tough. I. Shulman
Starrett, Jack
 Cleopatra Jones. R. Goulart
 Slaughter. H. Clement
Staub, Ralph
 Mandarin Mystery. E. Queen; Chinese Orange Mystery
Steger, Julius
 Burden of Proof. V. Sardou; Diplomates
Stein, Paul L.
 Black Limelight. G. Sherry
 Poison Pen. R. Llewellyn
 Saint Meets the Tiger. L. Charteris; Meet the Tiger
Stevens, Robert
 Big Caper. L. White
 I Thank a Fool. A. E. Lindop
 Never Love a Stranger. H. Robbins
Stevenson, Robert
 Non-Stop New York. K. Attiwill; Sky Steward
 One of Our Dinosaurs Is Missing. D. Forrest; Great Dinosaur Robbery
 That Darn Cat. Gordons; Undercover Cat
 Ware Case. G. Pleydell
Stoloff, Ben
 Hidden Hand. Rufus King; Invitation to a Murder
 Two in the Dark. G. Burgess; Two O'Clock Courage
Stone, Andrew L.
 Cry Terror. A. L. Stone
 Decks Ran Red. A. L. Stone
 Julia. A. L. Stone
Stone, Oliver
 Hand. M. Brandel; Lizard's Tail
Storch, Wolfgang
 Two Faces in January. P. Highsmith
Storm, Jerome
 Brass Bowl. L. J. Vance
 Honor First. G. F. Gibbs; Splendid Outcast
Strayer, Frank R.
 I Ring Doorbells. R. Birdwell
 Murder at Glen Athol. N. Lippincott
Strick, Joseph
 Balcony. J. Genet
Sturgeon, Rollin S.
 Through the Wall. C. Moffett
 Whose Wife? C. H. Bullivant
Sturgis, John
 Bad Day at Black Rock. M. Niall
 Eagle Has Landed. J. Higgins
 Kind Lady. E. Chodorov
 McQ. A. Edwards
 People Against O'Hara. E. Lipsky
 Satan Bug. I. Stuart
 Sign of the Ram. M. Ferguson
Sullivan, Fred G.
 Cold River. W. Judson
Sullivan, Frederick
 Mr. Meeson's Will. H. R. Haggard
Summers, Walter
 At the Villa Rose. A. E. W. Mason
 Dark Eyes of London. E. Wallace
 House Opposite. J. L. Farjeon
 Limping Man. W. Scott; Man
 Return of Bulldog Drummond. H. C. McNeile; Black Gang
 Traitor Spy. T. C. H. Jacobs
 What Happened Then? L. T. Bradley
Suso, Henry
 Deathsport. W. Hughes
Sutherland, A. Edward
 Having Wonderful Crime. C. Rice
 Nine Lives Are Not Enough. J. Odlum
 One Night in the Tropics. E. D. Biggers; Love Insurance
Sykes, Peter
 To the Devil—a Daughter. D. Wheatley
Szwarc, Jeannot
 Enigma. M. Barak
Taggert, Errol
 Longest Night. C. Fitzsimmons; Whispering Window
 Sinner Take All. W. Chambers; Murder for a Wanton
Tannen, William
 Flashpoint. G. La Fountaine
Tarride, Jean
 Yellow Dog. G. Simenon; Face for a Clue
Tashlin, Frank
 Alphabet Murders. A. Christie; ABC Murders
 Caprice. J. Withers
 Glass Bottom Boat. B. Street
 Man from the Diner's Club. S. Baol
Taurog, Norman
 Fifty Roads to Town. F. Nebel
 Phantom President. G. F. Worts
Tavernier, Bertrand
 Clockmaker. G. Simenon; Watchmaker of Everton
 Population 1280. J. Thompson; Pop. 1280
Taylor, Donald
 Straw Man. D. M. Disney
Taylor, Henry Cockraft
 Jack Sheppard. W. H. Ainsworth
Taylor, Sam
 Cat's Paw. C. B. Kelland
Taylor, Stanner E. V.
 Dead Secret. W. Collins
 Lone Wolf. L. J. Vance
Taylor, William Desmond
 High Hand. J. Futrelle
 Witching Hour. A. Thomas
Tennyson, Pen
 There Ain't No Justice. J. Curtis
Terriss, Tom
 Dead Men Tell No Tales. E. W. Hornung
 Find the Woman. A. S. Roche
 Lion and the Mouse. A. Hornblow
 Mystery of Edwin Drood. C. Dickens
 Romance of a Million Dollars. E. Dejeans
 Third Degree. A. Hornblow
Terwilliger, George W.
 Fatal Hour. E. K. Chatterton; Marriages of Mayfair
Tetzlaff, Ted
 Window. W. Irish; Dead Man Blues
Tewkesbury, Peter
 Trouble with Girls. D. Keene; Chautauqua
Thom, Robert
 Angel, Angel, Down We Go. W. Johnston
Thomas, Gerald
 Solitary Child. N. Bawden
Thomas, Ralph
 Appointment with Venus. J. Tickell
 Campbell's Kingdom. H. Innes
 Deadlier Than the Male. H. Reymond
 High Bright Sun. I. S. Black
 High Commissioner. J. Cleary
 Hot Enough for June. L. Davidson; Night of Wenceslas
 Thirty-Nine Steps. J. Buchan
 Upstairs and Downstairs. R. S. Thorn
 Venetian Bird. V. Canning
Thompson, Frederick
 After Dark. D. Boucicault
Thompson, J. Lee
 Ambassador. E. Leonard; Fifty-Two Pickup
 Cape Fear. J. D. MacDonald; Executioners
 Chairman. J. R. Kennedy
 Evil That Men Do. R. L. Hill
 Eye of the Devil. P. Loraine; Day of the Arrow
 Guns of Navarone. A. MacLean
 Ice-Cold in Alex. C. Landon
 Murder Without Crime. J. L. Thompson
 Passage. B. Nicolaysen; Perilous Passage
 Reincarnation of Peter Proud. M. Ehrlich
 Return from the Ashes. H. Monteilhet
 St. Ives. O. Bleeck; Procane Chronicle
 Yield to the Night. J. Henry
Thomson, Chris
 Empty Beach. P. Corris
Thornby, Robert
 Girl in the Web. G. Bonner; Miss Maitland, Private Secretary
 Half a Chance. F. S. Isham
 On Dangerous Ground. B. E. Stevenson; Little Comrade
Thornton, F. Martin
 Belonging. O. Wadsley
 Diana and Destiny. C. Garvice
 Diana of the Islands. B. Bolt
 Man Who Bought London. E. Wallace
 Melody of Death. E. Wallace
 My Lord Conceit. Rita
 River of Stars. E. Wallace
 Splendid Coward. H. Townley
Thorpe, Jerry
 Venetian Affair. H. MacInnes
Thorpe, Richard
 Above Suspicion. H. MacInnes
 Cheating Cheaters. M. Marcin
 Earl of Chicago. B. Williams
 Green Eyes. H. Ashbrook; Murder of Steven Kester
 Horizontal Lieutenant. G. Cotler; Bottletop Affair
 House of the Seven Hawks. V. Canning; House of the Seven Flies
 King Murder. C. R. Jones
 Murder on the Campus. W. Chambers; Campanile Murders
 Night Must Fall. E. Williams
 Scorpio Letters. V. Canning
Till, Eric
 Walking Stick. Winston Graham
Tinling, James
 Great Hospital Mystery. M. G. Eberhart (headnote)
Tokar, Norman
 Candleshoe. M. Innes; Christmas at Candleshoe
Tomlinson, Lionel
 Death in High Heels. C. Brand
Tourneur, Jacques
 Ivory Snuff Box. A. Fredericks
 My Lady's Garter. J. Futrelle
Tourneur, Maurice
 Hand of Peril. A. Stringer
 White Circle. R. L. Stevenson; New Arabian Nights
Tournier, Jacques
 Experiment Perilous. M. Carpenter
 Fear Makers. D. L. Teilhet
 Leopard Man. C. Woolrich; Black Alibi
Treville, Georges
 Beryl Coronet. A. C. Doyle; Adventures of Sherlock Holmes
 Copper Beeches. A. C. Doyle; Adventures of Sherlock Holmes
 Musgrave Ritual. A. C. Doyle; Memoirs of Sherlock Holmes
 Mystery of Boscombe Vale. A. C. Doyle; Adventures of Sherlock Holmes
 Reigate Squires. A. C. Doyle; Memoirs of Sherlock Holmes
 Silver Blaze. A. C. Doyle; Memoirs of Sherlock Holmes
 Speckled Band. A. C. Doyle; Adventures of Sherlock Holmes
 Stolen Papers. A. C. Doyle; Memoirs of Sherlock Holmes
Trieschman, Charles
 Two. C. Trieschman
Tronson, Robert
 Man at the Carlton Tower. E. Wallace; Man at the Carlton
 Man Detained. E. Wallace; Debt Discharged
 Never Back Losers. E. Wallace; Green Ribbon
 Number Six. E. Wallace
 On the Run. E. Wallace (headnote)
Truffaut, Francois
 Bride Wore Black. C. Woolrich
 Let It Be Sunday. C. Williams; Long Saturday Night
 Mississippi Mermaid. W. Irish; Waltz into Darkness
 Shoot the Piano Player. D. Goodis; Down There
 Such a Lovely Kid Like Me. H. Farrell; Such a Gorgeous Kid Like Me
Truman, Michael
 Girl in the Headlines. L. Payne; Nose on My Face
Tuchner, Michael
 Fear Is the Key. A. MacLean
 Villain. J. Barlow; Burden of Proof
Tucker, George Loane
 Arsene Lupin. E. Jepson
 Called Back. H. Conway
 Folly of Desire. A. Askew; Shulamite
 Game of Liberty. E. P. Oppenheim
 Miracle Man. F. Packard
 Shulamite. A. Askew
 Sons of Satan. W. Lequeux
 Traffic in Souls. E. H. Ball
Tudor, F. C. S.
 Devil's Profession. G. de S. W. James
Tully, Montgomery
 Clash by Night. R. Croft-Cooke
 Diamond. M. Procter; Rich Is the Treasure
 Glass Cage. A. E. Martin; Outsiders
 House in Marsh Road. L. Meynell
 Long Knife. S. Truss; Long Night
 Man in the Shadow. S. Davis; One Man's Secret
 Man Who Was Nobody. E. Wallace
 No Road Back. F. L. Cary; Madam Tic-Tac
 Out of the Fog. B. Graeme; Fog of a Killer
 Price of Silence. L. Meynell; One Step from Murder
 Strange Awakening. P. Quentin; Puzzle for Fiends
 Way Out. B. Graeme
 Who Killed the Cat? A. Ridley; Tabitha
Turner, Otis
 Black Box. E. P. Oppenheim
 Called Back. H. Conway
 Gay Lord Waring. H. Townley
 Lady Audley's Secret. M. E. Braddon
 Pool of Flame. L. J. Vance
 Son of the Immortals. L. Tracy
 Spy. J. F. Cooper
Tuttle, Frank
 Benson Murder Case. S. S. Van Dine

Cry in the Night. W. Masterson; All Through the Night
Easy Come, Easy Go. O. Davis
Glass Key. D. Hammett
Greene Murder Case. S. S. Van Dine
Hell on Frisco Bay. W. P. McGivern; Darkest Hour
Hostages. S. Heym
Studio Murder Mystery. Edingtons
This Gun for Hire. G. Greene; Gun for Sale

Twist, Derek
Family Doctor. J. Fleming; Deeds of Dr. Deadcert

Ulmer, Edgar G.
Detour. M. M. Goldsmith

Urson, Frank
Chicago. M. Watkins

Vadim, Roger
Blood and Roses. J. S. Le Fanu; In a Glass Darkly
Pretty Maids All in a Row. F. Pollini

Vajda, Ladislav
It Happens in Broad Daylight. F. Duerrenmatt; Pledge

Vale, Travers
Aurora Floyd. M. E. Braddon
East Lynne. H. Wood
Ernest Maltravers. E. Bulver-Lytton
Ticket-of-Leave Man. T. Taylor
Woman of Mystery. G. Ohnet

Van, Wallie
Scarlet Runner. C. N. Williamson

Van Dyke, W. S., II
Destroying Angel. L. J. Vance
I Love You Again. O. R. Cohen
Pagan. J. Russell; In Dark Places
Penthouse. A. S. Roche
Rage in Heaven. J. Hilton
They Gave Him a Gun. W. J. Cowen
Thin Man. D. Hammett

Varnel, Marcel
Bones. E. Wallace
Silent Witness. J. De Leon

Varnel, Max
Question of Sixpence. R. Vickers (headnote)
Rivals. E. Wallace; Elegant Edward

Varney, Edward
Road to Fortune. H. Broadbridge; Moorland Terror

Veiller, Bayard
Ladyfingers. J. Gregory
Trial of Mary Dugan. B. Veiller

Vekroff, Perry
Cynthia-of-the-Minute. L. J. Vance

Verneuil, Henri
Big Grab. J. Trinian
Burglars. D. Goodis; Burglar
Forbidden Fruit. G. Simenon; Act of Passion
President. G. Simenon; Premier

Vernon, Richard
Street of Shadows. L. Meynell; Creaking Chair

Versini, Andre
See Venice and Die. R. Marshall; Mission to Venice

Vianey, Michel
Cops' Sunday. A. Coburn; Off Duty

Vidor, Charles
Blind Alley. J. Warwick
Double Door. E. McFadden
Ladies in Retirement. E. Percy
Muss 'Em Up. J. E. Grant; Green Shadow

Vidor, King
Beyond the Forest. S. Engstrand
Cynara. R. Gore-Brown; Imperfect Lover
Lightning Strikes Twice. M. Echard; Dark Fantastic

Viertel, Berthold
Wiser Sex. C. Fitch; Woman in the Case

Vignola, Robert G.
Under Cover. R. C. Megrue
Vicky Van. C. Wells
Woman Who Came Back. C. M. S. McLellan; Leah Kleschna

Villiers, David
Candidate for Murder. E. Wallace (headnote)

Vincent, James
Woman in Grey. A. M. Williamson

Visconti, Luchino
Obsession. J. M. Cain; Serenade

Vohrer, Alfred
All People Will Be Brothers. J. M. Simmel; Cain '67
And Jimmy Went to the Rainbow's Foot. J. M. Simmel; Caesar Code
Love Is Only a Word. J. M. Simmel; Love Is Just a Word
Only the Wind Knows the Answer. J. M. Simmel; Wind and the Rain
Soho Gorilla. E. Wallace; Dark Eyes of London
Sorcerer. E. Wallace; Ringer
Squeaker. E. Wallace

Stuff That Dreams Are Made Of. J. M. Simmel; Traitor Blitz
Waiting Room for the Other Side. R. Marshall; Mission to Siena

Von Sternberg, Josef
Crime and Punishment. F. M. Dostoevskii
Dishonored. F. Vreeland

Vorhaus, Bernard
Blind Justice. A. Ridley; Recipe for Murder
Dusty Ermine. N. Grant
Last Journey. J. J. Farjeon; Holiday Express
Ten Minute Alibi. A. Armstrong

Wadleigh, Michael
Wolfen. W. Strieber

Waggner, George
Climax. F. J. Lewis

Wajda, Andrzej
Ashes and Diamonds. J. Andrzeyevski

Walker, Norman
Hate Ship. B. Graeme

Walker, Stuart
Mystery of Edwin Drood. C. Dickens

Wallace, C. R.
Trooper O'Neill. G. Goodchild

Wallace, Edgar
Red Aces. E. Wallace
Squeaker. E. Wallace

Wallace, Richard
Fallen Sparrow. D. B. Hughes
Kick-In. W. Mack
Masquerader. K. C. Thurston
Night to Remember. K. Roos; Frightened Stiff

Walls, Tom
Plunder. B. Travers

Walsh, Raoul
Background to Danger. E. Ambler; Uncommon Danger
Colorado Territory. W. R. Burnett; High Sierra
From Now On. F. Packard
High Sierra. W. R. Burnett
Jump for Glory. A. McDonell
Me—Gangster. C. F. Coe
Northern Pursuit. L. T. White; 5,000 Trojan Horses
Red Dance. H. L. Gates; Red Dancer of Moscow
They Drive by Night. A. I. Bezzerides; Long Haul
Yellow Ticket. V. Morton

Wanamaker, Sam
File of the Golden Goose. J. Watson

Ward, Albert
Poison. A. Askew

Warde, Ernest C.
Devil to Pay. F. N. Greene
House of Whispers. W. Johnston
Woman in White. W. Collins

Warren, Charles Marquis
Back from the Dead. C. Turney; Other One

Warren, Mark
Come Back, Charleston Blue. C. Himes; Heat's On

Waschneck, Erich
His Official Wife. R. H. Savage; My Official Wife

Watkins, Peter
Privilege. John Burke

Webb, Kenneth
His Wife's Husband. A. K. Green; Mayor's Wife
How Women Love. I. L. Forrester; Dangerous Inheritance
Jim the Penman. C. L. Young
Secrets of Paris. E. Sue; Mysteries of Paris

Webb, Robert D.
Caribbean Mystery. J. W. Vandercook; Murder in Trinidad
Spider. F. Oursler
Way to the Gold. W. D. Steele; Way to Gold

Weber, Lois
John Needham's Double. J. Hatton
Mary Regan. L. Scott

Webster, Harry McRae
Jimmy Dale, Alias "The Grey Seal". F. Packard; Adventures of Jimmie Dale

Weeks, Stephen
I, Monster. R. L. Stevenson; Strange Case of Dr. Jekyll and Mr. Hyde

Weight, Harmon
Ramshackle House. H. Footner

Weine, Robert
Hands of Orlac. M. Renard

Weinstein, Marvin R.
Running Target. S. Frazee

Weir, Peter
Witness. W. Kelley

Weis, Don
Remains to Be Seen. H. Lindsay

Welles, Orson
Lady from Shanghai. Sherwood King; If I Die Before I Wake
Mr. Arkadin. O. Welles
Stranger. A. Veiller
Touch of Evil. W. Masterson; Badge of Evil

Wellman, William A.
Beggars of Life. J. Tully
Lady of Striptease. G. R. Lee; G-String Murders
Love Is a Racket. R. James
Night Nurse. D. Macy
President Vanishes. Anonymous
Public Enemy. K. Glasmon
Stingaree. E. W. Hornung

Wells, Jack
Lion Man. R. Parrish; Strange Case of Cavendish

Wenders, Wim
American Friend. P. Highsmith; Ripley's Friend
Hammett. J. Gores

Wendkos, Paul
Mephisto Waltz. F. M. Stewart

Werker, Alfred L.
Double Cross Roads. W. Lipman; Yonder Grow the Daisies
Repeat Performance. W. O'Farrell
Sherlock Holmes. W. Gillette
Young Don't Cry. R. Jessup

West, Langdon
Banker's Double. S. Campbell; Below the Dead-Line
Case of the Vanished Bonds. S. Campbell; Below the Dead-Line
Dickson's Diamonds. S. Campbell; Below the Dead-Line
Man Who Vanished. S. Campbell; Below the Dead-Line

West, Roland
Bat. M. R. Rinehart
Bat Whispers. M. R. Rinehart; Bat
Corsair. W. Green
Unknown Purple. Roland West

West, Walter
Brotherhood. E. Wallace; Double
Case of Lady Camber. H. A. Vachell
In the Blood. A. Soutar
Maria Marten. Anonymous
Sweeney Todd, the Demon Barber of Fleet Street. G. D. Pitt
Ware Case. G. Pleydell
When Greek Meets Greek. P. Trent

Weston, Harold
Mystery of a Hansom Cab. F. Hume

Wetherell, M. A.
Moorland Tragedy. B. Orczy; Unravelled Knots

Whale, James
Frankenstein. M. Shelley
Old Dark House. J. B. Priestley; Benighted
Remember Last Night? A. Hobhouse; Hangover Murders

Wharton, Leopold
Mr. Potter of Texas. A. C. Gunter

Wharton, Theodore
New Adventures of J. Rufus Wallingford. G. R. Chester; Get-Rich-Quick Wallingford

Whelan, Tim
Nightmare. M. Porlock; Mystery in Kensington Gore
Ten Days in Paris. B. Graeme; Disappearance of Roger Tremayne
This Was a Woman. Joan Morgan

White, George A.
My Gun Is Quick. M. Spillane

Whorf, Richard
Love from a Stranger. F. Vosper

Wicki, Bernhard
Morituri. W. J. Luddecke
Visit. F. Duerrenmatt

Widerberg, Bo
Man on the Roof. M. Sjowall; Abominable Man

Wiene, Robert
Raskolnikov. F. M. Doestoevskii; Crime and Punishment

Wilbur, Crane
Bat. M. R. Rinehart
Patient in Room 18. M. G. Eberhart

Wilcox, Herbert
Trent's Last Case. E. C. Bentley
Woman in White. W. Collins

Wilde, Cornell
Storm Fear. C. Seeley

Wilder, Billy
Double Indemnity. J. M. Cain
Private Life of Sherlock Holmes. Michael Hardwick
Witness for the Prosecution. A. Christie

Wilder, Gene
Adventure of Sherlock Holmes' Smarter Brother. G. Pearlman

Wilder, W. Lee
Spy in the Sky. A. S. Fleischman; Counterspy Express
Vicious Circle. H. Herald; Burning Bush

Wiles, Gordon
Gangster. D. Fuchs; Low Company

Willat, Irvin V.
  False Faces. L. J. Vance
  Fifty Candles. E. D. Biggers
  Guilty Man. F. Coppee
  Pawned. F. Packard
  Story Without a Name. A. Stringer
  Yellow Men and Gold. Gouverneur
    Morris
Williams, Brock
  Root of All Evil. J. S. Fletcher
Willis, Gordon
  Windows. H. B. Gilmour
Willoughby, Lewis
  Secret of the Moor. M. Gerard
Wilson, Andrew P.
  Fighting Snub Reilly. E. Wallace;
    Forty-Eight Short Stories
Wilson, Ben
  Brass Bullet. F. R. Adams; Pleasure
    Island
  Voice on the Wire. E. H. Ball
Wilson, Frank
  Grand Babylon Hotel. A. Bennett
  Turf Conspiracy. N. Gould
  Woman Wins. C. H. Bullivant
Wilson, Hugh
  Burglar. L. Block (headnote)
Wilson, Rex
  Quinney's. H. A. Vachell
Wilson, Richard
  Al Capone. J. Roeburt
  Big Boodle. R. Sylvester
Windom, Lawrence C.
  Modern Marriage. D. Vane; Lady
    Varley
Winner, Michael
  Big Sleep. R. Chandler
  Death Wish. B. Garfield
  Jokers. M. Sands
  Mechanic. L. J. Carlino
  Nightcomers. Michael Hastings
  Scorpio. M. Roote
  Sentinel. J. Konvitz
  Stone Killer. J. Gardner; Complete
    State of Death
Winslow, Dicky
  East Lynne. H. Wood
  Maria Marten. Anonymous
  Octoroon. D. Boucicault
Winston, Ron
  Don't Just Stand There. C. Williams;
    Wrong Venus
Wise, Herbert
  To Have and to Hold. E. Wallace
    (headnote)
Wise, Robert
  Audrey Rose. F. De Felitta
  Body Snatcher. R. L. Stevenson
  Born to Kill. J. Gunn; Deadlier Than
    the Male
  Game of Death. R. Connell; Variety
  Haunting. S. Jackson; Haunting of
    Hill House
  House on Telegraph Hill. D. Lyon;
    Frightened Child
  Odds Against Tomorrow. W. P. McGivern
Withey, Chet/Chester
  Pleasure Buyers. A. S. Roche
  Teeth of the Tiger. M. Leblanc
Witney, William
  Drums of Fu Manchu. S. Rohmer
  Juvenile Jungle. Firth Counsel
  Secret of the Purple Reef. D. Cot-
    trell; Silent Reefs
  Young and Wild. Morton Cooper
Wood, Sam
  Ivy. M. B. Lowndes; Story of Ivy
  Madame X. J. W. MacConaughy
  New Adventures of Get-Rich-Quick
    Wallingford. G. R. Chester; Get-
    Rich-Quick Wallingford
  Raffles. E. W. Hornung; Amateur
    Cracksman
  Under the Lash. A. Askew; Shulamite
  Within the Law. B. Veiller
Woods, Arthur
  Busman's Honeymoon. D. L. Sayers
  Dark Stairway. M. G. Eberhart; From
    This Dark Stairway
  Nursemaid Who Disappeared. P.
    MacDonald
  They Drive by Night. J. Curtis
Worne, Duke
  Devil's Chaplain. G. Bronson-Howard
  Man from Headquarters. G. Bronson-
    Howard; Black Book
  Mysterious Mr. Garland. W. Martyn
Worsley, Wallace
  Highest Bidder. M. Foster; Trap
Worthington, William
  Illustrious Prince. E. P. Oppenheim
  Silent Barrier. L. Tracy
  Tong Man. C. C. Westover; Dragon's
    Daughter
Wray, John Griffith
  Winding Stair. A. E. W. Mason
Wrede, Caspar
  Ransom. P. Wheeler
Wright, George A.
  Catspaw. W. H. Osborne

Wyler, William
  Collector. J. Fowles
  Dead End. S. Kingsley
  Desperate Hours. J. Hayes
  Detective Story. S. Kingsley
  How to Steal a Million. M. Sinclair
  Letter. W. S. Maugham
Yarbrough, Jean
  Challenge. H. C. McNeile
  Shed No Tears. D. Martin
Yates, Peter
  Bullitt. R. Pike; Mute Witness
  Eleni. N. Gage
  Eyewitness. J. Minahan
  For Pete's Sake. B. Street
  Friends of Eddie Coyle. G. V. Higgins
  Hot Rock. D. E. Westlake
Yorkin, Bud
  Thief Who Came to Dinner. T. L. Smith
Young, James
  Daughter of Two Worlds. L. Scott
  Hornet's Nest. W. Woodrow
  My Official Wife. R. H. Savage
  Notorious Miss Lisle. B. Reynolds
  On Trial. E. L. Reizenstein
Young, Terence
  Action of the Tiger. J. Wellard
  Amorous Adventures of Moll Flanders.
    D. Defoe; Fortunes and Misfortunes
    of the Famous Moll Flanders
  Bloodline. S. Sheldon
  Corridor of Mirrors. C. Massie
  Doctor No. I. Fleming
  From Russia with Love. I. Fleming
  From the Boys. R. Matheson; Ride the
    Nightmare
  Jigsaw Man. Dorothea Bennett
  Tall Headlines. A. E. Lindop
  Thunderball. I. Fleming
  Wait Until Dark. F. Knott
Young, Tony
  Hidden Homicide. P. Capon; Death at
    Shinglestrand
  My Death Is a Mockery. D. G. Baber
Yust, Larry
  Trick Baby. I. Slim
Zampi, Mario
  Fatal Night. M. Arlen; May Fair
Zanussi, Krzysztof
  Catamount Killings. J. H. Chase; I
    Would Rather Stay Poor
Zeisler, Alfred
  Amazing Quest of Mr. Ernest Bliss.
    E. P. Oppenheim
  Fear. F. M. Dostoevskii; Crime and
    Punishment
Zelnik, Fred
  I Killed the Count. A. Coppel
Zelnik, Friedrich
  Crimson Circle. E. Wallace
Zimmerman, Vernon
  Fade to Black. R. Renaud
Zinnemann, Fred
  Behold a Pale Horse. E. Pressburger;
    Killing a Mouse on Sunday
  Day of the Jackal. F. Forsyth
  Eyes in the Night. B. Kendrick; Odor
    of Violets
  Seventh Cross. A. Seghers
Zinner, Peter
  Salamander. M. West
Zito, Joseph
  Invasion U.S.A. J. Frost

JUN 2 6 1990